To my wife, Suzanne,
and our sons, John and Steven

Summary of Contents

CONTENTS		ix
TABLE OF FORMS AND TABLES		lvii
PREFACE		lxi
ACKNOWLEDGMENTS		lxiii
CITATION FORM AND REFERENCES		lxv
CHAPTER 1	An Overview of Estate Planning and the Elements of Professional Responsibility	1
CHAPTER 2	Basic Transfer Tax Laws and Estate Planning Strategy	91
CHAPTER 3	Concurrent Ownership and Nontestamentary Transfers	175
CHAPTER 4	Wills and Related Documents	241
CHAPTER 5	The Gift and Estate Tax Marital Deductions	345
CHAPTER 6	Life Insurance	441
CHAPTER 7	Planning Lifetime Noncharitable Gifts	603
CHAPTER 8	Gifts to Charitable Organizations	675
CHAPTER 9	Limiting Estate Size Through Intrafamily Transactions	741
CHAPTER 10	Trusts	835
CHAPTER 11	Closely-Held Business Interests	975
CHAPTER 12	Post-Mortem Planning	1067
GLOSSARY		1187
TABLE OF CASES		1205
TABLE OF INTERNAL REVENUE CODE SECTIONS		1223

TABLE OF INTERNAL REVENUE CODE SECTIONS	1223
TABLE OF TREASURY REGULATIONS	1243
TABLE OF INTERNAL REVENUE RULINGS	1249
TABLE OF MISCELLANEOUS FEDERAL CITATIONS	1257
TABLE OF STATUTES	1259
INDEX	1269

CONTENTS

TABLE OF FORMS AND TABLES lvii
PREFACE lxi
ACKNOWLEDGMENTS lxiii
CITATION FORM AND REFERENCES lxv

CHAPTER 1

AN OVERVIEW OF ESTATE PLANNING AND THE ELEMENTS OF PROFESSIONAL RESPONSIBILITY 1

A. Introduction 4
- §1.1. Scope 4
- §1.2. Professional Responsibility 5
  - §1.2.1. Professional Ethics: Origin of the Rules 5
  - §1.2.2. Basic Elements of Professional Ethics 6
- §1.3. Malpractice; Obligations to Intended Beneficiaries 6

B. The Role and Duties of Lawyers in Estate Planning 8
- §1.4. Client Relations 8
- §1.5. Communicate with Clients Effectively and Frequently 9
- §1.6. Be Efficient; Do Not Procrastinate 10
- §1.7. Duty of Competence; Involve Experts If Required 12
  - §1.7.1. Agreement Regarding Fees of Experts 13
  - §1.7.2. Original Lawyer Retains Overall Direction 13

§1.7.3. Lawyer Cannot Retain Referral Fees, Commissions, or Kickbacks 13
§1.8. Test the Competence of Clients and Make Housecalls 14
§1.8.1. Traditional Test for Testamentary Competence 15
§1.8.2. Options Where Competence Is Doubtful 16
§1.8.3. Help the Client Avoid Critical Decisions During Emotional Upset 17
§1.9. Be More Than a Mere Scrivener: Counsel Client Regarding Impact of Actions 17
§1.10. Put It in Writing 19
§1.10.1. Client Data Summary 19
§1.10.2. Client Document Summary 19
§1.11. Train and Supervise Subordinates 20
§1.12. Beware of Multijurisdictional Problems 20
§1.13. Legal Ethics and Taxes 22
C. Conflicts of Interest 25
§1.14. Representation of Multiple Parties 25
§1.14.1. Intergenerational Estate Planning 26
§1.14.2. Husband and Wife or Parties Contemplating Marriage or Cohabitation 28
§1.14.3. Lawyer as Intermediary 30
§1.14.4. Imputed Disqualification of Partners and Associates 30
§1.15. Do Not Subordinate the Client's Interests 31
§1.16. Do Not Accept Gifts from Clients Who Are Nonrelatives 31
§1.17. Do Not Enter into Any Business Transactions with a Client 33
§1.18. Scrivener Should Be Wary of Accepting Appointment as Fiduciary 34
D. Lawyer's Fees 36
§1.19. Discussions with the Client 36
§1.20. Determining the Amount for Lifetime Services 37
§1.21. Who Pays the Lawyer's Fee? 40
§1.22. Determining the Amount for Estate Administration Services 40

	§1.23.	Avoid Bequest in Satisfaction of Lawyer's Fee	42
	§1.24.	Income Tax Deductibility of Lifetime Estate Planning Fee	43
	§1.25.	Deductibility of Post-Mortem Estate Planning Fee	45
E.	Inter Vivos Estate Planning		45
	§1.26.	Introduction	45
	§1.27.	Stages of Inter Vivos Estate Planning	45
	§1.28.	Getting the Facts	46
	§1.29.	Initial Letter to the Client	48
		Form 1-1. Letter to Client Regarding Initial Conference	*49*
	§1.30.	Initial Interview with the Client	50
		§1.30.1. Getting Off to a Good Start	51
		§1.30.2. Office Arrangement	51
		§1.30.3. Encouraging Communication	52
		§1.30.4. Learning the Client's Objectives	52
		§1.30.5. Examining Documents	52
		§1.30.6. Engagement Letter	54
		Form 1-2. Letter to Client After Initial Conference	*54*
		§1.30.7. Associating Others	55
	§1.31.	Helping the Client Choose a Plan	56
		§1.31.1. Valuation of Assets	57
		§1.31.2. Tax Estimates	58
		§1.31.3. Record of Advice to the Client	59
	§1.32.	Letter Describing Recommended Plans; Tax Estimates	60
		Form 1-3. Letter to Client Describing Recommended Plan	*60*
		Form 1-4. Tax Estimates	*62*
	§1.33.	Producing the Documents	67
		§1.33.1. Develop and Use Estate Planning Forms	68
		§1.33.2. Establishing a Timetable	68
		§1.33.3. Transmitting Drafts to the Clients	69
		§1.33.4. Advanced Technology; Security Problems; Sources of Information	69
		Chart 1-1. Disposition of Husband's Estate	*70*

§1.34. Implementing the Plan 71
§1.34.1. Follow-up Instructions and Subsequent Services 72
§1.34.2. Subsequent Communications; Ethical Considerations 73
F. Post-Mortem Estate Planning 74
§1.35. Post-Mortem Estate Planning 74
§1.36. Lawyer's Relationship with Personal Representative and Beneficiaries 74
§1.37. Lawyer Must Avoid Personal Transactions with Estate or Beneficiaries 76
§1.38. Cash Projection and Tax Planning 77
§1.39. Tax Returns and Malpractice 77
§1.40. Closing the Estate 78
Form 1-5. Confidential Estate Planning Data Form *78*
Form 1-6. Federal Estate Tax Worksheet *84*

Bibliography 86

CHAPTER 2

Basic Transfer Tax Laws and Estate Planning Strategies 91

A. Introduction 94
§2.1. Scope 94
B. Unified Transfer Tax System 94
§2.2. Historical Note 94
§2.3. Unification Under the Tax Reform Act of 1976 and Subsequent Changes 96
Table 2-1. Increases in Unified Credit and Credit Equivalent *97*
Chart 2-1. Federal Estate and Gift Tax Rates Prior to 1993 *98*
C. Federal Gift Tax Highlights 100
§2.4. Basic Nature of the Federal Gift Tax 100
§2.4.1. Scope of Tax; Gifts by Nonresidents 101
§2.4.2. Gift Tax Exemption Replaced by Credit 101
§2.4.3. Completed Gifts 101
§2.5. Annual Gift Tax Exclusion, §2503(b) 102

	§2.5.1.	Present and Future Interests	102
	§2.5.2.	Gifts in Trust	103
	§2.5.3.	Gifts in Trust: *Crummey* Powers of Withdrawal	104
	§2.5.4.	Gifts in Trust: §2503(c) Trusts (Trusts for Minors)	105
	§2.5.5.	Gifts to Corporations	105
	§2.5.6.	Indirect Gifts by Controlling Shareholder	105
	§2.5.7.	Gifts to Partnerships	106
	§2.5.8.	Gifts to a Noncitizen Spouse, §2523(i)	107
§2.6.	Exclusion for Payment of Tuition and Medical Expenses, §2503(e)		107
§2.7.	Gift Splitting, §2513		108
§2.8.	Charitable Deduction, §2522		109
§2.9.	Marital Deduction, §2523		110
	§2.9.1.	Pre-1982 Marital Deduction	111
	§2.9.2.	Post-1981 Marital Deduction	111
	§2.9.3.	Marital Deduction: Some Planning Comments	113
§2.10.	Gift Tax Returns		113
	§2.10.1.	Community Property Gifts	114
	§2.10.2.	Manner and Time of Filing	114
	§2.10.3.	Changes in Valuation, §2504(c)	115
	§2.10.4.	Payment and Penalties	116
D. Federal Estate Tax Highlights			117
§2.11.	Nature and Computation of the Tax		117
§2.12.	Gross Estate		118
§2.13.	Valuation		120
§2.14.	Deductions		121
§2.15.	Credits		122
§2.16.	Transfer Within Three Years of Death, §2035		124
§2.17.	Retained Interests and Powers, §§2036, 2038		125
	§2.17.1.	Retained Voting Rights, §2036(b)	125
	§2.17.2.	Anti-Freeze Provision, Former §2036(c)	126
§2.18.	Annuities and Other Death Benefits, §2039		127
§2.19.	Joint Tenancies, §2040		127
	§2.19.1.	Joint Tenants Other Than Husband and Wife	127

	§2.19.2.	Husband and Wife as Joint Tenants: Qualified Joint Interests, §2040(b)	128
§2.20.	Powers of Appointment, §2041		129
	§2.20.1.	Exceptions	130
	§2.20.2.	Release of Post-1942 General Powers	130
	§2.20.3.	Lapses of General Powers; $5,000 or 5 Percent Power	130
§2.21.	Life Insurance, §2042		131
E.	Generation-Skipping Transfer Tax (GSTT)		131
§2.22.	Background		131
§2.23.	1986 GSTT		133
	§2.23.1.	Direct Skips and Skip Persons, §§2612(c), 2613	134
	§2.23.2.	Taxable Terminations, §2612(a)	135
	§2.23.3.	Taxable Distributions, §2612(b)	135
§2.24.	Application of GSTT; Inclusion Ratio; Applicable Fraction		136
§2.25.	GSTT $1 Million Exemption		138
§2.26.	Reverse QTIP Election, §2652(a)(3)		139
§2.27.	Allocation of Exemption; Deemed Allocation Rules		141
	§2.27.1.	Certain Inter Vivos Transfers	141
	§2.27.2.	Charitable Lead Trusts	142
	§2.27.3.	Default Allocation of GSTT Exemption	143
§2.28.	Exclusions, §§2611(b), 2642(c)		144
§2.29.	Valuation of Property		145
§2.30.	Taxable Amount of Generation-Skipping Transfers		146
	§2.30.1.	Direct Skips	146
	§2.30.2.	Taxable Distributions	147
	§2.30.3.	Taxable Terminations	147
§2.31.	Identifying and Changing the Transferor		148
§2.32.	Generational Assignments, §2651		150
§2.33.	Separate Trusts		151
§2.34.	Multiple Transfers, §2642(d)		151
§2.35.	Basis Adjustment, §2654(a)		152
§2.36.	Returns, §2662		153
	§2.36.1.	Direct Skips	153
	§2.36.2.	Trust Arrangements	154

	§2.36.3.	Deferral of GSTT on Direct Skips of Closely-Held Business Interests, §6166(h)	155
	§2.36.4.	Redemption of Stock to Pay GSTT, §303(d)	155
§2.37.	Return Due Dates		155
§2.38.	Effective Dates		155
§2.39.	$2 Million Exclusion, 1986 Act §1433(b)(3)		158
§2.40.	GSTT Planning Strategies		159
	§2.40.1.	Use Each Client's $1 Million GSTT Exemption	159
	§2.40.2.	Coordinate Use of GSTT Exemption, the Unified Credit, and the Marital Deduction	159
	§2.40.3.	Make Nontaxable Gifts, §2642(c)	160
	§2.40.4.	Make Inter Vivos Direct Skips	161
	§2.40.5.	Preserve Status of Trusts That Are Exempt Under Effective Date Rules	161
	§2.40.6.	Create and Administer Trusts in Light of Prior Use of GSTT Exemption	162
	§2.40.7.	Use the Orphan Grandchild Exclusion, §2612(c)	162
	§2.40.8.	Consider Authorizing Trustees to Make Distributions and to Amend Trust	163
F. Basic Lifetime Estate Planning Tax Strategies			164
§2.41.	Overview		164
§2.42.	Shift Income Within the Family		165
	§2.42.1.	Methods	166
	§2.42.2.	Assignment of Income Alone Is Ineffective for Income Tax Purposes	166
§2.43.	Reduce the Size of the Estate: Gifts and Valuation Games		167
	§2.43.1.	Make Gifts to Qualify for Valuation Discounts	169
	§2.43.2.	Make Gifts of Life Insurance	170
§2.44.	Freeze the Value of the Estate		170
§2.45.	Bypass the Estates of Survivors		171
§2.46.	Defer the Payment of Estate and GST Taxes		173
Bibliography			174

CHAPTER 3

Concurrent Ownership and Nontestamentary Transfers 175

A. Introduction 177
§3.1. Scope 177
B. Tenancy in Common 178
§3.2. Substantive Law Summary 178
§3.3. Creation 178
§3.4. Tenancy in Common in Community Property States 180
§3.5. Miscellaneous 181
§3.6. Creditor's Claims 182
§3.7. Gift Tax 182
§3.7.1. Termination 182
§3.7.2. Conversion of Community Property into Tenancy in Common 183
§3.7.3. Conversion of Tenancy in Common into Community Property 183
§3.8. Estate Tax 184
§3.9. Income Tax 185
§3.10. Use in Estate Planning 185
C. Joint Tenancy and Tenancy by the Entirety 186
§3.11. Introduction 186
§3.11.1. Advantages 187
§3.11.2. Disadvantages 187
§3.12. Features of Joint Tenancies 188
§3.12.1. Multiparty Financial Accounts 189
§3.12.2. Uniform TOD Security Registration Act 189
§3.12.3. Simultaneous Death 190
§3.12.4. Creditor's Rights 190
§3.12.5. Community Property 190
§3.13. Tenancy by the Entirety 191
§3.14. Gift Tax 193
§3.14.1. Revocable Transfers 194
§3.14.2. Pre-1982 Transfers of Real Property to a Spouse 195
§3.15. Estate Tax: General Rule, §2040(a) 196
§3.15.1. Contributions by Surviving Tenant 197
§3.15.2. Gifts to Decedent and Survivor as Joint Tenants 198

§3.16. Qualified Joint Interests, §2040(b) 199
§3.17. Estate Tax: Simultaneous Deaths 200
§3.18. Estate Tax: Termination of Joint Tenancies 201
§3.19. Disclaimers, §§2046, 2518 203
§3.20. Income Tax 203
§3.20.1. Income from Joint Tenancy Property 204
§3.20.2. Income Tax Deductions 204
§3.20.3. Basis; General Rule 205
§3.20.4. Special Basis Rule, §1014(e) 206
§3.20.5. Depreciation Adjustment to Basis, §1014(b)(9) 206
§3.20.6. Community Property in Joint Tenancy 207
§3.20.7. Community Property Transmuted into Separate Property Joint Tenancy 207
§3.20.8. Basis Planning with Joint Tenancies 208
§3.20.9. Termination of Joint Tenancies 208
§3.21. Planning with Joint Tenancies 209
D. Community Property 210
§3.22. Scope 210
§3.23. History 211
§3.24. Estate Planning with Community Property 212
§3.25. Preserve the Community or Separate Character of Property 212
§3.26. Preserve the Availability of Stepped-up Basis Under §1014(b)(6) 214
§3.27. Avoid Unnecessarily Increasing Size of Surviving Spouse's Estate 214
§3.28. Separate and Community Property 215
§3.28.1. Gifts of Separate Property 215
§3.28.2. Gifts of Community Property 215
§3.28.3. Tracing the Character of Property 216
§3.28.4. Presumption Favoring Community Property 216
§3.28.5. Special Problems of Characterization 217
§3.29. Agreements Regarding Character of Property 219
§3.30. Agreements Governing Disposition of Property at Death 220

§3.31. Survivorship Community Property 221
§3.32. Employee Benefit Plans; Terminable Interest Rule 222
§3.33. Estate Tax 223
§3.33.1. Deductions 224
§3.33.2. Marital Deduction 225
§3.33.3. Credits 225
§3.34. Gift Tax 226
§3.34.1. Transfer of Separate into Community Property 226
§3.34.2. Partition of Community Property into Separate Property 227
§3.34.3. Conversion of Future Income into Separate Property 227
§3.35. Income Tax 228
§3.35.1. No Gain or Loss on Transfers Between Spouses, §1041 228
§3.35.2. Conversion of Separate Property into Community Property 229
§3.35.3. Conversion of Community Property into Separate Property 230
§3.35.4. Basis Following Death of a Spouse 231
§3.35.5. Appreciated Property Acquired from a Decedent 233
§3.36. Conflict of Laws: Basic Rules 234
§3.37. Uniform Disposition of Community Property Rights at Death Act 235
§3.38. Quasi-Community Property 236
§3.39. Protecting the Property Interests of Migratory Spouses 238

Bibliography 238

CHAPTER 4

WILLS AND RELATED DOCUMENTS **241**

A. Introduction 245
§4.1. Overview 245

§4.2.	Federal Estate and Gift Taxes in Perspective		246
§4.3.	Statutory Wills		247
§4.4.	Avoiding Intestacy		248
	§4.4.1.	Succession in Common Law Property States	249
	§4.4.2.	Succession in Community Property States	250
§4.5.	An Estate Administration Proceeding May Protect the Survivors' Economic Interests		251
§4.6.	Income-Splitting Between Estate and Survivors		252
§4.7.	Contractual Wills		253
	§4.7.1.	Uncertain Tax Consequences	254
	§4.7.2.	Trusts Are Preferable	255
	§4.7.3.	Conditional Wills	255
B.	Organization and Content of Wills		256
§4.8.	General		256
		Chart 4-1. Disposition of Assets Under Will of John Q. Client	*257*
		Form 4-1. Table of Contents, John Q. Client Will	*257*
§4.9.	Introduction to Will		259
		Form 4-2. Introduction to Will	*259*
§4.10.	Revocation		260
		Form 4-3. Revocation of Prior Wills	*260*
§4.11.	Disposition of Remains		261
§4.12.	Payment of Debts		262
§4.13.	Extent of Testator's Property		262
§4.14.	Family Status and Definitions		263
		Form 4-4. Family Status and Definitions	*263*
§4.15.	Gift of a Specific Item of Personalty		265
		Form 4-5. Gift of Specific Item of Personalty	*265*
	§4.15.1.	Ademption	266
	§4.15.2.	Alternative Disposition	266
	§4.15.3.	Simultaneous Death	267
	§4.15.4.	Survivorship for Specified Period	267
		Form 4-6. General Survivorship Requirement	*267*
§4.16.	Cash Gifts		268
		Form 4-7. Cash Gift to Charity	*268*

	§4.16.1.	Charitable Deduction for Tax Purposes	269
	§4.16.2.	Satisfaction	269
	§4.16.3.	Distribution in Kind	270
	§4.16.4.	Forgiveness of Indebtedness	270
§4.17.	Tangible Personal Property		271
		Form 4-8. Gift of Tangible Personal Property	*271*
	§4.17.1.	Testamentary Gifts to Custodians for Minors	272
	§4.17.2.	Specific Gifts and Cash Legacies	272
	§4.17.3.	Nonspecific Gifts	273
§4.18.	Disposition of Tangible Personal Property in Accordance with Testator's Subsequent Directions		273
		Form 4-9. Gift of Tangible Personal Property by List	*273*
	§4.18.1.	Incorporation by Reference	274
	§4.18.2.	Facts or Acts of Independent Significance	274
	§4.18.3.	Bequest with Request	275
	§4.18.4.	Informal Lists	275
		Form 4-10. List of Gifts of Tangible Personal Property	*276*
§4.19.	Gifts of Corporate Securities		277
		Form 4-11. Gift of Corporate Securities	*277*
§4.20.	Gifts of Residence, Policies of Life Insurance, and Employee Benefits		278
		Form 4-12. Gift of Residence, Life Insurance, and Employee Benefits	*278*
	§4.20.1.	Exoneration	278
	§4.20.2.	Insurance on Realty and Personalty	279
	§4.20.3.	Insurance on the Lives of Others	279
	§4.20.4.	Testamentary Changes of Beneficiary Designations on Life Insurance Policies	279
	§4.20.5.	Revocation by Change of Circumstances	280
	§4.20.6.	Interest in Retirement Plans	280

§4.21.	Residuary Gift		281
		Form 4-13. Residuary Gift	*281*
	§4.21.1.	Should the Residuary Clause Exercise All Powers of Appointment?	282
	§4.21.2.	All to the Surviving Spouse?	284
	§4.21.3.	A "Pot" Trust or a Separate Trust for Each Child?	285
	§4.21.4.	Consolidate the Client's Property in One Trust	286
		Form 4-14. Pour-Over to Inter Vivos Trust	*287*
	§4.21.5.	Discretionary Distributions	287
	§4.21.6.	Trust for Minor Descendants	288
	§4.21.7.	Ultimate Disposition of Residue	288
§4.22.	Trust Provisions		289
		Form 4-15. Trust for Descendants	*289*
		Form 4-16. QTIP Trust	*291*
§4.23.	Trust for Minors		293
		Form 4-17. Trust for Minor Distributees	*293*
§4.24.	Provisions Applicable to All Trusts		294
		Form 4-18. Trust Administrative Provisions	*294*
	§4.24.1.	Successor Trustees	295
	§4.24.2.	Waive Bond	296
	§4.24.3.	Trustee's Powers	296
	§4.24.4.	Unified Management of Trust Assets	298
	§4.24.5.	Investment Criteria	298
	§4.24.6.	Authority to Terminate Uneconomical Trusts	299
	§4.24.7.	Merger and Division of Trusts	300
	§4.24.8.	Spendthrift Clause	300
§4.25.	Guardian of Minor Children		301
		Form 4-19. Appointment of Guardian	*301*
§4.26.	Appointment of Executors		302
		Form 4-20. Appointment of Executors	*302*
		Form 4-21. Waiver of Confidentiality by Executor	*304*

	§4.26.1.	Lawyer-Fiduciary	304
	§4.26.2.	Corporate Fiduciary	305
	§4.26.3.	Family Member Fiduciary	306
	§4.26.4.	Coexecutors	307
	§4.26.5.	Alternate or Successor Executor	307
	§4.26.6.	Exculpatory Clause	307
		Form 4-22. Exculpatory Clause	*308*
	§4.26.7.	Executor's Bond	308
	§4.26.8.	Compensation of Executors	308
	§4.26.9.	Authority to Settle Estate Without Court Supervision	309
§4.27.	Directions Regarding Debts, Expenses of Administration, and Taxes		309
		Form 4-23. Payment of Debts, Taxes, and Expenses	*309*
	§4.27.1.	Source of Funds to Pay Federal Estate Tax	310
	§4.27.2.	QTIP and §2207A	311
	§4.27.3.	§2207B	312
	§4.27.4.	Clarity	312
	§4.27.5.	Preserving Qualification for Redemption Under §303	313
	§4.27.6.	Power to Make Non-Pro Rata Distributions	313
	§ 4.27.7.	Tax Payments and the Marital and Charitable Deductions	314
	§4.27.8.	Payment of State Inheritance Tax	314
	§4.27.9.	Statutes Relating to Payment of Federal Estate Tax	315
	§4.27.10.	Power to Make Tax Elections	315
§4.28.	Wills Not Pursuant to Contract		316
		Form 4-24. Wills Not Contractual	*316*
§4.29.	No Contest Clause		316
§4.30.	Execution		317
		Form 4-25. Execution Clause	*317*
		Form 4-26. Attestation Clause	*318*
§4.31.	Self-Proving Affidavit		318
§4.32.	Execution Ceremony		319
§4.33.	Letter of Transmittal to Client		321
		Form 4-27. Letter of Transmittal	*321*

C. Additional Documents			323
§4.34.	General		323
§4.35.	Durable Powers of Attorney		324
	§4.35.1.	Creation, Recordation, and Revocation	325
	§4.35.2.	Scope and Use	326
		Form 4-28. Power to Represent Principal with Respect to Federal Tax Matters	*327*
	§4.35.3.	Health Care Decisions and *Cruzan*	327
		Form 4-29. Power to Make Health Care Decisions	*328*
	§4.35.4.	Additional Powers to Deal with Property	329
		Form 4-30. Power to Make Gifts to Family Members	*329*
	§4.35.5.	Durable Power to Transfer Property to Revocable Trust	330
	§4.35.6.	Limitations	330
	§4.35.7.	"Springing Powers"	331
		Form 4-31. Date Power Becomes Effective	*331*
	§4.35.8.	Conclusion	331
§4.36.	The Living Will and Natural Death Acts		332
	§4.36.1.	Who May Make a Living Will	333
	§4.36.2.	Immunity Against Civil or Criminal Prosecution	334
	§4.36.3.	Uniform Rights of the Terminally Ill Act (1989)	334
		Form 4-32. Declarations Under the Uniform Rights of the Terminally Ill Act (1989)	*335*
	§4.36.4.	Conclusion	336
§4.37.	Sources of Information		336
§4.38.	Anatomical Gifts		336
	§4.38.1.	Summary of 1968 V.A.G.A.	338
	§4.38.2.	Donees	338
	§4.38.3.	Ways of Making a Gift	338
	§4.38.4.	Revocation and Amendment	339
	§4.38.5.	Action by Others	339
	§4.38.6.	Planning	340

§4.38.7. Donor Card 340
Form 4-33. Uniform Donor Card (Anatomical Gifts) *341*
§4.38.8. Conclusion 341
Bibliography 342

CHAPTER 5

THE GIFT AND ESTATE TAX MARITAL DEDUCTIONS **345**

A. Introduction 348
§5.1. Scope 348
§5.2. The Past 349
§5.2.1. 1942 Legislation 349
§5.2.2. 1948 Adoption of Marital Deduction and Joint Income Tax Returns 350
§5.2.3. 1976 Liberalization of Marital Deduction 351
§5.3. 1981 Quantitative and Qualitative Liberalization 353
§5.3.1. Quantitative Change: Unlimited Marital Deduction 353
§5.3.2. Qualitative Changes: Additional Interests Qualify for Marital Deduction 354
§5.3.3. Transitional Rule for Pre-1982 Formula Gifts 354
§5.4. The Future 357
B. Planning for Use of the Marital Deduction 357
§5.5. Approaching the Planning Job 358
§5.5.1. Tax Estimates 359
§5.5.2. Valuation of Property 359
§5.6. General Objectives 359
§5.7. Equalizing the Spouses' Estates and Minimizing Overall Taxes 360
§5.7.1. Equalization Clauses 361
§5.7.2. Community Property Estates Are Already Equalized 362
§5.8. Minimize Taxes — Defer Payments 363
§5.9. Taking Advantage of the Unified Credits of Both Spouses 364
C. How to Qualify for the Marital Deduction 365

§5.10.	Basic Requirements		365
§5.11.	Gift Tax		366
§5.12.	Decedent Was Citizen or Resident		366
§5.13.	Inclusion in Gross Estate		367
§5.14.	Surviving Spouse		367
§5.15.	Surviving Spouse Was Citizen or Property Distributed to Qualified Domestic Trust (QDT)		368
§5.16.	Interests Passed to Surviving Spouse		369
	§5.16.1.	Family Awards and Allowances	370
	§5.16.2.	Disclaimers	371
§5.17.	A Deductible Interest (i.e., Not a Nondeductible Terminable Interest)		371
	§5.17.1.	Terminable Interest	373
	§5.17.2.	Interest Passed to Another Person	373
	§5.17.3.	Subsequent Enjoyment	374
	§5.17.4.	Executor Purchase Rule	374
	§5.17.5.	Unidentified Asset Rule	375
	§5.17.6.	Contractual Wills	375
§5.18.	Exceptions to Terminable Interest Rule		376
§5.19.	Limited Survivorship		377
§5.20.	Simultaneous Death		380
§5.21.	Estate Trust		381
§5.22.	Life Interest General Power of Appointment Trust, §2056(b)(5)		384
	§5.22.1.	Specific Portion	386
	§5.22.2.	Frequency of Payment of Income	387
		Form 5-1. Payment of Income to Surviving Spouse (§2056(b)(5) Trust)	*390*
	§5.22.3.	Power of Appointment	390
		Form 5-2. Surviving Spouse's General Testamentary Powers of Appointment (§2056(b)(5) Trust)	*390*
§5.23.	Qualified Terminable Interest Property (QTIP)		392
	§5.23.1.	What Is QTIP	393
	§5.23.2.	Qualifying Income Interest for Life	394
	§5.23.3.	Additional Interests Surviving Spouse May Be Given in QTIP Trust	395

§5.23.4. Partial QTIP Election 396
§5.23.5. Annuity Interests 397
§5.23.6. Transfer to Lifetime QTIP to Equalize Estates or to Preserve Use of Unified Credit 399
§5.23.7. QTIP with Charitable Remainder 400
§5.23.8. Use in Connection with Disclaimers 400
§5.23.9. Election and Authorization to Make Election 401
Form 5-3. Executor Authorized to Make Partial or Total QTIP Election *403*
§5.23.10. Disposition of Qualifying Income Interest in QTIP, §2519 403
§5.23.11. Estate Tax on Surviving Spouse's Death 404
§5.24. Current Interest in Charitable Remainder Trust, §2056(b)(8) 405
§5.25. Qualified Domestic Trust (QDT), §§2056(d), 2056A 406
§5.25.1. QDT 407
§5.25.2. Tax on Distributions from QDT 407
§5.25.3. Surviving Spouse Becomes Citizen 408
§5.26. Which Form of Trust — Summary 409
§5.27. Savings Clause 409
Form 5-4. Marital Deduction Savings Clause *410*
D. The Gift Tax Marital Deduction 410
§5.28. Overall Considerations 410
§5.29. General Objectives of Inter Vivos Gifts 411
§5.30. Equalizing Estates by Lifetime Gifts 412
§5.31. Using Lifetime Gifts to Take Advantage of the Poorer Spouse's Unified Credit 412
E. Expressing a Marital Deduction Gift — Formula and Nonformula Gifts 413
§5.32. Overview 413
Form 5-5. Nonformula Pecuniary Nonmarital Deduction Gift *416*

§5.33.	An Assessment of Formula Provisions		416
§5.34.	Formula Pecuniary Gift		418
	§5.34.1.	Credits	419
	§5.34.2.	Charge Nonmarital Share for Principal Expenses for Which No Estate Tax Deduction Is Claimed	420
§5.35.	Formula Pecuniary Marital Deduction Gift		421
		Form 5-6. Formula Pecuniary Marital Deduction Gift	*421*
§5.36.	Model Formula Pecuniary Nonmarital Deduction Gift		422
		Form 5-7. Formula Pecuniary Nonmarital Deduction Gift	*422*
§5.37.	Directions Regarding Funding a Formula Pecuniary Gift		423
	§5.37.1.	Valuation of Assets Distributed in Kind	423
	§5.37.2.	Value on the Date of Distribution ("True Worth")	424
		Form 5-8. Date of Distribution (True Worth) Funding Clause	*426*
	§5.37.3.	Estate Tax Value; Revenue Procedure 64-19	426
	§5.37.4.	Estate Tax Value: "Minimum Value" Provisions	428
		Form 5-9. Minimum Worth Funding Clause	*429*
	§5.37.5.	Estate Tax Value: "Fairly Representative"	429
		Form 5-10. Estate Tax Value, Fairly Representative Funding Clause	*429*
	§5.37.6.	Directions Regarding Allocation of Assets to Pecuniary Formula Marital Deduction Gifts	430
§5.38.	Planning and Drafting a Formula Fractional Share Gift		431
	§5.38.1.	Expressing the Fraction	433
	§5.38.2.	Formula Fractional Share Gift	433
		Form 5-11. Formula Fractional Share Marital Deduction Gift	*433*

§5.38.3. Directions Regarding Allocation of Income and Capital Gains and Losses 434
§5.38.4. Why Use a True Residue Provision? 435
§5.39. Income Tax Aspects of a Formula Fractional Share Gift 437
§5.40. Summary — Choosing Between a Formula Pecuniary Gift and a Formula Fractional Share Gift 438
Bibliography 439

CHAPTER 6

LIFE INSURANCE 441

A. Introduction 446
§6.1. Scope 446
§6.2. Terminology; Insurable Interest 448
§6.3. Data Collection 450
§6.4. Basic Functions of Life Insurance 451
§6.5. How Much Life Insurance? 452
§6.6. Spouse Insurance 453
§6.7. Basic Planning Techniques 454
§6.8. Types of Life Insurance 454
§6.9. Cash Value Insurance 455
§6.9.1. Whole Life 455
§6.9.2. Limited-Pay Life 455
§6.9.3. Endowment Insurance 456
§6.9.4. Universal Life 456
§6.9.5. Variable Life 457
§6.10. Term Insurance 458
Graph 6-1. Annual Premium, Five-Year Renewable $250,000 Term Policy *459*
§6.10.1. Decreasing Term 460
§6.10.2. Group-Term 460
§6.11. Common Policy Riders 461
§6.11.1. Accidental Death 461
§6.11.2. Waiver of Premium 461
§6.12. Participating and Nonparticipating Policies 462
§6.13. Life Insurance Agents 462
§6.14. Financial Condition of Insurers 463
§6.15. Community Property 464

	§6.15.1.	Inception-of-Title Rule	464
	§6.15.2.	Apportionment Rule	465
	§6.15.3.	Risk Payment Doctrine	466
B.	Planning with Life Insurance		467
§6.16.	Introduction		467
§6.17.	Combined Marital Estates of Less Than $600,000		468
§6.18.	Combined Marital Estates of Less Than $1.2 Million (Two Credit Equivalents)		468
	§6.18.1.	Protect Minor Children	469
	§6.18.2.	Use Trusts	470
	§6.18.3.	Plan Based upon a Revocable Trust	471
		Chart 6-1. Disposition of Property Upon Death of Married Insured	*472*
	§6.18.4.	Plan Based upon a Testamentary Trust	472
§6.19.	Choosing Between a Revocable Trust and a Testamentary Trust		473
§6.20.	Combined Marital Estates of More Than $1.2 Million: Eliminating the Insurance from the Estate of the Insured		473
§6.21.	Ownership by an Individual Other Than the Insured		474
	§6.21.1.	Cross-Owned Insurance	474
	§6.21.2.	Applications and Assignments	475
	§6.21.3.	Community Property	475
	§6.21.4.	Premium Payments	475
	§6.21.5.	Beneficiary Designations	476
	§6.21.6.	Successive Ownership	476
§6.22.	Marital Deduction Planning		477
	§6.22.1.	Beneficiary Designations	477
	§6.22.2.	Premium Payments	478
	§6.22.3.	Successive Ownership	478
§6.23.	Irrevocable Life Insurance Trusts		479
	§6.23.1.	Estate Tax	479
	§6.23.2.	Gift Tax	481
	§6.23.3.	Survivorship Policies	481
	§6.23.4.	GSTT	482
	§6.23.5.	Drafting Considerations	484
	§6.23.6.	Community Property	486
§6.24.	Other Types of Life Insurance Trusts		489
	§6.24.1.	Community Property Widow's Election Life Insurance Trust	489

§6.24.2. Business Uses 491
§6.24.3. Charitable Uses 492
C. Estate Taxation of Life Insurance 492
§6.25. History 492
§6.26. Life Insurance Receivable by or for the Benefit of the Estate, §2042(1) 493
§6.27. Incidents of Ownership, §2042(2) 495
§6.27.1. Policy Facts and Intent Facts 496
§6.27.2. Incidents of Ownership 497
§6.27.3. Power to Change Beneficiaries by Divorce, Birth, or Adoption 498
§6.27.4. Power to Terminate Membership in Group Plans 498
§6.27.5. Power to Convert Group Insurance to Ordinary Insurance 499
§6.27.6. Right to Prevent Cancellation by Purchasing Employer Owned Life Insurance 499
§6.27.7. Power to Remove and Replace Trustee 500
§6.27.8. Negative or "Veto" Powers 500
§6.27.9. Incidents of Ownership Under Extraneous Contract 502
§6.27.10. Reversionary Interests, §2042(2) 502
§6.27.11. Incidents of Ownership Held in a Fiduciary Capacity 504
§6.28. Attribution of Incidents of Ownership 506
§6.28.1. Stock Held as Community Property 507
§6.28.2. Insurance Owned by a Partnership 508
§6.29. Reciprocal Trust Doctrine and Life Insurance 509
§6.30. Transfer of Interests in Insurance Within Three Years of Death, §2035 510
§6.31. §2035; Pre-1982 Law 511
§6.32. §2035; Post-1981 Law 511
§6.32.1. Insured Transfers Owned Insurance 512
§6.32.2. Controlled Corporation or Other Noninsured-Owner Transfers Insurance Within Three Years of Insured's Death 512

§6.32.3. Pre-1982 Law: Insured Transfers Funds Used to Purchase Insurance 513
§6.32.4. Post-1981: Insured Transfers Funds Used to Purchase Insurance 515
§6.32.5. Exchange of Policies Owned by Others Within Three Years of Insured's Death 516
§6.33. Insurance Acquired with Joint or Community Property Funds 517
§6.34. Sale of Life Insurance by Insured Within Three Years of Death, §2035 517
§6.35. Exclusion of Part of Proceeds to the Extent Premiums Paid by Others 519
§6.36. Insurance on the Life of a Person Other Than the Decedent, §2035 520
§6.37. Premiums Paid Within Three Years of Death; Pre-1982 Law, §2035 520
§6.38. Transfer of Incidents of Ownership Within Three Years of Death, §2035 521
§6.39. Retained Life Interest, §2036 522
§6.40. State Death Taxes 524
§6.41. Generation-Skipping Transfer Tax (GSTT) 525
§6.41.1. GSTT Exemption for Nontaxable Gifts 526
§6.41.2. GSTT $1 Million Exemption 527
D. Gift Taxation of Life Insurance 527
§6.42. General 527
§6.43. Valuation of Policies 528
§6.43.1. Term and Group-Term Insurance 528
§6.43.2. Single-Premium and Paid-Up Policies 529
§6.43.3. Other Policies — Interpolated Terminal Reserve 529
§6.43.4. Policy Subject to a Loan 530
§6.43.5. Physical Condition of Insured 530
§6.43.6. Form 712, Life Insurance Statement 530
§6.44. Annual Exclusion 531
§6.44.1. Multiple Donees 531
§6.44.2. Transfer to Trusts 531
§6.44.3. GSTT 532
§6.45. Transfer of a Policy 533

	§6.45.1.	Irrevocable Beneficiary Designation	533
	§6.45.2.	Charitable and Marital Deductions	533
§6.46.	Payment of Premiums		534
§6.47.	Payment of Proceeds		535
E.	Income Taxation of Life Insurance		537
§6.48.	Introduction		537
§6.49.	Life Insurance Defined, §7702		537
		Table 6-1. Cash Corridor Test of §7702(d)(2)	*539*
§6.50.	Modified Endowment Contract, §7702A		539
§6.51.	Payment of Proceeds, §101(a)(1)		540
	§6.51.1.	Deferred Payment of Proceeds, §101(c), (d)	541
	§6.51.2.	Proceeds Paid to Shareholder-Beneficiary	541
§6.52.	Settlement Options, §101(c), (d)		541
§6.53.	Transfer for Value, §101(a)(2)		542
	§6.53.1.	Exceptions	543
	§6.53.2.	First Exception, §101(a)(2)(A)	543
	§6.53.3.	Second Exception, §101(a)(2)(B)	544
§6.54.	Policy Purchased by a Qualified Plan		545
§6.55.	Premium Payments		546
	§6.55.1.	Premium Payments Deductible as Alimony	546
	§6.55.2.	Premium Payments as Charitable Contributions	546
	§6.55.3.	Premium Payments at a Discount	547
§6.56.	Premiums Paid by Employers Are Deductible		547
§6.57.	Cost of Insurance Protection Provided by Qualified Plans, §72(m)(3)		547
§6.58.	Grantor Trusts, §677(a)(3)		548
§6.59.	Policy Loans		549
	§6.59.1.	Loans on Policies Other Than Modified Endowment Contracts	549
	§6.59.2.	Loans on Modified Endowment Contracts	551
	§6.59.3.	Loan Rates and Dividends	551
§6.60.	Deductibility of Interest on Policy Loans: General		552

	§6.60.1.	Who Is Entitled to Deduct Interest Paid	552
	§6.60.2.	Interest on Policy Loans: Limitations of §264	553
	§6.60.3.	Exceptions to §264(a)(3)	554
§6.61.	Dividends		555
§6.62.	Sale, Surrender, or Exchange of Insurance Policies: General		556
§6.63.	Sale of Policy — Gain and Loss		556
	§6.63.1.	Sale or Other Disposition of Encumbered Policy	557
	§6.63.2.	"Loss" on Sale	557
§6.64.	Surrender of Policies		557
§6.65.	Exchange of Policies Under §1035		559
	§6.65.1.	What Constitutes an Exchange	559
	§6.65.2.	Exchange of Assignable Policies	559
	§6.65.3.	Exchange of Nonassignable Policies	560
§6.66.	Exchanges Within §1035; Permissible Exchanges		561
§6.67.	Costs of Exchanges — Exercise Care and Study the Economics		562
§6.68.	Exchange of Policies Not Within §1035		562
§6.69.	Alternative Minimum Tax, §56(g)(4)(B)(ii)		563
F. Special Types of Life Insurance			564
§6.70.	Introduction		564
§6.71.	Split-Dollar Life Insurance: General		564
	§6.71.1.	Reverse Split-Dollar	566
	§6.71.2.	Income Tax Consequences	567
		Table 6-2. Uniform One-Year Term Premiums for $1,000 Life Insurance Protection	*568*
	§6.71.3.	Gift Tax Consequences	569
	§6.71.4.	Estate Tax Consequences	570
§6.72.	Employer-Provided Group-Term Life Insurance: General		571
	§6.72.1.	Planning with Group-Term Insurance	572
	§6.72.2.	Insurance on Spouses and Children	572
	§6.72.3.	Nondiscrimination Rules	573
	§6.72.4.	Nondiscrimination Rules as to Eligibility	573

§6.72.5. Nondiscrimination Rules as to Benefits 574
§6.72.6. Basic Requirements 574
§6.72.7. Plans That Include Permanent Benefits 575
§6.72.8. Who Are "Employees"? 575
§6.72.9. Determining the Amount Includible in Income 576
Table 6-3. Uniform Premiums for $1,000 of Group-Term Life Insurance Protection 576
§6.72.10. Assignment 577
§6.72.11. Estate Tax 577
§6.72.12. Gift Tax 580
§6.72.13. Group-Term Life Insurance: Retired Lives Reserve (RLR) 581
§6.73. Minimum-Deposit Life Insurance Plans 582
§6.74. Single-Premium Whole Life 583
§6.75. Second-to-Die or Survivorship Whole Life 584
§6.76. Leased Life Insurance 585
§6.77. Veterans' Life Insurance 586
§6.78. Death Benefit Only Plans 587
§6.78.1. Estate Tax, General 587
§6.78.2. §2033 588
§6.78.3. "Transfer" §§2035-2038 588
§6.78.4. §2035 589
§6.78.5. §2036 589
§6.78.6. §2037 590
§6.78.7. §2038(a)(1) 590
§6.78.8. Gift Tax 591
§6.78.9. Income Tax 593
§6.78.10. Installment Payment of Death Benefit Taxed as Annuity 594
§6.78.11. Reasonable and Necessary Payments are Deductible by Employer 595
§6.78.12. ERISA 595
§6.79. Gifts of Life Insurance Under the Uniform Transfers to Minors Act 595
§6.80. Life Insurance and the Uniform Simultaneous Death Act 597
Bibliography 599

CHAPTER 7

PLANNING LIFETIME NONCHARITABLE GIFTS 603

A. Introduction 606
§7.1. Scope 606
§7.2. Nontax Considerations 606
§7.2.1. Economic Position 607
§7.2.2. Age and Health 608
§7.2.3. Emotional and Family Circumstances 608
B. Local Property Law 610
§7.3. Significance of Local Law 610
§7.4. Inter Vivos Gifts and Gifts Causa Mortis 610
§7.5. Elements of Inter Vivos Gifts 610
§7.5.1. Delivery 611
§7.5.2. Acceptance 611
§7.6. Gifts of Community Property 612
C. Tax Objectives of Gifts 612
§7.7. General 612
§7.8. Eliminate Further Appreciation in Value from the Donor's Estate 613
§7.8.1. Annual Exclusion and Unified Credit Gifts 613
§7.8.2. Carryover of Donor's Basis 614
§7.9. Shift Income from Donor to Donee 614
§7.9.1. Kiddie Tax 615
§7.9.2. Shifting Capital Gains 615
§7.10. Reduce Nonbusiness Holdings of Donor in Order to Qualify for Benefits of §§303, 2032A, or 6166 616
§7.11. Minimize State Transfer Tax Costs 616
Table 7-1. Table of Statutory Benefits Under §303, 2032A, and 6166 *617*
D. Tax Factors Involved in Selecting Property to Give 619
§7.12. Give Appreciated Property? 619
§7.13. Do Not Give Property Subject to an Encumbrance in Excess of Its Basis 621
§7.14. Do Not Give Property with a Basis That Exceeds Its Current Fair Market Value 621
§7.15. Do Not Give Property with Positive Tax Characteristics 622

	§7.16.	Give Property That Reduces the Value of Assets Retained by the Donor	622
	§7.17.	Do Not Make a Gift That Will Have Adverse Income Tax Consequences for the Donor	623
E.	Specialized Gift Techniques		624
	§7.18.	Introduction	624
	§7.19.	Small Below-Market Loans	625
	§7.20.	Payment by One Spouse of Entire Income or Gift Tax Liability	626
	§7.21.	Grantor Pays Income Tax on Grantor Trust	626
	§7.22.	Free Services and Free Use of Property	627
	§7.23.	Gift of a Residence with Continued Occupancy by Donor	627
	§7.24.	Installment Gifts: Periodic Forgiveness of Transferee's Notes	629
	§7.25.	Net Gifts	630
		§7.25.1. Income Tax	631
		§7.25.2. Gift Tax	633
		§7.25.3. Estate Tax	634
	§7.26.	Gifts of Encumbered Property	635
	§7.27.	Part Gift and Part Sale	636
F.	Gifts to Minors		638
	§7.28.	Importance of Gifts to Minors	638
	§7.29.	Outright Gifts	639
		§7.29.1. Gift Tax	639
		§7.29.2. Estate Tax	639
		§7.29.3. Income Tax	640
	§7.30.	Series EE Bonds	640
		§7.30.1. Minor as Sole Owner	641
		§7.30.2. Minor as Coowner	642
		§7.30.3. Minor as Beneficiary	642
	§7.31.	Payable-on-Death (POD) Bank Accounts	643
	§7.32.	Savings Account or Totten Trust	643
	§7.33.	Joint Bank or Securities Accounts	644
		§7.33.1. Joint Bank Accounts	645
		§7.33.2. Joint Securities Accounts	645
	§7.34.	Gifts Under the Uniform Acts	646
		§7.34.1. Gift Tax	647
		§7.34.2. Estate Tax	647
		§7.34.3. Income Tax	648
	§7.35.	Gifts in Trust	649
	§7.36.	Section 2503(c) Trusts	650
		§7.36.1. Property or Income	650
		§7.36.2. No Substantial Restrictions	651
		§7.36.3. Payable at 21	651

	§7.36.4.	Payable to Donee's Estate or As Donee Appoints	652
	§7.36.5.	Terms of §2503(c) Trust	653
		Form 7-1. Distributive Provisions of §2503(c) Trust	*653*
	§7.36.6.	Estate Tax	654
	§7.36.7.	Income Tax	655
	§7.36.8.	GSTT	656
	§7.36.9.	Conclusion	656
§7.37.	Discretionary Trust with *Crummey* Powers		656
	§7.37.1.	Gift Tax	657
	§7.37.2.	Limit the Amount Subject to Withdrawal?	658
	§7.37.3.	Authorize Each Donor to Restrict the Amount Subject to Withdrawal?	661
		Form 7-2. Limitation of Power of Withdrawal	*661*
	§7.37.4.	Hanging Power: A Power of Withdrawal That Lapses at 5 or 5 Annual Rate	661
		Form 7-3. Annual Lapse of Hanging Power	*662*
	§7.37.5.	How Many Beneficiaries May Hold a Power of Withdrawal?	663
	§7.37.6.	Notice to the Beneficiary	664
	§7.37.7.	Must the Trust Have Liquid Assets to Satisfy a Withdrawal?	665
	§7.37.8.	How Long Should the Power Be Exercisable?	666
	§7.37.9.	Separate Trusts or One Trust for Multiple Donees?	667
	§7.37.10.	Income Tax	668
	§7.37.11.	Estate Tax	669
	§7.37.12.	Model *Crummey* Power	669
		Form 7-4. Crummey *Power for Trust with One Beneficiary*	*669*
§7.38.	Mandatory Distribution of Income Trust, §2503(b)		670
	§7.38.1.	Nontax Considerations	671
	§7.38.2.	Tax Considerations	671
§7.39.	Irrevocable Short-Term Trusts		672

Bibliography 672

CHAPTER 8

Gifts to Charitable Organizations 675

A. Introduction 677
§8.1. Scope 677
B. Federal Tax Consequences of Outright Gifts 679
§8.2. Qualified Charities, §170(c) 679
§8.2.1. Foreign Charities 680
§8.2.2. Cumulative List of Charitable Organizations; Requests for Rulings 681
§8.3. Public Charities, §170(b)(1)(A) 681
§8.4. Nonpublic Charities 683
§8.4.1. Gifts for the Use of a Charitable Organization 683
§8.4.2. Gifts of Services and the Use of Property 684
§8.5. Charitable Contributions Carryover, §170(d)(1) 685
§8.6. When Is a Gift Made? — Reg. §1.170A-1(b) 685
§8.7. Appraisals, Substantiation, and Valuation of Gifts, Reg. §§1.170A-1(c), 1.170A-13(b)(2)-(4); §6662 686
§8.7.1. Substantiation Rules 688
§8.7.2. Penalty for Underpayment of Tax 688
§8.7.3. Report of Disposition of Property by Charity 689
§8.8. Gifts of Depreciated Property 689
§8.9. Gifts of Ordinary Income Property, §170(e)(1)(A) 689
§8.10. Gifts of Capital Gain Property; General §§170(b)(1)(C), (D); 170(e) 690
§8.11. Gifts of Capital Gain Property: Election to Reduce Amount of Gift, §§170(b)(1)(C)(iii), 170(e) 692
§8.12. Gifts of Capital Gain Property: Tangible Personal Property, §170(e)(1)(B)(i), (ii) 695
§8.13. Gifts of Future Interests in Tangible Personal Property, §170(a)(3), Reg. §1.170A-5 696
C. Gifts of Partial Interests 697

§8.14. General 697
§8.15. Remainder Interest in Personal Residence or Farm 697
§8.15.1. Life Estate Transferred to Spouse or Others 698
§8.15.2. Charitable Gift of Remainder in Part of Farm or Residence 699
§8.15.3. Sale Required Upon Termination of Life Estate 699
§8.15.4. Depreciation and Depletion 699
§8.16. Undivided Portion of Donor's Entire Interest 701
§8.17. Donor's Entire Interest in Property 703
§8.18. Transfers Subject to a Condition or Power 704
D. Gifts in Trust 704
§8.19. General Limitations 704
§8.20. Charitable Remainder Trusts in General, §664(d) 706
§8.20.1. Double Deductions 706
§8.20.2. Diversification of Investments 707
§8.20.3. Wealth Replacement Plans 707
§8.20.4. Substitute for Tax-Exempt Retirement Plan 708
§8.20.5. Marital Deductions 708
§8.21. Charitable Remainder Annuity Trust (CRAT) 709
§8.22. Charitable Remainder Unitrust (CRUT) 711
§8.23. Sample Declarations of Trust 712
§8.24. Income Taxation of Charitable Remainder Trusts 714
§8.25. Valuing Charitable Remainders 715
§8.26. Private Foundation Rules 717
§8.27. Requests for Rulings 717
§8.28. Advantages of Charitable Remainder Trusts 718
§8.29. Comparison of CRATs and CRUTs 719
§8.30. Pooled Income Fund, §642(c)(5) 720
§8.31. Gifts to Charitable Lead Trusts, §§170(f)(2)(B), 2055(e)(2)(B), 2522(c)(2)(B) 723
§8.32. Guaranteed Annuity Interests and Unitrust Interests 725
§8.33. Gifts of Income Interests 726
§8.34. Payments to Charity from a Trust upon Death of Grantor 728
§8.35. Salvaging Charitable Deductions for Nonqualifying Interests 729

E. Special Types of Transfers 731
§8.36. Bargain Sales to Charity, §1011(b) 731
§8.37. Charitable Gift Annuities 733
§8.38. Gift and Redemption of Appreciated Stock 736
§8.39. Gift of Life Insurance 737
§8.40. Charitable Pledges 738

Bibliography 738

CHAPTER 9

LIMITING ESTATE SIZE THROUGH INTRAFAMILY TRANSACTIONS **741**

A. Introduction 744
§9.1. Overview 744
§9.2. Professional Responsibility 746
B. The Installment Sale 747
§9.3. General 747
§9.4. Gift Tax Consequences 750
§9.5. Estate Tax Consequences 751
§9.6. Income Tax Consequences 752
§9.6.1. Payments Received 754
§9.6.2. Alternative Minimum Tax (AMT) 755
§9.6.3. Inter Vivos Disposition of Obligation 756
§9.6.4. Disposition at Death 757
§9.6.5. Imputed Interest or Original Issue Discount 758
Table 9-1. Applicable Federal Rates *759*
Table 9-2. Applicable Federal Rates for November, 1991 *760*
§9.6.6. Sale of Land to Family Member 760
§9.7. Resale by Related Person, §453(e) 760
§9.7.1. Related Person 761
§9.7.2. What Dispositions Constitute Resales? 761
§9.7.3. Involuntary Transfers 762
§9.7.4. Marketable Securities 763
§9.8. Self-Cancelling Installment Note (SCIN) 763
§9.8.1. Estate Tax 764
§9.8.2. Income Tax 765

§9.9.	Installment Sales to Nonresident Aliens		765
C.	The Private Annuity		765
§9.10.	General		766
	§9.10.1.	Transfer to Trust in Exchange for Annuity	766
	§9.10.2.	Planning Considerations	767
§9.11.	Nontax Considerations		768
§9.12.	Income Tax Consequences of Transfer		769
§9.13.	Income Taxation of Annuitant		770
§9.14.	Income Taxation of Transferee		773
	§9.14.1.	Depreciation	774
	§9.14.2.	Gain or Loss	775
§9.15.	Gift Tax Consequences		776
§9.16.	Estate Tax Consequences		776
D.	The Gift or Sale and Leaseback		777
§9.17.	General		777
§9.18.	Overall Consequences		779
§9.19.	Income Tax Consequences of Transfer		781
§9.20.	Income Tax Consequences of Rental Payments		781
	§9.20.1.	Economic Reality	783
	§9.20.2.	No Equity Interest	783
	§9.20.3.	Tax Court Requirements	784
	§9.20.4.	Suggested Approach	784
	§9.20.5.	Grantor Trust Rules	785
§9.21.	Gift Tax Consequences		785
§9.22.	Estate Tax Consequences		787
	§9.22.1.	Outright Gift and Leaseback	787
	§9.22.2.	Sale and Leaseback	788
E.	The Widow's Election in Community Property and Common Law States		788
§9.23.	Introduction		788
§9.24.	Testamentary Elections		790
§9.25.	Widow's Election Described		790
§9.26.	Typical Widow's Election Plan		792
§9.27.	Inter Vivos or Post-Mortem Election?		793
§9.28.	"Voluntary" Widow's Election		793
§9.29.	Nontax Consequences of a Forced Election		794
§9.30.	Gift Tax Consequences		795
	§9.30.1.	Powers of Appointment	796
	§9.30.2.	Voluntary Election	797
§9.31.	Income Tax Consequences		797
	§9.31.1.	The Trustee	798
	§9.31.2.	The Widow	801

§9.32. Income Tax Consequences of Trust Distributions 803
§9.33. Estate Tax: The Husband's Estate 805
§9.34. Estate Tax: The Widow's Estate 805
§9.35. GSTT 807
§9.36. Widow's Election Variations 811
§9.37. Widow's Election Insurance Trust 813
§9.38. State Tax Consequences 813
§9.39. Widow's Election Planning 814
F. Dividing Interests: Sale of Remainders, Joint Purchases, GRITs, and Qualified Personal Residence Trusts 815
§9.40. Introduction 815
§9.41. Sale of Remainder Interest 816
§9.41.1. Gift Tax Consequences 817
§9.41.2. Estate Tax Consequences 819
§9.41.3. Income Tax Consequences 820
§9.42 Joint Purchases 821
§9.42.1. Gift Tax Consequences 821
§9.42.2. Estate Tax Consequences 823
§9.42.3. Income Tax Consequences 824
§9.43. GRITs (Grantor Retained Interest Trusts) 824
§9.43.1. Gift Tax Consequences 826
§9.43.2. Qualified Interests 826
§9.43.3. Personal Residence Trusts 828
§9.43.4. Estate Tax Consequences 832
§9.43.5. Income Tax Consequences 833
§9.44. Conclusion 833

Bibliography 834

CHAPTER 10

TRUSTS 835

A. Introduction 840
§10.1. Scope 840
§10.2. Encourage Flexibility 841
§10.3. Avoid Sham Trusts and Trusts with No Economic Substance 841
§10.4. Income Tax Summary 843
§10.4.1. Grantor Trust Rules, §§671-677 844
§10.4.2. Nongrantor Treated as Owner, §678 845

	§10.4.3.	Distributable Net Income, §643(a)	845
	§10.4.4.	Income Tax Consequences of Distributions, §§651, 652, 661, 662	847
	§10.4.5.	No Standard Deduction; Personal Exemptions	848
	§10.4.6.	Two Percent Floor on Miscellaneous Itemized Deductions, §67	848
	§10.4.7.	Passive Activity Losses (PALs)	849
	§10.4.8.	Rules Applicable to Simple Trusts, §§651, 652	851
	§10.4.9.	Rules Applicable to Complex Trusts, §§661, 662	853
	§10.4.10.	Throwback Rules, §§665-667	855
	§10.4.11.	Sale of Appreciated Property Within Two Years, §644	859
	§10.4.12.	Recognition of Loss, §267	859
	§10.4.13.	Section 1244 Stock	860
	§10.4.14.	S Corporation Stock	860
	§10.4.15.	Redemptions Under §303	862
	§10.4.16.	Taxable Year of the Trust	862
	§10.4.17.	Payment of Income Tax by Fiduciary	863
	§10.4.18.	Estimated Income Tax Payments	863
§10.5.	Gift Tax Summary		864
§10.6.	Estate Tax Summary		865
	§10.6.1.	Right to Vote Stock of Controlled Corporation, §2036(b)	865
	§10.6.2.	Benefits Under Qualified Plans, §2039	866
	§10.6.3.	General Power of Appointment, §2041	867
	§10.6.4.	Life Insurance Proceeds, §2042	867
	§10.6.5.	Alternate Valuation Date	867
	§10.6.6.	Deduction of Expenses Under §2053	868
	§10.6.7.	Deferral of Estate Tax	868

	§10.6.8.	Discharge of Executor and Other Fiduciaries from Personal Liability for Estate Tax	868
	§10.6.9.	Flower Bonds	869
B.	The Revocable Trust		870
§10.7.	Scope		870
§10.8.	Reserving the Power to Revoke		871
		Form 10-1. Reserved Power to Amend or Revoke	*872*
§10.9.	Nontestamentary Nature of Revocable Trusts		873
§10.10.	Validity of Pour-Over to Revocable Trust		874
		Form 10-2. Residuary Clause for Pour-Over Will	*875*
§10.11.	Claims of Creditors Against Grantor		875
§10.12.	Principal Advantages of Revocable Trusts		875
§10.13.	Principal Disadvantages of Revocable Trusts		881
§10.14.	Summary of Tax Consequences		882
§10.15.	Income Tax Considerations		883
§10.16.	Gift Tax Considerations		884
§10.17.	Estate Tax Considerations		884
C.	Planning the Beneficiary's Interests in an Irrevocable Trust		886
§10.18.	Scope		886
		Table 10-1. Income Tax Rates Applicable to Trusts and Estates, 1991	*886*
		Table 10-2. Income Tax Rates Applicable to Trusts and Estates, 1990	*887*
§10.19.	Multiple Trusts		887
§10.20.	Mandatory or Discretionary Distributions?		888
	§10.20.1.	Distribution or Accumulation of Income	889
	§10.20.2.	Sprinkling of Income	890
	§10.20.3.	Powers Held by Independent Trustee	890
	§10.20.4.	Powers Limited by an Ascertainable Standard, §674(d)	892
	§10.20.5.	Grantor as Trustee	892
	§10.20.6.	Beneficiary as Trustee	893
	§10.20.7.	"Absolute" or "Uncontrolled" Discretion	893

§10.20.8.	Standards to Guide the Exercise of Discretion	894
§10.20.9.	Transferability of the Beneficiary's Interest	894
§10.20.10.	Discretionary Distribution Form	895
	Form 10-3. Discretionary Distributions	*895*
§10.21.	Spendthrift Clauses — Restricting the Transfer of a Beneficiary's Interests	896
§10.21.1.	Form of Spendthrift Clause	897
	Form 10-4. Spendthrift Clause	*897*
§10.21.2.	Self-Settled Trusts	897
§10.22.	General Powers of Appointment	898
§10.23.	Special Powers of Appointment	899
	Form 10-5. Special Testamentary Power of Appointment	*901*
§10.24.	$5,000 or 5 Percent Power of Withdrawal	901
	Form 10-6. 5 or 5 Power of Appointment	903
§10.24.1.	Income Tax	903
§10.24.2.	"Hanging Power"	905
	Form 10-7. Hanging Power of Withdrawal	906
§10.25.	Power to Withdraw Trust Assets Limited by an Ascertainable Standard	907
	Form 10-8. Power of Withdrawal Limited by an Ascertainable Standard	908
§10.26.	Other Nongeneral Powers of Appointment	908
§10.27.	Beneficiary as Trustee	909
§10.27.1.	Income Tax	910
§10.27.2.	Gift Tax	911
§10.27.3.	Estate Tax	912
§10.28.	Removal and Replacement of Trustee	913
§10.29.	Planning Summary	914
D.	Planning the Grantor's Interests in an Irrevocable Trust	914
§10.30.	Scope	915
§10.31.	Basic Income Tax Rules	915
§10.31.1.	Adverse Party	917
§10.31.2.	Jointly Exercisable Powers	918
§10.32.	Grantor Treated as Owner of Trust Under Subchapter J	918

	§10.32.1.	Grantor Makes Free Gift of Income Tax on Trust	919
	§10.32.2.	Trust Holds S Corporation Stock	920
	§10.32.3.	Trust Holds Installment Obligations	920
	§10.32.4.	Grantor Trust Not Subject to Throwback Rules	920
	§10.32.5.	Capital Gains of Grantor Trust Offset by Grantor's Losses	921
	§10.32.6.	Exclusion of Gain on Sale of Grantor's Principal Residence	921
	§10.32.7.	Nonrecognition of Gain on Certain Dispositions	921
	§10.32.8.	No Gain on Sale of Trust Property to Grantor	922
	§10.32.9.	Grantor Trust May Sell Stock to ESOP	922
§10.33.	Basic Gift Tax Rules		922
	§10.33.1.	Annual Exclusion	923
	§10.33.2.	Charitable Deduction	925
§10.34.	Powers That Result in Transfers Being Incomplete		925
	§10.34.1.	Joint Power to Make Discretionary Distributions	926
	§10.34.2.	Joint Power to Terminate Trust	926
	§10.34.3.	Retained Testamentary Special Power to Appoint Remainder	926
	§10.34.4.	Retained Testamentary Power to Revoke Successive Private Interest	927
§10.35.	Basic Estate Tax Rules		927
	§10.35.1.	§2036	928
	§10.35.2.	§2037	929
	§10.35.3.	§2038	929
§10.36.	Retained Reversionary Interest		930
	§10.36.1.	Income Tax Consequences	930
	§10.36.2.	Gift Tax Consequences	930
	§10.36.3.	Estate Tax Consequences	931
§10.37.	Retained Control of Beneficial Enjoyment		931
	§10.37.1.	Income Tax Consequences	932
	§10.37.2.	Gift Tax Consequences	934
	§10.37.3.	Estate Tax Consequences	934

§10.38. Administrative Powers 934
§10.38.1. Income Tax Consequences 935
§10.38.2. Gift Tax Consequences 937
§10.38.3. Estate Tax Consequences 937
§10.39. Power to Revest Title in Grantor 938
§10.39.1. Income Tax Consequences 938
§10.39.2. Gift Tax Consequences 939
§10.39.3. Estate Tax Consequences 939
§10.40. Retained Income Interest 940
§10.40.1. Income Tax Consequences 940
§10.40.2. Gift Tax Consequences 942
§10.40.3. Estate Tax Consequences 943
§10.41. Power to Appoint Successor Trustees 943
§10.41.1. Revenue Ruling 79-353 943
§10.41.2. Power to Remove Trustee and Appoint Self 944
§10.41.3. Factors in Planning Power to Appoint Successor Trustee 945
§10.41.4. Independent Trustee or Cotrustee 945
§10.41.5. Extent of Trustee's Discretionary Power or Authority to Make Distributions That Satisfy Legal Obligations 946
§10.41.6. Prohibit Distributions That Satisfy Legal Obligations 947
§10.41.7. Income Tax Consequences of Distributions for Support 948
§10.41.8. Drafting Power of Grantor or Beneficiary to Remove and Replace Trustee with Tax-Sensitive Powers 949
§10.41.9. Prohibit Self-Appointment by Grantor or Beneficiary 950
§10.41.10. Disclaimers 952
§10.41.11. Releases 952
§10.41.12. Eliminating Powers by Court Order 953
E. Additional Issues 953
§10.42. Introduction 953
§10.43. Selection of Trustee 953
§10.43.1. Corporate Fiduciary 954
§10.43.2. Lawyer as Trustee 955
§10.43.3. Grantor as Trustee 956

§10.43.4. Beneficiary as Trustee 957
§10.43.5. Cotrustees 957
§10.43.6. Removal of Trustees 958
§10.44. Selection of Property to Transfer in Trust 958
§10.45. Provisions Regarding Trust Investments 960
§10.45.1. Investment Standard 960
§10.45.2. Trustees with Greater Skill 962
§10.45.3. Additional Directions Regarding Specific Assets 963
§10.45.4. Investment Advisor 964
§10.46. Exculpatory Clauses 964
§10.47. Power to Allocate Between Principal and Income 965
§10.47.1. Stock Splits and Stock Dividends 966
§10.47.2. Amortization of Bond Premium and Accumulation of Discount 966
§10.47.3. Depreciation 967
§10.47.4. Unproductive and Underproductive Property 968
§10.47.5. Annuity Trusts or Unitrusts 969
§10.48. Perpetuities Savings Clause 971
Form 10-9. Perpetuities Savings Clause *971*

Bibliography 973

CHAPTER 11

Closely-Held Business Interests 975

A. Introduction 977
§11.1. Overview 977
§11.2. Nontax Features of Corporations 979
§11.3. Income Taxation of Subchapter C Corporations 980
§11.4. Subchapter S Corporations 981
§11.4.1. One Class of Stock 983
§11.4.2. Election to Be S Corporation 983
§11.4.3. Termination of S Corporation Status 984
§11.4.4. Income, Distributions, and Basis 984
§11.4.5. Pre-1987 S Corporation Strategy 985

§11.5. Partnerships 985
B. Buy-Sell Agreements 987
§11.6. Overview 987
§11.7. Nontax Considerations 990
§11.8. Entity Purchase or Cross-Purchase? 991
§11.9. Redemptions by C Corporations 994
§11.10. Redemptions by S Corporations 995
§11.11. Valuation 997
§11.12. Funding the Purchase 999
§11.12.1. Installment Payments 1000
§11.12.2. Medium of Payment 1001
§11.12.3. Accumulated Earnings Tax 1001
§11.13. Ethical Considerations 1002
§11.14. Community Property Aspects 1002
C. Redemptions Under §303 1003
§11.15. Overview 1003
§11.16. Introduction to §303 1004
§11.17. Thirty-five Percent Requirement, §303(b)(2)(A) 1007
§11.18. Stock in Two or More Corporations, §303(b)(2)(B) 1008
§11.19. Maximum Amount Redeemable, §303(a) 1009
§11.20. Time Limit on Redemptions, §303(b)(1), (4) 1010
§11.21. What May Be Distributed 1010
§11.22. Inter Vivos Planning for Redemptions Under §303 1011
§11.23. Worksheet for §303 1011
§11.24. Redemptions That Do Not Qualify Under §303 1014
§11.24.1. Redemption Not Essentially Equivalent to a Dividend, §302(b)(1) 1014
§11.24.2. Substantially Disproportionate Redemption, §302(b)(2) 1016
§11.24.3. Complete Termination of Interest, §302(b)(3) 1017
§11.24.4. No Waiver of Entity Attribution 1019
D. Deferral of Estate Tax Under §6166 1020
§11.25. Overview 1020
§11.26. Closely-Held Business 1022
§11.26.1. Who Is Counted as a Partner or Shareholder 1022
§11.26.2. Trade or Business 1023
§11.26.3. Passive Assets, §6166(b)(9); Farmhouses, §6166(b)(3) 1025

§11.26.4. Partnerships and Stock That Is Not Readily Tradeable, §6166(b)(7) 1025
§11.26.5. Holding Companies, §6166(b)(8) 1026
§11.27. Qualification Under §6166 1028
§11.27.1. Protective Election 1028
§11.27.2. Acceptance or Rejection of Election 1028
§11.27.3. Overpayments 1029
§11.27.4. Deficiencies 1029
§11.28. Installment Payments Under §6166 1029
§11.29. Acceleration Under §6166(g) 1031
§11.29.1. Distribution Under Will, §6166(g)(1)(D) 1031
§11.29.2. Withdrawals of Money or Other Property, §6166(g)(1) 1032
§11.29.3. Estate Has Undistributed Income, §6166(g)(2) 1033
§11.29.4. Failure to Pay Income and Principal on Time, §6166(g)(3) 1033
§11.30. Worksheet for Making §6166 Calculations 1034
E. Recapitalizations 1036
§11.31. Overview 1036
§11.32. Application and Effect of §2701 1038
§11.33. Scope and Effect of §2704 1039
§11.34. Income Tax Treatment of Recapitalizations 1041
§11.34.1. Business Purpose of Recapitalization 1042
§11.34.2. Boot 1042
§11.34.3. Section 306 Stock 1042
§11.34.4. Section 305 Problems 1044
§11.34.5. Redemption Premium, §305(c) 1045
§11.35. Recapitalization Tax Freezes Not Subject to §2701 1047
§11.35.1. Valuation Problems 1048
§11.35.2. Gift or Additional Compensation? 1049
§11.36. Other Tax Considerations 1050
§11.37. Recapitalization Strategies 1050
F. Family Partnerships and Partnership Freezes 1051
§11.38. Overview 1052
§11.38.1. Suitable Assets 1052
§11.38.2. Income Tax Advantages 1053

§11.38.3. Tax Uncertainties 1053
§11.38.4. Valuation Problems and Costs 1054
§11.38.5. Scrutiny by IRS 1054
§11.38.6. Ethical Considerations 1055
§11.39. Creation of Partnership Is Not a Taxable Event 1055
§11.40. Family Partnership Rules 1057
§11.40.1. Capital as a Material Income-Producing Factor 1058
§11.40.2. Trustees and Minors as Partners 1058
§11.40.3. Allocation of Income 1059
§11.40.4. Retained Control by Donor 1059
§11.41. Planning a Frozen Partnership Interest 1060
§11.41.1. Liquidation Preference 1060
§11.41.2. Income Interest 1061
§11.41.3. Management and Control 1062
§11.42. Conclusion 1063

Bibliography 1063

CHAPTER 12

POST-MORTEM PLANNING **1067**

A. Introduction 1071
§12.1. Scope 1071
§12.2. Initial Steps 1073
§12.2.1. Memorandum for the Personal Representative 1073
§12.2.2. Cash Needs 1073
§12.2.3. Federal Tax Notices 1074
§12.2.4. Extensions of Time 1074
B. Income Tax 1075
§12.3. The Decedent's Final Income Tax Return: General 1075
§12.3.1. Election to File a Joint Return 1076
§12.3.2. Advantages of Filing a Joint Return 1076
§12.3.3. Disadvantage of Filing a Joint Return 1078
§12.3.4. Deduction of Medical Expenses, §213 1078
§12.3.5. Passive Activity Losses, §469 1079

	§12.3.6.	Miscellaneous Itemized Deductions, §67	1080
	§12.3.7.	Election to Report Accrued Interest as Income, §454	1080
§12.4.	Subchapter S Election, §1362		1081
§12.5.	Partnership Elections, §§754, 732(d)(4)		1082
	§12.5.1.	Extensions to Make Election, Reg. §1.9100	1084
	§12.5.2.	Section 732 Election	1084
	§12.5.3.	Partnership Agreements	1085
§12.6.	Declaration and Payment of Estimated Tax		1086
§12.7.	Selection of a Taxable Year for an Estate or Trust, §441		1087
§12.8.	Waiver of Fees		1090
C.	Estate Tax and Income Tax Deductions		1091
§12.9.	General		1091
§12.10.	Deductions in Respect of a Decedent		1093
§12.11.	Deductions Allowed Only for Estate Tax Purposes		1094
§12.12.	Deductions Allowed Only for Income Tax Purposes		1095
§12.13.	Deductions Allowable Either for Income or Estate Tax Purposes		1096
	§12.13.1.	Miscellaneous Itemized Deductions, §67	1097
	§12.13.2.	Expenses of Sale: Capital Gain Offset or Estate Tax Deduction, §642(g)	1097
	§12.13.3.	Planning Considerations	1098
	§12.13.4.	IRS Access to Attorney's Time Records	1098
	§12.13.5.	Comparative Tax Benefits of Deductions	1098
	§12.13.6.	Community Property Administration Expenses	1100
§12.14.	Equitable Adjustments		1100
D.	Elections Affecting Estate and GST Taxes		1103
§12.15.	Alternate Valuation Method, §2032		1103
	§12.15.1.	Limits on Use of Alternate Method	1104
	§12.15.2.	Income Tax Impact of Using Alternate Method	1104
	§12.15.3.	Property Affected by Alternate Method	1105
	§12.15.4.	Effect on Special Use Valuation	1106

	§12.15.5.	Alternate Valuation Election	1107
	§12.15.6.	Distributed, Sold, Exchanged, or Otherwise Disposed of	1107
	§12.15.7.	Alternate Method and GSTT	1108
§12.16.	Penalties for Incorrect Valuation of Assets on Returns Due Prior to January 1, 1990		1109
		Table 12-1. Penalties for Underpayment of Estate or Gift Tax	*1109*
		Table 12-2. Penalty for Underpayment of Income Tax, Pre-1990	*1110*
§12.17.	Incorrect Valuation of Assets on Estate or Gift Tax Returns Due After 1989, §6662		1111
§12.18.	Avoid Incurring Valuation Penalties		1111
§12.19.	Special Use Valuation, §2032A		1112
	§12.19.1.	Election	1113
	§12.19.2.	Protective Election	1113
	§12.19.3.	Maximum Reduction in Value of Property	1113
	§12.19.4.	Basic Requirements	1114
	§12.19.5.	De Minimis Interests Passing to Nonqualified Heirs	1114
	§12.19.6.	Ownership, Use, and Material Participation	1115
	§12.19.7.	Cropshare Leases	1115
	§12.19.8.	Special Use Valuation Methods	1116
	§12.19.9.	Recapture	1116
	§12.19.10.	Additional Tax	1117
	§12.19.11.	Involuntary Conversion and Like Kind Exchanges	1117
	§12.19.12.	Personal Liability	1118
	§12.19.13.	Special Lien	1118
	§12.19.14.	Practical Concerns	1118
	§12.19.15.	Planning for Special Use Valuation and Marital Deduction	1118
	§12.19.16.	Impact of Special Use Valuation on Other Provisions	1119
§12.20.	Marital Deduction QTIP Election, §2056(b)(7)		1120
	§12.20.1.	Partial Election	1120
	§12.20.2.	Formula Elections	1121
		Form 12-1. Formula QTIP Election	*1122*

	§12.20.3.	Making the QTIP Election	1123
	§12.20.4.	Protective Election	1124
	§12.20.5.	Professional Responsibility	1124
§12.21.	Marital Deduction QDT Election, §2056A		1124
§12.22.	Reverse QTIP Election for GSTT Purposes, §2652(a)(3)		1126
§12.23.	Allocation of GSTT Exemption, §2631(a)		1127
§12.24.	Consent to Split Gifts, §2513		1129
	§12.24.1.	Time of Consent	1129
	§12.24.2.	Revocation of Consent	1130
	§12.24.3.	Deceased Spouse Was Donor	1130
	§12.24.4.	Gifts Not Included in Decedent's Gross Estate	1130
	§12.24.5.	Surviving Spouse Was the Donor	1132
§12.25.	Qualified Plan Benefits		1133
	§12.25.1.	Special Exceptions	1134
	§12.25.2.	Lump Sum Distribution to Surviving Spouse	1134
	§12.25.3.	Income Taxation of Lump Sum Distribution	1135
	§12.25.4.	Five-Year Forward Averaging	1135
§12.26.	Tax on Excess Distributions and Excess Accumulations of Qualified Plans, §4980A		1136
	§12.26.1.	Grandfather Election	1137
	§12.26.2.	Lump Sum Distributions	1137
	§12.26.3.	Excess Accumulations	1138
	§12.26.4.	No Deductions or Credits Allowable	1138
	§12.26.5.	Computation of Tax on Excess Accumulations	1139
§12.27.	Life Insurance Proceeds		1139
E.	Reordering the Distribution of Property		1140
§12.28.	General		1140
§12.29.	Family Awards and Allowances		1141
	§12.29.1.	Estate Tax	1142
	§12.29.2.	Income Tax	1142
§12.30.	Widow's Election		1142
§12.31.	Disclaimers: General		1144
§12.32.	Qualified Disclaimers, §2518		1146
	§12.32.1.	Powers	1146
	§12.32.2.	Disclaimer of Benefit of Tax Clause	1147
	§12.32.3.	Pre-1977 Transfers	1147
	§12.32.4.	Statutory Requirements for Qualified Disclaimers	1147

Form 12-2. Acknowledgment for Receipt of Disclaimer 1148
§12.32.5. Disclaimers Not Recognized by Local Law 1150
§12.33. Disclaimer of Joint Tenancy Interests 1150
§12.33.1. Revocable Transfers 1151
§12.33.2. Property Subject to Partition 1152
§12.34. Disclaimer of Partial Interests 1152
§12.35. Disclaimer Planning 1154
F. Planning Estate Distributions 1156
§12.36. General 1156
§12.36.1. Basic Rule 1157
§12.36.2. Distributable Net Income (DNI) 1158
§12.36.3. Tier System 1158
§12.36.4. Specific Gifts 1159
§12.36.5. Timing of Distributions 1159
§12.36.6. Distributions to Trusts 1160
§12.36.7. In Kind Distributions 1161
§12.37. Distributions That Do Not Carry Out DNI, §663(a)(1) 1161
§12.37.1. Annuities and Similar Payments from Income 1162
§12.37.2. Specifically Devised Real Property 1162
§12.38. Distributions in Kind 1163
§12.39. Non-Pro Rata Distributions 1164
§12.39.1. Fiduciary Duty of Impartiality 1166
§12.39.2. Community Property 1166
§12.40. Trapping Distributions 1168
G. Payment of Estate and GST Taxes 1169
§12.41. Introduction 1169
§12.42. Source of Payment of Estate Tax 1170
§12.42.1. Recovery of Estate Tax from Estate and Beneficiaries, §2205 1170
§12.42.2. Recovery of Estate Tax from Insurance Beneficiaries, §2206 1170
§12.42.3. Recovery of Estate Tax from Property Subject to General Power, §2207 1171
§12.42.4. Recovery of Estate Tax on QTIP, §2207A 1171
§12.42.5 Recovery of Estate Tax on §2036 Property, §2207B 1172

	§12.42.6. Transferee Liability	1173
§12.43.	Extension of Time to File Estate Tax or GSTT Return, §6081	1173
§12.44.	Extension of Time to Pay Estate Tax, §6161	1174
§12.45.	Deferral of Estate Tax on Reversions and Remainders, §6163	1174
§12.46.	Estate Tax Deferred Under Former §6166A	1175
§12.47.	Deferral of Estate and GST Taxes Under §6166	1176
§12.48.	Payment of Estate Tax with "Flower Bonds"	1177
	§12.48.1. Bonds Purchased by an Agent for an Incompetent Principal	1177
	§12.48.2. Income Tax Consequences and Community Property Issues	1179
	§12.48.3. Community Property Planning	1179
	§12.48.4. List of Redeemable Bonds	1180
	§12.48.5. Procedure for Redemption	1180
§12.49.	Release from Liability for Taxes	1180
	§12.49.1. Request for Prompt Determination of Estate Tax, §2204	1181
	§12.49.2. Request for Discharge from Personal Liability for Income and Gift Taxes, §6905	1182
	§12.49.3. Request for Prompt Assessment of Income and Gift Taxes, §6501(d)	1182
§12.50.	Checklist of Post-Mortem Matters	1182

Bibliography 1184

GLOSSARY 1187
TABLE OF CASES 1205
TABLE OF INTERNAL REVENUE CODE SECTIONS 1223
TABLE OF TREASURY REGULATIONS 1243
TABLE OF INTERNAL REVENUE RULINGS 1249
TABLE OF MISCELLANEOUS FEDERAL CITATIONS 1257
TABLE OF STATUTES 1259
INDEX 1269

Table of Forms and Tables

Form 1-1.	Letter to Client Regarding Initial Conference	49
Form 1-2.	Letter to Client After Initial Conference	54
Form 1-3.	Letter to Client Describing Recommended Plan	60
Form 1-4.	Tax Estimates	62
Form 1-5.	Confidential Estate Planning Data Form	78
Form 1-6.	Federal Estate Tax Worksheet	84
Table 2-1.	Increases in Unified Credit and Credit Equivalent	97
Form 4-1.	Table of Contents, John Q. Client Will	257
Form 4-2.	Introduction to Will	259
Form 4-3.	Revocation of Prior Wills	260
Form 4-4.	Family Status and Definitions	263
Form 4-5.	Gift of Specific Item of Personalty	265
Form 4-6.	General Survivorship Requirement	267
Form 4-7.	Cash Gift to Charity	268
Form 4-8.	Gift of Tangible Personal Property	271
Form 4-9.	Gift of Tangible Personal Property by List	273
Form 4-10.	List of Gifts of Tangible Personal Property	276
Form 4-11.	Gift of Corporate Securities	277
Form 4-12.	Gift of Residence, Life Insurance, and Employee Benefits	278
Form 4-13.	Residuary Gift	281
Form 4-14.	Pour-Over to Inter Vivos Trust	287
Form 4-15.	Trust for Descendants	289
Form 4-16.	QTIP Trust	291
Form 4-17.	Trust for Minor Distributees	293
Form 4-18.	Trust Administrative Provisions	294
Form 4-19.	Appointment of Guardian	301
Form 4-20.	Appointment of Executors	302
Form 4-21.	Waiver of Confidentiality by Executor	304

Form 4-22.	Exculpatory Clause	308
Form 4-23.	Payment of Debts, Taxes, and Expenses	309
Form 4-24.	Wills Not Contractual	316
Form 4-25.	Execution Clause	317
Form 4-26.	Attestation Clause	318
Form 4-27.	Letter of Transmittal	321
Form 4-28.	Power to Represent Principal with Respect to Federal Tax Matters	327
Form 4-29.	Power to Make Health Care Decisions	328
Form 4-30.	Power to Make Gifts to Family Members	329
Form 4-31.	Date Power Becomes Effective	331
Form 4-32.	Declarations Under the Uniform Rights of the Terminally Ill Act (1989)	335
Form 4-33.	Uniform Donor Card (Anatomical Gifts)	341
Form 5-1.	Payment of Income to Surviving Spouse (§2056(b)(5) Trust)	390
Form 5-2.	Surviving Spouse's General Testamentary Powers of Appointment (§2056(b)(5) Trust)	390
Form 5-3.	Executor Authorized to Make Partial or Total QTIP Election	403
Form 5-4.	Marital Deduction Savings Clause	410
Form 5-5.	Nonformula Pecuniary Nonmarital Deduction Gift	416
Form 5-6.	Formula Pecuniary Marital Deduction Gift	421
Form 5-7.	Formula Pecuniary Nonmarital Deduction Gift	422
Form 5-8.	Date of Distribution (True Worth) Funding Clause	426
Form 5-9.	Minimum Worth Funding Clause	429
Form 5-10.	Estate Tax Value, Fairly Representative	429
Form 5-11.	Formula Fractional Share Marital Deduction Gift	433
Table 6-1.	Cash Corridor Test of §7702(d)(2)	539
Table 6-2.	Uniform One-Year Term Premiums for $1,000 Life Insurance Protection	568
Table 6-3.	Uniform Premiums for $1,000 of Group-Term Life Insurance Protection	576
Table 7-1.	Statutory Benefits Under §§303, 2032A, and 6166	617
Form 7-1.	Distributive Provisions of §2503(c) Trust	653
Form 7-2.	Limitation of Power of Withdrawal	661
Form 7-3.	Annual Lapse of Hanging Power	662
Form 7-4.	Crummey Power for Trust with One Beneficiary	669

Table of Forms and Tables

Table 9-1.	Applicable Federal Rates	759
Table 9-2.	Applicable Federal Rates for November, 1991	760
Form 10-1.	Reserved Power to Amend or Revoke	872
Form 10-2.	Residuary Clause for Pour-Over Will	875
Table 10-1.	Income Tax Rates Applicable to Trusts and Estates, 1991	886
Table 10-2.	Income Tax Rates Applicable to Trusts and Estates, 1990	887
Form 10-3.	Discretionary Distributions	895
Form 10-4.	Spendthrift Clause	897
Form 10-5.	Special Testamentary Power of Appointment	901
Form 10-6.	5 or 5 Power of Appointment	903
Form 10-7.	Hanging Power of Withdrawal	906
Form 10-8.	Power of Withdrawal Limited by an Ascertainable Standard	908
Form 10-9.	Perpetuities Savings Clause	971
Table 12-1.	Penalties for Underpayment of Estate or Gift Tax	1109
Table 12-2.	Penalties for Underpayment of Income Tax, Pre-1990	1110
Form 12-1.	Formula QTIP Election	1122
Form 12-2.	Acknowledgment for Receipt of Disclaimer	1148

PREFACE

This book is intended primarily for use by estate planning professionals as a resource and reference tool. In large measure it evolved from my book, Contemporary Estate Planning, that was published by Little, Brown and Company in 1983. The current book is longer, includes more forms, and deals more extensively with issues regarding the professional responsibility of estate planners. Each chapter includes a generous number of examples that illustrate the application of the principles being discussed. To some extent the content of the book reflects the suggestions and comments made by the teachers, students, and practicing estate planners who used my 1983 book. It also reflects my further experiences as a lawyer specializing in estate planning and administration in a large law firm and as a teacher of those subjects. Finally, the approach and content of the book expresses my concern that an estate planner provide clients with high quality personal services and comprehensive, fully integrated estate plans (what might be called "holistic" estate planning).

Several features distinguish the present book. First, it gives major consideration to the professional responsibility of lawyers engaged in estate planning. Second, it combines a technical consideration of the tax laws with a practical approach. While the book is not a form book, it contains a relatively large number of forms — ranging from a form of QTIP trust to forms of spendthrift and no contest clauses. Third, the book includes an extensive glossary of terms. Fourth, at appropriate points the text comments on practical issues regarding estate planning and includes suggested forms of letters to clients and worksheets. Finally, because of the migrant character of our population and the growing interest in community property and similar marital property regimes, the text includes discussions of community property considerations.

The book opens in Chapter 1 with an overview of estate planning and professional responsibility and concludes in Chapter 12 with a review of the increasingly important post-mortem phase of estate planning. In between, consideration is given to a wide range of important estate planning problems and techniques, extending from nontax topics, such as the use of durable powers of attorney and living wills, to sophisticated tax devices, such as the private annuity and the charitable remainder trust. Considerable attention is devoted to life insurance, which continues to offer important estate planning opportunities to clients. Constraints of time and space required some difficult decisions to be made regarding scope and coverage. Accordingly, the book does not presently include a separate consideration of two important subjects — premarital and marital dissolution planning and employee benefit plans. Those subjects are mentioned at various points, particularly in connection with professional responsibility and post-mortem planning. The treatment of those subjects will be expanded in forthcoming supplements to the book.

The examples, forms, checklists, and worksheets contained in the text are included for purposes of illustration only. Accordingly, they should, of course, not be used without the assistance of competent counsel. Neither the author nor the publisher makes any representation regarding their legal sufficiency or suitability in connection with the legal affairs of any person.

John R. Price

March 1992

ACKNOWLEDGMENTS

As with my 1983 book, a large and varied group contributed directly or indirectly to the completion of this book. Foremost, as always, were my wife, Suzanne, and our two sons, John and Steven, all of whom were a continual source of love, support, and encouragement. My achievements are also those of my brother, Professor H. Douglas Price, of the Department of Government, Harvard University, who from a very early point in our lives provided important support, affection, and an unmistakable example of high scholarly achievement.

Work on the book benefited greatly from the valuable counsel, assistance, and encouragement of colleagues in teaching at the University of Washington Law School and in practice at Perkins Coie in Seattle. Important help and stimuli were also provided by teachers and practicing estate planners across the country — many of whom badgered me over the years to write another book on estate planning. Of them all, I am particularly grateful to my colleagues at the University of Washington, Ron Hjorth and Jack Huston, and my colleagues at Perkins Coie, Bob Mucklestone, Reg Koehler, Jan Cunningham, Bruce Flynn, and Sandra Blair. I am also very grateful to my secretaries Patty Vye (1982-1989) and Grace King (1989-present) at the University of Washington, and Donna Kavanaugh at Perkins Coie. Patty Vye also played an important role in providing encouragement and support and creatively helping me find time to work on the book during the period I served as dean of the University of Washington School of Law, 1982-1989.

Students in my estate planning classes and seminars also helped in the development and refinement of the book. Their comments while students and following graduation have been useful and reassuring. I am particularly grateful to the research assistants who helped over the years with various portions of the text. Of them I am particularly grateful to Michael Tobiason, Sherri Anderson, and John Creahan.

Throughout the extended period over which the book was being written and prepared for publication, the editors and staff of Little, Brown and Company were most cooperative, encouraging, and patient — particularly the Executive Editor Monte Van Norden. The constructively critical analyses of Developmental Editor Sandy Doherty and her predecessor, Shana Wagger, were very helpful. The book also reflects the important and dedicated work of manuscript editor Bob Caceres and the creativity of design coordinator Kurt Hughes.

Cartoons from The New Yorker appear in Chapters 1 and 10 with the permission of The New Yorker Magazine, Inc. A cartoon from Momma appears in Chapter 4 with the permission of Field Enterprises, Inc. An excerpt in Chapter 5 from Professor Sheldon Kurtz's article, Allocation of Increases and Decreases to Fractional Share Marital Deduction Bequest, 8 Real Prop., Prob. & Tr. J. 450, 460 (1973), is reprinted by permission of the Real Property, Probate and Trust Section of the American Bar Association.

The work on the book was supported over the years by research grants from the University of Washington School of Law.

Citation Form and References

Citation form. Most citations follow widely used and perfectly orthodox forms, but for the sake of brevity some short forms are used. Thus, sections of the Internal Revenue Code of 1986 are referred to by citing the section number alone (*e.g.*, §267). Similarly, references to sections of the Treasury Regulations are made by citing "Reg." followed by the numbers of the sections. Private letter rulings and technical advice memoranda are cited "LR" followed by the documents' seven-digit numbers. Each LR is cited by reference to this number: the first two digits indicate the year of its publication, the next two the week of its publication, and the final three the order of its publication in that week. Thus, LR 9135001 is the first document of the set published in the thirty-fifth week of 1991. Also for brevity and convenience, major tax acts are cited simply by reference to the year of their enactment. Thus, the Tax Reform Act of 1976 is the "1976 Act," the Economic Recovery Tax Act of 1981 is the "1981 Act," the Technical Corrections and Miscellaneous Revenue Act of 1988 is the "1988 Act," and the Revenue Reconciliation Act of 1989 is the "1989 Act." References throughout the text regarding ethical issues are made to the Model Rules of Professional Conduct (MRPC) and to the Code of Professional Responsibility (CPR). (Disciplinary Rules are cited "DR"; Ethical Considerations, "EC.") Throughout the book cases are generally cited only to the most popular or widely available reporter in which they are printed.

Books, periodicals, and loose leaf services. Each chapter includes a bibliography that cites helpful books, articles, and other resource materials. Nonetheless, at this point it may be helpful to mention some of the books, periodicals, and services that are particularly helpful to estate planners. Special mention should also be made of the outstanding estate planning materials that are published by the California Continuing Education of the Bar.

A number of valuable texts and treatises are available that deal with various tax and nontax aspects of estate planning. They include the following, most of which are supplemented annually or more frequently:

T. Atkinson, Wills (2d ed. 1953)
Cal. C.E.B., Estate Planning Practice (1987)
A. J. Casner, Estate Planning (5th ed. 1986)
M. Ferguson, J. Freeland & R. Stephens, Federal Income Taxation of Estates and Beneficiaries (1970)
G. Hazard & W. Hodes, The Law of Lawyering (2d ed. 1990)
E. Hood, S. Kurtz & J. Shors, Closely Held Corporations in Business and Estate Planning (1982)
J. Horn, Planning and Drafting for the Generation-Skipping Transfer Tax (1990)
J. Kasner, Post Mortem Tax Planning (1982)
W. McGovern, S. Kurtz & J. Rein, Wills, Trusts and Estates (1988)
J. Munch, Financial and Estate Planning with Life Insurance Products (1990)
R. Powell, Real Property (rev. ed. 1975)
A. Scott, The Law of Trusts (W. Fratcher 4th ed. 1987)
R. Stephens, G. Maxfield & S. Lind, Federal Estate and Gift Taxation (5th ed. 1983)
C. Teitell, Deferred Giving (1982)
C. Teitell, Charitable Lead Trusts (1983)
C. Wolfram, Modern Legal Ethics (1986)

Papers presented at various tax institutes are also helpful in research and planning. Fortunately, the papers from several major institutes are reprinted each year, including those from the University of Miami's Philip E. Heckerling Institute on Estate Planning, New York University's Institute on Federal Taxation, and the University of Southern California's Tax Institute.

Current developments are discussed and articles of interest to estate planners appear regularly in a number of periodicals, including: Community Property Journal; Estate Planning; Journal of Taxation; Journal of Taxation of Estates and Trusts; Probate and Property; Real Property, Probate and Trust Journal; Tax Lawyer; Tax Advisor; Taxes; Tax Law Review; and Trusts and Estates. In addition, the BNA Tax Management portfolios include a number of very helpful volumes (*e.g.*, W. Streng, Estate Planning, 11-11th, BNA Tax Mgmt. Port. (1990); S. Simmons, Personal Life Insurance Trusts, 210-2nd, BNA Tax Mgmt. Portfolio (1980), and J. Pennell, Estate Tax Marital Deduction, 239-4th, BNA Tax Mgmt. Port. (1990). Finally, the statutes, regulations, rulings, and cases relating to estate and gift tax laws are available in electronic form through Lexis and Westlaw and are compiled in looseleaf services published by Commerce Clearing House and by Maxwell Macmillan, both of which also publish similar compilations of federal income tax laws.

PRICE ON
CONTEMPORARY ESTATE PLANNING

CHAPTER 1

An Overview of Estate Planning and the Elements of Professional Responsibility

A. Introduction

§1.1. Scope
§1.2. Professional Responsibility
    §1.2.1. Professional Ethics: Origin of the Rules
    §1.2.2. Basic Elements of Professional Ethics
§1.3. Malpractice; Obligations to Intended Beneficiaries

B. The Role and Duties of Lawyers in Estate Planning

§1.4. Client Relations
§1.5. Communicate with Clients Effectively and Frequently
§1.6. Be Efficient; Do Not Procrastinate
§1.7. Be Competent; Involve Experts If Required
    §1.7.1. Agreement Regarding Fees of Experts
    §1.7.2. Original Lawyer Retains Overall Direction
    §1.7.3. Lawyer Cannot Retain Referral Fees, Commissions, or Kickbacks
§1.8. Test the Competence of Clients and Make House Calls
    §1.8.1. Traditional Test for Testamentary Competence
    §1.8.2. Options Where Competence Is Doubtful
    §1.8.3. Help the Client Avoid Critical Decisions During Emotional Upset
§1.9. Be More Than a Mere Scrivener: Counsel Client Regarding Impact of Actions
§1.10. Put It in Writing

§1.10.1. Client Data Summary
§1.10.2. Client Document Summary
§1.11. Train and Supervise Subordinates
§1.12. Beware of Multijurisdictional Problems
§1.13. Legal Ethics and Taxes

C. Conflicts of Interest

§1.14. Representation of Multiple Parties
§1.14.1. Intergenerational Estate Planning
§1.14.2. Husband and Wife or Parties Contemplating Marriage or Cohabitation
§1.14.3. Lawyer as Intermediary
§1.14.4. Imputed Disqualification of Partners and Associates
§1.15. Do Not Subordinate the Client's Interests
§1.16. Do Not Accept Gifts from Clients Who Are Nonrelatives
§1.17. Do Not Enter into Any Business Transactions with a Client
§1.18. Scrivener Should Be Wary of Accepting Appointment as Fiduciary

D. Lawyer's Fees

§1.19. Discussions with the Client
§1.20. Determining the Amount for Lifetime Services
§1.21. Who Pays the Lawyer's Fee
§1.22. Determining the Amount for Estate Administration Services
§1.23. Avoid Bequest in Satisfaction of Lawyer's Fee
§1.24. Income Tax Deductibility of Lifetime Estate Planning Fee
§1.25. Deductibility of Post-Mortem Estate Planning Fee

E. Inter Vivos Estate Planning

§1.26. Introduction
§1.27. Stages of Inter Vivos Estate Planning
§1.28. Getting the Facts
§1.29. Initial Letter to the Client
Form 1-1. Letter to Client Regarding Initial Conference
§1.30. Initial Interview with the Client
§1.30.1. Getting Off to a Good Start
§1.30.2. Office Arrangement
§1.30.3. Encouraging Communication
§1.30.4. Learning the Client's Objectives
§1.30.5. Examining Documents

§1.30.6. Engagement Letter
Form 1-2. Letter to Client After Initial Conference
§1.30.7. Associating Others
§1.31. Helping the Client Choose a Plan
§1.31.1. Valuation of Assets
§1.31.2. Tax Estimates
§1.31.3. Record of Advice to Client
§1.32. Letter Describing Plan; Tax Estimates
Form 1-3. Letter to Client Describing Recommended Plan
Form 1-4. Tax Estimates
§1.33. Producing the Documents
§1.33.1. Develop and Use Estate Planning Forms
§1.33.2. Establishing a Timetable
§1.33.3. Transmitting Drafts to the Clients
Chart 1-1. Disposition of Husband's Estate
§1.33.4. Advanced Technology; Security Problems; Sources of Information
§1.34. Implementing the Plan
§1.34.1. Follow-up Instructions and Subsequent Services
§1.34.2. Subsequent Communications; Ethical Considerations

F. Post-Mortem Planning

§1.35. Post-Mortem Estate Planning
§1.36. Lawyer's Relationship to Personal Representative and Beneficiaries
§1.37. Lawyer Must Avoid Personal Transactions with Estate or Beneficiaries
§1.38. Cash Projection and Tax Planning
§1.39. Tax Returns and Malpractice
§1.40. Closing the Estate
Form 1-5. Confidential Estate Planning Data Form
Form 1-6. Federal Estate Tax Worksheet

Bibliography

> Estate planning is not susceptible of precise definition; it is as broad as the human imagination. It involves the use and arrangement of property for and among the members of a family group under a planned design affording the greatest enjoyment to the whole group commensurate with sufficient conservation. It is still one of the privileges of this Republic. J. Farr & J. Wright, An Estate Planner's Handbook 1 (4th ed. 1979).

A. INTRODUCTION

§1.1. Scope

Estate planning challenges the lawyer to counsel clients wisely regarding the effective and economical organization and disposition of their wealth. In order to do so properly the lawyer must combine interviewing and counselling skills with technical legal expertise in ways that fulfill the lawyer's professional responsibility. As counselor the lawyer must learn about the client's circumstances and goals, which usually focus on providing for the client's family, and educate the client about the various ways of carrying out the client's goals. Estate planning already encompasses a wide range of specialties. However, in the future the estate planning lawyer may assume a greater responsibility for advising clients regarding financial planning and management. Thus far few lawyers have sought to provide financial planning services to their clients — in effect, abandoning the field of financial planning to other advisors.

This chapter provides an overview of the professional responsibility of lawyers in estate planning and discusses the various phases of inter vivos and post-mortem estate planning. Along the way it suggests how to establish and maintain successful relations with clients. It also includes samples of some letters and other documents that might be sent to clients during various phases of the estate planning process. This chapter includes a relatively comprehensive discussion of professional responsibility. Having established that base, throughout the remainder of the book issues of professional responsibility are discussed

"And please protect me from the appearance of wrongdoing."
Drawing by Lorenz; ©1982 The New Yorker Magazine, Inc.

as another facet of the particular subject under consideration. Such a "pervasive" approach is suggested by the ubiquitousness of professional responsibility problems.

§1.2. Professional Responsibility

Professional responsibility encompasses two overlapping areas that are often treated as entirely separate: professional ethics and standards of professional performance (malpractice). Rules of professional ethics, which vary somewhat from state to state, establish the standards that govern the conduct of lawyers among themselves and toward clients, the courts and administrative agencies, and the public. A violation of professional ethics may result in disciplinary action or a reduction by the court in the amount of the fee requested by the lawyer for representing a fiduciary. Violation of the professional ethical standards may be referred to in a malpractice action, but a violation does not give rise to an independent cause of action. The second area is malpractice — the liability of lawyers to clients or to others for failures to exercise the requisite degree of professional skill. In some cases the same conduct may violate the ethical standards of the profession and result in malpractice liability. For example, a lawyer's failure to draft a will properly may at once violate the lawyer's fundamental ethical duty of competence and constitute actionable malpractice. In short, the lawyer must *both* be aware of the ethical demands of an estate planning practice and alert to avoid acts of professional malpractice.

§1.2.1. Professional Ethics: Origin of Rules

Most states adopted the ethical rules contained in the Model Code of Professional Responsibility (CPR) that was adopted by the American Bar Association (ABA) in 1969. The CPR consists of three related parts: Nine Canons, which are very general "statements of axiomatic norms"; Ethical Considerations (ECs), which are aspirational in nature; and Disciplinary Rules (DRs), which are mandatory in character. According to the Preamble and Preliminary Statement, the Disciplinary Rules "state the minimum level of conduct below which no lawyer can fall without being subject to disciplinary action."

Many states now have adopted the Model Rules of Professional Conduct (MRPC), which were approved by the ABA in 1983. The MRPC consists of blackletter rules with explanatory comments that are intended to assist in the interpretation and application of the rules. The comments are not intended to impose any additional rules.

§1.2.2. Basic Elements of Professional Ethics

The Preamble to the MRPC summarizes the principal functions of the lawyer and the rules that apply in the discharge of the lawyer's responsibilities. The following passage from the Preamble touches on several of the lawyer's most important duties, which are also critical to maintaining successful client relations — being competent, exercising diligence (*i.e.,* avoiding procrastination), maintaining effective communications, and preserving the confidences of clients:

> In all professional functions a lawyer should be competent, prompt and diligent. A lawyer should maintain communications with a client concerning the representation. A lawyer should keep in confidence information relating to representation of a client except so far as disclosure is required or permitted by the Rules of Professional Conduct or other law.

Among other duties, a lawyer must also avoid conflicts of interest and charge fees that are reasonable.

§1.3. Malpractice; Obligations to Intended Beneficiaries

The advent of new forms of property, the burgeoning importance of will substitutes, and the growing complexity of the income and transfer tax laws have broadened the scope of estate planning to include much more than the preparation of a will. An appropriate estate plan for a client may now involve a variety of documents including a will, a revocable or irrevocable trust, a durable power of attorney, a directive to physicians (or "living will"), and an instrument of transfer under the Uniform Anatomical Gifts Act. A plan may also call for creating or terminating cotenancies, making gifts outright or in trust, changing beneficiary designations of life insurance policies or employee benefit plans, acquiring new life insurance policies or transferring old ones, and changing investments or the form of a business enterprise. Accordingly, the lawyer must be competent in a number of important areas of substantive and tax law.

If a gift in a will or trust fails for some reason, the disappointed beneficiary may bring a malpractice action against the lawyer for the deceased client. Such actions fail in some states because of the lack of privity between the beneficiary and the lawyer. *E.g., Copenhaver v. Rogers,* 384 S.E.2d 593 (Va. 1989); *Elam v. Hyatt Legal Services,* 541 N.E.2d 616 (Ohio 1989) (finding plaintiff met Ohio's curious requirement that there be privity between the deceased client and intended beneficiary); *St. Mary's Church of Schuyler v. Tomek,* 325 N.E.2d 164 (Neb. 1982). However, the imposition of a privity requirement is considered by many courts and commentators to have been erroneously borrowed from contract law. Indeed, courts in several states have seriously eroded or eliminated it. In addition, actions rarely fail because of the statute of limitations: It usually does not begin to run until the death of the client, when the injury to the beneficiary becomes unavoidable.

Privity has generally been abandoned in favor of a multipart test drawn from a California Supreme Court decision involving a malpractice action against a notary public who prepared and supervised the unwitnessed execution of the decedent's will. *Biakanja v. Irving,* 320 P.2d 16 (Cal. 1958). The test, as it has evolved, balances the need to protect the intended beneficiaries against the need to protect lawyers and the courts from too much litigation. In *Biakanja,* the elements of the test were described as follows:

> The determination of whether in a specific case the defendant will be held liable to a third person not in privity is a matter of policy and involves the balancing of various factors, among which are the extent to which the transaction was intended to affect the plaintiff, the foreseeability of harm to him, the degree of certainty that the plaintiff suffered injury, the closeness of the connection between the defendant's conduct and the injury suffered, the moral blame attached to the defendant's conduct and the injury suffered, and the policy of preventing future harm. Id. at 19.

Later cases in California and other jurisdictions have varied the elements somewhat, sometimes omitting reference to the moral blame associated with the defendant's conduct. *See, e.g., Lucas v. Hamm,* 364 P.2d 685 (Cal. 1961), *cert. denied,* 368 U.S. 987 (1962). In states adopting the California approach, an action may be maintained by an intended beneficiary against a lawyer whose negligence caused the intended beneficiary to suffer an economic loss. *See, e.g., Auric v. Continental Casualty Co.,* 331 N.W.2d 325 (Wis. 1983) (will improperly witnessed); *Arnold v. Carmichael,* 524 So. 2d 464 (Fla. App. 1988) (lawyer omitted residuary clause from revised will); *Ross v. Caunters,* [1979] 3 All E.R. 580 (will witnessed by spouse of beneficiary).

A few states have retained privity, but have adopted a third-party beneficiary exception to the privity requirement. "In general terms, a third party beneficiary contract arises when two parties enter into an agreement with the intent to confer a benefit on a third party, allowing the third party to sue on the contract despite the lack of privity. Several jurisdictions, including Illinois and Pennsylvania, have adopted this particular approach." *Flaherty v. Weinberg,* 492 A.2d 618, 622 (Md. 1985). A similar result was reached in Oregon. *Hale v. Croce,* 744 P.2d 1289 (Or. 1987) (lawyer omitted $300,000 gift from new will and trust for client). Virginia has made it very difficult for a disappointed beneficiary to bring a third-party beneficiary claim. *Copenhaver v. Rogers,* 384 S.E.2d 593 (Va. 1989).

B. THE ROLE AND DUTIES OF LAWYERS IN ESTATE PLANNING

§1.4. Client Relations

The technically proficient work of a lawyer may be unappreciated or underappreciated by a client unless attention is also paid to the client's personal feelings and concerns. Adherence to simple rules of courtesy, consideration, and confidentiality provides a good starting point in dealing with clients and helps the lawyer avoid the most common failures in lawyer-client relations. Lawyers should also communicate effectively, be prompt, and avoid condescension.

A lawyer must also be aware of the psychological dimensions of estate planning. Clients are often fearful of lawyers, reluctant to face their own mortality, and anxious about the cost of the lawyer's services. They are typically asked to make a complete disclosure of personal and financial information that is often not discussed in the same detail with anyone else, including members of their families. In addition, clients may be asked to confront and deal with difficult subjects and relationships. For example, a husband and wife must decide the extent to which property will pass to the survivor of them and whether it will pass outright or in trust. Similarly, the clients must decide whether his, her, or their children will all be treated equally. Particularly when one or both spouses have children by prior marriages, the extent to which the surviving spouse will be free to dispose of their property is a matter of serious concern. *See Oursler v. Armstrong,* 179 N.E.2d 489 (N.Y. 1961) (surviving spouse of author Fulton Oursler not contractually obligated to leave to his children any of the property she received from him).

Perhaps more than other areas of practice, estate planning calls upon the lawyer to provide personal services that meet the needs of the whole client. The nature of the services requires the lawyer to recognize and respect the individuality of each client. Clients deserve individual attention — they are not inanimate objects being processed on an assembly line. The lawyer may have dozens of clients, but the client probably has only one lawyer, who may be the first lawyer the client has ever consulted professionally.

§1.5. Communicate with Clients Effectively and Frequently

> A more effective communications process between estate planners and their clients would result in more informed decision making by the owners of wealth and written documents which more accurately reflect the transferor's wishes. Schwartz, Whose Wealth Is It Anyway: Impediments to the Realization of an Owner's Plan of Disposition, 25 Ariz. L. Rev. 671, 686 (1983).

In the estate planning process the lawyer should focus on the disposition the client wishes to make of his or her property. Accordingly, it is most appropriate to learn the client's wishes first without encumbering the discussion with technical tax considerations. An exploration of the client's wishes normally evolves into one that touches on the devices that are available to carry out those wishes. As counselor the lawyer has a role to play in helping the client decide how to dispose of his or her property, but the client is the one who is ultimately responsible for making the decision. Thus, as the comments to MRPC 1.2 state, "The client has ultimate authority to determine the purposes to be served by legal representation, within the limits imposed by law and the lawyer's professional obligations."

The lawyer sometimes plays a valuable role in helping the client decide whether or not to make the same provision for each of the client's children. *See* §1.9. Differences in the circumstances of the children may justify leaving one child more than another or leaving one child an outright gift while placing the share of another child in trust. For example, one child may be a professional with a high income while another is a less well-compensated single parent. Also, illness or disability may cause some children to have greater or different needs. A Wyoming practitioner has noted the risks that arise when all children do not receive equal shares: "Since Biblical times parents have often chosen one child over another as the object of their bounty. Quite predictably parental favoritism can lead to extreme jealousy among siblings, and the potential for a will contest may not be as obvious to the parent as it is to the attorney." Warnick, The Ungrateful Living: An Estate Planner's Nightmare, the Trial Lawyer's Dream, 24 Land & Water L. Rev. 401, 411 (1989). In some circumstances, the potential for discord is reduced or eliminated if the client discusses the subject fully with the children. However, many clients do not wish to discuss death or the disposition of their property with their families. Some reasons militate against doing so: The discussion may precipitate disagreement and ill feelings, or the client's plans may change. In some cases a family discussion promotes family understanding and solid support for the parent's plan. How to proceed in any given case is highly fact-specific — it is impossible to articulate general rules about how to proceed.

The need for timely and effective communication with a client is emphasized by MRPC 1.4:

> (a) A lawyer shall keep a client reasonably informed about the status of a matter and promptly comply with reasonable requests for information.
>
> (b) A lawyer shall explain a matter to the extent reasonably necessary to permit the client to make informed decisions regarding the representation.

MRPC 1.4 can be viewed as requiring sufficient communication to allow a client to make informed judgments regarding estate planning. Indeed, some academicians have suggested that a failure to inform clients sufficiently should be actionable. *See, e.g.,* Andersen, Informed Decisionmaking in an Office Practice, 28 B.C. L. Rev. 225 (1987).

The task of providing a client with sufficient information regarding complex legal matters may be made simpler if the client is provided with examples and, perhaps, a written explanation of the devices and techniques under consideration. Some firms provide written explanations for this purpose and some have prepared videotapes. A clearly written pamphlet of reasonable length that provides the client with basic information about estate planning can make the inter vivos estate planning process more efficient and economical. However, regardless of the economic pressures, the lawyer must allow adequate time for counseling the client.

Throughout the representation courtesy, consideration, and professional ethics require a lawyer to keep a client informed regarding the status of a matter. Communication is particularly necessary if the lawyer will be unable to meet the established schedule for completion of the work.

Neither the MRPC nor its comments indicate the extent to which the lawyer for a fiduciary should communicate directly with the beneficiaries of the trust or estate, who are generally not clients of the lawyer. Some communication with them is necessary; more may be desirable. However, in communicating with the beneficiaries the lawyer for the fiduciary should point out that he or she does not represent them — at least not directly. In order to protect their interests adequately the beneficiaries may need to obtain independent representation.

§1.6. Be Efficient; Do Not Procrastinate

A lawyer should work with the client at the outset to establish a realistic timetable for the submission of draft documents to the client and the ultimate completion of the work. Delay in performing estate planning services is inefficient and irritates clients. Extended intervals between the times a client's file is worked on requires the lawyer to spend time reviewing the file before resuming work. Efficiency is increased by working on drafts as soon as practicable after the conference at which the lawyer and client agree upon a plan. *See* §1.33. In order to maintain an efficient pace the client should be encouraged to review and respond to the drafts promptly.

In extreme cases, delays may result in disciplinary or malpractice actions or both. For example, in *Colorado v. James,* 502 P.2d 289 (Colo. 1972), a lawyer who had been previously disciplined for derelictions of duties to clients was disbarred for "failure to prepare a will for at least eight months after [being] employed to do so" by an aged and infirm client. The court stated that the lawyer "was grossly negligent and showed a total lack of responsibility."

In addition, an intended beneficiary who suffers a loss because the lawyer failed to prepare a will or trust for a client within a reasonable time may bring a malpractice action against the lawyer. Of course, in some jurisdictions such an action would be dismissed for lack of privity between the lawyer and the intended beneficiary. *Krawczyk v. Stingle,* 543 A.2d 733 (Conn. 1988) (attorney's negligent failure to arrange for timely execution of estate planning documents does not allow intended beneficiaries to pursue a cause of action for legal malpractice); *Victor v. Goldman,* 74 Misc. 2d 685, 344 N.Y.S.2d 672 (N.Y. Sup. Ct. 1973).

Timely performance (and billing) by the lawyer is more efficient and more remunerative. It is also required by MRPC 1.3, which states:

> A lawyer shall act with reasonable diligence and promptness in representing a client.

The seriousness of the problem is indicated by the comment that accompanies MRPC 1.3:

> Perhaps no professional shortcoming is more widely resented than procrastination. . . . Even when the client's interests are not affected in substance, however, unreasonable delay can cause a client needless anxiety and undermine confidence in the lawyer's trustworthiness.

A study of the 285 decisions of court approved disciplinary decisions in California from June 1988 through June 1989 indicated that 46 percent of the cases involved "a failure to perform for or communicate with clients." Evans, Lawyers at Risk, 9 Cal. St. B.J. 45 (Oct. 1989).

§1.7. Be Competent: Involve Experts If Required

The CPR and the MRPC both require the lawyer to represent a client competently. DR 6-101; MRPC 1.1. The requirement is stated concisely in MRPC 1.1: "A lawyer shall provide competent representation to a client. Competent representation requires the legal knowledge, skill, thoroughness and preparation reasonably necessary for the representation." On the malpractice side, *Horne v. Peckham,* 158 Cal. Rptr. 714 (Cal. Ct. App. 1979), concerned an action involving the liability of a general practitioner for damages resulting from the ineffectiveness of a short-term reversionary trust to relieve the grantor from the income tax liability for patent license payments made to the trustee by a corporation controlled by the grantor. The California Court of Appeal upheld a jury instruction that stated,

> It is the duty of an attorney who is a general practitioner to refer his client to a specialist or recommend the assistance of a specialist if under the circumstances a reasonably careful and skillful practitioner would do so.

It upheld a judgment of almost $65,000 against the lawyer-draftsman for legal malpractice in connection with the preparation of the trust instrument. Comment, General Practitioners Beware: The Duty to Refer An Estate Planning Client to a Specialist, 14 Cum. L. Rev. 103 (1983).

A number of options are open to a lawyer who lacks the competence to handle a matter. First, the lawyer may refer the client to an expert. Of course, a lawyer who is concerned about the long-term retention of the client may be reluctant to make such a referral. Second, the lawyer may ask the client to approve associating an expert. The client's approval is required because the association will almost inevitably involve disclosure of confidential information regarding the client. Third, the lawyer may, at his or her own expense, retain a consultant. Problems of confidentiality are avoided if the consultant is only provided with "sanitized" documents that do not disclose the identity of the client. A lawyer should not be reluctant to recommend the association of insurance advisors, accountants, trust officers, or others whose expertise may assist the client.

Lawyers who wish to minimize the risk of losing a client may ask another lawyer to serve as a consultant for the limited purpose of reviewing the will or other documents that are prepared for the client. In order to preserve confidentiality all names must be deleted from the document. The consultant is at a disadvantage in such a case to the extent the relevant facts are not all disclosed to him or her.

§1.7.1. Agreement Regarding Fees of Experts

In considering the association of an expert, the lawyer and client must take into account the cost involved and the billing and payment procedures that will be followed. The expert will often prefer to bill and be paid promptly by the lawyer. In any case, the lawyer and client should agree regarding the payment of the expert's fee. The retention of the expert and the amount and method of payment of his or her fee should be confirmed in writing with a copy to the client.

> A client is not bound to pay for the services of an assisting attorney whom he did not employ unless he has authorized the employment or consented to it in some binding fashion. *Estate of Anderson v. Smith,* 316 N.E.2d 592, 594 (Ind. App. 1974).

§1.7.2. Original Lawyer Retains Overall Direction

In most cases the original lawyer should exercise overall supervision of the estate planning process even though other lawyers are associated (or serve as consultants) or advisors from other disciplines become involved. If the client has been referred to another lawyer, the responsibility of the original lawyer may be greatly reduced or entirely eliminated: Still, the original lawyer should oversee the formulation and execution of the estate plan because of its predominantly legal nature and because the original lawyer is generally free of the self-interest that may affect the judgment of other members of the estate planning team. Retention of the overall control of the process is appropriate also because of the probability that he or she will be liable for doing so in any case.

§1.7.3. Lawyer Cannot Retain Referral Fees, Commission, or Kickbacks

Without the full knowledge and consent of a client, the lawyer may not accept or retain any referral fee, commission, rebate, or discount from anyone on account of his or her dealings with the client. DR 5-107(A). The client is entitled to the benefit of any commission, rebate, or discount that is paid to the lawyer. *See, e.g.,* N.Y. Bar Assn., Formal Ethics Op. 107 (1969); N.Y. Bar Assn., Formal Ethics Op. 107(a) (1970). The same conclusion was reached in San Diego County Bar Assn., Ethics Op. 1989-2, which held it improper for a lawyer to seek a referral fee in exchange for engaging a real estate broker to sell property of a decedent's estate: "In the situation presented the lawyer may be more concerned about recovering an attractive referral fee than obtaining the most competent broker and highest price for the property. The demand, therefore, is unacceptable."

§1.8. Test the Competence of Clients and Make House Calls

Before proceeding with an estate planning matter the lawyer should be satisfied that the client is competent and not acting under duress or a discoverable form of undue influence. Particular care must be exercised if the representation is initially arranged by a person other than the client, especially when the client is aged, ill, or of diminished capacity. *See* C. P. Snow, In Their Wisdom (1974). If a lawyer drafts a will for one client that significantly benefits another client, a presumption of undue influence may arise. *E.g., Haynes v. First National Bank,* 432 A.2d 890 (N.J. 1981). In any case, the lawyer should personally interview the client out of the presence of the person who initiated contact. The duties owed to such a client were summarized as follows:

> I would suggest that in this day of speedy methods of transportation there should be no occasion when a solicitor should prepare a will without receiving his instructions from the testator. It is certainly improper for the solicitor to draft a will without taking direct instructions from the testator and then not to attend personally when the will is executed. For example, a son of an old client might come to the solicitor's office and advise that his father, a widower, is in hospital and wants a will leaving his whole estate equally among his children. In such circumstances, the solicitor might properly, for convenience, engross such a will and attend on the testator, but should — under no circumstances — say to the testator: "I understand you want a will leaving your property thus and so and I have drawn such a will. Is this satisfactory?" This, especially with older people, is a dangerous practice and the solicitor should, on attending the testator, say: "I understand you want a will drawn and will you tell me how you wish your estate to go on your death." The asking of leading questions by a solicitor obtaining instructions from an elderly testator is a practice to be avoided. Too often the elderly person, if asked leading questions, will reply in the affirmative, but if simply asked "What property do you have?" or "How do you wish your estate to go on your death?" may exhibit complete lack of comprehension. *Re Worrell,* 8 D.L.R.3d 36, 42-43 (Ont. Surr. Ct. 1969).

Serious conflicts of interest may arise when a lawyer is asked by a child to prepare estate planning documents for an elderly parent. For example, a Wisconsin lawyer was disciplined in two matters in which he was retained by an adult child to prepare estate planning documents on behalf of an aged parent. *In re Disciplinary Proceedings Against John W. Strasburg,* 452 N.W.2d 152 (Wis. 1990). In both instances he performed the services the child requested but charged the parent without the client's consent. He was found to have charged excessive fees, represented conflicting interests without complete disclosure and client consent, and failed to communicate in a timely fashion with the client. The court described the lawyer's conduct with respect to one of the clients as follows:

> Even though all of the documents he prepared directly affected the woman's interests, Attorney Strasburg never spoke to or met with her concerning the effect of those documents. Moreover, he never sought or obtained the woman's consent to act on matters directly affecting her and never sought to explain to her the effect of an irrevocable and complete divestiture of her assets, which amounted to approximately $100,000. His stated reason for not doing so was that he did not make "house calls." Id. at 154.

§1.8.1. Traditional Test for Testamentary Competence

In the case of a disabled client or a "deathbed" will, the lawyer should use the meetings with the client to test for the presence of at least the minimum degree of competence required for the execution of a will. Most statutes, including the Uniform Probate Code, allow a will to be made by "any person 18 years of age or older who is of sound mind." U.P.C. §2-501, 8 U.L.A. 102 (1983). The typical test of testamentary capacity requires the testator to understand "(1) The nature and extent of his property, (2) The persons who are the natural objects of his bounty, and (3) The disposition which he is making of his property." T. Atkinson, Wills §51 (2d ed. 1953); McGovern, Kurtz & Rein, Wills, Trusts and Estates 274 (1988). Discussions with doctors, nurses, family members, and friends may provide additional useful information regarding the testator's mental condition. As a precautionary measure the lawyer may take statements from some of them regarding the testator's condition and use more witnesses than necessary when the will is executed. In order to establish the competency of the testator and the proper execution of the will, a videotape may be made of an interview of the testator and the execution of the will. While such a videotape is not a will, it may be admissible if the validity of the will is contested. *Estate of Reed,* 672 P.2d 829 (Wyo. 1983).

If the lawyer concludes that the client lacks the necessary testamentary capacity, some commentators believe that the lawyer must refuse to draw the will. H. Drinker, Legal Ethics 93 (1953). Others point out that if the lawyer refuses to draw a will for a marginally competent client, the lawyer inappropriately deprives the client of having a court determine the client's competency and the validity of the will. Of course, if a will is drawn for the client of uncertain competency, there is no assurance that the validity of the instrument will ever be considered by a court. After the client has died, it would be unusual, and perhaps inappropriate, for the scrivener to inform interested parties of the testator's uncertain competency. In *Morgan v. Roller,* 794 P.2d 1313 (Wash. App. 1990), the court held that a lawyer did not have a duty to disclose his views of a client's disability to the client's intended beneficiaries.

> Certainly the benefit of all doubt should be given to the client and the determination of the fact left to the courts. In most such situations there is sufficient doubt to justify drafting the will. But where the lawyer is convinced that the client lacks the capacity he should not assume responsibility for preparing the will. To do so would give false assurance to the client and would be apt to cause litigation that might otherwise not occur. Miller, Functions & Ethical Problems of the Lawyer in Drafting a Will, 1950 U. Ill. L. Rev. 415, 426.

A liberal approach is also encouraged by MRPC 1.14(a): "When a client's ability to make adequately considered decisions in connection with the representation is impaired, whether because of minority, mental disability or for some other reason, the lawyer shall, as far as reasonably possible, maintain a normal client-lawyer relationship with the client."

If the client is incompetent the lawyer should assist in protecting the client's interests. Thus, MRPC 1.14 indicates that the lawyer may act on the client's behalf to obtain the appointment of a conservator or guardian. *See* §1.8.2. The matter is delicate and requires the lawyer to avoid the conflicts of interest that may easily arise.

§1.8.2. Options Where Competence Is Doubtful

In cases where there is some doubt regarding a client's competence, the lawyer should retain, or advise the client to retain, previously executed wills. If a new will is executed, special care may be taken to preserve evidence regarding the client's competence and the execution ceremony. *See* §4.32. In a few states the validity of a will may be determined during the testator's lifetime. In particular, Arkansas, North Dakota, and Ohio provide for the ante-mortem probate of wills. In the absence of such a binding determination, the lawyer should preserve the prior will or wills of a client who may lack testamentary capacity.

Under MRPC 1.14, a lawyer may seek the appointment of a guardian in order to protect the interests of a client if it is reasonably believed that the client cannot act adequately in his own interests. In contrast, California Formal Ethics Opinion 1989-112 concluded that the lawyer's duty of confidentiality precludes the lawyer from instituting conservatorship proceedings to protect the interests of a client:

> By instituting conservatorship proceedings, the attorney will not only be disclosing such client secrets to the court, but also to any necessary third parties (including family members) called upon to act in the conservatorship role. An attorney is absolutely prohibited from divulging the client's secrets gained during the attorney-client relationship, and from acting in any manner whereby the attorney is forced to use such secrets to the client's disadvantage. (*Stockton Theatres v. Palermo,* [264 P.2d 72 (Cal. App. 1953)].) The Committee thus concludes that the attorney may not divulge what the attorney has observed of the client's behavior.

The MRPC position is preferable to the exceptionally narrow California view, which exalts maintaining absolute confidentiality over serving the actual interests of the client. California law, as reflected in Opinion 1989-112, unnecessarily prohibits a lawyer from acting reasonably to protect the interests of a client. In this connection note that the opinion assumes that disclosure of information regarding the client's condition would be to the client's disadvantage.

§1.8.3. Help Client Avoid Critical Decisions During Emotional Upset

The lawyer should also discourage a client from making decisions regarding the disposition of property when the client is emotionally distraught or may be suffering from an "insane delusion." For example, a bereaved widow or widower should defer making large gifts or establishing irrevocable trusts. Here some procrastination may be justified: The lawyer may delay the preparation and execution of a new will or other dispositive documents until the client has had a chance to think things over and there has been an opportunity to reason with the client. An alert lawyer may be able to dissuade the client from taking unwise action. As the comments to MRPC 1.4 recognize, "In some circumstances, a lawyer may be justified in delaying transmission of information when the client would be likely to react imprudently to an immediate communication. Thus, a lawyer might withhold a psychiatric diagnosis of a client when the examining psychiatrist indicates that disclosure would harm the client."

§1.9. Be More than a Mere Scrivener: Counsel the Client Regarding Impact of Actions

Both the CPR and the MRPC encourage lawyers to counsel clients regarding the consequences of their actions. EC 7-8 states that it is often "desirable for a lawyer to point out those factors which may lead to a decision that is morally just as well as legally permissible. He may emphasize the possibility of harsh consequences that might result from assertion of legally permissible positions." MRPC 2.1 is similarly explicit: "In representing a client, a lawyer shall exercise independent professional judgment and render candid advice. In rendering advice, a lawyer may refer not only to law but to other considerations such as moral, economic, social and political factors, that may be relevant to the client's situation."

As mentioned in §1.5, the lawyer may help the client reach a conclusion regarding the manner in which the client's children will share in the client's estate. Economic success, educational considerations, domestic instability, and physical or mental disabilities are among the factors that may motivate a client not to provide for each child in the same way. Indeed, some children may suggest to their parents that they receive smaller shares than other children who have greater needs. Neither the lawyer nor the client should underestimate the hurt that may be felt by a child who unexpectedly receives a smaller share than a sibling or siblings. If unequal provision is to be made, the client should consider discussing it in advance with the children. Likewise, if a client plans to make a major lifetime or testamentary charitable gift, family understanding may be promoted if the client first discusses the plan with his or her children: As the "natural objects" of the client's bounty, they are the ones who are most likely to be surprised and hurt. By discussing the matter openly and perhaps making the charitable gift in the name of the entire family the client may avoid a will contest and family strife.

If the client insists that the lawyer help with a plan that is unjust, unwise, or vulnerable to being set aside, the lawyer is faced with a difficult choice: "Shall I assist my client in carrying out an unwise plan, or refuse to participate and probably lose the client?" The ethical rules do not provide a clear answer to the question. The response of any given lawyer will be colored by the lawyer's concept of morality, the lawyer's perception of the duties owed to a client, the nature of the plan, and the lawyer's own economic security. From an economic perspective, it is easier for a prosperous lawyer to refuse a client than it is for a new, financially insecure lawyer to do so. Hopefully even a financially insecure lawyer will have high enough standards to refuse a client rather than to help the client use the law to achieve questionable goals. Edmond Cahn, the late legal philosopher, wrote enthusiastically of the lawyer's exhilaration in refusing to represent a client who has asked the lawyer to do something wrong. Cahn, Introduction to Ethical Problems of Tax Practitioners, in Professional Responsibility in Tax Practice 15-16 (B. Bittker, ed., 1970).

§1.10. Put It in Writing

The initial agreement with the client regarding the services to be performed and other important communication should be written. An engagement letter may be useful to express the scope of the representation, the method of determining fees, and appropriate concerns about representing multiple clients. Advice regarding tax consequences and alternate methods of achieving the client's goals should also be provided in written form. A form of engagement letter that may be adapted for this purpose appears in §1.30.6. Finally, when the estate planning work has been completed, it may be useful to send the client an "exit" draft letter that describes the services performed, potential tax savings, and the services to be provided in the future, if any.

§1.10.1. Client Data Summary

A lawyer may find it helpful to maintain a summary form in each client file on which to record pertinent data about a client and the client's estate plan, including any estimate of fees that the lawyer may make. A comprehensive form of checklist that is suitable for this purpose is included in Francis Collin's article, A Post-Interview Estate Planning Checklist, 2 Prob. & Prop. 58 (Mar.–Apr. 1988). Ready access to such a form enables the lawyer to respond more rapidly and intelligently to telephone calls or unexpected visits from clients. A short summary of the client's family circumstances, property holdings, and estate plan can help the lawyer's recollection and save time that otherwise might be spent reviewing the complete documents in the file. Recording the estimated amount of the lawyer's fee may also help avoid the embarrassment of sending the client a statement that is not consistent with the estimate. Ideally, the lawyer could quickly call up such a client data summary on a computer terminal on the lawyer's desk.

§1.10.2. Client Document Summary

It is also important to keep, in a readily retrievable form, a summary of the salient features of the estate planning documents executed by a client. Data regarding the client's will would include, for example, the type of marital deduction gift used, directions regarding funding, and the identity of the trustee. Comparable data would be recorded, for example, regarding charitable gifts. By recording and maintaining such data in an electronically retrievable form the lawyer will be able to identify the clients affected by particular changes in the estate, gift, income, or generation-skipping transfer tax laws.

§1.11. Supervise Subordinates

The CPR and MRPC both require a lawyer to exercise control over subordinates. DR 4-101(D) provides that a lawyer "shall exercise reasonable care to prevent his employees, associates, and others whose services are utilized by him from discussing or using confidences or secrets of a client." MRPC 5.1 requires a lawyer with supervisory authority over other lawyers to make reasonable efforts to ensure that the other lawyers comply with the MRPC. In addition, MRPC 5.3 requires lawyers with supervisory authority over nonlawyers to make reasonable efforts to ensure that the conduct of the nonlawyers is compatible with the professional obligations of the lawyer. As noted in the comments to MRPC 5.3, a lawyer should "give such assistants appropriate instructions concerning the ethical aspects of their employment, particularly regarding the obligation not to disclose information relating to representation of the client, and should be responsible for their work product." Junior lawyers and nonlawyer staff members should be provided with instructional materials describing the ethical obligations of the lawyers and staff members. Distributing the material in written form, such as an office manual or series of memoranda, is useful as it permits staff members to refer to the material as required.

§1.12. Beware of Multijurisdictional Problems

> Entirely apart from questions of malpractice, the planner of multijurisdictional estates must be forever wary of unauthorized practice problems. These difficulties generally can arise in two situations. First, a client domiciled or residing in the state in which the attorney is admitted to the bar may have interests in property outside the state, or out-of-state parties may have interests in the client's assets. In order to represent his client properly, the attorney may have to travel to the foreign jurisdiction and make appearances in court or before an agency; alternatively, he may have to negotiate with other parties there or settle various disputes or claims on behalf of his client.
>
> The second situation in which issues of unauthorized practice arise is quite different. Here, the client is from a jurisdiction in which the attorney is not admitted to practice. In many ways, the problems presented in this setting are even more difficult and unsettled than those in the first situation, since the foreign jurisdiction has the added interest of protecting one of its residents from a locally unlicensed attorney. J. Schoenblum, 1 Multistate and Multinational Estate Planning §5.01 (1982).

As indicated in the foregoing passage, the lawyer must exercise particular care in dealing with out-of-state properties or clients. If a client owns real property that is subject to the law of another state or country, the estate plan may attempt to avoid the necessity of conducting an ancillary estate administration in those jurisdictions. The greater mobility and longevity of our population suggest that lawyers will encounter more clients who own real property in other states, each of which might require an ancillary proceeding. For example, a couple who retire to Arizona, California, or Florida may retain substantial interests in real property located in Iowa or Nebraska. In such a case their estate plan may seek to avoid the necessity of ancillary probate proceedings by transferring all of their out-of-state real property to a revocable trust. The estate plan for those clients might involve issues regarding the validity of the trust and of the deeds or other instruments of transfer and the extent to which property held in the trust is subject to the claims of creditors or to the statutory elective share of a surviving spouse.

In any case, the client's principal (domiciliary) lawyer is usually responsible for creating the client's overall estate plan and seeing that it is carried into effect. If significant issues of foreign law are concerned, the client (and the lawyer) may need the advice of qualified counsel in the other jurisdictions. As indicated by Professor Schoenblum, problems of foreign law may also arise when the lawyer is asked to advise a client who is domiciled in another jurisdiction with respect to issues of local law. While the client's principal lawyer might be able to learn and apply the law of the other jurisdictions, it may be inefficient and more costly for the lawyer to attempt to do so. "[I]n U.S. state jurisdictions, the estate planning lawyer is responsible to the client for recognizing the questions of foreign law. Once such a question is recognized or should be recognized, the lawyer is obliged either to deal competently with the foreign law point himself, or to advise his client that foreign or other local counsel expert in foreign law should be retained." Hendrickson, Ethical Considerations in Multi-Jurisdictional Estate Planning, 123 Tr. & Est. 31, 38 (1984).

The lawyer must also be alert to the possibility that his or her activities relating to other jurisdictions might constitute the unauthorized practice of law in those jurisdictions if he or she is not admitted to practice in all of the affected states. Unfortunately, as noted in the comment to MRPC, "The definition of the practice of law is established by law and varies from one jurisdiction to another." If the representation was not successful, the lawyer might face both malpractice and disciplinary proceedings. Under MRPC 5.5 a lawyer "shall not: (a) practice law in a jurisdiction where doing so violates the regulation of the legal profession in that jurisdiction." DR 3-101(B) of the CPR is to the same effect.

§1.13. Legal Ethics and Taxes

A lawyer must also be equipped to deal with the ethical issues that may arise in connection with giving clients advice regarding tax matters, preparing tax returns, or representing clients before the IRS. The lawyer's role is complicated by the fact that his or her conduct toward the government is subject to the provisions of Treasury Circular 230, 31 C.F.R. pt. 10 (1988) ("Circular 230"), and the CPR or MRPC. Thus, in tax practice the lawyer's conduct is governed by two sets of rules, which sometimes conflict. Of course, some conduct is clearly permissible under each and some is clearly prohibited by each, but unfortunately the requirements imposed by the federal tax laws and regulations and the ethical rules promulgated under the CPR and the MRPC are not the same. Put most succinctly, tax practitioners are concerned that the positions taken in the Internal Revenue Code and by the IRS are more demanding. *E.g.*, §6662(d)(2)(B).

Under §6662 a 20 percent penalty is imposed in the case of a substantial understatement of income tax unless the position taken by the taxpayer is supported by "substantial authority" or is adequately disclosed in the return or a statement attached to the return. §6662(d)(2)(B). The amended provision of Circular 230 requires lawyers to exercise "due diligence" with respect to the preparation and filing of returns, documents, affidavits, and other papers relating to IRS matters. 31 C.F.R. §10.22. The same due diligence requirement applies to oral and written representations made by the lawyer to the Department of the Treasury and to oral and written representations made by the lawyer to clients with regard to matters administered by the IRS.

Neither the CPR nor the MRPC deal explicitly with the professional responsibility of a tax lawyer. Both, of course, bar assisting a client in a criminal or fraudulent undertaking, relating to tax or other matters. Under DR 7-102(A)(5), "in his representation of a client, a lawyer shall not knowingly make a false statement of law or fact," and DR 1-102(A)(4) prohibits a lawyer from engaging "in conduct involving dishonesty, fraud, deceit, or misrepresentation." Such conduct is also banned by Circular 230, the violation of which may cause the lawyer to be disbarred or suspended from practice before the IRS. 31 C.F.R. §§10.51(a), (b), (d), & (j) (1988).

The provisions of MRPC 1.2(d) prohibit a lawyer from assisting a client to engage in criminal or fraudulent behavior. Some portions of MRPC 3.1–3.9, which deal with the role of the lawyer as advocate, are also relevant. In addition, MRPC 4.1 provides that a lawyer shall not knowingly:

> (a) make a false statement of material fact or law to a third person; or

(b) fail to disclose a material fact to a third person when disclosure is necessary to avoid assisting a criminal or fraudulent act by a client, unless disclosure is prohibited by Rule 1.6.

The CPR also provides, in DR 7-102(A)(1), that a lawyer may not "file a suit, assert a position, conduct a defense, delay a trial, or take other action on behalf of his client when he knows or when it is obvious that such action would serve merely to harass or maliciously injure another."

The provisions of the CPR and MRPC were the basis upon which two Formal Opinions have been issued by the ABA. The first, Opinion 314, concluded that the relationship of the lawyer for a client toward the IRS was adversarial, and that while false assertions of fact are not permitted, lawyers could emphasize the strong points and minimize the weak. In the preparation of returns the lawyer could encourage the client to take the most favorable positions "so long as there is *reasonable basis* for those positions." Id. (Emphasis added.) As one commentator has pointed out, Opinion 314 "drew a flawed analogy between the submission of a return and the statement of a position in an adversarial proceeding." Durst, The Tax Lawyer's Professional Responsibility, 39 U. Fla. L. Rev. 1027, 1034 (1987). The subject was reconsidered in Formal Opinion 85-352, which concluded that the lawyer could take a position in a return for which there was "some reasonable possibility of success if the matter is litigated." It also pointed out that the lawyer must advise the client of the penalties, such as those of §6662, that might be imposed if certain positions are taken. The fundamental difference in these duties is that Opinion 85-352 requires that there be a "reasonable basis" for positions taken, §6662 requires that a position be supported by "substantial authority," and Circular 230 requires that a lawyer exercise "due diligence."

When the facts or the law are uncertain, the ABA rules would allow the lawyer to take positions that favor the client. In contrast, §6662 would allow the lawyer to do so with respect to positions that were supported by substantial authority. Circular 230 would also require the lawyer to exercise due diligence.

None of the rules permits a lawyer to advise a client to claim deductions or credits that are clearly unwarranted. However, under the ethical rules a lawyer may advance an uncertain claim for which there is adequate support if the facts are sufficiently disclosed in the client's return. Hard questions sometimes arise regarding the extent of the disclosure that must be made. Although the ethic may not be perfectly adhered to in practice, the lawyer should recommend full and fair disclosure of the facts regarding questionable positions. *See* Paul, The Lawyer As Tax Adviser, 25 Rocky Mtn. L. Rev. 412 (1953), *reprinted in* Professional Responsibility in Federal Tax Practice 64, 79 (B. Bittker ed. 1970).

Ethical concerns and Circular 230 bar lawyers from advising their clients to play the "tax lottery" game by taking positions for which there is little or no legal support on the chance that their returns will not be audited by the IRS or the unsubstantiated position will not be discovered if their returns are audited. The complexity of the tax law, the relatively high tax rates, and the limited capacity of the IRS to audit returns all tempt lawyers and clients to participate in the tax lottery. Taxpayers may be attracted to the lottery because of the small number of individual returns that are audited and the limited economic risk to the taxpayer. "Finally, even if the odds in the lottery come up against the taxpayer and the case is lost, as long as his original position finds sufficient protective coloration against the background of a confused or uncertain statute, the taxpayer is in danger of no greater penalty than simple interest for the tax money 'borrowed' from the Government." Ferguson, Tax Complexity and Compliance — One View from the Department of Justice, U. So. Cal., 30th Tax Inst. 871, 874 (1978). Now, of course, the Code permits penalties to be imposed in a broader range of cases — for overvaluation or undervaluation of assets, for example.

Former Assistant Attorney General Ferguson also pointed out that the success of our system of self-assessment depends heavily upon the essential integrity and honesty of taxpayers and their professional advisors. "The system could not survive on a principle of hide-and-seek between the Service and taxpayers. If tax returns were to degenerate into mere first offers, signaling the beginning of a bargaining process, we might well be forced to abandon the income tax as our principal method of sharing the expense of government. Thus, the effective operation of our tax laws depends upon the lawyers, the accountants, and others engaged in the professional practice of tax counselling and return preparation to assure full and fair reporting of tax liabilities." Id. at 878.

Lawyers who are fair and reasonably open in their dealings with the tax authorities will find that their work and their words are more readily accepted than those of other lawyers. Here, in a sense, virtue is rewarded. Lawyers with a reputation of high integrity will also be rewarded by the esteem of their colleagues and the benefit of referrals from them. In order to protect their reputation, lawyers must insist on full and complete disclosure by their clients, some of whom may seek to take advantage of one's good reputation to sanitize a questionable position.

C. CONFLICTS OF INTEREST

§1.14. Representation of Multiple Parties

> Loyalty is an essential element in the lawyer's relationship to a client. An impermissible conflict of interest may exist before representation is undertaken, in which event the representation should be declined. If such a conflict arises after representation has been undertaken, the lawyer should withdraw from the representation. Model Rules of Professional Conduct Rule 1.7 comment (1983).

Conflicts arise in many settings, often where multiple clients are involved. While conflicts may be actual or prospective, as noted in the comment to MRPC 1.7, "A possible conflict does not itself preclude the representation." Also, slight conflicts are unlikely to jeopardize the lawyer's exercise of independent judgment:

> [T]here are many instances in which a lawyer may properly serve multiple clients having potentially differing interests in matters not involving litigation. If the interests vary only slightly, it is generally likely that the lawyer will not be subjected to an adverse influence and that he can retain his independent judgment on behalf of each client; and if the interests become differing, withdrawal is less likely to have a disruptive effect upon the causes of his clients. EC 5-15.

The representation by a single lawyer of parties with interests that seriously conflict is also undesirable because of its unseemly appearance. That is the thrust of Canon 9 of the CPR: "A lawyer should avoid even the appearance of professional impropriety."

As EC 5-17 points out, typically recurring situations involving potentially differing interests include representation of "beneficiaries of the estate of a decedent." Because of the potential for conflicts, in most instances a lawyer should not represent a fiduciary and one or more beneficiaries of the fidiciary estate. The reason is simple: The lawyer will be required to advise the fiduciary regarding tax and other matters about which the beneficiaries will almost certainly have conflicting interests (*e.g.,* tax elections regarding an estate and decisions regarding the timing and amount of distributions).

Representation of multiple parties, including family members and partners of other business associates, is often possible if the lawyer makes full disclosure and all parties consent. This is recognized by DR 5-105 and MRPC 1.7 and 2.2 (lawyer as intermediary). The parties are generally not in the position of adversaries. Instead, they may have common interests which do not seriously conflict.

> Conflict questions may also arise in estate planning and administration. A lawyer may be called upon to prepare wills for several family members, such as husband and wife, and, depending upon the circumstances, a conflict of interest may arise. In estate administration the identity of the client may be unclear under the law of a particular jurisdiction. Under one view, the client is the estate or trust, including its beneficiaries. The lawyer should make clear the relationship to the parties involved. MRPC 1.7, comment.

A lawyer must bear in mind that a conflict may exist at the outset or develop later. In either case, under DR 5-105 a lawyer may not represent clients with conflicting interests unless "it is obvious that he can adequately represent the interest of each and if each consents to the representation after full disclosure of the possible effect of such representation on the exercise of his independent professional judgment on behalf of each." *See* EC 5-16. Whether it is "obvious" that a lawyer can adequately represent each client is often in doubt, but where the interests of multiple clients do involve a significant conflict, a single lawyer cannot adequately represent all of them.

Maintaining the confidentiality of information disclosed by clients is also a major concern when multiple representation is involved, particularly in the case of family members. Future problems can be averted if the lawyer cautions the clients at the outset that there can be no secrets between them regarding the object of the representation. Thus, before undertaking to represent a husband and wife, the lawyer may explain that joint representation of them will preclude any undisclosed confidences between them. There must be open communication regarding the object of the representation although the communications remain confidential as to others. It is helpful to reiterate the point in writing as part of an engagement letter sent after the initial conference that defines, among other things, the scope of the representation, the manner of determining the lawyer's fee. *See* §1.30.6.

§1.14.1. Intergenerational Estate Planning

It is often most efficient and effective to provide estate planning services to several generations of family members. A common situation involves the representation of parents and of children who are entitled to receive distributions from trusts or custodianships under the Uniform Gifts to Minors Act or the Uniform Transfer to Minors Act. In such a case the lawyer should meet separately with the child and give him or her independent advice. As indicated in the rules, the child should be told who is paying the lawyer's fee. If the attitude or wishes of the parent(s) do not allow the lawyer to represent them and give the child independent advice, the lawyer faces a serious practical problem: How to educate them regarding the lawyer's professional responsibilities without offending the parent. Candid discussion with the parent(s) may result in a sufficient degree of autonomy for the lawyer and the child. Otherwise the lawyer may be unable to represent both the parent(s) and the child. Regardless of who is paying the lawyer's fee, the child is entitled to independent advice. Multigenerational planning is also particularly appropriate where a closely-held business is involved.

Most clients recognize the value of coordinated planning and freely consent to the same lawyer representing others in the client's family and communicating with the other family members regarding estate planning matters. Of course, without the client's consent a lawyer may not disclose to another family member, or any other person, the content of documents the lawyer has prepared for the client. *See* DR 4-101; EC 4-4; MRPC 1.6(a); H. Drinker, Legal Ethics, 94, 136 (1953). Without advance consent and waiver of confidentiality as to other family members, the representation of members of more than one generation can put the lawyer in difficult positions.

Example 1-1. Lawyer represented Father and Mother, whose original wills left all of their property outright to their 3 children upon the death of the surviving parent. Lawyer also prepared a will for Son, the terms of which were based on the assumption that Son would receive a share of his surviving parent's estate. Son later told Lawyer that he was heavily in debt and entering a drug treatment program. Lawyer has a continuing duty to Father and Mother that may require Lawyer to tell them of Son's circumstances. However, before doing so, Lawyer should attempt to persuade Son to inform Father and Mother of his problems, or authorize Lawyer to do so. Lawyer faces a similar problem of disclosure if Father and Mother were to decide to change their wills regarding the provision for Son.

Example 1-2. Lawyer has represented Father, Mother, and Daughter in connection with their personal estate planning and in relation to Family, Inc., all of the stock of which is owned by Father and Mother. Daughter is the chief executive officer of Family, Inc. Father and Mother have asked Lawyer to assist them in transferring shares of Family, Inc. to their other two children who reside in other states. The interests and plans of Father and Mother may conflict with those of Daughter, who is also a client. Indeed, Father and Mother may not wish their plans to be disclosed to Daughter at all. Again, if Lawyer discusses the conflict with Father and Mother, they may agree to review their plans with Daughter. Some conflicts that are more readily soluble may also arise if Lawyer is asked to represent Daughter regarding her salary or fringe benefits, for example, in negotiations with Family, Inc.

Representing more than one member of a family can give rise to serious conflicts of interest. *E.g., Haynes v. First National Bank,* 432 A.2d 890 (N.J. 1981). *See* §1.8. In particular, representing an adult child and an aged or infirm parent may involve the attorney in conflicts of interest and, possibly, charges of fraud, undue influence, or overreaching the parent. "Private consultation with the parent and provision of independent advice to, and loyal representation of, him or her is absolutely essential." Price, Professional Responsibility in Estate Planning: Progress or Paralysis?, U. Miami, 21st Inst. Est. Plan., ¶1802.1C (1987).

§1.14.2 Husband and Wife or Parties Contemplating Marriage or Cohabitation

Common representation of a husband and wife is typical in the estate planning setting and frequently does not involve any actual conflict of interest between the clients. While the spouses may have somewhat different estate planning objectives, their differences do not necessarily involve conflicts of interest that would require them to be separately represented. As suggested in §1.14, the common representation of husband and wife requires the complete disclosure of information to each party; the lawyer cannot withhold relevant information from either of them.

Some lawyers have suggested that a lawyer may undertake to represent husband and wife individually as *separate* clients in the hope that the confidences of each can be maintained without making any disclosure to the other. Such an arrangement is inconsistent with the lawyer's primary duty of loyalty: How could a lawyer adequately represent both spouses if he or she has agreed that the confidences of each would not be disclosed to the other?

Conflicts between a husband and wife or persons contemplating marriage may be so serious as to require them to be separately represented. For example, serious conflicts may arise regarding the characterization of property (who owns what) or their respective interests under wills and trusts, the sale or exchange of property between themselves, the designation of beneficiaries in life insurance policies and employee benefit plans, the selection of retirement options, and inter vivos and testamentary gifts between themselves or to third parties.

Example 1-3. Lawyer earlier planned the estate of Client, a woman who now asks Lawyer to advise her and her fiancé regarding an antenuptial agreement. Lawyer should be most reluctant to represent both Client and her fiancé, whose economic interests regarding the antenuptial agreement will necessarily conflict. In addition, although Lawyer may have completed the initial estate planning job for Client, Lawyer's duties to Client continue, which preclude Lawyer from using against Client's interests any information that was received by Lawyer in connection with the original representation. Because of the conflict of interest Lawyer should heed the advice of the Washington Court of Appeals:

> [P]arties interested in establishing an estate plan may be well advised to seek independent counsel, particularly in instances, such as this, where the wife is giving up certain rights. The utilization of independent counsel would forestall a challenge to the estate plan upon that basis. However, we decline to establish a requirement that independent advice must be sought or that a recommendation to seek independent counsel be expressed before such a plan is valid. *Seattle First National Bank v. Whitney,* 560 P.2d 360, 364 (Wash. App. 1977), *aff'd,* 579 P.2d 937 (Wash. 1978) (inter vivos widow's election to allow all of the community property to pass to testamentary trust under husband's will, of which wife was the life income beneficiary, is binding although the wife was not separately represented).

A lawyer who represents both parties to an antenuptial agreement or other agreement between spouses or cohabitants may violate the rules of professional responsibility. In addition, the joint representation of both spouses is a factor to be considered in determining the validity of the agreement. For example, in *Hale v. Hale,* 539 A.2d 247 (Md. App. 1988), the lawyer who represented both parties in connection with a separation agreement was found to have violated professional ethics and the agreement was set aside. However, in *Estate of Sumpter,* 419 N.W.2d 765 (Mich. App. 1988), the court held that an attorney who had previously represented the decedent and his spouse in connection with an antenuptial agreement was not precluded from acting as personal representative of the decedent's estate. That conclusion was reached although the opinion refers to another action which held that in representing both parties the lawyer had violated his duty to the surviving spouse. In most jurisdictions all of the circumstances will be considered in determining whether an agreement will be upheld or struck down. Although a party was not independently represented, an agreement may be enforced against that party if the agreement was fair or if the party was knowledgeable and there was complete disclosure by the other party. *See, e.g., Jackson v. Seder,* 467 So. 2d 422 (Fla. App. 1985). An agreement that is unfair or unreasonable will not be enforced by some courts unless the parties were separately represented. *See, e.g., Estate of Crawford,* 730 P.2d 675 (Wash. 1986). Statutes in some states provide that the fact that both parties were represented by the same counsel does not itself make the agreement invalid. *E.g.,* Wis. Stat. Ann. §766.58(8) (1988 Supp.); Ark. Stat. Ann. §9-11-402(2) (1987). Finally, under the Uniform Premarital Agreement Act, 9B U.L.A. 369 (1987), which has been enacted in over a dozen states, the absence of independent counsel is only one of the factors to be taken into account in determining the validity of the agreement.

§1.14.3. Lawyer as Intermediary

MRPC 2.2 deals with the role of the lawyer as intermediary, which involves the common representation of parties where the attorney's efforts are, as reflected in the comments, "to resolve potentially conflicting interests by developing the parties' mutual interests." A comment to MRPC 2.2 points out that "[t]he alternative can be that each party may have to obtain separate representation, with the possibility in some situations of incurring additional cost, complication, or even litigation. Given these and other relevant factors, all the clients may prefer that the lawyer act as intermediary." Because the lawyer is required to be impartial between commonly represented clients, the comment notes that "intermediation is improper when that impartiality cannot be maintained. For example, a lawyer who has represented one of the clients for a very long time period and in a variety of matters might have difficulty being impartial between that client and one to whom the lawyer has only recently been introduced." Some commentators have suggested that the representation of a husband and wife is not appropriately subject to the intermediary rule, but should be governed by the basic conflict rule of MRPC 1.7. *See* Brosterhous, Conflicts of Interest in Estate Planning and Administration, 123 Tr. & Est. 18 (1984). A more liberal interpretation, consistent with the role of estate planners as family counselors, should prevail.

§1.14.4. Imputed Disqualification of Partners and Associates

If separate counsel is required, it is insufficient to refer one of the parties to a partner or associate. This rule is stated explicitly in MRPC 1.10(a): "While lawyers are associated in a firm, none of them shall knowingly represent a client when any one of them practicing alone would be prohibited from doing so. . . ." *See also* Eckhardt, The Estate Planning Lawyer's Problems: Malpractice and Ethics, U. Miami, 8th Inst. Est. Plan. ¶606.3 (1974).

§1.15. Do Not Subordinate the Client's Interests

As a fiduciary the lawyer is not permitted to take advantage of the client. DR 5-104(A); MRPC 1.8(a). The lawyer should also be careful not to influence a client to appoint to a fiduciary office a business associate of the lawyer or an institution with which the lawyer has some connection. A corporate fiduciary should be recommended, for example, only when in the best interests of the client. Even then, if the client asks for a recommendation, the lawyer would do well to recommend more than one institution. Any documents that are drawn should protect the client's interests and not unduly favor the corporate fiduciary. Thus, the inclusion of a provision relieving the fiduciary from liability for its acts is suspect.

> In the past lawyers have too often been willing to subordinate the needs of their clients to the interests of the corporate fiduciary, particularly when the law firm has been recommended by the fiduciary. Whitman, Coping With Corporate Fiduciaries Declining to Serve, 115 Tr. & Est. 9, 52, n.7 (1976).

Along the same lines, if the client is considering the appointment of a corporate fiduciary, the lawyer should tell the client if the corporate fiduciaries have a practice of retaining the lawyer who prepares an instrument that names it as fiduciary. The client is entitled to know about such policies before a fiduciary is chosen. Also, as indicated in §1.7.3, the lawyer cannot accept rebates, kickbacks, or referral fees.

§1.16. Do Not Accept Gifts from Clients Who Are Nonrelatives

Conflicts of interest and a presumption of undue influence affect direct or indirect gifts made by a client to a lawyer who is not a close relative. The taint extends to gifts by a client to the spouse or children of the lawyer. *Matter of Peeples,* 374 S.E.2d 674 (S.C. 1988) (public reprimand upheld where the lawyer drafted will for client which made gifts to lawyer's daughters). A survivorship bank account between a lawyer and client is subject to the same presumption. *In re Estate of Mapes,* 738 S.W.2d 853 (Mo. 1987) (joint accounts were between client and his grand nephews, of whom one was his lawyer but neither was a beneficiary of his will). It also applies where the client gives the lawyer an interest in a trust, *Klaskin v. Klepack,* 534 N.E.2d 971 (Ill. 1989), or an option to purchase assets of the client's estate at a preferential price, *Matter of Rentiers,* 374 S.E.2d 672 (S.C. 1988) (public reprimand upheld where lawyer exercised option but later reconveyed the property).

The presumption of undue influence does not apply to gifts that are made to a lawyer by a competent client who is independently advised. Also, most commentators and courts agree that a lawyer may prepare a will that benefits the lawyer when the client is a close relative, provided that the gift to the lawyer does not exceed the portion of the relative's estate that the lawyer would have been entitled to receive if the will were not established. A lawyer who assists a relative in making disproportionately large gifts to him or her practically invites other children to challenge the validity of the gifts. *See Dunham v. Dunham,* 528 A.2d 1123 (Conn. 1987).

A lawyer who accepts a gift from a client or participates in the preparation of a will that names the lawyer as a beneficiary may be the subject of an action to invalidate the gift or bequest *and* a disciplinary action. *See, e.g., Magee v. State Bar of California,* 374 P.2d 807 (Cal. 1962). Los Angeles County Bar Association Formal Ethics Opinion 462 (1991) concludes that a lawyer may not prepare a will for a nonrelative which contains a gift to the lawyer. Opinion 462 also advises, "[I]f the client refuses to seek such [independent] advice, the attorney must not make the revisions requested by the client, or, if the attorney has already been retained, the attorney must withdraw under California Rule of Professional Conduct 3-700(B)(2)." The Opinion also "seriously questions whether an attorney is performing competently if he or she drafts or amends a will in which he or she receives a gift under circumstances reasonably suggestive of undue influence."

In the CPR, the subject of gifts by a client to a lawyer is addressed as follows:

> A lawyer should not suggest to his client that a gift be made to himself or for his benefit. If a lawyer accepts a gift from his client, he is peculiarly susceptible to the charge that he unduly influenced the client. If a client voluntarily offers to make a gift to his lawyer, the lawyer may accept the gift, but before doing so, he should urge that his client secure disinterested advice from an independent, competent person who is cognizant of all the circumstances. Other than in exceptional circumstances, a lawyer should insist that an instrument in which his client desires to name him as beneficiary be prepared by another lawyer selected by the client. EC 5-5.

A former president of the American Bar Association was disbarred because of having drafted, for an affluent client, a will under which he was the sole beneficiary of a large estate. *Committee on Professional Ethics v. Randall,* 285 N.W.2d 161 (Iowa 1979), *cert. denied,* 446 U.S. 946 (1980).

A stricter, more explicit, but still incomplete ban is imposed by MRPC 1.8(c):

> A lawyer shall not prepare an instrument giving the lawyer or a person related to the lawyer as a parent, child, sibling, or spouse any substantial gift from a client, including a testamentary gift, except where the client is related to the donee.

The comments to MRPC 1.8(c) indicate that a lawyer may accept a gift from a client, "if the transaction meets general standards of fairness" or where the gift is a simple holiday gift which is a token of appreciation. Substantial gifts can only be made to a nonrelated lawyer if the client is independently represented. Note that under MRPC 1.10(a) the client cannot be adequately represented by a lawyer who is associated with the lawyer-donee.

Unfortunately, the MRPC does not define what constitutes a "substantial" gift. It is presumably relative to the size of the client's estate, so a bequest of $5,000 by a client with a $5 million estate might be permissible. However, such a gift would be impermissible if the client's estate were only $50,000. The status of gifts made to the lawyer's favorite charity, of which the lawyer may also be a trustee, is also doubtful. Note also that MRPC 1.8(c) apparently permits a lawyer who is remotely related to the client to prepare a will which favors the scrivener over the client's closer relatives.

§1.17. Do Not Enter into Any Business Transactions with a Client

A lawyer must also avoid business transactions with a client that might create a conflict of interest with the client. *See* DR 5-104(A) and EC 5-3, which discourage lawyers from entering into business transactions with clients. MRPC 1.8 similarly discourages a lawyer from entering into business transactions with a client. The same proscription should extend to transactions between the lawyer and a client who is a fiduciary (personal representative or trustee) or a beneficiary of the fiduciary estate. *See* §1.37.

The comment to MRPC 1.8 notes, "As a general principle, all transactions between client and lawyer should be fair and reasonable to the client. In such transactions a review by independent counsel on behalf of the client is often advisable." The best rule is not to enter into any business transactions with a client other than routine ones that do not involve a lawyer-client feature. A lawyer may, of course, purchase office supplies from a business owned by a client, or borrow from a bank that is a client.

"Neither a borrower, nor a lender be." The Bard's admonition is appropriate: The relative frequency of disciplinary cases that deal with lawyers who have borrowed from clients indicates the extent to which clients are victimized by lawyers with financial problems. A lawyer should not borrow from a client — at least not without the client obtaining independent legal advice. Lawyers who do so may be subject to a disciplinary proceeding. *Giovanazzi v. State Bar of California,* 619 P.2d 1005 (Cal. 1980). The Oregon Supreme Court has stated that "[i]t is axiomatic that attorneys should not borrow or accept gifts from their clients unless the client has had advice from independent counsel or a knowledgeable person. The transaction should be reduced to writing, fully explaining the circumstances." *In re Hendricks,* 580 P.2d 188, 190 (Or. 1978).

§1.18. Scrivener Should Be Wary of Accepting Appointment as Fiduciary

Most jurisdictions permit a lawyer to prepare for an unrelated client a will that appoints the scrivener to a fiduciary office. *See also* §4.26.1. Indeed, it is generally considered to be proper for the client to appoint a lawyer-scrivener as a fiduciary when the lawyer has been a long-time friend, confidante, advisor, or otherwise brings special qualifications to the fiduciary office. Appointment of the lawyer-scrivener as fiduciary is permitted by the CPR so long as the lawyer did not seek the appointment.

> A lawyer should not consciously influence a client to name him as executor, trustee, or lawyer in an instrument. In those cases where a client wishes to name his lawyer as such, care should be taken by the lawyer to avoid even the appearance of impropriety. EC 5-6.

The provision is directed primarily at problems of solicitation and appearances of impropriety. However, the more serious problems involve conflicts of interest. The appointments of some scriveners as fiduciaries have been struck down by the courts. For example, in *Estate of Weinstock,* 351 N.E.2d 647 (N.Y. 1971), the appointment of a father and son team of lawyers was struck down because they overreached the 82-year-old client in obtaining the appointment. In *Estate of Paul J. DeMarco,* N.Y. L.J., Mar. 1, 1988, at 15, Surrogate Laurino found the scrivener-executor nominee unqualified to act as executor; the lawyer failed to explain to the testator the cost of appointing him as executor of a $925,000 liquid estate that was left entirely to the testator's sister, who was competent and was nominated as successor executor. "As a consequence of his engagement as decedent's attorney, there arose a confidential relationship which imposed on the petitioner a special obligation of both full disclosure and fair dealing. The record before this court indicates that such obligation was not met and to such extent that petitioner is guilty of a constructive fraud on the testator."

A decision of the Michigan Court of Appeals, *Matter of Green Charitable Trust,* 431 N.W.2d 492 (Mich. Ct. App. 1988), illustrates the risks that face the lawyer who undertakes to act both as lawyer and fiduciary. Quoting from another Michigan case, the court stated, "A lawyer who is also a fiduciary bears a doubly high degree of responsibility and accountability." Id. at 503. The lawyer in *Green* acted as cotrustee of the charitable trust that was selling a large tract of land, attorney for the trustees, and attorney for the purchaser. The lawyer-fiduciary was found liable with the corporate cotrustee for $1.9 million in damages for selling trust property for an inadequate price, despite a clause which exculpated them for acts done in good faith. Liability was imposed on the lawyer although he declined to participate as cotrustee with respect to the offer made by the buyer-client and obtained the consent of the other trustees to his dual representation. The lawyer's disclosures were inadequate because the other trustees "were not fully informed of [the lawyer's] past representations of [the purchaser.]" Id. at 503. As the court noted, "in a conflict situation as was involved here, it would be prudent for the trustee electing to proceed in any capacity to both fully inform the beneficiaries and seek court approval." Id. at 505.

Unfortunately, even the limited guidance provided by EC 5-6 was omitted from the MRPC. Instead of dealing directly with this issue, the MRPC relies upon the general rule of MRPC 1.8(c), which bars a lawyer from entering into a business transaction with a client unless it is fair and reasonable, entered into with full knowledge of the client who has an opportunity for independent representation and receives the written consent of the client. In this connection, a lawyer who relies upon having made full disclosure to a client, "should state the disclosures in writing." *In re Germundson,* 723 P.2d 793 (Or. 1986). One informal opinion concluded that the MRPC does not prohibit a lawyer from preparing a will for a client that names the lawyer as executor if the appointment is the express wish of a fully informed client:

> The lawyer should disclose to the client the duties and obligations of an executor, the fees which the lawyer will charge for performing those services, the fees alternative executors would probably charge, and should advise the client that he or she is free to seek the advice of independent counsel. This disclosure should be in writing to ensure that the client understands its significance and to establish conclusively that it occurred. Wash. State B. Assn. Rules of Professional Conduct Committee, Informal Op. 86-1, 2 Wash. State B. Resources 96 (Apr. 1988).

The informal opinion suggests that a lawyer who is appointed to a fiduciary office should be prepared to show that the client was informed of the relative advantages and disadvantages of appointing the lawyer, another individual, or a corporate fiduciary and should also have pointed out the conflicts that might arise when the lawyer also acts as fiduciary, particularly with respect to fees. Thus, as the court cautioned in *In re Coe,* 731 P.2d 1028, 1037-1038 (Or. 1987), "Before undertaking that dual role [as personal representative and attorney for the personal representative], and any specific actions thereunder, every attorney would be well advised to carefully peruse Disciplinary Rule 5-101, et seq." The lawyer should not underestimate the legal, ethical, and practical problems that may arise if the lawyer serves as a fiduciary. *See* Laurino, The Duties and Responsibilities of the Attorney/Fiduciary, U. Miami, 19th Inst. Est. Plan., ¶1603 (1985). All of the conduct of a lawyer-fiduciary may be subject to the rules of professional conduct. *Layton v. State Bar,* 789 P.2d 1026 (Cal. 1990). In *Layton,* the lawyer-executor was disciplined for willful failure to use reasonable diligence in estate matters. "Where an attorney occupies a dual capacity, performing, for a single client or in a single matter, along with legal services, services that might otherwise be performed by laymen, the services that he renders in the dual capacity all involve the practice of law, and he must conform to the Rules of Professional Conduct in the provision of all of them." Id. at 1034.

Finally, designation in a will of the lawyer-scrivener to serve as attorney for a fiduciary is also a questionable practice. There is usually no justification for such a designation. Moreover, as a technical matter such a designation generally does not bind the personal representative, who is free to employ the lawyer of his or her choice.

D. LAWYER'S FEES

§1.19. Discussions with the Client

The CPR encourages, and the MRPC requires, the lawyer to discuss fees with a client at an early point. In particular, EC 2-19 calls for the discussion to be "as soon as possible after a lawyer has been employed." MRPC 1.5(b) provides that "when the lawyer has not regularly represented the client, the basis or rate of the fee shall be communicated to the client, preferably in writing, before or within a reasonable time after commencing the representation." The mandatory approach of MRPC 1.5(b) is justified because of the lawyer's dominant position and the reluctance many clients have to broach the subject of fees even though they may be very concerned about the amount they will be charged. If the lawyer's fee will exceed $1,000, California requires a written contract for services, specifying the hourly rate and other charges, the nature of the legal services to be provided, and the respective responsibilities of the lawyer and the client. Cal. Bus. & Prof. Code §6148 (West 1990). Failure to comply with the requirements of the California statute makes the contract voidable at the option of the client, in which case the lawyer is entitled to a reasonable fee.

EC 2-19 recommends that fees be discussed as soon as feasible *after* the lawyer is employed. It is preferable that such a discussion *precede* the actual employment of the lawyer.

> As soon as feasible after a lawyer has been employed, it is desirable that he reach a clear agreement with his client as to the basis of the fee charges to be made. Such a course will not only prevent later misunderstanding, but will also work for good relations between the lawyer and the client. It is usually beneficial to reduce to writing the understanding of the parties regarding the fee, particularly when it is contingent. A lawyer should be mindful that many persons who desire to employ him may have had little or no experience with fee charges of lawyers, and for this reason he should explain fully to such persons the reasons for the particular fee arrangement he proposes. Id.

At an early point in the initial conference with a prospective client the manner in which the lawyer's fee will be determined should be reviewed. The lawyer may also want to indicate that at the conclusion of their meeting he or she will be in a position to make some recommendations and to provide an estimate of the overall cost of providing the services. If a prospective client declines to proceed, lawyers generally do not make any charge for the conference. On the other hand, if the lawyer is engaged to provide the services, the lawyer should mention the estimate in his or her follow-up letter to the client. In this connection see the sample letter at §1.30.6. The estimate should also be recorded at a convenient and obvious place in the client's file.

As the work for a client progresses the lawyer should keep the estimate in mind. If the client's affairs are more complicated than expected or additional work is undertaken for the client, the lawyer should let the client know if the estimate will be exceeded. In that way the client will be better prepared to receive a statement for a larger amount.

§1.20. Determining the Amount for Lifetime Services

> Hourly rates, for decades the mainstay of law firms' fee structures, continue to be gradually supplanted by more creative ways of putting a price tag on a case.
>
> Task-based, or value billing — a system in which the lawyer and client negotiate an agreed-upon fee for a case — is meeting broader acceptance by many firms and corporate in-house counsel.
>
> Premium billing — adding a surcharge to an amount deter-

> mined by a firm's hourly rate when a good result is obtained, or charging a higher-than-usual rate for complex cases — is used less widely, but has worked for lawyers handling high-priced deals such as mergers and acquisitions. Cook, Hourly Billing: A Thing of the Past?, 1989 A.B.A. Sec. Econ. of Law Prac. 29.
>
> To value a lawyer's service to a client based primarily on hours spent ignores the true worth of the lawyer's services and rewards incompetence. It is unfair to both client and lawyer to do so. Reed, Responsibility, Expertise, Productivity: The True Measure of Value of a Lawyer's Services, 1989 A.B.A. Sec. Econ. of Law Prac. 77.

The lawyer's fee for estate planning services is usually based either on a fixed fee (*e.g.,* $500 for reciprocal wills with marital deduction trusts for a husband and wife; $100 additional for durable powers of attorney) or on an hourly time charge (*e.g.,* $125 per hour for the lawyer's time and $50 per hour for the time of a senior legal assistant). Bills based on time charges are calculated according to the actual time spent, but some lawyers bill on the basis of time units allocated to particular tasks that take into account the time required for research and development of forms and systems (*e.g.,* a durable power of attorney or a living will is charged at 1.0 hours). A growing number of lawyers also charge for word processing, for computer-based legal research, and for a portion of costs previously incurred in creating forms and systems. In cases involving unusual demands and responsibilities some lawyers bill their time at premium rates.

In any particular case the fee may take into account the factors enumerated in EC 2-18 and MRPC 1.5(a). According to EC 2-18 the fees "of a lawyer will vary according to many factors, including the time required, his experience, ability, and reputation, the nature of the employment, the responsibility involved, and the results obtained." Other factors are often considered including the fee customarily charged in the locality for similar services, the novelty and difficulty of the work, and time constraints imposed by the client.

Historically, compensation for lifetime estate planning services was inadequate. The nominal charges that were made in early years reflected the practice of using wills as "loss leaders" (*i.e.,* the lawyer's present loss in drafting a will would be made up by the future compensation to be received when the lawyer acted as counsel for the client's personal representative). That practice led some critics to charge that lawyers did not adequately inform their clients about inter vivos trusts and other will substitutes that might eliminate the need for estate administration proceedings. The charge may have some substance in states such as California, in which the compensation of the personal representative's lawyer is based on the amount of the estate subject to administration.

Lawyers are now usually compensated better for lifetime estate planning services. It is desirable that the fee for estate planning work approximate the fee the lawyer would charge for other types of work of similar duration and complexity. If the fees are comparable, the lawyer is more likely to devote the same effort to estate planning work, which should improve the quality of estate plans and of the documents produced. Of course, clients who were accustomed to paying only a small fee for estate planning services (the proverbial $50 wills for husband and wife) are not pleased with the trend. However, at least the more affluent clients will probably adjust to the change; they are unlikely to become clients of lawyers who produce $50 wills.

The lawyer's fee should reflect the cost of providing services to the client, including the research and development of will and trust forms, the cost of word processing, and the use of legal assistants. When a fee is based on an hourly charge it is common to include a charge, at lower hourly rates, for the work of estate planning legal assistants. In preparing and presenting a statement, the lawyer should consider that clients are more willing to pay substantial fees for estate planning services if they understand how the planning will reduce administrative costs and taxes. Of course, some of the projected savings may not occur until the death of the client or the client's spouse. Tax estimates can be used to illustrate the savings that will result from a plan recommended by the lawyer. The client's reaction may also be more favorable if it shows the portion of the fee that is deductible for income tax purposes, subject to the two percent floor applicable to miscellaneous itemized deductions. §67.

Executive Estate Planning. A growing number of private employers pay the cost of providing estate planning services to some executives. In some instances the services are provided by a single law firm, which may achieve some economies of scale by representing several executives with generally the same set of employee benefits. Such a program may include periodic seminars for the executives as a group. Law firms that are interested in expanding their estate planning practices may make attractive Executive Estate Planning packages available to business clients. Under another approach the employer simply reimburses the executive for the cost of the services, not to exceed a specified annual maximum.

Group Meetings with Clients; Providing Clients with Videotapes. The amount of time a lawyer is required to spend with individual clients and the resultant cost of estate planning services may be reduced by two other approaches. First, the lawyer may provide some basic information to clients or potential clients as a group prior to meeting with them individually. Such an approach may be appropriate in the case of members of an organization, such as a union, that might sponsor the group meeting. Second, following a brief initial meeting the client might be provided with a videotape that includes a basic explanation of common estate planning techniques.

A major Seattle firm, Foster Pepper & Shefelman, uses audio tapes and workbooks to make the estate planning process more efficient.

> The firm's Estate Planning Plus package includes cassettes and a workbook that help prepare the client for meeting with an attorney, explaining procedures, documents and estate planning steps clients should take. The result is less time — and money — to prepare an estate plan.
>
> Efficiency and better organization allow Foster Pepper to offer fixed fees of $675–$900 for a couple, depending on the size of the estate. Drake [an estate planner in the Foster Pepper firm] estimates that other firms are charging as much as $4,000 for the same service. Seattle Daily J. Commerce, June 12, 1991, at 19.

§1.21. Who Pays the Lawyer's Fee

One person may pay the cost of preparing a will or providing other legal services to another person. Thus, an employer, child, or parent may pay the cost of estate planning services provided to another. The person for whom the will is prepared or the other services are rendered is the client, and he or she is the person to whom the lawyer is responsible. Under DR 5-107(B), "[a] lawyer shall not permit a person who recommends, employs, or pays him to render legal services for another to direct or regulate his professional judgment in rendering such legal services." MRPC 1.8(f) has the same general effect — payment by another is allowed with the client's permission if the arrangement does not jeopardize the client's confidences nor compromise the lawyer's independence of judgment.

§1.22. Determining the Amount for Estate Administration Services

Until the Supreme Court's decision in *Goldfarb v. Virginia State Bar,* 421 U.S. 773 (1975), in many states the compensation of the lawyer for a personal representative was usually based upon a fee schedule published by the local bar association. In other states, including California, fees of the personal representative and the lawyer for the personal representative were based upon statutory fee schedules. In either case, the fees determined under the schedules sometimes bore little or no relation to the time or expertise required or the results obtained. *Goldfarb* held a minimum fee schedule promulgated by a county bar association and sanctioned by the state bar association was not exempt from the Sherman Antitrust Act under the "learned profession" or "state action" exceptions. Instead, the schedule was found to have violated the Act because it resulted in the fixing of prices that affect interstate commerce. The Court pointed out, however, that a different issue would be involved in the case of a "purely advisory fee schedule issued to provide guidelines, or an exchange of price information without a showing of an actual restraint on trade." Id. at 781.

In *Goldfarb,* the Court did not pass on the legality of fee schedules prescribed by the state; however, the opinion did recognize the interest of the state in regulating the legal profession. A fee schedule applicable to the ordinary services of the personal representatives and their attorneys remains in effect in California. Cal. Prob. Code §§901, 910 (West 1991 Supp.). The validity of the schedule was upheld in *Matter of Effron's Estate,* 173 Cal. Rptr. 93 (4th Dist. 1981), as within the state action exception to the Sherman Act. The California schedule provides for a fee of four percent on the first $15,000, three percent of the next $85,000, two percent of the next $900,000, one percent on the next $9 million, one-half of one percent on the next $15 million, and a reasonable fee on the amount over $25 million. In most other states the fee of the personal representative's attorney is usually based on the allowance of an hourly fee which the local law often requires to be "reasonable" in amount. A hearing on the amount of fees may be required if interested parties object to the amounts sought by the personal representative or the lawyer for the personal representative. In an extreme case, a 5-4 majority of the Washington Supreme Court upheld objections to the lawyer's fees including one made on the ground that the fees related to tasks that could have been performed by legal assistants. *Estate of Larson,* 694 P.2d 1051 (Wash. 1985). (In order to avoid disallowance under this approach must a lawyer use a word processing system to produce court documents or form letters instead of using dictating equipment or handwriting drafts of document?) In *Larson,* the court also held that if the lawyer's fees were challenged the lawyer could not recover any of the costs of justifying the fees, even if the challenge was rejected by the court.

When a petition for the allowance of fees is filed, the court, or court commissioner, often requires the lawyer to file an affidavit regarding the time spent representing the estate. Some also require the lawyer to file copies of time records or a summary of the records. Even apart from such a requirement it is important for the lawyer to keep accurate time records, which describe in some detail the work performed.

Concern over the amount of fees charged in estate administration proceedings led to the adoption of the Statement of Principles Regarding Probate Practices and Expenses by the Real Property, Probate and

Trust Section of the American Bar Association. The statement, which appears at 8 Real Prop., Prob. & Tr. J. 293 (1973), is intended to provide guidelines to legislatures, courts, and bar associations when investigating, evaluating, and establishing standards with respect to the fees of personal representatives. Approved by the ABA House of Delegates in 1975, it evidences the shift away from strict adherence to fee schedules and emphasizes the desirability of basing the compensation of lawyers upon the value of services each actually renders. It calls for significant weight to be given to the following factors:

1. The extent of the responsibilities assumed and the results obtained;
2. The time and labor required, the novelty and difficulty of the questions involved, and the skills required to perform the services properly; and
3. The sufficiency of assets properly available to pay for the services.

These factors are among those specified in DR 2-106(B) for use in determining the reasonableness of a lawyer's fee. The Statement also recognizes that a personal representative or lawyer is entitled to compensation for services that must be rendered in connection with nonprobate property even though the owner of the property did not request the services. Accordingly, the personal representative could charge a surviving joint tenant with some of the cost of valuing and determining taxes on joint tenancy property. Point 4 of the statement allows a lawyer to serve as personal representative and to be compensated for services in both capacities, but some states, including California, do not.

§1.23. Avoid Bequest in Satisfaction of Lawyer's Fee

In some cases clients have agreed to make specified testamentary gifts to their attorneys in lieu of paying for the services currently. Arrangements of that type should generally be avoided because of the uncertainty of payment at any time (*e.g.,* the client may change his or her will), possible ethical violations, and the absence of any tax advantages. For example, *Wolder v. Commissioner,* 493 F.2d 608 (2d Cir. 1974), held that a specific gift to a lawyer pursuant to a contract with the decedent was income to the lawyer and deductible by the estate for estate tax purposes. "A transfer in the form of a bequest was the method that the parties chose to compensate Mr. Wolder for his legal services, and that transfer is therefore subject to taxation, whatever its label whether by federal or by local law may be." Id. at 612. Other barter arrangements also generate reportable income for the lawyer and involve similar ethical concerns.

§1.24. Income Tax Deductibility of Lifetime Estate Planning Fees

A portion of the lawyer's fee for estate services may be deductible by the client under §212, subject to the two percent floor on the deductibility of miscellaneous itemized deductions imposed by §67. In the case of an individual §212 allows a deduction for ordinary and necessary expenses incurred during the taxable year,

> (2) for the management, conservation, or maintenance of property held for the production of income; or
> (3) in connection with the determination, collection, or refund of any tax. §212(2)-(3).

Some part of the lawyer's fees incurred in connection with the establishment and administration of a revocable trust composed of income-producing property may be deductible under §212(2). However, the creation of the trust may be for personal reasons and not in the nature of investment advice for the management of income-producing property. *Arthur K. Wong,* 58 T.C.M. 3519 (1989). However, as indicated in *Wong,* the portion of the lawyer's fees attributable to tax advice regarding the establishment and administration of such a trust should be deductible under §212(3). The IRS generally takes a narrow view of the deductibility of legal fees under §212.

There is considerable tension between §§212 and 262. Section 262 disallows deductions for "personal, living, or family expenses" not otherwise allowed. The Regulations under §212 reflect the narrow view the IRS has generally taken regarding the deductibility of fees for lifetime estate planning services. However, the courts have been more generous to taxpayers. *See, e.g., Carpenter v. United States,* 338 F.2d 336 (Ct. Cl. 1964); *Nancy R. Bagley,* 8 T.C. 120 (1947), *acq.,* 1947-1 C.B. 1. The IRS position was relaxed somewhat in Rev. Rul. 72-545, 1972-2 C.B. 179, which held that a deduction was allowable under §212(3) for the portion of a lawyer's fee attributable to advice regarding the federal income, gift, and estate tax consequences of a divorce. Despite the ruling the IRS has often not allowed deductions for advice regarding the tax consequences of donative transfers.

Fees incurred in connection with a trade or business are deductible under §162. However, personal, living, and family expenses are not deductible by reason of §262. It has long been established that the cost of preparing a will is a nondeductible personal expense. *Estate of Helen*

S. Pennell, 4 B.T.A. 1039 (1926). The same rule should apply to the preparation of other documents that do not relate to the management of income-producing property, such as durable powers of attorney or living wills. Expenses incurred in connection with the defense or perfection of title to property are generally not deductible. *See* §263 (capital expenditures) and Reg. §1.212-1(k). Under the latter authority, "Expenses paid or incurred in protecting or asserting one's rights to property of a decedent as heir or legatee, or as beneficiary under a testamentary trust, are not deductible." The Tax Court has disallowed a deduction for lawyer's fees for advice regarding the use of a revocable trust to insulate the taxpayer's property from potential liability arising from litigation in which the taxpayer sought to recover an interest in the estate of Howard Hughes. *Estate of Platt W. Davis,* 79 T.C. 503 (1982).

The lawyer's statement to a client for services rendered should specify the portion that is tax deductible. In order to support such an allocation adequate records of the time devoted to various work performed for a client should be kept. It is not enough to show that the work performed had some tax consequences. Instead, "the plaintiff must show that there is a reasonable basis for allocating a portion of his legal fees to tax counselling advice. [T]his court has found that a good faith allocation by the attorney who performed the services may be sufficient to meet plaintiff's burden." *Hall v. United States,* 78-1 U.S.T.C. ¶9126, 41 A.F.T.R.2d 78-367 (Ct. Cl. 1978).

In *Wong,* the taxpayer had claimed a deduction for the amount, $5,408, that the law firm attributed on its bill to "tax counsel." The firm had charged a total of $5,660, of which it stated $208 was for the preparation of wills and $44 for xeroxing and recording. The Tax Court disallowed the deductions under §212(1) and (2), but allowed 20 percent under §212(3) as expenses incurred for tax counsel. Most of the charges related to the establishment of a revocable trust to which taxpayers transferred their residence, life insurance policies, and income-producing property. The Tax Court held that the establishment of the trust was unrelated to the production or collection of taxable income, which is the basis upon which a deduction would be allowed under §212(1). It also held that no amount was deductible under §212(2): "Expenses incurred, however, for rearranging title to income-producing property, for planning one's personal and family affairs or for retaining ownership of property are not deductible under section 212(2), but are nondeductible personal expenditures within the meaning of section 262." Id. at 3520-3521. Because of the failure of the law firm to provide an itemization of the work performed, the court held that only 20 percent of the fee was for tax advice and deductible under §212(3). The *Wong* opinion relied upon the following passage from *Sidney Merians,* 60 T.C. 187, 189 (1973):

> A complete analysis of an estate involves more than a consideration of tax consequences; in fact, it is basically concerned with transferring

> the client's property to the persons he wishes to receive it. The client's financial condition, the nature of his property, the extent to which he wants various persons to share in his estate, the needs and capacity of each intended beneficiary, the details of State law, and the need for flexibility are among the multitude of factors which are considered in establishing a plan to dispose of a client's wealth.

The *Wong* opinion helps to clarify the extent to which the Tax Court will uphold the deductibility of the legal fees incurred in connection with the establishment of revocable trusts. Some further guidance is provided by *Merians*.

§1.25. Deductibility of Post-Mortem Estate Planning Fees

The fees of the personal representative and of the lawyer for the personal representative are deductible for income *or* estate tax purposes, but not for both. *See* §12.13. Under the Regulations, a portion of a deduction may be claimed for income tax purposes and the remainder for estate tax purposes. Reg. §1.642(g)-2. Under §2053 the fees are deductible whether they are incurred with respect to property subject to claims or not subject to claims. Reg. §§20.2053-3(c)-20.2053-8. However, fees incurred by beneficiaries are generally not deductible by the estate (they are not administration expenses) or by the beneficiaries (they are personal in nature).

E. INTER VIVOS ESTATE PLANNING

§1.26. Introduction

Parts E and F adopt a functional approach in describing and analyzing the steps involved in the inter vivos and post-mortem estate planning processes. The inter vivos and post-mortem phases, discussed separately in the following pages, are intimately related: The plan that is adopted during the inter vivos planning phase determines the disposition of the client's property that will be made at death and establishes the framework within which post-mortem planning must take place.

§1.27. Stages of Inter Vivos Estate Planning

The inter vivos estate planning process consists of at least four functionally distinct stages. In chronological sequence they are: (1) getting the facts, (2) helping the client choose a plan, (3) producing the required documents, and (4) implementing the plan. A fifth stage, (5) providing continuing guidance, may be present depending on the nature of the plan that is adopted. In any case, the lawyer should encourage clients to review their plans periodically.

Stages of Inter Vivos Estate Planning

1. *Getting the facts.* In this stage the lawyer collects data by interviewing the client, examining documents, and gathering information from other sources.
2. *Helping the client choose a plan.* Here the lawyer analyzes the data, prepares tax estimates, and counsels the client regarding the choice of plan.
3. *Producing the required documents.* Drafting the necessary documents and submitting them to the client and others for review are the main features of this stage.
4. *Implementing the plan.* In this stage the lawyer supervises execution of documents, transfers of property, and submission of necessary tax returns and advises the client and the fiduciaries regarding their duties to beneficiaries and others.
5. *Continuing guidance.* Finally, the lawyer provides advice to the client and the fiduciaries regarding accountings, tax returns, and changes in the law.

Each stage is important and presents the lawyer with a different set of challenging opportunities and responsibilities. However, the first stage is often considered to be the most important.

§1.28. Getting the Facts

> [T]he chief fault with most estate plans is that they are based upon incomplete facts and that emphasis is wrongly placed; insufficient attention is given to those things which in human affairs ought to come first. J. Farr & J. Wright, An Estate Planner's Handbook 2 (4th ed. 1979).

The lawyer cannot begin to advise the client regarding an estate plan until the lawyer has relatively complete information regarding the client's family, assets, and planning objectives. Without the basic data the lawyer will not know what assets the client owns and how they are held. In short, the lawyer would not know what assets are subject to testamentary disposition.

Example 1-4. Husband and Wife had living parents but no children. They wished all of their property to be available to the survivor of them for life and ultimately distributed one-half to each set of parents. Lawyer drew reciprocal wills for them under which the surviving spouse would receive a life estate and the remainder would go in equal shares to their parents. Husband died survived by Wife. Lawyer then discovered that all of their property was held in joint tenancies with rights of survivorship. If the tenancies were validly created there was no property which would be subject to Husband's will except to the extent she might disclaim the right to Husband's interest in the property. *See Lambert v. Peoples National Bank,* 574 P.2d 738 (Wash. 1978) (joint tenancies not validly created, securities were community property of which half was subject to husband's will); *Estate of Fletcher v. Jackson,* 613 P.2d 714 (N.M. Ct. App. 1980) (joint tenancies upheld). If the joint tenancies are upheld, the remaindermen may assert a claim against Lawyer for loss of their interests in the securities.

The necessary information can be collected more efficiently and effectively if the lawyer makes prudent use of legal assistants, questionnaires, and checklists. A reliable questionnaire or checklist to guide the client and to remind the lawyer of all of the information needed is indispensable. One expert put the case for using questionnaires in these terms: "To elicit the requisite facts takes more than a good memory. Only a written questionnaire covering these facts in depth will do the job. There is simply too much that needs to be known, and memory, however good, is always fallible." Bush, Estate Planning: The Client Interview, N.Y.U., 33rd Inst. Fed. Tax. 3, 4 (1975).

The job of collecting the necessary information may be helped along if the lawyer sends a new estate planning client a letter that confirms the appointment for the initial interview and suggests the main points that the client should consider in advance. The letter may also describe the types of information that will be needed and the documents that the client should bring to the meeting. In appropriate cases, it may also ask the client to complete a questionnaire with basic data regarding the client's family and finances. However, a questionnaire that is too detailed or too demanding may deter the client from going forward and result in a cancelled appointment. Perhaps for that reason or out of personal preference, some lawyers prefer to obtain the necessary data from the client during the initial interview. Still others leave the collection of the data to a legal assistant who interviews the client before he or she meets with the lawyer.

Clients generally react favorably to the use of legal assistants in estate planning, but they should not be involved beyond the level that is acceptable to the client. Also, some clients are more reluctant to disclose intimate family and financial matters to a legal assistant than to a lawyer. In any case, the client may be more willing to provide the necessary information if he or she is assured that the information will be held in strictest confidence by the lawyer and the lawyer's office staff. Both the CPR and the MRPC require the exercise of reasonable care to prevent other lawyers or staff members from violating the confidences of a client or other professional obligations. *See* §1.11.

The success of the first stage depends largely upon the ability of the lawyer to obtain the necessary information from the client — what the late Joseph Trachtman called "a benign species of cross examination." J. Trachtman, Estate Planning 5 (1968). The task is facilitated if the physical arrangement of the lawyer's office and the lawyer's approach are designed to encourage communication between the client and the lawyer. Overall, the lawyer should strive to eliminate any features of the office or his or her demeanor that may interfere with the establishment of a good relationship: Comfort, privacy, and the lawyer's undivided attention are all conducive to effective communication. *See* A. Watson, The Lawyer in the Interviewing and Counselling Process 75 (1976). Of course, communication can be more difficult if it touches on painful subjects such as failed marriages or strained relationships with family members. The lawyer must be alert to the verbal and nonverbal cues that a subject is difficult for a client or may need more explorations. Communication regarding a painful subject may be helped if the lawyer listens attentively and is empathetic. The task can also be helped if the lawyer tells the client in advance about information that will be needed.

A growing number of firms are striving to make the estate planning process more efficient by doing more to assist clients before their initial meeting. For example, at least one firm offers free educational meetings on one evening of each month for prospective estate planning clients. As described in §1.20, one Seattle firm provides estate planning clients with educational audio tapes, pamphlets, and workbooks. Such approaches reduce the amount of time required to provide basic estate planning information to a client.

§1.29. Initial Letter to the Client

Sending a letter to a prospective client confirming the initial appointment helps establish a good relationship. If appropriate the lawyer may enclose a confidential estate planning data form. As indicated in the following sample, the letter can suggest some of the points the client should think about prior to the initial conference. It can also list some of the documents that the client should bring to the meeting.

Form 1-1. Letter to Client Regarding Initial Conference

Mr. and Mrs. Joseph L. Client
1500 Evergreen Lane, N.E.
Our Town, XX 00000

Dear Mr. and Mrs. Client:

This confirms the appointment we have to meet in my office at 2:00P.M. next Thursday, November 16. As I mentioned in my telephone conversation with Mr. Client, my office is located on the fourth floor of the Exchange Building. Although you might be able to park on the street, you may find it more convenient to park in the lot located on the north side of our building.

Enclosed is a copy of the Confidential Estate Planning Data Form that I mentioned when I spoke with Mr. Client. Please complete the form, as best you can, and bring it along to our meeting next Thursday. Although the form looks complicated I believe you will be able to complete the pertinent items without too much difficulty. As you will see, some of the questions call for readily available data but others may require some digging to complete. In any case, you will not need to complete all of the items. Please bring to our meeting copies of various documents mentioned in the form, including your present wills, deeds, insurance policies, and trusts in which you have an interest. It will be important for me to see the documents at some point. However, do not be concerned if they are not all available when we meet.

Prior to our meeting please give some thought to the persons you will each want to appoint as fiduciaries (executors, guardians, and trustees). Each will should designate an executor and a successor executor (the executor is the person who will be in charge of administering your property and carrying out the terms of your will). Husband and wives often designate each other as executor. Although the need may not arise, it is desirable to name a relative, trusted friend, or financial institution to serve as successor if required. Also, your wills should name individuals to serve as guardian and successor guardian of the person of your minor children should neither of you be able to act. An individual or corporate trustee may serve as guardian of the estate (property) of a minor.

In the unlikely event that you both die leaving minor children, you will probably want to leave your property in trust for their benefit. If your wills do not include contingent trusts for your children, any property that becomes distributable to a minor child would be received and managed for the child by a guardian of the

> child's estate. A trust is preferred to a guardianship, which is generally more cumbersome and expensive to administer. If you go the trust route, your wills should name one or more trustees to invest and manage the trust property and make distributions to, or for the benefit of, your children. The same person could serve as guardian of the person of your minor children and as trustee. However, a corporate trustee cannot act as guardian of the person. The provisions of a trust can be very flexible regarding the distribution of the trust's income and principal. It is possible to create a separate trust fund for each child from the outset. However, many parents prefer to have only a single trust fund until all of the educational expenses of the youngest child are met, which may require a disproportionate portion of the income and principal. When the youngest child's education is completed (or when the youngest child attains a specified age), the trust fund may be divided into separate shares and distributed to the children, or retained in trust for their benefit for an additional period.
>
> You might also give some thought to any gifts you might want to make to other relatives, special friends, or charities. Please also consider how you would like your property distributed if none of your children or grandchildren survive the two of you.
>
> Looking forward to seeing you next week, I am,
>
> Sincerely yours,

A sample of a comprehensive estate planning data collection form appears as Form 1-5 at the end of this chapter. The form may be edited to create a shorter, simpler, and more concise form that may be more suitable for some clients. For another data collection form, see Streng, Estate Planning, 11-11th Tax Mgmt. Port. (1991).

§1.30. Initial Interview with the Client

An interview with a lawyer may be intimidating for the prospective client. Accordingly, the lawyer should make the physical and psychological setting as welcoming and unthreatening as possible, and consider minimizing or eliminating barriers that may arise because of the dominant position that lawyers generally occupy in dealing with clients. Unsophisticated clients may perceive themselves to be dependents in need of help and the lawyer to be the powerful professional.

The lawyer should be aware of the risks of transference:

> The person being helped projects certain feelings and attributes onto the helper. This projection or transference may extend to the client's superficial dependence on the lawyer. The tendency of clients to become dependent or hooked on lawyers is related to the perception of the lawyer as an authority or parental figure. In addition to the transference of positive feelings that encourage dependency, the client may project negative feelings onto the lawyer, causing the client to be hostile and uncooperative. Elkins, The Legal Persona: An Essay on the Professional Mask, 64 Va. L. Rev. 735, 752-753 (1978).

The relationship between the lawyer and client may develop better if they "interact openly and on an equal basis [which allows] both [to] seek recognition, appreciation, respect, and value in the other as a total being." Id. at 754.

§1.30.1. Getting Off to a Good Start

The prospective client's first impression of the lawyer, created by their initial meeting, will influence the direction of their relationship. In particular, the establishment of a positive image is essential if they are to communicate easily and effectively. Meeting the prospective client in the reception area and extending a warm greeting will help to get their relationship off to a good start. If the client is brought to the lawyer's office by a receptionist or secretary, the lawyer should at least come forward to meet the client instead of remaining behind a desk or table.

§1.30.2. Office Arrangement

Achieving the desired rapport may be quickened if office furniture is thoughtfully arranged; where possible, the lawyer should be able to sit with the client. A desk, another symbol of the lawyer's power and authority, generally suggests an undesirable degree of separation. The lawyer and client should sit together at a table instead. Many lawyers use a round table for this purpose, which permits more flexible seating than a square or rectangular table. Natural and artificial lighting should also be considered when the seating is arranged; a client should be spared direct sunlight and other harsh glares. Finally, the lawyer should ensure that the conference will not be interrupted by telephone calls or other intrusions. The client deserves the lawyer's undivided attention during the interview.

§1.30.3. Encouraging Communication

Communication by the client is facilitated if the lawyer is "tolerant and non-judgmental, neutral as to the subject matter, concerned as to the person. . . . You should certainly avoid what clients complain of most, appearing bored or indifferent or exhibiting a superior attitude." H. Freeman & H. Weihofen, Clinical Law Training: Interviewing and Counseling 18 (1972). A client may be discouraged (or angry) if the lawyer is condescending or uses technical terms or concepts that are unknown to the client. Generally the flow of information from the client is encouraged if the lawyer is attentive and responds to the client's statements with conversation facilitators — words, gestures, and expressions that indicate that a statement has been heard and understood. A short verbal or nonverbal response, such as a nod, is generally sufficient. The flow of information may also be encouraged by responding at appropriate points with a question, such as "When did you move here?"

As a rule a client will tell the lawyer what he or she believes to be important. Be alert for verbal or nonverbal indications of a subject that may need to be explored in more detail. For example, a failure to discuss one child may indicate a dissatisfaction with that child or with the child's perceived attitude toward the client. Sometimes the lawyer's benign cross-examination can help the client better understand his or her own feelings — which may lead to an improvement in family relations.

§1.30.4. Learning the Client's Objectives

It is axiomatic that the client's overall planning objectives should be established first and without regard to the tax consequences. At this stage the lawyer needs to acquire an accurate picture of the client's objectives and feelings about family members and the disposition of property. Throughout the process the emphasis should be on sound planning for the client and the client's family; this is an aim that may not be entirely consistent with tax minimization. Counseling the client regarding the tax and nontax effects of attempting to achieve the client's objectives in various ways occurs in the next stage.

§1.30.5. Examining Documents

In most cases the lawyer will need to examine a variety of documents, including trusts in which the client has an interest, decrees of divorce or separate maintenance that affect the client or the client's spouse, summaries of employee benefit plans that include the client, and insurance policies on the client's life or in which the client has an interest. Gift tax returns should also be examined if the client has made taxable gifts in prior years. In some cases the lawyer may need to see copies of recent income tax returns. In some cases, a law-trained person will need to examine deeds, stock certificates, and other documents that affect title to property. It is necessary to do so because the average lay client cannot be expected to characterize properly the nature or extent of interests in property, being generally unaware of the distinctions between various forms of property ownership and the important substantive and tax law consequences that turn upon them. The need for reliable information regarding the manner in which clients hold title to property is illustrated by this example:

> **Example 1-5.** *B* told Lawyer that he and his sister *S* owned Blackacre as joint tenants. *B* wanted *S* to own Blackacre if she survived him. *B* intended to leave his residuary estate to those of his other siblings who survive him. Lawyer drew a will in accordance with *B*'s instructions. *B* died shortly after executing the will, survived by *S* and two other siblings, *C* and *D*. Blackacre was actually owned by *B* and *S* as tenants in common. Accordingly, *B*'s one-half interest in Blackacre would pass as a part of *B*'s residuary estate to *C* and *D*. Note that *B*'s interest in Blackacre might pass to *S* if *C* and *D* were to disclaim their right to receive any interest in it by will or by intestacy. (Disclaimers are explained at §§12.31-12.35.)

The breadth of the lawyer's duty to collect data is suggested by *Smith v. Lewis,* 530 P.2d 589 (Cal. 1975), in which the California Supreme Court upheld a malpractice award of $100,000 against a lawyer for failure to assert the community character of military pension rights in a divorce action that took place in 1967. (Ironically, the U.S. Supreme Court later held that military pension rights were not subject to division or equitable distribution under community property laws. *McCarty v. McCarty,* 453 U.S. 210 (1981).) The extent of the lawyer's duty expressed in *Smith v. Lewis* remains valid. *Aloy v. Mash,* 212 Cal. Rptr. 162 (1985). In *Smith v. Lewis* the court said an attorney "is expected . . . to possess knowledge of those plain and elementary principles of law which are commonly known by well informed attorneys, and to discover those additional rules of law which, although not commonly known, may readily be found by standard research techniques." 530 P.2d at 595. An analogous obligation to exercise diligence in ascertaining the existence of property and powers over the disposition of property and the state of beneficiary designations probably exists in the field of estate planning.

§1.30.6. Engagement Letter

A letter confirming the work to be done by the lawyer, the rates of compensation, and other details might be sent to the client following the initial conference. The letter might be along the lines of Form 1-2.

Form 1-2. Letter to Client After Initial Conference

Mr. and Mrs. Joseph L. Client
1500 Evergreen Lane, N.E.
Our Town, XX 00000

Dear Mr. and Mrs. Client:

This is the letter I promised during our initial meeting to send to you. It will, I hope, provide a helpful summary of some of the matters we discussed and will also be useful for your later reference. The letter first confirms the basis upon which the fee for our estate planning services will be determined. Next, it lists the general nature of the estate planning services that we will perform for you. Finally, it points out that the information you provide to me will be confidential as to others, but not as between yourselves.

You will be billed for our estate planning services after our work is completed [monthly, quarterly]. Our fee for preparing a durable power of attorney, a living will, and a will with a marital deduction trust, for each of you will probably be in the range of $800 to $1,200. However, as I mentioned to you, the fee for our work will be based upon the time actually required to prepare and implement your estate plan. As supervising attorney I will be responsible for seeing that the work is carried out in an efficient and economical manner. To that end I may be assisted by other attorneys and legal assistants in our office. In that connection, perhaps I should say that my associates and legal assistants are also bound to you by duties of loyalty and confidentiality. My time will be billed at $ ______ per hour. The hourly rates of my associates and legal assistants are considerably lower — currently $ ______ and $ ______ respectively. [Alternately: Our time is currently billed at rates of between $ ______ and $ ______ per hour. As I mentioned to you, our hourly rates are usually adjusted each year effective July 1.]

Based upon our preliminary discussion, you agreed that we should undertake such of the following services as we believe are reasonably required to prepare and implement your plan:

1. Review and analyze your existing wills and other dispositive documents (trusts, life insurance policies, etc.);

2. Review and analyze the property now owned by either or both of you, including consideration of its origin, manner in which title is held, and tax bases;
3. Consult with you regarding the manner in which each of you wishes to dispose of property over which you have any power of disposition;
4. Estimate the tax consequences of implementing your goals and advice regarding alternative methods by which those goals may be carried out;
5. Prepare the documents necessary to implement your plans, including drafts of wills, trust, property status agreements, and other documents that may be required;
6. Supervise the execution of documents and implementation of your plan.

The execution of documents and implementation of your estate plan will conclude our active role as your lawyers. However, in order to remind you to review your will periodically we will send annual reminder letters to you, beginning on the third anniversary of the execution of your wills.

Each of you may develop independent plans for the disposition of your property. Some couples establish plans that are mirror images of each other, but others do not. It is entirely possible that there may be some differences between you regarding the disposition of your property. Such differences would not prevent me from representing both of you. However, as I explained, I will not be able to represent both of you if it becomes necessary to negotiate and define your respective property interests in a property status agreement or if other conflicts of interest develop.

You have each agreed that there will be a complete and full disclosure and exchange of all information that we receive from either or both of you. That understanding applies regardless of whether we obtain such information in conferences with both of you, including conferences that may have taken place before the date of this letter.

As we go along, please let me know if you have any questions or need any additional assistance.

Sincerely,

§1.30.7. Associating Others

As indicated in §1.7, if a client's affairs involve legal matters beyond the competence of the lawyer, he or she should recommend associating counsel who are qualified to advise the client competently. This course of action is dictated by the needs of the client, ethical considerations, and by a concern for the lawyer's potential liability if the client does not receive competent advice.

§1.31. HELPING THE CLIENT CHOOSE A PLAN

> In assisting his client to reach a proper decision, it is often desirable for a lawyer to point out those factors which may lead to a decision that is morally just as well as legally permissible. He may emphasize the possibility of harsh consequences that might result from assertion of legally permissible positions. In the final analysis, however, the lawyer should always remember that the decision whether to forego legally available objectives or methods because of non-legal factors is ultimately for the client and not for himself. In the event that a client in a non-adjudicatory matter insists upon a course of conduct that is contrary to the judgment and advice of the lawyer but not prohibited by the Disciplinary Rules, the lawyer may withdraw from the employment. EC 7-8.

After the facts are collected and analyzed, the lawyer will be in a position to counsel the client regarding the adoption of a plan for the organization and disposition of the client's property. Because the client's objectives may often be achieved by various methods, the lawyer should advise the client regarding the overall consequences of each of the principal methods under consideration. The relative convenience, reliability, flexibility, cost, and fairness of each should be explained in accordance with MRPC 1.4(b): "A lawyer shall explain a matter to the extent reasonably required to permit the client to make informed decisions regarding the representation." EC 7-8 similarly states that a lawyer should "exert his best efforts to insure that decisions of his client are made only after the client has been informed of relevant considerations." In devising a plan the client should consider the need and circumstances of the family and how the family members might react to the plan. *See* §1.5 regarding the problems that may arise if children are not treated equally.

The lawyer and the client should also understand that the adoption of a plan that minimizes state and federal taxes is not morally objectionable. As Judge Learned Hand pointed out, "Anyone may so arrange his affairs that his taxes shall be as low as possible; he is not bound to choose that pattern which will best pay the Treasury; there is not even a patriotic duty to increase one's taxes." *Helvering v. Gregory,* 69 F.2d 809, 810 (2d Cir. 1934), *aff'd,* 293 U.S. 465 (1935). As indicated in the comments to MRPC 1.2, the choice of a plan is a matter for the client and not the lawyer to decide. In particular, the lawyer should not attempt to force a tax-saving plan on a client.

The lawyer should also be sure that the client gives adequate consideration to the nontax consequences of the plans under consideration.

> In considering tax avoidance devices in estate planning the client should be counseled to consider not only tax-saving effects of any proposed scheme, but also its soundness in terms of flexibility. An inter vivos disposition, as by irrevocable trust, may give away assets that the client ought to retain against possible future needs, of himself or his widow in old age or in an emergency. The human, personal effects should also be considered. Although the scheme may save money, is it likely to disappoint children or other potential heirs, or otherwise create family discord? Is the tax liability that may be avoided worth the anxiety caused over whether the scheme may be questioned by the Internal Revenue Service, and perhaps held illegal? H. Freeman & H. Weihofen, Clinical Law Training: Interviewing and Counseling 306 (1972).

The lawyer may properly attempt to dissuade a client from a course of conduct that may hurt or disadvantage others. As stated in EC 7-8, it is permissible, desirable, and thoroughly professional for a lawyer to point out to a client the "factors which may lead to a decision which is morally just as well as legally permissible. He may emphasize the possibility of harsh consequences that might result from assertion of legally permissible positions."

§1.31.1. Valuation of Assets

The proper valuation of assets is important in order to prepare tax estimates for a client and to advise the client properly regarding estate planning matters. In doing so, the lawyer must keep in mind the difference between the income tax basis of an asset and its value for gift and estate tax purposes.

The income tax basis of an asset is most frequently its cost, adjusted for depreciation and other factors. Also, see §1016 regarding adjustments to basis. Income tax values are used to determine the consequences of the sale of an asset or in helping to select property to give to a family member or to a charity. Of course, the fair market value of an asset is often used to determine the amount of a charitable deduction for income tax purposes. The gift or estate tax value of an asset is also determined by its fair market value. That value is used to calculate the amount of a gift for gift tax purposes and the amount that is includible in the gross estate for estate tax purposes. In this connection, note that discounts may be allowed, or required, in valuing closely-held stock and fractional interests in property. *See* §2.43.1.

Fair market value is defined as "the price at which the property would change hands between a willing buyer and a willing seller, neither being under any compulsion to buy or sell and both having reasonable knowledge of relevant factors." Reg. §§20.2031-1(b), 25.2512-1. The Regulations also provide detailed instructions for the valuation of particular types of assets for gift and estate tax purposes. For example, Reg. §§20.2031-2 and 25.2512-2 describe the way in which stocks and bonds are valued and Reg. §§20.2031-8 and 25.2512-6 govern the valuation of life insurance and shares in open-end investment companies (mutual funds). The value of closely-held stock may be affected by the terms of a buy-sell agreement. *See* §§11.6-11.14. Life estates, remainders, annuities, and other limited interests transferred after April 30, 1989 are valued according to interest rates that change monthly and actuarial tables that were updated in 1989 as required by §7520. *See* IRS Publications 1457 and 1458. The values of such split interests were determined previously according to actuarial tables based upon fixed rates of interest (unisex ten percent tables for transfers made after November 30, 1983, Reg. §§20.2031-7, 25.2512-5; sex-based six percent tables for transfers made between December 31, 1970 and December 1, 1983, Reg. §§20.2031-10, 25.2512-9; and unisex three-and-one-half percent tables for transfers prior to January 1, 1971).

§1.31.2. Tax Estimates

If an individual client's gross estate is, or the combined estates of a husband and wife are, likely to exceed $600,000 the lawyer should prepare estimates of the transfer tax consequences that would result from the implementation of each of the plans under consideration. The detail and formality of the estimates will depend upon the size and complexity of the client's estate. Fortunately, computer programs are available that can produce detailed estimates efficiently and economically based on various assumptions regarding, for example, the growth in value of assets. Estate planning (tax calculation) programs are frequently reviewed in periodicals including *Probate and Property,* published by the ABA section on Real Property, Probate, and Trust Law, and *Trusts and Estate Magazine*. For a helpful discussion see Boyle, Estate Planning Software: Brain Transplants for the Estate Planner, U. Miami, 23rd Inst. Est. Plan., ch. 21 (1989). As an alternative the lawyer can use a standard form to prepare such estimates. *See* Form 1-6. The estimates will indicate the tax cost of each plan and can be used to show the net amount of property that would remain under each for distribution to the beneficiaries. Whether the client is given only a summary of the tax consequences or is also given the worksheets themselves will depend in large measure on the sophistication and interest of the client. In any case, the client should be given an oral or written description of the plans under consideration and the overall tax consequences of implementing each of them. In some cases it is also important to point out their cash flow consequences. Written descriptions have obvious advantages should a dispute arise regarding the nature and sufficiency of the lawyer's tax advice.

The primary purpose of estimating the tax consequences of various plans is to enable the client to make an informed choice among them. In some cases the estimates should be amplified to indicate how particular assets would be disposed of under the various plans. For example, life insurance proceeds and joint tenancy assets might pass outright to a surviving spouse under one plan, whereas under another plan they might pass into a trust for the surviving spouse. By tracing the disposition of significant assets under various plans, the lawyer will be in a better position to advise the client regarding the provisions that should be included in a will or trust. Such an analysis may indicate that most of the client's property will pass to his or her spouse outside the will, which may make it uneconomical to create a testamentary trust for the spouse. As an alternative the client might change the manner of holding title to some property to eliminate the survivorship feature.

§1.31.3. Record of Advice to Client

> Another reason to inform the client of the cost of deferring taxes is to protect the lawyer. If the surviving spouse dies shortly after the first spouse to die, the decision to defer taxes may prove costly. Sometimes the credit on prior transfers, a disclaimer or other post mortem planning may reduce the extra tax cost, but not always. The next generation of beneficiaries might well ask, in a hostile manner, if the deceased estate planning clients were informed of the overall tax cost of deferring estate taxes. If the lawyer did the math and explained it to the clients (and preserved copies of the computer generated reports in the file), the question can be answered "yes." By giving the client a copy of the computer generated report and explaining it to a client, a potentially dangerous situation is avoided. Boyle, Estate Planning Software: Brain Transplants for the Estate Planner, U. Miami, 23rd Inst. Est. Plan ¶2102.9 (1989).

It is important for the lawyer to make a contemporaneous written record of the advice that is given to a client and of the client's instructions to the lawyer, particularly if the client selects a plan that does not minimize the overall tax costs. For example, in order to provide a surviving spouse with the maximum degree of freedom, a married client with a large estate may choose to give all of his or her property to the surviving spouse outright. Such a disposition wastes the deceased spouse's unified credit, which may unnecessarily increase the estate tax that will be payable by the surviving spouse's estate. Other clients who are similarly situated may choose not to make any substantial gift to the surviving spouse in a form that qualifies for the marital deduction. In either case, it may be helpful to give the client a written description of the tax consequences of the plan as compared with other more tax effective plans. Without contemporaneous written evidence it may be very difficult to persuade the surviving spouse, the beneficiaries, or a court that the client received competent legal advice and that the plan that was chosen did not minimize death taxes. In other contexts the courts have often acknowledged that wills are commonly planned with the intent of reducing taxes: "[I]t is well known that wills and testamentary trusts are customarily prepared in light of their probable tax consequences, and that, particularly where the testator is married, they are usually written to take advantage of the marital deduction." *Mittleman v. Commissioner,* 522 F.2d 132, 139 (D.C. Cir. 1975) (will construed to qualify for marital deduction). Similar risks exist if property is given to the surviving spouse in a way that will unnecessarily subject it to taxation upon his or her death. *See Bucquet v. Livingston,* 129 Cal. Rptr. 514 (1976).

§1.32. Letter Describing Plan; Tax Estimates

Here are samples of the type of letter and tax estimates that might be sent to a client following the initial conference. The letter and form of the estimates can be tailored to meet the needs of a particular client.

Form 1-3. Letter to Client Describing Recommended Plan

Mr. and Mrs. Joseph L. Client
1500 Evergreen Lane, N.E.
Our Town, XX 00000

Dear Mr. and Mrs. Client:

As agreed at our initial conference last week I have prepared estimates of the federal estate taxes and related costs that might be imposed on your estates under your current plan and the plan we discussed. The estimates rely heavily upon the data provided by the Confidential Estate Planning Data Form that you brought to our meeting. Copies of the estimates are enclosed for your review and reference. For purposes of the estimates, we have assumed that the value of assets would remain constant and that the estate tax law would not change (including the amount of the credit that is allowable for estate tax purposes, $192,800). The estimates indicate that about $240,000 in taxes and expenses will be saved by substituting the plan we discussed for the one you now have.

Under your existing wills when one of you dies, all of the decedent's property would pass outright to the survivor. As I explained at our meeting, in such a case no federal estate tax would be payable upon the death of the first of you to die because an unlimited marital deduction is allowed for the value of property that passes to a surviving spouse. However, passing all of the property outright to the surviving spouse would unnecessarily increase the amount of estate tax payable by his or her estate. In particular, if Joe dies first, the present plan will require the payment of about $240,000 in additional estate tax and expenses on Mary's death.

Part A of Estimate 1 shows that no tax will be due on Joe's death. However, as shown in Part B, state and federal taxes totaling over $301,000 would be due from Mary's estate. Under the alternate plan we discussed, which involved leaving your property in trust for Mary's benefit, Mary's estate would pay only about $71,000 in death taxes. In the latter case, we estimate that the expenses of administering Mary's estate would be reduced by $10,000. Accordingly, the total saving in taxes and expenses would be about $240,000.

Estimate 2 shows the federal estate taxes that would be due if you adopt the alternate plan we discussed. Under it each of you would leave most of your property to a trust of which the survivor is entitled to receive all of the income and limited distributions of principal. In addition, the survivor could be given the power to control the distribution of the property among your descendants upon the survivor's death. The trust is particularly attractive because the surviving spouse can elect how much of the trust is claimed as a marital deduction in computing the estate tax on the deceased spouse's estate. The election gives the plan additional flexibility without affecting the actual interests of the survivor in the trust. Of course, to the extent the marital deduction is claimed in the first estate the property of the trust is includible in the estate of the survivor. Again, no estate tax will be due if Joe dies first. More important, the estate tax payable on Mary's death would be dramatically reduced. As indicated above, the total amount of taxes and expenses would be reduced by about $240,000.

If Mary dies first, no federal estate tax will be due unless the value of her total estate exceeds $600,000. However, the estate tax that will be due on Joe's death will be increased to the extent

Mary leaves property to him outright or in other ways that would cause it to be included in his estate for tax purposes when he dies. Under the present circumstances any property that is added to Joe's estate will be subject to a marginal estate tax of at least 39 percent. Accordingly, Mary may want to leave her property in ways that will insulate it from taxation on Joe's death. For example, she might leave her jewelry outright to your children and her stocks and bonds to a trust for Joe and your children.

Please call me after you have reviewed the enclosures and are ready to meet again. At our next meeting you may be able to settle upon the details of your estate plan, after which we can begin to prepare drafts of the necessary documents.

Sincerely yours,

Form 1-4. Tax Estimates

Estimate 1. Federal Estate Tax
Mr. and Mrs. Joseph L. Client

This part of the memorandum estimates the amount of the estate taxes that will be due upon deaths of Mr. and Mrs. Client, assuming that Mr. Client dies first, leaving all of his property outright to Mrs. Client.

Part A. Tax on Mr. Client's Estate

1. Gross Estate		
Annuity (Employee Benefit Plan)	$ 300,000	
Residence	150,000	
Stocks and bonds	390,000	
Cash	50,000	
Tangible personal property	50,000	
Life insurance	200,000	
Total Gross Estate		$1,140,000
2. Deductions		
Debts, funeral expenses, etc. (est.)	$ 10,000	
Administration expenses (est. at about 3% of gross estate)	30,000	

Marital deduction (value of property passing to Mrs. Client)	1,100,000	
Total Deductions		$1,140,000
3. Taxable Estate (Gross Estate less Deductions)		$ 0
4. Federal Estate Tax		
Adjusted taxable gifts	$ 0	
Taxable Estate	0	
Total Tax Base		$ 0
Tentative Tax		$ 0
Less:		
Unified credit	$ 0	
Credit for state death taxes	0	
Total credits		$ 0
Estate Tax Due		$ 0
5. Amount available to beneficiaries from Mr. Client's estate:		
Total Gross Estate		$1,140,000
Less:		
Debts and expenses	$ 40,000	
State death taxes	0	
Federal estate tax	0	40,000
Net Amount Available		$1,100,000

Part B. Tax on Mrs. Client's Estate

1. Gross Estate		
Inherited from Mr. Client	$1,100,000	
Mrs. Client's stocks and bonds	300,000	
Jewelry and personal effects	25,000	
Total Gross Estate		$1,425,000
2. Deductions		
Debts, funeral expenses, etc. (est.)	$ 10,000	

Administration expenses (est. at about 3% of gross estate)	35,000	
Total Deductions		$ 45,000
3. Taxable Estate (Gross Estate less Deductions)		$1,380,000
4. Federal Estate Tax		
Adjusted taxable gifts	$ 0	
Taxable estate	1,380,000	
Total tax base		$1,380,000
Tentative tax		504,200
Less:		
Unified credit	$ 192,800	
Credit for state death taxes	60,560	263,360
Estate Tax Due		$ 240,840
5. Amount available to beneficiaries from Mrs. Client's estate:		
Total Gross Estate		$1,425,000
Less:		
Debts and expenses	$ 45,000	
State death taxes	60,560	
Federal estate tax	240,840	346,400
Net Amount Available		$1,078,600

Estimate 2. Federal Estate Tax
Mr. and Mrs. Joseph L. Client

Below are estimates of the estate taxes that will be due from the estates of Mr. and Mrs. Client, assuming that Mr. Client dies first leaving a will creating a trust for Mrs. Client that qualifies for the marital deduction under §2056(b)(7) (a "qualified terminable interest property trust" or QTIP trust). The portion of the trust with respect to which the election is made will be included in Mrs. Client's estate, but the balance will not.

Part A. Tax on Mr. Client's Estate. Mr. Client's executor can make an election under §2056(b)(7) that will eliminate any estate tax on his estate yet shelter an amount equal to the credit equivalent ($600,000) from inclusion in Mrs. Client's estate.

1. Gross Estate (as in Estimate 1, Part A, above)		$1,140,000
2. Deductions		
Debts, funeral expenses, etc.	$ 10,000	
Administration expenses (est. at about 3% of gross estate)	30,000	
Marital deduction (election to claim this portion of trust as qualified terminable interest property under §2056(b)(7))	500,000	
Total Deductions		$ 540,000
3. Taxable Estate (Gross Estate less Deductions)		$ 600,000
4. Federal Estate Tax		
Adjusted taxable gifts	$ 0	
Taxable Estate	600,000	
Total Tax Base		$ 600,000
Tentative tax		$ 192,800
Less:		
Unified credit		$ 192,800
Estate Tax Due		$ 0
5. Amount available to beneficiaries from Mr. Client's estate:		
Total Gross Estate		$1,140,000
Less:		
Debts and expenses	$ 40,000	
State death taxes	0	
Federal estate tax	0	40,000
Net Amount Available		$1,100,000*

*The trust for Mrs. Client will be funded with the full $1,100,000 of which $500,000 is assumed to be includible in her estate under Code §2044 by reason of the election Mr. Client's executor made under Code §2056(b)(7). Actually, her estate will be required to include 5/11th of the value of the trust ($500,000/$1,100,000) at the time of her death. The other $600,000 (6/11th) is not includible in her estate.

Part B. Tax on Mrs. Client's Estate.

1. Gross Estate		
Marital deduction interest in trust under Mr. Client's will	$500,000	
Mrs. Client's stocks and bonds	300,000	
Jewelry and personal effects	25,000	
Total Gross Estate		$825,000
2. Deductions		
Debts, funeral expenses, etc. (estimated)	$ 10,000	
Administration expenses (estimated at about 3% of gross estate)	25,000	
Total Deductions		$ 35,000
3. Taxable Estate (Gross Estate less Deductions)		$790,000
4. Federal Estate Tax		
Adjusted taxable gifts	$ 0	
Taxable estate	790,000	
Total tax base		$790,000
Tentative tax		$263,900
Less:		
Unified credit (1987 amount)	$192,800	
Credit for state death taxes	25,200	218,000
Estate Tax Due		$ 45,900
5. Amount available to beneficiaries from Mrs. Client's estate and trust under Mr. Client's will:		
(a) From Mrs. Client's estate		
Total Gross Estate	$825,000	
Less:		
Debts and expenses	$ 35,000	
State death taxes	25,200	
Federal estate tax	45,900	106,100

Net Amount Available		$ 718,900
(b) From trust under Mr. Client's will		
Net amount distributable under Mr. Client's will (Estimate 2, Part A 5)	$1,100,000	
Less:		
Marital deduction gift to trust for Mrs. Client	500,000	
Net Amount Available		$ 600,000
(c) Total from estate and trust ((a) & (b))		$1,318,900

(d) Comparison with plan described in Estimate 1. If all of Mr. Client's property is left outright to Mrs. Client, a total of $1,078,600 will be available for distribution on her death. See Estimate 1, Part B 5. Under the plan described in this estimate the distributees will receive $1,318,900 or about $240,300 more.

§1.33. Producing the Documents

> How to get the document on paper and to the client for execution is generally not covered by any course in law school. "Clinical studies in law schools would expose law students to the many books and articles on the subject. The average lawyer newly admitted to practice opens his career with limited knowledge of the existence of systems and procedures that can be used in his estate planning practice, or even be adapted to his preferences."
>
> There is a great difference between what attorneys actually do in their practice of drawing wills for clients and what they could do, or what they should do. They are well aware of what they could or should do, but don't do. Boucher, THE WILL-sey REPORT in Estate Planning: Systems and Technology 3, 4 (ABA Sections of Econ. of Law Prac. and of Real Prop., Prob. and Tr. Law, 1978).

One of the greatest opportunities for improving the lawyer's performance exists in the third stage — the production of documents. Computerbased document assembly systems and advanced word processing software allow lawyers to produce documents quickly and economically. The objectives of automation in estate planning are well summarized in this passage from a relatively early article:

> The objectives of the estate planner in installing a system of automation are: (1) cost control in increasingly complex computations and documents; (2) quality control over such computations and documents; (3) freeing himself for the highest functions for which he was trained and should be paid; (4) improving service to clients by delivery of advice and documents in shorter turn around time; (5) increasing his own professional and job satisfactions by gaining time for doing those things which caused him to select the estate planning specialty. Brink, Automation in Estate Planning, N.Y.U., 32d Inst. Fed. Tax. 1, 4 (1974).

§1.33.1. Develop and Use Estate Planning Forms

For reasons of efficiency, economy, and accuracy, a lawyer should develop and use a reliable set of forms whether or not an automated document production system is used. It may be more convenient and cost-effective to store forms in a computer, but some lawyers prefer to use more traditional methods that rely upon less sophisticated systems, such as "cut-and-paste" forms that may be photocopied. Some formbooks are available commercially from publishers or through financial institutions that sponsor the publication of the books. The discussion accompanying the forms in some formbooks provides valuable insight regarding their use. The forms contained in the books must, of course, be reviewed carefully. Unacceptable risks are involved if the lawyer uses or alters forms without understanding their purpose or the effect of the alterations.

It is inefficient, costly, and downright dangerous to create each document from scratch. Too much time is required and there are too many opportunities unintentionally to include or exclude a provision or to draft a provision improperly. Developing and maintaining a repertoire of interchangeable forms also helps the lawyer understand the purpose and function of each interrelated part as well as the whole.

§1.33.2. Establishing a Timetable

As noted in §1.6, as soon as practicable the lawyer and client should agree on a tentative timetable. It should be possible to establish a reasonable timetable once the client has chosen the principal elements of his or her estate plan. The plan should include target dates for the submission of drafts to the client and for final execution of the documents. The interests of the client and the lawyer are best served if the lawyer drafts the documents as soon as possible after the lawyer and client agree upon a plan. In order to avoid the type of lengthy delays about which clients often complain, the lawyer can calendar reminders to prepare the documents. From the lawyer's perspective it is most economical and efficient to produce documents promptly. Maintaining an efficient pace may be easier if the client is encouraged to review and respond to the drafts promptly. Again, as noted in §1.6, an unreasonable delay in providing services to the client may result in disciplinary or malpractice actions or both.

§1.33.3. Transmitting Drafts to the Clients

How forceful are right words. Job 6:25 (King James).

Most clients will better understand the draft documents if they are written in understandable language. The task of understanding a will (or other document) is made easier if it is accompanied by a table of contents which includes a general description of the provisions of the document(s). *See* §4.8. Some lawyers also send graphs or flowcharts, which show how various items of property will be passed under the plan. The letter should, of course, explain any substantial differences between the tax results described in previous letters and the results that will flow from the drafts. A chart or graph depicting the dispositions under the will of a husband which leaves all of the property to his wife if she survives him, otherwise to a contingent trust for minor children might look like Chart 1-1, *infra*.

§1.33.4. Advanced Technology; Security Problems; Sources of Information

The use of advanced technology based upon optical scanners and computers is growing. The relatively large capital cost involved in some new systems may lead individual lawyers or small law firms, in the interest of economy, to share the use of computers, facsimile machines, and other equipment. If this is done, the lawyers must be sure that the system protects the confidentiality of their clients' information.

The methods available to retrieve and reproduce forms are constantly evolving, but the particular method that a lawyer uses is relatively unimportant. Many systems are capable of quickly producing documents of acceptable quality and appearance. Information regarding computer hardware is available from vendors, consultants and a variety

Chart 1-1
Disposition of Husband's Estate

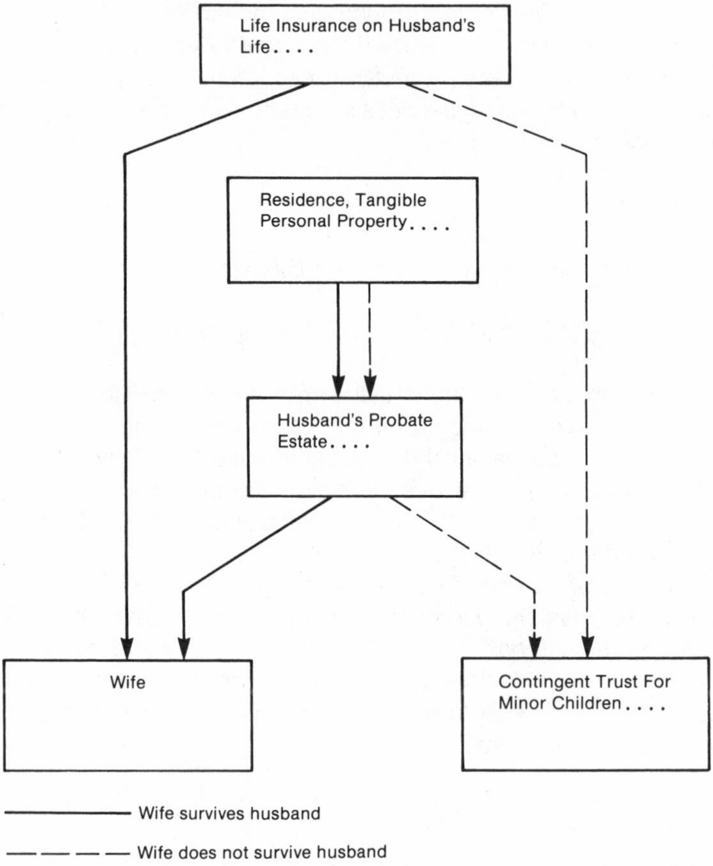

of publications. Likewise, information regarding software programs is available from a wide variety of sources, including publications of sections and committees of the ABA, and state and local bar associations, in particular the Real Property, Probate and Trust Section of the American Bar Association (the Section Journal and Probate and Property). *See also,* Boyle, Estate Planning Software: Brain Transplants for the Estate Planner, U. Miami, 23rd Inst. Est. Plan., ch. 21 (1989); Wilkins, Document Drafting in the 1990s, U. Miami, 23rd Inst. Est. Plan., ch. 8 (1989); Bilter, The Computer Connection: Estate Planning, Probate and the PC, U. Miami, 20th Inst. Est. Plan., ch. 19 (1986). Vendors of various computer systems can also usually arrange for visits to offices that have systems in operation.

§1.34. Implementing the Plan

When the time comes to implement the plan, the lawyer should remain in charge although the client's estate planning team may have many members. In particular, the lawyer should oversee the execution of documents, the transfer of property, and the filing of tax returns. Because of the possibility that documents might be altered or incorrectly executed, the lawyer should not ordinarily entrust them to clients for execution. A lawyer may advise an out-of-town client regarding the proper method of executing a will, but allowing a legal assistant to supervise the execution of a will may violate DR 3-101(A), which states that "A lawyer shall not aid a non-lawyer in the unauthorized practice of law." N.Y. Bar Assn. Formal Ethics Op. 347 (1974). If a document prepared by a lawyer is not properly executed, the lawyer may be the subject of a malpractice action. *See, e.g., Ward v. Arnold,* 328 P.2d 164 (Wash. 1958). The lawyer should also supervise title transfers, assignments and changes of beneficiary designations in insurance policies, and other acts necessary to implement the plan.

> **Example 1-6.** Client executed an irrevocable trust in Lawyer's office in the presence of Client's insurance agent, Agent. Under Client's estate plan, the existing life insurance policies on Client's life were to be assigned to the trustee of the trust. Agent, who assisted in the acquisition of the policies, agreed to arrange their transfer. The policies were not transferred promptly. Client died more than 3 years after the creation of the trust but within 3 years of the time the policies were transferred to the trustee. As a result, the life insurance proceeds were included in Client's gross estate under §2042. *See* §6.32.1.
>
> Lawyer may or may not be liable for the additional estate tax imposed on Client's estate because of the failure promptly to transfer the policies to the trustee, but in either case the beneficiaries of the trust will almost certainly be unhappy with Lawyer's performance. In other instances the lawyer may be held liable for the loss caused by the failure of an insurance advisor to prepare and have the client execute a change of beneficiary form in accordance with the plan. *See* Eckhardt, The Estate Planning Lawyer's Problems: Malpractice and Ethics, U. Miami, 8th Inst. Est. Plan. ¶607.2. (1974).

Because of the lawyer's position of leadership on the estate planning team, the lawyer may be held liable for the failure of another team member to carry out a portion of the estate planning program competently.

§1.34.1. Follow-up Instructions and Subsequent Services

After the documents are executed arrangements must be made for the custody of the originals and for the distribution of copies as appropriate. If the lawyer retains the originals, which may be the safest and most convenient arrangement for the client, he or she should provide the client with an appropriate receipt indicating that the original is held at the latter's request and subject to his or her order. Some commentators believe it is inappropriate for the lawyer to retain the original documents because of the advantage it gives the lawyer-custodian when it comes time to select a lawyer for the testator's personal representative. *See* Johnston, An Ethical Analysis of Common Estate Planning Practices — Is Good Business Bad Ethics?, 45 Ohio St. L.J. 57 (1984). The practice was also criticized by the Wisconsin Supreme Court in *State v. Gulbankian,* 196 N.W. 2d 733 (Wis. 1972). However, the practice should be upheld if the client chooses to leave his or her will with the scrivener after full disclosure of the advantages and disadvantages of doing so.

The letter sending the client copies of the documents should also cover a number of other subjects, including the nature and extent of the fiduciary duties that the client assumes currently under the plan (*e.g.,* service as trustee of an irrevocable trust for the benefit of children). A relatively simple form of transmittal letter which cautions the client not to make changes in beneficiary designations or forms of property ownership appears at §4.33. For a helpful form letter that describes the duties of a fiduciary see Leimberg & Plotnick, A Sample Letter to Clients on Their Duties as Executors and Trustees, 32 Prac. Lawyer 23 (Sept. 1986). The letter should also remind the client to file appropriate tax returns, such as a gift tax return reporting gifts that were made. Ordinarily, the lawyer should assist in preparing any gift tax returns or other tax returns that are required at the time. The letter should also define the extent of any obligations the lawyers may have to provide continuing supervision or services.

With the implementation of the plan the lawyer might want to emphasize that the active phase of the estate planning work has been concluded. As indicated in the sample engagement letter at §1.30.6, the letter might indicate that the lawyer will send a reminder letter to the client at the end of two or three years suggesting that the client review the will. Such an approach, or a more direct one, might reduce or eliminate any responsibility the lawyer might have to inform the client of subsequent changes in the law. As a matter of client relations the lawyer would probably want to communicate with any clients who might be affected by future changes in the law, but he or she should be reluctant to undertake any affirmative responsibility to do so. If the duty is undertaken the letter should clearly describe that responsibility and the charges that will be made for the services.

> If the lawyer is willing to assume that burden, he is justified in charging for the service. If the client is not willing to pay for this service, the lawyer need not bear the burden. If the lawyer is not willing to assume that burden even with annual retainer, he should so advise the client. Eckhardt, The Estate Planning Lawyer's Problems: Malpractice and Ethics, U. Miami, 8th Inst. Est. Plan. ¶P611 (1974).

In order to render a service of that type, the clients who may be affected by a particular change in the law must be readily identifiable. The lawyer will have this capacity if the contents of dispositive instruments are classified and recorded in a readily retrievable form, such as the "Client Document Summary" described in §1.10.2. A retrieval system may be used for other purposes in the office, such as providing reminders of dates upon which tax returns are due or other important events. Understandably, some lawyers prefer to limit their role to providing clients with periodic reminders that their estate plans should be reviewed.

§1.34.2. Subsequent Communications; Ethical Considerations

It is ethically appropriate to provide clients with advice regarding changes in the law or reminders to review their wills. For example, the ABA Committee on Professional Ethics and Grievances has stated:

> It is our opinion that where the lawyer has no reason to believe that he has been supplanted by another lawyer, it is not only his right, but might even be his duty, to advise his client of any change of fact or law which might defeat the client's testamentary purpose as expressed in the will. Periodic notices might be sent to the client for whom a lawyer has drawn a will suggesting that it might be wise for the client to re-examine his will to determine whether or not there has been any change in his situation requiring a modification of his will. A.B.A. Comm. on Professional Ethics and Grievances, Formal Op. 210 (1941).

The same conclusion was reached by the New York Bar Association: "An attorney may call the attention of his clients to facts which inure to their benefit in relation to matters regarding which he has been consulted, and the attorney may, in fact, have a duty to do so." EC 2-1, 3 and 4; DR 2-104(A)(1); *cf.* A.B.A. Committee on Professional Ethics, Op. No. 210 (1941). There is no ethical objection to the will review program proposed [reminder that will is five years old and recommendation that it be reviewed.] N.Y. Bar Assn. Formal Ethics Op. 188 (1971).

F. POST-MORTEM PLANNING

§1.35. Post-Mortem Estate Planning

Creative post-mortem planning can maximize the benefits the survivors will derive from a decedent's estate. *See* Chapter 12. The process is a challenging one that requires the lawyer to explore all of the opportunities state and federal laws (substantive and tax) offer to minimize taxes and protect property from creditors. In a large estate the help of a competent accountant can be very valuable. In order not to lose any tax-saving opportunities it is important to begin planning for the administration of an estate as soon after death as possible.

The stages of the post-mortem estate planning process roughly parallel those of the inter vivos process. At the beginning an extensive amount of information must be collected regarding the decedent and the decendent's property. *See, e.g.,* Abel & Price, First Steps in Handling Decedent's Property, 1 Cal. Decedent Est. Admin. 207 (Cal. CEB 1970). If an estate administration proceeding is required, the lawyer will prepare the documents necessary to obtain appointment of the personal representative. At the outset of the administration the lawyer should provide the personal representative with a lengthy letter or printed statement that provides a comprehensive guide to the steps involved in the administration of the estate and of the personal representative's duties. After the appointment, the lawyer will help the personal representative marshal and protect the decedent's property, publish notice to creditors, and other duties. Later stages involve the formulation of plans for the administration of the estate, including the sale of assets, distributions, and the closure of the estate.

§1.36. Lawyer's Relationship to Personal Representatives and Beneficiaries

In the context of estate administration the lawyer is most appropriately considered to represent the personal representative as a fiduciary and not as an individual. However, views diverge, as is pointed out in the comments to MRPC 1.7: "In estate administration the identity of the client may be unclear under the law of a particular jurisdiction. Under one view, the client is the fiduciary. Under another view the client is the estate or trust, including its beneficiaries." In *Steinway v. Bolden,* 460 N.W.2d 306 (Mich. Ct. App. 1990), the court held that "although the personal representative retains the attorney, the attorney's client is the estate, rather than the personal representative."

The lawyer is generally not considered directly to represent the beneficiaries or creditors, whose interests may conflict with each other or the overall interests of the estate. However, under the better view the lawyer is considered to owe fiduciary duties to the beneficiaries. As a fiduciary the lawyer for a personal representative or trustee is obligated to deal fairly and openly with the beneficiaries, to respect their interests, and to be impartial in making decisions affecting the beneficiaries.

> In probate, the attorney-client relationship exists between the attorney and the personal representative of the estate. . . . The personal representative stands in a fiduciary relationship to those beneficially interested in the estate. He is obligated to exercise the utmost good faith and diligence in administering the estate in the best interests of the heirs. . . . The personal representative employs an attorney to assist him in the proper administration of the estate. Thus, the fiduciary duties of the attorney run not only to the personal representative but also to the heirs. *Estate of Larson,* 694 P.2d 1051 (Wash. 1985).

> An attorney who acts as counsel for a trustee provides advice and guidance as to how that trustee may and must act to fulfill his obligations to all beneficiaries. It follows that when an attorney undertakes a relationship as adviser to a trustee, he in reality also assumes a relationship with the beneficiary akin to that between trustee and beneficiary. *Morales v. Field,* 160 Cal. Rptr. 239, 244 (Cal. App. 1979).

Some courts have adopted a narrower view of the lawyer's responsibility to the beneficiaries of an estate. For example, a California decision based such a conclusion to some extent on the lack of contractual privity between the lawyer and the beneficiaries. In a malpractice action brought by the beneficiaries of a decedent's estate against the lawyer for the personal representative, *Goldberg v. Frye,* 266 Cal. Rptr. 483 (4th Dist. 1990), the court concluded that the lawyer did not owe any duty to the beneficiaries. While noting that the attorney must communicate with the beneficiaries, "the attorney by definition represents only one party: the fiduciary." Id. at 1269. The court apparently believed that in the absence of an attorney-client relationship between the lawyer and the beneficiaries the lawyer does not have any duty to the beneficiaries. According to the court, "It would be very dangerous to conclude that the attorney, through performance of his service to the administrator and by way of communication to estate beneficiaries, subjects himself to claims of negligence from the beneficiaries. The beneficiaries are entitled to evenhanded and fair administration by the fiduciary. They are not owed a duty directly by the fiduciary's attorney." Id. at 1269. *See also, Elam v. Hyatt Legal Services,* 541 N.E.2d 616 (Ohio 1989) (requisite privity existed under Ohio law).

Although the lawyer may not represent the fiduciary in an individual capacity, it is appropriate for the fiduciary to be informed regarding the tax and other consequences that would follow if a timely waiver of the right to receive a fee is made. In any case the lawyer should advise the fiduciary fully regarding the fiduciary's duties (*e.g.,* impartiality toward beneficiaries, undivided loyalty).

The lawyer may communicate directly with the beneficiaries at the outset of the administration of the estate or trust regarding matters of interest to them. Indeed, if they consider themselves to be represented by the lawyer, the lawyer may have a duty to communicate with them. For example, in *Linck v. Barokas & Martin,* 667 P.2d 171 (Alaska 1983), the court held that the failure of attorneys to advise the beneficiary-clients of the availability and consequences of a disclaimer by the surviving spouse was actionable malpractice. Unlike *Linck,* most cases will not involve beneficiaries who were also clients of the lawyer and who (apparently) looked to him or her for advice. Because of the potential for serious conflicts of interest, the lawyer for the personal representative should not also represent a beneficiary who wishes to explore the possibility of disclaiming an interest. In such a case the conflict is greater if the lawyer also represents a beneficiary whose interest might be enhanced by the disclaimer. The initial letter to the beneficiaries should point out that the lawyer does not represent them in connection with the estate.

The lawyer-beneficiary may represent the fiduciary "unless, because of the factual situation surrounding the estate and the bequest, a conflict of interest (E.C. 5-5) or an appearance of impropriety (Canon 9) will arise." N.Y. Formal Ethics Op. 356 (1974).

Regular communication with the beneficiaries regarding the progress in the administration of the estate may be desirable. Such a practice may forestall the common complaint that lawyers fail to inform beneficiaries regarding estate matters. *See* M. Sussman, J. Cates & D. Smith, The Family and Inheritance (1970).

§1.37. Lawyer Must Avoid Personal Transactions with Estate or Beneficiaries

Neither the fiduciary nor the lawyer for the fiduciary is free to purchase assets of the fiduciary estate or to acquire interests of beneficiaries. In some instances transactions between the fiduciary and the estate or trust may be valid and formally unobjectionable if they are approved by a court upon full disclosure. IIA A. Scott, Trusts §§170-170.11 (4th ed. 1987); A.B.A. Comm. on Professional Ethics, Informal Ethics Op. C-804 (1964). However, as a general rule the lawyer should not enter into any personal transactions with a fiduciary or a beneficiary of a trust or estate.

§1.38. Cash Projection and Tax Planning

In this stage the lawyer must analyze the data that have been collected and project the amount of cash the estate will need to, for example, support dependents and pay legacies, debts, taxes, and expenses. The projection will be used to determine the estate's liquidity and to plan for the sale of assets, borrowing, or other steps that should be taken to meet any cash shortfall. Early in this stage the lawyer and fiduciary should consider the adoption of a tax year for the estate and the elections that must be made for tax purposes. The entire process requires a continuous consideration of the state and federal tax consequences of actions planned or taken. The sale and distribution of assets may begin in this stage, depending upon the circumstances of the estate and the beneficiaries.

§1.39. Tax Returns and Malpractice

> The number of legal malpractice decisions between 1970 and 1980 was four times greater than reported in the prior decade. Moreover, the number of claims since 1980 continues to increase at the rate of almost 20 percent a year. It is now estimated that a claim for legal malpractice will be filed against one of every seventeen lawyers this year. Portuonodo, Malpractice Risks of Tax Practitioners, N.Y.U., 46th Inst. Fed. Tax. ¶18.1 (1988).

In the third stage, filing the estate tax return and making the more important sales and distributions of assets take place. When the return is prepared the lawyer and fiduciary must make some decision regarding the available elections (*e.g.,* alternate valuation of assets, QTIP election, use of alternatively deductible expenses). The considerations involved in making the elections are described in Chapter 12. Throughout the proceedings the lawyer must also consider the options available under the local law, including the use of family awards, allowances, and disclaimers.

The lawyer may be liable for any additional taxes, penalties, or interest that must be paid because a tax return is filed late. *Cameron v. Montgomery,* 225 N.W.2d 154 (Wis. 1975); *Lohn's Estate,* 269 A.2d

451 (Pa. 1970). However, a lawyer is not negligent in advising a client regarding an estate tax matter in accordance with the current understanding of the law among competent lawyers in the community, although the advice is subsequently determined to be incorrect. *Smith v. St. Paul Life & Marine Ins. Co.,* 366 F. Supp. 1283 (M.D. La. 1973), *aff'd per curiam,* 500 F.2d 1131 (5th Cir. 1974) (erroneous advice that a judgment of possession under Louisiana law did not constitute a distribution for alternate valuation date purposes under the federal estate tax law). The lawyer "is not required to exercise perfect judgment in every instance." *Ramp v. St. Paul Fire & Marine Ins. Co.,* 269 So. 2d 239, 244 (La. 1972).

§1.40. Closing the Estate

The final stage of the post-mortem process involves the audit of the estate's tax returns, the preparation of the necessary estate fiduciary accountings, and the closure of the estate. The lawyer must see that the fiduciary provides the beneficiaries with the necessary information regarding distributions and the bases of assets, that receipts are received for distributions, and that the fiduciary is properly discharged. If distributions are made to guardians or trustees, the lawyer should also provide them with some guidance regarding their duties.

Form 1-5. Confidential Estate Planning Data Form

I. General Information

	Husband	*Wife*
Name	______________	______________
Citizenship	______________	______________
Soc. Sec. No.	______________	______________
Occupation	______________	______________
Date and place of birth	______________	______________
Home address:	______________________________	
	______________________________	
Telephone	______________	______________
Bus. telephone	______________	______________

Date and place of marriage ______________________

Length of residence in this state ______________________

Prior residences during marriage ______________________

Prior marriages

(Attach a copy of decree of dissolution and other documents regarding property settlement and custody of children.)

Property Agreement. Attach a copy of any agreement between husband and wife regarding property (ante-nuptial or post-nuptial agreements).

II. Children

1.	2.
Name ________________	Name ________________
Date and place of birth and age ________________	Date and place of birth and age ________________
Soc. Sec. No. ___________	Soc. Sec. No. ___________
Address ________________	Address ________________
________________	________________
Occupation ___________	Occupation ___________
Name of spouse ___________	Name of spouse ___________
Names and ages of children ___________	Names and ages of children ___________
___________	___________
Special needs of this child ___________	Special needs of this child ___________
Note if adopted, divorced, or separated ___________	Note if adopted, divorced, or separated ___________

[Add further blanks for other children as required.]

III. Parents, Brothers, and Sisters

1. Parents

	Husband		*Wife*	
Names	________________		________________	
	________________		________________	
Address	________________		________________	
	________________		________________	
Health	M_______	F_______	M_______	F_______
Age or date of death	M_______	F_______	M_______	F_______
Estimated size of estate	M_______	F_______	M_______	F_______

2. Brothers and Sisters

	Husband	*Wife*
Names and ages (or dates of death)	________	________
	________	________
	________	________

3. Are any persons other than minor children dependent on husband or wife? If so, describe relationship and degree of dependency.

____

____

IV. Gifts and Inheritances
(Attach Copies of any Gift Tax Returns Previously Filed by Husband or Wife)

1. Describe the date and amount of any large* gifts that have been made to husband or wife.________________________
____
2. Describe any inheritance that husband or wife has received from any person.________________________
____
3. Describe any gifts or inheritances that husband or wife expects to receive from any person.________________________
____
4. Describe any large* gifts that husband or wife has made to any person in any one year.________________________
____
5. Describe any gifts that husband or wife expects to make to any person in any one year.________________________
____

V. Wills and Trusts

1. Attach a copy of any trust under which husband or wife is a beneficiary or holds any power of appointment.
2. Attach a copy of any will or trust agreement that has been executed by client or client's spouse.

*For purposes of this form a "large" gift is one of more than $3,000 if made prior to 1982 or more than $10,000 if made after 1981. This ties in to the amount of the allowable annual per donee federal gift tax exclusion.

VI. Asset Information

1. Real property. At some point we will need to see copies of all deeds in order to verify the manner in which title to the property is held by husband and wife. Details regarding each parcel of real property may be written on a separate sheet of paper and attached to this form. In each case indicate the net value of the asset.

	Husband	*Wife*
a. Residence	________	________
b. Recreational property	________	________
c. Investment property	________	________
Total value of real property	________	________

2. Publicly traded stocks and bonds. Details regarding each issue of stock or series of bonds may be provided on an attachment. Again, we will need to verify the manner in which title to the securities is held.

	Husband	*Wife*
Common stocks	________	________
Preferred stocks	________	________
Bonds and debentures	________	________
Tax-exempt bonds	________	________
Total value of stocks and bonds	________	________

3. Closely-held stock. Give details regarding any interests husband or wife has in a corporation that is closely held (*i.e.*, the stock is not publicly traded).

4. Accounts in financial institutions.

	Husband	*Wife*
Checking		
Bank name and location	________	________
Approximate balance	________	________
Savings		
Bank name and location	________	________
Approximate balance	________	________
Certificates of deposit		
Bank name and location	________	________
Amounts	________	________

5. Life insurance.

	On Life of Husband	On Life of Wife
Company and policy number	______	______
Face amount	______	______
Annual amount	______	______
Loans outstanding on policy and interest rate	______	______
Type (term, ordinary life, etc.)	______	______
Dividend option selected	______	______
Disability waiver	______	______
Owner of policy and designated successor, if any	______	______
Beneficiaries designated in policy,	1. ______	1. ______
	2. ______	2. ______
Location of policy		

[Repeat blanks as required for additional policies.]

6. Tangible personal property.

	Husband	*Wife*
Jewelry	______	______
Antiques	______	______
Art objects	______	______
Automobiles	______	______
Boats	______	______
Stamps, coins, or other collections	______	______

7. Employee Benefit Plans and IRAs. Describe any employee benefit plans, including IRAs, in which husband or wife has an interest. Attach a copy of the plan description if one is available and the most recent report of your interest in the plan. Indicate whether or not the plans are qualified plans under the federal income tax law, the approximate value of interests in the plans, and how payments will be made in the event of the death or retirement of the participant.

Husband: ______________________________

____

____

Wife: ______________________________
____
____

8. Describe any interests that husband or wife has in any other deferred compensation contracts or plans.

9. Describe any other assets in which husband or wife may have an interest.

10. Describe any debts of husband or wife that are not reflected in any of the lists of assets.

11. What is the approximate present net worth of husband and wife, excluding life insurance.
Husband: ____________
Wife: ____________

12. Location of any safe deposit boxes maintained by husband or wife.

Husband	*Wife*
____________	____________
____________	____________
____________	____________

13. List club memberships of husband and wife, including their resale value.
Husband: ______________________________
____
Wife: ______________________________
____

VII. Advisors

Please list the names, addresses, and telephone numbers of other persons who serve as advisors to husband or wife.

	Husband	*Wife*
Other lawyers	____________	____________
	____________	____________
Stockbroker	____________	____________
	____________	____________
Investment counselor	____________	____________
	____________	____________

Life insurance	________________	________________
	________________	________________
Accountant	________________	________________
	________________	________________
Real estate advisors	________________	________________
	________________	________________
Physician	________________	________________
	________________	________________
Dentist	________________	________________
	________________	________________
Minister, priest, rabbi, or other religious counselor	________________	________________
	________________	________________

Form 1-6. Federal Estate Tax Worksheet

The letter designation of items on this worksheet corresponds to their designation in the federal estate tax return (Form 706). If an estate does not include any community property, all entries in Part I should be made in the column headed "Total."

	One-half of Community Property	*Separate Property*	*Total*
I. Gross Estate:			
A. Real Property			
B. Stocks and bonds			
C. Mortgages, notes, and cash			
D. Insurance on decedent's life			
E. Jointly owned property			
F. Miscellaneous assets			
G. Transfers during lifetime			
H. Powers of appointment			
I. Annuities	__________	__________	__________
Total	$	$	$
Total gross estate			$______

II. *Less* Deductions:
- J. Funeral expenses (§2053) (The amount allocable to decedent's estate differs from state to state where community property is involved) and expenses administering property subject to claims (§2053) (Entire amount attributable to tax matters, including costs of appraisal, etc.) $______
- K. Debts, mortgages, and liens (§2053) (One-half of community property debts, etc., and usually pro rata share of joint note where others are also liable) ______
- L. Casualty losses (§2054) and expenses administering property not subject to claims ______
- M. Marital deduction (§2056) ______
- N. Charitable deduction (§2055) ______

  Total deductions −$______

III. Computation of Estate Tax:
- A. Taxable estate (total gross estate less total deductions) $______
- B. Post-1976 taxable gifts other than gifts includible in gross estate +$______
- C. Total of (A) and (B) $______
- D. Tentative tax on (C) from rate schedule (§2001(c)) $______
- E. *Less:*
  1. Gift taxes paid on post-1976 gifts $______
  2. Unified credit (§2010) ______
  3. Credit for state death taxes (§2011) ______
  4. Credit for gift tax on pre-1977 gifts includible in gross estate (§2012) ______

5. Credit for tax on prior transfers (§2013)	________	
6. Credit for foreign death taxes (§2014)	________	−$________
F. Estate tax liability	________	$________

The payment of the federal estate tax may be extended for reasonable cause, §6161, or to the extent attributable to a reversionary or remainder interest, §6163. *See* §§12.44-12.55. Payments may be extended over a 15-year period to the extent the tax is attributable to an interest in a closely-held business (*see* worksheet for §6166, §11.30, and §12.47). Also, stock included in the decedent's estate may be redeemed under §303 (*see* worksheet for §303, §11.23).

A few United States Treasury bonds that remain outstanding may be redeemed at par plus accrued interest in payment of the federal estate tax to the extent they are included in the decedent's gross estate. *See* §12.48.

BIBLIOGRAPHY

I. Legal Interviewing and Counselling:

Freeman, H. & Weihofen, H., Clinical Law Training: Interviewing and Counseling (1972)

Hoffman, Rabow & Watenmaker, Estate Planning: A Client-Based Approach, U.S. Cal., 39th Inst. Fed. Tax., ch. 18 (1987)

Schwartz, Whose Wealth Is It Anyway: Impediments to the Realization of an Owner's Plan of Disposition, 25 Ariz. L. Rev. 671 (1983)

Shaffer, T. & Redmount, R., Legal Interviewing & Counseling (1980)

Watson, A., The Lawyer in the Interviewing and Counseling Process (1976)

Zabel, Time Out for the Human Side of Estate Planning, 127 Tr. & Est. 8 (May 1988)

II. Collection of Estate Planning Data:

Bush, Estate Planning: The Client Interview, N.Y.U., 33rd Inst. Fed. Tax., ch. 3 (1975) (includes an extensive form of questionnaire)

Cohen, Using Legal Assistants in Estate Planning, 30 Prac. Lawyer 73 (Oct. 1984)

Mucklestone, The Legal Assistant in Estate Planning, 10 Real Prop., Prob., & Tr. J. 263 (1975)

Wilkins, How an Attorney Can Use a Checklist to Better Organize an Estate Planning Practice, 5 Est. Plan. 30 (1978)

III. Malpractice:

Adams & Abendroth, Malpractice Climate Heats Up for Estate Planners, 126 Tr. & Est. 41 (April 1987)

Comment, General Practitioners Beware: The Duty to Refer An Estate Planning Client to a Specialist, 14 Cum. L. Rev. 103 (1983)

Johnston, Avoiding Malpractice Claims that Arise out of Common Estate Planning Situations, 63 Taxes 780 (1985)

Portuonodo, Malpractice Risks of Tax Practitioners, N.Y.U., 46th Inst. Fed. Tax., ch. 18 (1988)

Stern, Reducing Malpractice Risk, 72 A.B.A. J. 52 (June 1986)

Warnick, The Ungrateful Living: An Estate Planner's Nightmare; the Trial Attorney's Dream, 24 Land & Water L. Rev. 401 (1989)

IV. Professional Responsibility:

American College of Trust and Estate Counsel, Guidelines for Estate Planners, 13 Prob. Notes 7 (1987)

Bruce & Springs, Marital Agreements in the Estate Planning Context, U. Miami, 21st Inst. Est. Plan., ch. 7 (1987)

Comment, Considerations of Professional Responsibility in Probate Matters, 51 Neb. L. Rev. 456 (1972)

Committee Report, Developments Regarding the Professional Responsibility of the Estate Planning Lawyer: The Effect of the Model Rules of Professional Conduct, 22 Real Prop., Prob. & Trust J. 1 (1987)

deFuria, A Matter of Ethics Ignored: The Attorney-Draftsman as Testamentary Fiduciary, 36 U. Kan. L. Rev. 275 (1988)

Drinker, H., Legal Ethics (1953)

Durst, Tax Lawyer's Professional Responsibility, 39 U. Fla. L. Rev. 1027 (1987)

Eckhardt, The Estate Planning Lawyer's Problems: Malpractice & Ethics, U. Miami, 8th Inst. Est. Plan., ch. 6 (1974)

Freedman, The Creation of the Attorney-Client Relationship: An Emerging View, 22 Cal. W.L. Rev. 209 (1986)

Hazard, G. & Holdes, The Law of Lawyering: A Handbook on the Model Rules of Professional Conduct (1985)

Holden, Standards of Practice and Treasury Circular 230, N.Y.U., 46th Inst. Fed. Tax., ch. 46 (1988)

Johnston, An Ethical Analysis of Common Estate Planning Practices: Is Good Business Bad Ethics?, 45 Ohio St. L.J. 57 (1984)

Miller, Functions and Ethical Problems of the Lawyer in Drafting a Will, 1950 U. Ill. L. Forum 415

Pennell, Professional Responsibility: Reforms Are Needed to Accommodate Estate Planning and Family Counselling, U. Miami, 25th Inst. Est. Plan., ch. 18 (1991)

Price, Professional Responsibility in Estate Planning: Progress or Paralysis?, U. Miami, 21st Inst. Est. Plan., ch. 18 (1987)

Professional Responsibility in Federal Tax Practice (B. Bittker ed. 1970)

Symposium on Education in the Professional Responsibilities of Lawyers, 41 U. Colo. L. Rev. 303 (1969)

Tate, Handling Conflicts of Interest That May Occur in an Estate Planning Practice, 16 Est. Plan. 32 (Jan.-Feb. 1989)

Vollmar, V., Professional Responsibility in Estate Planning and Administration (Oregon State Bar 1988)

Wade, When Can a Lawyer Represent Both Husband and Wife in Estate Planning?, 1 Prob. & Prop. 13 (March-April 1987)

Wolfman, B. & Holden, J., Ethical Problems in Federal Tax Practice (2d ed. 1985)

Wolfram, C., Modern Legal Ethics (1986)

IV. Determination and Deductibility of Estate Planning Fees:

ABA Sec. Econ. of Law Prac., Beyond the Billable Hour (R. Reed, ed., 1989)

Allington, Deductibility of Estate Planning Fees, 60 A.B.A.J. 482 (1974)

Comment, Considerations of Professional Responsibility in Probate Matters, 51 Neb. L. Rev. 456 (1972)

Gibbs, Post-Gilmore — Recent Trends in the Deductibility of Professional Fees, 23 S.W.L.J. 644 (1969)

Grisham, Deductibility of Legal Expenses for Income Tax Purposes, 26th U. So. Cal., 26th Tax Inst. 875 (1974)

Horn, Setting and Deducting Fees in an Estates Practice, U. Miami, 24th Inst. Est. Plan., ch. 3 (1990)

Symposium on Education in the Professional Responsibilities of Lawyers, 41 U. Colo. L. Rev. 303 (1969)

Weaver, The Merians Decision: What Are Its Implications for Tax Planning Deductions, 39 J. Tax 348 (1973)

Wormser, Charging for Estate Planning — Methods and Problems, U. Miami, 10th Inst. Est. Plan., ch. 8 (1976)

V. Grief and Grieving:

Cain, L., Widow (1974)

Kubler-Ross, on Death and Dying (1969)

Limberg & Plotnick, What a Probate Attorney Must Know About the Psychological Aspects of Death and Dying, 32 Prac. Law. 33 (Aug. 1986)

Report, Task Force on Counseling the Bereaved — Grief: An Analysis and Explanation, 15 Prob. Notes 15 (Fall, 1989) (with bibliography of books and treatises)

CHAPTER 2

Basic Transfer Tax Laws and Estate Planning Strategies

A. Introduction

§2.1. Scope

B. Unified Transfer Tax System

§2.2. Historical Note
§2.3. Unification Under the Tax Reform Act of 1976 and Subsequent Changes
Table 2-1. Increases in Unified Credit and Credit Equivalent
Graph 2-1. Federal Estate and Gift Taxes Prior to 1993

C. Federal Gift Tax Highlights

§2.4. Basic Nature of the Federal Gift Tax
§2.4.1. Scope of Tax; Gifts by Nonresidents
§2.4.2. Gift Tax Exemption Replaced by Credit
§2.4.3. Completed Gifts
§2.5. Annual Gift Tax Exclusion, §2503(b)
§2.5.1. Present and Future Interests
§2.5.2. Gifts in Trust
§2.5.3. Gifts in Trust: *Crummey* Powers of Withdrawal
§2.5.4. Gifts in Trust: §2503(c) Trusts (Trusts for Minors)
§2.5.5. Gifts to Corporations
§2.5.6. Indirect Gifts by Controlling Shareholder
§2.5.7. Gifts to Partnerships
§2.5.8. Gifts to a Noncitizen Spouse, §2523(i)
§2.6. Exclusion for Payment of Tuition and Medical Expenses, §2503(e)
§2.7. Gift Splitting, §2513
§2.8. Charitable Deduction, §2522

§2.9. Marital Deduction, §2523
§2.9.1. Pre-1982 Marital Deduction
§2.9.2. Post-1981 Marital Deduction
§2.9.3. Marital Deduction: Some Planning Comments
§2.10. Gift Tax Returns
§2.10.1. Community Property Gifts
§2.10.2. Manner and Time of Filing
§2.10.3. Changes in Valuation, §2504(c)
§2.10.4. Payment and Penalties

D. Federal Estate Tax Highlights

§2.11. Nature and Computation of the Tax
§2.12. Gross Estate
§2.13. Valuation
§2.14. Deductions
§2.15. Credits
§2.16. Transfer Within Three Years of Death, §2035
§2.17. Retained Interests and Powers, §§2036, 2038
§2.17.1. Retained Voting Rights, §2036(b)
§2.17.2. Anti-Freeze Provision, former §2036(c)
§2.18. Annuities and Other Death Benefits, §2039
§2.19. Joint Tenancies, §2040
§2.19.1. Joint Tenants Other Than Husband and Wife
§2.19.2. Husband and Wife as Joint Tenants: Qualified Joint Interests, §2040(b)
§2.20. Powers of Appointment, §2041
§2.20.1. Exceptions
§2.20.2. Release of Post-1942 General Powers
§2.20.3. Lapses of General Powers; $5,000 or 5 Percent Power
§2.21. Life Insurance, §2042

E. Generation-Skipping Transfer Tax (GSTT)

§2.22. Background
§2.23. 1986 GSTT
§2.23.1. Direct Skips and Skip Persons, §§2612(c), 2613
§2.23.2. Taxable Terminations, §2612(a)
§2.23.3. Taxable Distributions, §2612(b)
§2.24. Application of GSTT; Inclusion Ratio; Applicable Fraction
§2.25. GSTT $1 Million Exemption
§2.26. Reverse QTIP Election, §2652(a)(3)
§2.27. Allocation of Exemption; Deemed Allocation Rules
§2.27.1. Certain Inter Vivos Transfers
§2.27.2. Charitable Lead Trusts
§2.27.3. Default Allocation of GSTT Exemption

§2.28. Exclusions, §§2611(b), 2642(c)
§2.29. Valuation of Property
§2.30. Taxable Amount of Generation-Skipping Transfers
§2.30.1. Direct Skips
§2.30.2. Taxable Distributions
§2.30.3. Taxable Terminations
§2.31. Identifying and Changing the Transferor
§2.32. Generational Assignments, §2651
§2.33. Separate Trusts
§2.34. Multiple Transfers, §2642(d)
§2.35. Basis Adjustment, §2654(a)
§2.36. Returns, §2662
§2.36.1. Direct Skips
§2.36.2. Trust Arrangements
§2.36.3. Deferral of GSTT on Direct Skips of Closely-Held Business Interests, §6166(h)
§2.36.4. Redemption of Stock to Pay GSTT, §303(d)
§2.37. Return Due Dates
§2.38. Effective Dates
§2.39. $2 Million Exclusion, 1986 Act §1433(b)(3)
§2.40. GSTT Planning Strategies
§2.40.1. Use Each Client's $1 Million GSTT Exemption
§2.40.2. Coordinate Use of the GSTT Exemption, the Unified Credit, and the Marital Deduction
§2.40.3. Make Nontaxable Gifts, §2642(c)
§2.40.4. Make Inter Vivos Direct Skips
§2.40.5. Preserve Status of Trusts That Are Exempt Under Effective Date Rules
§2.40.6. Create and Administer Trusts in Light of Prior Use of GSTT Exemption
§2.40.7. Use the Orphan Grandchild Exclusion, §2612(c)
§2.40.8. Consider Authorizing Trustees to Make Distributions and to Amend Trust

F. Basic Lifetime Estate Planning Tax Strategies

§2.41. Overview
§2.42. Shift Income Within the Family
§2.42.1. Methods
§2.42.2. Assignment of Income Alone Is Ineffective for Income Tax Purposes
§2.43. Reduce the Size of the Estate: Gifts and Valuation Games
§2.43.1. Make Gifts to Qualify for Valuation Discounts
§2.43.2. Make Gifts of Life Insurance
§2.44. Freeze the Value of the Estate
§2.45. Bypass the Estates of Survivors
§2.46. Defer the Payment of Estate and GST Taxes

Bibliography

A. INTRODUCTION

§2.1. Scope

This chapter opens with an historical review and summary of the main features of the federal gift and estate taxes. Next, a longer look is given to the generation-skipping transfer tax (GSTT). The chapter concludes with a classification and discussion of the most important basic estate planning tax strategies. Depending upon the reader's background, the chapter may serve either as an initial orientation to the federal transfer taxes or as a refresher. In either case, the chapter introduces the remainder of the book. Later chapters explore the federal taxes in more detail and examine the various devices that can be used to carry out the basic planning strategies. The income taxation of trusts and estates is summarized in Chapters 10 and 12 and relevant income tax considerations are discussed throughout the book. Later materials also consider the major nontax considerations that bear on the selection and implementation of various estate planning techniques.

B. UNIFIED TRANSFER TAX SYSTEM

§2.2. Historical Note

Federal inheritance taxes were imposed for three short periods between 1797 and 1902 in order to meet temporary fiscal emergencies. The federal estate tax was adopted in 1916, largely to finance the cost of military preparations for participation in World War I. *See* Eisenstein, The Rise and Decline of the Estate Tax, 11 Tax L. Rev. 223, 230-231 (1956). It has remained essentially the same, although refinements have been made over the years to meet new challenges and to deal with changed circumstances. For example, important changes have been made in the taxation of powers of appointment, §2041, and of life insurance, §2042. The adoption of a limited marital deduction in 1948, §2056, was perhaps the single most important change made between 1916 and 1976. The most sweeping changes in the federal transfer tax laws were made by the 1976 Act, which unified the gift and estate tax structure, the 1981 Act, which removed the quantitative limits on the amount of the marital deduction, and the 1986 Act, which imposed a new form of GSTT.

The first federal gift tax was adopted in 1924 and repealed two years later. That short-lived tax was seriously flawed by the fact that it was calculated annually on a noncumulative basis. It was also weakened by a large annual exemption. In 1932, the existing graduated, cumulative gift tax was adopted in more or less its present form. It was intended to help bolster federal tax revenues, which had sagged with the onset of the Great Depression, and to supplement the income and estate taxes. A gift tax provides valuable protection for income and estate taxes by imposing a tax on transfers that would deplete the amount of his or her income and the size of the donor's estate. Perhaps because it was adopted at a later time, the gift and estate taxes were largely independent of each other until their unification in 1976.

Unification was spurred by the extraordinary preferences the dual system accorded to inter vivos gifts, which were attributable to three of its basic features. First, although the gift and estate tax rate schedules had identical brackets, at each interval the gift tax was only 75 percent of the estate tax rate. Second, the gift tax was based upon only the net value of the property transferred (*i.e.,* the gift tax on a transfer was not "grossed up" and included in the tax base). In contrast, the estate tax was based upon the total amount of the decedent's gross estate (*i.e.,* the amount of the estate tax itself was included in the tax base). Third, inter vivos gifts were usually not included in the donor's gross estate or otherwise included in the estate tax base.

Although the gift tax was calculated on the cumulative total of gifts made by the donor after June 6, 1932, gifts completed more than three years prior to death were generally not included in the donor's estate tax base. Where an inter vivos gift was included in the donor's gross estate, the donor's estate was allowed a credit for any gift tax paid (or due) on the gift. Despite the allowance of the credit, the amount of the gift tax was not included in the estate tax base. In fact, a deduction was allowed for any gift tax that was due but unpaid at the time of death. Deathbed gifts were strongly encouraged by the availability of the credit and the failure to include the amount of the gift tax in the donor's estate tax base.

The operation of the dual transfer tax system under the pre-1977 law is illustrated by Example 2-1.

Example 2-1. *X* and *Y* each owned property worth $2,000,000. *X* made no gifts during his lifetime. Accordingly, when he died, his entire estate was subject to the old estate tax. Under the old rates an estate tax of $726,200 would have been due from *X*'s executor, leaving his family $1,273,800. *Y* made a lifetime gift of $1,000,000 to her family, which would have been subject to a gift tax of $227,625. The remaining $772,385 would have been subject to an estate tax of $220,035 when she died. Thus, taxes of $447,660 would have been paid with respect to *Y*'s transfers, leaving $1,552,340 for her family. By giving half of her estate away during her lifetime *Y* could pass almost $280,000 more to her family than *X*, who made no inter vivos gifts.

Commentators frequently charged that the preference shown for inter vivos gifts was unjustified and discriminatory and proposed various remedial steps, including the adoption of a unified transfer tax system. A form of unified transfer tax was advanced in the 1969 tax reform proposals that were published by the Treasury Department. Tax Reform Studies and Proposals, 91st Cong., 1st Sess. (Comm. Print 1969).

In 1976 Congress concluded that the dual transfer tax system was inequitable and undesirable, and sought to remedy the situation by unifying the existing gift and estate tax systems. Staff of Joint Comm. on Taxn., General Explanation of the Tax Reform Act of 1976, 94th Cong., 2d Sess., 526 (1976). The unification largely eliminated the features of the dual system that preferred inter vivos gifts. However, the changes do not require the gift tax paid on a transfer made more than three years prior to death to be grossed up and included in the tax base. The 1976 Act also left intact the annual gift tax exclusion, which sheltered annual gifts of $3,000 or less per donee from both the gift and the estate tax. The 1981 Act increased the amount of the annual exclusion to $10,000 per donee. By regularly making gifts within the amount of the exclusion an individual can transfer a substantial amount of property to the donees completely free of tax. The remaining incentives for making lifetime gifts are discussed in detail in Chapter 7.

§2.3. Unification Under the Tax Reform Act of 1976 and Subsequent Changes

The transfer tax system was unified by adopting a single progressive rate schedule that applies to the cumulative total of lifetime and deathtime taxable transfers. As a result, nearly the same amount of tax will be paid by taxpayers who make taxable transfers of equal total amounts, whether or not any of the transfers are made inter vivos. Thus, the large disparity in the tax imposed on the two taxpayers described in Example 2-1, above, is eliminated. A preference remains for gifts, however, on which the tax is computed on a tax-exclusive basis (*i.e.*, the amount of the gift tax is not included in the base on which the tax is computed). Any retroactive effect of unification was avoided by cumulating only the amount of post-1976 gifts. §2001(b)(2).

The unified rate schedule adopted in 1976, §2001(c), opens at a higher rate than the prior one but the rates increase more slowly and end at a lower rate than before. Also, the 1976 Act substituted a single unified credit for the separate lifetime $30,000 gift tax and $60,000 estate tax exemptions. The unified credit, which applies to lifetime or deathtime transfers, increased in roughly equal annual increments from

$30,000 in 1977 to $47,000 in 1981, which was equal to the tax imposed on a taxable transfer of $175,625. The amount of a taxable transfer sheltered by the credit is called the *credit equivalent.* The adoption of the unified credit eliminated the estate tax on about two-thirds of the estates that would otherwise have been required to file estate tax returns. The 1981 Act increased the unified credit in unequal annual stages from $47,000 in 1981 to $192,800 in 1987 and thereafter, which greatly diminished the number of estates required to file estate tax returns.

The increases in the unified credit and the credit equivalent are shown in Table 2-1. The increase in the amount of the unified credit also affects the lowest marginal rate at which any tax will be due from an estate. Specifically, the marginal rate was 32 percent for 1982; 34 percent for 1983, 1984, and 1985; and 37 percent for 1986 and later.

Table 2-1
Increases in Unified Credit and Credit Equivalent

Year	*Unified Credit*	*Credit Equivalent*
1981	$ 47,000	$175,625
1982	62,800	225,000
1983	79,300	275,000
1984	96,300	325,000
1985	121,800	400,000
1986	155,800	500,000
1987 and later	192,800	600,000

The 1981 Act also reduced the maximum gift and estate tax rates by five percent annually for the following four years. Between 1981 and 1984 the maximum rate decreased from 70 percent to 55 percent. In an attempt to help control the size of the federal deficit the scheduled reduction in the maximum rate to 50 percent was deferred in 1984 and again in 1987. The reduction to 50 percent is now scheduled to take effect in 1993. Although the maximum rate was reduced substantially, no reductions were made in the rates payable by estates of $2.5 million or less. The unified transfer tax rates applicable to amounts in excess of $250,000 other than the five percent surtax applicable to amounts in excess of ten million dollars are portrayed in Graph 2-1, *infra.*

Between 1981 and 1987 the "spread" between the lowest marginal rate at which any estate tax is payable and the maximum estate tax rate shrank from 38 percent (70 percent − 32 percent) to only 18 percent (55 percent − 37 percent), or 23 percent, taking account of the five percent surtax applicable to taxable estates in excess of ten million dollars. This shrinkage increased the advantages of deferring the payment of any estate tax and decreased the advantages of equalizing the sizes of the spouses' estates. A consideration of the relative advantages of deferral and equalization must take other factors into

Graph 2-1
Federal Estate and Gift Tax Rates Prior to 1993
(excluding surtax)

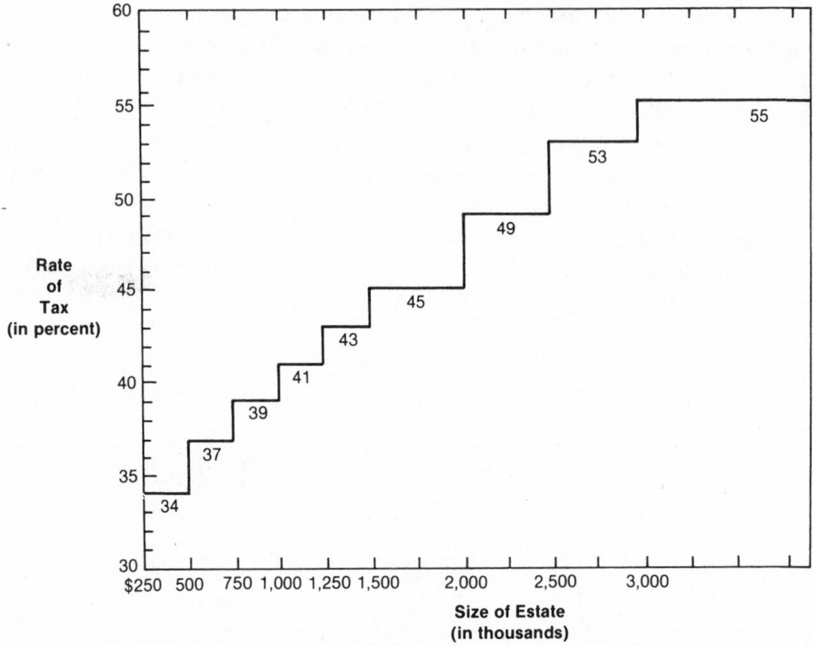

account, including the effect of inflation on the amount of property subject to tax and the yield that can be earned on the amount of any taxes that are deferred.

Section 2001(c)(3), added by the 1987 Act, imposes a five percent surtax on estates in excess of $10 million. It applies to the extent necessary to phase out the benefits of the unified credit and of the lower rates that apply to the first $3 million ($2.5 million after 1992). The surtax, which applies to amounts between $10 million and $21,040,000 ($18,340,000 in 1993 and later, when the maximum rate is 50 percent), generates a maximum additional tax of $552,000. That amount is equal to the $192,800 unified credit plus the $359,200 benefit of the lower rates that apply to the first $3 million of a taxable estate. After 1992 the maximum surtax will be $417,000 ($192,800 + $224,200).

The effect of the unification is most evident when it comes to calculating the estate tax due from the estate of a person who made taxable gifts after December 31, 1976. First, a "tentative tax" is determined by applying the unified rate schedule to the sum of the post-1976 taxable gifts and the taxable estate. §2001(c). Then the estate tax is determined by subtracting the amount of gift tax on post-1976 gifts. (Pre-1977 gifts are not included in the tax base at death and no credit is allowed for any gift tax paid with respect to them.) The amount of the estate tax thus calculated is then reduced by the unified credit allowable for the year of the decedent's death. §2010(a). The unified credit is always allowed in the full amount because all post-1976 taxable gifts are included in the base upon which the estate tax is calculated, either as an adjusted taxable gift or as an item included in the donor's gross estate. Credits are also allowed against the estate tax for state death taxes, §2011, taxes paid on prior transfers, §2013, and for foreign death taxes, §2014.

Example 2-2. *T* made taxable gifts of $250,000 prior to 1977 and taxable gifts of $500,000 in 1990. *T* paid a gift tax of $16,700 on the 1990 gifts, which is the amount by which the tax on the gifts ($209,500) exceeded the amount of *T*'s unified credit ($192,800). The gift tax liability is calculated as follows:

Taxable gifts prior to 1977	$250,000
Plus Taxable gifts in 1990	500,000
Lifetime total of taxable gifts	$750,000
Tentative tax on total taxable gifts	$248,300
Less: Tax on pre-1977 gifts	38,000
Gift tax on 1990 gifts	$209,500
Less: Unified credit	192,800
Gift tax payable for 1990	$ 16,700

T died in 1991 leaving a taxable estate of $1,500,000 including the gift tax of $16,700 that was paid within 3 years of death. *See* §2035(c).

An estate tax of $506,900 is due from T's estate, calculated as follows:

Post-1976 taxable gifts		$ 500,000
Plus Taxable estate		1,500,000
Tax base		$2,000,000
Tentative tax		780,800
Less: Gift tax paid on post-1976 gifts		16,700
Estate tax		$ 764,100
Less: Unified credit	$192,800	
State death tax credit*	64,400	257,200
Estate tax payable		$506,900

*All states impose a death tax sufficient to absorb the maximum credit that is allowable under the federal estate tax law.

The unification of the gift and estate tax and the adoption of the GSTT (*see* §§2.22-2.40) improved the overall equity of the transfer tax system. Changes made since 1976 also sealed some important loopholes. At the same time the increases in the unified credit relieved the vast majority of estates of the obligation to file an estate tax return and to pay any federal transfer tax. Unfortunately, changes made since 1976 have increased the complexity of the transfer tax laws, which inevitably increases the compliance costs and the potential for estate planning malpractice. Alas, neither simplicity nor stability is a hallmark of the federal transfer tax system.

C. FEDERAL GIFT TAX HIGHLIGHTS

§2.4. Basic Nature of the Federal Gift Tax

This part presents a basic overview of the main features of the federal gift tax law. The tax and other considerations involved in making noncharitable gifts are reviewed in Chapter 7 and those concerning charitable gifts are explored in Chapter 8.

The federal gift tax is an excise tax imposed on the transfer of property by a gift during any calendar year. §2501(a)(1). It applies although the identity of the donee may not be known or ascertainable at the time of the gift. The donor is primarily liable for payment of the tax. §2502(d).

Neither the Code nor the Regulations attempt to define the term "gift"; however, the latter explains that the term includes "all transactions whereby property or property rights or interests are gratuitously passed or conferred upon another, regardless of the means or device employed." Reg. §25.2511-1(c). The tax applies to all gratuitous transfers, whether direct or indirect, whether outright or in trust, and whether the property transferred is real or personal, tangible or intangible. §2511(a); Reg. §25.2511-1(a).

Example 2-3. Father, *F,* sold 1,000 shares of XYZ, Inc. common stock to his daughter, *D,* for $10 per share on a day when the mean price of the stock on an established exchange was $25 per share. *F* made a gift to *D* of $15 per share — the difference between the mean price of $25 per share and the price he received. The transaction was part sale, part gift, and not a bona fide business transaction. *D*'s carryover basis in the stock is determined under §1015. No income tax deduction is allowable when there is a "loss" on the sale or exchange of property between related taxpayers. §267.

§2.4.1. Scope of Tax; Gifts by Nonresidents

The gift tax applies to essentially all gifts that are subject to U.S. jurisdiction for purposes of taxation and, except as otherwise provided by treaty, to all gifts made by citizens or residents and to gifts by nonresident aliens of property that has a situs in the United States. In general, it applies to gifts by nonresidents except ones of intangible personal property. Under §2501(a)(2) the gift tax does not apply to "the transfer of intangible property by a nonresident not a citizen of the United States." In addition, §2511(a) provides that "in the case of a nonresident not a citizen of the United States" the tax applies only "if the property is situated within the United States."

§2.4.2. Gift Tax Exemption Replaced by Credit

With respect to gifts made prior to 1977, the donor could elect to use all or part of the lifetime gift tax exemption of $30,000 at any time. As a part of the unification of the gift and estate tax laws in 1976 the exemption was replaced by the unified credit, which *must* be used by the donor as a credit against the tax on gifts as they are made. Rev. Rul. 79-398, 1979-2 C.B. 338. This rule has particular significance in planning "net" gifts. *See* §7.25.

§2.4.3. Completed Gifts

The gift tax applies only to completed gifts. A gift is complete as to any property over which the donor has so parted with dominion and control as to leave the donor with no power to change its disposition. *See* Reg. §25.2511-2. Thus, a gift is incomplete if the transferor retains a lifetime or testamentary general or special power to appoint the property. In such a case the gift is completed if the transferor releases the retained power. *See Estate of Sanford v. Commissioner,* 308 U.S. 39 (1939). In some circumstances a client may wish to transfer property to an irrevocable trust over which he or she has retained sufficient powers to make the transfer incomplete for gift tax purposes. *See* PLR 8940008 (trustor retained power to revoke the trust with the consent of an independent trustee); §10.34. Of course, retention of such a power would require inclusion of the property in the testator's estate. The retention of only a power to change the manner or time of enjoyment, such as a power to accelerate the time of distribution to a trust beneficiary, does not make the gift incomplete. Reg. §25.2511.2(d).

A gift of a check or note is not completed by its mere delivery: the gift of a note is complete when it is paid or transferred for value and the gift of a check is complete when it is paid, certified, accepted by drawee, or is negotiated for value to a third person. Rev. Rul. 67-396, 1967-2 C.B. 351. Under the relation back doctrine a gift of a check to a charity which subsequently negotiates the check may be treated as a completed transfer at the time it was delivered to the charity. *See* §8.6. The relation back doctrine does not apply to noncharitable gifts.

§2.5. Annual Gift Tax Exclusion, §2503(b)

The continuing availability of the annual gift tax exclusion of $10,000 per donee is a major reason for the popularity of inter vivos gifts. Under §2503(b) the first $10,000 of property or interests in property, other than future interests, given to each person is excluded in computing the donor's taxable gifts for the year. (Prior to 1982 the exclusion was $3,000 per donee.) The exclusion extends to gifts of interests to a minor in a trust that meets the requirements of §2503(c), but not to "future interests." *See* §§2.5.1., 2.5.4. A donor is not required to file a gift tax return with respect to gifts that are within the exclusion of §2503(b) or qualify for the marital deduction under §2523. *See* §6019(a); §2.10. In most other cases the donor must file a return. A return must also be filed for a donor to split gifts with his or her spouse under §2513 or to claim a gift tax marital deduction for qualified terminable interest property or a charitable deduction.

§2.5.1. Present and Future Interests

For the purposes of §2503 the term *future interest* "includes reversions, remainders, and other interests or estates, whether vested or contingent, and whether or not supported by a particular interest or estate, which are limited to commence in use, possession or enjoyment at some future date or time." Reg. §25.2503-3(a). Thus, if *X* transfers Blackacre to *A* for life, remainder to *B,* the life interest transferred to *A* is a present interest, but the remainder transferred to *B* is a future interest. No annual exclusion is available with respect to the future interest given to *B* although it is indefeasibly vested, may be of great value, and is freely alienable by *B*.

The question of whether or not a particular interest constitutes a present or a future interest is primarily determined by the nature and extent of the transferee's interest and not by the character of the property. As the Regulations explain:

> The term has no reference to such contractual rights as exist in a bond, note (though bearing no interest until maturity), or in a policy of life insurance, the obligations of which are to be discharged by payments in the future. But a future interest or interests in such contractual obligations may be created by the limitations contained in a trust or other instrument of transfer used in effecting a gift. Reg. §25.2503-3(a).

Thus, an outright gift of a note on which payments are due in the future is a gift of a present interest. In contrast, a gift of such a note to a trust, the beneficiaries of which have no present right to receive distribution from the trust, is a future interest. *See* §2.5.2.

The annual exclusion for gifts to each donee is renewable, but not cumulative. One $10,000 exclusion is available annually to each donor with respect to gifts to a particular donee, whether or not gifts were made to the donee in any preceding years. Thus, gifts of present interests having a value of $10,000 or less are generally not subject to the gift or the estate tax.

§2.5.2. Gifts in Trust

The present interest/future interest dichotomy is most difficult to resolve in the case of transfers in trust. For gift tax purposes a transfer in trust is treated as made to the beneficiaries and not to the trust or the trustee. *Helvering v. Hutchings,* 312 U.S. 393 (1941). A transfer in trust qualifies for the annual exclusion to the extent the beneficiaries have the unrestricted right to the immediate use, possession, or enjoyment of the property or the income from it. Reg. §25.2503-3(b). The donee of an income interest in a trust that requires its income to be distributed currently has a present interest in the income. The value of such an income interest, or a remainder or other limited interest in a trust, is ordinarily determined under actuarial tables issued by the Internal Revenue Service in accordance with §7520. However, use of the tables is "not appropriate in the case of *non*income yielding investment. . . ." *Berzon v. Commissioner,* 534 F.2d 528, 532 (2d Cir. 1976). The IRS has consistently ruled that no annual exclusion is allowable with respect to the income beneficiary's interest in a trust funded with a gift of nonincome producing stock. LR 83200007 (TAM). Also, no annual exclusion is allowable with respect to the income interest in a trust if the trust reflects an intention that the trustee invest for future growth rather than current income. Rev. Rul. 69-345, 1969-1 C.B. 225. The use of the actuarial tables to value the life interest of a beneficiary is not appropriate if the beneficiary is terminally ill. Rev. Rul. 80-80, 1980-1 C.B. 194. The donor's retained term interest in a trust may be valued at zero under the rules of §2702.

The interest of the beneficiary of a discretionary trust is not a present interest — any distribution to the beneficiary is dependent upon the trustee's subsequent exercise of discretion.

§2.5.3. Gifts in Trust: *Crummey* Powers of Withdrawal

The present interest requirement is satisfied to the extent the beneficiary has a presently exercisable power to withdraw property that is transferred to the trust. The power, sometimes called a *Crummey* power, is discussed at §7.37. Giving a *Crummey* power to the beneficiaries of an irrevocable life insurance trust is particularly useful. *See* §6.23.4. Depending upon the terms of the trust, the lapse of a *Crummey* power may constitute a completed gift by the power holder of a future interest in the property subject to the power. However, if the holder of the power which lapses continues to hold a power to direct the disposition of the property, such as a special testamentary power of appointment, any gift resulting from the lapse is incomplete and not then subject to the gift tax. *See* §2.4.3.

> **Example 2-4.** *T* transferred $10,000 to a trust for the benefit of *B*. The trust required the trustee to notify *B* of the transfer. Within 30 days following notification of a transfer of property to the trust *B* has the noncumulative right to withdraw the transferred property. The income and principal are distributable to *B* in the discretion of the trustee. Upon *B*'s death the trust property will be distributed to whomever *B* appoints by will. The $10,000 transferred by *T* to the trust qualifies for the annual gift tax exclusion because of *B*'s *Crummey* power. The lapse of the power does not involve any gift by *B* because the trust property is subject to *B*'s testamentary power of appointment.

An annual exclusion gift made to a *Crummey* trust is not subject to the GSTT if the beneficiary is the only person to whom income or principal may be distributed during the beneficiary's lifetime and the trust will be included in the beneficiary's estate if the beneficiary dies before receiving distribution of the trust property. §2642(c)(2). *See* §2.40.3.

§2.5.4. Gifts in Trust: §2503(c) Trusts (Trusts for Minors)

A transfer of property to a trust for the benefit of a minor also qualifies for the annual exclusion if the requirements of §2503(c) are met. *See* §7.37. In brief, a trust meets the requirements of §2503(c) if the trustee is empowered to distribute the income or principal of the trust to the minor without the imposition of any substantial restriction and the property is distributable to the minor at age 21. A Technical Advice Memorandum holds that a gift of nonincome producing stock to a §2503(c) trust qualifies for the annual gift tax exclusion because of the trustee's power to use all of the property for the benefit of the minor and to distribute the balance to the beneficiary at age 21. LR 8320007 (TAM).

§2.5.5. Gifts to Corporations

A gift to a corporation is considered to be made to its shareholders. Reg. §25.2511-1(h)(1). Such a gift is not a present interest unless the shareholders have a power similar to a *Crummey* power to withdraw the property or an immediate right to use the property. *See* LR 9104024. Otherwise, shareholders do not have a direct right or interest in property that is transferred to the corporation. *See, e.g., Heringer v. Commissioner,* 235 F.2d 149 (9th Cir.), *cert. denied,* 352 U.S. 927 (1956); *CTUW Georgia Ketteman Hollingsworth,* 86 T.C. 91 (1986); LR 7935115.

A gift by the controlling shareholder of stock of a closely-held corporation to key employees is treated as proportionate gifts of future interests to the other shareholders and as compensation to the employees. LR 9114023. Such treatment is based upon the fundamental distinction between the corporate entity on the one hand and the shareholder-owners on the other. A gift to a corporation may enhance the value of the stock owned by the shareholders, but it is almost never treated as a transfer of a present interest to them.

> **Example 2-5.** *T* transferred real property worth $750,000 to a closely-held corporation in exchange for a $500,000 note. *T* has made a gift of $250,000 to the shareholders: Each gift is in proportion to the shareholder's ownership of the corporation's stock. The gifts are future interests. *CTUW Georgia Ketteman Hollingsworth,* 86 T.C. 91 (1986).

§2.5.6. Indirect Gifts by Controlling Shareholder

A gift to other shareholders may result from the action or inaction of the controlling shareholder. A gift of stock by the controlling shareholder to key employees is a pro rata gift to other shareholders. LR 9114023. Indirect gifts to other shareholders may arise in a variety of settings. For example, in LR 89403010 the controlling shareholder made a gift to the other common shareholders by permitting the corporation to fail to pay the required dividends on his noncumulative preferred stock in order to pay dividends on the common stock.

There are ways of making gifts to the shareholders of a closely-held corporation that do qualify for the annual exclusion. A donor might transfer the property to the corporation in exchange for additional stock and give those shares of stock to the donees. Another approach would be to give the property to the donees, who then transfer their interests to the corporation in exchange for shares of stock. Either of these approaches might have been used to good effect in Example 2-5, *supra*.

§2.5.7. Gifts to Partnerships

A gift of an ownership interest in a partnership is analogous to a gift of shares of stock in a corporation and qualifies for the annual exclusion under the same rules. For example, outright gifts and gifts to *Crummey* trusts of interests in limited partnerships qualify for the annual gift tax exclusion. The annual exclusion is allowable for gifts of limited partnership interest although the donor was the general partner and, as such, held extensive powers of management LR 9131006 (TAM). Under state law, the general partner was bound by strict fiduciary duties in exercising those powers. LR 8445004 (TAM); LR 8611004 (TAM). Importantly, the transferred interests are not includible in the donor's estate under §§2036 or 2038 because the donor's powers were exercisable in a fiduciary capacity. That conclusion is based upon an application of the rationale of *United States v. Byrum,* 408 U.S. 125 (1972). LR 9131006 (TAM).

Gifts to the capital account of a partner are superficially analogous to gifts to a corporation. The annual exclusion is available for gifts to a partner's capital account if the partner has the unrestricted right to withdraw amounts from his or her capital, which a partner has under the Uniform Partnership Act. *Wooley v. United States,* 1990-1 U.S.T.C. ¶60,013 (S.D. Ind. 1990). The existence of such a right of withdrawal, analogous to a *Crummey* power of withdrawal, supported the allowance of the annual exclusion in *Wooley*. *See* LR 9104024. In order to avoid any questions regarding the availability of annual exclusions, gifts of interests in a partnership should be made before any significant restrictions on the transfer or disposition of interests are imposed. Problems are also minimized if the donor gives property directly to the donees, who then join to form the partnership.

§2.5.8. Gifts to a Noncitizen Spouse, §2523(i)

The marital deduction is not allowed with respect to gifts made on or after July 14, 1988 to a spouse who is not a citizen of the United States. Instead, the annual gift tax exclusion allowed under §2503(b) is increased to $100,000 for transfers to a noncitizen spouse. §2523(i). Of course, the donative property may or may not be included in the donee spouse's gross estate depending on the circumstances that exist at the time of his or her death. For example, if the noncitizen spouse is a resident of the United States at the time of death, all of his or her property is subject to the federal estate tax. On the other hand, if the noncitizen spouse dies a nonresident, only the property that has a situs in the United States is subject to the federal estate tax. Marital deduction planning considerations relevant for persons married to citizens and noncitizen spouses are discussed in Chapter 5.

§2.6. Exclusion for Payment of Tuition and Medical Expenses, §2503(e)

Section 2503(e), which was added by the 1981 Act, allows gift tax exclusions for tuition payments made directly to educational institutions described in §170(b)(1)(A)(ii) and payments of medical expenses (including medical insurance) made directly to the individuals or organizations providing the services. Rev. Rul. 82-98, 1982-1 C.B. 141. The exclusions are allowable regardless of the relationship or absence of relationship between the donors and the donees. Note that only direct payments can be excluded: A reimbursement of such expenses made to the donee as intermediary does not qualify. Reg. §25.2503-6(c), example 4. Insofar as educational expenses are concerned, the exclusion extends only to tuition payments, although a strong argument can be made for broadening it to cover other associated costs (*e.g.,* books, supplies, and room and board). The exclusion for medical expenses extends to those described in §213. However, medical expense payments are excludable regardless of the percentage limitation of §213. The exclusion is helpful because most taxpayers were probably unaware that payments of educational or medical expenses constituted a gift under the prior law except to the extent the payor was legally obligated to make the payments.

Note that the GSTT does not apply to transfers that would qualify for this exclusion if made by an individual. §2611(b)(1).

§2.7. Gift Splitting, §2513

In order to equalize the gift tax on gifts of community and noncommunity property, §2513 permits married persons to elect to treat all gifts made to third parties during a calendar year as made one-half by each. However, the option to split gifts is only available if both spouses were citizens or residents of the United States at the time of the gift. §2513(a) (1). For estate tax purposes the actual donor and not the consenting spouse is regarded as the transferor. *English v. United States,* 284 F. Supp. 256 (W.D. Fla. 1968) (§2035). The privilege of splitting gifts does not apply to community property because it is naturally "split" between the spouses from the outset: When a gift of community property is made to a person outside the community, each spouse is necessarily the donor of one-half of the property. Each spouse is considered to be the donor of one-half of the total value of community property gifts even in states that permit one spouse alone to make gifts of community property. Rev. Rul. 56-408, 1956-2 C.B. 600. However, as a matter of practice both spouses should join in making gifts of community property in order to avoid any uncertainty regarding the effectiveness of the gift.

Gift splitting is also recognized for GSTT purposes. In particular, §2652(a)(2) provides that if a gift is split under §2513, each spouse will be treated as a transferor of one-half of the property for GSTT purposes. This opportunity makes it easier to use each spouse's $1 million GSTT exemption.

In effect, §2513 doubles the exclusions available for gifts of noncommunity property made by a husband and wife to third parties. Gift splitting also allows the spouses to equalize the unified transfer tax rates that are applicable to each of them. Prior to the adoption of the unlimited marital deduction, which allows free interspousal gifts, gift splitting was more important.

In order to split gifts, both spouses must signify their consent to split gifts for the period in question. If only one spouse is required to file a return, the consent of both spouses must be signified on that return. The same result can be achieved by making a tax-free gift from one spouse to the other, after which each makes equal gifts to third parties.

> **Example 2-6.** *H* transferred $20,000 of his separate property to his son, *S,* on December 30. Neither *H* nor *W* made any other gifts during that year. The gift to *S* must be reported on *H*'s gift tax return for the calendar year. The short form of the gift tax return, Form 709A, may be filed in such a case. If *W* signifies her consent on *H*'s gift tax return the amount of the gift will be completely offset by the annual exclusions available to *H* and *W* and no gift tax will be due. *W* is not required to file a return because

she did not make any gifts during the year, and the gift she is considered to have made to *S* did not exceed her annual exclusion of $10,000 and was not a future interest. *See* Reg. §25.2513-1(c).

When both spouses are required to file gift tax returns, the consent of each spouse to split gifts may be signified on either return. Reg. §25.2513-2(a)(1)(i). A decedent's personal representative may consent to split gifts made prior to the decedent's death. *See* §12.24.5.

None of the property actually transferred by the donor spouse is includible in the gross estate of the consenting spouse. For estate tax purposes, the consenting spouse is not treated as the transferor of property that was actually transferred by the other spouse. Thus, property held by a consenting spouse as custodian under the Uniform Transfers to Minors or the Uniform Gifts to Minors Act at the time of death is not includible in his or her gross estate when the custodial property was actually transferred to the minor by the other spouse and the consenting spouse was only treated as the donor for gift tax purposes. Rev. Rul. 74-556, 1974-2 C.B. 300 (involving §2038). However, the amount of taxable gifts, including split gifts, is taken into account in computing the consenting spouse's gift and estate tax liability.

Where the state gift tax law also permits gift splitting, the state and federal elections can be made independent of each other (*i.e.,* gifts made by a couple may be split for federal, but not for state, tax purposes). In states that determine the gift tax in part according to the relationship between the donor and donee, the state gift tax may be lower in some cases if the gift is not split. Such a result may occur, for example, where the donor spouse is closely related to the donee, but the consenting spouse is unrelated to the donee. Thus, if a donor makes a gift to his or her parents, the state gift tax may be lower if the gift is not split with the donor's spouse, who probably would be considered to be unrelated to the donor's parents.

§2.8. Charitable Deduction, §2522

The income, gift, and estate tax rules applicable to charitable gifts are reviewed in detail in Chapter 8. In brief, §2522 allows an unlimited deduction for the value of gifts made by a citizen or resident of the United States to charities described in §2522(a). Gifts made by a nonresident alien are governed by the same rules as those applicable to citizens, except that they are subject to two additional restrictions: (1) Gifts made to a corporation qualify only if it is created or organized under the laws of the United States or a state or territory of the United States, and (2) gifts such as those to a trust or community chest qualify only if they must be used within the United States exclusively for religious, charitable, educational, scientific, or literary purposes, including the encouragement of art and the prevention of cruelty to children or animals. Reg. §25.2522(b)-1. With slight variations the same organizations are qualified donees under the income, gift, and estate tax laws. *See* §8.2.

Planning outright gifts to charitable organizations is usually simple enough, although the valuation of some assets can present a problem. However, that problem is eased considerably and the risk that a penalty might be imposed for overvaluation of the property is virtually eliminated if the donor obtains a contemporaneous appraisal of the property by a qualified expert. Planning becomes much more complex when the charitable gift consists of less than the donor's entire interest in the property. A deduction is generally allowed for gifts of split interests only if it takes the form of (1) a charitable remainder trust or pooled income fund (*see* §§8.20-8.30), (2) a guaranteed annuity interest or unitrust interest (*see* §§8.31-8.32), (3) a nontrust remainder interest in a personal residence or a farm (*see* §8.15), or (4) an undivided portion of the donor's entire interest (*see* §8.16).

> **Example 2-7.** *D* transferred securities to the trustee of an irrevocable trust, the income of which is payable to her daughter, *X,* for life, with the remainder to a charity described in §2522(a). The gift of the remainder interest to the charity is not deductible for income, gift, or estate tax purposes because it is not in one of the approved forms. Prior to the changes made by the 1969 Act, federal tax deductions would have been allowed for the value of the charitable remainder interest. If *X* made a qualified disclaimer of her income interest, the charitable remainder would accelerate and the donor would be entitled to a gift tax charitable deduction for the full value of the property transferred to the trust. Likewise, a charitable deduction will be allowed if the trust is reformed to conform to the requirements of §2522. §2522(c)(4).

Because of the complexity of the income, gift, and estate tax rules, gifts of split interests must be planned very carefully.

§2.9. Marital Deduction, §2523

Section 2523 allows an unlimited marital deduction for qualifying gifts made by a citizen or resident of the United States to a spouse who is a citizen of the United States. As indicated above, the marital deduction for gifts made on or after July 14, 1988 is limited to gifts made to citizens of the United States. §2523(i). However, an annual exclusion of

$100,000 is allowable for gifts made to a spouse who is not a citizen of the United States. §2523(i)(2).

For gifts made prior to 1977 the marital deduction was limited to half of the value of the gift. The 1976 Act amended §2523 to allow a full deduction for the first $100,000 of noncommunity property given to a spouse after 1976. §2523(a)(2)(A). No deduction was allowed for the next $100,000 of post-1976 taxable gifts. Thereafter (*i.e.,* to the extent post-1976 taxable gifts exceeded $200,000) a deduction of 50 percent was allowed. §2523(a)(2)(B). No gift tax marital deduction was allowable for gifts of community property made prior to January 1, 1982, §2523(f), or of nonqualifying terminable interests, §2523(b). Beginning in 1982 a deduction was allowed on an elective basis for gifts of qualifying terminable interest property (QTIP). §2523(f). *See* §5.23.

§2.9.1. Pre-1982 Marital Deduction

Between 1977 and 1982, the marital deduction was fully allowable for the first $100,000 of noncommunity property given to spouse. No deduction was allowable for the next $100,000. Thereafter, a 50 percent deduction was allowable. In addition, the gift tax marital deduction was coordinated with the estate tax marital deduction by reducing the amount of the estate tax deduction where the deductions allowable under §2523 exceeded 50 percent of the value of the post-1976 gifts.

Example 2-8. *H* and *W* are both citizens of the United States. In 1979 *W,* who had not previously made any gifts, gave her husband, *H,* noncommunity property worth $103,000. No gift tax was due on the gift because of the combined effect of the annual exclusion ($3,000) and the marital deduction ($100,000). When *W* gave *H* an additional $103,000 in property in 1980, the annual exclusion sheltered the first $3,000 from tax, but the remaining $100,000 was subject to tax. *W*'s unified credit offset the tax on the gift. If *W* made any other pre-1982 gifts to *H,* a 50 percent marital deduction would have been available. Thus, if *W* had given *H* another $103,000 in 1981, she would have been entitled to a marital deduction of $51,500 and an annual exclusion of $3,000, which would have resulted in a taxable gift of $48,500.

§2.9.2. Post-1981 Marital Deduction

Gifts made after December 31, 1981 qualify for the unlimited marital deduction if the donee spouse receives a sufficient interest in the property. The deduction is available on an elective basis for gifts of QTIP.

See §5.23. Again, however, no marital deduction is allowable with respect to gifts made to a noncitizen spouse after July 13, 1988.

The overall gift and estate tax consequences of various interspousal gift programs should be estimated and given to the client for consideration before any substantial gifts are made. The estimates should indicate the tax consequences of making gifts of various amounts assuming, alternatively, that the donor predeceases the donee and vice versa. Although the effect of the gifts may seem obvious, the preparation of estimates provides a valuable check that may lead to a refinement of the plan.

Because of the progressive nature of the federal transfer tax, the overall gift and estate tax burden may be minimized if the sizes of the spouses' estate are equalized. A plan can easily provide for equalization if the wealthier spouse happens to die first. Lifetime interspousal gifts provide a hedge against the possibility that the poorer spouse will die first. These gifts may be in the form of a QTIP trust in which the donee spouse receives only a life estate. §2523(f). If the donee spouse receives a life income interest plus a general power of appointment, the donor spouse may retain a successive life estate without requiring the property to be included in his gross estate if the donee spouse predeceases him. *See* LR 8944009. Thus, the sizes of the estates can be equalized for estate tax purposes although the donor spouse "hedges" the gift by retaining a successive life estate. Of course, if the gift tax marital deduction is claimed with respect to the gift, the property is includible in the donee spouse's estate under §2044. Equalization is of little value unless the estate of one spouse is much larger than the estate of the other because the tax brackets are relatively large and the increase in rates is quite gradual after $100,000. For example, a rate of 37 percent applies to the amount of a transfer between $500,000 and $750,000, and a rate of 39 percent applies to the amount between $750,000 and $1,000,000. Also, apart from the surtax applicable to amounts in excess of $10 million, the "spread" between the marginal rate applicable to amounts in excess of the credit equivalent (37 percent) and the maximum rate (55 percent) is now only 18 percent and will come down to 13 percent after 1992.

The 1981 Act generally enhanced the advantages of deferral and decreased the importance of equalization. The expanded unified credit gives each married couple the opportunity to pass up to $1.2 million free of any federal gift or estate tax. If gifts are made for purposes of equalization, the donee's estate should be planned so as to dispose of the donative property in a way that will not cause the property to be included in the donor's estate if the donee dies before the donor. For example, the donee might leave the donor spouse a limited interest in the property or leave the property to their children or to a bypass trust for the benefit of the donor.

Substantial interspousal gifts are sometimes made to the poorer spouse so that the donee's estate can use the full amount of the unified credit and the GSTT exemption should the donee predecease the donor. As indicated above, the gifts might be made to a QTIP trust of which the poorer spouse is given only a life income interest. Unless such gifts are made, the unified credit of the donee spouse may be wasted if he or she predeceases the wealthier spouse. The estate of a poorer spouse can be built up without federal transfer tax cost by making gifts to him or her. A program of outright gifts might be undesirable, however, for other reasons, such as the possibility of marital dissolution.

§2.9.3. Marital Deduction: Some Planning Comments

Gifts to a spouse are usually made in order to (1) equalize the sizes of the spouses' estates and (2) create an estate for the "poorer" spouse as a hedge against the donee's earlier death and consequent loss of the marital deduction to the donor. As noted in §2.9.2., gifts to the poorer spouse may be made to preserve the benefit of the donee's unified credit and GSTT exemption. Where the spouses' estates are entirely community, an interspousal lifetime gift program is seldom indicated. In that case their estates are equalized naturally, which eliminates most of the tax advantages of making interspousal gifts. Of course, in any case the tax on the death of the first spouse can be completely deferred under the unlimited marital deduction.

Inter vivos gifts to a spouse are not generally made for income tax purposes because the advantages of income splitting are already available by filing joint income tax returns. However, during periods that capital gains are taxed at a substantially lower rate than ordinary income gifts may be helpful. For example, a sale at the more favorable capital gains rates may be facilitated by transferring the property from one spouse, in whose hands the property is not a capital asset, to the other spouse, in whose hands it will be. *See* §7.9.2. The general tax factors discussed in §§7.12-7.17 should also be considered in selecting property transfer to a spouse.

§2.10. Gift Tax Returns

A federal gift tax return (Form 709) is filed individually and not jointly or collectively with other taxpayers. §6019. However, no return is required for gifts that are not included in total gifts for the year by reason of §2503(b) (annual gift tax exclusion) and §2503(e) (qualified transfers to an educational institution or health care provider) or for gifts that qualify for the marital deduction under §2523. §6019(a). A short form

(Form 709A) can be used where a return is required only to split gifts between the spouses and the resulting gifts are within the amount of the allowable annual exclusions. As noted in §2.7, it is necessary to file gift tax returns in order to take advantage of gift splitting under §2513. A return must be filed on or before April 15 of the year following the close of the calendar year in which the gifts were made. However, a return for the year that includes the death of the donor must be filed no later than the time for filing the donor's estate tax return (*i.e.,* nine months after death). §6075(b)(3).

Example 2-9. *T* made a gift of $50,000 to *X* on January 1 and died on January 15. A gift tax return reporting the gift to *X* is due at the same time as *T*'s estate tax return, that is, October 15.

§2.10.1. Community Property Gifts

A gift of community property to a person outside the marital community is considered to be two gifts — each spouse is treated as having made a gift of one half of the whole value of the property. Accordingly, where community property is given to a third party, each spouse may be required to file a gift tax return. However, neither spouse is required to file a gift tax return where the gift is a present interest that does not exceed $20,000 in value.

Example 2-10. *H* and *W* gave their daughter, *D,* $20,000 of community property cash last year. Because each of them is considered to have made a gift of $10,000 to *D,* they are not required to file any gift tax return respecting the gift. *H* and *W* would be required to file returns on or before April 15, however, if they had made any other gifts to *D* during the year. In January of this year *H* and *W* gave *D* community property worth $25,000. *H* and *W* are each required to file a return reporting a gift of $12,500 on or before April 15 of next year.

§2.10.2. Manner and Time of Filing

The donor should file a gift tax return with the Internal Revenue Service Center with which the donor's federal income tax return is or would be filed. Instructions for Form 709 (rev. Dec. 1988). Otherwise, the return may be handcarried to the office of the district director for the district in which the donor resides. *See* §6091(b)(4).

Under §7503, if the last day prescribed for filing is a Saturday, Sunday, or legal holiday, the time is extended to the next succeeding day that is not a Saturday, Sunday, or legal holiday. A return is considered timely filed if it is mailed within the time allowed. The pertinent regulations provide generally that a document is deemed filed on the date of the postmark stamped on the cover in which it was mailed. Reg. §301.7502-1(a). If the date of mailing or receipt is important, returns and other documents mailed to the IRS should be sent by certified or registered mail, return receipt requested.

An addition to tax of five percent per month for each month a gift tax return is delinquent to a maximum of 25 percent will also be imposed under §6651(a)(1) unless the failure to pay the tax was for reasonable cause.

§2.10.3 Changes in Valuation, §2504(c)

> It is believed that once the value of a gift has been accepted for purposes of the [gift] tax by both the Government and the taxpayer, this value should be acceptable to both in measuring the tax to be applied to subsequent gifts. For this reason the bill provides that the value of a gift as reported on a taxable gift tax return for a prior year is to be conclusive as to the value of the gift (after the statute of limitation has run) in determining the tax rate to be applied to subsequent gifts. This substantially increases certainty in the gift tax area. H.R. Rep. 1337, 83d Cong., 2d Sess. 93 (1954).

Section 2504(c) bars the IRS from revaluing gifts for gift tax purposes after the tax has been paid and the statute of limitations has run. The bar only applies, however, when a tax "was assessed or paid." Thus, it does not bar revaluation where the donor's unified credit was used to offset the tax. When the gift and estate taxes were unified in 1976 the IRS should have been prohibited from revaluing gifts in connection with the determination of the estate tax. Under §2001(b) the amount of post-1976 taxable gifts is included in the tax base and a credit is allowed for gift taxes payable on such gifts.

The IRS has sought to avoid the bar of §2504(c) by arguing that it does not prohibit a revaluation of the amount of taxable gifts in connection with the determination of a deceased donor's estate tax liability. The argument was rejected in *Boatmen's First National Bank v. United States,* 705 F. Supp. 1407 (W.D. Mo. 1988), which noted that the IRS was attempting to do indirectly what it could not do directly. "This approach, in practice, would extend the statutory limitations period on gift valuation indefinitely, limited only by how long the donor survived after giving a gift. Congress could not have intended this, in light of its clearly established three-year limitation." 705 F. Supp. at 1413. The Tax Court proved to be a somewhat more hospitable forum for the IRS. In *Estate of Frederick R. Smith,* 94 T.C. 872 (1990), the Tax Court held that §2504(c) did not bar revaluation of gifts for estate tax purposes. In doing so the Tax Court recognized that a revaluation of a decedent's gifts "requires the subtraction for gift taxes be adjusted to take into account any increase in the value of the previous gifts." 94 T.C. at 879. If such an adjustment were not made, the IRS would be permitted "to collect the barred gift taxes through the imposition of a higher estate tax without an offsetting adjustment." 94 T.C. at 880. Although an adjustment is made, the decedent's estate may be pushed into higher estate tax brackets.

The outcome in *Boatmen's National Bank* is preferable. Once the value of a gift is finally determined, in the absence of fraud or other independent grounds, it should not be changed for transfer tax purposes. Otherwise a deceased donor's estate might be required to defend the valuation of gifts made, and apparently accepted by the IRS, decades before. The simple solution is to amend §2001(b) to provide that the valuation of gifts as finally determined for gift tax purposes cannot be challenged when it comes to determining the estate tax.

§2.10.4 Payment and Penalties

Under §6151(a), the gift tax must be paid at the time the return is due, though an extension may be allowed under §6161 in cases of "undue hardship." *See* §6161(a); Reg. §25.6161-1(b). However, the donor's unified credit is available to offset the gift tax and must be used for that purpose to the full extent it remains available to the donor. Unlike the case of the $30,000 lifetime gift tax exemption that was available under §2521 prior to 1977 the donor has no option regarding the use of the unified credit.

Checks or money orders in payment of the tax should be drawn to the order of "Internal Revenue Service" and carry the donor's social security number.

Any tax that is not paid when due is subject to an interest charge at the floating annual rate established under §6621 until it is paid. §6601(a). The interest rate applicable to deficiencies after December 31, 1986, is the Federal shortterm rate plus three percent. §6621(a) (2). An interest rate one percent lower applies to tax overpayments. §6621(a)(1). Under §6651(a)(2) an addition to tax of one-half of one percent per month is imposed for a failure to pay the tax not to exceed 25 percent unless the failure was due to reasonable cause. In addition, a penalty of five percent of any underpayment resulting from negligence or disregard of rules shall be imposed under §6652(a)(1). If an underpayment is due to fraud a penalty of 75 percent of the underpayment shall be imposed, but no delinquency penalty under §6651. §6652(b)(d).

A penalty is imposed by §6662 with respect to an estate or gift tax underpayment of $5,000 or more that is due to the valuation of property on the return at 50 percent or less of its correct valuation. §6662(g). The penalty is an addition to tax of an amount equal to 20 percent of the underpayment attributable to the undervaluation. Under §6664(c) no penalty may be imposed if the underpayment was due to reasonable cause. *See* Prop. Reg. §1.6664-4. Presumably no penalty would be imposed if the donor's valuation of the property was based on a written appraisal by a qualified expert.

D. FEDERAL ESTATE TAX HIGHLIGHTS

> Death taxes are ancient taxes. They were known to the Egyptians, as well as the Romans and Greeks. Even the complaints against them have a venerable pedigree. Pliny the Younger provides as good an example as any. He is among the earliest critics who have left summaries of their complaints. Pliny eloquently argued that a tax on the shares of direct heirs "was an 'unnatural' tax, augmenting the grief and sorrow of the bereaved." Almost two thousand years later the same argument was still being heard. For in 1898 Senator Allen forcefully inquired whether it was right "to stand with the widow and children at the grave side of a dead father to collect a tax," and then he sympathetically referred to the widow "in weeds" and the children "in tears." Eisenstein, The Rise and Decline of the Estate Tax, 11 Tax L. Rev. 223 (1956).

§2.11. Nature and Computation of the Tax

The federal estate tax is "neither a property tax nor an inheritance tax." Reg. §20.0-2(a). Instead, it is an excise tax imposed on the transfer of the entire taxable estate of the decedent. §2001(a). A decedent's taxable estate is determined by subtracting the deductions allowable under §§2053-2056 from the decedent's gross estate. As explained at §2.3, the tentative amount of the estate tax is calculated by applying the unified rate schedule, §2001(c), to the sum of the decedent's taxable estate *plus* the amount of post-1976 taxable gifts made by the decedent. However, in order to avoid taxing the same property twice, gifts that are includible in the decedent's gross estate are not counted as post-1976 taxable gifts. *See* §2001(b). The gross amount of the estate tax is determined by subtracting the gift tax on the decedent's post-1976 taxable gifts from the amount of the tentative tax. The gross tax is then reduced by the unified credit allowable in the year of the decedent's death and any of the other credits that are allowable under §§2011-2014. Most estates involve only the unified credit and the credit for state death taxes allowed by §2011.

The taxable estate, together with the decedent's post-1976 taxable gifts, is the base on which the decedent's tax liability is determined. It is calculated by subtracting Deductions, §§2053-2056, from the Gross Estate, §§2033-2044.

§2.12. Gross Estate

The property and interests described in §§2033-2044 are included in the gross estate and valued in accordance with §§2031-2032A. Although the gross estate includes the property subject to administration in a decedent's estate under state law, the gross estate is a much broader and more inclusive concept. As explained below, it may include property that the decedent no longer owned at death.

The scope of §§2033-2044 and §2046 is described in the following paragraphs, which are largely adapted from Reg. §20.2031-1(a).

1. Owned Property, §2033. Property owned by a decedent at death is includible in the decedent's gross estate under §2033. The section extends to future interests as well as present possessory interests. Section 2034 merely provides that the property is includible in the decedent's estate even though the decedent's surviving spouse has an interest in the property, such as dower or curtesy.

2. Property Transferred During Lifetime, §§2035-2038. Property transferred within three years of death is generally not includible in the gross estate of a transferor who dies after December 31, 1981. A contrary rule applied to the estates of persons dying prior to 1982. §2035.

Other lifetime transfers are includible under §§2036-2038 unless the transferor received full and adequate consideration for the transfer in money or money's worth. In general, §2036 requires the inclusion of property with respect to which the decedent retained either the use or income from the property or the power to designate who would receive its use or income. Property transferred by the decedent is includible under §2037 if it could be enjoyed by others only if they survive the decedent and the decedent retained a reversionary interest, the value of which immediately before the decedent's death exceeded five percent of the value of the property. The scope of §2038 is essentially the same as that of §2036 although §2038 speaks specifically of a power, retained by the decedent, to alter, amend, revoke, or terminate the transfer.

3. Annuities; Joint Interests; Powers of Appointment and Life Insurance, §§2039-2042. Sections 2039 through 2042 deal with special types of property and powers of appointment held by the decedent. Section 2039 requires the inclusion of certain interests in annuities and other payments made pursuant to a contract or other agreement under which the decedent had a right to receive payments for life or for a period not ascertainable without reference to his or her death. Section 2040 governs the inclusion of interests in joint tenancies and tenancies by the entirety. Property subject to certain powers of appointment is includible in the power-holder's estate under §2041. Finally, §2042 requires the inclusion of insurance receivable by the insured's executor or over which the insured retained any incident of ownership.

4. Consideration Offset, §2043. Under §2043 the amount includible in a decedent's estate under §§2035-2038 and 2041 is reduced by the amount of consideration in money or money's worth that the decedent received in exchange for the transfer of the property or the release or exercise of the power. This section deals with cases in which the decedent received insufficient consideration in money or money's worth for the transfer, release, or exercise. The amount of consideration received by the decedent is "frozen" at the time of the transfer, while the value of the property transferred by the decedent is determined on the appropriate valuation date, *i.e.,* the value of the property included in the transferor's estate may increase or decrease after the date of the transfer, but the amount of the consideration is fixed on that date). Section 2045 merely directs that unless otherwise provided the rules of §§2034-2042 apply to transfers, interests, and powers whenever made, created, exercised, or relinquished.

5. QTIP, §2044. Under §2044 a decedent's gross estate includes any property that was transferred to the decedent and for which a marital deduction was allowed as qualified terminable interest property under §2523(f) (gift tax) or §2056(b)(7) (estate tax). *See* §5.23.

6. Qualified Disclaimers, §2046. The estate tax recognizes that a qualified disclaimer under §2518 does not constitute a transfer for purposes of the estate tax. §2046.

The scope and application of §§2035, 2036, and 2038-2041 are examined in more detail in §§2.16-2.20. Particular attention is given to some of the traps created by those sections and how to avoid them. Some other provisions explored at greater length are the life insurance section, §2042, in Chapter 6, and the marital deduction sections, §§2044, 2056 and others, in Chapter 5.

§2.13. VALUATION

For estate and gift tax purposes, property is generally valued at its fair market value, which is the "price at which the property would change hands between a willing buyer and a willing seller, neither being under any compulsion to buy or sell and both having reasonable knowledge of the relevant facts." Reg. §§20.2031-1(b), 25.2512-1. The effect of revaluation of taxable gifts made by a decedent is discussed in §2.10.3. A client should be fully informed about the ways in which the client's assets might be arranged so as to control or depress their value. Shrinking or freezing the value of the estate is an important estate planning strategy. *See* §2.43-2.44. Substantial discounts are frequently allowed in valuing minority interests in a business enterprise or undivided interests in real property. Note that the IRS will insist that gifts of such interests to charity be subject to the same discounts. The same interests may also qualify for a discount for lack of marketability. Thus, in *Harwood Investment Co.,* 82 T.C. 239 (1984), *aff'd without opinion,* 786 F.2d 1174 (9th Cir.), *cert. denied,* 479 U.S. 1007 (1986), a discount of 50 percent was allowed in valuing gifts of interest in a family limited partnership. Conversely, in some cases an interest that carries control of a business may be valued at a premium. For example, a premium was attached to the 51 percent of a business that qualified for the marital deduction in *Estate of Dean E. Chenoweth,* 88 T.C. 1577 (1987).

Under §2031(a), property included in a decedent's gross estate is valued on the date of the decedent's death. Extensive regulations issued under §2031 describe the manner in which various types of property are to be valued, including annuities, life estates, terms for years, and remainders. *See* Reg. §20.2031-10. The valuations are made utilizing the actuarial tables issued pursuant to §7520. *See* I.R.S. Publications 1457 and 1458 (1989). However, §2032 allows the executor to elect to value a decedent's gross estate on an alternate valuation date if the election will result in a decrease in the value of the gross estate *and* in the total amount of the estate and GST tax. §2032(c). If the election is made, any assets that are distributed, sold, exchanged, or otherwise disposed of within six months following death must be valued on the date of distribution, sale or exchange. Any assets that are not distributed, sold, or exchanged within six months following death must be valued as of the date six months following the decedent's death. Changes in value due to the mere lapse of time are not taken into account for purposes of the alternate valuation. Section 2032A allows certain closely-held farm and business real property to be valued specially at less than its fair market value. Alternate valuation and special use valuation under §2032A are described more fully in §§12.15-12.19.

The 1987 Act added an extraordinarily complex provision,

§2036(c), that was intended to prevent the use of preferred stock recapitalizations, multitiered partnerships, and other estate tax freezing techniques to reduce or to eliminate value from a transferor's estate at little or no gift tax cost. The 1990 Act replaced §2036(c) with Chapter 14, §§2701-2704, which is designed to prevent the depressed valuation of interests that are transferred inter vivos to family members. Chapter 14, which is considered in more detail in Chapters 9 and 11, *infra,* prescribes special gift tax rules for the valuation of retained interests in family corporations and partnerships, §2701; options and buy-sell agreements, §2703; and the effect of lapses of voting and liquidation rights, §2704. The special rules of §2702 apply to the valuation of retained interests in trusts other than personal residence trusts.

§2.14. Deductions

Sections 2053 to 2057 describe the deductions that are allowed against the gross estate in calculating a decedent's taxable estate. In brief, the sections provide as follows:

1. Funeral and Administration Expenses, §2053. Deductions are allowed for funeral and administration expenses and claims against the estate, including certain taxes and charitable pledges. Essentially the same deductions are allowable whether or not there is an estate administration. The personal representative may elect to deduct administration expenses either on the estate tax return or on the estate's income tax return. This, and other important post-mortem elections, are described in Chapter 12.

2. Losses, §2054. A deduction is allowed for the amount of uncompensated losses suffered during administration of the estate on account of fires, storms, shipwrecks or other casualties, or from theft.

3. Charitable Transfers, §2055. Section 2055(a) allows a deduction for the value of charitable transfers of property included in the decedent's estate. However, if a transfer is made for both a charitable and a noncharitable purpose, a deduction is allowed for the value of the charitable interest only if the transfer takes one of the forms described in §2055(e)(2). The allowance of charitable deductions for such "split interests" is explored in more detail in Chapter 8.

4. Marital Deduction, §2056. Section 2056 allows a decedent's estate an unlimited marital deduction for property or qualifying interests in property that are transferred to a surviving spouse who is a U.S. citizen. All of the property of a married person may be passed, free of tax, to or for the benefit of his or her surviving spouse. Also, beginning in 1982, the deduction was made available on an elective basis for part or all of the value of property in which the surviving spouse is given a qualifying income interest for life. §2056(b)(7). At the same time a marital deduction first became available for the current interest in a qualifying charitable remainder trust given to a surviving spouse. §2056(b)(8). Prior to the 1981 Act §2056 allowed only a limited deduction for the value of property or interests in property that were included in the decedent's gross estate and passed from the decedent to the surviving spouse. In the case of a surviving spouse who is not a U.S. citizen the marital deduction is allowable only to the extent the decedent's property passes to a qualified domestic trust for the benefit of the surviving spouse. §§2056(d), 2056A. *See* §5.25.

A planner must have a good grasp of the rules regarding the charitable and marital deductions in order to advise clients competently regarding the formulation of estate plans. A comprehensive understanding of the deductions is also necessary in order to do an effective job of post-mortem planning. Of course, in some cases the inter vivos or post-mortem planning may require the assistance of an expert on the particular subject.

§2.15. Credits

Sections 2010 through 2016 describe the credits that are allowable against the federal estate tax. The most important is the unified credit that §2010 allows the estate of each citizen or resident. The credit of $192,800 is equal to the tax imposed on a transfer of $600,000. Although the same rate schedule applies to the estates of nonresident aliens, a credit of only $13,000 (equal to the tax on a transfer of $60,000) is allowed unless otherwise required by treaty. §§2101-2102. In addition to the unified credit, credits are allowed for:

1. State Death Tax Credit, §2011. A credit is allowed for state death taxes actually paid with respect to property included in the decedent's gross estate. The credit ranges from an opening rate of .8 percent to 16 percent on a taxable estate in excess of $10,100,000. A large number of states impose a "pick-up" tax, which is a death tax equal to the amount of the allowable federal credit.

2. Credit for Gift Tax on Pre-1977 Gifts, §2012. A credit is allowed for gift taxes paid on gifts made prior to January 1, 1977, when the same property is included in the donor's gross estate. In determining the amount of the estate tax the amount of gift tax attributable to post-1976 gifts is deducted from the tentative tax. *See* §2001(b).

3. Previously Taxed Property Credit, §2013. Section 2013 allows a credit for the estate tax paid with respect to the transfer of property to the decedent by or from a person who died within ten years before or two years after the death of the decedent. The transferred property is not required to be identified in the estate of the later decedent, nor must it be in existence at the time of his or her death. The amount of the credit is limited to the lesser of (1) the amount of the tax attributable to the interest in the estate of the transferor and (2) the amount of the tax attributable to the interest in the estate of the present decedent. The full amount of the credit is allowable if the later decedent died within two years of the time the property was transferred to him or her. Thereafter the amount of the credit diminishes by 20 percent every two years, so that no credit is allowable if the transferor died more than ten years preceding the death of the later decedent.

A substantial credit may be allowed with respect to the value of a life income interest that the decedent received from the estate of a prior decedent. Such an interest is valued under the actuarial tables as of the date of the death of the transferor (the prior decedent). The credit is allowable although the life estate or other transferred property is not included in the estate of the transferee (the later decedent). Rev. Rul. 59-9, 1959-1 C.B. 232. Of course, no credit is allowed to the extent the marital deduction was claimed by the estate of the prior decedent in connection with the transfer. §2013(d)(3); *United States v. Denison,* 318 F.2d 819 (5th Cir. 1963). No credit is allowable for a purely discretionary income interest which permits distributions to be made to other beneficiaries as well. LR 8944005 (TAM).

4. Foreign Death Tax Credit, §2014. A credit may be allowed for the amount of death taxes actually paid to any foreign country with respect to property situated in that country and included in the decedent's gross estate. The allowance of the credit may be affected by the terms of a gift and estate tax treaty between the United States and the foreign country imposing the tax.

5. Credit for Deferred State and Foreign Death Taxes, §2015. This section concerns the allowance of the credits for state and foreign death taxes attributable to remainder or reversionary interests with respect to which the payment of the estate tax has been deferred under §6163(a). In essence, the section allows credits for the state and foreign death taxes if they are paid within the time for payment of the deferred portion of the estate tax. Note that the provisions of this section do not apply to deferrals under §6166.

6. Notification of State and Foreign Death Tax Credits, §2016. A person who receives a refund of any state or foreign death tax that was claimed as a credit under §2011 or §2014 must notify the district director of the refund within 30 days of its receipt. The amount of the estate tax is then redetermined and the amount of any additional tax due by reason of the redetermination must be paid by the executor.

The unified credit is particularly important in planning relatively small estates. However, in some instances the other credits offer important planning opportunities. The previously taxed property credit that is allowed for a portion of the tax paid with respect to a life estate, §2013, can be particularly valuable. Of course, for many estates the credits are only significant in connection with the preparation of the federal estate tax returns.

§2.16. Transfers Within Three Years of Death, §2035

Property transferred within three years of death generally is not includible in the estate of a transferor who dies after December 31, 1981. §2035(d). However, the value of such property may be included for the purpose of determining the qualification of the deceased transferor's estate for special treatment under §§303, 2032A, and 6166. §2035(d)(3). Thus, a donor cannot make use of deathbed gifts of nonbusiness property in order to qualify his estate for the benefits of §§303, 2032A and 6166. Insurance on the life of the transferor and certain other property transferred within three years of her death are includible under the provisions of §2035(d)(2). Section 2035(c) requires the inclusion of the amount of any gift tax paid by the decedent or the decedent's estate on any gift made by the decedent or the decedent's spouse within three years of the decedent's death. Prior to 1977 the law strongly encouraged deathbed gifts because it did not require such a "gross up." The application of §2035 is illustrated by the following example:

> **Example 2-11.** In 1991 *X* gave stock worth $10,000 to her daughter, *D.* She also gave a $250,000 policy of insurance on her life that had a present value of $2,500 to her son, *S. X* died in 1993 when the stock was worth $50,000. *S* received the insurance proceeds of $250,000. None of the value of the stock is includible in *X*'s gross estate. The entire proceeds of the life insurance policy are includible by reason of §2035(d)(2) because the proceeds would have been includible in the estate of the insured under §2042 had the policy not been transferred.

§2.17. Retained Interests and Powers, §§2036, 2038

Property transferred during lifetime is includible in the transferor's estate under §2036(a) to the extent the decedent retained "for his life or for any period not ascertainable without reference to his death or for any period which does not in fact end before his death — (1) the possession or enjoyment of, or the right to the income from, the property, or (2) the right, either alone or in conjunction with any person, to designate the persons who shall possess or enjoy the property or the income therefrom." Thus, this section extends to transfers, in trust or otherwise, under which the transferor retained the use or enjoyment of property or the right to designate the persons who could possess or enjoy the property or the income from it. The scope of §2038 is essentially the same as that of §2036(a)(2) and specifically extends to any interest in property transferred by the decedent, in trust or otherwise, if the enjoyment of the property was subject at the date of the decedent's death to change through the exercise of a power by the decedent to alter, amend, revoke, or terminate the interest. Inclusion is also required if the decedent relinquished the power within the three-year period ending on the date of the decedent's death. *See* §2038(a)(1); Reg. §20.2035-1(b).

> **Example 2-12.** *T* purchased securities that were registered in *T's* name as custodian under the Uniform Gifts to Minors Act for *T's* 10-year-old nephew, *N*. The registration of the securities constituted an irrevocable gift subject to the gift tax. If *T* dies while acting as custodian, the securities are includible in *T's* gross estate under §2038 because of *T's* power under the Uniform Act to distribute the securities to *N* prior to the time when custodianship would otherwise terminate. *See* §7.34.2.

§2.17.1. Retained Voting Rights, §2036(b)

Section 2036 was broadened in 1976 and 1978 to require inclusion of stock in a "controlled corporation" that was transferred during lifetime if the transferor retained, directly or indirectly, the right to vote the stock alone or in conjunction with any person. The provision was adopted in order to overcome the effect of *United States v. Byrum,* 408 U.S. 125 (1972), which held that the power to control a corporation through a retained power to vote its stock did not require inclusion of the stock under §2036. A controlled corporation is one in which the transferor at any time after the transfer of the property, and within three years of death, owned or had the right to vote stock that represented at least 20 percent of the combined voting power of all classes of stock.

§2036(b)(2). The attribution rules of §318 apply for the purpose of determining whether the transferor owned the requisite interest in the stock. Thus, the stock owned by the transferor's spouse and children are taken into account in determining the percentage of stock owned by the transferor. Also, for purposes of applying §2035, the relinquishment or cessation of voting rights is treated as a transfer of property made by the decedent. §2036(b)(3). Section 2036(b) does not require the inclusion of nonvoting Class B common stock transferred by the decedent prior to death although the decedent retained all of the Class A voting common stock. LR 9004009.

The provisions of §2036(b) create a trap for the unwary and raise a host of complex issues that will require litigation to resolve. *See* McCord, The 1978 Anti-*Byrum* Amendment: A Cruel Hoax, U. Miami, 14th Inst. Est. Plan., ch. 12 (1980). A serious trap exists because §2036(b) requires inclusion of stock in a controlled corporation with respect to which the decedent retained the right to vote in any capacity. For example, the section extends to stock over which the transferor held the right to vote solely in a fiduciary capacity — as trustee or custodian under the Uniform Gifts to Minors Act.

§2.17.2. Anti-freeze Provision, Former §2036(c)

Former §2036(c), added by the 1987 Act and repealed by the 1990 Act, was designed to eliminate the estate tax advantages of most "estate freezes" entered into after December 17, 1987. In brief, the provision required inclusion in the donor's estate of an interest in an enterprise that was transferred to a family member during the donor's lifetime if the transferred interest carried a disproportionately large share of the potential appreciation and the donor retained an interest in the income or other rights of the enterprise. The provision was aimed at techniques such as the preferred stock recapitalization or the multitiered partnership by which the members of a senior generation transferred the future growth in the equity of a family enterprise to the younger generations at little or no transfer tax cost. *See* Chapter 11. However, the broad scope of the subsection threatened some gifts and other relatively innocent transactions that were not related to any objectionable attempt to shift future appreciation to others. In short, §2036(c) was objectionably overbroad. Some clarifying amendments were made by the 1988 Act, which also added some important safe harbor provisions. As noted in §2.13, *supra,* §2036(c) was repealed in 1990 and a different approach was taken by its replacement, §§2701-2704. *See* Chapter 9.

§2.18. Annuities and Other Death Benefits, §2039

Section 2039 requires the inclusion of an annuity or other payment receivable by any beneficiary by reason of surviving the decedent under the terms of certain contracts or agreements to the extent that the annuity is attributable to contributions made by the decedent or the decedent's employer. The estate tax consequences of the inclusion of an annuity are offset in many cases by the availability of the marital deduction. Under §2056(b)(7)(C) the marital deduction is available with respect to an annuity under which only the decedent's surviving spouse has the right to receive payments.

§2.19. Joint Tenancies, §2040

Joint tenancies and tenancies by the entirety are widely used (particularly by married persons) to hold title to property because each of the tenancies carries a right of survivorship. That is, upon the death of one tenant the decedent's rights in the property terminate and all rights in the property are owned by the survivor. The estate tax disadvantage of spouses holding property in joint tenancy form was largely eliminated by the adoption of the unlimited marital deduction.

§2.19.1. Joint Tenants Other Than Husband and Wife

The two basic rules that govern the taxation of joint tenancies are stated in §2040(a). First, where the joint tenancy was acquired by the decedent and the other joint owner by gift, devise, or inheritance, the decedent's fractional interest in the property is included in the decedent's gross estate. This rule is simple and logical in its application, at least in states that permit a joint tenant to sever the joint tenancy and convert it into a tenancy in common with no right of survivorship. The second rule includes the entire value of the property in the decedent's gross estate except to the extent it is attributable to the contributions in money or money's worth made by the other tenant. For this purpose, the contributions of the other tenant are not taken into account to the extent they are attributable to money or other property acquired from the decedent for less than full and adequate consideration.

> **Example 2-13.** *T*'s will left Blackacre to *T*'s children, *A* and *B,* as joint tenants with right of survivorship. *T* also left a cash gift of $100,000 to *A,* which A used to purchase Whiteacre in the name of *A* and *B* as joint tenants. The purchase of Whiteacre

involved a gift from *A* to *B* of $50,000 (half of its total value). If *A* dies survived by *B,* a half interest in Blackacre and the whole interest in Whiteacre are includible in *A*'s estate under §2040(a). Because the value of Whiteacre is included in *A*'s gross estate, the amount of the prior taxable gift is not taken into account in computing the estate tax. *See* §2001(b). Otherwise, the same property would be taxed twice.

§2.19.2. Husband and Wife as Joint Tenants: Qualified Joint Interests, §2040(b)

In 1976 Congress added §2040(b), under which only half of the value of a qualified joint interest is includible in the gross estate. A *qualified joint interest* is an interest in property held by the decedent and the decedent's spouse as tenants by the entirety or as joint tenants with right of survivorship, but only if they are the sole tenants. Only half of a qualified joint interest is includible in the decedent's gross estate regardless of which spouse provided the consideration for the acquisition of the property. A marital deduction is allowable under §2056 for the amount included in the decedent's estate as a qualified joint interest. Again, the benefits of §2040(b) are not available if the decedent's surviving spouse is not a citizen of the United States. §2056(d)(1)(B). Under §2523(i)(3) the rules of former §§2515 and 2515A apply to the transfer of property into joint tenancy with a spouse who is not a citizen. According to former §2515, the creation of a joint tenancy in real property does not involve a gift, but under §2515A each spouse is considered to have an equal interest in a joint tenancy in personal property.

The partial inclusion rule of §2040(b) is fair, simple to understand, and easy to administer. It is also consistent with the adoption of the unified transfer tax system that substantially reduced the advantages of making lifetime gifts. However, §2040(b) originally applied only to a joint tenancy created after 1976 by one or both spouses that was treated as a gift. In addition, only the spouses could be parties to the tenancy. The 1978 Act added provisions that allowed conversion of pre-1976 joint tenancies into qualified joint interests. *See* former §§2040(d)-(e). The 1981 Act repealed §§2040(c)-(e), and made the qualified joint interest rule applicable to all joint tenancies between a husband and wife in which there was no other joint tenant.

The estate of the spouse first to die includes only half of the total value of qualified joint interests, including post-gift appreciation. Of course, the entire value of the property is includible in the estate of the surviving joint tenant.

For historical purposes it should be noted that the 1978 Act also added §2040(c), permitting the efforts of the decedent's spouse to be taken into account in determining the amount of jointly held farming or business property includible in the decedent's gross estate. This cumbersome elective provision allowed the value of the gross estate to be reduced by (1) the adjusted consideration of the spouse and (2) by two percent of the excess of the value of the property over the total adjusted consideration provided by both spouses for each year that the decedent's spouse participated materially in the operation of the farm or other business. The *adjusted consideration* was defined as the consideration furnished by a spouse plus interest computed at six percent per year from the date the consideration was furnished until the date of the decedent's death. The provision was intended to give a surviving spouse reasonable credit for the increase in the value of the joint tenancy property due to the surviving spouse's efforts.

§2.20 POWERS OF APPOINTMENT, §2041

The flexibility of an estate plan is increased substantially by giving survivors powers of appointment that can be used to alter the distribution of income and principal in light of changed future circumstances. However, transactions involving powers of appointment must be carefully planned because of their important tax consequences, particularly for estate tax purposes. Section 2041 defines the extent to which the property subject to a power of appointment is includible in the estate of the power holder, but it does not apply to powers that a transferor retains over property that he or she transfers to others. *See* Reg. §20.2041-1(b)(2). In such a case the property is subject to inclusion in the transferor's estate under §§2036 and 2038.

Under §2041, property over which a decedent possessed, exercised, or released a general power of appointment is usually includible in the decedent's gross estate. A general power of appointment is one that is exercisable in favor of "the decedent, his estate, his creditors, or creditors of his estate." §2041(b)(1).

Property subject to a nongeneral power of appointment is not includible in the gross estate of the holder of the power under §2041. In light of that rule, wills and trusts are frequently drafted to give a surviving family member the power to appoint the property to and among a limited class or a class that includes everyone *other than* the holder of the power, his creditors, his estate, and the creditors of his estate. Unfortunately, powers are often created that are too restrictive. For example, a power may exclude the spouses of descendants from the class of persons to whom appointments might be made. Of course, such a restricted power does prevent the property from being appointed out of the family line.

§2.20.1. Exceptions

There are some important exceptions to the basic rules regarding the taxation of powers under §2041. To begin with, property subject to a general power of appointment created before October 22, 1942 is not includible in the decedent's gross estate unless the power is exercised. §2041(a)(1). Also, a power is not considered to be a general power of appointment if the power is exercisable only with the consent or joinder of (1) the creator of the power or (2) a person having a substantial adverse interest. §2041(b)(1)(C). Finally, a power limited by an ascertainable standard relating to the health, education, support, or maintenance of the power-holder is not a general power of appointment. §2041(b)(1)(A). These exceptions are explained in Chapter 10.

§2.20.2. Release of Post-1942 General Powers

Property subject to a post-October 21, 1942 general power of appointment is also includible in the decedent's estate if the power was exercised or released in such a way that the property would have been includible in the decedent's estate under §§2035-2038 had it been a transfer of property owned by the decedent. §2041(a)(2). Thus, property that had been subject to a general power of appointment is includible in the power-holder's estate if the power-holder released the power and retained the income, use, or control of the property.

> **Example 2-14.** After October 21, 1942 *G* transferred property in trust to pay the income to *X* for life, then to distribute the principal to *Y*. The trust gave *X* a power to withdraw the trust principal whenever *X* chose to do so. *X* irrevocably released the power. The property of the trust is includible in *X*'s gross estate under §2041(a)(2) and is treated as if *X* had transferred property to the trust and reserved the income in the property for life. Of course, the release also involved a gift to *Y* of the value of the remainder interest. §2514(b).

§2.20.3. Lapses of General Powers; $5,000 or 5% Powers

The lapse of a general power created after October 21, 1942 is treated in the same way as a release. §2041(b)(2). Thus, property subject to a general power that lapses is includible in the power-holder's estate if the power-holder retains an interest or power in the property described in §§2036-2038. However, lapses of powers during any calendar year are treated as releases only to the extent that the property subject to the power exceeds the greater of $5,000 or five percent of the value of the property out of which the exercise of the power could have been satisfied. Thus, a person can be given the noncumulative annual right to withdraw the greater of $5,000 or five percent of the value of the trust without causing the property to be included in the power holder's gross estate other than for the property subject to withdrawal under the power at the time of the power holder's death. This rule, together with the exception for powers limited by ascertainable standards, allows an individual to hold important powers of withdrawal without requiring any substantial part of the trust principal to be included in his or her gross estate. These rules are explored in more detail in Chapter 10.

§2.21. Life Insurance, §2042

Insurance proceeds "receivable" by the insured's executor are includible in the estate of the insured under §2042(1). This rule applies although the insured never owned or had any interest in the underlying insurance policy. It extends also to proceeds that are "receivable by another beneficiary but are subject to an obligation, legally binding upon the other beneficiary, to pay taxes, debts, or other charges enforceable against the estate." Reg. §20.2042-1(b).

Insurance proceeds are includible in the insured's estate under §2042(2) if, at the time of death, the insured possessed any incident of ownership in the policy, exercisable alone or in conjunction with any other person. The term "incidents of ownership" is not defined in the Code. However, the Regulations indicate that it refers generally to "the right of the insured or his estate to the economic benefits of the policy. Thus, it includes the power to change the beneficiary, to surrender or cancel the policy, to assign the policy, to revoke an assignment, to pledge the policy for a loan, or to obtain from the insurer a loan against the surrender value of the policy." Reg. §20.2042-1(c)(2). The mysteries of incidents of ownership are examined in more detail in §6.27.

E. GENERATION-SKIPPING TRANSFER TAX (GSTT)

§2.22. Background

The need for a GSTT arises from the fact that by transferring property in trust the transferor may insulate the property from the reach of the estate and gift taxes for several generations. The opportunity to pass property through successive generations free of federal transfer taxes arose largely because the estate tax only applies to property that was owned or transferred by a decedent or with respect to which the decedent had a significant power or incident of ownership: It does not require a decedent's estate to include any interest in property in which the decedent held a life interest created by others. The difference in tax cost between leaving property to a child outright or to a generation-skipping trust for the benefit of a child and successive generations of beneficiaries is illustrated by the following example:

> **Example 2-15.** *T* died in 1950, leaving a will that transferred $1,000,000 to a testamentary trust. The income of the trust was payable at the discretion of the trustee to *T*'s son *S* for life and thereafter for successive generations of the descendants of *S*. Twenty-one years after the death of the last of *T*'s descendants who were living at the time of *T*'s death the trust will terminate and the principal will be distributed by right of representation among those of *S*'s descendants who are then living. The property that *T* transferred to the trust was subject to the estate taxation when *T* died. When *S* died in 1982 the trust had a value of $20,000,000. None of the trust, which now benefits *S*'s children, was included in his gross estate. Indeed, the trust property will not again be subject to a federal transfer tax until after the trust terminates and the property has been distributed to *T*'s descendants. Had the trust terminated in 1982 the beneficiaries would have received $20,000,000. The termination of life interests and the shifting of beneficial interests from generation to generation are not subject to the estate tax.
>
> *T*'s will also left $1,000,000 outright to his daughter, *D*. The property, which was worth $20,000,000 when *D* died in 1982, was included in her estate. A tax of over $12,000,000 was paid with respect to the property. Only $8,000,000 was available for distribution to *D*'s beneficiaries.

As a general rule neither the estate tax nor the gift tax applies to the distribution of property from a trust to a beneficiary.

Generation-skipping trusts were widely used by very wealthy families to provide for successive generations of descendants without subjecting the property to estate or gift taxes. Of course, once property is distributed from a trust it is subject to the estate and gift taxes in the hands of the distributee.

Troubled by the relatively widespread use of generation-skipping trusts, Congress struck back in 1976 by enacting a complex form of GSTT. The tax was intended to be substantially equivalent to the gift and estate taxes that would have been imposed had the property been transferred outright once in every generation. However, the 1976 version of the GSTT did not apply to any transfer that was subject to the estate or gift tax, but instead only applied to a taxable termination of a trust or trust equivalent or a taxable distribution from a generation-skipping trust or trust equivalent. The GSTT was imposed at the marginal estate or gift tax rate applicable to the "deemed transferor," who was most often the parent of the transferee most closely related to the grantor. Pursuing this theme, the unused portion of the deemed transferor's unified credit could be offset against the tax on transfers that took place at or after the death of the deemed transferor. The 1976 version was complex and difficult to understand and imposed substantial recordkeeping requirements.

The potential effectiveness of the 1976 version of the GSTT was eroded by several important loopholes. First, the GSTT only applied to generation-skipping trusts and trust equivalents and not to outright transfers. Thus, substantial amounts could be given outright to the members of each generation of descendants without incurring any GSTT liability. Second, the GSTT did not apply to trusts all of the beneficiaries of which belonged to the same generation. This rule encouraged the creation of separate trusts for each generational level of beneficiaries ("layered" trusts). Third, the GSTT did not apply to distributions of income. Finally, the GSTT allowed a grandchildren's exclusion of $250,000 for transfers to trusts for the children of each child of the deemed transferor.

> **Example 2-16.** *G*'s will made bequests of $1,000,000 outright to her grandchild *X* and to *X*'s children, *Y* and *Z*. The outright transfers to *X, Y,* and *Z* were subject to the estate tax in *G*'s estate, but they were not subject to the 1976 version of the GSTT. The transfers would be subject to the 1986 version of the GSTT.
>
> *G* also left $1,000,000 in trust to distribute the income to her niece *N* and grandniece *GN,* for so long as they or the survivor of them should live. Distributions of income to *GN* would not have been subject to the GSTT. When *N* died the GSTT would have applied at the marginal rate applicable to her estate.

§2.23. 1986 GSTT

In 1986 Congress repealed the 1976 GSTT retroactively and replaced it with a slightly less complex, more workable version. For GSTT purposes, the transferor of a generation-skipping transfer is the decedent in the case of a transfer subject to the estate tax and the donor in the case of a gift. Unlike the 1976 version, the new GSTT applies to a generation-skipping transfer *in addition to* the gift or estate taxes that apply to the transfer. Each individual has a $1 million GSTT exemption, which may be allocated by the individual (or his or her executor) to any transfer of which the individual is the transferor. §2631(a).

The 1986 GSTT applies to three types of generation-skipping transfers: direct skips, taxable terminations, and taxable distributions.

§2.23.1. Direct Skips and Skip Persons, §§2612(c), 2613

A *direct skip* is a transfer that is subject to the estate or gift tax made to a skip person. A *skip person* is either (1) a natural person who is assigned to a generation which is two or more generations below the generation of the transferor or (2) a trust in which all interests are held by skip persons or a trust in which no person holds an interest and from which no distribution may be made to a nonskip person. §2613(a). Not surprisingly, a *nonskip person* is a person who is not a skip person. §2613(b). Thus, the grandchildren and more remote descendants of a transferor are skip persons, but the transferor's spouse, siblings, or children are nonskip persons. In this connection note that a transfer that skips a single generation is taxed in the same way as one that skips several generations.

> **Example 2-17.** *T*'s will left gifts of $1,000,000 to his child *C, C*'s son *GS, GS*'s daughter *GGD,* and *GGD*'s daughter *GGGD. C* is not a skip person, but *GS, GGD,* and *GGGD* are. Accordingly, the transfers to *GS, GGD,* and *GGGD* are subject to the GSTT. The transfers to *GS, GGD,* and *GGGD* are all taxed in the same way although the transfers skip 1, 2, and 3 generations respectively. (The method of making generational assignments is described in §2.32.)

The full value of a gift to a skip person for life, remainder to the transferor's child (a nonskip person), is subject to the GSTT, LR 9105006 (TAM). The transfer was treated as a deemed trust. *See* §2.30.1.

Under a special "orphan grandchild's" exception a transfer to a grandchild of the transferor is not a direct skip if the parent who is a lineal descendant of the transferor (or the transferor's spouse or former spouse) is dead at the time of the transfer. §2612(c)(2). Thus, a gift to a grandchild is not a direct skip if the transferor's child who was a parent of the donee is not living at the time of the gift. Under this rule outright gifts made by a great-grandparent to great-grandchildren were treated as gifts to children where the parents and grandparents of the donees were deceased at the time of the gifts. LR 9114024.

Example 2-18. *T* died leaving a will which gave $1,000,000 to her grandchild *GC*. *T*'s daughter, *D,* the mother of *GC,* died before *T*. The transfer to *GC* is not a direct skip. A bequest by *T* to a child of *GC* would be a direct skip.

§2.23.2. Taxable Terminations, §2612(a)

A taxable termination is the "termination (by death, lapse of time, release of power, or otherwise) of an interest in property held in trust" unless immediately afterwards a nonskip person has an interest in the property or at no time thereafter may a distribution be made to a skip person. §2612(a). *Interest* is defined as a *present* right to receive income or corpus from the trust. §2652(c). Also, a person, other than a charitable organization, who is a permissible distributee of income or principal has an interest in the trust.

Example 2-19. *T* left $2,000,000 in trust to pay the income to her son *S* for life. Following the death of *S* the trust is to continue for the benefit of his children and grandchildren. The life income interest of *S* is an interest in the trust that terminates upon the death of *S,* following which only skip persons hold interests in the trust. Thus, the death of *S* constitutes a taxable termination that would be subject to the GSTT except to the extent that *T*'s $1,000,000 exemption was allocated to the trust.

The death of *S* would not constitute a taxable termination if the income of the trust had been distributable to *S* and his sister *D,* who survived him. In that case a nonskip person, *D,* would have an interest in the property following the death of *S*. Instead, a taxable termination would take place upon the death of *D.*

§2.23.3. Taxable Distributions, §2612(b)

A taxable distribution occurs when property is distributed from a trust to a skip person which is not "a taxable termination or a direct skip." §2612(b). Distributions of income or principal to a skip person are subject to the GSTT, but because of the quoted limitation, a distribution that also fits the definition of a taxable termination is classified as such and not as a taxable distribution. Likewise, a distribution that constitutes a direct skip is classified as such and not as a taxable distribution.

Example 2-20. *T*'s will established a testamentary trust which authorized the trustee to sprinkle income among *T*'s descendants. A distribution of income to a skip person, such as one of *T*'s grandchildren, is a taxable distribution. Note that for income tax purposes distributees can deduct the GSTT imposed on distributions of income as a tax. §164(a), (b)(4).

§2.24. Application of GSTT; Inclusion Ratio; Applicable Fraction

The GSTT is imposed at the applicable rate, which is determined by multiplying the maximum federal estate tax rate at the time of the transfer by the inclusion ratio. §2641(a). Until 1993 the maximum rate is 55 percent. §2001(b)(2)(D). Thereafter it is scheduled to be 50 percent. In turn, the inclusion ratio is defined in §2642 as the amount by which 1 exceeds the applicable fraction. The inclusion ratio, once determined, remains effective for the trust, subject to adjustments for such things as additions to the trust.

The numerator of the applicable fraction is the amount of the transferor's GSTT exemption allocated to the trust (or to the property transferred in a direct skip). §2642(a)(2)(A). The denominator is the value of the transferred property less the amount of federal and state taxes recovered from the trust attributable to such property and any charitable deduction allowed for gift or estate tax purposes with respect to the property. §2642(a)(2)(B). The time at which the fraction is determined is important because the value of the transferred property will vary over time. In general, it is best to fix the fraction as soon as possible.

> **Example 2-21.** *T* transferred $500,000 to her daughter *D* as trustee for *D*'s son *GS*. *T* allocated $500,000 of her GSTT exemption to the transfer. The applicable fraction is 1 ($500,000 ÷ $500,000), the inclusion ratio is zero (1 − 1) and the applicable rate is zero (55% × 0). *T* later made an outright gift of $1,000,000 to *GS*, to which *T* allocated the $500,000 balance of her GSTT exemption. The applicable fraction for this transfer is ½ ($500,000 ÷ $1,000,000), the inclusion ratio is ½ (1 − ½), and the applicable rate is 27.5% (55% × ½).

When determining the inclusion ratio, the manner in which the unused portion of the transferor's exemption is allocated or is deemed to have been allocated may affect the time the property is valued for purposes of calculating the applicable fraction. The applicable fraction may be smaller and the inclusion ratio higher if the denominator has increased in size (*i.e.*, if the value of the transferred property has increased). In particular, the time at which the allocation is made may affect the adequacy of the exemption to shield the property from application of the GSTT.

The rules prescribed by the statute are these: If the donor's exemption is allocated to a gift on a timely filed gift tax return, the value of the property determined for gift tax purposes also establishes its value for purposes of the GSTT exemption. §2642(b)(1). If such an allocation is not made on a timely filed return, or deemed made at that time, the value of the property is determined (for purposes of the GSTT exemption) by its value at the time the allocation is filed with the Secretary. §2642(b)(3). A delay in making the allocation can be costly.

Example 2-22. On December 31, 1991 *T,* a widower, made a gift of $2,000,000 to grandchild *GC,* whose parents were both living at the time of the gift. *T* allocated his entire $1,000,000 exemption to the gift. The applicable fraction is $1,000,000 divided by $2,000,000, or ½. Accordingly, the inclusion ratio is ½ (1 − ½) and the applicable rate is 27.5% (55% × ½). In the case of a direct skip such as this, the amount subject to tax is the amount received by the donee. §2623. Accordingly, a GSTT of $550,000 is due on the gift ($2,000,000 × 27.5%). Note that the amount of the GSTT is taken into account in calculating the gift tax on a direct skip. §2515.

Example 2-23. On June 30, 1991 *W,* a widow, made a gift of $2,000,000 to a trust in which her daughter *D* had a life income interest, *D*'s children were the successive life income beneficiaries, and their children were the ultimate remaindermen. *W* allocated her entire $1,000,000 exemption to the transfer on a timely filed gift tax return. Throughout its existence the trust will have an inclusion ratio of 50% regardless of the growth in value of the principal. Accordingly, the tax rate applicable to each generation-skipping transfer will be half of the maximum federal estate tax rate at the time of the transfer. Note the *W*'s allocation of her exemption to the transfer fixed the value of the denominator. Because *W* allocated her exemption to the transfer in a timely filed gift tax return, the value of the denominator was fixed at the gift tax value of the property. §2642(b)(1). If the allocation of the exemption had not been made, or been deemed made, until later, the value of the denominator (the value of the property transferred) would have been determined at the time of the allocation. Thus, an increase in the value of the property would have resulted in an increase in the inclusion ratio. §2642(b)(3). For example, if *W*'s $1,000,000 exemption were allocated to the trust at the time of her death, when the trust property had a value of $4,000,000, the applicable fraction would have been ¼ ($1,000,000 ÷ $4,000,000) and the inclusion ratio would have been 75%.

A delay in allocating the exemption may be advantageous if the value of the property will decline. Thus, the donor may wish to delay allocating any part of the GSTT exemption to gifts made to an irrevocable trust that will use the funds to buy an insurance policy, which will be worth considerably less than the amount of the initial premium payments. For example, the donor may give $100,000 to the trust each year, which will be used to pay premiums on a $2 million policy on the donor's life. However, after the second premium payment the policy may have a value of only $40,000. The trust would have an inclusion ratio of zero if the donor allocated $40,000 of his or her GSTT exemption to the trust at the end of the second year, which would "save" $160,000 of the donor's GSTT exemption. In future years the donor might choose to allocate the GSTT exemption as additional funds were transferred to the trust. Of course, such a delay would be disastrous if the donor were to die prior to allocating his or her GSTT exemption to the trust. In such a case the amount of the insurance proceeds would be included in the value of the trust as a result of which the donor's GSTT exemption could shelter only one-half of the trust from the GSTT.

§2.25. GSTT $1 Million Exemption

As indicated above, each individual is allowed a $1 million exemption from the GSTT, which may be allocated by the individual to any property of which the individual is the transferor. §2631(a). An allocation, once made, is irrevocable. §2631(b). Because each spouse has an exemption of $1 million, the GSTT is of limited concern to couples whose combined estates are substantially less than $2 million. Planning for the use of the exemption by a husband and wife with $2 million or more is easier if each of them owns one-half of their total property, which is often the case in community property states. Of course, under other circumstances the unlimited gift tax marital deduction allows a couple to equalize the sizes of their estates without tax cost. Also, the GSTT recognizes the effect of splitting gifts under §2513. §2652(1)-(2).

> **Example 2-24.** *W* made an inter vivos gift of $2,000,000 to her grandchild *GC,* whose parent *P* is living. *W*'s husband *H* consented to be treated as donor of half of the gift for gift tax purposes. *W* and *H* may entirely insulate the gift from the GSTT by allocating their $1,000,000 exemptions to the gift.

As explained in §2.27, the allocation of the exemption determines the rate at which the GSTT will apply to a generation-skipping transfer.

§2.26. Reverse QTIP Election, §2652(a)(3)

> The consequence of a reverse QTIP election is that the decedent who was the creator of the QTIP trust (the first spouse to die) remains the transferor of the particular QTIP trust with respect to which the election is made. As a result, that decedent's GSTT exemption may be allocated to that QTIP trust, and the denominator of the applicable fraction is determined by reference to the value of the trust property in the gross estate of that decedent. LR 9002014.

Under §2044 the property of a QTIP trust is includible in the gross estate of the surviving spouse. Accordingly, the surviving spouse would be treated as the transferor of the property for GSTT purposes, which might cause part or all of the GSTT exemption of the first spouse to die to be wasted. Section 2652(a)(3) allows the donor (in the case of an inter vivos transfer) or the estate of the first spouse to die to elect to treat all of the property in such trust for GSTT purposes "as if the election to be treated as qualified terminable interest property had not been made." If such a reverse QTIP election is made, the first spouse to die is treated as the transferor of the trust for GSTT purposes. Unfortunately, §2652(a)(3) does not permit a partial reverse election to be made. The inability to make a partial reverse QTIP election contrasts sharply with §2056(b)(7), which *allows* a partial QTIP election. The ban on partial elections requires careful planning to maximize the benefit of the GSTT exemptions of both spouses. As reflected below in the discussion of LR 9002014, the prohibition on partial elections is avoided if the instrument gives the fiduciary authority to divide a trust into two or more identical trusts.

Example 2-25. *W* died last year leaving an estate of $4,000,000, of which $600,000 passed to a credit shelter trust for the benefit of her children and their descendants. The balance of *W*'s estate passed to a trust for the benefit of her husband *H* who survived her. The trust for *H* qualified for the QTIP marital deduction under §2056(b)(7). *W*'s executor allocated $600,000 of *W*'s GSTT exemption to the credit shelter trust and the balance to the trust for *H*. *W*'s executor also elected to claim the marital deduction with respect to the entire value of *H*'s trust. The portion of *W*'s exemption that *W*'s executor allocated to the trust for *H* ($400,000) was wasted because the entire value of the trust will be included in his gross estate under §2044. For GSTT purposes the value of the property included in *H*'s estate under §2044 is fixed by its value in his estate. §2652(6)(4). *W*'s executor could have made a reverse QTIP election under §2652(a)(3). However, as a result of such an election for GSTT purposes *W* would have been treated as the transferor of the entire trust. Accordingly, *H* could not allocate any of his GSTT exemption to the trust.

The full benefit of the exemptions of both spouses may be utilized if a separate QTIP trust is created for the surviving spouse in an amount equal to the amount of the unused portion of the GSTT exemption of the first spouse (*i.e.,* the portion that remains after the allocation of a portion of it to the credit shelter trust). Thus, the will of the first spouse to die may direct the creation of a discretionary credit shelter trust ($600,000) for the benefit of his or her spouse and issue *and* the creation of two QTIP trusts. The deceased spouse's executor would allocate $600,000 of the decedent's GSTT exemption to the credit shelter trust, giving it an inclusion ratio of zero. The first QTIP would be funded with an amount equal to the difference between the previously unused portion of the decedent's GSTT exemption and the amount of the GSTT exemption allocated to the credit shelter trust. Typically, that amount would be $400,000 ($1,000,000 − $600,000). The decedent's executor would make a reverse QTIP election under §2652(a)(3) with respect to this trust. The residue of the decedent's estate would pass to the other QTIP trust. Under §2044 the value of both QTIP trusts would be includible in the estate of the surviving spouse for estate tax purposes. However, by reason of the reverse QTIP election for GSTT purposes the predeceased spouse would continue to be treated as the transferor of the QTIP trust with respect to which the election was made. The surviving spouse would be treated as transferor of the other QTIP trust. The executor of the surviving spouse could allocate any unused portion of his or her GSTT exemption to that trust.

The IRS has indicated that for purposes of §2652(a)(3) it will recognize the division of trusts made by an executor or trustee prior to the due date of the estate tax return of the first spouse to die. LR 9002014. The IRS ruled that

> the division of a single QTIP into two QTIP trusts for the purpose of making a reverse QTIP election with respect to one of such trusts is permissible when, as in this case, the property transferred to the reverse QTIP trust is fairly representative of the net appreciation or depreciation in the value of all property available for such use. We conclude that such a division is not precluded by section 2654(b) of the Code.

After such a division the trusts will be treated as separate trusts for GSTT purposes. Wills and trusts should give the fiduciary authority to divide trusts into two or more identical trusts in order to facilitate optional use of the decedent's GSTT exemptions.

Wills and trusts should be drafted in ways that facilitate reverse

QTIP elections. For example, the fiduciary might be authorized to divide any trust into two or more trusts with identical terms. In order to reduce the potential for a dispute with the IRS over the valuation of the property for purposes of allocating the deceased spouse's exemption, the trust should direct that the property is to be valued according to a method that meets the requirements of Rev. Proc. 64-19, 1964-1 C.B. 682. Thus, the trust might direct that property allocated to the trust should be valued according to values current at the time of the division. Note also that the division of a trust may be helpful from a trust administration point of view.

§2.27. Allocation of Exemption; Deemed Allocation Rules

If a transferor does not make a timely election regarding the allocation of his or her GSTT exemption, the Code prescribed how the exemption will be allocated. The unused portion of the transferor's exemption is generally allocated to lifetime direct skips to the extent necessary to reduce the inclusion ratio to zero: "If the amount of the direct skip exceeds such unused portion, the entire unused portion shall be allocated to the property transferred." §2632(b). Note, however, that an individual may elect not to apply these rules to a transfer. §2632(b)(3). That is, unlike the unified credit for gift tax purposes, GSTT permits the transferor to elect to preserve the exemption for allocation to later transfers.

§2.27.1. Certain Inter Vivos Transfers

The 1988 Act added §2642(f) which provides that the inclusion ratio for certain inter vivos transfers is not determined at the time of the initial transfer. Specifically, if the transferred property would be included in the transferor's gross estate (other than by reason of §2035), the GSTT exemption cannot be allocated to the property until the end of the estate tax inclusion period. The *estate tax inclusion period* is the period after the transfer during which the property would be included in the transferor's estate if the transferor died. §2642(f)(3). In any case, the period does not extend beyond the earlier of the date of the transferor's death or the date of a generation-skipping transfer of the property. Subsection 2642(f) eliminates the opportunity to leverage the GSTT exemption by allocating it to a transfer in which the transferor retained an interest. Thus, the grantor of a trust in which the grantor retained a term interest cannot allocate his GSTT exemption to the transfer until the end of the estate tax inclusion period (*i.e.*, the date on which the transferor dies, the term of the transferor's retained interest ends, or else there is a generation-skipping transfer). In the absence of a provision such as §2642(f) the transferor's GSTT exemption might be allocated to such a trust at the time it was created. If so, in calculating the applicable fraction, the denominator would be the *present* value of the remainder interest.

Example 2-26. *T* transferred $2,000,000 to a trust in which he retained a term interest that was valued at $1,000,000 under §2702. The property of the trust would be included in *T*'s gross estate under §2036(a) if *T* dies during the term of the retained interest. For purposes of determining the inclusion ratio of the trust, the value of the property will be determined at the end of the estate tax inclusion period (*i.e.*, *T*'s death or the end of *T*'s term interest). Without such a rule the allocation of the exemption to the trust might result in a large applicable fraction (*i.e.*, the denominator would be only the value of the remainder that *T* transferred). If *T* died prior to the end of the term, when the trust had a value of $4,000,000, the estate tax inclusion period would end and the full $4,000,000 value of the trust would be the denominator of the applicable fraction.

§2.27.2. Charitable Lead Trusts

As explained in §8.31, income, gift, and estate tax deductions are allowed for a gift to charity of the current interest in a trust in the form of a guaranteed annuity or unitrust interest.

The 1988 Act also eliminated the possibility that the protection provided by the GSTT exemption could be leveraged by transferring property to a charitable lead trust. A special rule now applies to determine the inclusion ratio for charitable lead annuity trusts created by transfers made after October 13, 1987. §2642(e). Previously the value of the exemption would have been leveraged to the extent the value of the property transferred to the trust increased by a rate greater than the rate used to compute the value of the charitable interest. Under §2642(e) the amount of the numerator (the exemption allocated to the transfer) is increased by the interest rate that was applied in determining the value of the gift or estate tax charitable deduction claimed with respect to the transfer for the actual duration of the charitable lead annuity. The denominator is the value of all the property of the trust immediately after the termination of the charitable lead annuity. Thus computed the formula adjusts for the over- or underperformance of the investments of the trust — there is no leverage.

§2.27.3. Default Allocation of GSTT Exemption

Under §2632(c) any portion of an individual's exemption that is not allocated on or before the date the individual's estate tax return is due is deemed to be allocated

1. To property which is the subject of a direct skip occurring at such individual's death, and
2. To trusts with respect to which such individual is the transferor and from which a taxable distribution or a taxable termination might occur at or after such individual's death.

Note that the "default" allocation of the exemption specified in the statute may not achieve optimal tax results. The loss of the benefit of the exemption may be particularly sharp if the exemption is allocated pro rata among trusts as provided by the default rules of §2632(c)(2)(A).

Example 2-27. *T*'s will left $1,000,000 to a trust, the income of which could be sprinkled among *T*'s spouse *S*, children, and grandchildren. *T* left the residue of his estate ($1,000,000) to a marital deduction trust, the income of which is payable to *S*. Upon the death of *S* the remainder of the marital deduction trust will be distributed to *T*'s then living children and to the issue of deceased children. If *T*'s exemption is not allocated by his executor it will be allocated under the default rules. Under §2632(c)(2) the exemption would be allocated pro rata between the trusts ($500,000 to each). Accordingly, each would have a 50% inclusion ratio. The entire exemption should be allocated to the discretionary trust, all of the distributions of which might be made to skip persons otherwise subject to the GSTT. In contrast, the income distributions of the marital deduction trust and distributions to children are not subject to the GSTT. The marital deduction trust is includible in the estate of *S* under §2044. If appropriate, *S*'s $1,000,000 exemption might be allocated to the marital deduction trust.

The application of the rules regarding the allocation of exemptions to inter vivos transfers is illustrated by the following example.

Example 2-28. On July 30, 1991 *T* transferred $2,000,000 to a trust the income of which was payable to her son *S* for life and thereafter to his children for their lives. Upon the death of the last of *S*'s children to die the trust principal would be distributed by right of representation to those of the issue of *T* who were then living. *T* did not allocate any part of her exemption to the trust. *T* allocated her entire $1,000,000 exemption to the trust on January 1, 1993 when the trust property was worth $4,000,000. The applicable fraction is $1,000,000 ÷ $4,000,000 or ¼. Accordingly, the inclusion ratio is 75% (1 − ¼).

Because the transfer was not a direct skip, under the rules of §2632(b) no part of *T*'s exemption was deemed allocated to the transfer at the time it was made. (Had *T* either allocated or been deemed to have allocated her full $1,000,000 exemption to the trust, the trust would have had an inclusion ratio of 50%.) The value of the denominator of the applicable fraction (the transferred property) is determined at the time the exemption is allocated to a transfer. §2642(b)(2).

§2.28. Exclusions, §§2611(b); 2642(c)

Under §2611(b) the term "generation-skipping transfer" does not include "any transfer which, if made inter vivos by an individual, would not be treated as a taxable gift by reason of section 2503(e) (relating to exclusion of certain transfers for educational or medical expenses)." Accordingly, distributions from exempt trusts for those purposes would be wasteful. Instead, the trustee of a nonexempt trust should be authorized to pay the tuition and medical care expenses of skip persons such as the transferor's grandchildren. For example, those expenses might be paid out of a nonexempt trust that the transferor created for his or her children instead of out of a separate exempt trust of which grandchildren and more remote issue were the beneficiaries.

The sting of the GSTT can also be reduced by making direct skips that qualify for gift tax exclusions, thereby giving them a zero inclusion ratio under §2642(c). Direct skips that are nontaxable gifts have an inclusion ratio of zero. §2642(c)(1). For this purpose a nontaxable gift is one that is within the annual exclusion of §2503(b) (taking into account the gift splitting possibilities of §2513) or that is a qualified transfer under §2503(e) (*i.e.,* a direct payment of tuition to an educational institution or of medical care expenses to a health care provider). Thus, each year a grandparent may transfer $10,000 outright to a grandchild free of both the gift tax *and* the GSTT. However, under §2642(c)(2) the exclusion only applies to a donee's interest in a trust if (1) during the life of the donee none of the income or principal could be used for the benefit of any other person, and (2) the property will be included in the donee's estate if he or she dies before the trust terminates. The requirements of §2642(c)(2) were added by the 1988 Act in order to limit the extent to which property transferred to a trust could be insulated from the GSTT by giving the beneficiaries *Crummey* powers. However, the IRS has recognized that single-beneficiary *Crummey* trusts have a zero inclusion ratio. LR 8922062. A single trust can be drafted so the separate share of each grandchild will meet the requirements of §2642(c).

A §2503(c) trust for a minor meets the requirements of §2642(c)(2). Accordingly, transfers to the trust have a zero inclusion ratio to the extent annual gift tax exclusions were allowed under §2503(b) with respect to the transfers. That is, transfers to such a trust are nontaxable gifts to the extent annual gift tax exclusions were allowed.

Example 2-29. This year *GF* and *GM* gave $20,000 to each of their 5 grandchildren. They also paid $20,000 in tuition to the colleges the grandchildren attend. The GSTT does not apply to any of the $200,000 in gifts made by *GF* and *GM,* all of which qualifies for gift splitting and an exclusion under §2503. Accordingly, the gifts all have zero inclusion ratios under §2642(c).

Example 2-30. *GF* and *GM* transferred $20,000 to separate trusts for each of their grandchildren. For GSTT purposes the gifts are direct skips. The beneficiary of each trust has a noncumulative power to withdraw the property transferred to the trust within a limited time following notification of the transfer. Distributions may only be made to the beneficiary of each trust during his or her lifetime. If the beneficiary dies prior to termination of the trust the beneficiary may appoint the trust property to creditors of his or her estate. The gifts made by *GF* and *GM* to the trusts qualify for gift splitting and annual gift tax exclusions under §2503(b). The trusts also meet the requirements of §2642(c)(2). Accordingly, each trust has an inclusion ratio of zero. The exclusion offered by such a trust is particularly valuable if it invests in life insurance, the ultimate value of which may be many times the amount of the transfers to the trust.

§2.29. VALUATION OF PROPERTY

Property subject to a generation-skipping transfer is valued at the time of the transfer. §2624. However, in the case of a direct skip of property included in the transferor's gross estate, the value of the property will reflect the alternate valuation or special use valuation of the property under §§2032-2032A. §2624(b). Also, if a taxable termination occurs at the same time and as the result of the death of an individual, an election may be made to value the property on the alternate valuation date. §2624(c). Finally, the amount of the property transferred is reduced by any consideration provided by the transferee. §2624(d).

Example 2-31. *H,* who had already used all of his GSTT exemption, left Blackacre to his grandson, *GS.* This was subject to a requirement that *GS* pay $1,000,000 to *X,* the former wife of *GS. GS,* his parents, and *X* all survived *H*. Blackacre was valued at $5,000,000 for federal estate tax purposes in *H*'s estate. The devise involved a generation-skipping transfer of $4,000,000 to *GS* (the $5,000,000 value of Blackacre less the $1,000,000 that *GS* was obligated to pay to *X*). Presumably, the transfer of $1,000,000 to *X* will also be treated as a generation-skipping transfer by *H.*

§2.30. Taxable Amount of Generation-Skipping Transfers

The base on which the GSTT is computed varies depending upon the type of generation-skipping transfer. In the case of a direct skip the taxable amount is determined on a tax exclusive basis. §2623. That is, the tax is imposed only with respect to the value of the property received by the transferee. In contrast, the GSTT on taxable distributions and taxable terminations is determined on a tax inclusive basis. §§2621, 2622. In those cases, the tax base includes the amount of GSTT imposed on a taxable distribution or a taxable termination.

§2.30.1. Direct Skips

The GSTT on a direct skip is determined according to the value of the property received by the transferee. For this purpose note that the transferee may be a trust or trust equivalent. Thus, in LR 9105006 (TAM), the IRS held that the transferor had made a direct skip of the full value of property in which a life estate was given to a friend who was 40 years younger than the transferor (a skip person) and the remainder was given to the transferor's daughter (a nonskip person). By not including the amount of the GSTT in the tax base of an inter vivos direct skip the GSTT resembles the gift tax — in neither case is the amount of the tax included in the tax base. Note, however, that under §2515 the amount of any GSTT paid with respect to a direct skip is included in the gift tax base.

Example 2-32. *T,* who had already used her $1,000,000 GSTT exemption and was in the maximum unified tax bracket, made a gift of $1,000,000 to *GC,* her grandchild, whose parents were both living. The transfer was subject to a GSTT of $550,000. The gift of $1,550,000 was subject to a gift tax of $852,500. Thus, the gift "cost" *T* a total of $2,402,500 ($1,550,000 + $852,500).

Example 2-33. *T*, the donor described in Example 2-32 above, died leaving a bequest of $1,000,000 to *GC*, whose parents both survived *T*. In order to make a net bequest of $1,000,000 to *GC* the estate of *T* must expend $3,444,444:

Amount required	$3,444,444
Estate Tax (55% rate)	1,894,444
Amount net of estate tax	$1,550,000
Bequest to *GC*	$1,000,000
GSTT on $1 million	550,000
Total bequest & GSTT	$1,550,000

§2.30.2. Taxable Distributions

The tax base of a taxable distribution is the value of the property received by the transferee less the value of the expense incurred by the transferee with respect to the distribution. §2621. Under §2603(a)(1) the transferee is obligated to pay the GSTT on a taxable distribution, so the tax is computed on a tax inclusive basis: The GSTT is computed on the gross amount received by the distributee *before* the GSTT is paid.

Example 2-34. On January 1, 1992 a trust made a taxable distribution of $100,000 of income to *X*. The trust has an inclusion ratio of 1. The tax base is $100,000 of which *X* is obligated to pay a GSTT of $55,000. *X* is left with $45,000 after paying the GSTT. Note that for income tax purposes *X* is entitled to deduct the amount of the GSTT as a tax under §164 unless the distribution was a throwback distribution subject to §666. §164(b)(4).

§2.30.3. Taxable Terminations

In the case of a taxable termination the taxable amount is also determined on a tax inclusive basis. It includes the value of all property with respect to which the taxable termination has occurred including the amount of the GSTT, but is reduced by the amount of indebtedness, expenses, and taxes. §2622. The deduction is to be "similar to the deduction allowed by section 2053 (relating to expenses, indebtedness, and taxes) for amount attributable to property with respect to which the taxable termination has occurred." §2622(b).

Example 2-35. *W* died on October 31, 1990. She left $2,000,000 to a trust for the benefit of *D*, her daughter, for life after which the trust would continue for the benefit of *D*'s issue. *T*'s executor allocated *T*'s $1,000,000 exclusion to the trust. Accordingly, the trust has an inclusion ratio of .50. *D* died on January 1, 1992, survived by children and grandchildren. The trust had a value of $5,000,000 at the time of *D*'s death, so a taxable termination of property worth $5,000,000 took place when *D* died. No deductions were allowable under §2622(b) for expenses, indebtedness, or taxes. A GSTT of $1,375,000 was payable by the trustee, which was calculated by multiplying $5,000,000 by the maximum estate tax rate times the inclusion ratio (55% × .50). Under §2654(a)(2) the basis of the property is "adjusted in a manner similar to the manner provided under section 1014(a); except that, if the inclusion ratio with respect to such property is less than 1, any increase or decrease shall be limited by multiplying such increase or decrease (as the case may be) by the inclusion ratio."

§2.31. IDENTIFYING AND CHANGING THE TRANSFEROR

Under the basic rule, the decedent is treated as the transferor of any property that is subject to the estate tax. §2652(a)(1)(A). Similarly, the donor is treated as the transferor of any property that is subject to the gift tax. §2652(a)(1)(B). In some cases the overall transfer tax costs may be reduced if the identity of the transferor is shifted to another person whose unified credit or GST tax exemption might otherwise be unused. For example, an independent trustee might be authorized either to distribute the trust property outright to a child or other beneficiary who is a nonskip person or to amend the trust to give a general power of appointment to such a person. The distribution of the property to the beneficiary or the beneficiary's possession of the general power of appointment would cause the property to be included in the beneficiary's estate. Accordingly, the beneficiary would become the transferor for GSTT purposes. In order to protect the estate plan of the original transferor the beneficiary might be given the least control possible (*e.g.,* the power to appoint the property to the creditors of his or her estate with the concurrence of a nonadverse party, §2041(b)(1)).

Example 2-36. *T,* who had already used his GSTT exemption, left $1,000,000 to a trust, the income of which was to be used for the benefit of *S,* his son. Following the death of *S* the income was payable to the issue of *S. S* and several of his children survived *T.* Under the trust an independent trustee had discretion to amend the trust to give *S* the testamentary power to appoint the property to the creditors of his estate. (Some transferors might prefer to allow the beneficiary's power to be exercisable only with the joinder of the trustee.) *S* owned no other property and was not indebted to any creditors. When he was terminally ill the trustee amended the trust to give him the testamentary power to appoint the trust property to his creditors. When he died, the trust was includible in his gross estate. Accordingly, *S* became the transferor of the trust. As a result, *S*'s death did not involve a direct skip, a taxable distribution, or a taxable termination. If the trust were included in *S*'s estate at a value of $1,000,000, it would result in the imposition of an estate tax of $153,000 ($345,800 − $192,800). Presumably *S*'s executor would allocate his $1,000,000 exemption to the trust. Thereafter the trust will be completely exempt from the GSTT.

An alternative technique for shifting the transferor is available in states which allow a special power of appointment to be exercised by creating a general power of appointment. As a result of such an exercise of the special power, the vesting of interests may be postponed "for a period ascertainable without regard to the date of the creation of the first power." *See* 3A A. J. Casner, Estate Planning §12.2.5 (5th ed. 1986); Blattmachr & Pennell, Using "Delaware Tax Trap" to Avoid Generation-Skipping Taxes, 68 J. Tax. 242 (1988). The exercise of such a post-1942 power will cause the property to be included in the estate of the holder of the special power under §2041(a)(3). For purposes of the Rule Against Perpetuities a presently exercisable general power of appointment is treated as the equivalent of outright ownership of the property.

Section 2041(a)(3) is called the "Delaware Tax Trap" because it was designed to prevent the use of Delaware law to create trusts that could indefinitely avoid imposition of the estate tax. In particular, §2041(a)(3) requires the inclusion of property subject to a post-1942 power that is exercised to postpone the vesting of an interest or to suspend the absolute power of alienation for a period that is ascertainable without reference to the date of the creation of the first power. Under Delaware law the period of the Rule Against Perpetuities with respect to the exercise of a special *or* general power of appointment runs from the date the power is exercised. Del. Code Ann. Tit. 25, §501 (1989). Accordingly, the Delaware Rule Against Perpetuities would allow the creation and exercise of successive special powers of appointment.

The transferor is also changed if there is a generation-skipping transfer of property that remains in trust. §2653(a). For subsequent GSTT purposes the property which was subject to the transfer is treated as if "the transferor of such property were assigned to the 1st generation above the highest generation of any person who has an interest in such trust immediately after the transfer." Id. Although there is a change in the transferor the exclusion ratio of the trust remains the same. §2653(b).

> **Example 2-37.** *T,* who has previously used her $1,000,000 GSTT exemption, died in 1991 leaving her residuary estate in trust for the benefit of *C,* her child, for life. Following *C*'s death the income of the trust was payable to the children of *C* in equal shares. Upon the death of each child of *C* a proportionate part of the trust is distributable outright to his or her issue. *C* died in 1992 survived by 3 children. *C*'s death constituted a taxable termination subject to GSTT. Thereafter *C* will be treated as the transferor of the trust. When each child of *C* dies the GSTT will apply to the amount of the taxable distribution to such decedent's issue.

§2.32. Generational Assignments, §2651

The application of the GSTT turns on the identification of skip persons, defined in §2613(a) as natural persons two or more generations below the generation assignment of the transferor. A lineal descendant of a grandparent of the transferor is assigned to "that generation which results from comparing the number of generations between the grandparent and such individual with the number of generations between the grandparent and the transferor." §2651(b)(1). Thus, the transferor and the siblings of the transferor are both two generations below their grandparents. The same rules apply in determining the generational assignment of the descendants of the grandparents of the transferor's spouse. §2651(b)(2). Adopted persons and persons related by the halfblood are treated in the same way as full blood relations. A person who was at any time married to the transferor is assigned to the transferor's generation. §2651(c)(1). Similarly, a person who was at any time married to a lineal descendant of a grandparent of the transferor or the transferor's spouse is assigned to the same generational level as such person. §2651(c)(2).

> **Example 2-38.** *T* gave $100,000 to her niece, *N,* and to *N*'s daughter, *GN. N* is assigned to a generation (3) only one below that of *T* (2). Thus, *N* is not a skip person. *GN* is assigned to a generation (4) that is two below that of *T.* Accordingly, *GN* is a skip person. The gift of $100,000 to *GN* is a direct skip that is subject to the GSTT.

Persons who are not descendants of the grandparents of the transferor or the transferor's spouse are assigned to generational levels based upon their dates of birth. A person born not more than 12½ years after the date of birth of the transferor is assigned to the same generational level as the transferor. §2651(d)(1). A person whose date of birth is more than 12½ years, but not more than 37½ years after the date of birth of the transferor is assigned to the first generational level below that of the transferor. §2651(d)(2). The generational assignments of persons born more than 37½ years after the transferor are made on the basis of successive 25-year generational periods. Thus, a person between 37½ and 62½ years younger than the transferor is assigned to the same generation as are the grandchildren of the transferor. *See, e.g.,* LR 9105006 (TAM).

§2.33. Separate Trusts

Portions of a trust attributable to transfers from different transferors are treated as separate trusts for GSTT purposes. §2654(b)(1). In addition, substantially separate and independent shares of different beneficiaries in a trust are treated as separate trusts. §2654(b)(2). In this connection, note that for GSTT purposes the IRS has recognized the division, prior to the time the estate tax return was due, of a single QTIP trust into two substantially similar QTIP trusts. *See* §2.26.

§2.34. Multiple Transfers, §2642(d)

If additional property is transferred to a trust, the applicable fraction for the trust is recalculated. First, the value of the property in the trust immediately before the present transfer is multiplied by the applicable fraction for the trust. The product is the "nontax portion" of the trust. Second, the numerator of the new applicable fraction is calculated by adding the GSTT exemption allocated to the present transfer to the nontax portion of the trust. Third, the denominator of the fraction is determined by adding the value of the property transferred to the trust to the value of all property held in the trust immediately before the transfer. For this purpose the value of the property transferred to the trust is reduced by the sum of the death taxes paid from the property and the amount of the gift or estate tax charitable deductions allowed with respect to the transfer.

Example 2-39. In 1991 *T* transferred $1,000,000 to a trust to which she allocated her $1,000,000 exemption. Thus, the trust had an applicable fraction of 1 and an inclusion ratio of zero. In 1992 *T* transferred an additional $1,000,000 to the trust. Immediately prior to the second transfer the property of the trust had a value of $1,500,000. The applicable fraction of the trust, recalculated as provided in §2642(d), is 3/5 ($1,500,000 ÷ $2,500,000).

§2.35. BASIS ADJUSTMENT, §2654(a)

Subsection 2654(a) provides for adjustments to the bases of property similar to the adjustments that are made in the case of transfers that are subject to the gift and estate taxes. That is, property that is transferred in a taxable termination at the death of an individual is adjusted in a manner similar to the manner provided in §1014(a) (*i.e.,* the federal estate tax value of the property becomes its basis). §2654(a)(2). However, in the case of the GSTT adjustment, if the inclusion ratio is less than one, the increase or decrease in basis is limited by multiplying the increase or decrease by the inclusion ratio. The following example illustrates how the basis adjustment should be computed for a taxable termination which occurs at the same time and as the result of the death of an individual.

> **Example 2-40.** *T* died leaving $1,000,000 in securities in trust to pay the income to *S,* his son, for life, after which the income would be paid to *S*'s children for their lives. *T*'s executor allocated $500,000 of *T*'s GSTT exemption to the trust. Accordingly, the trust had an inclusion ratio of 50%. When *S* died the securities had a basis of $1,000,000 and a fair market value of $2,000,000. The basis of the securities is increased by $500,000 (the excess of the fair market value of the securities ($2,000,000) over their basis ($1,000,000) multiplied by the inclusion ratio (50%)). A GST tax of $550,000 would be paid with respect to the taxable termination resulting from *S*'s death ($2,000,000 × (55% × 50%)).

In other cases (*i.e.,* direct skips, taxable distributions, and taxable terminations that do not result from the death of an individual), the basis of property transferred in a generation-skipping transfer is increased by an amount of the GSTT attributable to the excess of the fair market value of the property over its adjusted basis immediately before the transfer. §2654(a)(1). The adjustment is made after any basis adjustment under §1015, which calls for a similar adjustment to be made with respect to the gift tax attributable to the net appreciation in a post-1976 gift (*i.e.,* the amount by which the fair market value of the property exceeds the donor's basis immediately before the gift). §1015(d)(6). Presumably the adjustment would only be made with respect to the amount of the gift (*i.e.,* the adjustment would not take into account the portion of the gift attributable to the GSTT paid with respect to the gift).

While the amount of the GSTT is included in the base of the gift tax, the tax is paid in cash, for which no basis adjustment is possible. Cash presumably has a basis equal to its face amount.

Example 2-41. *T,* who had previously used his entire $1,000,000 GSTT exemption and his unified credit made a gift of $1,000,000 to *GD,* his granddaughter. Earlier in the year *T* made an annual exclusion gift of cash to *GD. T* paid a gift tax of $580,550 on the taxable gift of $1,550,000 (the amount of the gift plus the amount of the GSTT paid). The gift property had an adjusted basis of $500,000 immediately before the gift. The basis of the property would be increased by $187,274, calculated as follows: $580,550 (gift tax) × $500,000 (appreciation) ÷ $1,550,000 = $187,274. After the adjustment for the gift tax the basis of property would be $687,274. *T* also paid a GSTT of $550,000 with respect to the $1,000,000 gift. The basis of the property would be increased by an additional $166,499 ($550,000 (GSTT) × $302,726 ÷ $1,000,000). Thus, the final adjusted basis of the property would be $853,773 ($687,274 + $166,499).

§2.36. RETURNS, §2662

In general, GSTT returns must be filed by the person liable under §2603(a) for the payment of the tax. §2662(a) (1). The following table indicates the persons who are required under Temp. Reg. §26.2662-1(c) to make the necessary return and pay the tax:

Type of Transfer	*Person Responsible*	*Type of Return*
Taxable Distribution	Transferee	706GS(D)
Taxable Termination	Trustee	706GS(T)
Inter Vivos Direct Skip	Transferor	709
Direct Skips at Death		
Subject to Estate Tax	Transferor's Executor	706 (Sched. R)
Direct Skip from Trust	Trustee	706 (Sched. R-1)

§2.36.1. Direct Skips

Generation-skipping transfers of property that are included in the decedent's gross estate are divided between Schedules R and R-1. A direct skip that is not made from a trust is reported by the executor on

Schedule R. The GSTT on such a transfer is paid by the estate. On the other hand, a direct skip from a trust is reported on Schedule R-1, which serves as a payment voucher for the trustee to remit the GSTT to the IRS. Schedule R-1 is used whether the direct skip is made to an individual or to another trust.

> **Example 2-42.** *S* was the beneficiary of a QTIP trust for which a marital deduction was claimed by the executor of her deceased husband's will. When *S* died the trust terminated and the property was distributed outright to her adult grandchildren, whose parents were living. The trust was included in *S*'s estate by reason of §2044. The distribution of the trust property to *S*'s grandchildren involved direct skips. Accordingly, the transfers are reported by the trustee on Schedule R-1. *See* Temp. Reg. §26.2662-1(c)(1)(iv), (v).

§2.36.2. Trust Arrangements

In the case of property held in "trust arrangements" at the time of the transferor's death, the executor is liable for the tax and for making the return if the total value of the property involved in direct skips with respect to the same trustee is less than $100,000. Temp. Reg. §26.2662-1(c)(2)(iii). A *trust arrangement* is any arrangement other than an estate, which although not an explicit trust, has the same effect as an explicit trust. As indicated in the Instructions for Form 706, "[T]rust includes life estates with remainders, terms for years, and insurance and annuity contracts." (Jul. 1990 Rev., p.18.) The responsibility for making the return and paying the tax is illustrated in the following example from the Temporary Regulations:

> *Example (1).* On August 1, 1988, *A,* the insured under an insurance policy, died. The proceeds ($95,000) were includible in *A*'s gross estate for federal estate tax purposes. *A*'s grandchild, *GC,* was named the sole beneficiary of the policy. The insurance policy is treated as a trust under section 2652(b)(1), and the payment of the proceeds to *GC* is a transfer "from a trust" for purposes of Chapter 13. Therefore, the payment of the proceeds to *GC* is a direct skip. Since the proceeds from the policy ($95,000) are less than $100,000, the executor is liable for the tax imposed by Chapter 13 and is required to file Form 706. Temp. Reg. §26.2662-1(c).

The Temporary Regulations empower the executor to recover the tax from the trustee if the property continues to be held in trust, otherwise from the recipient of the property. Temp. Reg. §26.2662-1(c)(2).

§2.36.3. Deferral of GSTT on Direct Skips of Closely-Held Business Interests, §6166(h)

Under §6166(h) the GSTT on interests in closely-held businesses that are the subject of a direct skip as a result of the decedent's death is subject to deferral. According to the House Report on the bill that became the 1986 Act, "The special rules under which estate tax attributable to interests in certain closely-held businesses may be paid in installments also apply to direct skips occurring as a result of death." 1986-3 C.B. Vol. 2, 828.

§2.36.4. Redemption of Stock to Pay GSTT, §303

If the stock of a corporation is subject to a generation-skipping transfer at the same time and as a result of the death of an individual, the redemption of the stock may qualify under §303 as a distribution made in exchange for the stock. Again, according to the House Committee Report, "The provision permitting tax-free redemptions of stock to pay estate tax is amended to permit those redemptions to pay generation-skipping transfer tax in the case of such transfers occurring as a result of death." Id.

§2.37. Return Due Dates

In the case of a direct skip other than from a trust, the GSTT return is due on or before the date on which the gift or estate tax return is required to be filed with respect to the transfer. §2662(a)(2)(A). The return for all other generation-skipping transfers is due on or before the fifteenth day of the fourth month after the close of the taxable year of the person required to make the return.

§2.38. Effective Dates

The amended generation-skipping transfer tax applies to transfers after the date of enactment (October 22, 1986), subject to the following exceptions:

1. Inter vivos transfers occurring after September 25, 1985, are subject to the amended tax;
2. Transfers from trusts that were irrevocable before September 26, 1985, are exempt to the extent that the transfers are not attributable to additions to the trust corpus occurring after that date;

> 3. Transfers pursuant to wills in existence before the date of enactment of the Act (October 22, 1986) are not subject to tax if the decedent died before January 1, 1987 [this exception was extended by the 1988 Act to transfers made before January 1, 1987 under revocable trusts executed prior October 22, 1986]; and
>
> 4. Transfers under a trust to the extent that such trusts consist of property included in the gross estate of the decedent or which are direct skips which occur by reason of the death of any decedent if the decedent was incompetent on the date of enactment of this Act (October 22, 1986) and at all times thereafter until death. General Explanation, Tax Reform Act of 1986, 1267-68.

The basic GSTT effective date rules are relatively simple: The GSTT applies to generation-skipping transfers made after October 22, 1986. However, it does not apply to generation-skipping transfers made by trusts that were irrevocable before September 26, 1985 *except* to the extent attributable to property added to the trust after September 25, 1985 (or made out of income attributable to property added to the trust after September 25, 1985). Under the Temporary Regulations the irrevocability of a trust on September 25, 1985 will be determined in some cases according to estate tax principles. In particular, a trust is not considered to be irrevocable to the extent it is includible in the grantor's gross estate under §2038 (*i.e.,* the grantor retained a power to amend, revoke or terminate the trust). Temp. Reg. §26.2601-1(b)(ii)(B). Similarly, a policy of life insurance that is treated as a trust under §2652(b) is not considered to be an irrevocable trust to the extent the insured possessed any incidents of ownership that would have caused the insurance proceeds to be included in the insured's estate under §2042.

Estate plans should take into account the value of preserving the exemption provided by the effective date rules. Thus, assets should not be added to preexisting trusts, distribution plans should maximize the benefit of the exemption, and the exemption should be continued as long as possible. A grandfathered trust can be reformed in ways that do not affect its substantive provisions without subjecting it to the GSTT. *E.g.,* LR 9043061 (amendments allow trust to qualify as GSTT). *See* §2.40.5.

Note that a party may be treated as having constructively added property to a trust by satisfying an obligation of the trust. "For example, where an estate fails to exercise the right of recovery available under §2207A for federal estate tax paid on the value of property includible in the estate under section 2044, the beneficiaries of the estate are considered to have added an amount equal to such federal estate tax attributable to such property to the trust at the time the right of recovery lapses." Temp. Reg. §26.2601-1(b)(1)(v)(C).

Example 2-43. On a date prior to September 26, 1985, *T* transferred property to an irrevocable trust for the benefit of her descendants. The trustee has discretion to distribute income and principal among *T*'s children and their issue. The exempt status of the trust should be protected. In particular, no property should be added to the trust. Distributions from the trust should be coordinated with distributions from other trusts in order to maximize the benefit of the exemption. Thus, distributions from this trust might be made to *T*'s grandchildren or more remote descendants while distributions to *T*'s children and other nonskip persons are made from nonexempt trusts.

The Regulations illustrate how the GSTT is applied where property is added to a preexisting trust. Temp. Reg. §26.2601-1(b)(iv). Following an addition the trust consists of a nonChapter 13 portion (the preexisting portion of the trust) and a portion subject to Chapter 13 (the addition to the trust). The inclusion ratio of the nonChapter 13 portion is zero and the inclusion ratio of the Chapter 13 portion is determined under §2642 as in other cases. When a taxable termination or a taxable distribution occurs the portion attributable to the Chapter 13 portion is determined by multiplying the amount of the termination or distribution by the "allocation fraction." The numerator of the allocation fraction is the amount of the addition to the trust and the denominator is the value of the trust immediately after the addition was made. Temp. Reg. §26.2601-1(b)(1)(v).

Example 2-44. On January 1, 1985, *T* transferred property worth $500,000 to an irrevocable trust, the income of which was distributable to his child, *C,* for life, then to *C*'s child, *GC,* for life. When *GC* dies the trust will terminate and the trust property will be distributed to *GC*'s issue. On January 1 of this year *T* transferred an additional $500,000 to the trust. Immediately after the transfer the trust property was worth $1,500,000. The allocation fraction is ⅓ ($500,000 ÷ $1,500,000). Accordingly, one-third of the amount of generation-skipping transfers made from the trust after January 1 of this year will be attributed to the Chapter 13 portion and will be subject to the GSTT. Of course, the inclusion ratio of the Chapter 13 portion of the trust would be zero if *T* made a timely allocation of $500,000 of his GSTT exemption to the addition to the trust.

§2.39. $2 Million Exclusion, 1986 Act §1433(b)(3)

The so-called Gallo Amendment allowed a GSTT exclusion of $2 million per grandchild for property transferred prior to January 1, 1990. 1986 Act §1433(b)(3). The exclusion applied to outright transfers and certain transfers in trust. In the case of a transfer in trust that met the requirements described below the exclusion also prevented application of the GSTT to either a taxable termination on the death of the grandchild or a taxable distribution to the grandchild. The transfer to a grandchild was, of course, subject to the gift tax. The exclusion encouraged very wealthy individuals to give substantial amounts of property to grandchildren at a sharply reduced transfer tax cost.

Example 2-45. *T,* who was subject to the maximum gift tax rate and had already used her $1,000,000 GSTT exemption, made a gift of $2,000,000 to her grandchild, *GC. T* paid a gift tax of $1,000,000 on the gift, so her estate was reduced by $3,100,000.

If *T* instead made a testamentary gift of $3,100,000 to *GC* that did not qualify for the $2,000,000 exclusion, *GC* would receive much less. First, the gift would be subject to an estate tax of $1,705,000, leaving $1,395,000. Second, the remainder would be subject to a GSTT of $767,250. Thus, only $627,750 would remain for distribution to *GC* ($1,395,000 − $767,250).

A comparison of the net amount received by *GC* is telling: The inter vivos transfer that qualified for the $2,000,000 exclusion left *GC* with $2,000,000 while the testamentary gift of $3,100,000 that did not qualify for the $2,000,000 exclusion left *GC* with only $627,750.

Under amendments made by the 1988 Act transfers in trust qualified for the $2 million exclusion only if the following requirements were met:

1. During the lifetime of the grandchild no portion of the corpus or income of the trust may be distributed to or for the benefit of any other person.
2. If the grandchild dies prior to termination of the trust the assets of the trust will be included in the grandchild's gross estate.
3. After the grandchild becomes 21 all of the trust income will be distributed to or for the benefit of the grandchild at least annually.

The third requirement does not apply to transfers made before June 11, 1987.

§2.40. GSTT PLANNING STRATEGIES

GSTT planning for a particular client is not done in isolation. Instead, it must be carried out in light of the client's wishes and the constraints imposed by other relevant taxes, particularly the federal income, gift, and estate taxes. Most GSTT planning will involve the application of the basic strategies described in the following subsections.

§2.40.1. Use Each Client's $1 Million GSTT Exemption

The most basic and important strategy is to make full use of each client's $1 million GSTT exemption. In the case of a couple, one of whom is wealthy and the other is not, the clients may wish to assure that the GSTT exemption of each spouse will be used. In order to guard against the possibility that the exemption of the poorer spouse might be wasted if he or she were the first to die, the wealthy spouse might make a lifetime gift to the poorer spouse or to a QTIP trust for the benefit of the poorer spouse.

> **Example 2-46.** *W,* who is very wealthy, made a gift of $1,000,000 to a QTIP trust for her relatively poor husband *H.* Upon the death of *H* the trust will continue for the benefit of their issue. The value of the trust will be included in *H*'s estate under §2044. Accordingly, *H* will be treated as the transferor of the trust for GSTT purposes. His executor may allocate *H*'s $1,000,000 GSTT exemption to the trust. Of course, if the value of the trust property is greater than $1,000,000 at the time of *H*'s death, *H*'s exemption will not be sufficient to reduce the trust's inclusion ratio to zero.

Making full use of an individual's GSTT exemption may involve creating separate exempt trusts (*i.e.,* trusts with inclusion ratios of zero) for skip persons and separate nonexempt trusts for nonskip persons.

§2.40.2. Coordinate Use of the GSTT Exemption, the Unified Credit, and the Marital Deduction

The plan for a client should take into account GSTT and estate tax considerations in order to maximize the benefit of the GSTT exemption, the unified credit, and the unlimited marital deduction. An estate plan for the wealthier spouse may involve creating three trusts: (1) a credit shelter trust for the benefit of skip persons (the trustee might also be given discretion to distribute income to the surviving spouse) to which

$600,000 of the decedent's GSTT exemption would be allocated; (2) a QTIP trust funded with an amount equal to the balance of the deceased spouse's GSTT exemption, which would be allocated to this trust (presumably $400,000); (3) a residuary QTIP trust. Instead of providing explicitly for the creation of a QTIP trust in an amount equal to the unused portion of the decedent's GSTT exemption, the will of the first spouse to die might simply authorize his or her executor to divide the residuary QTIP into two or more trusts with identical provisions. *See* §2.26; LR 9002014. The deceased spouse's GSTT exemption would be allocated to the unified credit trust and the smaller QTIP trust. The full benefit of the GSTT exemption of the deceased spouse might be preserved by providing that any distributions of principal to the surviving spouse should be made from the nonexempt residuary QTIP.

In order to preserve the full benefit of the GSTT exemption of the deceased spouse a reverse QTIP election would be made with respect to the smaller QTIP trust, so it will have an inclusion ratio of zero. The deceased spouse's will might also provide that the exempt trusts continue for the benefit of skip persons (grandchildren or great-grandchildren) following the death of the surviving spouse. In addition, the surviving spouse might be given a special power of appointment over the exempt unified credit and smaller QTIP trusts that would preserve the benefit of the deceased spouse's GSTT exemption. Upon the death of the surviving spouse distributions might be made from the nonexempt trust to children or other nonskip persons.

§2.40.3. Make Nontaxable Gifts, §2642(c)

Clients should make inter vivos gifts that are treated as nontaxable for GSTT purposes to or for the benefit of skip persons. Under §2642(c) direct skips that are nontaxable have a zero inclusion ratio. Nontaxable gifts are ones that qualify for the annual gift tax exclusion (including gifts that are split with a spouse under §2513) and qualified transfers (*i.e.,* tuition paid directly by the donor to an educational institution and expenses of medical care paid directly by the donor to the person providing the care, §2503(e)). *See* §2.28. Gifts in trust qualify as nontaxable gifts if (1) distributions of income and principal can only be made for the benefit of the donee during his or her lifetime, and (2) the assets of the trust will be included in the donee's estate if he or she dies prior to receiving distribution of the trust assets. §2642(c)(2).

A client might take advantage of this strategy by making outright annual exclusion gifts to skip persons (grandchildren or great-grandchildren) *and* by paying the cost of their tuition or the expenses of their medical care. As an alternative, gifts might be made to separate trusts that qualify for the annual gift tax exclusion and meet the additional requirements of §2642(c)(2). Presumably such gifts can be made to a single trust, a separate share of which is held for each beneficiary. Maximum leverage might be obtained by making annual exclusion gifts to irrevocable life insurance trusts that meet the requirements of §2642(c)(2).

§2.40.4. Make Inter Vivos Direct Skips

The cost of making generation-skipping transfers is lowest for GSTT inter vivos direct skips (*e.g.*, outright gifts to grandchildren and great-grandchildren). This is because the GSTT is determined on a tax exclusive basis. Also, making gifts early maximizes the shelter provided by the GSTT exemption. In particular, the strategy avoids subjecting further growth in value to the GSTT.

§2.40.5. Preserve Status of Trusts That Are Exempt Under Effective Date Rules

Care should be exercised to preserve the status of trusts that are exempt under the effective date rules. Insofar as possible, planning should be done in ways that take advantage of the existence of preexisting exempt trusts. Additional property should not be transferred to a preexisting trust that is exempt from the GSTT. Also, a preexisting trust should not be amended in any way that affects the beneficial interests in the trust.

> **Example 2-47.** In 1984 *T* transferred $1,000,000 to an irrevocable trust which gave the independent trustee discretion to distribute income and principal, from time to time, to those of *T*'s issue who are living. Under the effective date rules the trust is exempt from application of the GSTT. *T,* who has already used his $1,000,000 GSTT exemption, now wishes to make additional property available to his issue. Property should not be added to the 1984 trust because it is wholly exempt from the GSTT. Instead, *T* might transfer an equivalent amount to a similar trust. In order to minimize GSTT costs the trustee could make distributions from the exempt trust to skip persons and from the new trust to nonskip persons.

Note that under Prop. Reg. §26.2601-1(b)(v)(A), the exercise of a special power of appointment (*i.e.,* one that is not a general power under §2041) is generally not treated as a constructive addition to a grandfathered trust.

Direct skips made under instruments executed prior to October

22, 1986 are not subject to Chapter 13 if the transferor was incompetent on that date and did not regain competency prior to his or her death. Temp. Reg. §26.2601-1(b)(3). In some instances this rule can be effectively coupled with the use of disclaimers. For example, the IRS concluded that the GSTT would not apply to direct skips made to grandnephews and grandnieces as a result of disclaimers made by nephews of the right to receive the outright distribution of property under a will executed prior to October 22, 1986 where the testator was incompetent on that date and at all subsequent times. LR 9111011.

§2.40.6. Create and Administer Trusts in Light of Prior Use of GSTT Exemption

Trusts should be created and administered in ways that maximize the benefit of the allocation that has been made of the transferor's GSTT exemption. In particular, gifts might be made to, or separate trusts might be created for, each generation of beneficiaries (*i.e.,* the gifts might be "layered"). Making gifts to or for the exclusive benefit of children is desirable because gifts to children (or to the children of deceased children under the orphan grandchild exclusion) are not subject to the GSTT. Distributions made from nonexempt trusts to children are also not subject to the GSTT. Thus, distributions from exempt trusts should be made to skip persons and distributions from nonexempt trusts should be made to nonskip persons. Note, however, that property of a nonexempt trust could be used to pay the tuition and medical care expenses of skip persons without incurring any GSTT liability. Under §2611(b) such distributions are not generation-skipping transfers. Planning at all stages should take into account the orphan grandchild exclusion. *See* §2612(c)(2).

§2.40.7. Use the Orphan Grandchild Exclusion, §2612(c)

Wills and trusts should be planned in ways that permit appointments and distributions to be made in light of the "orphan" grandchild exclusion of §2612(c)(2). If the transferor's child is deceased at the time a transfer is made, the children of the deceased child and more remote descendants move up one generation. Thus, a child of the deceased child is treated as the transferor's child. The rule applies in classifying direct skips.

Example 2-48. *W* died in 1991 leaving $600,000 to a credit shelter trust, $400,000 to a QTIP trust, and her residuary estate of $2,000,000 to another QTIP. *W*'s $1,000,000 GSTT exemption was allocated to the credit shelter trust and the $400,000 QTIP trust. *W* was survived by *H,* her husband, and their two children *A* and *B.* A reverse QTIP election was made with respect to the smaller QTIP trust. Both the credit shelter and the smaller QTIP trusts have inclusion ratios of zero.

A died recently survived by his two children *GS* and *GD* and *H.* Accordingly, when *H* dies *GS* and *GD* will be treated as his children (*i.e.,* nonskip persons) for GSTT purposes. *W*'s GSTT exemption would be wasted to the extent the property of the unified credit and smaller QTIP trusts is distributed to *B,* a nonskip person. *GS* and *GD* are skip persons as to *W,* who remained the transferor of those trusts for GSTT purposes. The value of *W*'s GSTT exemption could be fully preserved if *H* had a special power of appointment over the trusts. The exercise of the power should be made in light of two important GSTT considerations: (1) that *B, GS,* and *GD* are all nonskip persons as to *H,* and (2) that the unified credit and smaller QTIP trusts created by *W* are exempt from the GSTT. Accordingly, *H* might exercise a special power over the exempt trusts in a way that maximizes the benefit of their exempt status. Thus, *H* might appoint the property of those trusts to *GS* and *GD* and make compensating gifts to *B* or act to continue the trusts for as long as possible. *H*'s GSTT exemption could be used to shelter outright gifts to the children of *B* or the establishment of trusts for their benefit.

§2.40.8. Consider Authorizing Trustees to Make Distributions and to Amend Trust

Trusts can be drafted to allow trustees to take advantage of the unified credits and GSTT exemptions of first generation beneficiaries. In particular, trusts can permit trustees to make outright distributions to the transferor's children or other nonskip persons. As a result of the distributions the children (or other distributees) would own the property *and* the original transferor would no longer be connected with it for GSTT purposes. The same goal can be achieved if an independent trustee exercised the power to amend the trust to give a child or another nonskip person a general power of appointment over the property of a trust. The power given to the child could be the narrowest that would cause the property to be included in the child's estate and cause the child to become the transferor of the property for GSTT purposes. Thus, the child might be given the power, exercisable jointly with the trustee or another nonadverse party to appoint the property to the creditors of the child's estate. As an alternative the holder of a special power of appointment might investigate the consequences of exercising the power to create a presently exercisable general power of appointment. *See* §2041(a)(3). *See also* §2.31.

F. BASIC LIFETIME ESTATE PLANNING TAX STRATEGIES

§2.41. OVERVIEW

This part describes the general strategies or approaches that describe the specific estate planning components of most estate plans. A general strategy can often be achieved in a variety of ways, some of which may have different tax and nontax consequences. In some instances the use of a specific technique may serve more than one general goal. For example, the gift of an income-producing asset achieves two goals: (1) shifting future income to the donee and (2) reducing (or freezing) the size of the donor's estate for transfer tax purposes. The details of the estate plan for a client must be based upon the client's wishes. To the extent consistent with that goal it should be formulated in light of important tax considerations, which include the gift tax and GSTT exclusions, the unified credit, and the GSTT exemption. The details of the client's program should take full advantage of the gift tax annual exclusion, the exclusions for the direct payment of the tuition or medical expenses of a donee (which are also available for GSTT purposes), gift splitting between the client and the client's spouse, and the marital deduction. A substantial gift program might consume the unified credits of the client and the client's spouse. Many estate planning devices were affected by the 1986 Act, which reduced and compressed the income tax rates and eliminated most of the income tax advantages of the "sophisticated" income tax shelters that proliferated in the early 1980s. Some relatively simple income tax shelters remain, such as tax-exempt municipal bonds and retirement funds. Post-mortem planning strategies are considered in detail in Chapter 12.

The following lifetime strategies are discussed in this part:

1. Shift income within the family
2. Reduce the size of the estate
3. Freeze the value of the estate
4. Bypass the estates of survivors, and
5. Defer the payment of estate taxes.

As mentioned above, each of these general strategies can usually be carried out in a variety of ways. For example, several relatively simple techniques remain available by which the value of a client's estate may be frozen, such as gifts (outright or in trust), installment sales, and transfers of property in exchange for a private annuity. *See* Chapters 7 and 9. The estate planning techniques that will be recommended to a particular client will vary, of course, depending upon his or her overall circumstances. As always, the content of an estate plan should be designed to carry out the client's tax and nontax objectives.

§2.42. SHIFT INCOME WITHIN THE FAMILY

The 1986 Act compressed individual income tax rates to the point that relatively little income tax advantage is produced by shifting income within the family. However, the strategy can produce some limited income tax benefits and can shift some wealth from the donor to others. Shifting income is also worth considering because of the possibility that future income tax rates may be more progressive. In brief, a family unit may enjoy an income tax benefit if investment income is divided among more family members, particularly ones with little or no other income. A shift of income from family members who are subject to the maximum rate to ones subject to lower rates results in an increase in the family's after-tax income.

> **Example 2-49.** Mother, *M,* is subject to a marginal income tax rate of 31%. Her two children, 15 and 17, each have taxable incomes of $10,000. A 15% income tax rate applies to the first $19,450 of the taxable income of unmarried individuals other than surviving spouses and heads of households. Taxable income in the band between $19,450 and $47,050 is subject to a 28% rate. If *M* could deflect $9,450 of taxable income to each of her children, the family's overall annual income tax liability might be cut by $3,024 ($18,900 × (31% − 15%)).

Of course, under the "Kiddie Tax," which was added as a part of the 1986 Act, the unearned income of children under 14 is taxed at the maximum rate applicable to the parents. §1(i). Accordingly, the opportunity to shift taxable unearned income to children has been severely restricted.

A variation on the basic approach involves creating additional taxpayers (trusts and corporations) with whom the family income may be split. However, only the first $3,300 of the income of a trust or estate is subject to the lowest rate (15 percent). In addition, the benefit derived from the use of trusts as separate taxpayers is limited by the throwback rules. §§665-667, under which distributions of accumulated income are taxed as if the beneficiary had received the income as it was accumulated. See §10.4.1.

§2.42.1. Methods

Clients can select from a variety of methods by which income can be shifted within the family. However, most require the donor to give up the property permanently. They are, consequently, beyond the means of most taxpayers. An outright gift to a donee is an example of such a gift. *See* §7.2.1. Of course, where the donee is a minor, the gift should be made in a way that avoids the necessity of a guardianship. For example, the gift might be made to a custodian under the Uniform Transfer to Minors Act (or the Uniform Gift to Minors Act) or to the trustee of a trust for the minor. *See* §§7.34-7.36. Income may also be shifted by more indirect means, such as by deflecting business or investment opportunities to a child. *See* §7.18.

Prior to the 1986 Act income could be shifted by several methods by which the donor retained an interest in the property. The most popular was the short-term trust in which the grantor retained a reversionary interest that would take effect after ten years or more. However, an amendment to §673(a) eliminated that opportunity. Now the grantor is treated as the owner of any portion of a trust in which the reversionary interest of the grantor or the grantor's spouse has a value of five percent or more at the inception of the trust. *See* §10.4.1.

The 1986 Act similarly ended the opportunity for clients with a surplus of cash to shift income by making interest-free demand loans to their children, other family members, or to trusts. §7872. Also, the decision in *Dickman v. Commissioner,* 465 U.S. 330 (1984), recognized that interest-free demand loans result in a taxable gift of the use of the transferred funds.

§2.42.2. Assignment of Income Alone Is Ineffective for Income Tax Purposes

> But this case is not to be decided by attenuated subtleties. It turns on the import and reasonable construction of the taxing act. There is no doubt that the statute could tax salaries to those who earned them and provide that the tax could not be escaped by anticipatory arrangements and contracts however skillfully devised to prevent the salary when paid from vesting even for a second in the man who earned it. That seems to us the import of the statute before us and we think that no distinction can be

> taken according to the motives leading to the arrangement by which the fruits are attributed to a different tree from that on which they grew. *Lucas v. Earl,* 281 U.S. 111, 114-115 (1930).

As indicated by a host of Supreme Court decisions, an assignment of income alone is not effective to shift the tax incidence from the assignor to the assignee. *E.g., Helvering v. Horst,* 311 U.S. 112 (1940) (father taxable on bond interest where interest coupon detached and given to son prior to payment date); *Lucas v. Earl, supra* (husband remained taxable on personal service income that he contracted to give to his wife). In general, the law distinguishes between a gift of property, which is usually effective to shift the income from the property, and a gift of the "mere" right to receive income, which is usually not effective to shift the income. That distinction is the origin of the famous fruit and tree analogy that appears in the above quotation from *Lucas v. Earl.* However, differentiating between "property" and a "right to income" can be difficult in some cases. Because of that problem some arbitrary rules have grown up, as illustrated by the tax consequences of the assignment of the income interest in a trust.

In *Blair v. Commissioner,* 300 U.S. 5 (1937), the Supreme Court held that a life income beneficiary's gratuitous assignment of his interest in the trust income constituted a transfer of an equitable property interest sufficient to shift the income to the assignee. In a subsequent case the Court ruled that the transfer of one year's trust income was not sufficient to shift the income to the assignee. *Harrison v. Shaffner,* 312 U.S. 579 (1941). It reasoned that the donor "has parted with no substantial interest in property other than the specified payments of income which, like other gifts of income, are taxable to the donor." Id. at 583. Several later decisions held that assignments of trust income for ten years or more would shift the income to the assignee. *E.g., Hawaiian Trust Co. v. Kanne,* 172 F.2d 74 (9th Cir. 1949). In 1955 the IRS adopted that view, ruling that the trust income would be taxed to the assignee where it was transferred for a period of at least ten years. Rev. Rul. 55-38, 1955-1 C.B. 389. The ruling was consistent with prior form of §673 under which the grantor would not be treated as owner of the trust if the reversionary interest of the grantor would not take effect for a period of ten years or more.

§2.43. Reduce the Size of the Estate: Gifts and Valuation Games

> [M]any actions taken by taxpayers in positioning their investment and business assets secure significant transfer tax advantages because those acts depress the value of the property interests

involved. This occurs, for example, whenever a deed of real estate splits the ownership of the asset into two or more parts. Wallace, Now You See It, Now You Don't — Valuation Conundrums in Estate Planning, U. Miami, 24th Inst. Est. Plan. ¶805.6 (1990).

Reducing the amount of property that is potentially includible in a client's gross estate is a primary estate planning strategy. Outright lifetime gifts are the simplest and most direct way of achieving such a reduction. Of course, as a result of the unification of the gift and estate taxes in 1976, the amount of post-1976 taxable gifts is included in the tax base at the time of the donor's death. The unification of the taxes increased the importance of reducing one's estate by making inter vivos gifts that qualify for the gift tax annual exclusion. Under the unified transfer tax rate table, each $10,000 annual exclusion can be expected to save at least $3,700 in estate taxes ($10,000 × 37 percent, the lowest marginal unified tax rate applicable to amounts in excess of the credit equivalent). Importantly, even deathbed gifts may be excluded from the donor's gross estate. Under §2035 gifts other than interests in life insurance, made within three years of death, generally are not included in the donor's estate.

Taxable gifts (*i.e.,* ones in excess of the annual exclusion) can also help control the size of a client's gross estate. Although the amount of a taxable gift is includible in the donor's tax base, any subsequent appreciation in value of the transferred property is excluded. The future income from the property is also excluded from the donor's estate. Finally, any gift tax paid more than three years prior to death is not included in the donor's estate. Note that taxable gifts within the amount of the credit equivalent do not require any out of pocket tax cost.

Example 2-50. In 1991 Donor, *D,* made a gift of stock worth $610,000 to her son, *S.* The gift did not require the payment of any gift tax — $10,000 was allowed as a gift tax exclusion and the tax on $600,000 was offset by *D*'s unified credit. When *D* died in 1993 the stock she gave to *S* was worth $1,000,000. Because *D* made the gift of stock her transfer tax base was $400,000 smaller than it would have been without the gift. Of course, any income derived from the stock after the gift was made was also excluded from *D*'s estate. By making the gift the estate tax payable by *D*'s estate was reduced by at least $153,000 ($400,000 × the applicable marginal rates, 37% and 39%).

§2.43.1. Make Gifts to Qualify for Valuation Discounts

The difficulty of valuing property according to a hypothetical sale between a willing buyer and a willing seller at the time of a death or gift is referred to in the following passage from a British tax case:

> The result is that I must enter into a dim world peopled by the indeterminate spirits of fictitious or unborn sales. It is necessary to assume the prophetic vision of a prospective purchaser at the moment of death of the deceased, and firmly to reject the wisdom which might be provided by the knowledge of subsequent events. *Holt v. Inland Revenue Commissioners,* (1953) 2 All E.R. 1499, 1501.

Undivided interests in real estate and minority interests in businesses qualify for discounts that make their valuation particularly difficult.

Gifts of interests in some types of property may result in a disproportionately large reduction in value of the donor's estate. This may occur, for example, where a gift reduces the donor's stock holding in a closely-held business to a minority interest. Minority interests generally qualify for a substantial discount from the pro rata value of the stock. The same interest may also be discounted for lack of marketability. Similarly, a gift of an undivided interest in real property may reduce the value of the donor's retained interest. The IRS is understandably reluctant to recognize any discount from the pro rata value of stock or real property in the case of gifts to noncharities. It is now more vigilant and vigorous in asserting the value of gifts to charities should reflect appropriate discounts. Despite IRS challenges to the valuation of noncharitable gifts, courts frequently allow substantial discounts that are supported by expert appraisals. *See* Bringardner, Discounting the Value of Undivided Interests in Realty, 72 J. Tax. 12 (1990) (includes table showing discounts allowed in selected cases) and Harris, Valuation of Closely Held Partnerships and Corporations: Recent Developments Concerning Minority Interest and Lack of Marketability Discounts, 42 Ark. L. Rev. 649 (1989).

The possibility that a gift may result in a disproportionately large reduction in the value of the donor's retained interest exists because the value of a transfer for gift tax purposes is measured by the value of the property transferred and not the amount by which the transfer reduces the value of the donor's estate. §2512. Securing the proper discount depends upon obtaining reliable appraisals by qualified experts. As a matter of strategy some estate planners hire the appraiser or appraisers most often used by the IRS in valuing the particular type of property that is involved. The following examples illustrate the operation of the existing valuation rules:

Example 2-51. *T* owned 60 of the 100 outstanding shares of the common stock of T, Inc. In 1991 *T* gave 11 shares of T, Inc. stock to her child *C.* The proper valuation of the 11 shares will reflect the fact that they constitute a small minority interest and that they would be difficult to market. By making the gift *T* has reduced her ownership of T, Inc. stock to a minority interest that should later qualify for the same discounts. (Discounts for minority interests were denied by the Tax Court in *Estate of Ralph E. Lenheim,* 60 T.C.M 356 (1990), and *Estate of Elizabeth B. Murphy,* 60 T.C.M. 645 (1990), where the transfers that reduced the decedent's ownership interests to minority status were made shortly prior to their deaths.) From time to time legislation has been proposed that would require the undiscounted pro rata valuation of minority interests. On the other extreme, under the United Kingdom's former Capital Transfer Tax the amount of a chargeable transfer was the amount by which the transfer reduced the value of the transferor's estate. Finance Act 1975, §20(2). The special valuation rules of Chapter 14 do not apply where, as in this example, the retained interest is of the same class as the transferred interest. *See* §2701(a)(2)(B).

Example 2-52. *O* gave an undivided one-tenth interest in Blackacre to each of her 6 grandchildren. Each gift qualifies for the annual gift tax exclusion. In addition, each would qualify for a discount because of the undivided ownership of the property. An expert appraisal would probably sustain a discount of at least 15%. *See, e.g., Estate of Propstra,* 680 F.2d 1248 (9th Cir. 1982).

§2.43.2. Make Gifts of Life Insurance

The prospective size of a client's gross estate can often be reduced substantially by making gifts of insurance on the client's life, which may have little or no value for gift tax purposes. The assignment of term or group-term insurance can produce quite favorable results because of its low present value. *See* §6.43.1. Greater overall estate tax savings may result if the insurance is transferred, or initially acquired by, an irrevocable trust and the insurance is also insulated from inclusion in the estate of the insured's spouse. *See* §6.23.

§2.44. Freeze the Value of the Estate

Many wealthy or prospectively wealthy clients seek to prevent any further growth in value of appreciating assets by utilizing one or more devices that prevent any future growth in the value of the asset from being included in their estates. Because these devices "freeze" the value that is includible in the owner's estate they are called "estate freezes." The transfer tax advantages of estate freezes were limited by former §2036(c), which was adopted in 1987 and repealed retroactively in 1990. *See* §2.17.2.

Estate freeze techniques range from relatively simple approaches, such as inter vivos gifts or installment sales, to more complex ones, such as transfers of property to retained interest trusts. The uses of noncharitable gifts are reviewed in Chapter 7. The other principal methods of accomplishing an estate freeze are reviewed in Chapter 9. They include the installment sale, the private annuity, and the sale and leaseback. Of them, the installment sale is probably the least controversial and the most widely used. In an installment sale the owner exchanges an asset with significant potential for appreciation for a promissory note, the value of which is fixed. Changes made by the Installment Sales Revision Act of 1980 removed some of the income tax ploys that were formerly used. The private annuity is used less often, perhaps because of its more controversial nature and more uncertain tax consequences. A typical private annuity transaction involves the transfer by a senior family member of appreciated property to a junior family member in exchange for the latter's unsecured promise to pay the transferor a specified annual amount for life. The sale and leaseback usually involves the sale of an office or office equipment by a doctor or other professional to family members or a trust for family members, from whom the property is leased back. Although it has some estate-freezing characteristics, it is primarily intended to redistribute income within the family.

§2.45. Bypass the Estates of Survivors

Transferring property in a way that will not subject it to taxation upon the death of the transferee is one of the most fundamental strategies for limiting estate taxes. For example, the estates of married persons are often planned so the surviving spouse will receive the benefit of a portion of the deceased spouse's estate that will not be included in the survivor's estate. A qualified terminable interest property (QTIP) trust is perhaps the most popular and effective way to accomplish that result. The trust property is includible in the surviving spouse's estate only to the extent an election is made to claim the marital deduction in the estate of the first spouse to die. The balance of the property "bypasses" the surviving spouse's estate. Leaving the surviving spouse a legal life estate in the property is generally a much less flexible and satisfactory way of reaching this result than using a trust.

A bypass trust is simply one in which the surviving spouse or other beneficiary is given substantial interests, but not ones that are sufficiently extensive to cause the trust property to be included in the beneficiary's estate. The beneficiary is commonly given a life income interest in the trust, although others are sometimes given the right to receive discretionary distributions of income or principal. (Of course, a trust that allows any distributions to others during the lifetime of the surviving spouse cannot qualify for the marital deduction.) In addition, the beneficiary may be given a limited power to invade corpus and a special testamentary power of appointment.

A bypass trust may be used to provide for the grantor's descendants. However, the tax incentive to attempt to bypass one or more generations of descendants is eroded somewhat by the GSTT. Prior to the adoption of the GSTT, wealthy individuals frequently established trusts that were designed to provide lifetime benefits to two or more generations of descendants without subjecting the trust property to taxation in the estates of the intermediate generations. Of course, the number of generations of estate tax levies that could be "skipped" by a trust was limited to some extent by the applicable Rule Against Perpetuities. Nonetheless, it is quite easy to draft a trust that skips one generation.

> **Example 2-53.** Parent *P* created a trust to pay the income to her child *C* for life. Upon the death of *C* the trust property is distributable to *C*'s children who survive her. The GSTT would apply to the distribution of principal to the issue of *C* when she dies. However, the distribution would not be taxable for GSTT purposes to the extent (1) *P* applies her $1,000,000 exemption to the property that she transferred to the trust, or (2) the trust is included in *C*'s gross estate.

Bypass trusts for grandchildren or more remote descendants of the transferor will escape the GSTT only to the extent they are sheltered by an exclusion or exemption. Accordingly, clients should consider plans that maximize the value of their $1 million exemptions and the limited exclusions that are available. In particular, the exemption should be used in connection with trusts that would otherwise be entirely subject to the GSTT. Part of the value of the exemption is wasted if it is allocated to a QTIP trust or other trust that will make distributions to nonskip persons such as the transferor's spouse or children. Instead, the transferor might create separate trusts for the benefit of his or her children and for grandchildren or more remote descendants. The reason is simple: Distributions from trusts for the exclusive benefit of children are not subject to the GSTT. On the other hand, distributions from trusts for the exclusive benefit of grandchildren and more remote descendants are entirely subject to the GSTT.

> **Example 2-54.** *T* wishes to put $2,000,000 in trust for the benefit of his children and grandchildren. *T* should consider establishing a $1,000,000 discretionary trust for *T*'s children and a separate $1,000,000 trust for *T*'s grandchildren. All distributions from the trust for grandchildren will be free of the GSTT if *T*'s $1,000,000 exemption is allocated to it. In contrast, if *T* had established a single $2,000,000 discretionary trust for children and grandchildren, the allocation of the full amount of *T*'s exemption to the trust would shelter only half of the amount of generation-skipping transfers from the GSTT.

§2.46. DEFER THE PAYMENT OF ESTATE AND GST TAXES

Substantial savings can be achieved by deferring payment of estate and GST taxes. The estate tax marital deduction, which is discussed in detail in Chapter 5, is the most important deferral option. In essence it allows the payment of the estate tax on a married person's entire estate to be deferred until the death of the surviving spouse. In the interim, the funds that would have been paid in estate tax on the death of the first spouse are available for use by the surviving spouse. The estate and gift tax marital deductions can also be used to equalize the sizes of the spouses' estates and possibly reduce the overall estate tax burden because of the progressive nature of the estate tax.

> **Example 2-55.** *W* has an estate of $2,000,000, but her husband *H* owns only a nominal amount of property. If *W* dies in 1992, leaving all of her property in a form that does not qualify for the marital deduction, her estate will have to pay state and federal death taxes of at least $588,000 ($780,800 less the unified credit of $192,800). Of course, in that case the property would probably not be subject to the estate tax when *H* dies. On the other hand, if *W* leaves all of her property to *H* in a form that qualifies for the marital deduction, such as a QTIP, no tax need be paid by her estate. Ideally, *W*'s unified credit would be used to shelter $600,000 of the property from taxation on *H*'s death. If $600,000 were effectively sheltered by use of *W*'s unified credit, only $1,400,000 will be subject to tax in *H*'s estate. A tax of $320,000 ($512,800 − $192,800) would be imposed on *H*'s estate. Thus, the combined use of the marital deduction and unified credits might

reduce the overall estate tax cost of passing property from *H* and *W* to their children by $268,000 (from $588,000 to $320,000).

A limited deferral opportunity is extended to the estates of persons who own substantial interests in closely-held businesses. Where the interest in a closely-held business comprises a large enough part of a decedent's estate, the estate tax attributable to that interest may be paid over a maximum of 15 years under §6166. Deferral under §6166 is particularly attractive because the tax attributable to the first $1 million in value of the business is only subject to a four percent interest rate. *See* §6601(j). *See also* §12.41. The balance of the deferred tax is subject to the Federal Short Term Rate plus three percentage points. §6621(a)(2).

Section 6166 allows the executor to defer making any payment on the principal amount of the tax until five years after the due date of the estate tax return, after which the tax is payable in equal annual installments over a period of not more than ten years. As indicated in §2.36.3, the GSTT imposed on direct skips of closely-held business interests may be deferred under §6166. *See* §6166(h).

Lifetime planning decisions for clients who own interests in closely-held businesses should take into account the opportunity for deferral under §6166. For example, a client's gift program might be planned in a way that will leave a client's estate with a sufficient interest in the business to meet the requirements of §6166. *See* §7.10 and Chapters 11-12. The same considerations may lead a client to transfer additional property to a corporation in order to increase the value of the client's stock holding and to reduce the nonbusiness portion of the client's estate.

BIBLIOGRAPHY

Bringardner, Discounting Undivided Interests in Realty, 72 J. Tax. 12 (1990)

Frankel, Exceptions and Exclusions in Generation-Skipping: Planning Considerations, N.Y.U., 48th Inst. Fed. Tax., ch. 15 (1990)

Horn, J., Planning and Drafting for the Generation-Skipping Transfer Tax (1991)

Pennell, Income Shifting After TRA '86, N.Y.U., 46th Inst. Fed. Tax., ch. 50 (1988)

Peschel, J. & Spurgeon, E., Federal Taxation of Trusts, Grantors and Beneficiaries (2d ed. 1991)

Wallace, Now You See It, Now You Don't — Valuation Conundrums in Estate Planning, U. Miami, 24th Inst. Est. Plan., ch. 8 (1990)

CHAPTER 3

Concurrent Ownership and Nontestamentary Transfers

A. Introduction

§3.1. Scope

B. Tenancy in Common

§3.2. Substantive Law Summary
§3.3. Creation
§3.4. Tenancy in Common in Community Property States
§3.5. Miscellaneous
§3.6. Creditor's Claims
§3.7. Gift Tax
§3.7.1. Termination
§3.7.2. Conversion of Community Property into Tenancy in Common
§3.7.3. Conversion of Tenancy in Common into Community Property
§3.8. Estate Tax
§3.9. Income Tax
§3.10. Use in Estate Planning

C. Joint Tenancy and Tenancy by the Entirety

§3.11. Introduction
§3.11.1. Advantages
§3.11.2. Disadvantages
§3.12. Features of Joint Tenancies
§3.12.1. Multiparty Financial Accounts
§3.12.2. Uniform TOD Security Registration Act
§3.12.3. Simultaneous Death

§3.12.4. Creditor's Rights
§3.12.5. Community Property
§3.13. Tenancy by the Entirety
§3.14. Gift Tax
§3.14.1. Revocable Transfers
§3.14.2. Pre-1982 Transfers of Real Property to a Spouse
§3.15. Estate Tax: General Rule, §2040(a)
§3.15.1. Contributions by Surviving Tenant
§3.15.2. Gifts to Decedent and Survivor as Joint Tenants
§3.16. Qualified Joint Interests, §2040(b)
§3.17. Estate Tax: Simultaneous Deaths
§3.18. Estate Tax: Termination of Joint Tenancies
§3.19. Disclaimers, §§2046, 2518
§3.20. Income Tax
§3.20.1. Income from Joint Tenancy Property
§3.20.2. Income Tax Deductions
§3.20.3. Basis; General Rule
§3.20.4. Special Basis Rule, §1014(e)
§3.20.5. Depreciation Adjustment to Basis, §1014(b)(9)
§3.20.6. Community Property in Joint Tenancy
§3.20.7. Community Property Transmuted into Separate Property Joint Tenancy
§3.20.8. Basis Planning with Joint Tenancies
§3.20.9. Termination of Joint Tenancies
§3.21. Planning With Joint Tenancies

D. Community Property

§3.22. Scope
§3.23. History
§3.24. Estate Planning with Community Property
§3.25. Preserve the Community or Separate Character of Property
§3.26. Preserve the Availability of Stepped-up Basis Under §1014(b)(6)
§3.27. Avoid Unnecessarily Increasing Size of Surviving Spouse's Estate
§3.28. Separate and Community Property
§3.28.1. Gifts of Separate Property
§3.28.2. Gifts of Community Property
§3.28.3. Tracing the Character of Property
§3.28.4. Presumption Favoring Community Property
§3.28.5. Special Problems of Characterization
§3.29. Agreements Regarding Character of Property
§3.30. Agreements Governing Disposition of Property at Death
§3.31. Survivorship Community Property
§3.32. Employee Benefit Plans; Terminable Interest Rule
§3.33. Estate Tax
§3.33.1. Deductions
§3.33.2. Marital Deduction

§3.33.3. Credits
§3.34. Gift Tax
§3.34.1. Transfer of Separate Property into Community Property
§3.34.2. Partition of Community Property into Separate Property
§3.34.3. Conversion of Future Income into Separate Property
§3.35. Income Tax
§3.35.1. No Gain or Loss on Transfers Between Spouses, §1041
§3.35.2. Conversion of Separate Property into Community Property
§3.35.3. Conversion of Community Property into Separate Property
§3.35.4. Basis Following Death of a Spouse
§3.35.5. Appreciated Property Acquired from a Decedent
§3.36. Conflict of Laws: Basic Rules
§3.37. Uniform Disposition of Community Property Rights at Death Act
§3.38. Quasi-Community Property
§3.39. Protecting the Property Interests of Migratory Spouses

Bibliography

A. INTRODUCTION

§3.1. Scope

This chapter focuses on the three principal forms of coownership of legal interests in property other than the partnership form. They are, in order of discussion: the tenancy in common, the joint tenancy and the tenancy by the entirety, and community property. Each part discusses the characteristics of the form, the methods by which it is created, the federal tax consequences of transactions involving its use, and its use in estate planning. Rules regarding survivorship forms of ownership of deposits in financial institutions and of United States savings bonds are considered in connection with the discussion of joint tenancies. The chapter also includes references to the use of survivorship arrangements authorized by U.P.C. §6-101 (formerly U.P.C. §6-201) and similar statutes authorizing nontestamentary transfers that are in effect in a growing number of states. Other forms of will substitutes, including life insurance and trusts, are discussed in later chapters.

Throughout the chapter dominant consideration is given to coownership of property by a husband and wife, who are more likely than others to own property together. Because of the differences in substantive and tax law treatment, an estate planner must be aware of the characteristics of the principal forms of coownership. Community property is discussed in some detail because of its importance to present or past residents of the nine community property states. Planners in noncommunity property states must also be aware of the basic characteristics of community property because of the migrant nature of our population. Under basic conflicts of law rules, the nature of a couple's interests in property is generally fixed at the time of acquisition and does not vary although they later move to a state with a different marital property regime.

B. TENANCY IN COMMON

§3.2. Substantive Law Summary

A tenancy in common is a form of concurrent ownership between two or more persons in which each cotenant owns an undivided fractional interest in the property. The interests are presumed to be equal unless otherwise specified in the instrument creating the tenancy. Whether or not the interests are equal, each tenant has an equal right to occupy the whole of the property.

The interest of each tenant is freely transferable and devisable. In the ordinary case there is no right of survivorship between tenants in common. However, the instrument creating the tenancy may provide for survivorship interests. Although most states follow the general rules regarding tenancies in common, there are some variations. For example, Wisconsin recognizes a tenancy in common with an indestructible right of survivorship. *Zander v. Holly,* 84 N.W.2d 87, 96 (Wis. 1957); Sheedy & Sullivan, Nature of Cotenancies and Their Taxation — Death and Gift, 56 Marq. L. Rev. 3, 5 (1972). Oregon takes a similar approach as to interests in real property. Or. Rev. Stat. §93.180 (1990); *Holbrook v. Holbrook,* 403 P.2d 12 (Or. 1965).

A corporation, trust, or other artificial legal entity may be a tenant in common, but not a joint tenant.

§3.3. Creation

A tenancy in common may be created by the express terms of a will, conveyance, or other instrument of transfer ("to *X* and *Y* as tenants in common"). However, more often it results from a transfer to two or more persons that does not specify the type of tenancy the transferor intended to create or the extent of each transferee's interest (*e.g.*, "to *A, B,* and *C*"). A tenancy in common also results when property passes to two or more persons under the intestate succession law. In most states, a transfer to two or more persons creates a tenancy in common and not a joint tenancy unless the instrument of transfer expressly declares an intent to create a joint tenancy. *E.g.*, Cal. Civ. Code §683 (West 1991 Supp.); Nev. Rev. Stat. §111.060 (1987); N.Y. Est. Powers & Trusts Law §6-2.2(a) (McKinney 1991 Supp.). Those states have reversed the ancient constructional preference that favored joint tenancies. In them a conveyance "to *X* and *Y* jointly" would probably be characterized as a tenancy in common and not as a joint tenancy. Of course, property gratuitously transferred to a husband and wife may create a tenancy by the entirety in common law states that recognize that form of ownership. N.Y. Est. Powers & Trusts Law §6-2.2(b) (McKinney 1991 Supp.). Property transferred to a "husband and wife" who are not married typically creates a tenancy in common. *Marriage of Smith,* 705 P.2d 197 (Or. 1985). However, under New York law a transfer of realty to "a husband and wife" who are not married creates a joint tenancy unless it is expressly declared to be a tenancy in common. N.Y. Est. Powers & Trusts Law §6-2.2(c) (McKinney 1991 Supp.). Also, except where a transfer is sufficient to create a tenancy by the entirety, under Florida law, a transfer to two or more persons creates a tenancy in common unless the instrument expressly creates a right of survivorship. Fla. Stat. Ann. §689.15 (West 1991 Supp.).

A tenancy in common may also be created when a joint tenancy is severed, as it is when one joint tenant transfers an interest in the joint tenancy property to a third party. *E.g.*, Cal. Civ. Code §683.2 (West 1991 Supp.).

Example 3-1. *X* devised Blackacre to his daughters *A* and *B* as joint tenants, which was sufficient to constitute them as joint tenants with right of survivorship. Prior to the death of either of them, *B* conveyed her interest to her stepsister, *C*. Following the conveyance *A* and *C* owned Blackacre as tenants in common (*i.e.*, the transfer from *B* to *C* severed the joint tenancy and terminated the right of survivorship). Thereafter *A* and *C* were each free to dispose of her interest in the property by deed or will.

Also, property owned by a husband and wife as joint tenants or tenants by the entirety may be converted into a tenancy in common if their marriage is dissolved and the property is not otherwise disposed of in the decree of dissolution. As pointed out in §3.4, unless otherwise provided in the decree of dissolution, former spouses generally hold as tenants in common the community property they owned at the time of divorce. *E.g.,* Wis. Stat. Ann. §766.75 (West 1991 Supp.). Under the laws of Michigan and Ohio and the 1990 version of U.P.C. §2-804, joint tenancies between a husband and wife are severed upon their divorce. Mich. Stat. Ann. §552.102 (1984); Ohio Rev. Code Ann. §5302.20(c)(5) (Page 1989).

A joint tenancy may also be converted into a tenancy in common by an agreement of the tenants or a decree of a court that directly or indirectly terminates the right of survivorship. *E.g., McDonald v. Morely,* 101 P.2d 690 (Cal. 1940) (separation agreement that terminating right of survivorship severed the joint tenancy); *Reilly v. Sageser,* 467 P.2d 358 (Wash. App. 1970) (agreement eliminating survivorship feature); *Mann v. Bradley,* 535 P.2d 213 (Colo. 1975) (divorce property settlement agreement providing for sale of premises and division of proceeds upon occurrence of certain events evidences intent no longer to hold the property in joint tenancy). As suggested by *Mann* and other cases, property settlement agreements incident to marital dissolutions should provide expressly for the disposition of all the spouses' property.

§3.4. Tenancy in Common in Community Property States

Community property states allow married persons to hold title to property as tenants in common. The interests of the spouses in tenancy in common property have traditionally been treated as separate, not community, property. However, some community property states presume that property held by husband and wife as tenants in common is their community property. Cal. Civ. Code §4800.1 (West 1991 Supp.); N.M. Stat. Ann. §40-3-8B (1990).

In some states property that is gratuitously transferred to a husband and wife ("to *H* and *W*") is treated as their community property. *Estate of Salvini,* 397 P.2d 811 (Wash. 1964). In Texas, property conveyed in that manner probably would be owned by the husband and wife as tenants in common. W. deFuniak & M. Vaughn, Principles of Community Property §69 (2d ed. 1971). In California, property acquired during marriage by a husband and wife in joint form (*i.e.,* as tenants in common, joint tenants, or tenants by the entirety) is presumed to be their community property upon the marriage's dissolution. Cal. Civ. Code §4800.1(b) (West 1991 Supp.). Some commentators believe that the courts will apply the statutory presumption at death as well.

Upon the death of a spouse, the property formerly owned as community property may be owned by the surviving spouse and the deceased spouse's successors as tenants in common. This result occurs where the community property interest of the deceased spouse is devised to a person other than the surviving spouse or where the deceased spouse dies intestate and the surviving spouse is not entitled to receive all of the deceased spouse's share in the community property under the local law. *See, e.g.,* Wis. Stat. Ann. §861.01(2) (West 1990 Supp.); *Pritchard v. Estate of Tuttle,* 534 S.W.2d 946 (Tex. Civ. App. 1976).

> **Example 3-2.** *H* and *W* owned Whiteacre as community property. *H*'s will devised his interest in Whiteacre to their daughter, *D.* Following *H*'s death *W* and *D* own Whiteacre as tenants in common.

The community property of a couple may also be converted into a tenancy in common owned as separate property in equal shares upon the termination of their marriage, either according to the express terms of a decree of dissolution or by a decree of dissolution that does not dispose of the community property.

> If the marital relationship between the parties is dissolved, the prerequisite to community property is gone. Therefore, the former community property, if not changed from its community status by a transfer while the two were married and if not allocated by the court in the dissolution action, will be held by the former spouses as equal tenants in common. Cross, The Community Property Law in Washington (revised 1985), 61 Wash. L. Rev. 13, 113 (1986).

The same rule is followed in other community property states, including California, *Tarien v. Katz,* 15 P.2d 493 (Cal. 1932), and Texas, *Fox v. Smith,* 531 S.W.2d 654 (Tex. Civ. App. 1975). In the *Fox* case the decedent and his former wife were treated as having owned a profit-sharing plan as tenants in common where contributions were made to the plan only during the marriage and the plan was not allocated in the divorce decree. Community property interests in employee benefit plans are discussed at §3.32. All forms of existing or inchoate community property that are not allocated by decree, including employee benefits and insurance policies, are generally owned by the former spouses as tenants in common. Accordingly, it is important to provide for the disposition of all of the community property of a husband and wife upon dissolution of their marriage.

§3.5. Miscellaneous

The fractional interests of tenants in common in real property may be voluntarily or involuntarily partitioned into individually owned parcels in a court proceeding. If a partition is not practical, a sale of part or all of the property may be required. Although the provisions vary somewhat from state to state, all states provide a form of action for partition of real property. 4A R. Powell, Real Property ¶609 (rev. ed. 1975). Personal property may also be partitioned by voluntary or involuntary action.

§3.6. Creditor's Claims

The interest of a tenant in common is usually subject to creditor's claims to the same extent as other individually-owned property. That is, a creditor may reach the fractional interest of the debtor-tenant, but not the interest of any other tenant. A creditor who forecloses on the debtor's interest in the tenancy becomes a tenant in common in place of the debtor.

§3.7. Gift Tax

The creation of a tenancy in common may constitute a gift, depending upon the manner of creation and the extent of each tenant's interest in the property. A gift results when the tenants contribute unequally toward the purchase price. However, it would qualify for the annual gift tax exclusion. The acquisition of an asset in the names of both spouses as tenants in common would qualify for the unlimited gift tax marital deduction if the donee spouse is a U.S. citizen. If the donee spouse is not a U.S. citizen, no marital deduction is allowed. However, an annual exclusion of $100,000 is available. §2523(i).

> **Example 3-3.** *T* provided the entire purchase price of Greenacre. Title was taken in the names of *T* and *X*, who are not married. Under the local law *T* and *X* own Greenacre as tenants in common. When *T* purchased Greenacre, *T* made a gift of half of the purchase price to *X*. If *X* was a U.S. citizen and was married to *T*, the gift would qualify for the gift tax marital deduction under §2523.

Apart from the marital deduction, the creation of a tenancy in common between spouses is treated in the same way as the creation of the tenancy between unrelated parties.

§3.7.1. Termination

No gift occurs upon the termination of a tenancy in common if each tenant receives a share of the property or its proceeds proportional to his or her ownership interest in the tenancy. A gift does occur, however, if a tenant receives less than his or her proportional share.

Example 3-4. *X* and *Y* each contributed half of the cost of acquiring Blackacre as tenants in common. They recently sold Blackacre for $100,000, of which *X* received $60,000 and *Y* received $40,000. The unequal division of the proceeds involves a gift of $10,000 from *Y* to *X* unless it was made in the ordinary course of business. *See* Reg. §25.2512-8.

§3.7.2. Conversion of Community Property into Tenancy in Common

The conversion of community property into a tenancy in common owned as separate property in equal shares by a husband and wife does not involve a taxable transfer for federal gift or estate tax purposes. *Commissioner v. Mills,* 183 F.2d 32 (9th Cir. 1950); Rev. Rul. 55-709, 1955-2 C.B. 609. In some community property states a husband and wife may hold community property in tenancy in common form. Wis. Stat. Ann. §766.60(4)(a) (West 1991 Supp.). Also, as indicated at §3.4, upon dissolution of marriage property held by a husband and wife as tenants in common is presumed to be community property in California. Cal. Civ. Code §4800.1 (West 1991 Supp.). If a conversion from community property to a tenancy in common is effective, each spouse may be free to dispose of his or her interest in the property by reason of the general rule that one spouse may transfer separate property without the consent of the other spouse. In contrast, neither husband nor wife has the right to make gifts of community property. *See* §3.28.2. Because of the fiduciary relationship between the spouses, a conversion procured by fraud, undue influence, or other inequitable means is vulnerable to challenge by the disadvantaged spouse.

Example 3-5. *H* induced *W* to consent to the formal conversion of their community property ranch into a tenancy in common for "tax reasons." Shortly thereafter, *H* transferred all of his interest in the ranch to his nephew and instituted dissolution proceedings against *W.* The conversion would not involve any gift by *H* or *W.* However, the conversion might be subject to challenge by *W* if it was to her disadvantage.

§3.7.3. Conversion of Tenancy in Common into Community Property

The conversion of separate property held by a husband and wife in a tenancy in common into a community property form of ownership should not involve a gift because the conversion does not alter the value of the interests owned by the husband and wife. Each spouse owned a half interest in the property before and after the transfer. *See* Rev. Rul. 77-359, 1977-2 C.B. 24. As a general rule, no gift occurs where the value of the property interests owned by each spouse does not change as a result of the transfer.

§3.8. Estate Tax

In general, the interest of each tenant is includible in the tenant's gross estate under §2033 in accordance with basic estate tax principles.

> **Example 3-6.** *T* left Blackacre by will "to *A* and *B* in equal shares." Under the local law the devise was effective to constitute *A* and *B* as equal tenants in common. The interests of *A* and *B* are freely transferable. Upon the death of either *A* or *B,* the value of a half interest in Blackacre is includible in his or her estate.

The interest of the surviving tenant in common ordinarily is not includible in a deceased tenant's estate. However, if the deceased tenant died prior to 1982, the entire value of the property was includible in the decedent's estate under §2035(a) if the decedent created the tenancy with his or her own property within three years of death.

The potential inclusion of all of a decedent's joint tenancy property under §2040(a) may be blunted by converting the joint tenancies into tenancies in common. The conversion would eliminate the survivorship feature of the joint tenancy. Particularly in the case of such conversion, each tenant in common should understand that his or her interest in the property is subject to disposition by will. In this connection, note that the unlimited marital deduction and the qualified joint interest rule of §2040(b) make it unnecessary for married joint tenants to attempt to avoid the application of §2040(a).

The courts and the IRS seem to agree that §2040(a) applies only to property held in joint tenancy form at the time of a decedent's death. *See, e.g., Glaser v. United States,* 306 F.2d 57 (7th Cir. 1962); Rev. Rul. 69-577, 1969-2 C.B. 173. Accordingly, the amount of property includible in a joint tenant's estate may be limited by converting a joint tenancy into a tenancy in common prior to the joint tenant's death. As indicated above, such a conversion occurs if one of the tenants transfers an interest in the property to another person or the survivorship feature is eliminated by agreement or judicial action. This rule applies even when the severance is made with three years of death.

> **Example 3-7.** *X,* who was not married to *Y,* paid the entire cost of acquiring Blackacre. Title was taken in the names of "*X* and *Y* as joint tenants with right of survivorship." The purchase of

the property involved a gift from *X* to *Y* of half of the value of Blackacre. If the title remains in that form, the entire value of Blackacre is includible in *X*'s estate under §2040(a). However, only half of the value of Blackacre is includible in *X*'s estate if the joint tenancy is terminated prior to *X*'s death. The necessary termination might occur if *Y*'s interest is transferred or if the tenants agree to hold the property as tenants in common.

§3.9. INCOME TAX

Neither the creation nor the termination of a tenancy in common usually involves any recognition of gain or other income tax consequences. The income from property owned as tenants in common is taxed to the tenants in accordance with their respective rights to the income under the local law. In the absence of a contrary agreement, each tenant is ordinarily entitled to a part of the income proportionate to his or her ownership interest in the property. No gain or loss is recognized on the transfer of property from one spouse to another if the transferee spouse is a U.S. citizen. §1041.

§3.10. USE IN ESTATE PLANNING

The tenancy in common is used infrequently in planning and organizing the ownership of family wealth. However, individuals sometimes wish to convey or devise interests in real or personal property to children or other family members as tenants in common. The transfer of property to multiple parties as tenants in common is often preferable to its transfer to them as joint tenants with right of survivorship. Indeed, some states bar the creation of joint tenancies and some others have abolished the incident of survivorship. *See* §3.12. In rare cases a testator may leave property to several individuals as tenants in common in order to force them to cooperate with each other — at least minimally. For example, Canadian lawyer Charles Millar left his home in Jamaica to three acquaintances "who each had an abiding dislike for one another, so naturally Millar thought it would be a good idea if they lived together." R. S. Menchin, The Last Caprice 28 (1963).

The management and operation of the property and the relations between parties are often complicated by joint ownership. Those factors may be relieved if each transferee receives a fee interest in a separate parcel of property instead of owning a larger parcel as cotenants. It is often best to transfer the property to a trustee who can provide unified management for the benefit of multiple donees.

If a client contemplates transferring property to multiple parties as tenants in common the planner should alert the client to the difficulties that can arise regarding the management and disposition of undivided interests in real property. Also, the relationship between cotenants with divergent views can be aggravated by the difficulty of extricating themselves from a tenancy in common. The cost and delay involved in obtaining a satisfactory partition or liquidation of one tenant's interest can be very frustrating. The potential for additional problems is increased if the interests of the tenants are further fractionalized upon their deaths.

Because the tenancy in common lacks a survivorship feature, it does not have the popular appeal of the joint tenancy or some of the other will substitutes. An inter vivos or testamentary trust often provides a far more flexible and intelligent method of arranging title than a tenancy in common.

Individuals sometimes choose to take title to investment property as tenants in common. Those who do should enter into an agreement regarding the property's management and disposition if one or more tenants wish to terminate their coownership. Also, individuals associated in a professional practice may purchase an office building as tenants in common. For example, partners in a medical practice may acquire real property initially as tenants in common. *Perry v. United States,* 520 F.2d 235 (4th Cir. 1975), *cert. denied,* 423 U.S. 1052 (1976). However, the ownership of such a building by the partnership, or a corporation or trust created by the parties, is more typical.

All in all, the creation of a tenancy in common probably results more often from the absence of effective estate planning than from an intelligently formulated plan.

C. JOINT TENANCY AND TENANCY BY THE ENTIRETY

§3.11. INTRODUCTION

The joint tenancy with right of survivorship has long been a popular form of coownership, particularly by husbands and wives. Hines, Personal Property Joint Tenancies: More Law, Fact and Fancy, 51 Iowa L. Rev. 582 (1966). The popularity of the joint tenancy is primarily attributable to the right of survivorship, which makes it a simple and effective probate avoidance device. Because of the survivorship feature, when a joint tenant dies the surviving joint tenant or tenants own the entire interest in the property by operation of law. Thus, a deceased tenant's interest is not subject to disposition by will or administration in the decedent's estate. However, under the U.P.C. joint tenancy property is included in a deceased spouse's augmented estate for purposes of the surviving spouse's right of election. U.P.C. §2-202(b).

§3.11.1. Advantages

A comprehensive article by Professor Regis Campfield, Estate Planning for Joint Tenancies, 1974 Duke L.J. 669, 671-673, identified the following commonly recognized advantages of the joint tenancy:

1. Jointly held property oftentimes enjoys preferential treatment for state death tax purposes;
2. Jointly held property is free from the claims of creditors of either spouse;
3. Joint property expresses the idea of partnership in a marriage and reinforces family security and harmony;
4. Joint property reduces administration costs;
5. Joint property avoids probate delays;
6. Joint property avoids publicity;
7. Joint property is convenient; and
8. Joint property avoids fragmentation of ownership.

In recent years some of the advantages have declined in importance and others have been eliminated. The repeal of separate state death tax systems has virtually eliminated the preferential tax treatment of joint tenancies. Similarly, under U.P.C. §6-215 the personal representative of a deceased party to a multiparty account in a financial institution may recover the decedent's interest in the account "to the extent needed to pay claims against the estate and statutory allowances to the surviving spouse and children."

§3.11.2. Disadvantages

The principal disadvantages of joint tenancies spring from their general inflexibility and the inability of tenants to dispose of the property by will except upon the death of the survivor. The potentially adverse estate tax consequences of joint ownership by spouses were largely eliminated by the adoption of the unlimited marital deduction in the 1981 Act. However, the excessive use of joint tenancies may deprive a decedent's estate of needed cash, thereby causing problems of liquidity. It also deprives the survivors of income-tax-splitting opportunities to the extent the estate is eliminated as a separate income-tax-paying entity. *See* §4.6. The principal vice of the joint tenancy is that the entire interest in the property passes to the surviving tenant outright — which makes it all subject to inclusion in his or her estate.

Joint tenancies are not complete will substitutes and should not be taken as such. It is almost invariably necessary for the tenants to have wills to dispose of other assets or all of the property if the testator is the survivor, and to appoint guardians for minor children.

Overall, the joint tenancy is neither an estate planning panacea nor a disaster. It is reasonable for some persons with small estates to hold all of their property in joint tenancies and for most persons to hold some of their property, such as checking or savings accounts, in one. "All joint tenancies are not cursed. Ordinarily, there would not seem to be any real harm in spouses holding their house as joint tenants, or maintaining their household bank account in that manner." Manning, Planning for Problems Created by Various Types of Property and Ownership, N.Y.U., 30th Inst. Fed. Tax 623, 660 (1972).

§3.12. Features of Joint Tenancies

Most states allow two or more individuals to hold real or personal property in joint tenancy, under which each tenant owns an equal, undivided interest in the property. The joint tenancy is distinguished from the tenancy in common primarily by the right of survivorship. As mentioned above, the right of survivorship operates upon the death of one tenant so that the surviving tenant (or tenants) becomes the exclusive owner (or owners) of the property. Because of the survivorship feature, an artificial legal entity, such as a corporation, cannot be a joint tenant. However, individual fiduciaries — trustees or personal representatives — may hold fiduciary property as joint tenants. In a few states joint tenancies between a husband and wife are severed if they are divorced. *See* §3.3.

Joint tenancies were once favored by the law; however, now they are generally disfavored by both judicial decisions and legislative enactments. The law of many states provides that a joint tenancy may only be established by a written instrument that expressly declares the interest created to be a joint tenancy. *E.g.,* Cal. Civ. Code §683 (West 1990 Supp.); Nev. Rev. Stat. §111.060 (1987); N.Y. Est. Powers & Trusts Law §6-2.2(a) (McKinney 1990 Supp.); Wash. Rev. Code §64.28.087 (1989). The courts have generally required complete compliance with such statutes in order to create a valid joint tenancy. Accordingly, a conveyance "to *A* and *B* jointly" would probably not create a joint tenancy. Instead, *A* and *B* would probably hold the property as tenants in common. *See* §3.3. Joint tenancies in land have been abolished in some states. *E.g.,* Or. Rev. Stat. §93.180 (1990). Statutes in some other states abolish survivorship as an incident of joint tenancies. N.C. Gen. Stat. §41-2 (1989).

§3.12.1. Multiparty Financial Accounts

Joint accounts in financial institutions are generally subject to special statutory provisions that impose different requirements. The accounts are often called "joint tenancy accounts," but they ordinarily would not qualify under the common law definition for failure to satisfy the four unities. Unfortunately, the law in most states regarding joint accounts is confusing and unclear. The law regarding multiparty accounts is effectively rationalized and clarified by Article VI, Part 2 of the Uniform Probate Code. 8 U.L.A. 142 (1990 Supp.). An earlier version of Part 2 has been widely adopted. In general, the Uniform Probate Code recognizes that a joint account belongs to the parties in proportion to their respective net contributions to the account. U.P.C. §6-211. Under this approach, the interest of a party *passes* at death to the surviving account holder or holders. U.P.C. §6-212(a). It rejects the joint tenancy theory that each tenant was seized of the whole from the inception of the joint tenancy. Even apart from the U.P.C., in the case of joint accounts the courts may be more willing to treat an ambiguous account as carrying a right of survivorship. For example, in a case involving the question of whether a right or survivorship attached to an account in the name of "*A* or *B*," the Washington Court of Appeals stated that "[w]e think the modern policy favors the avoidance of probate administration by use of joint tenancy survivorship rights." *In re Estate of Bonness,* 535 P.2d 823, 833 (Wash. App. 1975).

§3.12.2. Uniform TOD Security Registration Act

The 1989 revision of U.P.C. Article VI includes the Uniform Transfer on Death (TOD) Security Registration Act. 8 U.L.A. §6-301 *et seq.* (1990). The TOD provisions authorize securities to be registered in a "beneficiary form," which indicates the owner of the security and "the intention of the owner regarding the person who will become the owner of the security upon the death of the owner." U.P.C. §6-301(1). The requisite intent is shown by registration use of the words "transfer on death," or TOD, "pay on death," or POD. *See* U.P.C. §6-310. Under U.P.C. §6-302, "multiple owners of a security registered in beneficiary form hold as joint tenants with right of survivorship, as tenants by the entireties, or as owners of community property held in survivorship form, and not as tenants in common."

§3.12.3. Simultaneous Death

Section 3 of the Uniform Simultaneous Death Act, 8A U.L.A. 575 (1983), provides, in substance, that the tenancy is severed in case the joint tenants die simultaneously. Under it the undivided interest of each tenant is distributed as if he or she had survived the other.

> **Example 3-8.** *A* and *B,* who own Blackacre as joint tenants, die simultaneously. The right of survivorship is inoperative. That is, one half of Blackacre will be distributed in the estate of *A* as if *A* were the surviving joint tenant and the other half will be distributed similarly in the estate of *B.*

The estate tax consequences of the simultaneous death of joint tenants are discussed at §3.17.

§3.12.4. Creditor's Rights

The creditors of a joint tenant can ordinarily reach the tenant's undivided interest in the property until the tenant's death. (If a joint tenant's interest is taken in satisfaction of a tenant's debt, the joint tenancy is severed and the holding shifts to a tenancy in common.) The common law does not allow the creditors of a deceased joint tenant to reach the property unless an action was commenced prior to the tenant's death or the property was transferred into the joint tenancy in fraud of creditors. Of course, the limitation on the reach of creditors is meaningful only if the deceased tenant's estate is insolvent or the property of the decedent's estate is otherwise exempt from the reach of creditors. *Rupp v. Kahn,* 55 Cal. Rptr. 108, 113 (Cal. App. 1966), concluded that "the entire title held by a surviving joint tenant resulting from a conveyance by an insolvent without consideration, is subject to the debts of the transferor." The alleged insulation of joint tenancy property from the claims of creditors is often illusory.

§3.12.5. Community Property

Community property states typically allow spouses to acquire and hold property in joint tenancy form. Historically, and analytically, if a valid joint tenancy was created the interest of each spouse was properly characterized as separate property. Following that approach, courts in several community property states held that the joint tenancy and community property forms of ownership were mutually exclusive. In *Estate of Cooke,* 524 P.2d 176 (Idaho 1974), the court put it succinctly:

"[P]roperty held in a joint tenancy between husband and wife is not community property. If a true joint tenancy exists, created according to statute, each spouse owns his or her respective interest as separate property." The same rule was followed in Arizona, California, and New Mexico. *Collier v. Collier,* 242 P.2d 537 (Ariz. 1952); *King v. King,* 236 P. 912 (Cal. 1915); former N.M. Stat. Ann. §40-3-8(6) (1978).

The law of most community property states allows community property to be transmuted into separate forms of ownership, including joint tenancies. However, the policy favoring community property generally requires the proponent of a transmutation to prove it by clear and convincing evidence. *Estate of Bogert,* 531 P.2d 1167 (Idaho 1975).

In recent years several states have adopted statutes under which property held in joint tenancy by husbands and wives is presumed to be community property. *E.g.,* Cal. Civ. Code §4800.1 (West 1990 Supp.); N.M. Stat. Ann. 40-3-8B (1989); Wash. Rev. Code §64.28.040 (1989). Other states now allow community property to be held in survivorship form, including Nevada, Texas, and Wisconsin. Nev. Rev. Stat. §111.064 (1987); Tex. Fam. Code Ann. §451, *et seq.* (Vernon 1990 Supp.); Wis. Stat. Ann. §766.60(5) (West 1990 Supp.). Under Texas Family Code §452 spouses may create a right of survivorship in community property by a writing signed by both of them. The liberality reflected in the statutes adds desirable flexiblity to estate planning. The statutes were intended to allow a survivorship feature to be attached to community property without sacrificing the full step-up in basis that is allowed with respect to community property under §1014(b)(6) on the death of either spouse. Revenue Ruling 87-98, 1987-2 C.B. 206, indicates that the IRS will give effect to the state law and allow the full step-up in basis.

If the interests of a husband and wife in property held by them in joint tenancy are not community property, presumably each is free to make a gratuitous transfer of his or her interest to a person outside the marital community. In contrast, some community property states do not allow a spouse to make an inter vivos gift of community property without the consent of the other spouse. *See* §3.28.2.

§3.13. Tenancy by the Entirety

A tenancy by the entirety is a concurrent estate between husband and wife that was traditionally viewed as "held in its entirety — without undivided shares — by the marital unit of husband and wife." 4A R. Powell, Real Property ¶621(3) (rev. ed. 1990). It resembles a joint tenancy in that both require the four unities and carry a right of survivorship, but it was classically not subject to partition between the spouses and terminated upon dissolution of the marriage. While the tenancy by the entirety form was once favored by the law, it has declined in importance and is now recognized by only 25 states and the District of Columbia. Id., ¶621[4].

The tenancy by the entirety is usually created in land, although some states permit personal property to be held in the same manner. Its characteristics vary from state to state, particularly regarding the rights of the wife. In some states the husband alone is entitled to the income from the property and the wife cannot convey any interest in the property or cause a partition of it. The characteristics of the tenancy, of course, have an impact on its treatment for tax purposes. Thus, under the prior North Carolina law, a gift to a husband and wife did not qualify for the annual exclusion as to the wife's interest because she had no enforceable interest in the rents, income, or profits from the property during coverture. Rev. Rul. 75-8, 1975-1 C.B. 309. Legislation that became effective on January 1, 1983 gave wives in North Carolina an equal interest in tenancy by the entirety property. N.C. Gen. Stat. §39-13.3 (1984).

The tenancy is usually created by a conveyance of real property to a husband and wife, designated as such in the instrument of conveyance. For example, in states that recognize the tenancy, a conveyance of land "to *H* and *W,* husband and wife" is effective to create a tenancy by the entirety between them in the property. The outcome is less certain when other language is used or additional persons also receive interests under the conveyance. When an instrument is ineffective to create a tenancy by the entirety, the transferees usually hold the property as tenants in common. However, under N.Y. Est. Powers & Trusts Law §6-2.2(c) (McKinney 1990 Supp.) a transfer of real property to a "husband and wife" who are not married creates a joint tenancy unless expressly declared to be a tenancy in common.

None of the community property states recognize the tenancy by the entirety. It is mentioned in a Washington statute that expressly abolishes the right of survivorship as an incident of the tenancy by the entirety, Wash. Rev. Code §11.04.071 (1989), but it is not referred to in another statute that lists the permissible forms of joint ownership, Wash. Rev. Code §64.28.020 (1989). Statutes of the latter type have been construed as evidencing the unavailability of the tenancy by the entirety in the jurisdiction. *Swan v. Walden,* 103 P. 931 (Cal. 1909).

At best the common law tenancy by the entirety is an anachronistic duplication of the joint tenancy; at worst it is an unjustifiable form of discrimination against women. The extent to which it will survive, and the characteristics it will have in the future, are uncertain. The characteristics of the tenancy favoring the husband were attacked in several federal court actions. *Klein v. Mayo,* 367 F. Supp. 583 (D. Mass. 1973), *aff'd mem.,* 416 U.S. 953 (1974); *D'Ercole v. D'Ercole,* 407 F. Supp. 1377 (D. Mass. 1976). Although the attacks were unsuccessful, the Massachusetts statute was subsequently amended to eliminate the discrimination against wives.

For estate planning purposes the significance of the tenancy depends upon its characteristics under the governing law. In most cases it will produce the same tax consequences as a joint tenancy, which may or may not meet the needs of a particular couple. The tenancy may also effectively shield the property from the claims of creditors of either spouse. It can be used to obviate the necessity of an estate administration proceeding in another state in which the client owns real property or immovable personalty, but it does not eliminate the need for a proceeding on the death of the surviving tenant. Overall, a revocable trust is better suited to help clients avoid ancillary estate administration proceedings.

§3.14. Gift Tax

The gift tax consequences of creating a joint tenancy or a tenancy by the entirety depend upon whether the tenants are married to each other, the nature and valuation of the interests of the tenants, and the amount each tenant contributes toward the acquisition of the property. Property transferred into joint tenancy form qualifies for the unlimited gift tax marital deduction if the donee spouse is a U.S. citizen. §2523(d). In most states one tenant acting alone can sever the joint tenancy, thereby terminating the right of survivorship and converting the holding into a tenancy in common. Accordingly, in those states each tenant is considered to have an equal interest in the joint tenancy property regardless of age. In contrast, interests must be valued actuarially where the joint tenancy is not unilaterally severable.

> **Example 3-9.** *X,* a 78-year-old unmarried female, conveyed Blackacre into joint tenancy with right of survivorship with *Y,* a 45-year-old male. Under the local law (Michigan), when express words of survivorship are used a joint tenancy may be severed only with the consent of all of the joint tenants. The value of an interest dependent upon the continuation of more than one life is determined by using a special factor which is available from the IRS upon request. Based upon the 6% sex-based tables in effect in 1978 the special factor to be used to value *X*'s retained interest was .21388. Accordingly, the value of *X*'s gift to *Y* is .78612 times the value of Blackacre. *See* LR 7946080 (Michigan law).

In states that allow the unilateral severance of joint tenancies, the creation of a joint tenancy does not involve a gift if each tenant makes an equal contribution toward the acquisition of the property. For example, no gift occurs if community property is used to acquire an asset in joint tenancy. However, a gift of half of the value of the property would occur where one person transfers previously owned property into a joint tenancy without any contribution by the other tenant or tenants. The same result occurs where one person provides the funds with which an asset is purchased and title is taken in the name of the donor and another as joint tenants.

Example 3-10. *X,* an unmarried man, purchased stock with his own funds, the certificates for which were issued in the names of *X* and *Y* as joint tenants with right of survivorship. The purchase of the shares involved a gift to *Y* of half of the fair market value of the stock. The gift tax consequences would have been the same if *X* had transferred the title of stock that he had already owned into the names of *X* and *Y* as joint tenants with right of survivorship.

The interest transferred to the donee constitutes a present interest that qualifies for the annual gift tax exclusion. As noted above, the interest qualifies for the marital deduction where the donor and donee are married and the donee spouse is a U.S. citizen. Section 2523(d) provides expressly that the survivorship interest of the donor and the right of severability do not constitute a retained interest for purposes of determining whether the interest was terminable under §2523(b).

Example 3-11. *W* paid $50,000 of her noncommunity property for securities that were issued in the names of *W* and *H* as joint tenants with right of survivorship. The total gift to *H* was $25,000, which qualifies for the annual exclusion and the marital deduction.

§3.14.1. Revocable Transfers

There is an important exception to the basic rule that a transfer of property by a donor into joint tenancy with a donee is a present gift. It treats the creation of a joint tenancy in certain types of assets as a revocable transfer that does not involve a present gift. In those cases the donor has the right to recover the entire interest in the property at any time without obligation to the donee. Within this exception are joint bank accounts; joint U.S. savings bonds (*i.e.,* ones acquired in the names of "donor or donee"), Reg. §25.2511-1(h)(4); and joint accounts with brokerage firms where the securities are held by the firm in "street name" (*i.e.,* the securities are registered in the name of the firm's nominee), Rev. Rul. 69-148, 1969-1 C.B. 226.

Example 3-12. *X* deposited funds in a joint account in the name of *X* and *Y* at a financial institution. Under the local law *X* may withdraw the entire fund without the consent of *Y. X* did not make a gift at the time of the deposit of the funds. However, a gift occurs at any time *Y* withdraws funds without any obligation to account to *X*.

In general, where a donor places funds in a joint tenancy that allows the donor to withdraw the full amount without obligation to the donee, no gift takes place until the donee withdraws the funds for his or her own account.

§3.14.2. Pre-1982 Transfers of Real Property to a Spouse

Prior to 1982 the creation of a joint tenancy in real property between husband and wife was not deemed a transfer for gift tax purposes regardless of the proportion of the consideration furnished by each spouse unless the donor elected to treat the transaction as a gift by filing a timely gift tax return. *See* former §2515(a), (c). If the donor spouse did not treat the creation of the joint tenancy as a gift, the donor was treated as owner of the entire property for most gift and estate tax purposes. Thus, a gift took place if the joint tenancy was later terminated and the donor spouse did not receive all of the proceeds of the termination. Former §2515(b).

Example 3-13. In 1979 *W* provided all of the funds used to purchase Blackacre. Title was taken in the names of *H* and *W* as joint tenants with right of survivorship. *W* did not file a gift tax return treating the purchase of Blackacre as a gift. *H* and *W* sold Blackacre in 1981 for $100,000, half of which was paid to each of them. The sale constituted a termination of the joint tenancy under former §2515(b) and the payment of $50,000 to *H* was treated as a gift. Of course, the gift qualified for the gift tax exclusion and the pre-1982 gift tax marital deduction under §2523.

Note that under §2523(i)(3) the creation of a joint tenancy between a husband and wife in real property is subject to the pre-1982 law where the donee spouse is not a U.S. citizen, except that donor cannot elect to treat the transfer as a gift. Thus, the full amount of the property is subject to inclusion in the donor spouse's estate under §2040(a).

Under former §2515(a) additions to the value of the joint tenancy property or reductions in the indebtedness thereon were subject to the same election.

Under the pre-1982 law an election under §2515(c) also had important estate tax consequences. If creation of the joint tenancy was reported as a gift, each spouse was treated as owning a half-interest in the property for estate tax purposes. Former §2040(b). Otherwise, the entire value of the joint tenancy property was includible in the donor spouse's estate if the donor died first. Former §2040(a). None of the value was includible in the estate of the donee spouse if he or she died first. As illustrated by the following example, reporting the creation of the joint tenancy as a gift was disadvantageous in some cases.

Example 3-14. In 1978 *W* paid the entire $100,000 cost of acquiring Blackacre, title to which was taken in the name of "*H* and *W* as joint tenants with right of survivorship." *W* elected to report the creation of the joint tenancy as a gift under §2515. Because *W* had already made gifts of more than $100,000 to *H,* the purchase of Blackacre resulted in a taxable gift of $47,000 (½ × $100,000 − $3,000 annual exclusion). When *H* died in 1981, half of the value of Blackacre was included in his gross estate. Thereafter, *W* owned the entire interest in Blackacre — all of which is includible in her estate. Under the pre-1982 law *W*'s election under §2515 caused the same one-half interest to be subject to transfer tax three times.

Under the pre-1982 law if one spouse provided all of the consideration for the acquisition of *personal property* in joint tenancy with the other spouse, the donor spouse was considered to have made a gift to the donee spouse of half of the value of the property. Former §2515A. In such a case the donor spouse had no election: The donor spouse was treated as having made a gift of half of the value of the property. The rule of §2515A applies to gifts made to a spouse who is not a U.S. citizen. Note that the qualified joint interest rule of §2040(b) does not apply where the donee spouse is a noncitizen at the time of the donor spouse's death. §2056(d)(1).

§3.15. ESTATE TAX: GENERAL RULE, §2040(a)

Under the general rule of §2040(a) a decedent's estate includes the full value of property held with others in a joint and survivorship form except to the extent the property is traceable to contributions made by others. The rule is fleshed out in Reg. §20.2040-1(a), which requires the inclusion of

> [P]roperty held jointly at the time of the decedent's death by the decedent and another person or persons with right of survivorship, as follows:
>
> (1) To the extent that the property was acquired by the decedent and the other joint owner or owners by gift, devise, bequest, or inheritance, the decedent's fractional share of the property is included.
>
> (2) In all other cases, the entire value of the property is included

> except such part of the entire value as is attributable to the amount of the consideration in money or money's worth furnished by the other joint owner or owners. . . .

In particular, the entire value of jointly held property is included in the estate of a deceased joint tenant "unless the executor submits facts sufficient to show that property was not acquired entirely with consideration furnished by the decedent, or was acquired by the decedent and the other joint owner or owners by gift, bequest, devise, or inheritance." Reg. §20.2040-1(a)(2).

§3.15.1. Contributions by Surviving Tenant

If the survivor contributed toward the acquisition of the joint tenancy, a proportionate part of its value is excluded from the decedent's estate. This "proportionate contribution" rule applies whether or not the creation of the joint tenancy was treated as a gift. The proportionate contribution rule continues to apply to all joint tenancies *other than* qualified joint interests (*i.e.,* a tenancy by the entirety or a joint tenancy of which the decedent and his or her spouse were the only tenants, §2040(b)). *See* §3.16.

The application of the basic rule is illustrated in the following example.

> **Example 3-15.** *O* and *P* each contributed half of the cost of purchasing securities. Certificates were issued in their names as joint tenants. Upon the death of either *O* or *P,* half of the value of the securities is includible in the decedent's gross estate.

However, if the decedent had given the survivor the money or other property that the survivor contributed toward the cost of acquiring the property, the entire value of the property is includible in the decedent's gross estate. The rule is the same where the property contributed by the survivor toward the acquisition increased in value between the date of the gift to the survivor and the acquisition of the joint tenancy property. Reg. §20.2040-1(c)(4).

The contribution of the surviving joint tenant toward the cost of acquiring joint tenancy property, although derived from a gift received from the decedent, is taken into account in some cases. Specifically, any income received by the survivor on property given to him or her by the decedent and applied toward the acquisition of the join tenancy property is counted as a contribution by the survivor. Reg. §20.2040-1(c)(5). Gain received by the survivor on property given to him or her by the decedent is also taken into account. Thus, "[w]hen the transfer to the joint tenancy consists of proceeds realized by the survivor upon a sale of property acquired with monies transferred from the decedent, the sale proceeds attributable to appreciation in value during the survivor's ownership of the acquired property are considered the survivor's individual contribution to the joint tenancy for purposes of section 2040." Rev. Rul. 79-372, 1979-2 C.B. 330. *See also Estate of Marcia P. Goldsborough,* 70 T.C. 1077 (1978).

The basic proportionate contribution rule and not the special rule of §2040(b) applies if the decedent's surviving spouse is not a U.S. citizen. §2056(d)(1)(B). Thus, a decedent's estate must include the full value of a joint tenancy to which an alien surviving spouse made no contribution. However, under §7815(d)(16) of the 1989 Act, an alien surviving spouse is treated as having contributed to the joint tenancy to the extent the survivor received an interest in the property by gift prior to July 18, 1988. The House Committee Report explained the provision in the following passage:

> A gift made by creating a joint tenancy in property prior to July 14, 1988 is treated as consideration belonging to the surviving spouse for purposes of determining the value of the tenancy includible in the decedent spouse's estate. Accordingly, the amount of joint tenancy property included in the spouse's estate is reduced proportionately by the amount of the gift. H.R. Rep. No. 101-247, 101 Cong., 1st Sess. 1429.

The effect of the 1989 change is illustrated in the following example:

> **Example 3-16.** In 1987 *W* paid $100,000 for Blackacre, title to which was taken in the name of *W* and her alien husband, *H.* The gift of a one-half interest in Blackacre was reported on a gift tax return filed by *W* for 1987. An annual gift tax exclusion of $10,000 and a marital deduction of $40,000 were claimed on the return. *W* died in 1991 when Blackacre was worth $200,000. *W* was survived by *H,* who remained an alien. For purposes of §2040(a) *H* is treated as having contributed half of the cost of acquiring Blackacre. Accordingly, $100,000 is includible in *W*'s gross estate. A marital deduction is allowable for this amount only if *H* transfers the property to a qualified domestic trust. *See* §2056A. *See also* §5.25.

§3.15.2. Gifts to Decedent and Survivor as Joint Tenants

If an asset was gratuitously transferred to the decedent and others as joint tenants, only the decedent's pro rata share of the property is includible in his or her estate. For example, if Blackacre was devised to *A* and *B* as joint tenants, only half of the value of Blackacre is included in the estate of the first of them to die. *See* Reg. §20.2040-1(c), examples 7-8. The proportionate interest includible in the gross estate of a deceased tenant is increased, however, if he or she made subsequent unreimbursed contributions in connection with the property (*e.g.,* additions or improvements).

§3.16. Qualified Joint Interests, §2040(b)

> In view of the unlimited marital deduction adopted by the committee bill, the taxation of jointly held property between spouses is only relevant for determining the basis of property to the survivor (under sec. 1014) and the qualification for certain provisions (such as current use valuation under §2032A, deferred payment of estate taxes under secs. 6166 and 6166A, and for income taxation of redemptions to pay death taxes and administration expenses under sec. 303). Accordingly, the committee believes it appropriate to adopt an easily administered rule under which each spouse would be considered to own one-half of jointly held property regardless of which spouse furnished the original consideration. H.R. Rep. No. 97-201, 97th Cong., 1st Sess. 160 (1981).

The 1976 Act added §2040(b), which introduced the concept of the "qualified joint interest" between husband and wife (half of which is includible in the estate of the spouse who dies first). For purposes of §2040 a qualified joint interest is a joint tenancy (or tenancy by the entirety) in which the husband and wife are the only tenants. The 1981 Act eliminated the requirement, initially imposed by the 1976 Act, that the creation of the joint tenancy must have been treated as a gift for gift tax purposes. Providentially, the more complex rules of §§2040(c)-(e) were repealed by the 1981 Act. Note that §2040(b) does not apply unless the surviving spouse is a U.S. citizen. §2056(d)(1)(B).

Treatment as a qualified joint interest under §2040(b) usually results in no particular advantage because the unlimited marital deduction is available to the estate of the spouse who dies first. Of course, it does result in a stepped-up basis of *only* the portion included in the decedent's estate.

Example 3-17. In 1987 *W* paid $50,000 for stock that was issued in the name of "*H* and *W* as joint tenants with right of survivorship." The purchase of the stock resulted in a gift of $25,000 to *H,* which qualified for the annual gift tax exclusion and the marital deduction. When *W* died in 1991, survived by *H,* the stock was worth $200,000. Half of the value of the stock, $100,000, was included in *W*'s gross estate, which qualified for the estate tax marital deduction. The basis of the one-half interest in the stock included in *W*'s estate was adjusted under §1014; *H* retains the unadjusted basis of $25,000 in the other half. When *H* dies, the full value of the stock will be includible in his estate. The results would have been the same had *H* predeceased *W*.

Essentially the same tax treatment applies to property acquired by the spouses as tenants in common where the interest of the spouse who dies first is left to the surviving spouse. In such a case the interest of the spouse first to die is included in his or her estate, but an offsetting marital deduction is allowable.

§3.17. Estate Tax: Simultaneous Deaths

Adverse estate tax consequences may occur if joint tenants other than a husband and wife die simultaneously. Under §3 of the Uniform Simultaneous Death Act, "[w]here there is no sufficient evidence that two cotenants or tenants by the entirety have died otherwise than simultaneously the property so held shall be distributed one-half as if one had survived and one-half as if the other had survived." 8A U.L.A. 575 (1983). In two Revenue Rulings the IRS has asserted that if this act is applicable, the entire value of the property is includible in the gross estate of the tenant who provided all of the consideration paid to acquire the property and one-half is includible in the estate of the other tenant. Rev. Rul. 66-60, 1966-1 C.B. 221; Rev. Rul. 76-303, 1976-2 C.B. 266. Presumably the IRS analysis does not apply to qualified joint interests which are subject to the special rule of §2040(b). In other cases the adverse effect should be reduced by the availability of the previously taxed property credit under §2013. The rule also could be avoided if the sole contributor were deemed to be the survivor.

In Revenue Ruling 66-60, the government asserted that the full value of the property was includible under §2040 in the gross estate of the tenant who provided the full consideration (*H*) and one-half was includible under §2033 in the estate of the other tenant (*W*) because under the Uniform Simultaneous Death Act the survivor had the power to dispose of one-half of the property. The analysis was changed by Revenue Ruling 76-303, which held that §2040 applies only if the other tenant survives. Accordingly, only the value of the one-half of the property with respect to which *W* was considered to have survived was includible in *H*'s estate under §2040. The full value of that half was includible because there was no evidence that *W* had furnished any consideration for the acquisition of the property. However, none of the value of the one-half interest with respect to which *H* was deemed to be the survivor was includible in *W*'s estate under §2040 because *H* provided all of the consideration for the property.

Revenue Ruling 76-303 also held that half of the value of the property was includible in each tenant's gross estate under §2033: "[S]ince each is considered to have survived as to one-half of the property, each is considered to have acquired an absolute, sole ownership interest in one-half of the property before death. Thus, the value of one-half of the property is includible in each of their gross estates under section 2033 of the Code." Under this approach the one-half interest included in *H*'s estate should have qualified for the marital deduction. In other instances a previously taxed property credit should be available to the survivor's estate under §2013.

Of course, these rulings antedated the adoption of the qualified joint interest rule of §2040(b). Accordingly, they only involved the proportionate contribution rule and did not indicate that any different result would occur if the joint tenants were husband and wife. In the case of the simultaneous deaths of a husband and wife after 1981, presumably half of the total value of the joint tenancy property would be included in each spouse's estate under §2040(b). If each such interest is disposed of as if the decedent's spouse did not survive, then no marital deduction would be available. In such a case it would be difficult to uphold the inclusion of any additional amount of the property in either spouse's estate. On the other hand, if a marital deduction were allowed for the one-half included in one spouse's estate, then the full value of the property should be included in the other spouse's estate under §2033.

The position taken in Revenue Ruling 76-303 might also be contested on the basis of the Tax Court's holding in *Estate of Nathalie Koussevitsky,* 5 T.C. 650 (1945), *acq.,* 1945 C.B. 4, that when §2040 is applicable no section other than §2035 may also be applied. The contest might be assisted by the general hostility of the courts to the operation of §2040.

§3.18. Estate Tax: Termination of Joint Tenancies

As noted above, the proportionate contribution rule of §2040(a) is restricted if the joint tenancy is terminated, even though the termination occurs within three years of death. Section 2040 applies to property "held jointly at the time of the decedent's death by the decedent and another person or persons with right of survivorship." Reg. §20.2040-1(a). Most important, the courts have held that §2040 has no application to property transferred before the decedent's death. *E.g., Glaser v. United States,* 306 F.2d 57 (7th Cir. 1962). If the creation of the joint tenancy is treated as a gift, a severance allows one-half of the post-gift appreciation to escape taxation on the death of the donor. Of course, this result will occur without a severance where the tenants are husband and wife and the joint tenancy is a qualified joint interest under §2040(b). *See* §3.16. A severance can backfire if the donee tenant predeceases the donor. In such a case the proportionate contribution rule of §2040(a) no longer applies and the full value of the donee's interest in the property is includible in the donee's estate.

In the past some commentators complained that the treatment given terminated joint tenancies was unduly favorable and was based on an unnecessarily narrow construction of the statute. *See* C. Lowndes, R. Kramer & J. McCord, Federal Estate & Gift Taxes 284-285 (3d ed. 1974); Campfield, Estate Planning for Joint Tenancies, 1974 Duke L.J. 669, 707-708. Given the unification of the transfer tax system and the adoption of the unlimited marital deduction, it is hard to become too concerned over the issue. However, the present treatment is undesirable in the sense that it represents a triumph of form over substance and places a premium on obtaining sophisticated estate planning advice. The law would be simpler and more straightforward if it simply required the inclusion of a proportionate interest in the property upon the death of any joint tenant.

Example 3-18. *X* paid the full $100,000 cost of acquiring Blackacre. Title was taken in the name of *X* and his brother, *Y*, as joint tenants with right of survivorship. The purchase of Blackacre resulted in a gift of $50,000 from *X* to *Y* which qualified for the annual gift tax exclusion. The joint tenancy in Blackacre was severed a week before *X* died, when it had a value of $200,000. As a result, *X* and *Y* held Blackacre as tenants in common. The severance did not result in a gift, because *X* and *Y* each already owned a full one-half interest in Blackacre. *Estate of Sullivan v. Commissioner,* 175 F.2d 657 (9th Cir. 1949). *X*'s estate includes half of the value of Blackacre at the time of his death ($100,000). The amount of the original taxable gift is probably includible in *X*'s tax base as a post-1976 adjusted taxable gift. *See* §2001(b).

Example 3-19. The facts are the same as in Example 3-18, *supra.* However, instead of severing the joint tenancy and holding Blackacre as tenants in common, *X* and *Y* transferred their interests to a trust from which each was entitled to receive one-half of the income and to dispose of one-half of the principal. Only one-half of the trust property is includible in *X*'s gross estate under §2036 on account of his reserved life estate. Rev. Rul. 69-577, 1969-2 C.B. 173. The same result would follow if they transferred Blackacre to other parties, reserving life estates to themselves.

United States v. Heasty, 370 F.2d 525 (10th Cir. 1966). Presumably the adoption of §2035(d) does not affect the outcome in this case.

§3.19. Disclaimers, §§2046, 2518

Effective post-mortem planning may call for a surviving joint tenant to disclaim the right to become the sole owner of the property that was held in joint tenancy. The use of disclaimers in connection with joint tenancy interests is discussed in detail in §12.33. For example, a surviving spouse may disclaim some joint tenancy interests in order to "fine tune" the amount of property passing to him or her for purposes of achieving the optimum estate tax marital deduction. The disclaimer may allow the survivors to salvage the benefits of a carefully constructed estate plan that would otherwise be jeopardized by the parties' unwitting transfer of too much of their property into joint tenancies. Joint tenancies and the benefits of other survivorship arrangements may also be disclaimed in order to make the decedent's fractional interest subject to his or her will. Thus, the right to receive the decedent's fractional interest in the property may be disclaimed in favor of its passage under the decedent's will to a charity or other beneficiaries or to a trust.

§3.20. Income Tax

The creation of a joint tenancy does not ordinarily have any immediate income tax consequences. However, the transfer of some special types of assets may generate an income tax liability. In particular, the transfer of property into joint tenancy probably constitutes at least a partial disposition of installment obligations under §453B and investment recapture ("section 38") property under §47(a). The creation of a joint tenancy ordinarily should not involve recapture of depreciation under §§1245 or 1250 because recapture does not take place in the case of transfers by gift. No gain or loss is recognized on any transfer between spouses or incident to a divorce provided the trransferee is a U.S. citizen. §§47(e), 453B(g), 1041.

In some unusual cases the creation of a joint tenancy may be treated as a taxable event and result in the recognition of gain by one or more taxpayers. As one author indicates, "[t]axable gain may also be realized upon creation of the joint tenancy if it is created by an exchange of property owned by one of the joint tenants where the property exchanged does not constitute a like kind property within section 1031 — for example, where corporate stock owned by one joint tenant is exchanged for real estate which is conveyed in joint tenancy." Young, Tax Incidents of Joint Ownership, 1959 U. Ill. L. Rev. 972, 977.

> **Example 3-20.** *X,* who owned ABC stock with a basis of $100 and a fair market value of $1,000, converts that stock into a joint tenancy with *Y;* in exchange *Y* converts XYZ stock, which has a basis and a fair market value of $1,000, into joint tenancy with *X.* In effect *X* transfers an asset with a basis of $50 (a one-half interest in the ABC stock) in exchange for an asset worth $500 (a one-half interest in the XYZ stock). Presumably the gain is taxable to *X* at the time of the exchange. *Y* has no gain or loss as a result of the transaction.

If the exchange involved stock in the same corporation, the transaction might not be taxable by reason of §1036. *See* Rev. Rul. 66-248, 1966-2 C.B. 303 (the conversion by a husband and wife of equal amounts of common stock in the same corporation from separate to community was nontaxable). Although a transfer between husband and wife would not be taxable by reason of §1041, the holding of Revenue Ruling 66-248 should shield other taxpayers from any recognition of gain or loss.

§3.20.1. Income from Joint Tenancy Property

In the absence of an agreement to the contrary, each joint tenant is usually entitled under the local law to an equal share of the income from joint tenancy property. *E.g., Lipsitz v. Commissioner,* 200 F.2d 871 (4th Cir.), *cert. denied,* 350 U.S. 845 (1955) (Maryland law). The income attributable to each tenant is determined by reference to the state law — not necessarily according to the extent of the contributions the tenant made toward acquiring the asset. As indicated above, an unequal distribution of income may constitute a taxable gift from one tenant to the other.

§3.20.2. Income Tax Deductions

Conceptually a tenant should be entitled to deduct the taxes and interest the tenant pays only to the extent it exceeds the tenant's right to reimbursement from other tenants. *See* 3 A. J. Casner, Estate Planning 34 (5th ed. 1986). However, a tenant may be entitled to deduct the amount of taxes and interest he or she actually pays on joint tenancy property where the tenants are jointly and severally liable to make the payments. Revenue Ruling 71-268, 1971-1 C.B. 58, followed such a rule in the case of a tenancy by the entirety where the husband and wife filed separate income tax returns. On the other hand, the ruling may merely evidence a more liberal policy of allowing deductions to married persons who make payments without regard to any right of reimbursement. *See* Young, Tax Incidents of Joint Ownership, 1959 U. Ill. L. Rev. 972, 988. Where the joint tenants are husband and wife, the allocation of income and expenses is unnecessary if they file a joint income tax return.

§3.20.3. Basis; General Rule

The basis of the joint tenants is determined according to the ordinary rules applicable to acquisitions by purchase, §1012, gift, §1015, and inheritance, §1014.

> **Example 3-21.** *X* provided the entire purchase price of Redacre. Title was taken in the name of *X* and *Y* as joint tenants. *X* has made a gift of a half-interest in Redacre to *Y*. *Y*'s basis in the property is one-half of *X*'s cost basis, increased under §1015(d)(6) by the portion of any gift tax paid that is attributable to the appreciation element. However, in no event can *Y*'s basis exceed the fair market value of the interest on the date of the gift.

Under §1014(b)(9) the basis of a surviving joint tenant is determined by the federal estate tax valuation in the decedent's estate to the extent that the property is includible in the decedent's estate. Rev. Rul. 56-215, 1956-1 C.B. 324.

> **Example 3-22.** *F* and *G* each paid $5,000 as the cost of acquiring Whiteacre, title to which was taken in their names as joint tenants. The property increased in value from $10,000 at the time of acquisition to $20,000 on the date of *F*'s death. Half of the then value of Whiteacre, $10,000, is includible in *F*'s gross estate. *G*'s basis in the property is $15,000, a composite of *G*'s cost basis, $5,000, and the federal estate tax valuation of the interest included in *F*'s estate, $10,000.

Section 2040 cannot be used by a survivor to gain an unwarranted increase in basis. That is, a survivor will not receive an increased basis in the whole of joint tenancy property merely by failing to rebut the presumption of §2040(a) that all of the property is includible in the gross estate of the first tenant to die. *Richard v. Madden,* 52 T.C. 845 (1969), *aff'd per curiam,* 440 F.2d 784 (7th Cir. 1971). Also, an estate cannot elect to use the alternate valuation date unless (1) the decedent's estate was required to file an estate tax return, and (2) the election decreases the value of the gross estate and the sum of the estate and generation-skipping transfer taxes. §2032(c); Reg. §20.2032-1(b); Rev. Rul. 56-60, 1956-1 C.B. 443.

§3.20.4. Special Basis Rule, §1014(e)

Under §1014(e), which was added in 1981, the basis of appreciated property transferred by gift to a decedent within one year prior to death is not adjusted where the property passes directly or indirectly from the donee-decedent to the donor or the donor's spouse. Thus, the rule would bar a step-up in the basis of appreciated property that a donor transferred into joint tenancy with a donee within a year prior to the donee's death. Of course, the amount included in the deceased donee's estate would be limited by §2040(a) in any case. Note that the bar of §1014(e) applies to property that passes directly or indirectly from the donee to the donor *or* the donor's spouse. Accordingly, there is no step-up in basis of appreciated property transferred by the donor into a joint tenancy with the donee and the donor *or* the donor's spouse. The application of this rule to community property is discussed at §3.35.5.

§3.20.5. Depreciation Adjustment to Basis, §1014(b)(9)

Under §1014(b)(9) a survivor's basis in property acquired from a decedent prior to death *and* included in the decedent's estate is reduced to the extent the deductions were allowable to the survivor "for exhaustion, wear and tear, obsolescence, amortization, and depletion on such property before the death of the decedent." §1014(b)(9). Note that a reduction is made only with respect to the basis of an interest that is included in a decedent's gross estate. In most states, as between two joint tenants, each is entitled to half of the income and is chargeable with half of the expenses of joint tenancy property. Accordingly, the survivor's basis in the property would be reduced by half of the depreciation deductions that were allowable following the creation of the joint tenancy. Under the prior law of some states all of the income of a tenancy by the entirety was allocable to the husband. In such a case on the death of the husband no adjustment was required under §1014(b)(9) because the survivor was not entitled to any of the income or deductions with respect to the property. *See, e.g.,* Rev. Rul. 75-142, 1975-1 C.B. 256 (tenancy by the entirety, Michigan law).

Example 3-23. In 1985 *X* paid $100,000 for depreciable property. Title was taken in the names of *X* and her brother, *B,* as joint tenants with right of survivorship. Depreciation deductions of $5,000 were allowable annually to *X* and *B*. *X* died in 1990, survived by *B*, when the property was worth $150,000. The full value of the property, $150,000, was included in *X*'s gross estate. *B*'s basis in the property is the federal estate tax value of the property in *X*'s estate, $150,000, *less* $25,000 — the amount of depreciation allowable to *B* for the period between the creation of the joint tenancy and the death of *X*. If *X* had been entitled to all of the income under the state law, the basis of *B* would not be reduced under §1014(b)(9). Rev. Rul. 75-142, 1975-1 C.B. 256.

§3.20.6. Community Property in Joint Tenancy

> If property held in a common law estate is community property under state law, it is community property for purposes of section 1014(b)(6) of the Code, regardless of the form in which title was taken. Rev. Rul. 87-98, 1987-2 C.B. 207.

As noted in §3.12.5, Wisconsin and several of the other community property states allow community property to be held in survivorship form. Others presume that property held by a husband and wife in joint tenancy or community property form is their community property. In either case Revenue Ruling 87-98 indicates that the property would be recognized as community property entitled to a fully adjusted basis under §1014(b)(6) on the death of either spouse. The survivor's interest in community property is considered to have been acquired from the decedent and, hence, its basis is determined by reference to the federal estate tax value of the decedent's interest. When the federal estate tax value in the decedent's estate exceeds the otherwise determined basis of the survivor in the property (*e.g.*, its cost), the rule of §1014(b)(6) operates in the taxpayer's favor. In such cases the survivor's basis is increased without any tax cost whatever. A higher basis is of obvious advantage, for example, in the case of depreciable property or in the case of sale.

Because planners have focused on the use of the rule to increase the survivor's basis, it is commonly referred to as the "free step-up" of the survivor's basis.

§3.20.7. Community Property Transmuted into Separate Property Joint Tenancy

In most community property states a husband and wife may transmute community property into any form of separate property, including a joint tenancy or tenancy in common. If community property is transmuted into a "true" joint tenancy between husband and wife, the property is equally owned by them as their separate property. Under §2040 only half of the property is includible in the estate of the spouse first to die. The basis of that one-half of the property is adjusted under §1014 — the basis of the survivor's one-half interest is not adjusted. As noted above, §3.12.5, earlier decisions by courts in several community property states held that community property transferred to a validly created joint tenancy lost its character as community property. In addition, federal tax cases applying California law held that the basis of the surviving spouse is not affected by the death of a spouse in the case of community property converted to joint tenancy property, (*Bordenave v. United States,* 150 F. Supp. 820 (N.D. Cal. 1957) or tenancy in common property, *Murphy v. Commissioner,* 342 F.2d 356 (9th Cir. 1965). In *Murphy,* the Ninth Circuit said "[W]e think Congress did not intend that the surviving spouse in a community property state should get a new basis for the one-half separate interest that the survivor owns in former, but converted, community property. There will, however, in such case be a new basis for the one-half interest that is in the decedent's estate, just as is true in Dr. Murphy's estate." 342 F.2d at 360.

§3.20.8. Basis Planning with Joint Tenancies

Placing community property in joint tenancy form may jeopardize a tax-free increase of the survivor's basis in the property. On the other hand, if it appears that the federal estate tax value of community property on the death of one spouse will be lower than its adjusted basis, a "step-down" of the survivor's basis in the property could be averted if the property is transferred into a true joint tenancy, partitioned, or otherwise converted into a tenancy in common. *See* §3.26.

§3.20.9. Termination of Joint Tenancies

The conversion of joint tenancy property into property held as tenants in common or otherwise equally owned by the tenants probably does not constitute a taxable event. Dickinson, Federal Income Tax Treatment of Divisions of Property: Marital Property Settlements, Estate and Trust Distributions and Other Transactions, 18 U. Kan. L. Rev. 193, 229 (1970). This view is supported by Rev. Rul. 56-437, 1956-2 C.B. 507, which held that "[t]he conversion, for the purpose of eliminating a survivorship feature, of a joint tenancy into a tenancy in common is a nontaxable transaction for Federal income tax purposes." Also, a termination involving a transfer of the entire interest in the property to one tenant would not involve any immediate income tax consequences if it were treated as a gift under §102. Of course, a transfer between spouses or incident to divorce does not involve the recognition of any gain or loss. §1041.

§3.21. Planning with Joint Tenancies

Tax and nontax considerations dictate that joint tenancies should be used cautiously, if at all. The advantages of joint tenancies must be balanced against the disadvantages, including the virtually unlimited control that a joint tenant has over at least half of the joint tenancy property. Indeed, the interests of a client may best be served by holding title to property in forms that do not give anyone else any control over the property. The client's needs may be met by utilizing the multiparty bank accounts and other nontestamentary survivorship arrangements that are available under the U.P.C. and the law of many states. *See* U.P.C. §6-101.

A husband and wife may wish to hold their home and some bank accounts in joint tenancy form. However, in order to avoid bloating the survivor's estate they may not want the survivor to receive large amounts of property outright — by joint tenancy or otherwise. They may instead prefer to hold their property in ways that do not involve survivorship features. For example, a husband or wife may choose to leave most of his or her property to a trust for the survivor of them and, possibly, other beneficiaries. Effectuating such a plan may require rearranging the title to property including the termination of some existing joint tenancies.

On the other hand, joint tenancies and other forms of survivorship may meet the basic needs of a couple whose combined estates are likely to have a value of less than the credit equivalent ($600,000). In any case, each spouse should have a backup will provide for the disposition of (1) any assets not held in joint tenancy in case the testator dies first, (2) the testator's share of the assets in case of simultaneous death, and (3) all of the assets in case the testator is the survivor.

There are some valid nontax reasons for a couple to hold title to the family home and some accounts at financial institutions in joint tenancy form. First, holding property in that form expresses confidence in the marriage and in the ability of the survivor to deal with the property. Second, joint tenancy bank accounts are seldom "frozen" on the death of a tenant and, thus, are fully and immediately available to the surviving spouse. Third, in some states the fees of the personal representative and the personal representative's attorney are based upon the amount of property accounted for in the estate proceeding, which does not include joint tenancy property, life insurance, and other property that passes outside of the proceeding.

Terminating a joint tenancy may reduce the amount of property that is includible in the estate of a tenant who provided more than a proportionate part of the cost of acquiring the property. *See* §3.18. On the income tax side the position of the parties may be improved by creating or terminating a joint tenancy. As a rule of thumb the client should attempt to preserve the adjusted basis of property that has declined in value by taking steps to prevent it from being included in the client's estate. Conversely, within the limits of §1014(e), the client may wish to take steps to cause the inclusion in the client's estate of property that has substantially appreciated in value and will qualify for the marital deduction.

> **Example 3-24.** In 1987 *X* paid $500,000 for Blackacre. Title was taken in the names of *X* and her brother, *B,* as joint tenants with right of survivorship. *X* filed a gift tax return which reported a gift of a one-half interest in Blackacre, $250,000, to *B.* Early in 1991 Blackacre was appraised at $300,000 and *X* was diagnosed as being terminally ill. If title to Blackacre remains in the names of *X* and *B* as joint tenants, its entire $300,000 value will be included in *X*'s gross estate. However, if the value of *B*'s one-half interest in Blackacre were included in *X*'s gross estate, the tentative tax on *X*'s estate would be calculated without including the amount of the taxable gift that *X* made to *B* when Blackacre was acquired. §2001(b). Under §1014 *X*'s basis in Blackacre would be limited to $300,000. *B*'s position would be improved if the joint tenancy were converted into a tenancy in common. *X* might then execute a codicil leaving her interest in Blackacre to *B.* If the joint tenancy were terminated, half of its value and the amount of the 1987 taxable gift would be included in the tax base of *X*'s estate. *B* would retain his original basis of $250,000 in his half. *B* would take an adjusted basis of $150,000 in the other one-half, which would pass to him under *X*'s will. If the joint tenancy were severed, *X*'s tax base *and B*'s basis in Blackacre would be $400,000 ($250,000 + $150,000).

D. COMMUNITY PROPERTY

§3.22. Scope

This part presents a broad overview of the community property laws in effect in nine American states, including their origins, basic characteristics, and tax consequences. It does not present a detailed analysis of the law of any particular state. The relationship of community property to specific subjects is considered in later portions of the book. For example, the community property aspects of the gift and estate tax marital deductions are discussed in Chapter 5, community property issues concerning life insurance are covered in Chapter 6, and the use of the community property widow's election is explored in Chapter 9. In general, each chapter includes a separate discussion of the relevant community property considerations.

§3.23. History

Community property concepts were introduced in this country by early settlers from France and Spain. Curiously, community property was not adopted by Florida, which was first settled by the Spanish in 1565 — before any other settlement in North America. Of course, after two centuries of Spanish rule Florida became a British colony not long before the Revolutionary War. When the colonies of France and Spain were ultimately freed of foreign rule all except Florida retained the civil law marital property system. Curiously, all but Louisiana abandoned the civil law in favor of the English common law as their basic system of jurisprudence. Community property systems were adopted later in Idaho and Washington, perhaps due to the influence exerted by California.

Community property marital property systems have long been in effect in eight southern and western states: Arizona, California, Idaho, Louisiana, Nevada, New Mexico, Texas, and Washington. Short-lived community property systems were adopted in several other states in the 1940s in order to split the income of an employed spouse between husband and wife. The systems were abandoned soon after the federal income tax law was changed to permit spouses to file joint returns, which in effect provides for income splitting. Wisconsin adopted a community property system based on the Uniform Marital Property Act, 9A U.L.A. 97 (1987), effective January 1, 1986. Wis. Stat. Ann. §766.01 *et seq.* (West 1990 Supp.). The Wisconsin law refers to property acquired during marriage in which each spouse has an equal share as "marital property" rather than "community property." However, Wis. Stat. Ann. §766.001(2) states, "It is the intent of the legislature that marital property is a form of community property."

Despite their common origin in the marital property laws of Spain and France, the community property law of each community property state has developed into a unique body of law. Of all of the states Louisiana adheres most closely to the original civil law rules. Elsewhere, notably California, there have been infusions of English common law principles and extensive statutory "modernization" to meet changing economic and social conditions. W. Reppy & W. de Funiak, Community Property in the United States v (1975).

Community property states all treat a husband and wife as partners who are presumed to own equal one-half interests in property acquired during marriage. In all nine states a husband and wife own equal interests in property onerously acquired during marriage. Of course, the marital community ceases to exist upon the death of a spouse or dissolution of the marriage. Until relatively recent times a husband generally had greater managerial powers over community property than his wife. Sweeping legislative changes made in the 1970s gave each spouse essentially the same powers to manage and control community property.

§3.24. Estate Planning with Community Property

Important property rights and tax consequences are affected by the characterization of property as separate or community property. Accordingly, one of the lawyer's first jobs is to determine the character of the property owned by a married person. If the character of some items is uncertain, the husband and wife may wish to enter into an agreement specifying their respective interests in those items. Of course, the lawyer should be alert to the tax consequences of interspousal agreements as well as the ethical implications of representing both spouses. The lawyer may also recommend that the status of some items be changed by agreement, conveyance, or partition. Thus, steps may be taken to assure that assets held in joint tenancy will be treated as community property in order to preserve the step-up in basis that is available for all of the community property on the death of one spouse. *See* §3.20.6 and §3.26. For essentially the same reason a husband and wife moving to a community property state may wish to convert their property to community property. Conversely, in order to prevent a full step-down in the bases of assets that have declined in value the planner may recommend that they be converted into equally owned forms of separate property ownership (*e.g.*, tenancy in common or a true separate property joint tenancy).

§3.25. Preserve the Community or Separate Character of Property

Once the character and ownership of the items is properly arranged, the spouses should be counselled regarding the importance of maintaining the arrangement. In particular, they should be advised to keep the separate and community property completely segregated. Thus, separate and community property funds should be kept in separate bank accounts and securities registered in proper forms. They should also avoid changing the way in which they hold title to property.

Extra care is required in Idaho, Louisiana, Texas, and Wisconsin, which characterize the income derived from separate property as community property. In those states, the interest paid on a separate property bank account should be withdrawn at regular intervals and deposited in a community property account. Otherwise all or a substantial portion of the original account might later be treated as community property as a result of commingling the community property income with the separate property principal. Caution must also be exercised with respect to the reinvestment of the dividends on separately owned mutual funds shares. Note that in Louisiana and Wisconsin a spouse may reserve as separate property the income from his or her separate property by executing a written declaration. La. Civ. Code Ann. art. 2339 (West 1985); Wis. Stat. Ann. §766.59(1) (West 1990 Supp.).

The transfer of property to a revocable inter vivos trust is often the best way to preserve its separate or community property character. The transfer of community property to a properly drafted revocable trust should not cause any change in its character. Revocable trusts are discussed in some detail at §§10.7-10.17. The Wisconsin law expressly recognizes that the transfer of property to a trust does not by itself change the classification of the property. Wis. Stat. Ann. §766.31(5) (West 1990 Supp.). However, in order to preserve the character of the property the trust agreement should specify that the property transferred to the trust will retain its character as community or separate property. The provisions of the trust regarding revocation, distribution of income, and other matters should, of course, be consistent with the character of the property transferred to the trust. Thus, a trust of community property ordinarily should be revocable by the joint action of husband and wife, the income should be payable to them as community property, and the property should retain its community character in the event of revocation. As an alternative one spouse could hold, with respect to community property, a power of revocation that would be exercisable on behalf of both spouses.

Under California law community property transferred to a revocable inter vivos trust retains its character if the trust "provides that the trust is revocable as to that property during the marriage and the power, if any, to modify the trust as to the rights and interests in that property during the marriage may be exercised only with the joinder or consent of both spouses." Cal. Civ. Code §5110.150(a) (West 1990 Supp.). *See also,* Rev. Rul. 66-283, 1966-2 C.B. 297 (California law); *Katz v. United States,* 382 F.2d 723 (9th Cir. 1967) (California law). Idaho law also allows community property that is placed in a revocable trust to retain its character. Idaho Code §32-906A (1983).

§3.26. Preserve the Availability of Stepped-Up Basis Under §1014(b)(6)

A major goal of estate planning in community property states is to achieve a step-up in the income tax basis of all appreciated community property under §1014(b)(6) upon the death of either spouse. A second goal, discussed at §3.27, is to avoid unnecessarily increasing the size of the surviving spouse's estate.

As noted above, upon the death of either spouse the bases of all of the community property are changed to their values on the federal estate tax valuation date applicable to the deceased spouse's estate. §1014(b)(6). Accordingly, attaining this goal simply requires that the spouses establish and maintain the community property character of appreciated property. This is assisted by legislation in several community property states which establish a presumption that property held by husband and wife in joint tenancy form is community property. *E.g.*, Wash. Rev. Code §64.28.040 (1989); Cal. Civ. Code §4800.1 (West 1990 Supp.) (by its terms the California statute only applies upon dissolution of marriage by divorce). As indicated above, the spouses should consider taking steps to preserve the basis of property that has declined in value in order to avoid a downward adjustment of basis upon the death of either spouse. Thus, depreciated community property should be partitioned into equal separately owned interests or switched into separate property forms of ownership (*e.g.*, tenancies in common and "true" separate property joint tenancies).

From a tax perspective it is generally desirable for a husband and wife who are domiciled in a community property state to hold their property as community property. Accordingly, a husband and wife with a stable marriage who move from a common law state to a community property state may consider entering into an agreement changing their property into community property. *See* §3.29. That step is clearly preferable to having the property characterized as quasi-community property, which is generally treated for tax purposes as the separate estate property of the spouse who acquired it. *See* §3.38.

§3.27. Avoid Unnecessarily Increasing Size of Surviving Spouse's Estate

The estate plan for a husband and wife in a community property state is typically drafted to avoid subjecting an unnecessarily large amount of property to taxation upon the death of the surviving spouse. Such a plan usually also seeks to preserve the benefit of each spouse's unified credit. The allowance of the marital deduction that is available for property transferred to a qualified terminable interest property (QTIP) trust has made it relatively simple to achieve this goal. In brief, QTIP property is included in a surviving spouse's estate only to the extent the marital deduction is claimed in the estate of the first spouse to die. *See* §§2044 and 2056(b)(7). *See also* §5.23. Some clients attempt to reduce the amount of property subject to tax on the surviving spouse's death and gain some other tax advantages by using a community property widow's election plan. *See* §§9.21-9.29. However, a widow's election plan is unsuitable for most clients because of its rigidity, complexity, and somewhat uncertain tax consequences. *See* §9.29.

§3.28. Separate and Community Property

In simple terms, separate property ("individual property" under Wisconsin law) is property owned by a spouse prior to marriage and all property acquired after marriage by gift, inheritance, devise, or bequest. All other property acquired during marriage by a husband or wife is their community property. This "negative" definition of community property is simple to understand and provides the key to answering most questions regarding the characterization of property. It is important to note that marriage itself does not cause any previously owned property to become community property. Quite the contrary: Property owned prior to marriage retains its separate character unless it is changed by agreement or conduct of the parties. Thus, "Property owned at a marriage which occurs after 12:01 A.M. on January 1, 1986, is the individual property of the owning spouse. . . ." Wis. Stat. Ann. §766.31(6) (West 1990 Supp.).

§3.28.1. Gifts of Separate Property

Each spouse is generally free to dispose of his or her separate property inter vivos or at death without restriction. However, the "quasi-community property" concept, adopted by several community property states, including California, Idaho, Washington, and Wisconsin gives the nonacquiring spouse an interest at death or dissolution of marriage in property that was acquired during marriage while the couple resided in a noncommunity property state which would have been community property had they been domiciled in the community property state. Quasi-community property is discussed further at §3.38.

§3.28.2. Gifts of Community Property

Each spouse owns an equal, undivided one-half interest in all community property. *E.g.*, Wis. Stat. Ann. §766.31(3) (West 1990 Supp.). Consistent with that concept of ownership, each spouse has the power of testamentary disposition over only half of the community property — the other half belongs to the other spouse. California, Idaho, and Washington prohibit one spouse from making a gift of community property without the consent of the other spouse. Cal. Civ. Code §5125(b) (West 1990 Supp.); Wash. Rev. Code §26.16.030(2) (1989); *Koenig v. Bishop,* 409 P.2d 102 (Idaho 1965). Wisconsin permits a spouse to make a gift to a third party of marital property that is subject to the donor spouse's management and control if the gifts to the donee do not exceed "$1,000 in a calendar year, or a larger amount if, when made, the gift is reasonable in amount considering the economic position of the spouses." Wis. Stat. Ann. §766.53 (West 1990 Supp.). The other community property states appear to permit a spouse to make reasonable gifts of community property that do not injure or defraud the other spouse. W. Reppy & W. de Funiak, Community Property in the United States 338-344 (1975); W. de Funiak & M. Vaughn, Principles of Community Property §122 (2d ed. 1971). In order to reduce the potential for conflict, both spouses should consent in writing to any significant gifts of community property.

§3.28.3. Tracing the Character of Property

The character of property as separate or community generally persists through sales, changes in form, and reinvestments. Thus, the proceeds from the sale of an item of separate property and any property purchased with the proceeds is separate property. In all states the income derived from community property is community. Likewise, in some community property states the income from separate property is separate. However, in Idaho, Louisiana, Texas, Wisconsin, and perhaps Arizona, the income from separate property is community property. Idaho Code §32-906(1) (1983); La. Civ. Code Ann. art. 2339 (West 1985 Supp.); Wis. Stat. Ann. §766.31(4) (West 1990 Supp.). Until 1980 Texans could not overcome that rule, which caused some estate tax complications under §2036. However, under a 1980 amendment to the Texas constitution, the income from the spouses' separate property is community property unless the spouses otherwise agree in writing. Tex. Const. art. XVI, §15(1980). *See* Vaughn, Texas Amends Its Constitution and Its Community Property System, 8 Community Prop. J. 59 (1981).

§3.28.4. Presumption Favoring Community Property

Community property states presume that property acquired during marriage, or owned at the time of dissolution of the marriage, is community property. Rebuttal of that presumption generally requires clear, cogent, and convincing evidence to the contrary. The presumption is the basis of the rule that commingled property is community in nature (*i.e.,* any separate property component is lost if it cannot be traced). "In the absence of any statutory qualification, this presumption in favor of community property is given effect regardless of whether the title to the property is taken in the name of one or the other or both of the spouses. Doctrines of the common law relative to presumptions existing when property is purchased by one spouse and taken in the name of the other or in the names of both are not entitled to recognition under a system in which the presumption is that an acquisition is community property of husband and wife." W. de Funiak & M. Vaughn, Principles of Community Property §60 (2d ed. 1971).

§3.28.5. Special Problems of Characterization

Certain types of property present particularly difficult problems of characterization. Perhaps the most serious involves the characterization of the appreciation in value during marriage of a closely-held business that was owned by one spouse prior to marriage. The marital community is entitled to the fruits of the labor of the spouses during marriage. Accordingly, most community property states "first attempt to ascertain whether the community estate has been fairly compensated for the community efforts, by way of salary or otherwise. If this is the case, the entire appreciation will be awarded to the owner-spouse's separate estate." Weekley, Appreciation of a Closely-Held Business Interest Owned Prior to Marriage — Is It Separate or Community Property?, 7 Community Prop. J. 261, 279 (1980). If the community was not fairly compensated for the owner-spouse's efforts, some part of the appreciation will be treated as community property. In *Jensen v. Jensen,* 665 S.W.2d 107 (Texas 1984), the Supreme Court of Texas discussed two theories: the "reimbursement" theory, under which the community is entitled to be reimbursed for the reasonable value of the time and effort of both spouses, and the "community ownership" theory, under which the increase in value of separate property due to the efforts of the owner spouse is allocated to the community. In *Jensen,* which was the last of three opinions written by the Texas Supreme Court in the same case, the court adopted the reimbursement theory.

Sticky problems can also arise where mixed separate and community funds are used to acquire an asset. In community property states (with the possible exception of Louisiana), when an asset is purchased with a lump sum payment that is made up of community and separate funds, proportionate interests in the asset are held as community and separate property respectively.

Example 3-25. Blackacre was purchased by *H* and *W* for $10,000, of which $3,000 was community and $7,000 was *W*'s separate property. Absent a contrary agreement, in most community property states *H* and *W* would own a 30% interest in Blackacre as their community property. The balance would be the separate property of *W*.

Different results may occur where a spouse contracts to buy an asset prior to marriage but some postmarriage payments on the asset are made from community property. In some states the asset would be treated as separate because it was separate at the time the purchasing spouse first acquired an interest in it (this is called the "inception of title" rule). In those states the expenditure of community funds is seldom treated as a gift to the spouse who owns the separate property. Instead, the community has a right of reimbursement for the payments made from community property. *E.g., McCurdy v. McCurdy,* 372 S.W.2d 381 (Tex. Civ. App. 1963), *writ refused.* Although the community may be reimbursed, it is generally not entitled to recover any interest on the community funds that were invested in the property. Id. In contrast, other states apply the proportionate ownership rule to property acquired with mixed deferred payments, just as in the case of lump sum payments. *E.g., Gudelj v. Gudelj,* 259 P.2d 656 (Cal. 1953). Thus, if community funds are used to make one-third of the payments on property that was originally acquired as the separate property of one spouse, a one-third interest in the property is held as community property.

The characterization of life insurance acquired with mixed community and separate funds also varies among the states. *See* §6.15. California and Washington generally characterize cash value life insurance according to the proportion of the premiums paid from each source, while the other states usually follow an inception of title approach under which the insurance retains its original character. However, in the latter case, the other estate would be entitled to reimbursement for premiums paid from it.

The Wisconsin law regarding the characterization of life insurance is quite different from that of the other community property states. Wis. Stat. Ann. §766.61 (West 1990 Supp.). Under it, interests in policies of the lives of married persons and the proceeds of the policies are determined in accordance with three general rules. First, a policy issued after the determination date (*i.e.,* date of marriage, date on which both spouses become domiciled in Wisconsin, or on January 1, 1986) that lists the insured spouse as owner is marital property regardless of the character of funds used to pay premiums. Wis. Stat. Ann. §766.61(b)(3) (West 1990 Supp.). Second, a policy that lists the noninsured spouse as owner is the individual property of the noninsured spouse regardless of the character of funds used to pay premiums. Wis. Stat. Ann.

§766.61(c) (West 1990 Supp.). Third, a policy that lists a third person as owner is partially marital property if any premium is paid from marital property. "The marital property component of the ownership interest and proceeds is the amount which results from multiplying the entire ownership interest and proceeds by a fraction, the numerator of which is the period during marriage that the policy was in effect after the date on which a premium was paid from marital property and the denominator of which is the entire period the policy was in effect." Wis. Stat. Ann. §766.61(d) (West 1990 Supp.).

§3.29. Agreements Regarding Character of Property

The community property states generally allow a husband and wife to enter into agreements regarding the character of their property. *See, e.g.,* Cal. Civ. Code §§5103, 5110.730 (West 1990 Supp.); Nev. Rev. Stat. §123.070 (1979); Wash. Rev. Code §26.16.120 (1989). Wisconsin law also recognizes that "a marital property agreement may vary the effect of this chapter. Wis. Stat. Ann. §766.17(1) (West 1990 Supp.). The restrictions formerly imposed by the Texas constitution were largely removed by a 1980 amendment of Article XVI, Section 15. *See* Vaughn, Texas Amends Its Constitution and Its Community Property System, 8 Community Prop. J. 59 (1981). Some of the states also recognize oral agreements regarding the ownership of personal property. However, in California a change in the character of property made after 1984 must be "in writing by an express declaration that is made, joined in, consented to, or accepted by the spouse whose interest in the property is adversely affected." Cal. Civ. Code §5110.730 (West 1990 Supp.).

Spouses may use an agreement to change the character of property from separate to community or vice versa. Such changes may have important tax consequences. Of course, spouses may also partition community property into equally owned units of separate property. Perhaps most important, an agreement can be used to clarify the rights of the spouses in their property where its separate or community property character is uncertain. An agreement could be used, for example, to establish the character of commingled property or the separate or community character of property that is nominally joint tenancy. Because of the inherent conflict in the spouses' economic interests, each party to an agreement should be encouraged to obtain independent counsel. Criteria by which the validity of a property agreement will be determined generally include its voluntariness, fairness, adequacy of financial disclosures, and the opportunity for independent legal advice. *See, e.g.,* Wis. Stat. Ann. §766.58(6) (West 1990 Supp.).

§3.30. Agreements Governing Disposition of Property at Death

Idaho, Texas, and Washington have statutes that expressly permit a husband and wife to enter into written agreements regarding the disposition of property at death. Idaho Code §15-6-201 (1979); Tex. Prob. Code Ann. §§451-462 (Vernon 1990 Supp.); Wash. Rev. Code §26.16.120 (1989). The Wisconsin law allows a marital property agreement to provide that the property of either or both of the spouses passes upon the death of either spouse "without probate to a designated person, trust or other entity by nontestamentary disposition." Wis. Stat. Ann. §766.58(f) (West 1990 Supp.). In addition, Nevada and Wisconsin allow a right of survivorship to be attached to community property. Nev. Rev. Stat. §111.064; Wis. Stat. Ann. §766.60(5) (West 1984). *See* §3.31. Under Wisconsin law the first deceased spouse may not dispose at death of any interest in survivorship marital property. Wis. Stat. Ann. §766.60(5)(a) (West 1990 Supp.). An agreement subject to the Idaho and Wisconsin laws may extend to separate *and* community property, but the statutes in the other states apparently apply only to community property. The Texas law provides that an agreement that satisfies the statutory requirements is effective without an adjudication. Tex. Prob. Code Ann. §458 (Vernon 1990 Supp.). However, it establishes a procedure by which a surviving spouse or the personal representative of a deceased spouse may apply to the court for an order "stating that the agreement satisfies the requirements of this code and is effective to create a right of survivorship in community property." Tex. Prob. Code Ann. §456(a) (Vernon 1990 Supp.). Use of the adjudication procedure may be required by transfer agents and others involved in the registration of title to property. Proof of death and a declaration of the facts necessary to establish the validity of the survivorship arrangement may be required in the other four states. Their statutes do not provide for an estate administration proceeding or any process for adjudicating the validity of the arrangement. The Idaho statute is simply an expanded version of U.P.C. §6-101 (formerly §6-201), which treats as nontestamentary a variety of arrangements that were previously often challenged as testamentary in nature. Professor Richard Effland has suggested that the amended form of U.P.C. §6-101 adopted in Arizona will sustain interspousal agreements regarding the status and disposition of property at death. Estate Planning Under the New Arizona Probate Code, 1974 Ariz. St. L.J. 1, 19. In contrast, the Texas statute was added in 1989 to implement the 1987 amendment of Article XVI, Section 15 of the Texas Constitution. Of course, Texas also adopted an amended form of U.P.C. §6-101. Tex. Prob. Code Ann. §450 (Vernon 1990 Supp.).

A survivorship arrangement of the type under discussion is not itself a sufficient estate plan, even for a couple with a relatively small estate. The arrangement is similar to a joint tenancy between spouses — it needs to be supplemented with a will to dispose of any property not subject to the agreement and to dispose of all of the property upon the death of the survivor. Also, such an arrangement is not a complete substitute. It probably cannot be used, for example, to nominate guardians for minor children, direct apportionment of taxes, exercise powers of appointment, dispose of property subject to administration in other states. Finally, property subject to such an arrangement probably cannot be set apart to a surviving spouse as a family award or family allowance that is exempt from creditors. Presumably a surviving spouse could disclaim the right to receive the decedent's interest in the property subject to the agreement, which would subject the property to administration in the deceased spouse's estate. *See* §2518. *See also* §§12.31-12.35.

Spouses in community property states are generally free to contract regarding the content or revocability of their wills. However, contractual wills often give rise to serious tax and nontax problems. *See* §4.7. In most cases clients should be encouraged to use another device, such as an inter vivos trust, instead of contractual wills.

§3.31. Survivorship Community Property

Survivorship community property is created in Nevada when the instrument of transfer expressly declares that the husband and wife take the property as community property with right of survivorship. In Wisconsin registration of property as "survivorship marital property" is effective to vest ownership of the property in the surviving spouse. Presumably the registration of community property as survivorship community property does not have any present tax consequences.

The law regarding survivorship community property will probably emulate the law applicable to joint tenancies. Thus, a dissolution of the parties' marriage would terminate the survivorship feature and constitute the parties tenants in common with respect to the property. Under the Nevada statute the survivorship feature is extinguished if either spouse transfers his or her interest in the property. However, as in Wisconsin it is doubtful that the spouse first to die could overcome the survivorship feature by a provision in his or her will. The statutes also do not deal with any rights a deceased spouse's creditors may have against the property. They do provide a shortcut to pass community property to the surviving spouse without the necessity of an estate administration proceeding, which would be required to pass community property to the survivor by will or under the intestate succession law. They also allow the spouses to avoid the possible income tax basis disadvantage of putting their property into joint tenancy form. *See* §3.35.4.

§3.32. Employee Benefit Plans; Terminable Interest Rule

> [W]e hold that in light of the settled marital property rule in Texas that a spouse has a community property interest in that portion of the retirement benefits of the opposite spouse earned during their marriage, the retirement benefits in this case were properly characterized as community property, and thus, one-half of such benefits was properly included in the wife's estate. *Allard v. French,* 754 S.W.2d 111, 114 (Tex. 1988), *cert. denied,* 109 S. Ct. 788 (1989).

The idea that the nonemployee spouse may dispose of an interest in the employee spouse's retirement benefits will surprise many clients. However, as indicated in the above quotation, employee benefits accrued during marriage are generally treated as deferred compensation that is appropriately characterized as community property. Vested and nonvested interests are apportioned between community and separate property if they accrued in part during marriage in a community property state and in part while the employee-spouse was unmarried.

In most states the interest of the nonemployee spouse in employee benefit plans is recognized upon dissolution of the community upon divorce. Recognition of the community character of interests in an employee benefit plan that accrued during marriage is appropriate in the context of divorce. It is arguably less appropriate that the interest of the nonemployee spouse be recognized upon his or her death. In such a case should not the survivor, the employee spouse, be entitled to receive all of the benefits? Nonetheless, most states have held that an interest in the benefits is includible in the estate of the nonemployee spouse and subject to disposition by him or her.

Wisconsin has adopted a "terminable interest" rule under which the interest of the nonemployee spouse in employee benefits terminates if he or she predeceases the employee-spouse. In particular, the Wisconsin law provides, "[T]he marital property interest of the non-employee spouse in a deferred employee benefit plan terminates at the death of the nonemployee spouse if he or she predeceases the employee spouse." Wis. Stat. Ann. §766.31(3) (West 1990 Supp.). A terminable interest rule was judicially adopted in California. However, it was legislatively repealed — at least in the divorce setting. *See* Cal. Civ. Code §4800.8 (West 1990 Supp.). After some equivocal decisions, in *Allard* the Texas Supreme Court refused to adopt the terminable interest rule. This rule was also judicially rejected in Washington. *Farver v. Department of Retirement Systems,* 644 P.2d 1149 (Wash. 1982).

Qualified Plans. Although a nonemployee spouse has a community property interest in the employee spouse's qualified plan, ERISA may prevent the nonemployee spouse from disposing of it. In particular, the extent to which the nonemployee spouse's interest in a qualified plan is subject to disposition as an asset is not finally settled. In two advisory opinions issued in 1990, A.O. 90-46A and A.O. 90-47A, the Department of Labor ruled that the administrator of a qualified plan was not bound by the order of a state probate court directing the disposition of the nonemployee spouse's community property interest in the plan. The opinions reasoned that the federal prohibitions against alienation of an employee's interest in a qualified plan barred all dispositions except qualified domestic relations orders, which do not include orders of a probate court disposing of the community property interest of the nonemployee spouse: "We find no indication that Congress contemplated that the QDRO provisions would serve as a mechanism in which a non-participant spouse's interest derived only from state property law could be enforced against a pension plan." A.O. 90-46A. The same result was reached in *Ablamis v. Roper,* 937 F.2d 1450 (9th Cir. 1991), which held that ERISA preempted any state community property law that would provide a predeceasing nonemployee spouse with a transmissible interest.

The estate plan for the nonemployee spouse should be prepared in light of his or her interest in employee benefits. In particular, in states other than Wisconsin the nonemployee spouse needs to understand that his or her will may dispose of an interest in the other spouse's employee benefit plan. Of course, the disposition of the nonemployee spouse's interest may appropriately be the subject of an ante-nuptial or post-nuptial property agreement.

§3.33. Estate Tax

Community property is includible in the estate of a deceased spouse to the extent of the decedent's one-half interest. In this connection it is important to note that the characterization of property is governed by the applicable state law and not by federal rules. For example, the amount of property includible in the estate of a deceased spouse may be affected by the terms of a property agreement between the spouses if such agreements are allowed under the local law, as they generally are. Of course, an agreement between the spouses is effective to characterize their property only if the requirements of state law are satisfied. Some states demand more than others to overcome the presumption that property acquired during marriage is community property. In some states an oral agreement may suffice, but in others more is required. For example, *Kern v. United States,* 491 F.2d 436 (9th Cir. 1974), held that under Washington law the presumption was overcome only if the evidence of separate property ownership was clear, definite, and convincing.

The estate tax regulations include some special rules regarding the inclusion of community property in the gross estate in order to preserve the equity of the estate tax. In particular, the regulations recognize that only half of the proceeds of community property life insurance is ordinarily includible in the estate of the insured spouse. Reg. §20.2042-1(b)(2). Similarly, where the noninsured spouse dies first, only half of the value of a community property policy is includible in the decedent's estate. Reg. §20.2042-1(c)(5). Although it is largely no longer of much significance by reason of the unlimited marital deduction, the IRS earlier recognized that only half of the value of joint tenancy property acquired with community property funds is includible in a deceased spouse's estate. Rev. Rul. 55-605, 1955-2 C.B. 328 (Nevada). The nonemployee spouse's interest in an employee benefit plan is includible in his or her estate under §2033. However, a marital deduction is available to the extent the nonemployee spouse's interest passes to the employee spouse.

§3.33.1. Deductions

Deductions are allowable under §2053 for expenses of administration, funeral expenses, and debts, to the extent they are chargeable to the decedent's share of the community property under the local law. Thus, where only the decedent's half of the community property is subject to administration, the estate is allowed a deduction for the full amount of the administration expenses. On the other hand, if all interests in the community property are administered, the deduction is limited to one-half of the expenses of administration that are not specifically allocable to the decedent's share of the community property. Expenses that relate only to the decedent's share of the community property are *fully* deductible. Thus, the attorney's fees and other expenses incurred in connection with the determination of federal and state death taxes are fully deductible. *Lang's Estate v. Commissioner,* 97 F.2d 867 (9th Cir. 1938). Likewise, the costs of appraising the decedent's interest in the community property are fully deductible. *Ray v. United States,* 385 F. Supp. 372 (S.D. Tex. 1974), *aff'd per curiam on other issues,* 538 F.2d 1228 (5th Cir. 1976). In *Ray* the court upheld the deductiblity of 95 percent of the attorney's fees.

Funeral expenses are deductible under §2053 only to the extent the decedent's estate is liable for their payment. Accordingly, half of the funeral expenses are deductible in a state that makes them a charge against the entire community property. *Lang's Estate, supra;* Rev. Rul. 70-156, 1970-1 C.B. 190. The IRS has ruled that the expenses are fully deductible in the states that changed their laws to provide that funeral expenses are charged entirely to the decedent's share of the community property. Rev. Rul. 71-168, 1971-1 C.B. 271 (California); Rev. Rul. 69-193, 1969-1 C.B. 222 (Texas).

Deductions for losses and charitable transfers are of course limited to the decedent's interest in the lost or transferred property. *See* §§2054, 2055.

§3.33.2. Marital Deduction

An unlimited marital deduction is allowable to the estates of decedents dying after December 31, 1981 regardless of the community or separate character of the decedent's property. The marital deduction allowable to the estates of decedents dying prior to 1982 was subject to qualitative and quantitative limitations. Prior to 1977 no marital deduction was allowable to an estate composed entirely of community property. Technically, the deduction was limited to 50 percent of the adjusted gross estate, which was defined as the gross estate reduced by the sum of (1) the §2053 and §2054 deductions attributable to the decedent's separate property and (2) the decedent's interest in community property. A limited marital deduction was allowed with respect to community property for decedents dying after 1977 and before 1982. In that period the marital deduction was limited to the greater of 50 percent of the adjusted gross estate or $250,000. §2056(c)(1)(A). However, the alternate $250,000 amount was reduced to the extent the community property included in the decedent's estate exceeded its pro rata share of the §2053 and §2054 deductions. §2056(c)(1)(C). Accordingly, no marital deduction was allowable if the decedent's share of the community property estate had a value of $250,000 or more, net of §2053 and §2054 deductions.

§3.33.3. Credits

The unified credit and the credits for state death taxes, taxes on prior transfers, and foreign death taxes are allowable with respect to property included in the decedent's estate regardless of its community or separate nature.

§3.34. Gift Tax

Taxable gifts may result from transfers of community property to third parties. In addition, transactions between spouses that affect their respective ownership interests in community property may also result in gifts between the spouses. Interspousal gifts generally qualify for the gift tax marital deduction if the donee spouse is a U.S. citizen. §2523. For federal and state gift tax purposes, a gift of community property to a person outside the community is treated as two gifts — one by each spouse and each for one-half of the total value of the property transferred. Accordingly, each spouse is treated as a donor of the property, whose transfer may qualify for the annual gift tax exclusion.

> **Example 3-26.** In 1991 *H* and *W* gave $20,000 of community property cash to their daughter, *D*. For gift tax purposes *H* and *W* are each considered to have made a gift of $10,000 to *D*. The gifts involve present interests that qualify for the annual gift tax exclusion. Accordingly, if neither *H* nor *W* makes any other gifts to *D* in 1991, neither is required to report the gifts to *D* on a federal gift tax return.

A gift also takes place if one spouse transfers all of his or her interest in a community property asset to the other spouse, who then owns the entire interest in the asset as separate property. Such a transfer of community property qualifies for the gift tax annual exclusion and the marital deduction if the donee spouse is a U.S. citizen. It would be unnecessary to file a gift tax return with respect to such a gift. §6019.

§3.34.1. Transfer of Separate Property into Community Property

When one spouse transfers separate property into community property, the transferor makes a gift to the other spouse of an amount equal to half of the value of the transferred property. That results because after the transfer each spouse owns a one-half interest in the property. When both spouses transfer separate property into community property, "a single gift will take place with respect to the conversion of the separately owned properties and the value of the single gift will be the net difference between the value of the husband's (or the wife's) separate property before its conversion into community property and the value of the husband's (or the wife's) interest in the community property resulting from the conversion." Rev. Rul. 77-359, 1977-2 C.B. 24. Such a gift should qualify for the gift tax annual exclusion and marital deduction if the donee spouse is a U.S. citizen. Louisiana law was changed in 1981 to permit spouses to transmute separate property into community property. La. Civ. Code Ann. art. 2443.1 (West 1985).

> **Example 3-27.** *W* transferred $100,000 of her separate property cash into a community property form of ownership with her husband, *H,* who is a U.S. citizen. The transfer involved a gift from *W* to *H* of half of the amount transferred ($100,000 × ½ = $50,000). Such a transfer qualifies for the gift tax annual exclusion and marital deduction. If *H* had also transferred $50,000 of his separate property into a community property form of ownership with *W,* the transfers by *W* and *H* would be aggregated for purposes of determining the gift tax consequences. After the transfers were made each spouse would own a community property interest worth $75,000 (½ × ($100,000 + $50,000)). *H* would not have made a gift since he transferred property worth $50,000 and received interests worth $75,000. *W* would have made a gift of $25,000, since she transfered property worth $100,000 and received an interest worth only $75,000.

§3.34.2. Partition of Community Property into Separate Property

The partition of community property into equal shares of separate property does not involve a gift because each spouse continues to own an interest of equivalent value. Probably no gift occurs if each spouse receives either an equal interest in each asset or the whole interest in assets of the same total value. As indicated in §3.35.3, either type of division should not require any recognition of gain. The result should be the same regardless of the type of separate property ownership. Thus, a transfer of community property into joint tenancy or tenancy in common does not involve a gift. In 1981 Louisiana changed its laws to allow spouses voluntarily to partition community property into separate property. La. Civ. Code Ann. arts. 2336, 2341 (West 1985). Upon the death of a spouse only the basis in the deceased spouse's interest in the former community property is changed; the separate property interest of the surviving spouse is not affected. Rev. Rul. 68-80, 1968-1 C.B. 348 (community property in New Mexico real property traded for tenancy in common real property in Virginia).

§3.34.3. Conversion of Future Income into Separate Property

An agreement that the future income of each spouse will be his or her separate property may constitute a gift. The gift might not take place when the agreement is executed because of the impossibility of valuing the interests involved. *Cf.* Rev. Rul. 69-346, 1969-1 C.B. 227. Presumably gifts would occur over time as income is earned by one or both spouses. Here, again, the analysis is largely of academic interest since gifts to a spouse who is a U.S. citizen will qualify for the gift tax marital deduction. As explained in §3.35.1, the transfer of interests between spouses is not a taxable event. §1041(a).

Example 3-28. *H* and *W* entered into an agreement, valid under the local law, that the employment income of each spouse will be the separate property of the spouse who earns it. It was impossible to determine the gift tax consequences at the time the agreement was made. In the following year *H* was unemployed and *W* received employment income of $25,000. *H* may be treated as having made a gift of $12,500 to *W* if the agreement was effective to cause the entire $25,000 to be treated as *W*'s separate property. Such a gift should qualify for the gift tax annual exclusion and marital deduction.

§3.35. Income Tax

In general the income tax law follows the state law characterization of income and expenditures. Thus, the income earned by a married couple in a community property state is naturally "split" between them. When the income tax rates were more progressive, the split of community property income between the spouses was of great advantage to couples who lived in community property states so long as the federal law required each spouse to file a separate income tax return. The significance of community property in that regard was largely eliminated in 1948 when Congress enacted a legislative package that sought to equalize the overall tax treatment of community and noncommunity property. Part of that package gave married persons the option to report their combined income on a single ("joint") income tax return, where it would be taxed at preferential rates.

§3.35.1. No Gain or Loss on Transfers Between Spouses, §1041

No gain or loss is recognized on a transfer of property made after July 18, 1984 from an individual to, or in trust for the benefit of, his or her spouse. §1041(a). Instead, the transfer is treated as a gift, with the basis of the transferor carrying over to the transferee. §1041(b). The same rules apply to transfers to a former spouse that are made incident to divorce.

> The transferor of property under section 1041 recognizes no gain or loss on the transfer even if the transfer was in exchange for the release of marital rights or other consideration. This rule applies regardless of whether the transfer is of property separately owned by the transferor or is a division (equal or unequal) of community property. Reg. §1.1041-T(d), Q-10.

However, the nonrecognition rule does not apply "if the spouse of the individual making the gift is a nonresident alien." §1041(d).

The rules with respect to the income tax consequences for the transferee are stated in the response to Q-11 of Temp. Reg. §1.1041-T(d):

> The transferee of property under section 1041 recognizes no gain or loss upon receipt of the transferred property. In all cases, the basis of the transferred property in the hands of the transferee is the adjusted property in the hands of the transferor immediately before the transfer. Even if the transfer is a bona fide sale, the transferee does not acquire a basis in the transferred property equal to the transferee's cost (the fair market value). This carryover basis rule applies whether the adjusted basis of the transferred property is less than, equal to, or greater than its fair market value at the time of transfer (or the value of any consideration provided by the transferee) and applies for the purpose of determining loss as well as gain upon the subsequent disposition of the property by the transferee. Id., Q-11.

§3.35.2. Conversion of Separate Property into Community Property

Under §1041 the conversion of separate property into community property is not a taxable event. Prior to its adoption such a conversion might have resulted in the realization of gain. A conversion by only one spouse was a gift by that spouse, which was not a taxable event. However, a conversion by both spouses of separate property into community property might have been treated as a taxable exchange, which could have resulted in the recognition of gain. No gain was realized, however, if the separate conversions by husband and wife were determined to be gifts under §102. LR 7821150. Most conversions probably satisfied the requirement of *Commissioner v. Duberstein,* 363 U.S. 278 (1960), that a gift in the statutory sense of §102 must proceed from a detached and disinterested generosity out of affection, respect, admiration, charity, or like impulses. If a conversion qualified as a gift under §102, no gain was realized and, presumably, each spouse had a basis in the assets equal to half of the sum of the adjusted bases of the assets that were formerly held as separate property. Such a conversion could not result in a loss because of §267, which bars the deduction of a loss on transfers between related taxpayers including spouses.

§3.35.3 Conversion of Community Property into Separate Property

Under §1041 conversions of community property into separate property also do not constitute a taxable event. A conversion might involve a sale or exchange, a gift by one spouse to the other, or an equal division. Presumably the rule extends to those types of assets, such as installment obligations, the disposition of which would otherwise trigger the recognition of gain or loss. *See* §453B. Under the prior law the conversion of a community property asset into one that the spouses owned as equal tenants in common or as joint tenants was not taxable. *See Commissioner v. Mills,* 183 F.2d 32 (9th Cir. 1932); Rev. Rul. 56-437, 1956-2 C.B. 507 (conversion of joint tenancy in stock into tenancy in common or partition and issuance of separate stock certificates is not taxable). Similarly, under the prior law a division of community property by which each spouse received the entire interest in assets of approximately equal value was not taxable. LR 8016050. An unequal in kind division of community property was also nontaxable if the transfer of the excess property to one spouse was regarded as a gift under §102.

Most of the prior law regarding the taxability of conversions of community property was generated by cases involving the consequences of marital dissolutions. That law is summarized in Rev. Rul. 76-83, 1976-1 C.B. 213, which held that no gain or loss resulted from the approximately equal division of the fair market value of community property. *See also Jean C. Carrieres,* 64 T.C. 959 (1975), *aff'd per curiam,* 552 F.2d 1350 (9th Cir. 1977), *acq. in result,* 1976-2 C.B. 1. The ruling involved an agreement that called for each spouse to receive community property of equal value. "However, certain community assets cannot feasibly be partitioned between the taxpayers because the nature of the assets makes them incapable of division, they are associated with a particular liability, or they are part of a business venture that can be managed by only one of the taxpayers. Under the terms of the settlement agreement, certain assets will be assigned to the husband and certain other assets of approximate equal value will be assigned to the wife. The remaining community assets will be equally partitioned between the taxpayers." Id. Insofar as the basis of assets is concerned, the ruling held that an asset allocated entirely to one spouse retains its community basis. It continued to say that each spouse's basis in a partitioned asset was equal to the percentage of the asset received by the spouse multiplied by the community property basis of the asset. "For example, if corporate stock that has a community basis of $15,000 is partitioned so that the husband receives 40 percent of the stock and the wife receives the remaining 60 percent of the stock, the basis of the stock received by the husband will be $6,000 (40 percent of $15,000) and the basis of the stock received by the wife will be $9,000 (60 percent of $15,000)." Presumably the same result would obtain under §1041.

§3.35.4. Basis Following Death of a Spouse

The characterization of property as community or separate is also important when it comes to determining the basis of property following the death of a spouse. Under §1014(b)(6), both shares of the community property have a basis equal to its fair market value on the valuation date applicable to the deceased spouse's estate for federal estate tax purposes (*i.e.,* either on the date of the decedent's death or on the alternate valuation date under §2032). Thus, the survivor's share of the community property benefits from a free "step-up" in basis where the community property has appreciated in value, but suffers a decrease in basis ("step-down") if the estate tax value in the decedent's estate is below its adjusted basis at the time of the decedent's death. In contrast, the basis of the surviving spouse in his or her separate property is not changed by reason of the decedent's death. It is readily apparent, then, that the survivor's basis in a jointly owned asset depends upon whether it was held as community property or as equally owned units of separate property (*e.g.,* a separate property tenancy in common or joint tenancy). In Rev. Rul. 68-80, 1968-1 C.B. 348, the IRS ruled that the surviving spouse's basis in her undivided one-half interest in Virginia property that she held with her deceased husband as tenants in common was not affected by his death. Revenue Ruling 68-80 was concerned with a husband and wife who, "In 1965 . . . moved to Virginia and traded their community property in New Mexico for real property in Virginia to which they took title as tenants in common." The ruling treated the Virginia property as equally owned by the husband and wife as their separate property. Merely taking title to the Virginia property as tenants in common should not have resulted in a change in the character of the property from community to separate. Under basic conflicts of law principles the Virginia property should have been characterized as community property regardless of the manner in which title was held. *See* §3.36.

It is generally advantageous to hold an appreciated asset in community property form, which allows the basis in both halves of it to be stepped-up on the death of the first spouse to die. Presumably the step-up is available with respect to any property that is characterized as community property under the applicable state law. *See* Rev. Rul. 87-98, 1987-2 C.B. 206. *See also* §3.20.6. As indicated in §3.26, in some community property states all property held in joint form between husband and wife is presumed to be community property. Of course, a "full" step-up in basis is also available where the entire interest in an asset is included in a deceased spouse's estate.

Example 3-29. *H* and *W* purchased 100 shares of stock at $10 per share with their community property funds. At the same time *H* purchased an additional 100 shares with his separate property. *H* bequeathed his interest in the 200 shares of stock to *W*, a U.S. citizen, who survived him. The stock had a value of $100 per share on the estate tax valuation date applicable to *H*'s estate. Insofar as the community property stock was concerned, *H*'s estate included a value of $5,000 attributable to the stock (½ × $100 × 100). As a result, its basis was increased to $5,000. *W*'s one-half interest in the stock was also increased to $5,000 under §1014(b)(6). Accordingly, *W* has a basis of $10,000 in the 100 shares that were formerly held as community property. *H*'s estate included the full value ($10,000) of the 100 shares that were acquired as his separate property. However, in both cases the value of the stock included in *H*'s estate was fully offset by the marital deduction allowable to his estate.

In the case of separate property, only the decedent's interest in the property is affected by §1014. Thus, the survivor's bases in assets that stood in joint tenancy form will vary according to whether they are treated as true separate property joint tenancies or as their community property. As stated in Revenue Ruling 87-98, "If property held in a common law estate is community property under state law, it is community property for purposes of section 1014(b)(6) of the Code, regardless of the form in which title was taken." On the other hand, only the decedent's interest in a "true" (*i.e.*, separate property) joint tenancy is affected by the decedent's death. *See Murphy v. Commissioner*, 342 F.2d 356 (9th Cir. 1965); *Bordenave v. United States*, 150 F. Supp. 820 (N.D. Cal. 1957). A community property characterization might result if a presumption that joint tenancies between husband and wife are community property is not overcome, the attempt to establish the joint tenancy fails to comply with the requirements of the local law, or the joint tenancy form was used for convenience without intending to create a valid joint tenancy with right of survivorship. By way of illustration, had the stock in Example 3-29, *supra*, been held by *H* and *W* in a true separate property joint tenancy, *W* would have had a basis of only $5,500 in the stock following *H*'s death. That figure is the sum of *W*'s share of the original cost basis ($500) plus the basis of *H*'s one-half share determined under §1014 ($5,000).

When the value of community property has declined below its adjusted basis, §1014(b)(6) could cause a decrease in the basis of both halves of the property. However, that result can be avoided by partitioning the property prior to the death of a spouse. If that is done, the survivor's basis in half of the property is unaffected by the decedent's death. Only the decedent's one-half share of the property suffers a decrease in basis. The IRS has recognized this opportunity:

> There is nothing in the Internal Revenue Code or regulations that would indicate that section 1014(b)(6) of the Code relating to "community property held" was intended to include separate property that had previously been converted from community property to separate property. Accordingly, *W*'s unadjusted basis in her undivided one-half interest in the Virginia property held as tenant in common at *H*'s death is her cost. Her unadjusted basis in the undivided one-half interest she acquired by inheritance from *H* is its fair market value at the time of *H*'s death. Rev. Rul. 68-80, 1968-1 C.B. 348.

An inter vivos gift of one spouse's share in community property that has declined in value would produce essentially the same result: The donee's original interest in the property would retain its adjusted basis unaffected by the gift or the donor's death and the donee's basis in the gifted share would be limited to its fair market value on the date of the gift for the purpose of determining loss. *See* §1015(a).

The effect of §1014(b)(6) on a client's estate plan should be carefully considered, particularly if the client is terminally ill. An appropriate shift into or out of a community property form of ownership may leave the surviving spouse with a higher basis in the property.

§3.35.5. Appreciated Property Acquired from a Decedent

The 1981 Act added §1014(e), which provides that the stepped-up basis rules of §1014 do not apply to appreciated property acquired by the decedent by gift within a year of death where the property passes directly or indirectly from the donee-decedent to the original donor or the donor's spouse. The Ways and Means Committee recommended this provision because of a concern that §1014 would otherwise encourage taxpayers to transfer appreciated property to a terminally ill person in hopes of receiving the property back upon the death of the donee, complete with a stepped-up basis. The concern was more acute because of the adoption of the unlimited marital deduction.

> The donor-heir might pay gift taxes on the fair market value of the gift (unless it qualified for the marital deduction or the amount of the gift is less than the donor's annual exclusion or unified credit) but will pay no income tax on the appreciation. . . . [U]pon the death of the donee-decedent, the donor-heir could receive back the property with a stepped-up basis equal to its fair market value. The stepped-up basis would permanently exempt the appreciation from income tax. H.R. Rep. No. 97-201, 97th Cong., 1st Sess. 188 (1981).

Section 1014(e) may bar any step-up in the basis of the surviving spouse in separate property that he or she transferred into community property within a year preceding the death of the donee spouse.

Example 3-30. *W* owned separate property with a basis of $50,000 and a fair market value of $500,000. Within a year preceding *H*'s death *W* transferred the property into a community property form of ownership with *H.* Thereafter *H* owned a one-half interest with a basis of $25,000 and a value of $250,000. When *H* died he left to *W* his one-half interest in the community property created by *W*'s transfer. *H*'s one-half interest ($250,000) was includible in his estate under §2033, but by reason of §1014(e) *W*'s basis in it may remain $25,000. If *W*'s basis in *H*'s half of the property is increased, presumably the basis of *W*'s one-half interest would be stepped-up under §1014(b)(6).

The basis in *H*'s half of the property would have been stepped-up if *H* had left it outright to someone other than *W.* In such a case presumably *W*'s one-half interest in the property would also receive a stepped-up basis. It is unclear whether the basis of either share would be stepped-up if *H* left his one-half interest to a trust in which *W* had an interest.

§3.36. Conflict of Laws: Basic Rules

> A marital property interest in a chattel, or right embodied in a document, which has been acquired by either or both of the spouses, is not affected by the mere removal of the chattel or document to a second state, whether or not this removal is accompanied by a change of domicile to the other state on the part of one or both of the spouses. The interest, however, may be affected by dealings with the chattel or document in the second state. Restatement (Second), Conflict of Laws §259 (1971).

Under basic conflict of laws principles the character of property acquired by a husband and wife while domiciled in one state is not changed if they move to another state. However, their rights in the property may be affected by the move, as indicated in the discussion of quasi-community property in §3.38.

Applying the basic rule, property acquired as community property in California is recognized as community property if the couple move to a noncommunity property state such as Colorado. *People v. Bejarano,* 358 P.2d 866 (Colo. 1961). Other noncommunity property states may improperly treat imported community property as converted into a more familiar common law form of ownership, such as a tenancy in common. *Edwards v. Edwards,* 233 P. 477 (Okla. 1924); *Depas v. Mayo,* 49 Am. Dec. 88 (Mo. 1848). That approach may lead to an acceptable resolution of some tax and nontax problems if the couple's new domicile recognizes that each spouse has a one-half interest in the imported community property. Under such an approach, only the decedent's basis in the imported community property may be increased upon the death of one spouse. *See* Rev. Rul. 68-80, 1968-1 C.B. 348, discussed at §3.35.4. Unfortunately, the tax authorities and courts have not always recognized the ownership interest of each spouse in the imported community property. *See, e.g., Commonwealth v. Terjen,* 90 S.E.2d 801 (Va. 1956). (The court recognized that property imported from California retained its community character, but erroneously failed to recognize the wife's interest in the property because it was a "mere expectancy.")

§3.37. Uniform Disposition of Community Property Rights at Death Act

Several noncommunity property states have addressed the problem of providing for the proper disposition of community property upon the death of a spouse by adopting the Uniform Disposition of Community Property Rights at Death Act, 8A U.L.A. 121 (1983). The Act, which was approved as a Uniform Act in 1971, has been adopted by an important minority of states, including Alaska, Arkansas, Connecticut, Hawaii, Kentucky, Michigan, Montana, New York, Oregon, Virginia, and Wyoming. It defines the rights, at death, of a married person in community property that was acquired before the couple became domiciled in a noncommunity property state. In brief, it recognizes the right each spouse has under the community property law to dispose at death of half of the community property, the other half of which belongs to the surviving spouse. The Commissioners' Prefatory Note states that the Act was intended "to preserve the rights of each spouse in property which was community property prior to the change of domicile, as well as in property substituted therefore where the spouses have not indicated an intention to sever or alter their 'community' rights. It thus follows the typical pattern of community property which permits the deceased spouse to dispose of 'his half' of the community property while confirming the title of the surviving spouse in 'her half.' " 8A U.L.A. 121 (1983). Professor Stanley Johanson has argued persuasively that the Act provides an appropriate solution for the most commonly encountered problems regarding imported community property. Johanson, The Migrating Client: Estate Planning for the Couple from a Community Property State, U. Miami, 9th Inst. Est. Plan. ¶831 (1975).

§3.38. Quasi-Community Property

When a couple move from a noncommunity property state to a community property state, the property formerly owned by each spouse is generally characterized as his or her separate property. Thus, property acquired with the earnings of a husband while the couple was domiciled in a noncommunity property state is generally treated as his separate property following their move. This treatment works well enough in most instances. However, as a result of the move, the nonacquiring spouse usually loses any right to dower, curtesy, or an elective share that was provided by the state of their former domicile. In order to deal with that problem, California, Idaho, Washington, and Wisconsin have adopted the quasi-community property concept. Wisconsin gives a surviving spouse the right to elect to take a one-half interest in "deferred marital property" (the Wisconsin equivalent of quasi-community property) in lieu of what the surviving spouse would have otherwise received from the decedent. Wis. Stat. Ann. §861.055 (West 1990 Supp.).

In brief, quasi-community property is property acquired during marriage while the spouses were domiciled in a noncommunity property state that would have been community property had they been domiciled in the state of the decedent's domicile at the time of acquisition. Cal. Civ. Code §4803 (West 1983); Idaho Code §15-2-201(b) (1979); Wash. Rev. Code §§26.16.220-.250 (1989). Several community property states apply the same concept to the characterization of property upon dissolution of marriage. Ariz. Rev. Stat. §25-318 (West 1989 Supp.); Tex. Fam. Code Ann. §3.63 (Vernon 1988 Supp.). Upon termination of the marriage by dissolution or death of the acquiring spouse, each spouse is generally treated as having a one-half interest in the quasi-community property. Wisconsin gives the surviving spouse the right to claim an elective share in "deferred marital property," which is "property acquired while spouses are married and . . . which would have been marital property under ch. 766 if it were acquired when ch. 766 applied."

Wis. Stat. Ann. §851.055 (West 1990 Supp.). The quasi-community property concept is not extended to dissolutions in Washington: The courts are authorized to make an equitable division of all of the community and separate property in marital dissolution actions.

Upon the death of the acquiring spouse, half of the quasi-community property is subject to the decedent's disposition and the other half belongs to the surviving spouse. Cal. Prob. Code §101 (West 1991 Supp.); Idaho Code §15-2-201(a) (1979); Wash. Rev. Code §26.16.230 (1987). In Wisconsin the surviving spouse may elect to receive not more than a one-half interest in any or all items of deferred marital property. Wis. Stat. Ann. §861.02 (West 1990 Supp.). The validity of the California statute was upheld in *Addison v. Addison,* 399 P.2d 897 (Cal. 1965). Note that neither the quasi-community property nor the Wisconsin deferred marital property approach allows the nonacquiring spouse to dispose of any portion of the property if he or she predeceases the acquiring spouse. Indeed, in *Paley v. Bank of America,* 324 P.2d 35 (Cal. App. 1958), the court held that a statute was unconstitutional which gave the nonacquiring spouse power of testamentary disposition over quasi-community property during the lifetime of the acquiring spouse.

Community property states could deal with the problem of protecting the nonacquiring immigrant spouse by giving him or her the same rights in the property that he or she would have had under the law of the place of acquisition. As pointed out by Professor Thomas Andrews, "such a borrowed-law approach can be found in Arizona, New Mexico, Nevada, and Idaho, where such an approach was taken to deal with the problem of migration at divorce." Washington's New Quasi-Community Property Act: Protecting the Immigrant Spouse, 15 Community Prop. J. 50, 52 (1988). However, such an approach is more complicated and almost necessarily involves difficult tracing of assets. Tracing would be particularly difficult if a couple had lived in several noncommunity property states prior to their move to California, Idaho, or Washington. California earlier tried to deal with the problem by adopting a statute that converted the separate property of a married person to community property when they established a domicile in California. That approach was struck down in *Estate of Thornton,* 33 P.2d 1 (Cal. 1934), as an unconstitutional taking of the acquiring spouse's property without due process of law and as a violation of the acquiring spouse's privileges and immunities by penalizing the acquiring spouse for making a change of domicile.

For federal tax purposes quasi-community property is treated as the separate property of the acquiring spouse. Accordingly, the entire interest in quasi-community property is includible in the gross estate of the acquiring spouse. *Estate of Frank Sbicca,* 35 T.C. 96 (1960).

§3.39. PROTECTING THE PROPERTY INTERESTS OF MIGRATORY SPOUSES

Preserving the character of the property owned by a husband and wife is often an important goal of estate planning, particularly when they are moving from a state with one type of marital property law to another. However, in some instances the husband and wife may wish to change the character of their property — particularly if they are moving to a community property state. In any case a migratory couple should understand that a move from a community property state to a common law state or from a common law state to a community property state may affect their property interests and the manner in which their property is treated for tax purposes. First, the courts or administrative agencies of the state of the couple's new domicile may mischaracterize their property interests as the IRS appears to have done in Rev. Rul. 68-80, 1968-1 C.B. 348. Second, as indicated in §3.38, married couples moving to some community property states are not protected by the quasi-community property concept. Instead, the property accumulated by a deceased spouse prior to moving to the community property state will probably be characterized as his or her separate property — in which the surviving spouse has no interest and limited rights to family awards and allowances. Thus, the move to a community property state may involve an exchange by the nonacquiring spouse "of a *mere* expectancy for *no* expectancy." Cantwell, Protecting Spousal Rights in a Domicile Change, 14 Community Prop. J. 72, 75 (Jan. 1988).

The methods by which the character of property may be preserved are discussed at §3.25. They include the proper registration of titled assets, the transfer of assets to revocable trusts, and deposit of assets with a financial institution as agent (custodian or agency accounts). The object of the methods is simply to segregate assets of a particular character and to prevent them and their income from being intermixed with assets of a different character.

BIBLIOGRAPHY

I. GENERAL

Committee Report, Property Owned with Spouse: Joint Tenancy, Tenancy by the Entireties and Community Property, 11 Real Prop., Prob. & Tr. J. 405 (1976)

II. Joint Tenancy

Barton, Jointly Owned Spousal Properties, N.Y.U., 41st Inst. Fed. Tax., ch. 41 (1983)

Campfield, Estate Planning for Joint Tenancies, 1974 Duke L.J. 669

Gabrielson, Joint Tenancy Property, 131-2nd BNA Tax Management Portfolio (1989)

Maxfield, Some Reflections on the Taxation of Jointly Held Property, 34 Tax Law. 47 (1980)

III. Community Property

Andrews, Washington's New Quasi-Community Property Act: Protecting the Immigrant Spouse, 15 Community Prop. J. 50 (1988)

Cantwell, Protecting Spousal Rights in a Domicile Change, 14 Community Prop. J. 72 (Jan. 1988)

Crehore, Community Property — Quasi-Community Property — A Caveat for Common Law Practitioners, N.Y.U., 34th Inst. Fed. Tax. 1685 (1976)

Dionisopoulos, The Wisconsin Marital Property Law and Its Effect on Estate Planning, 13 Community Prop. J. 62 (July 1986)

Hilker, Planning for the Married Couple Moving Into or Out of Community Property States, 14 Est. Plan. 212 (1987)

Huston & Mucklestone, Community Property: General Considerations, 212-3rd BNA Tax Management Portfolio (1985)

Johanson, The Migrating Client: Estate Planning for the Couple from a Community Property State, U. Miami, 9th Inst. Est. Plan., ch. 8 (1975)

Kasner, Termination of the Community by Death: The California Perspective, 15 Community Prop. J. 64 (July 1988)

CHAPTER 4

Wills and Related Documents

A. Introduction

§4.1. Overview
§4.2. Federal Estate and Gift Taxes in Perspective
§4.3. Statutory Wills
§4.4. Avoiding Intestacy
§4.4.1. Succession in Common Law Property States
§4.4.2. Succession in Community Property States
§4.5. An Estate Administration Proceeding May Protect the Survivors' Economic Interests
§4.6. Income-Splitting Between Estate and Survivors
§4.7. Contractual Wills
§4.7.1. Uncertain Tax Consequences
§4.7.2. Trusts Are Preferable
§4.7.3. Conditional Wills

B. Organization and Content of Wills

§4.8. General
Chart 4-1. Disposition of Assets Under Will of John Q. Public
Form 4-1. Table of Contents, John Q. Client Will
§4.9. Introduction to Will
Form 4-2. Introduction to Will
§4.10. Revocation
Form 4-3. Revocation of Prior Wills
§4.11. Disposition of Remains
§4.12. Payment of Debts
§4.13. Extent of Testator's Property
§4.14. Family Status and Definitions
Form 4-4. Family Status and Definitions
§4.15. Gift of a Specific Item of Personalty
Form 4-5. Gift of Specific Item of Personalty

§4.15.1. Ademption
§4.15.2. Alternative Disposition
§4.15.3. Simultaneous Death
§4.15.4. Survivorship for Specified Period
Form 4-6. General Survivorship Requirement
§4.16. Cash Gifts
Form 4-7. Cash Gift to Charity
§4.16.1. Charitable Deduction for Tax Purposes
§4.16.2. Satisfaction
§4.16.3. Distribution in Kind
§4.16.4. Forgiveness of Indebtedness
§4.17. Tangible Personal Property
Form 4-8. Gift of Tangible Personal Property
§4.17.1. Testamentary Gifts to Custodians for Minors
§4.17.2. Specific Gifts and Cash Legacies
§4.17.3. Nonspecific Gifts
§4.18. Disposition of Tangible Personal Property in Accordance with Testator's Subsequent Directions
Form 4-9. Gift of Tangible Personal Property by List
§4.18.1. Incorporation by Reference
§4.18.2. Facts or Acts of Independent Significance
§4.18.3. Bequest with Request
§4.18.4. Informal Lists
Form 4-10. List of Gifts of Tangible Personal Property
§4.19. Gifts of Corporate Securities
Form 4-11. Gift of Corporate Securities
§4.20. Gifts of Residence, Policies of Life Insurance, and Employee Benefits
Form 4-12. Gift of Residence, Life Insurance, and Employee Benefits
§4.20.1. Exoneration
§4.20.2. Insurance on Realty and Personalty
§4.20.3. Insurance on the Lives of Others
§4.20.4. Testamentary Changes of Beneficiary Designations; Life Insurance Policies
§4.20.5. Revocation by Change of Circumstances
§4.20.6. Interest in Retirement Plans
§4.21. Residuary Gift
Form 4-13. Residuary Gift
§4.21.1. Should the Residuary Clause Exercise All Powers of Appointment?
§4.21.2. All to the Surviving Spouse?
§4.21.3. A "Pot" Trust or a Separate Trust for Each Child?
§4.21.4. Consolidate the Client's Property in One Trust
Form 4-14. Pour-Over to Inter Vivos Trust
§4.21.5. Discretionary Distributions
§4.21.6. Trust for Minor Descendants

§4.21.7. Ultimate Disposition of Residue
§4.22. Trust Provisions
Form 4-15. Trust for Descendants
Form 4-16. QTIP Trust
§4.23. Trust for Minors
Form 4-17. Trust for Minor Distributees
§4.24. Provisions Applicable to All Trusts
Form 4-18. Trust Administrative Provisions
§4.24.1. Successor Trustees
§4.24.2. Waive Bond
§4.24.3. Trustee's Powers
§4.24.4. Unified Management of Trust Assets
§4.24.5. Investment Criteria
§4.24.6. Authority to Terminate Uneconomical Trusts
§4.24.7. Merger and Division of Trusts
§4.24.8. Spendthrift Clause
§4.25. Guardian of Minor Children
Form 4-19. Appointment of Guardian
§4.26. Appointment of Executors
Form 4-20. Appointment of Executors
Form 4-21. Waiver of Confidentiality by Executor
§4.26.1. Lawyer-Fiduciary
§4.26.2. Corporate Fiduciary
§4.26.3. Family Member Fiduciary
§4.26.4. Coexecutors
§4.26.5. Alternate or Successor Executor
§4.26.6. Exculpatory Clause
Forrn 4-22. Exculpatory Clause
§4.26.7. Executor's Bond
§4.26.8. Compensation of Executors
§4.26.9. Authority to Settle Estate Without Court Supervision
§4.27. Directions Regarding Debts, Expenses of Administration, and Taxes
Form 4-23. Payment of Debts, Taxes, and Expenses
§4.27.1. Source of Funds to Pay Federal Estate Tax
§4.27.2. QTIP and §2207A
§4.27.3. §2207B
§4.27.4. Clarity
§4.27.5. Preserving Qualification for Redemption Under §303
§4.27.6. Power to Make Non-Pro Rata Distributions
§4.27.7. Tax Payments and the Marital and Charitable Deductions
§4.27.8. Payment of State Inheritance Tax
§4.27.9. Statutes Relating to Payment of Federal Estate Tax
§4.27.10. Power to Make Tax Elections

§4.28. Wills Not Pursuant to Contract
Form 4-24. Wills Not Contractual
§4.29. No Contest Clause
§4.30. Execution
Form 4-25. Execution Clause
Form 4-26. Attestation Clause
§4.31. Self-Proving Affidavit
§4.32. Execution Ceremony
§4.33. Letter of Transmittal to Client
Form 4-27. Letter of Transmittal

C. Additional Documents

§4.34. General
§4.35. Durable Powers of Attorney
§4.35.1. Creation, Recordation, and Revocation
§4.35.2. Scope and Use
Form 4-28. Power to Represent Principal with Respect to Federal Tax Matters
§4.35.3. Health Care Decisions and *Cruzan*
Form 4-29. Power to Make Health Care Decisions
§4.35.4. Additional Powers to Deal with Property
Form 4-30. Power to Make Gifts to Family Members
§4.35.5. Durable Power to Transfer Property to Revocable Trust
§4.35.6. Limitations
§4.35.7. "Springing Powers"
Form 4-31. Date Power Becomes Effective
§4.35.8. Conclusion
§4.36. The Living Will and Natural Death Acts
§4.36.1. Who May Make a Living Will
§4.36.2. Immunity Against Civil or Criminal Prosecution
§4.36.3. Uniform Rights of the Terminally Ill Act (1989)
Form 4-32. Declarations Under the Uniform Rights of the Terminally Ill Act (1989)
§4.36.4. Conclusion
§4.37. Sources of Information
§4.38. Anatomical Gifts
§4.38.1. Summary of the 1968 U.A.G.A.
§4.38.2. Donees
§4.38.3. Ways of Making a Gift
§4.38.4. Revocation and Amendment
§4.38.5. Action by Others
§4.38.6. Planning
§4.38.7. Donor Card

Form 4-33. Uniform Donor Card (Anatomical Gifts)
§4.38.8. Conclusion

Bibliography

> While it is increasingly popular to support the estate plan in its main parts upon inter vivos instruments, particularly the revocable living trust, the historic keystone of the arch is the will. Of all legal instruments the will is probably the most familiar; almost every person ought to have one, and every member of the bar is likely to be required, from time to time, to prepare one. Thus the estate plan may consist only of a will: for a person of modest means and "normal" family, possibly a simple will; for a person of moderate or substantial means, with or without some family member needing special attention, possibly a will with trust provisions. The estate plan may consist of several instruments, including a revocable or irrevocable trust; but there always is a will. J. Farr & J. Wright, An Estate Planner's Handbook 129 (4th ed. 1979).

A. INTRODUCTION

§4.1. Overview

This chapter opens with a review of some of the main reasons why most adults should have wills, followed by a discussion of some of the advantages of conducting an estate administration proceeding and the disadvantages of joint or contractual wills. The main portion of the chapter consists of an examination of a form of a will for a married person with a contingent trust for the testator's children. Each provision of the will is followed by comments regarding relevant tax and nontax considerations. More complex dispositive devices, such as marital deduction trusts, widow's election trusts, irrevocable life insurance trusts and charitable remainder trusts, are discussed in later chapters. The chapter concludes with a discussion of some of the other documents a client may wish to execute along with a will, including the durable power of attorney, §4.35, the so-called living will, §4.36, and the gift of bodily parts under the Uniform Anatomical Gift Act, §4.38.

As the quotation from Farr and Wright indicates, almost every adult should have a will. Even though the bulk of a client's wealth may pass under the terms of inter vivos trusts, retirement plans, life insurance policies, joint tenancies, and other will substitutes, a will is needed to provide backup protection. A will can control the disposition of assets that are not effectively disposed of by will substitutes, dispose of after-acquired assets, and perform some important functions that other instruments often cannot perform. For example, a will — and often no other instrument — may be used to:

1. Disinherit children in favor of a spouse, or otherwise deviate from the local intestate succession law;
2. Appoint guardians of the person and estate of minor children;
3. Consolidate assets in inter vivos or testamentary trusts for post-mortem management;
4. Exercise testamentary powers of appointment;
5. Direct the source from which debts and death taxes should be paid;
6. Achieve income and transfer tax savings by giving survivors limited interests in testamentary trusts;
7. Dispose of the proceeds of policies of insurance on the life of the testator if the beneficiary does not survive the testator; and
8. Vary the consequences of simultaneous death or require the beneficiaries to survive the testator for a limited period.

Under the existing law the terms of a will generally do not affect the disposition of nonprobate property. For example, amounts payable under multiparty bank accounts, employee benefit plans, life insurance policies, and other nontestamentary devices are not subject to change by will. In some cases, however, the courts have upheld changes of beneficiary or other dispositions of nonprobate property that were made by will. *See* §4.18.4. In the future the Uniform Probate Code (U.P.C.) may give recognition to the concept of a "super will" by which the testator could affect the disposition of some types of property that are not usually subject to estate administration. Legislation might authorize a testator, by express testamentary reference, to designate a new beneficiary of a life insurance policy or preretirement death benefit. Such authorization is probably consistent with the intention of most testators and would promote the orderly administration and disposition of property without serious hazard to insurers or financial institutions.

§4.2. Federal Estate and Gift Taxes in Perspective

Because the unified credit shelters up to $600,000 from the federal estate and gift taxes they are of little concern to most American families.

Indeed, the data indicate that estate tax returns were filed in 1988 for only about 2.4 percent of the number of deaths in 1987. 1989 Statistical Abstract of the United States 61 (death data); 1988 Annual Report of the Commissioner of Internal Revenue 7 (estate tax return data); Johnson, Estate Tax Returns, 1986-88, 9 Statistics of Income Bulletin 27 (no. 4, 1990) (data for 1968); McCubbin & Rosenfeld, Introducing an IRS Data Base for Estate Tax Research, 128 Tr. & Est. 62 (Mar. 1989) (data regarding returns filed for estates of persons who died in 1984). Likewise, because of the $1 million exemption, the Generation-Skipping Transfer Tax (GSTT) is of concern to relatively few individuals.

Most clients have modest wealth and relatively simple estate plans. For example, the principal goals of the estate plan of a married couple who have young children are usually (1) to transfer all of their property to the surviving parent or, if neither of them survives, to a contingent trust for their children; and (2) to appoint guardians of the person for their minor children. Their needs may be met by a "simple" will which includes a contingent trust for children (or provision for distribution to a custodian for each child under the Uniform Transfer to Minors Act), a durable power of attorney, and a living will. Those documents are explored in later parts of this chapter.

§4.3. Statutory Wills

In the long run statutory forms of wills and trusts may simplify estate planning for clients of modest means. Work on forms of statutory wills proceeded along two lines in the 1980s. The work of a committee of the Real Property, Probate, and Trust Section of the American Bar Association, chaired by John A. Perkins, culminated in the Uniform Statutory Wills Act, approved by the National Conference of Commissioners on Uniform State Laws in 1984, 8A U.L.A. 196 (1990 Supp.).

> The Uniform Statutory Wills Act is a proposed statute to provide a scheme of testamentary disposition of broad utility. This Act contemplates that a testator will *adopt* the statutory *will through incorporation by reference* in a "simple will." This Act does not provide a battery of optional schemes or provisions, but it does permit modifications and additions to be made by the will which adopts the statutory will scheme generally or for some portion of the testator's estate. The statutory will may be the entire will of a testator and thus apply to all of the testator's testamentary estate, or it is adaptable to apply to a portion of the testator's estate as part of a will which includes other devises. . . .
>
> The approach of this Act is to provide attorneys a simple will embodying an estate plan workable for many clients, a will that can be prepared quickly, that can be adapted easily to special situations, and that guards against common drafting errors, all at minimum cost to the

client and productive use of the lawyer's time. Although the Act is thus helpful to the legal profession, its intended and true beneficiaries are the public in terms of economical and expeditious legal services. Prefatory Note, 8A U.L.A. 196, 197 (1990 Supp.).

Another approach was taken in California, which adopted two complete statutory will forms. *See* Cal. Prob. Code §§6220-6247 (West 1991 Supp.). Copies of the statutory will may be ordered from: State Bar of California, 555 Franklin Street, San Francisco, California 94102. A similar approach has been taken in some other states, including Maine, Michigan, and Wisconsin. Me. Rev. Stat. Ann. tit. 18-A, §2-514 (1990); Mich. Stat. Ann. §27.5122 (Callaghan 1980); Wis. Stat. Ann. §§853.50-853.62 (1990 Supp.). There is some risk that individuals may misunderstand or misuse the statutory forms. The point was made by the National Commissioners in their Prefatory Note, *supra:* "With statutory wills act that are enacted with a statutory form, there seems to be a contemplation that the forms will be used by persons without the advice of an attorney. Although the forms include several notices or caveats, one of which encourages the user to consult an attorney, it is believed that the forms will be used without consulting an attorney and if used that way, the forms are fraught with opportunities for misunderstanding and mistake by the unwitting." Overall, however, the statutory forms provide the public with important tools which are unquestionably superior to the printed will forms that were formerly available.

§4.4. Avoiding Intestacy

Although transfer taxes are not a major concern for most individuals, they do need to be concerned about providing in the most economical and efficient way for their spouses, children, and other dependents. Indeed, proper estate planning may be most important for those with the smallest estates — the persons whose dependents can least afford incurring unnecessary costs or delays.

If neither parent survives, the welfare of minor children is generally best served by consolidating all of the parents' wealth in either an inter vivos trust (through the use of a "pour-over" will) or in a testamentary trust. Through proper beneficiary designations and contractual arrangements life insurance proceeds and other nonprobate assets may also be made payable to the trustee of an inter vivos or testamentary trust. In any event, the expense, delay, and inconvenience of a guardianship of a minor's share of an estate should be avoided. These plans are discussed in more detail in connection with the residuary clause of the model will. *See* §4.21.

Most married persons who die testate transfer all of their property at death to the surviving spouse, whether they reside in a community or a common law property state. M. Sussman, J. Cates & D. Smith, The Family and Inheritance 89-90, 143-144 (1970); Price, the Transmission of Wealth at Death in a Community Property Jurisdiction, 50 Wash. L. Rev. 277 (1975). Wills are usually needed to achieve that result because under many states' intestate succession laws a surviving spouse is not entitled to all of a deceased spouse's property. A surviving spouse is entitled to a deceased spouse's entire share of the community property in all cases under the law of some community property states — California, Idaho, Nevada, New Mexico, Washington — but not of others. For example, a surviving spouse is entitled to all of the community property under the intestate succession law of Arizona only if all of the surviving descendants are descendants of the surviving spouse. In Texas, the surviving spouse takes all of the community property only if the decedent is not survived by descendants.

§4.4.1. Succession in Common Law Property States

Most common law property states limit the intestate share of the surviving spouse if the decedent was also survived by issue of any degree. *E.g.,* Fla. Stat. Ann. §732.102 (West 1988). Under the Florida law the estate of an intestate decedent would be divided between a surviving spouse and the decedent's grandchildren or other more remote descendants. Indeed, in many common law property states a decedent's parents and their descendants are entitled to a share of the property in preference to the decedent's surviving spouse. *E.g.,* N.Y. Est. Powers & Trusts Law §4-1.1 (McKinney 1990 Supp.). In contrast, studies have repeatedly demonstrated that the overwhelming majority of married persons who die testate leave all of their property to their surviving spouses or wish to do so. *E.g.,* M. Sussman, J. Cates & D. Smith, The Family and Inheritance 133 (1970); Dunham, The Method, Process and Frequency of Wealth Transmission at Death, 30 U. Chi. L. Rev. 241 (1963); Fellows, Simon & Rau, Public Attitudes About Property Distribution at Death and Intestate Succession Laws in the United States, 1978 Am. Bar. Found. Res. J. 319. *See also,* Price, The Transmission of Wealth at Death in a Community Property Jurisdiction, 50 Wash. L. Rev. 277 (1975). Perhaps believing that the studies reflect the wishes of most individuals, the U.P.C. and a growing number of states have increased the intestate shares of the surviving spouse. In a few common law property states the surviving spouse is entitled to all of a deceased spouse's intestate property unless the decedent left issue who were not issue of the surviving spouse. *E.g.,* Iowa Code

Ann. §§633.211-633.212 (West 1990 Supp.); Mont. Code Ann. §72-2-202(1) (1989).

Under the U.P.C. if an intestate married decedent is survived by a spouse and descendants, all of whom are also descendants of the surviving spouse, the survivor is entitled to receive the first $200,000 and three-fourths of the balance of the decedent's estate. U.P.C. §2-102 (1990). (If some of the decedent's descendants are not also descendants of the surviving spouse, the surviving spouse is limited to $100,000 and half of the estate.) Florida law is to the same effect except the dollar amount is $20,000. Fla. Stat. Ann. §732.102(1) (West 1988).

Under basic conflict of laws principles, when married persons move from a community property state to a common law property state the community property they bring with them should retain that character. However, courts have encountered some difficulty in properly characterizing the property. *See* Johanson, The Migrating Client: Estate Planning for the Couple from a Community Property State, U. Miami, 9th Inst. Est. Plan., ch. 8 (1975). Under the Uniform Disposition of Community Property Rights at Death Act, 8A U.L.A. 121 (1983), which has been adopted by several common law property states, half of the community property brought into a common law property state is confirmed to the surviving spouse and half is subject to the deceased spouse's power of testamentary disposition. *See* §3.37.

§4.4.2. Succession in Community Property States

Under community property law each spouse owns a one-half interest in the community property. The same is true of marital property under §4(c) of the Uniform Marital Property Act. The death of one spouse does not impair the surviving spouse's ownership of one-half of the community property. Only the deceased spouse's one-half interest in the community property and his or her separate property is subject to his or her will or to distribution under the intestate succession law. The succession law of most community property states and the alternate provisions of the U.P.C. recommended for adoption in community property states give the surviving spouse all of a deceased spouse's share of the community property. *E.g.,* Cal. Prob. Code §6401(a) (West 1991 Supp.); Wash. Rev. Code §11.04.015(1)(a) (1989); Wisc. Stat. Ann. §852.01 (West 1990 Supp.) (entire net estate); U.P.C. §2-102A. In most community property states the noncommunity property of a deceased spouse is divided between the surviving spouse and, in order of priority, the decedent's surviving descendants, parents, and issue of parents. Under the alternate provisions of the

U.P.C. a surviving spouse is also entitled to all of the decedent's noncommunity property if the decedent was not survived by descendants or parents.

Again, under basic conflict of laws principles, when married persons move from a common law property state to a community property state, or vice versa, the property they owned prior to the move retains its original character in the absence of some action on their part to change it. *See* §3.36. This typically means that in a move from a common law property state to a community property state, the imported property is treated as the separate property of the acquiring spouse — in which the nonacquiring spouse has no interest. However, in California, Idaho, and Washington the surviving spouse is entitled to a share of the quasi-community property (property acquired during marriage while residing in a noncommunity property state that would have been community property had the couple resided in a community property state at the time the property was acquired). *See* §3.38.

§4.5. An Estate Administration Proceeding May Protect the Survivors' Economic Interests

A client may assume that it is best to "avoid probate" entirely. However, in many states the additional cost of conducting an estate proceeding may be relatively slight — often more than offset by the advantages of such a course. For example, having such a proceeding makes it mandatory for the claims of creditors to be filed within a statutory period (typically four months from the first publication of notice to creditors) or they are forever barred. *See, e.g.,* Cal. Prob. Code §§9051, 9100 (West 1991 Supp.); U.P.C. §3-803. Of course, creditors will only be barred if the notice to creditors procedure meets the due process requirements of *Tulsa Professional Collection Services, Inc. v. Pope,* 485 U.S. 478 (1988).

The protection against creditors may be particularly valuable in the case of a decedent engaged in business or professional activities that might generate lingering contract or tort liabilities. In some cases a lawyer may be negligent if he or she fails to advise a client that creditors' claims may be barred by conducting an estate proceeding and publishing the requisite notice. Also, family awards and allowances that are available to a surviving spouse and minor children under the law of most states insulate a small amount of property from creditors' claims. *See* §12.30. Finally, in recent years the cost and delay of estate administration proceedings have been reduced by the U.P.C. and other streamlined estate administration procedures.

§4.6. Income-Splitting Between Estate and Survivors

Conducting an estate administration proceeding is advantageous because a decedent's estate is treated as a separate taxable entity for income tax purposes. "Splitting" the family's income among the decedent's estate and the survivors usually produces some income tax savings. Although the compressed income tax rate structure that was adopted in 1986 limits the advantages, income-splitting retains some importance. First, an estate is entitled to a $600 deduction in lieu of a personal exemption. §642(b). Second, the income tax rates have some progressivity, at least until a taxable income of $10,350 is reached. The income tax rates applicable to estates and trusts in 1991, reflecting the adjustment for inflation, are:

Taxable Income	*Tax*
$0 — $3,450	15% of Taxable Income
$3,450 — $10,350	$518 plus 28% on excess over $3,450
$10,350 and over	$2,450 plus 31% on excess over $10,350

The amount of the potential savings depends largely upon the income tax position of the beneficiaries. For example, beneficiaries whose income is subject to a marginal rate of 28 percent could save as much as $527 each year ($600 (deduction) plus $3,450 (lowest bracket) times 13 percent (bracket differential)). In addition, through proper planning any excess deductions of the estate can be carried out to the beneficiaries for whom it will produce the largest income tax savings.

It is important to understand that the income tax does not "track" the estate tax in a very important respect: The income from an asset included in the gross estate is not necessarily taxed to the estate. The post-mortem income from property that passes to a survivor without estate administration is normally taxed entirely to the survivor and not to the decedent's estate. A leading text explains the point in this way:

> During the estate's recognized period of existence, the property treated as a part of the estate for income tax purposes does not necessarily include all assets in which the decedent had some interest at death. However, property subject even temporarily to administration is usually within the Subchapter J estate. Thus, many of the tax consequences . . . hinge not so much on the nature of the decedent's interests in property generating income after his death as on the degree to which the property is subject to the custody or management of his personal representative. C. Ferguson, J. Freeland & R. Stephens, Federal Income Taxation of Estates and Beneficiaries 11 (1970).

Thus, the post-mortem income generated by property that the decedent and a survivor held as joint tenants is taxed entirely to the survivor. For most nontax purposes joint tenancy property is also not considered to pass through the decedent's estate. An asset held in joint tenancy and the income generated by it belong exclusively to the survivor by reason of the form of ownership. The same is true of property that is subject to other survivorship arrangements (*e.g.,* Totten trusts, survivorship accounts in financial institutions).

The post-mortem income from the decedent's share of the community property that is subject to an administration proceeding is taxed to the decedent's estate. The remaining half is taxed to the surviving spouse. That rule applies even if the local law subjects all of the community property to administration upon the death of one spouse.

The message is relatively short and simple — if there is no estate administration there is no separate taxable entity and no opportunity for income-splitting.

§4.7. Contractual Wills

A husband and wife, siblings, or other relatives often ask for wills that contain more or less reciprocal provisions. In such cases the clients need to decide the extent to which they want to restrict the survivor's right to dispose of the property inter vivos or change the dispositive provisions of his or her will. *See* Form 4-24 (Article Sixteen), §4.28 *infra.* This subject should be raised, although the lawyer should conduct the discussion in a tactful way that does not promote discord between the clients or generate undue suspicions or concerns. The lawyer must also be alert to the conflict-of-interest problems that may arise if the parties wish to bind the survivor in some respect. In a word, their interests may be adverse. *See* §1.14.

In any case, wills that contain reciprocal provisions should generally state whether or not they were executed pursuant to any agreement. If so, the agreement should be set forth in the wills or in a supplemental instrument. The same practice should be followed whether the parties execute separate instruments with reciprocal provisions (mutual wills) or a single instrument (a joint will). The statement should be made even though the governing law may, like the U.P.C., make it difficult to prove will contracts. Under U.P.C. §2-514 (1990) will contracts entered into after its effective date may "be established only by (1) provisions of a will stating material provisions of the contract; (2) an express reference in a will to a contract and extrinsic evidence proving the terms of the contract; or (3) a writing signed by the decedent evidencing the contract. The execution of a joint will or mutual wills does not create a presumption of a contract not to revoke the will or wills." Statutes in some states are more stringent. For example, Fla. Stat. Ann. §732.701 (West 1988) provides that an agreement to make a will or not to revoke a will is enforceable only if "the agreement is in writing and signed by the agreeing party in the presence of two attesting witnesses." The same Florida statute provides that the execution of a joint will or mutual wills does not create a presumption of a contract to make a will or not to revoke the will or wills. Despite the best efforts of the testators to clarify their intentions, when contractual wills are executed the potential for litigation remains high.

§4.7.1. Uncertain Tax Consequences

The uncertain federal and state tax consequences of contractual wills also make them generally undesirable. For example, the interests in property that pass to a surviving spouse under a contractual will may or may not qualify for the marital deduction. However, the interest of the surviving spouse will frequently qualify for the elective QTIP marital deduction under §2056(b)(7). Dobris, Do Contractual Will Arrangements Qualify for Qualified Terminable Interest Property Treatment Under ERTA?, 19 Real Prop., Prob. & Tr. J. 625 (1984). *See* §5.23. No deduction was available to the estate of a person dying before 1982 if the survivor received an interest only equivalent to a life estate in the decedent's property with a power to consume. *Estate of Opal v. Commissioner,* 450 F.2d 1085 (2d Cir. 1971). In such a case the surviving spouse received a terminable interest that was not deductible.

Upon the death of the first spouse to die, the surviving spouse may be treated as having made a taxable gift of a future interest in his or her property to the beneficiaries named in the contractual wills. *Grimes v. Commissioner,* 851 F.2d 1005 (7th Cir. 1988); *Pyle v. United States,* 766 F.2d 1141 (7th Cir. 1985), *cert. denied,* 475 U.S. 1015 (1986). *See also* LR 7810001. Under Illinois law, applied in *Grimes* and *Pyle,* the surviving spouse is under an obligation to preserve the property and distribute what remains in accordance with the provision of the joint will. "Joint wills permit the surviving spouse to invade the corpus only for limited purposes." *Grimes,* 851 F.2d at 1007. In *Pyle* the Seventh Circuit Court of Appeals said, "The state court's linking the word 'comfort' to the words 'health, support, and maintenance' in its construction of the will, while imposing strict limits on Grace's power to alienate her property, convinces us that the will limited her discretion by an ascertainable standard." In *Estate of Lidbury v. Commissioner,* 800 F.2d 649 (7th Cir. 1986), another Illinois case involving a joint and mutual will, the Seventh Circuit held that no gift took place upon the death of the wife because of the limited restrictions that the agreement placed upon the surviving husband's use and disposition of the property: "The contract executed by William and Rose allowed William to incur debts and alienate the property with only slight restrictions." 800 F.2d at 654. Presumably other courts would reach the same conclusion if the survivor were relatively free to use and consume the property.

The imposition of a gift tax at the time of the death of the first spouse to die is also consistent with Rev. Rul. 69-346, 1969-1 C.B. 227, which holds that in the case of a binding inter vivos widow's election, a gift of the survivor's remainder interest in the community property takes place at the time of the husband's death, when it is first possible to value the remainder interest in the property that she became obligated to transfer at the time she executed the election. *See* §9.24. Presumably no gift takes place if the survivor retains a power to consume or appoint his or her share of the property. *See* Reg. §25.2511-2(c). If there is a completed gift at the time of the death of the first spouse to die, §2702 may apply. If so, the retained life interest of the surviving spouse may be valued at zero, as a result of which she will be considered to have made a gift of her entire interest in the property. *See* §9.42.3.

§4.7.2. Trusts Are Preferable

In view of the substantive law problems and uncertain tax consequences of contractual wills, an inter vivos or testamentary trust is almost invariably a better way to provide for survivors. More important, a trust may avoid the uncertainty that inheres in contractual arrangements regarding a variety of matters, including the scope of the survivor's authority to dispose of assets during his or her lifetime. Also, in the case of a trust, the legal title to the trust property is vested in the trustee, who may manage and invest the assets in accordance with the terms of the trust. A trust may also more effectively limit the control that one of the parties may exert over the property. Of course, a trust may also avoid the necessity of establishing a guardianship should one or both of the parties become incompetent. However, in such a case the trustee must be given sufficient discretionary powers to distribute income and principal to the survivors in order to meet their needs.

§4.7.3. Conditional Wills

The effectiveness of a will, or of a provision of a will, may be made conditional on the occurrence or nonoccurrence of a specific event. Conditional wills should generally be avoided, however, because of their potential for litigation. Reflecting the presumption favoring testacy, a "condition" may be construed by a court as an indication of the reason the will was made rather than as a condition. Generally a client's needs are better met by a "regular" will, which may include conditional bequests. *See* T. Atkinson, Wills §83 (2d ed. 1953).

B. ORGANIZATION AND CONTENT OF WILLS

§4.8. General

Professionally prepared wills are usually arranged so that the articles, or paragraphs, that deal with related subjects appear together. A will typically contains a series of articles that, successively, (1) identify the testator and the members of the testator's family, revoke earlier wills, and define terms; (2) dispose of the testator's property; (3) appoint fiduciaries including guardians and trustees; (4) enumerate the powers and duties of fiduciaries and contain directions regarding the payment of debts and taxes; and (5) provide for execution by the testator and witnesses. Some lawyers prefer to locate the articles appointing fiduciaries and enumerating their powers in the fore part of the will, before the dispositive provisions, on the theory that the identity of the fiduciaries and the extent of their powers should be dealt with at the outset. In any case the substance — not the particular order of these materials — is most important.

The following sections present the provisions that might be included in a "typical" will for a married client of modest means. After making some specific gifts, the will gives all of the client's property to his wife if she survives him, otherwise to a contingent trust for their children. Each provision is followed by a comment concerning its substantive and tax law consequences. The comments also point out why some other commonly encountered provisions should be used sparingly, if at all. The provisions are presented for the purpose of discussion and analysis and are not intended for use without the professional assistance of a competent lawyer.

As a convenience some lawyers attach a table of contents to the wills and trusts that they prepare. A table of contents is particularly helpful to a client if it includes a brief summary of the content of each article of the will or trust. Some lawyers also attach a chart to each will or trust they prepare, which shows how various types of property will be disposed of under the client's estate plan. A simple chart for John Q. Client appears as Chart 4-1. *See* Chart 1-1, §1.33.3, *supra.*

A table of contents may refer to all of the provisions of the will or only to the principal dispositive provisions.

Chart 4-1
Disposition of Assets
Under Will of John Q. Client

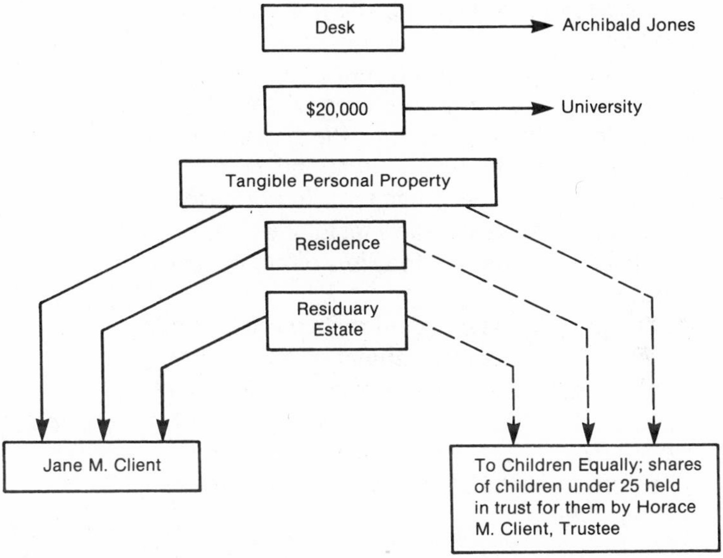

Jane M. Client appointed Executor and Horace M. Client as Successor
Horace M. Client appointed Guardian of Minor Children and Louise Client Smith as Successor
Horace M. Client appointed Trustee and ____________ as Successor

——————— Jane M. Client survives John Q. Client

— — — — — Jane M. Client does not survive John Q. Client

Form 4-1. Table of Contents, John Q. Client Will

Article One. Revocation of prior wills. p. ____
Article Two. Description of family members. Definition of descendants. p. ____
Article Three. Specific gift of antique desk. p. ____
Article Four. Cash gift of $20,000 to University. p. ____
Article Five. Gift of tangible personal property to wife if she survives, otherwise to children equally, having due regard for preferences of each child. p. ____
Article Six. Gift of jewelry to wife to dispose of in accordance with my wishes [or by list]. p. ____

Article Seven. Gift of 100 shares of XYZ, Inc. stock to brother Horace M. Client if he survives testator. p. ____

Article Eight. Gift of residence and associated policies of insurance to wife if she survives. p. ____

Article Nine. Give of remainder of estate to wife if she survives, otherwise in equal shares to children who survive. The share of each child under 25 will be held in trust until he or she reaches that age. If neither wife nor children survive, then one-half to testator's nearest relations and one-half to wife's nearest surviving relations. p. ____

Article Ten. Terms of trust for children, including provision for reimbursement of guardian for additional expenses incurred in caring for children. p. ____

Article Eleven. Simple trust to hold property otherwise distributable to a beneficiary under 25. p. ____

Article Twelve. Appointment of Horace M. Client as trustee of each trust, ________________ as successor. Waiver of any requirement that trustee post bond. Clause preventing beneficiaries from transferring, or their creditors reaching, their interests in the trust(s). p. ____

Article Thirteen. Appointment of Horace M. Client as guardian of minor children and Louise Client Smith as successor. p. ____

Article Fourteen. Appointment of wife as executor and Horace M. Client as successor. Waiver of any requirement that executor post bond. Authorization for executor to hire accountants, lawyers, and other assistants and to settle estate without intervention of any court to the maximum degree permitted under local law. p. ____

Article Fifteen. Direction to pay all expenses of administration and death taxes from assets of the residuary estate (Article Nine). Authorization to make various tax elections. p. ____

Article Sixteen. Statement that wills of husband and wife are reciprocal in nature, but not contractual. Survivor is free to revoke his or her will. p. ____
Execution and attestation clauses. p. ____
Self-proving affidavit. To enable will to be admitted to probate without personal appearance of witnesses. p. ____

§4.9. Introduction to Will

Form 4-2. Introduction to Will

WILL OF JOHN Q. CLIENT

I, John Q. Client, also known as John Quincy Client, a resident of ________________ (*city*), ________________ (*state*) declare this to be my will.

The introduction (or exordium clause) of a will indicates the name or names by which the testator is known. This may help the personal representative to identify, collect, and transfer the testator's property. The declaration may also help establish the place of the decedent's residence. Although not determinative, it is some indication of the testator's understanding and intent. T. Atkinson, Wills §147 at 819 (2d ed. 1953). The recitation may be helpful in dealing with procedural issues, such as the jurisdiction and venue of courts. Normally the courts of the state of a decedent's domicile have jurisdiction over most estate administration matters. Within a state the venue is generally laid in the county in which the decedent was domiciled.

The determination of domicile is sometimes also significant for death tax purposes. In general, the state of a decedent's domicile has jurisdiction to tax all of the decedent's property except real property and tangible personal property located in other states. Most states have enacted laws that are intended to relieve the double tax burdens that might be imposed if two or more states determine that the decedent was a domiciliary. However, if at all possible the potential for conflict regarding the place of a client's domicile should be eliminated through advance planning.

Attention must also be given to the citizenship of the testator because of tax and administrative considerations. Citizenship is particularly important because the marital deduction is now generally limited to transfers to spouses who are U.S. citizens or deathtime gifts that are in the form of qualified domestic trusts. *See* §5.24. Also, if a testator owns property in another country consideration should be given to executing one will covering assets with a situs in the United States and another for each other country in which assets are held.

The declaration that the instrument is the testator's will indicates that the testator is aware of the character and purpose of the instrument and evidences the requisite testamentary intent. The introduction may also include a clause revoking all prior wills, but a revocation clause is perhaps more properly the subject of a separate article. In either case the revocatory provision is equally effective.

Some lawyers favor more elaborate captions and clauses, perhaps to satisfy clients' expectations regarding the formality and quality of their wills. Thus, the caption may read "LAST WILL AND TESTAMENT OF JOHN Q. CLIENT," and the exordium may read, "IN THE NAME OF GOD, AMEN, I, JOHN Q. CLIENT, also known as JOHN QUINCY CLIENT, a resident of ____________, ____________, being of sound mind and body and sound and disposing memory and not acting under fraud, duress, or undue influence, do make, publish, and declare the following to be my last will and testament, to wit. . . ." A recitation setting forth the soundness of the testator's mind is of little value and may even create suspicion that the testator's lawyer was uncertain about his or her testamentary capacity. Nonetheless, language of that kind still crops up in form books . . . and wills.

© Mell Lazarus
By permission of Mell Lazarus and Creators Syndicate

§4.10. Revocation

Form 4-3. Revocation of Prior Wills

Article One: I revoke all wills and codicils previously made by me.

A complete disposition of the testator's property in a later will revokes the provisions of a former one by inconsistency. However, it is more straightforward and orderly to include an express revocation of earlier testamentary documents. There is ordinarily no virtue in leaving the issue even slightly uncertain when it can easily be nailed down.

The lawyer may wish to omit a revocation clause if the effectiveness of the will is uncertain or may be dependent upon the testator surviving for a specified period of time following execution of the will. A revocation clause might be omitted, for example, from a will that repeats a charitable bequest that was contained in an earlier will if the local law includes a mortmain statute which denies effect to charitable gifts unless the testator survives for a specified period following execution of the will. Otherwise, if the testator were to die prior to passage of the required length of time, the charitable bequest might be denied any effect; the bequest in the later will would be invalid under the mortmain statute and the earlier will would be ineffective because of the revocation clause. Of course, some courts might save the day by applying the doctrine of dependent relative revocation in a way that denied effect to the revocation clause, at least with respect to the charitable bequest. *In re Kaufman's Estate,* 155 P.2d 831 (Cal. 1945).

§4.11. Disposition of Remains

Directions regarding funeral arrangements and the disposition of remains are sometimes included in a will. The inclusion of directions ordinarily does no harm; however, they should also be included in a letter or other writing more readily accessible than the will. Perhaps the best solution is for the client to give a separate statement to the executor named in the will or to another reliable person. The statement, and perhaps the client's will, should refer to any burial plot the client owns and any funeral arrangements the client has made. As one commentator has observed, the will is perhaps the worst place to put directions regarding the disposition of the testator's remains. "Most families, when stricken by the death of a close relative, will abstain from reading the will until after the funeral. This is the result of grief, appearances, decency or ritual." T. Shaffer, The Planning and Drafting of Wills and Trusts 176 (2d ed. 1979).

If a client wishes to make a gift of part or all of his or her body for medical research or organ transplantation, the intended donee institution should be consulted regarding the acceptability of the intended gift, the form in which the gift should be made, and any other requirements the donee may impose. All states have enacted some form of the Uniform Anatomical Gift Act. Section 4 of the Act authorizes gifts to be made by will, card, or other writing signed by the donor and two witnesses in the donor's presence. 8A U.L.A. 15, 43 (1983). *See* §4.38.

§4.12. Payment of Debts

Wills frequently include a direction that "my executor shall pay all of my just debts as soon as practicable after my death." Such a direction is better omitted. It is superfluous and can lead to a variety of wholly unnecessary disputes. For example, a controversy may arise concerning the necessity of exonerating requests of encumbered property or of paying debts that are barred by the statute of limitations. With respect to exoneration, U.P.C. §2-607 (1990) provides that "[a] specific devise passes subject to any mortgage interest existing at the date of death, without right of exoneration, regardless of a general directive in the will to pay debts." As indicated below, designating the source of funds that should be used to pay debts, expenses of administration, and taxes may be desirable, rather than relying on the local law regarding abatement. *See* Form 4-23, *infra.* Such a specification is permissible under U.P.C. §3-902 (1990).

§4.13. Extent of Testator's Property

If a husband and wife have had some contact with a community property state during their marriage, their wills might include provisions that specify the extent to which they believe their property, or specific items of it, is community in nature. Although such a recitation is not determinative of the property's character, it is some evidence of the testator's understanding. Also, a discussion of the matter of community property, if it had not been previously broached between the lawyer and involved parties, is encouraged by such a provision. In order to fortify the effect of any other oral or written agreement between a husband and wife, it may be desirable to include a statement in their wills regarding the character of the property they own. The statement may be particularly appropriate where their property is entirely community in nature. For example, the will might state, "I declare that all of the property in which I have an interest is the community property of my wife and me." Except in cases in which there is an intent to put a surviving spouse to an election, the will might also recite, "I hereby declare that I do not intend to put my wife to any election regarding the disposition of her interest in our community property and I expressly confirm to her the one-half interest therein that belongs to her by reason of law." The community property widow's election device is explained in Chapter 9.

Uncertain language may require the surviving spouse either to elect whether to accept the benefits provided under the decedent's will and consent to the decedent's disposition of the entire community interest in a particular asset, or to reject the benefits and retain a one-half interest in all of the community property. An election may be required if, for example, the will leaves "all items of property which bear both my name and my wife's name to my wife" and "all other property to my children." In *Estate of Patton,* 494 P.2d 238 (Wash. App. 1972), the court held that such provisions required the wife to elect whether (1) to receive the entire interest in assets that stood in both their names and consent to the transfer of the entire interest in all other community property to the decedent's children, or (2) to retain her half of the community property and receive no benefits under the will. If a surviving spouse elects against the will, the local law should bar the surviving spouse from receiving an intestate share in any of the property that is undisposed of by the will as a result of the election.

In some community property states, property that is held in joint tenancy by a husband and wife is presumed to be their community property. The will may also confirm that the residence of the husband and wife is held by them as joint tenants and that he intends the property to belong exclusively to her if she survives him. The provision is particularly appropriate if the will leaves the testator's residuary estate to persons other than the surviving spouse — such as children by a prior marriage. The residue would be increased to the extent of half of the value of the residence if it was determined to be held by them as tenants in common or owned by them as community property. For example, under the law of some community property states, assets that are acquired in joint tenancy form with community property funds may remain the community property of the spouses.

§4.14. Family Status and Definitions

Form 4-4. Family Status and Definitions

Article Two: I declare that I am married to Jane Martin Client ("my wife") and that I now have three children, namely, Karen Ann Client (born August 1, 1978), Samuel Martin Client (born April 15, 1982), and John Rogers Client (born November 7, 1985). References in this will to "my children" are to them and any children later born to or adopted by me.

The term "descendants" refers to all naturally born or legally adopted descendants of all degrees of the person indicated.

The introduction and identification of the testator's spouse and children establishes the testator's family circumstances at the time the will was executed. It also helps a reader by clarifying the relationship of the persons mentioned in the will, resolves ambiguities that might otherwise be caused by the use of terms such as "wife" and "children," and avoids the pretermission of children by naming all existing children and using a class term to include children who are later born to or adopted by the testator. The recitation also tends to establish that the testator knew "the objects of his bounty" at the time the will was executed, which is one of the elements of the traditional test of testamentary capacity. By including the dates of the children's births the client and the lawyer will be led to consider problems that might arise by reason of their minority, such as the need for guardians of their persons. The dates may also be helpful to the court, tax authorities, and others who may be called upon to deal with the instrument. The possible pretermission of descendants of a testator's deceased children under the law of some states suggests the desirability of also mentioning the testator's grandchildren by name or class (*e.g.,* descendants).

The term "descendants" is used in the instrument rather than "issue" because the former term is more understandable by lay persons. It is defined to include both naturally born and adopted persons of all degrees. A client may wish to exclude either all adopted persons or ones who are adopted after a specified age, such as 18. In some cases a restriction may be appropriate in order to prevent an adult from being adopted primarily for the purpose of qualifying to receive property under a will or trust. The definition is broad enough to include children born to unmarried parents. Under §2 of the Uniform Parentage Act, 9A U.L.A. 287 (1987), and similar laws, a child's status is recognized regardless of whether the child's parents ever intermarry. Accordingly, it may be wise expressly to include or exclude children born to unmarried parents in order to avoid their pretermission. Unless a term such as "descendants" or "issue" is adequately defined it may require construction by a court — a form of resolution that should be avoided.

In general, "heirs" is a term that should not be used in any dispositive instrument. It is inappropriate because the testator usually intends to describe a definite, more limited class of persons (*e.g.,* children or descendants). Even if the term appears to be proper, a more precise description of the intended beneficiaries is preferable. Finally, "heirs" should not be used in order to avoid any lingering possibility that the Rule in Shelley's Case or the testamentary branch of the Doctrine of Worthier Title might be applied to gifts made in the will.

§4.15. Gift of a Specific Item of Personalty

Form 4-5. Gift of Specific Item of Personalty

Article Three: I give my antique mahogany desk by Samuel McIntyre to my friend Archibald Jones if he survives me. However, if the desk is not a part of my estate at the time of my death for reasons other than an inter vivos gift to Archibald Jones, I give him the sum of Five Thousand Dollars ($5,000) in place of the desk if he survives me. If Archibald Jones does not survive me no property shall pass under this Article.

A gift to an individual beneficiary should ordinarily be expressly conditioned, as here, upon the beneficiary surviving the testator. Under such a provision, if the beneficiary does not survive the testator and the gift is not "saved" by the anti-lapse statute, the property will be disposed of as a part of the testator's residuary estate. An anti-lapse statute usually does not apply if the testator indicates that it should not. For this purpose most courts accept that such an intention is evidenced if the bequest is conditioned on the beneficiary surviving the testator. W. McGovern, S. Kurtz & J. Reid, Wills, Trusts and Estates §10.4 (1988). Unfortunately, the 1990 version of the U.P.C. adopts a contrary rule: that conditioning a bequest on survivorship is not itself sufficient evidence of an intention that the anti-lapse statute should not apply. U.P.C. §2-603(b)(3) (1990). In any case, most anti-lapse statutes only apply to gifts that are made to a relative of the testator who predeceases the testator leaving lineal descendants who survive the testator. *See, e.g.,* U.P.C. §2-605 (1990); N.Y. Est. Powers & Trusts Law §3-3.3 (McKinney 1990 Supp.) (only applies to issue and siblings of the testator); Wash. Rev. Code §11.12.110 (1989). If a specific gift not conditioned on survivorship fails because the beneficiary predeceases the testator and the anti-lapse statute does not apply, the subject of the gift becomes a part of the testator's residuary estate under the common law and under the provisions of many statutes. U.P.C. §2-604(a) (1990).

In order to be consistent and avoid unnecessary problems, specific gifts of tangible personal property, such as Article Three, should be excluded from the coverage of a general gift of tangible personal property, such as made by Article Five. Form 4-8, §4.17, *infra.*

Example 4-1. *T* died leaving a will that included a bequest of "my gold watch to my uncle Harold" and gave the entire residuary estate to a charitable organization. Harold did not survive the testator, but his wife, Wilma, and two children, Adam and

Claude, did. Under a typical form of anti-lapse statute the watch would pass to Harold's children. They would, in effect, stand in the place of their parent, who was related to and predeceased *T.* If a beneficiary validly disclaims the right to receive a bequest, the beneficiary is usually treated as having predeceased the testator. *See* §12.28. Thus, if Harold survived *T,* but disclaimed the bequest of the watch, in most states it would pass to Harold's children.

§4.15.1. Ademption

Under the common law, a specific gift is adeemed and fails entirely if the property does not exist at the time of the testator's death. Thus, if the property is lost, sold, stolen, destroyed, or otherwise disposed of prior to the testator's death, the gift fails and the beneficiary is not entitled to receive any other property in its place. Where the property was insured, the right to any insurance recovery generally becomes an asset of the residuary estate. However, under some statutes the legatee of a specific gift is entitled to any proceeds unpaid at the time of the testator's death on fire or casualty insurance on the property. *E.g.,* U.P.C. §2-606 (1990); N.Y. Est. Powers & Trusts Law §3-4.5 (McKinney 1990 Supp.). In all cases in which a client indicates a desire to make a specific gift, the lawyer should ask whether he or she wishes to make any alternative gift to the beneficiary if the particular property is not owned by the client at his or her death. In appropriate cases, the will should include a substitutional gift, as in Form 4-5. The testator's intent regarding the matter should be specified in the will even if the same result might be reached under existing statutes or decisional law. The reasons why these should not be relied upon are obvious — the law might change or the testator might be domiciled in another jurisdiction at the time of death.

§4.15.2. Alternative Disposition

The lawyer also needs to know how the client would want the property to pass if the intended beneficiary does not survive the client. It is unwise to count on the survivorship of the intended beneficiary or the sufficiency of the local anti-lapse statute. One cannot assume that (1) the named beneficiary will survive the testator or (2) a distribution in accordance with the provisions of the local law (or the testator's intent as determined by the court) will serve the interests of the client or the client's family. An early Connecticut decision described the problem as follows:

> It frequently happens that legatees die during the lifetime of the testator. The testatrix could have provided for such a contingency by giving it to the survivors, or to other parties. She did neither. There is, therefore, some presumption that she intended that the law should settle the matter. That presumption is strengthened by the fact that she had an opportunity to change her will after one or more of the legatees had died, and failed to do so. *Bill v. Payne,* 25 A. 354 (Conn. 1892).

In short, a will should include appropriate provisions dealing with the premature death of the beneficiaries.

§4.15.3. Simultaneous Deaths

A will should also include some direction regarding the disposition of the property in the event of the simultaneous deaths of the testator and the intended beneficiary. In that way the client's intent will be clear, constructional problems will be avoided, and the lawyer will be protected against serious criticism and liability for failure to draft an unambiguous bequest.

A direction that the client's spouse should be deemed to survive the client in the event of their simultaneous deaths may be appropriate if it is important for the client's estate to qualify for the federal estate tax marital deduction. For marital deduction purposes the estate tax regulations allow survivorship to be governed by a presumption provided by the instrument or the local law in the event of simultaneous deaths. Reg. §20.2056(e)-(2). *See* §5.14.

§4.15.4. Survivorship for Specified Period

Many lawyers routinely recommend that testamentary gifts be conditioned upon the beneficiary surviving the testator by a specified number of days. In general the practice is a good one. The condition may be imposed with respect to an individual gift or all gifts. For example, a will might contain a provision such as that found in Form 4-6.

Form 4-6. General Survivorship Requirement

For the purposes of this will a beneficiary is deemed to survive me only if the beneficiary is living on the sixtieth day following my death.

This type of survivorship requirement prevents the same property from being subjected to the cost and delay of multiple estate administrations and possibly greater tax burdens if the beneficiary dies soon after the testator. It also prevents the property from passing in an uncontrolled manner in such cases. For example, without such a provision under Article Three (Form 4-5), if Archibald Jones survives the testator for one day, the antique desk would be distributed from Client's estate to Jones' personal representative. The desk would then be disposed of as an asset of Jones' estate, totally uncontrolled by John Q. Client's will. The item might pass to a person who had no appreciation of or use for it. Of course, where the deaths of the testator and beneficiary occur close together in time, a survivorship clause might prevent a life or term interest from passing to the beneficiary, which would deprive the beneficiary's estate from claiming an otherwise allowable previously taxed property credit under §2013. The loss of the credit could be very costly, particularly in the case of a life interest such as a QTIP that would support a credit although no principal was includible in the beneficiary's gross estate. *See* §5.23.

Survivorship of more than 180 days is usually not required because (1) distributions are often made within 180 days following death and (2) a gift to a spouse may qualify for the marital deduction if it is conditioned on the death of the surviving spouse within six months of the testator's death and the surviving spouse survives that period. Reg. §20.2056(b)-3(a). A lengthier survivorship period would disqualify the gift for the marital deduction. §2056(b)(3).

Note that the U.P.C. requires survivorship of 120 hours in the case of intestate succession, U.P.C. §2-104 (1990), and testate dispositions unless otherwise provided in the will, U.P.C. §2-702 (1990). The requirement alleviates some of the problems of the "almost simultaneous death," but does not deal with the problems that arise if the beneficiary survives for more than five days.

§4.16. Cash Gifts

Form 4-7. Cash Gift to Charity

Article Four: I give Twenty Thousand Dollars ($20,000) to the Regents of the University of ____________________, to be used for such of the general educational purposes of the University as they deem proper. However, if the total inventory value of the property of my estate subject to administration less liens and encumbrances is less than Five Hundred Thousand Dollars ($500,000), then the amount of this gift shall be reduced to an amount that bears the same relation to Twenty Thousand Dollars

> ($20,000) as such adjusted inventory value of my estate bears to Five Hundred Thousand Dollars ($500,000).

The aggregate amount of cash gifts generally should be limited in a way that protects the residuary estate from undue diminution if the testator's estate shrinks in value after the will is executed. Without this safeguard an unexpectedly large part of the estate might be required to pay cash gifts if the client's estate shrinks in value because of business reversals, large unforeseen expenses, lifetime gifts, or any other reason. If the will contains a number of cash bequests, the limitation can be modified to apply to all of them. In the case of multiple cash gifts, the limitation could be expressed as a percentage of the testator's net estate subject to administration. In such a case, it should also provide for a pro rata reduction of each legacy if the percentage limit is exceeded.

§4.16.1. Charitable Deduction for Tax Purposes

A gift to a charity of less than the taxpayer's entire interest in the property qualifies for the estate tax charitable deduction only if the gift takes the form of an undivided portion of the property, a remainder interest in a personal residence or farm, a charitable remainder trust, a charitable income interest, or a pooled income fund. §2055(e)(2). In order to qualify for a charitable deduction, a gift of a remainder interest in trust must meet the stringent rules of §664. *See* §8.20. A gift of a life estate to a surviving spouse, remainder to charity, qualifies for the elective marital deduction under §2056(b)(7), but does not qualify for a charitable deduction in the testator's estate. The property is includible in the surviving spouse's estate under §2044 to the extent the marital deduction is claimed. The survivor's estate is entitled to an offsetting charitable deduction under §2055 for the value of the property included in her estate under §2044(a), which is considered to have passed from her for estate and GSTT tax purposes. §2044(b). LR 9043016. A gift, not in trust, of a remainder interest in a personal residence or farm does qualify for the charitable deduction. *See* §8.15.

§4.16.2. Satisfaction

A cash gift or other general legacy may be satisfied in whole or in part by an inter vivos gift to the legatee. Under the U.P.C. satisfaction occurs only if the will provides for a deduction of the lifetime gift, or the testator declares in a contemporaneous writing that the gift is to be deducted from the devise or is in satisfaction of the devise, or the devisee acknowledges in writing that the gift is in satisfaction. U.P.C. §2-609 (1990). If a client intends to discharge a bequest included in his or her will with an inter vivos transfer, the client should execute a new will or a codicil rather than rely on the proper application of this doctrine.

§4.16.3. Distribution in Kind

Commentators disagree about the extent to which an executor should be authorized to distribute estate assets in kind in satisfaction of pecuniary legacies. Such authority does give the executor more flexibility. However, if assets are distributed in kind in satisfaction of a pecuniary gift, the estate will realize a taxable gain in the amount by which the date of distribution value of the property exceeds its estate tax value. Reg. §1.661(a)-2(f)(1). A distributee will take a basis in the property equal to the amount of the pecuniary claim that was discharged by the distribution. *See, e.g., Lindsay C. Howard,* 23 T.C. 962, 966 (1955), *acq.* 1955-2 C.B. 6.

If it appears that a testator's estate may not be sufficiently liquid to pay pecuniary gifts without difficulty, it may be preferable to avoid making pecuniary gifts rather than to burden the executor with the problem of deciding whether and how to make distributions in kind in satisfaction of the pecuniary gifts.

> **Example 4-2.** *T*'s will made a cash bequest of $10,000 to *B,* who survived *T.* The will gave *T*'s executor authority to satisfy cash gifts by distributing assets in kind. The executor distributed 100 shares of ABC, Inc. stock to *B* in satisfaction of the gift. The shares, which had been purchased by *T* several years before for $2,000, had a value of $8,000 on the estate tax valuation date and $10,000 on the date of distribution. The estate realized a gain of $2,000 when the shares were distributed, which is the difference between their value on the date of distribution, $10,000, and the estate's basis in the shares, $8,000.

§4.16.4. Forgiveness of Indebtedness

A debt owed the testator may be forgiven conditionally or unconditionally by an appropriate provision in the will. Because the forgiveness is essentially equivalent to a cash bequest, the former debtor may be obligated to contribute toward the payment of the state death tax and, depending upon the provisions of the testator's will and the local law, a portion of the federal estate tax. If the estate is insolvent a forgiveness directed in the will may not be effective. However, where the note or other obligation provides for forgiveness of the debt, it might be an effective nontestamentary provision. *See* U.P.C. §6-201 (1990).

The testator might, as an alternative, bequeath the note to the obligor. Keep in mind, however, that the forgiveness or other cancellation of an installment obligation triggers recognition of gain under the installment sale rules. *See* §691(a)(5). *See also* §9.6.

§4.17. Tangible Personal Property

Form 4-8. Gift of Tangible Personal Property

Article Five: I give all of my clothing, furniture, furnishings and effects, automobiles, and other tangible personal property of every kind except jewelry and gifts of specific items of tangible personal property made under other provisions of this will to my wife if she survives me. If my wife does not survive me, I give such tangible personal property excluding automobiles to those of my children who survive me, to divide among themselves as they may agree. If my children do not agree regarding the disposition of the personal property within sixty (60) days of my death, I direct my executor to divide the property among them in shares as nearly equal in value as practicable, having due regard for the personal preferences of each child. The share of any child who is a minor at the time the property is distributed may be delivered without bond to the child's guardian or to any suitable person with whom the child resides or who has custody or control of the child.

The disposition of the testator's interest in tangible personal property may pose problems if a number of beneficiaries must agree upon its distribution. If the property might pass to a minor the will should attempt to obviate the need to have a guardian of the estate appointed for the minor. For example, the will might provide that the property otherwise distributable to a minor may be delivered to the guardian of the minor's person or to other suitable persons. Where minors are involved, the client should consider excluding automobiles, boats, and airplanes from the gift. Because of jewelry's high value and its unsuitability for distribution to minors, it is excepted from this Article Five and is disposed of expressly in Article Six. *See* Form 4-9, §4.18, *infra*. Otherwise, jewelry could be included within the scope of this article.

The executor or another responsible adult may be authorized to sell such of the items of a minor's share of the personal property as he or she believes is in the best interest of the child. In that way the insurance, storage, and other costs of retaining "white elephants" can be avoided and the proceeds invested for the minor, possibly in conjunction with a contingent testamentary trust.

The scope of Article Five may be further refined by specifically excluding money, precious metals (including coins) and unmounted gems held for investment, evidences of indebtedness, documents of title, and securities and property used in trade or business. Otherwise some beneficiaries might contend that those items are included in a bequest of "tangible personal property."

§4.17.1. Testamentary Gifts to Custodians for Minors

Section 5 of the Uniform Transfer to Minors Act (U.T.M.A.) and the version of the Uniform Gifts to Minors Act (U.G.M.A.) adopted in some states authorize testamentary gifts to custodians for minors. *E.g.,* Cal. Prob. Code §3905 (West 1991 Supp.); N.Y. Est. Trusts & Powers Law §7-4.9 (McKinney 1990 Supp.). Under the former all types of property may be given to a custodian for a minor. In contrast, statutes based on the U.G.M.A. usually authorize only gifts of a security, life insurance policy, annuity contract, or money to a custodian for a minor. *E.g.,* Fla. Stat. Ann. §710.102 (West 1988). Under both Uniform Acts each gift must be made to one minor — there cannot be multiple beneficiaries of a custodianship. The device is particularly useful in making gifts of small amounts of cash or securities to minors without requiring a full-blown trust or the appointment of a guardian for the minor.

If there is no will or the will or trust does not include a gift to a custodian for a minor the U.T.M.A. and the laws of some states allow the fiduciary to distribute property to a custodian for a minor. U.T.M.A. §6, 8A U.L.A. 254 (1990 Supp.); N.Y. Est. Powers & Trusts Law §7-4.9 (McKinney 1990 Supp.).

§4.17.2. Specific Gifts and Cash Legacies

Casting gifts in the form of specific bequests or cash legacies will prevent a distribution of the property from carrying out the distributable net income of the estate to the beneficiaries. §663(a)(1). *See* §12.37. Such gifts may be distributed to the beneficiaries without adverse income tax consequences and without affecting the estate's income-splitting role.

Specific gifts to a surviving spouse are particularly useful to preserve income-splitting in community property states where the income from community property is naturally divided between the estate of the deceased spouse and the surviving spouse.

Example 4-3. *H* died survived by his wife, *W,* leaving a will that gave *W* a cash legacy, his interest in their tangible personal property, and the residue of his estate. Cash in satisfaction of the legacy and the personalty may be distributed to *W* without carrying out to her any of the estate's distributable net income for federal income tax purposes. In contrast, a distribution of the residue to *W* would carry out to her the distributable net income of the estate for the year of distribution, which would be taxed to her rather than to the estate. *See* §§12.37-12.38.

§4.17.3. Nonspecific Gifts

The estate may elect whether or not to report gain or loss on the distribution of property in kind in satisfaction of nonspecific gifts. §643(e)(3). *See* §12.38.

§4.18. Disposition of Tangible Personal Property in Accordance with Testator's Subsequent Directions

Form 4-9. Gift of Tangible Personal Property by List

Article Six: I give all of my jewelry to my wife, which I request her to dispose of as she believes would be in accordance with my wishes. I do not intend this Article in any way to obligate my wife to dispose of the jewelry to any other persons.

[*Alternative Article Six for U.P.C. states and others that allow reference to a list to be prepared in the future:* I give my jewelry to the persons and in the shares designated on a written list I intend to leave.]

The problem of drafting provisions designed to control the disposition of a large number of items of personalty to a changeable number of beneficiaries is troublesome in states that do not recognize holographic wills and do not have a specific statute, such as U.P.C. §2-513 (1990), that authorizes reference to a list prepared later by the testator. In those states a client is generally faced with the necessity of executing codicils to effectuate changes or to transfer the property to a trust which can be more easily changed.

§4.18.1. Incorporation by Reference

Most jurisdictions other than New York allow a testator to incorporate in the will an extrinsic writing by reference, provided the writing is in existence at the time the will is executed, is adequately described, and is mentioned in the will with the intent to incorporate it. *E.g.,* U.P.C. §2-510 (1990). Thus, this theory allows a will to incorporate a list or other existing writing that the testator intends to govern the distribution of property. For a survey of the doctrine, see Incorporation by Reference — The Latter Days, 7 Real Prop., Prob. & Tr. J. 502 (1972). Writings that are incorporated cannot be effectively changed after execution of the will unless the changes comply with the required testamentary formality. Uncertainties regarding the law and the risk that the incorporated document may be altered or destroyed suggest that private documents should generally not be incorporated. However, such things as statutes and regulations may be incorporated to good effect — particularly if the testator wants to "freeze" the provision in its present form.

§4.18.2. Facts or Acts of Independent Significance

An alternate doctrine allows a testator to control the disposition of property by appropriate reference to facts or acts of independent significance. U.P.C. §2-512 (1990). Under this doctrine a testator could provide for a gift to a particular legatee of "all of the art objects listed on the fine arts rider to my fire and casualty insurance policy." Subsequent changes in the items listed on the rider would generally be recognized in making distribution of the testator's estate because of the independent significance of the list. Similarly, the identity of a beneficiary may be determined by independently significant facts, such as employment: "I give one hundred dollars ($100) to each person who is employed by J. Q. Client, Inc. at the time of my death."

Overall, incorporation by reference and reference to acts of independent significance are probably less satisfactory in dealing with the problem than the execution of a new testamentary instrument when the testator wishes to make changes in the disposition of the property. However, the preparation of a codicil or a new will may involve unacceptable additional cost. Also, codicils can cause considerable confusion where the testator leaves several — particularly if they are not entirely consistent.

§4.18.3. Bequest with Request

Some clients prefer to leave their tangible property to one person with a request that the beneficiary dispose of it as the beneficiary believes is in accordance with the testator's wishes. Under this approach the testator's wishes regarding the disposition of the property are usually expressed to the beneficiary in letters or other writings that may be changed by the testator from time to time. Although the gift does not impose a legal obligation on the person to dispose of the property in the way indicated by the testator, the approach generally works and clients are usually satisfied with it.

The state and federal transfer taxes are generally computed on the theory that the beneficiary named in the will receives outright ownership of the personalty. If the beneficiary gives some of the property to others, the beneficiary has made a gift, which may produce some gift tax liability. Consistent with that approach, the beneficiary and not the estate will be entitled to a charitable deduction for any property the beneficiary transfers to charity.

§4.18.4. Informal Lists

In states that have adopted the U.P.C. or have a similar statute, the disposition of tangible personalty may be dealt with by the following direct, yet informal, method:

> Whether or not the provisions relating to holographic wills apply, a will may refer to a written statement or list to dispose of items of tangible personal property not otherwise specifically disposed of by the will, other than money. To be admissible under this section as evidence of the intended disposition, the writing must be signed by the testator and must describe the items and the devisees with reasonable certainty. The writing may be referred to as one to be in existence at the time of the testator's death; it may be prepared before or after the execution of the will; it may be altered by the testator after its preparation; and it may be a writing which has no significance apart from its effect upon the dispositions made by the will. U.P.C. §2-513 (1990).

If a client intends to utilize this procedure, the lawyer should provide the client with written instructions regarding the preparation and alteration of the list. Also, the client should be warned that the list may be ineffective if the client resides in a non-U.P.C. state at the time of death. Coins and currency should not be disposed of under this provision because the section applies to items "other than money." If the section were construed narrowly the informal disposition of items of numismatic value might be ineffective. The client should keep any statement of this type with the will, or in a place known to the lawyer and the person named as executor. If a client wishes to change the disposition that is provided for in a list, a new one should be prepared and signed and the old one destroyed in order to avoid any uncertainties regarding the intent of the change or the identity of the person who made it.

As a precaution, items of substantial value should not be disposed of by an informal list. For example, valuable jewelry should be disposed of in the will and any changes made by codicil. If that is done, the transfer tax consequences will also be more straightforward.

An informal list of gifts made pursuant to authorization in a will might look like Form 4-10.

Form 4-10. List of Gifts of Tangible Personal Property

My will states that I may leave a list that disposes of certain items of my jewelry [tangible personal property]. I make the gifts of the jewelry [tangible personal property] listed below to the persons named. The survivorship provisions of my will apply also to these gifts.

Item of Property	*Beneficiary*
____________________	____________________
____________________	____________________
____________________	____________________

This list was made on ____________________, 199____

____
Testator

The reference in the testator's will and the list should be consistent. Accordingly, consistent with the terms of Article Three (Form 4-5, *supra*), the above list refers only to items of jewelry. The will and the list might instead refer to all types of tangible personal property.

A list may be effective to make a life insurance beneficiary designation. In *Burkett v. Mott,* 733 P.2d 673 (Ariz. App. 1986), the court held that the designation of the beneficiary of life insurance made in a list that was appropriately referred to in the insured's will was effective to change the beneficiary. The disposition was effective because the insurance policy was not among the types of property that were specifically excluded from the statute authorizing the disposition of property in a list. *See also* §4.20.4.

§4.19. Gift of Corporate Securities

Form 4-11. Gift of Corporate Securities

Article Seven: I give one hundred (100) shares of the common stock of ZYX, Inc., which I now own, as the same may be hereafter increased or decreased by reason of stock dividends, stock splits, mergers, consolidations, or reorganizations (but disregarding rights to purchase stock, whether exercised or not), to my brother Horace M. Client if he survives me. If I do not own a sufficient number of shares of the stock at the time of my death to satisfy this gift in full, then the gift shall be limited to the number of shares, if any, owned by me. If my brother Horace M. Client does not survive me, no property shall pass under this Article.

A gift of securities should specify whether the testator intends to give the legatee only the particular securities then owned by the testator (a specific bequest) or the specified quantity of the named securities whether or not the testator owns any at the time of his death (a general bequest). A specific gift of the type illustrated above, or as indicated by the use of the possessive pronoun "my" in describing the shares, typically carries with it any lifetime increase in the quantity of securities attributable to stock splits. If the gift were characterized as general rather than specific many courts would limit the gift to the original number of shares. The courts are divided as to whether a specific gift carries with it shares that were received as stock dividends. *See* T. Atkinson, Wills §135 (2d ed. 1953); McGovern, Kurtz & Rein, Wills, Trusts & Estates §10.1 (1988).

The terms of this article generally parallel the provisions of U.P.C. §2-605 (1990) under which a specific gift of securities carries with it additional securities received by reason of action initiated by the issuer other than shares received as a result of the exercise of purchase options. However, even though the existing law may carry out the client's present intent without elaboration, the will should specify the effect that should be given to changes in the number of shares owned by the client. If the will contains multiple gifts of the same issue of securities the testator may wish to reduce them all proportionately if the quantity of securities owned at death is insufficient to satisfy all of the gifts in full.

§4.20. Gift of Residence, Life Insurance, and Employee Benefits

Form 4-12. Gift of Residence, Life Insurance and Employee Benefits

Article Eight: If my wife survives me, I give her all of my interest in

(a) any property we use as our principal place of residence at the time of my death that does not otherwise pass to her upon my death by right of survivorship or otherwise, together with my interest in all policies of insurance thereon including the right to receive the proceeds of all claims thereunder that are unpaid at the time of my death;

(b) all policies of insurance on her life and on the lives of our children, and

(c) all qualified and unqualified benefit plans resulting from her employment, including self-employment.

It is not strictly necessary to include a specific devise of residential real property to the surviving spouse who is also the residuary legatee. However, a specific devise may reassure the testator's spouse that he or she will receive their residential property and continue to have the right to occupy it regardless of whether title to it is held by them in a survivorship form. Such a devise may also provide some greater flexibility in making distributions to the survivor from the estate. In this connection consider the effect of §663, discussed at §4.17.2.

§4.20.1. Exoneration

The will should also specify whether or not an encumbrance on any specifically bequeathed or devised property should be satisfied. If so, the will should also designate the source from which the payment should be made — typically the assets of the residuary estate. Under the U.P.C. and the law of most states, an encumbrance need not be exonerated unless the testator specifically directs that the obligation be paid. U.P.C. §2-607 (1990) provides that "[a] specific devise passes subject to any mortgage interest existing at the date of death, without right of exoneration, regardless of a general directive in the will to pay debts."

§4.20.2. Insurance on Realty and Personalty

The testator's interest in insurance on real or personal property should also be given to the beneficiaries in order to give them the benefit of paid-up insurance and to provide them with continued protection. The will should also specify whether the devisee is entitled to receive the proceeds of insurance claims that exist, but are unpaid at the time of the testator's death. U.P.C. §2-606(a)(3) (1990) and statutes in some states give the beneficiary the right to the unpaid insurance proceeds in such cases. *See, e.g.,* N.Y. Est. Powers & Trusts Law §3-4.5 (McKinney 1990 Supp.). The provision could also deal specifically with the disposition of the proceeds of any sale or condemnation of the property that remain unpaid at the time of the testator's death.

§4.20.3. Insurance on the Lives of Others

A testator's interest in policies of insurance on the lives of others should also receive special attention, particularly if the insured also owns an interest in the policies. Of course, if the noninsured spouse holds the entire interest in the policies for the purpose of keeping the proceeds out of the gross estate of the insured spouse, the noninsured spouse should leave the policies to a trust or a person other than the insured spouse. The insured generally should not serve as trustee of a trust that owns policies on the insured's life, which might cause inclusion of the proceeds of the policies in the insured's gross estate. *See* §6.27.11. Ordinarily minors should not be given an outright interest in life insurance policies or proceeds, because a guardian might have to be appointed to deal with the insurance on their behalf. If the testator's interest is given to a trustee of a trust in which the insured does not have an interest, the insured might also transfer his interest to the trustee in order to reduce the size of his gross estate. Techniques for dealing with the life insurance in estate planning are discussed in more detail in Chapter 6.

§4.20.4. Testamentary Changes of Beneficiary Designations; Life Insurance Policies

An attempt to change a life insurance beneficiary designation by will is generally not effective. Even if a local decision permits the testamentary change of beneficiaries, it is unwise to rely upon a testamentary change alone. Beneficiary designations and changes of beneficiary designations made by will have been recognized in some interpleader cases where the insurers did not object to the insureds' failure to make the changes of beneficiary in the manner required by the policies. Those decisions emphasize that by recognizing the beneficiary designations the court gives effect to the insured's expressed intention. *See, e.g., Sears v. Austin,* 292 F.2d 690 (9th Cir. 1961), *cert. denied,* 368 U.S. 929 (1961) (federal employees group insurance); *Doss v. Kalas,* 383 P.2d 169 (Ariz. 1963); §4.18.5.

The current beneficiary designations on policies in which the client has an interest must be examined. The lawyer should also advise the client to review the sufficiency of the beneficiary designations if any of the named beneficiaries dies or if the circumstances of the testator or the beneficiaries change substantially. Under the law of most states a life insurance beneficiary designation is not affected by a change in the insured's family circumstances. *See* Parotaud, Should Implied Revocation Be Applied to a Life Insurance Beneficiary Designation, 25 Fed. Ins. Couns. Q. 357 (1975). However, under the laws of Michigan, Ohio, Oklahoma, and Texas and the 1990 version of U.P.C. §2-804, the designation of the spouse of the insured as beneficiary is revoked if they are divorced. Mich. Stat. Ann. §25.131 (1991 Supp.); Ohio Rev. Code Ann. §1339.63 (1990 Supp.); Okla. Stat. Ann. tit. 15, §178 (1992 Supp.); Tex. Fam. Code Ann. §§3.632-3.633 (Vernon 1991 Supp.).

§4.20.5. Revocation by Change of Circumstances

Divorce and annulment are the only changes in family circumstances that revoke testamentary provisions under U.P.C. §2-804 (1990). However, in most states a prenuptial will is revoked as to a surviving spouse who is not mentioned or provided for in the will or in a property settlement agreement. A will for a person who is contemplating marriage should mention or provide for the intended spouse in a way that will protect the will from revocation if the marriage takes place and the testator predeceases his or her spouse. "A reasonably prudent attorney should appreciate the consequences of a post-testamentary marriage, advise the testator of such consequences, and use good judgment to avoid them if the testator so desires." *Heyer v. Flaig,* 449 P.2d 161, 165 (Cal. 1969).

§4.20.6. Interest in Retirement Plans

In community property states the nonemployee spouse may have a transmissible interest in the employee spouse's retirement plans. The portion of the retirement plan attributable to employment during marriage is community property. *See* §3.32. As such, some states recognize that the nonemployee spouse has a transmissible interest. *E.g., Farver v. Department of Retirement Systems,* 644 P.2d 1145 (Wash. 1982). In light of this possibility, the nonemployee spouse may wish to leave his or her interest to the employee spouse. As indicated in §3.32, Wisconsin legislatively adopted a "terminable interest" rule under which the marital property interest of the nonemployee spouse terminates if he or she predeceases the employee spouse. With regard to a nonemployee spouse's interest in a qualified plan, Advisory Opinions issued by the Department of Labor (A.O. 90-46A and A.O. 90-47A) and a split decision by the Ninth Circuit Court of Appeal, *Ablamis v. Roper,* 937 F.2d 1450 (9th Cir. 1991), hold that ERISA preempts state community property laws and prevents a predeceasing nonemployee spouse from transferring his or her interest. *See* §3.32.

§4.21. Residuary Gift

Form 4-13. Residuary Gift

Article Nine: I give all of my property that is not effectively disposed of by the foregoing provisions of this will, including all property over which I hold a power of appointment [excluding all property over which I only hold a power of appointment] (my "residuary estate"), as follows:

(1) If my wife survives me, I give my residuary estate to her. [If my wife survives me, but disclaims the right to receive outright any portion of my residuary estate, I give the disclaimed portion to my trustee to hold in trust for the benefit of my wife as provided in Article __________.]

(2) If my wife does not survive me, but I am survived by one or more children who are under the age of twenty-five (25) years at the time of my death, I give my residuary estate to my trustee to hold in trust for the benefit of my descendants as provided in Article Ten.

(3) If I am survived by descendants, but not by my wife or any children who are under twenty-five (25) years of age at the time of my death, I direct my executor to divide my residuary estate into as many shares of equal value as are required to carry out the following provisions:

(a) I give one (1) such share to each of my children who survives me and has attained twenty-five (25) years of age at the time of my death; and

(b) I give one (1) such share to the descendants who survive me of any child of mine who fails to survive me, such descendants to take by right of representation subject, however, to the provisions of trust for minors described in Article Eleven of this will.

(4) If I am not survived by my wife or by any of my descendants, I give one-half (½) of my residuary estate to the persons entitled to receive the property of my wife under the laws of the State of ______________________ now in effect, as if she had died intestate at the time of my death not survived by a spouse, the shares of such persons also to be determined by said laws; and I give one-half (½) of my residuary estate to the persons entitled to receive my property under the laws of the State of ______________________ now in effect, as if I had died intestate, not survived by any spouse, the shares of such persons also to be determined by said laws now in effect.

§4.21.1. Should the Residuary Clause Exercise All Powers of Appointment?

The residuary estate is described in Article Nine (Form 4-13, *supra*) in a way that attempts to exercise any power of appointment the testator may have. If that approach is adopted some lawyers would prefer to include the word "appoint" *viz,* "I give, devise, bequeath, and appoint . . ."). The bracketed alternate language should be used if the lawyer and client conclude that the attempt should not be made. Most commentators do not favor the blind exercise of powers of appointment. However, as Professor Edward Rabin suggests, the exercise of unknown powers could be made dependent upon their nontaxability for federal estate tax purposes. *See* Rabin, Blind Exercises of Powers of Appointment, 51 Cornell L. Rev. 1 (1965). A client who is given the choice may prefer to attempt the exercise in order to pass the absolute maximum amount of property to the beneficiaries he or she has selected and named.

There is some danger that a blind exercise may cause additional property to be included in the testator's gross estate. Property subject to a pre-1942 general power of appointment is not includible in the donee's gross estate unless the power is exercised. §2041(a). Of course, in some instances, a pre-1942 power may be exercised by the donee's will although the will does not manifest any intent to exercise the power. *Stewart v. United States,* 512 F.2d 269 (5th Cir. 1975). Such results are attributable to the overly broad language of the instrument that created the power regarding the manner in which it could be exercised.

The effect of the inclusion may be ameliorated if the executor recovers the estate tax attributable to inclusion of the appointive property from the recipients of the property. *See* §2207, §12.42.3. However, the recovery of a proportionate amount of the estate tax will not completely offset the increase in estate taxes where the inclusion of the property drives the taxable estate into higher brackets, increasing the marginal rate and the overall effective rate of the tax.

Many lawyers oppose preparing a will that exercises powers without knowing what the tax effects of the exercise will be and what provisions the donor of the power may have included in the instrument for disposition of the property in default of exercise of the power. If a client holds an interest in a trust, the lawyer should review the terms of the trust carefully in order to ascertain the extent of the client's interest and whether or not the client holds a power of appointment over the trust property. A lawyer cannot safely rely upon a client's impression regarding the extent of his or her interest in a trust or the existence of a power of appointment.

Whatever decision is made regarding the blind exercise of powers, the will should state expressly whether or not the testator intends to exercise any powers. Under the majority American rule a residuary clause does not exercise a power of appointment unless the clause makes specific reference to the power or otherwise expresses an intention to exercise the power. U.P.C. §2-608 (1990); Cal. Prob. Code §6142 (West 1991 Supp.); Cal. Civ. Code §1386.2 (West 1990 Supp.); Fla. Stat. Ann. §732.607 (West 1988). However, under New York law a testamentary power of appointment is presumably exercised by a residuary clause. *See* N.Y. Est. Powers & Trusts Law §10-6.1(a)(4) (McKinney 1990 Supp.). The will should eliminate any opportunity for a court to clamber into the testator's armchair in order to ascertain the testator's intent on the subject. Although the law of the testator's domicile may not recognize a residuary clause as effective to exercise a power, it may be recognized as effective by the law of the jurisdiction in which the trust is being administered. For example, in *Estate of Coffin,* 499 P.2d 223 (Wash. App. 1972), a garden variety residuary clause was recognized by the trustee of a Massachusetts trust as effective to dispose of property that was subject to a general testamentary power of appointment. At the time the Massachusetts law permitted a general power of appointment to be exercised by a residuary clause. For a general discussion of the subject, *see* French, Exercise of Powers of Appointment: Should Intent to Exercise be Inferred from a General Disposition of Property?, 1979 Duke L.J. 747.

§4.21.2. All to the Surviving Spouse?

Article Nine (Form 4-13) gives the entire residuary estate to the testator's wife if she survives him. Such a disposition is in accordance with the wishes of most testators. However, it will cause all of the couple's property to be subject to taxation upon the surviving spouse's death. If the combined estates of the spouses are large enough to generate any federal estate tax liability on the survivor's death, the will might allow the surviving spouse to disclaim the right to receive part or all of the residuary estate in order to make use of the deceased spouse's unified credit. The bracketed language in Form 4-13 is suitable for that purpose. Under the bracketed alternative if the testator's wife survives, any part of the residuary estate she disclaims will pass to a trust which would not necessarily be includible in her estate. The trust could take the form of either a QTIP trust, from which the surviving spouse must have the right to all of the income (*see* Form 4-16 and §5.23) or a family trust in which the trustee has discretion to distribute income to and among the surviving spouse and children. In either case the trust would not terminate prior to the death of the surviving spouse.

Under the disclaimer-QTIP approach any portion of the residuary bequest that is disclaimed by the surviving spouse would pass to a trust in which the surviving spouse would have a qualifying income interest for life. The executor would then be free to claim the QTIP marital deduction with respect to an appropriate portion of the trust. Of course, the portion of the trust with respect to which the QTIP election is made is includible in the surviving spouse's estate under §2044, but the balance of the trust (*e.g.,* an amount equal to the deceased spouse's credit equivalent) would not be included in his or her estate.

A legal life estate may constitute a qualified income interest for life for purposes of the elective marital deduction under §2056(b)(7). *See* §5.23. However, under almost all circumstances the use of a legal life estate with remainder over is a less satisfactory way of disposing of interests in real or personal property. Legal life interest create wholly avoidable problems of defining the rights of the owners *inter se* and of managing and disposing of the property. Also, the remaindermen may contest the ability of the life tenant to sell, lease, or otherwise dispose of the property and demand security and accountings. *See, e.g., Lehner v. Estate of Lehner,* 547 P.2d 365 (Kan. 1976). A trust is almost always a better choice because of its flexibility and the variety of interests that can be given to the surviving spouse.

Tax considerations aside, the maximum degree of flexibility might be achieved (and the interests of the surviving spouse protected) if the trustee were authorized to distribute the income of the trust to and among the surviving spouse and children. Of course, the marital deduction is not allowable with respect to such a trust.

Importantly, a surviving spouse may be given additional powers over the trust without jeopardizing its qualification under §2056(b)(7). *See* §5.23. Specifically, a surviving spouse may be given the following powers: (1) to draw down the greater of $5,000 or 5 percent of the trust corpus annually; (2) to appoint the corpus of the trust by will to and among the testator's descendants; (3) to invade corpus (to provide the surviving spouse with support in the survivor's accustomed manner of living, with education, including college and professional education, and with medical, dental, hospital, and nursing expenses). *See* Reg. §20.2041-1(c)(2). An independent trustee could also be given a discretionary power to invade trust corpus for the benefit of the surviving spouse or children without adverse impact.

Under the law of some states the need for estate administration and attendant costs are virtually eliminated if the surviving spouse is entitled to receive all of the decedent's property. Cal. Prob. Code §13500 *et seq.* (West 1991 Supp.); Tex. Prob. Code Ann. §155 (Vernon 1991 Supp.). Texas law provides several alternatives to formal administration of a decedent's estate, including the admission of a will to probate as a muniment of title. Tex. Prob. Code Ann. §89 (Vernon 1991 Supp.).

§4.21.3. A "Pot" Trust or a Separate Trust for Each Child?

The testator's will could adopt any of a variety of patterns for distributing the residuary estate to descendants if the testator's spouse does not survive. For a parent with a modest-sized estate a single "pot" trust for minor children is preferable to a separate trust for each child. Article Nine places the entire residuary estate in a single trust if any of the testator's children are under 25 at the time of the testator's death. The trust will continue until the youngest living child is 25. Some clients will want to provide for such a trust if any of their children are under another age, say 30 or 35. The concept is more important than the particular age chosen.

Under the trust's distributive provisions, Article Ten, the trustee is free to use the entire income and principal of the trust flexibly to meet the needs of the testator's descendants. Form 4-14, §4.22. However, the primary emphasis is to provide for the support and education of the children who are under 21 at the time. The older children will probably be more self-sufficient and more nearly through with their formal education. A modified approach may be called for if the testator has a child with special needs. In particular, the client may wish to provide for the continuation of the trust for the lifetime benefit of a disabled child. Most clients will want the trust to provide benefits to the child that are not otherwise available from public agencies. Thus, the benefits of the trust would be supplemental to, and not in lieu of, public support. The object is to insulate the property of the trust from claims by public agencies for reimbursement for the support they provide. A trust that gives the trustee broad discretion to provide for the beneficiary is perhaps the best approach. Lombard, Planning for Disability: Durable Powers, Standby Trusts and Preserving Eligibility for Governmental Benefits, U. Miami, 20th Inst. Est. Plan. ¶1710 (1986).

A testator with sufficient wealth to provide amply for the needs of each child may prefer to divide the residuary estate into equal shares for the children at the time of the testator's death. That may also be an acceptable plan if the testator's children are older, their educational expenses have been substantially met, and they are more or less independent. Under this approach, one share could be distributed outright to each child over, say, 25, and one share held in a separate trust for each child under that age. However, in order to reduce the potential for conflict between children who would be entitled to distributions at different times, some clients prefer to provide that distributions of principal be made to all children at the same time (*e.g.,* five years after the testator's death). In any case the lawyer should describe the alternatives fully to the clients and counsel them regarding the choice that seems best suited to their needs. The lawyer should not routinely squeeze clients into a particular type of estate plan or a particular form of trust that the lawyer happens to have available.

§4.21.4. Consolidate the Client's Property in One Trust

Upon the death of the surviving parent, the most economical and efficient management of the property for the benefit of the children will result if the probate assets are consolidated with life insurance proceeds and other nonprobate property. Under one approach the client's will creates a testamentary trust for the benefit of minor children if the client's spouse does not survive and the policies of insurance on the client's life are made payable to "the trustee named or to be named" in the will as contingent beneficiary. State statutes typically permit such a beneficiary designation to be made without losing otherwise available exemptions of the insurance from creditors' claims and the local death tax. *E.g.,* Cal. Prob. Code §6324 (West 1991 Supp.); Fla. Stat. Ann. §732.513 (West 1988 Supp.); Ill. Ann. Stat. ch. 110½, §4-5 (Smith-Hurd 1978); Tex. Ins. Code Ann. §3.49-3 (Vernon 1981); Wash. Rev. Code §48.18.452 (1989).

If the local law does not expressly permit a testamentary trustee to be named as beneficiary, the desired consolidation could be achieved by establishing an inter vivos trust and naming the trustee as secondary beneficiary of the life insurance policies. Such a trust is generally recognized as valid although the trust is not funded during the lifetime of the insured and the trustee merely has the right to receive the insurance proceeds upon the insured's death. *See* §6.18.2. If such a trust is created, the testator's residuary estate should be "poured over" to the trust if the testator's spouse does not survive.

Statutes authorizing pour-overs, modeled on the Uniform Testamentary Additions to Trust Act, are in force in most states. U.P.C. §2-511, 8A U.L.A. 599 (1990). *E.g.,* Fla. Stat. Ann. §733.808 (West 1991 Supp.). A paragraph like that in Form 4-14 might be included in the will when a pour-over plan is used.

Form 4-14. Pour-Over to Inter Vivos Trust

(b) If my wife does not survive me and I am survived by any of my descendants, I give my residuary estate to the trustee, acting at the time of my death, of the trust created by the agreement dated January 1, 1990, between me as trustor and Horace M. Client as trustee, as the trust shall exist at the time of my death, to be added to and administered in all respects as property of the trust. I expressly direct that the trust shall not be considered to be a testamentary trust.

Other nonprobate assets, such as the balance due on notes, might also be made payable to the trustee if the testator's spouse does not survive. Such a provision for payment is treated as nontestamentary by U.P.C. §6-101 (1990), but may be required to comply with testamentary formalities in other states.

§4.21.5. Discretionary Distributions

The total income tax burdens of the beneficiaries may be lighter if one trust is created and the trustee is given the power to "sprinkle" the income among them. Ordinarily a beneficiary should not serve as trustee of a discretionary trust because of the potentially adverse income, gift, and estate tax consequences. *See* §10.27. In determining the time and amount of distributions the trustee can take into account the income tax position of the beneficiaries. The income tax bite may be smaller if most of the income is distributed to children who are over 14 (*i.e.,* not subject to the "Kiddie Tax") and have relatively little other income. If such distributions are made the trust will be left with little taxable income. The fact that the throwback rules do not apply to income accumulated prior to the time the beneficiary attains 21 is helpful in this regard. §665(b). Of course, in some cases that fact will favor the establishment of separate trusts. The discretionary nature of the trust also allows the trustee to distribute property in kind, which may be useful in some cases.

§4.21.6. Trust for Minor Descendants

Under the provisions of Article Nine (Form 4-13, *supra*), if none of the testator's children is under 25, one share of the residuary estate will go to each living child and one share to the descendants of each deceased child. The share allocable to the descendants of a deceased child who are under 21 is subject to a very simple minors' trust under Article Eleven. Form 4-17, §4.23, *infra.* This approach should obviate the necessity of establishing a guardianship of the estate of a minor descendant. In states that have adopted the U.T.M.A., the will might instead provide that the share of a minor would be distributed to a custodian under the Uniform Act. "A personal representative or trustee may make an irrevocable transfer pursuant to Section 9 to a custodian for the benefit of a minor as authorized in the governing will or trust." U.T.M.A. §5, 8A U.L.A. 215 (1989 Supp.). The custodian may be designated in the will or trust, otherwise the personal representative or trustee may designate the custodian from those eligible to serve as such. Id. Such a custodianship terminates when the beneficiary becomes 21. U.T.M.A. §20, 8A U.L.A. 237 (1989 Supp.).

§4.21.7. Ultimate Disposition of Residue

Most wills should include a "waste-basket clause," such as Article Nine (4), that disposes of the testator's residuary estate in the event the testator's spouse, descendants, and other specifically designated beneficiaries fail to survive the testator. Form 4-13, §4.21, *supra.* If neither spouse nor descendants survive, a client may wish to divide the residuary estate equally between the client's surviving relations and those of the client's spouse. This article includes a form that gives half of the residue to the persons who would have been entitled to succeed to the wife's property by intestate succession had she died unmarried at the time of the testator's death, and the other half to the testator's intestate successors. Some clients will prefer to provide for some gifts to charity if none of the members of their immediate family survive.

In effect, the gift recognizes the contribution each spouse made to acquiring the property and makes a logical division of the property between the surviving relatives of each spouse. The form avoids the problems that could arise if the gift were made to the "heirs" of the client and the client's spouse: It specifies (1) the time at which the class of persons is to be ascertained, (2) the law that is to govern the identification of class members, and (3) the shares they are to take. The identification of the persons and shares should be made under the law in effect at the time the will is executed, which is known, rather than the law as it may exist at a later time, which is unknown. The testator might choose to base the distribution upon the intestate succession law of another state. *See* U.P.C. §2-703 (1990). However, a lawyer should hesitate to draft such a provision unless he or she knows exactly what the result will be.

The disposition of half of the residuary estate to the persons who are entitled to receive the testator's noncommunity property under the intestate succession law in effect at the time the will is executed might be subject to the testamentary branch of the Doctrine of Worthier Title. However, the doctrine has been abolished in many states either legislatively or judicially and the Restatement, Property §312(2) (1940) states that it is no longer a part of American law. In any event, the application of this branch of the doctrine would very seldom have any significance.

§4.22. Trust Provisions

Form 4-15. Trust for Descendants

Article Ten: The property I have given to my trustee to hold for the benefit of my descendants as provided in this Article shall be held and administered as follows:

(1) The trustee shall pay to or apply for the benefit of my children and their respective spouses and descendants so much of the net income and principal of the trust as the trustee shall deem proper for their support, education, and general welfare. In making decisions regarding distributions of income or principal, or both, the trustee shall take into account other sources of funds known to the trustee to be available to them for such purposes. Further, in making decisions regarding distributions, I direct the trustee to prefer children of mine who are under twenty-one (21) years of age at the time of any payment or application of trust funds and to consider that the preservation of principal for ultimate distribution to my beneficiaries is of secondary importance. I direct the trustee to reimburse fully the guardian of the person of a child of mine for all reasonable expenses incurred by the guardian in

caring for and sheltering the child. In short, I do not intend the guardian to bear any financial burden whatsoever by reason of acting as such.

The trustee may pay or apply the income and principal of the trust unequally among my children and their respective spouses and descendants and may exclude one or more of my children and their respective spouses and descendants in making any payment or application of trust funds.

Any net income of the trust that is not expended pursuant to the provisions of this paragraph shall be accumulated and added to the principal of the trust at such times as the trustee determines.

(2) The trust shall terminate when there are no living children of mine under twenty-five (25) years of age ("then"). When the trust terminates I direct the trustee then to divide the property of the trust into as many shares of equal value as are required to carry out the following provisions:

(a) I give one (1) such share to each of my children who is then living;

(b) I give one (1) such share to then living descendants of each of my children who is then deceased, such descendants to take by right of representation subject, however, to the provisions of Article Eleven. [A child might be given a special testamentary power to appoint to and among a limited class. *See* §10.23 and Form 10-5, *infra.*]

Provided, however, if none of my descendants are then living, I give all such property to the persons and in the shares described in Article Nine (4), as if my wife and I had died at the time of termination of the trust.

Article Ten is designed to give the testator's children the maximum protection the testator can provide. Thus, the trustee is given very broad discretionary powers to use both the income and principal of the trust for the support and education of the testator's children and their dependents. In making distributions, however, the trustee is instructed to consider particularly the needs of minor children. The trustee is also directed to consider other funds that are available to the beneficiary from any source. Finally, the trustee is directed to reimburse the guardian of the person of a child for all reasonable expenses incurred by reason of the guardianship. Some clients may wish to provide expressly that the trustee should pay the costs incurred by the guardian in acquiring furniture or enlarging, remodeling, or renovating the guardian's residence to accommodate the testator's minor children.

This article also provides that the trust will terminate when there are no living children of the testator under 25, but a client could just as well choose 30 or 35. Alternatively, the testator could provide for termination of the trust at the end of five or ten years following the testator's death. Upon termination an equal share of the trust property will be distributed to each living child of the testator and to the living descendants of deceased children. Under another approach the trust might be divided into separate shares at a certain point (*e.g.,* when the youngest child reaches 25), after which portions of each trust would be distributed to its beneficiary. For example, one-third at 25, one-half of the balance at 30, and the balance at 35.

The article does not provide a share for the surviving spouses of deceased children, but some clients may wish to give each child a special testamentary power to appoint some or all of the child's share to a surviving spouse (or to and among the child's surviving spouse and children). Unfortunately, the needs of the spouses of deceased children are often overlooked in the planning process. As indicated in the bracketed material in the form, a child might be given a special power to appoint the property to and among members of a limited class if the child dies prior to termination of the trust. *See* §10.23. If no descendants survive, the ultimate substitutional takers are the persons, determined in accordance with Article Nine (4), who would be the intestate successors of the testator and his wife as of the time of termination. Form 4-13, §4.21.

Form 4-16. QTIP Trust

Article ______. Qualified Terminable Interest Property Trust. All property that shall pass to my trustee as a result of a disclaimer by my wife or otherwise shall be held and administered as follows:

(1) The trustee shall pay the net income of the trust to my wife in quarterly or more frequent installments.

Any income that is accrued or received but undistributed at the time of my wife's death shall be paid to her personal representative.

My wife shall have the power to compel the trustee to convert any unproductive or underproductive property and to invest it in income-producing property within a reasonable time.

(2) My executor shall have the power to elect to claim the marital deduction with respect to part or all of the trust. If a marital deduction is claimed with respect to part of the trust, I direct that the trustee hold that share as a separate marital deduction trust (the marital deduction trust) and the other share as a separate nonmarital deduction trust (the nonmarital deduction trust). All additional death taxes imposed on my wife's estate by reason of the inclusion of the marital deduction trust in the base of such

taxes shall be paid from the property of that trust unless my wife expressly provides otherwise in her will.

[(3) My wife shall have the power in each calendar year to withdraw from the principal of the marital deduction trust, an amount not to exceed the greater of $5,000 or five percent of the value of the principal of the trust determined as of the end of the calendar year. This power may be exercised in whole or in part each year by a written notice delivered to the trustee. The power of withdrawal is noncumulative, so that the power of withdrawal with respect to a particular calendar year can only be exercised during the calendar year.

In addition, my wife shall have the power to withdraw from the principal of the marital deduction trust so much as may be required to provide for her support and maintenance in health and reasonable comfort taking into account all income and property available to my wife from other sources. If the trust under this Article ______ is divided into a marital deduction share and a nonmarital deduction share, I direct that no principal may be withdrawn or expended from the nonmarital deduction trust until all of the funds held in the marital deduction trust are exhausted.]

(4) Upon the death of my wife ("then") the trust or trusts under this Article shall terminate. Upon such termination I direct the trustee to divide the property of the trust or trusts into as many shares of equal value as are required to make the following distributions, which I direct the trustee to make: [Instead, the surviving spouse might be given a special power to appoint the property of the trust or trusts to and among the members of a limited class, such as those of the testator's descendants and their respective spouses who shall survive his wife.]

(a) Distribute one (1) such share to each of my then living children who is 25 years of age or older;

(b) Distribute one (1) share to a separate trust under Article Ten for each then living child of mine who is under 25 years of age, provided that this share shall be added to the principal of any separate trust previously established hereunder for the benefit of such child; and

(c) Distribute one (1) such share to the then living descendants of each child of mine who is then deceased, to take by right of representation, subject however, to the provisions of Article Eleven.

(5) I intend that the trust established under this Article will qualify for the federal estate tax marital deduction to the extent my executor elects. Accordingly, I direct that all provisions of this will shall be interpreted and applied in a manner that is consistent with my intention. I authorize and direct my trustee to amend the

provisions of this trust to the extent required in order to sustain the marital deduction to the extent of my executor's election.

Form 4-16 is a simple form of QTIP trust which could be incorporated in the will and established to the extent the surviving spouse disclaims the right to receive any part of the testator's residuary estate. The first bracketed optional provision of paragraph 3 gives the surviving spouse a 5 or 5 power of withdrawal which provides some additional comfort and possibly a greater credit under §2013 if the surviving spouse dies within ten years following the death of the testator. The IRS has recognized that giving the surviving spouse a 5 or 5 power does not prevent a trust from meeting the requirements of §20556(b)(7). *E.g.,* LR 8943005 (TAM). The other provision gives the surviving spouse a power of withdrawal limited by an ascertainable standard related to her health, education, support or maintenance and a special testamentary power of appointment. Note that if a partial QTIP election is made, withdrawals of principal must first be made from the marital deduction trust. These and other points are discussed in Chapter 5, which considers marital deduction planning in depth. QTIP trusts are discussed at §5.23.

§4.23. Trust for Minors

Form 4-17. Trust for Minor Distributees

Article Eleven: If the property of a trust or any of my residuary estate would be distributable to a person who is under the age of twenty-one (21) at such time, then I direct that, in lieu of being paid or distributed to such person, the property shall be held or retained by my trustee, in trust, as a separate trust fund for such person ("the beneficiary").

The trustee shall pay or apply so much of the income and principal of the trust for the benefit of the beneficiary as the trustee shall deem proper for the support, maintenance, and education of the beneficiary. In making such determinations the trustee shall take into account all other funds available for such purposes that are known to the trustee.

The trust shall terminate when the beneficiary attains the age of twenty-one (21) or sooner dies. Upon termination, the trustee shall distribute the property of the trust to the beneficiary if he or she is then living. If the beneficiary is not then living, the trustee shall distribute the trust property to the then living descendants of the beneficiary, by right of representation. If the beneficiary leaves no then living descendants, then the trust property shall be distributed to the persons and in the shares described in Article Nine (4), as if my wife and I had died at the time of termination of the trust.

Article Eleven (Form 4-17, *supra*) establishes a simple but very flexible trust to receive and administer property that would otherwise be distributed to persons under the age of 21. As indicated in §4.21.6, the U.T.M.A. and some states' versions of the U.G.M.A. permit the share of a minor beneficiary to be distributed to a custodian for the benefit of the minor.

In large measure this trust is intended to eliminate the need to appoint guardians of the estates of minor beneficiaries and to provide them with the benefit of a more flexible property arrangement. Article Eleven is added out of an excess of caution — its provisions will come into play very rarely. Under most circumstances the testator's estate will be distributed either to the testator's surviving spouse or to their children.

The provisions of this article do not give rise to any problem under the common law Rule Against Perpetuities. The interests will all ultimately vest when a beneficiary (whose parent was a life in being at the time of the testator's death) attains age 21 or sooner dies. If a greater age is used, the provisions may cause a violation of the Rule. Hence, a savings clause might be included in such cases. *See* §10.48.

§4.24. Provisions Applicable to All Trusts

Form 4-18. Trust Administrative Provisions

Article Twelve: (1) I appoint my brother, Horace M. Client, as trustee of each trust hereunder. If he shall fail or cease to act for any reason, I appoint ____________________ to serve as trustee in his place. I authorize my trustee to employ, at the expense of the trust, such attorneys, custodians, accountants, investment advisors, or other professionals as my trustee believes is in the best interest of the trust.

(2) I direct that no bond shall be required of my trustee or any successor trustee for any purpose.

(3) I expressly confirm to the trustee named herein and any successor trustee, all of the powers contained in Chapter _____ of the laws of the State of ____________________, as they

now exist, which I incorporate by reference. In addition, I confer upon my trustee the following additional powers. . . .

(4) If more than one trust is created by this will, I authorize the trustee to hold, manage, and invest the assets of the trusts as one unit, maintaining the separateness of the trusts by bookkeeping and not a physical segregation of assets.

(5) I authorize the trustee to invest in property of all kinds. In making investment decisions the trustee is directed to take into account the overall investment strategy of the trust, the duration of the trust, the needs of the beneficiaries, the tax circumstances of the trust and the beneficiaries, economic conditions, and the other investments of the trust.

(6) If the value of the principal of any trust (including the combined value of all trusts with identical terms and beneficiaries) is less than Twenty Thousand Dollars ($20,000), I authorize the trustee to terminate the trust and distribute the trust property in accordance with the terms of the trust. If a distributee is under the age of 21 at the time of such distribution I authorize the trustee to distribute the property to a custodian for the beneficiary under the Uniform Transfers to Minors Act [Uniform Gifts to Minors Act].

(7) I authorize the trustee to merge two or more substantially identical trusts which have the same beneficiary or beneficiaries.

I authorize the trustee to divide one trust into two or more trusts with identical provisions. In particular, I encourage the trustee to do so if the trustee believes the division will maximize the benefits of the allocation of my generation-skipping tax exemption. A division may be made by the trustee either on the basis of the value of each asset on the date of the division or by allocating to each trust a fractional interest in each asset.

(8) I direct that no interest of any beneficiary in the income or principal of any trust created by this will may be anticipated, assigned, or encumbered, or be subject to any creditor's claims or legal process prior to its actual distribution to the beneficiary.

§4.24.1. Successor Trustees

If a will or trust appoints an individual as trustee, it generally should appoint a successor or provide a mechanism for the selection of a successor. The first-named individual may not survive the testator or termination of the trust. Of course, the adult beneficiaries could be given the power to appoint someone other than one of themselves as successor trustee. (If taxes are not a consideration or the trustee did not hold any "tax sensitive" powers, the beneficiaries could be given the power to appoint one of their number as successor trustee.) The appointment of a successor could involve some delay and unpleasantness unless one is named in the will. Also, where multiple trustees are appointed, the survivor(s) could be given the power to fill any vacancy in the trusteeship. The power to replace a trustee with a person other than a beneficiary should not cause any problems. In contrast, the IRS might contend that a power to *remove and replace* the trustee should cause the beneficiaries to be treated as holding the powers of the trustee. *See* Rev. Rul. 79-353, 1979-2 C.B. 325 (involving §2038, not §2041); §10.41.

§4.24.2. Waive Bond

Article Twelve (3) waives any requirement that a bond be required of the trustee. The provision accords with the probable intent of most testators, who prefer to save the cost of a fiduciary bond and rely upon the good faith of the trustee they have selected. State statutes commonly exempt corporate trustees from posting bonds. A client might wish to require a bond of a successor trustee in a case such as this, where a successor is not named in the will. Again, this is a matter that should be put to the client for decision.

§4.24.3. Trustee's Powers

This will meets the problem of defining the trustee's powers by incorporating the existing state statutory provisions. This approach is satisfactory if the statutes give adequate powers to trustees. If the local law gives a trustee adequate powers, it is not necessary to incorporate them. However, some lawyers prefer to do so in order to "freeze" the applicable law at the time and to call the powers to the attention of the trustee and others. The latter objective is, of course, better served by including a complete statement of powers in the will. If the local law does not provide an adequate list of powers, the will may incorporate either the laws of another state or the Uniform Trustees' Powers Act, which has served as a model for statutes adopted in many states in recent years. *See* Horowitz, Uniform Trustees' Powers Act, 41 Wash. L. Rev. 1 (1966). The jurisdictions that have enacted the Uniform Act or statutes based on it are listed in the latest supplement to 7B U.L.A. 741 (1985). Before a lawyer drafts a will that incorporates a list of powers, he or she should review the list carefully to determine whether it is necessary to make any additions or deletions based upon the needs of the particular client.

The trustee will often need additional powers if he or she is expected to deal with special situations or special types of property, such as agricultural property, mineral interests, income-producing real property, or a business that may be continued following the testator's death. Also, it may be necessary to include special provisions regarding the allocation of receipts and disbursements between principal and income, particularly where income-producing real property is involved, and to give some specific directions to the trustee regarding depreciation and other charges. In some cases, clients will also want small stock dividends allocated to income instead of to principal as provided in the Uniform Principal and Income Act §6(a) (1962 Revised Act), 7B U.L.A. 145 (1985). *See* §10.47.

Special provisions may also be required in order to relieve the trustee from conflicts of interest. For example, an instrument may waive conflicts that might arise if (1) the fiduciary and the testator are partners or shareholders in a closely-held business; (2) the fiduciary and the testator are parties to a buy-sell agreement respecting stock owned by each of them; or (3) the fiduciary is a broker who might provide services to the estate.

Insofar as deletions are concerned, an informed client may wish to negate the provisions of statutes that authorize a trustee to retain all assets transferred to the trustee, including stock issued by a corporate trustee. *See* Uniform Principal and Income Act §3(c)(1) (1962 Revised Act), 7B U.L.A. 145 (1985). The client also may not wish to relieve the trustee of the duty to diversify investments, Nev. Rev. Stat. §163.280 (1987), or to allow the trustee to invest in common trust funds and shares of regulated investment companies.

It is questionable whether a professional fiduciary should be insulated from liability for the retention of assets however they were acquired by the trust. After all, a trustee is compensated in part to provide prudent management and investment of the trust assets. Also, because of the potential conflict of interest, in most cases a corporate trustee should not be authorized to acquire or retain its own stock. If a client owns particular assets that the client desires the trustee to retain, his or her wishes should be expressed clearly in the will. In such a case the lawyer should not rely upon the general statutory authorization.

Clients may or may not wish to permit the trustee to invest in mutual funds or common trust funds. Such investments can provide broad diversification and relatively low transaction costs. On the other hand, some argue that such investments involve a double layer of management fees — the fee charged by the trustee *and* the one charged by the mutual fund manager. Whatever the state law may be on the point, the client should consider including an express provision in the will. Giving specific authorization removes any doubt regarding the issue and alerts the trustee to the existence of the authority. If the authority to invest in common trust funds is denied to a corporate fiduciary it may refuse to serve or charge substantially higher fees. For a discussion of trust investment provisions, see §§4.24.5 and 10.45.

A lawyer may prefer to set forth the trustee's powers in full in the will. The provisions of the Uniform Trustees' Powers Act or the statutory provisions of a state such as Florida, New York, or Virginia could serve as a good base from which to work. Once evolved, basically the same statement of powers could be modified as required and used in other wills. As in the case of other forms, it should be used intelligently and not mindlessly included as boilerplate.

§4.24.4. Unified Management of Trust Assets

Paragraph (4) of Article Twelve (Form 4-18, *supra*) authorizes the trustee to hold and manage the assets of trusts under the will as a single unit. In this way the trustee may achieve some economies of scale and greater diversification of the assets of each trust. The necessary segregation of the assets of the trusts can be adequately maintained on the books of the trust. In addition, the assets of the trusts may always be physically segregated if it becomes desirable to do so.

§4.24.5. Investment Criteria

A client may wish to give the trustee broader authority and additional direction regarding the investments of the trust, allowing the trustee to pursue more promising investment strategies without liability. Article Twelve (5) is intended to permit the trustee to make individual investment decisions in light of all relevant factors, including the other assets of the trust, economic conditions, and the tax positions of the trust and its beneficiaries. This provision should free the trustee from the unreasonable application of the prudent person standard of investments.

The prudent person standard of investments originated in an early Massachusetts decision, *Harvard College v. Amory,* 26 Mass. (9 Pick.) 446 (1830). Under it trustees must "observe how men of prudence, discretion, and intelligence manage their own affairs, not in regard to speculation, but in regard to the permanent disposition of their funds, considering the probable income, as well as the probable safety of the capital to be invested." The standard, which draws an unreasonably sharp distinction between "speculation" and "safety," has generally been applied to individual investments without regard to the other investments of the trust under consideration. The text of the standard is also premised on distinguishing income from principal. It is unreasonable and unfair to fail to consider the role of a particular investment in a trust's overall portfolio.

The desirability of taking other factors into account has influenced some courts and has lead some states to adopt investment standards that allow other factors to be considered. For example, Cal. Prob. Code §16040(b) (West 1991 Supp.), authorizes the trustee to make individual investment decisions in light of "the general economic conditions and the anticipated needs of the trust and its beneficiaries" and "as a part of an overall investment strategy." Other statutes explicitly provide that the tax consequences may be taken into account. *E.g.,* Del. Code Ann. tit. 12, §3302(a) (1987). Legislation adopted in Washington authorizes investment decisions to be made in light of the trust's overall portfolio of assets. Wash. Rev. Code §11.100.020 (1989). Subject to the overall investment standards, the Washington law allows the trustee to invest up to ten percent of the value of the trust "in new, unproven, untried, or other enterprises with a potential for significant growth whether producing a current return, either by investing directly therein or by investing as a limited partner in one or more commingled funds which in turn invest primarily in such enterprises." Wash. Rev. Code §11.100.23 (1989).

Two factors frequently require trustees to consider the impact of investments upon the income and principal interests in a trust. First, the prudent person standard required the trustee to consider investments in light of their probable income as well as their safety. Second, the beneficial interests in trusts are typically divided between beneficiaries who are entitled to receive the net income of the trust and ones who are entitled to the principal. The importance of the distinction is diminished if the trustee has discretion to distribute income or principal, or both, to the current beneficiaries. In those instances, the trustee is not compelled by the bifurcation of beneficial interests to make investments designed to generate income to be distributed currently to the income beneficiaries. Instead, the trustee can focus on the overall potential of the investments for growth and security. The importance of the distinction between income and principal is also largely eliminated if the current beneficiary is entitled each year to receive a unitrust amount — a fixed percentage of the principal value of the trust, determined on a specified date. For example, the current beneficiary might be entitled to receive each calendar year periodic distributions equal to six percent of the fair market value of the trust assets as determined on the first business day of the year.

§4.24.6. Authority to Terminate Uneconomical Trusts

In order to prevent the trust administration expenses from becoming too large in relation to the size of the trust, a provision might also be included that would authorize the trustee to terminate any trust if its principal value falls below a specified minimum amount, say, $20,000, at the end of any accounting period. If a trust is terminated for that reason, the trustee could be directed to distribute the fund to each beneficiary who is 21, otherwise to a custodian for the beneficiary under the U.T.M.A. A guardianship should be avoided because the associated expenses could easily exceed the costs of continuing the trust. California authorizes judicial modification or termination of an uneconomical trust upon petition of the trustee or any beneficiary. Cal. Prob. Code §15408 (West 1991 Supp.). In addition, the cited provision of the California Probate Code allows termination if the principal falls below $20,000 in value.

§4.24.7. Merger and Division of Trusts

In order to facilitate tax planning and to permit the more economical administration of trusts, the client may wish to authorize the trustee to merge substantially identical trusts that have the same beneficiaries. Such a provision may be sufficient alone, or with the approval of the court, to merge similar trusts, which could reduce overall trust administration expenses. California allows a trust to be merged or divided by the court upon petition of a beneficiary or trustee. Cal. Prob. Code §§15411-15412 (West 1991 Supp.).

It is also desirable to authorize the trustee to divide one trust into two or more identical trusts. Giving the trustee authority to make such a division is particularly important if the executor makes a reverse QTIP election for GSTT purposes. *See* §2.26.

§4.24.8. Spendthrift Clause

The last provision of Article Twelve (Form 4-18, *supra*) makes the interest of each beneficiary inalienable to the extent permitted by local law. Most states recognize spendthrift restrictions to some extent. In some states income and principal interests can be made spendthrift, while in others only income, or some portion of income, can be protected in this way. Although the interest of a beneficiary may be inalienable because of its discretionary character, it may be desirable to make it spendthrift as well. The addition of this paragraph somewhat increases the probability that the beneficiaries will receive the intended benefits of the trust. Also, in the case of modest estates, there are usually no countervailing tax considerations that would support the omission of a spendthrift provision. The use of spendthrift clauses is reviewed in §10.21.

§4.25. Guardian of Minor Children

Form 4-19. Appointment of Guardian

Article Thirteen: If my wife does not survive me, or for any reason fails to qualify or ceases to act as guardian of the person of any of my children who are minors at the time, I appoint my brother, Horace M. Client, as guardian of the person [and estate] of each such minor child. If he fails to qualify or ceases to act as such guardian at any time during the minority of any of my children, I appoint my sister, Louise Client Smith, now of San Francisco, California, as guardian of the person [and estate] of such minor children. I direct that no bond be required of the guardian for any purpose. I expressly authorize the guardian to change the place of residence of any minor child of mine from time to time to any place within or without the state in which the child resides at the time of my death or later.

The law of many states permits a surviving parent to appoint a guardian for a minor child by will. U.P.C. §5-202 (1990); Tex. Prob. Code Ann. §117 (Vernon 1980); Wash. Rev. Code §11.88.080 (1989). For obvious reasons, only individuals may serve as guardians of the person. Although a trust or custodianship is used to provide for the management of the minor's property, a guardian of the minor's estate may be appointed to deal with additional assets that are excluded from the trust or custodianship. The person serving as trustee or custodian, another individual, or a corporate fiduciary may be appointed guardian of the minor's estate. The appointment of a guardian of the person of a child is normally not required if a parent survives — a surviving parent is ordinarily entitled to the care and custody of a minor child.

Although the law of most states does not require a bond of the guardian of a minor's person, the imposition of a bond should be expressly waived in order to settle the matter clearly. The Texas law does require a bond of the guardian of the person. Tex. Prob. Code Ann. §193 (Vernon 1980). Because of the possibility of the death of both parents as a result of a common accident, it is wise for clients to consider appointing guardians for their minor children. Before their wills are prepared the clients should discuss the subject with the prospective guardians. If the prospective guardians are not family members, the clients must consider whether the provisions of the will should be disclosed to family members. A discussion might relieve problems that could arise if, for example, the family members contested the appointment made in the will. On the other hand, broaching the subject of appointing a nonfamily member could generate a controversy within the family.

State law often allows a minor over the age of 14 to participate in guardianship proceedings and to nominate a person to serve as his or her guardian. If the clients' children are 14 or older at the time the wills are prepared, the clients may wish to discuss the subject with them. Such a discussion can provide a valuable opportunity for the family members to examine their feelings about each other, family friends, and, importantly, about death. Some clients will readily accept this suggestion — others will reject it or merely not follow through.

Some jurisdictions allow the appointment of nonresident guardians. If the local law does not permit such an appointment, it may be difficult to meet the needs of some clients. However, a possible solution is to appoint a resident as coguardian with the nonresident. The authorization to change the place of residence of a minor child may provide some additional flexibility, although it is given to guardians by some existing statutes. *See, e.g.,* U.P.C. §5-209(c)(2) (1990).

§4.26. Executors

Form 4-20. Appointment of Executors

Article Fourteen: I appoint my wife as executor of this will. If my wife does not survive me or otherwise fails or ceases to act as executor, I appoint my brother, Horace M. Client, to serve as executor in her place. I authorize my executor to employ, at the expense of my estate, such attorneys, custodians, accountants, investment advisors, or other professionals as my executor believes are in the best interests of my estate. In addition, I authorize my executor to serve without bond and to administer and to settle my estate independently, without the participation or supervision of any court, to the maximum extent permitted by the applicable law. If an ancillary administration of my estate is required in other jurisdictions, I authorize my executor to serve in each such jurisdiction or to designate an executor to serve in each such ancillary jurisdiction.

The lawyer can help a client select an executor by explaining both the role of an executor in an estate administration and the pros and cons of having an individual executor, a corporate executor, or coexecutors.

One factor to bear in mind is the cost. If a family member is appointed, either the executor will waive the right to receive a fee or the fee paid will remain within the family. If a nonfamily member is appointed, a substantial fee may pass outside the family.

> Where a decedent's personal representative was compensated, the cost was often substantial. However, in most cases in the sample the personal representative was a relative of the decedent who served without compensation. Sometimes a personal representative related to the decedent was paid — perhaps to minimize the aggregate estate and income taxes payable by the estate and the survivors. Even in those cases, the funds stayed within the decedent's family. Unrelated persons served as personal representatives in a small number of cases. Price, The Transmission of Wealth at Death in a Community Property Jurisdiction, 50 Wash. L. Rev. 277, 324-325 (1975); *see also* Kinsey, A Contrast of Trends in Administrative Costs in Decedents' Estates in a Uniform Probate Code State (Idaho) and a Non-Uniform Probate Code State (North Dakota), 50 N.D.L. Rev. 523, 524-527 (1974).

A fiduciary may waive the right to compensation without adverse gift or income tax consequences, provided it is done in a timely fashion. *See* §12.8. For federal tax purposes the necessary intention to serve gratuitously is indicated if the fiduciary makes a formal waiver of any right to compensation within six months of appointment. *See* Rev. Rul. 66-167, 1966-1 C.B. 20; Rev. Rul. 70-237, 1970-1 C.B. 13. Of course, when the lowest marginal estate tax rate is higher than the highest marginal income tax rate, some overall tax saving will result if the fiduciary is compensated.

The basic fee of a corporate fiduciary is typically determined by applying a percentage scale to some measure of the value of the property for which it must account, such as the inventory value. Current fee schedules can usually be obtained upon request by a lawyer from corporate fiduciaries. A typical schedule establishes a minimum fee and rates that range from .6 percent or more for the first $100,000 or $200,000 to .35 percent on amounts in excess of $1,000,000. Some corporate fiduciaries use schedules that base their fees in part according to an hourly charge for the time of trust department personnel at rates comparable to those of junior lawyers.

In most jurisdictions the extent to which the lawyer for a fiduciary may disclose the misconduct of the fiduciary to the beneficiaries of the fiduciary estate or to the court is uncertain. *See* MRPC 1.6. Accordingly, the testator may wish to condition the appointment of the executor and other fiduciaries upon their consent to the disclosure of any breaches of trust by their counsel. It is particularly appropriate to do so in the case of a corporate or other professional fiduciary. Indeed, the testator may also wish to condition the appointment of the lawyer for the fiduciary upon the lawyer's agreement to make such disclosures. However, if the fiduciary has filed the required waiver of confidentiality, the lawyer will be inclined to make the necessary disclosures in order to avoid liability for losses caused by a failure to do so. This approach is based upon a recognition that the purpose of the lawyer's services in drawing the will and representing the fiduciary is to benefit the beneficiaries designated in the will. It would be anomalous to permit the fiduciary to use the rules of professional responsibility to prevent disclosure of breaches of trust. Accordingly, the testator may wish to include a provision like that found in Form 4-21, *infra.*

Form 4-21. Waiver of Confidentiality by Executor

I enjoin my executor of my will and counsel selected by my executor faithfully to discharge their duties in the administration of my estate. In furtherance of my intention, I expressly condition the appointment of my executor upon the executor executing and filing with the court a document which permits counsel for the executor to disclose to the court and to the beneficiaries under this will any acts or omissions that might constitute a breach of trust by the executor, including breaches discovered through disclosures of information by the executor.

§4.26.1. Lawyer-Fiduciary

The lawyer who prepares a will should be reluctant to accept appointment as a fiduciary under the wills. *See* §1.13. In this connection, EC 5-6 provides that a lawyer shall not suggest directly, or indirectly that the will appoint him or her as a fiduciary. Surrogate Laurino has cautioned that, before undertaking to serve as fiduciary, a lawyer should consider the "grave legal, ethical and practical problems that he may have to overcome in order to perform his duties as a fiduciary and as an attorney." Laurino, The Duties and Responsibilities of the Attorney/Fiduciary, 19th U. Miami, Inst. Est. Plan., ch. 16 (1985).

The lawyer should also explain to a client that the appointment of an individual as executor or trustee may require the lawyer to do more post-mortem legal work, as a result of which the lawyer's compensation might be greater than if a corporate fiduciary were appointed. On the other hand, the additional cost of legal services may be less than the cost of using a corporate fiduciary.

Although the lawyer does not serve as personal representative, some states recognize that he or she owes fiduciary duties to the beneficiaries, which may be enforced by them in appropriate cases. In *Estate of Larson,* 694 P.2d 1051 (Wash. 1985), the court discussed the origin of the lawyer's fiduciary duties to the beneficiaries:

> In probate, the attorney-client relationship exists between the attorney and the personal representative of the estate. . . . The personal

> representative stands in a fiduciary relationship to those beneficially interested in the estate. He is obligated to exercise the utmost good faith and diligence in administering the estate in the best interests of the heirs. . . . The personal representative employs an attorney to assist him in the proper administration of the estate. Thus, the fiduciary duties of the attorney run not only to the personal representative but also to the heirs.

While the rationale expressed by the Ohio Supreme Court in *Elam v. Hyatt Legal Services,* 541 N.E.2d 616 (1989), was unusual, the court concluded that the attorney for the fiduciary of an estate is liable to the beneficiary of a vested interest for damages caused by the attorney's negligence. In addition, the lawyer is obligated to act with candor toward the court. MRPC 3.3. Some courts conclude that the lawyer for the fiduciary represents the fiduciary and owes few, if any, duties to the beneficiaries. *See* §1.36.

If a lawyer serves as fiduciary, in most states he or she may also serve as attorney, or engage his or her firm to provide legal services. Service in both capacities is approved by the Statement of Probate Principles promulgated by the Real Property, Probate and Trust Law Section of the American Bar Association. It is expressly permitted by statute in New York. N.Y. Surr. Ct. Proc. Act Law §2111 (McKinney 1967). However, it may be unwise for an attorney to serve as a fiduciary. *See* §1.18. In California, Wisconsin, and some other states, a lawyer who acts in both capacities is not entitled to compensation both as executor and as lawyer for the estate. *See* Lombard & Gother, Choosing Your Executor and Trustee, 8 Probate Notes 246 (1983).

§4.26.2. Corporate Fiduciary

It is impossible to generalize about the desirability of appointing a corporate fiduciary. The quality of a corporate fiduciary's performance depends in large measure on the ability and personality of the individual or individuals who are assigned to the estate or trust. The lawyer can influence the fiduciary's performance to some degree, but, after all, the lawyer is retained by the fiduciary, not vice versa. In order to enable the client to make an informed selection of fiduciaries, the lawyer should tell the client of any policy the corporate fiduciaries under consideration may have regarding the employment of lawyers who draw instruments appointing them as fiduciaries. The client should also understand that a corporate fiduciary may decline appointment, particularly if it did not review and approve of the terms of its appointment prior to the testator's death.

A corporate fiduciary is particularly appropriate where the client intends to create one or more large trusts that may continue for a substantial period of time, the services of an independent trustee are needed, or the client otherwise wishes to use a professional fiduciary. Also, when other potential appointees may be seriously affected by conflicts of interest the selection of an independent corporate fiduciary may be helpful. A client may ask the lawyer to recommend a corporate fiduciary. If so, the lawyer might suggest that the client interview trust officers at a select group of institutions and choose from among them. Of course, the client may wish to use a particular corporate fiduciary with which the client has a substantial existing relationship. With the client's approval the lawyer may inform the corporate fiduciary that it is named in the clients' will. In some instances a corporate fiduciary may be asked to review a client's will and related documents. If a corporate fiduciary has reviewed and approved the documents, it may feel obligated to serve as fiduciary. Otherwise it is not under an obligation to accept an appointment.

§4.26.3. Family Member Fiduciary

The availability, willingness, and ability of a family member to serve as executor must also be considered. After the death of a family member, the grief of a surviving spouse or other family member may be relieved by devoting some time to the details of the executor's job. In some cases the lawyer can play a valuable role by assigning the survivors a reasonable amount of information gathering and other work. Clients often decide to name a surviving spouse as executor, recognizing that he or she may decline to serve in favor of a child or other alternate named in the will. The lawyer should recognize that a surviving spouse or other client may become emotionally attached to and overly dependent on the lawyer and his or her advice. A lawyer should be sympathetic, while at the same time discouraging the development of such dependence.

An individual may be less reluctant to serve as a fiduciary if he or she is given express authority to retain attorneys, accountants, investment counselors, or other professionals whose services might assist in the administration of the estate. In essence, the services of a corporate fiduciary can be approximated if an individual executor is authorized to employ sufficient professional assistance. Indeed, many corporate fiduciaries have "unbundled" and make their custodial and investment management services available to individual fiduciaries. It is particularly appropriate to authorize the employment of professional advisors if the will names as fiduciary a family member who is unlikely to accept a fee.

§4.26.4. Coexecutors

The relationship between coexecutors can be a difficult one. A common cause of conflict involves the division of responsibilities and compensation. The advantages of having coexecutors, including continuity in the event one dies or otherwise ceases to serve, should be balanced against the potential disadvantages, including possible disputes over the custody and management of assets and over fees. A corporate fiduciary understandably wants custody of all of the estate's assets and to receive full compensation for its services. In some states such as New York *each* coexecutor is entitled to a full statutory commission. *See* N.Y. Surr. Ct. Proc. Act Law §§2307, 2309 (McKinney 1967). Under the New York law if the estate exceeds $300,000 a full commission is payable to as many as three fiduciaries. If there are more than three fiduciaries, the commission for three is divided among them.

The law commonly requires the concurrence of both (or all) coexecutors to bind the estate, which can cause some delays and require the reference of some matters to the court for instructions. Some problems are avoided if the will authorizes one executor to act during the absence or disability of the other.

§4.26.5. Alternate or Successor Executor

An alternate or successor executor should be appointed in wills that name individual executors. The first-named executor may not survive the testator, may decline to serve, or may not complete the administration of the estate. The need to name a successor is indicated by the fact that roughly ten percent of the individual executors named in a sample of Washington wills failed to survive the testator. Price, The Transmission of Wealth at Death in a Community Property Jurisdiction, 50 Wash. L. Rev. 277, 325 n.130 (1975). Although a corporate executor might decline to serve or later resign, it is less necessary to name a successor to a corporate fiduciary. If a successor is not named, the will should establish a procedure for the selection of one (*e.g.,* "a successor executor may be designated by a majority of my surviving adult children").

§4.26.6. Exculpatory Clause

A testator may wish to exculpate an individual personal representative from liability for official acts except in cases of willful misconduct or gross negligence. As a general proposition, corporate fiduciaries and other professionals who are fairly compensated for their services should not be relieved of liability for their acts or omissions. Of course, a lawyer may not enter into an agreement with a client that relieves the lawyer from liability for his or her acts or omissions. MRPC 1.8(h).

Form 4-22. Exculpatory Clause

Excepting acts of gross negligence and willful misconduct I relieve my Executor of any liability to my estate or any person interested in my estate for actions taken as personal representative.

§4.26.7. Executor's Bond

In most instances no bond is required of a personal representative under the U.P.C. *See* U.P.C. §3-603 (1990). Under New York law no bond is required except where required by the will, the nominee is a nondomiciliary, or the nominee does not possess the degree of responsibility required of a fiduciary. N.Y. Surr. Ct. Proc. Act Law §710 (McKinney 1967). In many states a bond is still routinely required of individual personal representatives unless it is waived. Cal. Prob. Code §8480 (West 1991 Supp.); Tex. Prob. Code §§194, 195 (Vernon 1980). However, statutes generally excuse corporate fiduciaries from the requirement of posting bond. Fiduciary bonds, which cost from $5 to $10 per $1,000 annually, are often an unnecessary expense that may deprive the surviving family members of needed funds. A client should, of course, be given the option of requiring a bond of fiduciaries but, in most cases, the additional cost should be avoided.

§4.26.8. Compensation of Executors

A will may specify the amount of compensation to be paid to a fiduciary. A fiduciary who accepts appointment of a will containing such a provision without objection is bound by it. Under some circumstances, it may be desirable to include such a provision in the will. However, the fiduciary may choose not to accept appointment or may seek to be freed of the restriction.

The states have a wide variety of arrangements for establishing the compensation of fiduciaries. For example, California and New York have statutory rate scales, while other states expect the courts to establish the "reasonable" compensation of executors and trustees.

Under Reg. §20.2053-3(b)(2), a bequest in lieu of commissions is not deductible by the estate. However, an amount of compensation fixed in the will is deductible to the extent it does not exceed the amount allowable under the local law. The payment but probably not the bequest will be income to the executor. In recent years the IRS has shown greater interest in monitoring the amounts paid as commissions and challenging amounts that it considers to be unreasonable or unnecessary. *See* §12.13.4.

§4.26.9. Authority to Settle Estate Without Court Supervision

Unsupervised administration of estates is the norm under the U.P.C. without any specific form of authorization. The expanded powers given to personal representatives under U.P.C. §3-715 (1990), and recent changes in the laws of many states, largely eliminate the need to set forth the powers of the decedent's personal representative. Again, however, in special cases it may be desirable to give the personal representative specific powers with regard to particular assets. Some lawyers confer upon the personal representative the same powers that are given the trustee.

The powers of personal representatives in California were expanded by enactment of the Independent Administration of Estate Act, but no truly independent administration is authorized. *See* Cal. Prob. Code §10500, *et seq.* (West 1991 Supp.). For over a century the law of Texas has allowed a testator to provide that his or her estate be settled without any action of the court other than the probating and recording of the will and the return of an inventory, appraisement, and list of claims against the estate. Tex. Prob. Code §145 (Vernon 1980). Commentators have observed that virtually all well-drafted wills prepared in Texas direct that the estate be settled by independent administration. The Washington experience with the unsupervised administration of estates has also been very good. Because of the mobility of our population and the possible enactment of similar legislation in other states, Article Fourteen authorizes the executor to settle the estate without court intervention. *See* Form 4-20, *supra.*

§4.27. Directions Regarding Debts, Expenses of Administration, and Taxes

Form 4-23. Payment of Debts, Taxes, and Expenses

Article Fifteen: (1) I direct my executor to pay all expenses of administration and all inheritance, estate, succession, and similar taxes ("death taxes") imposed upon my estate by reason of

> my death, other than any generation-skipping transfer tax and any estate tax attributable to property included in my gross estate by reason of I.R.C. §2044, from the assets of my residuary estate, whether or not the expenses of administration or death taxes are attributable to property passing under this will.
>
> (2) I authorize my executor to exercise all elections available under federal and state laws with respect to (a) the date or manner of valuation of assets, (b) the deductibility of items for state or federal income or death tax purposes, (c) the marital deduction, (d) the generation-skipping transfer tax exemption and (e) other matters of federal or state tax law, in accordance with what my executor believes to be in the best interests of my estate. I relieve my executor of any duty to make any adjustment to the shares or interest of any person who may be adversely affected by such elections and from any liability for making any such elections.

A properly drawn will or trust should include a provision definitely establishing the fund from which expenses of administration and death taxes should be paid. This important subject may involve numerous taxes, multiple jurisdictions, and a high degree of complexity. *See* Pennell, Tax Payment Provisions and Equitable Apportionment, U. Miami, 22d Inst. Est. Plan., ch. 18 (1988). In order to enable the lawyer and client to make informed plans regarding the allocation of tax burdens, the amounts of the various taxes and expenses should be estimated. Giving consideration to the estimates increases the probability that the client's dispositive plan will not be frustrated by the manner in which the taxes are charged. The appropriate directions should be included particularly if they are not consistent with the underlying local law.

The tax clause generally should not assume any obligation to pay the estate tax attributable to QTIP that is included in the testator's estate by reason of §2044. It is generally preferable for the tax on §2044 property to be recovered from the recipient as provided in §2207A. Similarly, the obligation to pay the GSTT generally should not be imposed on the residuary estate.

§4.27.1. Source of Funds to Pay Federal Estate Tax

The executor is obligated to pay the federal estate tax, §2002, but the source from which the tax is paid is generally determined by state law. Many states follow the common law rule that calls for payment of the entire amount of the tax from the decedent's residuary estate. Others have adopted rules that require the tax to be apportioned among the recipients of the decedent's property. Though some states have adopted them by judicial decision, apportionment rules are usually statutory. *E.g.,* U.P.C. §3-916 (1990); Cal. Prob. Code §20100 *et seq.* (West 1991 Supp.); N.Y. Est. Powers & Trusts Law §2-1.8 (McKinney 1991 Supp.). A more comprehensive apportionment statute was adopted by California and is effective with respect to decedents dying after 1986. It also apportions the additional estate tax on excess retirement accumulations and the GSTT.

All states recognize that a testator may direct the tax to be satisfied from a different source by appropriate direction in the will. A will provision dealing with the subject must be carefully drafted in order to prevail over the local rule.

> [A]pportionment of the taxes is the general rule to which exception is to be made only when there is a clear and unambiguous direction to the contrary. Ambiguities are to be resolved in favor of apportionment. *In re Armstrong's Estate,* 366 P.2d 490, 494 (Cal. 1961).

While apportionment may be the general rule, the goals of a client with a relatively simple estate and an uncomplicated dispositive plan are served by providing that the death taxes are to be paid from the client's residuary estate.

§4.27.2. QTIP and §2207A

QTIP is includible in the estate of the surviving spouse to the extent a QTIP marital deduction was claimed by the estate of the spouse first to die. §2044. Unless otherwise provided in the surviving spouse's will, his or her executor may recover any additional estate tax attributable to the QTIP from the recipient of the property. §2207A. In most cases, the surviving spouse-beneficiary does not have any control over the ultimate distribution of the property of the QTIP trust. For that reason the surviving spouse usually chooses not to direct that the estate tax on the QTIP be paid from his or her own property. Accordingly, as a general rule the will of the surviving spouse should not provide for payment of the estate tax imposed on section 2044 property. *See* §12.42.4.

The payment of the federal estate tax from the surviving spouse's estate may constitute an addition to the trust for GSTT purposes. *Cf.,* Temp. Reg. §26.2601-1(b)(1)(v) (the failure to assert the right to recovery available under §2207A for estate tax paid on property included in the survivor's estate under §2204 is a constructive addition to the trust). The temptation to do so might arise if a reverse QTIP election were made and the GSTT exemption of the predeceased spouse were allocated to the QTIP trust.

§4.27.3. §2207B

A decedent's personal representative is entitled to recover a portion of the estate tax attributable to the inclusion of property by reason of §2036 (relating to transfers with retained life estates). §2207B. The amount of tax recoverable is based upon the ratio of the value of the §2036 property to the total value of the taxable estate. Although the inclusion of the property will require the payment of tax at a higher marginal rate, the right of recovery is based upon the average rate. The right of recovery does not exist if the decedent provides otherwise in a will or revocable trust specifically referring to §2207B. §2207B(a)(2).

§4.27.4. Clarity

The substantial volume of litigation regarding the effect of particular tax clauses indicates the problems lawyers have had in drafting adequate provisions. For example, the term "estate" often appears in tax clauses without specifying whether it refers to the gross estate for tax purposes, the "probate" estate, or some other measure of property. Unfortunately the cost of the litigation is almost always borne by the hapless beneficiaries and not the lawyer who drafted the inadequate provision.

If multiple dispositive instruments are involved, all of the directions for the payment of taxes should be consistent and comply with the requirements of local law. Inconsistent provisions contained in a will and a trust may cause problems in tax and substantive law that require judicial resolution. *Estate of Brenner,* 547 P.2d 938 (Colo. App. 1976). The local law may deny effect to directions regarding payment of taxes if they are not included in the will. For example, a provision of an inter vivos trust that directs the trustee to pay "any and all of the Federal Estate Tax for which no other provision for payment has been made" may not be given effect. *Hill v. Nevada National Bank,* 545 P.2d 293, 294 (Nev. 1976). The problem of inconsistent directions in multiple instruments is addressed by a New York statute that provides that any direction in an instrument only relates to property passing thereunder unless otherwise provided. N.Y. Est. Powers & Trusts Law §2-1.8(d) (McKinney 1991 Supp.). It also provides that:

> (1) any such direction in a will which is later in date than a prior nontestamentary instrument which contains a contrary direction shall govern provided the later will specifically refers to the direction in such prior instrument;
> (2) any such direction provided in a nontestamentary instrument which is later in date than a prior will or nontestamentary instrument and which contains a contrary direction shall gov-

ern provided the later instrument specifically refers to the direction in such prior will or instrument;

(3) any such direction provided in a nontestamentary instrument only relates to the payment of the estate tax from property passing thereunder and such direction shall not serve to exonerate such nontestamentary property from the payment of its proportionate share of the tax even if otherwise directed in the nontestamentary instrument.

In addition, this section provides that a general direction to pay taxes does not apply to the tax imposed by reason of the death of a life tenant of QTIP or the additional estate tax imposed on excess retirement accumulations.

§4.27.5. Preserving Qualification for Redemption Under §303

In drafting a provision regarding the payment of taxes it should be borne in mind that stock that is entirely relieved of the obligation to pay death taxes and funeral and administration expenses may not qualify for redemption under §303. For that reason closely-held stock that might be redeemed should not be used to satisfy a marital deduction bequest or be treated as QTIP under §2056(b)(7). In some instances, the problem can be avoided by making the closely-held stock expressly subject to a pro rata portion of taxes and expenses. Such a provision might be effective even as to stock that does not stand in the decedent's name (*e.g.*, in a joint tenancy or a trust). *See United States v. Goodson,* 253 F.2d 900 (8th Cir. 1958) (Minnesota law construed to allow will to impose obligation of contributing to the estate tax on trust beneficiaries and joint tenants).

§4.27.6. Power to Make Non-Pro Rata Distributions

In general, the executor should be authorized to make non-pro rata distributions to beneficiaries who are entitled to share equally in a pool of assets (*e.g.,* the residuary estate). The IRS has recognized that an equal, but non-pro rata, distribution to beneficiaries was not a taxable event where the decedent's will authorized such a distribution. LR 8119040. If a non-pro rata distribution is made with the consent of the beneficiaries, but without authorization by the testator or by the governing law, the beneficiaries may be treated as having made a taxable exchange. Rev. Rul. 69-486, 1969-2 C.B. 159. *See* §12.39.

> **Example 4-4.** *T*'s will give his residuary estate equally to *A* and *B* but did not authorize his executor to make non-pro rata distributions. In accordance with an agreement between *A* and *B,* asset 1 was distributed entirely to *A* and asset 2 was distributed entirely to *B*. Following the approach of Revenue Ruling 69-486, *supra, A* is treated as having exchanged a one-half interest in asset 2 for *B*'s one-half interest in asset 1.

The same concern regarding non-pro rata distributions applies to trusts as well. As pointed out in Chapter 5, the issue recurs in connection with distributions in satisfaction of fractional share marital deduction gifts. *See* §5.46.

§4.27.7. Tax Payments and the Marital and Charitable Deductions

Special care should also be exercised in drafting directions regarding the payment of taxes if the client is passing property that is intended to qualify for the federal estate tax marital deduction to a surviving spouse:

> In the determination of the value of any property interest which passed from the decedent to his surviving spouse, there must be taken into account the effect which the Federal estate tax, or any estate, succession, legacy, or inheritance tax, has upon the net value to the surviving spouse of the property interest. Reg. §20.2056(b)-4(c)(1).

The marital deduction is allowable only to the extent of the net value of property passing to the surviving spouse. Reg. §20.2056(b)-4(a). The allowance of the charitable deduction is similarly limited: "Section 2055(c) in effect provides that the deduction is based on the amount actually available for charitable uses, that is, the amount of the fund remaining after the payment of all death taxes." Reg. §20.2055-3(a). The typical apportionment statute meets the problem by providing that allowances shall be made for exemptions and deductions that are available by reason of the relationship of the recipient to the decedent or by reason of the purposes for which the gift is made. *See, e.g.,* U.P.C. §3-916(e)(2) (1990).

§4.27.8. Payment of State Inheritance Tax

State inheritance taxes are usually payable by the decedent's executor but are charged against the interest of each person who receives property from the decedent. Thus, they are naturally apportioned. However, a testator may direct that the inheritance tax should be borne instead by the residuary estate. If so, the provision will probably be treated as an additional gift to the beneficiaries whose obligation to pay the inheritance tax is relieved. If the rules are adequately explained to clients, they will often choose to relieve specific gifts from the burden of inheritance taxes.

§4.27.9. Statutes Relating to Payment of Federal Estate Tax

The laws regarding the source of payment of the federal estate tax are reviewed in §12.42 in connection with the discussion of post-mortem planning. As indicated above, the testator is free to choose the way in which the tax burden is allocated. In the absence of contrary direction the executor may collect a portion of the federal estate tax from insurance beneficiaries and others. *See* §§2205-2207B.

§4.27.10. Power to Make Tax Elections

The second clause of Article Fifteen (Form 4-23) is intended to alert the executor to valuable tax elections that should be considered, to authorize the executor to make the election, and to relieve the executor from the obligation of making adjustments to interests affected by the elections. In the absence of such a provision the executor might be required to make an equitable adjustment if alternatively deductible expenses, paid from the residuary estate, were claimed on the fiduciary income tax return rather than on the estate tax return. *See* §12.14. The authorities generally indicate that the residuary estate should be reimbursed for the additional estate tax that results from the election to claim the expenses as income tax deductions. Even so, the persons entitled to the income will receive some benefit from the election in many instances. The provision in the will merely relieves the executor from any obligation of making the adjustment, which could require a complicated accounting, and does not preclude making the adjustment.

Clauses (c) and (d) specifically authorize the executor to make elections regarding the marital deduction, such as a QTIP election under §2056(b)(7) and to allocate the testator's GSTT exemption.

§4.28. Wills Not Pursuant to Contract

Form 4-24. Wills Not Contractual

Article Sixteen: The terms of this will and the will executed on the date hereof by my wife are essentially reciprocal in nature. That is, my wife is the principal beneficiary of this will and I am the principal beneficiary of my wife's will. However, the wills are not executed pursuant to any agreement between us. Accordingly, they may be changed or revoked at any time as each of us chooses.

The lawyer may wish to counter the uncertainty that may arise regarding the revocability of reciprocal wills by including a clarifying statement in the wills. Of course, if the clients intend to have a binding agreement for the disposition of their wealth upon the death of the survivor, a different course of action is called for. In such a case the interests of a couple might be better served by establishing an inter vivos trust of substantially all of their property, which could become partially or totally irrevocable upon the death of the first spouse to die. This arrangement parallels the widow's election will that is sometimes used in community property states. *See* §§9.23-9.39. In the typical widow's election will, the survivor receives the entire benefit of the property in the trust for life, with the remainder to others upon the survivor's death. An independent individual or corporate fiduciary could assure that the survivor receives the intended benefits, yet protect the interest of the remaindermen. Even if a trust were utilized, it is difficult to provide the remaindermen with the intended degree of protection and adequately provide for the surviving spouse. However, the trustee could be given the power to invade the corpus of the trust for specified needs of the survivor. Of course, the income, gift, and estate tax consequences of such an alternative must be carefully considered.

§4.29. No Contest Clause

An "in terrorem" clause, which invalidates gifts to a beneficiary who contests the will, is routinely included by many lawyers. Courts have generally upheld such provisions, at least insofar as they prohibit contests that are not made in good faith or have no reasonable cause. Under the U.P.C. such a provision is unenforceable "if probable cause exists for instituting proceedings." U.P.C. §3-905 (1990). Some states bar the enforcement of all such provisions. *E.g.,* Fla. Stat. Ann. §732.517 (West 1976).

In general, such a clause should not be included. The reason is simple: An in terrorem clause is unlikely to protect the integrity of the testator's actual will. Indeed, such a provision may be placed in a will by a person who does exercise undue influence over a testator and wants to deter a contest.

§4.30. EXECUTION

Form 4-25. Execution Clause

In witness whereof, I have signed this will on __________, 19______, at ______________________________.

____
John Q. Client

____
____
____
(witnesses)

The testimonium clause should indicate both the date and place of execution. Those facts, while not required, are often helpful in passing on the validity and effect of the instrument.

All states require that there be two witnesses to nonholographic wills, except South Carolina and Vermont, which require three. Accordingly, in most states wills are witnessed by two persons. Some lawyers in states other than South Carolina and Vermont use three witnesses, increasing the probability that at least one witness will survive the testator and be available to testify if needed. South Carolina and Vermont both recognize the validity of a will executed in accordance with the law of the place of execution or domicile of the testator. The U.P.C. provides a conflicts rule which recognizes the validity of wills that were executed in accordance "with the law at the time of execution of the place where the will was executed, or of the place where at the time of execution or at the time of death the testator is domiciled, has a place of abode, or is a national." U.P.C. §2-506 (1990).

Totally disinterested adults should serve as witnesses. The U.P.C. does not invalidate a gift to an interested witness. Specifically, U.P.C. §2-505(b) (1990) provides, "The signing of a will by an interested witness does not invalidate the will or any provision of it." In contrast, the law of most states deprives an interested witness of benefits under the will except to the extent the witness would receive property from the decedent if the will were not established. Of course, in any case the credibility of a witness may be affected if the witness is also a beneficiary under the will. The lawyer who drew the will and the persons appointed as fiduciaries generally are not disqualified from acting as witnesses, but may prefer not to do so.

An attestation clause, such as Form 4-26, *infra,* should be provided for signature by the witnesses if the local law does not provide for the use of self-proving affidavits or if one is not used for some reason. The clause is not necessary for the validity of the will, but the recitation it contains of the facts required to establish due execution supports a presumption that the instrument was validly executed. The use of such a clause also makes it difficult for the witnesses later to disavow the facts of due execution recited in it.

Form 4-26. Attestation Clause

On the date last above written John Q. Client declared to us that the foregoing instrument, consisting of ______ pages including this page, was his will and requested us to act as witnesses thereto. He thereupon signed his will in our presence, all of us being present at the same time. At his request and in the presence of each other we signed our names as witnesses thereto and signed this attestation clause.

____
Address: ______________________
____

____
Address: ______________________
____

____
Address: ______________________
____

§4.31. Self-Proving Affidavit

Many states now allow a will to be proved by an affidavit of the witnesses or declaration of the witnesses under penalty of perjury which shows that the requirements of the statute of wills are satisfied. *See* U.P.C. §2-504 (1990). The laws vary among the states, however, with some requiring that the witnesses sign the will as witnesses *and* complete the affidavit. The affidavit may be completed either at the time the will was executed or at a later time. Under some statutes the testator and the witnesses sign the affidavit, while under others only the witnesses sign it.

The content of the affidavit will vary according to whether the witnesses sign both the will and the affidavit or only the affidavit. Completion of the affidavit simplifies the proof of the will by recording the necessary facts in a form that is admissible as evidence. In lieu of an affidavit some states permit the use of a declaration of the witnesses made under penalty of perjury. A self-proved will may be admitted to probate without the testimony of the subscribing witnesses. The specific content of the form must comply with the applicable law, which varies somewhat.

§4.32. EXECUTION CEREMONY

The execution ceremony should be conducted by the lawyer in a way that meets the requirements of the law of the place of execution and the law of the most demanding state currently in effect. It should also be done in a manner that satisfies the client's expectations: What may be routine for the lawyer is for most clients an extremely significant event. Finally, special precautions should be taken if the lawyer believes there is a risk that the will may be contested. Extra care may be called for if an elderly, ill, or otherwise vulnerable testator is leaving a substantial portion of property to charities or to persons other than the natural objects of his or her bounty. *See* §§1.8-1.9. If the lawyer believes there is such a risk, the witnesses should be carefully selected for their independence and credibility, consideration should be given to videotaping the execution ceremony, and the ceremony should be conducted in a way that clearly demonstrates the testator's capacity to the witnesses. Note in this connection that some states now authorize the use of a videotape as evidence of the proper execution of a will. Ind. Code Ann. §29-1-5-3(c) (Burns 1989). In order to demonstrate the testator's capacity, he or she might be asked to identify his or her major property holdings, to name his or her nearest relatives, and to describe how the will disposes of his or her property.

Two or more adults who are not beneficially interested in the will should be asked to serve as witnesses and be present throughout the entire execution ceremony. In order to establish the authenticity of the document and its integration as one document, the client should initial each page in the margin or at the bottom of the page and also fill in the date and place of execution in the testimonium clause. The lawyer should then ask the testator, "Do you declare this to be your will and ask the two [three] persons present with us to act as witnesses to the will and to your signature?" The testator should answer affirmatively in a voice clearly audible to all witnesses.

After having declared the document to be his or her will and asked the persons present to act as witnesses, the testator should sign the will in the space provided at the end of the instrument in full view of all of the witnesses. Then each witness should sign the will in the space provided immediately below the testator's signature. The testator and all of the witnesses should observe each other's signatures. However, under the U.P.C. it is not necessary for (1) the witnesses to see the testator sign the will (if the testator acknowledges the signature to them), (2) the testator to observe the witnesses sign, or (3) the witnesses observe each other sign. U.P.C. §2-502 (1990).

If a separate attestation clause is used, the witnesses should then complete and sign it. If the local law provides for making a will self-proving by the use of an affidavit or declaration of due execution, it should be executed by the witnesses in lieu of an attestation clause. In the case of an affidavit a notary must acknowledge the witnesses' signatures, and in some cases the testator's signature as well. The execution of affidavits such as this is facilitated if one or more persons in the lawyer's office is a notary public.

The lawyer may retain the original will for safekeeping if requested by the client to do so. If it is retained, the lawyer should give the client a receipt and make the document available to the client upon request. Some courts and bar association ethics committees have disapproved of lawyers retaining original wills. *E.g., State v. Gulbankian,* 196 N.W.2d 733 (Wis. 1972). Professor Johnston objects to the practice on the ground that it may unfairly advantage the lawyer who drew the will when it comes time to employ a lawyer to represent the personal representative. Johnston, An Ethical Analysis of Common Estate Planning Practice — Is Good Business Bad Ethics?, 45 Ohio St. L.J. 57 (1984). The problem could be avoided by explaining the "risk" to the client, who might nonetheless choose to leave the will with the lawyer. In any case, the personal representative is free to employ as counsel whomever the personal representative chooses. Overall, the retention of wills by lawyers is a valuable service that should be made available to clients. In this way the client's will is safeguarded, yet is readily available to the client or the executor named in the will.

Only one copy of a will should be executed by the testator and the witnesses. It should be placed by the person having custody of it, usually the testator or the lawyer, in a safe place known to others. Multiple copies should not be executed because of the difficulty of accounting for all of them and the presumption of revocation that may arise if all of the executed copies cannot be produced. However, at least in Oklahoma, "[t]he modern practice of executing duplicate wills . . . is to be encouraged." *Estate of Shaw,* 572 P.2d 229, 232 (Okla. 1977) (presumption of revocation of will caused by disappearance of duplicate traced to testator's possession is overcome by production of other executed copy and proof of due execution). On the other hand, it may be desirable for the testator to execute multiple copies of the durable power of attorney and living will. In that way executed copies can be provided to various persons as required.

Photocopies of the will, or conformed copies of the will with the date, place of execution, and signature blocks typed in, should be sent to the testator for reference. With the testator's approval copies could be sent to the individuals or organizations named as fiduciaries. Because of the likelihood that changes will be made in the will, copies should not routinely be sent to beneficiaries — at least not to all beneficiaries. If the testator is given the original document, he or she should be cautioned not to attempt to make changes in it or to execute a subsequent instrument intended to have testamentary effect without professional assistance. The testator should also be reminded of the necessity of reviewing the will periodically and of considering the need for changes if the testator's family or economic circumstances change substantially.

§4.33. Letter of Transmittal to Client

The lawyer should send copies of the documents to the clients as soon as possible after the execution ceremony. In addition to serving as a letter of transmittal, the letter can be used to remind the clients regarding the necessity of reviewing the wills periodically, communicating with the lawyer if there are changes in circumstances, and avoiding changes of title or beneficiary designations that might adversely affect their estate plans. While practices vary, lawyers often send a statement for services separately.

Form 4-27. Letter of Transmittal

Mr. and Mrs. John Q. Client
1000 Green Street
Your City, XX, XXXXX

Dear Mr. and Mrs. Client:

Enclosed is a folder that contains photocopies of the documents you executed in my office yesterday. They are: your Wills, Directives to Physicians and Durable Powers of Attorney. The folder also includes a roster of the names, addresses, and telephone numbers of your principal advisors including your accountants, doctors, and brokers. In accordance with your instructions we have placed the original executed copies of the documents in our safe deposit box [office vault] for safekeeping. The documents are, of course, available to you at any time. As you requested, we have mailed one executed set of your living wills to your principal physician, Dr. Martin A. Smith.

Periodic Review. We have now completed the active phase of our estate planning work for you. Accordingly, until we hear from you again our role will be limited to sending you periodic reminders of the desirability of reviewing your will. As I mentioned to you, we recommend that you review your wills and basic estate plan every three to four years to be sure that they continue to meet your needs. I have made a note on my calendar to send you a reminder in three years if I don't hear from you in the meantime. Please be sure to let me know if you want to make any changes in the wills or other elements of your estate plan before then.

Changes in Circumstances. We also recommend that you review your wills and basic estate plan if there are any substantial changes in your personal or financial circumstances. Such a review should be made, for example, if there are any changes in your family as a result of births or deaths, marriages or divorces. A review is also indicated if you plan to move to another state or if the size or composition of your estate changes substantially. You should also be alert for any events that might affect the suitability or availability of the executors, trustees, and guardians who are named in your wills.

Forms of Property Ownership. In order for your estate plan to be effective, you should continue the present methods of property ownership and the present beneficiary designations in your life insurance and employee benefit plans. The transfer of property into another form of ownership, such as a joint tenancy with right of survivorship (*e.g.,* John Q. and Jane M. Client, as joint tenants with right of survivorship), or the change of beneficiary designations could affect the distribution of your property and could have adverse tax consequences. Please check with me before you acquire or dispose of substantial assets, including life insurance.

Gifts. Please also let me know if you plan to make any gifts which total more than $10,000 in value to one person in any calendar year. Substantial gifts must be carefully planned in order to produce the optimum tax results. Particular attention should be given to the method by which gifts are made (*e.g.,* outright or in trust), the selection of the property to be transferred, and the time at which the gifts are made.

Please call me if you have any questions or would like to consult with me further regarding your plans.

Sincerely,

C. ADDITIONAL DOCUMENTS

§4.34. General

The lawyer should counsel clients regarding a variety of additional documents they may wish to consider. Three that have come into prominence in recent years are discussed in the following pages: the power of attorney that either becomes effective (or, if presently effective, does not terminate) if the principal becomes incompetent (the so-called durable power of attorney); the living will (or directive to physicians authorized by natural death acts in some states); and an instrument of gift under the original 1968 or the revised 1987 version of the Uniform Anatomical Gift Act.

The durable power of attorney, which is available in a growing number of states, provides some protection against the necessity of a guardianship if the principal becomes incompetent. The Uniform Durable Power of Attorney Act, 8A U.L.A. 88 (1991 Supp.), has been adopted in a number of states and the District of Columbia. The National Conference of Commissioners on Uniform State Laws (NCCUSL) has also adopted a Statutory Form Power of Attorney Act, which includes a provision making it "durable." 8A U.L.A. 151 (1991 Supp.). Executing a statutory form of power of attorney confers upon the attorney-in-fact the powers described in more detail in §§3-5 of the act. Importantly, in some states the principal may give the attorney-in-fact authority to make health care decisions for the principal during any period of incapacity. A few states expressly authorize a durable power of attorney for health care.

Many clients are also anxious to execute a living will or similar document that expresses their wishes regarding the medical care they should receive in the event they become terminally ill and incompetent. The scope and content of such a document depends upon the local law and should be compatible with any durable power of attorney the client may execute. Unfortunately, the scope of a living will is often limited. In many states it cannot be used to authorize another person to make health care decisions for the maker. The NCCUSL has approved the Uniform Rights of the Terminally Ill Act, 9B U.L.A. 609 (1987), which is a form of natural death act, which has been adopted in a few states including Alaska, Arkansas, Iowa, Maine, Missouri, Montana, and Oklahoma. The Uniform Act, having a narrow scope, simply authorizes an adult to execute a declaration "instructing a physician to withhold or withdraw life-sustaining treatment in the event the person is in a terminal condition and is unable to participate in medical treatment decisions." Prefatory Note, 9B U.L.A. 609 (1987).

Clients are also often interested in making gifts of their bodies or parts of their bodies for medical education, research, or transplantation.

Advances in medical technology make it possible to relieve a wide range of illnesses and diseases by transplants, grafts, or other procedures. The Uniform Anatomical Gift Act provides a useful way of carrying out a client's wish to assist others.

§4.35. Durable Powers of Attorney

> The National Conference included Sections 5-501 and 5-502 in Uniform Probate Code (1969) (1975) concerning powers of attorney to assist persons interested in establishing noncourt regimes for the management of their affairs in the event of later incompetency or disability. The purpose was to recognize a form of senility insurance comparable to that available to relatively wealthy persons who use funded, revocable trusts for persons who are unwilling or unable to transfer assets as required to establish a trust. Commissioners' Prefatory Note, Uniform Durable Power of Attorney Act, 8A U.L.A. 275 (1983).

According to Francis J. Collin, Jr. of Napa, California, one of the leading practitioners in the field, "All 50 states and the District of Columbia have durable power of attorney statutes. However, . . . only a few states have specific statutory authority for a DPAHC [Durable Power of Attorney for Health Care]. This does not mean that a DPAHC cannot be used in those jurisdictions which do not have specific statutory authority." Collin, Planning and Drafting Durable Powers of Attorney for Health Care, U. Miami, 22nd Inst. Est. Plan. ¶504.5 (1988).

In brief, the durable power statutes allow a person to execute a power of attorney that will not be affected by any future physical disability or mental incapacity. Although the laws vary somewhat from state to state, they are largely traceable to the sections of the U.P.C. that provide for a durable power of attorney. *See* U.P.C. §§5-501 *et seq.* (1990). In 1979 the NCCUSL promulgated a separate act, the Uniform Durable Power of Attorney Act, which is identical to the revised provisions of the U.P.C. Slight revisions were made in the Uniform Act in 1984 and 1987. Revised forms of the Durable Power of Attorney Act have been adopted in many important states, including California, Indiana, Pennsylvania, and Wisconsin.

Collin argues persuasively that the Uniform Act permits the attorney-in-fact to be given authority to make health care decisions for the principal. He points out that the subsequent adoption of the Model Health-Care Consent Act by the NCCUSL in 1982 recognized that the power to designate an individual to make health care decisions "exists in jurisdictions that have statutes similar to the Uniform Durable Power of Attorney Act." Collin, *supra,* at ¶504.5C.

Under the U.P.C. a person may specify that the power will become or remain effective in the event the maker should later become disabled. U.P.C. §5-501 (1990). In the absence of such a statute, the usefulness of a power of attorney in estate planning is limited by the common law rule that a power of attorney is terminated by the death *or* incompetency of the principal. All states have now adopted a form of durable power of attorney that makes it possible to provide for the management of the principal's property in the event the principal becomes incompetent without subjecting the property to management by a guardian or custodian. The durable power is superior to other devices because it avoids the publicity, delays, and expense that are otherwise incurred. The power also eliminates the need to account to the court and to obtain court approval for actions concerning the sale or other use of the principal's assets. A durable power is also superior to joint bank accounts and similar arrangements, which may spawn conflicting claims to the funds on deposit — even prior to the principal's death.

The death of the principal terminates a durable power just as it would an ordinary power. However, actions taken in good faith by the attorney-in-fact under a durable or nondurable power without knowledge of the principal's death bind the successors in interest of the principal. U.P.C. §5-504(a) (1990). Also, "[t]he disability or incapacity of a principal who has previously executed a written power of attorney that is not a durable power does not revoke or terminate the agency as to the attorney in fact or other person, who, without actual knowledge of the disability or incapacity of the principal, acts in good faith under the power." U.P.C. §5-504(b) (1990). Note that a dissolution of the marriage of the principal and the attorney-in-fact may not revoke a power of attorney — particularly one that has been recorded. *See Puget Sound National Bank v. Burt,* 786 P.2d 300 (Wash. App. 1990).

§4.35.1. Creation, Recordation, and Revocation

Some states require that a durable power be executed with the same formality as a will and that it be recorded. *E.g.,* S.C. Code Ann. §62-5-501(C) (Law Co-op. 1990 Supp.). Presumably recording is required because the attorney-in-fact may transfer or acquire interests in real property. In other jurisdictions a durable power may not be recorded unless the attorney-in-fact does enter into transactions involving real property. The possibility that the attorney-in-fact may engage in real estate transactions suggests the desirability that the document be acknowledged by a notary.

In order to create a durable power the U.P.C. simply requires that the attorney-in-fact be designated in a writing that contains "the words 'This power of attorney shall not be affected by subsequent disability or incapacity of the principal,' or 'This power of attorney shall become effective upon the disability or incapacity of the principal,' or similar words showing the intent of the principal that the authority conferred shall be exercisable notwithstanding the principal's subsequent disability or incapacity." U.P.C. §5-501 (1990).

Under the U.P.C. if a conservator, guardian, or other fiduciary of the principal's estate is appointed after the execution of a durable power of attorney, the attorney-in-fact is required to account to the appointee. In order to avoid conflicts and unnecessary expense, the principal may nominate a guardian in the durable power — who may be the same person as the attorney-in-fact.

The principal may revoke a durable power at any time. In addition, a person appointed as conservator, guardian, or other fiduciary of the principal's estate has all of the powers the principal would have had to revoke, suspend, or terminate the power of attorney. U.P.C. §5-503(a) (1990). The potential for conflict between the attorney-in-fact and the conservator or guardian is reduced if the attorney-in-fact is also nominated in the durable power to serve as the principal's conservator or guardian. *See* U.P.C. §5-503(b) (1990). Such a nomination will discourage others from applying for appointment as conservator or guardian and will secure the authority of the attorney-in-fact against upset in the event it becomes necessary or desirable to appoint a conservator or guardian for the principal. It is often wise to designate one or more successor attorneys-in-fact lest the first-named person predecease the principal or otherwise be unable to act.

§4.35.2. Scope and Use

A durable power may confer as few or as many powers on the attorney-in-fact as the principal wishes. However, in the absence of express statutory authorization, a durable power probably cannot authorize the attorney-in-fact to exercise powers that are personal and nondelegable, such as the power to make a will or to exercise a power of appointment. Because a power of attorney is useful only to the extent it can be used to carry out transactions with other persons, many clients will choose to give the attorney-in-fact broad general powers to act with respect to their property. The acceptability of such a power of attorney is generally enhanced if it includes both a statement of the general powers that the attorney-in-fact may exercise and a list of the specific powers that the attorney-in-fact is most likely to need. A durable power of attorney may include authority to act for the principal with regard to federal income tax matters. Under Reg. §601.504(a), a power of attorney

> [S]hould clearly express the taxpayer's intention as to the scope of the authority of the representative, and must show the type of tax involved,

> the federal tax form number, and the year(s) or period(s) involved. . . . A power of attorney or tax information authorization thus may relate to more than one matter as, for example, a tax information authorization which relates to a taxpayer's income taxes for several different taxable years. . . . [A] . . . general power of attorney authorizing the representative to perform any and all acts the taxpayer can perform with respect to specified tax matters may be used.

Thus, a durable power might include a provision like that found in Form 4-28.

Form 4-28. Power to Represent Principal with Respect to Federal Tax Matters

The attorney-in-fact is authorized to perform any and all acts the taxpayer can perform with respect to (1) federal income tax matters, including filing and amending Form 1040, filing refund claims and representing principal in audits, conferences, and litigation, with respect to the years 1991 through 2025; (2) federal gift tax matters, including filing and amending Form 709, filing refund claims and representing principal in audits, conferences, and litigation, with respect to the years 19__ through 2025; and (3) federal generation-skipping tax matters, including filing and amending forms relating to the tax, filing refund claims, and representing principal in audits, conferences, and litigation.

§4.35.3. Health Care Decisions and *Cruzan*

> The recent U.S. Supreme Court decision in the *Cruzan* case poignantly highlights the fact that health care decision making by surrogates works best when the individual has acted in advance of incapacity by preparing a written medical directive and appointing a proxy to make health care decisions in the event of incompetency. These mechanisms, sometimes referred to as "advance directives," are now recognized in most states in the form of either "living will" laws or health care power of attorney laws. Joint Statement by L. Stanley Chauvin, Jr., President American Bar Association and Nancy W. Dickey, M.D., Member Board of Trustees, American Medical Association and former Chair, AMA Council on Ethical and Judicial Affairs.

In light of the Supreme Court decision in *Cruzan v. Director, Missouri Dept. of Health,* 110 S. Ct. 2841 (1990), clients should be given the opportunity to execute a durable power of attorney which expresses their wishes regarding health care matters. The form of DPAHC presented and discussed in Collin's comprehensive article (see §4.35, *supra*) includes extensive directions regarding the principal's health care and the designation of a proxy to make decisions within the parameters of those directions. *See* §4.36.3, Uniform Rights of Terminally Ill Act (1989).

Cruzan explicitly recognized a constitutionally protected right of a competent person to refuse medical treatment. However, it also held that a state could impose a high standard of proof where another person wishes to exercise that right on behalf of an incompetent person. In particular, the Court held that a state could require clear and convincing proof of the wishes of an incompetent where a guardian sought to discontinue nutrition and hydration. (Note, in this connection, that the majority opinion assumed that nutrition and hydration were properly considered to be medical treatment.) Importantly, Justice O'Connor's concurring opinion suggests that a patient's constitutional liberty interest in refusing medical treatment may require states to effect surrogate decision-making laws. Thus, a DPAHC that specifically authorizes the attorney-in-fact to exercise the principal's right to refuse medical treatment should be recognized as a legitimate exercise of the principal's constitutionally protected rights. The opinion suggests that no one is in a position to exercise the right to refuse medical treatment on behalf of persons who have never been competent or who never clearly expressed their wishes.

A durable power of attorney can be drafted to express the principal's wishes regarding medical treatment in detail or in a more general way. A general expression of wishes with a broad delegation of authority to the attorney-in-fact is more flexible and potentially more useful. In addition, a DPAHC can also include a statement of the principal's wishes regarding other related matters, such as the principal's desire to remain at home rather than being institutionalized. A simple version of the provision might read along the lines suggested in Form 4-29.

Form 4-29. Power to Make Health Care Decisions

The attorney-in-fact is authorized to make health care decisions for Principal and to give informed consent to health care on behalf of Principal. Principal intends that the attorney-in-fact exercise Principal's constitutionally protected right to refuse medical treatment, including nutrition and hydration. In making health care decisions for Principal, attorney-in-fact shall be guided by the following statement of the Principal's wishes. . . .

See §4.36.3, especially the text of §2(c) of the Uniform Rights of the Terminally Ill Act (1989).

As pointed out by Collin, a DPAHC is superior to a living will because of its potentially greater scope and flexibility. "One major distinction between a DPAHC and a Living Will (whether statutory or otherwise) is that the DPAHC can be used for a broad range of health decisions. It need not be limited to the withholding or withdrawing of life-sustaining treatment. Quite the contrary, a DPAHC may be used to authorize maximum medical treatment under all circumstances and without regard to cost if that happens to be the desires of the principal." Collin, *supra,* at ¶504.3.

§4.35.4. Additional Powers to Deal with Property

Although relatively few bonds remain available that are redeemable at par in payment of the federal estate tax, a durable power of attorney might include specific authority to take certain actions including the acquisition of "flower bonds." *See* §12.48.

Also, in appropriate cases the client may wish to authorize the attorney-in-fact to make gifts to specified donees or classes of donees. For example, the attorney-in-fact might be authorized to make gifts that are within the amount of the annual gift tax exclusion and ones that qualify for exclusion under §2503(e). Gifts that qualify for those exclusions are exempt from the GSTT. §2642(c)(3). Such a provision might read like Form 4-30.

Form 4-30. Power to Make Gifts to Family Members

The attorney-in-fact is authorized (1) to make annual gifts to each descendant of the principal, which in any calendar year do not exceed the amount of the annual federal gift tax exclusion and (2) to pay directly the tuition and medical expenses of each such descendant to the extent such payments constitute qualified transfers for federal gift tax purposes.

In order to avoid creating gift and estate tax problems under §§2514 and 2041, the power should prohibit the attorney-in-fact from making gifts to himself or herself, or to or for the benefit of any person he or she is legally obligated to support. Alternatively, the power may be drafted to authorize a special agent to make gifts to or for the benefit of the attorney-in-fact and his or her dependents. If the client has created an irrevocable life insurance trust, he or she may wish to authorize the attorney-in-fact to continue to make annual transfers to the trust. Otherwise, there may be no practical source of funds with which to pay the premiums.

A power may enable a couple to make transfers between themselves, which may be desirable for a variety of purposes. Interspousal transfers, which are fully sheltered by the unlimited marital deduction, can be used to maximize the governmental benefits that are available and to utilize fully each spouse's unified credit and GSTT exemption.

§4.35.5. Power to Transfer Property to Revocable Trust

The needs of some clients are best met by a limited form of durable power that merely authorizes the attorney-in-fact to fund a revocable trust of which the principal and the principal's spouse are the current beneficiaries. The typical plan involves a revocable trust, a pour-over will, and a limited durable power of attorney. If the principal becomes incapable of managing property, the attorney-in-fact is authorized to transfer the principal's assets to the trustee for administration in accordance with the terms of the trust. Any additional assets of the principal that may be subject to testamentary disposition will be added to the trust under the terms of the principal's pour-over will. Under an alternative plan, the revocable trust only serves as a management vehicle during the principal's lifetime; upon the principal's death the trust property "pours back" to the principal's estate to be disposed of as provided in the principal's will.

There are two other common approaches to establishing a trust under a durable power of attorney. Under the first approach, the trust agreement is presently executed and the trust is either funded with some assets or the trustee is named as beneficiary of policies of insurance on the client's life. In this case the durable power authorizes the attorney-in-fact to add the client's other assets to the trust. Under the second approach, a form of revocable trust agreement is attached to the durable power of attorney, which the attorney-in-fact is authorized to execute on behalf of the principal in the event of his or her incompetency. In such a case the durable power also authorizes the attorney-in-fact to transfer the principal's assets to the trustee to be held and managed as a part of the trust. Either approach should be satisfactory, although the former is, perhaps, more in accord with prior practice.

§4.35.6. Limitations

In some instances it is desirable to impose express limits on the power of the attorney-in-fact. John Lombard has pointed out that where a husband and wife execute reciprocal durable powers of attorney, the documents should limit the power of an insured spouse to deal with policies of insurance owned by the noninsured spouse. Lombard, Planning for Disability: Durable Powers, Standby Trusts and Preserving Eligibility for Governmental Benefits, U. Miami, 20th Inst. Est. Plan. ¶1705.3 (1986). Otherwise, if the insured spouse dies first, the IRS may argue that he or she held incidents of ownership over the insurance. Also, there is always the possibility that the IRS may harden its position regarding the significance of incidents of ownership that are only exercisable in a fiduciary capacity. *See* §6.27.11.

§4.35.7. "Springing Powers"

Under the U.P.C. it is possible to execute a durable power of attorney that will become effective upon the incapacity of the principal. U.P.C. §2-501 (1990). Such a "springing power" is helpful to clients who want the protection that a durable power provides, yet are reluctant to execute a presently effective power. The problem remains of defining when the principal becomes incapacitated. That problem is typically addressed by making the power effective when the attorney-in-fact receives a written certification of incapacity from one or more persons designated in the instrument (*e.g.,* the principal's attending physician). A second certificate is often required, commonly from another physician, the principal's spouse, or another relative.

Form 4-31. Date Power Becomes Effective

The attorney-in-fact is authorized to act on behalf of principal and to exercise all powers under this Durable Power of Attorney when the attorney-in-fact receives written certification by two physicians that Principal is for any reason unable to manage his property, or to care for himself, or both.

§4.35.8. Conclusion

Virtually every client should be given the opportunity to execute an appropriate durable power of attorney. A durable power of attorney can provide a client with important, low cost protection against the legal complications of physical or mental incapacity. Moreover, the attorney-in-fact can be authorized as the principal's proxy to make gifts and take other important actions to carry out the principal's wishes and minimize tax and other burdens. *Cruzan* suggests that clients may express their constitutional right to refuse medical treatment in a durable power that designates a proxy to make health care decisions for them. Even before the *Cruzan* decision many commentators believed that in the absence of statutory restrictions a durable power could authorize the attorney-in-fact to make health care decisions for the principal. As noted above, under the provisions of some acts the principal may nominate a guardian in a durable power of attorney.

§4.36. THE LIVING WILL AND NATURAL DEATH ACTS

> The principle that a competent person has a constitutionally protected liberty interest in refusing unwanted medical treament may be inferred from our prior decisions. . . .
> But for purposes of this case, we assume that the United States Constitution would grant a competent person a constitutionally protected right to refuse lifesaving hydration and nutrition. *Cruzan,* 110 S. Ct. at 2851, 2852.

> Despite their grand title, living wills are very limited in scope. Two limits are critically important. First, in most states they can only be used to refuse extraordinary, life-prolonging care. Second, they are effective to refuse care only after a patient has become terminally ill — or even, in some states, when death is very near. They are not advance directives through which treatment can be refused more generally. Francis, The Evanescence of Living Wills, 24 Real Prop., Prob. & Tr. J. 141, 145 (1989).

Living wills naturally fall into two broad categories — those executed in compliance with state enabling legislation and those that are not. The latter category encompasses ones executed in states that have not adopted legislation authorizing living wills and ones that do not comply with the local legislation. In all cases, living wills provide important evidence of the makers' intentions regarding medical treatment — even in states which have not given legislative recognition to any form of living will. Importantly, *Cruzan* may impart greater status to living wills than they previously had — particularly in states that have not adopted enabling legislation.

Most states have enacted legislation that gives limited recognition to the right of a competent adult to refuse medical care. The statutes generally authorize directives that express a patient's intention that life-sustaining measures be terminated, or not commenced, if the maker is incompetent and death is imminent. Unfortunately, the laws are far from uniform. However, in general, they permit a competent adult to direct in writing that in the event of terminal illness his or her life shall not be prolonged by artificial, extraordinary, or extreme medical treatment. The laws thus sanction a form of passive euthanasia or antidysthanasia, which is defined as the failure to take positive action to prolong the life of an incurably ill patient. Because death results naturally from the failure to provide medical care, the acts are often called Natural Death Acts.

Although a document may lack express statutory recognition, under *Cruzan* it may be recognized as a sufficient expression of the maker's constitutional right to refuse medical treatment. Living wills have been recognized as providing persuasive evidence of the intentions of an incompetent patient. For example, in *John F. Kennedy Memorial Hospital v. Bludworth,* 452 So. 2d 921 (Fla. 1984), the court held that a close family member or guardian could exercise an incompetent patient's right to refuse treatment without court intervention. According to the court,

> If such a person, while competent, had executed a so-called "living" or "mercy" will, that will would be persuasive evidence of that incompetent person's intention and should be given great weight by the person or persons who substitute their judgment on behalf of the terminally ill incompetent. 452 So. 2d at 926.

While some living will statutes do not expand the common law right of patients to refuse medical treatment, they give important legal status to written expressions of intention that conform to their requirements. Perhaps more important, they generally cloak health care providers with immunity from civil or criminal liability for actions taken in conformity with the statutes.

A DPAHC described in §4.35.3 can be far broader than a simple living will. Most important, it can be used to designate a surrogate decision maker and to express the principal's intentions regarding the manner in which health care decisions should be made.

§4.36.1. Who May Make Living Will

Under *Cruzan* presumably any competent adult can make an advance directive that must be recognized by the state. Thus, it may override statutes which only allow advance directives to be made by persons who are terminally ill or which limit the period during which directives are valid. Similarly, *Cruzan* casts doubt on statutes that prescribe the text of the directive to physicians that must be used. It is important to note that, consistent with *Cruzan,* statutes do not permit anyone to execute a living will on behalf of a minor or incompetent person. Thus, the statutory procedures are generally inapplicable if a patient did not execute a living will prior to incompetency. However, it may be possible for a patient's family to move the patient from a health care facility in a state with restrictive policies to a state with more liberal policies.

Section 4206 of the Omnibus Budget Reconciliation Act of 1990, P.L. 101-508, 104 Stat. 1388-115, requires hospitals, skilled nursing facilities, home health agencies, and hospice programs to provide information to each patient regarding an individual's right under state law to make decisions regarding health care, "including the right to accept or refuse medical or surgical treatment and the right to formulate advance directives. . . ." In a later provision the term "advance directive" is defined to mean "a written instruction, such as a living will or durable power of attorney for health care . . . relating to the provision of such care when the individual is incapacitated."

§4.36.2. Immunity Against Civil or Criminal Prosecution

Natural death acts generally provide immunity against civil or criminal liability for specified persons who carry out the patient's instructions. However, the persons to whom immunity is given and the circumstances under which it is given vary considerably. "Some statutes provide immunity only for physicians; other provide it for physicians, nurses and medical institutions; whereas others, such as the Arkansas statute, provide immunity to any person who acts in reliance on the living will." Panel Discussion, Legal Problems of the Aged and Infirm — The Durable Powers of Attorney — Planned Protective Services and the Living Will, 13 Real Prop., Prob. & Tr. J. 1, 23 (1978). Also, some statutes prescribe penalties for the concealment, destruction, falsification, or forgery of a living will.

§4.36.3. Uniform Rights of the Terminally Ill Act (1989)

> The best solution would be adoption by all states of the Uniform Rights of the Terminally Ill Act, as recently revised by the National Conference of Commissioners on Uniform State Laws. This excellent legislation covers almost every aspect in clear prose that anyone can understand and follow. It was approved by the American Bar Association on February 13, 1990. Warnock, Living Wills: The Need for Uniform State Laws, 5 Prob. & Prop. 52 (May-June 1991).

The original Uniform Act authorized a competent adult to execute a declaration, witnessed by two individuals, instructing a physician to withhold or withdraw life-sustaining treatment if the maker is likely to die within a reasonably short time and is no longer able to participate in medical care decisions. The 1989 Act, 9B U.L.A. 79 (1991 Supp.), changed the provision slightly and added subsection §2(c) that allows a competent adult to designate another person to make decisions regarding the withholding or withdrawal of life-sustaining treatment. Section 2 of the 1989 Act includes forms of declarations that may, but need not, be used. The forms, which are generally helpful, could be expanded to include reference to more specific matters.

Form 4-32. Declarations Under the Uniform Rights of the Terminally Ill Act (1989)

[(b) A declaration directing a physician to withhold or withdraw life-sustaining treatment may, but need not, be in the following form:]

If I should have an incurable and irreversible condition that, without the administration of life-sustaining treatment will, in the opinion of my attending physician, cause my death within a relatively short time, and I am no longer able to make decisions regarding my medical treatment, I direct my attending physician, pursuant to the Uniform Rights of the Terminally Ill Act of this State, to withhold or withdraw treatment that only prolongs the process of dying and is not necessary to my comfort or to relieve pain. . . .

[(c) A declaration that designates another individual to make decisions governing the withholding or withdrawal of life-sustaining treatment may, but need not be, in the following form:]

If I should have an incurable and irreversible condition that, without the administration of life-sustaining treatment, will, in the opinion of my attending physician, cause my death within a relatively short time, and I am no longer able to make decisions regarding my medical treatment, I appoint ______________ or, if he or she is not reasonably available or is unwilling to serve, ______________________, to make decisions on my behalf regarding withholding or withdrawal of treatment that only prolongs the process of dying and is not necessary for my comfort or to alleviate pain, pursuant to the Uniform Rights of the Terminally Ill Act of this State.

Subsection 2(c) continues with the following optional language:

[If the individual(s) I have so appointed is not reasonably available or is unwilling to serve, I direct my attending physician, pursuant to the Uniform Rights of the Terminally Ill Act of this State, to withhold or withdraw treatment that only prolongs the process of dying and is not necessary for my comfort or to alleviate pain.]

§4.36.4. Conclusion

The laws and the problems the natural death acts address are complex and controversial. Nonetheless, most clients appreciate being advised regarding the extent to which they can control the medical care they will be given during their terminal illness if they become incompetent. The likelihood that health care providers will comply with an advance directive is enhanced if the directive complies with the local law. Compliance is also enhanced if family members support the principal's directive — which suggests the importance of discussing the matter with family members. *See* Zinberg, Decisions for the Dying: An Empirical Study of Physician's Responses to Advance Directives, 13 Vt. L. Rev. 445 (1989). If a local form is not mandated, a client may prefer to use a form of living will such as the very popular one published by the Euthanasia Educational Council, New York, N.Y. In light of *Cruzan,* a sufficiently specific form should be adequate to support discontinuance of some medical treatment, including artificial hydration and nutrition.

The execution of a living will provides a valuable expression of the client's wishes that is useful even in jurisdictions which do not authorize them statutorily. A living will helps provide the maker's family members and attending physicians with the guidance they need. As a matter of routine more than one copy should be executed. An executed copy may be given to the client, another sent to the client's regular physician, and another retained by the lawyer. If that is done, a copy of the document should be readily available in the event of illness or emergency. In addition, some members of the maker's family should also be told about the document.

§4.37. Sources of Information

Information regarding living wills and suggested forms are available from a variety of sources, including the following:

Society for the Right to Die 250 West 57th Street New York, NY 10107	Concern for Dying 250 West 57th Street New York, NY 10107

§4.38. Anatomical Gifts

If the subject is raised, some clients will wish to donate part or all of their bodies to be used following their deaths to help the living and to contribute to medical education and research. Advances in medical science have made it possible to use a variety of a decedent's body parts, including corneas, kidneys, pituitary glands, and skin. Making such gifts is facilitated by the 1968 and 1987 versions of the Uniform Anatomical Gift Act, 8 U.L.A. 15 (1983) and 8A U.L.A. 7 (1991 Supp.) (U.A.G.A.). The 1987 Act has been adopted in several states including Arkansas, California, Connecticut, Hawaii, Idaho, Montana, Nevada, North Dakota, Rhode Island, Utah, Vermont, Virginia, and Wisconsin. The 1968 Act is in effect in the other states and the District of Columbia. The U.A.G.A. helps significantly by estalishing legal procedures for making anatomical gifts and by providing for the resolution of conflicting interests. However, the acts do not attempt to deal with some issues, such as the time at which death occurs. Despite the acts, the number of organs available for transplant falls far short of the need. Under the existing U.S. laws, in the absence of consent the organs of cadavers may not be transplanted. Some European countries, in contrast, presume consent to cadaveric transplants. Mehlman, Presumed Consent to Organ Donation: A Reevaluation, 1 Health Matrix 31 (1991).

The prefatory Note to the 1987 Act describes the changes that were incorporated in it:

> The proposed amendments simplify the manner of making an anatomical gift and require that the intentions of a donor be followed. For example, no witnesses are required on the document of gift (Section 2(b)) and consent of next of kin after death is not required if the donor has made an anatomical gift (Section 2(h)). The identification of actual donors is facilitated by a duty to search for a document of gift (Section 5(c)) and of potential donors by provisions for routine inquiry (Section 5(a)) and required request (Section 5(b)). A gift of one organ, e.g., eyes, is not a limitation on the gift of other organs after death, in the absence of contrary indication by the decedent (Section 2(i)). Revocation by a donor of an anatomical gift that has been made is effective without communication of the revocation to a specified donee (Section 2(f)). Hospitals have been substituted for attending physicians as donees of anatomical gifts (Section 6(b)), and they are required to establish agreements or affiliations with other hospitals and procurement organizations in the region to coordinate the procurement and utilization of anatomical gifts (Section 9). If a request for an anatomical gift has been made for transplant or therapy by a person specified in the Act and if there is no contrary indication by the decedent or known objection by the next of kin to an anatomical gift the [coroner] [medical examiner] or [local public health official] may authorize release and removal of a part subject to specific requirements (Section 4(a) and (b)). The categories of persons that may remove anatomical parts are expanded to include eye nucleators and certain technicians (Section 8(c)). The sale or purchase of parts is prohibited (Section 10). Persons who act, or attempt to act, in good faith in accordance with the terms of the

> Act are not liable in any civil action or criminal proceeding. The categories of persons covered by this exemption are specified (Section 11(c)).

The 1987 version of the U.A.G.A. also adds an important provision that insulates the donor and the donor's estate from any injury or damage that may result from the making or use of the anatomical gift. §11(c).

§4.38.1. Summary of the 1968 U.A.G.A.

The 1968 Act is in effect in most states. Under §2(a) an individual 18 years of age and of sound mind may give all or any part of his or her body to certain specified donees. Further, in the absence of actual notice of the decedent's contrary intention, certain other persons may give all or part of the decedent's body to the specified donees. In order of priority the other persons are (1) spouse; (2) adult children; (3) parent; (4) adult brother or sister; (5) guardian of the deceased; or (6) person authorized or obligated to dispose of the body. §2(b). A donee may not accept the gift if (1) the donee has actual knowledge that the gift was opposed by the decedent or (2) if the gift is made by another person, the donee may not accept the gift if it is opposed by a member of the same or a prior class. Thus, the wishes of the decedent are recognized as paramount.

§4.38.2. Donees

The donees to whom gifts may be made under the U.A.G.A. include hospitals, surgeons, dentists, medical or dental schools, organ banks, or storage facilities for the purpose of education, research, therapy, or transplantation. Under §3 a gift may be made to a specified individual for therapy or transplantation. Also, a gift may be made without specifying the donee, in which case the attending physician may accept the gift. §4(c). However, in order to avoid any conflict of interest in the latter case the attending physician is prohibited from participating in the removal or transplantation of a part.

§4.38.3. Ways of Making a Gift

There are several ways of making a gift under the U.A.G.A. The donor may make an anatomical gift by will, which is effective immediately upon death without the need for probate. Indeed, such a gift is effective even though the will is found to be invalid for testamentary purposes. §4(a). A gift may also be made by a document signed by the donor in the presence of two witnesses who must sign the document in the donor's presence. §4(b). As in the case of a will, the document need not be delivered during the donor's lifetime. Importantly the document may be in the form of a card designed to be carried on the person. §4(b). A suitable form is printed on the back of driver's licenses in some states. Survivors who are authorized to make gifts of a decedent's body may do so by a signed document, or by telegraphic, recorded telephonic, or other recorded message. §4(e). Finally, the document or will may designate the physician or surgeon to carry out the appropriate procedures. §4(d).

Donee organizations such as eye banks, hospitals, and medical schools will usually supply donor cards and literature regarding anatomical gifts upon request. The cards typically have space for the donor to designate a gift of "any needed organs or parts" or "only the following organs or parts." They also usually permit a whole body donation for medical education or research purposes.

§4.38.4. Revocation and Amendment

There are also several means by which a gift may be revoked or amended. Where the will or other document has been delivered to the donee, the donor may revoke or amend the gift by (1) a signed statement delivered to the donee, (2) an oral statement made in the presence of two witnesses and communicated to the donee, (3) a statement made during a terminal illness or injury to a physician and communicated to the donee, or (4) a signed card or document found on the donor's person or among the donor's effects. §6(a). Where the will or other document has not been delivered, the gift may be revoked in any of the same four ways, or by mutilation, cancellation, or destruction of the document and all executed copies thereof. §6(b). Finally, any gift may be revoked or amended in the same manner that a will may be revoked or amended. §6(c).

§4.38.5. Action by Others

A donee may accept or reject an anatomical gift. §7(a). If the donee accepts a gift of the entire body, subject to the terms of the gift the donee may arrange for embalming or other funeral services. If only part of the body is accepted, the donee is required to remove the part without unnecessary mutilation. After the removal of a part or parts of the decedent's body the remainder is subject to the control of the surviving spouse, next of kin, or other person who is obligated to dispose of the decedent's body. Id. Under §7(b), the physician who determines the time of death may not participate in the removal or transplantation of any part. The Act further provides that good faith compliance with the terms of the Act precludes any civil or criminal liability. §7(c). Finally, the Act provides that it is subject to the laws regarding autopsies. §7(d).

§4.38.6. Planning

Many clients are understandably squeamish when it comes to discussing anatomical gifts and the disposition of their remains. At the same time, however, they may appreciate receiving an explanation of the power they have over the post-mortem disposition of their bodies. The subject is typically discussed during an initial office conference or in an early letter to the client. In order to avoid any uncertainty or conflict, the client's wishes should be recorded in an appropriate instrument whether or not the client plans to make any anatomical gifts. As explained in §4.9, a client's wishes regarding the disposition of his or her body should usually be contained in an instrument other than a will that may not be read until after funeral or memorial services are held and cremation or burial has taken place. Also, the client may be more willing to communicate his or her wishes to family members and others if they are set forth in a document other than a will. A client should be encouraged to inform close relatives and intended donees of his or her plans. The disclosure is particularly important if the client intends to provide a bodily part for purposes of transplantation, which may require some ante-mortem preparation and prompt post-mortem action. Also, a donee may be reluctant to accept an anatomical gift where it appears that the spouse or next of kin may object.

§4.38.7. Donor Card

A simple donor card is usually sufficient to record a client's anatomical gifts. Cards are free, easy to complete, and convenient. A copy of the card should be given to the executor named in the client's will, to the client's spouse, and, perhaps to the client's parents or adult children. The client may also want to record his or her wishes regarding funeral or memorial services. Such a document, which may be captioned "burial instructions" or "direction for disposition of remains," may be executed at the same time as the will. At a minimum it should be dated and signed by the client. Although witnesses are not required by local law, many lawyers have it witnessed by the same persons who witnessed the client's will. The text of a common form of a donor's card that complies with the provisions of the Act is set forth below:

Form 4-33. Uniform Donor Card (Anatomical Gifts)

UNIFORM DONOR CARD

Print or type name of donor

In the hope that I may help others, I hereby make this anatomical gift, if medically acceptable, to take effect upon my death. The words and marks below indicate my desires. I give

(a) ☐ any needed organs or parts
(b) ☐ only the following organs or parts

Specify the organ(s) or part(s) for the purpose of transplantation, therapy, medical research, or education.

(c) ☐ my body for anatomical study if needed.

Limitations or special wishes, if any

[Reverse side]

Signed by the donor and the following 2 witnesses in the presence of each other.

Signature of Donor ______________________________
Date of Birth of Donor ____________ Date Signed ____________
City and State ______________________________
Witness ______________________________
Witness ______________________________

§4.38.8. Conclusion

The Uniform Anatomical Gifts Act helps to relieve the need for the body parts suitable for transplantation. However, there is a serious shortage of suitable anatomical gifts. The problem is noted in the Preface to a report by the Hastings Center, Ethical, Legal and Policy Issues Pertaining to Solid Organ Procurement (Oct. 1985):

> An overriding problem common to all organ transplantation programs as well as to the well-established programs in tissue banking (for corneal, skin and bone transplantation) is the serious gap between the need for organs and tissues and the supply of donors. Despite substantial support for transplantation and a general willingness to donate organs and

> tissues after death, the demand far exceeds the supply. At any one time, there are an estimated 8,000 to 10,000 people waiting for a donor organ to become available. Prefatory Note, 8A U.L.A. 3 (1991 Supp.).

Curiously, despite the shortage, a donee is not obligated to accept a gift. Also, the gift of a body or organs may not eliminate the responsibility of the decedent's estate or of surviving family members to pay the cost of cremation or burial.

BIBLIOGRAPHY

I. Wills

Atkinson, T., Wills (2d ed. 1953)
California Will Drafting (Cal. CEB 1965)
Estate Planning for the General Practitioner (Cal. CEB 1979)
Estate Planning Practice (2 vols., Cal. CEB 1987)
Hess, The Federal Transfer Tax Consequences of Joint and Mutual Wills, 24 Real Prop., Prob. & Tr. J. 469 (1990)
Martin, The Draftsman Views Wills for a Young Family, 54 N.C.L. Rev. 277 (1976)
McGovern, Kurtz & Rein, Wills, Trusts and Estates (1988)
Report, A Sample Simple Will, 15 Real Prop., Prob. & Tr. J. 569 (1980)
———, Proposed Uniform Acts for a Statutory Will, Statutory Trust and Statutory Short Form Clauses, 15 Real Prop., Prob. & Tr. J. 837 (1980)
———, The Role of the Probate Lawyer in a Changing Environment, 22 Real Prop., Prob. & Tr. J. 753 (1987)
Shaffer, Non-estate Planning, 42 Notre Dame Law. 153 (1966)
———, The Planning and Drafting of Wills and Trusts (2d ed. 1979)
Squires & Mucklestone, A Simple "Simple" Will, 57 Wash. L. Rev. 461 (1982)

II. Durable Powers of Attorney

Collin, Planning and Drafting Durable Powers of Attorney for Health Care, U. Miami, 22nd Inst. Est. Plan., ch. 5 (1988)
Collin, F. J., Jr., Lombard, J. J., Moses, A. L., Spitler, H., Drafting the Durable Power of Attorney (1987)

Fowler, Appointing A Medical Agent, 84 Col. L. Rev. 985 (1984)

Lombard, Planning for Disability: Durable Powers, Standby Trusts and Preserving Eligibility for Governmental Benefits, U. Miami, 20th Est. Plan. Inst., ch. 17 (1986)

Lombard, Health Care Decisions — Right to Terminate Medical Treatment — Proxy Decision Making: Trends in the Law, 12 Prob. Notes 265 (1987)

Neuwirth, Steps a Client Can Take to Plan for Future Medical Treatment Decisions, 12 Est. Plan. 14 (1985)

III. Anatomical Gifts

Best, Transfers of Bodies and Body Parts Under the Uniform Anatomical Gift Act, 15 Real Prop., Prob. & Tr. J. 806 (1980)

Comment, Consent and Organ Donation, 11 Rutgers Computer & Tech. L. J. 559 (1985)

Naylor, The Role of Family in Cadaveric Organ Procurement, 65 Ind. L. J. 167 (1989)

Quay, Utilizing Bodies of the Dead, 28 St. Louis L. J. 889 (1984)

Silver, The Case for a Post-Mortem Organ Draft and a Proposed Model Organ Draft Act, 68 B.U.L. Rev. 681 (1988)

IV. Living Wills

Brink, A Glimpse Through the Planning Window of the Young, Terminal Client, U. Miami, 25th Inst. Est. Plan., ch. 6 (1991)

Buckley, Videotaping Living Wills: Dying Declarations Brought to Life, 22 Val. U. L. Rev. 54 (1987)

Francis, The Evanescence of Living Wills, 24 Real Prop., Prob. & Tr. J. 141 (1989)

Kolb, Indiana's Living Wills and Life Prolonging Procedures Act, 19 Ind. L. Rev. 285 (1985)

Leflar, Liberty and Death: Advance Health Care Directives and the Law of Arkansas, 39 Ark. L. Rev. 446 (1986)

Warnock, Living Wills: The Need for Uniform State Laws, 5 Prob. & Prop. 52 (May-June 1991)

Zartman, The Legacy of *Cruzan,* 5 Prob. & Prop. 13 (May-June 1991)

CHAPTER 5

The Gift and Estate Tax Marital Deductions

A. Introduction

§5.1. Scope
§5.2. The Past
§5.2.1. 1942 Legislation
§5.2.2. 1948 Adoption of Marital Deduction and Joint Income Tax Returns
§5.2.3. 1976 Liberalization of Marital Deduction
§5.3. 1981 Quantitative and Qualitative Liberalization
§5.3.1. Quantitative Change: Unlimited Marital Deduction
§5.3.2. Qualitative Changes: Additional Interests Qualify for Marital Deduction
§5.3.3. Transitional Rule for Pre-1982 Formula Gifts
§5.4. The Future

B. Planning for Use of the Marital Deduction

§5.5. Approaching the Planning Job
§5.5.1. Tax Estimates
§5.5.2. Valuation of Property
§5.6. General Objectives
§5.7. Equalizing the Spouses' Estates and Minimizing Overall Taxes
§5.7.1. Equalization Clauses
§5.7.2. Community Property Estates Are Already Equalized
§5.8. Minimize Taxes — Defer Payments
§5.9. Taking Advantage of the Unified Credits of Both Spouses

C. How to Qualify for the Marital Deduction

§5.10. Basic Requirements
§5.11. Gift Tax
§5.12. Decedent Was Citizen or Resident
§5.13. Inclusion in Gross Estate
§5.14. Surviving Spouse
§5.15. Surviving Spouse Was Citizen or Property Distributed to Qualified Domestic Trust (QDT)
§5.16. Interests Passed to Surviving Spouse
§5.16.1. Family Awards and Allowances
§5.16.2. Disclaimers
§5.17. A Deductible Interest (*i.e.*, Not a Nondeductible Terminable Interest)
§5.17.1. Terminable Interest
§5.17.2. Interest Passed to Another Person
§5.17.3. Subsequent Enjoyment
§5.17.4. Executor Purchase Rule
§5.17.5. Unidentified Asset Rule
§5.17.6. Contractual Wills
§5.18. Exceptions to Terminable Interest Rule
§5.19. Limited Survivorship
§5.20. Simultaneous Death
§5.21. Estate Trust
§5.22. Life Interest General Power of Appointment Trust, §2056(b)(5)
§5.22.1. Specific Portion
§5.22.2. Frequency of Payment of Income
Form 5-1. Payment of Income to Surviving Spouse (§2056(b)(5) Trust)
§5.22.3. Power of Appointment
Form 5-2. Surviving Spouse's General Testamentary Power of Appointment (§2056(b)(5) Trust)
§5.23. Qualified Terminable Interest Property (QTIP), §2056(b)(7)
§5.23.1. What Is QTIP
§5.23.2. Qualifying Income Interest for Life
§5.23.3. Additional Interests Surviving Spouse May Be Given in QTIP Trust
§5.23.4. Partial QTIP Election
§5.23.5. Annuity Interests
§5.23.6. Transfer to Lifetime QTIP to Equalize Estates or to Preserve Use of Unified Credit
§5.23.7. QTIP with Charitable Remainder
§5.23.8. Use in Connection with Disclaimers
§5.23.9. Election and Authorization to Make Election
Form 5-3. Executor Authorized to Make Partial or Total QTIP Election
§5.23.10. Disposition of Qualifying Income Interest in QTIP, §2519
§5.23.11. Estate Tax on Surviving Spouse's Death

§5.24. Current Interest in Charitable Remainder Trust, §2056(b)(8)
§5.25. Qualified Domestic Trust (QDT), §§2056(d), 2056A
§5.25.1. QDT
§5.25.2. Tax on Distributions from QDT
§5.25.3. Surviving Spouse Becomes Citizen
§5.26. Which Form of Trust — Summary
§5.27. Savings Clause
Form 5-4. Marital Deduction Savings Clause

D. The Gift Tax Marital Deduction

§5.28. Overall Considerations
§5.29. General Objectives of Inter Vivos Gifts
§5.30. Equalizing Estates by Lifetime Gifts
§5.31. Using Lifetime Gifts to Take Advantage of the Poorer Spouse's Unified Credit

E. Expressing a Marital Deduction Gift — Formula and Nonformula Gifts

§5.32. Overview
Form 5-5. Nonformula Pecuniary Nonmarital Deduction Gift
§5.33. An Assessment of Formula Provisions
§5.34. Formula Pecuniary Gift
§5.34.1. Credits
§5.34.2. Charge Nonmarital Share for Principal Expenses for Which No Estate Tax Deduction Is Claimed
§5.35. Formula Pecuniary Marital Deduction Gift
Form 5-6. Formula Pecuniary Marital Deduction Gift
§5.36. Model Formula Pecuniary Nonmarital Deduction Gift
Form 5-7. Formula Pecuniary Nonmarital Deduction Gift
§5.37. Directions Regarding Funding a Formula Pecuniary Gift
§5.37.1. Valuation of Assets Distributed in Kind
§5.37.2. Value on the Date of Distribution ("True Worth")
Form 5-8. Date of Distribution (True Worth) Funding Clause
§5.37.3. Estate Tax Value; Revenue Procedure 64-19
§5.37.4. Estate Tax Value: "Minimum Value" Provisions
Form 5-9. Minimum Worth Funding Clause
§5.37.5. Estate Tax Value: "Fairly Representative" Requirement
Form 5-10. Estate Tax Value, Fairly Representative Funding Clause
§5.37.6. Directions Regarding Allocation of Assets to Pecuniary Formula Marital Deduction Gifts
§5.38. Planning and Drafting a Formula Fractional Share Gift
§5.38.1. Expressing the Fraction

§5.38.2. Formula Fractional Share Gift
Form 5-11. Formula Fractional Share Marital Deduction Gift
§5.38.3. Directions Regarding Allocation of Income and Capital Gains and Losses
§5.38.4. Why Use a True Residue Provision?
§5.39. Income Tax Aspects of a Formula Fractional Share Gift
§5.40. Summary — Choosing Between a Formula Pecuniary Gift and a Formula Fractional Share Gift

Bibliography

> The achievement of the purposes of the marital deduction is dependent to a great degree upon the careful drafting of wills. *Jackson v. United States,* 376 U.S. 503, 511 (1964).

> We are not aware of any cases or guidelines establishing in a civil case a standard for the reasonable, diligent and competent assistance of an attorney engaged in estate planning and preparing a trust with a marital deduction provision. We merely hold that the potential tax problems of general powers of appointment in inter vivos or testamentary marital deduction trusts were within the ambit of a reasonably competent and diligent practitioner from 1961 to the present. *Bucquet v. Livingston,* 129 Cal. Rptr. 514, 521 (Cal. App. 1976).

A. INTRODUCTION

§5.1. Scope

The gift and estate tax marital deduction provisions are among the most important and the most complex provisions of the federal transfer tax laws. Our nomadic population and the fundamental importance of the marital deduction provisions make it necessary for lawyers in common law and community property states to know when and how to make inter vivos and deathtime gifts that qualify for the marital deduction.

The first part of this chapter reviews the history and the general contours of the marital deduction provisions. The next part examines the underlying strategies of utilizing the marital deduction, including a discussion of the general objectives of testamentary and inter vivos marital deduction gifts and the advantages and disadvantages of the principal types of formula marital deduction clauses. A related subject, the community property widow's election, is discussed in Chapter 9 in connection with an overall review of transfers for consideration. The last part considers the basic requirements of the deductions in detail, with special attention to the terminable interest rule and its most important exceptions — the life income-general power of appointment trust, the estate trust, and the qualified terminable interest property (QTIP) trust.

§5.2. The Past

From the inception of the estate tax in 1916 until 1942, the estate tax burdens imposed on residents of common law states and those imposed on residents of community property states were not equal. The inequality arose from the federal recognition of the natural "estate splitting" of property onerously acquired by couples who lived in the community property states. For example, if a family's material wealth was all attributable to a husband's earnings during marriage, only half of it was subject to the estate tax on his death if it had been earned in a community property state. In contrast, all of it was taxed if he had earned it during marriage in a common law state.

On the income tax side, couples who lived in community property states benefited from the natural splitting of their income: Each spouse was taxed on half of the community property income. In contrast, the income of each spouse living in a common law state was fully taxable to the recipient alone. The advantage offered by estate-splitting was enough to lead six jurisdictions to adopt community property systems between 1945 and 1947 (Hawaii, Michigan, Nebraska, Oklahoma, Oregon, and Pennsylvania). The "new" community property jurisdictions all reverted to common law systems soon after the Revenue Act of 1948 was passed. It extended the principal tax benefits enjoyed by residents of community property states to residents of common law states. Equalization of advantages, the heart of the marital deduction provisions from 1948 through 1981, proved to be more acceptable and durable than equalization of the disadvantages.

§5.2.1. 1942 Legislation

In 1942 Congress attempted to equalize estate tax burdens of residents of community and common law states by bringing the treatment of residents of community property states more into line with that imposed on residents of common law states. The estate tax amendments enacted that year required all of the community property to be included in the gross estate of the spouse first to die except to the extent it was attributable to the services or property of the survivor. This approach ordinarily required all of the community property to be included in the gross estate of the husband. If the wife died first, one-half of the community property was ordinarily includible in her gross estate because of a provision that called for the inclusion of community property over which a decedent held a power of testamentary disposition. The 1942 solution was unpopular with couples in community property states and did not improve the position of couples in common law states.

§5.2.2. 1948 Adoption of Marital Deduction and Joint Income Tax Returns

The 1948 changes affected the transfer taxes and the income tax. For estate tax purposes only the decedent's one-half interest in the community property was includible in his or her gross estate. Estate tax parity was achieved by allowing a deduction for transfers to a surviving spouse, limited ordinarily to 50 percent of the noncommunity property included in the deceased spouse's estate. Technically, the deduction was limited to half of the decedent's adjusted gross estate. (The adjusted gross estate was a concept that existed solely for the purpose of determining the maximum allowable marital deduction. *See* former §2056(c).) The adjusted gross estate was defined as the gross estate less (1) the value of all community property included in the decedent's estate and (2) the portion of §2053 and §2054 deductions allocable to the noncommunity property.

Example 5-1. *H* died in 1981 leaving a gross estate of $800,000 in noncommunity property. A total of $40,000 in deductions was allowed under §2053. *H* left $25,000 to a charity, for which a deduction was allowable under §2055, and the balance of his estate to his wife, *W*. The maximum allowable marital deduction was limited to $380,000 (one-half of *H*'s adjusted gross estate) computed as follows:

Gross estate	$800,000
Less:	
Deductions under §2053	40,000
Adjusted gross estate	760,000
Maximum marital deduction	$380,000

If the expenses allowable as deductions under §2053 were not claimed on *H*'s estate tax return, *H*'s adjusted gross estate would have been $800,000 and the maximum allowable deduction $400,000.

In general, a deduction was allowable with respect to property transferred to a surviving spouse if the interest transferred to the survivor was sufficient to cause it to be includible in his or her gross estate. By taking advantage of these provisions, a married person could halve the amount of noncommunity property that would be subject to tax when he or she died.

The 1948 gift tax changes allowed a couple to "split" gifts made by either or both to third parties and treat the gifts as made one-half by each. They also introduced a deduction for up to 50 percent of the value of gifts of noncommunity property made to the donor's spouse. Finally, the 1948 Act allowed couples to reduce their income tax liability by filing a joint return on which their combined income was taxed at preferential rates.

The following passage recounts the purpose of the 1948 legislation:

> The 1948 tax amendments were intended to equalize the effect of the estate taxes in community property and common-law jurisdictions. Under a community property system, such as that in Texas, the spouse receives outright ownership of one-half of the community property and only the other one-half is included in the decedent's estate. To equalize the incidence of progressively scaled estate taxes and to adhere to the patterns of state law, the marital deduction permits a deceased spouse, subject to certain requirements, to transfer free of taxes one-half of his non-community property to the surviving spouse. Although applicable to separately held property in a community property state, the primary thrust of this is to extend to taxpayers in common-law States the advantages of "estate splitting" otherwise available only in community property States. The purpose, however, is only to permit a married couple's property to be taxed in two stages and not to allow a tax-exempt transfer of wealth into succeeding generations. Thus, the marital deduction is generally restricted to the transfer of property interests that will be includible in the surviving spouse's gross estate. *United States v. Stapf,* 375 U.S. 118, 128 (1963).

As the quotation indicates, the estate tax marital deduction adopted in 1948 allowed a portion of the tax otherwise payable upon the death of one spouse to be deferred until the death of the survivor. It did not allow the tax to be entirely avoided.

§5.2.3. 1976 Liberalization of Marital Deduction

The 1976 Act relaxed the quantitative limits on the marital deduction, which remained in effect until the unlimited marital deduction was adopted, effective January 1, 1982. Congress liberalized the marital deduction provisions in 1976 in order to increase the amount of property an individual could leave to a surviving spouse free of estate tax and to allow freer interspousal lifetime transfers. The 1976 Act amended §2056(c) to allow a new minimum marital deduction of $250,000. Under the amendment an estate was allowed to claim a deduction of $250,000 or 50 percent of the adjusted gross estate, whichever was larger. The $250,000 minimum deduction, reduced by the amount of community property included in the gross estate, was available to estates composed entirely of community property. However, because of the reduction, the $250,000 minimum deduction was not a major factor in planning community property estates.

The 1976 Act also amended §2523 to allow a greater current deduction for post-1976 gifts to a spouse. Under the change, a full marital deduction was allowed for the first $100,000 of qualifying transfers to a spouse, no deduction was allowed with respect to the next $100,000, and a maximum deduction of 50 percent was allowed to the extent the post-1976 gifts exceeded $200,000. §2523(a). As before, no gift tax marital deduction was allowed for transfers of community property. Former §2523(f). Finally, the maximum allowable estate tax deduction was reduced by the amount by which the gift tax marital deduction that had been allowed the decedent under §2523 exceeded 50 percent of the value of the property transferred (*i.e.,* where the post-1976 gifts were less than $200,000). Former §2056(c)(1)(B).

The approach taken in 1976 represented a compromise between the proponents of an unlimited marital deduction of the type proposed in the Treasury Department's 1969 gift and estate tax reform proposals, U.S. Treas. Dept., Tax Reform Studies and Proposals, 91st Cong., 1st Sess., pt. 3 at 357 *et seq.* (Comm. Print 1969), and those who wanted little or no change in the deductions. Proponents argued that an unlimited deduction would leave more property for the support of the surviving spouse, provide more flexibility in planning transfers, and simplify the law. Opponents countered that an unlimited deduction would merely increase the tax benefits already available to wealthy taxpayers, whose surviving spouses were amply protected by the existing law. They noted that even under the pre-1977 law a substantial amount of property could be transferred to a spouse inter vivos and at death without incurring any federal transfer tax liability. As noted below, the proponents of the unlimited marital deduction carried the day in 1981 when their proposal was adopted effective with respect to decedents dying after December 31, 1981.

§5.3. 1981 Quantitative and Qualitative Liberalization

With relatively little fanfare the 1981 Act removed all quantitative limits on the marital deduction and relaxed the qualitative restrictions to allow two additional types of interests to qualify for the gift and estate tax deductions. The changes closely parallel two of the key recommendations made in the Treasury Department's 1969 tax reform proposals.

> It does not appear, then, that transfers of property between husband and wife are appropriate occasions for imposing tax. An especially difficult burden may be imposed by the tax when property passes to a widow, particularly if there are minor children. The present system of taxing transfers between spouses does not accord with the common understanding of most husbands and wives that the property they have accumulated is "ours." Furthermore, the distinctions drawn by existing law between transfers which qualify for the marital deduction and those which do not qualify have generated drafting complexities, artificial limitations upon dispositions, and considerable litigation.
>
> Under the [proposed] unified transfer tax there will be an exemption for the full amount of any property that passes to a spouse, either during the life of the transferor spouse or at his or her death. However, property received by the transferee spouse will, of course, become part of his or her taxable estate, unless consumed. U.S. Treas. Dept., Tax Reform Studies and Proposals, 91st Cong., 1st Sess., pt. 3, 358 (Comm. Print 1969).

§5.3.1. Quantitative Change: Unlimited Marital Deduction

The quantitative change was brought about by repealing §2056(c) (which limited the amount of the estate tax deduction as noted above), §2523(a)(2) (which limited the amount of the gift tax deduction), and §2523(f) (which disallowed any gift tax deduction for gifts of community property). Accordingly, beginning in 1982, gift and estate tax marital deductions became allowable for the full value of property that passes to a spouse in a qualifying way. As a result of the repeals, the gift and estate tax marital deduction provisions no longer differentiate between community and noncommunity property. Deferral of the tax on the death of the first spouse to die is a very valuable option.

§5.3.2. Qualitative Changes: Additional Interests Qualify for Marital Deduction

Important qualitative changes were also made by the 1981 Act. Most important, the Act added §§2056(b)(7) and 2523(f), which allow elective marital deductions with respect to qualified terminable interest property (QTIP). In brief, QTIP is property in which the donee spouse is given a "qualifying income interest for life." To constitute such a qualifying income interest the donee spouse must be entitled to all of the income from the property for life, payable annually or at more frequent intervals, and no person can have the power to appoint any of the property to any person other than the surviving spouse during his or her lifetime. §§2056(b)(7)(B)(ii), 2523(f)(2). In essence the changes allow a marital deduction for a simple life income interest, provided that no one can divert any of the property to another person during the surviving spouse's lifetime. The lifetime and post-mortem planning opportunities created by the adoption of the QTIP changes are enhanced by the fact that the deductions are not automatically allowable with respect to qualifying income interests for life. Instead, the donor, or the decedent's executor, can elect whether or not to claim a marital deduction with respect to the property in which the donee spouse has a qualifying income interest for life. Such an election can be made with respect to all or a specific portion of the property. §2056(b)(7)(B)(iv). The elective feature makes it possible to "fine tune" the amount of the estate tax marital deduction after the death of a spouse, when much more is known about the circumstances of the decedent's estate and of the surviving spouse. Of course, the portion of the property for which a deduction is claimed is includible in the donee spouse's estate under §2044 unless the property is disposed of during his or her lifetime.

The 1981 Act also added provisions that allow gift and estate tax deductions for current interests in charitable remainder trusts that are transferred to a spouse. §§2056(b)(8), 2523(g). *See* §5.24. Since the inception of the charitable remainder trust rules in 1969, gift and estate tax deductions have been allowed for the value of qualifying charitable remainder interests. *See* §§2055(e)(2), 2522(c)(2). *See also* §8.20. However, prior to 1982 no deductions were allowable with respect to the noncharitable current interest in such trusts. Given the shift to an unlimited marital deduction, Congress thought it was desirable to extend the deduction to this type of interest.

§5.3.3. Transitional Rule for Pre-1982 Formula Gifts

> Congress was not concerned with clauses that *merely mention* the maximum marital deduction, but with clauses under which

> the amount of property transferred to the surviving spouse is determined *solely* by reference to the maximum marital deduction. *Estate of Samuel I. Levitt,* 95 T.C. 289, 298 (1990).

The changes in the marital deduction provisions made by the 1981 Act generally apply with respect to gifts made, or decedents dying, after December 31, 1981. However, under §403(e)(3) of the 1981 Act, Pub. L. 97-34, 95 Stat. 305 (1981), the unlimited marital deduction generally does not apply to property passing under a will or trust executed prior to September 13, 1981 "which contains a formula *expressly* providing that the spouse is to receive the maximum amount of property qualifying for the marital deduction allowable by Federal law." (Emphasis added.) Congress enacted the transitional rule in order to avoid the constructional problems that would otherwise exist, the resolution of which might frustrate the testator's intent. "The committee is concerned that many testators, although using the formula clause, may not have wanted to pass more than the greater of $250,000 or one-half of the adjusted gross estate (recognizing the prior law limitation) to the spouse." S. Rep. 97-144, 97th Cong., 1st Sess. 128 (1981). The statute deals essentially with the amount of property that will pass under a maximum marital deduction formula clause, which is more appropriately a state law concern.

By reason of §403 the pre-1982 law may apply to formula marital deduction gifts contained in "old" instruments (*i.e.,* the marital deduction will be limited to the greater of one-half of the adjusted gross estate or $250,000). However, the unlimited marital deduction applies to pre-September 13, 1981 instruments if (1) the formula is amended after September 12, 1981, to refer to the unlimited marital deduction or (2) the state enacts a statute "which construes this type of formula as referring to the [unlimited] marital deduction allowable by Federal law." §403(e)(3)(C)-(D). Note that the first alternative requires that the formula be amended after September 12, 1981. The requirement is not met by the republication of the will by a codicil that does not amend the formula. *Matter of Hickok,* 530 N.Y.S.2d 983 (Surr. Ct. Orange County 1988), *aff'd,* 552 N.Y.S.2d 49 (App. Div. 2d Dept. 1990).

Some states have enacted statutes that make the unlimited marital deduction available to decedents whose instruments executed prior to September 12, 1981 included formula gifts based upon the maximum allowable marital deduction. La. Rev. Stat. Ann. §9:2439 (West 1991); Okla. Stat. Ann. tit. 84, §186 (West 1990) (held to be effective in LR 8341007 (TAM)); Utah Code Ann. §§75-2-613, 75-7-501 (1991 Supp.); Wash. Rev. Code §11.108.040 (1989). Most states were reluctant to enact such a statute because of the palpable uncertainty regarding the decedent's intention in such a case. Reflecting that concern, a few states have adopted statutes that provide for a contrary result (*i.e.,* unless otherwise provided, a reference to the maximum marital deduction in a pre-1982 will is deemed to refer to the maximum marital deduction that was allowable under §2056 prior to the 1981 changes. *E.g.,* Cal. Prob. Code §21523 (West 1991 Supp.); Va. Code Ann. §64.1-64.1 (1987). A statute in Alaska provides that a reference in a testamentary gift to the marital deduction provisions of the Code and Regulations "is construed to contemplate the marital deduction allowable under the Internal Revenue Code and regulations on the date of the death of the decedent making the gift." Alaska Stat. §13.11.277 (1985).

Decisions by the Courts of Appeal and the Tax Court provide some guidance regarding the meaning and application of the transitional rule. Of course, the outcome in any given case depends upon the language of the instrument involved. The outcomes in two broad categories of cases are relatively clear. The transition rule applies to the first category, exemplified by *Liberty Natl. Bank & Trust Co.,* 88-1 U.S.T.C. ¶13,760 W.D. Ky. 1988), *aff'd,* 867 F.2d 302 (6th Cir. 1989), in which the marital deduction gift is expressed by reference to the maximum marital deduction allowable. In contrast, the transition rule does not apply to cases such as *Estate of Francis L. Bruning,* 57 T.C.M. 88 (1988), *aff'd per curiam,* 888 F.2d 657 (10th Cir. 1989), which mention the maximum marital deduction, but provide that the marital deduction gift should be the smallest amount required to eliminate any federal estate tax liability. The IRS will no longer contend that the transition rule applies to cases "in which the decedent makes reference to a formula designed to pass only the lesser of (a) the maximum marital deduction, and (b) the minimum marital deduction which, after the application of the unified credit, will result in no estate tax." A.O.D. 1990-14.

Some decisions are difficult, if not impossible, to reconcile. For example, differing constructions may be given to a direction that the marital deduction be determined in accordance with the law in effect at the time of the testator's death. In particular, an Indiana court held that an unlimited marital deduction was available (*i.e.,* the transition rule did not apply) with respect to a trust executed in 1972 which provided that the marital deduction would be determined "under the law in effect at the time of Settlor's death." *Unborn Beneficiaries v. Kreigh,* 554 N.E.2d 1167, 1168 (Ind. App. 1990). The IRS follows the Indiana approach. *E.g.,* LR 9048001 (TAM) (unlimited marital deduction allowed for formula gift of maximum marital deduction allowable under the "United States Internal Revenue Code of 1954 as now existing or hereafter amended"). A contrary result was reached in *Hickok,* which provided for funding the marital deduction trust with "that fractional part of my residuary estate which shall be needed to obtain the maximum marital deduction allowable in determining the Federal Estate Tax payable by my estate under the laws in effect at the time of my death. . . ." 530 N.Y.S.2d at 984.

§5.4. The Future

While making predictions is hazardous, it seems unlikely that the basic contours of the marital deduction will change in the near future. In particular, the liberalized provisions adopted in 1981 will probably remain in place. However, under budgetary pressure it is possible that Congress may impose a limit on the maximum amount of the marital deduction. That step might be taken because it would slightly increase tax collections in the short run, although it would probably decrease them in the longer term. One hopes that at some point the complexity of the provisions will be reduced, particularly those relating to marital deduction trusts and the qualified domestic trust. The October, 1991 version of the estate tax return (Form 706) helps by eliminating the necessity of checking a separate box in order to elect to claim a QTIP marital deduction. Now, if Schedule M includes property that meets the requirements of §2057(b)(7), the executor is deemed to have made the necessary election. Finally, while some of the fine distinctions between deductible and nondeductible interests were relaxed by the 1981 Act, some of the remaining distinctions are hard to justify in terms of equity, administrative convenience, or other considerations of tax policy. The excessive technicalities of the law are particularly objectionable because of the hazards and substantial direct and indirect compliance costs they impose on taxpayers. The difficulties of complying with the technicalities are sometimes compounded by the "hidebound position taken by the Commissioner." *Estate of Smith v. Commissioner,* 565 F.2d 455, 458 (7th Cir. 1977). The principal direct costs are payments of additional fees to personal representatives and attorneys in connection with disputes spawned by the present law. The indirect costs, which are generated by the additional loads placed upon the IRS, the Department of Justice, and the courts are also substantial.

B. PLANNING FOR USE OF THE MARITAL DEDUCTION

> It is important to keep in mind the main objectives — always to chart a plan which keeps foremost the special needs and personalities and relationship of the interested parties. The practitioner does not deal with symbols *H* and *W* and estates of dollars in cash. He is concerned with particular individuals and their families and particular combinations of assets and liabilities. Much of the "buzzing, blooming confusion" about taking or not taking the marital deduction and how to do it may disappear if

> taxes are considered after, and not before, the main objectives are analyzed. What would the testator want to do apart from the marital deduction? How far is he led away from that by the tax law? J. Trachtman, Estate Planning 82 (rev. ed. 1968).

§5.5. Approaching the Planning Job

In formulating an estate plan, the lawyer and the client should give priority to sound planning for the welfare and security of the client and his or her family. A host of primarily nontax factors need to be considered in the process, including the age, health, ability, marital status, wealth, and feelings of the members of the client's family. For example, in some cases all of a client's estate will need to be made available to the surviving spouse for his or her support and in others it will not. The circumstances of the client and the client's family will also determine whether gifts to the surviving spouse are to be made outright or in trust and what choice of assets is made to fund the gifts. After the general contours of a plan are worked out, the lawyer and client should give more direct attention to tax planning, including the use of the marital deduction, to conserve the family's property.

In order to make the necessary tax analysis, the lawyer needs to know the size and composition of the estates of both spouses and the objectives of their dispositive plans. Those factors influence to a great degree the extent to which overall tax benefits will result from the use of the marital deduction and from other dispositions of the client's property. Consideration must be given to the effect of a plan upon the amount of estate tax due upon the death of each spouse, including the five percent surtax that applies to the taxable estate between $10,000,000 and $21,040,000 ($18,350,000 for decedents dying after 1992) under §2001(c)(3) and various income tax matters, including the bases of assets. The availability of the credit for property previously taxed, §2013, should also be taken into account.

> **Example 5-2.** *W*'s estate is worth $2,000,000 and *H*'s is worth $600,000 or less. Under the existing law *H*'s unified credit is sufficient to shelter his estate from the imposition of any estate tax. Accordingly, no estate tax would be due upon *H*'s death whether or not *W* survives. However, any property *H* leaves to *W* will be subject to a marginal estate tax rate of at least 49% when she dies. *H*'s unified credit is wasted to the extent his property passes in a way that will require it to be included in *W*'s estate. Of course, *H* and *W* may not be concerned about the size of the survivor's estate, particularly if all of their property will pass to charity upon the death of the survivor.

§5.5.1. Tax Estimates

The lawyer should prepare estimates of the state and federal tax consequences of the plans under consideration. The estimates, which should take into account the possibility that either spouse may die first or that they will die simultaneously, provide a good check on the merits of a plan from the transfer tax perspective. While estimates are helpful for purposes of analysis, the lawyer and client need to remember that they are only *estimates* — informed guesses about exceedingly uncertain future events. Estimates can be prepared most efficiently by using an available software program, which can produce estimates that include projected changes in value over time.

§5.5.2. Valuation of Property

Planners must recognize that the same factors that justify discounting the value of an interest in property passing in a way that does not qualify for a charitable or marital deduction may require discounting the value of a similar interest passing in a way that qualifies for one of the deductions. The IRS is increasingly alert to the propriety of discounting the value of minority or fractional interests that pass to charity or to the surviving spouse. In short, planning should be done in light of the discounts that may apply to the assets included in the client's estate *and* to the interests that pass to the surviving spouse. Planners must recognize that an estate may be advantaged or disadvantaged by a valuation that takes into account the appropriate premiums or discounts. Thus, a 51 percent interest in a closely-held business that passes to a marital deduction gift may be valued at a premium. *Estate of Dean A. Chenoweth,* 88 T.C. 1577 (1987). Of course, the transfer of a controlling interest to a marital deduction trust may result in the inclusion of that controlling interest in the estate of the surviving spouse. On the flip side, the IRS has ruled that a discount applies to the valuation of a minority interest that passes to a marital deduction trust. LR 9050004 (TAM) (decedent's will divided his 100 percent interest in a closely-held company between a trust for his son (51 percent) and a trust for his surviving spouse (49 percent)).

§5.6. General Objectives

Identifying and reviewing general objectives of marital deduction tax planning may be helpful in formulating and analyzing estate plans that involve use of marital deduction gifts. The objectives are:

1. To equalize the sizes of the spouses' estates and to pay the least total amount of estate tax (including minimization of the surtax applicable to estates over $10,000,000 in vaule);
2. To defer the payment of any estate tax until the death of the surviving spouse; and
3. To insure that the estates of both spouses will take full advantage of the unified credit.

The objectives are not equally important and are not always entirely compatible. For example, equalizing the sizes of the spouses' estates may not minimize the amount of tax due on the death of the first spouse to die. The value of the objectives should also be kept in mind. They merely suggest general approaches that may reduce tax costs, but which must yield to the circumstances and desires of particular clients.

§5.7. Equalizing the Spouses' Estates and Minimizing Overall Taxes

The tax advantage that flows from equalizing the amount of property subject to tax in each spouse's estate is a product of the progressivity of the unified tax rate schedule, §2001. From the transfer tax standpoint the optimum result is achieved when both estates are subject to the same marginal tax rate. A greater combined estate tax is paid if one of the estates is subject to a higher marginal rate than the other. However, the importance of equalization is often overemphasized: The transfer tax brackets are generally quite broad, the rates increase rather slowly, and the gap between the lowest rate at which any tax will be paid and highest marginal rate has narrowed considerably. It must also be balanced against the importance of deferring the payment of any tax until the death of the surviving spouse. However, equalization may allow a couple to avoid imposition of the five percent surtax on estates over $10 million. For example, if *W* has an estate of $18 million and *H* has an estate of $1 million, their estates might be planned in a way that allows them to be equalized in size if *W* dies first. By implementing such a plan their estates could be equalized at an amount ($9.5 million) below the threshold of the surtax. The interest given to *H* under such a plan should be crafted with a view to the §2013 credit that is allowable for a portion of the tax paid by a prior estate with respect to the actuarially determined value of an interest passing to a transferee who dies within ten years of the first decedent. The availability of the unlimited gift and estate tax marital deductions allow the estates of a husband and wife to be equalized by making inter vivos *or* deathtime gifts.

§5.7.1. Equalization Clauses

The size of the gross estates of the spouses may be closely equalized as of the appropriate valuation date if the wealthier spouse dies first, leaving the surviving spouse an amount equal to the difference in value of their estates on the estate tax valuation date applicable to the decedent's estate. A proper simultaneous death clause can be combined with an equalization clause to provide the optimum tax result if the spouses die simultaneously. The necessary equalization can also be achieved through the use of a QTIP trust, which does not require an election to be made until the estate tax return is filed (*i.e.,* at least nine months after death). *See* §5.23. Disclaimers can also be used to adjust the amount of property received by the surviving spouse, which presumably will be included in his or her estate. *See* §§12.31-12.35.

The IRS first contended that the interest given the survivor under an equalization clause is a terminable interest. However, the contention was rejected by the courts. *Estate of Charles W. Smith,* 66 T.C. 415, *nonacq.,* 1978-1 C.B. 3, *withdrawn and acq. substituted,* 1982-2 C.B. 1, *aff'd,* 565 F.2d 455 (1977); *Estate of Fritz L. Meeske,* 72 T.C. 73 (1979), *aff'd sub nom. Estate of Laurin v. Commissioner,* 645 F.2d 8 (6th Cir. 1981, consolidated appeal). The courts considered that the necessary interest unquestionably passed to the survivor and would be included in her gross estate. In their view only the value of the interest depends upon the subsequent valuation of assets. In early 1982 the IRS abandoned the contention and conceded that a marital deduction gift subject to an equalization clause was not a terminable interest. Rev. Rul. 82-23, 1982-1 C.B. 139.

The key clause of the will upheld in the *Smith* case read as follows:

> (b) There shall then [after allocation of the Residual Portion] be allocated to the Marital Portion that percentage interest in the balance of the assets constituting the trust estate which shall when taken together with all other interests and property that qualify for the marital deduction and that pass or shall have passed to Settlor's said wife under other provisions of this trust or otherwise, obtain for Settlor's estate a marital deduction which would result in the lowest Federal estate taxes [on] Settlor's estate and Settlor's wife's estate, on the assumption Settlor's wife died after him, but on the date of his death and that her estate were valued as of the date on (and in the manner in) which Settlor's estate is valued for Federal estate tax purposes; Settlor's purpose is to equalize, insofar as possible, his estate and her estate for Federal estate tax purposes, based upon said assumptions. Smith, 66 T.C. at 418.

As noted above, the use of an equalization clause or a QTIP trust is particularly appropriate where both spouses are expected to die within a relatively short time period. The payment of estate tax in the estate of the first to die may support a substantial previously taxed property credit in the second estate, which is particularly valuable if the interest that passed to the transferee's estate is not includible in the transferee's estate (*e.g.*, a life estate in QTIP).

§5.7.2. Community Property Estates Are Already Equalized

The ownership of community property is naturally equalized by operation of state laws. Accordingly, in most cases the total estate tax burden on community property is minimized if little or no property is passed to a surviving spouse in a way that will cause it to be included in the survivor's gross estate. However, many clients prefer to transfer enough of their community property to the surviving spouse in order to defer payment of any estate tax until the death of the survivor.

Under one of the most common plans a client with a substantial community property estate leaves most of it to a QTIP trust (*i.e.*, one that meets the requirements of §2056(b)(7), described in more detail in §5.23). The interests given to the surviving spouse are not sufficient to cause the property to be included in his or her gross estate apart from the portion with respect to which the executor elects to claim the marital deduction. §2044. Thus, the surviving spouse receives a life income interest in the trust. Importantly, the survivor may also be given: the noncumulative right to draw down the greater of $5,000 or five percent of the value of the trust each year, §2041(b)(2); the power to invade the corpus of the trust limited by an ascertainable standard relating to the survivor's health, education, support, or maintenance, §2041(b)(1)(A); and a testamentary power to appoint the trust property to a limited class of persons, excluding herself, her creditors, her estate, and creditors of her estate, §2041(b)(1). Note that the last-mentioned power should not be exercisable with respect to property which passed into the trust as the result of a disclaimer by the surviving spouse. The reason is simple — a disclaimer is not a qualified disclaimer under §2518 if the disclaiming party retains a discretionary power over the disposition of the property. Of course, in any case a trustee other than the surviving spouse can be given the power to make discretionary distributions of corpus to the surviving spouse. Under this approach the executor can elect to claim a marital deduction for a portion of the property transferred to the trust according to the circumstances as they exist at the time the estate tax return is filed for the spouse who died first.

§5.8. Minimize Taxes — Defer Payments

The needs of a family of modest wealth may be served best by a plan that defers payment of any estate tax until the death of the surviving spouse. With the unlimited marital deduction, it is relatively easy to achieve that goal. However, such a deferral may unreasonably delay the time at which any of the property will be available to the client's children or other younger generation beneficiaries. In most cases the client will not want to "waste" the unified credit of the spouse first to die by giving all of his or her property outright to the surviving spouse. Of course, such a waste could be avoided to the extent the surviving spouse disclaims interests in the property. The goal may be more securely achieved, however, by using a QTIP trust or a marital deduction formula clause. In either case the plan preserves the maximum amount of property during the surviving spouse's lifetime. Also, by eliminating the need to pay any tax, the estate of the first spouse to die is relieved of the necessity to liquidate additional assets, which could require the recognition of capital gains.

If both spouses own a substantial amount of property, the total amount of transfer taxes ultimately payable by their estates may be increased by deferring the payment of any tax until the death of the surviving spouse. First, an increase might result because of the progressivity of the estate tax. However, the progressivity of the tax was greatly reduced by the 1981 Act, which dramatically increased the amount of the unified credit and decreased the progressivity of the tax. The maximum rate of 55 percent is scheduled to be reduced to 50 percent in 1993. Thus, after 1992 the spread between the lowest marginal rate at which any tax will be payable and the maximum rate will be only 13 percent. *See* §2.3. Second, the tax might be greater on the surviving spouse's death because of an increase in the value of the assets or because of his or her accumulation of income. This risk is easily exaggerated — it is impossible to foresee the composition or value of the surviving spouse's estate or the rates or other provisions of the tax laws that will be in effect at the time of his or her death. In this connection recall that the substantial transfer tax changes made by the 1976 and 1981 Acts were largely unanticipated even in the years they were adopted. Also, the amount and value of property includible in the surviving spouse's estate may be controlled by careful estate planning, including gifts, installment sales, and other strategies. In this connection it should be noted that the unified credit currently allows a relatively large amount of property to escape taxation entirely.

After 1992, when the highest marginal estate tax rate will be 50 percent, the largest amount of additional tax that could result from the use of the unlimited marital deduction is $129,200 if the values remain constant. That amount represents the difference between the tentative tax on an estate of $2.5 million ($1,025,800) and the tentative tax on two estates of $1.25 million ($448,300 × 2 or $896,600). Of course, the value of the unified credit and progressive rates is phased out for estates of more than $10 million. §2001(c)(3).

Example 5-3. *H* died leaving an estate of $1,000,000 to a trust in which *W* has a qualifying income interest for life. No tax will be due from *H*'s estate if his executor elects to claim a deduction with respect to $400,000 of the property passing to the trust (40% of the total trust). If the value of the trust does not exceed $1,500,000 at the time of *W*'s death and no other property is includible in her estate, *W*'s unified credit is sufficient to offset the tax on her estate. The result would be the same if the trust had a value of $1,000,000 at the time of her death, of which $400,000 would be includible in her estate, and up to $200,000 of other property was includible in her estate.

§5.9. Taking Advantage of the Unified Credits of Both Spouses

In general a spouse should not provide in his or her will for a larger gift to the other spouse than is necessary to eliminate the testator's estate tax liability. That is, none of a client's unified credit should be wasted. Instead, the estate of each spouse should make maximum use of the "shelter" provided by his or her unified credit. Of course, this point generally concerns only married clients whose combined gross estates are likely to exceed the amount of the credit equivalent allowable to one person ($600,000).

Example 5-4. *H* died leaving an estate of $600,000 to *W,* who owned about $400,000 in property. No estate tax was due from *H*'s estate which was within the credit equivalent ($600,000). However, it is includible in *W*'s estate. If the value of the property remains constant an estate tax of $153,000 will be due from *W*'s estate. No tax would have been due had *H* used his unified credit to shelter his property from taxation upon *W*'s death. For example, *H* might have left his entire estate to a QTIP trust with respect to which the shelter could have been preserved by an appropriate election by *H*'s executor.

As indicated by Example 5-4, the "shelter" provided by the unified credit may be preserved in a variety of ways. Some clients prefer to make a formula gift of an amount equal to the credit equivalent in a way that insulates the property from tax on the death of the surviving spouse. Others prefer to leave substantially all of their property outright to their surviving spouses and to rely upon them to adjust the amount of the gifts through the use of disclaimers. Probably the most popular approach is based on a QTIP trust, in which the surviving spouse has a qualifying income interest for life. Its success of course depends upon the decedent's executor making an appropriate election under §2056(b)(7).

If one spouse has a relatively large estate and the other spouse has an estate significantly smaller than the amount of the credit equivalent, the wealthier spouse may make inter vivos gifts to the poorer spouse in order to assure the use of the donee-spouse's full unified credit. For example, under one approach the wealthier spouse makes a gift to a QTIP trust for the benefit of the poorer spouse. In this connection note that if the donee spouse is given a general power of appointment over the property, the donor spouse can retain a successive life income interest in the trust without causing the property to be included in his estate. The IRS has recognized that the retention of such an interest will not require the property to be included in the donor's estate whether or not the donor survives the donee. LR 8949009. Alternatively, if property were transferred to a QTIP trust with respect to which the donee spouse had a special power of appointment, the donee could appoint the property to a QTIP trust for the benefit of the donor spouse. Presumably the property of the latter trust would be included in the estate of the donor spouse only to the extent the QTIP marital deduction was claimed by the donee's spouse's executor. Of course, the basis of the property is not increased under §1014 if the donee spouse dies within one year of the original gift and leaves the property to the donor spouse. §1014(e).

C. HOW TO QUALIFY FOR THE MARITAL DEDUCTION

§5.10. Basic Requirements

Five requirements must be met in order for a gift of an interest in property to qualify for the estate tax marital deduction. Listed in more or less ascending order of complexity and capacity for creating problems, they are as follows:

1. The decedent was a U.S. citizen or resident;
2. The interest in property is included in the decedent's gross estate;

3. The decedent is survived by a spouse who is a citizen of the United States;
4. The interest "passes" to the decedent's surviving spouse; and
5. The interest is a deductible one (*i.e.,* it is not a nondeductible terminable interest).

The first three requirements ordinarily do not pose any particularly difficult problems. However, if the surviving spouse is not a citizen of the United States, the marital deduction is only available for transfers to a qualified domestic trust (QDT). §2056(d). *See* §5.25. Sometimes disputes regarding the allowability of a marital deduction are generated by the fourth and more often the fifth requirements. In part the volume of litigation reflects the extent to which the IRS has insisted upon full compliance with some very technical provisions of the law.

If a timely QDT or QTIP election is not made, the executor may apply for an extension of time under Temp. Reg. §301.9100-1T. An extension may be granted if the request is made within a reasonable time and granting it will not jeopardize the interests of the government. See §12.2.4.

§5.11. Gift Tax

Section 2523 imposes similar requirements in connection with the gift tax marital deduction. However, the 1988 Act amended §2523(a) to eliminate the prior requirement that the donor spouse be a citizen or resident. As a result a marital deduction is available for a gift by a nonresident alien of property with a situs in the United Sates if the donee is a U.S. citizen. Under the 1988 changes no marital deduction is allowable for a gift to a spouse who is not a U.S. citizen. §2523(i)(1). Instead, an annual exclusion of $100,000 is allowable. §2523(i)(2). The annual exclusion is only available for a gift to a noncitizen spouse to the extent the gift constitutes a present interest under §2503(b).

In order to qualify for the gift tax marital deduction the donor and the donee must be validly married at the time of the transfer. This places a premium on knowing when a gift is complete, particularly in cases that involve antenuptial agreements. The main differences between the gift and estate tax deductions are mentioned in the course of a detailed review of the estate tax provisions.

§5.12. Decedent Was Citizen or Resident

The citizenship and residence of a client are usually clear and will not be the subject of controversy upon his or her death. The overall consequences of establishing citizenship and residence should be carefully considered when a client has ties to more than one country. In general, ambiguous relationships should be resolved one way or another before a problem arises — either by firmly establishing the relationship or by clearly severing it. The existing tax treaties do not completely eliminate the additional transfer taxes that may result if a client has ties to two or more countries. The ownership of assets in more than one jurisdiction could result in tax complications. The cautious use of trusts and corporations allows some multijurisdictional problems to be avoided. *See* §10.12.

§5.13. Inclusion in Gross Estate

The includibility of property in a decedent's gross estate is also usually clearly determined under other Code sections. Although an otherwise qualifying interest passes to the surviving spouse in a requisite way, no deduction is allowed unless the interest is included in the decedent's gross estate and is not otherwise deductible. For example, amounts for which a deduction is allowed under §2053 for commissions paid to the surviving spouse as personal representative are not also deductible under §2056. Reg. §20.2056(a)-2(b)(2).

> **Example 5-5.** *W* is the designated beneficiary of a policy of insurance on *H*'s life, which is owned by *W*. The insurance proceeds received by *W* are deductible only to the extent they are included in *H*'s gross estate. Of course, the policy would be includible in *H*'s estate under §2042(2) if he held any incident of ownership in the policy at the time of his death.

No estate tax deduction is allowed for property the decedent gave inter vivos to his or her spouse unless the property is included in the decedent's gross estate.

§5.14. Surviving Spouse

Neither the Code nor the Regulations define "surviving spouse." However, it is clear that the decedent and the transferee must be married at the time of the decedent's death. In that connection the IRS has ruled that "[t]he marital deduction is not allowed with respect to transferred property if the decedent was not married to the transferee at the time of death even though the decedent may have been married to the transferee at the time of the transfer." Rev. Rul. 79-354, 1979-2 C.B. 334 (gift made to spouse within three years of decedent's death, but donee predeceased donor). The same Ruling allowed a marital deduction for a gift made within three years of the donor's death to a person other than the donor's spouse where the donor and donee were married at the time of the donor's death.

For federal estate tax purposes the marital status of a decedent is determined under the law of the state of his or her domicile. *Estate of Goldwater v. Commissioner,* 539 F.2d 878 (2d Cir.), *cert. denied,* 429 U.S. 1023 (1976); *Estate of Spalding v. Commissioner,* 537 F.2d 666 (2d Cir. 1976); *Estate of Steffke v. Commissioner,* 538 F.2d 730 (7th Cir.), *cert. denied,* 429 U.S. 1022 (1976).

Example 5-6. *H* married *W* in 1946. *H* obtained a Mexican divorce from *W* in 1958. In 1959 *H* participated in a marriage ceremony with *R*. A court of the state in which *H* was domiciled later declared the Mexican divorce to be invalid. Thereafter *H* died, leaving his entire estate of $1,000,000 to *R*. *W* claimed and received an elective share of $700,000 from *H*'s estate. The marital deduction is limited to the amount that passed to *W*, who was *H*'s surviving spouse under the applicable state law (*i.e.*, no marital deduction is allowable for the property left to *R*).

As the example indicates, questions of status are extremely important in resolving issues both of tax law and of substantive property law. Presumably the marital relation will be recognized for tax purposes although the spouses are living apart if their marriage has not been formally dissolved.

§5.15. Surviving Spouse Was Citizen or Property Distributed to Qualified Domestic Trust (QDT)

A decedent's estate is not entitled to a marital deduction for property passing to a surviving spouse who is not a citizen of the United States. However, there are two important exceptions to the general rule. First, under §2056(d)(4) the marital deduction is allowable for an otherwise qualified gift to the surviving spouse if he or she becomes a U.S. citizen before the day on which the decedent's estate tax return is due and the surviving spouse was a U.S. resident at all times between the date of the decedent's death and the date the surviving spouse becomes a citizen. Second, a marital deduction is allowable with respect to property transferred to a qualified domestic trust (QDT or QDOT), if an election is made on the decedent's federal estate tax return. §2056A.

The marital deduction is only allowable for a transfer to a trust if the trust is a QDT *and* meets the basic requirements of §2056. The trust must be an estate trust, a life interest and general power of appointment trust, a QTIP trust, or a charitable remainder trust. *See* §§2056(b)(5), 2056(b)(7), and 2056(b)(8). *See also* §§5.21-5.24. To qualify as a QDT the trust instrument must require (1) at least one trustee of the trust be an individual citizen of the United States or a domestic corporation, and (2) that such trustee have the right to withhold the estate tax imposed by §2056A from any distribution of principal. §2056A(a)(1). In addition, the executor must elect to treat the trust as a QDT. QDTs are discussed in more detail at §5.25.

§5.16. INTERESTS PASSED TO SURVIVING SPOUSE

A deduction is allowed only for interests that "pass" to the surviving spouse. The ways in which interests in property are considered to pass to a surviving spouse are listed in §2056(c). They include interest passing by (1) bequest or devise; (2) inheritance; (3) dower or curtesy; (4) inter vivos transfer; (5) joint tenancy or right of survivorship; (6) the exercise or nonexercise of a power of appointment; and (7) policies of insurance on the decedent's life. A decedent commonly passes property to a surviving spouse in several of the ways listed in the statute.

A controversy involving the passing requirement may arise if a surviving spouse elects against the decedent's will or, less commonly, when he or she receives (or surrenders) an interest in a decedent's estate in connection with a will contest. Any dower, statutory share, or other property a surviving spouse receives as a result of an election against the will is considered to pass from the decedent to him or her. However, any interest a surviving spouse is required to give up as a result of an election is not considered to pass from the decedent to him or her. Reg. §20.2056(e)-2(c). The value of the right of a surviving spouse to elect against the decedent's will and to receive a statutory share of the decedent's estate is not includible in the surviving spouse's gross estate if the surviving spouse dies without making the election. Rev. Rul. 74-492, 1974-2 C.B. 298. The cited ruling holds that the right is neither a property interest includible under §2033 nor a general power of appointment includible under §2041. Under it, "the election to take under the husband's will is treated as a disclaimer or renunciation of the alternative rights of the widow provided under state statute." Id. The tax consequences of a surviving spouse's election to claim (or not to claim) dower or an elective share are explored in some detail in §12.30.

An interest is also considered to pass from the decedent to the surviving spouse if it is received as a result of a bona fide recognition of his or her enforceable rights in the estate. The necessary showing is ordinarily provided by a court decree upon the merits in an adversary proceeding following a genuine and active contest. Consistently, an interest in property is not considered to have passed to the surviving spouse to the extent he or she assigns or surrenders it in settlement of a controversy. *See* Reg. §20.2056(e)-2(d).

The Regulations point out that the surviving spouse must receive the beneficial interest in the property in order to qualify for the deduction. Reg. §20.2056(e)-2(a). Thus, no deduction is allowed for property transferred to the spouse as trustee for others. Along the same lines, the deduction is limited to the net value of the interests that pass to the spouse or to the marital deduction trust. *See, e.g.,* LR 8834005 (TAM). Section 2056(b)(4) requires the amount of death taxes, encumbrances, and any other obligations imposed by the decedent with respect to the passing of an interest to be deducted in computing the value of the interest received by the surviving spouse. This limitation on the amount of the deduction is discussed in *United States v. Stapf,* 375 U.S. 118 (1963). In *Stapf* the Court properly concluded that a deduction was allowable only to the extent the value of the interests received by the decedent's widow exceeded the value of the interests she was required to transfer to others.

§5.16.1. Family Awards and Allowances

The regulations recognize that a widow's allowance or other family award payable during the administration of an estate constitutes property that passes from a decedent to the recipient. However, as explained in §5.17, no deduction is permitted if the allowance is a nondeductible terminable interest. *See* Reg. §20.2056(b)-1(g)(8). For example, in *Jackson v. United States,* 376 U.S. 503 (1964), the Court concluded that the California widow's allowance was not a deductible interest because the widow "did not have an indefeasible interest in property at the moment of her husband's death since either her death or remarriage would defeat it." 376 U.S. at 507. Family allowances typically do not qualify for the deduction under the terminable interest rule. Note, Widow's Allowance and Marital Deductions — The Date-of-Death Rule, 63 Mich. L. Rev. 924 (1965). However, homestead allowances and awards in lieu of homestead that vest immediately at death and are not terminable do qualify for the marital deduction. *See, e.g.,* Rev. Rul. 72-153, 1972-1 C.B. 309 (Washington); Comment, Federal Estate and State Inheritance Tax Aspects of the Family Allowance, the Homestead and the In Lieu of Homestead Awards, 37 Wash. L. Rev. 435 (1962). In contrast, homestead awards that are terminable by abandonment are not deductible. *Estate of Henry H. Kyle,* 94 T.C. 829 (1990) (Texas).

The IRS has ruled that the Arizona homestead allowances of a cash sum and the exempt property allowance, which are based on the former version of U.P.C. §§2-401 and 2-402, both qualify for the marital deduction. Rev. Rul. 76-166, 1976-1 C.B. 287. Note that they qualify although the surviving spouse must survive the decedent by 120 hours and must elect to claim them. In contrast, the value of a family allowance made to a surviving spouse under U.P.C. §2-404 is a terminable interest that does not qualify for the deduction.

§5.16.2. Disclaimers

The use of disclaimers in post-mortem planning is reviewed in some detail at §§12.31-12.35. At this point it is sufficient to note that the amount passing to the surviving spouse may be increased or decreased by "qualified disclaimers." Under §§2046 and 2518 qualified disclaimers are recognized for purposes of the estate, gift, and GST taxes.

A "qualified disclaimer" is defined in §2518(b) as a written, unequivocal, and unqualified refusal to accept an interest in property (including a power with respect to property) that is received by the transferor of the interest or the transferor's legal representative not later than nine months after the day on which the transfer creating the interest was made. A disclaimer is not qualified if the disclaimant accepted the property or any benefits from it prior to making the disclaimer. As a result of the disclaimer, the interest must pass to the decedent's surviving spouse or a person other than the disclaimant. Also, the disclaimant cannot direct the transfer of the property to another person.

Qualified disclaimers may prevent a surviving spouse from receiving "too much" property from the decedent's estate. In particular, disclaimers can adjust the amount of property that passes to the surviving spouse so the decedent's unified credit is not wasted and the surviving spouse's estate is not unnecessarily enlarged. They may also be used to increase the amount of property passing to the surviving spouse in ways that qualify for the marital deduction. Property that the surviving spouse becomes entitled to receive as a result of qualified disclaimers is recognized as passing from the decedent to the surviving spouse. Reg. §20.2056(d)-1(b).

§5.17. A Deductible Interest (*i.e.,* Not a Nondeductible Terminable Interest)

> [W]hile the terminable interest rule is, indeed, a thicket, the Congressional purpose of disqualifying terminable bequests was certainly not to elevate form above substance. It was, instead, to prevent the wholesale evasion of estate taxes which the skillful employment of terminable interests could have easily achieved. *Allen v. United States,* 359 F.2d 151, 153-154 (2d. Cir.), *cert. denied,* 385 U.S. 832 (1966).

The so-called terminable interest rule of §2056(b) is intended to assure that property for which a marital deduction is allowed in the estate of the spouse first to die will be included in the gross estate of the surviving spouse, except to the extent the surviving spouse consumes or disposes of it during his or her lifetime. Accordingly, where the interest involved will be includible in the surviving spouse's estate, some courts have declared that "the Commissioner's dependence on any literal statutory language arguably contrary should not prevail, for in such an instance, form may not be elevated over substance." *Estate of Smith v. Commissioner,* 565 F.2d 455, 459 (7th Cir. 1977).

The basic terminable interest rule bars a deduction for an interest in property only where (1) the interest passing from the decedent to the surviving spouse is terminable (*i.e.,* it will terminate on the occurrence or nonoccurrence of an event or contingency), (2) the decedent also passed an interest in the same property to another person for less than adequate and full consideration in money or money's worth, *and* (3) the other person or his or her successors may possess or enjoy the property *after* the surviving spouse's interest terminates. §2056(b)(1). The rule does not bar a deduction unless all three of the elements are present. Practically the same rule applies to inter vivos transfers. *See* §2523(b).

Properly drafted formula marital deduction bequests and equalization clause bequests (*i.e.,* ones that give the surviving spouse interests in the deceased spouse's property sufficient to equalize the sizes of their respective taxable estates) do not violate the terminable interest rule. In the case of the equalization clause, the interest that the surviving spouse receives is not terminable — its value is simply not determined until the survivor's estate is valued, just as the value of a formula gift is not determined until certain post-mortem valuations are made.

A deduction may not be allowed to the extent that the property passing to an otherwise qualifying marital deduction trust is subject to an option held by a person other than the surviving spouse to purchase the property at a bargain. In LR 9139001 (TAM) the IRS ruled that a trust did not meet the requirements of a QTIP where the decedent's son held an option to purchase the closely-held stock at its book value. *See* §5.23. The IRS reasoned that the surviving spouse did not have a qualifying income interest for life because by exercising the option the decedent's son could, in effect, withdraw a portion of the trust for his benefit. In addition, according to the IRS, the surviving spouse did not have a qualifying income interest in any specific portion of the trust — as a result of which no marital deduction was allowable. Essentially the same issue also arose in LR 9147065 (TAM), in which the IRS denied the marital deduction to the extent of the closely-held stock that was subject to an option held by the decedent's children to purchase the stock at a bargain price.

§5.17.1. Terminable Interest

The first requirement of the rule is satisfied only if the interest given the surviving spouse is a terminable interest. Under the Regulations "[a] 'terminable interest' in property is an interest which will terminate or fail on the lapse of time or on the occurrence or failure to occur of some contingency. Life estates, terms for years, annuities, patents, and copyrights are therefore terminable interests." Reg. §20.2056(b)-1(b). In contrast, "a bond note, or similar contractual obligation, the discharge of which would not have the effect of an annuity or a term for years, is not a terminable interest." Id.

Example 5-7. *H* devised Blackacre to *W* for life, remainder to his son *S*. The life interest that *H* passed to *W* is a nondeductible terminable interest because it will terminate upon *W*'s death and Blackacre will be owned by *S* or his successors, who did not pay fair and adequate consideration for the remainder interest. However, the life interest may constitute a qualifying income interest for life, for which *H*'s executor might elect to treat as QTIP under §2056(b)(7). *See* §5.23.

§5.17.2. Interest Passed to Another Person

The second requirement is met only if an interest in the same property passes for less than full and adequate consideration from the decedent to a person other than the surviving spouse. §2056(b)(1)(A). For the purposes of the terminable interest rule, "it is immaterial whether interests in the same property passed to the decedent's spouse and another person at the same time, or under the same instrument." Reg. §20.2056(b)-1(e)(1).

Example 5-8. *H* gave Blackacre to *S,* reserving the use of the property for a 20-year term. *H* died during the term and bequeathed his interest to his surviving spouse, *W*. The interest passed to *W* is a nondeductible terminable interest because *S,* who did not pay full and adequate consideration for his interest in Blackacre, will possess it after the term expires.

Example 5-9. *H* sold a remainder interest in Blackacre to his son, *S,* for full and adequate consideration, reserving a joint and survivor life estate to himself and his wife *W*. If *W* survives *H,* the interest *W* received from *H* is a deductible terminable interest. Although *W*'s interest is terminable and the property will be enjoyed by *S* or his successors upon her death, *S* paid full and adequate consideration for the interest he received from *H*.

Example 5-10. *H* bequeathed a patent to his wife *W*. The interest given *W* will terminate upon the lapse of time. However, it is a deductible interest because no other person received any interest in the patent from *H*.

This requirement of the rule is not satisfied if the surviving spouse exercises the right to claim an absolute interest in the decedent's property, whether the elective right is conferred by the decedent's will or by state statute. In such cases the interest is not terminable and no interest in the property passes to any other person. *Estate of Neugass v. Commissioner,* 555 F.2d 322 (2d Cir. 1977) (will provision); Rev. Rul. 72-8, 1972-1 C.B. 309 (Florida award of absolute dower interests).

§5.17.3. Subsequent Enjoyment

The third requirement is present only if the other person to whom an interest was transferred or that person's successors may possess or enjoy the property *after* the termination of the surviving spouse's interest. §2056(b)(1)(B). Thus, a deduction may be allowed where the surviving spouse will possess or enjoy the property upon the termination of another interest.

Example 5-11. *H* devised Blackacre to *S* for life, remainder to his wife *W*. *H*'s estate will be allowed a deduction for the value of the remainder interest determined in accordance with the applicable actuarial tables. The interest devised to *S* is terminable, but the interest transferred to *W* is not: No one is entitled to possess or enjoy the property *after W* as a result of *H*'s transfer.

§5.17.4. Executor Purchase Rule

Two subsidiary rules also restrict the allowability of a marital deduction. The first is the executor purchase rule, which prohibits a deduction for any terminable interest that "is to be acquired for the surviving spouse pursuant to the directions of the decedent, by his executor or by the trustee of a trust." §2056(b)(1)(C). As indicated in the following example, the rule can be easily avoided. Given its lack of effectiveness, it is largely a trap for the unwary. Equity and simplicity support its repeal.

Example 5-12. *H* bequeathed $100,000 to his wife *W* subject to a direction that his executor use the funds to purchase an annuity for *W.* The bequest is a nondeductible interest. If *H* had purchased a joint and survivor annuity under which payments were to be made to *W* after his death, the interest of *W* would be deductible. Reg. §20.2056(b)-1(g), example 3. There is no justification for the difference in treatment. Note that the marital deduction would be allowed for an outright bequest to *W* that she used to purchase an annuity.

If the executor is directed to purchase a terminable interest for the surviving spouse, the last two requirements of the terminable interest rule are not satisfied. Nonetheless, because of the special rule of §2056(b)(1)(c), no deduction is allowed.

§5.17.5. Unidentified Asset Rule

The other rule, often called the unidentified or "tainted" asset rule, is also intended to assure that interests for which a marital deduction is allowed will be included in the surviving spouse's gross estate. §2056(b)(2). Under this rule a deduction is not allowed to the extent that an interest given the survivor may be satisfied with assets (or their proceeds) that are nondeductible. For example, Reg. §20.2056(b)-2 indicates that a bequest to a surviving spouse of one-third of the decedent's residuary estate does not qualify for the marital deduction to the extent the residuary estate includes nondeductible interests that might be assigned to the surviving spouse. A marital deduction gift can be insulated from challenge under this rule if the will or other governing instrument prohibits the fiduciary from satisfying the gift with nondeductible interests.

§5.17.6. Contractual Wills

As indicated in §4.7, since the tax consequences of contractual wills are uncertain, they should be used with great caution. Accordingly, if it is important to obtain a marital deduction upon the death of the first spouse to die, the clients should adopt a plan that produces tried and true results. Because the outcome in a contractual will case depends upon the particular language used and the peculiarities of the local law, it is preferable to avoid using one. "The treatment of transfers under joint and mutual wills as gifts is an artifact of an unusual rule of common law in Illinois, and we suspect that neither the attorneys who draft these wills nor the couples who execute them understand their tax consequences." *Grimes v. Commissioner,* 851 F.2d 1005, 1010 (7th Cir. 1988). For an extensive treatment of joint and mutual wills, *see* Hess, The Federal Transfer Tax Consequences of Joint and Mutual Wills, 24 Real Prop., Prob. & Tr. J. 469 (1990).

The deductibility of an interest passing under a contractual will depends upon the nature of the interest passing to the surviving spouse and the terms of the contract. Under the pre-1982 law interests that passed to the surviving spouse under a contractual will frequently failed to qualify for the marital deduction because of the terminable interest rule. For example, in *Estate of Opal v. Commissioner,* 450 F.2d 1085 (2d Cir. 1971), no deduction was allowed for the interest that passed to the surviving spouse under a joint will because the interest was essentially a life estate with a power to consume. No marital deduction was allowed because the survivor did not have the requisite power to appoint to herself or to her estate. Of course, had the decedent died after 1981, presumably the decedent's executor could have elected to treat the property as QTIP and claimed a marital deduction under §2056(b)(7). *See* §5.23. Likewise, a marital deduction would be allowable in cases such as *Grimes* to the estate of the first spouse to die for at least a portion of the value of the life estate received by the surviving spouse. The amount of the deduction would be limited, however, to the extent the survivor was required to give up other property in exchange. *See* §2056(b)(4); *United States v. Stapf,* 375 U.S. 118 (1963). *See also* §9.33.

§5.18. Exceptions to Terminable Interest Rule

Several important exceptions to the terminable interest rule allow transfers to a surviving spouse to qualify for the marital deduction although all three elements of the rule are present. The exceptions apply to transfers under which:

1. The interest of the surviving spouse will terminate if he or she dies within six months of the decedent or as a result of a common disaster, §2056(b)(3), §5.19;
2. The entire interest in the property will pass to the surviving spouse *or* to his or her estate (the so-called estate trust exception), §2056(b)(1) and Reg. §20.2056(e)-2(b), §5.21;
3. The surviving spouse will receive all of the income from the property for life and will have a general power of appointment over it (the "life interest-general power of appointment" exception), §2056(b)(5), §5.22. Another subsection of the Code allows a deduction where the surviving spouse receives similar

interests in the proceeds of insurance on the decedent's life, §2056(b)(6);

4. The surviving spouse will receive all of the income from the property for life and no one, including the surviving spouse, has the power to appoint any part of the property to any person other than the surviving spouse during the surviving spouse's lifetime. §2056(b)(7), §5.23; or
5. The surviving spouse is the only noncharitable beneficiary of a charitable remainder annuity trust or a charitable remainder unitrust as defined in §664. §2056(b)(8), §5.24.

The exceptions permit much greater flexibility in providing for the surviving spouse than would otherwise be possible. The fourth of the listed exceptions, for QTIP, offers an appealing way of providing for the surviving spouse in a manner that allows a deduction for an elective amount. It is also appealing because the surviving spouse need not be given any control over the disposition of the property following his or her death. In any case, great care must be taken in planning and drafting marital deduction trusts to be sure that the exacting requirements of the Code and Regulations are met. Much of the litigation related to the exceptions involves instruments that include either inappropriate boilerplate or otherwise appropriate provisions that have been altered in an uninformed way.

§5.19. Limited Survivorship

Under §2056(b)(3), a limited survivorship requirement may be imposed upon a transfer to a surviving spouse without jeopardizing the marital deduction. An interest will not be considered a terminable interest "if (1) the only condition under which it will terminate is the death of the surviving spouse within six months after the decedent's death, or her death as a result of a common disaster which also resulted in the decedent's death, and (2) the condition does not in fact occur." Reg. §20.2056(b)-3(a). The provision allows an individual to provide for an alternate disposition of property if the testator's spouse survives for only a short period of time. If the spouse does not survive the specified period, the testator's will and not the will of the surviving spouse controls the disposition of the property. Such a provision can be used to avoid the additional costs that would be incurred if the same property were to pass through two successive estates.

Example 5-13. *H* died leaving a will that gave his residuary estate to *W* if she survived him by 6 months, otherwise to *X*. If *W* survives *H* by less than 6 months *H*'s estate will not be entitled to a marital deduction with respect to the residuary estate. However, if *W* survives *H* by 6 months, the contingent interest of *X* is extinguished and *W* is the only person to whom *H* transferred an interest in the property. In such a case, the residuary gift qualifies for the marital deduction under the exception provided for in §2056(b)(3).

For the purposes of this rule the IRS has indicated that a month is measured from a given day in one calendar month to the corresponding numbered day in the next month. Rev. Rul. 70-400, 1970-2 C.B. 196. The ruling allowed a marital deduction for a gift to a surviving spouse which was conditioned upon survivorship for six months where the decedent died on January 1 and his widow died on July 2 (*i.e.,* the spouse survived the decedent by more than six months).

The exception also permits the use of a gift that will equalize the size of the spouses' taxable estates if they die within six months of each other. However, the objective of equalizing the sizes of the spouses' estates may be better achieved by giving the surviving spouse interests with respect to which a QTIP election can be made. Under §2056(b)(7) the deceased spouse's executor is allowed to elect a marital deduction with respect to part or all of the interests on the estate tax return of the spouse who died first (*i.e.,* the election need not be made until nine months after his or her death). In effect, §2056(b)(7) allows the estates to be equalized if the spouses die within nine months of each other. Of course, taking into account the credit for property previously taxed, §2013, a considerable saving may result if the deceased spouse's executor elects to pay some tax on the decedent's estate. A credit will be allowed in the surviving spouse's estate for the portion of the tax paid by the estate of the predeceased spouse with respect to the surviving spouse's life income interest although the life interest is not includible in the surviving spouse's gross estate. The credit available with respect to life income interests makes it particularly important that the interest of the surviving spouse is *not* conditioned on survivorship for any period.

Example 5-14. *W* died on June 1, 1992 leaving an estate of $1,000,000 entirely to a trust for the benefit of *H* for life, remainder to their children. The trust met the requirements of §2056(b)(7). *H,* who was 65 years of age at the time of *W*'s death, survived her by only 3 months. *H* left his estate of $1,000,000 to their children. *W*'s executor may elect to claim a $400,000 marital deduction with respect to the trust for *H,* as a result of which no federal estate tax would be payable by her estate. In that case, *H*'s gross estate would be $1,400,000. Disregarding any deductions, *H*'s estate would be subject to an estate tax of $320,000.

On the other hand, if *W*'s executor did not elect to claim the marital deduction with respect to any portion of the trust, a much better result would be achieved because of the previously taxed property credit of §2013. In that event, *W*'s estate would pay a tax of $153,000. However, assuming that a 10% rate applied under §7520, *H*'s life estate in the trust under *W*'s will would have a value of .71213. Applying that factor to the net amount passing into the trust for *H* ($847,000), *H*'s life estate would have a value of $603,174. The estate tax credit allowed to *H*'s estate for the tax paid by *W*'s estate is determined by multiplying the amount of the tax ($153,000) by a fraction, the numerator of which is the value of the interest transferred to *H* ($603,174) and the denominator of which is the net value of *W*'s estate ($847,000). The result is a credit of $108,956. The estate tax on *H*'s estate is $153,000 against which a credit of $108,956 is allowable, requiring a payment of only $44,044. The total estate tax on both estates is $197,044. If the estates were equalized and no credit were allowable, each would pay $153,000 or a total of $306,000. As indicated above, if a marital deduction of $400,000 were claimed in *W*'s estate, *H*'s estate would be subject to an estate tax of $320,000.

Some states have enacted statutes that are intended to reduce to six months the length of any administrative contingency that is annexed to a marital deduction gift. For example, the California statute provides as follows:

> (a) If an instrument that makes a marital deduction gift includes a condition that the transferor's spouse survive the transferor by a period that exceeds or may exceed six months, other than a condition described in subsection (b), the condition shall be limited to six months as applied to the marital deduction gift. Cal. Prob. Code §21525 (West 1991 Supp.)

In *Estate of Heim v. Commissioner,* 914 F.2d 1322 (9th Cir. 1990), the court held that the California statute only applies to provisions that indicate the transferor's intention to make a marital deduction gift. The gift in *Heim,* which required that the decedent's wife "survive distribution," was not saved by the statute, since it was a simple outright gift that made no reference to the marital deduction. According to the court, the statute could not "operate to reform the survivorship requirement in decedent's will, since there is insufficient evidence that decedent intended the gift to qualify for a marital deduction." 914 F.2d at 1329. The decision is a harsh one. Instead, the court should have presumed the decedent intended an outright gift to his surviving spouse to qualify for the marital deduction.

§5.20. Simultaneous Death

In the event of the spouses' simultaneous deaths, the Regulations provide that a presumption of survivorship provided by the local law, the decedent's will, or otherwise will be respected for marital deduction purposes.

> If the order of the deaths of the decedent and his spouse cannot be established by proof, a presumption (whether supplied by local law, the decedent's will, or otherwise) that the decedent was survived by his spouse will be recognized as satisfying paragraph (b)(1) of §20.2056(a)-1, but only to the extent that it has the effect of giving to the spouse an interest in property includible in her gross estate under Part III of subchapter A of Chapter 11. Reg. §20.2056(e)-2(e).

Under the basic rule of §1 of the Uniform Simultaneous Death Act, if there is no sufficient evidence that persons have died otherwise than simultaneously and no contrary directions were given by the decedents, the property of each decedent is disposed of as if he or she survived the other. 8A U.L.A. 561 (1983).

> **Example 5-15.** *H* and *W* died under such circumstances that there was no sufficient evidence that they died other than simultaneously. In the absence of the contrary direction in the will of *H,* his property will be disposed of as if he survived *W.* Similarly, the property of *W* will be disposed of as if she survived *H.* As a result neither estate is entitled to a marital deduction. However, the IRS would respect a provision in the will of either spouse that the other spouse should be deemed to have survived the testator in the event of their simultaneous deaths.

A substantial tax savings can be achieved through the proper use of such a clause (*e.g.,* if the gross estate of one spouse is much larger than that of the other and the will of the wealthier spouse makes gifts to the poorer spouse that equalize the sizes of their taxable estates). Where the dispositive plans of a husband and wife are harmonious, the wealthier spouse should consider including a simultaneous death clause sufficient to equalize the sizes of their taxable estates in such event. The approved language for a survivorship provision is, "if she [he] shall survive me for a period of six months." *See* Rev. Rul. 70-400, 1970-2 C.B. 196.

In the case of simultaneous deaths it is unlikely that a credit will be allowed under §2013 for the value of a life interest that was treated as having passed from one spouse to the other. For example, in *Estate of Andrew P. Carter,* 921 F.2d 63 (5th Cir. 1991), the court held that where the husband and wife died simultaneously the usufructuary interest of the one that was treated as the survivor under Louisiana law had no value. In doing so the court refused to apply the actuarial tables "to those situations in which the transferee and transferor of an indeterminate interest such as a usufruct die in a common disaster." The same result was reached in *Estate of Lion v. Commissioner,* 438 F.2d 56 (4th Cir.), *cert. denied,* 404 U.S. 870 (1971) and *Everard W. Marks, Jr.,* 94 T.C. 720 (1990). In *Marks,* which also involved Louisiana law, the Tax Court said that "it would be improper to ignore reality by placing (for tax purposes) a mythical value on the deemed surviving spouse's usufructuary interest." 94 T.C. at 729.

The U.P.C. extends the concept of requiring survivorship for a limited period to provide that an heir, and in the absence of a contrary direction a devisee, will be deemed to have predeceased a decedent unless the heir or devisee survives the decedent by 120 hours or more. U.P.C. §§2-104, 2-702 (1990). The provisions of both the Uniform Simultaneous Death Act and the U.P.C. may be overridden by a contrary direction in an individual's will. Neither provision jeopardizes the allowance of a marital deduction for interests that pass to the decedent's spouse. Rev. Rul. 76-166, 1976-2 C.B. 287.

The marital deduction is not preserved under §2056(b)(3) if the gift is contingent upon an event other than survivorship for a period of six months or less or death as the result of a common disaster. Specifically, no deduction is allowed if the gift is conditioned upon the occurrence or nonoccurrence of an administrative contingency such as admission of the decedent's will to probate or distribution of the decedent's estate.

> A decedent devised and bequeathed his residuary estate to his wife if she was living on the date of distribution of his estate. The devise and bequest is a nondeductible interest even though distribution took place within six months after the decedent's death and the surviving spouse in fact survived the date of distribution. Reg. §20.2056(b)-3(d), example 4.

A gift intended to qualify for the marital deduction should not require survivorship for more than six months or survivorship of the occurrence or nonoccurrence of an event.

§5.21. Estate Trust

> Although the trustee may accumulate the income during the surviving spouse's lifetime and retain unproductive property, the bequest to the Trust nevertheless qualifies for the marital

> deduction because the principal and any accumulated income is to be paid to the estate of the surviving spouse upon her death. LR 9109003 (TAM).

A second and possibly unintended exception to the terminable interest rule allows a marital deduction for interests that pass entirely to the surviving spouse or to his or her estate. The basic terminable interest rule denies a marital deduction for an interest passing to a surviving spouse *only* if an interest in the same property also passed "from the decedent to any person other than such surviving spouse (or the estate of such spouse)." §2056(b)(1). The parenthetical language has led to an interpretation of §2056 that allows a marital deduction for the full value of an interest that passes from the decedent to the estate of a surviving spouse, although the survivor receives little, if any, lifetime benefit from the property.

> [T]here are two types of transfers that may qualify a limited interest passing to the surviving spouse, such as a life estate, for the marital deduction. The first, which is illustrated in examples (i), (ii), and (iii) of section 20.2056(e)-2(b)(1) of the regulations, is the estate trust, that is a trust that provides that the income is payable to the surviving spouse for a term of years, or for life, or is to be accumulated, with all of the undistributed trust property passing to the surviving spouse's executor or administrator at her death. In these cases the interest to the surviving spouse qualifies for the marital deduction for the reason that she does not get a nondeductible terminable interest. No one other than the surviving spouse or her estate takes any interest in the property passing from the decedent. Rev. Rul. 72-333, 1972-2 C.B. 530.

Thus, a deduction is allowed for interests transferred in trust although the lifetime benefits of the surviving spouse are limited provided that the trust property is ultimately distributable to the surviving spouse's personal representative. The rule salvages the marital deduction where the trustee of a trust for a surviving spouse is given the discretionary power to accumulate the income of the trust or to retain unproductive assets. Rev. Rul. 68-554, 1968-2 C.B. 412.

The IRS disallowed the marital deduction for a trust the corpus of which was payable to the testamentary appointee of the surviving spouse, and in default of exercise thereof to his or her estate. Rev. Rul. 75-128, 1975-1 C.B. 308. According to the ruling the trust failed to qualify because the surviving spouse held a testamentary power of appointment over the property. Under Reg. §20.2056(e)-3 the possible appointees of such a power are considered persons to whom the deceased spouse passed an interest in the property.

The operation of Revenue Ruling 75-128 might be avoided if the decedent's will were construed to pass the absolute interest in the trust property to the personal representative of the surviving spouse, subject to the general testamentary power (*i.e.,* if the power were considered to be a "power appendant"). In such event the power should not be recognized at all. Where a person is given an absolute interest in property, any power also given to the same person is an invalid power appendant or a "lesser included interest," which may be disregarded. *See, e.g.,* V American Law of Property §23.13 (1952); Restatement, Property §325 (1940); Note, Appendant Powers of Appointment in the United States, 50 Harv. L. Rev. 1284 (1937). In any event, note that the deduction might be preserved in such a case if the surviving spouse disclaimed the power. The disclaimer would not be a qualified disclaimer under §2518 because of the surviving spouse's continuing power to dispose of the property by will. However, that power would prevent the disclaimer from having any adverse gift tax consequences. There is no evident policy or revenue reason to support the unnecessarily technical position taken in Revenue Ruling 75-128.

Thus far the estate trust exception has functioned most often to "save" the marital deduction for trusts that do not qualify for the life estate-power of appointment exception because of deficient draftsmanship. *See, e.g.,* Rev. Rul. 72-333, 1972-2 C.B. 530. However, the estate trust can be very useful in some cases. As mentioned above, it allows a trustee to be directed to retain unproductive property, such as recreational real property or interests in a family business, without jeopardizing the allowance of the marital deduction. Rev. Rul. 68-554, 1968-2 C.B. 412. In contrast, no deduction is allowable where the trustee of a life interest power of appointment trust is directed to retain unproductive property, unless the surviving spouse could compel the trustee to make the property productive or to convert it within a reasonable time. Reg. §20.2056(b)-5(f)(4) and (5).

An estate trust is also attractive because of the limitless range of provisions it allows to be made for the lifetime benefit of the surviving spouse. If the surviving spouse is expected to have a large income, the potential income tax savings of an estate trust make it preferable to an outright gift or a life interest power of appointment trust. The spouse could be adequately protected if the trustee were authorized to make discretionary distributions of income to him or her as needed to provide for care and support and to meet emergencies. Of course, any income accumulated by the trustee would be initially taxed to the trust and subject to the throwback rules when it is distributed to the surviving spouse or to his or her estate. *See* §§665-667. Under those rules an accumulation distribution is taxed as if the distributee had received equal amounts of the accumulated income in the years it was accumulated. *See* §10.4.10. Where an accumulation distribution is made to the surviving spouse's estate, little or no additional income tax is likely to be due because (1) the estate did not exist during the accumulation period and it necessarily had no other income and (2) the estate is entitled to a credit for the income tax paid by the trust on the accumulation distribution.

Under the prior rules regarding the in-kind distribution of appreciated property the trustee of an estate trust could make distributions that resulted in a tax-free increase in the basis of property. The opportunity was eliminated by the enactment of §643(e), under which the basis of property in the hands of a distributee is the estate's basis plus any gain recognized on the distribution at the election of the estate. Thus, an increase in the basis of the distributee is available only if the estate elects to recognize gain or loss upon all distributions made during the taxable year in the same manner as if the property had been sold to the distributees at fair market value.

For a variety of reasons the estate trust is not widely used. First, most lawyers are not familiar with the device. Second, some commentators are concerned about the validity and effect of a gift to the estate of a named person. *See* Fox, Estate: A Word to Be Used Cautiously, If at All, 81 Harv. L. Rev. 992 (1968); Huston, Transfers to the "Estate of a Named Person," 15 Syracuse L. Rev. 463 (1964); Browder, Trusts and the Doctrine of Estates, 72 Mich. L. Rev. 1507, 1517 (1975).

Third, and most important, the required distribution of the trust property to the surviving spouse's personal representative has some serious disadvantages. Most arise from the fact that the property will be subject to (1) claims of creditors against the estate of the surviving spouse, (2) claims of a subsequent spouse to an elective share under the law of common law property states should the surviving spouse remarry, (3) family awards, and (4) increased costs of estate settlement (particularly executor's commissions and attorney's fees). A distribution of property to the estate of the surviving spouse also involves some risk that the property will ultimately go to unintended takers (*e.g.,* the intestate successors of the surviving spouse). In addition, property distributed to the surviving spouse's estate may be subject to the state death tax although it might not be taxed under other circumstances (*e.g.,* if the surviving spouse held only a qualifying income interest for life and no power of appointment). Finally, a spouse may react negatively to a plan that does not assure him or her of all of the trust's income, but instead gives the trustee the discretionary power to make distributions.

§5.22. Life Interest General Power of Appointment Trust, §2056(b)(5)

Section 2056(b)(5) was unquestionably the most important exception to the terminable interest rule until the 1981 Act's addition of the exception for QTIP. *See* §5.23. Under this exception a deduction is allowed for an interest that passes to a surviving spouse to the extent the surviving spouse is entitled for life to all of the income from it (or a determinable portion of it) and the surviving spouse also holds a general power of appointment over it (or a corresponding part of it). As stated in Reg. §20.2056(b)-5(a), this exception applies only if all of the following five requirements are met:

1. The surviving spouse is entitled for life to all of the income from the entire interest, or a specific portion of the entire interest, or to a specific portion of all the income from the entire interest;
2. The income is payable to the surviving spouse annually or at more frequent intervals;
3. The surviving spouse is given the power to appoint the entire interest or the specific portion to himself or herself or to his or her estate;
4. The power in the surviving spouse is exercisable by him or her alone and (whether exercisable by will or during life) must be exercisable in all events; and
5. The entire interest or the specific portion is not subject to a power in any other person to appoint any part to any person other than the surviving spouse.

The exception is available whether the interests involved are legal or equitable (*i.e.*, in trust). As a matter of planning, however, the exception is used almost exclusively in connection with trusts. Under a comparable provision a marital deduction is allowable for insurance proceeds from which installment (or interest) payments are made to the surviving spouse, who also has a general power to appoint all amounts that remain at the time of his or her death. §2056(b)(6).

The use of this type of trust calls for very careful draftsmanship. A failure to satisfy any one of the requirements completely will deprive the estate of the spouse first to die of the deduction, although the surviving spouse is given sufficient interests in the property to cause it to be included in his or her estate.

Example 5-16. *H* died leaving his residuary estate to a trust in which *W* had the requisite life income interest. Under the trust *W* held a power exercisable jointly with her son, *S*, to appoint the corpus of the trust to whomever she wished. The power is not exercisable by *W* alone and in all events. Accordingly, under the pre-1982 law *H*'s estate was not entitled to a marital deduction, but the corpus of the trust would be included in *W*'s gross estate under §2041. If *S* made a qualified disclaimer of his power to join in appointing the corpus of the trust presumably the marital deduction would be allowable. No deduction would be allowable under the post-1981 law unless the power to appoint to persons other than *W* during her lifetime was effectively disclaimed and *H*'s executor elected to treat the property as QTIP under §2056(b)(7).

§5.22.1. Specific Portion

If the right to income or the power of appointment or both is limited to a specific portion of the property passing from the decedent, the marital deduction is allowable only to the extent of the specific portion. Prop. Reg. §20.2056(b)-5(c)(1). Bowing to the Supreme Court decision in *Northeastern Pennsylvania National Bank & Trust Co. v. United States,* 387 U.S. 213 (1967), the proposed Regulations recognize that a specified amount of income payable annually or more frequently out of the property and its income that is not limited by the income of the property constitutes a specific portion. Prop. Reg. §20.2056(b)-5(c)(3).

The Tax Court has allowed the marital deduction where the surviving spouse's power of appointment was limited to a specified dollar amount. *Estate of C. S. Alexander,* 82 T.C. 39 (1984), *aff'd in unpublished opinion* (4th Cir. 1985). Because of the possibility that all future appreciation in the value of the trust would be excluded from the estate of the surviving spouse, the IRS refuses to follow *Alexander.* The IRS position is made clear by Prop. Reg. §20.2056(b)-5(c)(3), which states that "no deduction will be allowable under section 2056(b)(5) except to the extent the surviving spouse has the required power of appointment *over a fractional or a percentile share* of the property." Id.

Example 5-17. *W* left her residuary estate of $1,000,000 to a trust for *H.* Under the terms of the trust *H* was entitled to all of the income and held a testamentary general power of appointment over "one-half" of the property of the trust. For purposes of §2056(b)(5) the marital deduction would be limited to one-half of the value of the property transferred to the trust. In this connection note that if a QTIP election were made, the marital deduction might be allowable for the entire value of the trust under §2056(b)(7). If *H* had been given a testamentary general power of appointment over only a specified dollar amount of the trust the outcome would be uncertain. The regulations indicate that no deduction is allowable under §2056(b)(5) in such a case. However, the Tax Court reached a contrary result in *Alexander, supra.* Here, again, note that a marital deduction might be allowable under §2056(b)(7) for the entire value of the trust.

The marital deduction is not allowed to the extent the property might be applied by a fiduciary in satisfaction of debts, taxes, or other expenses even though none of it is actually used for those purposes. *Estate of Wycoff v. Commissioner,* 506 F.2d 1144 (10th Cir. 1974), *cert. denied,* 421 U.S. 1000 (1975); Rev. Rul. 79-14, 1979-1 C.B. 309. For that reason, the governing instrument usually prohibits charging any taxes or expenses against the marital deduction gift.

The IRS has ruled that no deduction was allowable with respect to an otherwise qualifying marital deduction trust whose income was to be used to accumulate $10,000 within two years of the decedent's death to provide for the education of his grandchildren. Rev. Rul. 77-444, 1977-2 C.B. 341. "Unlike *Northeastern Pennsylvania National Bank* and [*Gelb v. Commissioner,* 298 F.2d 544 (2d Cir. 1962)], it is not possible in the instant case to determine any 'specific portion' as to which the income right of the surviving spouse relates." Id.

In some cases it may be advantageous and economical for a client to establish a single trust (a so-called "one lung" trust), a specific portion of which qualifies for the marital deduction under §2056(b)(5) and the remainder of which does not. Of course, this result is routinely reached by creating a QTIP trust with respect to which the decedent's executor elects to claim a partial marital deduction with only a bookkeeping segregation of the marital and nonmarital shares. If only one trust is created, savings in trustee's fees and administrative costs may result and greater diversification of investments may be possible. However, care must be exercised in funding the trust and allocating interests in it. Specifically, the surviving spouse's share should not include interests that do not qualify for the marital deduction.

§5.22.2. Frequency of Payment of Income

A trust instrument should ordinarily require income to be paid to the surviving spouse more often than annually for the convenience and protection of the beneficiary as well as to qualify for the marital deduction. For example, a trust might provide that "the trustee shall pay the net income of the trust to my surviving spouse in quarterly or more frequent installments." The marital deduction may be available although an instrument does not include any express direction regarding frequency of payment of the income to the surviving spouse. Under the Regulations, "silence of a trust instrument as to the frequency of payment will not be regarded as a failure to satisfy the condition . . . that income must be payable to the surviving spouse annually or more frequently unless the applicable law permits payment to be made less frequently than annually." Reg. §20.2056(b)-5(e). The statutory requirements are satisfied if the surviving spouse is given "substantially that degree of beneficial enjoyment of the trust property during her life which the principles of the law of trusts accord to a person who is unqualifiedly designated as the life beneficiary of a trust." Reg. §20.2056(b)-5(f). In some states the requirement is met by a statute that requires the income of a trust for a surviving spouse to be paid at least annually.

Delay in Payment. In general, the Regulations require the income to be distributed currently. Reg. §20.2056(b)-5(f)(8). An interest will not satisfy this requirement to the extent that the income must be or may be accumulated. Reg. §20.2056(b)-5(f)(7). Thus, no deduction is allowed with respect to a testamentary trust that provides that, after the net income from the trust for the past year has been determined, "such income shall be quarterly paid to my wife as long as she may live. . . ." Rev. Rul. 72-283, 1972-1 C.B. 311. A deduction will not be denied, however, "merely because the spouse is not entitled to the income from the estate assets for the period before distribution of those assets by the executor, unless the executor is . . . authorized or directed to delay distribution beyond the period reasonably required for administration of the decedent's estate." Reg. §20.2056(b)-5(f)(9). Consistent with that Regulation, a deduction was allowed for interests in a trust to be funded upon the settlor's death with assets from an inter vivos trust, where the trust instrument delayed funding the trust for a reasonable time until after the payment of all probate expenses and death taxes. Rev. Rul. 77-346, 1977-2 C.B. 340. In such cases, the delay in payment of the income is taken into account in valuing the interest passing to the surviving spouse. Reg. §20.2056(b)-4(a).

Income Distribution Must be Mandatory and Not Terminable. The surviving spouse's right to income cannot be directly limited by the trustee's discretion or otherwise. However, a trustee may be given some indirect control through the exercise of administrative powers, such as ones concerning the allocation of receipts and disbursements between principal and income. Reg. §20.2056(b)-5(f)(3). The determination of whether a particular trust meets the statutory requirement is based upon an overall consideration of the terms of the trust. A facility of payment clause that allows the trustee to pay the income to the surviving spouse or to apply it for his or her benefit is permissible. In contrast, no marital deduction is allowed if the distribution of income to the surviving spouse is discretionary in the event the survivor becomes incompetent. *See, e.g., Estate of Frank E. Tingley,* 22 T.C. 402 (1954), *aff'd sub nom. Starrett v. Commissioner,* 223 F.2d 163 (1st Cir. 1955). Similarly, no deduction is allowed if the amount of income payable to the surviving spouse may be reduced. Thus, no deduction was allowed where the surviving spouse was entitled to all of the income except such amounts as the trustee considered to be necessary to maintain the decedent's parents in their customary standard of living. Rev. Rul. 79-86, 1979-1 C.B. 311. In such a case the surviving spouse does not have an unqualified right to receive all of the income from any specified portion of the trust — an undetermined amount of the income could be diverted from the surviving spouse to the decedent's parents.

A marital deduction is not allowed if the distribution of income to the survivor will terminate or become discretionary upon the occurrence of some event such as the remarriage of the surviving spouse, his or her bankruptcy, or the attempted alienation of the beneficiary's interest in the trust. However, the deduction is not threatened merely because the instrument contains an orthodox spendthrift clause (*e.g.,* "that the right of the surviving spouse to the income shall not be subject to assignment, alienation, pledge, attachment or claims of creditors." Reg. §20.2056(b)-5(f)(7)).

Exercise Caution in Authorizing Retention of Unproductive Assets. Care should also be exercised in drafting provisions that direct or authorize the trustee to retain the assets transferred in trust. As previously indicated, such a provision may jeopardize the deduction to the extent of the unproductive assets. *See* Reg. §20.2056(b)-5(f)(4), (5). The deduction is allowable, however, if the instrument or the local law gives the surviving spouse power to require the trustee to "make the property productive or convert it within a reasonable time." Reg. §20.2056(b)-5(f)(4). The deduction is not jeopardized by a provision that permits the retention of "a residence or other property for the personal use of the spouse." Reg. §20.2056(b)-5(f)(4).

Give Spouse Power over Undistributed Income. The income that is accrued but undistributed at the time of the surviving spouse's death (the so-called "stub" income) must be subject to disposition by the surviving spouse. Reg. §20.2056(b)-5(f)(8). That requirement is satisfied if the stub income is either distributable as the surviving spouse appoints or as an asset of the surviving spouse's estate. Again, some states have enacted statutes that give the surviving spouse a power of appointment over stub income unless otherwise provided in the trust instrument. Note that the surviving spouse need not have such a power to dispose of the stub income of a QTIP trust. *Estate of Howard v. Commissioner,* 910 F.2d 633 (9th Cir. 1990), *rev'g* 91 T.C. 329 (1988). The decision in *Howard* upholds Prop. Reg. §20.2056(b)-7(c)(ii) which provides that "an income interest will not fail to constitute a qualifying income interest for life solely because income between the last distribution date and the date of the surviving spouse's death is not required to be distributed to the surviving spouse or the surviving spouse's estate."

Form 5-1. Payment of Income to Surviving Spouse (§2056(b)(5) Trust)

The entire net income of the trust shall be paid in quarterly or more frequent installments to my wife/husband. Any income that is received or accrued in the period between the date of the last distribution to my wife/husband and the date of her/his death shall be paid to the personal representative of her/his estate [shall be distributed as my wife/husband shall appoint]. My wife/husband may require the trustee to make productive any unproductive property of the trust or to convert it to productive property.

§5.22.3. Power of Appointment

The surviving spouse must have a power of appointment exercisable alone (without the required joinder of any other person) and in all events (not contingent upon any event), "in favor of such surviving spouse, or of the estate of such surviving spouse, or in favor of either, whether or not in each case the power is exercisable in favor of others." *See* §2056(b)(5); §2523(e). A power will satisfy the requirement if it is exercisable during the lifetime of the surviving spouse (*e.g.,* an unlimited power to invade), by will, or by a combination of inter vivos and testamentary powers. The Regulations recognize that the requirement may be satisfied by a combined power:

> [T]he surviving spouse may, until she attains the age of 50 years, have a power to appoint to herself and thereafter have a power to appoint to her estate. However, the condition that the spouse's power must be exercisable in all events is not satisfied unless irrespective of when the surviving spouse may die the entire interest or a specific portion of it will at the time of her death be subject to one power or the other (subject to the exception in §20.2056(b)-3, relating to interests contingent on survival for a limited period). Reg. §20.2056(b)-5(g)(1)(iii).

Form 5-2. Surviving Spouse's General Testamentary Power of Appointment (§2056(b)(5) Trust)

My wife/husband shall have the power by her/his last will to appoint all of the property of the trust, including all income then accrued but not yet received and all income received but not yet distributed, to or for the benefit of such persons, including her/his estate and creditors of her/his estate, upon such terms and conditions as she/he chooses, either outright or upon further trust.

Surviving Spouse May Hold Additional Powers of Appointment. If the surviving spouse has a power of the type required by the statute, it is immaterial that the survivor also holds other powers over the interest, such as a noncumulative power like that described in §§2041(b)(2) and 2514(e) to draw down the larger of $5,000 or five percent of the corpus each year (a "5 or 5" power). In addition, the trustee may hold powers to distribute trust principal to the surviving spouse. Additional powers should be planned with care, particularly if the trustee is also a beneficiary of the trust, whose interests may be affected by the exercise of the powers.

A 5 or 5 power to draw down provides the survivor with some additional independence and protection. A noncumulative 5 or 5 power given to a surviving spouse constitutes a power sufficient to support a marital deduction equal to the greater of 5 percent of the corpus of the trust or $5,000 even though the survivor is not given any other power of appointment over the trust corpus. *Estate of Jean C. Hollingshead,* 70 T.C. 578 (1978). Although the surviving spouse was entitled to all of the income of the trust for life, the deduction was limited to the amount subject to appointment under the 5 or 5 power at the time of the decedent's death because "any excess over 5 percent is not 'exercisable . . . in all events.' " 70 T.C. at 580. No marital deduction is allowable where the surviving spouse holds a 5 or 5 power and no income interest. LR 8202023.

A presently exercisable 5 or 5 power of withdrawal allows the surviving spouse to reduce the amount of property includible in his or her gross estate by withdrawing property and making annual gifts within the annual gift tax exclusion. Although all of the trust property may be included in the surviving spouse's estate in any case, the testator may wish to limit the survivor's right of withdrawal in order to assure the preservation of the trust principal and the continued source of support for the survivor. As the entire ordinary income of the trust will be taxed to the surviving spouse, the existence of a limited power of withdrawal will not be disadvantageous for income tax purposes. *See* §678. The income tax flexibility of the trust is reduced if the surviving spouse is given an unlimited inter vivos general power of appointment. In that event the capital gains of the trust will also be taxed to him or her. *See* §678(a)(1).

In the ordinary case the surviving spouse is given a general testamentary power of appointment over the entire trust. Accordingly, giving the surviving spouse a 5 or 5 power does not increase the amount of the trust that is includible in his or her estate. Consistently, the existence of the power does not increase the amount of the previously taxed property credit under §2013.

Mental Competency to Exercise Power Not Required. The mental incapacity of the surviving spouse under state law to exercise the power of appointment does not affect the allowance of the deduction under §2056(b)(5). If the trust otherwise qualifies, "the fact that the spouse is presently incapable of exercising a power of appointment over the interest by virtue of State law regarding legal incapacity does not require disallowance of the deduction." Rev. Rul. 75-350, 1975-2 C.B. 366 (testamentary power). *See* Rev. Rul. 55-518, 1955-2 C.B. 384 (inter vivos power). The former ruling is based upon a determination that the phrase "in all events does not refer to those events that State law has determined to be sufficient to deprive a person of control of his or her property during a period of physical or mental incompetency. Otherwise, in view of the fact that any given person may become legally incompetent during his or her lifetime, no trust could ever qualify under §2056(b)(5)." 1975-2 C.B. at 368. However, if the existence of the power is restricted by the terms of the instrument, the trust would not satisfy the requirements of §2056(b)(5).

In *Fish v. United States,* 432 F.2d 1278, 1280 (1970), the Court of Appeals for the Ninth Circuit held "the matter of the decedent's competency to be immaterial." *See also Estate of Alperstein v. Commissioner,* 613 F.2d 1213 (2d Cir. 1979), *cert. denied sub. nom. Greenberg v. Commissioner,* 446 U.S. 918 (1980); *Estate of Bagley v. United States,* 443 F.2d 1266 (5th Cir. 1971); *Estate of Gilchrist v. Commissioner,* 630 F.2d 340 (5th Cir. 1980); *Pennsylvania Bank & Trust Co. v. United States,* 597 F.2d 382 (3d Cir.), *cert. denied,* 444 U.S. 980 (1979). The same conclusion has been reached in cases concerning the inclusion of property in the estate of a minor under §2041. *Estate of Rosenblatt v. Commissioner,* 633 F.2d 176 (10th Cir. 1980); Rev. Rul. 75-351, 1975-2 C.B. 368 (property includible in estate of minor who held general testamentary power of appointment even though the minor could not execute a will under local law).

§5.23. Qualified Terminable Interest Property (QTIP), §2056(b)(7)

As noted above in §5.3, the 1981 Act also created new gift and estate tax exceptions to the terminable interest rule for property in which the transferor's spouse is given a qualifying income interest for life. §§2056(b)(7), 2523(f). In simple terms this exception allows decedent's executor to elect to claim a marital deduction for part or all of the value of property in which the transferee spouse is given a qualifying income interest for life. The deduction is allowable only if all of the income is payable to the surviving spouse annually or more frequently for life and no one has the power to appoint any of the property to a person other than the surviving spouse during his or her lifetime. A simple form of QTIP trust appears as Form 4-14 in §4.22.

The QTIP exception has two important features: (1) It can be claimed with respect to part or all of the transferred property in which the transferee spouse has the right to the income for life; (2) the surviving spouse need not be given any power of appointment over the trust. Naturally, any property for which an estate or gift tax marital deduction is claimed is includible in the estate of the transferee spouse. §2044. The basis of the property included in the donee spouse's estate under §2044 is stepped up under §1014. §1014(b)(10).

Overall, the QTIP exception is most similar to the one for a life interest general power of appointment trust. §2056(b)(5). *See* §5.22. However, in the case of a QTIP, the donee spouse need not be given any control over the ultimate disposition of the property. This makes the device particularly attractive to spouses who have children by previous marriages. For example, one spouse may be glad to provide a life income interest to the other spouse, provided that the property will ultimately pass to the descendants of the original owner.

As noted in §5.17, the IRS may disallow the marital deduction to the extent the property is subject to another person's option to purchase at a price other than fair market value. Accordingly, particular care must be exercised in planning marital deduction trusts if either spouse owns property that is subject to an option, including a buy-sell agreement.

§5.23.1. What is QTIP

"Qualified terminable interest property" is defined as property passing from the decedent in which the surviving spouse receives a qualifying income interest for life and with respect to which the decedent's executor makes an election under §2056(b)(7). §2056(b)(7)(B)(i). If the interest passing to the surviving spouse is a qualifying income interest for life, a deduction should be allowable — neither the passing nor the election requirement should pose any particular difficulty. Note, however, that the election "shall be made by the executor, on the return of tax imposed by Section 2001. Such an election, once made, shall be irrevocable." §2056(b)(7)(B)(v). For this purpose, the definition of the term "executor" provided in §2203 controls. Under it, the decedent's personal representative is the executor; if none is appointed, qualified, or acting, then the executor is any person in actual or constructive possession of the decedent's property. The election must be made on the return; it is not required to be made by the time fixed for filing the return (*i.e.,* normally nine months after the decedent's death). In LR 8335033, the IRS indicated that the trustee of a funded revocable trust could make the QTIP election where no personal representative of the decedent's estate had been appointed.

§5.23.2. Qualifying Income Interest for Life

Under §2056(b)(7)(B)(ii) a qualifying income interest for life must satisfy two basic requirements. First, the surviving spouse must be entitled for "life to all of the income from the entire interest, or all of the income from a specific portion thereof, payable annually or at more frequent intervals." H.R. Rep. 97-201, 97th Cong., 1st Sess. 161 (1981). Income interests for a term of years or until remarriage do not satisfy this requirement. However, a legal life estate or other nontrust interest may qualify if it gives the surviving spouse "rights to income which are sufficient to satisfy the rules applicable to marital deduction trusts under present [pre-1982] law." Id. Consistently, Prop. Reg. §20.2056(b)-7(c) provides for the application of the principles of Reg. §20.2056(b)-5(f) relating to whether the spouse is entitled for life to all of the income from the entire interest or a specific portion of the entire interest. Accordingly, care should be exercised if the trustee is authorized or directed to retain unproductive property (*e.g.,* unimproved real property, closely-held stock). In such a case the surviving spouse should be given the power to require the trustee to dispose of unproductive property or to convert it to productive property within a reasonable time. Note, however, that under Reg. §20.2056(b)-5(f)(4), "[A] power to retain a residence or other property for the personal use of the spouse will not disqualify the interest passing in trust."

Second, no one (including the transferee spouse) can have a power to appoint any part of the property subject to the qualifying income interest to any person other than the transferee spouse during his or her lifetime. As the House Ways and Means Committee pointed out, "This rule will permit the existence of powers in the trustee to invade corpus for the benefit of the spouse but will insure that the value of the property not consumed by the spouse is subject to tax upon the spouse's death (or earlier disposition)." H.R. Rep. 97-201, 97th Cong., 1st Sess. 161 (1981). Powers to appoint corpus to others are permissible provided that they are "exercisable only at or after the death of the surviving spouse." §2056(b)(7)(B)(ii). Note that the limitation restricts the time a power is exercisable and the nature of the interest subject to the power.

Example 5-18. *W* died leaving a trust from which her husband *H* was entitled to receive all of the income payable annually or at more frequent intervals. In addition, *H* was given the power, exercisable by deed or will, to appoint the remainder following his life income interest. The text of §2056(b)(7)(B)(ii) and of the House Committee Report both indicate that the possible exercise of the power during the surviving spouse's lifetime would bar a deduction from being allowed for the property unless he or she effectively disclaimed the power or its lifetime exercise.

§5.23.3. Additional Interests Surviving Spouse May Be Given in QTIP Trust

Giving the transferee spouse an unlimited power of withdrawal or other general power of appointment could negate the effect of a partial QTIP election with respect to a trust in which the surviving spouse was given a qualified income interest for life. In particular, an undisclaimed general power of appointment probably would require all of the property subject to the power to be included in the transferee spouse's estate under §2041. Indeed, if the transferee spouse's interest in the trust meets the requirements of both §2056(b)(5) and §2056(b)(7), it is not clear that the decedent's executor could elect to treat the property as QTIP under §2056(b)(7). Such a choice should be permitted, as there is no compelling reason to hold that the exceptions are mutually exclusive. In any event, under §2041 all property over which a decedent held a general power of appointment is includible in his or her estate. Such inclusion might result although the deceased spouse's executor claimed a marital deduction with respect to only part of the trust. §5.23.2. That is, the provisions of §2041 might override those of §2044 in such a case. Caution should be exercised in this regard until the uncertainties are clarified by Regulations or otherwise.

Example 5-19. *H* died in 1991 leaving his entire $1,000,000 estate to a trust from which *W* was entitled to receive all of the income for life. In addition, *W* was given a testamentary general power of appointment over the trust. *H*'s executor elected under §2056(b)(7) to claim a marital deduction with respect to 40% of the trust ($400,000). The tax on the other $600,000 was offset by *H*'s unified credit of $192,800. When *W* died a few years later the trust property was worth $2,000,000. If §2041 controls, the full $2,000,000 is includible in *W*'s estate. On the other hand, if §2044 controls, only $800,000 of the trust is includible in *W*'s estate (40% × $2,000,000).

The surviving spouse may be given nongeneral powers such as a 5 or 5 power of withdrawal. LR 8943005 (TAM) (upholding a 5 or 5 power to withdraw or to appoint the same to whomever she designates). Likewise, the deduction is not jeopardized if the surviving spouse is given a lifetime power of withdrawal limited by an ascertainable standard relating to the surviving spouse's health, education, support, or maintenance and a limited power over the ultimate disposition of the trust fund. In addition, the surviving spouse could safely be given a testamentary power to appoint the QTIP among a limited class of persons, such as those of the transferor's issue who are living at the time of the transferee spouse's death. Of course, as noted above, in order to be QTIP no one can have the power to appoint it to anyone other than the transferee spouse during his or her lifetime.

The Regulations also recognize that the trustee may be given power to distribute the principal of a QTIP trust to the donee spouse. "An income interest in a trust will not fail to constitute a qualifying income interest for life solely because the trustee has a power to distribute corpus to or for the benefit of the surviving spouse." Prop. Reg. §20.2056(b)-7(c)(1). The surviving spouse may feel more secure if he or she is given the power to make withdrawals subject to an ascertainable standard permitted by §§2041(b)(1)(B) and 2514(c)(1), or limited each year to the greater of $5,000 or five percent of the principal value of the trust under §§2041(b)(2) and 2514(e). *See* §§10.24-10.25.

§5.23.4. Partial QTIP Election

If the surviving spouse has a qualifying income interest for life in the entire trust, the executor may make a partial election in order to preserve the benefit of the deceased spouse's unified credit. However, the mandatory payment of all of the income to the surviving spouse may be disadvantageous. The payment to the surviving spouse of the income from the nonmarital share of the trust may unnecessarily subject it to high income taxes or increase the size of the surviving spouse's estate. Of course, the size of the surviving spouse's estate can be controlled to some extent by making annual exclusion gifts. If a client does not wish to require the payment of all of the income to the surviving spouse, he or she may prefer to establish a separate credit shelter trust whose income can be sprinkled among the client's surviving spouse and children by an independent trustee.

> **Example 5-20.** *H* left his entire estate in trust, the income from which is payable to *W* for life, remainder to those of their issue who survive *W*. *H*'s executor can elect to claim a marital deduction with respect to a specific portion of the property by making a timely election under §2056(b)(7). If the trust provided that *W* was entitled only to receive the income from the portion of the trust with respect to which *H*'s executor made a QTIP election, no deduction would be allowable under §2056(b)(7). In such a case *W*'s right to the income would be dependent on the election by *H*'s executor, who, in effect, holds a special power of appointment over the property.

If the executor makes a partial QTIP election with respect to a trust, the election must "relate to a fractional or percentile share of the property so that the elective part will reflect its proportionate share of the increment or decline in the whole of the property for purposes of applying sections 2044 and 2519." Prop. Reg. §20.2056(b)-7(a). A partial election should be made by use of a formula. *See* §12.20.2. If a partial election is made, the trust may be divided into separate trusts provided the fiduciary is required by the instrument or local law to make the division according to the fair market value of the assets of the trust at the time of the division. Once the division is made the trustee may direct that any distributions of principal to the surviving spouse should first be made from the marital deduction share. Prop. Reg. §20.2056(b)-7(e), example 11. This approach reduces the amount includible in the surviving spouse's estate under §2044.

A partial election is possible only if the surviving spouse has the requisite income interest with respect to the entire trust. In particular, the interest of the surviving spouse cannot be dependent upon the executor's election.

> [A]n income interest (or life estate) that is contingent upon the executor's election under paragraph (b)(3) of this section is not a qualifying income interest for life, regardless of whether the election is actually made. Prop. Reg. §20.2056(b)-7(c)(1); *see also* Reg. §20.2056(b)-7(e), example 7.

§5.23.5. Annuity Interests

If the surviving spouse is the only person to whom the decedent transferred an interest in an annuity, the interest is a deductible terminable interest. *See* §5.17.1. However, if an interest in an annuity may pass to another person upon the death of the surviving spouse, the interest of the surviving spouse may be treated as a qualified income interest under §2056(b)(7)(C). The issue may arise in connection with (1) an annuity payable the surviving spouse or (2) an annuity payable to a QTIP trust.

Under §2056(b)(7)(C), the surviving spouse's interest in an annuity that was included in the decedent's estate under §2039 is treated as a qualifying income interest if the surviving spouse is the only person entitled to receive any payment prior to the surviving spouse's death. §2056(b)(7)(C). Thus, a QTIP marital deduction would be allowable for an annuity that was payable to the surviving spouse for life with any balance at her death payable to other beneficiaries, such as their children. Note that under §2056(b)(7)(C)(ii) the executor is treated as having made a QTIP election with respect to such an annuity unless a contrary election is made on the decedent's estate tax return. The deductible interest is "the specific portion of the property (including an annuity contract) that, assuming the interest rate generally applicable for the valuation of annuities at the time of the decedent's death would produce income equal to the minimum amount payable annually to the surviving spouse for life." Prop. Reg. §20.2056(b)-7(c)(2). Accordingly, the value of the surviving spouse's annuity, determined according to the appropriate interest rate under §7520, may be more or less than the amount that was included in the decedent's estate under §2039. Thus, a portion of the amount included in the decedent's estate may be subject to the estate tax. The method of determining the deductible amount is illustrated by Prop. Reg. §20.2056(b)-7(e), examples 12-13.

A QTIP marital deduction is available where the surviving spouse is entitled to receive the remaining annual installments that are due under an IRA, which include all of the income earned on the remaining principal in the account plus a portion of the principal. Prop. Reg. §20.2056(b)-7(e), example 10. Also, a QTIP marital deduction is allowable with respect to an IRA, payments from which include all of the income earned by the IRA are made to a QTIP trust for the benefit of the surviving spouse. This opportunity was acknowledged by the IRS in Revenue Ruling 89-89:

> A decedent's executor can elect under section 2056(b)(7) of the Code to treat a decedent's IRA as qualified terminable interest property if (a) the decedent elected an IRA distribution option requiring the principal balance to be distributed in annual installments to a testamentary QTIP trust and the income earned on the undistributed balance of the IRA to be paid annually to the trust and (b) the trust requires that both the income earned on the undistributed portion of the IRA which it receives from the IRA and the income earned by the trust on the distributed portion of the IRA be paid currently to the decedent's spouse for life. Rev. Rul. 89-89, 1989-2 C.B. 231.

In this instance the marital deduction is available with respect to the entire amount of the IRA and not merely an amount determined in accordance with Prop. Reg. §20.2056(b)-7(C)(2). Note, however, that in order to meet the requirements of a QTIP, the payments from the IRA must be made to the surviving spouse beginning immediately after the decedent's death. Otherwise, distributions could be deferred until required by the minimum distribution rules.

Following Revenue Ruling 89-89, LR 9038015 holds that the QTIP marital deduction is allowable with respect to an IRA that is payable to a QTIP trust. In the letter ruling the executor was required to make the QTIP election with respect to the IRA, all of the income of which was directed to be payable to the QTIP trust and, from the QTIP trust, to the surviving spouse.

A slightly different approach was taken in LR 9043054, which involved the transfer of a portion of an IRA to a separate trust (IRA trust), distributions of which were required to be made to a QTIP trust (QTIP trust) of the greater of all of the income from the share of the IRA held in trust or the minimum amount that the IRA was required to distribute. In turn the QTIP trust was required to distribute all of the income received from the IRA trust to the surviving spouse. The ruling holds that the QTIP marital deduction is allowable with respect to the IRA trust and the QTIP trust. It appears that under the arrangement the QTIP trust was not required to distribute to the surviving spouse any distribution received from the IRA trust that was in excess of the income from the share of the IRA it held. In particular, any principal that was required to be distributed by the IRA would not have to be distributed to the surviving spouse.

§5.23.6. Transfer to Lifetime QTIP to Equalize Estates or to Preserve Use of Unified Credit

If one spouse is wealthier than the other, the overall gift, estate, and GSTT picture may be improved if the wealthier spouse makes a lifetime transfer to the poorer spouse, or to a QTIP trust for him or her. In particular, transfers to a QTIP can be used to equalize the sizes of their estates to enable the full use of the poorer spouse's unified credit or to make use of the poorer spouse's GSTT exemption.

> **Example 5-21.** *W*'s estate is worth $2,000,000 and her husband *H*'s only $200,000. *H,* who is terminally ill, intends to leave his property to their children. In order to avoid wasting part of *H*'s unified credit, *W* might transfer $400,000 to a trust in which *H* is given a qualified income interest for life, remainder to their children. If *H* were given a general power of appointment over the QTIP property *W* might retain a successive income interest in it.

Letter Ruling 8944009 indicates that a donor spouse can retain a successive life estate in the QTIP without causing it to be included in the donor spouse's gross estate, provided that the donee spouse is given a general power of appointment over the property. The ruling concludes that the trust would not be included in the donor spouse's estate under §2036(a). Apparently giving the donee spouse the power to appoint the property by will to creditors of her estate was sufficient to cut off the donor spouse's status as transferor for purposes of §2036(a).

§5.23.7. QTIP with Charitable Remainder

A marital deduction is allowable under §2056(b)(7) where the surviving spouse is given a qualifying income interest for life and the remainder is given to a charity. This possibility was noted in the following footnote in the House Committee Report:

> The general rules applicable to qualifying income interests may provide similar treatment where a decedent provides an income interest in the spouse for her life and a remainder interest to charity. If the life estate is a qualifying income interest, the entire property will, pursuant to the executor's election, be considered as passing to the spouse. Therefore, the entire value of the property will be eligible for the marital deduction and no transfer tax will be imposed. Upon the spouse's death, the property will be included in the spouse's estate but, because the spouse's life estate terminates at death, any property passing outright to charity may qualify for a charitable deduction. H.R. Rep. 97-201, 97th Cong., 1st Sess., 162, n.4 (1981).

Under §2044(c), property that is includible in the decedent's estate by reason of a QTIP election having been made is treated as having passed from the decedent for gift, estate, and GST tax purposes. Accordingly, the surviving spouse's estate should be entitled to a charitable deduction under §2055 for the value of the property included in his or her estate under §2044 that passes to a charity upon his or her death. LR 9008017, *Estate of John T. Higgins,* 91 T.C. 61 (1988) (dicta), *aff'd on other issues,* 897 F.2d 856 (6th Cir. 1990).

Note that a QTIP election is probably not permissible where the donee spouse is given an annuity interest in a charitable remainder trust. Under §2056(b)(7)(C) QTIP treatment is limited to annuities that were included in the decedent's estate under §2039. In such a case a marital deduction is exclusively allowable under §2056(b)(8).

§5.23.8. Use in Connection with Disclaimers

The opportunity to disclaim property exists independent of the §2056(b)(7) QTIP election. Thus, the surviving spouse may disclaim the right to receive property outright and cause the property to fall into a trust in which he or she has a qualifying income interest for life and with respect to which the executor can make a §2056(b)(7) election. Of course, a surviving spouse could also disclaim part or all of his or her interest in the trust. The disclaimed interest would pass according to the terms of the trust or, if there are none, according to the local law. Of course, it is essential for the surviving spouse and the executor to coordinate their planning with regard to the use of disclaimers and the §2056(b)(7) election. *See* §§12.31-12.35.

Example 5-22. *W* died in 1989 leaving her entire $900,000 estate to her husband *H* outright, provided that any property *H* disclaimed would pass to a QTIP trust for his benefit. The trust provided that upon *H*'s death the trust would terminate and the trust property would be distributed to their then living issue by right of representation. *H* disclaimed the right to receive any of *W*'s estate outright. Accordingly, all of her property passed to the trust. *H* also disclaimed all rights in 60% of the trust, which had a value equal to the credit equivalent ($600,000). Accordingly, a 60% interest in the trust property passed outright to the issue of *H* and *W*. The remainder of *W*'s property remained in trust for *H*. *W*'s executor elected under §2056(b)(7) to claim a marital deduction with respect to all of the property ($400,000) received by the trust. When *H* dies all of the trust property will be includible in his gross estate under §2044.

In some cases disclaimers may be used to eliminate powers or interests that otherwise prevent a trust from meeting the requirements of a QTIP. For example, a trust may fail to qualify because the trustee, the surviving spouse, or others have the power, during the lifetime of the surviving spouse, to cause income or principal to be distributed to persons other than the surviving spouse. *See, e.g.,* LR 8935024 (surviving spouse disclaimed lifetime power to appoint principal to children). If a disclaimer is not made in such a case no marital deduction would be allowable with respect to the trust. *See, e.g., Estate of Roger Bowling,* 93 T.C. 286 (1989) (QTIP marital deduction not available where trustee had power, during the lifetime of the surviving spouse, to invade principal for the benefit of the surviving spouse and others — no disclaimer attempted). A marital deduction was allowed in LR 8443005 (TAM) where the children disclaimed the right to receive discretionary distributions of income during the surviving spouse's lifetime. As a result the surviving spouse held a qualifying income interest. A fiduciary's attempt to disclaim a power to make discretionary distributions to persons other than the surviving spouse may not be recognized for gift and estate tax purposes — at least not a disclaimer that is not authorized by local law. Rev. Rul. 90-110, 1990-2 C.B. 209.

§5.23.9. Election and Authorization to Make Election

The election to claim the marital deduction with respect to part or all of the property that meets the requirements of §2056(b)(7) is made by the decedent's executor on the federal estate tax return. Considerations regarding the use of the election and the procedure for making the election are discussed in detail in §12.20. The Regulations recognize that the amount of the election can be expressed in a formula. The use of a formula guards against the necessity of paying some estate tax, which might otherwise result if the amount of the taxable estate were increased because of a change in the valuation of assets included in the gross estate or if some deductions were disallowed. *See* §12.20.2. For similar reasons, although the decedent's estate might not be required to pay any federal estate tax according to the federal estate tax return as filed, the decedent's executor might make a protective election. *See* §12.20.4.

A decedent's executor probably has the authority to make a QTIP election whether or not the executor is expressly given the power by the controlling instrument. However, it is desirable to eliminate any doubt by giving the executor such authority. It is also generally desirable to give the executor some guidance regarding the considerations that should govern the exercise of the power. Finally, the executor should be relieved from any liability that might otherwise result from exercise of the power. In this connection note that some states have enacted statutes that recognize the executor's right to make the election. Indeed, some statutes expressly relieve the executor from liability arising from a good faith exercise of the power. *E.g.,* Cal. Prob. Code §21526 (West 1991 Supp.) ("A fiduciary is not liable for a good faith decision to make any election or not to make any election referred to in Section 2056(b)(7) or Section 2523(f) of the Internal Revenue Code.") The inclusion of a provision that expressly empowers the executor to make the election should reduce the potential for conflict among the survivors and should insulate the executor from liability resulting from an exercise of the election.

Although the decedent may direct the executor to make the election with respect to all or some part of the property, it is unwise to do so because of the possibility that the unexpected may occur. For example, the surviving spouse may die shortly after the decedent. In such a case a directed election that resulted in the payment of no estate tax by the estate of the first spouse to die would prevent the estates from minimizing the overall estate tax burden through the use of the previously taxed property credit. On balance it is preferable to authorize the executor to make the necessary election and to give the executor some guidance regarding the criteria that should be considered in making the decision. A provision directing exercise of the election gives the executor less flexibility in planning post-mortem strategy. *See* Form 5-3. For other examples, see Ascher, The Quandary of Executors Who Are Asked to Plan the Estates of the Dead: The Qualified Terminable Interest Election, 63 N.C. L. Rev. 1, 48 (1983); Pennell, BNA 239-4th Tax Mgmt. Portfolio, Estate Tax Marital Deduction 45 (1990).

Form 5-3. Executor Authorized to Make Partial or Total QTIP Election

I authorize my executor, in her/his discretion, to elect to claim the federal estate tax marital deduction with respect to part, all, or none of the property that passes to the trust for the benefit of my wife/husband. My executor may make the election regardless of the impact that the election may have upon her/his interests, those of my wife/husband, or of any other person. In particular, I exonerate my executor from liability to anyone that results from a good faith exercise of her/his election, which shall be binding and conclusive upon all parties. I intend my executor to be free to make the election that she/he believes is in the best interests of my estate and its beneficiaries. In making the election I request that my executor consider the overall estate, gift and generation-skipping transfer tax increase or decrease that the election may have upon my estate and the estate of my wife/husband in light of her/his apparent financial status, health and life expectancy. My executor may also consider the amounts of property passing to my wife/husband and other beneficiaries of the trust under this will and pursuant to other arrangements.

§5.23.10. Disposition of Qualifying Income Interest in QTIP, §2519

Under §2519(a), if the donee spouse transfers all or any portion of the qualifying income interest, the donee will be treated as having transferred all of the QTIP. The transfer does not qualify for the annual gift tax exclusion. Of course, the transfer of the qualifying income interest itself also constitutes a gift, which does qualify for the annual gift tax exclusion. Any tax paid by the donor with respect to such a transfer may be recovered from the person receiving the transfer. §2207A(b). If the tax is entirely offset by the donor's unified credit it is unclear whether the statute gives the donor the right to recover any amount. Where some tax is recoverable, presumably the transaction will be taxed as a net gift (*i.e.,* the amount of the gift will be reduced by the gift tax paid by the donee). *See* §7.25.

The problem caused by the transfer of an interest in a qualifying income interest is illustrated by the following example from Prop. Reg. §25.2519-1(h):

Example (1). Assume that a decedent, *D,* owned at the time of death a personal residence valued at $250,000 for estate tax purposes; that such property passed under *D*'s will to *D*'s surviving spouse, *S,* for life and after *S*'s death to *D*'s children; and that *D*'s executor elected to treat that property as qualified terminable interest property on the estate tax return for *D*'s estate. During 1988, *S* makes a gift of all of *S*'s interest in the property to *D*'s children, at which time the fair maket value of the property is $300,000 and the value of *S*'s life interest in the property is $100,000. Pursuant to section 2519, *S* is treated as making a gift in the amount of $200,000 (which is the fair market value of the qualified terminable interest property less the fair market value of the life interest in such property). In addition, *S* is treated pursuant to section 2511 as making a gift of $100,000 (which is the fair market value of *S*'s income interest in the property). *See* §§25.2511-2 and 25.2514-1(b)(2).

In order to guard against inadvertently subjecting the property to the gift tax, the trust might prohibit the surviving spouse from disposing of all or any part of the income interest without the consent of the trustee or another responsible party. The inclusion of such a spendthrift provision is permitted by the Regulations in the case of life interest-general power of appointment trusts, Reg. §20.2056(b)-5(f)(7), and has been permitted in some letter rulings dealing with QTIP trusts. *E.g.,* LR 8521155; LR 8532006. Spendthrift clauses are discussed in detail at §4.24.8.

§5.23.11. Estate Tax on Surviving Spouse's Death

Unless otherwise directed in the surviving spouse's will, the estate tax attributable to the property included in his or her estate under §2044 is recoverable by his or her executor from the recipients of the property. §2207A(a). Thus, the inclusion of the property in the surviving spouse's estate ordinarily will not increase the amount of estate tax payable from the surviving spouse's property. Under §2207A(a)(1) the surviving spouse's executor has the right to recover the entire additional amount of tax incurred by reason of the inclusion of the QTIP in the surviving spouse's gross estate. The right of recovery extends to any penalties and interest attributable to the additional taxes. §2207(c). Where the §2044 property is distributed to more than one person, the right of recovery may be asserted against each of them. §2207A(d). New York and some other states provide that a general direction to pay all taxes due by reason of the testator's death is not to be construed to apply to the taxes imposed on QTIP property includible in the surviving spouse's estate under §2044. N.Y. Est. Powers & Trusts Law §2-1.8 (McKinney 1990 Supp.).

Example 5-23. *H* died in 1988 leaving an estate of $1,000,000 to a QTIP trust. His executor elected to claim the marital deduction with respect to $400,000 of the property. Accordingly, no estate tax was paid by *H*'s estate. When his wife *W* died in 1992 her taxable estate of $1,100,000 included $500,000 that was includible in her estate under §2044 (40% of the value of the trust in 1992, $1,250,000). *W*'s will did not contain any directions regarding the source of payment of the estate tax. The tax on *W*'s $600,000 in property was entirely offset by the unified credit of $192,800. *W*'s estate is subject to a tax of $194,000, all of which is recoverable by *W*'s executor from the distributees of the QTIP property.

Tax on estate of $1,100,000	$386,800
Less:	
Tax payable without inclusion of QTIP property	192,800
Tax payable by QTIP distributees	$194,000

As noted before, a similar right of recovery applies with respect to the gift tax imposed on the inter vivos disposition of part or all of a qualifying income interest. §2207A(b). It is recoverable by the transferee spouse (the donor of the qualifying income interest) from the recipients of the property.

§5.24. CURRENT INTEREST IN CHARITABLE REMAINDER TRUST, §2056(b)(8)

> If any individual transfers property outright to charity, no transfer taxes generally are imposed. Similarly, under the unlimited marital deduction provided in the committee bill, no tax generally will be imposed on an outright gift to the decedent's spouse. As a result, the committee finds no justification for imposing transfer taxes on a transfer split between a spouse and a qualifying charity. Accordingly, the bill provides a special rule for transfers of interest in the same property to a spouse and a qualifying charity. H.R. Rep. 97-102, 97th Cong., 1st Sess., 162 (1981).

The 1981 Act also created an exception to the terminable interest rule for the current interest in charitable remainder trusts where the surviving spouse is the only noncharitable beneficiary. §2056(b)(8). A corresponding gift tax exception applies where the donor's spouse and the donor are the only noncharitable beneficiaries. §2523(g). Accordingly, a transfer to a charitable remainder unitrust qualifies for a charitable deduction under §2055 (or §2522) for the value of the charitable remainder interest and a marital deduction under §2056 (or §2523) for the value of the current (annuity or unitrust) interest. A gift tax return is not required on account of the marital deduction gift, but one probably is required to claim the charitable deduction. Note that an inter vivos gift of this type will also qualify for an income tax charitable deduction under §170. Unlike the QTIP, under this approach upon the death of the donee spouse nothing is includible in his or her gross estate by reason of the existence of the charitable remainder trust.

§5.25. Qualified Domestic Trust (QDT), §§2056(d), 2056A

Under the general rule of §2056(d), the estate tax marital deduction is not allowable for transfers to a surviving spouse for which the marital deduction would otherwise be available if the surviving spouse is not a U.S. citizen. The intention of this rule is to assure that the property for which the marital deduction is allowed in a decedent's estate will be subject to the gift or estate tax. The several exceptions to the rule are all fashioned to provide the necessary assurance. In brief, the restriction imposed by the basic rule is lifted with respect to otherwise qualifying transfers if any of the alternative requirements discussed below are satisfied.

The first allows the deduction if the surviving spouse was a U.S. resident at all times following the decedent's death and becomes a citizen before the decedent's estate tax return is filed. §2056(d)(4). A failure to become a citizen before the return must be filed eliminates this option. LR 9021037. However, note the opportunity under §2056A(b)(12), discussed below, to escape from §2056A if the surviving spouse later becomes a citizen.

Under the second, the deduction is available with respect to property that passes from the decedent to a QDT. §2056(d)(2)(A). Property passing to the surviving spouse is treated as having passed to a QDT if either the property is transferred to a QDT before the decedent's tax return is filed or the property is irrevocably assigned to a QDT before the return is filed. §2056(d)(2)(B). Property that the surviving spouse receives as surviving joint tenant, beneficiary of life insurance or employee benefit plans, or by bequest may be transferred to a QDT. LR 8952005; LR 9044072 (life insurance proceeds). Note, however, that the transfer of property to a QDT might subject the remainder interest to the gift tax unless the surviving spouse retains a power sufficient to make the transfer incomplete under Reg. §25.2511-2.

Finally, the determination of whether or not a trust is a QDT is made on the date the decedent's return is filed. However, if a reformation action is filed on or before that date, the changes made to the trust in that proceeding will be taken into account. §2056(d)(5)(A). According to the IRS a trust reformation will be recognized only if the marital deduction would have been allowable with respect to the trust but for the citizenship of the surviving spouse. LR 9043070.

§5.25.1. QDT

Under §2056A(a) a QDT trust must require that

1. At least one trustee must be an individual citizen of the United States or a domestic corporation; and
2. No distribution (other than income) can be made unless the trustee who is a citizen of the United States or a domestic corporation has the right to withhold from the distribution the tax on distributions imposed by §2056A.

In addition, the trust must meet such requirements as the Secretary may by regulation prescribe in order to assure the collection of any tax imposed by §2056A(b). In light of this requirement, the trust might authorize the trustee to amend the trust from time to time as required to comply with regulations issued pursuant to §2056A. Finally, the decedent's executor must make an irrevocable election on the decedent's estate tax return to treat the trust as a QDT. §2056A(d). No election can be made on a return filed more than one year after the time prescribed for filing the return, including extensions. Bear in mind that the marital deduction is only allowable if the trust also meets the requirements of §2056(b) (*e.g.,* a life interest-general power of appointment trust, an estate trust, or QTIP trust).

§5.25.2. Tax on Distributions from QDT

In general any distribution from a QDT made before the death of the surviving spouse and any property remaining in a QDT at the time of the death of the surviving spouse is subject to an estate tax at the marginal rate applicable to the estate of the deceased spouse who created the trust. §2056A(b). Upon the death of the surviving spouse the benefits of §§303, 2011, 2014, 2032, 2032A, 2055, 2056, 6161, and 6166 are available. Recognizing that the QDT may attract a §2056A tax and a regular estate tax imposed on the estate of the surviving spouse, §2056(d)(3) allows a credit under §2013 for the §2056A tax without regard to the date of the death of the first spouse to die.

Example 5-24. *H* died in 1990 leaving $2,000,000 to a QDT for his wife, *W. W* was not a U.S. citizen. *H* also left $600,000 to a trust for his children by a prior marriage. *H*'s estate paid no estate tax. In 1991 $400,000 of principal was distributed to *W* from the QDT. The distribution was subject to a §2056A estate tax of $153,000. In 1992 *W* died a resident of the United States and left an estate of $2,000,000 including the QDT. *W*'s estate is entitled to a credit under §2013 for the tax paid pursuant to §2056A in connection with the distribution of property to her.

The §2056A estate tax does not apply to any distribution of income to the surviving spouse or to any distribution to the surviving spouse on account of hardship. §2056A(b)(3). Although hardship is not defined in the statute, some guidance is provided by the Regulations under §401(k). For example, "a distribution is on account of hardship only if the distribution both is made on account of an immediate and heavy financial need of the employee and is necessary to satisfy such financial need." Reg. §1.401(k)-1(d)(2). An immediate and heavy financial need might occur in connection with the funeral expenses of a family member, but not to pay for recreational expenses such as the purchase of a boat.

The §2056A tax on distributions is due on April 15 of the year following the calendar year in which the distribution was made. §2056A(b)(5)(A). The tax on the death of the surviving spouse is due nine months after the date of death. §2056A(b)(5)(B). Each trustee is personally liable for the tax. §2056A(b)(6). A lien for the §2056A tax is imposed for ten years under §6324 as if the tax were an estate tax. §2056A(b)(8).

§5.25.3. Surviving Spouse Becomes Citizen

A trust is no longer subject to the §2056A tax if the surviving spouse becomes a citizen and the following requirements of §2056A(b)(12) are met:

1. The surviving spouse was a U.S. resident at all times after the date of death of the decedent and before the surviving spouse became a citizen; and
2. No §2056A tax was imposed on distributions before the surviving spouse became a citizen, *or,* the surviving spouse elects to treat any taxable distributions as taxable gifts made by her for purposes of the gift and estate taxes.

§5.26. Choosing the Form of the Trust — Summary

The particular circumstances of the clients and their desires will determine which form of marital deduction trust, if any, should be used. Since 1981 the QTIP trust has become the dominant form of marital deduction trust, displacing almost entirely the life interest-general power of appointment trust. Both types of trust eliminate the necessity of administering the trust property upon the death of the surviving spouse. Two main factors account for the popularity of the QTIP form of trust. First, in the case of a QTIP the surviving spouse need not be given any power over the ultimate disposition of the property. Second, the amount of the marital deduction claimed with respect to a trust that meets the requirements of §2056(b)(7) is elective. Also, clients with large estates that may involve the GSTT may benefit from the flexibility provided by the possibility of making a reverse QTIP election for GSTT purposes under §2652(a)(3). Finally, lawyers probably feel more comfortable using a trust of the QTIP variety because it more closely resembles the traditional form of family trust.

On the other hand, the estate trust is useful in some circumstances, particularly where the surviving spouse does not need to be assured of additional lifetime income. The charitable remainder trust may be attractive to clients in special circumstances (*e.g.,* ones with no children and a strong desire to benefit one or more charities). Of course, all four types of trusts provide for the management of property during the surviving spouse's lifetime. With the exception of the estate trust the trusts also generally insulate the trust property corpus from the surviving spouse's creditors.

§5.27. Savings Clause

The IRS and the courts give some recognition to clauses that express the decedent's intent that the provisions of the instrument be interpreted and applied so as to sustain the allowance of the marital deduction. Such a clause may save a marital deduction where a particular power, duty, or discretion of the trustee might otherwise bar the deduction. For example, Rev. Rul. 75-440, 1975-2 C.B. 372, held that a disqualifying power to invest in nonincome-producing property applied to the residuary trust but not to the marital deduction because of the decedent's intent as expressed in a savings clause. Consistently, LR 8440037 held that the marital deduction was available because a savings clause prevented the application to the marital deduction trust of a boilerplate provision that allowed the trustee to invest in or retain unproductive property. However, a savings clause is generally ineffective to overcome the effect of a disqualifying power that is clearly applicable to the trust intended to qualify for the marital deduction. The IRS and some courts have refused to recognize "condition subsequent" clauses that purport to revoke powers that apply to the trust in the event the powers are determined to prevent allowance of the marital deduction. Thus, in Rev. Rul. 65-144, 1965-1 C.B. 442, the IRS refused to give effect to a clause that attempted to revoke the powers of the trustee to the extent necessary to make the interest deductible for federal tax purposes.

Overall, it is worthwhile to include a savings clause in an instrument that is intended to generate a marital deduction. *See* Johanson, The Use of Tax Savings Clauses in Drafting Wills and Trusts, U. Miami, 15th Inst. Est. Plan., ch. 21 (1982). The clause provides some assurance that the instrument will be interpreted and applied in a sympathetic way. However, such a clause should not be relied upon to provide any protection against disqualifying provisions that clearly apply to the gift intended to support the marital deduction. A savings clause might be drafted along these lines:

Form 5-4. Marital Deduction Savings Clause

I intend that the property passing from me to the trustee of the trust for the benefit of my wife/husband shall qualify for the federal estate tax marital deduction. Accordingly, I direct that all provisions of this will shall be interpreted and applied in a manner consistent with my intention.

D. THE GIFT TAX MARITAL DEDUCTION

§5.28. Overall Considerations

Two changes made by the 1981 Act sharply reduced the tax advantages of making inter vivos gifts to a spouse. They were (1) the adoption of the unlimited marital deduction and (2) the enactment of a much larger unified credit. Together the changes compressed the estate and gift tax rates. Prior to 1982 lifetime gifts to a spouse were frequently used to equalize the size of the estates of the donor and donee and to maximize the amount of property that could be passed to a spouse free of tax. Despite the 1981 changes, lifetime gifts to a spouse retain some tax advantages, particularly where the estates of the spouses are of widely disparate sizes. The potential for savings is more obvious if the estate of one spouse is below the amount of the credit equivalent.

Of course, the desirability of making substantial gifts to a spouse should depend in large measure upon nontax factors, including the stability of the marriage. In the nature of things few individuals will make outright gifts of a substantial portion of their wealth to a spouse under any circumstances. In some cases a large gift may help to cement the relationship between the spouses by providing tangible evidence of the donor's affection for, and confidence in, the donee. The desirability of each spouse's having control over some assets and of holding others in the names of both spouses should also be recognized. However, an unanticipated dissolution proceeding may negate the "tax advantages" of gifts, including: inter vivos assignments of life insurance policies, *Moser v. Moser,* 572 P.2d 446 (Ariz. 1977); private annuities, *Stanger v. Stanger,* 571 P.2d 1126 (Idaho 1977); and other estate planning devices, *Marriage of Hadley,* 565 P.2d 790 (Wash. 1977) (agreements regarding status of assets as community or noncommunity property). A lawyer who participates in a plan which involves substantial gifts from one spouse to the other should be alert to the conflict of interest that exists if both parties look to the lawyer for advice.

§5.29. General Objectives of Inter Vivos Gifts

Some of the general objectives of making inter vivos gifts also apply in planning gifts to a spouse. First, an interspousal gift removes from the donor's estate any future appreciation in value of the property transferred. Of course, the significance of this objective was reduced by the adoption of the unlimited marital deduction — tax-free gifts can be made to a spouse at any time regardless of their value. Second, such a gift may reduce the value of the nonbusiness assets owned by the donor so the business holdings retained by the donor will constitute a large enough proportion of his estate to qualify for the special tax benefits of §§303, 2032A, or 6166. However, gifts made within three years of the donor's death are brought back into the donor's estate for purposes of §§303, 2032A, and 6166. §2035(d)(3). Third, inter vivos gifts to a spouse can also serve to equalize the sizes of the spouses' estates and to create an estate for the poorer spouse in order to take advantage of the donee spouse's unified credit should he or she predecease the donor. This advantage may be secured by making a gift to a QTIP trust for the poorer spouse. As indicated above, a letter ruling indicates that the donor may retain a successive life estate in the trust without requiring the property to be included in the donor's estate under §2036 if the donee spouse is given a general power of appointment over the property. LR 8943005. A gift to the poorer spouse may also preserve the use of the poorer spouse's GSTT $1 million exemption.

Gifts to a spouse generally yield little, if any, income tax benefit because married persons usually benefit from filing joint income tax returns.

§5.30. Equalizing Estates by Lifetime Gifts

The general importance of equalizing the sizes of the spouses' estates is reviewed in §5.7. Lifetime equalization may be undertaken to ensure that the wealthier spouse will be able to transfer some property at lower tax cost via the poorer spouse's estate. If inter vivos gifts are made, the spouses' dispositive instruments should be reviewed to be sure the provisions are compatible with the gifts. For example, it may be necessary to scale down the amount of the gifts made to the donee in the donor's will to avoid unduly increasing the donee's estate. Also, the donee should plan to dispose of the gifted property in a tax-sensitive way consistent with their overall dispositive goals. For example, the donee spouse's will should be drafted so the gifted property will not return to the donor or otherwise be included in the donor's gross estate.

As a result of the adoption of the unlimited marital deduction, it is ordinarily no more advantageous to make lifetime equalizing gifts during lifetime than it is to do so at death if the wealthier spouse dies first. However, inter vivos gifts are an effective hedge against the possibility that the opportunity to equalize will be lost by the unexpected prior death of the less wealthy spouse.

The sizes of the estates may be equalized without depriving the donor of assets of substantial current value by making gifts of life insurance. For example, the spouse with the smaller estate may be given policies of insurance on the other spouse's life or funds with which to acquire new policies. Alternatively, the insurance might be transferred to an irrevocable life insurance trust. *See* §§6.16-6.24.

§5.31. Using Lifetime Gifts to Take Advantage of the Poorer Spouse's Unified Credit

Where the estate of one spouse substantially exceeds the amount of the credit equivalent and the estate of the other is substantially less than the credit equivalent, steps should be taken to assure that the shelter provided by the poorer spouse's credit is fully utilized.

Example 5-25. *W*'s estate is worth $1,000,000 while her husband *H*'s estate is worth only $50,000. If *H* predeceases *W*, most of his unified credit will be wasted. *W* should consider making a substantial gift to *H*, which he could leave to a QTIP trust for the benefit of *W* if he predeceases her.

There may be some tax advantages to transferring property to a terminally ill spouse whose estate is less than the credit equivalent. However, the bases of appreciated assets given to the decedent within a year of death are not increased if the decedent transfers them back to the original donor (or his or her spouse). §1014(e). Care should also be exercised in discussing transfers to or from a terminally ill spouse because of the possibility that the clients will react negatively to using tax advantages they perceive as derived from the spouse's illness and death. Also, if such a gift is made, it may be necessary to change the content of the donee's will in order to take full advantage of the tax savings plan. The lawyer and client must also consider how the gifts would affect other dispositive plans and how they would be viewed by other members of the donor's family.

If the technique is used, highly appreciated assets (*i.e.,* ones with low bases) should normally be transferred to the terminally ill spouse. Their bases would be increased the most by the stepped-up basis the assets would acquire under §1014 upon the donee's death.

E. EXPRESSING A MARITAL DEDUCTION GIFT — FORMULA AND NONFORMULA GIFTS

§5.32. Overview

Property may pass to a surviving spouse in a variety of ways that qualify for the marital deduction. *See* §2056(c) and §5.16. Because property commonly passes to a surviving spouse and others under several will substitutes (*e.g.,* joint tenancies, life insurance beneficiary designations, multiparty bank accounts), the lawyer should assist the client in reviewing, analyzing, and organizing the client's property. Estate plans often use a formula to define the portion of the transferor's estate that will pass to the surviving spouse in a way that qualifies for the marital deduction. The formulas used for this purpose are designed to assure that the plan will make use of the transferor's unified credit to shelter a portion of the transferor's estate from inclusion in the surviving spouse's estate. Prior to the adoption of the unlimited marital deduction the formulas were usually designed to give the surviving spouse a portion of the transferor's estate equal to the maximum allowable marital deduction.

Two basic formulas were developed in response to the problem of transferring precisely the right amount of property to the surviving spouse (or to a qualifying trust) to support the maximum marital deduction. The formulas generally sought to avoid "overfunding" the marital deduction gift. Both formulas gave the surviving spouse property equal in value to the maximum allowable marital deduction *less* the value of all other property for which the deduction was available. One formula gave the surviving spouse *an amount* of property equal to the maximum allowable marital deduction (the *pecuniary formula*); the other gave the survivor *a fractional interest* in a designated portion of the testator's estate (the *fractional share formula*). Both types of formula have been adapted for use in connection with the unlimited marital deduction. *See* §§5.33-5.40. The revised formulas are designed to preserve the testator's unified credit by limiting the amount of property passing to the surviving spouse in ways that would require the inclusion of the property in the estate of the surviving spouse.

Before turning to a consideration of the formulas it should be noted that it is unnecessary to use formula marital deduction gifts in some cases. First, it is unnecessary to use a formula when the shelter provided by the testator's unified credit will not be needed (*i.e.,* where the value of the spouse's combined estates is likely to be less than the amount of a single credit equivalent ($600,000) when the surviving spouse dies). In such a case the testator may choose to leave all of his or her estate outright to the surviving spouse. Thus, the plan for a young couple whose estates are small may provide for an outright gift of all of the testator's property to the surviving spouse with a contingent gift to a trust for their minor children. Such a plan is discussed in detail in Chapter 4. Of course, this approach involves some speculation about the value the couple's property will have and the amount of the unified credit that will be available to the surviving spouse's estate.

Second, although the spouses' estates may be large enough to generate some tax on the death of the surviving spouse, the testator may choose to rely upon the surviving spouse's use of qualified disclaimers to adjust the amount of property that passes to him or her. In its simplest form this approach merely involves an outright gift of the testator's entire estate to the surviving spouse with no special provision for the disposition of any property disclaimed by the surviving spouse. In such a case the distribution of any disclaimed property would be determined by the local law. For example, if the surviving spouse disclaims a one-half interest in the testator's residuary estate, the interest would pass to the testator's intestate successors. In order to assure that the disclaimed property will pass to others, the surviving spouse must also disclaim the right to receive any interest in the property by intestate succession. It should be recognized that the surviving spouse may be incompetent to execute a valid disclaimer, which can jeopardize the plan unless an effective disclaimer can be made by a guardian or other personal representative. Also, the surviving spouse may be unwilling to disclaim any property because it will pass outright to others and will not be directly available to support him or her.

Under a more sophisticated approach, the testator's will provides for the disposition of any property disclaimed by the surviving spouse. The will might call for any disclaimed property to pass outright to designated persons or to a QTIP trust (*i.e.,* one in which the surviving spouse has a qualifying income interest for life). If the disclaimed property passes to a QTIP trust, the testator's executor can control the amount of the marital deduction through exercise of the QTIP election under §2056(b)(7). As a further embellishment such a plan might provide that if the surviving spouse also disclaims any interest in the QTIP trust, that portion of the property will pass outright to designated persons (or to trusts for their benefit).

A formula is also unnecessary if the transferor wishes to leave the bulk of his or her estate to a QTIP trust, thus relying upon the executor's election under §2056(b)(7) to produce the optimum tax result. Here again, the testator could provide for the disposition of any interest in the trust that is disclaimed by the surviving spouse.

Example 5-26. *W,* who died in 1991, left her $1,500,000 estate outright to her husband *H* if he survived her, otherwise to those of their adult children who survive her. *W* was survived by *H* and their two adult children, *S* and *D. H* disclaimed the right to receive property from *W*'s estate that had a value equal to the amount of the credit equivalent available to *W*'s estate ($600,000). The disclaimed property passed directly to *S* and *D.* Accordingly, it will not be includible in *H*'s gross estate. *W*'s unified credit offset the amount of tax due from her estate on the disclaimed property. The $900,000 remainder passed to *H.* Unless disposed of by *H* during his lifetime it will be included in his estate.

Example 5-27. *H* died in 1992, leaving his estate of $750,000 to a trust in which his wife *W* had a qualifying income interest for life. *H*'s executor elected under §2056(b)(7) to claim a marital deduction with respect to an interest in the trust that had a value of $150,000 (a 20% interest). The election took advantage of *H*'s unified credit by sheltering most of the trust from inclusion in *W*'s estate (*i.e.,* 80% of the trust will not be included in *W*'s estate).

Finally, the testator may choose to approximate the effect of a formula clause by making a pecuniary nonmarital deduction (or "credit shelter") gift of an amount equal to the credit equivalent and leaving the balance of his or her estate to the surviving spouse. While this approach may not yield the optimum tax result, it is simple and easy to understand. The nonmarital pecuniary gift might be expressed along the lines suggested in Form 5-5.

Form 5-5. Nonformula Pecuniary Nonmarital Deduction Gift

If my husband/wife survives me, I give to A, B, & C Trust Company, in trust, subject to the terms of Article Ten [a nonmarital trust], property of my estate equal in value to $600,000, or such greater or lesser amount as may be equal to the federal unified credit equivalent allowable at the time of my death.

The amount of such a gift would more closely approximate the credit equivalent if it were reduced by the amount of the testator's adjusted taxable gifts (*i.e.,* taxable gifts made after 1976) and other dispositions or expenses that are not deductible in computing the federal estate tax (*e.g.,* expenses of administration that are not claimed as federal estate tax deductions).

Overall, perhaps the most flexible plan involves the creation of a QTIP trust for the surviving spouse with provision for the disposition of any interest in the trust that he or she disclaims. This disclaimed interest might pass into a family trust with respect to which the trustee would have discretion to distribute the income, and perhaps the principal, to a class consisting of the surviving spouse and the testator's descendants. Note that the surviving spouse's disclaimer would not be a qualified disclaimer if the surviving spouse held discretionary powers over the distribution of the income or principal. *See* Reg. §25.2518-2(e)(5), example 5. *See also* §12.32.4. The use of a QTIP trust allows the choice regarding the size of the marital deduction to be made after the testator's death when many more facts are known. However, unless the surviving spouse is able to disclaim the credit equivalent amount into a family trust, the use of a QTIP trust may cause the surviving spouse to receive too much income. In this connection recall that the surviving spouse *must* receive all of the income from a QTIP, which may increase the overall income tax burden and may bloat the size of the surviving spouse's estate.

§5.33. An Assessment of Formula Provisions

Both the pecuniary and the fractional share clauses automatically adjust for changes in the composition and value of the testator's estate prior to death and in the amount of property that passes under will substitutes. The use of a formula clause is a reasonably effective way to ensure the proper division of property between transfers that are designed to preserve the testator's unified credit and ones to the surviving spouse that qualify for the marital deduction. Although a formula clause is capable of producing good results, it is not a universal panacea and is no substitute for careful planning and drafting. The use of a formula clause does not relieve the lawyer of the obligation to review, analyze, and organize the client's estate in a careful and deliberate way.

It is also important to appreciate the limitations of formula provisions: No mere formula clause can provide absolute protection against transferring too little or too much property to the surviving spouse. Too little may be transferred to the surviving spouse if the bulk of a client's estate passes to other persons under will substitutes and the probate estate is inadequate to satisfy the formula gift to the surviving spouse. Conversely, too much may pass to the surviving spouse if assets in excess of the amount necessary to eliminate the decedent's estate tax liability pass to the surviving spouse under will substitutes that are not subject to the limitations expressed in the formula clause. Of course, disclaimers are often used to cure some problems of overfunding or underfunding the marital deduction. §12.34.

Caution must also be exercised because the amount of property that passes under a formula provision may be too small to warrant the establishment of a trust. For that reason the planner should consider providing that the gift will pass to the surviving spouse outright if its value is below a certain amount. A small trust can be a nuisance, involving unnecessary expenditures of time and money preparing accountings, keeping records, and filing fiduciary income tax returns. The expense could be considerable if a trustee were appointed that required payment of a large annual fee.

To put matters further into perspective, the general disadvantages of formula provisions should be mentioned. First, by their very nature formula clauses are complicated and difficult to draft, explain, understand, and administer. Because of their complexity it is relatively easy to make a costly mistake at any step along the way. Second, the use of a formula marital deduction clause may require multiple valuations of assets and more complex accountings that can delay settlement of an estate and impose additional costs of administration. Delays could also occur because the exact amount of the gift may not be known until the valuation of property included in the gross estate is finally determined upon audit of the estate tax return. Third, the use of a formula may cause controversies between the surviving spouse and other beneficiaries regarding the proper exercise of elections by the fiduciary that affect the amount of the gifts to the surviving spouse and others. Among these elections are those regarding the use of the alternate valuation date, §2032; the specific use valuation of assets, §2032A; the use of the decedent's $1 million GSTT exemption; and, the return upon which alternatively deductible items are claimed for tax purposes, §642(g). As noted in §5.34, an election to claim an alternatively deductible item as an income tax deduction will affect the amount of a nonmarital pecuniary formula gift.

§5.34. Formula Pecuniary Gift

A formula pecuniary gift is generally simpler to understand and easier to administer than a formula fractional share gift. Personal observation and experience indicate that formula pecuniary gifts are used more often than fractional share gifts, probably because they are simpler and less expensive to administer. The IRS has agreed that a pecuniary formula can be used to express the amount of *either* the marital or nonmarital pecuniary gift that is to be satisfied according to values on the date or dates of distribution. As explained below, a pecuniary gift may be satisfied by two other forms of distribution: "fairly representative" and "minimum worth." §§5.37.4-5.37.5. In Rev. Rul. 90-3, 1990-1 C.B. 176, the IRS allowed a marital deduction based upon estate tax values where a pecuniary nonresiduary gift was satisfied according to date of distribution values. Because of a decline in the value of the assets of the estate, the marital share received distribution of assets worth only $55,000 although the residuary marital share had a value of $250,000 according to federal estate tax values. Until this Revenue Ruling was issued, it was not entirely clear that the IRS would accept a pecuniary nonmarital gift that could be funded according to date of distribution values. While some letter rulings had indicated that the approach was acceptable, the IRS remained free to change its mind. The question was significant primarily because, as indicated by Revenue Ruling 90-3, the amount of the pecuniary gift remains fixed although the overall value of the estate may increase or decrease. Viewed conversely, the gains or losses will all be allocated to the nonpecuniary share (usually the residuary estate). The difference is illustrated by the following simplified example:

> **Example 5-28.** *W*'s will made a formula pecuniary gift to her husband *H* and left the residue of her estate to a discretionary trust for *H* and their children. *W*'s estate had a federal estate tax value of $1,000,000, of which *H* was entitled to receive $400,000 by reason of the formula gift. Under the terms of *W*'s will, the gift to *H* could be satisfied by distributing assets in kind provided they were valued for that purpose according to their values on the date of distribution. The value of the assets of the estate increased to $2,000,000, on the date of distribution. None of the increase is allocable to *H*'s gift. Thus, *H* received only $400,000 and the residuary trust received $1,600,000. Note, however, that a decrease in the value of the estate's property would reduce the amount passing under the nonmarital gift (*i.e.,* the portion in the trust, sheltered by *W*'s unified credit).

It is also significant that gain is realized on the transfer of appreciated property in kind in satisfaction of a pecuniary gift. *See* §5.37.1.

Accordingly, a larger gain may be realized where the amount passing under the formula pecuniary gift is greater than the amount passing under the residuary clause. For that reason it is preferable to use formula pecuniary language to describe the share (marital or non-marital) that is expected to be smaller.

§5.34.1. Credits

In computing the amount of a pecuniary marital deduction gift the formula should take into account the decedent's unified credit. As indicated below, in some jurisdictions it is appropriate also to consider the credit for state death taxes. In contrast, marital deduction formulas should not take into account the credits for gift taxes and foreign death taxes paid. Indeed, the formula clauses suggested in a leading treatise only take into account the unified credit. 4 A. J. Casner, Estate Planning §§13.4.3, 13.4.5 (5th ed. 1988). The instrument should generally direct that property which qualifies for the foreign death tax credit cannot be distributed in satisfaction of the marital deduction gift. Such a direction will allow the estate to make the maximum use of the foreign death tax credit — the credit will not be reduced because the assets could have been used to satisfy the marital deduction. Moore, Recognition and Uses of Federal Estate Tax Credits in Estate Planning and Administration, U. Miami, 21 Inst. Est. Plan. ¶809.2 (1987).

It may be appropriate to provide that the state death tax credit should be taken into account. However, as Richard Covey suggests, whether or not the state death tax credit should also be taken into account depends upon the nature of the local death tax. R. Covey, Marital Deduction and Credit Shelter Dispositions and the Use of Formula Provisions 32-33 (2d ed. 1984).

If the jurisdiction imposes only a "pick-up" tax, equal to the maximum allowable state death tax credit, then the state death tax credit should be taken into account only to the extent doing so will not require an increase in the amount of tax payable to any state. In the states that only impose a pick-up tax, no state death tax need be paid on a taxable estate of $600,000, the federal tax on which is completely offset by the unified credit of $192,800. Taking the state death tax credit into account in those states would require the payment of $15,697 in state death taxes ($15,697 is the state death tax credit allowable on a taxable estate of $642,425). In such a case no additional federal estate tax would be due because the gross amount of the estate tax on a taxable estate of $642,425 is $208,497 ($192,800 + $15,697). The payment of a state tax of $15,697 would shelter only an additional $26,728. That is, the state death tax of $15,697 would be included in the taxable estate, which would reduce the additional sheltered amount to $26,728 ($42,425 − $15,697). While this approach would reduce the amount of the marital deduction and the amount subject to tax on the death of the surviving spouse by $42,425, the state death tax would consume $15,697 of that amount.

In states which impose a state death tax other than a pick-up tax, an overall saving may be achieved if the formula takes the state death tax credit into account. As indicated above, a state death tax credit of $15,697 is allowable with respect to a taxable estate of $642,425. The state death tax imposed on a taxable estate of $600,000 may approach or exceed that figure. In such a case taking the state death tax credit into account may shelter an additional amount at little or no additional state death tax cost. Except for that additional cost, giving recognition to the state death tax credit would allow an additional $42,425 to be diverted from the marital deduction share and sheltered from taxation on the death of the surviving spouse.

Example 5-29. *H* died leaving an estate of $1,000,000. His will made a formula pecuniary gift to his wife *W* of the smallest amount which, if allowable as a marital deduction, would result in the payment of no federal estate tax, taking into account all other deductions, the unified credit, and the state death tax to the extent the state death tax credit did not increase the amount of tax payable to any state. The residue of *H*'s estate was left to a nonmarital trust. *H*'s estate was entitled to no deductions apart from the marital deduction. In a jurisdiction which only imposed a death tax equal to the maximum credit allowable under §2011, the total amount that could be sheltered would be $600,000. However, if the jurisdiction imposed a state death tax that was not a pick-up tax, payment of some state tax might produce an overall saving. For example, if the state death tax were $16,000 if the taxable estate were $600,000 and only $20,000 if the taxable estate were $642,425 the payment of an additional $4,000 in tax could shelter an additional $38,425. If the formula did not permit an increase in the state death tax credit only $584,000 would pass to the residuary credit shelter trust ($600,000 − $16,000). On the other hand, $622,425 would pass to the residuary trust ($642,425 − $20,000) if the formula allowed the payment of an additional $4,000 in state death taxes.

§5.34.2. Charge Nonmarital Share for Principal Expenses for Which No Estate Tax Deduction Is Claimed

A marital deduction is allowable only with respect to the net amount passing to the surviving spouse. §2056(b)(4). That rule does not cause a problem where the formula gift to the surviving spouse includes a proper adjustment for deductions charged against principal and *allowed* for federal estate tax purposes. *See* §5.32. Administration expenses and other items that are deductible for federal estate tax purposes should not be taken into account to the extent they are claimed on the estate's income tax return. A formula that takes "allowable" expenses into account could cause some estate tax liability to arise because it required too much property to be allocated to the nonmarital share.

> **Example 5-30.** *H* died leaving an estate of $1,000,000. His will contained a pecuniary formula marital deduction gift to his wife *W* and left the residue of his estate to a nonmarital trust. The formula provided that the amount of the marital gift should be calculated by taking into account the unified credit and all other deductions *allowed* to his estate. *H'* s estate paid a total of $50,000 in administration expenses and other items that were deductible under §2053. However, all of the items were claimed as deductions on the estate's income tax return. The amount of the pecuniary marital deduction gift ($400,000) is equal to the difference between the gross estate ($1,000,000) and the amount of the credit equivalent ($600,000). Had the expenses been claimed as deductions on the estate tax return, the marital gift would have been reduced to $350,000, which represents the excess of the gross estate over the sum of the deductions allowed for estate tax purposes ($50,000) and the credit equivalent ($600,000). If the formula had provided that *allowable* deductions would be taken into account, some estate tax would have been due had the items been claimed as income tax deductions (*i.e.,* too much property would have passed to the nonmarital trust).

§5.35. Formula Pecuniary Marital Deduction Gift

A formula pecuniary marital deduction gift could be expressed in a variety of ways. Language such as the following reflects the points discussed above and should suffice as a preresiduary formula gift.

Form 5-6. Formula Pecuniary Marital Deduction Gift

If my wife/husband survives me, I give to [her/him or to a trust for her/his benefit] the smallest amount, which if allowable as a marital deduction for federal estate tax purposes in the matter of my estate will result in no federal estate tax being due from my estate, taking into account all other deductions allowed to my estate for federal estate tax purposes and the amount of the

> unified credit and the state death tax credit. However, the state death tax credit shall only be taken into account to the extent that it does not increase the amount of tax payable to any state.

A preresiduary formula pecuniary marital deduction gift is often used if the value of property passing under it is likely to be lower than the value of the nonmarital residuary gift and the gift is to be funded by distributing assets in kind, valued according to their date of distribution values. Such a funding approach minimizes the possibility that gain will be recognized when assets are distributed in satisfaction of the formula gift. Under either the fairly representative or the minimum worth funding provisions the distribution of assets in kind would not give rise to the recognition of gain. Accordingly, if either such funding provision is used, no gain will be realized whether the marital or nonmarital share is defined by the formula.

§5.36. Model Formula Pecuniary Nonmarital Deduction Gift

Where the size of the marital share will exceed the nonmarital share and the gift will be funded at date of distribution values, it may be desirable to make a formula pecuniary gift of the nonmarital share. In that way the potential for the recognition of capital gain is decreased. However, if the formula nonmarital gift will be funded at date of distribution values, all of the appreciation or depreciation will be allocated to the residuary marital gift. Again, under a fairly representative or minimum worth funding provision, no gain is recognized when appreciated assets are distributed in satisfaction of the gift.

A formula nonmarital deduction gift could be expressed along these lines:

> **Form 5-7. Formula Pecuniary Nonmarital Deduction Gift**
>
> If my wife/husband survives me, I give to [the nonmarital trust or other beneficiaries] an amount equal to the excess of (1) the amount upon which the tentative tax calculated under I.R.C. §2001(c) is equal to the sum of the unified credit and the state death tax credit (but the state death tax credit shall be taken into account only to the extent that it does not increase the amount of tax payable to any state) over (2) the amount of post-1976 taxable gifts made by me other than gifts includible in my gross estate; the amount of property includible in my gross estate for which no charitable or marital deduction or casualty loss deduction is allowed; and the amount of administration expenses and other ex-

> penses incurred in connection with the settlement of my estate that are charged against principal and are not allowed as deductions for federal estate tax purposes.

In this case the formula should also be fleshed out by appropriate provisions regarding funding and valuation of property.

§5.37. Directions Regarding Funding a Formula Pecuniary Gift

Various options are available for specifying the manner in which a formula pecuniary gift should be satisfied. If nothing is said on the subject, local law may require the gift to be satisfied in cash. The liquidation of assets that would ordinarily be required to do so might be inconvenient and cause the estate to incur unnecessary capital gains taxes. Whatever the local law may be, it is generally desirable to authorize the fiduciary to satisfy the gift by distributing assets in kind. The fiduciary needs the flexibility that such a provision provides in order to be able to select and distribute the most appropriate assets, taking into account the circumstances of the estate and the beneficiaries.

Stock distributed in kind in satisfaction of a pecuniary marital deduction bequest is redeemable "only to the extent that the interest of the shareholder is reduced directly (or through a binding obligation to contribute) by any payment of" death taxes and funeral and administration expenses. §303(b)(3). The scope and operation of this limitation, applicable to the "interests of the shareholder," which would ordinarily be the decedent's executor or trustee, is uncertain. Until it is clarified the safest course is to direct that neither stock redeemed pursuant to §303 nor the proceeds of a redemption of stock that meets the requirements of §303 should be distributed in satisfaction of the marital deduction.

§5.37.1. Valuation of Assets Distributed in Kind

The fiduciary should be given some guidance regarding the valuation of any assets that are distributed in kind in satisfaction of a formula pecuniary bequest. Of necessity some specific value must be assigned to each asset. The principal valuation methods and the income and estate tax consequences of each are described in the following sections.

Thus far the IRS has not required the income tax basis of an asset to be taken into account in valuing the asset in connection with an in kind distribution. Accordingly, neither the value of an asset nor the amount of the marital deduction has been adjusted merely because the asset will have a basis in the hands of the distributee that is less than its value for purposes of distribution. Similarly, no adjustment has been required when the assets distributed included a component of income in respect of a decedent. Thus, a marital deduction has been allowed without reduction for future income tax liability that might arise upon payment of installment notes distributed in satisfaction of the marital deduction gift. LR 7827008. Consistent with that result the Tax Court has not allowed a decedent's estate to discount the value of installment notes on account of the possible income tax payable on collections made on the notes in the future. *Estate of G. R. Robinson,* 69 T.C. 222 (1977).

At some point the IRS might require the distribution of assets that fairly reflect the overall appreciation or depreciation in value of all assets available for distribution. Beyond that, the tax consequences are probably too speculative and uncertain to take into account. Thus, future tax consequences are generally disregarded in marital dissolution planning. However, they are sometimes taken into account for other purposes. *See* Hjorth, The Effect of Federal Tax Consequences on Amount of Property Allocated to Spouses in State Court Dissolution Proceedings, 24 Fam. L. Q. 247 (1990).

§5.37.2. Value on the Date of Distribution ("True Worth")

Unless a fiduciary is directed to value the assets that are distributed in kind in some other manner, general fiduciary principles may require the fiduciary to value them at their fair market values on the date or dates of distribution. Such a requirement is imposed by some states. It is also the funding method most frequently imposed by the terms of a will or trust. In operation, a true worth provision assures that the value of the property distributed in satisfaction of the gift will have a total market value on the date or dates of distribution exactly equal to the amount of the marital deduction. It imposes both a ceiling and a floor on the value of assets distributed in satisfaction of a marital deduction gift. If the assets of the estate appreciate in value, the method imposes a ceiling on the value of assets that can be distributed; if they decline, it acts as a floor. A true worth provision can be used in connection with a pecuniary marital *or* nonmarital gift.

Example 5-31. *W* died leaving an estate that consisted of assets A, B, C, and D. Each of the assets was worth $200,000 on the estate tax valuation date and $300,000 on the date of distribution. *W* made no taxable gifts during her lifetime and her taxable estate is $800,000. Her will made a "true worth" pecuniary formula gift to her husband *H* of the smallest amount that, if allowed as a marital deduction, would result in no estate tax being due from *W*'s estate, taking into account the unified credit and the state death tax credit to the extent it did not require the payment of any additional state death tax. *W* resided in a state that only imposed a pick-up tax. *W*'s executor determined that the formula required a marital deduction of $200,000. The assets distributed to *H* in satisfaction of the marital deduction formula gift must have a total value on the date or dates of distribution equal to the marital deduction of $200,000 that was claimed by *W*'s estate. If a pecuniary nonmarital gift were used, the estate would be obligated to distribute property worth $600,000 on the date of distribution in satisfaction of the gift. The use of a pecuniary marital deduction gift, rather than a formula nonmarital gift, limits the amount of gain that might be realized by the estate if appreciated property must be distributed in satisfaction of the formula gift.

As noted in §5.32, if the assets of the estate appreciate substantially in value between the estate tax valuation date and the date of distribution, a true worth marital deduction gift prevents the marital gift from sharing in the appreciation. By limiting the value of property that can be distributed in satisfaction of the marital deduction gift the method helps control the size of the surviving spouse's estate. In such a case the benefit (or burden) of the appreciation passes under the other provisions of the will or trust. Of course, if the assets of the estate decline in value, the floor comes into effect and a smaller amount passes to the other beneficiaries.

"Sale" at a Gain. Under the true worth approach assets that are distributed in satisfaction of the gift must be valued again on the date or dates of distribution. The extra valuation may be time-consuming and costly where the estate includes items that are difficult to value. A trust or estate recognizes gain if a pecuniary gift is satisfied by distributing an asset that has a date of distribution value greater than the asset's estate tax value. The gain is generally limited to the amount by which the fair market value of the property on the date of distribution exceeds its estate tax value. Note that §1040 limits the amount of gain taxed to a trust or estate when special use property is distributed to a qualified heir in satisfaction of a pecuniary bequest. In such a case the gain is limited to the amount by which the date of distribution value of the property exceeds its estate tax value, determined without regard to §2032A (*i.e.,* its fair market value on the estate tax valuation date). §1040(a). Where such a distribution is made, the qualified heir's basis in the property is equal to the basis of the estate or trust immediately before the distribution plus the amount of gain recognized by the estate or trust as a result of the distribution. §1040(c).

Language of this type could be used to express a true worth valuation requirement:

Form 5-8. Date of Distribution (True Worth) Funding Clause

> I authorize my executor to satisfy this gift by making distributions in cash or in kind, or part in cash and part in kind, provided that each asset that is distributed in kind shall be valued at its fair market value on the date it is distributed.

"Sale" at a Loss — §267. If the value of an asset is lower on the date of distribution than its basis, the fiduciary must decide whether to sell the asset to a third party or distribute it to a beneficiary in a transaction that will be treated as a sale. In the former case the fiduciary may unquestionably take advantage of the loss on the fiduciary income tax return, while in the latter case the deduction may be prohibited by §267. That section bars a deduction for a loss incurred in a sale or exchange directly or indirectly between related taxpayers, including a fiduciary of a trust and a beneficiary of the trust. However, it does not bar a deduction for a loss on a sale between an estate and a beneficiary of the estate. *Estate of Hanna v. Commissioner,* 320 F.2d 54 (6th Cir. 1963); Rev. Rul. 77-439, 1977-2 C.B. 85.

The true worth provision is probably used more often than any other, although it requires an additional valuation of assets and may result in recognition of gain by the fiduciary. Planners are attracted by its relative simplicity. When a true worth requirement is used in conjunction with a pecuniary marital deduction gift, the surviving spouse is provided with protection against a decline in the value of the marital deduction share. However, as explained below, greater protection may be provided by a "minimum value" funding provision. *See* §5.37.4.

§5.37.3. Estate Tax Value; Revenue Procedure 64-19

Some wills and trusts attempt to provide additional tax planning flexibility by directing that assets distributed in satisfaction of a marital deduction gift must be valued at their respective estate tax values. Under such a provision a distribution does not result in gain or loss because each asset is deemed to have a value equal to its federal estate tax value — its basis under §1014. However, the rule tempted fiduciaries to allocate assets that had declined in value to the marital share and assets that had increased in value to the other beneficiaries. Such an allocation was intended to minimize the amount of property includible in the estate of the surviving spouse. (In the case of a pecuniary nonmarital gift the fiduciary would be tempted to make the reverse allocation.) The IRS responded by issuing Rev. Proc. 64-19, 1964-1 C.B. 682, which enumerates the conditions under which a marital deduction will be allowed for a pecuniary gift that the fiduciary is authorized to satisfy by distributing assets in kind at their federal estate tax values.

Revenue Procedure 64-19 provides that when an instrument allows or requires a fiduciary to distribute assets in kind in satisfaction of a pecuniary marital deduction gift and specifies that the assets distributed in kind must be valued at their values as finally determined for federal estate tax purposes, a marital deduction will be allowed only if (1) the fiduciary "must distribute assets, including cash, having an aggregate fair market value at the date, or dates, of distribution amounting to no less than the amount of the pecuniary bequest or transfer, as finally determined for Federal estate tax purposes," or (2) the fiduciary "must distribute assets, including cash, fairly representative of appreciation or depreciation in the value of all property thus available for distribution in satisfaction of such pecuniary bequest or transfer." In effect, federal estate tax values can only be used if the integrity of the marital deduction is protected by the alternative requirements quoted above. Presumably the principles of Revenue Procedure 64-19 will apply where a pecuniary formula is used to express the nonmarital gift.

Revenue Procedure 64-19 also noted that the problem it addressed did not arise in some other cases. In particular, it noted that the problem was not present:

> 1. In a bequest or transfer in trust of a fractional share of the estate, under which each beneficiary shares proportionately in the appreciation or depreciation in the value of assets to the date, or dates, of distribution.
>
> 2. In a bequest or transfer in trust of specific assets.
>
> 3. In a pecuniary bequest or transfer in trust, whether in a stated amount or an amount computed by the use of a formula, if:
>
> (a) The fiduciary must satisfy the pecuniary bequest or transfer solely in cash, or
>
> (b) The fiduciary has no discretion in the selection of assets to be distributed in kind, or
>
> (c) Assets selected by the fiduciary to be distributed in kind in satisfaction of the bequest or transfer in trust are to be valued at their respective values on the date, or dates, of their distribution.
>
> §4.01, Rev. Proc. 64-19, 1964-1 C.B. at 684.

However, Revenue Procedure 64-19 does not approve the use of devices in those cases that may operate to diminish the value of the interests that are transferred in satisfaction of a marital deduction gift.

In particular, it does not authorize the fiduciary to select and distribute assets on a non-pro rata basis in satisfaction of a formula fractional share gift.

Under Revenue Procedure 64-19, a fiduciary may be given authority to satisfy a pecuniary marital deduction gift that requires the use of the federal estate tax value of the assets by one of two approved methods. The fiduciary may not be given a choice between them. Many commentators favor the "minimum value" method. *E.g.,* Polasky, Marital Deduction Formula Clauses in Estate Planning — Estate and Income Tax Considerations, 63 Mich. L. Rev. 809, 832 (1965) (cited hereafter as Polasky). The other method, which is commonly called either the "fairly representative" or "ratable sharing" provision, is more cumbersome and is less well understood by planners, courts, and the IRS.

§5.37.4. Estate Tax Value: Minimum Value Provisions

Under the "minimum value" method, assets distributed in kind must have an aggregate fair market value on the date or dates of distribution of no less than the amount of the pecuniary marital deduction gift. The effect of this approach is to specify a floor beneath which the value of the assets distributed in kind cannot fall (an amount equal to the pecuniary gift), but no ceiling. No gain is realized from a distribution of assets in kind in satisfaction of a minimum worth gift because such a distribution is valued at the *lower* of its basis or value at the date of distribution. Note that a minimum worth provision should not be used in connection with a pecuniary formula nonmarital gift because of the possibility that the value of a residuary marital deduction gift could be eroded by allocating "too much" to the pecuniary nonmarital gift.

> **Example 5-32.** *H*'s estate is composed of 10 assets. Each has an estate tax value of $100,000 and a date-of-distribution value of $200,000. *H*'s will makes a formula pecuniary gift to his wife *W* of an amount that is determined to be equal to $400,000. Under an estate tax minimum value provision, assets worth at least $400,000 on the date of distribution must be transferred in satisfaction of the gift. However, assets having a date-of-distribution value of as much as $800,000 could be distributed. On the other hand, if the assets fell to a value of $50,000 each on the date of distribution, the fiduciary would still be obligated to distribute to *W* assets with a total date-of-distribution value of at least $400,000.

A minimum worth provision can be used in conjunction with a pecuniary marital deduction gift, especially when a client wishes to permit the fiduciary to allocate some of the increase in value of assets to the marital deduction gift. However, it should not be used if a client does not want to put the fiduciary in the position of having to decide whether the marital deduction gift or other beneficiaries will benefit from an increase in the value of the estate's property. If it is used the fiduciary should be protected against liability for a good faith exercise of the power.

Form 5-9. Minimum Worth Funding Clause

I authorize my fiduciary to satisfy this gift by making distributions in cash or in kind or part in cash and part in kind, provided that the aggregate fair market value of the cash and other assets on the date or dates of distribution shall be no less than the amount of the gift as finally determined for federal estate tax purposes.

A minimum value marital deduction gift complies with Revenue Procedure 64-19. It should also eliminate the possibility that the estate will realize gain upon the distribution of assets in kind. According to Professor Polasky, no gain or loss occurs because "the ultimate value of the bequest is not ascertainable until distribution; and the receipt of assets cannot be said to be in satisfaction of a fixed dollar amount bequest or claim." Polasky at 867.

§5.37.5. Estate Tax Value: Fairly Representative Requirement

A requirement that the assets distributed in satisfaction of the marital deduction gift fairly reflect the appreciation and depreciation in value of the estate's assets may be imposed by the local law or the instrument itself. In either case, the requirement satisfies the Revenue Procedure 64-19. A fairly representative clause is safe to use in conjunction with a formula pecuniary marital or nonmarital gift. *See* Form 5-10.

Form 5-10. Estate Tax Value, Fairly Representative Funding Clause

I authorize my fiduciary to select and distribute in satisfaction of this gift assets included in my gross estate (or the proceeds of their disposition), including cash, which have an aggregate fair market value fairly representative of the distributee's proportionate share of the appreciation or depreciation in value, to the date or dates of distribution, of all property then available for distribution.

A fairly representative clause assures that the marital deduction gift *and* other gifts will be treated fairly when it comes to making distributions: All will share ratably in any overall increase or decrease in the value of the assets available for distribution. However, a ratable allocation is most important where the surviving spouse will not also receive the benefit of the nonmarital share. In contrast, where the surviving spouse will receive the benefit of both shares, it is more efficient from the tax perspective to use a clause that permits the distribution to the marital deduction share of assets having as low a value as possible. By doing so the size of the surviving spouse's gross estate is minimized.

The primary disadvantage of the fairly representative approach is its difficulty of application, particularly where distributions are made at different times to multiple beneficiaries. It is administratively more complex, which increases the responsibilities of the fiduciary, which may increase the fees of the fiduciary and of the attorney.

> **Example 5-33.** *H*'s will contains a formula pecuniary marital deduction gift to his wife *W* that directs it to be satisfied by distributing assets at their federal estate tax values, provided they must be fairly representative of the change in value of all assets between the federal estate tax valuation date and the date or dates of distribution. *H*'s gross estate consisted of the assets that had a total federal estate tax value of $1,250,000. Expenses of administration and other costs of $50,000 will be deducted for federal estate tax purposes. If *H* lived in a state that imposed only a pick-up tax and had made no prior taxable gifts, *H*'s estate would claim a marital deduction of $600,000. Thus, *W*'s share would be equal to half of the net amount available for distribution according to their federal estate tax values. If the assets available for distribution had an aggregate value of $1,800,000 on the date of distribution, *W* would be entitled to receive assets which had a total value of $900,000. No gain would be realized as a result of the distribution of appreciated assets. Had the value of the assets declined to $900,000 in value on the date of distribution, *W* would have been entitled to receive ones worth a total of $450,000.

§5.37.6. Directions Regarding Allocation of Assets to Pecuniary Formula Marital Deduction Gifts

The amount of the marital deduction is subject to reduction under the terminable interest rule if any disqualified assets (or their proceeds) could be distributed in satisfaction of the marital deduction gift. *See* §5.17.5. Accordingly, instruments that include a formula gift typically require the fiduciary to satisfy the marital deduction portion by distributing only assets that qualify for the deduction. For example, an instrument might provide, "This gift shall be satisfied only with assets or the proceeds of assets with respect to which a federal estate tax marital deduction is allowable." Without such a provision, the marital deduction would be disallowed to the extent that nondeductible interests were included in the pool of assets from which the gift could be satisfied.

Special directions should be included if the client owns stock that it might be desirable to redeem under §303. *See* §§5.37 and 5.39.

A will or trust might also contain a direction regarding the allocation of income in respect of a decedent (IRD). A concern arises because a distribution in satisfaction of a pecuniary bequest will trigger recognition of income by the estate. Under §691(a)(2) income must be reported if an IRD item is sold or exchanged. However, income is not triggered by the distribution of an IRD item in satisfaction of a specific bequest. Thus, a planner has some flexibility in planning for the distribution of IRD items. In some cases it may be preferable to have the estate bear the tax and permit the surviving spouse to receive the income free of tax. In other cases it is preferable for the surviving spouse to be taxed on the income, which in effect reduces the size of his or her estate.

The income tax cost of IRD is ameliorated somewhat by the deduction that is available under §691(c) for the estate tax paid with respect to the IRD. Of course, if a marital deduction formula works properly the estate will pay no estate tax.

§5.38. Planning and Drafting a Formula Fractional Share Gift

The beneficiary of a fractional share gift is entitled to receive a fractional interest in each asset that is included in the pool against which the fraction is applied. The beneficiary is also entitled to receive a proportionate part of the income generated by the asset pool.

> **Example 5-34.** *H* bequeathed half of his residuary estate to his wife *W*. When *H*'s estate is distributed, *W* is entitled to receive an undivided one-half interest in each asset included in *H*'s residuary estate, together with half of the income derived from it. If the death taxes, costs of administration, and like items are payable from the nonmarital share of the residue, *W* may be entitled to a larger proportionate interest in each asset and a larger proportion of the income after those items are paid.

A nonformula fractional share gift (*e.g.,* half of my residuary estate) may have a value that is more or less than the amount of the optimum marital deduction. Also, such a gift does not include any mechanism for adjusting the amount of the fraction on account of property that passes outside the will or trust. The absence of a self-adjusting mechanism makes this type of gift too unreliable for general use in marital deduction planning.

In contrast, a formula fractional share gift produces a marital deduction that is precisely equal to the amount necessary to eliminate the payment of any estate tax by the decedent's estate. Exceptions occur if either the gift is overfunded by nontestamentary transfers or the pool of assets against which the fraction is applied is too small to fund the gift fully. A formula fractional share gift also allows each beneficiary to participate in any overall change in the value of the residuary estate or other pool of assets from which the gift will be satisfied. Thus, the fraction serves two purposes.

First, it describes the proportionate share of the residuary estate that is to be qualified for the marital deduction. Necessarily this will produce an *amount,* expressed in dollars, to be claimed on the estate tax return. Second, once constituted, the fraction will be applied to allocate the aliquot shares of the described residuary estate to the marital and nonmarital trusts at the distribution date. Polasky at 841.

As the composition and value of a residuary estate will inevitably change between the estate tax valuation date and the date or dates of distribution, the value of the assets actually distributed in satisfaction of the gift may be more or less than the amount of the marital deduction.

> **Example 5-35.** *W* died leaving a will that made a formula fractional share gift to her husband *H.* According to the federal estate tax value of the assets of *W*'s estate, which governed for the purpose of the formula gift, *H* was entitled to receive five-ninths of *W*'s residuary estate. Accordingly, *H* was entitled to receive a five-ninths fractional interest in each asset, regardless of its value on the date or dates of distribution.

A fractional share gift should be used sparingly where community property is involved. The management of the property could be complicated if it is fractionalized further by distributing part of a deceased spouse's share to a marital deduction trust for the surviving spouse and part to others or to another trust. Where community property is involved, a pecuniary formula is generally preferable.

Drafting a formula fractional share gift requires the lawyer to focus on two problems: (1) formulating the language with which to express the fraction itself, and (2) determining and describing the residue or other pool of assets against which the fraction will be applied (the multiplicand).

§5.38.1. Expressing the Fraction

The fraction itself may be referred to in several ways that qualify for the marital deduction. Most often, the numerator is the amount of property to be passed to the surviving spouse. Of course, a "reverse" formula could be used that would be based upon the maximum amount of property that could be passed to persons other than the surviving spouse or charities without incurring any estate tax. The denominator is the residuary estate or other pool of assets against which the fraction is applied. In order to preserve the fractional character of the gift, the denominator must also reflect the estate tax value of the assets. *See* Polasky at 842, n.116. In drafting the gift, the lawyer must be sure that the same definition of the residue is used both for the denominator and the multiplicand. If so, the value of the gift will be the same whether the residue is constituted before the payment of cash legacies, expenses, debts, and taxes; before the payment of taxes (a "pre-tax" provision); or after the payment of all of those items (a "true residue" provision).

§5.38.2. Formula Fractional Share Gift

Form 5-11. Formula Fractional Share Marital Deduction Gift

If my wife/husband survives me, I give to [her/him or to a trust for her/his benefit] a fraction of my residuary estate, determined after payment of all pecuniary gifts, expenses of administration, debts, and death taxes that are properly chargeable against my residuary estate. The numerator of the fraction shall be the smallest amount which, if allowable as a marital deduction for federal estate tax purposes in the matter of my estate, will result in no federal estate tax being due from my estate, taking into account post-1976 taxable gifts made by me and all other deductions allowed for federal estate tax purposes, the unified credit, and the state death tax (but only to the extent that the latter credit does not increase the state death tax payable to any state). The denominator of the fraction shall be the federal estate tax value of my residuary estate so determined. For the purposes of this gift, my residuary estate shall include only assets that would qualify for the federal estate tax marital deduction if they were distributed outright to my spouse.

Of course, a fractional share gift can be made outright to the surviving spouse or in trust. As explained below, most fractional share formula clauses are based on the "true residue." That is, the multiplicand and the denominator are defined as the residuary estate *after* the payment of all pecuniary gifts, expenses of administration, debts, and death taxes (a true residue provision). The final sentence of the gift is included to prevent loss of any portion of the deduction under the unidentified (tainted) asset rule if the residue includes any terminable interests. Again, some commentators suggest using a formula that only takes into account the unified credit. 4 A. J. Casner, Estate Planning §13.4.5 (5th ed. 1988).

§5.38.3. Directions Regarding Allocation of Income and Capital Gains and Losses

The manner in which the income and capital gains and losses will be allocated under a formula fractional share gift is usually not clear under the local law. Accordingly, the governing instrument should contain specific directions. Without them, fiduciaries adopt different approaches regarding the allocation of income.

> [A]n informal survey of corporate fiduciaries suggests varying approaches not necessarily keyed to the particular definition of the residue. Some apply the fraction produced by the formula while others allocate to the marital share only that amount of income which the average rate of return would produce on the calculated marital share. Polasky at 849-850.

> **Example 5-36.** *W* left an estate that was valued at $1,300,000 for federal estate tax purposes and a will that made a formula fractional share gift of her residuary estate to her husband *H.* Expenses of administration and debts of $100,000 were paid at the same time from the residue. *H*'s fractional share was one-half under the true residue provision that was contained in *W*'s will. Income of $50,000 was earned by the estate prior to the payment of the expenses and debts. To be equitable, the nonmarital share should receive all of the income that was generated by the assets used to pay expenses, debts, and taxes. Accordingly, the nonmarital share should be entitled to 7/13ths of the income earned prior to payment of those items. Income earned thereafter should be allocated according to the formula fraction (*i.e.,* one-half to the marital share and one-half to the other residuary beneficiaries). Of course, convenience tempts the fiduciary to allocate all of the income on the basis of a single fraction.

In an actual case the allocation is likely to be complicated by the payment of debts, expenses, and other items at various times and by the receipt of income at intervals that do not nicely coincide with those times. The same problem exists with respect to the allocation of capital gains and losses, which are frequently incurred to raise funds with which to pay expenses, debts, and taxes.

If the fiduciary is directed to allocate all income and capital gains according to the fraction determined under a true residue provision, the marital share will receive more of those items than it would under the strictly equitable approach. In operation, such a provision will inflate the survivor's gross estate to the extent of the excess. However, this approach is infinitely simpler to administer than one that calls for allocation according to the equitable approach and requires almost continuous revision. A provision that allocates income according to a formula based upon a residue constituted prior to the payment of expenses, debts, and taxes would overcompensate the nonmarital share.

§5.38.4. Why Use a True Residue Provision?

Use of a true residue provision is generally preferable to any other definition of the residue for purposes of the fractional share gift. In general, the use of a true residue provision increases the fiduciary's ability to select and dispose of assets in satisfaction of pecuniary legacies, expenses of administration, debts, and taxes. The increased flexibility that such a provision allows the fiduciary can be very useful. The effect of using a true residue is described in the following passage:

> Shrinking the residue to which the fraction is to be applied obviously increases the percentage interest of the marital share in the remaining available assets, since the numerator stays the same while the denominator diminishes. Further, shrinking the defined residue gives the executor an increasing power to choose assets to satisfy the general pecuniary legacy and other non-residue obligations and a concomitant power to affect the makeup, in terms of the specific assets remaining, of the pool to which the fractional share will be applied. . . . Polasky at 844-845.

Also, a true residue provision requires fewer adjustments to the fraction and is generally easier to adminster. Finally, the need to trace assets of the estate for purposes of distribution can be eliminated if a true residue provision is used. In other cases it might be necessary to trace all of the assets that were originally included in the residuary estate in order to determine the portion of each asset that should be distributed to the marital and nonmarital shares. *See* 4 A. J. Casner, Estate Planning §13.5.4 (5th ed. 1988).

The fraction will change regardless of the residuary definition if a non-pro rata distribution is made to a residuary beneficiary. For that reason, disproportionate distributions should generally be avoided when a fractional share gift is used in an instrument. If a true residue provision is used, the fraction will not have to be adjusted when pecuniary legacies, expenses of administration, debts, and taxes are paid. Adjustments are required, however, if the fraction is originally computed according to the value of the residuary estate prior to the payment of those items. In such a case the payment of each such item is in effect a distribution to the nonmarital share, which is chargeable with such payments. Accordingly, the fraction must be adjusted every time the estate pays an item that is properly chargeable to the residue.

The complexity of recomputing the fraction discourages many planners from using formula fractional share gifts. The steps involved in determining the initial and final fractions have been described as follows:

> 1. Determine the initial fraction. The numerator and denominator are based upon estate tax values as of the decedent's death if the executor does not elect the alternate valuation method. The denominator must be reduced by all administration expenses, whether or not claimed as an estate tax deduction and, if a true residuary clause is utilized, by estate taxes. If the executor elects the alternate valuation method, the assets of the residuary estate must be valued as of the appropriate alternate valuation date.
>
> 2. Divide the numerator by the denominator in order to determine the initial percentage interest of the marital share in increases and decreases of the estate until the first tax payment or distribution, whichever occurs first if a pre-tax residuary clause is utilized, or the first distribution if a true residuary clause is utilized.
>
> 3. As of the date of any tax payment or distribution, determine the fair market value of the undistributed residuary estate, including cash, and subtract therefrom any unpaid administration expenses taken into account in determining the initial denominator. Determine any net appreciation or depreciation by subtracting therefrom in the case of the first revaluation the denominator of the initial marital fraction or, in the case of any revaluation other than the first, the denominator of the initial marital fraction increased or decreased by any tax payments, distributions, increases or decreases taken into account in all prior revaluations resulting in a change in the denominator. Allocate to the marital share its percentage interest in the difference, if any, applicable to the period during which such appreciation or depreciation occurs.
>
> 4. Subtract from the denominator the amount of the tax payment if a pre-tax residuary clause is utilized or, in the case of distributions, subtract from the denominator the total amount of distributions (whether or not made to the surviving spouse) and from the numerator only that amount of the distribution passing to the surviving spouse.

5. After allocating the increases or decreases and subtracting the tax payments or distributions, divide the resulting numerator by the resulting denominator to determine the revised fractional interest of the marital share in the undistributed assets of the residuary estate.

6. With each succeeding tax payment or distribution, apply the principles set out in 3, 4 and 5 above. Kurtz, Allocation of Increases and Decreases to Fractional Share Marital Deduction Bequest, 8 Real Prop., Prob. & Tr. J. 450, 460 (1973).

As indicated in the foregoing passage, the fraction must be recomputed "at each tax payment and distribution in the case of a pre-tax residuary clause and at each distribution in the case of a true residuary clause." Id. at 460.

Example 5-37. *H* died earlier this year in a state that only imposed a pick-up tax. *H* left a will that made a formula fractional share gift to his wife *W* of the type described in §5.38.2. He gave the balance of his residuary estate to a nonmarital trust. His gross estate had a value of $1,200,000 for federal estate tax purposes, including a house held in joint tenancy with *W* that had a total value of $200,000, survivorship bank accounts with *W* in the amount of $25,000, and life insurance payable to *W* in the amount of $75,000. In addition, *H* had made post-1976 taxable gifts of $100,000. Debts, costs of administration, etc., payable from the residuary estate, that will be claimed as deductions for federal estate tax purposes amounted to $100,000. *W*'s fractional interest is four-tenths. The fraction represents a numerator of $400,000 ($1,300,000 − ($100,000 for the qualified joint tenancy in the residence + $100,000 expenses + $25,000 in survivorship bank accounts + $75,000 of life insurance + $600,000 credit equivalent)) over a denominator of $1,000,000 ($1,300,000 − ($100,000 for the qualified joint tenancy + $100,000 in expenses + $25,000 in the survivorship bank account and $75,000 in life insurance)).

§5.39. Income Tax Aspects of a Formula Fractional Share Gift

A distribution in satisfaction of a fractional share gift does not cause the fiduciary to recognize any gain or loss. Reg. §§1.661(a)-2(f)(1), 1.1014-4(a)(3). This rule is generally beneficial for taxpayers and is an important reason for using a fractional share formula. Of course, its benefit depends upon the nature of the property involved and the relative income tax positions of the surviving spouse and the estate. A distribution in satisfaction of a fractional share gift does carry out the distributable net income of the estate which may increase the distributee's basis in the property. Reg. §1.661(a)-2(f)(3).

As noted in §5.37, stock may be redeemed under §303 only to the extent that the interest of the redeeming shareholder is reduced by payment of death taxes and funeral and administration expenses. The marital share, of course, is not reduced by the payment of those items. Accordingly, stock that the parties may wish to redeem under §303 should not be included in the pool of assets subject to a marital deduction formula gift.

Under a hybrid approach the fiduciary is authorized to make non-pro rata distributions in satisfaction of fractional share interests. In such a case the value of the fractional share interest is determined on the date of distribution. Then the gift is satisfied by distributing assets in kind equal in value on the date of distribution to the amount of the gift. Such a distribution should not be treated as a taxable exchange that would give rise to the recognition of any gain or loss. This conclusion rests in part upon the implications of Rev. Rul. 69-486, 1969-2 C.B. 159. *See* §12.39. In Revenue Ruling 69-486, the IRS concluded that the non-pro rata distribution of trust property to the two beneficiaries upon termination of the trust involved a taxable exchange between them where the trust instrument did *not* authorize the trustee to make such a distribution. According to the ruling, "Since the trustee was not authorized to make a non-pro rata distribution of property in kind but did so as a result of the mutual agreement between *C* and *X*, the non-pro rata distribution by the trustee is equivalent to a distribution to *C* and *X* of the notes and common stock pro rata by the trustee, followed by an exchange between *C* and *X* of *C*'s pro rata share of common stock for *X*'s pro rata share of notes." Id. The IRS has also held that no taxable exchange takes place when there is a non-pro rata distribution of community property as a result of which each party receives property of equal value. Rev. Rul. 76-83, 1976-1 C.B. 213. The same result was reached in LR 8016050 which involved spouses each of whom received the entire interest in assets of approximately equal value.

§5.40. Summary — Choosing Between a Formula Pecuniary Gift and a Formula Fractional Share Gift

A fractional share formula has a slight edge when it comes to fairness and security against manipulation. Under a formula fractional share gift the share of each beneficiary fluctuates with changes in the composition and value of the residue, rather than being based upon a fixed amount. Of course, the actual value of the items distributed in satisfaction of a pecuniary gift depends in part upon the type of valuation clause that is used. From the income tax perspective the fractional share gift has the advantage because the distribution of assets does not involve the realization of any gain. However, when appreciated assets are distributed in kind in satisfaction of a pecuniary gift, only the gain in value that takes place between the estate tax valuation date and the date of distribution is realized. The fractional share gift also enjoys an advantage if a portion of the income taxes attributable to sales made in order to generate funds with which to pay debts, expenses of administration, and taxes can be absorbed by the marital share without requiring any adjustment.

The formula fractional share gift has two major disadvantages. First, the fiduciary does not have as broad a power to select and allocate assets to the marital share as in the case of the pecuniary gift. This shortcoming may be alleviated if the fiduciary is given authority to make non-pro rata distributions of assets in kind. However, the tax consequences of giving the fiduciary such authority are uncertain: The IRS could argue that it converts the gift into a pecuniary one, which would require the fiduciary to recognize gain or loss upon the distribution of assets. *See* Rev. Rul. 60-87, 1960-1 C.B. 286. Second, the administration and accounting for a fractional share gift is much more complicated.

> The fraction itself is easily arrived at — initially. The problem is, that each time a non-pro rata distribution is made the fraction must be recalculated. The numerator and denominator are originally computed using federal estate tax values. The estate is then revalued at each partial distribution, reduced by all unpaid principal charges, and the fraction then recast in terms of current market values. The numerator is reduced by distributions to the spouse and the denominator is reduced by distributions to the spouse and other beneficiaries, payment of expenses (whether or not deductible), and the like. A new fraction is then arrived at which is to be used for the period until the next partial distribution. Rosen, How to Select the Proper Formula Clause to Fit Testator's Desires and Minimize Taxes, 3 Est. Plan. 20, 25 (1975).

In contrast, the administration of a formula pecuniary gift is usually very simple. Often the only complication is that the assets distributed in kind in satisfaction of the gift must be valued again at the time of distribution.

BIBLIOGRAPHY

Casner, A. J., Estate Planning (5th ed. 1988)

Cornfeld, A Tin Cup for QTIPs — The Tenth Anniversary of the Unlimited Marital Deduction, U. Miami, 26th Inst. Est. Plan., ch. — (1992)

Covey, R., Marital Deduction and Credit Shelter Dispositions and the Use of Formula Provisions (2d ed. 1984)

Gutierrez, Godzilla Meets Rodan: Generation-Skipping Transfer/Marital Deduction Planning, U. Miami, 23rd Inst. Est. Plan., ch. 9 (1989)

Hilker, The Marital Deduction, ch. 2 in 1 CEB Estate Planning (1988)

Karp, Estate Planning for the Alien — The Danger of the Mixed Marriage, U. Miami, 24th Inst. Est. Plan., ch. 9 (1990)

Kurtz, Impact of the Revenue Act of 1978 and the 1976 Tax Reform Act on Estate Tax Marital Deduction Formulas, 64 Iowa L. Rev. 739 (1979)

Llewellyn, Levin & Richmond, Computing the Optimum Marital Deduction: Is a Zero-tax Formula Appropriate?, 24 Real Prop., Prob. & Tr. J. 331 (1989)

Pennell, Estate Tax Marital Deduction, 239-4th BNA Tax Mgmt. Portfolio (1990)

Plaine & Siegler, The Federal Gift and Estate Tax Marital Deduction for Non-United States Citizen Recipient Spouses, 25 Real Prop., Prob. & Tr. J. 385 (1990)

Polasky, Marital Deduction Formula Clauses in Estate Planning — Estate and Income Tax Considerations, 63 Mich. L. Rev. 809 (1965)

Trapp, Appreciation, Depreciation, and Basis in Drafting and Funding Marital Deduction Formula Bequests, U. Miami, 13th Inst. Est. Plan., ch. 3 (1979)

CHAPTER 6

LIFE INSURANCE

A. Introduction

§6.1. Scope
§6.2. Terminology; Insurable Interest
§6.3. Data Collection
§6.4. Basic Functions of Life Insurance
§6.5. How Much Life Insurance?
§6.6. Spouse Insurance
§6.7. Basic Planning Techniques
§6.8. Types of Life Insurance
§6.9. Cash Value Insurance
§6.9.1. Whole Life
§6.9.2. Limited-Pay Life
§6.9.3. Endowment Insurance
§6.9.4. Universal Life
§6.9.5. Variable Life
§6.10. Term Insurance
Graph 6-1. Annual Premium, Five-Year Renewable $250,000 Term Policy
§6.10.1. Decreasing Term
§6.10.2. Group-Term
§6.11. Common Policy Riders
§6.11.1. Accidental Death
§6.11.2. Waiver of Premium
§6.12. Participating and Nonparticipating Policies
§6.13. Life Insurance Agents
§6.14. Financial Condition of Insurers
§6.15. Community Property
§6.15.1. Inception-of-Title Rule
§6.15.2. Apportionment Rule
§6.15.3. Risk Payment Doctrine

B. Planning with Life Insurance

§6.16. Introduction

§6.17. Combined Marital Estates of Less Than $600,000
§6.18. Combined Marital Estates of Less Than $1.2 Million (Two Credit Equivalents)
§6.18.1. Protect Minor Children
§6.18.2. Use Trusts
§6.18.3. Plan Based upon a Revocable Trust
Chart 6-1. Disposition of Property upon Death of Married Insured (Moderate-size Estates)
§6.18.4. Plan Based upon a Testamentary Trust
§6.19. Choosing Between a Revocable Trust and a Testamentary Trust
§6.20. Combined Marital Estates of More Than $1.2 Million: Eliminating the Insurance from the Estate of the Insured
§6.21. Ownership by an Individual Other Than the Insured
§6.21.1. Cross-Owned Insurance
§6.21.2. Applications and Assignments
§6.21.3. Community Property
§6.21.4. Premium Payments
§6.21.5. Beneficiary Designations
§6.21.6. Successive Ownership
§6.22. Marital Deduction Planning
§6.22.1. Beneficiary Designations
§6.22.2. Premium Payments
§6.22.3. Successive Ownership
§6.23. Irrevocable Life Insurance Trusts
§6.23.1. Estate Tax
§6.23.2. Gift Tax
§6.23.3. Survivorship Policies
§6.23.4. GSTT
§6.23.5. Drafting Considerations
§6.23.6. Community Property
§6.24. Other Types of Life Insurance Trusts
§6.24.1. Community Property Widow's Election Life Insurance Trust
§6.24.2. Business Uses
§6.24.3. Charitable Uses

C. Estate Taxation of Life Insurance

§6.25. History
§6.26. Life Insurance Receivable by or for the Benefit of the Estate, §2042(1)
§6.27. Incidents of Ownership, §2042(2)
§6.27.1. Policy Facts and Intent Facts
§6.27.2. Incidents of Ownership
§6.27.3. Power to Change Beneficiaries by Divorce, Birth, or Adoption
§6.27.4. Power to Terminate Membership in Group Plans
§6.27.5. Power to Convert Group Insurance to Ordinary Insurance

§6.27.6. Right to Prevent Cancellation by Purchasing Employer Owned Life Insurance
§6.27.7. Power to Remove and Replace Trustee
§6.27.8. Negative or "Veto" Powers
§6.27.9. Incidents of Ownership Under Extraneous Contract
§6.27.10. Reversionary Interests, §2042(2)
§6.27.11. Incidents of Ownership Held in a Fiduciary Capacity
§6.28. Attribution of Incidents of Ownership
§6.28.1. Stock Held as Community Property
§6.28.2. Insurance Owned by a Partnership
§6.29. Reciprocal Trust Doctrine and Life Insurance
§6.30. Transfer of Interests in Insurance Within Three Years of Death, §2035
§6.31. §2035; Pre-1982 Law
§6.32. §2035; Post-1981 Law
§6.32.1. Insured Transfers Owned Insurance
§6.32.2. Controlled Corporation or Other Noninsured-Owner Transfers Insurance Within Three Years of Insured's Death
§6.32.3. Pre-1982 Law: Insured Transfers Funds Used to Purchase Insurance
§6.32.4. Post-1981 Law: Insured Transfers Funds Used to Purchase Insurance
§6.32.5. Exchange of Policies Owned by Others Within Three Years of Insured's Death
§6.33. Insurance Required with Joint or Community Property Funds
§6.34. Sale of Life Insurance by Insured Within Three Years of Death, §2035
§6.35. Exclusion of Part of Proceeds to the Extent Premiums Paid by Others
§6.36. Insurance on the Life of a Person Other Than the Decedent, §2035
§6.37. Premiums Paid Within Three Years of Death; Pre-1982 Law, §2035
§6.38. Transfer of Incidents of Ownership Within Three Years of Death, §2035
§6.39. Retained Life Interest, §2036
§6.40. State Death Taxes
§6.41. Generation-Skipping Transfer Tax (GSTT)
§6.41.1. GSTT Exemption for Nontaxable Gifts
§6.41.2. GSTT $1 Million Exemption

D. Gift Taxation of Life Insurance

§6.42. General
§6.43. Valuation of Policies

§6.43.1. Term and Group-Term Insurance
§6.43.2. Single-Premium and Paid-Up Policies
§6.43.3. Other Policies — Interpolated Terminal Reserve
§6.43.4. Policy Subject to a Loan
§6.43.5. Physical Condition of Insured
§6.43.6. Form 712, Life Insurance Statement
§6.44. Annual Exclusion
§6.44.1. Multiple Donees
§6.44.2. Transfer to Trusts
§6.44.3. GSTT
§6.45. Transfer of a Policy
§6.45.1. Irrevocable Beneficiary Designation
§6.45.2. Charitable and Marital Deductions
§6.46. Payment of Premiums
§6.47. Payment of Proceeds

E. Income Taxation of Life Insurance

§6.48. Introduction
§6.49. Life Insurance Defined, §7702
Table 6-1. Cash Corridor Test of §7702(d)(2)
§6.50. Modified Endowment Contract, §7702A
§6.51. Payment of Proceeds, §101(a)(1)
§6.51.1. Deferred Payment of Proceeds, §101(c), (d)
§6.51.2. Proceeds Paid to Shareholder-Beneficiary
§6.52. Settlement Options, §101(c), (d)
§6.53. Transfer for Value, §101(a)(2)
§6.53.1. Exceptions
§6.53.2. First Exception, §101(a)(2)(A)
§6.53.3. Second Exception, §101(a)(2)(B)
§6.54. Policy Purchased by a Qualified Plan
§6.55. Premium Payments
§6.55.1. Premium Payments Deductible as Alimony
§6.55.2. Premium Payments as Charitable Contributions
§6.55.3. Premium Payments at a Discount
§6.56. Premiums Paid by Employers Are Deductible
§6.57. Cost of Insurance Protection Provided by Qualified Plans, §72(m)(3)
§6.58. Grantor Trusts, §677(a)(3)
§6.59. Policy Loans
§6.59.1. Loans on Policies Other Than Modified Endowment Contracts
§6.59.2. Loans on Modified Endowment Contracts
§6.59.3. Loan Rates and Dividends
§6.60. Deductibility of Interest on Policy Loans: General
§6.60.1. Who Is Entitled to Deduct Interest Paid
§6.60.2. Interest on Policy Loans: Limitations of §264
§6.60.3. Exceptions to §264(a)(3)

§6.61. Dividends
§6.62. Sale, Surrender, or Exchange of Insurance Policies: General
§6.63. Sale of Policy — Gain and Loss
§6.63.1. Sale or Other Disposition of Encumbered Policy
§6.63.2. "Loss" on Sale
§6.64. Surrender of Policies
§6.65. Exchange of Policies Under §1035
§6.65.1. What Constitutes an Exchange
§6.65.2. Exchange of Assignable Policies
§6.65.3. Exchange of Nonassignable Policies
§6.66. Exchanges Within §1035; Permissible Exchanges; Basis
§6.67. Costs of Exchanges — Exercise Care and Study the Economics
§6.68. Exchange of Policies Not Within §1035
§6.69. Alternative Minimum Tax, §56(g)(4)(B)(ii)

F. Special Types of Life Insurance

§6.70. Introduction
§6.71. Split-Dollar Life Insurance: General
§6.71.1. Reverse Split-Dollar
§6.71.2. Income Tax Consequences
Table 6-2. Uniform One-Year Term Premiums for $1,000 Life Insurance Protection
§6.71.3. Gift Tax Consequences
§6.71.4. Estate Tax Consequences
§6.72. Employer-Provided Group-Term Life Insurance: General
§6.72.1. Planning with Group-Term Insurance
§6.72.2. Insurance on Spouses and Children
§6.72.3. Nondiscrimination Rules
§6.72.4. Nondiscrimination Rules as to Eligibility
§6.72.5. Nondiscrimination Rules as to Benefits
§6.72.6. Basic Requirements
§6.72.7. Plans That Include Permanent Benefits
§6.72.8. Who Are "Employees"?
§6.72.9. Determining the Amount Includible in Income
Table 6-3. Uniform Premiums for $1,000 of Group-Term Life Insurance Protection
§6.72.10. Assignment
§6.72.11. Estate Tax
§6.72.12. Gift Tax
§6.72.13. Group-Term Life Insurance: Retired Lives Reserve (RLR)
§6.73. Minimum-Deposit Life Insurance Plans
§6.74. Single-Premium Whole Life
§6.75. Second-to-Die or Survivorship Whole Life
§6.76. Leased Life Insurance

§6.77. Veterans' Life Insurance
§6.78. Death Benefit Only Plans
§6.78.1. Estate Tax, General
§6.78.2. §2033
§6.78.3. "Transfer" §§2035-2038
§6.78.4. §2035
§6.78.5. §2036
§6.78.6. §2037
§6.78.7. §2038(a)(1)
§6.78.8. Gift Tax
§6.78.9. Income Tax
§6.78.10. Installment Payment of Death Benefit Taxed as Annuity
§6.78.11. Reasonable and Necessary Payments Are Deductible by Employer
§6.78.12. ERISA
§6.79. Gifts of Life Insurance Under the Uniform Transfers to Minors Act
§6.80. Life Insurance and the Uniform Simultaneous Death Act

Bibliography

A. INTRODUCTION

§6.1. Scope

Estate planners seldom see a client whose life is not insured under at least one policy of life insurance. Indeed, for many families life insurance is the largest single investment apart from the family residence. Life insurance proceeds are commonly the largest single liquid asset that is available upon the death of the head of a family. Life insurance may also play an important role in the business context, from funding buy-sell agreements to providing death benefits to the families of deceased employees.

Irrevocable life insurance trusts remain one of the most attractive opportunities for sheltering a substantial amount of property from the federal transfer taxes. The use of irrevocable life insurance trusts is aggressively marketed as providing "wealth replacement" for the amounts the insured will be required to pay in death taxes. "Life insurance is a viable answer for the high net worth client faced with replacing assets lost to estate taxation. The client should get past his philosophical objections and understand that use of this product in his estate plan is an investment decision rather than a life insurance buying decision." Wilshinsky, Life Insurance: A New Dimension in Estate Planning, 130 Tr. & Est. 10 (June 1991). Because of the important role that life insurance plays in estate planning, it is important for the planner to be familiar with the basic substantive and tax law regarding life insurance.

A good grasp of the basic tax laws is necessary to advise clients regarding the consequences of both simple and complex insurance transactions. The existing federal tax laws offer some important opportunities for removing a very substantial amount of life insurance from the gross estate of the insured at little or no gift or income tax cost. Indeed, the tax advantages of the irrevocable life insurance trust has made it a common element of estate plans in many circumstances. *See* §6.23. Benefits paid under so-called death benefit only plans may also be excluded from the estate of a deceased employee. *See* §6.78. Life insurance continues to play an important role in estate planning despite the adoption of the unlimited marital deduction and of the relatively large unified credit. Indeed, the ability to defer the payment of the estate tax until the death of the second spouse to die makes it possible to provide for payment of the tax through the use of a policy that matures on the death of the second spouse to die. Such policies carry premiums much lower than would be payable on policies that matured on the death of one spouse. For a discussion of last-to-die or survivorship life insurance, which is particularly attractive when used in conjunction with an irrevocable trust, *see* §6.75. The GSTT exemption and exclusions for nontaxable gifts can be used to shelter a large amount of life insurance from the GSTT. *See* §§2.25, 2.27.

Estate planners also need to know the basic types of life insurance policies, the advantages and disadvantages of different forms of ownership, and different types of beneficiary designations. The estate plan recommended for a client may involve the transfer, surrender, exchange, or retention of existing policies, or it may involve the acquisition of additional ones. Lawyers should recognize their own limitations, however, and should be reluctant to assume the role of insurance or investment advisor. The increased complexity of both cash value life insurance contracts (which reflects a growing emphasis on their investment features) and the tax law make it important for clients and lawyers to have the advice of competent experts. Experts can help in selecting among available policies and in many other ways, including the selection of a financially sound insurer. In keeping with the practices of lawyers and accountants, many insurance advisors now charge hourly fees for their services. The recommendations regarding life insurance will depend upon a variety of factors, including the client's age, health, family circumstances, and investment and planning objectives.

This chapter includes a review of the basic types of life insurance; a consideration of the basic objectives and techniques of planning with life insurance; a discussion of the gift, estate, and income tax consequences of transactions involving life insurance; and an examination of the characteristics of some special types of life insurance.

Basically, life insurance is a contractual arrangement for spreading among all members of a group the risk of suffering economic loss upon the death of any member of the group. This is accomplished by each person in the group paying a relatively small amount each year into a pool in consideration of the promise by the operator of the pool to pay a larger amount to designated persons upon the death of any group member during that year. In practice, the risk pools are operated by insurance companies subject to state laws and the supervision of state insurance commissioners.

The beneficiary designated in the insurance contract is ordinarily not subject to change by will. However, a contrary conclusion has been reached in a few cases. *See Connecticut General Life Insurance Co. v. Peterson,* 442 F. Supp. 533 (W.D. Mo. 1978). *See also* §4.18.4. In most states the right of a beneficiary to receive the proceeds of an insurance policy is not affected by a divorce of the insured and the beneficiary unless otherwise specified in the divorce decree. However, divorce revokes the beneficiary designation of a former spouse under the 1990 version of U.P.C. §2-804 and the laws of Michigan, Ohio, Oklahoma, and Texas. *See* §4.20.4.

§6.2. Terminology; Insurable Interest

Before going further it may be helpful to review the terms that are commonly used to designate the parties to a transaction involving life insurance and to consider the requirement that the person procuring life insurance have an insurable interest in the life of the insured.

The *insurer* is the company that issues a life insurance policy. The *insured* is the person whose life is insured and upon whose death a specified sum is payable under the terms of the policy. A life insurance policy is itself property as distinct from the proceeds payable at the death of the insured. An insured may or may not have been the *applicant* who originally applied for issuance of the policy and the *policy owner.* Upon the death of the insured the death benefit (policy proceeds) is payable to the *beneficiary* designated in the policy or in a change of beneficiary form. If the primary beneficiary is an individual, it is wise to designate a secondary, or contingent, beneficiary to whom the proceeds will be paid if the primary beneficiary does not survive the insured. Under the terms of modern policies the policy owner, who may or may not be the insured, has the unrestricted right to change the beneficiary unless the beneficiary has been irrevocably designated. A revocably designated beneficiary has no property interest in the policy — only a contingent interest in the proceeds. The policy owner owns and controls the policy, including the designation of the beneficiary. The irrevocable designation of a beneficiary in effect makes that person the owner of the policy. Such a designation is seldom desirable and seldom done because the substantive and tax law consequences are not entirely clear.

In order for a third party to acquire insurance on the life of another person, the third party must have an insurable interest in the life of the insured. The requirement is imposed in order to prevent insurance from being used for gambling purposes. The rule that limits the exclusion from income of the proceeds of life insurance paid under a policy that has been transferred for value, §101(a)(2), is imposed for a similar reason. *See* §6.53. "[T]he interest commonly sought is a financial interest adversely affected if the insured dies." J. Munch, Financial and Estate Planning with Life Insurance Products ¶7.1.2 (1990). Individuals related by blood or law are presumed to have an insurable interest engendered by love and affection. 40 Pa. Stat. Ann. §512 (Purdon 1971).

In LR 9110016 the IRS indicated that it would deny income, gift, and estate tax deductions with respect to an insurance policy that the insured-donor proposed to transfer to a charity. According to the IRS view the charity would not have an insurable interest in the life of the insured under the applicable state law, that of New York. The ruling concerned an individual who planned to (1) acquire a policy of insurance on his life, (2) assign irrevocably the policy to a charity, and (3) continue to pay premiums on the policy. The IRS concluded that the original acquisition of the insurance by the donor was intended to circumvent a state law requirement that the owner-beneficiary of a policy have an insurable interest in the life of the insured. If so, under New York law the insurer might deny liability upon the death of the insured or the insured's personal representative might recover the proceeds from the charity-beneficiary. Accordingly, the IRS concluded that no income or gift tax deductions were allowable with respect to the transfer or payment of premiums, that the insurance would be includible in the insured's estate and that no charitable deduction would be allowable for estate tax purposes. The IRS's reasoning, based on New York law, seems flawed. Once a policy is acquired by the insured, the insured should be free to transfer the policy to whomever he or she chooses. In addition, a charity should be presumed to have an insurable interest in the life of a donor. New York amended the law to eliminate the problem after which the IRS revoked LR 9110016. LR 9147040. The same issue could arise in other jurisdictions which have laws similar to former law of New York (*e.g.,* Washington, Wash. Rev. Code §48.18.030 (1989)), but will not in other states, such as Pennsylvania, that have statutes allowing a validly issued policy to be transferred to an assignee who does not have an insurable interest in the life of the insured. "If a policy of life insurance has been issued in conformity with this section, no transfer of such policy or any interest thereunder shall be invalid by reason of a lack of insurable interest of the transferee in the life of the insured or the payment of premiums thereafter by the transferee." 40 Pa. Stat. Ann. §512 (Purdon's 1971).

§6.3. Data Collection

As a rule an experienced lawyer or legal assistant should assemble data regarding all existing policies of insurance on the client's life for purposes of analysis and future reference. Reliable data regarding some items of information, such as the beneficiary designations, current policy values, and outstanding loan balances may only be available from the insurers. The necessary information is usually provided promptly by the insurer in response to a letter signed by the owner of the policy that encloses an appropriate data collection form. The use of a standard data collection form is convenient and assures that the necessary data will be obtained for each policy. With the approval of the client the data may be collected and submitted by the client's insurance advisor.

The following information should be collected regarding each policy:

1. insurer and number of policy;
2. type of policy (term, whole life, endowment, etc.);
3. face amount;
4. amount of premium and source of payment;
5. dividend option selected;
6. accidental death benefit;
7. waiver of premium in event of disability;
8. original applicant;
9. current owner of policy;
10. successive owner of policy (if designated);
11. current beneficiary designation;
12. current cash surrender value; and
13. amount of policy loans, if any, and interest rate.

The lawyer should also record the place where the client keeps the policies. *See* Form 1-5. Some additional data should be collected for special types of policies and when policies have been assigned to a trust. It is important to know the current status of beneficiary designations, policy loans, and the like in order to integrate life insurance fully into the client's estate plan. To preserve the integrity and value of a plan, the client should be cautioned not to change beneficiary designations, to assign policies, or to take other significant action with respect to life insurance without consulting the lawyer in advance.

§6.4. Basic Functions of Life Insurance

Life insurance is usually purchased in order to provide funds with which to (1) pay taxes, costs, and expenses of an illiquid estate; (2) satisfy a mortgage or other substantial indebtedness; (3) fund a buy-sell agreement or other business-related transaction; or (4) support the dependents of the insured. In addition, an investment in cash value life insurance may help provide investment diversification and provide wealth replacement as mentioned above at §6.1. In any case, the ownership and beneficiary designations can often be arranged so that none of the proceeds is includible in the insured's gross estate even though the insured paid the premiums.

Various types of cash value life insurance may be acquired as a personal investment because the earnings on the reserve attributable to a policy accumulate free of tax until withdrawal. The compounding of the tax-free accumulation of variable life policies can be particularly impressive. The increased emphasis on life insurance as a tax-advantaged investment led Congress to strike back in the 1988 Act, which imposed limits on some excesses. Finally, life insurance is often purchased in the business setting as an employee benefit. For example, an employer may provide all, or virtually all, employees with a limited amount of group term insurance as a fringe benefit. *See* §6.72. Additional insurance may be provided to key employees.

Additional insurance may be needed to fund the costs of the insured's final illness and funeral, debts, death taxes, and administration expenses. Life insurance is also a popular way for persons with illiquid estates to provide funds with which to meet those costs. In specific cases it may be purchased to avoid the forced liquidation of the decedent's interest in a closely-held business or other illiquid assets such as unimproved real property. Insurance may be needed although the immediate post-mortem demand for funds can be reduced through special use valuation under §2032A, redemption of stock under §303, or deferral of estate tax payment under §6166. *See* §§11.15-11.30, 12.19. Liquidity can, of course, be provided although the insurance is not includible in the insured's gross estate. An irrevocable life insurance trust is often used for this purpose. *See* §6.23.

Life insurance is also sometimes purchased in order to provide funds with which to finance the acquisition of the decedent's interest in a partnership, closely-held corporation, or other business enterprise. The amount needed for this purpose can be estimated and updated as required if the purchase price is fixed by the terms of a buy-sell agreement or is based upon a formula set forth in the agreement. Otherwise the amount may be more roughly estimated. Regardless of the form of the agreement (*e.g.*, cross-purchase or entity purchase), the ownership of the insurance and the beneficiary designations should be carefully arranged to preserve the available income and estate tax advantages. The use of buy-sell agreements is discussed at §§11.6-11.14.

§6.5. How Much Life Insurance?

Life insurance is often purchased to provide for the dependents of the insured following his or her death. For this purpose some companies and advisors recommend carrying insurance equal to five or six times annual earnings or spending "at least" a specified percentage of gross or net income for cash value insurance. Unfortunately, these simple formulas are not very helpful. An individual's annual income is not necessarily a reliable indicator of the actual financial needs or circumstances of his or her dependents. Similiarly, the emphasis on ordinary life insurance instead of term insurance is often misplaced.

The bias of some agents in favor of whole life insurance also contributes to the problem of some families being underinsured. In particular, the insurance needs of young families with modest incomes and small children are often best met through the purchase of less expensive term insurance. Of course, in later years term insurance may become too expensive to continue.

For the same premium, a much larger amount of term insurance can be purchased on the life of a relatively young person, which may better protect the economic security of a typical young family. By way of illustration, the annual premium cost of a $100,000 annually renewable and convertible term policy is about $165 for a male nonsmoker aged 35, while the annual premium on a cash value participating life policy of that amount is about $800. Also, note that the annual cost of group term insurance is often significantly lower than individual term. In any case, it pays to shop carefully before purchasing life insurance — the price of comparable policies may vary by as much as 300 percent.

The amount of insurance needed to protect a family can be based upon a projection of the family's needs and an estimate of the resources that will be available to the family. A rough estimate is the best we can do because we do not know when the insured will die or what the future will bring in terms of family circumstances or general economic conditions. The extent of the imponderables is illustrated by the difference between assuming the family's needs will be affected by a four-, six-, or ten percent rate of inflation. However, a fairly useful estimate can be made under the approach recommended by Consumers Union in a very helpful paperback book, Life Insurance: How to Buy the Right Policy from the Right Company at the Right Price 10-20 (1988). This approach is based on the preparation of a family balance sheet that includes estimates of what the family needs to maintain its standard of living if the insured were to die tomorrow and the resources, including

Social Security, pension payments, interest, and dividends that the family would have available to meet those needs. Funds needed at some future time (*e.g.,* for college expenses) are discounted to current value. Perhaps recognizing that most Americans are underinsured, insurance agents may offer to make essentially the same calculations for prospects who provide the necessary financial data. Programs of this type are generally helpful to clients because they take into account the latest developments that may not otherwise be readily known by individuals, such as changes in the Social Security benefit formulas.

Under the Consumers Union approach the family's needs are estimated first, including (1) the decedent's final expenses (*e.g.,* costs of last illness and funeral, debts, estate administration expenses, and death taxes); (2) the family's basic income requirements (*e.g.,* costs of food, clothing, recreation, net of Social Security benefits and pension payments); (3) the children's education fund (cost of making higher education available to children); and (4) the surviving spouse's retirement fund (to provide for retirement of surviving spouse). Some of the calculations are based only on uncertain projections. For example, the estimate of the family's income needs should reflect the different levels of Social Security benefits payable at various times since the amounts payable are related to the ages of the surviving spouse and children. It should reflect a discount (or inflation) factor that should be used when the needs are future ones, such as the cost of food and housing. The family assets are then estimated, including liquid assets, such as cash, securities, insurance proceeds and other death benefits, and illiquid assets such as equity in real estate. The income that could be generated by the family's liquid assets is estimated. The insurance needed by the family is the amount by which the family's estimated aggregate needs over time exceeds the estimated income and principal available to the family. Unfortunately, the estimates rapidly become obsolete because of changes in the family structure (number and age of children), the family fortunes, and in the provisions of retirement programs, including Social Security.

§6.6. Spouse Insurance

Some consideration should also be given to purchasing insurance on the life of a spouse, particularly one who devotes full, or nearly full, time to childcare. Insurance can be used to meet the liquidity needs that may arise if the caregiving spouse dies first, particularly where he or she owns an estate of substantial value that produces little income. Of course, the needs were reduced somewhat by the adoption of the unlimited marital deduction in 1981. The proceeds from this kind of insurance protection may also be excluded from the estate of the wage earning spouse where the policies are owned by their children or the trustee of an irrevocable life insurance trust. *See* §6.23. They may also help offset the additional costs that may be incurred by a surviving spouse for childcare and homemaking costs. If dependent children or stepchildren live with the surviving spouse, he or she may file income tax returns at joint return rates for two years and later as a head of household.

§6.7. Basic Planning Techniques

The basic life insurance planning techniques are discussed in Part B, §§6.16-6.24. They include ownership by a person other than the insured, the cross-ownership of insurance by a husband and wife, revocable and irrevocable life insurance trusts, and business-related insurance. Particularly impressive estate tax savings can result from the use of an irrevocable life insurance trust under which the proceeds of policies are excluded from the estates of both the insured and his or her spouse. Beneficial results are also available through plans that combine charitable gifts and life insurance.

§6.8. Types of Life Insurance

At base all life insurance policies are term insurance that provides insurance protection alone for the specified period, cash value insurance that combines insurance protection with an investment element, or a combination of the two. Term and cash value insurance are very different: Each meets the needs of some persons, but neither meets the needs of everyone. On the one hand, term insurance provides maximum current insurance protection for the premium dollar. On the other, cash value insurance provides insurance protection and a fund that is sheltered from creditors and that accumulates earnings in the hands of the insurer (the "inside" build-up) free of tax to the policy owner.

The main differences between term and cash value insurance arise from the fact that the premium on term pays only for the cost of insurance protection during the term, while the premium on cash value insurance includes an excess which is accumulated in a policy reserve that reduces the amount at risk in later years. The reserve supports the cash surrender value or loan value of the policy, which is available to the policy owner prior to maturity of the policy. Because mortality increases with age for adults, the cost of term insurance increases with the age of the insured. What is very economical term insurance protection at age 30 or 35 can become very expensive at age 60 or 65.

The premium cost of cash value insurance is initially much greater than term, but is typically much less in later years. However, because of the reserve fund, the premium on cash value insurance usually remains level or declines (in the case of participating policies). With favorable earnings the need to pay premiums on some cash value policies may disappear altogether after a few years. Another feature of the reserve fund in cash value insurance is that the amount at risk (the insurance element) decreases over time as the size of the reserve increases. In contrast, the entire amount of a term policy remains at risk throughout the term.

§6.9. Cash Value Insurance

The following sections describe the general types of cash value policies — whole life, limited pay life, and endowment contracts. It also reviews the basic characteristics of two innovations of the 1980s, Universal Life and Variable Life.

§6.9.1. Whole Life

The most common form of cash value insurance is whole life, which is also called straight life or ordinary life. Cash value policies are also sometimes called "permanent" insurance to distinguish them from term insurance that is issued for a specified term of years (*e.g.,* one, five, or ten years). Of course, term insurance is typically renewable without further evidence of insurability, at increasing premiums, until the insured reaches an advanced age. Historically in the typical whole life policy, both the amount of insurance and the premium usually remained level for the duration of the policy. Policies are now often designed with a wide range of variations, including lower initial premiums and increasing amounts of insurance. Premiums may be payable until the insured dies or the policy matures when the insured attains a very advanced age, usually 99 or 100. If the insured lives to maturity, the face amount of insurance is paid to the policy owner and the policy terminates. On the other hand, higher premiums may only be payable for a few years.

§6.9.2. Limited-Pay Life

Limited-pay life is a variation that involves payment of premiums for a limited period — usually a fixed number of years or until the insured attains a specified age. Policies on which premiums are payable for 20 years ("twenty-pay-life") or until the insured reaches age 65 ("pay-to-sixty-five") are common examples of limited-pay policies. The premium on a limited-pay policy is higher than on an old style whole life policy in the same amount, but the cash value of the limited-pay policy usually builds up faster.

§6.9.3. Endowment Insurance

The final initial category is the endowment policy. It is essentially a whole life policy with a maturity or endowment date that occurs after a certain number of years or at a certain age, usually 65 rather than 100. The purchaser of an endowment policy should understand that when a policy matures the amount by which the amount paid out exceeds the amount of premiums paid by the insured is includible in the insured's income. Premiums are typically payable on an endowment policy until the policy endows or the insured dies. Of course, if the insured dies prior to endowment, the face amount of insurance is payable to the designated beneficiary, just as with an ordinary life policy. Since an endowment policy matures more quickly than ordinary life and its cash value also equals its face value at maturity, the premiums must be substantially higher. Traditional endowment policies issued after June 21, 1988 may have difficulty meeting the requirements of §7702. At least some may be characterized as modified endowment contracts under §7702A. *See* §6.50.

§6.9.4. Universal Life

Each premium payment on a universal life policy is credited to the policy's cash value account. Deductions are made from the cash value account for an appropriate portion of the insurer's projected mortality costs (death claims) and expense charges (selling costs and commission payments). The remainder is credited with interest at a guaranteed minimum rate plus whatever higher rate may be earned and declared by the insurer. As some commentators have observed, a universal life policy resembles term insurance combined with a savings account. Of course, the internal build-up in value of the policy (the "interest" on the "savings account") is tax-free. The balance in the cash value account may be borrowed or may be withdrawn if the policy is surrendered. Expenses that are charged against the cash value account may include an initial fixed fee, a fixed dollar amount or a fixed or declining percentage of premiums, or some combination of them. As is the case with some mutual funds, some universal policies provide for a backload charge if the policy is surrendered. Backload charges typically decline each year and disappear after a specified number of years (eight, ten, or fifteen). Some policies guarantee a high rate of interest for an initial period, which may also be used for purposes of illustrations.

Universal life policies are usually available in forms that have a fixed death benefit (Option "A") or a death benefit that is composed of a fixed death benefit *plus* the balance of the cash value account (Option "B"). The cost of the latter type is naturally greater.

In comparing policy illustrations, the planner should be sure they involve the same premiums, death benefits, and interest rate assumptions. The planner should also examine the rates of interest that each company has actually credited to its universal life policies. Some illustrations indicate that the necessity of paying premiums will "vanish" after a relatively short term of years (seven or ten years are often used for illustrative purposes). However, the planner and the prospective policy owner should understand that the premiums will vanish and remain vanished only so long as the balance in the policy's cash value account is credited with interest that equals or exceeds the projected interest used in the illustration. Otherwise, the owner will be required to pay additional premiums. Policies issued by some companies tie the interest rate to an index, such as the 52-week Treasury bill rate.

Insurers frequently indicate a "target" premium that is intended to create a cash value sufficient to keep the policy in force for life. Because of the variability in the amount of charges against the account and interest credited to the account, payment of the target premiums might generate more or less than required to maintain the policy. Indeed, paying smaller premiums or skipping some premium payments might be sufficient to support the policy. Payments of larger premiums would create a larger reserve and cash value, which could remain invested or be borrowed by the policy owner.

§6.9.5. Variable Life

A variable life insurance contract is a type of whole life which usually has a fixed premium and a guaranteed minimum amount of insurance. It is called variable insurance because an additional amount of insurance may be provided under the policy, depending upon the investment performance of the fund or funds (usually mutual funds) selected by the policy owner. In this case, the product can be viewed as term insurance combined with a mutual fund. Importantly, the yield of an equity fund may significantly exceed the amount that would otherwise be credited to the policy based upon the investment performance of the insurer's general portfolio of assets (principally bonds). Again, the key to the popularity of variable life is that the internal build-up in value of policy is tax-free until it is withdrawn.

The owner of a variable life policy is usually free to allocate the cash value among one or more funds that reflect different investment philosophies. In effect this type of policy shifts the investment risk largely to the policy owner. If the arrangement is properly structured, the income, gain, or loss experienced by the fund is reportable by the insurer and not the policy owner. *E.g.,* LR 8427085. If the funds in which the cash value is invested produce a rate of return higher than the rate guaranteed in the policy, the excess may be used to purchase additional paid-up insurance. *E.g.,* LR 8349034. The variable life plans described in Rev. Rul. 79-87, 1979-1 C.B. 73, provide for the net annual premium to be allocated to a separate account, which is invested primarily in equity securities in the discretion of the insurer. The cash surrender value, and presumably the loan value, may also increase or decrease depending upon investment experience, but with no guaranteed minimum. In the long run variable insurance may provide an attractive way to make an additional investment in equity securities.

§6.10. Term Insurance

Term insurance, which may be issued either on an individual or a group basis, provides insurance protection for the period specified in the policy (usually a term of one, five, or ten years). It is often called "pure" insurance because it does not involve any investment component or nonforfeiture values. Unlike cash value insurance, term insurance does not provide any loan or surrender value that can be reached in case of financial emergency. Viewed in its simplest terms, the full face amount of the insurance is at risk each term.

If term insurance is guaranteed renewable, it may be continued for successive terms without further evidence of insurability until final termination of the coverage, which may not occur until an advanced age. If the amount of the term insurance remains the same, the premium will increase with each renewal as the insured grows older. If the insurance is not guaranteed renewable, the insurance protection will lapse at the end of the term and a new policy will be issued only upon showing evidence of insurability. Guaranteed renewability is desirable in order to enable the insured to continue the insurance regardless of the state of the insured's health.

Term insurance is also often convertible during the term into any regularly issued form of endowment or whole life policy issued by the insurer. In case of conversion the premium on the new policy is usually based upon the insured's attained age at the time of conversion and not the insured's age at the time the term policy was originally issued. A conversion right is also generally desirable because it can be used to continue the insurance on a permanent basis. Over the short term, renewable and convertible term insurance is usually the best buy for a relatively young person who wants to obtain the maximum amount of life insurance protection at the lowest cost. Over an extended period, such as fifteen years or more, a whole life policy may be a better buy.

At base, the cost of term insurance is determined by the amount of death benefits the insurer expects to pay for the group of insured lives according to its mortality tables and the projected amount of other costs and expenses. Because the mortality rate for adults increases with age, the cost of a fixed amount of life insurance increases as the insured grows older. By way of illustration, based upon the Commissioner's 1958 Standard Ordinary Mortality Table, an insurer would expect three persons out of a group of one thousand aged 35 to die over a one-year period. Accordingly, the insurer would have to charge a premium of $30 merely to cover the cost of death benefits that would be payable under $10,000 one-year term policies issued to a group of

Graph 6-1
Annual Premium, Five-Year Renewable $250,000 Term Policy, nonsmoking Male Insured

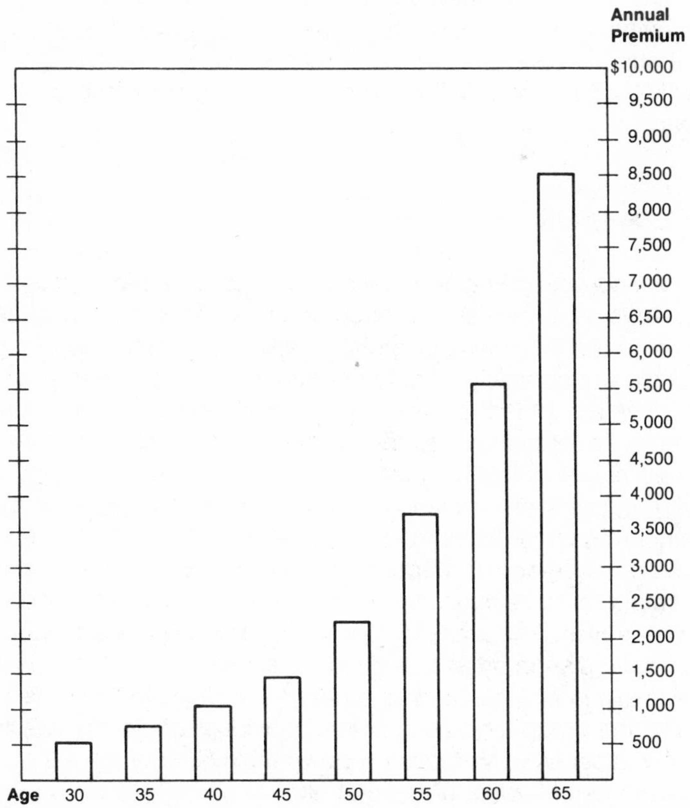

one thousand persons of that age. Based upon the same table the insurer would expect four persons to die in a year out of a group of one thousand persons aged 40; six persons out of a group aged 45; nine out of a group aged 50; thirteen out of a group aged 55, and twenty out of a group aged 60. In order to cover the death benefit alone, the annual premium on a $10,000 one-year term policy would be at least $40 at age 40, $60 at age 45, $90 at age 50, $130 at age 55, and $200 at age 60. A mortality table based upon the 1980 census, upon which various actuarial computations are based for tax purposes, was published by the IRS in 1989. IRS Pub. No. 1457, Table 80CNSMT, p. 6-1.

§6.10.1. Decreasing Term

In the case of decreasing term insurance the premium remains the same over time, but the face amount of insurance decreases. Decreasing term is often used to provide for payment of the balance of a mortgage if the primary breadwinner in a family dies prior to its satisfaction. Terms of from five to thirty years are usually available for this purpose, depending somewhat upon the age of the insured at the time of issue. It is usually less expensive for an individual to buy decreasing term directly than it is to buy the insurance through the mortgagor or other creditor.

§6.10.2. Group-Term

Very economical guaranteed renewable and convertible group-term insurance is often available through an employer, professional association, or other membership group. Many group plans do not require evidence of insurability for persons who buy a limited amount of group-term coverage when the plan is first made available or during some subsequent enrollment periods. In many cases group-term insurance fits well into an estate plan because of its low cost, its general assignability, and its slight value for gift tax purposes. However, in the case of employer provided group-term insurance, the continuation of the insurance coverage is dependent upon the continued existence of the employment relationship and the employer's continuation of the insurance plan. For example, the employer may decide to terminate a group-term plan in order to reduce expenses. Also, if the employment relationship ends, the former employee may have only the right to convert the group-term coverage to individual whole life, which could be very expensive. Moreover, a new employer may have a less generous group-term plan, or none at all.

§6.11. Common Policy Riders

Insurers typically offer at least two riders that can be added at a small increase in cost to most term and cash value policies: the accidental death benefit rider and the waiver of premium rider. Each of them is discussed below. A third rider that is frequently available with respect to cash value policies allows the owner to purchase term insurance on the life of the spouse or children of the insured, or both. The need for insurance on the lives of dependents and its relative cost should be considered by the client before taking advantage of the family term insurance rider.

§6.11.1. Accidental Death

Under the accidental death benefit rider, commonly called the "double indemnity clause," an additional death benefit equal to the face amount will be paid in the event the insured dies as the result of an accidental injury. Some clauses provide for triple indemnity if the insured dies as a result of injuries suffered while riding on a bus, train, plane, or other licensed public conveyance. The cost of the rider is usually about $1 per year for each $1,000 of accidental death benefit, but it is questionable whether it is a wise purchase for most persons. In truth, a double indemnity rider does not provide insurance protection that can be relied upon to meet the needs of the survivors. Instead, it is essentially a gamble that the insured will die as the result of an accident, which is highly unlikely in any given case.

§6.11.2. Waiver of Premium

The typical waiver of premium rider provides that the insurer will waive payment of all premiums falling due under the policy while the insured is totally and permanently disabled prior to a certain age (usually 65). This type of rider also typically comes into effect only if the disability occurs prior to age 60 or 65 and it lasts for six months or more. The value of the rider depends largely upon the limitations applicable to it and its cost, both of which vary substantially from policy to policy. Stripped to its essentials, the rider is a minidisability policy. The cost of the rider varies with the age and occupation of the insured and from company to company. Some advisors consider the rider to provide useful additional protection against disability. However, the same coverage might be available at lower cost by increasing the amount of disability insurance carried by the insured instead of purchasing the waiver of premium provision.

§6.12. Participating and Nonparticipating Policies

Policies upon which the insurer may pay annual dividends, usually beginning after the second or third policy year, are called *participating* policies. They include most cash value policies issued by mutual insurance companies and some issued by stock companies. Some term policies are also participating, but many are not. Although participating policies generally do not guarantee that any dividends will be paid, dividends that are paid can be quite substantial.

The initial premium on participating policies is generally higher than for nonparticipating policies, but the long run cost of participating policies is often much lower. In effect, the dividends represent a refund of excess premiums previously paid on a policy and part of the income derived from investing the excess. Consistent with that analysis, dividends are not taxable income until the amount recovered by the policy owner exceeds the premiums or other consideration paid for the policy. *See* §6.61. For purposes of setting the premium on nonparticipating policies, some insurers assume a low rate of return; as a result, the premium on a nonparticipating policy may actually exceed the premium on participating policies after a short time. Participating cash value policies generally give the policy owner five options regarding the use of the dividends: (1) to receive payment of the dividend in cash; (2) to apply the dividends against current premium costs; (3) to leave the dividends with the company at interest; (4) to use the dividends to purchase additional paid-up insurance; or (5) to use the dividends to purchase one-year term insurance equal to the cash value of the policy. The fifth dividend option is a key feature of some plans, such as the minimum deposit plans discussed at §6.73, and is very useful, particularly if the option can be exercised without further evidence of insurability.

It is often tempting to take dividends in cash or to apply them in reduction of the amount of the premium necessary to continue a policy. These may be poor choices. Instead, the dividends might better be used to buy additional paid-up insurance or one-year term insurance that will help maintain the real value of the insurance protection provided by the policy against the attrition of inflation. There is usually little or no reason to leave dividends at interest with the insurer at a low guaranteed rate of interest, especially since the interest is fully taxable.

§6.13. Life Insurance Agents

Life insurance agents typically recommend that prospects buy whole life insurance instead of term insurance. This recommendation often reflects a sincere belief in the superior quality of whole life insurance and on the importance of life insurance as an investment. Whole life and term are different types of insurance, but both are generally sold by the same companies, which indicates that they are both reliable. Objectively speaking, it is doubtful that (1) whole life is inherently superior or (2) cash value life insurance is a wise investment for a young family with a need for large amounts of insurance during the years the children are dependent. Also, traditional whole life has been a questionable investment, particularly during periods of high inflation. The needs of young families and some other individual life insurance purchasers might be better met if they bought much larger amounts of term insurance. The difference between the higher cost of whole life and the cost of term might be invested or used for other family purposes. Of course, some purchasers of term insurance would not save the difference, and, of those who did, some would make poor investments. In contrast, cash value life insurance involves forced savings that are readily available in case of need (or investment opportunity). It is, in effect, a form of forced saving.

Agents are also inevitably influenced to some degree by the higher commissions paid on sales of cash value life insurance. The commission on a whole life policy is a much higher percentage of the initial premium than it is for a term policy. Because the premium rate for ordinary life is often several times that of term insurance, agents have a powerful incentive to prefer sales of whole life insurance. Most states have anti-kickback laws which prohibit an agent from returning any portion of the premium. However, rebates or discounts are permitted in a few states, including California and Florida. As a result, some planners suggest that large cash value policies be purchased through agents in those states who offer discounts.

§6.14. Financial Condition of Insurers

When evaluating a life insurance plan, it is important to obtain some assurance regarding the financial responsibility of the insurers. At a minimum the planner should obtain information regarding the rating of the insurers by leading rating companies. The four leading services that rate insurers and the general categories they use are: A. M. Best Company, rankings from A+ (superior) to C, C− (fair); Duff & Phelps, Inc., rankings from AAA (highest) to CCC (risk of inability to pay claims); Moody's Investor Services, rankings from Aaa (exceptional) to C (lowest); and Standard and Poor's Corporation, rankings from AAA (extremely strong) to D (default).

A. M. Best, the best known service, publishes two large volumes of reports that are available in many public libraries. One report is on life insurance companies and the other on property liability companies.

Insurance advisors typically recommend that insurance only be placed with one of the 200-300 companies that has received an A+ ranking from A. M. Best, and should provide the highest degree of safety. In addition, advisors commonly recommend that a large amount of coverage be divided among two or more insurers. Diversification reduces some of the risks associated with insurance, including the investment performance of the insurer.

§6.15. Community Property

If a married client lived in a community property jurisdiction at any time during marriage, the lawyer must be aware of the need to characterize the client's life insurance as separate or community property. The proper characterization is important for tax and nontax purposes. For example, under the law of most community property states the character of a policy determines the extent to which the insured spouse has the power, acting alone, to designate the beneficiary. The character of a policy may also affect the disposition of the policy in the event the marriage is dissolved. Perhaps most important, it determines the extent to which the interests in the policy, or its proceeds, are subject to state and federal gift and death taxes. In general, the state law characterization of a policy is accepted and followed for federal tax purposes. *E.g., Scott v. Commissioner,* 374 F.2d 154, 157 (9th Cir. 1967).

Happily, insurance is often characterized without difficulty: It is either entirely community or entirely separate under the rules of all community property states. By way of illustration, a policy purchased by the insured prior to marriage is entirely separate property if the insured makes all subsequent premium payments from separate property. Conversely, a policy purchased during marriage is entirely community property if all premiums are paid with community funds.

Serious problems of characterization may arise when premiums on a policy are paid partly with separate funds and partly with community funds. In those cases the community property states apply a variety of rules. The three main rules are: (1) the inception-of-title rule, (2) the apportionment rule, and (3) the risk payment doctrine. A lawyer who understands the basic features of those rules will be able to recognize and deal with most common problems of characterization — even though the law in most states is still evolving and the outcome in certain circumstances is uncertain.

§6.15.1. Inception-of-Title Rule

The inception-of-title rule is generally applied by Arizona, Louisiana, New Mexico, and Texas to determine the character of cash value life insurance. Under it an insurance policy and its proceeds retain the original character of the policy regardless of the source of subsequent premium payments. Thus, if a policy is acquired prior to marriage, the policy remains separate property although some later premiums are paid with community property funds. However, in such a case the community is usually entitled to reimbursement out of the insurance proceeds for premiums that were paid with community funds. *See, e.g., McCurdy v. McCurdy,* 372 S.W.2d 381 (Tex. Civ. App., 1963), *writ refused.* The community's claim for reimbursement is reflected as a reduction in the amount of the insurance that is includible in the insured's gross estate. Thus, where the community paid $12,000 of the premiums on a $100,000 separate policy, $88,000 was includible in the insured's estate as insurance (§2042) and $6,000, representing half of the reimbursement, was includible as "owned" property (§2033). Rev. Rul. 80-242, 1980-2 C.B. 276. On the other hand, if the separate property funds of one spouse are used to pay premiums on a community owned policy without the intention of making a gift to the other spouse, the spouse whose funds were used is entitled to reimbursement for half of the amount of the payments. Comment, Community and Separate Property Interests in Life Insurance Proceeds: A Fresh Look, 51 Wash. L. Rev. 351, 356 (1976).

The inception-of-title rule is criticized in W. deFuniak & M. Vaughn, Principles of Community Property §79 (2d ed. 1971), as inconsistent with basic principles of community property. The authors favor the apportionment rule, which allocates interests in a policy according to the portion of the premiums that were paid with separate and community funds respectively.

§6.15.2. Apportionment Rule

California apportions both cash value and term insurance between separate and community according to the character of the funds used to pay the premiums. *Biltoft v. Wootten,* 157 Cal. Rptr. 581 (Cal. App. 1979), following *Modern Woodman of America v. Gray,* 299 P. 754 (Cal. App. 1931). Washington apportions cash value insurance, but not term insurance. *Aetna Life Ins. Co. v. Wadsworth,* 689 P.2d 46 (Wash. 1984). The application of this rule to cash value policies is consistent with the basic principle that "where separate or community property is used to acquire other property, the latter partakes of the same nature as that of the property used for its acquisition." W. deFuniak & M. Vaughn, Principles of Community Property §79 (2d ed. 1971). It is questionable whether the same rule should apply to term policies. The payment of a premium on a term policy merely provides insurance protection for that period — when the term ends the policy has no value in the ordinary case. Of course, the renewal right may have substantial value if the insured is terminally ill or is no longer insurable. Logically, at the expiration of the term there is no asset that is properly subject to apportionment. As explained below, the risk payment doctrine does a more satisfactory job of characterizing the proceeds of term insurance.

> **Example 6-1.** *H,* a resident of California, purchased a $25,000 nonparticipating cash value life insurance policy on which he paid five annual premiums prior to his marriage to *W.* Five subsequent premiums were paid with their community property funds. Under the apportionment rule at the end of ten years the policy is one-half the separate property of *H* and one-half the community property of *H* and *W.*

Thus far neither Idaho nor Nevada has adopted a general characterization rule. Often in the past Idaho courts have followed California or Washington precedents while Nevada courts have frequently followed Texas law.

§6.15.3. Risk Payment Doctrine

Idaho, Washington, and the inception-of-title states (Arizona, Louisiana, New Mexico, and Texas) characterize the proceeds of term insurance under the risk payment doctrine. Under that doctrine life insurance proceeds are characterized as separate or community according to the source of the last premium payment. For example, if the last premium on a term policy was paid with community property funds, the proceeds of the policy are characterized as entirely community property. This approach recognizes that the current protection provided by term insurance depends entirely upon the last premium payment. *See Aetna Life Ins. Co. v. Wadsworth,* 689 P.2d 46 (Wash. 1984); *Phillips v. Welborn,* 552 P.2d 471 (N.M. 1976). "Premium payments in years gone by are not considered important. This is in contrast to the necessity of knowing the sources of past years' premium payments before applying the inception of title and apportionment rules." Comment, Community and Separate Property Interests in Life Insurance Proceeds: The Risk Payment Doctrine in State Courts and Its Federal Estate Tax Consequences, 52 Wash. L. Rev. 67, 69 (1976). Because each premium payment provides only insurance protection for the period and does not contribute cumulatively to the value of a term policy, it seems more appropriate to apply the risk payment doctrine.

> **Example 6-2.** *W* had been employed by XYZ, Inc. for five years prior to her marriage to *H.* XYZ has provided *W* with $50,000 of group-term insurance coverage from the time she was first

employed by it. *W* died five years after her marriage to *H. W* had designated her mother, *M,* as beneficiary of the group-term insurance without *H*'s participation or consent. Under the risk payment doctrine the entire proceeds are community property, of which *H* is entitled to claim half ($25,000). In contrast, under the apportionment rule, the policy was one-half the separate property of *W* (attributable to five years of premium payments by *W*'s employer prior to *W*'s marraige to *H*) and one-half community property. Accordingly, in an apportionment state, *H* is entitled to claim only one-quarter of the proceeds ($12,500).

B. PLANNING WITH LIFE INSURANCE

§6.16. Introduction

Planning for the ownership, premium payments, and beneficiary designations of life insurance is a critical but often neglected aspect of estate planning. The overall objective is to integrate life insurance fully into the client's estate plan, which requires that it be coordinated with the client's will and other elements of the plan. As always, the federal tax considerations are important, but they should not dominate the planning.

The tax attributes of life insurance make it uniquely valuable in estate planning for clients with large estates. The initial value of life insurance policies is often a very small fraction of the death benefits payable under the policies, allowing them to be transferred at little or no gift tax cost. Also, the proceeds of life insurance policies are generally not subject to the income tax. Through proper planning a large amount of insurance proceeds can be made available to the insured's family at little or no tax cost. Importantly, such planning generally does not require the client to give up the lifetime use of any assets of substantial present value. For example, the proceeds of life insurance may be made available for the support of the insured's surviving spouse through an irrevocable life insurance trust; of these proceeds, little, if any, will be includible in the estate of the insured or the surviving spouse.

The nominal value and low cost of group-term insurance generally makes it the most economical type to transfer or to acquire for a trust of a person other than the insured. Split-dollar insurance is also popular for essentially the same reason. Finally, the benefits payable under a death benefit only plan are generally not included in the decedent's gross estate. *See* §§6.78.

§6.17. Combined Marital Estates of Less Than $600,000

The insurance plan for a married couple whose estates have a combined value that does not exceed the amount of the credit equivalent ($600,000) can be quite simple. Because no estate tax will be due on the death of either spouse it is unnecessary to attempt to eliminate the insurance proceeds, or other assets, from their gross estates. Because of the $1 million GSTT exemption, the GSTT is likewise not a concern. For such clients the principal question is simply how best to settle the insurance proceeds for the benefit of the insured's dependents.

When estate taxes are not a consideration, the surviving spouse is usually named as primary beneficiary. Depending upon the ages of the insured's children they, or a trust for their benefit, will be named as the contingent beneficiaries. The lawyer may only need to verify that the beneficiary designations are consistent with the plan. When the clients' wills include a contingent trust for children, the trustee of the trust is normally designated as the contingent beneficiary. The use of such a trust is described in §§4.21.3-4.21.4, and the text of a suitable form of trust for minors appears in §4.20. Chart 1-1, §1.33.3, depicts the disposition of the couple's assets under such a plan.

Attention must also be given to the disposition of any interest that the noninsured spouse has in the insurance. In most cases the interest of the noninsured spouse will pass to the insured spouse by specific bequest or by the residuary clause of the noninsured spouse's will. Complications arise if the noninsured spouse dies intestate and some interests in the policies pass to the children or parents of the noninsured spouse. Of course, where transfer taxes are a concern, the noninsured spouse should consider disposing of his or her interests in the policies in a way that will not cause them to be included in the insured's gross estate. For example, the noninsured spouse may leave his or her interests in the policies to persons other than the insured (*e.g.,* their adult children) or to a trust for their benefit.

§6.18. Combined Marital Estates of Less Than $1.2 Million (Two Credit Equivalents)

When somewhat larger estates are involved, the noninsured spouse is also often named as beneficiary. However, the potential of unnecessarily subjecting property to the estate tax on the death of the surviving spouse at marginal rates of 37 percent or more is an important countervailing factor. In such cases the clients should consider taking steps to assure that each spouse will be able to take full advantage of the unified credit, which can shelter up to $600,000 from taxation on the death of the surviving spouse.

If the proceeds are paid outright to the insured's surviving spouse, the unlimited marital deduction would allow the estate tax on the proceeds to be deferred until the death of the surviving spouse. However, such an approach may unnecessarily increase the size of the surviving spouse's gross estate. Inclusion of the proceeds in the noninsured spouse's gross estate is avoided if he or she is given only a limited interest in the proceeds either under a settlement option selected by the insured or under an inter vivos or testamentary bypass trust established by the insured. When an option is selected by the insured the proceeds are not includible in the beneficiary's gross estate, but when the option is selected by the beneficiary they are includible. *See* §6.39. The cost of making the proceeds payable to the surviving spouse outright is illustrated in Example 6-3.

> **Example 6-3.** *H* died leaving an estate of $400,000, including $100,000 in insurance, all of which passed outright to his surviving spouse, *W*. No estate tax was payable by *H*'s estate because of the unified credit available to his estate. Whatever remains of the $400,000 will be includible in *W*'s estate when she dies. If *W*'s taxable estate exceeds $600,000, some estate tax will be due from her estate. On the other hand, no tax would be due from *W*'s estate if her taxable estate is $600,000 or less. For example, *H* could leave the proceeds to a trust for *W*'s benefit or elect a settlement option under which periodic payments would be made to her, neither of which would require the proceeds to be included in her estate.

Some clients will prefer to give the proceeds outright to the surviving spouse although it may cause the payment of some estate tax by the estate of the surviving spouse. They may choose to do so in order to give the survivor more freedom and greater control over the proceeds. After all, they reason, the surviving spouse may consume the proceeds for support or may substantially eliminate them from his or her estate by making gifts prior to death. Of course, the lawyer should discuss with the client the tax and nontax consequences of settling the proceeds in various ways consistent with his or her basic objectives.

§6.18.1. Protect Minor Children

The interests of the insured's minor children may be protected if the noninsured spouse survives the insured and the proceeds are paid outright to the survivor. If the noninsured spouse does not survive the insured, the proceeds should not be made payable outright to minor children, which might necessitate the appointment of a guardian to collect and manage the proceeds. Instead, the proceeds should either be left with the insurer under a settlement option or be made payable to the trustee of a contingent testamentary trust for the children. *See* §4.21.4. A trust is generally preferable because it is more flexible and can provide greater protection for the children in the event of emergency. Also, a trust may produce a greater current yield than is received under settlement options. In some other instances the insured may wish to leave the proceeds in trust. For example, if the noninsured spouse is not a parent of the insured's children, the insured may wish to use a trust to secure an interest in the proceeds for his or her children. Overall, the children are best provided for if the assets are concentrated in one trust for their benefit, rather than being held in two or more trusts. *See* §4.21.3.

§6.18.2. Use Trusts

The cost of preparing an inter vivos insurance trust or a will containing a trust is usually greater than the fee for preparing a nontrust will. However, a trust better meets the needs of the family. In addition, it may save some estate administration expenses and possibly some income, inheritance, and estate taxes.

If the plan calls for establishing a trust for the benefit of the insured's surviving spouse and children, a funded or unfunded revocable trust or a testamentary trust might suffice. For estates in this range the creation of an irrevocable life insurance trust is usually unnecessary. Including the insurance in the estate of the insured is not the problem — controlling the size of the surviving spouse's estate is. Also, an irrevocable trust is less flexible and may place some assets that may be needed beyond the client's control.

Before making a recommendation the lawyer needs to be sure that the local law permits the trustee of an unfunded revocable trust or a testamentary trust to be designated as beneficiary of life insurance policies. Either designation might be challenged if it is not authorized by statute or judicial decision. Fortunately, many states have adopted statutes that permit the designation of the trustee of an unfunded trust as beneficiary. *E.g.,* Ind. Code Ann. §27-1-12-16 (Burns 1986); N.Y. Est. Powers & Trusts Law §13-3.3(a)(1) (McKinney 1991 Supp.); Wash. Rev. Code §48.18.450 (1989). A larger number of states specifically authorize the designation of the trustee named or to be named in the insured's will as beneficiary. *E.g.,* Cal. Prob. Code §§6320-6330 (West 1991 Supp.); Ill. Ann. Stat. ch. 110½, §4-5 (Smith-Hurd 1978);

Ind. Code Ann. §27-1-12-15(C) (Burns 1986); N.Y. Est. Powers & Trusts Law §13-3.3(a)(2) (McKinney 1991 Supp.); Wash. Rev. Code §48.18.452 (1989). On the other hand, the designation of the trustee of a funded revocable trust is no doubt valid in all states.

§6.18.3. Plan Based upon a Revocable Trust

A plan based upon a revocable trust involves the preparation and execution of a trust agreement and the designation of the trustee as beneficiary of the insurance. The insurance policies may either be assigned to the trustee or be retained by the insured. As a matter of convenience the insured often retains ownership of the policies rather than assigning them to the trust. In either case the insured is usually responsible for payment of premiums on the policies. Of course, the trust may be funded by transferring some other assets to the trust. If that is done, the trust is not vulnerable to challenge as a "dry" trust. A token fund of $10, for example, is probably sufficient for this purpose. Nonetheless, some lawyers recommend that a significant amount of assets be transferred to the trustee. Funding the trust, of course, makes dealing with the assets a bit more cumbersome. Also, the grantor-insured will be treated as owner of the property of the trust for income tax purposes under §§676 and 677.

If the trustee charges a substantial minimum annual fee to administer funded trusts, it may not be economical to create a trust with a nominal fund. On the other hand, where the trust is unfunded, a corporate trustee may charge only a nominal acceptance or review fee for executing the trust agreement and agreeing to serve following the death of the insured. Often, no other fee is charged until after the insured's death. The use of a trust is attractive in part because of the extensive discretionary powers that can be given to an independent trustee without tax risk. *See* §10.12. If the trustee is given such powers, a beneficiary of the trust cannot act as trustee without adverse tax consequences.

An inter vivos trust can be the vehicle used to consolidate the insured's assets and to provide for their unified management following his or her death. This can be accomplished by "pouring over" the client's residuary estate into the trust. The pour-over technique is validated by the Uniform Testamentary Additions to Trust Act, 8A U.L.A. 599 (1983), which is incorporated in the U.P.C. as §2-511 and is in effect in almost all states and the District of Columbia. Under a common plan the client's residence and tangible personal property are left to the surviving spouse by will and the life insurance and residuary estate pass into the trust. The plan is depicted in Chart 6-1, *infra. See* §10.10 for a more detailed discussion of pour-over provisions.

Chart 6-1
Disposition of Property upon Death of Married Insured
(Moderate Size Estates)

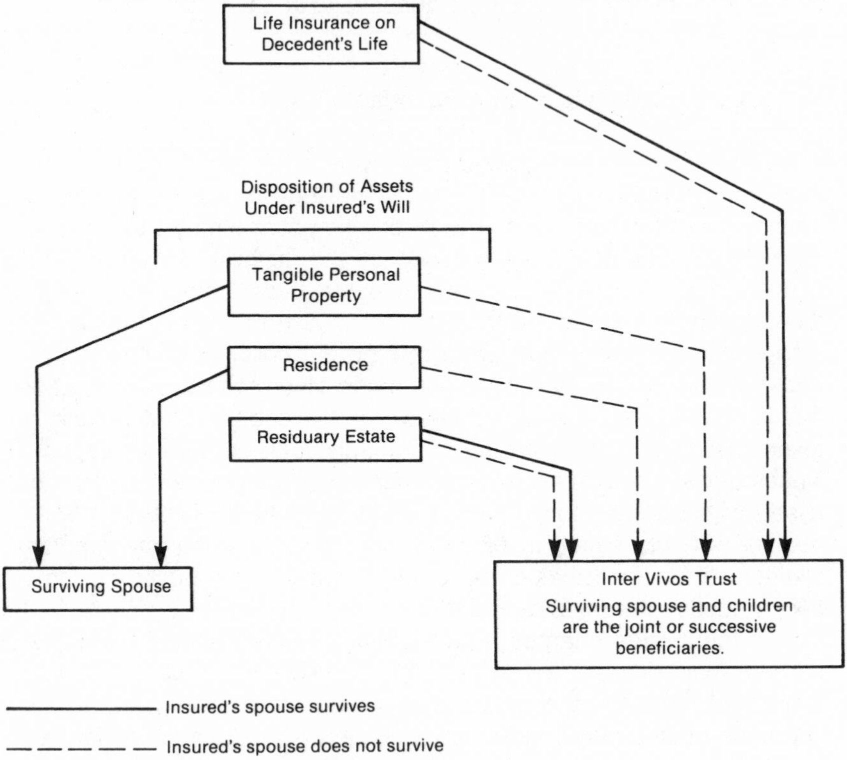

§6.18.4. Plan Based upon a Testamentary Trust

When the plan is based upon a testamentary trust, the life insurance proceeds are made payable to the trustee of the trust established by the will of the insured. The beneficiary designation is valid in states such as California, Illinois, Indiana, New York, and Washington that have adopted statutes specifically authorizing it. In some states the designation may be vulnerable to challenge as a testamentary transfer because the trustee cannot be ascertained and appointed until after the death of the insured.

An old Massachusetts decision, *Frost v. Frost,* 88 N.E. 446 (Mass. 1909), invalidated an assignment to the trustees named in the will because it was considered to be a testamentary disposition that failed to comply with the requirements of the wills act. Although most courts would strain to uphold the designation of a testamentary trustee as beneficiary, prudence suggests adopting a more reliable approach in states that do not specifically authorize such a designation.

The chart for a plan based upon a testamentary trust would be practically identical to Chart 6-1. The trusts are essentially the same except for the time of creation and that a testamentary trust would be a "court" trust subject in some states to continuing supervision by the probate court.

§6.19. Choosing Between a Revocable Trust and a Testamentary Trust

Where the local law permits the designation of the trustee of an unfunded inter vivos trust or the trustee of a testamentary trust as beneficiary of life insurance, the choice between them is a close one. In either case the surviving spouse or other beneficiary can be given substantial interests in the trust and extensive powers over the trust property without causing it to be included in his or her gross estate.

The preparation of an inter vivos trust and a complementary will may cost more than a will with a testamentary trust. However, the testamentary trust may generate higher costs of administration because of local law requirements regarding the reports and accounts the trustee must file. The trustee of an inter vivos trust is generally not required to file reports and accounts with the court. On the other hand, the testamentary trust may have the edge when it comes to having ready access to the court for instructions. In some states no mechanism is available to the trustee of an inter vivos trust by which to obtain such instructions.

A testamentary trust generally lacks the secrecy of an inter vivos trust because it is contained in a will, which is a public record after it is filed with the probate court. Also, the actual operation of a testamentary trust may be deferred for some time until the trustees are appointed and qualify to serve. Finally, the designation of a testamentary trustee as a beneficiary of life insurance could jeopardize the extent to which the proceeds are exempt from creditor's claims and the local death tax. Those risks do not arise in states that preserve the exemption for insurance paid to the trustees named in a will. *E.g.,* Ill. Ann. Stat. ch. 110½ §4-5 (Smith-Hurd 1978); Ind. Code Ann. §27-1-12-16 (Burns 1986); N.Y. Est. Powers & Trusts Law §13-3.3 (McKinney 1991 Supp.).

§6.20. Combined Marital Estates of More Than $1.2 Million: Eliminating the Insurance from the Estate of the Insured

Estate plans for wealthier clients often attempt to insulate the proceeds of life insurance from the imposition of any estate tax on the death of the insured. The plan may be a relatively simple one which involves ownership of the insurance by a person other than the insured. The proceeds would not be included in the insured's estate if the proceeds are not paid to the insured's estate, the insured held no incidents of ownership in the insurance, and any interest the insured owned in the insurance was transferred more than three years prior to his or her death. Of course, the payment of the estate tax is deferred if the insurance is paid to or for the benefit of the surviving spouse in a way that qualifies for the marital deduction. *See* §6.22. The use of the marital deduction does not eliminate the insurance from the insured's estate for purposes of determining whether his or her estate satisfies the requirements of §§303, 2032A, and 6166. For purposes of those sections a better result is produced if the insurance is excluded from the insured's estate. More ambitious plans may insulate the proceeds from inclusion in the estates of both spouses through the transfer of the insurance to an irrevocable trust. *See* §6.23. Irrevocable insurance trusts can, of course, be created for beneficiaries other than the insured's spouse.

§6.21. Ownership by an Individual Other Than the Insured

The proceeds of insurance policies originally acquired by an individual other than the insured, or assigned by the insured more than three years prior to death, are not included in the insured's estate. However, they are includible in the estate of a beneficiary who survives the insured. In effect, the ownership of the policies by a person other than the insured allows the tax on the proceeds to be deferred until the death of the owner-beneficiary.

§6.21.1. Cross-Owned Insurance

Prior to the adoption of the unlimited marital deduction the estate plan for a husband and wife often involved "cross-ownership" of insurance (*i.e.,* each spouse owned the insurance policies on the life of the other). If the noninsured spouse were to die first, the plan usually also called for him or her to leave the insurance on the surviving spouse's life in a way that would not require it to be included in the estate of the insured spouse. Thus, the wife's will might leave all of her interests in insurance on the life of her husband to their children or to a trust for the benefit of their children.

A cross-ownership plan under which the noninsured spouse, who is also the policy owner, is the designated beneficiary of each policy remains very advantageous if the spouses die simultaneously. In such a case, under the Uniform Simultaneous Death Act the beneficiary spouse is deemed to have predeceased the insured spouse. Hence, only the lifetime value of the policy and not the proceeds is included in the estate of the noninsured spouse. Nothing is included in the estate of the insured. *See* §6.80.

§6.21.2. Applications and Assignments

When the noninsured spouse originally applies for the insurance, the application and policy should clearly indicate that both spouses intend the applicant to own all interests in the insurance. The lawyer should review the application and the policy to be sure that the insured will not have any incidents of ownership in the policy. Similar precautions must be taken when the insured assigns his or her interest in the insurance to another person.

§6.21.3. Community Property

Particular attention must be given to ownership problems in community property states, where the presumption favoring community property may cause insurance acquired during marriage to be treated as community property absent clear evidence to the contrary. An oral agreement that the insurance is the separate property of the noninsured spouse may overcome the presumption in some states. *E.g., Kroloff v. United States,* 487 F.2d 334 (9th Cir. 1973) (Arizona law). Some others require the agreement to be evidenced by a writing apart from the policy. *Kern v. United States,* 491 F.2d 436 (9th Cir. 1974) (Washington law). The seriousness of this problem is reduced by the availability of the unlimited marital deduction. However, characterizing the insurance as community property may be disadvantageous in some circumstances.

§6.21.4. Premium Payments

The insured makes a gift to the owner to the extent he or she pays a premium directly or indirectly on a policy owned by another person. Reg. §25.2503-3(c), example 6; Rev. Rul. 76-490, 1976-2 C.B. 300 (employee-insured makes an indirect gift when the employer pays a premium on a group-term insurance the employee had assigned to a trust). Depending upon the terms of the trust the premium payment may be a gift of a present interest that qualifies for the annual exclusion. The annual exclusion is available when the insurance is owned by another individual. Reg. §25.2503-3(c), example 6; *see also* §6.46. The gift marital deduction may be available where the owner is the employee's spouse.

§6.21.5. Beneficiary Designations

The noninsured owner is usually designated as the primary beneficiary of the insurance. He or she may need the proceeds for support or to make the proceeds available to the insured's estate to meet taxes, debts, or expenses of administration. An individual beneficiary may choose to use the proceeds for purchase of assets from the insured's estate or otherwise provide funds with which to pay the taxes and other expenses of the insured's estate. However, in some cases the beneficiary does not do so.

When the proceeds are payable to an independent trustee there is more of an assurance that the plan will be followed and the proceeds will be made available to the insured's estate. The trustee should be authorized to loan the proceeds to the executor of the insured's estate or to use them to buy assets from his or her estate.

Gift Tax. If the owner survives the insured, the owner's acquiescence in the payment of the insurance proceeds to any other person involves a gift by the owner to the payee. *See* §6.47.

Contingent Beneficiaries. In any case, a contingent beneficiary should be designated in each policy to prevent payment of the proceeds to the estate of the insured, which might unnecessarily increase the insured's gross estate and eliminate any otherwise applicable state death tax exemptions.

§6.21.6. Successive Ownership

As noted above, the plan should also provide for disposition of the noninsured owner's interest in the insurance if the owner predeceases the insured. Generally speaking, the insurance should pass under the owner's will and not by the designation of a successive owner in the policy itself, which could be overlooked when later changes are made in the owner's estate plan.

In order to avoid subsequent inclusion of the insurance in the estate of the insured, the policy should not be left to the insured, nor should the insured be given any incidents of ownership in it. Instead, the noninsured owner should consider bequeathing the policy to adult children or to the trustees of a trust for the benefit of minor children.

If the insured is named as executor of the noninsured owner's will, his or her power over the policy should be limited in order to avoid any risk that the insurance would be in the insured's estate should the insured die during administration of the owner's estate. Also, if a policy is left in trust, the insured should not hold any incidents of ownership in the policy in any capacity. *See* §6.27.11, *infra.* Because of the possibility that inclusion might result if the insured holds an incident of ownership in other fiduciary capacities, a policy should not be given to the insured as custodian for a minor child. For the same reason, the insured should not serve as guardian for an incompetent person who owns a policy on his or her life.

§6.22. Marital Deduction Planning

The proceeds of life insurance paid to the insured's surviving spouse or to a marital deduction trust will escape taxation until the death of the surviving spouse. Such an approach has the advantage of allowing the insured to continue to own and control the policy until his or her death. Under this plan the surviving spouse can make insurance proceeds directly available to meet estate obligations without estate tax disadvantage — the proceeds are already includible in the estate of the insured. Of course, this amount is offset by the marital deduction when the insurance is payable outright to the surviving spouse. Where the insurance is payable to a QTIP trust (*i.e.,* one that meets the requirements of §2056(b)(7)), the insured's executor may elect to claim the marital deduction with respect to all or part of the insurance. *See* §5.23. Use of the marital deduction allows the estate tax on the insurance to be deferred until the death of the surviving spouse.

§6.22.1. Beneficiary Designations

Under the simplest approach the insured's spouse is designated as primary beneficiary and the insured's children as contingent beneficiaries. However, from the tax perspective the plan has greater flexibility if the insurance is payable to a trust in which the surviving spouse has an interest sufficient to support a QTIP election under §2056(b)(7). Under a variant the insurance may be payable to the insured's spouse or to the QTIP trust if he or she disclaims the right to receive the proceeds outright. It is less desirable to leave the proceeds on a settlement option with the company. Where community property is involved, the one-half interest of the noninsured spouse is generally paid to him or her outright, although it could be disposed of in another way.

§6.22.2. Premium Payments

The payment of premiums on policies owned by the insured does not involve gifts because the insured is the owner. Nor does it involve a gift to the beneficiaries, whose interests are revocable. There is a gift to the insured, however, if a premium is paid by another person. There is no gift where community property funds are used to pay the premiums on a community property policy. *See* §6.46.

§6.22.3. Successive Ownership

Where the insured owns the entire interest in a policy there is no need to provide for disposition of the policy upon death — the policy matures at that time.

Community Property. In the case of a community property policy, the interest of the noninsured spouse should be left in a way that does not increase the insured's gross estate if the noninsured spouse dies first. As mentioned above, this usually involves leaving the noninsured spouse's interest to adult children or to the trustees of a trust for the benefit of minor children. In such a case, if the noninsured spouse dies first, the ownership interests of the insured spouse and the recipients of the noninsured spouse's interest in the policy are equal at the outset and will remain so if each contributes equally to premium payments following the death of the noninsured spouse. If one of the owners pays more than half of the subsequent premiums without intending to make a gift to the other owner, the payor's interest in the policy will increase proportionately in the states that follow the apportionment rule. *Scott v. Commissioner,* 374 F.2d 154 (9th Cir. 1967). The ownership interests probably remain equal in inception-of-title states, and the party who paid more than his or her share of the premiums will have a right of reimbursement for any excess he or she may have paid.

> **Example 6-4.** *H*'s life was insured under a $100,000 nonparticipating cash value policy that was issued 20 years ago and was owned by *H* and his wife *W* as their community property until *W*'s death 10 years ago. *W* bequeathed her interest in the policy to their children, *A* and *B,* who made *all* subsequent premium payments on the policy without intending to make a gift to *H.* Half of the value of the policy, determined under Reg. §20.2031-8, was includible in *W*'s gross estate. When *H* died this year, the proceeds were paid outright to *A* and *B.* In states that follow the apportionment rule, *H*'s gross estate includes only the interest attributable to his one-half share of the premiums that were paid on the policy

up to the time of *W*'s death (one-half of $50,000 or $25,000). The other $75,000 is attributable to the ownership interests received from *W* ($25,000) and to the premium payments made by *A* and *B* after *W*'s death ($50,000). Half of the proceeds is probably includible in *H*'s estate in an inception-of-title state, subject to a claim by *A* and *B* for half of the premiums they paid following *W*'s death.

§6.23. Irrevocable Life Insurance Trusts

The irrevocable life insurance trust is one of the most significant and popular estate taxsaving devices that remains available. A properly planned and drafted trust can:

1. Remove the life insurance proceeds from the estates of both the insured and noninsured spouses;
2. Incur little or no gift tax upon creation of the trust and payment of subsequent premiums;
3. Preserve the income tax exclusion for the insurance proceeds;
4. Make the proceeds available to the insured's estate for the payment of taxes, debts and expenses;
5. Preserve flexibility through the use of an independent trustee who can be given broad discretionary powers over the trust; and
6. Reduce or eliminate GSTT problems by using annual gift tax exclusions and the GSTT exemption.

§6.23.1. Estate Tax

The goal of excluding the proceeds of the insurance from the estates of the insured and noninsured spouses is most easily achieved if existing insurance policies are not transferred to the trustee. The reason is simple: If existing policies are transferred, the insured must survive the transfer by three years or more in order to avoid inclusion under §2035. §2035(d)(2). Also, in order to avoid inclusion of the trust in the estate of the noninsured spouse under §2036, the noninsured spouse generally should not transfer any property to the trust if he or she is a beneficiary of the trust. (The widow's election life insurance trust described in §6.24.1 is an exception to this rule.)

Yielding to three adverse appellate decisions, the IRS will no longer contend that §2035(d)(2) requires inclusion in the insured's estate of insurance purchased by a trustee with funds transferred to the trustee within three years of the insured's death. A.O.D. 1991-12; *Estate of Eddie L. Headrick v. Commissioner,* 918 F.2d 1263 (6th Cir. 1990); *Estate of Joseph Leder v. Commissioner,* 893 F.2d 237 (10th Cir. 1989); *Estate of Frank M. Perry v. Commissioner,* 927 F.2d 209 (5th Cir. 1991). The conclusion reached in the trilogy of cases is based upon a literal reading of §2035(d)(2). Such a narrow reading of §2035(d)(2) may be overturned by Congress. Against this possibility irrevocable life insurance trusts should be planned and drafted with the care that was required by the pre-1981 version of §2035. Accordingly, the trustee should be formally free to invest the funds that the grantor transfers to the trust as the trustee chooses. In particular, the transfer of funds to the trust should not be tied to the purchase of insurance on the grantor's life.

Cases arising under the broader pre-1981 version of §2035 indicate the precautions that should be taken in order to prevent the proceeds from being included in the estate of the insured under §2035 when the insured created the trust and transferred cash to it within three years of death. Exclusion of the proceeds in such a case is likely if the trust is established in accordance with the following points:

1. An independent individual or institution is appointed as trustee of the trust.
2. The trustee is authorized to use the funds that the grantor transfers to the trust to make any type of investment. *Hope v. United States,* 691 F.2d 786 (5th Cir. 1982). That is, the trustee should not be expressly or impliedly obligated to use the funds to buy insurance on the grantor's life.
3. The grantor transfers more cash to the trustee than is required to make the anticipated initial premium payment. The client should be cautioned to avoid the mistake made by Mr. Kurihara, who gave the trustee a check in the exact amount of the insurance premium which noted that it was for payment of an insurance premium. *Estate of Tetsuo Kurihara,* 82 T.C. 51 (1984).
4. Neither the title nor terms of the trust indicate that the trustee is expected to use the funds contributed by the grantor to purchase policies of insurance on the grantor's life. Specifically, the trust should not be titled "Life Insurance Trust."

Inclusion under §2042(1) is avoided if the trustee is not obligated to use the proceeds for the benefit of the insured's estate. *Do not* require the trustee to make the proceeds available to the personal representative of the insured's estate or otherwise subject the proceeds to the insured's debts or taxes. The reach of §2042(2) is avoided if the insured has no direct or indirect control over the "incidents of ownership" of the insurance and no reversionary interests in any insurance formerly owned by the insured. Accordingly, despite a more relaxed attitude on the part of the courts and the IRS, the insured should not serve as a fiduciary if that might entail any power over the incidents of ownership. Also, the insured should not have the unlimited power to remove the trustee and designate a successor; the IRS considers this power cause to treat the insured as holding the powers of the trustee, which include powers over the policy that are incidents of ownership. *See* LR 8922003. *See also* §10.41.5.

The proceeds will not be included in the estate of the noninsured spouse if he or she neither made any transfers to the trust (which avoids the reach of the transfer sections, §§2035-2038) nor had a general power of appointment over the property of the trust.

§6.23.2. Gift Tax

The gift tax cost of establishing an irrecovable life insurance trust and of making subsequent transfers to it can be minimized or eliminated entirely by including provisions that support the allowance of the annual gift tax exclusion for the transfers. Where an existing policy is transferred to the trust, the value of the policy can be reduced prior to the transfer by taking out a loan against the policy. By giving each trust beneficiary a *Crummey* power of withdrawal, discussed at §7.37, transfers to the trust will qualify for multiple annual gift tax exclusions. Group-term insurance and split-dollar insurance policies are particularly attractive candidates for transfer to an irrevocable life insurance trust. The assignment of either type usually involves little or no gift tax liability and does not deprive the insured of the use or control of an asset with substantial current value that the insured might later need. Also, there is little current economic loss if the insured's employer or other financing party ceases making premium payments. If others ceased making premium payments, however, the continuation of the insurance could impose a substantial burden on the insured. Where group-term insurance is assigned to the trust, the assignment should include any replacement or renewal insurance and any increase in the amount of coverage.

§6.23.3. Survivorship Policies

The diminished need for liquidity on the death of the first spouse to die that resulted from the adoption of the unlimited marital deduction has lead to the development and popularity of so-called joint life or survivorship policies under which the proceeds are payable upon the death of the latter of two persons to die. *See* §6.75. Survivorship policies are also frequently acquired by the trustees of irrevocable trusts. Because of that feature the premiums are significantly lower than the premiums on a policy that insures only one life. Rates, of course, vary among insurers and the particular provisions of the policies. With proper planning the proceeds of survivorship policies can be available to meet liquidity needs when the surviving spouse dies without being included in the estate of either of the insured parties.

§6.23.4. GSTT

Life insurance and trusts holding life insurance are subject to the GSTT. Under §2652(b)(1), "The term 'trust' includes any arrangement (other than an estate) which, although not a trust, has substantially the same effect as a trust." Section 2652(b)(3) further provides that "Arrangements to which this subsection applies include arrangements involving life estates and remainders, estates for years, and insurance and annuity contracts." On the planning side it is very important to plan irrevocable life insurance trusts in light of the available exemptions from the GSTT, particularly the limited exemption under §2642(c) for transfers that qualify as nontaxable gifts and the $1 million exemption. *See* Brody & Reilly, GSTT, Planning Opportunities Continue After TAMRA, 128 Tr. & Est. 24 (1989). *See also* §6.41.

Section 2642(c) Exclusion. The nontaxable gift exclusion of §2642(c) for transfers in trust is allowed for a trust with *Crummey* powers of withdrawal if two additional requirements are met: (1) during the lifetime of the beneficiary no portion of the corpus or income may be distributed to or for the benefit of any other person, and (2) the property of the trust is includible in the beneficiary's estate if the beneficiary dies before the trust terminates. In order to qualify for the exclusion a separate share or subtrust should be established for each beneficiary, of which no portion of the principal or income may be expended for any other person during the beneficiary's lifetime. Each beneficiary should also be given a power of appointment over his or her separate share sufficient to require inclusion in the beneficiary's estate under §2041. The client may choose to give the beneficiary a broad power in order to provide greater flexibility. On the other hand, the client may prefer a power that is very limited, such as a power to appoint to creditors of the beneficiary. Even so, some clients prefer to limit the power that is exercisable jointly with another person, who must be a nonadverse party in order to assure inclusion in the beneficiary's estate under §2041. As indicated below, consideration should be given to using the grantor's $1 million GSTT exemption to the extent the transfers to the trust are not entirely sheltered by this exemption.

Under §2642(c)(2), an individual for whom a separate share or subtrust is established must be the only person entitled to receive any distribution from it during his or her lifetime. Note, however, that the trustee is not required to distribute any income or principal. Of course, if the beneficiary dies before termination of the trust, the entire value of the beneficiary's share is includible in his or her gross estate. If the beneficiary predeceases the insured, only a small amount may be includible, depending largely upon the type and value of the policies owned by the trustee. If the beneficiary survives the insured, a large amount may be includible in the beneficiary's estate. In such a case the beneficiary's executor may have the right under §2207 to recover a proportionate part of the estate tax from the recipients of the property subject to the power.

$1 Million Exemption. If the trust might be subject to the GSTT, the grantor should consider allocating his or her GSTT exemption to cover transfers to the trust. Specifically, the grantor could allocate a sufficient part of his or her GSTT exemption to insulate each transfer to the trust from the GSTT. If such allocations are made the trust will not be subject to the GSTT. In general the grantor's GSTT exemption should be allocated to a transfer on the gift tax return for the year in which the transfer was made. Under §2642(b)(1) if an allocation is made on a timely filed gift tax return, the inclusion ratio for that transfer is determined according to the gift tax value of the transferred property. Thus, the inclusion ratio for a transfer of $10,000 would be zero if the grantor allocated $10,000 of his or her GSTT exemption to the transfer on a timely filed gift tax return. If the allocation were not made until after the death of the grantor-insured, the inclusion ratio would be determined according to the post-death value of the property — possibly the entire amount of the insurance proceeds. Clients should also consider establishing "layered" insurance trusts. For example, one trust might be for the exclusive benefit of the insured's spouse and children, which would not involve any generation-skipping transfers in any case (*i.e.,* it is wholly free from the GSTT). Another trust might be for the exclusive benefit of the insured's grandchildren and more remote descendants — all distributions from which would involve generation-skipping transfers. The insured might insulate the latter trust from the GSTT by making timely allocations of his or her GSTT exemption sufficient to cover the amount of transfers made to the trust (*i.e.,* the trust would have an inclusion ratio of zero).

The value of the grantor's GSTT exemption can be highly leveraged by allocating it to cover transfers to an irrevocable life insurance trust that will involve generation-skipping transfers otherwise subject to the GSTT. The leverage results because of the small amount transferred to the trust each year to pay premiums relative to the large amount of insurance proceeds payable to the trust.

§6.23.5. Drafting Considerations

A trust agreement should be carefully drawn to prevent the insured from holding any incident of ownership in the insurance in any capacity. This requires that all interests in preexisting policies of insurance must be completely and effectively assigned to the trustee and that the insured must not have any control over any other insurance the trustee may acquire on his or her life. The best approach is to avoid a dispute with the IRS regarding the effect of holding incidents of ownership in a fiduciary capacity. Thus, the insured should not have any control over the insurance. Perhaps the most comprehensive protection is provided if the trust instrument prohibits the insured from acting as trustee or successor trustee. Also, to guard against inclusion in the insured's gross estate under §2036, the trust should not permit the assets to be applied in satisfaction of the insured's obligations including the support of dependents. Finally, the agreement should completely dispose of all interests in the insurance so the insured will not have any reversionary interests in it.

Although the following discussion focuses on an irrevocable trust created in part for the benefit of the insured's spouse, many of the points are equally applicable to trusts of which other persons are the beneficiaries.

The trust may safely give the trustee discretion to loan the proceeds to the insured's executor or to use them to purchase assets from the insured's estate. *See* §6.26. A broad form of authorization is useful to free the proceeds to be used to meet the cash requirements of the insured's estate. The provision should be carefully drafted because the proceeds are includible in the insured's estate to the extent they "are subject to an obligation, legally binding . . . to pay taxes, debts, or other charges enforceable against the estate." Reg. §20.2042-1(b).

More aggressive planners may give an independent trustee discretion to pay such debts, expenses, taxes, and other obligations of the insured's estate as may be requested by the insured's executor. Such a use of the proceeds should not cause them to be included in the insured's gross estate. In particular, the proceeds should not be includible under §2042(1) ("receivable by the executor"). *See* §6.25. The power is, in effect, a special power to appoint the proceeds to the persons whose interests in the probate estate are augmented by payment of the expenses by the trust. The power might constitute a general power of appointment if it were held by a person who would benefit from its exercise. In such a case, part or all of the proceeds could be included in the gross estate of the power holder.

If the trust is structured to meet the requirements of §2056(b)(7), the insured's executor may elect to claim a marital deduction with respect to any of the insurance that is included in the insured's estate. Such a trust is ordinarily includible in the surviving spouse's estate only to the extent a marital deduction was claimed in the estate of the deceased spouse. *See* §2044. *See also* §5.23. The survivor may be given the income from the trust and a special testamentary power to appoint the trust property to and among a limited class, such as his or her issue. The surviving spouse should not be given an unlimited power of withdrawal, a general power of appointment, or any other control that would cause trust assets to be included in her gross estate under §2041. Although the surviving spouse could act as trustee, it is preferable to have an independent trustee or at the least an independent cotrustee. One important reason for using one is the broad range of discretionary powers that can safely be given to an independent trustee but not to a beneficiary who is also a trustee. A cotrustee may also provide important continuity if the surviving spouse resigns or ceases to act as trustee because of death or incompetence.

If existing policies are to be included in the trust, they must be assigned to the trustee. In order to eliminate any possibility that the insured retained any control over the insurance, the policies themselves should be held by the trustee. Similiarly, the trustee should have possession of any policies that are subsequently issued or assigned to the trustee. Also, the trustee must be designated as primary beneficiary under the policies.

The trust assets are includible in the estate of the noninsured spouse under §§2036 or 2038 to the extent he or she is treated as a grantor of the trust and is entitled to its income or holds a power over the disposition of its income or corpus. *See* §6.39. Accordingly, the noninsured spouse should not have any interest in the policies that are transferred to the trust. In the ideal case the policies are acquired by the trustee with funds initially contributed by a person other than the insured or the insured's spouse.

The noninsured spouse is treated as a grantor of the trust under §2036(a)(1) to the extent he or she pays premiums on the insurance or otherwise contributes property to the trust. A noninsured spouse who pays any premiums may be treated as having transferred a proportionate part of the insurance to the trust and not merely the amount of the premiums. This problem is avoided if the premiums are paid with funds in which the noninsured spouse does not have any interest. The insured might pay the premiums from his or her own property, recognizing that the payments constitute gifts. In this connection remember that premium payments made by the insured's employer are treated as having been made by the employee. Rev. Rul. 76-490, 1976-2 C.B. 300. Of course, if the trust is funded, the premium payments may be made by the trustee. Funding requires that someone make more substantial gifts to the trust. Also, if the insured provides the funds, the income of the trust will be taxed to him or her under §677(a) to the extent the income could be used without the consent of an adverse party to pay the cost of insurance on the insured's life or that of his or her spouse. In some cases a family member other than the noninsured spouse may pay the premiums, which involves gifts by that person but does not increase the risk that the proceeds will be included in the estate of the noninsured spouse.

Some of the rigidity of an irrevocable trust is ameliorated if the trustee or another independent party has the power to terminate the trust at any time it would be in the best interests of the beneficiary to do so. The trustee might also be specifically authorized to terminate the trust if it became uneconomical to continue it. Upon termination the trustee would be authorized to distribute the trust property to the current beneficiaries. For example, the property might be distributed to the persons currently entitled to receive distributions of income, to be divided among them in the discretion of the trustee or by right of representation. The insured should not hold the power to terminate and distribute the trust property because that would cause the trust property to be includible in the insured's estate under §§2038 and 2042(2). Cautious advisors also counsel against giving such a power to the spouse of the insured. A potential distributee should not hold such a power because of the potential inclusion of the trust property in the power holder's estate under §2041. Beyond those considerations, the tax effects of such a "safety valve" are not at all clear. If the safety valve is controlled by an independent party, it should not cause estate tax complications, since there would be no basis for inclusion in the estate of the insured or of the beneficiaries. However, the risk of inclusion would increase if the power holder were subservient to the insured and the insured were treated as holding the power. Finally, if the trustee is given any power to make discretionary distributions, the planner must be alert to potential GSTT problems.

As a matter of routine a trust should include a provision authorizing the trustee to receive, purchase, and maintain policies of insurance on the life of the grantor, the beneficiaries, and any person in whom the beneficiaries have an insurable interest. Such a provision will help assuage any concerns the trustee or the insurer may have regarding the propriety of the trustee's acceptance, acquisition, or continuation of life insurance policies.

§6.23.6. Community Property

The noninsured spouse's interest in community property insurance held in a trust is particularly vulnerable to inclusion in his or her estate under §2036. Where the noninsured spouse has a life income interest in the trust the effect of inclusion may be ameliorated by claiming a consideration offset for the actuarial value of that interest. As in the widow's election cases (*see* §9.31.2), the noninsured spouse may be considered to have exchanged a remainder interest in his or her community share of the proceeds for a life income interest in the other share of the proceeds. In this connection see the discussion regarding the use of the community property life insurance widow's election trust approach. §6.24.1.

Gifts to the Insured. Some optimistic insurance advisors suggest that the possibility of inclusion in the noninsured spouse's estate under §2036 can be avoided if the noninsured spouse first makes a gift of his or her interest in the insurance to the insured. As a second step the insured would transfer the insurance policies to the trust. Unfortunately, this two-step process may not satisfy the IRS, which may insist that the noninsured spouse actually transferred his or her interest in the policy to the trust. It would argue that the noninsured spouse is the transferor and the intermediate transfer to the insured spouse served no purpose apart from attempting to avoid the estate tax upon the noninsured spouse's death. The argument is buttressed by the fact that the courts are committed to determining the tax consequences of transactions according to their substance and not their form: "The substance of a transaction rather than its form must ultimately determine the tax liabilities of individuals. . . . When one overall transaction transferring property is carried out through a series of closely related steps, courts have looked to the essential nature of the transaction rather than to each separate step to determine tax consequences of the transfer." *Johnson v. Commissioner,* 495 F.2d 1079, 1082 (6th Cir.), *cert. denied,* 419 U.S. 1040 (1974). The gift approach stands a greater chance of success if the gift and the transfer to the trust are separated in time, suggesting they are not related. Note that the full amount of the insurance will be includible in the insured's estate under §2035 if the insured dies within three years of transferring the entire interest in the insurance to the trust.

Sale of Policies to the Insured. There is perhaps a greater possibility of avoiding inclusion in the noninsured spouse's estate if the noninsured spouse's interest in the insurance is sold to the insured. Of course, in order to produce the desired result, the insured must make the purchase with noncommunity funds, which the insured may already have or which may be generated by partitioning some community property funds into equal units separately owned by the husband and wife. Again, there is some risk that the sale will be ignored unless the taxpayers can establish an independent (*i.e.,* nontax) purpose for it. Otherwise the IRS may argue that in substance the noninsured spouse has transferred his or her interest to the trust and reserved a life interest in the proceeds. Here also the risk of inclusion in the noninsured spouse's estate is lower where the sale and transfer are separated in time and are not directly related. Again, if the insured dies within three years of the transfer to the trust, the insurance is all includible in his or her estate. Note, however, that the trust can be structured to qualify for the marital deduction if the insurance is included in the insured's gross estate. Of course, the use of the marital deduction only defers the time at which the tax must be paid. The sale of the noninsured spouse's interest to the insured would not cause the proceeds to be included in the recipient's income. Although the transfer is made for consideration, it is within the exclusion of §101(a)(2)(B), which exempts transfers "to the insured, to a partner of the insured, to a partnership in which the insured is a partner, or to a corporation in which the insured is a shareholder or officer."

> **Example 6-5.** *H* purchased *W*'s one-half community property interest in a policy on his life with separate funds that resulted from the equal partition of community assets. Subsequently *H* transferred the policy to an irrevocable trust of which *W* was the life income beneficiary. If *H* dies within three years of making the transfer the entire proceeds will be included in his gross estate. However, if the trust is properly drawn, the insured's executor may elect to claim a marital deduction with respect to part or all of the proceeds. Of course, if such an election is made, a corresponding part of the trust would be included in *W*'s estate under §2044.

If *H* lived more than three years following the transfer of the policy to the trust in Example 6-5 none of the proceeds would be included in his gross estate and possibly none of the trust property attributable to the proceeds would be included in *W*'s estate.

Sale of Policies to the Trustee. A sale of the noninsured spouse's community property interest to the trustee is generally not feasible for two reasons. First, the trust is usually not funded with enough assets to support the purchase. Second, and more important, the sale would be a transfer of the policy for value, which could subject the proceeds to the income tax when they are paid. *See* §6.53. Because of the transfer for value rule it is generally undesirable to sell a policy to the trustee.

Aggressive clients may be willing to take the risks involved in giving or selling the noninsured spouse's interest in policies to the insured spouse for addition to the trust. The decision is theirs, but the lawyer should be sure they understand the risks and appreciate the irrevocable nature of the trust. Because the trust is irrevocable its provisions cannot be changed after it is established.

§6.24. Other Types of Life Insurance Trusts

The inherent flexibility of the trust device challenges planners to adapt it to meet the specialized needs of particular clients. Within the limits imposed by the insurance and tax laws, there are many ways in which an insurance trust may be crafted to help a client. Some arrangements are appropriate only for clients who are willing to assume the risk of being successfully challenged by the IRS.

§6.24.1. Community Property Widow's Election Life Insurance Trust

If the surviving spouse will be the beneficiary of an irrevocable life insurance trust, consideration should be given to structuring the trust in a way that minimizes the amount includible in his or her gross estate. Specifically, the amount of the insurance includible in the surviving spouse's estate may be reduced by a consideration offset under §2043(a) if the trust is properly structured. The approach, which is more fully described in Price, The Uses and Abuses of Irrevocable Life Insurance Trusts, U. Miami, 14th Inst. Est. Plan. ¶1111.3 (1980), is based on a variation of the widow's election that involves community property life insurance and results in the inclusion of none of the insurance in the estate of the insured. The plan involves the following steps:

1. Community property life insurance policies are transferred to a trust with the noninsured spouse retaining the right to revoke the trust with respect to the interest he or she contributes to it. The insured holds no interest in or control over the trust, which is irrevocable as to the interest he or she contributed. Accordingly, none of the proceeds is includible in the insured's estate if the insured survives the creation of the trust by three years or more. Indeed, if the trust is funded with cash that is later used by the trustee to acquire policies on the life of the insured, the proceeds should escape inclusion in the estate of the insured even if the insured dies within three years. *See* §6.32.4. Because of the noninsured spouse's retained power of revocation, the transfer of property to the trust by the noninsured spouse does not involve a gift. The transfer of the insured's interest may involve a substantial gift, depending on the value of the property transferred to the trust (cash or existing policies). Any *Crummey* power of withdrawal given to the noninsured spouse should be limited to the greater of $5,000 or five percent in order to avoid later inclusion of an unnecessarily large amount in the survivor's estate under §2041. *See* §10.24. Consideration should be given to planning the trust to take advantage of the limited

exemption from the GSTT that is available for gifts in trust that qualify for the annual gift tax exclusion. *See* §2642(c)(2). *See also* §6.23.4.

2. Upon the death of the insured, the noninsured spouse may elect to remove from the trust the portion of the proceeds attributable to his or her contributions (*i.e.*, half of the proceeds) or leave that portion of the proceeds in the trust. In the latter case, the noninsured spouse will be entitled to receive all of the income from the trust. With the exception of that election, the trust becomes irrevocable upon the death of the insured spouse. Note that the trust may use a formula to limit the value of the property that the surviving spouse must transfer to the trust to the actuarially determined value of the life estate in the decedent's share of the proceeds. Gutierrez & Thomas, Group Life Insurance — Special Problems, U. Miami, 15th Inst. of Est. Plan. ¶1904.1 (1981). If a formula is not used, the election may involve a gift by the surviving spouse of a portion of the remainder interest in his or her share of the proceeds. For gift tax purposes, the value of the remainder interest is offset by the value of the life interest received in the share of the proceeds attributable to the insured spouse. *Commissioner v. Siegel,* 406 F.2d 332 (9th Cir. 1957). The relatively high rates of return that are used under §7520 to calculate the value of life and other term interests operate to reduce the amount of the gift. Unless §2702 applies to the transaction, in most cases the gift (if any) will be small. If §2702 applies, the term interest retained by the surviving spouse will be disregarded unless it is a qualified interest. *See* §9.30. A gift would occur unless the value of the life interest received by the noninsured spouse was not less than the entire value of the property transferred to the trust by the noninsured spouse.

3. If the noninsured spouse predeceases the insured, the trust would become irrevocable at that time. Because of the noninsured spouse's retained power of revocation, a portion of the value of the trust property would be includible in his or her estate (*i.e.,* half of the interpolated terminal reserve of the policies).

If the insured spouse dies first, a portion of the trust property may ultimately be included in the estate of the surviving spouse under §2036. Of course, no part of the trust is includible in the estate of the noninsured spouse if he or she survives the insured and receives consideration equal to or greater than the value of the property the surviving spouse transferred to the trust. For this purpose an exclusion may result only if the consideration received by the noninsured spouse (the value of the noninsured spouse's life income interest in the insured spouse's share of the proceeds) had a value equal to the entire value of the share of the trust contributed by the noninsured spouse (*i.e.,* the half of the insurance proceeds attributable to the community property interest of the noninsured spouse). *See Gradow v. United States,* 1987-1

USTC ¶13,711, 11 Ct. Cl. 808 (1987), *aff'd,* 897 F.2d 516 (Fed. Cir. 1990). *See also* §9.34. Note that nothing would be includible in the estate of the surviving spouse if the right of the surviving spouse to receive the income from the portion of the trust property attributable to the insured (*i.e.,* half of the proceeds) were conditioned upon the surviving spouse electing to allow proceeds of an exactly equivalent actuarial value to remain in the trust. Under the *Gradow* approach a portion of the trust is includible in the estate of the surviving spouse under §2036 if the value of the one-half interest in the proceeds left in the trust by the surviving spouse exceeds the actuarial value of the life interest in the insured's share of the proceeds in the trust. In such a case the amount includible in the surviving spouse's estate is the value of the interest transferred to the trust by the surviving spouse determined on the federal estate tax valuation date applicable to the surviving spouse's estate *less* the actuarial value of the life estate in the insured's share of the proceeds that is determined on the federal estate tax valuation date applicable to the insured spouse's estate. This "frozen dollar" approach toward the determination of the value of the consideration received by the surviving spouse can be a serious disadvantage.

4. Neither the surviving spouse nor the trustee should realize any gain when the insured dies and the surviving spouse is considered to have transferred his or her interest in exchange for a life interest in the insured's share of the proceeds. Each of them has a basis in the proceeds equal to the amount of cash received under the insurance policies. Moreover, §1001(e) should not require any gain to be realized by the trust because the transferor's basis in the proceeds is not determined under §§1014 or 1015.

5. For income tax purposes the surviving spouse should be entitled to amortize the cost of a term interest acquired prior to July 28, 1989. *E.g., Christ v. United States,* 480 F.2d 171 (9th Cir. 1971). *See* §9.31. Under §167(r), added by the 1989 Act, no amortization or depreciation deduction is allowable with respect to a term interest in property if the remainder is held by a related taxpayer. For interests acquired prior to July 28, 1989 the decision in *Manufacturer's Hanover Trust Co. v. Commissioner,* 431 F.2d 664 (2d Cir. 1970), indicates that the purchaser of a life income interest in a trust is allowed an amortization deduction. In that case amortization was allowed although all of the income received from the trust was tax exempt.

§6.24.2. Business Uses

Insurance trusts have a wide range of applications where closely-held businesses are involved. For example, the insurance proceeds paid to the trustee can be used to buy the insured's stock from the insured's executor. The terms of the trust could reflect the interests and activities of family members. For example, a child who is active in the business could be given the right to vote the shares held by an independent trustee. The insured's other children could be beneficiaries of the trust without involving them directly in the management of the company.

§6.24.3. Charitable Uses

An irrevocable life insurance trust can also be used as a vehicle for making charitable contributions. Presumably the trustee of a trust established by the insured has an insurable interest in the life of the insured at least where the insured originally acquired the insurance and transferred it to the trustee. *See* §6.2. If the trust is properly drawn, current premium payments are deductible for income and gift tax purposes. Depending on the terms of the trust the insurance proceeds might be includible in the insured's gross estate. Inclusion would result, for example, if the insured retained the right to designate the charities that would receive the proceeds. *See* §2038. The insured's estate would be entitled to an offsetting charitable deduction. However, the inclusion of the proceeds in the insured's estate could make it more difficult for it to satisfy the percentage tests of §§303, 2032A, and 6166.

C. ESTATE TAXATION OF LIFE INSURANCE

§6.25. HISTORY

Since 1918 life insurance has been subject to special estate tax rules that were substantially changed in 1942 and 1954. In brief, between 1918 and 1942 the proceeds of life insurance policies were includible in the estate of the insured if the insurance had been taken out by the insured decedent. Proceeds receivable by the executor of the insured were fully includible, but the first $40,000 receivable by others was not includible. Because of uncertainties about the criteria that should be used in determining when insurance had been taken out by the decedent, that requirement was repealed by the Revenue Act of 1942. At the same time Congress repealed the $40,000 exemption and changed the law regarding the inclusion of life insurance receivable by other beneficiaries to require inclusion if the insured had paid premiums on the insurance or held incidents of ownership in the policy at the time of death. Under the first ground of inclusion, called the premium payment test, insurance was includible in the insured's gross estate in the proportion that premiums paid by the insured bore to the total premiums paid on the policy.

> **Example 6-6.** in 1943 *X* paid the first $1,000 premium on a $50,000 policy on his life and then irrevocably assigned all of his interests in it to *Y*. Afer the assignment *X* paid 4 more annual premiums and *Y* paid 5. When *X* died in 1952 the $50,000 proceeds were paid to *Y*. Under the premium payment test half of the proceeds were includible in *X*'s gross estate because he had paid half of the total premiums. Under the current provisions of §2035 none of the premiums paid by *X* would be included in *X*'s gross estate and none of the proceeds would be included under §2042. As noted below, the proceeds of life insurance transferred by the insured within 3 years of death is included in the insured's estate under §2035(d)(2).

The 1954 Code eliminated the premium payment test but retained the incidents of ownership rule (with one minor change). Accordingly, since 1954 insurance receivable by beneficiaries other than the insured's executor has not been includible in the insured's gross estate merely because the insured paid some of the premiums. This change created an important opportunity which allows an insured to pay the premiums on life insurance owned by a trust or other individuals without causing any of the insurance to be included in the insured's gross estate. Under most plans the allowable annual gift tax exclusions shield the premium payments from any gift tax liability. Of course, where the premium payments are subject to the gift tax, the unification of the gift and estate tax laws in 1976 reduced the tax advantages of this approach. Under the unified tax structure the amount of any post-1976 taxable gifts, including ones that result from premium payments during the lifetime of the insured, are included in the donor's tax base at death. Also, the proceeds of policies transferred by the insured within three years of death are included under §2035. (Note that §2035 does not require the insured's estate to include insurance transferred by another person within three years preceding the death of the insured.) Under the changes made by the 1981 Act premiums paid by the insured within three years of death generally are not included.

§6.26. Life Insurance Receivable by or for the Benefit of the Estate, §2042(1)

Insurance on a decedent's life is included in the insured's gross estate to the extent it is "receivable by the executor." §2042(1). However, insurance is not includible if it is payable to the estate in form and the state law requires it to be paid to the insured's surviving spouse or children. *Webster v. Commissioner,* 120 F.2d 514 (5th Cir. 1941).

Section 2042(1) requires the inclusion of insurance proceeds payable to or for the benefit of the insured's executor even though the insured neither held any incidents of ownership in a policy nor paid any premiums on it. Thus, the proceeds of a policy owned and controlled by a third party are includible to the extent they are payable to the decedent's personal representative for the benefit of the estate. *Draper v. Commissioner,* 536 F.2d 944 (1st Cir. 1976). The rule is inconsistent with the basic estate tax approach of taxing only property that was owned by the decedent at death or transferred inter vivos with some retained interest or control.

Example 6-7. *X* purchased a policy on the life of her brother, *B,* and paid all of the premiums on the policy until *B*'s death. The proceeds were paid to *B*'s personal representative in accordance with the terms of the policy. The proceeds are fully includible in *B*'s gross estate although he neither paid any premiums on the policy nor held any incidents of ownership in the policy.

Insurance is considered to be receivable by the executor if it is paid to a creditor in satisfaction of a loan or other indebtedness of the insured. *Bintliff v. United States,* 462 F.2d 403 (5th Cir. 1972); Reg. §20.2042-1(b)(1). Thus, the proceeds of "creditor" life insurance are includible in the gross estate of the insured to the extent they are applied in satisfaction of the insured's debts.

Proceeds receivable by other beneficiaries are includible under §2042(1) to the extent the beneficiaries are subject to a legally enforceable obligation to apply the proceeds for the benefit of the estate. Thus, although the property of a trust is not otherwise includible in the insured's gross estate, the insurance proceeds received by the trustee are includible to the extent they must be used to pay debts, taxes, and other expenses of the insured's estate. Reg. §20.2042-1(b). In such a case the proceeds are not includible if the trustee is merely authorized, or given discretion, to expend the corpus of the trust in satisfaction of the estate's obligations. *Estate of Charles Howard Wade,* 47 B.T.A. 21 (1942); *Old Colony Trust Co.,* 39 B.T.A. 871 (1939); *cf.* Rev. Rul. 73-404, 1973-2 C.B. 319 and *Estate of Joseph E. Salsbury,* 34 T.C.M. 1441 (1975) (both cases dealt with a comparable issue involving exclusion of qualified plan proceeds under the provisions of former §2039(c)). In order to preserve the estate tax benefit of an insurance trust, the trustee should be prohibited from using the proceeds to pay obligations of the insured's estate. *See* §6.23.5.

Insurance owned by a person other than the insured and payable to a revocable trust created by the insured is not includible in the insured's gross estate under §§2041 or 2042. *Margrave v. Commissioner,* 618 F.2d 34 (8th Cir. 1980); Rev. Rul. 81-166, 1981-1 C.B. 477. The cited ruling recognizes that the policy owner's revocable designation of the trustee of a trust created by the insured as beneficiary of the insurance does not constitute a gift. It also points out that the payment of the proceeds to a trust in which persons other than the policy owner have beneficial interests involves a gift by the policy owner to them. Where the policy owner is an income beneficiary of the trust, the portion of the trust corpus attributable to his or her contributions to the trust (*i.e.,* the policy proceeds) will be includible in his or her gross estate under §2036(a)(1). Rev. Rul. 81-166, *supra.*

To the extent a policy was owned by a husband and wife as community property, only the one-half interest of the deceased insured is generally includible in his or her estate under §2042(1). Reg. §20.2042-1(b)(2). The other half of the proceeds is not includible because it always belonged to the surviving spouse. However, if the full amount of the proceeds of a community policy is paid to the insured's personal representative for the benefit of the estate, the full amount is includible in the insured's gross estate under §2042(1). This issue could arise in a variety of ways. For example, inclusion of the entire proceeds would be required if the noninsured spouse had consented to the designation of the insured's personal representative as beneficiary and the proceeds were all available for payment of debts, taxes, and expenses of the estate. In contrast, the share of the proceeds attributable to the surviving spouse's community interest in a policy is not includible in the insured's gross estate when the survivor has the right to recover it from the estate. *See* Reg. §20.2042-1(b)(2).

§6.27. Incidents of Ownership, §2042(2)

> *Horticultural Analogies*
>
> Congress through §2042 has given discrete statutory treatment to policies of insurance. Sections 2036, 2037, 2038, 2041, and 2042 may be consanguineous, but each has an individual personality with genetic variations. These provisions developed from a common design to tax testamentary harvests, and they reach common sorts of decedent controls. As the caselaw cross-pollination — or pari materia interpretations — establish: Rose the insured and the possessor of incidents of ownership is Rose, even though garlanded by leaves of trusteeship. Each section is not identical, however. Life insurance is a specie of its own, it occupies a special place in the tax field, and we cannot simply graft terms from one provision onto another. Whether the insurance sheaves found in the decedent's hands are selected stalks

> from once-larger bundles, or whether they represent all that the taxpayer ever cultivated from the seed he had, the Congressional direction is to tax whatever is possessed at the end of the season. *Rose v. United States,* 511 F.2d 259, 265 (5th Cir. 1975).
>
> We hold that estate tax liability for policies "with respect to which the decedent possessed at his death any of the incidents of ownership" depends on a general, legal power to exercise ownership, without regard to the owner's ability to exercise it at a particular moment. *Commissioner v. Estate of Noel,* 380 U.S. 678, 684 (1965).
>
> The very phrase "incidents of ownership" connotes something partial, minor, or even fractional in its scope. It speaks more of possibility than probability. *United States v. Rhode Island Hospital Trust Co.,* 355 F.2d 7, 10 (1st Cir. 1966).

Insurance proceeds are includible in the insured's gross estate under §2042(2) if, at the time of death, the insured possessed *any* incident of ownership in the policy that was exercisable alone *or* in conjunction with any other person. Note that inclusion is required under §2042(2) if the insured *possessed* incidents of ownership. "Retention" of the incidents of ownership is not required. Inclusion does not require that the insured have ever owned the insurance and retained the incidents of ownership. *Rose, supra.*

The most common problems encountered under §2042(2) have been concerned with determining what constitutes an incident of ownership and under what circumstances an incident is considered to be exercisable by the insured.

§6.27.1. Policy Facts and Intent Facts

Whether or not an individual possesses an incident of ownership in a policy is determined in most instances according to the terms of the policy (the "policy facts") and not the intention of the parties (the "intent facts"). *Commissioner v. Estate of Noel,* 380 U.S. 678 (1965). Accordingly, if a policy permits the insured to exercise an incident of ownership, the proceeds of the policy are includible in the insured's gross estate. Some courts have recognized an exception, however, where the insurance contract does not reflect the instructions of the parties, "as where an agent, on his own initiative, inserts a reservation of right to change a beneficiary contrary to the intentions which had been expressed to him." *United States v. Rhode Island Hospital Trust Co.,* 355 F.2d 7, 13 (1st Cir. 1966). Similarly, LR 8610068 recognized that the decedent held no incidents of ownership over a policy which erroneously named him as owner instead of the corporation in which he owned a minority interest and of which he was president.

§6.27.2. Incidents of Ownership

The term "incidents of ownership" is not defined in the Code, but the Regulations describe the type of interests that are treated as incidents of ownership for purposes of §2042(2):

> [T]he term "incidents of ownership" is not limited in its meaning to ownership of the policy in the technical legal sense. Generally speaking, the term has reference to the right of the insured or his estate to the economic benefits of the policy. Thus, it includes the power to change the beneficiary, to surrender or cancel the policy, to assign the policy, to revoke an assignment, to pledge the policy for a loan, or to obtain from the insurer a loan against the surrender value of the policy, etc. Reg. §20.2042-1(c)(2).

The portion of the Regulation that links incidents of ownership to the economic benefits of a policy has caused some confusion. In one view a power is not an incident of ownership unless it can be exercised for the economic benefit of the insured. A competing view is that a power can constitute an incident of ownership although it cannot be exercised in a way that economically benefits the insured or the estate of the insured. For example, the courts have divided on the question of whether the bare power to select a settlement option under an employer-provided insurance plan is an incident of ownership. In *Estate of Lumpkin v. Commissioner,* 474 F.2d 1092 (5th Cir. 1973), the proceeds of a group-term policy were included in the gross estate of the insured because he had the power to vary the time at which the benefits would be paid. The court reasoned that inclusion under §2042 was justified by analogy to §§2036 and 2038 (which require the inclusion of property over which a decedent retained the power to vary the time of enjoyment). Critics hastened to point out that §§2036 and 2038 deal with property transferred by a decedent and that the insured in *Lumpkin* had never held or transferred any interest in the policy. Inclusion of the proceeds of the same group-term policy was rejected by the Third Circuit, which held that the insured's right "to select a settlement option with the mutual agreement of his employer and the insurer did not give him a substantial degree of control sufficient to constitute an incident of ownership." *Estate of Connelly v. Commissioner,* 551 F.2d 545, 552. The IRS will not follow the *Connelly* decision outside the Third Circuit. Rev. Rul. 81-128, 1981-1 C.B. 469.

§6.27.3. Power to Change Beneficiaries by Divorce, Birth, or Adoption

A change of beneficiary which results from an independently significant act of the insured does not require the insurance to be included in the insured's estate. For example, in LR 8819001 (TAM) the trust created by the insured provided that the interest of his wife would terminate if they became divorced. As the IRS concluded,

> The act of divorcing one's spouse is an act of independent significance, the incidental and collateral consequence of which is to terminate the spouse's interest in the trust. Thus, we do not believe the decedent possessed an "incident of ownership" in the insurance policy as a result of the trust provision which would terminate the interest of the decedent's spouse in the event of a divorce. Id.

Letter Ruling 8819001 relies upon Rev. Rul. 80-255, 1980-2 C.B. 273, "which holds that a trust provision for the inclusion of after-born and after-adopted children as beneficiaries is not the equivalent of the settlor's retention of a power to change the beneficial interests of the trusts within the meaning of sections 2036(a)(2) and 2038(a)(1)." Similarly, the grantor trust rules allow after-born or after-adopted children to be added as beneficiaries of a trust without requiring the grantor to be treated as owner of the trust. *See* §674(b)(5).

A client creating an irrevocable life insurance trust may wish to provide for the addition or deletion of beneficiaries based upon changes in family circumstances. In some instances the grantor may wish to make the additions or deletions contingent upon other factors, such as the size of the trust, the status of the individual as beneficiary of other trusts, or the concurrence of an independent party.

§6.27.4. Power to Terminate Membership in Group Plans

The power to cancel employer-provided insurance by terminating employment is not an incident of ownership. *Landorf v. United States,* 408 F.2d 461 (Ct. Cl. 1969). Revenue Ruling 69-54, 1969-1 C.B. 221, indicated otherwise but the position was abandoned. Rev. Rul. 72-307, 1972-1 C.B. 307. The latter ruling recognized that "[a]n insured's power to cancel his insurance coverage by terminating his employment is a collateral consequence of the power that every employee has to terminate his employment." Id. It continued to say that "[t]he examples in section 20.2042-1(c) of the regulations, on the other hand, concern powers that directly affect the insurance policy or the payment of its proceeds without potentially costly related consequences. Where the power to cancel an insurance policy is exercisable only by terminating employment, it is not deemed to be an incident of ownership in the policy." Id.

In contrast, the power to terminate group life insurance by terminating membership in a voluntary organization through which the insurance was acquired might properly be viewed as an incident of ownership. The issue could arise in connection with group insurance purchased by an alumna through her university's alumnae association. The insurance would remain in effect so long as the insured remains a member of the association and pays the required premiums. In such a case the irrevocable assignment of the insurance to others more than three years prior to the insured's death might not suffice to remove the insurance from her estate. Specifically, the power to terminate the insurance by terminating membership in the alumnae organization probably would constitute an incident of ownership sufficient to require inclusion of the insurance in the insured's estate. The outcome might be different if the policy were acquired through a group in which the insured was required to retain membership in order to practice a profession (*e.g.,* membership in an integrated bar).

§6.27.5. Power to Convert Group Insurance to Ordinary Insurance

As noted in Revenue Ruling 72-307, *supra,* the IRS recognized that the insured's right to cancel group insurance coverage by terminating employment was not an incident of ownership. Despite that enlightened approach, the IRS later contended that an employee's right to convert group insurance to individual insurance upon the termination of employment was an incident of ownership. However, the contention was rejected by the Tax Court, which said that "[i]f quitting one's job is too high a price to pay for the right to cancel an insurance policy, it is likewise too high a price to pay for the right to convert to another policy." *Estate of James Smead,* 78 T.C. 43, 52 (1982). Ultimately, the IRS conceded that the power to convert group-term life insurance to ordinary insurance upon termination of employment was not an incident of ownership. Rev. Rul. 84-130, 1984-2 C.B. 194.

§6.27.6. Right to Prevent Cancellation by Purchasing Employer Owned Life Insurance

In Rev. Rul. 79-46, 1979-1 C.B. 303, the IRS ruled that an employee's power to prevent cancellation of insurance coverage by purchasing the policy from his employer for its cash surrender value if the employer elected to terminate the policy was an incident of ownership. That position was rejected in *Estate of John Smith,* 73 T.C. 307 (1979), because of the contingent nature of the power: "Whatever rights Smith may have acquired under paragraph seven of his employment agreement were contingent ones dependent on an event which never occurred and over which he had no control." Of course, had Smith controlled his corporate employer through direct or indirect ownership of more than 50 percent of its stock, the incidents of ownership held by it would have been attributed to him. *See* Reg. §20.2042-1(c)(6). *See also* §6.28. A contingent power of the type involved in *Smith* must be distinguished from a power that is jointly exercisable by the insured and another person. *See, e.g., Commissioner v. Estate of Karagheusian,* 233 F.2d 197 (2d Cir. 1956). Inclusion *is* required under §2042(2) if any of the incidents of ownership were exercisable by the insured "either alone or in conjunction with any other person."

§6.27.7. Power to Remove and Replace Trustee

Revenue Ruling 79-353, 1979-2 C.B. 325, holds that a grantor who retains the power, without cause, to remove *and* replace a corporate trustee with another corporate trustee is treated as having reserved the powers held by the trustee. *See* §10.41.1. It is doubtful that this ruling would survive court challenge. However, a client may wish to avoid raising the issue. If so, an insured should not hold the power to remove and replace the trustee of a trust which holds policies insuring his or her life.

In LR 8922003 the IRS held that the proceeds of insurance policies owned by a trust created by the insured were includible in the insured's estate because the insured retained the right to remove the trustee and appoint a successor trustee. Following Revenue Ruling 79-353, the IRS held that the power to replace the trustee caused the incidents of ownership held by the trustee to be attributed to the insured grantor. However, because the trust was created prior to the date Revenue Ruling 79-353 was published, October 28, 1979, under Rev. Rul. 81-51, 1981-1 C.B. 458, the insurance was not included in the insured's estate.

§6.27.8. Negative or "Veto" Powers

A negative power, such as a power to prevent another person from changing the beneficiary, surrendering the policy, or exercising another incident of ownership, is itself an incident of ownership. *Eleanor M. Schwager,* 64 T.C. 781 (1975); Rev. Rul. 75-70, 1975-1 C.B. 301. In

Estate of Rockwell v. Commissioner, 779 F.2d 931 (3d Cir. 1985), the court recognized that a veto power may constitute an incident of ownership where it gives the insured control over the designation of the beneficiary. However, because of the extremely limited nature of the veto power retained by the insured, the *Rockwell* court concluded that the power was not an incident of ownership. There, the insured assigned the policies to his wife and retained the power to veto any beneficiary designation of, or assignment to, any person other than to a designated corporate trustee who did not have an insurable interest in his life. His wife later assigned the policies to a revocable trust of which she and the insured's children were the beneficiaries. The trust permitted the trustee to assign the trust property, which included the insurance policies, if the assignments were for the sole benefit of the beneficiaries. The veto power retained by the insured was redundant when he transferred the insurance policies to his wife and she transferred them to the trust. At the time the governing state law (Pennsylvania) prohibited the assignment of a life insurance policy to a person who did not have an insurable interest in the life of the insured. In passing upon the significance of the power the court in effect disregarded a later change in the state law which eliminated the prohibition. Moreover, when the insured's wife died in 1965 the trust became irrevocable, which effectively precluded the assignment of the insurance policies to any persons other than the beneficiaries of the trust — each of whom had an insurable interest in the life of the insured. The mere possibility that the insured's retained power might have been called into play had the trustee wished to assign the insurance policies to a person lacking an insurable interest in the insured's life in order to secure a loan was insufficient to require the insurance to be included in the insured's estate. According to the court, "Whatever vitality, if any, the veto power may have had at one time, Clara's death and the terms of the trust excluded Rockwell from any possible economic benefit. Congress' purpose in requiring the inclusion of policies in a gross estate when the decedent retains incidents of ownership is to prevent taxpayers from enjoying property without paying tax on it."

Consistently, an earlier case held that the insured's retained power to veto a sale of assets by the trustee of an irrevocable life insurance trust was not an incident of ownership. *Estate of Carlton v. Commissioner,* 298 F.2d 415 (2d Cir. 1962). In view of the trustee's fiduciary obligations and the terms of the trust, the power could not be exercised in a way that would economically benefit the insured.

In order to avoid risk of inclusion in the insured's estate, the insured should not have the power to veto any action with respect to an insurance policy, including a change of beneficiary, a surrender of the policy, or an assignment of it. If a veto power must be included in a trust, it should not extend to matters directly affecting the insurance on the power-holder's life because of the possibility that it would be considered to be an incident of ownership in policies held by the trustee.

§6.27.9. Incidents of Ownership Under Extraneous Contract

The insured may hold incidents of ownership in a policy owned by another person and with respect to which the insured holds no direct control. For example, in *Estate of James O. Tomerlin,* 51 T.C.M. 831 (1986), the proceeds of a policy owned by the insured's employer were included in the insured's estate because of the incidents of ownership held by the insured under a contract between the insured and his employer. Although the insured's employer (a corporation in which the insured owned 50 percent of the stock) was the owner of the policy, the insured was contractually entitled to designate the beneficiary, to veto a change of beneficiary or assignment of the policy, and to cancel and repurchase the policy at its cash surrender value. *Tomerlin* indicates the adverse tax results that may arise because of the terms of an extraneous contract, such as a split-dollar agreement. Similarly, an insured has an incident of ownership in a policy that he or she has the option to purchase from the owner. LR 9128008.

§6.27.10. Reversionary Interests, §2042(2)

The term "incidents of ownership" includes a reversionary interest in a policy or its proceeds, whether it arises by the express terms of the policy or other instrument or by operation of law, if the value of the reversionary interest exceeded five percent immediately before the death of the insured. §2042(2). However, the insured is not considered to have an incident of ownership in a policy if the power to obtain the cash surrender value existed in some other person immediately before the insured's death and was exercisable by such other person alone and in all events. Reg. §20.2042-1(c)(3). The Regulations also provide that the terms "reversionary interest" and "incidents of ownership" do not include the possibility that the decedent might receive a policy or its proceeds through the estate of another person, or as a surviving spouse under a statutory right of election or a similar right. Id.

Inclusion may be required if the insured retains reversionary interests in life insurance under the terms of a decree of dissolution. *E.g.,* Rev. Rul. 76-113, 1976-1 C.B. 277 (policies would revert to insured if former spouse predeceased him or remarried, the possibility of which exceeded five percent at time of insured's death; ruling notes the possibility of an offsetting deduction under §2053). Effective with respect to transfers made after July 18, 1984, a deduction may be allowed under §2043(b) to the extent the payment under the decree is in settlement of the noninsured spouse's marital or property rights or is to provide a reasonable allowance for the support of minor children of the marriage. §§2516 and 2043(b).

In Revenue Ruling 76-113, 1976-1 C.B. 277, the marital property settlement agreement required the insured to name his former spouse as beneficiary of several life insurance policies for so long as she lived and remained unmarried. Under its terms the policies would return to the insured or to his estate or would be subject to a power of disposition by him if his former spouse predeceased him or remarried prior to his death. When the insured died the proceeds were paid to his former spouse as beneficiary. The IRS held that the proceeds of the policies were includible in the insured's gross estate because the possibility that his former spouse would predecease him or remarry prior to his death exceeded five percent immediately prior to his death. The Ruling recognized that in some cases an offsetting deduction is allowable under §2053 when the proceeds are includible in the insured's estate. In the case of decedents dying after July 18, 1984, a transfer of property made pursuant to a property settlement agreement as provided in §2516(1) is considered to be made for full consideration in money or money's worth. §§2043(b), 2053(e).

When a divorce decree requires the payment of a specified sum upon the insured's death to a former spouse and the insured provided for payment of the obligation by purchasing insurance, a deduction is allowable under §2053(a)(3) as a claim against the insured's estate. Also, where the insurance proceeds that are included in the decedent's estate are paid to a former spouse in satisfaction of an indebtedness created in settlement of the decedent's marital obligations, the obligation is deductible under §2053(a)(4). If the obligation to provide the insurance is embodied not in a divorce decree, but in a property settlement agreement, a deduction is allowed only if the agreement was contracted bona fide and for an adequate and full consideration in money or money's worth, as required by §2053(c)(1). *Gray v. United States,* 541 F.2d 228 (9th Cir. 1976). Where the divorce court lacks power to alter the terms of the settlement, the obligation is deemed to be created by the property settlement agreement and not by the divorce decree. Id. In this connection recall that transfers made to a spouse after July 18, 1984, are deemed to be made for adequate and full consideration to the extent they are pursuant to settlements that satisfy the requirements of §2516.

Revenue Ruling 78-379, 1978-2 C.B. 238, denied a deduction under §2053 for insurance proceeds that were paid to the insured decedent's minor children pursuant to a property settlement agreement and divorce decree under which the decedent's obligation to provide child support terminated at death. However, the Ruling recognized that a deduction is allowable if the divorce court has power to change the property settlement agreement because it is then a judicially-imposed obligation. Similarly, a deduction should be allowed if an obligation to provide life insurance is imposed in a support decree. LR 8128005.

In order to avoid the reach of the reversionary interest rule a trust or other instrument governing the ownership of the policy should preclude the insurance from returning to the insured or becoming subject to the insured's control. For example, a rider might be added to the policy specifying that the policy will pass to a person other than the insured if the former spouse dies or remarries prior to the death of the insured. Note, too, that a decree of divorce or a property settlement agreement may sufficiently divest the insured spouse of the incidents of ownership so that the policy proceeds will not be includible in his or her gross estate. *Estate of Theodore E. Beauregard, Jr.,* 74 T.C. 603 (1980).

§6.27.11. Incidents of Ownership Held in a Fiduciary Capacity

> [A] decedent will not be deemed to have incidents of ownership over an insurance policy on decedent's life where decedent's powers are held in a fiduciary capacity, and are not exercisable for decedent's personal benefit, where the decedent did not transfer the policy or any of the consideration for purchasing the policy to the trust from personal assets, and the devolution of the powers on the decedent was not part of a prearranged plan involving the participation of the insured. Rev. Rul. 84-179, 1984-2 C.B. 195.

Prior to the issuance of Revenue Ruling 84-179, the IRS had consistently argued for a per se rule under which the insured's mere possession of incidents of ownership in a fiduciary capacity was sufficient to require inclusion in the insured's estate. Moreover, the IRS insisted that the rule should apply even in cases in which the incidents of ownership could not be exercised for the benefit of the insured-fiduciary. That position was supported by a minority of decisions, including ones by the Fifth Circuit. *See Rose v. United States,* 511 F.2d 259 (1975); *Terriberry v. United States,* 517 F.2d 286 (1975), *cert. denied,* 424 U.S. 977 (1976). Other courts upheld inclusion in the estate of the insured-fiduciary *only* if the powers could be exercised in a way that would benefit the insured-fiduciary. *Estate of Skifter v. Commissioner,* 468 F.2d 600 (3d Cir. 1972); *Estate of Fruehauf v. Commissioner,* 427 F.2d 80 (6th Cir. 1970); *Hunter v. United States,* 624 F.2d 833 (8th Cir. 1980); *Estate of Gesner v. United States,* 600 F.2d 1349 (Ct. Cl. 1979).

The change of position announced in Revenue Ruling 84-179 was presaged by the government's brief in *Estate of Harry Bloch, Jr.*, 78 T.C. 850 (1982), which abandoned the per se rule. The Tax Court ruled that insurance held in a trust established by the father of the insured-trustee was not includible in the insured's estate. The insurance involved was purchased by the insured-trustee after the trust was established. Inclusion was not required although the trust instrument gave the insured-trustee broad powers over the trust; according to the Tax Court the exercise of the powers was circumscribed by the insured's fiduciary duties. Interestingly, the Tax Court also concluded that the insured's breach of his fiduciary duties by pledging the insurance policies as collateral for a personal loan did not require inclusion.

In Revenue Ruling 84-179 the insured, *D,* originally acquired the insurance in 1960. However, in the same year he assigned the policy to his wife who named their child as beneficiary. In an unrelated transaction, *D*'s wife executed a will leaving her residuary estate to *D* as trustee of a trust for the benefit of their child. *D*'s wife died in 1978 and was survived by the insured. The policy of insurance on *D*'s life passed to the residuary trust. The Ruling concluded that the powers that *D* held as trustee were insufficient to cause the insurance to be included in his estate: The establishment of the testamentary trust was unrelated to the assignment of the insurance to *D*'s spouse and *D* could not benefit from the exercise of any of the powers that he held as trustee. Thus, although the insured served as trustee, the insurance was not includible in his estate. The Ruling was followed in LR 9111028 in which the insured served as trustee of a trust established by his wife but was barred from exercising any power with respect to insurance on his life.

Revenue Ruling 84-179 benefits taxpayers and helps to clarify the law. However, it is important to note that the Ruling requires inclusion where decedent held powers in a fiduciary capacity and had transferred to the trust either the policy or any of the consideration for maintaining the policy. In addition, according to the Ruling, inclusion is required if the powers could be exercised for the benefit of the insured. Although Reg. §20.2042-1(c)(4) continues to require the inclusion of the proceeds of a policy over which the insured held an incident of ownership as trustee, whether or not the incident could be exercised for the insured's own economic benefit, Revenue Ruling 84-179 provides that the Regulation will be interpreted in accordance with its provisions. Note also that it revoked an earlier Ruling that took a contrary position, Rev. Rul. 76-261, 1976-2 C.B. 276.

The government might also seek inclusion in the estate of the insured under §2042(2) if the insured held incidents of ownership over a policy as custodian for a minor whom the insured was legally obligated to support. A similar risk exists if an insured serves as guardian for an incompetent. All in all, it is safer not to appoint the insured to any fiduciary office with respect to policies on his or her life.

The insured should not hold any incidents of ownership in a policy as a fiduciary. Powers over a policy on the life of a trustee should be vested solely in a cofiduciary or some other party.

§6.28. Attribution of Incidents of Ownership

Under Reg. §20.2042-1(c)(6) incidents of ownership held by a corporation of which the decedent was the sole or controlling shareholder are attributed to the decedent to the extent the proceeds are not paid to or applied for the benefit of the corporation. However, the regulation provides that the power to surrender or cancel group-term life insurance as defined in §79 will not be attributed to a decedent "through his stock ownership."

In general, the proceeds of a policy are includible in the gross estate of a sole or controlling shareholder to the extent that they are paid to a personal beneficiary rather than to the corporation. Rev. Rul. 76-274, 1976-2 C.B. 278, situation 1. In applying §2042(2) it makes no difference whether the decedent was the sole shareholder or the controlling shareholder, since in either case the decedent held the power to affect the disposition of the proceeds through exercise of control over the corporation. *Estate of Milton L. Levy,* 70 T.C. 873 (1978) (the full amount of proceeds paid to a personal beneficiary was included in the estate of the 80.4 percent shareholder).

> **Example 6-8.** *D* owned a controlling interest in ABC, Inc., which owned 2 policies of insurance on *D*'s life. When *D* died the proceeds of Policy One were paid to her father, *F,* in accordance with the beneficiary designation in the policy. The proceeds of Policy Two were paid to ABC, Inc. Under §20.2042-1(c)(6) the proceeds of Policy One are includible in *D*'s gross estate. The proceeds of Policy Two are not; they are taken into account in valuing *D*'s shares of ABC, Inc. stock. The proceeds along with other corporate assets are subject to any applicable discount that is applied in valuing *D*'s shares. *Estate of John L. Huntsman,* 66 T.C. 861 (1976), *acq.,* 1977-1 C.B. 1. Under the analysis of Rev. Rul. 90-21, 1990-1 C.B. 172 and LR 8906002 (TAM) if *D* had transferred Policies One and Two and the controlling interest in ABC, Inc. within 3 years of death, Policy One would be included in *D*'s estate but not Policy Two. *See* §6.32.2.

In effect, the provisions of §2042(2) and §2031 are mutually exclusive — the proceeds of a policy may be includible under either but not both.

For purposes of §2042 a decedent is the controlling shareholder only if the decedent owned stock that represented more than 50 percent of the combined total voting power of the corporation. In making that determination, a decedent is treated as owning only the stock the legal title to which was held at the time of death by (1) the decedent, or an agent or nominee of the decedent, (2) the decedent and another person jointly (but only to the extent that the decedent furnished the total consideration for purposes of §2040), (3) the trustee of a voting trust to the extent of the decedent's interest, and (4) the trustee of any other trust of which the decedent was treated as the owner under §§671-678. Reg. §20.2042-1(c)(6).

Where incidents of ownership are attributed to a controlling shareholder, the fiduciary duties owed by the controlling shareholder to other shareholders or creditors may not prevent the insurance proceeds from being included in his or her estate. *Estate of Milton L. Levy,* 70 T.C. 873 (1978). A controlling shareholder owes fiduciary duties to minority shareholders and creditors, but some incidents held by the corporation over the insurance could be exercised in a variety of significant ways without violating those duties (*e.g.,* the right to borrow against the policy). In this respect the outcome differs from the Supreme Court's decision in *United States v. Byrum,* 408 U.S. 125 (1972), in which the transferor's fiduciary duties prevented the transferor's retained right to vote stock from requiring it to be included in his estate under §2036(a). The decision in *Byrum* lead to the adoption of §2036(b), which reversed it. *See* §2.17.1.

§6.28.1. Stock Held as Community Property

Where the stock of a corporation is all owned by a husband and wife as their community property, it is doubtful that either spouse will be considered to be a controlling shareholder for purposes of attributing the incidents of ownership by the corporation. In *Estate of Elizabeth Lee,* 69 T.C. 860 (1978), *nonacq.,* 1980-1 C.B. 2, the Tax Court held that the decedent's one-half community interest in 80 percent of the stock of a closely-held corporation would be valued separately as a 40 percent minority interest. A contrary result reached by a panel of the Fifth Circuit, *Estate of Bright v. Commissioner,* 619 F.2d 407 (5th Cir. 1980), was overturned when the issue was considered en banc, 658 F.2d 999 (5th Cir. 1981). Consistent with those decisions, *Propstra v. United States,* 680 F.2d 1248 (9th Cir. 1982), upheld the allowance of a discount in valuing the decedent's one-half community interest in real property. However, despite the foregoing decisions, the IRS may continue to raise the issue.

In the case of community property, less value may be included in a shareholder's gross estate if corporate-owned insurance is paid to the shareholder's personal beneficiaries than if it were payable to the corporation. The reason is simple: Only the insured's one-half interest in the community property shares should be taken into account in applying Reg. §20.2042-1(c)(6). Accordingly, neither husband nor wife would be a *controlling* shareholder where all of the shares of stock are owned by them as their community property. In such a case, the proceeds of corporate-owned insurance that are paid to personal beneficiaries may escape inclusion under §2042 or any other section of the Code. In contrast, the proceeds of corporate-owned insurance that are paid to the corporation would be taken into account under §2031 in valuing the decedent's interest in the stock. Under the Tax Court decision in *John L. Huntsman,* 66 T.C. 861 (1976), the proceeds of insurance payable to a corporation are included along with other assets in valuing the stock, which is subject to whatever discount may apply to its valuation. In *Huntsman,* the Tax Court rejected the government's contention that the full amount of the proceeds should be added after valuing the corporation exclusive of the proceeds.

The proceeds of corporate-owned insurance may be used to fund the redemption of the shares of an insured stockholder under a stock redemption agreement. *See* §11.8. If the proceeds exceed the amount required to fund the redemption, the excess is includible in the estate of the insured under §2038 if the insured voluntarily entered into the agreement and had control of the disposition of the excess. LR 8943082. According to that ruling the excess is taxable income to the extent it exceeds the $5,000 exclusion allowed by §101(b).

§6.28.2. Insurance Owned by a Partnership

Insurance owned by a partnership is not includible in the gross estate of a deceased partner where the proceeds are applied for the benefit of the partnership. *Estate of Frank H. Knipp,* 25 T.C. 153 (1955), *aff'd,* 244 F.2d 436 (4th Cir.), *cert. denied,* 355 U.S. 827 (1957) (appeal involved other issues); *nonacq. on insurance issue,* 1956-2 C.B. 10, *withdrawn and acq. in result substituted,* 1959-1 C.B. 4. If the proceeds are instead payable to a personal beneficiary designated by the insured partner, they are includible. Rev. Rul. 83-147, 1983-2 C.B. 158. However, where more than three years prior to death a partner assigned all interests in group-term insurance that would have qualified as §79 insurance had the partner been an employee, by analogy to Reg. §20.2042-1(c)(6), the insured partner is not treated as having possessed any incidents of ownership in the insurance. Rev. Rul. 83-148, 1983-2 C.B. 157. The reciprocal trust doctrine, discussed in §6.29, probably does not require inclusion of policies that are cross-owned by partners. Rev. Rul. 56-397, 1956-2 C.B. 599.

§6.29. Reciprocal Trust Doctrine and Life Insurance

The "reciprocal trust" or "crossed trust" doctrine was developed to determine who would be treated as the grantor of related trusts for tax purposes. Under the doctrine, where two or more trusts are created by related parties and the nominal grantor of one trust is the beneficiary of another trust, the trusts are uncrossed. That is, each person is treated as the grantor of the trust of which he or she is the beneficiary if the trusts are "interrelated, and . . . the arrangement, to the extent of mutual value, leaves the settlors in approximately the same economic position as they would have been in had they created trusts naming themselves as life beneficiaries." *United States v. Estate of Grace,* 395 U.S. 316, 324 (1969).

> **Example 6-9.** *H* transferred 1,000 shares of ABC, Inc. to a trust of which *W* was named trustee and income beneficiary. At the same time *W* transferred 1,000 shares of ABC, Inc. to an identical trust of which *H* was the trustee and income beneficiary. The children of *H* and *W* were the remaindermen of both trusts. Upon the death of either grantor the trusts will be "uncrossed" by the reciprocal trust doctrine and *H* will be treated as the grantor of the trust of which he was the trustee and income beneficiary and *W* will be treated as the grantor of the other trust. Upon *H*'s death the property of the trust of which he is treated as the grantor is includible in his gross estate under §2036(a)(1).

The doctrine may be applied although the grantors do not retain any economic interest in the trusts. Thus, the doctrine was applied in *Estate of Bruno Bischoff,* 69 T.C. 32 (1977), where each nominal grantor appointed the other as trustee with discretion to distribute trust property to the beneficiaries, who were the grandchildren of the grantors. It has also been applied where donors appoint each other as custodians of gifts made under the Uniform Gifts to Minors Act. *See* §7.34.2.

The government has argued that the reciprocal trust doctrine applies where a husband and wife each buy and own a policy of insurance on the other's life. The doctrine was applied where a husband and wife domiciled in Texas each used community property funds to purchase substantially identical policies of insurance on each other's life and designated the uninsured spouse as the owner and beneficiary. Rev. Rul. 67-228, 1967-2 C.B. 331. The Ruling concluded that, in such circumstances,

> [T]he presumption under Texas law that the policies are community property will prevail unless it is clearly shown that the transfers were not reciprocal and that gifts were intended. Accordingly, as a community asset, one-half of the value of the property received as insurance on the life of the husband upon his death is includible in his gross estate under the provisions of section 2042 of the Code. Furthermore, one-half of the value of the policy on the life of the wife is includible in his gross estate under section 2033 of the Code as his interest in the community asset. 1967-2 C.B. at 333.

In *Estate of Dorothy C. Wilmot,* 29 T.C.M. 1055 (1970), the court refused to consider a belated argument by the government that the reciprocal trust doctrine should be applied to policies each spouse owned on the life of the other.

It is reasonable to apply the reciprocal trust doctrine where the insured and another person acquire similar policies on each other's lives and the insured in fact has the power to designate the beneficiary of the policy that is nominally owned by the other person. The doctrine should not apply where the policies are owned by business associates in connection with a buy-out agreement. Rev. Rul. 56-397, 1956-2 C.B. 599. These rules roughly parallel the ones under which the incidents of ownership held by a corporation or partnership are attributed to the insured. It is questionable whether the doctrine should apply merely because a husband and wife, or two other parties, each purchase a policy on the life of the other. As some commentators have pointed out, the mutual acquisition of life insurance policies by a husband and wife involves the acquisition of new wealth and not the rearrangement of existing wealth. Eliasberg, The Estate Taxation of Life Insurance: A Survey of Recent Developments, U. So. Cal., 26th Tax Inst. 1, 62-66 (1974). The cross-ownership of life insurance policies should be recognized as a legitimate estate planning tool. As indicated in §6.21.1, some incentives remain for the cross-ownership of insurance by a husband and wife. However, the most prominent incentive was eliminated by the adoption of the unlimited marital deduction.

§6.30. Transfer of Interests in Insurance Within Three Years of Death, §2035

> The case law which has been developed in respect to the applicability of section 2035 to life insurance has not been the model of clarity, at least insofar as policies taken out within 3 years of the death of the insured are concerned. *Estate of Tetsuo Kurihara,* 82 T.C. 51, 53 (1984).

> Section 2035(a) itself is unchanged since 1976. Section 2035(d) is simply an added sieve through which transactions must pass before the transfer may even be tested under the 3-year rule. Although section 2035(d)(1) generally repeals the 3-year rule, perforations in the sieve are found in section 2035(d)(2) which allow the 3-year rule to be applied to a transfer of an interest in property which either (1) is included in the value of the gross estate under section 2042, or (2) would have been included under section 2042 had such an interest been retained by the decedent. *Estate of Leder,* 89 T.C. 235, 239 (1987), *aff'd,* 893 F.2d 237 (10th Cir. 1989).

§6.31. §2035; Pre-1982 Law

The 1976 Act amended §2035 to require the inclusion of gifts made within three years of death with the exception of gifts for which the donor was not required to file a gift tax return (*i.e.,* ones within the annual gift tax exclusion). Because the exception might result in the exclusion of large amounts of life insurance, the 1978 Act amended §2035(b) to provide that the exception did not apply "to any transfer with respect to a life insurance policy." The constitutionality of the retroactive 1978 amendment was upheld in several cases involving life insurance policies that were transferred in the post-1976 period before adoption of the 1978 amendment. *E.g., Estate of Ekins v. Commissioner,* 797 F.2d 481 (7th Cir. 1986); *Estate of Fein v. United States,* 730 F.2d 1211 (8th Cir.), *cert. denied,* 469 U.S. 858 (1984). The courts concluded that the due process clause does not bar changes in tax laws that are reasonably foreseeable and involve only fluctuations in the tax rates. Additionally, the changes were not so harsh or oppressive as to transgress the constitutional limitations.

§6.32. §2035; Post-1981 Law

Under §2035(d)(1), which was added by the 1981 Act, the rule of §2035(a) that required the inclusion of property transferred within three years of death does not apply to estate of decedents dying after December 31, 1981 except as otherwise provided in §2035(d)(2). That is, §2035(a) does not apply to post-1981 transfers made within three years of the donor's death except for those described in §2035(d)(2). By its terms, §2035(d)(2) requires that §2035(a) be applied to "a transfer of an interest in property which is included in the value of the gross estate under section 2036, 2037, 2038 or 2042 or would have been included under any of such sections if such interest had been retained by the decedent." The Tax Court and several courts of appeal have given the post-1981 law a literal reading; as a result, insurance purchased by an irrevocable trust with funds provided by the insured is not included under §2035 although the insured died within three years of the establishment of the trust. *See* §6.23.4. The IRS has stated that it will no longer litigate the issue. A.O.D. 1991-012.

§6.32.1. Insured Transfers Owned Insurance

Under §2035(d)(2) the proceeds of insurance policies that were transferred by the insured within three years preceding his or her death are included in the insured's estate. Such transfers are clearly within the reach of §2035(d)(2) because the proceeds of the policies would have been included in the insured's estate under §2042 had the policies not been transferred.

§6.32.2. Controlled Corporation or Other Noninsured-Owner Transfers Insurance Within Three Years of Insured's Death

Insurance policies owned by persons other than the insured that are transferred within three years of the insured's death are includible if the owner is merely the agent of the insured or if the owner's incidents of ownership are attributed to the insured. For example, Rev. Rul. 82-141, 1982-2 C.B. 209, held that the proceeds of insurance policies owned by the insured's controlled corporation were includible in the insured's estate where, within three years of the insured's death, the corporation transferred the policies to another person in a transaction that did not have a business purpose. Revenue Ruling 90-21, 1990-1 C.B. 172, amplified Revenue Ruling 82-141 to provide that inclusion under §2035(d)(2) is required in such a case when the insured also disposes of his or her controlling interest in the corporation within three years of death. According to LR 8906002, inclusion under the attribution rules and §2035(d)(2) is not required when, preceding the assignment of the insurance, the corporation was the designated beneficiary of the insurance. Exclusion follows in that case because Reg. §20.2042-1(c)(6) does not provide any basis for attributing ownership to the insured when insurance owned by the insured's corporation is payable to the corporation. Consistently, LR 8509005 required the inclusion of proceeds of a policy acquired by insured's wholly-owned corporation within three years of insured's death although the insurance was transferred by the corporation to an irrevocable trust prior to insured's death. Finally, inclusion was required under the pre-1981 form of §2035 when the insurance, in form owned by the insured's wife, was issued at his instance within three years preceding his death and all premiums on the insurance were paid by his controlled corporation. *Estate of Levine v. United States,* 10 Cl. Ct. 135 (1986).

In other cases inclusion does not result. For example, in *Estate of Leder,* 89 T.C. 235, *aff'd,* 893 F.2d 237 (10th Cir. 1989), the insurance acquired by the insured's spouse within three years of the insured's death was not includible although the insured's wholly-owned corporation paid all of the premiums. In the view of the Tax Court, the insured did not hold any incident of ownership directly or by attribution. The manner in which the insurance was acquired and other facts distinguish *Leder* from *Levine.* In *Leder,* the Tax Court reasoned that inclusion was not proper because under the governing state law (Oklahoma) the insured never held an interest in the policy or any incident of ownership in it. Thus, §2035(d)(2) did not apply to lift the bar of §2035(d)(1) and require inclusion under §2035(a).

As noted above, the IRS has ruled that inclusion is not required where the life insurance was acquired and all premiums were paid by a corporation which the insured controlled prior to her sale of all of her stock within three years of her death. LR 8906002. Because the insurance was payable to the corporation, the incidents of ownership in the policy were not attributed to the controlling shareholder under Reg. §20.2042-1(c)(6). "Thus, no basis exists either indirectly or directly, for including the policy proceeds in *A*'s gross estate under section 2042(2). Further, on the date of her death, *A* was not a shareholder in *X*." LR 8906002.

§6.32.3. Pre-1982 Law: Insured Transfers Funds Used to Purchase Insurance

Under the pre-1982 rules the courts reached inconsistent results where the insured provided funds that were used by a trustee or another person to purchase insurance within three years of the insured's death. Inclusion was generally not required when the funds were transferred to an independent trustee who was free to invest the funds as the trustee saw fit. *Hope v. United States,* 691 F.2d 786 (5th Cir. 1982).

> Although Beverly Hope did fill out the initial application form for the insurance policies, the court could not conclude from that fact alone that, in the language of *Bell* she "beamed the proceeds at her children." Such a conclusion would require a factual determination that the trustee, Byron A. Whitmash, had no discretion to invest the trust assets, but was in fact controlled by the decedent, acting as the decedent's agent when he paid the premiums. Nowhere, however, was it stipulated that the grantor controlled the trustee or that the trustee's powers were confined. On the

> contrary, the trust agreement is irrevocable and vests broad powers in the trustee, particularly with regard to investments. 691 F.2d at 789.

The same rule applies where the money was given to individuals who subsequently used the funds to purchase insurance on the donor's life. "If on the other hand, decedent had given money to her children, and they, entirely on their own volition, had chosen to purchase an insurance policy on her life, it would be equally clear that only the money would have been 'transferred.' " *Estate of Inez G. Coleman,* 52 T.C. 921, 923 (1969), *acq.,* 1978-1 C.B. 1.

Inclusion was required, however, where the insured was considered directly or indirectly to have acquired the policy. Thus, under the pre-1982 law the insured was frequently treated as having acquired and transferred a policy that was issued to a trust at the instance of the insured within three years of the insured's death and with respect to which the insured paid the premiums directly or indirectly. *See, e.g., Estate of Tetsuo Kurihara,* 82 T.C. 51 (1984) (inclusion of insurance issued to trustee within three years of death required where insured wrote check to trustee in the amount of the insurance premium, noting that it was "premium for Life Ins. No. 10010395 Columbian Mutual Life"; in fact the trustee did not act on its own).

> The purpose of section 2035 "is to reach substitutes for testamentary dispositions and thus to prevent the evasion of the estate tax." *United States v. Wells,* 283 U.S. 102, 117, 51 S. Ct. 446, 451, 75 L. Ed. 867 (1931). An insured pays the premiums on a life insurance policy in order to leave the proceeds to his beneficiaries; thus where a policy is both procured at the behest of the decedent within the statutory period and where all the premiums are paid by the decased in contemplation of death [within three years of death], the gift must necessarily be one of the property interest in the policy. . . . In short, what is intended with the purchase of a life insurance policy in circumstances like these is the passing of the proceeds at death. That is the equivalent of a testamentary disposition, and its taxation is precisely the object of section 2035. *First National Bank of Oregon v. United States,* 488 F.2d 575, 577 (9th Cir. 1973).

Cases consistent with *First National Bank of Oregon* include: *Schnack v. Commissioner,* 848 F.2d 933 (9th Cir. 1988); *Detroit Bank & Trust Co. v. United States,* 467 F.2d 964 (6th Cir. 1972), *cert. denied,* 410 U.S. 929 (1973); *Bel v. United States,* 452 F.2d 682 (5th Cir. 1971), *cert. denied,* 410 U.S. 929 (1972). Inclusion in such cases appropriately extends to the whole proceeds and not merely the amount of the premiums paid by the insured within three years of death.

§6.32.4. Post-1981 Law: Insured Transfers Funds Used to Purchase Insurance

Section 2035(d)(1) made the inclusionary rule of §2035(a) generally inapplicable to post-1981 transfers. However, under §2035(d)(2) the inclusionary rule of §2035(a) only applies to the post-1981 transfer "of an interest in property which is included in the value of the gross estate under section 2036, 2037, 2038, or 2042 or would have been included under any of such sections if such interest had been retained by the decedent." Thus, the insured's estate must include the proceeds of a life insurance policy transferred by the insured within three years of death. Had the policy been retained by the insured, the proceeds would have been included in the insured's estate under §2042. The Tax Court and several courts of appeal have held that under the 1981 amendments, no inclusion is required unless the insured held and transferred an incident of ownership in the insurance. *Estate of Joseph Leder,* 89 T.C. 235 (1987), *aff'd,* 893 F.2d 237 (10th Cir. 1989). In particular, the decisions have not required inclusion where within three years of death the insured transferred the funds that were used to purchase the insurance but did not actually transfer the insurance itself.

> In *Estate of Joseph Leder, supra,* we held that the proceeds from the policy in that case were not includible in the gross estate of the insured where the insured did not possess at the time of his death, or at any time within the three years preceding his death, any of the incidents of ownership in the policy because (1) the conditions of section 2042 were never met; (2) the section 2035(d) exception to section 2035(d)(1) is not applicable because the proceeds were not includible under section 2042 or the other sections cited in section 2035(d)(2); and (3) section 2035(d)(1) overrides section 2035(a). *Estate of Eddie L. Headrick,* 93 T.C. 171, 177 (1989), *aff'd,* 918 F.2d 1263 (6th Cir. 1990).

Estate of Frank M. Perry, 59 T.C.M. 65 (1990), *aff'd,* 927 F.2d 209 (5th Cir. 1991), followed *Leder* and *Headrick.* The taxpayer in *Perry* was awarded attorney's fees of $9,206 for handling the appeal by the IRS, which the Fifth Circuit court said was not "substantially justified." 931 F.2d 1044 (5th Cir. 1991). In the court's view the IRS was continuing "to whip a dead horse in circuit after circuit. . . ." Id. at 1046.

In an Action on Decision issued with respect to the appellate decision in *Headrick,* the IRS has stated that it will no longer litigate the issue. After reviewing the history of §2035(d)(2) and the adverse opinions in *Leder, Headrick,* and *Perry,* A.O.D. 1991-012 concluded: "Although we continue to believe that substance should prevail over form and that such indirect transfers should be included in a decedent's gross estate, in light of the three adverse appellate opinions set forth above, we will no longer litigate this issue." Of course, the IRS might prevail upon Congress to return to the pre-1982 rule or enact a more stringent one. Because of that possibility, trusts should be drafted with care as indicated in §6.23.1.

§6.32.5. Exchange of Policies Owned by Others Within Three Years of Insured's Death

An assignment of an existing life insurance policy should expressly include policies that may be issued in exchange for the existing policy and any changes in its terms and increases in the coverage. Although the IRS does not concede the validity of an anticipatory assignment, it did uphold the exclusion of the proceeds of a policy issued within three years of the insured's death in exchange for a preexisting policy that had been validly assigned by the insured more than three years prior to death. Rev. Rul. 80-289, 1980-2 C.B. 270. The IRS stated that "the [second] assignment will not be treated as a transfer under Section 2035 of the Code." Id. *See* §6.72.10. A similar result was reached in LR 8819001 (TAM), where the original policy was assigned by the insured to irrevocable trusts more than three years prior to death. Within three years of the insured's death the trustee exchanged the original policy for one that carried a lower premium and was issued by a separate company. The insured signed the application for the new policy, acknowledging that the representations in the application were correct. Within three years of the issuance of the second policy to the trustee the insured died. "Because the decedent owned no interest in the original policy at the time of the exchange and because the decedent's signature on the policy application was not essential to the exchange, we conclude that the decedent did not make a transfer of the insurance within three years of death for purposes of section 2035 of the Code." Id. A contrary result was reached in *American National Bank & Trust Co. of Rockford v. United States,* 832 F.2d 1032 (7th Cir. 1987), in which the original policy was assigned to the insured's wife more than three years prior to his death. However, the assignee was required to relinquish all interests in the assigned policy in connection with the issuance of a much larger policy that was not assigned to the insured's spouse. The court viewed the second policy as a different policy that was issued by a different insurer "only on condition that they terminated the earlier policy and thereby extinguished all the rights that Mrs. Olson had under it." Id.

§6.33. Insurance Acquired with Joint or Community Property Funds

Under the Regulations half of the proceeds of community property life insurance is includible in the insured's estate. Reg. §20.2042-1(b)(2). However, insurance acquired with community property (or jointly owned) funds more than three years prior to the insured's death may be entirely excluded if the husband and wife effectively agreed that the insurance was the separate property of the noninsured spouse. *See* §3.29. Where money that was originally community property (or jointly owned) is used within three years of the insured's death to purchase insurance, the courts have required inclusion in some cases, but not in others. The differing outcomes are difficult to reconcile.

In *Estate of Lee J. Clay,* 86 T.C. 1266 (1986), the Tax Court upheld complete exclusion of the insurance proceeds of a policy on which the premiums were paid from a joint account of the insured and his wife. The policy was issued to the insured's wife as owner within three years of the insured's death. In *Clay* the insured contributed 73 percent of the funds in the joint account, the use of which to pay premiums on the insurance constituted a transfer from the insured to his wife. The Tax Court rejected the tracing analysis, holding that "the mere payment of premiums with funds withdrawn from a joint account does not constitute payment by the nonwithdrawing tenant." Id.

Results contrary to *Clay* were reached in several cases involving community property. *Estate of Robert W. Hass,* 51 T.C.M. 453 (1986) (Nevada); *Estate of Mary Baratta-Lorton,* 49 T.C.M. 770 (1985) (California), *aff'd without opinion* (9th Cir. 1986). Moreover, in *Schnack v. Commissioner,* 848 F.2d 933 (9th Cir. 1988), the court required inclusion of one-half of the proceeds of a policy issued on the insured-wife's life within three years of death. Similar policies on the lives of husband and wife were issued simultaneously and paid for with community funds that had been deposited in a joint bank account. Analogizing the facts to those of *Kurihara,* the Ninth Circuit emphasized that the insured's release of her interest in the funds was for the specific purpose of paying the premiums on the policy. That is, the funds were not available to the insured's husband to use for whatever purpose he wished.

§6.34. Sale of Life Insurance by Insured Within Three Years of Death, §2035

The gross estate does not include property that is transferred within three years of death in "any bona fide sale for an adequate and full consideration in money or money's worth." §2035. The IRS has indicated that for purposes of the bona fide sale exception, it would follow *United States v. Allen,* 293 F.2d 916 (10th Cir. 1961), *cert. denied,* 368 U.S. 944 (1961) and *United States v. Past,* 347 F.2d 7 (9th Cir. 1965). LR 8806004 (TAM). It contends that those cases limit the exclusion for bona fide sales to consideration that is equal to the value at which the transferred property would otherwise be includible in the gross estate. Specifically, "any consideration received for such transfer is not adequate and full unless it is equal to the value at which such property would be included in the gross estate had it been retained by the decedent." Id. This position is consistent with the outcome in *Gradow v. United States,* 897 F.2d 516 (Fed. Cir. 1989), which is discussed at length at §9.34.

If adequate consideration is not received, the value of the transferred property is includible less the value of the consideration received. In the T.A.M. the IRS stated, "Even if [the consideration received] were equal to the reserve value of the policy at the time of transfer, the consideration received is still wholly inadequate since such consideration is measured against the value at which the property is includible in the decedent's gross estate, or $1,000,000. Accordingly, the entire value of the policy proceeds minus the value of any consideration received by the decedent's controlled corporation is includible in her estate."

It is doubtful that the position taken by the IRS in LR 8606004 would be upheld: *Allen* is an exceptional case that has not attracted a wide following. *Past* and similar cases dealing with the sufficiency of the consideration received in widow's election cases are of doubtful validity. *See* §9.30. Instead, the consideration received should be sufficient in the ordinary case if it were equal to the value of the policy determined under Reg. §20.2031-8(a)(2) (cost of comparable contracts or interpolated terminal reserve). However, the Regulation by its terms applies to the valuation of a life insurance policy on the life of a person other than the decedent. Under the primary regulation governing valuation, "all relevant facts and elements of value as of the appropriate valuation date shall be considered." Hence, it may be necessary to consider the physical condition and insurability of the insured at the time of transfer. For example, in *Estate of James Stuart Pritchard,* 4 T.C. 204 (1944), the terminally ill insured did not receive adequate or full consideration when he sold a $50,000 policy on his life to his wife for its cash surrender value of $10,483. Note that if a policy is sold, the income tax exclusion of the proceeds may be lost. *See* §101(a). *See also* §6.53.

§6.35. Exclusion of Part of Proceeds to the Extent Premiums Paid by Others

Part of the proceeds of a policy transferred within three years of death may be excluded from the insured's estate if some of the postassignment premiums are paid by a person other than the insured. Thus, the Tax Court has held that the insured's estate was not required to include a portion of the proceeds that bore the same relation to the total proceeds as the premium payments made by the assignee bore to the total amount of premium payments. *Estate of Morris R. Silverman,* 61 T.C. 338 (1973), *acq.,* 1978-1 C.B. 2, *other issues affirmed,* 521 F.2d 574 (2d Cir. 1975). In effect the court adopted the proportional premium payment rule that the government advanced in Rev. Rul. 67-463, 1967-2 C.B. 327, and abandoned in Rev. Rul. 71-497, 1971-2 C.B. 329. *Silverman* was followed in LR 8724014, which allowed exclusion of the proportion of the proceeds that was attributable to premium payments indirectly made by assignees who reimbursed the insured for premium payments withheld by his employer.

> **Example 6-10.** *D* irrevocably assigned a $100,000 policy on his life to his sister, *S,* within 3 years of his death. *D* paid 3 $1,000 premiums on the policy prior to the assignment and *S* paid 2 post-assignment premiums of $1,000 each. Following *D*'s death the proceeds were paid to *S*. Under *Silverman* only 3/5ths of the total policy proceeds are includible in *D*'s gross estate. The entire proceeds would have been includible if *D* had continued to pay the premiums.

It is curious that the government acquiesced in the Tax Court's decision in *Silverman* five years after it was decided. The Second Circuit opinion does not pass upon the proration issue because the government did not appeal that portion of the Tax Court's decision. Indeed, the appellate court admitted "some uneasiness about the proper basis for holding that . . . [the assignee's] payments in the last six months of his father's life changes the result from the situation where a decedent continues to pay the premiums until death." 521 F.2d at 577. It also questioned whether the assignee's payment of a portion of the premiums justified excluding a proportionate part of the proceeds rather than the actual amount the assignee paid in premiums. Where the insured dies within three years of making a gift of insurance on his or her life, a portion of the proceeds equal to the amount of any post-gift premiums paid by the assignee should be excluded from the insured's gross estate. The exclusion of a larger amount under the *Silverman* rule is difficult to justify.

§6.36. Insurance on the Life of a Person Other Than the Decedent, §2035

Insurance transferred by a decedent within three years of death is generally not includible in the decedent's gross estate where the insurance is on the life of another person. In such a case the insurance is not subject to the rules of §2042 that are made applicable to transfers within three years of death by §2035(d)(2). Instead, the insurance on the life of another person is subject to the same rules that apply to cash, securities, or other property transferred by the decedent within three years of death. A ruling issued prior to the 1981 Act reached a contrary conclusion, reasoning that the language of §2035(b) did not support exclusion of the insurance in such a case. Rev. Rul. 81-14, 1981-1 C.B. 456. The ruling was questionable and appears to be overturned by the provisions of §2035(d)(1). Insurance should be treated differently under §2035 according to the identity of the insured. The transfer of insurance on the transferor's life, which could reduce the size of the transferor's estate by an amount much larger than the value of the insurance at the time of transfer, should be subject to a more stringent rule. The transfer of insurance on the life of another person does not pose the same risk and should, therefore, be subject to the same rules that apply to the transfer of ordinary types of property.

§6.37. Premiums Paid Within Three Years of Death; Pre-1982 Law, §2035

Prior to amendment in 1976, §2035 required the inclusion of premiums paid within three years of death and in contemplation of death. "[T]he value of any premiums paid by the decedent in contemplation of death within three years of death [on policies transferred more than three years prior to death] is includible in his gross estate under section 2035 of the Code." Rev. Rul. 71-497, 1971-2 C.B. 329. This rule required inclusion whether or not the premium payments were within the annual gift tax exclusion. The 1976 Act amended §2035 to require inclusion of all transfers made within three years of death with the exception of gifts which were not required to be reported on a gift tax return (*i.e.,* gifts within the annual gift tax exclusion). §2035(b). If the exception were applicable to life insurance, it might allow the exclusion of large amounts of life insurance so long as the value of the transfers was within the amount of the gift tax exclusion. Because of that concern, the 1978 Act amended the exclusion to make it inapplicable retroactively to transfers "with respect to life insurance."

According to the Senate Finance Committee's Report on H.R. 6715, which contained the technical corrections to the 1976 Act, the limited exclusion allowed under §2035(b) was available with respect to "any premiums paid (or deemed paid) by the decedent within three years of death to the extent that such payments would not have resulted in the inclusion of the proceeds of the policy in the decedent's gross estate under prior law." S. Rep. No. 95-745, 95th Cong., 2d Sess. 87 (1978). The reference in the statement to the prior law is a bit confusing because the prior law was concerned with the subjective issue of whether the transfer was made in contemplation of death. However, the statement generally supports exclusion of premium payments made within three years of death.

Under the general rule of §2035(d)(1), mere premium payments made within three years of the donor's death are generally not includible in the donor's estate. That outcome reflects the general rule applicable to gifts and is simpler to understand and administer. Of course, inclusion would result if the premium payments were otherwise includible under §§2036, 2037, 2038, or 2042. *See* §2035(d)(2). *See also* §6.32.

§6.38. Transfer of Incidents of Ownership Within Three Years of Death, §2035

Section 2042(2) requires inclusion of the proceeds of policies over which the insured "possessed at his death any of the incidents of ownership." Inclusion is probably required under §2035 if, within three years of death, the insured transferred an incident of ownership that would otherwise require inclusion under §2042. Section §2035(d)(2) in effect provides that the general inclusionary rule of §2035(a) applies to "the transfer of an interest in property which is included in the gross estate under section 2036, 2037, 2038, or 2042 or would have been included under any of such sections if such interest had been retained by the decedent." *See* Rev. Rul. 90-21, 1990-1 C.B. 172 (insured estate includes proceeds of policy transferred to an individual beneficiary within three years of insured's death by corporation controlled by the insured).

Example 6-11. In 1991 *T,* a widow, transferred a $100,000 whole life policy to the independent trustee of an irrevocable life insurance trust of which *T*'s children were the beneficiaries. *T* retained the power to veto any disposition of the policy. In 1993 *T* irrevocably released the veto power. *T* died in 1995. Although *T* transferred ownership of the life insurance more than 3 years prior to death, she retained an incident of ownership over the policy which was sufficient to cause the insurance to be included in her estate under §2042(2). Presumably the insurance would also be includible in *T*'s estate under §2035(d)(2). One critical question would be whether such a release constituted a "transfer of an interest in property." As indicated below, the Regulations and a Technical Advice Memorandum indicate that the IRS takes that position.

First, Regulations issued prior to the adoption of the 1981 Act state that the proceeds are includible under §2035 if the insured transferred incidents of ownership over the policy in contemplation of death. Reg. §20.2042-1(a)(2). The position taken by the Regulation is sound and consistent with §2035(d)(2) and other Code provisions, such as §2038(a)(1). Second, LR 8806004 (TAM) states, "In order for §2035(d)(2) to apply the decedent must have possessed some incident of ownership in the life insurance policy at some time during the three year period before death and must have transferred this incident of ownership during the same period." As indicated by Rev. Rul. 90-21, *supra,* the rule extends to incidents of ownership that are attributed to the insured as the controlling shareholder. Indeed, Revenue Ruling 90-21 applied this rule to a situation in which the insured transferred the controlling interest in a corporation for less than full consideration within three years of death.

§6.39. Retained Life Interest, §2036

Insurance may be included in the gross estate of a person other than the insured who directly or indirectly transfers a policy in which the transferor retains a life interest. The insurance proceeds are includible, for example, when a noninsured owner transfers a policy to the trustee of a trust in which he or she has a life interest and the insured predeceases the transferor. Inclusion also results where the insurer holds the proceeds of a policy pursuant to an election made by the beneficiary to receive the income for life and to pay the principal to others following the beneficiary's death. *Pyle v. Commissioner,* 313 F.2d 328 (3d Cir. 1963). However, the insurance proceeds are not included in the beneficiary's estate where such a settlement option was chosen by the insured and not the beneficiary. *Estate of Idamay Swift Minotto,* 9 T.C.M. 556 (1950).

Example 6-12. *H*'s life was insured under 2 policies that he owned. Under Policy One the proceeds were payable outright to his wife, *W,* upon his death or according to a settlement option selected by her. After *H* died *W* elected an option under which she received the interest for life, remainder to their children. The proceeds of Policy Two were subject to the same option, which had been irrevocably selected by *H.* The proceeds of Policy One are includible in *W*'s gross estate, but not the proceeds of Policy

Two. In effect, *W* transferred the proceeds of Policy One to the insurer, but she did not transfer the proceeds of Policy Two.

Two decisions have allowed insurance proceeds to be excluded from the estate of a person other than the insured who paid premiums on policies in which he or she held substantial interests. In the first, *Goodnow v. United States,* 302 F.2d 516 (Ct. Cl. 1962), the insured's wife paid premiums on policies that the insured had transferred to a revocable trust in which the wife had a life interest. The insured predeceased his wife and the proceeds of the policies were paid to the trustee. Following the wife's death the Court of Claims upheld exclusion of the proceeds from her estate. In the court's view she did not retain an interest in the same property that she transferred to the trust (*i.e.,* the premiums). Although the analysis is shallow, it was followed in *City Bank of Cleveland v. United States,* 371 F.2d 13 (6th Cir. 1966). The insured had selected an option that called for the payment of interest to his wife for life, remainder to his children, and the insured's wife had the power during the lifetime of the insured to change the beneficiary designation and to exercise other incidents of ownership. The wife had paid most of the premiums but, the court said, "payment of [the] premiums by her did not make the insurance policies taxable as a transfer with a retained life income under §2036(a)(1)." 371 F.2d at 16.

The rationale of *Goodnow* and *City Bank of Cleveland* cannot reasonably be extended to the payment of premiums on policies held by an *irrevocable* trust in which the premiuim payor has a life interest. In such a case payment of the premiums is clearly a transfer with a retained life interest. Accordingly, in such cases where the insured predeceases the premium payor, the proceeds are properly includible in the gross estate of the premium payor.

In community property states a portion of the insurance is includible in the gross estate of the noninsured spouse when a community property policy is transferred to the trustee of an inter vivos trust in which the noninsured spouse holds a life income interest. *United States v. Gordon,* 406 F.2d 332 (5th Cir. 1969) (Texas law). In *Gordon* the court recognized that the noninsured spouse, who survived the insured, was a grantor of the trust to the extent of her community interest in the policy. Importantly, however, the court allowed her estate a consideration offset under §2043(a) that reduced the amount includible in her estate by the actuarial value of the life estate she received in the share of the insurance proceeds that the husband transferred to the trust. The court reasoned that a consideration offset was allowable here on the same theory that it is allowed in the more traditional widow's election cases — the surviving spouse exchanged a remainder interest in her share of the proceeds for a life income interest in the insured's share. *See* §9.34.

A special problem arises under the community property laws of some states. In Idaho and Louisiana the income from a spouse's separate property is characterized as community property; in Texas income from separate property is the spouses' community property unless they agree otherwise. *See* §3.29. In these states, if one spouse transfers a community property interest in a marital asset to the other spouse as the donee's separate property, the income subsequently generated by that asset is community property. The IRS had argued that the transfer of a community property interest to one's spouse under such circumstances was a transfer with a retained life estate under §2036(a)(1) because the income is still treated as community property. The Tax Court accepted this argument in several cases. *Estate of Charles J. Wyly,* 69 T.C. 227 (1977); *Estate of Winston Castleberry,* 68 T.C. 682 (1977); *Estate of Ray McKee,* 37 T.C.M. 486 (1978). It was rejected by the Fifth Circuit, which reversed both *Wyly* and *Castleberry.* The court held that §2036 does not require inclusion in such cases. *Estate of Wyly v. Commissioner,* 610 F.2d 1282 (1980). The IRS subsequently conceded the issue insofar as Texas is concerned. Rev. Rul. 81-221, 1981-2 C.B. 178.

The Fifth Circuit's reversal of *Wyly* and *Castleberry* was predicated upon two views. First, under Texas community property law, the donor's interest was not sufficient to be characterized as a "right" within the meaning of §2036(a)(1). Second, the donor's interest in the transferred property was brought about solely by operation of the Texas community property law and, thus, was not a "retention" within the meaning of §2036. The *Wyly* decision did not involve policies of life insurance, but the rationale is the same. In fact, the IRS raised, then abandoned, the application of the theory to life insurance in the *McKee* case, preferring instead to pursue an incidents of ownership argument under §2042(2). The problem for residents of Texas was also relieved by the 1980 amendment of Article XVI, Section 15 of the state constitution. 3 Tex. Const. Ann. (Vernon 1991 Supp.).

§6.40. State Death Taxes

Consideration must be given to the provisions of state income and death taxes in planning the disposition of life insurance. It is particularly important to do so in the states which impose a death tax potentially greater than the maximum credit allowable against the federal estate tax for state death taxes paid. For example, state death tax laws may provide that life insurance proceeds receivable by the insured's personal representative are subject to the tax, as they are for federal purposes under §2042(1). Proceeds paid to other beneficiaries may also be subject to tax as they are under federal law or they may be partly or totally exempt. Some states that allow an exemption expressly extend it to proceeds that are paid to the trustee of an inter vivos or testamentary trust except to the extent the proceeds are used for the benefit of the estate.

In some cases a state death tax saving may result from the careful selection and designation of the insurance beneficiary. A special opportunity exists, for example, in states that allow an exemption for insurance paid to a named beneficiary and calculate the tax according to the relationship of the decedent to the transferee of property. In those states insurance proceeds should be made payable to the person who would be subject to the highest inheritance tax rates upon the client's death. Thus, insurance proceeds should be made payable to more remotely related persons and assets that are subject to the tax should be bequeathed to closer relatives.

> **Example 6-13.** Client wishes to leave $50,000 to his cousin, *C,* and the residue of his estate to his wife and children. In states that impose an inheritance tax and allow an insurance exemption, the overall state death tax will be lower if $50,000 is paid to *C* as insurance proceeds rather than as a testamentary gift.

§6.41. Generation-Skipping Transfer Tax (GSTT)

Life insurance is generally subject to the same GSTT rules as is any other type of property. The rules apply to "arrangements involving life estates and remainders, estates for years, and insurance and annuity contracts." §2652(b)(3). Thus, the GSTT extends to the payment of life insurance proceeds to grandchildren of the insured or to other skip persons. *See* §§2612 and 2613.

> **Example 6-14.** The insurance proceeds payable by reason of *X*'s death were retained by the insurer under an option that called for the payment of interest only to the insured's nephew, *N,* for life and the payment of the principal sum to *N*'s children upon *N*'s death. The GSTT will apply when *N* dies.

The application of the GSTT to life insurance and annuity contracts requires that care be exercised in selecting a settlement option and the creation of trusts. The amount of GSTT may be reduced significantly or eliminated entirely by utilizing a properly created irrevocable life insurance trust.

> **Example 6-15.** In January 1991 *T* established an irrevocable trust in which his 2 grandsons (*X* and *Y*) held completely separate

interests. Under §2654(b), "substantially separate and independent shares of different beneficiaries in a trust shall be treated as separate trusts." During the lifetime of a beneficiary no distribution could be made to any other person. Each beneficiary held a general power of appointment over his separate share of the trust. *T* transferred $20,000 to the independent trustee of the trust for investment in accordance with the trustee's best judgment. Not surprisingly, the trustee purchased a $500,000 policy of insurance on *T*'s life and paid the premium of $19,000 per year. In later years *T* made similar transfers to the trust that were used to pay premiums. The *Crummey* powers held by *X* and *Y* were sufficient to support the allowance of annual gift tax exclusions with respect to the gifts that *T* made to the trust. The gifts made by *T* to the trust qualified as nontaxable gifts as a result of which the inclusion ratio of each separate trust is zero (*see* §2642(c)). Following *T*'s death in July, 1994, the insurance proceeds of $500,000 were received by the trustee and distributed to *X* and *Y* as directed by the trust. The insurance proceeds were neither included in *T*'s gross estate nor subject to the GSTT.

§6.41.1. GSTT Exemption for Nontaxable Gifts

Under the original version of §2642(c)(2), transfers made to a trust that were nontaxable by reason of the annual gift tax exclusion were exempt from the GSTT. Thus, gifts to irrevocable life insurance trusts under which the beneficiaries were given appropriate *Crummey* powers of withdrawal escaped both the gift tax and the GSTT. Section 2642(c) was amended effective with respect to transfers made after March 31, 1988 to limit the exclusion for transfers in trust.

Under §2642(c)(2), the exemption for nontaxable transfers made in trust is only available if:

> (A) During the life of such individual, no portion of the corpus or income of the trust may be distributed to (or for the benefit of) any person other than such individual, and
> (B) If such individual dies before the trust is terminated, the assets of such trust will be includible in the gross estate of such individual.

The change severely limits the utility of the exemption from the GSTT for traditional forms of irrevocable life insurance trusts. However, an irrevocable life insurance trust may be created which meets the requirements of §2642(c)(2). For example, a separate share of the trust can be set aside for each beneficiary from the inception of the trust. Under §2654(b) separate shares with different beneficiaries are treated as separate trusts. No other person would have any right to the corpus or income of that share during the beneficiary's lifetime. Upon the beneficiary's death the share would be subject to a testamentary power of appointment sufficient to require inclusion in the beneficiary's gross estate.

Transfers made to irrevocable life insurance trusts on or after April 1, 1988 may no longer qualify for the GSTT exemption. If they do not, the transferor should consider using a portion of his or her $1 million exemption to maintain the complete exemption of the trust.

§6.41.2. GSTT $1 Million Exemption

In large estates consideration should be given to applying the client's $1 million exemption against transfers to life insurance trusts of which only skip-persons are beneficiaries. The exemption is most productively applied against trusts that do not permit distributions to nonskip persons. Otherwise part of the exemption is wasted.

Application of the exemption to life insurance trusts provides significant leverage; the exemption can often be used to shelter proceeds of several million.

D. GIFT TAXATION OF LIFE INSURANCE

§6.42. General

A gift of an interest in life insurance is generally subject to the same gift tax rules as a gift of any other type of property. In particular, a gift may occur when a policy is assigned, when a premium is paid, or when the policy proceeds are settled. Reg. §25.2511-1(h)(8), 1(h)(9). The valuation of interests in life insurance is governed by special rules in the regulations, which have been upheld in litigation. Reg. §25.2512-6(a). No gift occurs when the policy owner revocably designates a beneficiary. Rev. Rul. 81-166, 1981-1 C.B. 477. Under §2702 the value of a term interest retained by the donor may be zero for gift tax purposes unless it is a qualified interest.

An annual gift tax exclusion is generally available for an outright transfer of life insurance or the payment of a premium on a policy owned by another person, but an exclusion is generally not available when insurance is transferred to an irrevocable trust. Reg. §25.2503-3(c), examples 2, 6.

An outright assignment of a policy may qualify for the gift tax charitable deduction, §2522, or marital deduction, §2523. Similarly, the payment of a premium on a policy owned by a charity or the payor's spouse qualifies for a gift tax charitable or marital deduction. The IRS may deny a charitable deduction unless the charitable donee has an insurable interest in the life of the donor. *See* §6.2.

§6.43. VALUATION OF POLICIES

For gift tax purposes the value of a life insurance policy is established by the cost of the particular policy or of comparable policies on the date of the transfer. Reg. §25.2512-6(a). The cost of a comparable new policy better reflects value than a policy's cash surrender value. *Guggenheim v. Rasquin,* 312 U.S. 254 (1941). As explained below, the values of term insurance or a cash value policy that has been in effect for some time are determined in other ways.

> **Example 6-16.** *X* paid $85,000 for a single-premium life insurance policy with a face amount of $250,000 and immediately assigned it to his daughter, *D.* The policy had a cash surrender value of $77,000 at the time of issue and transfer. For gift tax purposes *H* made a gift to *D* of property worth $85,000.

§6.43.1. Term and Group-Term Insurance

The valuation of term and group-term insurance presents a different problem. In the ordinary case the value of term insurance depends primarily upon the amount of the premium and the length of time for which the premium has been paid in advance. Of course, if the insured is terminally ill the value of renewable term insurance will approach the amount of insurance coverage.

> **Example 6-17.** On January 1 *X* paid the annual premium of $1,000 on a $150,000 term policy on his life. *X* assigned the policy to *Y* on June 30. For gift tax purposes the term policy will probably be considered to have a value of $500, which represents the portion of the premium that is attributable to the unexpired insurance coverage. If *X* were terminally ill, the insurance would probably have a much larger value.

In the case of employer-provided group-term insurance, the value of the gift may be determined according to the Table I cost of the insurance, Reg. §1.79-3(d)(2), which is used for income tax purposes. *See* Rev. Rul. 84-147, 1984-2 C.B. 201. Revenue Ruling 84-147 holds the employer's payment of a premium on employer-provided term insurance that had been assigned to a trust is determined under Table I if the plan is nondiscriminatory or the employee is not a key employee. It continues to say that, "If the employee chooses not to use Table I for this purpose, or if the plan is discriminatory and the employee is a key employee, the employee should use the actual cost allocable to the employee's insurance by obtaining the necessary information from the employer." *Cf.* Rev. Rul. 76-490, 1976-2 C.B. 300. *See* §6.72.12.

The use of Table I is a practical solution to the problem of valuing group-term insurance when it is not possible to identify the actual premium cost attributable to the particular insurance that was assigned. However, if it is possible to identify the actual cost of the insurance, a smaller cost may be incurred by basing the valuation on it.

§6.43.2. Single-Premium and Paid-Up Policies

A single-premium policy or a paid-up policy that has been in effect for some time has a value equal to the current cost of a policy of the same amount on the life of a person the age of the insured. Reg. §25.2512-6(a), example 3.

§6.43.3. Other Policies — Interpolated Terminal Reserve

The value of a policy that has been in effect for some time and on which further premium payments are to be made generally cannot be determined through the cost of comparable contracts. In such cases the Regulations provide that the value is determined by adding the interpolated terminal reserve on the date of the gift and the portion of the premium last paid that covers the period following the date of the gift. Reg. §25.2512-6(a). The application of that rule is illustrated by example 4 of that Regulation:

> A gift is made four months after the last premium due date of an ordinary life insurance policy issued nine years and four months prior to the gift thereof by the insured, who was 35 years of age at the date of issue. The gross annual premium is $2,811. The computation follows:

Terminal reserve at end of tenth year	$14,601.00
Terminal reserve at end of ninth year	−12,965.00
Increase	$ 1,636.00

One-third of such increase (the gift having been made four months following the last preceding premium due date) is	$ 545.33
Terminal reserve at end of ninth year	+12,965.00
Interpolated terminal reserve at date of gift	$13,510.33
Two thirds of gross premium ($2,811)	+1,874.00
Value of gift	$15,384.33

§6.43.4. Policy Subject to a Loan

The value of a policy is reduced by the amount of any loan outstanding against the policy, including accrued interest. Accordingly, a loan may be taken out against policies in advance of a gift in order to reduce the value of the gift to an amount within the allowable annual exclusions. In this connection note that the transfer of an encumbered policy is treated as a transfer for consideration. However, in some circumstances the income tax exclusion remains available. *See* §6.53.

§6.43.5. Physical Condition of Insured

For purposes of valuation, "all relevant facts and elements of value as of the time of the gift shall be considered." Reg. §25.2512-1. In some cases this may require the physical condition and insurability of the insured to be taken into account. *See United States v. Ryerson,* 312 U.S. 260, 262 (1941), *Estate of James Stuart Pritchard,* 4 T.C. 204 (1944) (an estate tax case discussed at §6.34).

§6.43.6. Form 712, Life Insurance Statement

The insurer should be asked to provide a completed copy of Form 712 for each policy that is transferred. A completed Form 712 contains detailed financial data regarding the policy that is used to value it for gift and estate tax purposes. The instructions for preparation of gift tax returns require that a Form 712 be attached to the gift tax return for each policy that is transferred.

§6.44. Annual Exclusion

The complete, irrevocable assignment of a life insurance policy to a single donee qualifies for the annual exclusion because it gives the donee all of the interests in the policy. An exclusion is available though the principal performance under the contract, payment of the face amount of insurance, will take place at a future time (if at all). Reg. §25.2503-3(a). As indicated by example 6 of that Regulation, the payment of a premium on a policy owned outright by another person also qualifies as a gift of a present interest.

§6.44.1. Multiple Donees

The transfer of a policy to multiple donees should qualify for the annual exclusion unless the donor has manifested an intent that the donees must act together in order to deal with the policy. *Skouras v. Commissioner,* 188 F.2d 831 (2d Cir. 1951) (no annual exclusions allowed where multiple donees must act together). Logically, an exclusion should be available if each donee has the right to transfer or otherwise deal with his or her interest in the policy independent of the other owners.

The multiple donee rule may prevent a transfer in trust from qualifying for the annual exclusion. When the policy is transferred to a trust, an annual exclusion is not available if the beneficiaries of the trust must act together in order to obtain the present use or benefit of the insurance or other assets that are transferred to the trust. *United States v. Ryerson,* 312 U.S. 405 (1941).

The GSTT exclusion for nontaxable transfers applies to transfers in trust that qualify for the annual exclusion and satisfy the additional criteria of §2642(c)(2) noted at §6.44.3.

§6.44.2. Transfer to Trusts

The general rules regarding the availability of an annual exclusion for interests in trusts apply in the case of insurance trusts. An annual exclusion is only available if the donee receives a present interest under the trust because the beneficiaries of a trust are the donees of property transferred to a trust. *Helvering v. Hutchings,* 312 U.S. 393 (1941). In order to qualify as a present interest the beneficiary must have the unrestricted right to the use, possession, or enjoyment of the trust property or its income. Reg. §25.2503-3(b). As indicated in Reg. §25.2503-3(c), example 2, an annual exclusion is not available if the benefits under the trust are payable only upon the death of the insured.

Although the beneficiary is given an immediate income interest in a trust, an annual exclusion is generally not available when the trust holds only life insurance policies which produce no income or where all of the income must be used to pay premiums. Rev. Rul. 69-344, 1969-1 C.B. 225; *Jesse S. Phillips,* 12 T.C. 216 (1949). However, an annual exclusion is available if the beneficiary may withdraw the principal of the trust at any time. *Harbeck Halsted,* 28 T.C. 1069 (1957), *acq.,* 1958-2 C.B. 5. An annual exclusion is also available to the extent the beneficiary holds a *Crummey* power that allows the beneficiary acting alone to withdraw property that is added to the trust within a limited period following its transfer to the trustee. *E.g.,* LR 8021058; LR 7935091. Note that the annual exclusion is limited to the lesser of (1) the amount that can be withdrawn under a *Crummey* power or (2) the amount of the annual exclusion allowed by §2503. Recognizing the possibility that the amount of the gift tax exclusion may be changed at some future time, the *Crummey* power may limit the amount that can be withdrawn by the beneficiary to "the lesser of (1) the value of the property transferred to the trust and (2) the amount allowable as an exclusion under IRC §2503(b) or its successor." Note that the lapse of a power to withdraw an amount that exceeds the greater of $5,000 or five percent of the principal value of the trust may involve a taxable gift. §2514(e). Accordingly, some trusts limit the amount that can be withdrawn by the beneficiary to that amount. The imposition of such a limitation bars the allowance of any annual exclusions in excess of that amount. The use of a "hanging power" may meet the needs of the donors and the power-holder by allowing withdrawal of the full amount transferred to the trust but limiting the annual lapse to the greater of $5,000 or 5 percent of the value of the trust. The use of hanging powers is discussed in more detail at §10.24.2.

The gift of a policy to a minor under the Uniform Gifts to Minors Act, the Uniform Transfers to Minors Act, or to a §2503(c) minor's trust that authorizes the distribution of principal qualifies for an annual exclusion. Prior to recommending the transfer of life insurance to a custodian, the planner should review the local legislation to be sure that such a transfer is authorized.

§6.44.3. GSTT

Direct skips that are nontaxable gifts by reason of the annual exclusion, §2503(b), or the exclusion for the direct payment of tuition or medical expenses, §2503(e), have inclusion ratios of zero. In effect, they are exempt from the GSTT. However, §2642(c)(2) requires that transfers in trust also satisfy two other requirements. First, during the lifetime of the beneficiary none of the trust property can be distributed to anyone other than the beneficiary. Second, if the beneficiary dies prior to termination of the trust, the trust must be includible in the beneficiary's estate. As indicated in §6.41.1, trusts can be structured to qualify for this exclusion.

§6.45. Transfer of a Policy

An irrevocable assignment is generally used to transfer interests in an existing policy from the present owner to the intended donee. Insurers will generally provide assignment forms upon request; however, the forms should be examined carefully to ensure that they comply with the policy's terms and will effectively transfer all incidents of ownership in it. If an insured-owner retains any interest in the insurance, an assignment may be incomplete *and* the policy proceeds may be includible in the insured's gross estate under §2042(2). If any part of the policy is, or may be, community property, both spouses should join in the assignment. Otherwise, in some community property states the nonconsenting spouse has the power to invalidate the gift — at least in part.

§6.45.1. Irrevocable Beneficiary Designation

The irrevocable designation of a beneficiary is sometimes used instead of an assignment, but it is less satisfactory because its effects are less certain. The economic interests of an irrevocably designated beneficiary are entitled to protection against unilateral action by the designated owner of the policy in most cases. However, the extent to which such a beneficiary may exercise control over the policy is not well defined in most states. "The law of West Virginia and other jurisdictions with regard to the right of irrevocably designated beneficiaries to exercise options of a life insurance policy without the consent of the insured is unclear at best." *Morton v. United States,* 457 F.2d 750, 754 (4th Cir. 1972). The IRS may assert that an insured who is named as owner of a policy has an incident of ownership although another person is irrevocably designated as the beneficiary.

§6.45.2. Charitable and Marital Deductions

A gift tax charitable or marital deduction is available if all the interests in a policy are transferred outright to a qualified donee with an insurable interest in the donor's life. No charitable deduction is available, however, where a charity is given a split interest in a policy. §2522(c)(2). In particular, no deduction is allowed where the charity is given the cash surrender value of a policy and the donor retains the right to designate the recipient of the difference between the face amount of the policy and the cash surrender value. Rev. Rul. 76-200, 1976-1 C.B. 308.

A marital deduction is generally not available for a policy transferred in trust unless the donee spouse has the requisite life income interest plus the right to compel the trustee to convert the policy into income-producing property. §2523(e)-(f); Reg. §25.2523(e)-1(f)(4). Of course, a marital deduction under §2523(e) is available only if the donee spouse also has a general power of appointment. However, a deduction is available under §2523(f) on an elective basis as QTIP where the donee receives a qualifying income interest for life. No marital deduction is allowed for a transfer to a spouse who is not a U.S. citizen.

§6.46. Payment of Premiums

The payment of a premium on a policy in which the premium payor has no interest constitutes a gift to the policy owner of an amount equal to the payment. There is a gift of that amount although benefits are payable under the policy only upon the death of the donor and the donee must survive the donor in order to receive the proceeds of the policy. Reg. §25.2511-1(h)(8). The value of the gift is the amount of the premium payment, not the resulting increase in the cash surrender value of the policy. There may be no gift, however, if the insured retains an interest in the policy or some control over it. The identity of the premium payor is largely irrelevant — the payment of a premium by a person other than the policy owner generally involves a gift.

> **Example 6-18.** The life of *X* is insured under a policy owned by his daughter, *D.* This year the annual premium of $5,000 was paid by *D*'s brother, *B.* By paying the premium *B* made a gift of $5,000 to *D.* The gift qualifies for the annual gift tax exclusion. Reg. §25.2503-3(c), example 6.

No gift is involved, however, where a premium is paid in order to protect the interests of the premium payor. Thus, there is no gift where the principal beneficiary of an insurance trust pays the premiums on policies held by the trustee in order to prevent lapse or diminution in the amount of insurance coverage. *Grace R. Seligmann,* 9 T.C. 191 (1947), *acq.,* 1947-2 C.B. 4.

The use of community property funds to pay premiums on a policy owned by one or both spouses as separate property ordinarily does not involve a gift. Under the apportionment rule, which is applied to cash value policies in California and Washington, the use of community property funds establishes a community property ownership interest in the policy in the absence of a contrary agreement. *See* §6.15.2. This is undesirable when the objective is to exclude all of the insurance from the estate of the insured. In the inception-of-title states — Arizona, Louisiana, New Mexico, and Texas — there is no gift because the community is entitled to reimbursement for premiums on separately owned policies that were paid with community funds. *See* §6.15.1.

> **Example 6-19.** *W* purchased a $250,000 ordinary life insurance policy on her life when she married *H* several years ago. *W* paid the initial $2,000 premium from her premarital earnings. *W*'s mother, *M,* is the revocably designated beneficiary of the insurance. Each year since their marriage, *H* has paid the annual premium of $2,000 from his earnings. If *H* and *W* live in a noncommunity state, *H*'s payment of the annual premiums involved gifts that qualified for the gift tax exclusion. The gift would, of course, qualify for the marital deduction, unless *W* is not a U.S. citizen. If *H* and *W* live in a community property state, *H*'s payment of the premiums would be treated as gifts if adequately documented. Otherwise, the payment of the premiums would not necessarily involve a gift. In the apportionment states, the premium payments made from *H*'s earnings, which were community property, could give rise to a community property interest in the insurance. In the inception-of-title states, the policy would be *W*'s separate property but the community could have an equitable claim to recover the amount of the premium payments that were made from *H*'s earnings.

A marital deduction may be allowed for the payment of premiums on a policy held in trust for the benefit of the premium payor's spouse if the trust otherwise meets the requirements of §2523. However, no deduction is available unless the donee has the right to compel the trustee to convert the policy into income-producing property. *Estate of Charles C. Smith,* 23 T.C. 367 (1954); Reg. §25.2523(e)-1(f)(4).

§6.47. Payment of Proceeds

When a policy is owned by a person other than the insured, a gift occurs if the proceeds are paid to a third person.

> **Example 6-20.** *X* owned a $100,000 policy on the life of *Y* that designated *X*'s daughter, *D,* as beneficiary. Upon *Y*'s death the $100,000 policy proceeds were paid to *D.* The payment of the proceeds constituted a gift of $100,000 from *X* to *D.* The gift qualifies for the annual exclusion. The mere revocable designation

of *D* as beneficiary did not involve a gift. The gift only took place when the insured died and *D*'s right to receive the proceeds became irrevocable.

The owner of a policy likewise makes a gift where the proceeds are paid to a trust for the benefit of other persons. *Goodman v. Commissioner,* 156 F.2d 218 (2d Cir. 1946); Rev. Rul. 81-166, 1981-1 C.B. 477. In that case the availability of the annual exclusion depends on the terms of the trust.

A gift may also take place when the proceeds of a community property life insurance policy are paid to a person other than the surviving spouse. This rule is stated in Reg. §25.2511-1(h)(9):

> Where property held by a husband and wife as community property is used to purchase insurance upon the husband's life and a third person is revocably designated as beneficiary and under the State law the husband's death is considered to make absolute the transfer by the wife, there is a gift by the wife at the time of the husband's death of half the amount of the proceeds of such insurance.

The Regulation was applied in *Cox v. United States,* 286 F. Supp. 761 (W.D. La. 1968), which held that the surviving spouse made a gift of one-half of the proceeds of community property life insurance policies to third-party beneficiaries. The result is consistent with the item theory of community property that recognizes that each spouse owns an undivided one-half interest in each community asset. However, the item theory approach was not applied in the later case of *Kaufman v. United States,* 462 F.2d 439 (5th Cir. 1972), where the surviving spouse received $175,000 in proceeds from community property policies on her husband's life and their daughter received $72,000 in proceeds from other community property policies. The government contended that the surviving spouse made a gift of $36,000 to the daughter by permitting the entire proceeds of $72,000 of community property policies to be paid to the daughter. The court rejected that argument and instead appeared to apply an aggregate theory of community property "since the wife received more than her share of the total community insurance proceeds, no gift can be constructively presumed." 462 F.2d at 441.

The risk that the payment of part of the proceeds of community property policies to a person other than the surviving spouse may involve a gift by the survivor is eliminated if the survivor receives at least half of the proceeds of each policy. The other portion of the proceeds is treated as a transfer by the decedent that does not involve a gift by the survivor.

Example 6-21. *H*'s life was insured under two $100,000 community property policies. One of the policies designated *H*'s wife, *W,* as beneficiary and the other designated his daughter, *D,* as beneficiary. Upon *H's* death $100,000 in proceeds was paid to *W* and $100,000 to *D.* Under the item theory applied in *Cox* the surviving spouse made a gift of $50,000 by permitting the full amount of the proceeds of the second policy to be paid to *D.* No gift would be involved, however, under the rationale of *Kaufman.* No gift would occur under either theory if the proceeds of each policy had been paid one-half to *W* and one-half to *D.* Similarly, no gift would have occurred if there had been only one $200,000 policy of which half of the proceeds would have been paid to *D* (*H's* half) and half to *W* (*W's* half).

The *Cox* approach is more consistent with the prevalent item theory of community property law, but the *Kaufman* approach is preferable because it is more equitable and treats similarly situated taxpayers in the same way.

E. INCOME TAXATION OF LIFE INSURANCE

§6.48. Introduction

Transactions involving life insurance often have important federal income tax consequences. This part discusses the income tax aspects of transactions involving life insurance, including the payment of policy proceeds, the payment of premiums, and the sale, surrender, or exchange of policies. The income tax aspects of split-dollar and group-term plans and certain other specialized arrangements are reviewed in Part F of this chapter, along with some of their other features.

§6.49. Life Insurance Defined, §7702

In 1984 Congress adopted §7702, which specifies the criteria which must be satisfied by contracts issued after 1984 in order to be treated as life insurance for purposes of the Code. In brief, §7702 requires that policies issued after 1984 both qualify as life insurance under local law and meet one of two other tests: the "cash value accumulation test" or a combination test consisting of the "guideline premium" and "cash value corridor" tests.

Under the *cash value accumulation test* the cash surrender value of the policy cannot at any time exceed the net single premium that would have been required to be paid in order to fund future benefits under the contract. §7702(b)(1). For the purposes of this test the calculations are made on the basis of: (1) interest at the greater of 4 percent or the rate guaranteed in the contract, §7702(b)(2)(A); (2) reasonable mortality charges and reasonable charges with respect to any qualified additional benefits, §7702(b)(2)(B); and (3) current and future death benefits and qualified additional benefits, §7702(b)(2)(C). Because of the nature of the data required to make the calculations, it is not ordinarily possible for an estate planner to determine whether or not the test has been satisfied.

The first element of the combination test is the *guideline premium test.* It is satisfied if the sum of the premiums paid under the contract does not at any time exceed the premium limitation as of such time. §7702(c)(1). The guideline limitation is the greater of (1) the guideline single premium (*i.e.,* the amount required to fund future benefits under the contract, taking into account relevant actuarial factors) and (2) the sum of guideline level premiums to date (the level annual amount payable over a period not ending before the insured reaches age 95, §7702(c)(4)).

The second element of the combination test is the *cash corridor test.* It is satisfied if the death benefit under the contract at any time is not less than the applicable percentage of the cash surrender value as shown in Table 6-1. For example, in order to satisfy the cash value corridor test, the death benefit on a policy with a cash surrender value of $100,000 on the life of a person aged 44 cannot be less than $215,000 (215% × $100,000).

If a contract fails to satisfy the tests specified by §7702, it will be treated as a combination of term insurance and a currently taxable deposit fund. Accordingly, the income on the contract would be treated as ordinary income in the year paid or accrued. §7702(g)(1)(A). For this purpose income on the contract is the sum of the increase in the cash surrender value over the year plus the cost of insurance provided for the year over the premium paid for the year. At death the excess of the amount paid by reason of the insured's death over the net cash surrender value of the contract is excluded from gross income under §101(a). §7702(g)(2). Thus, the beneficiary may be taxable on the remainder, except to the extent the beneficiary made an investment in the contract.

The 1986 Act amended §7702(f)(7) to provide that a withdrawal of funds within the first 15 policy years which involves a reduction in benefits under the policy is taxable under §72 (other than §72(e)(5)). Accordingly, a portion of the amount withdrawn would probably be included in the recipient's income under §72(e)(2)(B). The amount treated as income, however, may not exceed the recapture ceilings specified in the statute. After the first 15 policy years, presumably the investment made in the contract may be withdrawn first without any income tax consequences.

Table 6-1
Cash Corridor Test of §7702(d)(2)

In the case of an insured with an attained age as of the beginning of the contract year of:		The applicable percentage shall decrease by a ratable portion for each full year:	
More than:	*But not more than:*	*From:*	*To:*
0	40	250	250
40	45	250	215
45	50	215	185
50	55	185	150
55	60	150	130
60	65	130	120
65	70	120	115
70	75	115	105
75	90	105	105
90	95	105	100

§6.50. Modified Endowment Contract, §7702A

In 1988 Congress moved to limit the tax benefits of life insurance contracts with major lifetime investment characteristics. Specifically, the 1988 Act added §7702A which defined a class of life insurance contracts as "modified endowment contracts" that would be subject to the new rules under §72 regarding the distribution of amounts other than as annuity payments. In simplest terms, most amounts received under a modified endowment contract other than as an annuity (*e.g.,* as loans or dividends) are treated as income to the extent of the income on the contract. §72(e)(4)(A). However, for this purpose dividends retained by the insurer as a premium or other consideration paid for the contract are not includible in income. §72(e)(4)(B). Under §72(e)(2)(B), the income on the contract is the amount by which the cash surrender value of the contract immediately before the distribution exceeded the investment in the contract. A ten percent additional tax is imposed on taxable distributions from modified endowment contracts, except for ones made on or after the recipient attains age 59½, made as a result of the recipient's disability, or made as a part of a series of substantially equal payments made for the life of the taxpayer or of the taxpayer and a beneficiary. §72(v).

Under §7702A a modified endowment contract is a life insurance contract entered into after June 21, 1988 (or which is received in exchange for such a contract) that fails to meet a *7-pay test.* A contract fails the 7-pay test if the accumulated amount of premiums paid (less amounts distributed other than as an annuity and not included in the recipient's income) on the contract at any time during the first seven contract years exceeds the sum of the net level premiums which would have been paid on or before such time if the contract provided for paid-up future benefits after the payment of seven level premiums. A failure to satisfy the 7-pay test affects the taxation of distributions made in all contract years beginning with distributions made within two years preceding the failure. §7702A(d). Also, a material change in a contract causes it to be treated as a new contract subject to the 7-pay test as of the date of the material change. §7702A(c)(3).

§6.51. Payment of Proceeds, §101(a)(1)

In general, amounts received under a life insurance contract by reason of the death of the insured are not included in the recipient's gross income. §101(a)(1). However, part or all of the proceeds may be included where the policy was transferred for value, §101(a)(2), or the policy was held by a qualified retirement plan and paid to a beneficiary designated by the participant, §72(m)(3)(C). Also, the proceeds exclusion applies to the proceeds of a flexible premium policy issued before January 1, 1985 only if the premiums paid and cash value accrued meet the limitations of §101(f)(1)(A) or if the cash value accrued does not exceed the "single premium limitation" of §101(f)(1)(B).

Subject to the requirements of §7702, the general exclusion of §101(a) applies to all death benefits having the characteristics of life insurance, including endowment contracts, accident and health policies, double and triple indemnity provisions, and paid-up additions. *See* Reg. §1.101-1(a). The entire amount of the death benefit payable on a variable life insurance policy is excludable under §101(a) although the amount of the benefit may increase or decrease (but not below a stated minimum) in accordance with the investment experience of the separate account for the policy. Rev. Rul. 79-87, 1979-1 C.B. 73. The exclusion is available whether the payment is made to the estate of the insured or to another beneficiary. Likewise, it is available whether the payment is made directly to an individual or in trust. Id. Importantly, the exclusion is not dependent upon the proceeds being subject to the estate tax. Thus, the proceeds are excluded from the beneficiary's gross income whether or not they are included in the gross estate of the insured.

Example 6-22. *W*'s life was insured under a policy owned by her husband, *H,* which designated their child, *C,* as beneficiary.

The policy provided for the payment of an additional amount equal to the face amount of the policy if the insured died as the result of accidental injuries. *W* died in an automobile accident and *C* was paid the face amount of the policy plus the additional benefit. Although none of the insurance was included in *W*'s gross estate, the proceeds paid to *C* are excluded from *C*'s gross income.

The general exclusion extends only to the amount payable as a death benefit at the time of the insured's death. It does not apply to interest paid because of a delay in payment of the death benefit.

§6.51.1. Deferred Payment of Proceeds, §101(c), (d)

The exclusion under §101(a)(1) does not extend to additional amounts paid because of the deferred payment of the proceeds. §101(c), (d). Instead, the additional amounts are taxed as income to the recipient. The income tax treatment of the amount paid under policy options is described in §6.52.

§6.51.2. Proceeds Paid to Shareholder-Beneficiary

Insurance proceeds paid to a shareholder-beneficiary under a corporate-owned policy on which the corporation paid the premiums from its earnings and over which the corporation held the right to designate the beneficiary are taxed as a dividend to the recipient. Rev. Rul. 61-134, 1961-2 C.B. 250. The proceeds are only taxed under that rule where the recipient is a shareholder. LR 8144001.

§6.52. Settlement Options, §101(c), (d)

Most policies permit the insured or the beneficiary to elect to have the proceeds paid in a lump sum under one or more settlement options. The two principal options are the interest only option and the installment option. Under the former the beneficary is entitled to receive only interest on the proceeds at a guaranteed rate (which, under some policies, is augmented by "excess" interest) until the principal amount is withdrawn or paid out. The installment option usually provides for payment of a fixed amount either for a specified period (*e.g.*, $2,500 per month for ten years) or for the life of the beneficiary with a certain number of payments guaranteed.

When the proceeds are held subject to an option under which only interest is paid on a current basis, the beneficiary is taxed on the interest. §101(c). For this purpose it makes no difference whether the beneficiary has the right to withdraw the principal. This rule applies to payments made of interest earned on proceeds that are held without substantial diminution of principal during the period the interest payments were made or credited. Reg. §1.101-3(a). If the payments include a substantial amount of principal, the distributions are subject to §101(d) and not §101(c). Prior to 1987, former §101(d)(a)(B) allowed the surviving spouse of an insured to exclude up to $1,000 of the interest received in connecton with the deferred payment of the proceeds. This exclusion was only available with respect to payments subject to §101(d).

When payments are made under an installment option, the principal portion of each payment is not included in the beneficiary's income. §101(d). The principal component of each payment is determined by prorating the amount held by the insurer with respect to the beneficiary over the period for which payments will be made. The amount held by the insurer is usually the amount payable as a lump sum in discharge of the insurer's obligation under the policy; however, if the policy had been transferred for valuable consideration, the total amount held by the insurer cannot exceed the amount of consideration paid, plus any premiums or other amount subsequently paid by the transferee. Reg. §1.101-4(b)(3).

Example 6-23. The proceeds of a $100,000 policy on the life of *W* are payable to her mother, *M,* in 10 annual installments of $12,500 each. Under the basic rule of §101(d), $10,000 of each payment is excludable from *M*'s income ($100,000 ÷ 10 = $10,000). The other $2,500 of each payment is taxable as interest.

§6.53. Transfer for Value, §101(a)(2)

The proceeds of a policy that is transferred for value are generally includible in the recipient's income except to the extent of the consideration paid plus premiums and other amounts subsequently paid by the recipient. §101(a)(2). This limitation on the availability of the general exclusion was apparently intended to discourage trafficking in life insurance policies for profit. A provision with such a broad sweep is probably not necessary to achieve the desired purpose — a questionable object of the income tax law in any event. As it is, the transfer for value rule acts as a trap for the unwary and unsophisticated.

The statute only applies where there has been a transfer for value. Under Reg. §1.101-1(b)(4), the rule only applies where there is an enforceable right in the transferee to receive all or part of the proceeds of the policy. Thus, it does not apply if the insured has retained the exclusive right to designate the beneficiary. Rev. Rul. 74-76, 1974-1

C.B. 30 (shareholder-employee transferred policy to employer's profitsharing plan but retained power to designate the beneficiary). Undertaking a binding obligation to designate a beneficiary may constitute a transfer of the insurance for purposes of §101(a)(2). A transfer for consideration may take place where the shareholders of a closely-held corporation, who own insurance on each other's lives ("cross insurance"), agree to use the proceeds to buy the stock that belonged to a deceased shareholder. *Monroe v. Patterson,* 197 F. Supp. 146 (N.D. Ala. 1961); LR 7734048; LR 9045004.

§6.53.1. Exceptions

There are two important exceptions to the transfer for value rule. First, it does not apply when the basis of the policy for the purpose of determining gain or loss is determined in whole or in part by reference to the basis of the policy in the hands of the transferor. §101(a)(2)(A). Second, it does not apply when the transfer was made to the insured, a partner of the insured, a partnership of which the insured is a partner, or to a corporation in which the insured is a shareholder or officer. §101(a)(2)(B).

The question of whether the transfer of a policy subject to a loan involves a transfer for consideration is unsettled. Some commentators argue that the assignment of a policy subject to a loan is not a transfer for value because a policy loan merely allows the insurer to apply the policy proceeds first to discharge the loan and does not involve any personal liability on the part of the owner. Walker, Life Insurance from the Standpoint of the Federal Corporate and Personal Income Tax, Gift Tax and Estate Tax, U. So. Cal., 18th Tax Inst. 543, 576 (1966). On the other hand, the government apparently views the transfer of an encumbered policy as a transfer for value — perhaps based upon *Crane v. Commissioner,* 331 U.S. 1 (1947). Rev. Rul. 69-187, 1969-1 C.B. 45. In this ruling the insured transferred to his wife a policy that had a cash surrender value of $85,000 but was subject to a loan of $75,000. It concluded that the proceeds were not includible in the wife's gross income. This is unsettling because it stated that the policy had been transferred in part for consideration and in part as a gift (*i.e.,* the basis was determined in part by reference to the basis of the transferor).

§6.53.2. First Exception, §101(a)(2)(A)

The transfer for value rule does not apply to a transfer in which the basis carries over to the transferee. This shelters all transfers that have a gift element; thus, a transfer that is a part gift-part sale is within the exception. Rev. Rul. 69-187, 1969-1 C.B. 45. The exception also applies where a policy is transferred from one corporation to another in a tax-free reorganization, as a result of which the transferor's basis in the policy carries over to the transferee. Reg. §1.101-1(b)(5), example 4. Importantly, a transfer of insurance from the insured to a former spouse incident to a divorce is treated as a gift and not a transfer for value if neither spouse is a nonresident alien. §1041.

One commentator has suggested that the transfer of a policy subject to a loan in an amount greater than the owner's basis may not fall within this exception.

> In such a case, the transferor might be taxed for income tax purposes on the difference between his adjusted basis in the policy and the amount of the outstanding policy loan at the time of transfer. In addition, the IRS might conclude that the transferee's basis is not determined at least in part by the transferor's basis. Thus, the requirements of the carryover basis exception to the transfer for value rule would not be met, causing the transfer to be treated as a sale. As a sale, the death benefit proceeds received in excess of the transferee's basis would be reportable as income to the recipient. Cox, Gift of Life Insurance Policy with an Outstanding Loan Can Result in Two Taxes, 17 Est. Plan. 298 (1990).

§6.53.3. Second Exception, §101(a)(2)(B)

The second exception is particularly important in planning business transactions. Under it, the transfer for value rule does not apply when the transferee is the insured, a partner of the insured, a partnership in which the insured is a partner, or a corporation in which the insured is a shareholder or officer. §101(a)(2)(B). For example, the exemption for a transfer to a partnership of which the insured is a partner applied to policies on the lives of two partners that were transferrred by a corporation to the partnership in lieu of the payment of rent due to the partnership. LR 9012063. The transfers were made for consideration; however, they were made to an exempt entity. Beware, the superficial breadth of this exception is misleading — it does not protect a wide variety of fairly common transfers, among them:

1. Shareholder *A* transfers a policy insuring *A*'s life to Shareholder *B* in exchange for a similar policy on *B*'s life, or for other consideration;
2. An employee or director of a corporation who is not a shareholder or officer transfers a policy on his or her life to the corporation in exchange for cash or other valuable consideration; and,

3. A corporation sells a policy insuring the life of an employee to the employee's spouse for a cash payment. *See Estate of Rath v. United States,* 608 F.2d 254 (6th Cir. 1979).

Note that this exception does not protect transfers for value that are made to relatives of the insured. An exception for transfers to relatives would be desirable and would not conflict with the underlying purpose of §101(a)(2).

> **Example 6-24.** Father, *F,* applied for and paid the premiums on a $100,000 policy on the life of his daughter, *D.* Subsequently *F* transferred the policy to his son, *S,* in exchange for a cash payment equal to its cash surrender value of $5,000. *S* paid an additional $5,000 in premiums prior to *D*'s death. *S* will probably be taxed on $90,000 of the $100,000 in proceeds he received ($100,000 – $10,000). *Alcy S. Hacker,* 36 B.T.A. 659 (1937); *Bourne Bean,* 14 T.C.M. 786 (1955).

Of course, it is possible that a transfer that is not within the second exception may nonetheless fall within the scope of the first one. Thus, if any part of the transferor's basis carries over to the transferee, as it would in the case of a partial gift, the first exception would insulate the proceeds from taxation.

§6.54. Policy Purchased by a Qualified Plan

The proceeds of an insurance policy purchased by a qualified retirement plan on the life of an employee may not be included in the income of the plan beneficiary under §101(a) when they are distributed. However, they may be taxable under §72. If the employee paid the premiums, or the cost of the insurance was taxed to the employee under §72(m)(3)(B), the proceeds are excluded to the extent they exceed the cash surrender value of the policy immediately prior to the employee's death. §72(m)(3)(C). An amount of the proceeds equal to the cash surrender value qualifies for the $5,000 exclusion under §101(b) and the balance of it is taxable under the rules of §72. On the other hand, if the employee did not pay the premiums directly and they were not taxed to the employee under §72(m)(3), no part of the proceeds paid to the plan beneficiary as a death benefit qualifies for the exclusion under §101(a). Reg. §1.72-16(c)(4).

The rollover of a policy on an employee's life from one qualified plan to another does not constitute a transfer for value. LR 7906051.

§6.55. PREMIUM PAYMENTS

Premiums paid on personal (*i.e.,* nonbusiness) insurance are generally not deductible for income tax purposes. To begin with, premiums paid by a taxpayer on policies insuring the premium payor's life are considered to be nondeductible personal expenses. Reg. §1.262-1(b)(1). Premium payments made on policies insuring the lives of family members are also subject to that rule. In addition, premiums on policies insuring the life of another person are not deductible if the proceeds would be excluded from the premium payor's gross income under §101(a). §265(1); *Jones v. Commissioner,* 231 F.2d 655 (3d Cir. 1956).

§6.55.1. Premium Payments Deductible as Alimony

A deduction is allowed under §215 for premium payments that constitute income to a spouse or former spouse of the insured under §71. In order to obtain the deduction, the policy must generally have been assigned to the former spouse in connection with a legal separation, dissolution of marriage, or decree of separate maintenance. The mere designation of the former spouse as beneficiary is not sufficient. *Henry B. Kelsey,* 27 T.C.M. 337 (1968), *aff'd mem.,* 1969-2 U.S.T.C. ¶9619, 23 A.F.T.R.2d 69-1481 (2d Cir. 1969).

§6.55.2. Premium Payments as Charitable Contributions

Subject to the percentage limitations of §170, a charitable deduction is allowed for premiums paid on a policy that is owned by a charity or a charitable trust. *Eppa Hunton IV,* 1 T.C. 821 (1943), *acq.,* 1943 C.B. 12. When an income tax charitable deduction is sought the planner should not rely upon the mere irrevocable designation of the charity as beneficiary. *See* §6.45.1. Instead, the policy should be irrevocably assigned to the charity, which itself qualifies for the charitable deduction. In Rev. Rul. 80-132, 1980-1 C.B. 255, the IRS reached the uncertain conclusion that the gift to a private foundation of an insurance policy subject to an outstanding loan was an act of self-dealing under §4941(d)(i)(A) subject to tax under §4947(b). The rationale that the transfer of the policy relieved the donor of the obligation to repay the loan, pay interest on the loan as it accrued, or suffer continued diminution in value of the policy fails to notice the unique character of loans against life insurance policies. *See* §6.59. As indicated in §6.2, a charitable deduction is allowable only if the charity has an insurable interest in the donor's life, so it will be entitled to receive the proceeds when the donor dies.

§6.55.3. Premium Payments at a Discount

When a discount is given for premiums paid in advance, the interest earned on the advance payment or the increment in value is includible in the gross income of the premium payor in the year or years the premiums are due. Rev. Rul. 66-120, 1966-1 C.B. 14. On the other hand, an additional premium charge that is imposed when a premium is paid on a semiannual, quarterly, or monthly basis is not deductible as an interest charge under §163. Rev. Rul. 79-187, 1979-1 C.B. 95.

§6.56. Premiums Paid by Employers Are Deductible

Under §162 an employer may deduct the premiums paid on life insurance policies on the lives of its officers and employees. The premiums are deductible business expenses if (1) the payments are in the nature of additional compensation, (2) the total amount of compensation paid to an officer or employee is not unreasonable, §162(a), and (3) the employer is not directly or indirectly the beneficiary, §264(a)(1). Rev. Rul. 56-400, 1956-2 C.B. 116. No deduction is allowed for the payment of premiums on policies insuring lives of shareholders. Such payments constitute dividend distributions rather than the payment of compensation for services. In such cases, the amount of the dividends is includible in the shareholder's income. Also, no deduction is allowed if the employer is entitled to receive any of the proceeds of a policy under a split-dollar plan or otherwise. §264(a)(1); Rev. Rul. 66-203, 1966-2 C.B. 104.

In general, the premiums paid by an employer on a policy insuring the life of an employee are includible in the employee's gross income where the proceeds are payable to the beneficiary designated by the employee. Reg. §1.61-2(d)(2)(ii)(a). Under such circumstances the premiums paid by the employer constitute additional compensation to the employee. *N. Loring Danforth,* 18 B.T.A. 1221 (1930). Special provisions of §79 allow an employee to exclude the cost of up to $50,000 of employer-provided group-term insurance. *See* §6.72.

§6.57. Cost of Insurance Protection Provided by Qualified Plans, §72(m)(3)

The cost of current life insurance protection provided an employee under a qualified retirement plan is includible in the employee's income if the proceeds are payable directly or indirectly to the participant or the participant's beneficiary. §72(m)(3); Rev. Rul. 79-202, 1979-2 C.B. 31. If the trust has a right as a named beneficiary to retain any part of the proceeds, the premiums are not taxed to the employee. Under the Regulations, the proceeds are considered to be payable to the participant or the participant's beneficiary if "the trustee is required to pay over all of such proceeds to the beneficiary." Reg. §1.72-16(b)(1).

The amount of life insurance protection provided in any year is the excess of the death benefit payable over the cash surrender value of the policy. Reg. §1.72-16(b)(3). The cost of the protection is determined under the table of one-year term premiums set forth in Rev. Rul. 55-747, 1955-2 C.B. 228 (the "P.S. 58 cost").

> **Example 6-25.** The trustee of Employer's qualified pension plan, which provides a death benefit of $10,000, purchased a $10,000 ordinary life insurance policy on the life of Employee, who was 50 years old. The premium for the first year was $250, and at the end of that year the cash value of the policy was $0. The plan provided Employee's beneficiary with $10,000 of insurance protection. The P.S. 58 cost of $1,000 insurance for a person 50 years of age is $9.22. Employee must report $92.20 as income for the year (10 × $9.22).

§6.58. GRANTOR TRUSTS, §677(a)(3)

The income of a trust is taxed to the grantor of a trust to the extent it may be used without the consent of an adverse party to pay premiums on policies insuring the life of the grantor or the grantor's spouse except for policies irrevocably payable for charitable purposes. §677(a)(3). *See* §10.4.1. This rule is intended "to prevent the avoidance of tax by the allocation of income through a trust device to the payment of life insurance premiums, which are universally recognized as a normal expense of protecting dependents but which are personal, as distinguished from business, expenses, and are therefore not deductible from gross income." *Arthur Stockstrom,* 3 T.C. 664, 668 (1944). The income of the trust is not taxed to the grantor merely because the trustee is authorized to pay premiums on policies insuring the life of the grantor or the grantor's spouse. Rather, the application of the statute depends upon the actual existence of policies upon which premiums might have been paid from trust funds. *Corning v. Commissioner,* 104 F.2d 329 (6th Cir. 1939). The grantor will be treated as the owner of a trust that acquires insurance on the grantor's life although the trust agreement specifies that the premiums of policies on the life of the grantor may be paid only from the principal of the trust.

The deductibility of interest paid by a trustee on a policy loan is discussed in §6.60.1.

§6.59. Policy Loans

Under most cash value life insurance policies the owner may borrow up to the cash surrender value of the policy on the sole security of the policy. Although the payment to the owner is called a loan, there is no personal liability to repay it. The Tax Court commented on this feature of life insurance policies in *J. Simpson Dean,* 35 T.C. 1083, 1085 (1961), *nonacq.,* 1973-2 C.B. 4.

> Insurance policy loans are unique because the borrower assumes no personal liability to repay the principal or to pay interest on the amount borrowed. Such loans are based on the reserve value of the insurance policies involved. If either the principal or the interest is not repaid, it is merely deducted from the reserve value of the policy. Since the insurance company "never advances more than it already is absolutely bound for under the policy it has no interest in creating personal liability."

In *Williams v. Union Central Life Insurance Co.,* 291 U.S. 170, 179 (1934), the Supreme Court said, "While the advance is called a 'loan' and interest is computed in settling the account, 'the item never could be sued for,' and in substance 'is a payment, not a loan.' "

The transfer of an encumbered policy may give result in the realization of gain by the transferor. *See* §6.63.1.

§6.59.1. Loans on Policies Other Than Modified Endowment Contracts

A policy loan made with respect to a policy other than a modified endowment contract (defined in §7702A) is generally not treated as a distribution for income tax purposes. Accordingly, in the case of most policies, taking out a loan does not have any income tax consequences for the borrower. Under some circumstances, however, the excess of the amount borrowed on a policy over the premiums paid is includible in the borrower's gross income. The clearest case occurs when a policy is terminated for failure to pay on the loan or interest. Then the amount of the outstanding loan is an amount received under the contract for purposes of §72 and is includible in the borrower's gross income to the extent it exceeds the premiums and other amounts paid on the policy. Where the policy is not terminated or surrendered, the excess is not includible in the borrower's gross income if the transaction is treated as establishing a debtor-creditor relationship between the borrower and the insurer. In a related context the Tax Court held that a policy loan made against an employee annuity contract was not includible in the borrower-employee's income because it was not "an amount received under the contract" within the meaning of §72(e)(1)(B). *Robert W. Minnis,* 71 T.C. 1049 (1979), *nonacq.,* 1979-2 C.B. 2. The IRS has refused to follow *Minnis* and, in Rev. Rul. 81-126, 1981-1 C.B. 206, restated the position that was rejected by the Tax Court (*i.e.,* that money received by an employee as a loan against the value of an annuity contract prior to the annuity's starting date was a taxable advance).

As described in §6.60, after 1990 no income tax deduction is allowed for personal interest, such as interest paid on policy loans. §163(h). Accordingly, the owner of an insurance policy with a large outstanding loan against it may be concerned about the loan's overall cost because of the nondeductibility of interest on it. An owner who participated in an insurance plan that involved substantial borrowing against policies (*e.g.,* a minimum deposit plan, §6.73) may want to reduce or eliminate the relatively large nondeductible interest payments. On the other hand, an owner will be less concerned where the interest is paid by further borrowing against the cash value of the policy. The following options are available to the owner of a policy with an outstanding loan:

1. Pay off the loan — which may be economically unattractive.
2. Continue making interest payments although the interest is no longer deductible.
3. Allow the interest to be paid by borrowing against the remaining cash value of the policy.
4. Surrender the policy, which would require the owner to report as income the excess of the amount realized (including the outstanding loan) over the owner's investment in the contract (premium payments and other consideration paid). No deduction would be allowed if the policy owner receives less than the owner's investment in the contract.
5. Exercise an option to convert the remaining cash value of the policy (if any) into paid-up insurance or extended term insurance. The exercise of such an option might be treated as the equivalent of receiving the remaining value of the policy and subsequently purchasing the paid-up or term insurance. *See* Rev. Rul. 68-648, 1968-2 C.B. 49 (employee's election of extended life option available under a retirement income contract that had been purchased for him by his employer, a §501(c)(3) organization, was taxable). Of course, Revenue Ruling 68-648 deals with the exchange of contracts that would not qualify for nonrecognition under §1035 in any case — an annuity contract for a life insurance contract. *See* §6.65.
6. Exchange the policy for another under the nonrecognition provisions of §1035. An encumbered policy may be exchanged

for another similarly encumbered policy of the same type, insuring the same person. *See, e.g.,* LR 8604033. The terms of the new policy may make it economically attractive to make such an exchange. However, an exchange may involve additional costs including legal fees and the loading on the new contract. In addition, the exchange will probably start a new suicide and incontestability period, at least where different insurers are involved. Finally, the new policy may carry higher interest rates on loans.

§6.59.2. Loans on Modified Endowment Contracts

A loan received with respect to a modified endowment contract is treated as a distribution. §72(e)(4)(A). The loan proceeds are includible in gross income to the extent allocable to income on the contract. §72(e)(2)(B). For this purpose the income on the contract is the excess of the cash value of the contract over the investment in the contract (*i.e.,* the sum of premiums and other consideration paid less amounts received that were excludible from gross income, §72(e)(6)).

§6.59.3. Loan Rates and Dividends

Cash value policies issued prior to 1970 generally provide that loans carry an interest rate of five percent or less, while policies issued later commonly specify rates of eight percent or more or a floating rate. In order to discourage the outflow of funds when external interest rates are much higher, insurers now generally cut the dividend rate on participating policies against which there are outstanding loans at low rates unless the owners agreed to a policy amendment making a higher rate applicable to the loans. Of course, the income tax deduction for interest paid on personal loans, such as policy loans, was completely eliminated in 1991. §163(h). Because of the changes in dividend policy and in the income tax law, borrowing against a policy for purposes of making alternative investments is generally no longer economically attractive. However, for convenience, policy owners may borrow against their policies in order to pay policy premiums. In fact, many policies provide for an automatic loan, up to the remaining loan value of the policy, to pay any premium that is not timely paid. It is also common for an owner to borrow on a policy that the owner intends to transfer in order to reduce its value for gift tax purposes. Of course, there is some risk that the transfer of a policy subject to a loan equal to its full cash value might be treated as a transfer for value that would subject the proceeds to taxation under §101(a)(2). *See* §6.53.

§6.60. Deductibility of Interest on Policy Loans: General

Beginning in 1987 the deductible percentage of personal interest was reduced in stages. No deduction was allowed after 1990. (The deductible percentage of personal interest was 65 percent in 1987, 40 percent in 1988, 20 percent in 1989, and 10 percent in 1990.) §163(h)(5). In addition, no deduction is allowable with respect to interest paid on an indebtedness in excess of $50,000 on policies purchased after June 20, 1986 that insure the life of anyone who is an officer, employee, or person who is financially interested in the taxpayer's trade or business. §264(a)(4). However, the preexisting rules regarding the deductibility of interest on policy loans remains of some significance. For example, the old rules apply to loans of $50,000 or less with respect to business-related insurance.

Prior to the 1986 Act (and subject to the provisions of §264), interest payments made by a cash basis policy owner on an outstanding policy loan were generally deductible as interest under §163 in the year of payment. However, no deduction was allowed for interest paid on transactions that lacked economic substance apart from the possible benefit of an income tax deduction. *Knetsch v. United States,* 364 U.S. 361 (1960); *Carpenter v. Commissioner,* 322 F.2d 733 (3d Cir. 1963), *cert. denied,* 375 U.S. 992 (1964).

§6.60.1. Who Is Entitled to Deduct Interest Paid

Subject to §167(h)(5), a taxpayer is entitled to deduct interest that is paid or accrued during the time the taxpayer owns the policy. The owner's "obligation" to pay interest does not survive the assignment of the policy to another person. *J. Simpson Dean,* 35 T.C. 1083 (1961), *nonacq.,* 1973-2 C.B. 4. However, the assignee may not deduct interest that the assignee pays with respect to interest that accrued prior to the assignment. *Agnes I. Fox,* 43 B.T.A. 895 (1941).

Where a policy has been transferred to a trust, interest payments made by the trustee may be deductible by the grantor where the grantor is treated as the owner of the trust property under the grantor trust rules. This possibility was significant when personal interest was deductible and income tax rates were higher. Those conditions spawned the creation of "defective" trusts, that is, ones that contain provisions sufficient to cause the grantor to be treated as the owner under §§671 to 677 and thus report the items of income, deductions, and credits attributable to the trust. Defective trusts were drafted to produce that result without causing the trust to be included in the grantor's gross estate. In LR 7909031, for example, a nonadverse trustee was given the power to pay the income and principal of the trust to the grantor's wife, which was sufficient to require the grantor to be treated as owner of the trust assets under §677(a) but would not cause the assets to be included in the grantor's estate.

When interest is deducted from the original amount of the loan, or is unpaid and is added to the principal amount of the loan, an interest deduction is allowed to a cash basis taxpayer only when the interest is actually paid. Rev. Rul. 73-482, 1973-2 C.B. 44. This point is illustrated by Example 6-26.

Example 6-26. In 1991 *O,* a cash basis taxpayer, borrowed $10,000 against a cash value policy on the life of an employee of *O*'s business. At the time the insurer deducted $1,000 as interest on the loan for the first year and paid *O* the $9,000 balance. None of the $1,000 interest "payment" was deductible on *O*'s income tax return for 1991. In 1992 *O* paid the insurer $10,000 in full satisfaction of the loan. *O* was entitled to claim an interest deduction in 1992 for the $1,000 in business-related interest that was paid on the loan. If the interest paid by *O* had been characterized as personal interest under §167(h)(5) none of it would have been deductible. The same rule applies if the annual interest on a policy loan had not been paid and had instead been added to the principal amount of the loan: Interest is considered to have been paid when the full amount of principal and accumulated interest is paid.

If an interest deduction is otherwise allowable (*e.g.,* the interest is payable on business-related borrowings of $50,000 or less), the rule last described in Example 6-26 gives the taxpayer some flexibility in timing the interest deduction. For example, a business with little or no taxable income in one year might prefer to let the interest go unpaid and add it to principal until a later year in which an interest deduction would be more valuable for income tax purposes.

§6.60.2. Interest on Policy Loans: Limitations of §264

The rules of §264 bar a deduction for interest that would otherwise be deductible with respect to insurance-related loans. Under §264(a)(2) no deduction is allowed for amounts paid as indebtedness incurred directly or indirectly to purchase or continue in effect a single premium life insurance, endowment, or annuity policy purchased after March 1, 1954. A contract is considered to be a single premium one if substantially all of the premiums are paid within four years from the date on which it was purchased or if an amount is deposited after March 1,

1954 with the insurer for the payment of a substantial number of future premiums. Reg. §1.264-2. No deduction is allowed for interest paid on a bank loan secured by a single premium annuity policy purchased after 1954. Rev. Rul. 79-41, 1979-1 C.B. 124. As the ruling points out, "One who borrows to buy a single premium annuity contract and one who borrows against such a contract already owned are in virtually the same economic position."

Interest is also generally not deductible when paid in connection with a policy issued after August 6, 1963 under a purchase plan that contemplates the systematic direct or indirect borrowing of all or part of the increase in cash value of the policy. §264(a)(3). Even before the interest on personal loans became nondeductible, the limitation of §264(a)(3) reduced the attractiveness of the so-called financed life insurance or minimum deposit plan, which depended heavily upon the deductibility of interest payments made on indebtedness incurred to make premium payments. Minimum deposit plans are discussed at §6.73.

§6.60.3. Exceptions to §264(a)(3)

There are four exceptions to the general rule of §264(a)(3). The first and most important exception, the so-called *4-in-7 exception,* applies if any four of the first seven annual premiums are paid without incurring any indebtedness in connection with the policy. §264(c)(1). For this purpose a new seven-year period starts to run if there is a substantial increase in the amount of the premium. §264(c). This exception allows the deduction of interest paid on an indebtedness incurred in connection with fewer than four of the first seven annual premiums. Also, once the 4-in-7 exception is satisfied, the deductibility of interest on policy loans is not restricted by §264(a)(3). The IRS applies the 4-in-7 rule literally — it must be satisfied within the initial 7-year period without any violation of the rule. Thus, if *O* borrowed against a post-August 6, 1963 policy for four of the first seven years, the exception is not available even if the full amount of the loan is repaid within the seven-year period. Rev. Rul. 72-609, 1972-3 C.B. 199.

The second one is the *de minimis exception.* It applies if the total amount paid or accrued under plans that contemplate the systematic borrowing of cash values is $100 or less. §264(c)(2). It is obviously of limited significance.

Under the *unforeseen events exception,* a deduction is allowed for interest paid on indebtedness incurred because of an unforeseen substantial loss of income or an unforeseen substantial increase in financial obligations. §264(c)(3). For the purposes of this rule a loss of income or increase in financial obligations is not unforeseen if it was or could have been foreseen at the time the policy was purchased. Reg. §1.264-4(d)(3).

Lastly, the *trade or business exception* applies if the indebtedness was incurred in connection with the taxpayer's trade or business. §264(c)(4). However, the indebtedness must have been incurred to finance business obligations and not the acquisition of cash value life insurance. Specifically, borrowing to finance business life insurance, such as keyman, split-dollar, or stock redemption plans is not considered to be incurred in connection with the taxpayer's business. Reg. §1.264-4(d)(4). In contrast, borrowing to finance business expansion, inventory, or capital improvements does qualify under this exception.

§6.61. Dividends

As indicated previously, dividends generally constitute a partial premium refund. *See* §6-12. In the case of policies other than modified endowment contracts, a dividend is includible in the policy owner's income only to the extent that it, together with all previous excludible payments received under the policy, exceeds the total cost of the policy (*i.e.,* premiums and other consideration). Reg. §1.72-11(b)(1). Under that rule a dividend is not includible in gross income in most cases. Of course, excludable dividends are deducted from the consideration paid or deemed paid for the purpose of computing the exclusion ratio under §72. Id. Also, only the net amount of premiums paid is taken into account in determining gain on amounts not received as annuities under a policy. §72(e)(1). Dividends with respect to modified endowment contracts are not includible in gross income to the extent they are retained by the insurer as a premium or other consideration paid for the contract. §72(e)(4)(B).

Interest paid or credited on dividends left with the insurer is includable in the gross income of the policy owner for the year in which the owner may withdraw it. Reg. §1.61-7(d); Rev. Rul. 57-441, 1957-2 C.B. 45 (interest on dividends under converted U.S. Government Life Insurance or a National Service Life Insurance policy is not an exempt benefit within the meaning of the World War Veterans Act of 1924).

The distribution under a special reserve provision of a life insurance contract (additional amounts paid with respect to the policy for the first five years, which were distributable at the end of 20 years) was a nontaxable return of premiums where it was less than the total premiums paid under the policy. *Ned W. Moseley,* 72 T.C. 183 (1979), *acq.,* 1980-1 C.B. 1. In *Moseley,* the Tax Court refused to allocate the premiums paid by the taxpayer between the special reserve and the death benefit provisions.

§6.62. Sale, Surrender, or Exchange of Insurance Policies: General

The following general principles apply in determining the income tax consequences of transactions involving life insurance policies:

1. *Basis.* For the purpose of determining gain, the basis of a policy is the net amount of premiums or other consideration the taxpayer has invested in it. In contrast, for the purpose of determining loss the basis is the cash surrender value of the policy.
2. *Gain.* With the exception of the tax-free exchanges described in §1035, ordinary gain is recognized when one policy is exchanged for another policy.
3. *Loss.* The excess of premiums paid over the value of property received upon the sale, exchange, or surrender of personal insurance is not deductible.

§6.63. Sale of Policy — Gain and Loss

In the ordinary case, the excess of the proceeds received upon the sale of a policy over the net premiums paid (premiums paid less dividends received) is taxable as ordinary income. *Gallun v. Commissioner,* 327 F.2d 809 (7th Cir. 1964). For this purpose presumably the amount of policy loans outstanding against a policy would be treated as an amount received.

Premiums Paid
− Dividends Received
Net Premiums Paid

Analytically the courts have treated the excess as attributable to the earnings generated by the investment component of the policy essentially equivalent to interest and taxable as ordinary income. "[A]ccepting the effectiveness of the transaction as the sale of a capital asset, . . . we are, nevertheless, dealing here with the receipt as part of the purchase price — and in addition to any amount attributable to the property sold — of an amount representing income which has already been earned and which would have been ordinary income if and when received by the vendor." *Estate of Gertrude H. Crocker,* 37 T.C 605, 612 (1962). The gain that would have been ordinary income cannot be transformed into capital gain through the simple expedient of a sale or transfer. *First National Bank of Kansas City v. Commissioner,* 309 F.2d 587 (8th Cir. 1962).

Example 6-27. *X* had paid premiums of $12,000 on a policy that *X* sold to *Y* for $15,000. The $3,000 excess of the amount received over the premiums paid is ordinary income to *X*. Presumably the result would be the same if *X* had borrowed $10,000 against the policy and received $5,000 from *Y*.

§6.63.1. Sale or Other Disposition of Encumbered Policy

The sale or other disposition of an encumbered policy may result in a gain to the transferor depending upon the manner in which the policy loan is characterized. If it is treated as an ordinary loan, some taxable gain may result if the amount of the loan exceeds the transferor's basis. Thus, the donor of an encumbered policy may be treated as having realized an amount equal to the loan balance at the time the policy is transferred. The transfer of an encumbered policy may be treated as a discharge of indebtedness. Under Reg. §1.1001-2(a)(4)(i), "the sale or other disposition of property that secures a nonrecourse liability discharges the transferor from the liability."

§6.63.2. "Loss" on Sale

The excess of the net premiums paid for a policy over the amount realized upon the sale of the policy is not deductible. *Century Wood Preserving Co. v. Commissioner,* 69 F.2d 967 (3d Cir. 1934). The reason is simple — the excess is considered to be attributable to the nondeductible cost of insurance protection provided over the period preceding the sale. *Keystone Consolidated Publishing Co.,* 26 B.T.A. 1210 (1932). In essence, the courts have taken the position that there is no loss.

§6.64. Surrender of Policies

Ordinary income is realized to the extent the proceeds received upon surrender, refund, or maturity of a policy exceed the net amount of all premiums or other consideration paid. §72(e)(5)(E). If the taxpayer, within 60 days of the day a lump sum becomes payable under a contract, exercises an option to receive an annuity in lieu of the lump sum, then no part of the lump sum is includible in gross income at the time it became payable. §72(h). That is, the gain is not taxed currently if the policyholder elects, within 60 days of the time a lump sum becomes payable under the contract, to receive an annuity in lieu of a lump sum.

In the case of such an election, the annuity payments are taxed to the recipient in accordance with the basic income tax rules applicable to annuities (*i.e.,* a proportionate part of the total amount received each year is a tax-free return of capital and the balance is taxable income). §72(b).

When a policy is surrendered, the gain realized is ordinary income and not capital gain. The courts have reached that result because the surrender, refund, or maturity of a policy is not a sale or exchange. *Avery v. Commissioner,* 111 F.2d 19 (9th Cir. 1940) (maturity of endowment policy); *Bodine v. Commissioner,* 103 F.2d 982 (3d Cir.), *cert. denied,* 308 U.S. 576 (1939) (surrender of annuity policy). It is true that capital gain treatment is available under §1222 only when there is a sale or exchange of a capital asset. However, as indicated in §6.63, the sale of an insurance policy also generates ordinary income and not capital gain.

When a policy is surrendered the taxpayer may receive less than the total amount of the premiums and other consideration he or she paid for it. In general, no deduction is allowed for the difference. *London Shoe Co. v. Commissioner,* 80 F.2d 230 (2d Cir. 1935), *cert. denied,* 298 U.S. 663 (1936); *Standard Brewing Co.,* 6 B.T.A. 980 (1927). Some cases disallowed a deduction because the "loss" was not incurred in a transaction that was entered into primarily for profit as required by §165(c)(2). *Industrial Trust Co. v. Broderick,* 94 F.2d 927 (1st Cir.), *cert. denied,* 304 U.S. 572 (1938) (single premium nonrefund annuity contract was purchased for reasons of security and not profit); *Arnold v. United States,* 180 F. Supp. 746 (N.D. Texas 1959) (endowment policies purchased to provide life insurance protection until maturity when they would provide secure source of income); Rev. Rul. 72-193, 1972-1 C.B. 58. Deductions were denied in other cases because the cash surrender value was equal to the taxpayer's capital investment. *London Shoe Co., supra.* Any excess of premiums paid over cash surrender value represented the nondeductible cost of the insurance protection provided by policy. For example, in *Standard Brewing Co.,* the court said:

> To the extent that the premiums paid by the petitioner created in it a right to a surrender value, they constituted a capital investment. To the extent they exceeded the surrender value, they constituted a payment for earned insurance and were current expenses. . . . The surrender value of the policy was the measure of the investment and upon the surrender there was no capital lost. 6 B.T.A. at 984.

This result is consistent with the denial of a deduction for premiums paid on personal life insurance and on policies maintained on the lives of officers or employees of which the employer is a beneficiary.

§6.65. EXCHANGE OF POLICIES, §1035

Under the special nonrecognition rules of §1035, no gain or loss is recognized on certain exchanges of insurance policies where the policies exchanged relate to the same insured. Specifically, under §1035(a) no gain or loss is recognized in the following exchanges:

1. A contract of life insurance for another contract of life insurance or for an endowment or annuity contract (*e.g.,* LR 8604033 and LR 8816015); or
2. A contract of endowment insurance (a) for another contract of endowment insurance which provides for regular payments beginning at a date not later than the date payments would have begun under the contract exchanged, or (b) for an annuity contract; or
3. An annuity contract for an annuity contract (*e.g.,* LR 8501012 (variable annuity issued by one company exchanged for fixed annuity issued by another company)).

An exchange of a policy which insures one person for a policy insuring the life of another person is not tax-free under §1035. *See* Rev. Rul. 90-109, 1990-2 C.B. ____.

§6.65.1. What Constitutes an Exchange

Neither the Code nor the Regulations define "exchange." The existing authorities are helpful but not entirely consistent. In planning an exchange, the owner should avoid transactions that might involve a "surrender" of the existing policy, followed by a "reinvestment" in a second one.

§6.65.2. Exchange of Assignable Policies

The safest exchange transactions involve policies issued by the same insurer, with respect to which it is relatively simple to arrange an exchange. For example, in LR 8229107, a participating whole life policy with a low guaranteed interest rate was exchanged for a participating whole life policy issued by the same insurer on the life of the same insured with a higher guarantee.

When different insurers are involved it is safest to assign the existing policy to the company that will issue the new contract, being sure that there is no lapse in coverage. Rev. Rul. 72-358, 1972-2 C.B. 473. The IRS appears to accept that all such transactions qualify under

§1035. *E.g.,* LR 8604003 (encumbered whole life policy assigned to new insurer in exchange for insurance of similarly encumbered whole life policy on same insured) and LR 8433035 (single premium retirement annuity assigned in exchange for single premium deferred annuity contract). Without an assignment a transaction involving a readily transferrable annuity may be treated as a surrender and exchange of the proceeds in consideration for the second annuity. LR 8515063. In the view of the IRS such rollovers are likely not to qualify under §1035.

§6.65.3. Exchange of Nonassignable Policies

Annuity contracts issued under qualified plans are nonassignable by reason of §401(g). Accordingly, taxpayers wishing to exchange those contracts cannot do so by direct assignment. Fortunately, the IRS has generally approved transactions in which the taxpayer enters into a binding agreement with the new issuer which requires the taxpayer to surrender the existing contract and to direct the proceeds to be paid directly to the new issuer as consideration for the new contract. Rev. Rul. 73-124, 1973-1 C.B. 200. In addition, the owner would usually also agree to endorse in favor of the new issuer any check the owner receives from the original issuer. Such arrangements are usually held to involve a "single integrated transaction." *See* LR 8526038 (approving a transaction involving a transfer agreement between the annuity certificate holder and *either* his employer *or* the issuer of the new contract); LR 8424010; *contra* LR 8343010; LR 8310033 (holding the proposed transaction was a surrender and reinvestment although the taxpayer would enter into an agreement with the issuer of the new contract).

The IRS will generally not approve a transaction that does not involve a binding agreement between the insured and another party. However, the taxpayer may succeed in litigation. *Martin I. Greene,* 85 T.C. 1024 (1985), *acq. in result,* 1986-2 C.B. 1. *Greene* involved a taxpayer who purchased a nontransferable annuity from VALIC through a salary reduction agreement under §403(b). She surrendered the annuity contract in order to purchase a similar annuity contract through Charter, another insurer. VALIC would not pay the funds directly to Charter, instead issuing a check to the taxpayer. On October 28, 1980 VALIC issued a check to the taxpayer, which she endorsed in favor of Charter and submitted with her application on November 5, 1980. The IRS contended that the transaction did not constitute an "exchange" primarily because of the lack of a "binding agreement." Accordingly, the IRS argued that the taxpayer must report the entire proceeds of the original annuity contract as income. The Tax Court rejected the argument, holding the transaction was within Rev. Rul. 73-124, 1973-1 C.B. 200, which held:

> The fact that the employee first surrendered the original annuity contract to an insurer because of the restrictions required by section 401(g) of the Code does not prevent the transaction from being an exchange within the meaning of section 1035 of the Code provided the proceeds received upon surrender are applied immediately to the purchase of a second annuity contract for the same employee.

The transaction under consideration in Revenue Ruling 73-124 involved a binding agreement between the employee and his employer under which the employee was obligated to pay the employer an amount equal to any amount received under the first contract and the employer agreed to apply such amount to provide benefits for the employee under the second contract. This ruling did not state that such an agreement was required in order for the transaction to be within the scope of §1035.

The liberality of the approach taken in *Greene* may be attributed to the difficulties that taxpayers face in dealing with nontransferable contracts, which cannot be directly assigned to the new issuer. Also, had the first issuer (VALIC) agreed to pay the proceeds directly to the second (Charter), it is unlikely that any serious tax dispute would have arisen.

§6.66. Exchanges Within §1035; Permissible Exchanges; Basis

An exchange of one encumbered life insurance policy for another simiiliarly encumbered policy issued by another insurer relating to the same insured is within the scope of §1035. LR 8816015; LR 8604033. In such cases the "new" policy is considered to have been purchased on the date of the exchange — making §7702(f)(7) applicable to the policy. That is, if there is a reduction in benefits within the first 15 years as a result of which there is a cash distribution to the policyholder, the provisions of §72 other than §72(e)(5) apply to the distribution, not the "old" rules of §72 regarding the taxation of distributions.

The nonrecognition rule also applies when a life insurance endowment or fixed annuity policy is exchanged for a variable annuity policy. Rev. Rul. 68-235, 1968-1 C.B. 360. Likewise, a variable annuity contract issued by one company may be exchanged for a fixed annuity contract issued by another company. LR 8501012. Of course, for the nonrecognition rule to apply, the contracts must relate to the same insured, although they may be issued by different insurers. Rev. Rul. 72-358, 1972-2 C.B. 473.

When there is a tax-free exchange, the policy received has the same basis as the policy transferred. §1031(d). If other property is also received, the gain on the transaction must be realized by the taxpayer to the extent of the "boot" (cash or other property) received. The new contract has the same basis as the old one, adjusted as provided in §1031(d). Specifically, the basis is (1) decreased by the amount of money and the fair market value of other property received and (2) increased by the amount of gain recognized on the exchange. When a new policy and other property are received, any gain arising from the transaction is recognized but not in excess of the total value of the money and the other property received. §1031(b). In such an exchange no loss is recognized. §1031(c).

> **Example 6-28.** *T* exchanged a life insurance policy upon which *T* had paid premiums of $40,000 for a life insurance policy that had a replacement value of $40,000 and cash of $5,000. The full amount of *T*'s $5,000 gain is recognized in the year of the exchange. *T*'s basis in the new policy is $40,000 as indicated in Reg. §1.1031(d)-1(b). If *T* received no cash and the new policy were worth only $35,000, the $5,000 "loss" would not be recognized. Instead, the new policy would have a basis of $40,000.

§6.67. Costs of Exchanges; Exercise Care and Study the Economics

The exchange of policies may disadvantage the policy owner because of the additional costs involved in effectuating a transfer, including the loading on the new contract. Legal fees and other professional costs may also be incurred in connection with the transaction. In the case of life insurance, the exchange may also probably start a new suicide and noncontestability period, at least where different insurers are involved. Finally, the new policy may carry higher interest rates on loans.

§6.68. Exchange of Policies Not Within §1035

Exchanges not subject to §1035 are governed by the general rules regarding the recognition of gain or loss upon the sale or exchange of property. Thus, gain or loss is recognized when an endowment or annuity contract is exchanged for a life insurance contract. Gain or loss is also recognized when an annuity contract is exchanged for an endowment contract. Reg. §1.1035-1(c). Because of this rule, a taxpayer cannot avoid the taxation of earnings that have accrued on an endowment or an annuity policy by exchanging it for a life insurance policy.

The accrued earnings will be taxed to the owner unless the owner dies prior to the maturity of the policy. These rules reduce the flexibility a taxpayer has in dealing with investments in endowment or annuity policies, but they are consistent with other income tax principles.

> **Example 6-29.** In 1985 *T* paid $20,000 for a single premium endowment contract that would pay $35,000 to *T* in 1995 or to his beneficiary if he died before then. *T* exchanged the policy in 1994, when it had a cash value of $33,000, for a single premium paid-up life insurance policy that had a cash surrender value of $33,000. The same policy would cost $33,000 if purchased on the life of a person of *T*'s age, sex, and medical history. As a result of the exchange *T* must recognize a gain of $13,000.

Private Letter Ruling 8905004 involved the withdrawal of an amount equal to the original purchase price paid for an annuity, which was used to purchase a life insurance contract and the concurrent exchange of the taxpayer's residual interest in the original annuity contract for a new annuity. The transaction was treated as a tax-free exchange of one annuity contract for another. However, the life insurance contract was treated as taxable "boot" includible in the taxpayer's gross income.

For the purpose of determining gain, the fair market value of a single premium life insurance policy received by the taxpayer is the amount a person of the same age, sex, and condition of health as the insured would have to pay for a life policy with the same company at the date of the exchange. Here again, the measure of value is not the cash surrender value of the policy. *Charles Cutler Parsons,* 16 T.C. 256 (1951); *W. Stanley Barrett,* 42 T.C. 993 (1964), *aff'd,* 348 F.2d 916 (1st Cir. 1965) (matured endowment policies exchanged for paid-up life insurance policies); Rev. Rul. 54-264, 1954-2 C.B. 57 (exchange of single premium endowment policy for paid-up life insurance policy and cash).

§6.69. Alternative Minimum Tax, §56(g)(4)(B)(ii)

The alternative minimum tax of a corporation for taxable years beginning after 1989 must take into account the internal build-up in value of life insurance policies as determined under §7702(g) (*i.e.,* the increase in cash surrender value less the portion of any premium paid that is attributable to insurance coverage).

F. SPECIAL TYPES OF LIFE INSURANCE

§6.70. Introduction

The most important types of special life insurance and life insurance plans are described in this part, including split-dollar, group-term, and single premium plans. Others, such as minimum deposit plans, are discussed although tax changes have largely eliminated their appeal. Having some knowledge of these types of life insurance policies and plans is important to planners because they are often included in executive compensation packages and insurance proposals made to clients. Each type has some special advantages and is subject to some special tax rules. Second-to-die (or survivorship) life and death benefit only plans are also reviewed although the latter is not strictly life insurance. The part concludes with a discussion of gifts of life insurance under the Uniform Gifts to Minors Act and the application of the Uniform Simultaneous Death Act to life insurance.

§6.71. Split-Dollar Life Insurance: General

A split-dollar life insurance plan is most often used in the business setting to make a substantial amount of life insurance available to a key employee, or to the employee's assignee, at little or no cost to the employee. Descriptively, the plan is a permissible form of discriminatory nonqualified employee benefit under which key employees are preferred. The concept of split-dollar is based upon a division of the interests in a cash value policy between a financing party (usually an employer) and the insured (usually the employee). Under it, the cash surrender value is usually controlled by the financing party to the extent of premiums paid by it and the risk element (*i.e.,* the excess of the face amount of the insurance over the cash surrender value of the policy) is controlled by the insured or the insured's assignee. Although split-dollar may be used in a variety of contexts, it is most commonly used to provide a substantial amount of life insurance to key employees at a relatively low cost. Actually, before a limitation was imposed on the deductibility of interest paid by a business with respect to insurance on the life of an officer or employee, §264(a)(4), the employer frequently borrowed against its interest in life insurance in split-dollar plans. Specifically, the 1986 Act limited the deduction to the interest paid on $50,000 borrowed against policies issued after June 22, 1986 on the life of any employee. Id.

In a split-dollar arrangement, the financing party and the insured may split the premium cost between themselves in a variety of different ways — with the actual split affecting the income tax consequences as explained below. The financing party typically pays either the entire premium, an amount of the premium equal to the increase in cash value for the year, or the amount of the premium in excess of the employee's contribution, which is either the actual cost of the risk protection or the P.S. 58 cost (described below). In addition, if the financing party is the insured's employer, the employer may pay the insured employee a "bonus" equal to the portion of the premium paid by the employee — sometimes including the additional income tax the employee will be obligated to pay as a result of the plan. In order to prevent the risk portion from declining as the cash value increases, the dividends declared on participating policies may be applied under the fifth dividend option to buy term insurance equal to the increase in the financing party's interest in the cash value.

Under a split-dollar plan the financing party is entitled to recover some portion of the cash value of the insurance upon maturity of the policy or termination of the plan. The amount is typically: (1) the greater of the premiums paid or the cash surrender value of the policy, (2) the entire cash value regardless of the amount of premiums paid, or (3) the cash value of the policy to the extent of premiums paid.

The insured or the insured's assignee pays the portion of the premium (if any) not paid by the fiancing party and is entitled to name the beneficiary of the risk portion of the insurance (the difference between the face amount and the cash surrender value). Although the insured may be required to pay a large part of the premium in the first year or two, the insured's share of the premium rapidly decreases. Some policies are designed to build up cash value more rapidly to avoid this problem.

The two common types of split-dollar arrangements, the endorsement system and the collateral assignment system, are described in the following excerpt from Rev. Rul. 64-328, 1964-2 C.B. 11, 12:

> In the endorsement system, the employer owns the policy and is responsible for payment of the annual premiums. The employee is then required to reimburse the employer for his share, if any, of the premiums. Under the collateral assignment system, the employee in form owns the policy and pays the entire premium thereon. The employer in form makes annual loans, without interest (or below the fair rate of interest), to the employee of amounts equal to the increases in the cash surrender value, but not exceeding the annual premiums. The employee executes an assignment of his policy to the employer as collateral security for the loans. The loans are generally payable at the termination of employment or the death of the employee.

The arrangements for the ownership of the policy and premium payments can, of course, be tailored to meet the needs of the parties.

The "split" of the premium payments and the other details of a particular split-dollar plan can also vary according to the needs of the parties. The employee might, for example, pay only an amount equal to the P.S. 58 cost of the risk element. *See* §6.71.2. As indicated above, the employer might pay the employee a "bonus" equal to the portion of the premium taxed to the employee (the lower of the insurer's one-year term rate or the P.S. 58 cost). Of course, the interests of the financing party or of the insured can be held by a trust or an individual other than the insured. Also, the parties may enter into an agreement regarding the use of the proceeds (*e.g.,* to fund a stock purchase). Finally, dividends may be used in whole or in part to reduce the premium cost, to buy paid-up insurance, or to buy term insurance. As indicated above, if dividends are used to buy term insurance, the amount of insurance subject to the insured's control will not diminish as the cash value of the policy increases.

§6.71.1. Reverse Split-Dollar

In a reverse split-dollar plan the employee acquires cash value insurance over which the employer is given the right to designate the beneficiary in exchange for its payment of the cost of the risk element it controls. In effect, the employee benefits from the growth in the cash value of the policy and the amount of insurance provided in excess of the risk element controlled by the employer. The relatively low insurance protection provided to the employee in early years is a serious disadvantage of reverse split-dollar plans.

Following the general precepts applicable to split-dollar plans, the employer pays the portion of the premium attributable to the risk element. In a split-dollar plan the employee may be charged with either the P.S. 58 cost or the published cost of one-year term insurance available from the insurer. Rev. Rul. 66-110, 1966-1 C.B. 12. Advocates of reverse split-dollar plans point to the permissive language of Rev. Rul. 66-110 and argue that in the context of a reverse split-dollar plan the employer may pay the *greater* of the P.S. 58 cost or the one-year term cost. For example, the employer might choose to pay the P.S. 58 cost of the insurance if it exceeded the one-year term cost of the insurance. As a result, the employee-insured would contribute little, if anything, toward the actual premium payments. They may be wrong: If the corporation pays more than is required for the risk element it receives, the excess may constitute compensation to the employee. In the case of a closely-held corporation the excess payment may constitute a gift from the shareholders to the employee.

The objective of a reverse split-dollar plan is to provide an employee with increasing amount of life insurance protection and the benefit of the growth in the cash value of a policy. While the employer bears most, if not all, of the premium cost, the employer receives a declining amount of insurance protection and no interest in the cash value. Depending upon the terms of the "split," the employee, as the financing party, may be entitled to all increases in cash value.

A reverse split-dollar plan may be used as a key-person plan to provide substantial insurance proceeds to the employer upon the unanticipated early death of the employee. From the employee's perspective, the plan may involve a form of forced savings that involves contributions by the employer beyond the basic cost of comparable term insurance. Upon retirement the insurance may be assigned to the employee, for whom the policy could represent a major financial asset.

Of course, as described in detail in §6.71.2, the employer is not entitled to a deduction for the portion of the premium it pays. §264(a)(1). However, as a general rule any proceeds received by the employer would not be included in its income. §101(a)(1).

If the employee retains incidents of ownership in the insurance (*e.g.*, the right to borrow against the policy or designate the beneficiary), the entire proceeds are includible in the employee's estate. Accordingly, for estate tax purposes in a reverse split-dollar plan the insurance may be owned by the employee's spouse or by an irrevocable insurance trust.

§6.71.2. Income Tax Consequences

Since 1964 the economic value of an employer-provided split-dollar plan has been includible in the gross income of an insured employee. Rev. Rul. 64-328, 1964-2 C.B. 11. The value of the plan is equal to the one-year term cost of the life insurance protection provided to the employee less any amount paid by the employee. Because the plan is provided as an incident of employment, its value is includible in the employee's gross income though control over the risk portion has been assigned to the employee's spouse or another person. Rev. Rul. 78-420, 1978-2 C.B. 67. The value attributed to the employee must also include the amount of any dividend paid to the employee or applied toward the purchase of additional term or paid-up insurance. Rev. Rul. 66-110, 1966-1 C.B. 12. If the insured is a shareholder and not an employee, the value of the insurance protection is treated as a taxable distribution from the corporation to the shareholder. Rev. Rul. 79-50, 1979-1 C.B. 138.

The cost of the insurance protection provided under a split-dollar arrangement is based upon the P.S. 58 cost that is set forth in Rev. Rul. 55-747, 1955-2 C.B. 228. *See* Table 6-2. However, the insurer's actual one-year term rates may be used where the current published premium rates regularly charged by the insurer are lower than the P.S. 58 costs, which is often the case. Rev. Rul. 66-110, 1966-1 C.B. 12. (In the following discussion the lower of the P.S. 58 cost or the insurer's one-year term premium is referred to as the P.S. 58 cost unless otherwise indicated.) However, even where the actual rates are not lower, the insured employee receives a valuable benefit.

A premium paid by an employer who has an interest in the cash surrender value of a policy is not deductible because the employer is "directly or indirectly a beneficiary under such a policy" within the meaning of §264(a). Rev. Rul. 66-203, 1966-2 C.B. 104. In contrast, reasonable salary payments to employees are deductible. Accordingly, if the employer's marginal income tax rate is greater than that of the employee, the overall after-tax cost of a split-dollar plan may be lower if the employer increases the employee's salary and the employee uses the increase to pay a greater part of the premium. The optimum tax result is often produced when the employee pays an amount of the premium equal to the P.S. 58 cost of the insurance provided under the plan. If the employee pays such an amount none of the employer's

Table 6-2
Uniform One-Year Term Premiums for $1,000 Life Insurance Protection

Age	*Premium*	*Age*	*Premium*	*Age*	*Premium*
15	$1.27	35	$ 3.21	55	$13.74
16	1.38	36	3.41	56	14.91
17	1.48	37	3.63	57	16.18
18	1.52	38	3.87	58	17.56
19	1.56	39	4.14	59	19.08
20	1.61	40	4.42	60	20.73
21	1.67	41	4.73	61	22.53
22	1.73	42	5.07	62	24.50
23	1.79	43	5.44	63	26.63
24	1.86	44	5.85	64	28.98
25	1.93	45	6.30	65	31.51
26	2.02	46	6.78	66	34.28
27	2.11	47	7.32	67	37.31
28	2.20	48	7.89	68	40.59
29	2.31	49	8.53	69	44.17
30	2.43	50	9.22	70	48.06
31	2.57	51	9.97	71	52.29
32	2.70	52	10.79	72	56.89
33	2.86	53	11.69	73	61.89
34	3.02	54	12.67	74	67.33
				75	73.23

premium payment is included in the employee's income. An employer may cooperate by paying the employee a "bonus" equal to the portion of the premium to be paid by the employee or a "double bonus" equal to that amount plus the income tax that the employee must pay on it.

In the ordinary case the proceeds paid when the insured dies are not included in the gross income of the employer or the beneficiary. Rev. Rul. 64-328, 1964-2 C.B. 11. However, some portion of the proceeds may be taxable if the insurance has been transferred for value. §101(a)(2). Such a transfer might take place, for example, if the policy is sold by the employer to the spouse of the insured. *See Estate of Rath v. United States,* 608 F.2d 254 (6th Cir. 1979).

§6.71.3. Gift Tax Consequences

In the typical case neither the original acquisition of employer-provided split-dollar insurance nor the payment of subsequent premiums involves a gift for federal gift tax purposes. However, if the risk element has been assigned by the employee any subsequent premium payments made by the employee do involve gifts. Rev. Rul. 78-420, 1978-2 C.B. 67 (policy owned by spouse of employee). The gift in such a case may qualify for the annual exclusion. Rev. Rul. 76-490, 1976-2 C.B. 300; *but see* Rev. Rul. 79-47, 1979-1 C.B. 312. The payment of premiums may also involve gifts where a split-dollar plan is used in a nonbusiness setting.

> **Example 6-30.** Under a private split-dollar plan *M* pays a portion of the premium on an ordinary policy on the life of her daughter, *D,* equal to the increase in cash surrender value of the policy, and *D* pays the balance. As each premium is paid, *M* makes a gift to *D* of the P.S. 58 cost of the insurance protection over which *D* has control less the amount of the premium paid by *D.* If *D* had given her interest in the policy to another person, the subsequent premium payments would involve gifts by *M* and *D* to the owner of the policy.

The transfer of a split-dollar policy that has been in effect for some time involves a gift, as does the subsequent payment of premiums on the policy. Rev. Rul. 81-198, 1981-2 C.B. 188. In Revenue Ruling 81-198, the IRS ruled that an employee-donor made a gift equal to the total value of the policy (interpolated terminal reserve plus the unearned premium) *less* the value of the employer's interest in the policy. In such a case subsequent gifts are made by the employee as the employer, the employee, or both contribute to premium payments. The gift with respect to subsequent premium payments consists of two elements:

(1) the premium payment made by the employer to the extent it is treated as income to the employee and (2) the amount of the premium paid by the employee.

If all interests in the insurance are assigned to a qualified charity or charitable trust, presumably the assignment and the subsequent premium payments attributable to the employee qualify for the income and gift tax charitable deduction. In contrast, no deductions are allowed where the sole owner of a policy attempts to take advantage of the different interests in a policy by assigning only the cash surrender value to a charity. Thus, where the insured owned the entire interest in a policy, the irrevocable assignment of the cash surrender value does not qualify for the charitable deduction for income or gift tax purposes because only a portion of the donor's interest was transferred. The cash surrender value does not constitute an undivided interest as required in the case of split gifts of outright interests. Rev. Rul. 76-143, 1976-1 C.B. 63 (income tax); Rev. Rul. 76-200, 1976-1 C.B. 308 (gift tax). The rules applicable to charitable gifts are reviewed in detail in Chapter 8.

§6.71.4. Estate Tax Consequences

Upon the death of the employee none of the proceeds paid to the employer under a split-dollar plan is usually includible in the employee's estate. However, when the insured was the controlling shareholder of the employer corporation, the portion of the proceeds paid to the employer is included as an asset of the corporation in valuing the stock owned by the insured. Reg. §20.2031-2(f); *Estate of John Huntsman,* 66 T.C. 861 (1976), *acq.,* 1977-1 C.B. 1.

The proceeds attributable to the risk element of the policy are includible in the employee's estate under §2042(1) if they were paid to the employee's estate. In other cases inclusion is required under §2042(2) if the employee held any of the incidents of ownership at the time of death. In this connection note that for purposes of §2042(2) the incidents of ownership held by a corporation are attributed to the estate of the controlling shareholder. Reg. §20.2041-1(c)(6). Accordingly, the proceeds are includible in the estate of the controlling shareholder except to the extent the proceeds are payable to the corporation or are otherwise taken into account in valuing the insured's stock. *Estate of Alfred Dimen,* 72 T.C. 198 (1979), *aff'd mem.* (unpublished opinion) 633 F.2d 203 (2d Cir. 1980); Rev. Rul. 82-145, 1982-2 C.B. 213, *modifying* Rev. Rul. 76-274, 1976-2 C.B. 278, situation 3. The proceeds of a life insurance policy payable to the insured's wholly-owned corporation that are used pursuant to a stock redemption agreement to purchase a portion of the insured's stock are not includible in the insured's estate under §2042, but are instead reflected in the value of decedent's stock.

Rev. Rul. 82-85, 1982-1 C.B. 137. In contrast, the proceeds are includible in the estate of the insured-controlling shareholder where the proceeds are paid to another corporation that uses the proceeds for its own purposes. LR 8710004. The incidents of ownership of the controlled corporation are attributed to the insured because the proceeds of the insurance are neither payable to the corporation that owns the policy nor used for its business purposes. Id.

The proceeds of insurance held in an irrevocable trust under a "private" split-dollar plan are includible in the estate of an insured who retains the right to borrow against the cash surrender value of the policy. Rev. Rul. 79-129, 1979-1 C.B. 306. Specifically, the entire proceeds are includible in the estate of the insured when the insurance was assigned to an irrevocable trust but the insured retained the right to borrow against the insurance. However, the balance remaining at the time of the insured's death of the funds transferred by the insured to the trust to pay premiums is not includible in the insured's estate. Rev. Rul. 81-164, 1981-1 C.B. 458.

§6.72. Employer-Provided Group-Term Life Insurance: General

The relatively low cost of group-term insurance and the favorable income tax treatment it is given make it a common and important fringe benefit. First, the cost of employer-provided group-term insurance is generally deductible as a business expense under §162. Of course, the premium payments are not deductible if the employer is a beneficiary under the policy. §264(a). Second, the employee is not taxed on the cost of $50,000 of coverage. §79(a)(1). Third, the cost of group-term insurance in excess of $50,000, determined under the Table I rate schedule set out in Table 6-3 at §6.72.9, is includible in the gross income of an employee except to the extent the employee contributed to the cost of the coverage. The 1984 Act removed an exception that allowed an unlimited amount of group-term insurance to be provided to retired employees. Under a grandfather provision more than $50,000 of group term insurance can be provided under a plan that was in existence on or before January 1, 1984 with respect to an employee who was 55 on or before that date. Fourth, the cost of group-term insurance in excess of $50,000 is not includible when the employer or a charity is the beneficiary under the policy. §79(b)(2). However, no charitable deduction is allowable under §170 with respect to a policy that has been assigned or is payable to a charity. Reg. §1.79-2(c)(3). Fifth, the cost of group-term insurance in excess of $50,000 is not includible in the gross income of a disabled former employee. §79(b)(1). Of course, the preferential provisions of §79 do not apply to insurance in excess of the maximum amount of group-term insurance allowable under the applicable state law. Reg. §1.79-1(e).

The provisions of §79(a) govern the income taxation of the cost of group-term life insurance whether or not the employee has assigned his or her interest in the insurance. Rev. Rul. 73-174, 1973-1 C.B. 43. Each time the employer pays a premium on the insurance, the employee receives additional compensation. Rev. Rul. 76-490, 1976-2 C.B. 300 (gift tax).

§6.72.1. Planning with Group-Term Insurance

The current income, gift, and estate tax rules encourage the assignment of group-term insurance to an irrevocable life insurance trust. Accordingly, group-term insurance is often included among the policies that a client assigns to an irrevocable life insurance trust. However, a client should understand that group-term insurance is not a secure source of death benefits. Group plans may be terminated by the employer and coverage terminates if the employment relationship ends. An employer's payment of premiums on group-term insurance is compensation to the employee that continues to qualify for the limited exclusion under §79 although the insurance has been assigned. Little, if any, gift tax results from the assignment of group-term insurance to an irrevocable life insurance trust. First, group-term insurance usually has a low value — typically the remaining unearned premium. Second, the beneficiaries are usually given *Crummey* withdrawal powers sufficient to allow annual gift tax exclusions. The assignment of group-term insurance to a properly drafted irrevocable life insurance trust may insulate the proceeds from inclusion in the estates of the insured and the insured's spouse. Of course, if the insured dies within three years of assigning the insurance, the insurance proceeds are includible in the estate of the insured. (If the insured is the controlling shareholder, the employer's incidents of ownership will be attributed to the insured under Reg. §20.2042-1(c)(6) and the insurance will be included in the estate of the insured). If the insured dies within three years of transferring the insurance to the trust, the noninsured spouse is commonly given an interest in the trust sufficient to support a QTIP marital deduction in order to allow payment of the estate tax to be deferred until the death of the insured's spouse. Otherwise no portion of the trust should be included in the estate of the noninsured surviving spouse.

§6.72.2. Insurance on Spouses and Children

In general, the cost of employer-provided group-term life insurance on the life of an employee's spouse and children is includible in the employee's gross income. Here again, the cost is calculated under the Table I rate schedule. Reg. §1.79-3(d)(2). *See* Table 6-3 at §6.72.9. However, the cost of up to $2,000 of group-term insurance on their lives is considered incidental and is not includible in the employee's gross income. Reg. §1.61-2(d)(2)(ii)(b). The amount of group-term insurance on the life of the employee's spouse or children is not taken into account in applying the rules of §79 since it is not insurance on the life of the employee. Reg. §1.79-3(f)(2).

§6.72.3. Nondiscrimination Rules

In the case of a discriminatory group-term life insurance plan, §79(a)(1) does not apply with respect to any key employee. §79(d)(1). For this purpose a discriminatory plan is one that discriminates regarding either eligibility to participate or as to benefits. §79(d)(2). More particularly, §79(a)(1) would not apply to a plan that either (a) discriminated in favor of key employees as to eligibility to participate or (b) discriminated in favor of key employees as to the amount and type of benefits.

For the purposes of the nondiscrimination rules, a *key employee* is an employee who, at any time during the present year or any of the four preceding tax years was (or a retired employee who at the time of retirement was):

1. An officer of the employer whose annual compensation is more than $45,000;
2. One of the ten employees paid more than $30,000 per year and owning (applying the attribution rules of §318) the largest interests in the business;
3. A five percent owner of the employer, or;
4. A one percent owner of the employer who is paid more than $150,000 per year.

§6.72.4. Nondiscrimination Rules as to Eligibility

Under §72(d)(3)(a) the nondiscriminatory standards regarding eligibility are satisfied if the plan meets any of the following four criteria:

1. The plan benefits 70 percent or more of all employees;
2. At least 85 percent of all employees who participate are not key employees;
3. The plan benefits employees who qualify under a classification established by the employer and found by the Secretary not to be discriminatory; or

4. In the case of a plan that is part of a cafeteria plan, the requirements applicable to cafeteria plans, §125, are satisfied.

In determining whether the foregoing requirements are satisfied, §79(d)(3)(B) allows several classes of employees to be excluded from consideration. They are: employees who have not completed three years of service; part-time or seasonal employees; employees who are included in a collective bargaining agreement, if the benefits of the plan were the subject of bargaining between the employer and the employee group; and employees who are nonresident aliens and receive no earned income from within the United States.

§6.72.5. Nondiscrimination Rules as to Benefits

A group-term plan must make all of the benefits that are available to key employees available to all other employees. A plan does not discriminate as to benefits if the insurance made available to nonkey employees is a multiple of total or regular compensation that is equal to or greater than the multiple that applies to key employees. Reg. §1.79-4T, A-9.

Complex addititional requirements were imposed by §89, which was added by the 1986 Act and, providentially, repealed in 1989 by P.L. 101-140.

§6.72.6. Basic Requirements

In order to qualify as group-term life insurance it must be part of a group-term insurance plan that meets the technical requirements set out in the regulations issued under §79. Paraphrased, the basic requirements set forth in Reg. §1.79-1(a) are the following:

1. The insurance provides a general death benefit that is excludable from gross income under §101(a);
2. The insurance is provided to a group of employees;
3. The insurance is provided under a policy carried directly or indirectly by the employer;
4. The amount of insurance provided to each employee is computed under a formula that precludes individual selection (*i.e.*, the formula must be based on factors such as age, years of service, compensation, or position).

Health and accident insurance and other policies that do not provide a general death benefit do not satisfy the first requirement.

In general, the group life insurance must be provided to at least ten full-time employees in order to meet the second requirement. Reg. §1.79-1(c)(1). However, term insurance provided to a group of less than ten employees will qualify if (1) it is provided to all full-time employees, (2) the amount of insurance is computed either as a uniform percentage of compensation or on the basis of coverage brackets established by the insurer, and (3) evidence of insurability affecting an employee's eligibility is limited to a medical questionnaire completed by the employee. Reg. §1.79-1(c)(2). Term insurance provided to a group of less than ten employees will also qualify if (1) it is provided under a common plan of two or more unrelated employers, (2) the insurance is restricted to and mandatory for all employees who belong to or are represented by an organization (such as a union) that carries on substantial activities in addition to obtaining insurance, and (3) evidence of insurability does not affect an employee's eligibility. Reg. §1.79-1(c)(3).

In order to prevent individual selection, each element of the formula used to determine the amount of insurance must be structured so as to apply to more than one person. *William S. Towne,* 78 T.C. 791 (1982). In *Towne* the Tax Court upheld the disqualification of a plan that placed all employees but the president in one class, members of which were provided with life insurance coverage equal to their salary up to a maximum of $25,000, while the president was in a second class, members of which received an additional $500,000 of insurance coverage.

§6.72.7. Plans That Include Permanent Benefits

Prior to the revisions of the Regulations in 1979 and 1983, qualifying group-term insurance and permanent benefits were more frequently provided by an employer to key employees. The revised Regulations now define "permanent benefit," Reg. §1.79-0, impose certain requirements regarding the combination of group-term and permanent benefits, Reg. §1.79-1(b), and define the amount that an employee is required to include in income with respect to permanent benefits, Reg. §1.79-1(d). Of course, the nondiscrimination rules make it virtually impossible to provide tax advantaged permanent benefits to key employees in conjunction with a group-term plan. An employer is more likely, instead, to increase the compensation of a key employee in order to enable him or her to acquire additional permanent insurance.

§6.72.8. Who Are "Employees"?

Group-term life insurance may be provided only to employees. The common law rules for determining the existence of an employer-employee relationship provide the primary guide for resolving the question of whether or not a particular individual is an employee. Regs. §§1.79-0, 31.3401(c)-1. Clearly, a sole proprietor or partner is not an employee. A director of a corporation is also not an employee of the corporation. Reg. §31.3401(c)-1(f), *accord, M. A. Enright,* 56 T.C. 1261 (1971). Similarly, a trustee, executor, or other fiduciary is generally not considered to be an employee. Rev. Rul. 69-657, 1969-2 C.B. 189.

§6.72.9. Determining the Amount Includible in Income

For income tax purposes the cost of any group-term life insurance provided to an employee after 1988 is determined according to the Table I rate schedule set forth in Table 6-3 below and not by the actual cost of the insurance. The table appears in Reg. §1.79-3T. With respect to tax years beginning before 1989 the cost of group-term insurance provided to an employee over 64 was considered to be the same as the cost of insurance provided to persons in the five-year age bracket of 60 to 64. Former §79(c). For later years the cost of group-term insurance must be determined "on the basis of uniform premiums (computed on the basis of five-year age brackets) prescribed by regulations by the Secretary." §79(c). Table I, reflecting the cost of group-term insurance for years prior to 1989, is published in Reg. §1.79-3(d)(2).

Example 6-31 illustrates how the cost of group-term insurance is calculated under Table I (Table 6-3).

Table 6-3
Uniform Premiums for $1,000 of Group-Term Life Insurance Protection (Table I, Reg. §1.79-3T)

5-Year Age Bracket	*Cost per $1,000 of protection for 1-month period*
Under 30	.08
30 to 34	.09
35 to 39	.11
40 to 44	.17
45 to 49	.29
50 to 54	.48
55 to 59	.75
60 to 64	$1.17
65 to 69	$2.10
70 and above	$3.76

Example 6-31. Employer, Inc., pays the entire cost of a $100,000 group-term life insurance on the life of its general counsel, *X*, who is 45 years old. *X* has designated her husband as beneficiary of the insurance. The amount included in *X*'s gross income for the taxable year is calculated as follows:

Amount of group-term insurance	$100,000
Less: Tax-free amount	– 50,000
Amount of insurance subject to tax	$ 50,000
Table I cost of $1,000 of insurance per year (12 × $0.29) 3.48	
Amount includible in gross income (50 × $3.48)	$ 174

Any amount that *X* had contributed toward the cost of the insurance would be deducted from $174 in determining the amount includible in her gross income. None of the cost of the insurance would be taxed to her if the policy designated her employer or a charity as beneficiary.

§6.72.10. Assignment

The irrevocable assignment of group-term insurance is a particularly attractive estate planning tool because it permits a prospectively large item to be eliminated from the insured's gross estate at little or no gift tax cost. In general, group-term insurance is subject to the same gift and estate tax rules as other forms of life insurance. As indicated in §6.72.11, care must be exercised to determine that the group-term insurance is assignable under the group policy and the state law.

§6.72.11. Estate Tax

Some of the special estate questions that arise because of the particular characteristics of group-term insurance have been resolved by the IRS largely in the taxpayer's favor. To begin with, in 1968 the IRS ruled that the proceeds of an employer-provided group policy would not be included in the employee's gross estate under §2042 if the employee had irrevocably assigned all of his or her interests in the insurance prior to death. Rev. Rul. 68-334, 1968-1 C.B. 403, *restated and superseded,* Rev. Rul. 69-54, 1969-1 C.B. 221, *modified,* Rev. Rul. 72-307, 1972-1 C.B. 307. Following the issuance of Rev. Rul. 69-54, most states adopted statutes that expressly authorize the assignment of interests in group insurance. Unfortunately, however, some states limit the class of persons to whom such an assignment can be made. *E.g.,* Wash. Rev. Code §48.18.375 (1989). Even when assignments are permitted by state law, they may be barred by the terms of the master group policy. Before attempting to assign group-term insurance, the planner should be sure that assignments are permitted by the master policy. Unfortunately, it is not entirely safe to rely upon the description of the insurance contained in the certificate of insurance given to the insured employee. The certificate constitutes evidence of the insurance coverage but its terms may be subordinate to those of the master policy. *Poling v. North America Life & Casualty Co.,* 593 P.2d 568 (Wyo. 1979); *contra, Fittro v. Lincoln National Life Insurance Co.,* 757 P.2d 1374 (Wash. 1988) (group health coverage); *Estate of Max Gorby,* 53 T.C.80 (1969), *acq.,* 1970-1 C.B. xvi. If the master policy prohibits assignments, the employee may ask the employer to lift the prohibition. Employers and insurers commonly cooperate promptly to remove any restrictions on assignments.

Although Revenue Ruling 69-54 helped clear the air regarding the effect of assignments, some nagging doubts remained regarding the effectiveness of an assignment of annually renewable term insurance under §2035. Subsection 2035(d)(2) requires insurance to be included in the insured's gross estate if the insured dies within three years following a transfer of the insurance. *See* §6.30. Planners were concerned that the IRS might treat each annual renewal as giving rise to "new" insurance each year. If so, the insurance could not be assigned more than one year prior to death and the proceeds would be includible in the estate of the insured in all cases. That concern was largely alleviated by a T.A.M. issued in 1980. LR 8034017. It concluded that the proceeds of an annually renewable group-term policy were *not* includible in the insured's gross estate when the insured assigned the insurance more than three years prior to death. In 1982 the IRS ruled that an employer's renewal of a group-term policy by payment of the annual premium did not give the employee any new rights in the insurance. Rev. Rul. 82-13, 1982-1 C.B. 132. Accordingly, the insurance was not includible in the estate of an employee who effectively assigned all interests in the insurance more than three years prior to death. The result of the ruling hinged on the nature of the policy, which provided for automatic renewal upon payment of the annual premium. Of course, the mere payment of premiums on group-term insurance by the employer within three years of the employee's death does not cause inclusion of the premiums or the insurance.

A change of position by the IRS on another issue provides further encouragement for the assignment of group-term insurance. The IRS first ruled that an insured employee could not effectively assign an interest in group insurance that was provided at the time of the employee's death under a policy that was not in effect when the assignment was made. Rev. Rul. 79-231, 1979-2 C.B. 323. Revenue Ruling 79-231 involved an employee who, in 1971, assigned to his wife all of his interest in any life insurance that might be provided by his employer. The assignment was made more than three years prior to his death during a time when his group insurance was provided under a master policy issued by Company *Y.* In 1977 the employer terminated the master policy with Company *Y* and entered into a new master policy with Company *Z.* However, the terms of the master policies were identical in all relevant respects. Shortly after the master policy with Company *Z* became effective, the employee assigned all of his interest in it to his wife. As luck would have it, the employee died within three years of that assignment. Unhappily, the IRS ruled that the assignment that the employee made in 1971 was ineffective to transfer his rights in the insurance that was provided by the master policy subsequently issued by Company *Z.* According to the IRS, the employee could not make such an "anticipatory assignment" of insurance that was not in effect at the time. Accordingly, it held that the insurance was not assigned until 1977, as a result of which it was includible in the insured's estate under §2035.

Revenue Ruling 79-231 was revoked by the IRS less than a year after it was issued and a contrary ruling issued. Rev. Rul. 80-289, 1980-2 C.B. 270. The later ruling held upon identical facts that "the [second] assignment will not be treated as a transfer under Section 2035 of the code." Id. In it the IRS "maintains the view that the anticipatory assignment was not technically effective as a present transfer of the decedent's rights in the policy issued by Company *Z.* Nevertheless, the IRS believes that the assignment in 1977 to *D*'s spouse, the object of the anticipatory assignment in 1971, should not cause the value of the proceeds to be includible in the gross estate of the decedent under section 2035 where the assignment was necessitated by the change of the employer's master insurance carrier and the new arrangement is identical in all relevant aspects to the previous arrangement with Company *Y.*" Similar problems could arise if, subsequent to an assignment, a group policy is renewed or the amount of insurance is increased, as happens when the amount of coverage is tied to the employee's salary or position. The assignment of interests in existing group policies should attempt to deal with the problem by providing that the assignment covers all interests in the existing group insurance, all interests in group insurance provided by any renewal or replacement, and all changes in the amount of the insurance. Such an explicit assignment, if made more than three years prior to the assignor's death, should help insulate the proceeds of the insurance from inclusion in the insured's gross estate.

§6.72.12. Gift Tax

The amount of a gift resulting from the assignment of group-term insurance depends upon all of the circumstances, including the length of time for which the premiums have been paid, the extent to which the employer is obligated to make future payments, and the health of the insured. An assignment of group-term insurance may involve a gift composed of one or more of the following components:

1. An amount equivalent to the cost of a term policy for the unexpired portion of the period through which the premium on the group policy had been paid at the time of assignment (a proportionate part of the premium actually paid allocable to the cost of the unexpired period is an acceptable method of valuing this interest. Reg. §25.2512-6(a). Because that amount may be difficult or impossible to determine, it may be appropriate to use the Table I cost for this purpose);
2. The value of any right the assignment may carry with it to require the assignor or another person to make future premium payments; and
3. Any additional value the insurance may have because of the insured's poor health.

Further gifts will occur as later premiums are paid directly or indirectly by the employer or other third party. Thus, where the insured's employer is not obligated to pay future premiums on group-term insurance that the employee has assigned, any future premium payments involve future indirect gifts by the employee to the assignee. Rev. Rul. 76-490, 1976-2 C.B. 300. On the other hand, the assignment of a group-term policy on the last day of the premium payment period does not involve a present gift where the employer is not obligated to make further premium payments. Id.

Without any analysis Revenue Ruling 76-490 incorrectly concluded that the payment of future premiums on group-term insurance assigned to a trust would qualify for the annual gift tax exclusion. The conclusion is incorrect if, as indicated by the facts, the beneficiary was not entitled to any current benefits in the trust. Apparently, the trustee was required to retain the insurance until the death of the insured when the proceeds would be distributed to the beneficiary. A later ruling properly holds that an annual exclusion is not available with respect to the employer's payment of premiums when the trustee of the insurance trust will retain the proceeds in trust following the death of the insured. Rev. Rul. 79-47, 1979-1 C.B. 312. The availability of the annual exclusion for a transfer of insurance to a trust turns on the extent of the beneficiary's present interests in the trust and not on whether or not the proceeds are immediately distributable by the trustee when the insured dies. When a trustee is required to retain insurance and the beneficiary is not entitled to any current benefits under the trust, the beneficiary does not have a present interest in the insurance or in subsequent premium payments. *Commissioner v. Warner,* 127 F.2d 913 (9th Cir. 1942); Reg. §25.2503-3(c), example 2. Of course, the original transfer to the trust and the payment of subsequent premiums may qualify for the annual exclusion if the beneficiary has a *Crummey* power to withdraw property as it is added to the trust. *See* LR 8006109 and LR 8021058; *see also* §7.37.7.

§6.72.13. Group-Term Life Insurance: Retired Lives Reserve (RLR)

Retired lives reserve (RLR) plans, promoted in the 1970s and early 1980s, are of interest largely for historic reasons. RLR plans were intended to allow large amounts of post-retirement life insurance coverage to be provided to key employees at no tax cost. Under an RLR plan an employer paid the cost of providing current group-term insurance and made a contribution to a reserve fund or trust that would pay the cost of continuing the group-term insurance after an employee retired. The employer's contributions to the reserve fund, plus the tax-free income earned by the fund, were designed to be sufficient to pay the cost of providing group-term insurance to the retired employees covered by the plan. Thus, RLR plans were premised on the following assumptions: (1) that the employer's contributions to a reserve fund were currently deductible; (2) that the earnings of the reserve fund were nontaxable; (3) that disproportionately large amounts of life insurance could be provided to key employees; and (4) that none of the contributions or earnings of the plan would be included in the income of a retired employee. The 1984 Act dashed any hopes that the assumptions were justified. As matters now stand, deductions to reserve funds are limited, nondiscrimination rules apply to life insurance coverage, and the cost of group-term insurance in excess of $50,000 provided to retired employees is income to them. Group-term insurance to which §79 applies is not subject to §83. §83(e)(5). Specifically, contributions to a reserve account for post-retirement life insurance coverage is limited to the amount required to provide $50,000 of life insurance to the employee. §§419, 419A(c), 419A(e). In addition, §419A(e)(1) requires life insurance plans to comply with the nondiscrimination provisions of §505(b). The changes largely eliminated the attractiveness of RLR plans.

Insurance provided an employee under an RLR plan was probably assignable to the same extent as regular group-term insurance. *See*

§6.72.10. Accordingly, an employee should be able to remove the insurance from the employee's estate by an assignment made more than three years prior to death. However, the value of the insurance for gift tax purposes is uncertain. RLR proponents argued that the insurance had no greater value than group-term insurance that the employer was not obligated to continue. *See* Rev. Rul. 76-490, 1976-2 C.B. 300, discussed at §6.72.12. On the other hand, the insurance might have had significantly greater value, either at the time of the assignment or when the employee retires and the right to continued coverage provided by the reserve becomes fixed. The IRS might have contended that a gift of the insurance included a portion of the reserve fund already paid in and allocable to the insurance on the employee's life. Also, the gift might have had a greater value if the employer were obligated to make future premium payments and contributions to the reserve fund. In fact, if the employer were obligated to continue the insurance until the employee retires and to continue contributing to the reserve fund, a transfer of the insurance might be treated as a gift of the right to receive the face amount of the policy when the employee dies. The present value of the right to receive a specified amount upon the death of a person may be calculated by applying the appropriate actuarial factor. At the least, an employee who had assigned his or her RLR insurance made gifts as future premiums and contributions to the reserve fund were paid by the employer.

§6.73. Minimum-Deposit Life Insurance Plans

A minimum-deposit plan involves borrowing against the increase in cash value of a policy to pay part or all of the annual premiums. The attractiveness of minimum-deposit plans was based upon the availability of the cash value of a policy to fund substantial policy loans *and* the deductibility, for income tax purposes, of continually increasing interest payments. Of course, the amount of insurance protection was reduced by the amount borrowed against the policy. These problems plague any insurance plan that depends heavily on borrowing against policy values (the so-called "leveraged" plans). As one commentator has observed, "Some of its disadvantages (notably decreasing insurance) have been overcome by design improvements, but it still has problems. The most severe is that it does not produce policies that remain in force. At some point it becomes too cumbersome, too expensive, or both, and the insured cancels it." J. Munch, Financial and Estate Planning With Life Insurance Products, ¶21.2.2 (1990).

The attractiveness of minimum-deposit plans was virtually eliminated by changes in the Code that disallow a deduction for personal interest paid by individuals, §163(h), and for interest paid by businesses on loans of more than $50,000 against a policy on the life of an employee or officer, §264(a).

Prior to the 1986 Act, interest paid on loans that were directly or indirectly used to pay premiums on policies issued after August 6, 1963 was deductible only if the payment satisfied one of the exceptions to the general rule. In general the only reliable and useful exception for planning purposes was the "4-in-7" exception, which requires that at least four of the first seven premiums be paid with funds that are not borrowed. *See* §264(c)(1), discussed at §6.60.3. Accordingly, most minimum-deposit plans assumed that the owner will pay premiums for four of the first seven years without borrowing and that the interest payments would be deductible. The most advantageous illustrations assumed that premiums are paid without borrowing in the first, fifth, sixth, and seventh years. Hill & McKay, The Flowering of Financed Life Insurance, 118 Tr. & Est. 59, 62 (1979). Of course, in order to preserve their use of funds as long as possible, insurers generally preferred that the owner paid the first four premiums without borrowing.

§6.74. Single-Premium Whole Life

As its name suggests, a single large premium pays the entire cost of a single-premium policy. Until the 1988 Act changed the rules, including the phased-in elimination of the deduction for personal interest payments, single-premium policies were marketed aggressively because of their tax-free investment features. A policy typically provided for a guaranteed high rate of interest to be credited on the policy for an initial period (typically the first five years), which could be borrowed by the policy owner. For example, an individual might pay a single premium of $100,000 on a policy that guaranteed a return of ten percent. Under the old rules the owner could borrow the $10,000 increase in value each year tax-free and the interest paid with respect to the loan would be deductible. With respect to a single-premium policy issued after June 21, 1988, the owner would be required to include the loans in his or her income. In addition, the interest on most policy loans is entirely nondeductible after 1990. (This factor may cause the owner to explore ways of reducing the interest cost, which might be possible if the policy were exchanged for another policy with more favorable terms. *See* §6.65.) Perhaps of greater importance, a single-premium policy would be a modified endowment contract under §7702A. Accordingly, loans (or other distributions) would be treated as income under §72(e) to the extent the cash surrender value of the policy immediately before a loan exceeded the amount of the investment in the contract (*i.e.,* the single premium). *See* §§72(e)(2)(B), (3)(A), (4)(A), (10)(A).

Single-premium policies are subject to the normal gift and estate tax rules. Of course, in the case of such a policy, the gift tax value is likely to be high — except to the extent there have been loans against the policy.

§6.75. SECOND-TO-DIE OR SURVIVORSHIP WHOLE LIFE

The adoption of the unlimited marital deduction largely relieved the liquidity needs of the estate of the spouse first-to-die. However, use of the marital deduction simply defers the time for payment of the estate tax until the death of the survivor, when the effect of increases in value may require the payment of a substantially greater tax. The acquisition of a large amount of survivorship life insurance, under which the death benefit is payable on the death of the survivor of two insured persons, has become a popular way to provide liquidity upon the death of the survivor. Insurance advisors commonly recommend that large amounts of insurance be divided among two or more insurers. Such diversification lessens financial and investment risks and may reduce the underwriting requirements. Wilshinsky, Life Insurance: A New Dimension in Estate Planning, 130 Tr. & Est. 10, 16 (June 1991). Note, however, that serious complications can arise if the marriage of the husband and wife is dissolved. This problem is minimized if the policy or a rider allows the insurance to be split into two separate policies on the lives of the spouses. An additional charge may be made for such a rider. In the case of a split the contract or rider may require proof of insurability. The requirement is reasonable if one of the spouses was uninsurable.

The annual premium for a survivorship policy is significantly lower than that for either spouse alone. For example, the typical premium for a $1 million policy on the life of a nonsmoking male aged 65 and a nonsmoking female aged 60 are $35,000 and $22,000, respectively. The annual premium on a survivorship policy on the lives of a nonsmoking male (65) and a nonsmoking female (60) would be $13,000. Ford, Joint Life Insurance: It No Longer Matters Who Dies First, 3 Prob. & Prop. 42 (Nov./Dec. 1989).

Large survivorship policies are particularly attractive to couples with large estates that lack liquidity, such as estates that consist mainly of small businesses or other unique properties. In order to insulate the proceeds from the estate tax, survivorship policies are commonly acquired by or assigned to irrevocable life insurance trusts. Irrevocable life insurance trusts holding survivorship policies are usually designed so that gifts to the trust will qualify for sufficient annual exclusions to eliminate any gift tax liability. The trusts may be insulated from the GSTT by allocating the insured's GSTT exemption to the premium payments or assuring that the premium payments qualify as nontaxable transfers for purposes of §2642(c).

Because of the competitiveness of the market and the complexity of the options available with respect to the features of a survivorship policy, including the payment of premiums, it is prudent to consult with an expert life insurance advisor before advising a client with regard to the acquisition of a policy.

Under some charitable gift plans survivorship policies are used to "replace" the economic value of property that was contributed to charity. *See* §8.20.3. For example, a client may transfer substantially appreciated property that generates relatively little current income to a charitable remainder trust. The donor will benefit from a charitable deduction for income and gift tax purposes. In addition, the donor will receive a higher current income after the trustee sells the contributed property and reinvests the proceeds in property that produces a greater return. The donor then uses some of the income from the trust to fund premium payments on "replacement" policies owned by an irrevocable trust or by adult children.

§6.76. Leased Life Insurance

In the mid-1960s some promoters touted "leased life insurance" plans under which the owner of a policy assigned it to a leasing company in exchange for its cash surrender value but retained the right to designate the beneficiary. The company then "leased" the policy back to the assignor for a level annual charge in exchange for which the company agreed to pay the annual premiums and to pay the face amount of the policy to the designated beneficiary. The annual charge represented the difference between the increase in the cash surrender value and the premium, plus the sum of the interest expense incurred by the leasing company in borrowing the cash surrender value of the policy, the cost of other expenses, and a profit. Stripped to its bare essentials the plan represented a clever attempt to allow the owner of a policy to claim an interest deduction for the excess of the annual premium over the increase in the cash surrender value. In *Murray Kay,* 44 T.C. 660 (1965), the Tax Court considered the lessor to be the agent of the lessee and allowed a deduction for the portion of the annual charge that represented interest paid to the insurer. However, an interest deduction was later held not allowable when the agreement did not establish an indebtedness on the part of the lessee. Rev. Rul. 66-298, 1966-2 C.B. 48. Aside from the absence of tax advantages, a leased life insurance plan does not adequately protect the interests of the lessee. Snyder, Leading a Tax-Sheltered Life, N.Y.U., 25th Inst. Fed. Tax. 765, 776-779 (1976). Also, the unavailability of a deduction for personal interest would make the plan unattractive.

§6.77. Veterans' Life Insurance

The government has traditionally made a limited amount of life insurance available to members of the armed forces during active duty at little or no cost. Earlier programs allowed veterans to continue the insurance after separation from service under a variety of low cost term or cash value policies. The plan adopted by Congress in 1965 allowed members to purchase Servicemen's Group Insurance coverage of up to $15,000 from a large number of participating private insurance companies at a uniform premium cost. 38 U.S.C. §§765-776 (1988). However, until 1974 Servicemen's Group Insurance could only be converted into cash value policies that were available through the participating life insurance companies. 38 U.S.C. §768(c), *repealed by* Pub. L. 93-289 §5(a)(5), 88 Stat. 168 (1974). In 1974 Congress increased the maximum to $20,000 and authorized conversion to a new type of insurance, Veterans' Group Life Insurance. 38 U.S.C. §777. However, the only form of Veterans' Group Life Insurance available upon separation from service is a five-year nonparticipating and nonrenewable term policy. 38 U.S.C. §777(b) (1988).

The proceeds of life insurance policies issued under the World War Veterans' Act of 1924, the National Service Life Insurance Act of 1940, and the Servicemen's Indemnity Act of 1951 are includible in the estate of the deceased serviceperson or veteran. Rev. Rul. 55-622, 1955-2 C.B. 385. The proceeds of Servicemen's Group Life Insurance and Veterans' Group Life Insurance policies are also no doubt subject to inclusion in the gross estate of a deceased serviceperson or veteran. Inclusion of the proceeds of the latter types of policies in the gross estate of the insured under §2042(2) is inevitable because the insured is the only person who may designate a beneficiary and neither the insurance nor any of the benefits under it may be assigned. 38 C.F.R. §§9.16, 9.20 (1990).

In *Wissner v. Wissner,* 338 U.S. 655 (1950), the Supreme Court held in a 5-to-3 decision that the spouse of a member or veteran of the armed services did not acquire an interest in a National Service Life Insurance policy under a state's community property law. It reasoned that Congress intended to provide "a uniform and comprehensive system of life insurance for members and veterans of the armed forces" and to give the insured the exclusive right to name the beneficiary. Id. at 658. From that the Court concluded that it would frustrate the intent of Congress to recognize that a member's spouse had a community property interest in a government policy. The program was held to be a constitutional exercise of the congressional power over national defense. Because the proceeds of a veteran's policy are not community property they are fully includible in his or her gross estate under §2042(2). *Estate of Hugh C. Hutson,* 49 T.C. 495 (1968). Consistent with that rule, the proceeds of a veteran's policy were not treated as community property for purposes of calculating the pre-1982 maximum allowable marital deduction. *Hunt v. United States,* 59-2 U.S.T.C. ¶11, 891, 4 A.F.T.R.2d ¶6051 (E.D. Tex. 1959).

§6.78. Death Benefit Only Plans

Employment contracts sometimes provide for the payment of a lump sum or an annuity to the specified surviving family members of employees who die while actively employed. Unlike many other fringe benefits, the value of such death benefit only plans is seldom included in a deceased employee's estate. That result has followed whether the plan was one of a publicly-held corporation, such as IBM, or one provided by a closely-held company. There is, of course, less risk of inclusion if the plan is one provided by a large employer to certain classes of employees (a so-called "involuntary" plan). Death benefit only plans provided by closely-held companies involve more risk. Indeed, *Estate of Stanton A. Levin,* 90 T.C. 171 (1988), indicates that inclusion will result — at least where the employee was the controlling shareholder.

The death benefit paid under such plans is analogous to the group insurance provided by some employers that is payable to beneficiaries designated by the employer and not the employee. *See* §6.72. However, there is an important difference in the income taxation of the payments: Amounts payable under death benefit plans are taxed as income in respect of a decedent to the extent they exceed $5,000. *See* §§101(b), 691(a). Accordingly, substantially all of the amounts paid under a death benefit plan are included in the recipient's gross income. Of course, if the payments are included in the deceased employee's gross estate, the recipient is allowed an income tax deduction under §691(c) for the estate tax attributable to the benefits. In contrast, the proceeds of group-term insurance are generally not included in the recipient's gross income. *See* §101(a). *See also* §6.51.

§6.78.1. Estate Tax, General

The courts have rarely required pure death benefits to be included in the employee's gross estate. Inclusion is generally not required by §2039, which only applies to contracts or agreements under which the decedent was, or might become, entitled to receive an annuity or other lifetime benefit. For the purpose of determining whether or not the decedent held such a right, consideration is given to "any combination of arrangements, understandings or plans arising by reason of the decedent's employment." Reg. §20.2039-1(b)(ii). Note, however, that

§2039(a) is concerned only with post-retirement benefits. Contractual provisions for payment of a salary or disability benefits generally are not taken into account. *Estate of Schelberg v. Commissioner,* 612 F.2d 25 (2d Cir. 1979) (disability benefits); *Estate of Murray J. Siegel,* 74 T.C. 613 (1980) (disability benefits); *Estate of Firmin D. Fusz,* 46 T.C. 214 (1966), *acq.,* 1967-2 C.B. 2 (salary). More important, the IRS has ruled that benefits accruing under qualified plans are not to be considered together with rights arising under nonqualified plans (*e.g.,* death benefit only plans). Rev. Rul. 76-380, 1976-2 C.B. 270 (qualified retirement plan is not aggregated with nonqualified survivor's income benefit plan for purposes of determining includibility of the value of the survivor's benefits under §2039). Accordingly, insofar as §2039 is concerned, it is "safe" to provide an employee with a death benefit only plan and a qualified retirement plan.

§6.78.2. §2033

Courts have also generally not required inclusion of pure death benefits under §2033 whether or not the benefits were subject to the unilateral control of the employer (*i.e.,* benefits were revocable). In the typical case exclusion is based on the employee's lack of any property interest in the benefits and lack of control over their disposition following his or her death. *E.g., Estate of Tully v. United States,* 528 F.2d 1401 (Ct. Cl. 1976); *Kramer v. United States,* 406 F.2d 1363 (Ct. Cl. 1969). Even when the employee has a lifetime interest in the benefits, inclusion under §2033 is precluded because the interest terminates upon the employee's death. *See Estate of Edward H. Wadewitz,* 39 T.C. 925 (1963), *aff'd on other grounds,* 339 F.2d 980 (7th Cir. 1964) (inclusion required under §2039).

§6.78.3. "Transfer" Sections, §§2035-2038

Inclusion under one or more of the transfer sections, §§2035-2038, is possible if the decedent made the requisite transfer of an interest in the benefits and retained prohibited controls or interests. Several courts have found that the employee's agreement to render future services in exchange for a compensation package that included the death benefit constituted a transfer for purposes of these sections. *E.g., Estate of Tully v. United States,* 528 F.2d 1401 (Ct. Cl. 1976); *Estate of Stanton A. Levin,* 90 T.C. 171 (1988). The conclusion seems correct, but it does not itself require inclusion under any of the transfer sections. Indeed, more often than not the benefits have been excluded from the employee's estate for failure to satisfy other requirements of the transfer sections.

§6.78.4. §2035

Prior to the 1981 amendment of §2035, pure death benefits paid under contracts entered into within three years of death were potentially includible in the employee's gross estate under §2035. *See Estate of Bernard L. Porter,* 54 T.C. 1066 (1970), *aff'd,* 442 F.2d 915 (1st Cir. 1971) (death benefits paid under contracts entered into three weeks prior to decedent's death with three closely-held corporations were included under §2035). The changes made by the 1981 Act may preclude inclusion of such benefits. In the post-1981 era, transfers made within three years of death are includible only to the extent provided in §2035(d)(2). In the ordinary case, death benefits are not within the scope of §2035(d)(2). However, the risk of inclusion under §§2035 and 2038 exists for contracts entered into within three years of death does exist when the decedent was a controlling shareholder and a member of the board of directors. *See* §6.78.7.

§6.78.5. §2036

Pure death benefits may not be includible in the employee's gross estate under §2036. In 1987 the IRS seemed to concede as much in a T.A.M. that held that a death benefit payable to an irrevocable trust was not includible in the deceased employee's estate although he was the controlling shareholder and a member of the board of directors. LR 8701003 (TAM). In reaching that conclusion, the T.A.M. pointed out that the powers held by the majority shareholder were subject to fiduciary obligations to the other shareholders, citing *United States v. Byrum,* 408 U.S. 125 (1972). In addition, §2036(a)(1) may not appropriately apply to death benefit only plans because the employee cannot possess or enjoy any of the benefits during his or her lifetime — they only arise following death. Indeed, because the covered employees cannot enjoy any of the benefits the plans are sometimes called "pure" death benefit plans. The power of the employee to affect the beneficial enjoyment of the benefits by changing the terms of the employment agreement with the employer has not generally been recognized as sufficient to require inclusion under §2036(a)(2). However, the case for inclusion is stronger where the decedent was the controlling shareholder and a member of the board of directors. *Estate of Stanton A. Levin,* 90 T.C. 723 (1988), required inclusion under §2038 in such a case. *See* §6.78.7. Even in such a case, inclusion may not be proper because §2036(a)(2) "does not include a power over the transferred property itself which does not affect the enjoyment of the income received or earned during the decedent's life." Reg. §20.2036-1(b)(3).

§6.78.6. §2037

Inclusion under §2037 is possible if the employee retains a reversionary interest in the benefits, the value of which immediately before the employee's death exceeds five percent of the value of the benefits. §2037(a). Thus, LR 7802002 (TAM) held that death benefits were includible in the employee's estate where the benefits were payable to the employee's estate if he was not survived by a spouse. For purposes of §2037 a reversionary interest includes a possibility that the property transferred by the decedent will return to the transferor or the transferor's estate. §2037(b)(1). However, the reach of §2037 is avoided by precluding payment of the benefits to the employee's estate. Because the right to the benefits arises after the employee's death there is no need to bar their payment *to* the employee.

§6.78.7. §2038(a)(1)

Technical Advice Memorandum, LR 8701003, discussed in §6.78.5, does not require the inclusion of a death benefit plan in the estate of the deceased majority shareholder. Curiously, at about the same time LR 8701003 was issued the IRS took the contrary position in a case before the Tax Court. In *Estate of Stanton A. Levin,* 90 T.C. 171 (1988), the IRS successfully argued that §2038 required a pure death benefit to be included in the estate of a deceased employee because the employee held the power, exercisable alone or in conjunction with another person, to alter, amend, revoke, or terminate the enjoyment of the benefits. In *Levin* the decedent owned 80 percent of the voting stock of his employer, Marstan Industries, Inc., and was a member of its board of directors. The Tax Court held that the "Decedent's ability to amend or revoke the plan in conjunction with other Marstan board members is a sufficient 'power' to compel inclusion of the value of the post mortem annuity in the decedent's estate." 90 T.C. at 730-731. Note, however, that the effect of including the value of benefits payable to the employee's surviving spouse may be offset by the availability of a marital deduction. *See* §2056(b)(7). *See also* §5.23.

For purposes of §2038 an employee's power to affect the enjoyment of the benefits by a drastic action such as divorcing a spouse, terminating employment, or renegotiating the amount of his or her salary is probably not a retained power sufficient to require inclusion. *Estate of Tully,* 528 F.2d 1401 (Ct. Cl. 1976). The position taken by the Court of Claims in *Tully* is consistent with the IRS's concession that the power to cancel employer-provided group insurance by terminating employment is not an incident of ownership for purposes of §2042(2). *See* §6.27.4. However, the retention of such powers may prevent the entry into a death benefit only plan from involving a completed gift to the designated beneficiary: In *Levin* the Tax Court held that the decedent did not make an inter vivos gift to his wife because the decedent "retained control over his wife's right to the post mortem annuity because he could defeat the transfer by terminating his employment with Marstan prior to his death, by divorcing his spouse, or by agreeing to terminate the plan." *Levin,* 90 T.C. at 732. The *Tully* court also found that the mere possibility of bilateral contract modification did not constitute a §2038(a)(1) power. *Tully,* 528 F.2d at 1405. *See also Kramer v. United States,* 406 F.2d 1363 (Ct. Cl. 1969). The Tax Court has held that an express retention by the employer and employee of the power to modify the terms of the agreement required inclusion of the death benefit under §2038(a)(1). *Estate of Murray J. Siegel,* 74 T.C. 613 (1980). The includibility of the benefit should not turn on the question of whether or not the power to modify the contract was expressly reserved by the parties — a contract may generally be modified by the parties although they have not expressly reserved the right to do so.

§6.78.8. Gift Tax

Until 1981 the IRS did not attempt to subject death benefit only plans to the gift tax. However, in declining to apply the estate tax to such benefits, some courts suggested that the contract entered into between the decedent and his or her employer involved a gift. *E.g., Estate of Tully v. United States,* 528 F.2d 1401, 1040 (Ct. Cl. 1976) ("Tully in substance, if not in form, made a gift of part of his future earnings to his wife.") Of course, the gift tax can only be imposed if the employee made a transfer of value. Moreover, the imposition of the gift tax depends upon the time at which the transfer becomes complete, the valuation of the interests transferred, and the availability of the annual exclusion. Perhaps because of its lack of success in subjecting pure death benefits to the estate tax, the IRS ruled that the employee makes a completed gift of the amount of the death benefit at the time of his or her death, when the gift first became susceptible of valuation. Rev. Rul. 81-31, 1981-1 C.B. 475. The ruling also holds that the gift qualifies for the annual exclusion under §2503(b). In A.O.D. 1990-026 the IRS announced that it would acquiesce in result only in *Estate of Anthony*

F. DiMarco, 87 T.C. 653 (1986) and would no longer follow Revenue Ruling 81-31 because of its inconsistency with Reg. §25.2511-2(f).

The position taken by the IRS in Revenue Ruling 81-31 was rejected by the Tax Court in *DiMarco,* which involved an uninsured, unfunded, noncontributory survivors benefit plan under which IBM paid three times the annual salary of a deceased employee to specified survivors in semimonthly payments of 12.5 percent of the employee's final monthly salary. The plan covered essentially all regular employees of IBM other than a small group of top executives. An employee had no control over the plan, which could be changed or terminated by IBM at any time. DiMarco became employed by IBM in 1950 and earned a salary of $5,250 per month at the time of his death in 1979. The IRS contended that at the time of his employment he made a gift that was completed at the time of his death, when it first became possible to value the gift. The Tax Court held that under Reg. §25.2511-2(f), "transfers of property do not become complete for gift tax purposes by reason of the death of the donor." It also held that "property must be valued and the gift tax imposed at the time a completed transfer of the property occurs" regardless of the difficulty of valuation. Finally, the court held that DiMarco neither had a property interest in the plan nor took any action that could constitute a transfer. The conclusions reached by the Tax Court are entirely proper in light of the characteristics of the IBM plan.

DiMarco should not be read to insulate all death benefit plans from imposition of the gift tax on an employee's execution of an employment agreement. If the employee has a greater interest in the plan or control over the benefits payable under it, the execution of the contract may involve a transfer of value by the employee. As mentioned above, several courts have reached that conclusion in pure death benefit cases arising under the estate tax. However, the transfer may be incomplete at the time the contract is executed because of the expressly or impliedly reserved power of the employer and employee to change its terms. *See* Reg. §25.2511-2(e). The difficulty of valuing such a gift led the IRS to the questionable conclusion in Revenue Ruling 81-31: that the gift was completed at the time of the employee's death when the amount of the gift first became susceptible of valuation.

The protection provided by the death benefit may involve a continuing indirect gift by the employee analogous to the indirect gifts made by an employee each time his or her employer pays the premium on group-term insurance that is owned by another party. *See* Rev. Rul. 76-490. *See also* §6.72.12. However, such indirect gifts would be difficult to value and subject to dispute in virtually every case. Although the death benefit is somewhat analogous to employer-provided term insurance, it presents a different problem as it does not involve the payment of premiums (or other amounts indicative of its value). Any continuing indirect gifts that are found to take place might qualify for the annual gift tax exclusion, depending on the terms of the employment contract and the manner in which the benefits were payable. By analogy to the group-term insurance cases, the annual exclusion may be available where the benefits are payable outright to an individual or to a trust in which an individual has a sufficient present interest.

Revenue Ruling 81-31 held that the employee's gift of the death benefit was not completed until the employee died, when, according to the IRS, the amount of the gift first became susceptible of valuation. The approach reached the IRS objective of subjecting the death benefit to a transfer tax. However, as the Tax Court held in *DiMarco,* the IRS approach was not consistent with the basic thrust of the gift tax. First, the difficulty of valuing a transfer generally does not cause it to be incomplete. Second, the IRS approach is inconsistent with the fundamental concept that the gift tax only applies to completed inter vivos transfers. That concept is evidenced by Reg. §25.2511-2(f), which states, "The relinquishment or termination of a power to change the beneficiaries of transferred property, occurring otherwise than by the death of the donor (the statute being confined to transfers by living donors), is regarded as the event which completes the gift and causes the tax to apply." The Ruling will probably also be rejected by other courts.

§6.78.9. Income Tax

> The courts have uniformly held that post-death payments to an employee's widow are to be treated as "income in respect of a decedent" despite the fact that under the terms of the employment contract, the employee would never be entitled to actual receipt of the income. *Estate of Nilssen v. United States,* 322 F. Supp. 260, 265 (D. Minn. 1971).

The income taxation of pure death benefits is relatively simple. The payments are not includible in the income of a deceased employee who did not have the right to receive them during his or her lifetime. Instead, payments under a death benefit only plan are taxable to the recipient as income in respect of a decedent under §691. Such a characterization is appropriate because the payments are solely attributable to the decedent's lifetime services and are not subject to any other contingencies. *See* Rev. Rul. 73-327, 1973-2 C.B. 214. Accordingly, the payments are includible in the recipient's gross income except to the extent of the special $5,000 exclusion allowed under §101(b) for payments made by an employer on account of an employee's death.

Prior to the 1986 Act a totally voluntary payment to the members of a deceased employee's family might have constituted a nontaxable gift under §102. Certainly a voluntary payment would have been excludable if it satisfied the test articulated in *Commissioner v. Duberstein,* 363 U.S. 278 (1960), that the gift proceed from detached and disinterested generosity or out of affection, respect, admiration, charity, or like impulses. Id. at 285. However, payments made to an employee's widow because of a perceived moral obligation were not gifts. *See, e.g., Margaret L. Sweeney,* 1987 T.C.M. ¶87,550. The addition of §102(c) to the Code by the 1986 Act may have ended the possibility that payments by an employer might be excluded as gifts: "Subsection (a) shall not exclude from gross income any amount transferred by or from an employer to, or for the benefit of, an employee." The IRS will no doubt argue that payments made to the survivors of a deceased employee were made "for the benefit of, an employee."

§6.78.10. Installment Payment of Death Benefit Taxed as Annuity

Where a death benefit is paid in periodic installments, it is subject to the rules of §72. In such a case, the $5,000 exclusion allowed by §101(b)(2) is treated as the employee's investment in the contract. The recipient is entitled to exclude a portion of each payment that bears the same relationship to the total payment as the investment in the contract bears to the total value of the benefit to be received. §72(b). Under a rule that applied to payments which began prior to July 1, 1986, if the amount receivable in three years was equal to or exceeded the amount of the exclusion, the entire amount of each payment was excluded from the recipient's gross income until the $5,000 was excluded. Thereafter the full amount of each payment was includible in the recipient's gross income. §72(d); Rev. Rul. 58-153, 1958-1 C.B. 43. If the amount receivable in three years was less than $5,000, that amount was amortized over the period the payments will be made. For this purpose the annuitant's life expectancy was determined according to Table I of Reg. §1.72-9.

The estate tax treatment of the death benefit does not affect the amount includible in the recipient's gross income. Whether or not the death benefit is included in the employee's gross estate, its basis is not adjusted under §1014: "This section shall not apply to property which constitutes a right to receive an item of income in respect of a decedent under Section 691." §1014(c). However, where the death benefit is included in the employee's gross estate, the recipient is entitled to an income tax deduction for the additional estate tax imposed because of the inclusion of the death benefit. §691(c). In brief, the estate tax applicable to the employee's estate is computed with and without the inclusion of all items of income in respect of a decedent. The additional tax arising by reason of the inclusion of those items, for which the income tax deduction is allowed, is apportioned between them according to their respective estate tax values. Finally, a §691(c) deduction is allowable to the recipient of an item of income in respect of a decedent proportionately as the income from the item is reported as income by the recipient.

§6.78.11. Reasonable and Necessary Payments Are Deductible by Employer

Death benefit payments are deductible by the employer only if they are reasonable and necessary business expenses. In some cases no deduction is allowed. *See, M.S.D., Inc. v. United States,* 39 A.F.T.R.2d 77-1393 (N.D. Ohio 1977), *aff'd without opinion,* 611 F.2d 373 (6th Cir. 1979) (no deduction allowed for payments made by closely-held business to widow of deceased shareholder-officer, which were not necessary business expenses).

§6.78.12. ERISA

A properly structured death benefit only plan, which may provide benefits to the survivors of a group of key employees, should qualify for exemption from ERISA requirements on two grounds. First, the plan should be exempt as an unfunded excess benefit plan that is available only to certain employees. 29 U.S.C. §§1002(36), 1003(b)(5), 1051(7), 1081(a)(9), 1321(b)(8). Second, the plan should be exempt as an unfunded plan of deferred compensation for a select group of employees. 29 U.S.C. §§1051(2), 1081(a)(3), 1321(b)(6). Note, however, that for ERISA purposes a death benefit only plan which involves split-dollar life insurance policies on the lives of key executives may be held to be funded. *Dependhal v. Falstaff Brewing Corp.,* 491 F. Supp. 1188 (E.D. Mo. 1980), *aff'd on this issue,* 653 F.2d 1208 (1981), *cert. denied,* 454 U.S. 968 (1981). In order to avoid the result reached in *Dependhal* a death benefit only plan should not mention life insurance, the benefits payable under the plan should not be based upon the amount of insurance, and any policies owned by the employer should not be identified as having any relationship to the plan.

§6.79. Gifts of Life Insurance Under the Uniform Transfers to Minors Act

More than half of the states have adopted the Uniform Transfers to Minors Act, 8A U.L.A. 207 (1989 Supp.), §9 of which permits custodial property to be created when a life or endowment insurance policy is held in the name of a custodian for a minor. Specifically, the Uniform Act provides that a custodianship is created when a life or endowment policy is either

(1) registered with the issuer in the name of the transferor, an adult other than the transferor, or a trust company, followed in substance by the words: "as custodian for ____________ (name of minor) under the [Name of Enacting State] Uniform Transfers to Minors Act"; or
(2) assigned in a writing delivered to an adult other than the transferor or to a trust company whose name in the assignment is followed in substance by the words: "as custodian for ______________________ (name of minor) under the [Name of Enacting State] Uniform Transfers to Minors Act."

Most of the other states have versions of the 1966 revision of the Uniform Gifts to Minors Act that allow life insurance policies or annuity contracts on the life of a minor or a member of the minor's family to be given to the minor by registering them "in the name of the donor, another adult [an adult member of the minor's family, a guardian of the minor] or a trust company, followed, in substance, by the words: 'as custodian for (name of minor) under the [name of enacting state] Uniform Gifts to Minors Act.' " Id., §2(a)(4), 8A U.L.A. 345 (1983).

The federal tax consequences that generally flow from the transfer of property to a custodian for a minor also apply in the case of life insurance. *See* §7.34. In addition, the proceeds of a policy may be includible in the estate of the insured under §§2038 or 2042(2) if the insured is acting as custodian at the time of his or her death. The broad powers a custodian has to invest and reinvest the custodial property probably constitute incidents of ownership for purposes of §2042. Inclusion under §2042 might occur whether or not the policy had been given to the minor by the insured-custodian. In this connection recall the discussion of incidents of ownership held in a fiduciary capacity at §6.27.11. In contrast, §2038 would apply to the insurance only if the insured had transferred it to himself or herself as custodian for the minor.

The income from custodianship property is taxed to the minor except to the extent it is used to discharge the legal obligation of another person to support the minor. Of course, unearned income of a minor under 14 would be subject to the Kiddie Tax. Presumably the income will be taxed to the minor although it is used to pay premiums on a policy that insures the life of the donor or the donor's spouse. Of course, if a trust were involved, the income would be taxed to the grantor to the extent the income is or may be applied by the grantor alone, or without the consent of an adverse party, to payment of premiums on policies of insurance on the life of the grantor or the grantor's spouse. *See* §677(a)(3); *See also* §6.58.

§6.80. LIFE INSURANCE AND THE UNIFORM SIMULTANEOUS DEATH ACT

The Uniform Simultaneous Death Act, 8A U.L.A. 575 (1983), is in effect in almost all states. Under the basic rule of §1 of the Act, when devolution depends upon the priority of death of two persons and there is no sufficient evidence that they died otherwise than simultaneously, the property of each is disposed of as if he or she had survived the other. Thus, if a husband and wife die simultaneously, the husband's property is distributed as if he survived his wife and the wife's property is distributed as if she survived her husband. The parties may prescribe a different rule in the governing instrument that will control over the provisions of the Act.

Section 5 of the Act provides a special rule for distribution of life or accident insurance where the insured and the beneficiary die simultaneously. Under it the proceeds of a policy are distributed as if the insured had survived the beneficiary. In such event the proceeds are paid to any contingent beneficiary or beneficiaries who survive the insured. Of course, if no beneficiary survives the insured, the proceeds will be paid in accordance with the terms of the policy, which usually call for payment either to the estate of the insured or to the owner of the policy. Payment to the estate of the insured is generally undesirable because it may unnecessarily subject the proceeds to federal and state death taxes. Payment to the insured's estate may also subject the proceeds to claims of creditors against the insured. Accordingly, insurance should generally name both primary and contingent beneficiaries.

The estate tax advantage of naming a contingent beneficiary is illustrated by the cases in which the husband's life was insured under a policy owned by his wife that named her a primary beneficiary and their children as contingent beneficiaries. *Estate of Meltzer v. Commissioner,* 439 F.2d 798 (4th Cir. 1971); *Estate of Wein v. Commissioner,* 441 F.2d 32 (5th Cir. 1971); *Old Kent Bank & Trust Co. v. United States,* 430 F.2d 392 (6th Cir. 1970); *Estate of Chown v. Commissioner,* 428 F.2d 1395 (9th Cir. 1970). Under these decisions neither the policy nor its proceeds was includible in the gross estate of the insured. Moreover, none of the proceeds was includible in the wife's gross estate because she was deemed to have predeceased the insured. Only the interpolated terminal reserve value of the policy was includible in the wife's gross estate under §2033. As a result, the proceeds passed to the insured's children free of estate taxation except to the extent the value of the policy was included in the wife's estate.

> **Example 6-32.** *H*'s life was insured for $250,000 under a policy owned by his wife, *W*. *W* was named as primary beneficiary and their children *D* and *S* were named as contingent beneficiaries. *H* and *W* died simultaneously at a time when the interpolated terminal reserve value of the policy was $15,000. Under §5 of the Uniform Act, *W* (the beneficiary) is deemed to have predeceased *H* (the insured). Accordingly, only the interpolated terminal reserve ($15,000) is included in *W*'s gross estate. None of the proceeds is includible in *H*'s gross estate. Thus, the $250,000 proceeds are received by *D* and *S* at little or no estate tax cost.

Simultaneous Death: Community Property. A special problem may arise when a husband and wife die simultaneously owning a community property policy that insures the life of one of them and names the other as beneficiary. If no contingent beneficiary is named, the proceeds of the policy will be paid in accordance with the terms of the policy as if the insured had survived (*i.e.*, either in equal shares to the estates of the husband and wife as owners of the policy or entirely to the husband's estate as the insured under the policy). In California and Washington, the courts have incorrectly concluded that the presumption that the insured survived the beneficiary will persist through the distribution of the proceeds by their estates. *E.g., Estates of Saunders,* 317 P.2d 528 (Wash. 1957); *Wedemeyer's Estate,* 240 P.2d 8 (Cal. App. 1952). Under that approach the entire proceeds may be distributed to the beneficiaries named in the insured's will or to the intestate successors of the insured. The presumption that the insured survived should only apply to the beneficiaries — not to the ultimate distribution of payments to the policy owners.

> **Example 6-33.** *H* and his wife *W* died simultaneously owning a community property policy on *H*'s life that named *W* as sole beneficiary. Both *H* and *W* died intestate. *H* was survived by his father, *F*, and *W* was survived by her mother, *M*. Under the terms of the policy the proceeds were payable to the owner of the policy if no beneficiary survived the insured. Because the insured (*H*) is deemed to have survived the beneficiary (*W*), the proceeds will be paid in equal shares to the estates of *H* and *W*. Under the California approach, *W*'s one-half share will be distributed to *H*'s estate because he is deemed to have survived her. For the same reason *H*'s one-half share of the proceeds will not be distributed to *W*. Finally, the entire proceeds will be distributed as an asset of *H*'s estate (*i.e.*, to *F*), as *W* did not survive *H*. As a result the entire proceeds of the community property policy will be paid to

the relatives of the insured to the total exclusion of the relatives of the noninsured spouse. Of course, the wills of *H* and *W* could have controlled the distribution of the proceeds from their estates and could have directed that a different presumption of survivorship should govern the disposition of their estates.

This problem will not arise if the policy names a contingent beneficiary who survives the insured. It will also not arise in Arizona, New Mexico, Texas, and Wisconsin, which have adopted the substance of the amendment to §5 of the Uniform Act proposed by the Uniform Commissioners in 1953. The amendment provides that "if the policy is community property of the insured and his spouse, and there is no alternative beneficiary except the estate or personal representatives of the insured, the proceeds shall be distributed as community property under Section 4." 8A U.L.A. 581 (1983). Under §4 half of the community property is distributed as if the husband had survived and half as if the wife had survived. By way of illustration, §4 would require the proceeds of the policy described in Example 6-33 to be distributed one-half to *F* (*H*'s intestate successor) and one-half to *M* (*W*'s intestate successor). Consistent with that result, half of the proceeds would be included in the gross estate of each spouse. Rev. Rul. 79-303, 1979-2 C.B. 332 (Texas law).

BIBLIOGRAPHY

I. General Surveys of Insurance and Insurance Law

Chapman, Life Insurance as a Planning Tool — The Life Insurance Policy, N.Y.U., 33rd Inst. Fed. Tax., 723 (1975)

Consumers Union, Life Insurance: How to Buy the Right Policy from the Right Company at the Right Price (1988)

J. Munch, Financial and Estate Planning with Life Insurance Products (1990)

II. General Surveys of Taxation and Insurance

ABA Sec. of Real Prop. & Trust Law, Life Insurance Primer for Lawyers (1989)

ALI-ABA, Study Materials, Uses of Life Insurance in Estate and Tax Planning (1990)

Calleton, Current Uses and Abuses of Life Insurance in Estate Planning, U. So. Cal., 42nd Tax Inst. ch. 17 (1990)

Chasman, Life Insurance: A Sophisticated Estate and Financial Planning Tool, U. Miami, 22nd Inst. Est. Plan., ch. 4 (1988)

Jones, Uses of Life Insurance by Individual Taxpayers, N.Y.U., 45th Inst. Fed. Tax., ch. 35 (1987)

National Underwriter Law Services, Tax Facts on Life Insurance (published annually)

Simmons, Life Insurance — The More the Rules Change, The More They Stay the Same, U. Miami, 20th Inst. Est. Plan., ch. 6 (1986)

III. Specific Topics

Assignments

Kahn & Waggoner, Federal Taxation of the Assignment of Life Insurance, 1977 Duke L.J. 941

Death Benefit Only Plans

Swirnoff & Tolan, DBOs: Death Benefit Only Plans, Keeping Current (1986)

Wolk, The Pure Death Benefit: An Estate and Gift Tax Anomaly, 66 Minn. L. Rev. 229 (1982)

GSTT

Brody & Reilly, GSTT Planning Opportunities Continue After TAMRA, 128 Tr. & Est. 24 (1989)

Insurance Trusts

Blattmacher, Hastings & Slade, Irrevocable Life Insurance Trusts, Chase Review (Apr. 1988)

Keydel, Irrevocable Insurance Trusts: The Current Scene, U. Miami, 10th Inst. Est. Plan., ch. 5 (1976)

Lawrence, Structuring Irrevocable Trusts in Light of Tax Changes and Proposals, N.Y.U., 44th Inst. Fed. Tax., ch. 55 (1986)

Mirabello, Current Developments in Planning and Drafting Irrevocable Life Insurance Trusts, N.Y.U., 48th Inst. Fed. Tax., ch. 16 (1990)

Bibliography

Oshins, Planning with Irrevocable Life Insurance Trusts in Community Property Jurisdictions, 5 Community Prop. J. 97 (1978)

Price, The Uses and Abuses of Irrevocable Life Insurance Trusts, U. Miami, 14th Inst. Est. Plan., ch. 11 (1980)

Simmons, Irrevocable Life Insurance Trusts, U. So. Cal., 28th Tax. Inst. 23 (1976)

Survivorship Life Insurance

Ford, Joint Life Insurance: It No Longer Matters Who Dies First, 3 Prob. & Prop. 42 (Nov./Dec. 1989)

Saks, Survivorship Life Insurance Policies Continuing to Attract Increasing Attention, 15 Est. Planning 120 (1988)

Wilshinsky, Life Insurance: A New Dimension in Estate Planning, 130 Tr. & Est. 10 (June 1991)

Universal Life Insurance

Morlitz, Hamburg & Frankel, Universal Life Insurance: Where Do We Go From Here? N.Y.U., 46th Inst. Fed. Tax., ch. 54 (1988)

CHAPTER 7

Planning Lifetime Noncharitable Gifts

A. Introduction

§7.1. Scope
§7.2. Nontax Considerations
§7.2.1. Economic Position
§7.2.2. Age and Health
§7.2.3. Emotional and Family Circumstances

B. Local Property Law

§7.3. Significance of Local Law
§7.4. Inter Vivos Gifts and Gifts Causa Mortis
§7.5. Elements of Inter Vivos Gifts
§7.5.1. Delivery
§7.5.2. Acceptance
§7.6. Gifts of Community Property

C. Tax Objectives of Gifts

§7.7. General
§7.8. Eliminate Further Appreciation in Value from the Donor's Estate
§7.8.1. Annual Exclusion and Unified Credit Gifts
§7.8.2. Carryover of Donor's Basis
§7.9. Shift Income from Donor to Donee
§7.9.1. Kiddie Tax
§7.9.2. Shifting Capital Gains
§7.10. Reduce Nonbusiness Holdings of Donor in Order to Qualify for Benefits of §§303, 2032A, or 6166
Table 7-1. Statutory Benefits Under §§303, 2032A, and 6166
§7.11. Minimize State Transfer Tax Costs

D. Tax Factors Involved in Selecting Property to Give

§7.12. Give Appreciated Property?
§7.13. Do Not Give Property Subject to an Encumbrance in Excess of Its Basis
§7.14. Do Not Give Property with a Basis That Exceeds Its Current Fair Market Value
§7.15. Do Not Give Property with Positive Tax Characteristics
§7.16. Give Property That Reduces the Value of Assets Retained by the Donor
§7.17. Do Not Make a Gift That Will Have Adverse Income Tax Consequences for the Donor

E. Specialized Gift Techniques

§7.18. Introduction
§7.19. Small Below-Market Loans
§7.20. Payment by One Spouse of Entire Income or Gift Tax Liability
§7.21. Grantor Pays Income Tax on Grantor Trust
§7.22. Free Services and Free Use of Property
§7.23. Gift of a Residence with Continued Occupancy by Donor
§7.24. Installment Gifts: Periodic Forgiveness of Transferee's Notes
§7.25. Net Gifts
§7.25.1. Income Tax
§7.25.2. Gift Tax
§7.25.3. Estate Tax
§7.26. Gifts of Encumbered Property
§7.27. Part Gift and Part Sale

F. Gifts to Minors

§7.28. Importance of Gifts to Minors
§7.29. Outright Gifts
§7.29.1. Gift Tax
§7.29.2. Estate Tax
§7.29.3. Income Tax
§7.30. Series EE Bonds
§7.30.1. Minor as Sole Owner
§7.30.2. Minor as Coowner
§7.30.3. Minor as Beneficiary
§7.31. Payable-on-Death (POD) Bank Accounts
§7.32. Savings Account or Totten Trust
§7.33. Joint Bank or Securities Accounts
§7.33.1. Joint Bank Accounts
§7.33.2. Joint Securities Accounts

§7.34. Gifts Under the Uniform Acts
§7.34.1. Gift Tax
§7.34.2. Estate Tax
§7.34.3. Income Tax
§7.35. Gifts in Trust
§7.36. Section 2503(c) Trusts
§7.36.1. Property or Income
§7.36.2. No Substantial Restrictions
§7.36.3. Payable at 21
§7.36.4. Payable to Donee's Estate or As Donee Appoints
§7.36.5. Terms of 2503(c) Trust
Form 7-1. Distributive Provisions of §2503(c) Trust
§7.36.6. Estate Tax
§7.36.7. Income Tax
§7.36.8. GSTT
§7.36.9. Conclusion
§7.37. Discretionary Trust with *Crummey* Powers
§7.37.1. Gift Tax
§7.37.2. Limit the Amount Subject to Withdrawal?
§7.37.3. Permit Each Donor to Restrict the Amount Subject to Withdrawal?
Form 7-2. Limitation of Power of Withdrawal
§7.37.4. Hanging Power: A Power of Withdrawal That Lapses at 5 or 5 Annual Rate
Form 7-3. Annual Lapse of Hanging Power
§7.37.5. How Many Beneficiaries May Hold a Power of Withdrawal?
§7.37.6. Notice to the Beneficiary
§7.37.7. Must the Trust Have Liquid Assets to Satisfy a Withdrawal?
§7.37.8. How Long Should the Power Be Exercisable?
§7.37.9. Separate Trusts or One Trust for Multiple Donees?
§7.37.10. Income Tax
§7.37.11. Estate Tax
§7.37.12. Model *Crummey* Power
Form 7-4. Crummey *Power for Trust with One Beneficiary*
§7.38. Mandatory Distribution of Income Trust, §2503(b)
§7.38.1. Nontax Considerations
§7.38.2. Tax Considerations
§7.39. Irrevocable Short-Term Trusts

Bibliography

> Perhaps to assuage the feelings and to aid the understanding of affected taxpayers, Congress might use different symbols to describe the taxable conduct in the several statutes, calling it a "gift" in the gift tax law, a "gaft" in the income tax law, and a "geft" in the estate tax law. *Commissioner v. Beck's Estate,* 129 F.2d 243, 246 (2d Cir. 1942).

A. INTRODUCTION

§7.1. Scope

Lifetime gifts continue to play a major role in estate planning. The unification of the federal gift and estate taxes in 1976 and the adoption of compressed income tax rates in 1986 eliminated many, but not all, of the tax advantages of noncharitable inter vivos gifts that were formerly available. Small income tax savings may be available by giving income-producing property to family members. More important, gifts can be used to remove further appreciation in value from the donor's estate, to enable the donor's estate to qualify for some special tax elections, and to minimize the overall state and federal transfer tax burdens. *See* §§7.7-7.11. In particular, lifetime gifts may substantially reduce the GSTT cost of transferring property to descendants. *See* §2.40.

This chapter first reviews some of the main nontax considerations involved in counselling clients about gifts. After that it discusses the major tax objectives of gifts, the tax factors involved in selecting property to give, and the various methods of making gifts. The part dealing with methods of making gifts focuses on the various ways of making gifts to minors because of their importance and their illustrative value. Some references are made in the text to state gift tax laws that are in effect in a small but important minority of states, including Delaware, Louisiana, New York, North Carolina, Tennessee, and Wisconsin.

§7.2 Nontax Considerations

> Ingratitude, thou marble-hearted fiend,
> More hideous when thou showest thee in a child
> Than the sea-monster! . . .
> How sharper than a serpent's tooth it is
> To have a thankless child!
>
> — King Lear, Act 1, scene 4

Inter vivos gifts generally do not precipitate a family tragedy as they did in King Lear's case. However, before a client adopts a gift program, careful consideration should be given to the financial, family, and emotional circumstances of the client and the prospective donee. Those factors will sometimes suggest that one or both of them might suffer if a substantial gift were made.

Despite their tax advantages, gifts should only be made if they are consistent with the client's overall estate plan. The ultimate decision of whether or not to make a gift must be made by the client, but it is appropriate for the lawyer to make recommendations regarding gifts and other components of the estate plan. For example, a review of the client's affairs may lead the lawyer to recommend that the client make some noncharitable gifts as a part of the client's lifetime estate planning. Otherwise the client's annual exclusions may go unused and the estate tax payable upon the client's death may be unnecessarily high. The lawyer must be prepared for some rejections, however. Although all of the circumstances known to the lawyer may support the adoption of a gift program, the client may reject the idea because of other factual, emotional, or financial considerations. For example, a client may have philosophical convictions that are inconsistent with substantial lifetime noncharitable gifts or may be reluctant to make gifts because of memories of the Great Depression and a fear of becoming economically dependent on others.

§7.2.1. Economic Position

The economic position of the client is one of the most important factors in evaluating the desirability of a gift program. This factor involves a consideration of the client's net wealth and liquidity in view of his or her income, age, health, family obligations, and the extent to which future security is provided by employee benefit plans, medical and disability insurance, and other sources. Relatively small gifts or gifts for the support or education of a family member often have little adverse impact on the donor's economic position and are easily justifiable in many cases. For example, impressive tax reductions may result if a client makes annual exclusion gifts to children. Moreover, a grandparent's payment of the tuition for grandchildren or their medical expenses is neither subject to the gift nor the GST tax. §§2503(e), 2642(c)(3). However, a client may appropriately be discouraged from making substantial gifts that may jeopardize his or her economic independence or standard of living. A client must understand the irrevocable nature of a gift, which generally means that the property cannot be counted on for the client's use or support.

§7.2.2. Age and Health

The age and health of a client are also particularly significant factors. In general, an older client is in a better position to make substantial gifts than a younger client of equivalent wealth. A younger client faces a longer time during which he or she may become disabled, suffer economic losses, or have substantial increases in family obligations. For example, an elderly widow or widower with grown, independent children is generally in a better position to make substantial gifts than a young married person of equivalent wealth who has, or may have, dependent children. On the other hand, a young parent with a modest estate may prudently make gifts within the amount of the annual gift tax exclusion to a child under the Uniform Transfers to Minors Act (U.T.M.A.) or the Uniform Gifts to Minors Act (U.G.M.A.) or to a trust for the child in order to gain the benefits of income-splitting within the family and to accumulate an educational fund for the child at the lowest tax cost. Although the Kiddie Tax limits the opportunities of accumulating unearned income for children under 14, some possibilities still exist. *See* §§7.28-7.39 for a discussion of the major alternative methods of making gifts to minors. Sound planning may also suggest that life insurance should be transferred to another family member. Doing so may involve little risk if the insurance has little or no current economic value (e.g., group-term insurance or an employee's interest under a split-dollar plan) to a family member or to a family trust. In that way the size of the client's estate may be controlled without giving up an asset of substantial current value. *See* §§6.16-6.24 for a discussion of the basic plans for disposing of life insurance.

§7.2.3. Emotional and Family Circumstances

The emotional and family circumstances of the client and the client's family must also be considered in planning a gift program. The emotional attachment or identification that a client feels with respect to particular property, such as a collection of coins, stamps, paintings, or antiques may make it difficult for the client to give it to another person without feeling some anxiety or pain. Donees may not have the same appreciation for the property, which may lead them to neglect it — or sell it. Similarly, a client who has built up a successful business may be reluctant to give up its management or any significant ownership interest in it. Giving up the challenge and the responsibility of owning and operating a business could have a morbid effect on the client, because the client may consciously or unconsciously view it as a partial death. There are other circumstances in which the lawyer must be sensitive to the feelings of the client and the client's family. For example, in some circumstances tax benefits will be obtained if gifts are made by or to a dying person (*e.g.,* §§3.29, 5.7), but members of the client's family might take offense unless the topic is raised most tactfully.

The age, abilities, feelings, and financial circumstances of prospective donees and other family members must also be taken into account in formulating a gift program. For example, it may be unwise to make a substantial outright gift to a minor or a very elderly person. In either case the donee may be unable to make an effective sale or other transfer of the property without the appointment of a guardian. Along with some other problems, this may be overcome by making the gift in trust rather than outright. *See* §§7.35-7.39 for a discussion of trusts for minors and Chapter 10 for a general discussion of trusts. Care should be exercised in making substantial outright gifts to persons who have little or no financial or investment experience. Also, family discord may arise if a large gift is made to one child but not to others or if disproportionate gifts are made to children or other donees who are equally related to the client. Disproportionate gifts may be justified, however, when the needs of the donees differ and some face greater educational, medical, or other expenses than the others. Finally, a client may choose to pay some outstanding debts of a spendthrift, to whom the client may be reluctant to make a large outright gift.

Substantial gifts are most effective when they are coordinated with the donee's estate plan. In particular, a gift should generally be structured so that the gifted property will not return to the donor if the donee predeceases the donor. This problem is aggravated in the case of an outright gift to a minor or gift under the U.T.M.A. or the U.G.M.A. because minors generally lack the capacity to make a will. This is a serious disadvantage because such gifts would be subject to distribution as intestate property if the donee dies prior to attaining his or her majority. A minor donee's intestate property would usually pass to his or her surviving parent or parents. Of course, the probability that a minor will die prior to attaining majority is quite small. This problem is avoided entirely by making the gift to a trust under which the trust property will be distributed to persons other than the donor if the donee dies before the trust terminates. The annual exclusion is available for transfers to a trust insofar as the trust meets the requirements of §§2503(b) or (c). *See* §§7.36 and 7.38. An annual exclusion is also available to the extent the donee holds a *Crummey* power under which he or she can withdraw property that is transferred to the trust. *See* §7.37. If the trust contains a properly drafted *Crummey* power, the annual exclusion is available although the trust is a discretionary one (*i.e.,* the beneficiary does not have any fixed right to receive distributions of income or principal).

B. LOCAL PROPERTY LAW

§7.3. Significance of Local Law

In order to constitute a gift for federal gift tax purposes a transfer must be effective under local law to pass an interest in the property to the donee. The federal law describes the types of transfers that constitute taxable gifts, but the question of whether or not there has been an effective gift is decided under local law. "The sole criterion, for the purpose of the gift tax, is whether the particular conveyance is effective under the local law to transfer an interest in the property to a donee." Rev. Rul. 57-315, 1957-2 C.B. 624.

§7.4. Inter Vivos Gifts and Gifts Causa Mortis

Two general types of gifts are recognized for property law purposes: inter vivos gifts and gifts causa mortis. This chapter is concerned only with inter vivos gifts, which are usually immediately effective and irrevocable. In contrast, gifts causa mortis are made in contemplation of death and remain revocable until the death of the donor.

Gifts causa mortis are not used in estate planning because their revocable nature deprives them of any income, gift, or estate tax significance. In particular, the donor remains taxable on the income, §676, the gift is incomplete, Reg. §25.2511-2(c), and the property is includible in the donor's gross estate, §2038. In addition, gifts causa mortis are generally not favored by the courts because of their similarity to oral wills, which lack the formality and evidentiary reliability of written wills.

§7.5. Elements of Inter Vivos Gifts

For property law purposes a valid gift requires donative intent on the part of the donor, delivery to the donee or donee's agent, and some form of acceptance. In contrast, donative intent on the part of the transferor is not required in order to subject a transfer to federal gift taxation. Reg. §25.2511-1(g)(1). The local law may require a written instrument in order to transfer some interests in personal property and a deed is usually required to transfer interests in real property. Federal law governs the transfer of some types of property, such as U.S. Savings Bonds. *United States v. Chandler,* 410 U.S. 257 (1973).

A gift is not effective unless the donor is competent and not acting under fraud, duress, or undue influence. However, under the *substi-*

tution of judgment doctrine, a guardian, conservator, or committee of an incompetent may make gifts of the ward's property. Under this doctrine the court may authorize the fiduciary to make inter vivos gifts to the ward's relatives in order to reduce the overall transfer tax burden when it is consistent with the ward's estate plan and the property will not be needed for the ward's care and support. *See, e.g., In re Morris,* 281 A.2d 156 (N.H. 1971); *In re duPont,* 194 A.2d 309 (Del. Ch. 1963). In more recent years many states have passed legislation that allows a principal to authorize an attorney-in-fact acting under a durable power of attorney to make gifts of the principal's property. *See* §4.35 for a discussion of this point and a form authorizing the attorney-in-fact to make limited gifts.

§7.5.1. Delivery

The type of delivery that is required in order to complete a gift depends upon the nature and location of the property involved and the circumstances of the parties. Actual physical delivery of tangible personal property or of a stock certificate or other physical evidence of a chose in action is preferred, but other forms of delivery may suffice. For example, tangible personal property contained in a locked receptacle may be delivered constructively by giving the donee the key to the receptacle. Broadly speaking, tangible or intangible personalty may also be effectively delivered if the donee is given a writing evidencing the gift (a deed of gift in the case of tangible personalty or an assignment in the case of a chose in action).

Effective delivery may also be made through a third party. In general delivery to a third party is immediately effective if the third party represents the donee, but it is not effective until ultimate delivery to the donee where the third party represents the donor. This analysis is reflected in the gift tax regulations: "If a donor delivers a properly indorsed stock certificate to the donee or the donee's agent, the gift is completed for gift tax purposes on the date of delivery. If the donor delivers the certificate to his bank or broker as his agent, or to the issuing corporation or its transfer agent, for transfer into the name of the donee, the gift is completed on the date the stock is transferred on the books of the corporation." Reg. §25.2511-2(h).

§7.5.2. Acceptance

Acceptance by the donee is also a necessary element of a gift. However, the significance of this requirement is diminished by a presumption of acceptance by the donee. The presumption, which applies to all donees including minors and incompetents, facilitates the completion of gifts when delivery is made to the third party.

§7.6. Gifts of Community Property

> In Spanish law, the husband's powers of management over the community included the right to make reasonable gifts. A number of community property states have retained this principle. In such states, the issue is whether a particular gift is appropriate given its nature and the wealth of the parties. G. Blumberg, Community Property in California 423 (1987).

All of the community property states limit the power of one spouse, acting alone, to give community property to a third person. *See* §3.28.2. Some do not allow gifts to be made without the express or implied consent of the other. Cal. Civ. Code §5125(b) (West 1991 Supp.) (requires written consent); Wash. Rev. Code §26.16.030(2) (1989). The other states generally permit one spouse to make a gift of community property to a third party so long as the gift is not unfair or "constructively fraudulent." The question of whether or not a gift of community property to a third party is constructively fraudulent requires the court to consider a number of factors, including "the size of the gift in relation to the size of the community estate, the adequacy of the estate remaining to support the wife in spite of the gift, and the relationship of the donor to the donee." *Horlock v. Horlock,* 533 S.W.2d 52, 55 (Tex. Civ. App. 1975). The court in *Horlock* upheld the deceased husband's gift of over 13 percent of total estate to his teenage daughters where the community estate was large and the gifts resulted in tax savings. Gifts that are capricious, excessive, and arbitrary are constructively fraudulent although the donees are the children of the donor. *Logan v. Barge,* 568 S.W.2d 863 (Tex. Civ. App. 1978).

C. TAX OBJECTIVES OF GIFTS

§7.7. General

The main tax objectives of inter vivos gifts are discussed in this part. The objectives are largely independent, but some are inconsistent with others. For example, shifting ordinary income or capital gains from donor to donees as described in §7.9 may not be consistent with taking steps to qualify the donor's estate for the benefits of §§303, 2032A, or 6166 (discussed in §7.10). In order to accomplish the latter goal the donor might be required to make gifts that do not have the required characteristics. It is important to have the objectives in mind when it comes to helping the client choose the property to give. §§7.12-7.17. The objectives also help to identify which method should be used to make gifts to minors. §§7.27-7.39.

§7.8. Eliminate Further Appreciation in Value from the Donor's Estate

One of the common reasons for making an inter vivos gift is to remove from the donor's tax base any further appreciation in the value of the donated property. In effect, a gift freezes the amount that will be taxed to the donor at the value of the property on the date of the gift less the amount of the allowable gift tax exclusion. An inter vivos gift also removes from the donor's estate the future income generated by the donated property. The amount of any gift tax paid is also removed from the donor's tax base if he or she survives for three years. §2035(b). In considering a gift program, recall that in the case of donor's dying after December 31, 1981, outright gifts made within three years of death generally are not includible in the donor's estate under §2035. Of course, §2035(d)(2) may require the inclusion of gifts made from a revocable trust within three years of the trustor's death. *See* §10.17.

§7.8.1. Annual Exclusion and Unified Credit Gifts

Inter vivos gifts are particularly attractive to the extent they qualify for the annual gift tax exclusion. At the marginal estate tax rate, 37 percent, each $10,000 gift saves at least $3,700 in estate tax. Gifts in excess of the allowable exclusions are often useful, at least when the amount of the tax is offset by the donor's unified credit. Even when some gift tax must be paid by the donor, a gift program may save a substantial amount of transfer taxes. This result is clear where the property appreciates in value following the gift. As indicated above, a substantial tax saving may also result because the gift tax paid by the donor is not subject to the gift or estate tax unless the donor dies within three years and the amount of the gift tax is grossed up under §2035(c). In calculating the benefit of an inter vivos gift upon which a gift tax is paid, some consideration must be given to the effect of losing the use of the amount paid in tax. For a mathematical model that permits a comparison of the adjusted estate tax cost of retaining the property with the adjusted gift tax cost of making a present gift of it, *see* Officer & Banks, Estates vs. Gifts in a Period of Inflation, 58 Taxes 68 (1980).

§7.8.2 Carryover of Donor's Basis

In planning inter vivos gifts, it is also important to bear in mind that the donor's basis generally carries over to the donee under §1015. The basis of donative property is stepped up (or stepped down) when the donor dies only if it is included in his or her gross estate. §1014. The carryover of basis may be a negative factor when the donee is expected to sell the property after the donor's death; it is largely irrelevant if the donee is not expected to do so. Even if the donee sells the property, the capital gains tax payable on a sale may be much less than the additional estate tax that would be payable by the donor's estate if the gift were not made. Currently, the maximum rate applicable to capital gains is 28 percent, whereas the maximum estate tax rate is 55 percent. Also, the donee's basis in the property is increased by the amount of any gift tax paid with respect to the appreciation element of the gift (the excess of the fair market value of the property at the time of the gift over the donor's adjusted basis). §1015(d)(6).

> **Example 7-1.** An unmarried donor, *D,* had made taxable gifts in prior years that absorbed the full amount of *D*'s unified credit but did not require any gift tax to be paid. Earlier this year *D* gave a relative, *B,* $10,000 in cash. Before the end of the year *D* gave *B* 100 shares of stock that had an adjusted basis of $10 per share and a current market value of $100 per share. *D* must pay a gift tax by reason of the $10,000 gift of stock to *B,* of which 90% is attributable to the excess of the value of the shares over the donor's basis. *B* has a basis in the shares equal to *D*'s basis of $1,000, plus the gift tax paid by *D* with respect to the $9,000 of unrealized appreciation. The cash and the stock will be excluded from *D*'s estate. If *D* survives for 3 years the gift tax paid will also be excluded from his or her estate.

§7.9. Shift Income from Donor to Donee

"Income-splitting" within the family is another purpose of making inter vivos gifts. Its important varies according to the other income of the parties and the progressivity of the income tax rate schedule. The total family income tax burden may be reduced somewhat if income-producing assets are distributed among several family members rather than being concentrated in the hands of one or both parents.

§7.9.1. Kiddie Tax, §§1(g), 63(c)(5)

> .01 [Section 1(g)] of the Code provides that the tax on the net unearned income of a child under the age of 14 is computed at the marginal rate of the child's parent. Under [§1(g)(4)(A)(ii)] net unearned income generally equals unearned income less the sum of (I) the amount in effect for the taxable year under section 63(c)(5)(A), plus (II) the greater of the amount described in (I) or certain itemized deductions.
>
> .02 The amount in effect for 1991 under section 63(c)(5)(A) is $550. . . . Accordingly, for tax years beginning in 1991 the net unearned income will generally equal unearned income less the greater of $1,100 or $550 plus certain itemized deductions. Rev. Proc. 90-64, 1990-2 C.B. 674.

The potential income tax savings of transferring income-producing property to children are reduced by §§63(c)(5) and 1(g). Using the inflation-adjusted figures for 1991, §63(c)(5) limits the standard deduction to the greater of $550 or the earned income of dependents for whom a deduction is available to another taxpayer under §151. Under §1(g) the unearned income of a child under 14 in excess of $1,100 is taxed to the child at the top marginal tax rate applicable to the child's parents. A parent of a child under 14 may elect to report the unearned income of the child in excess of $1,000, up to $5,000, directly on his or her return by making an election under §1(g)(7). Because of the compressed rate structure adopted in 1986, only limited income tax savings will ordinarily result in any case. In order to avoid having the income of a person under 14 taxed to his or her parent, the property may be invested in forms that produce little or no current taxable income (*e.g.*, insurance policies) or ones that defer the recognition of income (*e.g.*, Series EE bonds). *See* §7.30. Importantly, the income of a trust is subject to the Kiddie Tax only to the extent it must be paid to the beneficiary or is distributed to him or her.

§7.9.2. Shifting Capital Gains

The capital gains tax on the sale of an appreciated asset may be reduced by transferring the property to a donee who either is in a lower income tax bracket or who can offset the gain with losses. The tax is computed at the rates applicable to the donor where appreciated property is transferred to a trust that sells it within two years. §644. For Kiddie Tax purposes the parent is treated as having paid any tax that is imposed on the trust under §644. §1(g)(3)(C).

A gift is also useful when the property will be sold and the gain on a sale would be ordinary income to the donor but capital gain to the donee. The benefit will depend upon the differential between the maximum rates applicable to ordinary income and to capital gains. Of course, the gift tax consequences of the transfer must be taken into account in deciding whether to make the gift. The combined gift and capital gains taxes may be less than the income tax that the donor would pay on the gain if it were all taxed to the donor as ordinary income.

> **Example 7-2.** A married donor, *D,* who is involved in real estate development and sales, gave his married, adult son *S* and *S*'s spouse a parcel of undeveloped real property that had an adjusted basis of $1,000 and a current value of $40,000. The entire gift to *S* and his spouse is sheltered by the available annual exclusions if the gift is split between *D* and his spouse. The donor's basis in the property ($1,000) carries over to the donees under §1015(a) as does the donor's holding period. *See* §1223(2) and Reg. §1.1223-1(b). Ordinarily the real property will be a capital asset in the hands of the donees and any gain they realize will be capital gain. However, if the sale was prearranged by *D,* the donees may be treated as *D*'s agents and the gain may be taxed to *D* as ordinary income. *See Salvatore v. Commissioner,* 434 F.2d 600 (2d Cir. 1970).

§7.10. Reduce Nonbusiness Holdings of Donor in Order to Qualify for Benefits of §§303, 2032A, and 6166

Gifts of nonbusiness assets may enable the donor's estate to meet the percentage tests of §303 (redemption of stock included in decedent's gross estate treated as payment in exchange for stock and not dividend), §2032A (special use valuation of farm or business assets), and §6166 (deferral and installment payment of estate tax attributable to closely-held business). However, note that transfers made within three years of death are generally brought back into the estate for purposes of determining whether an estate qualifies for the benefits of those sections. §2035(d)(3), (4). The percentage requirements of those sections and their basic limits are summarized in Table 7-1. For a more detailed discussion of them, *see* Chapters 11 and 12.

§7.11. Minimize State Transfer Tax Costs

Inter vivos gifts are also encouraged by the fact that a minority of states impose gift taxes while all states impose some form of death tax. The states imposing gift taxes are Delaware, Louisiana, New York, North

Table 7-1
Table of Statutory Benefits Under §§303, 2032A and 6166

Section	*Code Percentage Requirement*	*Nature of Benefit*
303	Stock included in gross estate must exceed 35% of excess of gross estate over deductions allowable under §§2053 and 2054. §303(b)(2)(A). Stock of 2 or more corporations may be aggregated if 20% or more of the value of the outstanding stock of each is included in decedent's gross estate. §303(b)(2)(B).	Redemption of stock treated as sale and not dividend to extent of total death taxes plus funeral and administration expenses allowable as deductions under §2053. §303(a).
2032A	Adjusted value of qualified real and personal property must exceed 50% of adjusted value of gross estate *and* adjusted value of qualified real property must exceed 25% of adjusted value of gross estate, which must pass to a qualified heir. §2032A(b)(1).	Value of qualified real property for estate tax purposes may be reduced by up to $750,000 based upon its valuation for farming or closely-held business purposes. §2032A(a)(2), etc.
6166	Closely-held business must constitute more than 35% of value of gross estate reduced by deductions allowable under §§2053 and 2054. §6166(a)(1). Two or more businesses may be aggregated for this purpose if 20% or more of the total value of each is included in decedent's gross estate. §6166(c). (Same test as for §303.)	Proportion of estate tax attributable to closely-held business may be deferred for 5 years and paid in installments over following 10 years. Interest on the tax imposed on the first $1 million in value of the closely-held business is subject to a 4% annual rate, §6601(j); the balance is subject to a variable rate.

Carolina, Tennessee, and Wisconsin. Thus, in most states the imposition of any state transfer tax may be avoided by making inter vivos gifts. Of course, gifts made within two or three years of death are often subject to state death taxation. Most states impose only a death tax equal to the maximum credit allowable under §2011 for state death taxes (a so-called "pick-up tax").

A state transfer tax saving often results from inter vivos gifts even in the states that have gift tax laws. First, the laws generally allow an annual exclusion or a similar exemption, which shelters modest-sized annual gifts from the tax. Many also allow gift-splitting, which permits a couple to transfer up to double the annual exclusion amount to each donee annually without incurring any gift tax liability. Second, the amount of state gift tax payable on a transfer is generally not included in the tax base in computing the gift tax (*i.e.*, it is not "grossed up"). Of course, the amount of the tax may be grossed up at death for state death tax purposes if the donative property is subject to the death tax and a credit is allowed for the gift tax. Third, the state transfer tax systems are not unified, which permits donors to take full advantage of the two sets of exemptions and low initial rates that are characteristic of dual transfer tax systems.

Any amount paid in state gift taxes on transfers made within three years of death is not grossed up and included in the donor's gross estate under §2035(c). That provision requires inclusion of only the federal gift tax paid by the decedent or the decedent's estate on gifts made by the decedent or his or her spouse within three years of death.

In 1981, the IRS finally conceded that a decedent's estate is not required to include the amount of a state death tax that was paid during a decedent's lifetime when the donative property subject to a state death tax and a credit is allowable for the previously paid state gift tax. Rev. Rul. 81-302, 1982-2 C.B. 170. Prior to the issuance of Revenue Ruling 81-302, the IRS contended that §2033 required inclusion of the state gift tax paid on an inter vivos gift where the property transferred was later included in the donor's inheritance tax base and a credit was allowed for the gift tax previously paid. Rev. Rul. 75-63, 1975-1 C.B. 294, *revoked by* Rev. Rul. 81-302, 1981-2 C.B. 170. In essence, the IRS viewed the gift tax in such a case as a prepayment of the donor's inheritance tax liability, which is not deductible under §2053. An earlier ruling had denied a deduction for state gift taxes unpaid at death to the extent a credit was allowable for them against the state death tax. Rev. Rul. 71-355, 1971-2 C.B. 334, *revoked by* Rev. Rul. 81-302, 1982-1 C.B. 170. However, the rulings in 1971 and 1975 did recognize that such indirect payments of state death taxes did qualify for the credit under §2011 for state death taxes. The IRS contentions were consistently rejected by the courts. For example, in *Estate of George E. P. Gamble,* 69 T.C. 942 (1978), *acq.*, 1981-2 C.B. 1, the Tax Court pointed out, "Because the decedent's lifetime payment of his State gift tax liability resulted in nothing that was capable of passing from him at the time of his death, respondent's reliance upon section 2033 to increase the value of his gross estate is misplaced." Id. at 950. In *Estate of Lang v. Commissioner,* 613 F.2d 770 (9th Cir. 1980), *aff'g in part and rev'g in part*, 64 T.C. 404 (1975), *acq.*, 1981-2 C.B. 2, the court held that a state gift tax paid after death remains a gift tax and is therefore deductible under §2053. Revenue Ruling 81-302 recognizes that state gift taxes on property that is later included in the donor's inheritance tax base are not assets of the estate when they were paid prior to death. It also concludes that state gift taxes are deductible if they were not paid prior to death. In the latter case Revenue Ruling 81-302 concludes that the state gift taxes that were unpaid at death do not qualify for the state death tax credit under §2011.

The transfer of property into a joint tenancy with another person can save state transfer taxes in states that treat joint tenancies favorably for tax purposes on the death of a joint tenant. In some states none of the joint tenancy property is taxed when a joint tenant dies; in others only the decedent's proportional interest is subject to tax. The overall saving will, of course, be less if the creation of the joint tenancy requires the payment of gift tax. However, in many cases there are strong tax and nontax reasons for not transferring assets into coownership with a spouse or others. For a more complete discussion of cotenancies, *see* Chapter 3.

D. TAX FACTORS INVOLVED IN SELECTING PROPERTY TO GIVE

§7.12. Give Appreciated Property?

In making an intrafamily gift, a client will generally prefer to give appreciated property rather than cash or property that has declined in value. When the donees are in lower income tax brackets than the donor, it may be advantageous to give them property with more, rather than less, built-in gain. As indicated below, a larger basis adjustment is allowable under §1015(d)(6) for gift tax paid on a gift of highly appreciated property than on a transfer of less appreciated property. The transfer of highly appreciated property is often desirable when the donees are expected to sell the property within a short time. Also, the capital gain that may be recognized by the donor on the sale of the property retained by the donor will be smaller if the donor retains assets that have appreciated less in value. On the other hand, where the donor is very elderly or in failing health, highly appreciated property might be retained in order to take full advantage of the tax-free step-up in basis at death that is available under §1014 for property that is included in the donor's gross estate.

If the gifts to a particular donee during the year will be large enough to require payment of some gift tax, they should be arranged to take maximum benefit of the adjustment that is available under §1015(d)(6). Under it the basis of the donee is increased by the portion of the gift tax that is attributable to the appreciation element. The amount of the adjustment will be higher if the donor transfers more highly appreciated property to the donee. The allocation formula under §1015(d)(6) is:

$$\frac{\text{Net appreciation in value of gift (fair market value less adjusted basis)}}{\text{Fair market value of the gift}} \times \text{Gift tax paid} = \text{Adjustment to basis}$$

When a donor plans to give a donee both cash (or unappreciated property) and appreciated property in the same year, a larger adjustment usually results if the donor transfers the cash or unappreciated property first. The annual exclusion applies to the first gift made to a donee during the year, Reg. §1.1015-5(b)(2), as a result of which any gift tax paid on gifts made to the same donee is allocable to later gifts.

Example 7-3. Donor, *D,* whose unified credit was used up by prior gifts, gave his son, *S,* $10,000 in cash on January 1, 1991, and 100 shares of XYZ, Inc. on December 30, 1991. The XYZ shares had an adjusted basis of $10 per share and a fair market value of $100 per share. The annual exclusion was applied to offset the gift of cash so the full amount of tax ($3,700) was imposed with respect to the gift of XYZ, Inc. stock. The donee's basis is $43.30 per share (the donor's basis of $10 per share plus the portion of the gift tax allocable to the appreciation element of each share, $33.30):

$$\frac{\$9,000}{\$10,000} \times \$3,700 = \$3,330$$

If the XYZ stock had been transferred first and the cash second, no tax would have been payable with respect to the gift of stock and there would have been no adjustment to basis under §1015(d). In that case the taxable gift would be limited to the amount of the cash gift. No adjustment would be allowable for two reasons. First, cash has no appreciation element. Second, cash has a carryover basis equal to its fair market value (face amount), which cannot be increased.

§7.13. Do Not Give Property Subject to an Encumbrance in Excess of Its Basis

In order to raise funds with which to pay the gift tax, a donor may borrow against appreciated property prior to making a gift of it. However, as explained in §7.26, the income tax consequences are neither entirely favorable nor entirely settled. A transfer of encumbered property will probably be treated as an exchange to the extent of the indebtedness, which will require the donor to realize gain if the indebtedness exceeds the donor's basis. *Johnson v. Commissioner,* 495 F.2d 1079 (6th Cir.), *cert. denied*, 419 U.S. 1040 (1974). A gift to charity of property subject to an encumbrance in excess of its basis is also treated as a sale or exchange — part gift and part sale in most instances. *See* §8.36.

A taxpayer contemplating a gift of encumbered property should consider other strategies, including a net gift of the property (*see* §7.25), a sale of it on the installment basis (*see* §§9.3-9.9), or an exchange of it for a private annuity (*see* §§9.10-9.16). For a comparative analysis of several methods, *see* Note, Part Gift-Part Sale, Net Gift and Gift of Encumbered Property — Specialized Strategies for Gifts of Unique Property, 50 Notre Dame L. Rev. 880 (1975).

§7.14. Do Not Give Property with a Basis That Exceeds Its Current Fair Market Value

The donor's basis in an asset carries over to the donee. §1015(a). However, for the purpose of determining loss the basis cannot exceed the fair market value on the date of the gift. Thus, in the case of a gift of an asset that has an adjusted basis of $10,000 and a fair market value of $5,000, the donee's basis is limited to $5,000 for the purpose of determining loss. Also, in such a case the donee's basis cannot be increased by any portion of the gift tax. None of the tax was imposed with respect to net appreciation — there wasn't any. *See* §1015(d)(6). A donor should not make a gift that involves losing the tax benefit of a loss. Instead, a donor should consider selling the depreciated property, taking advantage of the loss, and making a gift of the proceeds or of other property.

A terminally ill taxpayer may choose to sell assets that have declined in value in order to make use of the loss for income tax purposes. If depreciated assets are retained until death their bases are stepped down and no one will be entitled to claim a loss. §1014. Of course, §267 bars a deduction for the loss on a sale to certain related taxpayers.

§7.15. Do Not Give Property with Positive Tax Characteristics

A high bracket taxpayer should retain assets that generate tax-exempt income or that shelter other income. Thus, the donor should avoid making gifts of tax-exempt municipal bonds, depreciable assets, or other properties that are tax-exempt or generate deductions in excess of income. Instead, a donor should generally make gifts of appreciated assets that produce ordinary income.

Note, however, that a wealthy client may choose an estate plan that requires him or her to pay the income tax on income received by other family members from a trust established by the client. Such a payment is, in effect, a tax-free gift from the payor to the recipients of the income. Under the grantor trust rules the grantor may remain taxable on the income of the trust without subjecting the trust to inclusion in the grantor's estate. *See* §10.32.1.

§7.16. Give Property That Reduces the Value of Assets Retained by the Donor

Gifts may be used to reduce the donor's ownership interest in a closely-held business or a parcel of real estate to the point that it may be valued at a discount for estate tax purposes. *See* §2.43. For example, if a donor who owns 60 percent of the stock of a closely-held business gives 11 percent of the stock to others, the donor has retained a minority interest (49 percent) that may qualify for a discount. However, some cases have not allowed a minority discount in such cases, at least not when the gifts were made shortly before death. *See Estate of Elizabeth Murphy,* 60 T.C.M. 645 (1990). Of course, if the donor wants to preserve the benefits of §§303, 2032A, or 6166, it may be necessary to limit gifts of stock. *See* §7.10. Also, a fractional interest in real property may be valued at 15 to 25 percent less than a proportionate part of the total value, at least when a discount is supported by expert opinion. *Propstra v. United States,* 680 F.2d 1248 (9th Cir. 1982); *Nancy N. Mooneyham,* 60 T.C.M. — (1991); Wallace, Now You See it, Now You Don't — Valuation Conundrums in Estate Planning, U. Miami, 24th Inst. Est. Plan., ch. 8 (1990).

The IRS has resisted allowing a minority discount for shares owned by one person where his or her family retains a controlling interest in the corporation (interests included under §2035 were aggregated with decedent's other interests for purposes of evaluation). The so-called *family attribution* or *unity of ownership* theory was expressed in Rev. Rul. 81-253, 1981-2 C.B. 187, which denied a minority discount where the donor simultaneously gave all of the stock in a corporation in equal shares to his three children. *See also* Rev. Rul. 79-7, 1979-1 C.B. 294. However, the IRS position has been rejected by several courts, including the Tax Court. Indeed, in *Victor I. Minahan,* 88 T.C. 492, 500 (1987), the Tax Court held that the position of the IRS was unreasonable: "[W]e emphasize that we find respondent's position unreasonable only because, by espousing a family attribution approach, he seeks to repudiate a well-established line of cases of long and reputable ancestry, going back as far as 1940." Transfers to multiple donees were also not aggregated in related areas. *Rushton v. Commissioner,* 498 F.2d 88 (5th Cir. 1974) (blockage discount denied for gifts to several donees on the same day); *Mathilde B. Hooper,* 41 B.T.A. 114 (1940) (estate tax discount allowed for minority interest in family corporation), *acq. on valuation issue*, 1940-1 C.B. 3; *contra*, *Driver v. United States,* 38 A.F.T.R.2d 76-6315 (W.D. Wis. 1976) (gifts made within three days of each other were aggregated, no minority discount allowed).

§7.17. Do Not Make Gifts That Have Adverse Income Tax Consequences for the Donor

Most property can be transferred by gift without causing the donor to realize any income. However, gain will be realized when a gift is made of some special types of assets. For example, the gift of an installment obligation constitutes a disposition of the obligation under §453B, which requires the donor to realize gain or loss measured by the difference between its fair market value at the time of transfer and its basis. *See* Reg. §1.453-9. The transfer of an installment obligation does not constitute a disposition if the transferor continues to be treated as its owner for income tax purposes. *See* Rev. Rul. 74-613, 1974-2 C.B. 153 (transfer to revocable trust is not a disposition, grantor treated as owner under §§671-677).

A gift or other disposition of section 38 property (investment credit property) may require a recapture of a portion of the credit. Former §47(a). The disposition of investment credit property may trigger recapture although the basic provisions regarding the credit were repealed by the 1986 Act. The Regulations define "disposition" to include a transfer by gift. Reg. §1.47-2(a)(1). However, the term does not extend to a transfer by reason of death. Former §47(b)(1). Accordingly, a donor should be cautious about disposing of investment recapture property, particularly before the end of its useful life.

Gifts of some other types of recapture property do not have the same negative tax consequences. A gift of §1245 property (depreciable personal property) or §1250 property (depreciable real property) does not trigger recapture of depreciation. §§1245(b)(1), 1251(d)(1). Instead, the potential for depreciation recapture carries over to the donee. If a taxpayer plans to sell §§1245 or 1250 property, the taxpayer should consider giving it to one or more family members who are in lower income tax brackets prior to finalizing the sale. Spreading the income among several taxpayers may reduce the capital gain tax on the sale.

Care should also be exercised in making gifts of Subchapter S stock because of the limits on the number of shareholders. Under §1361(b)(1) a Subchapter S corporation cannot have more than 35 shareholders. In addition, only certain types of trusts are permitted to be shareholders.

E. SPECIALIZED GIFT TECHNIQUES

> "Transactions within a family group are subject to special scrutiny in order to determine if they are in economic reality what they appear to be on their face." . . . The presumption is that a transfer between closely related parties is a gift. *Estate of Pearl G. Reynolds,* 55 T.C. 172, 201 (1970).

§7.18. INTRODUCTION

Several specialized techniques of making gifts have evolved to meet the estate planning needs of wealthy clients. Among them are some arrangements that may not be treated as gifts for gift tax purposes: small below-market loans, the payment by the grantor of the income tax imposed on a grantor trust of which others are the beneficiaries, the payment by one spouse of the entire joint income or gift tax liability, and arrangements by which the donor performs services for others gratuitiously or allows them the free use of property. In addition, there are a variety of ways in which gifts can be structured to deal with particular types of property. They include the transfer of the donor's residence to a family member, the installment gift, the "net" gift, the gift of encumbered property, and the part gift and part sale. Individuals may also provide valuable assistance to family members in other ways that are not treated as gifts but which may help them to increase their estates. For example, a wealthy parent may tell children about investment opportunities rather than acting upon them himself or herself. Similarly, a wealthy individual may assist the investment program of other family members directly or by guaranteeing loans made to them by others. In a questionable private letter ruling, LR 9113009, the IRS held that a guarantee of the obligation of another family member made without adequate consideration was a present gift. In sum, there are many ways by which one person may help another increase his or her wealth without incurring any gift tax liability.

The taxation of a family's wealth can also be controlled by various types of intrafamily transfers for consideration that have donative overtones. *See* Chapter 9. Some of them, such as the sale of property on the installment method, can be used to "freeze" the value of the seller's estate. Others, such as the family annuity, seek broader tax benefits, including a reduction in the size of the seller's estate. In some circumstances a transfer for consideration may meet the client's needs better than a gift, with little or no reduction in the overall tax benefits.

§7.19. Small Below-Market Loans

The 1984 Act added §7872, which defines the income and gift tax consequences of demand and term loans that are made at below-market rates of interest. For purposes of this section a "gift loan" is a below-market loan where the forgoing of interest is in the nature of a gift. §7872(f)(3). No gift or income tax consequences flow from gift loans between individuals that do not exceed $10,000 unless the borrower uses the proceeds to purchase or carry income-producing assets. §7872(c)(2). Thus, a gift loan of $10,000 or less between individuals is totally ignored unless the proceeds are directly related to the purchase or retention of income-producing property.

Below-market loans of $100,000 or less between individuals result in imputed interest paid by the borrower to the lender for income tax purposes, but only to the extent of the "net investment income" of the borrower. §7872(d)(1)(A). For this purpose the net investment income of the borrower is only taken into account if it exceeds $1,000 for the year. Interest is imputed on the full amount of the loan if one of the principal purposes of the loan is tax avoidance. §7872(d)(1)(B).

For gift tax purposes a person making a below-market loan of more than $10,000 is treated as having made a gift to the borrower. That is, the $100,000 exception does not apply for gift tax purposes. In the case of a gift loan for a term, the lender is treated as having made a gift at the time the loan was made of the excess of the amount loaned over the present value of all payments to be made under the terms of the loan. §7872(b)(1). In the case of a gift demand loan the lender is treated as having made a gift of the forgone interest, calculated at the federal short-term rate, on the last day of the calendar year. §7872(a).

Example 7-4. On January 1 *M* made an interest-free demand loan of $100,000 to her daughter, *D,* who used the proceeds to purchase a residence. The loan remained outstanding throughout the entire year. *D* had no net investment income during the year. Under §7872(d) *D* is not considered to have paid and *M* is not considered to have received any interest on account of the loan. If the federal short-term rate were 11%, for gift tax purposes *M* would be treated as having made a gift of $11,000 to *D* on December 31.

§7.20. Payment by One Spouse of Entire Income or Gift Tax Liability

The payment by one spouse of the entire joint income tax liability for the year is not treated as a gift for gift tax purposes. Reg. §25.2511-1(d). Under that Regulation the same rule applies to the payment of the federal gift tax applicable to gifts that are split under §2513. Because of the adoption of the unlimited marital deduction, these exceptions now have little significance.

Example 7-5. *H* and *W,* who are both employed and have substantial incomes, filed a joint income tax return for the last year. *W,* the wealthier spouse, paid their entire income tax liability. In addition, *W* paid all of the gift taxes that were due on gifts she made during the year, which for gift tax purposes were split with *H* under §2513. Neither the payment of the income tax nor the gift taxes involved a gift from *W* to *H.*

§7.21. Grantor Pays Income Tax on Grantor Trust

As explained in §10.32.1, an irrevocable inter vivos trust may be structured so the grantor is treated as owner of the trust for income tax purposes, but the trust will not be included in the grantor's estate. By paying the income tax on income that is actually distributed to others the grantor is able to make a tax-free gift to them.

Example 7-6. Grantor *G* transferred income-producing property to a trust of which *G*'s children are the income beneficiaries. *G* retained the power, in a nonfiduciary capacity, to withdraw the principal and substitute property of equivalent value. Such a power causes *G* to be treated as the owner of the trust under §675(4)(C). *G* pays the income tax on the income of the trust although the income is actually distributed to *G*'s children. By paying the income tax *G* in effect makes a tax-free gift to the beneficiaries.

§7.22. Free Services and Free Use of Property

As yet the IRS has not sought to apply the gift tax to the free performance by one person of services for another. This position is consistent with dictum in *Commissioner v. Hogle,* 165 F.2d 352 (10th Cir. 1947), to the effect that the gratuitous performance of services does not constitute a taxable gift. It is also consistent with Rev. Rul. 66-167, 1966-1 C.B. 20, which held that a fiduciary's waiver of the right to receive statutory compensation did not constitute a gift where the fiduciary decided to serve gratuitously within a reasonable time after assuming office and the fiduciary thereafter took no action inconsistent with that position. However, a gift does take place where one person (the donor) pays another person to perform services for a third person (the donee).

Allowing another person the free use of property is more vulnerable to treatment as a gift. Perhaps the IRS has not sought to impose the gift tax on those transactions because of the valuation problems and other administrative difficulties. Providing another person with the free use of property no doubt confers a benefit upon the user, but defining the rules under which an arrangement of that type would be taxed would be exceptionally difficult. The difficulty is illustrated by the complex, yet somewhat inadequate, law on "free loans" adopted by the United Kingdom. Finance Act 1976, §§115 to 117.

> **Example 7-7.** *F* has been making annual cash gifts to his son *S* equal to the maximum allowable annual exclusion. This year *F* purchased a car for $15,000, and has allowed *S* to keep it at his apartment and drive it whenever *S* wished. In addition, *F* has paid the $1,200 annual cost of insurance on the car. *S* has made the car available to *F* when he needed one and during the periods that *S* was out of town. Under existing administrative practices, giving *S* the free use of the car and making the insurance payments are not treated as gifts to *S.*

§7.23. Gift of a Residence with Continued Occupancy by Donor

The gift of a residence to a family member is usually intended to remove any further appreciation in its value from the donor's estate. That goal may be achieved although the donor continues to occupy it until the time of death. However, the value of achieving that goal must be balanced against the tax and nontax risks the gift involves. Often the potential saving in taxes is outweighed by the risks. A trust in which the grantor retains the use of a personal residence for a term of years (the qualified personal residence trust described in §9.43) may be preferable because of its statutory recognition for tax purposes and better protection against the reach of creditors — at least during the term of the grantor's retained interest.

A basic problem with the transfer of a residence to family members is that the value of the residence will be included in the donor's gross estate if the donor dies while continuing to use or occupy it pursuant to an express or implied understanding or agreement. *Guynn v. United States,* 437 F.2d 1148 (4th Cir. 1971); Rev. Rul. 70-155, 1970-1 C.B. 189. For purposes of §2036 it is not necessary that the retained interest be expressed in the instrument of transfer or that the donor have a legally enforceable right to possession or enjoyment. *Estate of Emil Linderme, Sr.,* 52 T.C. 305 (1969). Continued co-occupancy of the residence by the donor and the donee-spouse does not of itself support an inference of an understanding or agreement regarding the retained use or enjoyment by the donor. *Estate of Allen D. Gutchess,* 46 T.C. 554 (1966). In contrast, exclusive occupancy of the residence by the donor is a very important factor in determining whether there was an understanding or agreement. *Estate of Adrian K. Rapelje,* 73 T.C. 82 (1979); *Linderme, supra*. As indicated by Rev. Rul. 78-409, 1978-2 C.B. 234, the IRS has a very expansive view of what constitutes an "understanding or agreement."

The case for exclusion of the residence from the donor's estate is improved where the gift is reported on a timely filed gift tax return and the donee pays the real estate taxes, insurance, and other costs of owning the residence. If the donor and the donee are married and both occupy the residence, it is not necessary for the donor to pay any rent for the donor's continued use of it. In other cases the donor should pay a fair rental. It is helpful if there is a written rental agreement that establishes the terms under which the donor occupies the premises.

The outright gift of a residence usually involves some other tax consequences that should also be taken into account. First, if the gift succeeds and the residence is not included in the donor's estate, the donee will take a carryover basis in the property determined under §1015 instead of an estate tax value determined under §1014. This factor is less significant if the donee does not intend to sell the residence. Second, as a result of the gift it may no longer be possible to exclude a substantial part of the gain under §121 if it is sold at a gain. That section allows a one-time exclusion of up to $125,000 of the gain realized on the sale of a principal residence by a person 55 or older. (If the donor retains a term interest in a personal residence trust the exclusion remains available because the donor is treated as the owner of the trust property for income tax purposes.) Third, the residence may no longer qualify for the preferential property tax treatment that may be allowed under local law for residential property owned and occupied by senior citizens.

On the nontax side there is always the risk that the donee might deprive the donor of any use of the property. Also, at some point the donor may no longer be able to pay the fair rental value of the property, which could jeopardize exclusion of the property from the donor's estate if the donor continued to occupy it. Perhaps more important, the gift makes the residence subject to disposition by the donee inter vivos and at death and reachable by the donee's creditors. Where a gift is made, the donee's will should dispose of the property in an acceptable manner should the donee predecease the donor.

§7.24. Installment Gifts: Periodic Forgiveness of Transferee's Notes

Various techniques are used to keep the value of a gift within the amount of the allowable annual exclusions. Thus, a donor may limit the amount of the gift made in a particular year by transferring a partial interest in an asset to the donee. However, under this approach the value of the interests retained by the donor may continue to appreciate in value. That risk can be avoided by transferring all of the donor's interests in a particular item of property in exchange for notes of the donee that have a value equal to the excess of the value of the transferred property over the amount of the allowable annual exclusions for the current year. In successive years the donor may forgive an amount of the notes equal to the annual exclusion. Of course, the forgiveness of the notes may trigger recognition of gain by the donor under the installment sales rules. *See* §9.6. An installment sale such as this should not be subject to the special valuation rules of §2702.

For gift tax purposes the amount of a gift is the value of the property transferred reduced by the value of notes or considerations received in exchange by the donor. §2512(b). "If a donor transfers by gift less than his entire interest in property, the gift tax is applicable to the interest transferred. The tax is applicable, for example, to the transfer of an undivided half interest in property, or to the transfer of a life estate when the grantor retains the remainder interest, or vice versa." Reg. §25.2511-1(e). For income tax purposes the transfer of property in exchange for a note would be treated as a sale to the extent of the consideration received, which could be very undesirable from the donor's point of view. Of course, the taxation of the gain may be deferred unless the seller opts not to use the installment sale method of reporting. In some cases the valuation of the transferee's note is a troublesome issue. For example, the IRS has indicated that a low-interest note that is due when the borrower's home is sold has no ascertainable value. LR 8103130. Accordingly, the full amount of the loan might be treated as a gift.

A promissory note given to the transferor by the donee may not be recognized by the IRS as consideration if it is systematically forgiven in annual increments equal to the annual gift tax exclusion. In such cases the IRS may argue that the notes must be disregarded and the transfer treated as a gift of the entire value of the property. That result must follow, according to the IRS, if the transferor intended from the outset to forgive the notes that he or she received. Rev. Rul. 77-299, 1977-2 C.B. 343. The issue has been most frequently litigated in the Tax Court, which has generally recognized valid, enforceable notes as consideration, particularly when they were secured. "This Court has held that when property is transferred in exchange for a valid, enforceable and secured legal obligation, there is no gift for Federal tax purposes." *Estate of I. W. Kelley,* 63 T.C. 321, 324 (1974), *nonacq.*, 1977-2 C.B. 2. *See also Selsor R. Haygood,* 42 T.C. 936 (1964), *acq. in result,* 1965-1 C.B. 4, *withdrawn and nonacq. substituted,* 1977-2 C.B. 2; *Nelson Story III,* 38 T.C. 936 (1962). The IRS succeeded in *Minnie E. Deal,* 29 T.C. 730 (1958), where the Tax Court found that the notes executed by the transferee-daughters "were not intended to be enforced and were not intended as consideration for the transfer by the petitioner, and that, in substance, the transfer of the property was by gift." 29 T.C. at 736. A gift may occur where the notes have a value less than their face amounts because the interest rate provided for in the notes is less than the market rate, *Gertrude H. Blackburn,* 20 T.C. 204 (1953), or because of other factors (*e.g., Estate of Pearl Gibbons Reynolds,* 55 T.C. 172 (1970)).

Notes can also be used to insulate transfers of cash from the gift tax. *See* §7.19. Under the approach generally taken by the Tax Court, such notes can be written down at an annual rate equal to the allowable annual exclusions without jeopardizing their status.

§7.25. Net Gifts

A *net gift* is a gift that is conditioned upon the donee's payment of the gift tax on the transfer. It is a useful planning technique, particularly when it is desirable for the donee to sell the property in order to generate funds with which to pay the tax. For example, the donor may not have sufficient funds to pay the tax and the tax on the gain would be less if the property were sold by the donee.

§7.25.1. Income Tax

A net gift generally does not have an adverse income tax consequence when the donor's basis in the property is equal to or greater than the gift tax to be paid by the donee. When the donor's basis is less than the tax, the income tax consequences of a net gift were uncertain until the Supreme Court's decision in *Diedrich v. Commissioner,* 457 U.S. 191 (1982). Under *Diedrich* it is clear that the donor realizes a gain in such a case. The gain is realized in the year the gift tax is paid, not in the year of the gift. *Estate of Weeden v. Commissioner,* 685 F.2d 1160 (9th Cir. 1982).

All along the IRS contended that this type of transaction involved a part gift and part sale in which the gift tax paid by the donee was an amount realized by the donor. LR 7752001. Under that approach the donor had a capital gain to the extent that the amount of the gift tax paid by the donee exceeds the donor's adjusted basis in the property. In *Diedrich* the Supreme Court accepted the IRS argument because the donor is statutorily liable for payment of the gift tax. §2502(d). Earlier cases had reached inconsistent outcomes.

Prior to *Diedrich* most courts held that a net gift transaction did not have any income tax consequences to the donor; the Tax Court found it difficult to see that the donor received anything as a result of the gift. *Richard H. Turner,* 49 T.C. 356 (1968), *aff'd per curiam,* 410 F.2d 752 (6th Cir. 1969), *nonacq.,* 1971-2 C.B. 4. The Sixth Circuit later purported to limit *Turner* to its peculiar facts in *Johnson v. Commissioner,* 495 F.2d 752 (6th Cir.), *cert. denied,* 419 U.S. 1040 (1974), which involved the transfer of encumbered property (*see* §7.25). In addition, *Turner* was followed in several other net gift cases: *Estate of Kenneth W. Davis,* 30 T.C.M. 1363 (1971), *aff'd per curiam*, 469 F.2d 694 (5th Cir. 1972); *Estate of Douglas Henry,* 69 T.C. 665 (1978); *Victor W. Krause,* 56 T.C. 1242 (1971).

While the Tax Court recognized that the IRS argument had a great deal of force, it asserted that "[t]hings have gone too far by now to wipe the slate clean and start all over again." *Edna Bennett Hirst,* 63 T.C. 307, 315 (1974), *aff'd,* 572 F.2d 427 (4th Cir. 1978). The IRS continued to litigate the issue, but was generally rejected in memorandum decisions that cited *Turner* and *Hirst* as conclusive and refused to reconsider the issue. *See, e.g., John T. Benson,* 37 T.C.M. 989 (1978); *Estate of Norman D. Weeden,* 39 T.C.M. 699 (1979).

The Eighth Circuit decision in the *Diedrich* case upheld the IRS. It rejected the *Turner-Hirst* line of cases and held that when a donor transfers appreciated property in exchange for the donee's promise to pay the resulting gift taxes, the donor realizes a gain to the extent that the gift taxes paid exceed the donor's adjusted basis in property. *Diedrich v. Commissioner,* 643 F.2d 499 (8th Cir. 1981), *rev'g Victory P. Diedrich,* 39 T.C.M. 433 (1979), and *Frances D. Grant,* 39 T.C.M. 1088 (1980). In addition, other courts of appeals, when urged to extend the *Turner-Hirst* rationale to other factual settings, refused to do so and strongly criticized the rationale itself. *See Estate of Levine v. Commissioner,* 634 F.2d 12 (2d Cir. 1980) and *Evangelista v. Commissioner,* 629 F.2d 1218 (7th Cir. 1980).

The holding period of the donee in net gift cases is unclear. *Citizens' National Bank of Waco v. United States,* 417 F.2d 675 (5th Cir. 1969), concluded that "tacking" of the donor's and donee's holding periods is allowable under §1223(2) because the donor's basis carried over to the donee under §1015. Thus, if a donee sells the property at a gain within a year of the transfer, the donor's holding period can be taken into account in determining whether or not the gain was long term. As noted below, where the gift is made to a trust, the gain on a sale made within two years of the transfer will be characterized as if the donor had made the sale and taxed to the trust at the donor's rates. Aside from §644, the IRS argues that the issue is governed by Reg. §1.1015-4(a)(1) where the transfer involves a part gift and part sale. Under it the donee's basis is the greater of the amount paid for the property *or* the donor's adjusted basis for the property *plus* an adjustment under §1015(d)(6) for gift tax paid with respect to the transfer. In the case of a net gift the donee's basis apparently includes both the amount paid by the donee (the amount of the gift tax) plus an increase in basis under §1015(b)(6) on account of the gift tax paid with respect to the appreciation element. Accordingly, the IRS will deny tacking under §1223(2) where the price paid by the donee exceeds the donor's basis. LR 7752001.

When the gift is made in trust, the gain on a sale made by the trustee within the following two years will be taxed under §644 as if the sale had been made by the donor. *See* §10.4.11. By its terms §644 applies to a sale made within two years, whether the transfer is characterized as a net gift or a part gift and part sale, if the fair market value of the property on the date of the transfer exceeds its adjusted basis in the hands of the trustee. In characterizing the proceeds of a sale the holding period of the grantor should be taken into account, §644(c), which could be important if tacking is not allowed.

A gift to a trust may also generate adverse income tax consequences where the trust income is used to pay the donor's gift tax. Prior to the adoption of the grantor trust rules, §§671-677, the courts held that the trust income was taxable to the donor as ordinary income under the *Clifford* doctrine. *Estate of A. E. Staley, Sr.,* 47 B.T.A. 260 (1942), *aff'd,* 136 F.2d 368 (5th Cir. 1943), *cert. denied,* 320 U.S. 786 (1945). Now, the income may be taxed to the grantor under §677 to the extent it is, or in the discretion of a nonadverse party may be, used to pay the donor's gift tax liability. *Estate of Craig R. Shaeffer,* 37 T.C. 99 (1961), *aff'd,* 313 F.2d 738 (8th Cir.), *cert. denied,* 375 U.S. 818 (1963). Note that the income of the trust is not taxable to the grantor on that theory after the donor's obligation is discharged by payment of the tax. Thus, when the trustee borrows the funds to pay the tax, the trust's subsequent income is not taxed to the donor even when it is used to repay the loan. Repayment of the loan discharges the trust's obligation and not that of the donor. *Estate of Annette S. Morgan,* 37 T.C. 981 (1962), *aff'd,* 316 F.2d 238 (6th Cir.), *cert. denied,* 375 U.S. 825 (1963); *Victor W. Krause,* 56 T.C. 1242 (1971). In general §677 does not apply if an encumbrance is paid with funds other than trust income. *See* Comment, Tax Consequences of Funding Trusts with Encumbered Property: The Demise of Section 677, 28 U. Fla. L. Rev. 708, 710 (1976).

The possibility that a net gift may result in some income tax liability to the donor should not deter most clients from using it. First of all, the net gift may reduce the total amount of gift tax that the donor must pay. *See* Example 7-8, *infra.* Thus, even though the donor might incur some income tax liability, the gift tax cost is reduced. Second, the recognition of gain by the donor may not result in a much larger income tax liability than if the donee sold the property. Where the gain will be taxed as long-term capital gain the maximum rate applicable to the donor (or the donee) may be lower than the rate applicable to ordinary income. Overall, the decision of whether to use a net gift should be made in light of the marginal income tax rates of the donor and the donee, the client's financial resources, and the other tax and nontax factors that are involved in deciding whether to make a gift.

§7.25.2. Gift Tax

On the gift tax side the IRS has been cooperative: It recognizes that where a gift is made subject to a condition that the donee pay the gift tax, the donor receives consideration equal to the amount of the gift tax the donee is obligated to pay. Rev. Rul. 75-72, 1975-1 C.B. 310 (including formula for computation of deduction); Rev. Rul. 76-49, 1976-1 C.B. 294 (including formula for computation of deduction where donee will pay both the federal and state gift taxes). In such cases the donor makes a gift of an amount equal to the value of the property less the amount of tax payable on the transfer. The method of calculating the amount of a net gift where state gift taxes are also involved is illustrated by Example D of IRS Publication 904 (rev. May 1985), Interrelated Computations for Estate and Gift Taxes.

Example 7-8. Donor, *D,* made a gift of property worth $110,000 to his son, *S,* in 1991 on condition that *S* pay the federal gift tax on the transfer. In prior years *D* had made taxable gifts of $600,000. The deduction is $27,007.30 based on the formula:

$$\frac{\text{Tentative Tax}}{1 + \text{Rate of Tax}} = \text{Tax Due}$$

First, the tax is calculated without regard to the condition, which indicates a tax of $37,000 (the "tentative tax"). Next, the formula calculation is made:

$$\text{Tax Due} = \frac{\$37,000}{1 + .37} = \$27,007.30$$

Finally, the calculation is proved by using the "true tax" to calculate *D*'s gift tax liability for the quarter in the ordinary way:

Gross transfer for year	$110,000.00
Less: Gift tax on transfer	−27,007.30
Net transfer	$82,992.70
Less: Annual exclusion	−10,000.00
Taxable gift for year	$72,992.70
Plus: Prior gifts by donor	+600,000.00
Total taxable gifts	$672,992.70
Tax on total gifts	219,807.30
Less: Tax on prior gifts	−192,800.00
Tax on gift for year	$27,007.30

Even in the case of a net gift, the donor's unified credit must be taken into account in computing the amount of the gift tax. Rev. Rul. 79-398, 1979-2 C.B. 338. The policy was explained in an earlier Private Letter Ruling as follows: "The unified credit must be used in computing the gift tax. The credit relates to the gift tax of the donor and consequently can only be used against the tax imposed upon the donor's transfers. The fact that a donee is going to satisfy the donor's primary obligation to pay the gift tax does not make the tax a tax on the donee's transfers. Therefore, the unified credit to be used is the donor's credit." LR 7842068. In the view of the IRS, no consideration flows from the donee to the donor for the amount of tax equal to the donor's available unified credit. Rev. Rul. 81-223, 1981-2 C.B. 189.

§7.25.3. Estate Tax

In most cases gifts made prior to the donor's death are includible in his or her estate. §2035(d)(1). However, under §2035(d)(2) policies of insurance on the donor's life are included in the donor's estate if the donor dies within three years of death. Of course, the gifted property is includable in the donor's estate under §§2036 and 2038 if the donor retained the use of the property or controls over its disposition.

§7.26. Gifts of Encumbered Property

When a donor makes a gift of encumbered property, only the excess of the value of the property over the amount of the encumbrance is generally subject to the gift tax. *D. S. Jackman,* 44 B.T.A. 704 (1941), *acq.,* 47-1 C.B. 9. This result is logical and consistent with the treatment of net gifts. See §7.25. However, if the donee can require the donor to satisfy the encumbrance out of other property, the value of the gift is not reduced by the amount of the encumbrance. *Estate of D. Byrd Gwinn,* 25 T.C. 31 (1955).

The income tax consequences for the donor of this type of gift also should be considered in advance. They are simple enough if the donor's basis exceeds the amount of the encumbrance — the donor does not realize any gain as a result of the gift. However, since 1971 the courts have recognized that the donor will realize gain when the amount of the encumbrance exceeds the donor's basis. *Crane v. Commissioner,* 331 U.S. 1 (1947). The trend began with *Malone v. United States,* 326 F. Supp. 106 (N.D. Miss. 1971), *aff'd per curiam,* 455 F.2d 502 (5th Cir. 1972). In *Malone* the donee, a trustee, formally assumed the donor's personal obligation for the mortgage indebtedness on the encumbered real property that was transferred to the trust. Because the indebtedness was assumed, the court readily concluded that the gift resulted in an economic benefit to the donor equal to the excess of the indebtedness over the donor's basis in the property.

The application of the *Crane* concept was significantly extended in *Johnson v. Commissioner,* 495 F.2d 1079 (6th Cir.), *cert. denied,* 419 U.S. 1040 (1974), which held that the donor received an economic benefit when encumbered stock was given to a trustee although the donor was not personally liable for the indebtedness and it was not assumed by the trustee. The taxpayer in *Johnson* borrowed $200,000 on a nonrecourse basis against stock that he gave to a trustee three days later. The stock had a basis of about $11,000 and a value of $500,000 at the time of the gift. Under those circumstances the donor realized a gain of $189,000 when the gift was made. The rule established in *Johnson* is logical, fair, and consistent with Reg. §1.1011-2(a)(3), which requires that the amount of an indebtedness be treated as an amount received for purposes of applying the bargain sale rules whether or not the transferee agrees to pay the debt.

Johnson was followed in *Estate of Aaron Levine,* 634 F.2d 12 (2d Cir. 1980), *aff'g* 72 T.C. 780 (1979), where the donor gave a trustee real property that was subject to encumbrances. These loans were entered into over a long period of years and came to a total amount that exceeded his basis. Although the timing of the loans in *Levine* did not evidence a plan to bail out the mortgage proceeds from the start, the donor nonetheless "reaped a tangible economic benefit from this transaction and such economic benefit is subject to tax under the rationale of [*Crane.*]" 72 T.C. at 792.

> **Example 7-9.** *D* owns 1,000 shares of XYZ, Inc. stock that have a basis of $1 per share and a current value of $100 per share. If *D* sells the stock for $100 per share *D* will realize a capital gain of $99 per share or a total of $99,000. If *D* borrows $75,000 against the stock *D* will not realize any gain until *D* disposes of the stock. However, under *Johnson* and *Levine* if *D* borrows on the stock and later makes a gift of it, *D* will realize a gain at the time of the gift.

When there is a gift of encumbered property the donee's basis will reflect both the gain realized by the donor and the portion of any gift tax paid that is attributable to the appreciation element of the gift. As the court explained in *Johnson,* Congress authorized increases in a donee's basis by both the amount of gain recognized in connection with gifts to trusts and the amount of gift tax paid, although that may superficially appear to be redundant.

Until the *Johnson* decision was handed down in 1974 a taxpayer might have borrowed against an appreciated asset, then given it away without ever being required to pay any income tax on the amount by which the loan exceeded his or her basis. If the transaction were carefully structured the obligation could be satisfied by the donee without any income tax liability to the donor. In the pre-*Johnson* era the grantor might be taxed on the income under §677 in the case of a gift to a trust. Even in the case of a trust, the reach of §677 was avoided if (1) the trustee assumed liability for the obligation, *Edwards v. Greenwald,* 217 F.2d 632 (5th Cir. 1954), or (2) the obligation was satisfied with funds other than trust income, *Estate of Annette S. Morgan,* 37 T.C. 981 (1962), *aff'd,* 316 F.2d 238 (6th Cir.), *cert. denied,* 375 U.S. 825 (1963).

§7.27. Part Gift and Part Sale

Under another approach the donor may sell part of the property to the intended donee in order to generate funds with which to pay the gift tax on a gift of the balance of the property. The plan may be implemented in either of two ways, which have substantially different income tax consequences. Under the first, the donor gives part of the property to the donee, who uses it as security to borrow funds with which to purchase the remainder of the property. In this case the gift and the sale relate to separate interests, which are respected for gift and income tax purposes. Under the second method all of the property is transferred to the donee for less than adequate and full consideration in money or money's worth (*i.e.,* a bargain sale). The owner's gift tax liability is the same under both approaches. However, under the first method the gain is computed separately for the property sold, while under the second gain is determined by reference to the transferor's basis in the entire property.

Example 7-10. *O* plans to transfer 1,000 shares of XYZ, Inc. stock to his daughter, *D,* in exchange for $15,000 which *O* will use to pay the taxes that will be due as a result of the transfer. The stock has a basis of $10 per share and a value of $50 per share. Whichever method is used, the transfer will involve a gift to *D* of property worth $35,000 for gift tax purposes.

Under the first method *O* would give *D* 700 shares outright, which involves a gift of $35,000 ($50 × 700). The gift would not cause *O* to recognize any gain unless the shares were encumbered. *D*'s basis in those shares would be *O*'s basis ($10) plus any gift tax paid with respect to the net appreciation in value of the shares. *See* §1015. Also, the time *O* held these shares could be taken into account in determining *D*'s holding period. *See* §1223(2). If *O* sells the remaining 300 shares to *D* for $50 each, *O* would have a capital gain of $12,000 ($50 × 300 − ($10 × 300)). Under §1012 *D*'s basis in those 300 shares would be their cost of $50 each, the holding period of which would begin with the date of purchase. Thus, if no gift tax were paid with respect to the gift of 700 shares, *D* would have a total basis of $22,000 in the 1,000 shares (700 × $10) + (300 × $50).

O's gain would be much smaller under the second method (*i.e.,* if *O* makes a part gift and part sale of the 1,000 shares to *D* for $15,000). In case of a part gift and part sale "the transferor has a gain to the extent that the amount realized by him exceeds his adjusted basis in the property." Reg. §1.1001-1(e)(1). Here the amount realized ($15,000) exceeds his basis ($10,000) by only $5,000. However, in this case *D*'s basis will be limited to the price paid ($15,000) plus the portion of the gift tax paid with respect to the net appreciation. *See* Reg. §1.1015-4(a). Accordingly, the IRS might argue that the time *O* held the shares could not be taken into account for holding period purposes. *See* LR 7752001.

As Example 7-10 indicates, income and gift tax consequences must be taken into account in choosing which method to use in effectuating a part gift and part sale. The outcomes should also be compared with the results produced by other techniques, such as the net gift. *See* §7.25. In this connection it is important to note that bargain sales to charity are subject to different rules. *See* §1011(b); *see also* §8.36.

F. GIFTS TO MINORS

§7.28. Importance of Gifts to Minors

Income tax changes, most notably the adoption of the Kiddie Tax, the compressed income tax rate schedule, and the elmination of the income-shifting potential of short-term trusts, limit the income-shifting advantages of making gifts to minors. However, gifts to minors remain important in estate planning. By making gifts to minors, the overall income tax burdens of a family may be lightened a bit. More important, the donor's estate will include neither the property's further appreciation in value nor the post-gift income from the property. Annual exclusion gifts to minors are a particularly advantageous way of reducing the donor's overall gift, estate and GST tax burdens.

Making gifts to a trust for a minor is made more attractive by the availability of annual exclusion if the beneficiary holds a properly drafted *Crummey* power. *See* §7.37. In planning trusts for minors, consideration must also be given to other income tax rules. For example, appreciation realized on the sale of appreciated property within two years following its transfer to the trust may be taxed at the grantor's marginal rate. §644. On the positive side, income accumulated before the beneficiary's birth or attainment of age 21 is excluded from the reach of the throwback rules. §665(b).

The sections that follow discuss the principal methods of transferring property to minors, including outright gifts, Series EE bonds, various forms of multiparty bank accounts, gifts under the U.G.M.A., 8A U.L.A. 317 (1983), or the U.T.M.A., 8A U.L.A. 243 (1990 Supp.) (hereinafter the "Uniform Acts"), and gifts in trust. The discussion points out the wide differences in tax and notax consequences that flow from different methods of making gifts to minors. For example, some transfers constitute completed gifts for gift tax purposes while others do not. Also, in the case of some gifts the subsequent income is taxed to the donor, while under others it is taxed to the donee or to a trust for the donee's benefit. Finally, in some cases the property is includible in the donor's gross estate, while in others it is not.

§7.29. Outright Gifts

The transfer of property directly into the name of a minor is generally unadvisable because of its nontax consequences. There is some risk that the minor donee might dissipate the property instead of saving it, which is usually what the donor has in mind. On the other hand, it may be necessary to obtain the appointment of a guardian in order to sell, exchange, lease, or otherwise deal with property that stands in the name of a minor. Also, if the donee dies prior to attaining the age of majority the property may return to the donor under the intestate succession law instead of passing to the donee's siblings or other relatives. Finally, even if a guardian is appointed, the donee will gain full control over the property when he or she attains the age of majority, which many clients consider to be far too soon.

If a minor owns stock, the transfer agent may require that assignments and other documents pertaining to the stock be signed by a duly appointed and acting agent. Transactions involving life insurance, real property, or other assets may also require the participation of a guardian. Local law and practice regarding the deposit and withdrawal of funds from accounts standing in the name of minors vary widely. Some institutions permit a minor to make small withdrawals if the minor is capable of writing his or her name and seems to understand the transaction, while others do not. As indicated below there is a simplified procedure for redemption of Series EE bonds that stand in the name of a minor.

§7.29.1. Gift Tax

The transfer of property into a minor's name is subject to state and federal gift taxes. However, the annual gift tax exclusion is available with respect to bona fide transfers except when the gift consists of a future interest in property.

§7.29.2. Estate Tax

Property that is given to a minor is includible in the minor's gross estate under §2033 and is not generally includible in the donor's gross estate under §2035. However, the property is includible in the donor's gross estate if the donor continues to use and control the property or expends it to satisfy a legal obligation to support the donee. §§2036 and 2038.

Overall, it is generally better to make small gifts to custodians under one of the Uniform Acts and larger ones under a carefully planned and drafted trust. Those methods do not involve the problems of management that may arise where an outright gift is made to a minor. However, gifts made under the Uniform Act do suffer from some of the same nontax disadvantages as outright gifts.

When an outright gift is made to a minor, a guardian may be appointed to participate in transactions affecting the property. However, a guardian cannot legitimately "undo" the gift and return the property to the donor or to a custodian under one of the Uniform Acts. Once an outright gift has been made to a minor, little can generally be done to relieve the situation.

§7.29.3. Income Tax

The income from property that is transferred into the name of a minor is taxed to the minor if it belongs to the minor and cannot be used to satisfy the donor's legal obligation of support. *See* Rev. Rul. 58-65, 1958-1 C.B. 13. Thus, dividends paid on stock given to a minor are taxed to the minor where they are reinvested for the minor's benefit and are not borrowed or otherwise used by the donors in any way. *Sandifur v. United States,* 64-2 U.S.T.C. ¶9817, 14 A.F.T.R.2d 5082 (E.D. Wash. 1964). However, the income is taxed to the donor when he or she continues to exercise control over the property and the income it generates. *Little v. United States,* 191 F. Supp. 12 (E.D. Tex. 1960); *Henry D. Duarte,* 44 T.C. 193 (1965). In sum, the income is taxed according to the economic reality of the situation and not necessarily according to the way title is held.

§7.30. Series EE Bonds

Funds are often invested for minors in Series EE (formerly Series E) bonds because of their security and ease of purchase. The applicable federal regulations require that "[t]he registration must express the actual ownership of, and interest in, the bond. The registration is conclusive of such ownership except [to correct an error in registration]." 31 C.F.R. §315.5 (1990). Under them bonds owned by natural persons may be registered only in the name of one person as sole owner ("*X*"), two persons as coowners ("*X* or *Y*," but *not* "*X* and *Y*"), or two persons as owner and beneficiary ("*X* payable on death to *Y*" or "*X* P.O.D. *Y*"). 31 C.F.R. §315.7(b) (1990). However, bonds owned by a minor may be registered in the name of the minor's guardian or in the name of a custodian under one of the Uniform Acts.

For income tax purposes the unreported increase in value of a bond is ordinarily not taxed until redemption or maturity. If one person obtains payment on a bond that is registered in the names of coowners, presumably the increase is taxed to that person alone. If the ownership of a bond is changed by reissue, the prior owner is liable for the income tax on the increase in value up to the date of reissue. *See* Rev. Rul. 54-327, 1954-2 C.B. 50. However, income is not realized where a bond is reissued at the request of the sole owner in his or her name and the name of another person as coowners. Rev. Rul. 70-428, 1970-2 C.B. 5. A change in ownership resulting from the death of an owner is also not a taxable event. Instead, the unreported increase in value to the date of death constitutes income in respect of a decedent that is subject to taxation under §691 when received by the owner. Rev. Rul. 64-104, 1964-1 C.B. 223.

In assessing the suitability of an investment in Series EE bonds, a client must consider their rate of return compared with the yields of other secure investments. An investment in Series EE bonds for a minor under 14 is attractive because the annual increase in value of the bond is not reportable as income unless an election is made under §454. Series EE bonds provide a safe and simple way to invest a relatively small amount on behalf of a minor. Also, they are easily purchased and redeemed. If a client intends to invest a small amount in Series EE bonds for a minor, consideration should be given to making the gift under one of the Uniform Acts. A large investment in Series EE bonds is generally not desirable.

§7.30.1 Minor as Sole Owner

The purchase of a bond in the name of a minor has the same tax consequences as any other outright transfer of property to a minor. As indicated in Rev. Rul. 68-269, 1968-1 C.B. 399, situation 3, the purchase constitutes a completed gift from the purchaser to the donee regardless of when the bond is actually delivered to the minor. Accordingly, it qualifies for the annual exclusion under §2503(b). The Regulations permit a minor to redeem a bond that is registered in the minor's name if the minor is sufficiently competent to sign a request for payment and understands the nature of the transaction. 31 C.F.R. §315.62 (1990). If the minor does not meet those requirements, a bond registered in the minor's name may be redeemed by a parent with whom the minor resides or who has legal custody of him or her. 31 C.F.R. §315.63 (1990). Otherwise, the bond may be redeemed by the person who is the primary source of support for the minor. Id.

If the minor dies owning the bond, it is includible in the minor's gross estate under §2033. Under ordinary circumstances the bond is not includible in the donor's estate.

The interest on a savings bond is ordinarily reported by a cash basis taxpayer when the bond is redeemed or reaches final maturity. Under §454(a), a taxpayer may elect to report the yearly increase in redemption value on the bond and all other appreciation-type securities. Taxpayers seldom elect to report the annual increase as it accrues because the election applies to all appreciation-type obligations and binds the taxpayer for all subsequent taxable years. Also, once the election is made, it can be changed only with the permission of the IRS.

§7.30.2. Minor as Coowner

Bonds purchased with the funds of a minor must be registered in the name of the minor without a coowner or beneficiary. However, bonds purchased with funds not belonging to a minor may be registered in the name of the minor as owner or coowner. 31 C.F.R. §315.6(c) (1990).

The purchase of a bond in the name of the purchaser and another individual in coownership form ("*X* or *Y*") does not constitute a completed gift. A completed gift does take place when a bond purchased by *X* is reissued in *Y*'s name alone, Rev. Rul. 55-278, 1955-1 C.B. 471, or when *Y* surrenders the bond for redemption without any duty to account to *X* for the disposition of the proceeds. Reg. §25.2511-1(h)(4); Rev. Rul. 68-269, 1968-1 C.B. 399, situation 5. When *X* provides the entire purchase price of the bond, none of the bond is includible in *Y*'s gross estate if *Y* predeceases *X*. Of course, if *X* dies first, the bond is includible in *X*'s estate under §2040 (*i.e.,* half of the value of the bond is included if *X* and *Y* are husband and wife, otherwise the full value is included). Generally, when either coowner dies, the bond belongs entirely to the survivor. 31 C.F.R. §315.70(b) (1990).

While both coowners are living, either of them may redeem the bond by separate request. 31 C.F.R. §315.37 (1990). In contrast, the bond may be reissued only upon the request of both owners. 31 C.F.R. §315.51 (1990). A gift from one coowner to the other is effective only if the bond is reissued in the name of the donee — mere physical delivery to the intended donee is insufficient. *United States v. Chandler,* 410 U.S. 257 (1973). As the Supreme Court explained in *Chandler,* "the regulations thus made the jointly issued bond nontransferable in itself and permitted a change in ownership, so long as both coowners were alive, only through reissuance at the request of both coowners." Id. at 260.

§7.30.3. Minor as Beneficiary

The registration of a bond in the name of "*X,* payable on death to *Y*" or "*X* P.O.D. *Y*" has the same tax consequences as registration in the coownership form ("*X* or *Y*"). Specifically, this type of registration does not involve a gift from *X* to *Y* and the bond is fully includible in the estate of *X* if *X* predeceases *Y.* When *X* and *Y* are not husband and wife and *Y* did not contribute to the purchase of the bond, nothing is includible in *Y*'s estate if he or she predeceases *X.* (When *X* and *Y* are husband and wife, presumably half of the value of the bond is includible under §2040(b) in the estate of the spouse first-to-die.) Also, the annual increase in redemption value of the bond is ordinarily not taxed on a current basis for income tax purposes. Income would be realized, however, when the bond is redeemed, finally matures, or is reissued in the name of an owner other than *X* (the original purchaser). The payable-on-death form of registration is an effective will substitute insofar as Series EE bonds are concerned.

§7.31. Payable-on-Death (POD) Bank Accounts

The payable-on-death (POD) form of multiparty account is recognized as nontestamentary in Part 2 of Article 6 of the U.P.C. (1990). However, the POD form must be used with more care in non-U.P.C. states. Although some non-U.P.C. states have enacted legislation validating POD accounts, some have not. In the latter POD accounts may be treated as testamentary transfers that are invalid unless they are executed in the manner required of wills. *E.g., Truax v. Southwestern College Oklahoma City, Oklahoma,* 522 P.2d 412 (Kan. 1974) (POD account invalid); *Blais v. Colebrook Guaranty Savings Bank,* 220 A.2d 763 (N.H. 1966) (POD account invalid); *but see Estate of Tonsik,* 235 N.E.2d 239 (Ohio App. 1968) (POD account upheld on basis of local statute).

When *X* deposits funds in an account that stands in the name of "*X* payable on death to *Y,*" the deposit does not have any significant federal tax impact: The interest on the account is taxable to *X,* the deposit does not constitute a gift because the funds may be freely withdrawn by *X,* and the account is includible in *X*'s gross estate. If *Y* predeceases *X* the account is not included in *Y*'s gross estate.

§7.32. Savings Account or Totten Trust

As revised in 1989 the U.P.C. "discourages creation of a Totten trust account and treats existing Totten trust accounts as POD designations." 8 U.L.A. 130 (1990 Supp.). A savings account or Totten trust is created when *X* opens an account in the name of "*X* as trustee for *Y.*" The term "Totten trust" is derived from the name of the case, *Matter of Totten,* 71 N.E. 748 (1904), in which the arrangement was upheld by the New York Court of Appeals. If *X* deposits funds to a Totten trust account for

Y ("*X* as trustee for *Y*"), *X* has the right to withdraw and use funds from the account without any duty to account to *Y*. *Y* is entitled to the balance of the account if *X* dies first. On the other hand, the trust is terminated if *Y* predeceases *X*. Fundamentally, the trust is a simple form of will substitute that does not involve a present completed gift to the named beneficiary.

A Totten trust does not have any present income, gift, or estate tax impact. The income is taxed to the depositor-trustee because the arrangement is completely revocable. §676. For the same reason, there is not a completed gift to the donee when the trustee deposits funds in the account. Reg. §25.2511-2(c). If another party deposits funds in the account, presumably the deposit constitutes a gift to the trustee and not a gift to the trust beneficiary. Such a deposit qualifies for the annual exclusion because of the trustee's right to use the account for his or her own benefit. Any balance on hand when the trustee dies is includible in the trustee's gross estate under §§2036 and 2038 to the extent the trustee funded the account. *Estate of Sulovich v. Commissioner,* 587 F.2d 845 (6th Cir. 1978). The portion of the account funded by others is includible in the trustee's estate under §2041 if the trustee had the power to withdraw the funds and use them without restriction. Of course, if the beneficiary survives the trustee, the account becomes the beneficiary's property and is includible in the beneficiary's gross estate at death. If the beneficiary predeceases the trustee, the account is not includible in the beneficiary's estate; instead, the trust terminates and the balance of the account is owned by the trustee.

The Totten trust is generally an unsatisfactory way to hold funds for a minor. Because of its revocable nature the tax consequences are not favorable. Overall, it is preferable to make a gift to the minor under one of the Uniform Acts or to a trust for the minor's benefit. Unfortunately, the personnel who handle new accounts at some financial institutions may push customers into Totten trusts because they are not sufficiently familiar with gifts to custodians under the Uniform Acts and other forms in which accounts might be opened.

§7.33. Joint Bank or Securities Accounts

The deposit of funds by one person in a joint account with another ("*X* or *Y*") may give the other person a present interest in the account. If it does, the deposit constitutes a present gift to the donee and each party has a duty to account to the other for disposition of the account. On the other hand, the deposit may be a revocable gift to the other party, in which case no gift results and there is no duty to account. It is not possible to generalize about joint accounts because the state laws regarding them vary substantially.

§7.33.1. Joint Bank Account

A joint bank account is often intended either to serve as a will substitute or to allow another person to make withdrawals as agent for the depositor. In neither case does the depositor intend that the other party will have a current beneficial interest in the account. The donor's probable intentions are recognized by U.P.C. §6-211(b), which provides that during the lifetime of all parties "an account belongs to the parties in proportion to the net contribution of each to the sums on deposit, unless there is clear and convincing evidence of a different intent." However, if the parties are married to each other, under the U.P.C. each is presumed to have contributed an equal amount to the account. Upon the death of one of the parties, the sums on deposit "belong to the surviving party or parties." U.P.C. §6-212(a). If two or more parties survive, and one is the surviving spouse of a deceased party, the portion of the account that belonged to the decedent immediately before death belongs to the surviving spouse. Otherwise, the surviving parties to an account share equally in the portion attributable to a deceased party to the account. Id. Under the U.P.C. a party to an account may designate a person to act as agent for the depositor or depositors. U.P.C. §6-205. The agent does not have an ownership interest in the account.

For gift tax purposes under the U.P.C. the deposit of funds in a joint account does not constitute a completed gift. *See* Reg. §25.2511-1(h)(4). The same result follows under other laws if the person making a deposit to a joint account has the power to withdraw all of the funds without being obligated to account to the other party. Consistently, in such a case a gift takes place when the donee withdraws funds from the account without any duty to account to the depositor. Id. Here, again, the income from the account is taxable to the depositor. Under the basic rule of §2040 the account is includible in the depositor's gross estate except to the extent it is traceable to funds contributed by others. On the other hand, if the sole depositors were husband and wife, only half of the account balance is included in the decedent's estate, which qualifies for the marital deduction. §§2040(b), 2056. The surviving tenant may make a qualified disclaimer of the right to receive the decedent's interest in a joint account. *See* §12.33.1.

A gift occurs at the time the deposit is made where the state law restricts the depositor's right to withdraw the funds for his or her own use.

§7.33.2. Joint Securities Accounts

Joint brokerage accounts with or without survivorship features may be established by complying with the requirements of local law. The transfer of property to such an account does not involve a gift unless the transfer gives the other party or parties an ownership interest in the account. In most circumstances transfers to joint brokerage accounts are revocable transfers that do not involve any gift to the other party. The income from the account will generally be taxed in accordance with the ownership interests of the parties. Likewise, the estate and GST tax consequences will track the ownership interests in the account.

In 1989 the Uniform TOD Security Registration Act was added to the U.P.C. as Part 3 of Article VI. 8 U.L.A. 142 (1990 Supp.). Under its provisions securities may be registered in "beneficiary form" under which the securities will belong to another person upon the death of the owner or owners. Section 6-305 provides that "Registration in beneficiary form may be shown by the words 'transfer on death' or the abbreviation 'TOD' or by the words 'pay on death' or the abbreviation 'POD,' after the name of the registered owner and before the name of the beneficiary." Registration in beneficiary form should not have any income, gift, estate or GST tax consequences.

§7.34. Gifts Under the Uniform Acts

In order to facilitate gifts to minors all states have adopted either U.G.M.A. in its original or revised form or U.T.M.A. The Uniform Acts, which vary somewhat from state to state, authorize gifts of certain types of property to be made to a minor under its provisions. The basic form of U.G.M.A. permits gifts of securities, life insurance policies, annuity contracts, or money to be made under it. Some states have expanded the types of assets that may be transferred to include other types of personal property and interests in real property. U.T.M.A. allows any type of property to be transferred to a custodian. In general, a gift is made under the Uniform Acts by registering the asset, or depositing the fund, in the name of the donor, another adult, or a trust company "as custodian for (name of minor) under the (name of state) Uniform Gifts to Minors Act." §2(a)(2), 8A U.L.A. 344 (1983); §9 U.T.M.A., 8A U.L.A. 257 (1990 Supp.). By complying with the statutory procedure the donor makes an irrevocable gift to the minor that incorporates the existing provisions of the Act. U.G.M.A. §3(b); U.T.M.A. §11(c). The custodian is a fiduciary whose investment and reinvestment of the property is governed by the "prudent person" standard. U.G.M.A. §4(e); U.T.M.A. §12(b). However, unlike property held in trust, the title to the property held by a custodian is vested in the minor and not the trustee. *Liberty National Life Ins. Co. v. First National Bank,* 151 So. 2d 225, 227-228 (Ala. 1963). U.G.M.A. §4(b) authorizes the custodian to pay over or apply any or all of the property for the support, maintenance, education, and benefit of the minor. U.T.M.A. §14(a) allows the custodian to pay or expend for the minor's benefit "so much of the custodial property as the custodian considers advisable for the use and benefit of the minor." In an effort to insulate the custodian from adverse tax consequences, U.T.M.A. §14(c) provides that, "A delivery, payment, or expenditure under this section is in addition to, not in substitution for, and does not affect any obligation of a person to support the minor." Property in the hands of the custodian must be distributed to the donee when he or she reaches the age specified in the statute, which is most often 21. If the minor dies prior to attaining that age, the property must be paid to the minor's estate. U.G.M.A. §4(d); U.T.M.A. §20.

§7.34.1. Gift Tax

A gift to a custodian for a minor under one of the Uniform Acts constitutes a completed gift that qualifies for the annual gift tax exclusion. Rev. Rul. 59-357, 1959-2 C.B. 212. The resignation of a custodian or the termination of the custodianship does not involve a further gift. Of course, a gift by a married person may be split between the donor and the donor's spouse under §2513. Gift-splitting does not apply to gifts of community property, which is already "split" between the spouses by reason of the form of ownership.

§7.34.2. Estate Tax

The custodial property is includible in the donor's gross estate if the donor is acting as custodian at the time of his or her death. Rev. Rul. 59-357, 1959-2 C.B. 212. In such a case the property is includible under §2038 because of the custodian's power to distribute the custodial property and, in effect, to terminate the custodial arrangement. *Stuit v. Commissioner,* 452 F.2d 190 (7th Cir. 1971). The same result follows if another person was the original custodian but the donor was acting in that capacity at the time of his or her death. Rev. Rul. 70-348, 1970-2 C.B. 193. The custodial property is not includible in the estate of the donor's spouse, although he or she elected to be treated as the donor of half of it under §2513 and was acting as custodian at the time of his or her death. Rev. Rul. 74-556, 1974-2 C.B. 300. That result is clearly correct under §§2036 and 2038 — the consenting spouse did not actually own or transfer any part of the property of which she was acting as custodian at the time of her death. Of course, half of the property would be includible in the custodian's estate if the gift had consisted of community property. Also, if the consenting spouse has the power as custodian to apply the property to discharge a legal obligation to support the minor, there is some risk that the property would be included in the consenting spouse's estate under §2041.

The reciprocal trust doctrine (*see* §6.29) applies when donors make related gifts under a Uniform Act and appoint each other as custodian. Thus, a deceased custodian's estate included the gifts nominally made by his spouse where they had made identical contemporaneous gifts to their minor children and named each other as custodian. *Exchange Bank & Trust Co. v. United States,* 694 F.2d 1261 (Fed. Cir. 1982).

The Uniform Acts provide an efficient and economical method of transferring limited amounts of certain types of property to minors. However, most clients are reluctant to make substantial gifts under them because the property must be paid over to the donee at an early age. Also, if the minor dies prior to attaining the age of majority, the property must be paid over to the donee's estate. Because a minor cannot make a will, the property would pass under the intestate succession law, which may be inconsistent with the donor's estate plan. Most often the donor is a parent who makes the gift to remove the property from his or her estate. Of course, the parent may disclaim succession to the deceased child's intestate property under §2045, but that might further frustrate the donor's estate plan. These disadvantages are avoided, however, if the gift is made to a properly drawn trust. *See* §§7.35-7.39.

§7.34.3. Income Tax

The income from the custodial property is taxed to the minor currently whether or not it is actually distributed or expended for his or her benefit. However, the IRS contends that to the extent the income is applied to discharge the legal support obligation of *any* person, the income must be taxed to that person. Rev. Rul. 56-484, 1956-2 C.B. 23, *approved in* Rev. Rul. 59-357, 1959-2 C.B. 212. Likewise, the income is taxable to the grantor to the extent it is used to satisfy the grantor's obligations. §677. For example, if the donor has assumed responsibility for paying the minor's private school tuition, the custodial income will be taxed to the donor to the extent it is used to meet that expense. *Morrill v. United States,* 228 F. Supp. 734 (D. Me. 1964) (irrevocable trust). A grantor-parent is also taxed on the income of a trust that is used to pay the private school tuition of a child if the parent is subject to that obligation under state law. *Christopher Stone,* 54 T.C.M. 462 (1987) (California); *Frederick C. Braun, Jr.,* 48 T.C.M. 210 (1984) (New Jersey).

The existence and extent of a parent's legal obligation to support a minor depends upon local law, which is often far from clear. *See* §10.40.1. Although children may be emancipated at 18, some parental obligations may persist, at least in the case of incompetent or dependent children. *See Braun, supra.* However, the income of a custodianship may be safely accumulated for the minor or expended for items of "super support" that parents are clearly not obligated to provide under the local law (*e.g.*, travel, private music or dance lessons). In one case, the IRS held that a trust beneficiary's power to appoint principal of a trust for "travel, camping trips, theater, ballet, music lessons, special schooling or instruction to enrich" the lives of the beneficiary's children was not a general power of appointment for purposes of §2041. LR 9030005.

A custodian may not execute a valid Subchapter S election. Rev. Rul. 66-116, 1966-1 C.B. 198. However, a guardian may do so and the IRS will recognize an election signed by a custodian if the same person is also the minor's guardian. Rev. Rul. 68-227, 1968-1 C.B. 381.

One additional risk should be taken into account where appreciated property is transferred under a Uniform Act and sold within two years. The IRS may contend that the sale is subject to §644 and the gain must be taxed to the minor as if the donor had sold the property. The contention should be rejected, however, because §644 only applies to sales or exchanges by a trust. Although a Uniform Act may be viewed as providing for a statutory trust, a custodianship is not treated as a trust for property law purposes or for other income tax purposes. A trustee holds legal title to trust assets whereas the minor holds "indefeasibly vested legal title" to property given to the minor under a Uniform Act.

§7.35. Gifts in Trust

Trusts are frequently used as vehicles for making gifts to minors because of their great flexibility. In order to maximize the tax savings that result from transfers in trusts, the trusts are usually drafted to qualify for the annual gift tax exclusion. That is particularly important because gifts within the annual exclusion are generally not included in the donor's transfer tax base at any time. Until the 1980s the most common method of qualifying for the annual exclusion was to draft the trust so that it met the requirements of §2503(c). The use of §2503(c) trusts is discussed in §7.36. Now, however, it is more common to use trusts that (1) continue past the donee's minority, (2) provide only for discretionary distributions to the donee, and (3) qualify for the annual exclusion by giving the minor a limited, noncumulative power to withdraw assets as they are added to the trust. Such a power of withdrawal is often called a *Crummey* power after *Crummey v. Commissioner,* 397 F.2d 82 (9th Cir. 1968), which allowed an annual gift tax exclusion for assets transferred to a discretionary trust for a minor. *See* §7.37. Some trusts require the trustee to distribute the income to the minor currently, the actuarially determined value of which constitutes a present interest under §2503(b). *See* §7.37.

§7.36. Section 2503(c) Trusts

The availability of the annual gift tax exclusion for interests transferred to a minor under a §2503(c) trust encourages their use. However, as explained below, a discretionary trust that gives the beneficiary a *Crummey* power of withdrawal (*see* §7.37) may better meet the needs of most clients. Under §2503(c) a transfer for the benefit of a donee under the age of 21 is not a future interest if the following requirements are met:

1. The property and the income may be expended by or for the benefit of the donee before the donee attains 21;
2. Any portion of the property not expended for the donee's benefit will pass to the donee when the donee attains 21; and
3. The property and its income will be payable to the donee's estate or as the donee may appoint under a general power of appointment if the donee dies prior to 21.

§7.36.1. Property or Income

Section 2503(c) literally requires both the property *and* its income to be expended or distributed in the prescribed manner. However, the IRS has acquiesced in decisions that allow an exclusion to the extent that either the income *or* the principal interest meets those requirements. *Arlean I. Herr,* 35 T.C. 732 (1961), *nonacq.,* 1962-2 C.B. 6, *withdrawn and acq. substituted,* 1968-2 C.B. 2, *aff'd,* 303 F.2d 780 (3d Cir. 1962); Rev. Rul. 68-670, 1968-2 C.B. 413.

Example 7-11. *X* transferred property to *T* as trustee of a trust for the benefit of *B,* a minor. The trustee was authorized to expend income, but not principal, for the support, comfort, and general welfare of *B* until *B* reached 21 or sooner died. At that time any accumulated income was payable to *B* if *B* was then living, otherwise to *B*'s estate. After *B* attained 21 the income was payable to *B* in the discretion of the trustee. The principal of the trust and any income accumulated after *B* attained 21 was payable to *B* at age 35. An exclusion under §2503(c) is available with respect to the actuarially determined value of the right to receive the income until *B* attains 21.

§7.36.2. No Substantial Restrictions

The requirement that the income or principal may be expended by or for the benefit of the donee prior to attaining 21 is met only if the trustee's discretion to expend funds is not subject to any "substantial restrictions," Reg. §25.2503-4(b)(1). Revenue Ruling 67-270, 1967-2 C.B. 349 holds that this requirement is met if the trust property may be expended during the donee's minority "for purposes which have no objective limitations (*i.e.,* 'welfare,' 'happiness' and 'convenience') and which provisions when read as a whole approximate the scope of the term 'benefit,' as used in section 2503(c) of the Code." In contrast, no annual exclusion is allowable if the trustee's power to make distributions is limited. Thus, no exclusion is allowable where the trustee can make distributions to the donee only if "his needs are not adequately provided for by his parents and only after his separate property has been expended." Rev. Rul. 69-345, 1969-1 C.B. 226. Similarly, no annual exclusion is available if the trustee is permitted to distribute property only for educational expenses or if the beneficiary is disabled. *Illinois National Bank of Springfield v. United States,* 91-1 U.S.T.C. ¶60,063 (C.D. Ill. 1991).

A trust that provides for the discretionary use of income for a minor until 21, at which time all the accumulated income is distributable to the beneficiary and all of the income is payable to the beneficiary thereafter, qualifies under §2503(c) only to the extent of the income interest for the beneficiary's minority. The right to receive the income after 21 is a future interest that cannot be combined with the pre-21 income interest for the purpose of the annual exclusion. The possible accumulation of the income prior to age 21 prevents the post-21 income interest from being a present interest for purposes of the annual exclusion. *Levine v. Commissioner,* 526 F.2d 717 (2d Cir. 1975).

§7.36.3. Payable at 21

Under the second requirement the interest must pass to the donee when he or she attains 21. In Rev. Rul. 73-287, 1973-2 C.B. 321, the IRS held that an annual exclusion was available under §2503(c) for a transfer under a version of the U.G.M.A. that provided for distribution to the donee at age 18 instead of 21. It reasoned that §2503(c) set the maximum restrictions that may be attached to gifts to minors: "Therefore, a provision that the custodial property be paid to the minor donee when he attains the age of 18 years will meet the requirement that the property pass to the donee at least by his attainment of age 21, and, hence, will satisfy the greater age requirement of section 2503(c) of the

Code." Id. Accordingly, an annual exclusion should be available for a gift to a trust that requires the necessary distributions be made to the donee before he or she becomes 21.

This requirement may be satisfied although the trust does not automatically terminate when the donee reaches 21. It is sufficient if the donee has the power to compel distribution upon reaching the age of 21, whether the power is a continuing one or is exercisable only for a limited period. Rev. Rul. 74-43, 1974-1 C.B. 285. However, the failure to exercise the power may cause the donee to be treated as the transferor of any interest that others have in the trust to the extent the amount that could be withdrawn exceeds the greater of $5,000 or five percent of the value of the property subject to the power. *See* §§2041 and 2514. Whether the lapse of the power constitutes a taxable gift depends upon several factors, including the extent to which the donee retains any power over disposition of the property.

§7.36.4. Payable to Donee's Estate or as Donee Appoints

If the donee dies prior to 21, any remaining interest must be payable to the donee's estate or as the donee appoints under a general power of appointment. Apparently, this requirement was imposed "to insure inclusion of the property, which had the benefit of a gift tax exclusion, in the gross estate of the beneficiary for estate tax purposes in the event that he dies prior to reaching age 21." *Cornelius A. Ross,* 71 T.C. 897, 900 (1979), *aff'd,* 652 F.2d 1365 (9th Cir. 1981). In *Ross* no annual exclusion was allowed under §2503(c) for a trust that provided for distribution of the property to the donee's "heirs at law" if he died prior to 21. The problem is, of course, that a distribution to the minor's "heirs at law" is not the equivalent of a distribution to the minor's estate. The requirement is satisfied if the donee is given a general testamentary power of appointment, although the donee is unable to exercise the power under the local law because of his or her minority. Reg. §25.2503-4(b). The possession of a general power of appointment is sufficient to cause the property to be included in the gross estate of the power-holder although he or she lacks the capacity to exercise it. §2041; Rev. Rul. 75-351, 1975-2 C.B. 368. This is consistent with the position that the IRS has taken in connection with the allowance of a marital deduction under §2056(b)(5). *See* §5.22.3. If the trust otherwise qualifies, a marital deduction is allowable although the surviving spouse is incapable of exercising the power of appointment because of legal incapacity. *See, e.g.,* Rev. Rul. 75-350, 1975-2 C.B. 366.

The annual exclusion is not available under §2503(c) if the trust itself imposes any restrictions on the exercise of the power. Thus, in *Gall v. United States,* 521 F.2d 878 (5th Cir. 1975), *cert. denied,* 425 U.S. 972 (1976), the exclusion was denied where the donee was required to be 19 in order to exercise the power and state law allowed persons of 19 years of age *and* younger married persons to execute wills.

§7.36.5. Terms of §2503(c) Trust

A §2503(c) trust must, of course, conform to the requirements of §2503(c). In addition, it ordinarily should include provisions that prohibit the trustee from exercising powers that would cause the grantor to be treated as owner of the trust under §675. *See* §10.38.1. The discretion the trustee must have to make distributions would require the trust to be included in the grantor's estate under §2038 if the grantor were serving as trustee. Accordingly, the grantor should not serve as trustee. *See* §10.37.3.

Form 7-1. Distributive Provisions of §2503(c) Trust

Until the beneficiary attains the age of 21 the trustee shall pay to or apply for the benefit of the beneficiary so much of the income and principal of the trust as the trustee believes is in the beneficiary's best interests.

Right of Withdrawal at Age 21. When the beneficiary attains the age of 21 the beneficiary shall have the right, by delivering written notice to the trustee, to require the trustee to distribute all of the property of the trust to the beneficiary. Such right of withdrawal shall lapse if the beneficiary does not deliver written notice to the trustee within 60 days after the beneficiary attains 21 years of age. The trust shall terminate to the extent the beneficiary withdraws property from the trust.

Distributions to the Beneficiary After Attaining Age 21. After the beneficiary attains 21 years of age the trustee shall distribute all of the net income to beneficiary in quarterly or more frequent installments. In addition, the trustee may make such distributions of principal to or for the benefit of the beneficiary as the trustee believes is in the best interests of the beneficiary. All of the property of the trust shall be distributed to beneficiary when she/he attains 35 years of age.

General Power of Appointment. If the beneficiary dies prior to termination of the trust, the trust property shall be paid outright or upon further trust to such person or persons, including the beneficiary's estate, as the beneficiary shall appoint by her/his last will. In default of exercise of such power the trust property shall be distributed in shares of equal value to those of the brothers and sisters of the beneficiary as shall survive her/him; provided, that the share of any brother or sister for whom a trust created by the grantor on the same date as this trust, remains in existence shall be added to and become a part of the property of the trust for the benefit of such brother or sister.

§7.36.6. Estate Tax

The trust property is includible in the donee's gross estate if it is payable to the donee's estate or if the donee holds a general power of appointment over it. It is also includible if the donee does not exercise a power to compel distribution of the trust property when he or she attains 21 and he or she remains a beneficiary of the trust until death. The failure to exercise the power of withdrawal constitutes a release and the property is includible in the donee's gross estate if the release results in a disposition "of such nature that if it were a transfer of property owned by the decedent, such property would be includible in the decedent's gross estate under sections 2035-2038, inclusive." §2041(a)(2). The failure to exercise the power might also involve a gift of an interest in the trust to other parties, such as contingent remaindermen who will be entitled to the property if the donee does not survive to a specified age or event.

Example 7-12. Parent, *P,* transferred property to a trust under which the principal and income could be expended by the trustee for the benefit of *P*'s daughter, *D,* until she reached 21. Under the trust *D* had the power to withdraw all of the trust assets by written notice delivered to the trustee within 60 days following her twenty-first birthday. The income from any property that is not withdrawn is payable to *D* annually and the principal is distributable to her when she reaches 45. If *D* dies prior to 21 the trust property is payable to her estate, but if she dies after reaching 21 and prior to 45, the trust property is payable to *P*'s then living descendants per stirpes.

The trust meets the requirements of §2503(c). Accordingly, an annual exclusion is available to *P* for property he transferred to the trust during *D*'s minority. *D*'s power to withdraw the property of the trust constitutes a general power of appointment under §2041. If she allows the power to lapse, or otherwise releases it, she has probably made a taxable gift of the contingent remainder interest. *See* Reg. §25.2514-3(c). However, under §2514(e) a lapse of a general power of appointment is subject to gift tax only to the extent that the property that could have been appointed by the donee of the power exceeds the greater of (i) $5,000 or (ii) 5% of the total value of the assets out of which the exercise of the lapsed power could have been satisfied. If the power lapses and *D* dies prior to attaining 45, a similar proportion of the trust assets is includible in her estate under §2041(a)(2). *See* Reg. §20.2041-3(d)(3), (4).

The trust property is subject to inclusion in the donor's estate under §2036(a)(2) or §2038(a)(1) if the trustee has the power to make discretionary distributions to the beneficiary and the donor is acting as trustee at the time of the donor's death. *See Lober v. United States,* 346 U.S. 335 (1953). The property might also be includible in the donor's estate under §2036(a) if the trust provides the beneficiary with types of support that the donor is obligated to provide under the local law. On the other hand, one leading decision holds that the property is not includible in the parent-donor's estate where there is an independent trustee and none of the property was ever used for the support of the child-donee. *Estate of Jack F. Chrysler,* 44 T.C. 55 (1965), *acq.,* 1970-2 C.B. xix, *rev'd on other issues,* 361 F.2d 508 (2d Cir. 1966).

§7.36.7. Income Tax

The income of a §2503(c) trust is taxed to the minor if it is distributed to the minor or used for the minor's benefit except to the extent the income is taxed to the grantor under §673-677. *See* §10.31. In other cases the income is taxed to the trust. Thus, the income from a §2503(c) trust for the benefit of a child under 14 is not subject to taxation at the marginal rate of the beneficiary's parent unless the income is actually distributed. In addition, income that is accumulated before the beneficiary reaches 21 is not subject to the throwback rules when it is distributed. §665(b). However, under §644, the gain on appreciated property that is sold within two years following its transfer to the trust is taxed as if the donor had made the sale.

The grantor may act as trustee of a §2503(c) trust without causing the income to be taxed to him or her. In particular, under §§674(b)(5)-(7) any person may hold discretionary powers to distribute or accumulate income during a beneficiary's minority or to distribute corpus to the income beneficiary of a trust so long as any distribution of corpus is charged to the beneficiary's proportionate interest in the principal of the trust. This allows considerable flexibility in income tax planning.

§7.36.8. GSTT

The transfer of property to a §2503(c) trust appears to qualify for the GSTT nontaxable transfer exclusion of §2642(c)(2). Briefly, under §2642(c)(1) a direct skip which is a nontaxable transfer has an inclusion ratio of zero. However, in the case of transfers in trust this exclusion is only available if the trust meets the requirements of §2642(c)(2). A §2503(c) trust can satisfy those requirements. Under §2642(c)(3) the term "nontaxable transfer" is defined as a transfer that is not treated as a taxable gift by reason of either §2503(b) (annual $10,000 exclusion allowed for gifts of present interests), taking into account the gift-splitting provisions of §2513, or §2503(e) (direct payments of tuition or of medical care are not gifts). Transfers that satisfy the requirements of §2503(c) are not future interests for purposes of §2503(b). Accordingly, if as required by §2642(c)(2) distributions can only be made from a §2503(c) trust to the minor during his or her lifetime and the trust will be includible in the minor's estate if he or she dies during its existence, transfers to the trust should be within the definition of nontaxable transfers under §2642(c)(3).

§7.36.9. Conclusion

A custom-made §2503(c) trust may better meet the needs of a client who wishes to make modest gifts to a minor than a gift under one of the Uniform Acts. For example, the trust can be drafted to prevent the property from returning to a donor-parent if the donee dies prior to 21. That is achieved by providing for payment of the trust property to another person or to a trust for another person if the donee dies prior to 21 without validly exercising a general testamentary power of appointment. The main shortcoming of a §2503(c) trust is the requirement that the interest pass to the donee upon attaining age 21. Most clients would be happier if the property were neither payable to the donee at 21 nor all subject to the donee's power of withdrawal. As indicated above, the power of withdrawal can cause gift and estate tax problems for the donee. For those reasons if a client wants the trust to continue after the donee attains 21, it is usually better to create a discretionary trust that gives the donee a *Crummey* power to withdraw assets for a limited time after they are transferred to the trust. As explained in the next section, neither the property nor the income of a *Crummey* trust is required to pass to the donee when he or she attains age 21.

§7.37. Discretionary Trust with *Crummey* Powers

A trust that gives the trustee discretion to make distributions of income and principal before and after the donee attains his or her majority is an excellent way to provide for the flexible management and distribution of family wealth. Although the beneficiary does not have any fixed right to receive distributions, the annual exclusion is available for transfers to the trust if the beneficiary is given a *Crummey* power. In addition, the throwback rules do not apply to income that is accumulated prior to the beneficiary's birth or the attainment of age 21. If the trust is properly drafted, the trust assets are not includible in the grantor's estate. In this connection the planner must not allow the grantor to retain any rights or controls that would require inclusion in the grantor's estate under §§2036 or 2038. In addition, the grantor should not transfer any policies of insurance on his or her life to the trust that would be includible in the grantor's estate under §2035(d)(2) if the grantor were to die within three years of the transfer. The trust can be drafted to terminate when the beneficiary attains a certain age or to continue after the beneficiary's death for the benefit of the beneficiary's children or others. Importantly, the trust can be drafted so that transfers that qualify for the annual gift tax exclusion will also qualify for the GSTT exclusion for nontaxable gifts under §2642(c).

§7.37.1. Gift Tax

The transfer of property to a discretionary trust usually constitutes a completed gift for gift tax purposes. The difficult problem is to draft the trust in a way that allows annual exclusions to be claimed for property that is transferred to the trust.

In the ordinary case property that is transferred to a discretionary trust does not qualify for the annual exclusion because the donee does not have a present interest in it. However, *Crummey v. Commissioner,* 397 F.2d 82 (9th Cir. 1968) (*Crummey*), held that a gift to a discretionary trust for a minor qualifies for the annual exclusion if the donee has the present right to demand distribution of the property. In late 1973 the IRS issued a revenue ruling that followed the holding in *Crummey*. Rev. Rul. 73-405, 1973-2 C.B. 321. The ruling recognized that "it is not the actual use, possession, or enjoyment by the donee which marks the dividing line between a present and a future interest, but rather the right conferred upon the donee by the trust instrument to such use, possession, or enjoyment." Accordingly, the annual exclusion is available when a minor donee is given the power to withdraw property transferred to the trust if there is no impediment under the trust or the local law to the appointment of a guardian who could exercise the power for the minor. For gift tax purposes the transfer of property to a trust that contains a properly drafted *Crummey* power is treated as if the property had been transferred outright to the donee.

The content of a *Crummey* clause will vary somewhat, depending upon the other provisions of the trust and the circumstances of the parties. For example, the form may differ if (1) there are multiple rather than single beneficiaries, (2) gifts may be made to the trust by more than one donor each year, or (3) the trust principal will be distributed to the donee at some point instead of remaining in trust for the donee's lifetime. In particular, the lawyer should consider the points that are raised in the following paragraphs.

§7.37.2. Limit the Amount Subject to Withdrawal?

Under a typical *Crummey* clause the donee is given a noncumulative power, exercisable within a limited period following notice of the transfer, to withdraw property that is transferred to the trust. The amount subject to withdrawal may be limited by the terms of the trust or by the terms of the transfer to the trust as described in §7.37.3. Considering the nature and purpose of the trust, it is generally undesirable to give the donee an unlimited power to make withdrawals, at least during the donee's minority. Although it is possible simply to allow each donor to define the amount subject to withdrawal, most instruments include a limit that will apply if the donor does not impose a limit in connection with an addition to the trust.

In deciding what limit to impose, consideration should be given to the tax *and* nontax effects of doing so. On the tax side the donor may wish to limit the amount subject to withdrawal to the amount for which an annual gift tax exclusion is allowable. The maximum annual exclusions will be allowed if the beneficiary has the power to withdraw "$10,000 per donor or such other amount as may be allowable as an annual gift tax exclusion at the time of the transfer to the trust." Such a provision is appropriate if the donor does not wish to allow the beneficiary to withdraw any more property than necessary to support the maximum annual gift tax exclusion. Also, a limit is imposed in many instruments in order to prevent the lapse of the power from resulting in adverse gift or estate tax consequences for the donee. The two most common limits on the amount that can be withdrawn by the donee each year are (1) $10,000 per donor and (2) $5,000 or five percent of the principal value of the trust (a "5 or 5" power of withdrawal). Sometimes the former limit is stated "not to exceed $10,000 per donor, or $20,000 per donor if the donor is married at the time the property is transferred to the trust." Such a provision assumes that the donor's spouse will consent to split the gift. The amount that can be withdrawn should not be made to depend upon whether the gift is split — which will not be determined until after the gift is made (*i.e.,* when a gift tax return is filed). To the extent a transfer is subject to such a qualification the gift constitutes a future interest for which no annual exclusion is available. LR 8022048.

The grantor may wish to express in the trust a limit on the amount that can be withdrawn during any year. The amount might be limited, for example, to the amount of the annual exclusion allowable to each donor. The imposition of such a limit protects the availability of the annual exclusion for all donors and protects against the adverse gift and estate tax consequences of a failure to exercise the power in a year when the transfers to the trust exceed the statutorily sheltered $5,000 or five percent amount. The limit may be expressed as a fixed dollar amount or by reference to "the annual exclusion allowable under IRC section 2503(b)."

If a 5 or 5 limit is imposed, the failure to exercise the power does not constitute a gift. §2514(e); LR 8003152. Also, the lapse of such a power will not cause any of the trust to be included in the donee's gross estate. §2041(b)(2). However, if a 5 or 5 limit is imposed, the annual exclusion is only available for that amount. Thus, the full amount of the annual exclusion would not be available to a donor who transfers $10,000 to the trust. Note, however, that the benefits of the annual exclusion and the shelter of the 5 or 5 limit of §2041(b)(2) may be obtained if the power lapses each year only to the extent of the 5 or 5 limit. The use of such a "hanging power" is discussed in §7.37.4.

> **Example 7-13.** The grantor, *G,* established a trust for the beneficiary, *B,* who was given the noncumulative right each year to withdraw property transferred to the trust during the year. Under the terms of the trust, the amount subject to withdrawal by *B* during a calendar year could not exceed the greater of $5,000 or 5% of the value of the property held in the trust. In 1991, *G* transferred property worth $10,000 to the trust. At the time of the transfer the property held in the trust had a value of $50,000. The annual exclusion is available only with respect to $5,000 of the amount that *G* transferred to the trust. Later in 1991 another donor, *D,* transferred property worth $10,000 to the trust. No annual exclusion is available to *D* with respect to the transfer *D* made to the trust. The maximum amount subject to withdrawal by *B* had already been exhausted by *G*'s transfer to the trust.

Where the client wants to preserve the annual exclusion for all transfers to the trust and the client is not concerned about the gift and estate tax consequences of a lapse of the power, the power can be drawn to allow the beneficiary to withdraw an unlimited amount of the property added to the trust during the year. As indicated below, it does not appear that the lapse of the power will have any adverse GSTT consequences. Alternatively, the trust might allow unlimited withdrawals, subject to any restriction imposed by the donor at the time a gift is made to the trust. *See* §7.37.3. Of course, the client should also recognize that the beneficiary might exercise such a power, which could discomfit the donor. The lapse of the power with respect to any particular addition will not result in any gift tax liability if the donee also holds a special testamentary power of appointment that prevents the lapse from constituting a complete gift. *See* Reg. §25.2511-2(b); LR 8517052; LR 8229097 (general power); LR 9030005. *See also* §10.24.

A transfer to a trust that is nontaxable under §2503(b) has a zero inclusion ratio for GSTT purposes if the beneficiary is the only person to whom distributions can be made during his or her lifetime and the property will be included in the beneficiary's estate if the beneficiary dies prior to termination of the trust. §2642(c)(2). The lapse of a *Crummey* power to withdraw property from such a trust does not have any negative gift, estate, or GST tax consequences. For gift and estate tax purposes, the nonexercise is sheltered to the extent of 5 or 5 by the terms of §§2041 and 2514. On the GSTT side, the lapse of such a power is not a direct skip, taxable termination, or taxable distribution. Also, to the extent the lapse does not involve a transfer that is taxable for gift or estate tax purposes the original donor remains the transferor — the lapse of the power does not cause the beneficiary to be treated as the transferor. §2652(a); Reg. §26.2601-1(b)(v)(A).

To the extent the lapse of the *Crummey* power is a taxable transfer for purposes of the gift or estate tax, presumably the power-holder would be treated as the transferor for tax purposes. A taxable gift of an interest in the trust would take place if the lapse resulted in a completed gift under Reg. §25.2511-2(b). Presumably the beneficiary would also become the transferor of the trust for GSTT purposes to the extent of the taxable gift. Of course, in most instances a *Crummey* trust is drafted so the lapse of the power *will not* result in a taxable gift. The beneficiary is typically given a testamentary power of appointment in order to avoid that result. A "hanging power" of withdrawal would similarly prevent a lapse from resulting in a taxable gift. (The annual lapse of a hanging power of withdrawal is subject to a 5 or 5 limit. *See* §7.37.4.) If a beneficiary whose power has lapsed over an amount in excess of the protected 5 or 5 amount dies prior to termination of the trust a portion of the property is includible in the beneficiary's gross estate under §2041(b)(2). The inclusion would cause the deceased beneficiary to become the transferor of the trust for GSTT purposes.

§7.37.3. Authorize Each Donor to Restrict the Amount That Is Subject to Withdrawal

A trust may include a provision that permits each donor to designate whether or not an addition of property made by him or her shall be subject to withdrawal. *See* Keydel, Irrevocable Insurance Trusts: The Current Scene, U. Miami, 10th Inst. Est. Plan. ¶508.1 (1976). Perhaps the best approach is to provide in the trust that transfers to the trust are subject to withdrawal unless otherwise provided in an instrument of transfer. *See* Moore, Tax Consequences and Uses of "Crummey" Withdrawal Powers: An Update, U. Miami, 22nd Inst. Est. Plan. ¶1103 (1988); LR 8003033; LR 8003152. While a person making a gift to the trust may have the inherent right to limit the amount that would be subject to withdrawal, if the client wishes donors to have such a power it is preferable to include an appropriate provision in the trust instrument. Authorizing donors to impose a limit on withdrawals should not cause any federal tax problems. Of course, the annual gift tax exclusion would not be available to the extent a donor provides that a transfer to the trust is not subject to withdrawal. Importantly, the power allows a donor to protect subsequent additions from withdrawal by the beneficiary and against the claims of his or her creditors.

A reserved power to designate whether or not additions to the trust are subject to withdrawal could be bothersome if additions to the trust may be made frequently, such as premium payments made by the insured's employer on group insurance held in the trust. However, that problem is eliminated if the additions are subject to withdrawal except as expressly provided in an instrument of transfer.

Form 7-2. Limitation of Withdrawal Power

Any person transferring property to the trust as a gift may, by a writing delivered to trustee at the time of the transfer, restrict or eliminate the beneficiary's right of withdrawal with respect to part or all of the transferred property.

§7.37.4. Hanging Power: A Power of Withdrawal That Lapses at 5 or 5 Annual Rate

In some instances it may be important for a power of withdrawal to achieve two somewhat inconsistent goals: (1) allowing donors to claim the annual exclusion with respect to all gifts to the trust, and (2) insulating the beneficiary from the potentially adverse tax consequences of the lapse of the power to withdraw an amount greater than $5,000 or five percent of the property subject to withdrawal. Both goals can be achieved if the trust provides that the power to withdraw property transferred to the trust will lapse each year only to the extent of the greater of the 5 or 5 limit. Of course, such a power may allow the beneficiary to make withdrawals over a longer period, which a donor may consider undesirable. In addition, such a power may cause the beneficiary to be treated under §678 as the owner of a larger portion of the trust than otherwise. *See* §7.37.10.

> **Example 7-14.** In 1991 the donor, *D,* transferred $10,000 to a trust with respect to which the beneficiary, *B,* had an unlimited power to withdraw gifts to the trust, provided that the power lapsed each year by an amount equal to the greater of $5,000 or 5% of the value of the property subject to withdrawal. Because of *B*'s unlimited power of withdrawal *D* was entitled to the annual exclusion for the full $10,000 transferred to the trust. *B*'s power of withdrawal lapsed as to $5,000 at the end of 1991. The lapse was within the amount sheltered by the provisions of §§2041 and 2514. Note, however, that the 5 or 5 limit is the total amount that is sheltered each year, counting lapses under all trusts or other arrangements. In 1992 *D* transferred an additional $10,000 to the trust. Accordingly, *B* could withdraw up to $15,000 of the $20,000 corpus of the trust. At the end of 1992 *B*'s power of withdrawal would lapse as to another $5,000. Thus, assuming that no gifts were made to the trust in 1993, *B* in that year would be entitled to withdraw $10,000 of the $20,000 corpus. At the end of 1993 *B*'s power would lapse as to another $5,000.

In LR 8901004 (TAM) the IRS held that the hanging power there involved was an impermissible condition subsequent that was invalid under *Commissioner v. Proctor,* 142 F.2d 824 (4th Cir. 1944). The problem identified in LR 8901004 can be avoided if the power is more carefully drafted. In particular, a power should avoid conditional expressions of the type included in that power: "if . . . the person holding the power will be deemed to have made a taxable gift for federal gift tax purposes, then such power . . . will not lapse."

A form providing for the annual lapse of a 5 or 5 portion of a hanging power appears as Form 7-3. For the complete text of a Hanging Power, *see* Form 10-7 at §10.24.2.

Form 7-3. Annual Lapse of Hanging Power

The beneficiary shall have the continuing cumulative right to exercise his or her power of withdrawal, provided, however, that the right of withdrawal shall lapse on December 31 of each calendar year with respect to a portion of the amount subject to withdrawal equal in value to the greater of $5,000 or 5% of the total value of the trust property on the last day of such calendar year (or such greater amount as a future amendment may specify in I.R.C. §2041(b)(2)). In no case shall a beneficiary's right to withdraw transferred property lapse until 30 days after notice to such beneficiary as provided above.

§7.37.5. How Many Beneficiaries May Hold a Power of Withdrawal?

The power of withdrawal may be given to any number of beneficiaries, including imcompetent persons, who have significant beneficial interests in the trust. Where there are multiple beneficiaries, each of them is usually given a power to withdraw a pro rata portion of property that is added to the trust each year, subject to whatever annual limit may be applicable to individual withdrawals. Of course, the number of annual exclusions that may be claimed is maximized if each beneficiary is given the power. In *Estate of Maria Cristofani,* 97 T.C. — (1991), the Tax Court has allowed the annual exclusion for each beneficiary holding the power, including contingent remaindermen (32 grandchildren). According to the Tax Court, the critical question is whether the beneficiaries had the legal right to exercise the power of withdrawal, not whether they held vested present or future interests in the trust. A fight with the IRS may be avoided if the donor is willing to settle for fewer annual exclusions; giving the power to the beneficiaries who hold current or vested interests in the trust, but not to the others. The IRS has refused to recognize a power of withdrawal given to persons with no beneficial interest in the trust (a "naked" *Crummey* power). LR 8727003. Similarly, the IRS has denied annual exclusions for *Crummey* powers held by persons with remote contingent interests. LR 9141008; LR 9045002 ("The purpose served by adding the 12 family members as beneficiaries was simply to avoid the federal gift tax through a proliferation of annual exclusions. The gifts were purportedly offered to the other 12 family members but the offers were never accepted.") Annual exclusions were allowed, however, in LR 8922062 for powers that were exercisable by beneficiaries who were only entitled to receive distributions for their support in accordance with an ascertainable standard. The IRS requirement that the power-holder have an interest in the trust apart from the power of withdrawal should be satisfied if each power-holder will ultimately receive, or have the power to appoint, an amount of property with a value at least equal to the total amount of the lapsed powers of withdrawal.

The IRS has also indicated that it will not recognize reciprocal powers of withdrawal. In particular, in the case of separate trusts created by two brothers for their issue, the "reciprocal" powers of withdrawal given by each grantor to the other were ignored. Rev. Rul. 85-24, 1985-1 C.B. 279.

§7.37.6. Notice to the Beneficiary

In order to qualify for the annual exclusion for property transferred to the trust, it is necessary for the beneficiary to have a reasonable opportunity to exercise the power of withdrawal prior to its lapse. Rev. Rul. 81-7, 1981-1 C.B. 474 (no annual exclusion for trust funded on December 29 and power lapsed on December 31). Letter Ruling 7946007 did not allow an annual exclusion where the adult beneficiary did not receive timely notice. Also, in LR 8006048 the IRS was unwilling to rule that the beneficiary had a present interest in the initial corpus of the trust where the trust instrument did not require the trustee to give the beneficiary notice of the power of withdrawal. In general, it is preferable to include a provision requiring the trustee to give the beneficiary prompt notice of additions to the trust. Even if the trust does not expressly require the trustee to give notice, the trustee of a *Crummey* trust should give prompt written notice to the beneficiary of any addition to the trust. Giving actual notice of each addition can be a nuisance, however, particularly where frequent additions are made to the trust, as may occur where the employer pays monthly premiums on group-term insurance held by the trustee. When employer-provided group-term insurance will be held in the trust perhaps the withdrawal clause could be drawn to permit a single annual notice, in advance, of premium payments that will be made during the year. Some commentators believe it is sufficient to provide a single notice at the creation of the trust that puts on the power-holder the burden of obtaining information about such things as future transfers. Moore, Tax Consequences and Uses of "Crummey" Withdrawal Powers: An Update, U. Miami, 23rd Inst. Est. Plan. ¶1102.3 (1988). The IRS has recognized that a donor does not have to give notice to himself as guardian for his minor children who held powers of withdrawal under the trust. LR 9030005.

Some planners are reluctant to include a provision in the trust requiring the trustee to give the beneficiary written notice of the receipt of additional property. They feel it is risky to include such a provision because of the possibility that the trustee might not comply exactly with its provisions, which could jeopardize the availability of the annual exclusion if the notice is not given. In their view it is preferable to advise the trustee separately that the trustee should give the beneficiary timely notice. The availability of the annual exclusion should depend upon whether or not the beneficiary receives notice of the transfer of the property to the trust and not upon the inclusion of a provision requiring notice. It may be better to require the trustee to give notice, however, because a direction contained in the trust puts the trustee on notice regarding the requirement and may be taken more seriously than the planner's advice regarding the current requirements of the tax law. Also, the inclusion of the requirement might satisfy an IRS examiner without the donor being required to prove that notice was in fact given to the beneficiary when property was added to the trust.

If a power of withdrawal is exercisable at the time of the power-holder's death, the amount subject to withdrawal is includible in the power-holder's estate, including the amount otherwise sheltered from inclusion by the 5 or 5 exclusion of §2041(b)(2). Some planners seek to avoid that result by providing that the power of withdrawal will lapse at the end of 30 days or one day prior to the death of the power-holder, whichever first occurs. LR 8922062. It is unclear whether the IRS will recognize the provision as effective to shield the 5 or 5 amount from inclusion in the power-holder's estate. The IRS might be troubled by the fact that the termination of the power caused by the death of the power-holder can only be determined retrospectively by reference to the date of his or her death. The provision is, in effect, a condition subsequent — on Day 2 the power would appear to be valid and exercisable until the time of the beneficiary's death, which would retrospectively invalidate an exercise of the power on Day 2.

§7.37.7. Must the Trust Have Liquid Assets to Satisfy a Withdrawal?

Some lawyers fear that an annual exclusion will not be available unless the trust has sufficient liquid funds to satisfy an exercise of the power of withdrawal. However, the IRS has not asserted such a requirement. Quite to the contrary, several letter rulings have allowed annual exclusions for gifts to *Crummey* trusts of term or group-term policies of insurance on the donor's life. *E.g.,* LR 7826050; LR 7935091; LR 8006048. In fact, the IRS has indicated that when the beneficiary holds a *Crummey* power an annual exclusion is allowable for the premium payment made by an employer on a group term life insurance policy that the employee had transferred in trust. LR 8006109. Logically, the right of withdrawal should be sufficient to create a present interest in the beneficiary whether the assets transferred to the trust are cash, securities, insurance, or tangible personal property; that is, the annual exclusion should be available whether or not the trustee has liquid assets on hand during the time the power is exercisable. The power could be satisfied by the transfer of an undivided interest in whatever assets are held in the trust. Helpfully, the IRS allowed annual exclusions in LR 8445004 (TAM) although the trust held only interests in limited partnerships. It was sufficient that the trust authorized the trustee to enter into a "sale, encumbrance, loan, mortgage, or other distribution" to raise funds with which to satisfy the power of withdrawal. Nonetheless, the conservative and safer practice is to fund the trust with sufficient liquid assets to support a withdrawal by the beneficiaries equal to the amount of the annual exclusion (*i.e.,* $10,000 each). The following example illustrates the safe sequence of events to follow in making a gift to an irrevocable life insurance trust.

Example 7-15. In 1991 the donor, *D,* established an irrevocable trust which gave the beneficiary, *B,* an effective *Crummey* power to withdraw additions to the trust by a writing delivered to the trustee that would expire 30 days following notice of an addition. Each year the trustee planned to use $9,000 on June 15 to pay the premium of an insurance policy on *D*'s life. On May 1, 1992 *D* transferred $9,000 to the trustee, who deposited the funds in the trust's bank account and promptly gave notice of the addition to *B. B* did not exercise the power of withdrawal. On June 15 the trustee used the funds to pay the premium.

§7.37.8. How Long Should the Power Be Exercisable?

In order to qualify for the annual exclusion the beneficiary or the guardian of a minor or incompetent beneficiary must have a reasonable time within which to exercise the power of withdrawal. A power of withdrawal that is exercisable for an unreasonably short period of time will be disregarded as illusory. Trusts usually permit the beneficiary to exercise the power either (1) for a specified number of days following notice of the transfer or (2) at any time during the calendar year in which the transfer was made, allowing a certain minimum period for withdrawals made near the end of the year. Annual exclusions were allowed in *Estate of Maria Cristofani,* 97 T.C. — (1991), in which the withdrawal power was only exercisable for only 15 days. Private letter rulings have upheld the allowance of the annual exclusion in cases that allowed withdrawals for 30 days, LR 8004172, or 60 days, LR 7947066, following the transfer, or at any time during the calendar year, LR 7935006. A power of withdrawal that was exercisable only after six months following the transfer prevented the gift from being treated as a present interest. LR 8433024 (annual exclusion denied with respect to property transferred to trust in September, where beneficiary's power to withdraw was only exercisable in March of the following year).

Permitting a withdrawal to be made only during the calendar year in which the property is added to the trust is less desirable for two reasons. First, the IRS may deny the annual exclusion when the transfer is made late in December on the ground that the beneficiary did not have a reasonable time within which to withdraw the property. Of course, in *Crummey* an exclusion was allowed where the trust contained such a provision and the transfer was made two weeks before the end of the year. That threat can be eliminated by providing that the power may be exercised by the beneficiary during a specified minimum period in any case. For example, the beneficiary could be authorized to withdraw property at any time during the calendar year in which the property is added to the trust, or for a period of 30 days following the addition of the property, whichever is longer. Of course, the power to withdraw a gift made after December 1 in any year would lapse in the following calendar year. Such a lapse would be aggregated with any others that take place during the same calendar year for purposes of applying the 5 or 5 limits of §§2041 and 2514. Some planners deal with the problem by prohibiting any additions from being made to the trust after a specified date, such as November 30. *See* LR 8006048. However, that approach unduly restricts the ability of prospective donors to make qualifying gifts to the trust.

Second, the use of a clause that permits the beneficiary to withdraw the property at any time during the calendar year may increase the liquidity requirements of the trust. Also, if the power exists throughout the entire year, the beneficiary may be treated as owner of a greater portion of the trust under §678 than if it existed only for a short time. The liquidity problem is particularly severe if the trustee must always have sufficient liquid assets on hand to satisfy all of the withdrawals that could be made at any time. Retaining that degree of liquidity should not be required in order to enable the donors to claim annual exclusions when they add property to the trust. Note also that the liquidity problem is substantially reduced if the power may be exercised only for a limited number of days following notice.

§7.37.9. Separate Trusts or One Trust for Multiple Donees?

In the case of multiple donees, it is usually simpler to create a separate trust for each of them than it is to create a single trust with multiple beneficiaries. Creation of separate trusts also makes it easier for transfers to the trusts to qualify as nontaxable transfers which have an inclusion ratio of zero for GSTT purposes. *See* §2642(c); *see also* §2.28. However, the donor is entitled to an annual exclusion for each trust beneficiary who has the right to withdraw a pro rata portion of the property that the donor transferred to the trust. Rev. Rul. 80-261, 1980-2 C.B. 279. Separate trusts can be easier to administer in some respects and are generally more beneficial from the income tax point of view because each trust is to some extent a separate taxpayer, allowing each trust a $100 exemption and separate use of the progressive rate schedule. When there are separate trusts, some economies of scale can be achieved if the assets of the trusts are managed as a unit, which can be authorized expressly in the trust instrument.

§7.37.10. Income Tax

A *Crummey* trust is usually subject to the same income tax rules as a §2503(c) trust. *See* §7.36.7. In addition, if the grantor is not treated as owner of the trust, the beneficiary is treated as the "owner" of the trust under the grantor trust rules to the extent the beneficiary holds a power to withdraw assets of the trust. §678(a)(1). The income is taxed to the beneficiary under §678 although the beneficiary is a minor and lacks the legal capacity to withdraw the property. "[I]t is the existence of a power rather than the capacity to exercise such a power that determines whether a person other than the grantor shall be treated as the owner of any part of the trust." Rev. Rul. 81-6, 1981-1 C.B. 385. *See also* Rev. Rul. 67-241, 1967-2 C.B. 225 (widow holding 5 or 5 withdrawal power is treated as partial owner of trust). Accordingly, under §678 a portion of the trust income will be taxed to the beneficiary in a year that property is added to the trust although no income is distributed to, or expended for, the benefit of the beneficiary. In LR 9034004, the IRS ruled that as each power of withdrawal lapsed the beneficiary would be treated as owner of an increasing portion of the trust. The formula to be used is:

$$\text{Increase} = \begin{array}{c}\text{Amount Subject}\\ \text{to Withdrawal}\end{array} \times \frac{\begin{array}{c}\text{Portion of Trust Not Already}\\ \text{Treated as Owned by Beneficiary}\end{array}}{\text{Total Value of Trust Corpus}}$$

Under §678(b) a beneficiary who holds a power of withdrawal is not treated as owner of the trust if the grantor is treated as owner under §§671-677. For example, the income is taxable to the grantor to the extent the grantor holds a power to control beneficial enjoyment under §674. Again, the trustee must also be aware that the gain on the sale of appreciated property within two years after it is added to the trust is taxed as if the grantor had made the sale unless the sale takes place after the grantor's death. *See* §644.

§7.37.11. Estate Tax

The estate tax consequences of a *Crummey* trust are generally the same as those of a §2503(c) trust. *See* §7.36.6. Inclusion in the donee's estate is usually limited to the amount in excess of the 5 or 5 limit with respect to which the donee's power of withdrawal has lapsed. *See* §2041(b)(2). Insofar as the donor is concerned, none of the trust should be included in the donor's estate unless either the trust income or property is used to discharge the donor's obligations or the donor is acting as trustee at the time of his or her death.

§7.37.12. Model *Crummey* Power

Form 7-4 might be used to express a *Crummey* power of withdrawal for a trust with one beneficiary. The creation of a separate trust for each beneficiary is administratively simpler and can more easily be drafted to meet the requirements of the GSTT exclusion for nontaxable gifts, §2642(c)(2). *See* LR 8922062.

Form 7-4. *Crummey* Power for Trust with One Beneficiary

Withdrawal rights. The beneficiary shall have the right to withdraw from the trust an amount of the property originally transferred to the trust not to exceed $20,000 in value by giving written notice, within 30 days of her/his receipt of a copy of this document, to the trustee of the exercise of such right. Trustee shall deliver a copy of the trust agreement to the beneficiary, or to her/his guardian, on the date the property is transferred to the trust.

Notice of Additional Transfers to Trust. The trustee shall promptly give written notice to the beneficiary of the receipt of any property that is gratuitously transferred to the trust by any donor ("additions to the trust").

Right to Withdraw Additions to Trust. The beneficiary may withdraw additions to the trust by giving written request to the trustee. Such right of withdrawal shall apply only to the property added to the trust and shall lapse if it is not exercised within 30 days following receipt of the trustee's notice that property has been transferred to the trust as a gift.

Limitation of Withdrawal Power. Any person transferring property to the trust as a gift may, by a writing delivered to the trustee at the time of the transfer, restrict or eliminate the beneficiary's power of withdrawal with respect to part or all of the transferred property.

Guardian for Minor or Incompetent Beneficiary. If the beneficiary is a minor on the date of this instrument or at the time of any subsequent transfer of property to the trust, or at any such time otherwise fails in legal capacity, the beneficiary's guardian may exercise on behalf of the beneficiary any right of withdrawal provided for in this article. If such right of withdrawal is exercised by the beneficiary or her/his guardian, the property received pursuant to such exercise shall be held for the use and benefit of the beneficiary.

§7.38. Mandatory Distribution of Income Trusts, §2503(b)

In order to qualify for the annual exclusion under §2503(b), a trust for a minor may be drafted to require the income to be distributed currently to the donee, the donee's guardian, or a custodian for the donee under one of the Uniform Acts. In those cases the annual exclusion is available for the value of the income interest determined in accordance with §7520. The remainder interest does not qualify for the annual exclusion: "[A] transfer of property in trust with income required to be paid annually to a minor beneficiary and corpus to be distributed to him upon his attaining the age of 25 is a gift of a present interest with respect to the right to income but is a gift of a future interest with respect to the right to corpus." Reg. §25.2503-4(c). Of course, the value of the remainder interest can be virtually eliminated by giving the beneficiary the income interest for life, with the power to terminate the trust and obtain the principal after attaining a specified age.

Example 7-16. Donor, *D,* transferred $10,000 to an irrevocable trust of which *D*'s 10-year-old child, *C,* was the income beneficiary. The income of the trust must be distributed each year to *D* until age 25 when the principal is distributable to C. Under Table B of IRS Publication 1457, based upon a 10% interest rate *C*'s right to receive the income for 15 years has a value of $7,606. The remainder, which is a future interest, has a value of $2,394.

If *C* were entitled to receive the income for life, with the power to terminate the trust at any time after age 25, under Table S(10.0) of Publication 1457, *C*'s interest would have a value of $9,881. The remainder interest would have a value of only $119.

§7.38.1. Nontax Considerations

From the nontax point of view a mandatory distribution trust is generally less desirable than a *Crummey* trust because of the difficulty of providing for current distribution of income in a satisfactory way. Direct payment of the income to the beneficiary is generally considered to involve an unacceptable risk of waste by the beneficiary. The other methods of distribution also have some disadvantages. Requiring the appointment of a guardian to receive distributions of income involves some additional complexity in drafting and operating the trust. More important, the conduct of a guardianship proceeding is cumbersome and expensive in most states. Distribution to a custodian under one of the Uniform Acts is a better choice, but it has several disadvantages: (1) the custodial property must be distributed to the minor when he or she becomes 21; (2) if the minor dies prior to 21 the custodial property will be distributed as an asset of the minor's estate — quite possibly defeating a major purpose of the gifts by being distributed to the minor's parents; and (3) the plan involves additional complexity in drafting and administering the trust.

§7.38.2. Tax Considerations

The transfer of property to a mandatory distribution trust is a completed gift unless the grantor retains a power to affect the beneficial interests in the trust (which is seldom done). As indicated above, in most cases the income interest in a mandatory distribution trust qualifies for the annual gift tax exclusion. However, the IRS may challenge the availability of the annual exclusion if the trustee is obligated to retain non-income-producing property.

The grantor of a mandatory distribution trust does not usually retain any interest or control that would require the trust to be included in the grantor's estate if the grantor dies before termination of the trust. In particular, the grantor does not retain any power to control the beneficial interests in the trust or to cause its termination or revocation. If the beneficiary dies prior to termination of the trust, the trust property will not be included in the beneficiary's estate unless the beneficiary held a general power of appointment. *See* §2041.

The income of a mandatory distribution trust is taxed to the beneficiary unless it is taxed to the grantor under the grantor trust rules of §§671-677. *See* §10.4.1. In this connection note that the income of the trust is taxable to the grantor under §677(b) only to the extent it is actually used to discharge the grantor's legal obligation to support the beneficiary. This risk can be eliminated by providing that the trustee may not make any distributions that will satisfy the grantor's obligations, including the obligation to support any person.

A properly planned mandatory distribution trust has three relatively minor tax disadvantages. First, the remainder interest in the property transferred to the trust does not qualify for the annual exclusion. Accordingly, the grantor would be required to file a gift tax return with respect to transfers to the trust. The grantor would also be required to pay some gift tax or use a portion of his or her unified credit in order to offset the tax attributable to the value of the remainder interest. Careful drafting can reduce the value of the remainder interest. *See* Example 7-16 at §7.38. Second, the income-splitting potential of the trust is limited where the distribution must be made to the minor or a custodian for him or her (income received by the custodian is taxed currently to the minor). In such a case the limited income tax saving potential of the trust is unavailable. Third, the distributions of income to or for the benefit of a child under 14 are subject to the Kiddie Tax.

§7.39. Irrevocable Short-Term Trusts

The adoption of the compressed income tax rate schedule and amendments to the grantor trust rules made by the 1986 Act virtually eliminated the income tax advantages of short-term reversionary trusts. Under §673 the grantor is treated as owner of the trust if the grantor or the grantor's spouse holds a reversionary interest in the income or principal that had a value of more than five percent of the value of the property at the time it was transferred to the trust. Prior to the 1986 Act, short-term trusts were frequently used by a taxpayer in a high income tax bracket to shift income to another family member temporarily, without permanently divesting himself or herself of all interests in the property. Importantly, the grantor could retain a reversionary interest in property transferred to the trust if the reversion would not, or was not reasonably expected to, take effect in possession or enjoyment within ten years following its transfer to the trust. Former §673(a).

BIBLIOGRAPHY

Adams, Powers of Withdrawal Held Individually or as a Fiduciary: A Pandora's Box of Tax Consequences, U. Miami, 23rd Inst. Est. Plan., ch. 19 (1989)

Atkinson, Gifts to Minors: A Roadmap, 42 Ark. L. Rev. 567 (1989)

Kasner, Gifts to Children and Grandchildren — With Particular

Emphasis on Educational Financing, N.Y.U., 48th Inst. Fed. Tax., ch. 22 (1990)

Moore, Tax Consequences and Uses of "Crummey" Withdrawal Powers: An Update, U. Miami, 22nd Inst. Est. Plan., ch. 11 (1988)

Muhs & Stikker, Lifetime Gifts and Transfers for Consideration, 1 Cal. CEB, Estate Planning Practice, ch. 6 (1988)

Price, Intrafamily Transfers: Blessed and More Blessed Ways to Give, U. Miami, 18th Inst. Est. Plan., ch. 6 (1984)

Report, Committee on Estate Planning and Drafting, What to Give Away, 18 Real Prop., Prob. & Tr. J. 678 (1983), 19 Real Prop., Prob. & Tr. J. 806 (1984)

CHAPTER 8

GIFTS TO CHARITABLE ORGANIZATIONS

A. Introduction

§8.1. Scope

B. Federal Tax Consequences of Outright Gifts

§8.2. Qualified Charities, §170(c)
§8.2.1. Foreign Charities
§8.2.2. Cumulative List of Charitable Organizations; Requests for Rulings
§8.3. Public Charities, §170(b)(1)(A)
§8.4. Nonpublic Charities
§8.4.1. Gifts for the Use of a Charitable Organization
§8.4.2. Gifts of Services and the Use of Property
§8.5. Charitable Contributions Carryover, §170(d)(1)
§8.6. When Is a Gift Made? Reg. §1.170A-1(b)
§8.7. Appraisals, Substantiation, and Valuation of Gifts, Reg. §§1.170A-1(c), 1.170A-13(b)(2)-(4); §6662
§8.7.1. Substantiation Rules
§8.7.2. Penalty for Underpayment of Tax
§8.7.3. Report of Disposition of Property by Charity
§8.8. Gifts of Depreciated Property
§8.9. Gifts of Ordinary Income Property, §170(e)(1)(A)
§8.10. Gifts of Capital Gain Property: General, §§170(b)(1)(C), (D); 170(e)
§8.11. Gifts of Capital Gain Property: Election to Reduce Amount of Gift, §§170(b)(1)(C)(iii), 170(e)
§8.12. Gifts of Capital Gain Property: Tangible Personal Property, §170(e)(1)(B)(i), (ii)
§8.13. Gifts of Future Interests in Tangible Personal Property, §170(a)(3), Reg. §1.170A-5

C. Gifts of Partial Interests

§8.14. General
§8.15. Remainder Interest in Personal Residence or Farm
§8.15.1. Life Estate Transferred to Spouse or Others
§8.15.2. Charitable Gift of Remainder in Part of Farm or Residence
§8.15.3. Sale Required upon Termination of Life Estate
§8.15.4. Depreciation and Depletion
§8.16. Undivided Portion of Donor's Entire Interest
§8.17. Donor's Entire Interest in Property
§8.18. Transfers Subject to a Condition or Power

D. Gifts in Trust

§8.19. General Limitations
§8.20. Charitable Remainder Trusts in General, §664(d)
§8.20.1. Double Deductions
§8.20.2. Diversification of Investments
§8.20.3. Wealth Replacement Plans
§8.20.4. Substitute for Tax-Exempt Retirement Plan
§8.20.5. Marital Deductions
§8.21. Charitable Remainder Annuity Trust (CRAT)
§8.22. Charitable Remainder Unitrust (CRUT)
§8.23. Sample Declarations of Trust
§8.24. Income Taxation of Charitable Remainder Trusts
§8.25. Valuing Charitable Remainders
§8.26. Private Foundation Rules
§8.27. Requests for Rulings
§8.28. Advantages of Charitable Remainder Trusts
§8.29. Comparison of CRATs and CRUTs
§8.30. Pooled Income Fund, §642(c)(5)
§8.31. Gifts to Charitable Lead Trusts, §§170(f)(2)(B), 2055(e)(2)(B), 2522(c)(2)(B)
§8.32. Guaranteed Annuity Interests and Unitrust Interests
§8.33. Gifts of Income Interests
§8.34. Payments to Charity from a Trust upon Death of Grantor
§8.35. Salvaging Charitable Deductions for Nonqualifying Interests

E. Special Types of Transfers

§8.36. Bargain Sales to Charity, §1011(b)
§8.37. Charitable Gift Annuities
§8.38. Gift and Redemption of Appreciated Stock

§8.39. Gift of Life Insurance
§8.40. Charitable Pledges

Bibliography

> [T]he words of such an act as the Income Tax, for example, merely dance before my eyes in a meaningless procession: cross-reference to cross-reference, exception upon exception — couched in abstract terms that offer no handle to seize hold of — leave in my mind only a confused sense of some vitally important, but successfully concealed, purport, which it is my duty to extract, but which is within my power, if at all, only after the most inordinate expenditure of time. Learned Hand, Thomas Walter Swan, 57 Yale L.J. 167, 169 (1947).

A. INTRODUCTION

§8.1. Scope

Historically, Americans have generously supported charitable causes. The social value of charitable gifts is recognized in the income, gift, and estate tax laws, each of which has allowed a deduction for charitable gifts from an early time in its history. Over the years these deductions are consistently among the most important to taxpayers, both in terms of dollars involved and the number of taxpayers who claim them.

The words Judge Hand wrote about the income tax law in general apply even more forcefully to the complex provisions that apply to some gifts to charities, including gifts of appreciated property and gifts of partial interests to charitable donees ("split gifts"). Fortunately, relatively simple rules govern the deductibility of outright gifts to churches, schools, and similar charitable organizations. In those cases only the first sentence of §170(a) is usually significant: "There shall be allowed as a deduction any charitable contribution (as defined in subsection (c)) payment of which is made within the taxable year." Pity the other donors, and their tax advisors, who must grapple with the remaining ten single-spaced pages of §170. In spite of the need for simplification, the fiscal realities, and the perceived need to encourage charitable gifts, the deduction will continue to be complex. *See, e.g.,* The President's Proposals for Fairness, Growth and Simplicity (1985).

The charitable deduction provisions of the income tax law, §170, the gift tax law, §2522, and the estate tax law, §2055, are similar in many respects. The principal differences are that the income tax law limits the amount of deductions and requires adjustments when certain types of property are transferred, whereas the gift and estate tax laws neither impose limits nor require adjustments. There are also slight differences in the types of organizations that qualify for the deductions under the three statutes. For example, the estate and gift taxes, but not the income tax, allow deductions for gifts to foreign charities. §§2055(a)(2), 2522(a)(2), 170(c)(2)(A). Nonresident aliens are generally allowed tax deductions only for contributions to domestic charities, or for use in the United States. §§873(b)(2), 2106(a)(2), 2522(b). Curiously, gifts to community chests are explicitly recognized as charitable in the income and gift tax laws, but not in the estate tax law. *Compare* §§170(c)(2) *and* 2522(a)(2) *with* §2055(a)(2). It is not possible to identify any policy that is served by the differences in the language of the three statutes.

In this chapter the federal tax consequences of outright gifts to charity are discussed first. The percentage limitations on income tax deductions and various types of charities are developed in the context of that discussion. Gifts of partial interests, gifts in trust, and special types of transfers are explored later in the chapter.

For income tax purposes, gifts to qualifying charitable organizations are deductible by individual taxpayers who itemize. However, the deductions are subject to the percentage limitations and adjustments required by §170. Depending upon the character of the charitable donee and the property donated, the deduction is limited to 20 percent, 30 percent, or 50 percent of the donor's adjusted gross income. Until 1982 a deduction was only allowed to taxpayers who itemized their deductions. From 1982 through 1986, a limited charitable contribution deduction was allowed on an experimental basis for taxpayers who did not itemize. This deduction was not extended when it expired in 1987. §§63(b), 170(i).

The allowance of an income tax deduction for charitable contributions has been criticized by some commentators who contend that the deduction should be replaced by a credit. They argue that a credit would be of equal value to all taxpayers whereas a deduction is of variable value, depending upon the donor's marginal income tax rate. Of course, the compression of the income tax rates that took place under the 1986 Act reduced the significance of the difference between a deduction and a credit for taxpayers who itemize. Other commentators contend that the income tax deduction should be unlimited, which would make it conform more closely to the gift and estate tax deductions.

The actual disparity in treatment of taxpayers is often increased because donors who do not itemize usually make cash contributions from earned income while wealthy donors frequently contribute appreciated property. Within the limits established by §170, a deduction is usually allowed for the full value of the appreciated property without requiring the donor to recognize any gain.

> **Example 8-1.** *D,* who is in the 31% income tax bracket, wishes to give $10,000 to a public charity. *D* has owned stock for more than 6 months that has a basis of $1,000 and a fair market value of $10,000. If *D* contributes $10,000 in cash, *D*'s tax will be reduced by $3,100. If *D* instead contributes the stock, the tax savings will be the same, but the unrealized gain of $9,000 will not be taxed to *D.*

Gifts of appreciated property must be carefully planned in view of the donor's contribution base (adjusted gross income), the nature of the property, the alternative minimum tax, and the character of the donee organization.

B. FEDERAL TAX CONSEQUENCES OF OUTRIGHT GIFTS

§8.2. Qualified Charities, §170(c)

For income tax purposes a charitable deduction is allowable only for gifts made "to or for the use of" an organization listed in §170(c). In the case of contributions by individuals the list includes:

1. A state or federal governmental unit, if the gift is made for exclusively public purposes (including an Indian tribal government, §7871(a));
2. A domestic corporation, trust, community chest, fund, or foundation that is organized and operated exclusively for religious, charitable, scientific, literary, or educational purposes, to foster national or international sports competition or for the prevention of cruelty to children or animals;
3. A post or other organization of war veterans;
4. A domestic fraternal organization, operating under the lodge system, but only if the gift is exclusively for religious, charitable, scientific, literary, or educational purposes, or for the prevention of cruelty to children or animals; and
5. A nonprofit cemetery company.

Gifts to or for the use of organizations listed in items 1, 2, and 3, and gifts to organizations listed in item 4 usually qualify for gift and estate tax deductions. *See* §§2055(a), 2522(a). Also note that gifts to or for the use of a fraternal organization qualify for the gift tax deduction. §2522(a)(3). A gift to a cemetery company (item 5) does not qualify for a gift or an estate tax deduction. *See Mellon Bank v. United States,* 762 F.2d 283 (3rd Cir. 1985), *cert. denied,* 475 U.S. 1032 (1986).

When a nonqualified entity collecting charitable contributions is simply acting as an agent for a qualified charity, the payment is treated as if it were made directly to the qualified charity. Rev. Rul. 85-184, 1985-2 C.B. 85. On the other hand, if a qualified domestic charity is collecting funds which will be used by a foreign charity (a nonqualified charity) and the domestic charity has control and discretion over the funds, and the funds are used in furtherance of specific purposes approved by the domestic charity, contributions are treated as made to the domestic charity. Rev. Rul. 66-79, 1966-1 C.B. 48. Also, "the statute does not preclude the deductibility of contributions to a domestic charitable corporation which uses its funds for a charitable purpose in a foreign country." Rev. Rul. 69-80, 1969-1 C.B. 65.

The estate of a nonresident alien is not entitled to an estate tax charitable deduction for a gift of works of art left to qualified charities to the extent they are not included in the decedent's gross estate. LR 9040003. Under §2055(d) deductions are allowable only for property that is included in a decedent's gross estate.

Qualified charities are themselves divided into two classes: (1) the so-called "public charities" described in §170(b)(1)(A) (also called 509(a)(1), (2) or (3) organizations), §8.3; and (2) all others, §8.4. Churches, hospitals, and schools are common examples of public charities. Gifts to public charities qualify for the maximum allowable income tax deduction, which is 30 percent or 50 percent of the donor's contribution base depending upon the nature of the property transferred. The term "contribution base" is defined as adjusted gross income, computed without regard to any net operating loss carryback under §172. §170(b)(1)(F). A ceiling of 30 percent applies to gifts made *to* other charities described in §170(c) such as cemetery companies, posts or organizations of war veterans, fraternal lodges, and private nonoperating foundations. It also applies to gifts made *for the use of* public charities.

§8.2.1. Foreign Charities

Contributions to foreign charities are not deductible for income tax purposes except for certain Canadian charities under the tax treaty between the United States and Canada. The deduction is also limited to the amount that would be allowed under Canadian law as if the taxpayer's Canadian source income were aggregate income. *See* Rev. Proc. 59-

31, 1959-2 C.B. 949; Convention Between the United States of America and Canada with Respect to Taxes on Income and Capital, Article XXI, par. 5.

§8.2.2. Cumulative List of Charitable Organizations; Requests for Rulings

A list of organizations that meet the requirements of §170(c) is published annually by the IRS. Cumulative List of Organizations Described in Section 170(c) of the Internal Revenue Code of 1954, I.R.S. Pub. No. 78. Additions, deletions, and changes are published in quarterly supplements. The Cumulative List is available on a subscription basis from:

Superintendent of Documents
U.S. Government Printing Office
Washington, D.C. 20402

A donor has some assurance that a deduction will be allowed for a gift made to an organization named in the Cumulative List. If the IRS subsequently revokes a letter ruling or determination letter previously issued to the organization, a deduction will generally be allowed for gifts made prior to publication in the Internal Revenue Bulletin of an announcement that gifts to the organization are no longer deductible. Rev. Proc. 82-39, 1982-1 C.B. 759. Accordingly, an estate tax charitable deduction was allowed for a gift to a charity that was listed in the Cumulative List at the time the decedent transferred a remainder in her personal residence to the charity and at the time of her death — the later revocation of the organization's exempt status does not bar the allowance of the deduction. LR 9005001 (TAM).

Requests for rulings must include a completed checklist of the type published in Rev. Proc. 91-14, 1991-1 C.B. —. The request must indicate that the applicant has read and complied with the procedures published each year in the first Internal Revenue Bulletin of the year, including the issues on which the IRS will not rule. Rulings should be requested with respect to unusual or complex nonfactual issues regarding the gift, estate, and generation-skipping transfer tax (GSTT) consequences of transfers involving charitable gifts.

§8.3. Public Charities, §170(b)(1)(A)

As indicated above, a larger income tax deduction is allowed for gifts made to a certain group of preferred charities, loosely called "public charities." In contrast, the estate and gift tax laws do not distinguish between the character of qualified charities.

In 1969 the maximum deduction was increased to 50 percent for a wide range of public charities described in §170(b)(1)(A)(i)-(viii). The charities that qualify include churches; schools with a regular faculty, curriculum, and student body; organizations that provide medical or hospital care or perform medical research or education; organizations that receive a substantial part of their support from federal and state sources and from the general public and use their funds for educational organizations owned or operated by a state or a state agency; and state or federal governmental units to the extent gifts are made exclusively for public purposes. §170(b)(1)(A)(i)-(v). Trusts, funds, or foundations described in §170(c)(2), such as publicly or governmentally supported museums, libraries, community centers, United Funds, and the American Red Cross, also qualify provided they receive a substantial amount of their support from a state or federal governmental unit or from the general public, §170(b)(1)(A)(vi) (commonly called "509(a)(1)" organizations). Three types of private foundations described in §170(b)(1)(E) also qualify for the 50 percent limitation. They are:

1. A private operating foundation described in §4942(j)(3); Reg. §§53.4942(b)-1 and 53.4942(b)-2;
2. A private nonoperating foundation that distributes all of the contributions it receives to public charities or makes certain other qualifying distributions within two and one-half months following the close of its taxable year (Reg. §1.170A-9(g)); and
3. A private foundation that pools contributions in a common fund and allows contributors (or their spouses) to designate the public charities that will receive the annual income and the portion of the fund attributable to their gifts. *See* Reg. §1.170A-9(h).

Finally, organizations described in §509(a)(2) or (3) are also treated as public charities for purposes of the 50 percent limit. §170(b)(1)(A)(viii). Importantly, organizations that qualify under §509(a)(1), (2) or (3) are not private foundations and are relieved from complying with the private foundation excise tax provisions of §§4940-4948. Section 509(a)(2) describes certain types of organizations that have broad public support, normally receive more than one-third of their support from gifts, grants, contributions, or membership fees, and do not receive more than one-third of their support from gross investment income. *See* Reg. §1.509(a)-3. A §509(a)(3) organization (a "supporting organization") is one that is organized and operated exclusively to support one or more specified public charities; operated, supervised, or controlled by or in connection with one or more public charities; and not controlled directly or indirectly by the donor or "disqualified" persons. *See* Reg. §1.509(a)-4. The use of supporting organizations as a vehicle for charitable gifts is popular because they are treated as public charities for income tax purposes and they are not subject to the private foundation rules.

§8.4. Nonpublic Charities

The deduction for gifts to private foundations and other charities not described in §170(b)(1)(A) is limited to the lesser of (1) 30 percent of the donor's contribution base for the year or (2) the excess of 50 percent of the donor's contribution base over the amount of the donor's gifts to public charities. §170(b)(1)(B). As indicated above, gifts "for the use of" all charities are subject to a 30 percent limit.

Example 8-2. During a year in which *D* had a contribution base of $25,000 he made cash gifts that totalled $10,000 to churches and schools described in §170(b)(1)(A). *D* also gave $5,000 in cash to the local post of the war veterans. The gift of $10,000 to public charities is fully deductible as it does not exceed 50% of *D*'s contribution base. Only $2,500 of the gift made to the war veterans' organization, a nonpublic charity, is deductible. The gift does not exceed 30% of *D*'s contribution base, but it does exceed the difference between 50% of his contribution base ($12,500) and the amount of his gifts to public charities ($10,000). The nondeductible portion of a gift to a nonpublic charity can be carried over and deducted in a later year. *See* §§170(b)(1)(B), 170(d). *See also* §8.5.

§8.4.1. Gifts for the Use of a Charitable Organization

For the purposes of §170 a gift of an income interest is considered to be a gift "for the use of" the charity, whether or not the gift is made in trust. In contrast, a gift of a remainder interest is a gift "to" the charity unless the remainder will be held in trust after the termination of the preceding interests, in which case it is a gift "for the use of" the donee. Reg. §1.170A-8(a)(2).

Example 8-3. *D* transferred Blackacre to the trustee of a charitable remainder annuity trust that meets the requirements of §664(d)(1). The trust provides that an annuity of 5% of the initial fair market value of the property transferred to the trust will be paid to *D* and, upon the death of *D,* Blackacre will be distributed to the H Hospital, a public charity that meets the requirements of §170(b)(1)(A). *D* made a gift of the charitable remainder interest "to" the H Hospital.

§8.4.2. Gifts of Services and the Use of Property

No deduction is allowed for the value of services performed for a charity. Thus, an attorney was not allowed a deduction for the fair market value of services he or she provided to a charity free of charge. W. W. Grant, 84 T.C. 809 (1985), *aff'd,* 800 F.2d 260 (4th Cir. 1986). However, a deduction is allowable for unreimbursed expenses incurred incident to rendering gratuitous services to a charitable organization. Such contributions are considered made "to" rather than "for the use of" the organization. Rev. Rul. 84-61, 1984-1 C.B. 40; *Rockefeller v. Commissioner,* 676 F.2d 35 (2d Cir. 1982).

A limited deduction is allowed for costs incurred to maintain a student in the donor's home under an organized program. The costs are treated as payments "for the use of" the organization. §170(g).

Unreimbursed out-of-pocket expenses incurred in activities for qualified charities may also be deductible, including mileage on passenger automobiles at a rate of 12 cents per mile. §170(j). *See also* Rev. Rul. 84-61, 1984-1 C.B. 40.

In *Davis v. United States,* 110 S. Ct. 2014 (1990), the Supreme Court resolved a split in the circuits regarding the deductibility, as contributions to a church, of travel and living expenses paid by the taxpayer on behalf of a son who is serving as a church missionary. The Court affirmed the Ninth Circuit decision in *Davis* denying a deduction for the expenses. 861 F.2d 558 (1988). According to the Court, such payments were not contributions "to" or "for the benefit of" the church. Moreover, the Regulations allow taxpayers to claim deductions *only* for expenditures made in connection with their own contribution of services. Reg. §1.170A-1(g); 110 S. Ct. at 2023. Decisions allowing deductions had been rendered in the Fifth and Tenth Circuits. *Brinley v. Commissioner,* 782 F.2d 1326 (5th Cir. 1986); *White v. United States,* 725 F.2d 1269 (10th Cir. 1984).

Travel expenses, whether paid directly or reimbursed, are not deductible if there is a significant element of personal pleasure, recreation, or vacation. §170(k).

The contribution of the use of a vacation home for a week to a charity auction does not qualify for a charitable contribution deduction. Rev. Rul. 89-51, 1989-1 C.B. 89. In the same ruling the IRS concluded that the individual who purchased the use of vacation home at an auction for the benefit of the charity was not entitled to a deduction: "A payment to a charity is not a contribution to the extent that valuable consideration is received in return." Finally, for purposes of determining the right of the owner to deduct expenses associated with the vacation home, the week contributed to charity is counted as a week of personal use by the owner.

§8.5. Charitable Contributions Carryover, §170(d)(1)

In general, contributions may be carried over for the next five taxable years to the extent they exceed the applicable percentage limit for the current year (20 percent, 30 percent, or 50 percent). §§170(b)(1)(B), 170(b)(1)(D)(ii), 170(d)(1). No carryover is allowed for a gift (1) "for the use of" a public charity or (2) "to or for the use of" a nonpublic charity (*e.g.,* private foundations).

> **Example 8-4.** *H* and *W,* who file joint returns, have a contribution base of $50,000 in Year 1 and $40,000 in Year 2. In Year 1 they made cash gifts of $30,000 to a public charity and $2,000 to a nonpublic charity. In Year 2 they gave $18,000 in cash to a public charity. Under §170(b)(1) they are entitled to a deduction of $25,000 for Year 1 (50% of their contribution base), which leaves a carryover under §170(d)(1) of $5,000 to Year 2. No deduction is allowed with respect to the $2,000 contribution to the nonpublic charity because of the 30% limit, but the contribution may be carried over to Year 2. §170(b)(1)(B). *H* and *W* are entitled to a deduction of $20,000 for Year 2 with respect to public charities ($18,000 plus $2,000 of the $5,000 carryover from Year 1). Their carryovers Year 3 will be $3,000 with respect to public charities, §170(d)(1), and $2,000 with respect to nonpublic charities, §170(b)(1)(B).

§8.6. When Is a Gift Made? Reg. §1.170A-1(b)

The time at which a gift is considered to be made can be of vital importance to the donor. It affects both the year in which a gift may be deducted and the total amount of gifts made in a particular year.

> Ordinarily a contribution is made at the time delivery is effected. The unconditional delivery or mailing of a check which subsequently clears in due course will constitute an effective contribution on the date of delivery or mailing. If a taxpayer unconditionally delivers or mails a properly endorsed stock certificate to a charitable donee or the donee's agent, the gift is completed on the date of delivery or, if such certificate is received in the ordinary course of the mails, on the date of mailing. If the donor delivers the stock certificate to his bank or broker as the donor's agent, or to the issuing corporation or its agent, for transfer into the name of the donee, the gift is completed on the date the stock is transferred on the books of the corporation. Reg. §1.170A-1(b).

A note given to a charity by its maker is a mere promise to pay, which is not deductible until it is paid. Rev. Rul. 68-174, 1968-1 C.B. 81. Similarly, a pledge made to a charity is deductible when it is paid, not at the time it is made. *Mann v. Commissioner,* 35 F.2d 873 (D.C. Cir. 1929); *cf.,* Rev. Rul. 78-129, 1978-1 C.B. 67. Further, a gift made to a charity by charging an amount against the donor's bank credit card is deductible in the year the charge is made even though the bank is not paid until the following year. Rev. Rul. 78-38, 1978-1 C.B. 67. For estate tax purposes a gift to a charity by check relates back to the date of delivery and is considered paid on that date if the payee promptly presents the check and it is duly paid by the bank. *Estate of Belcher,* 83 T.C. 227 (1984), *see also Estate of Elizabeth C. Dillingham,* 88 T.C. 1569 (1987), *aff'd,* 903 F.2d 760 (10th Cir. 1990).

§8.7. Appraisals, Substantiation, and Valuation of Gifts, Reg. §§1.170A-1(c), 1.170A-13(b)(2)-(4), §6662

In order to qualify for the charitable deduction the donor must satisfy the appraisal and substantiation requirements that were added by the 1984 Act. Under the Temporary Regulations individuals, closely-held corporations, personal service corporations, partnerships, and S corporations must file an appraisal summary (Form 8283, Noncash Charitable Contributions Summary) with respect to gifts after 1984 of property, other than money or traded securities, that have a claimed value of over $5,000. In addition, the taxpayer must obtain a qualified written appraisal of the property from a qualified appraiser, who must execute the certification of appraiser which is included on Form 8283. In the case of a charitable gift of nonpublicly traded stock, the value of which is not more than $10,000, Form 8283 must be filed but an appraisal is not required. In connection with the new requirements note that the value of similar property contributed to one or more charitable donees during the taxable year is aggregated. In addition, when similar items of property are contributed to more than one charitable organization, a separate Form 8283 must be filed with respect to each donee.

The abuses that the substantiation rules are intended to prevent are illustrated by *Peter J. Lio,* 85 T.C. 56 (1985). Dr. Lio purchased 150 unframed lithographs by an artist (Nelson) from the artist's sole publisher and distributor for $50 each. The agreement specified that "at the time of delivery, AAA will supply Dr. Lio with two 'independent appraisals' stating that the fair market value of each lithograph is not less than $150." It also provided that, "within 1 year after the investment portfolios are delivered to Dr. Lio, AAA shall, upon request, supply at no additional charge a list of charitable organizations which will accept a donation of the lithographs and two independent appraisals setting forth their then current fair market value." 85 T.C. at 59. After Dr. Lio had owned the lithographs for more than nine months, he contributed them, unframed, to a museum. In the same year two other individuals made similar gifts of 200 lithographs by the same artist to the museum. "The museum has not accessioned the Nelson lithographs to its permanent collection or displayed them, nor does it have a present intention to do so. The museum does not insure the lithographs." 85 T.C. at 59.

Dr. Lio claimed a charitable deduction of $24,688 for the 150 Nelson lithographs based upon a value of slightly over $164 each, which was the average of the appraisals he received from AAA. During the same year AAA sold 12,225 Nelson lithographs, "97% of which were sold for $50 or less." None of the lithographs from the five Nelson editions purchased by Dr. Lio was sold for more than $50. The Tax Court found that the relevant market for the lithographs was the market maintained by AAA and that the sale to Dr. Lio was, in effect, a sale to the ultimate consumer and the best evidence of the value of the lithographs. The appraisals submitted by Dr. Lio were not persuasive. There was no evidence that Dr. Lio received any special discount or that the lithographs had appreciated in value in the period following their purchase. Accordingly, the charitable deduction was limited to $50.

Example 8-5. During the same taxable year, *D* gave original prints valued at $2,000 to the M Museum and original prints worth $3,500 to the Art Department of the U University. *D* must obtain a qualified appraisal of the prints from a qualified appraiser. The appraiser must be a person who must hold himself out to the public as an appraiser and cannot be the donor, the donee, a party to the gift, employed by, or related to, any of the parties, or a person whose relationship to the parties would cause a reasonable person to question his independence. A separate Form 8283 must be completed with respect to each gift, acknowledged by an appropriate official of the donees, and the certification must be signed by the appraiser.

If a contribution is made in property other than money, the amount of the contribution is the fair market value of property at the time of the gift. Reg. §1.170A-1(c)(2), *Robert C. Chiu,* 84 T.C. 722, 730 (1985). For real property, fair market value is generally based on its highest and best use. However, reproduction cost is a relevant measure of value where the property is unique, its market limited, and there are no comparable sales. *Estate of Palmer v. Commissioner,* 839 F.2d 420,424 (1988). Because the valuation of art objects is often difficult, since the 1960s a panel of art experts has advised the IRS regarding valuation of art valued at $20,000 or more. Of course, where the property has a value in excess of its basis, the amount of the gift that is deductible for income tax purposes must be reduced in some cases. Reg. §1.170A-1(c). *See* §§8.9-8.12.

A gift of encumbered property qualifies for the charitable deduction only to the extent the fair market value of the property exceeds the amount of the encumbrances. *Winston F.C. Guest,* 77 T.C. 9 (1981).

§8.7.1. Substantiation Rules

Detailed rules govern the substantiation of deductions. Cash contributions require the donor to maintain a cancelled check, written receipt, or other reliable written records. Reg. §1.170A-13. Generally, a donation of property requires the donor to maintain a receipt from the donee which shows, among other things, the date, location, donee and the description and fair market value of the property. Temp. Reg. §1.170A-13(b)(1). In addition, if the deduction for a contribution of property exceeds $500, the donor's written records must show the manner of acquisition and the cost or basis of the property. Reg. §1.170A-13(b)(3). For property other than money or publicly traded securities, no deduction is allowable unless the donor obtains a qualified appraisal and attaches an appraisal summary (IRS Form 8283) to the tax return. Reg. §1.170A-13(c). A partially completed appraisal summary form suffices in certain cases, including gifts of nonpublicly traded stock worth between $5,000 and $10,000. Reg. §1.170A-13(c)(2)(B).

§8.7.2. Penalty for Underpayment of Tax

Under §6662, a penalty applies where there is any underpayment of $5,000 or more in income tax due to a substantial valuation overstatement. For this purpose a substantial valuation overstatement occurs if the value claimed is 200 percent or more of the correct valuation. §6662(e)(1). If the overstatement is 400 percent or more, the penalty is 40 percent. §6662(h)(1)(2). In order to avoid imposition of a penalty the taxpayer should obtain the required appraisals and make an independent inquiry into the value of the property. Under Prop. Reg. §1.6664-4(a), no penalty will be imposed under §6662 with respect to any portion of an underpayment for which there was reasonable cause. "Reliance on an information return, professional advice, or other facts, however, constitutes reasonable cause and good faith if, under all the circumstances, such reliance was reasonable and the taxpayer acted in good faith." Prop. Reg. §1.6664-4(b).

§8.7.3. Report of Disposition of Property by Charity

If a charitable donee sells or otherwise disposes of donated property (including similar property contributed to other donees), it must file an information return (Form 8282) with the IRS (with a copy to the donor) identifying the donor and providing information regarding the sale. §6050L. The reporting requirement applies when the value of the contributed property, other than cash and publicly traded securities, exceeds $5,000. Penalties apply under §6721 for failure to file the required report.

§8.8. Gifts of Depreciated Property

As a general rule, property with a basis in excess of its fair market value (depreciated property) should not be given to charity. The reason is simple: Property given to charity is valued at its fair market value for purposes of the charitable deduction. Reg. §1.170A-1(c). Also, no loss deduction is allowable under §165 where depreciated property is given to a charity. *Lavar Withers,* 69 T.C. 900 (1978).

Two rules prevent taking a loss deduction when depreciated property is given to charity. First, noncasualty losses of an individual are deductible only if they are incurred in a trade or business or in a transaction entered into for profit although not connected with a trade or business. §165(c)(1), (2). Charitable gifts are not made in either of those contexts. Second, a deduction is allowed only when a loss is "sustained," which requires that the loss be recognized for income tax purposes. Although a loss may be "realized" as a result of a gift to charity, no loss is "recognized." As *Withers* points out, a gift to charity constitutes a "sale or other disposition" that may cause a loss to be realized but does not constitute the "sale or exchange" necessary for a loss to be "recognized." *See also* §1001(a), (c); Reg. §1.1001-1(a).

§8.9. Gifts of Ordinary Income Property, §170(e)(1)(A)

A special rule applies to gifts of "ordinary income property" (*i.e.,* property that would not generate long-term capital gain if it were sold for its fair market value on the date of the transfer). Thus, it includes capital assets held for one year or less, property held for sale in the ordinary course of business, works of art and manuscripts created by the donor, depreciable tangible personal property or real property, §306 stock, and §341 stock of a collapsible corporation, and in some cases, partnership interests. *See* Reg. §1.170A-4(b)(1). When ordinary income property is given to a charity, the amount of the contribution is reduced to the extent the gain would not have been long-term capital gain had the property been sold by the donor at its fair market value on the date of the gift. *See* Rev. Rul. 80-33, 1980-1 C.B. 69 (contribution of §306 stock).

In effect, this rule puts the donor in the same position he or she would have been in had the property been sold for its fair market value and the proceeds contributed to charity.

> **Example 8-6.** *D* gave a charity ordinary income property that had a basis of $5,000 and a fair market value of $10,000. The contribution is reduced by $5,000, the amount of the gain that would not have been capital gain had *D* sold the property. Thus, *D* is treated as having made a gift of $5,000. The outcome would be the same if *D* had sold the property for $10,000 and given the proceeds to charity. In that case *D*'s income would have been $5,000 greater, but the amount of *D*'s contribution would be $10,000, unreduced under §170(e)(1)(A). Of course, in the latter case, *D* might not be entitled to deduct the full amount of the gift, depending upon the particular character of the donee and the size of the donor's contribution base.

Under §170(e) the deduction allowed to an artist who contributes to charity a work the artist created is limited to his or her basis in the work — the cost of materials. *Maniscalco v. Commissioner,* 632 F.2d (6th Cir. 1980).

In some cases, property that gives rise to ordinary income can be ideal for a charitable gift. For example, income in respect of a decedent is income that has accrued as of the date of death, but has not been paid. It is not includible in the decedent's final income tax return, but is taxable income to the estate or beneficiaries when received. It is also includible in the gross estate. Thus, when a charitable bequest is satisfied by a transfer of the right to receive income in respect of a decedent, both the estate tax and subsequent income tax will be avoided. Presumably the same rule applies where an installment sales obligation is distributed in satisfaction of a charitable gift.

§8.10. Gifts of Capital Gain Property: General, §§170(b)(1)(C), (D), 170(e)

Special rules also apply to a gift of property that would have produced long-term capital gain had it been sold for its fair market value on the date of the gift, including property used in a trade or business as defined in §1231(b). §170(b)(1)(C)(iv). In general, the charitable deduction for a gift of such "capital gain property" cannot exceed 30 percent of the donor's contribution base for public charities and 20 percent of the contribution base for nonpublic charities. Thus, a donor's gift of capital gain property to a public charity is generally subject to an overall 30 percent limit instead of the basic 50 percent limit.

Example 8-7. Last year, when *D* had a contribution base of $20,000, *D* made gifts of $10,000 in cash and $6,000 in capital gain property to public charities. *D*'s charitable deduction for the year is limited to $10,000 (50% × $20,000). *D* is entitled to carry over the $6,000 gift of capital gain property to the next year. If the entire $16,000 in contributions were 30% capital gain property, *D* could deduct $6,000 for last year and carry over the balance for the following 5 years. §170(d)(1) and Reg. §1.170A-10(c)(1)(ii).

A 50 percent limit applies if the donor elects to reduce the amount of the gift by the capital gain. *See* §8.11. Gifts of capital gain property to nonpublic charities remain subject to a 20 percent limit. In addition, the deduction for gifts of capital gain property to nonpublic charities is generally reduced to their adjusted bases by §170(e)(1). However, this limitation does not apply where publicly traded stock is contributed prior to 1995, and the contribution is not more than 10 percent of the total outstanding stock of the publicly traded corporation ("qualified appreciated stock"). §170(e)(5).

A contribution of 30 percent property is taken into account *after* gifts of other property, except that a contribution of 20 percent property is taken into account *after* gifts of 30 percent property. §§170(b)(1)(C)(i), 170(d)(1)(D)(i).

Alternative Minimum Tax. The alternative minimum tax (AMT) is designed to impart greater fairness to the tax system by requiring a tax payment from those individuals and entities (estates, trusts, and corporations) that otherwise might pay no federal income tax. The planner should be alert to the possibility that a substantial charitable gift of appreciated property could subject the donor to AMT.

Determination of AMT for an individual begins with the calculation of his or her alternative minimum taxable income (AMTI), which is taxable income adjusted as provided in §§56 and 58, and increased by the total of tax preference items described in §57. Under changes made by the 1986 Act the appreciation element in charitable gifts of appreciated capital gain property is a tax preference item. §57(a)(6). However, for this purpose property with respect to which an election has been made under §170(b)(1)(C)(iii) is not an item of tax preference. *See* §8.11. A tentative minimum tax is then computed (at 24 percent for individuals) based on the amount by which AMTI exceeds the applicable exemption. §55(b)(1). The exemption for a surviving spouse and persons filing joint returns is $40,000. §55(d)(1)(A). Note, however, that the amount of their exemption phases out at the rate of 25 percent of the amount by which AMTI exceeds $150,000. Thus, the exemption for that class phases out entirely when AMTI reaches $310,000 ($40,000 − (.25 × ($310,000 − $150,000)) = 0). The AMT is the amount by which the individual's tentative minimum tax exceeds the amount of regular tax for the taxable year.

Example 8-8. *H* and *W* had a taxable income of $150,000 in 1989 on which the regular income tax was $42,000. Taking into account the adjustments required by §§56 and 58 and tax preference items described in §57(a), including substantial charitable gifts of appreciated capital gain property, *H* and *W* had AMTI of $325,000 for 1989. The tentative minimum tax at the old rate of 21% was $68,230 ($325,000 × .21). (The $40,000 exemption available to individuals who file joint returns completely phased out at $310,000.) *H* and *W* were liable for AMT of $26,230 (AMT of $68,230 less regular tax of $42,000).

The application of the AMT may discourage individuals from giving highly appreciated property to charity. However, the reach of the AMT can be blunted by making gifts of undivided interests over a period of years. In such cases the charitable donee should take possession of the property or at least be entitled to possession of the property for a proportionate part of the year. *James L. Winokur,* 90 T.C. 733 (1988); LR 8333019. *See also* §8.16.

§8.11. Gifts of Capital Gain Property: Election to Reduce Amount of Gift, §§170(b)(1)(C)(iii), 170(e)

A donor may elect to have the 50 percent limit apply to all gifts of capital gain property made to public charities during the year. §170(b)(1)(C)(iii). However, if the election is made, the amount of the gifts must be reduced by the gain that would have been realized had the property been sold. §170(e)(1). The election can be used to increase the amount of the current deduction when the 30 percent ceiling would otherwise apply, but at the expense of losing the deduction for the appreciation on the property. In some cases the election may be used to increase the amount deductible in the current year and the amount deductible during the carryover period. That may occur where the gifts during the year far exceed the amount that could be deducted in that year and during the carryover period. The election does not apply to gifts of capital gain property to nonpublic charities.

Example 8-9. *D* expects to have an adjusted gross income of about $25,000 in this year and each of the following 5 years. Earlier this year *D* gave a parcel of real property that *D* had held for more than a year to a public charity. The property had a basis of $100,000 and a fair market value of $200,000. Without the election *D*'s deduction is limited to $7,500 per year (30% × $25,000) or a total of $45,000 over the 6-year period during which the deductions could be claimed. If *D* elects to reduce the amount of the gift by the gain component, *D*'s contribution deduction will be subject to the 50% limitation. By reducing the amount of the gift by $100,000, *D* could deduct $5,000 more each year. The deduction would be $12,500, which is 50% of *D*'s contribution base. Thus, by making the election, *D* could deduct a total of $75,000 instead of only $45,000.

It may also be useful to elect under §170(b)(1)(C)(iii) when a gift to a public charity exceeds 30 percent of the donor's contribution base, but the gain component is relatively small. Here again, if the donor reduces the amount of the gift by the gain, the limit on the amount of the deduction is increased from 30 percent to 50 percent.

Example 8-10. *D* had a contribution base of $50,000 in a year during which she made a gift of securities worth $25,000 to a public charity. The securities, which *D* had held for more than a year, had a basis of $24,500. Unless the election is made *D* could only deduct $15,000 for the year of the gift (30% × $50,000). The remaining $10,000 would be carried over to the next year. If *D* elects to reduce the amount of her gift by $500, she could deduct $24,500 this year, but would have no carryover to next year. The return earned on the tax saved by the additional $9,500 deduction this year will almost certainly more than offset the $500 reduction in the amount of the contribution.

If *D* does not want to make the election under §170(b)(1)(C)(iii) because of charitable deduction carryovers to the current year or some other reason, a similar result can be reached by selling the securities during the tax year and contributing the cash proceeds. In this case, *D* would realize a gain of $500 from the sale. However, she would be entitled to deduct the $25,000 cash contribution in full. Of course, the additional taxable income may affect her tax return in other ways, for example, by limiting her other itemized deductions. The additional income also raises her contribution base.

Finally, an election under §170(b)(1)(C)(iii) may be used to increase the amount of the deduction that can be taken on a decedent's final income tax return or by a terminally ill donor. The election may produce a saving because a decedent's excess contributions cannot be carried over to his or her successors. *See* §691(b). Of course, the unused portion of an excess contribution that is attributable to the surviving spouse may be carried over and used by the surviving spouse in a later year. *See* Reg. §1.170A-10(d)(4)(iii).

If the donor elects to have §170(b)(1)(C)(iii) apply to gifts of capital gain property, the amount of the gift is reduced for all purposes. Thus, the amount of the gift is reduced for the purpose of determining the amount of any carryover deductions. Also, when an election is made for a year subsequent to the gift (*i.e.*, a carryover year), the amount of the carryover must be recomputed. In some cases an election totally eliminates the carryover.

> **Example 8-11.** *D* gave a public charity stock he had owned for more than a year, which had a fair market value of $90,000 and a basis of $70,000. In the following year *D* gave the charity an additional $75,000 of stock he had also owned for more than a year and that had a basis of $65,000. In each year *D* had a contribution base of $200,000 and made no other charitable gifts. Ordinarily *D* would be entitled to deduct $60,000 each year (30% × $200,000). If *D* elects to subject the first gift to §170(e)(1), the charitable deduction for the first year would be increased to $70,000, but there would be no carryover. Specifically, under §170(e)(1) the $90,000 gift would be reduced by the $20,000 gain. If *D* instead makes the election only in the second year, the amount of the first year's gift would be recomputed under §170(e)(1) to determine whether there would be any carryover to the second year. In this case there would be a carryover of $10,000 since the basis of the gift ($70,000) exceeded the deduction claimed in the first year ($60,000). An election in both years would produce deductions of $70,000 and $65,000 respectively for Year 1 and 2, and no carryovers. Thus, *D* could choose between the various options on the basis of whether and the extent to which carryovers could be used in future years. If *D* chose to elect in Year 1, Year 2's results might be improved by a sale of the asset and contribution of the proceeds since the Year 1 carryover would be fully preserved.

Where a gift of capital gain property is planned or made, the lawyer should be alert to the consequences of making an election under §170(b)(1)(C)(iii). Once the election is made, it cannot be revoked after the original due date of the income tax return. *Jack J. Grynberg v. Commissioner,* 83 T.C. 255 (1984).

The foregoing examples illustrate the need to study the consequences of an election carefully before it is made. Ideally, the planning will precede the gift; however, the election is important to consider in all cases.

§8.12. Gifts of Capital Gain Property: Tangible Personal Property, §§170(e)(1)(B)(i), (ii)

The deduction for a gift of tangible personal property is not reduced when the donee's use of the property is *related* to its exempt functions. However, the amount of a gift of tangible personal property must be reduced by the gain component where the donee's use of the property is unrelated to the purpose for which its tax exemption was granted under §501(c). This rule applies independently of the overall 30 percent and 50 percent limitations on the amount of a donor's charitable deduction. The application of the rule is illustrated in the following passage: "For example, if a painting contributed to an educational institution is used by that organization for educational purposes by being placed in its library for display and study by art students, the use is not an unrelated use; but if the painting is sold and the proceeds used by the organization for educational purposes, the use of the property is an unrelated use." Reg. §1.170A-4(b)(3). *See also* LR 8143029. Applying this rule, the amount of the contribution was reduced where the donor gave an antique automobile to a college and could not show that the automobile would not be put to an unrelated use. LR 8009027.

A gift or estate tax deduction is available for the value of tangible personal property that is transferred outright to a charity. While gifts of less than the donor's entire interest generally do not qualify for a deduction (*see* Part C *infra*), a gift of a work of art to a charity whose use of the property is related to its exempt purpose is subject to a special rule added by the 1981 Act. *See* §§2055(e)(4), 2522(c)(3); Reg. §§20.2055-2(e)(1)(ii), 25.2522(c)-(3)(c)(1)(ii). Under it, the work of art and the copyright on the work of art are treated as separate properties. Thus, a charitable contribution deduction is allowable for the value of a work of art although the donor retains the copyright or transfers it to a noncharity (and vice versa). As noted in §8.16, a deduction is available for a charitable timeshare. The gift to a charitable donee of the possession and control of the property for a specified portion of each year qualifies as a gift of an undivided interest in property. Reg. §1.170A-7(b)(1)(i).

§8.13. Gifts of Future Interests in Tangible Personal Property, §170(a)(3), Reg. §1.170A-5

A present charitable deduction is usually not allowed for the transfer of a future interest in tangible personal property. Under §170(a)(3) a gift of a future interest in tangible personal property is treated as made only when all intervening interests in the property (1) have expired or (2) are held by persons other than the taxpayer or those standing in a relationship to the taxpayer described in §§267(b) or 707(b).

Example 8-12. Last year *D* transferred a painting to a museum by deed of gift, reserving a life (or term) interest in it. For purposes of §170 the gift was not complete at the time of the transfer. A gift of the painting will take place if *D* relinquishes all interest in the painting and transfers present possession of it to the museum. A charitable deduction would be available if *D* gave the museum the exclusive right to the possession and use of the painting for a specified period of each year. *See* §8.16.

As noted above, the deduction for a contribution of appreciated tangible personal property must be reduced where the donee's use of the property is unrelated to the purpose or function for which its exemption was granted under §501(c).

No gift or estate tax deduction is usually allowable for gifts of future interests in tangible personal property unless the interest is a remainder interest in a charitable remainder annuity trust or a charitable remainder unitrust. *See* Part D, *infra.* However, a marital deduction could be claimed with respect to the full value of tangible personal property in which the donor's spouse is given a qualifying income interest for life. *See* §2056(b)(7). Of course, in such a case the property would be includible in the donee spouse's estate under §2044. If the property passes to charitable remaindermen on the death of the donee spouse, his or her estate can claim a charitable deduction under §2055 for the value of the property passing to charities.

Example 8-13. *D* transferred a collection of antique dolls to a local museum by deed of gift, but retained the possession of them for life. The transfer does not qualify for an income tax deduction until *D*'s interest terminates. The transfer of a future interest in the dolls constituted a completed gift for gift tax purposes. Most important, no gift tax charitable deduction was allowable. §2522(c)(2). The value of the dolls is includible in *D*'s estate if *D* retains possession of them until his death. §2036. If so, *D*'s estate would be entitled to an equivalent deduction as an outright gift to the qualified charity. §2055(a). Double taxation is avoided by excluding from the estate tax base any taxable gifts that are included in a decedent's estate. §2001(b).

C. GIFTS OF PARTIAL INTERESTS

§8.14. General

The 1969 Act strictly limited the availability of income, gift, and estate tax deductions for gifts of partial interests to charities. In general, charitable gifts of less than the donor's entire interest in property do not qualify for a charitable deduction unless they are in the form of a charitable remainder trust, a pooled income fund, or a charitable lead trust. *See* Part D, *infra;* §§8.19-8.35. Two major exceptions to this rule allow deductions for gifts, not in trust, of (1) a remainder interest in a personal residence or a farm, or (2) an undivided portion of the donor's entire interest in property, including a qualified conservation contribution. *See* §§8.15-8.16. A deduction is also allowable for a gift of the donor's entire interest in property, even though it is a partial interest in the property. §8.17. However, no deduction is allowable for an interest that may be defeated by the occurrence of an act or event unless the possibility that the act or event will occur is so remote as to be negligible. §8.18.

§8.15. Remainder Interest in Personal Residence or Farm

A gift of a remainder interest in a personal residence or farm qualifies for the income, gift, and estate tax deductions. §§170(f)(3)(B)(i), 2055(e)(2), 2522(c)(2). The donor may retain a life estate or may transfer a life estate to another or others. Note that the IRS has restricted the deductions to *nontrust* gifts of remainder interests, although the availability of the deductions is not so limited by the statutes. Reg. §§1.170A-7(b), 20.2055-2(e)(2), 25.2522(c)-3(c)(2); *Ellis First National Bank of Bradenton v. United States,* 550 F.2d 9 (Ct. Cl. 1977); *Estate of Sara C. Cassidy,* 49 T.C.M. 580 (1985); Rev. Rul. 76-357, 1976-2 C.B. 285. The restriction is unwise because the interests of a remainderman are better protected when a trust is used. It also discourages the use of a trust to make a residence or farm available to an improvident or incompetent individual for life. The gift of a legal life interest to such a person might necessitate the appointment of a guardian, which is frequently cumbersome and expensive. So long as the IRS adheres to its present view charitable gifts of remainder interests in personal residences and farms should not be made in trust.

For purposes of the deductions, "personal residence" means any property used by the donor as a personal residence, even though it is not the donor's principal residence. Thus, a vacation home qualifies as a personal residence. The donor's stock in a cooperative housing corporation also qualifies as a personal residence if the donor used the unit as a personal residence. Reg. §§1.170A-7(b)(3), 20.2055-2(e)(2)(ii), 25.2522(c)-3(c)(2)(ii). Similarly, a condominium used by the donor as a personal residence qualifies under this exception. "Farm" is defined as "any land used by the taxpayer or his tenant for the production of crops, fruits, or other agricultural products or for the sustenance of livestock." Reg. §§1.170A-7(b)(4), 20.2055-2(e)(2)(iii), 25.2522(c)-3(c)(2)(iii). Buildings such as a house, barn, or other improvements located on a farm are included in the term.

Factors for the valuation of remainders in personal residences and farms are printed in IRS Pub. No. 1459, Actuarial Values, Gamma Volume (1989). The volume may be purchased from the Superintendent of Documents, U.S. Government Printing Office, Washington, D.C., 20402. The factors are also included in some charitable planning and federal tax software programs.

§8.15.1. Life Estate Transferred to Spouse or Others

The transfer of a presently possessory life estate to an individual donee qualifies for the annual gift tax exclusion. In contrast, a successive life estate is a future interest for which no annual exclusion is available. No gift tax would be imposed if a donor gave a life estate in a farm or residence to his or her spouse, remainder to a charity, provided the spouse was a U.S. citizen. A QTIP gift tax marital deduction is allowable with respect to the gift of a life estate to a citizen spouse. §2523(f). Note, however, that a successive life estate does not qualify for a QTIP marital deduction because the donee spouse's interest is not a qualified income interest (*i.e.,* the donee spouse is not entitled to all of the income (use of) the property for life). As suggested by Conrad Teitell, the donor may wish to retain a power to revoke the successive life estate in order for it to be an incomplete gift. Teitell, Charitable Gifts of Property — Tangible and Intangible, Real and Unreal, U. Miami, 20th Inst. Est. Plan., ¶918.3 (1986). If the donor exercises the power to revoke, the donor should be entitled to income and gift tax charitable deductions for the value of the life estate that was terminated in favor of the charitable remainderman.

§8.15.2. Charitable Gift of Remainder in Part of Farm or Residence

The exception for the gift of a remainder interest applies when the charity will receive the donor's entire interest in the personal residence or in a part of a farm upon termination of the preceding life or term interest. The exception applies even if state law requires the charity to dispose of the farm within ten years of acquisition. Rev. Rul. 84-9, 1984-2 C.B. 196. A gift of a remainder interest in a personal residence to a charitable organization (10 percent) and an individual (90 percent) as tenants in common qualifies for the charitable deduction. Rev. Rui. 87-37, 1987-1 C.B. 295, *revoking* Rev. Rul. 76-544, 1976-2 C.B. 285. As indicated in Revenue Ruling 87-37, "the value of the charitable interest must be reduced to reflect the appropriate valuation discount for the cotenancy arrangement." The amount of the discount would depend largely upon expert testimony, particularly as to comparable sales of partial interests. In an estate tax case involving the valuation of the decedent's one-half interest in real property, the Tax Court allowed a discount of 12.5 percent. *Estate of George W. Youle,* 56 T.C.M. 1594 (1989).

A gift of a remainder in a specified portion of the donor's farm acreage also qualifies for the deduction. Rev. Rul. 78-303, 1978-2 C.B. 122. That result follows because "farm" is defined in the Regulations as "any land" used for agricultural purposes. Accordingly, a gift of any portion that is so used meets the requirements of this exception.

§8.15.3. Sale Required upon Termination of Life Estate

The IRS has contended that no deduction is available when, under the terms of the gift, the personal residence or farm is to be sold upon the termination of the life estate. Rev. Rul. 77-169, 1977-1 C.B. 286. However, that position was rejected by the Tax Court in a case in which the state law gave the charitable remainderman the right to take the real property rather than the proceeds of sale. *Estate of Eliza W. Blackford,* 77 T.C. 1246 (1981), *acq. in result,* 1983-2 C.B. 1. *See also* Rev. Rul. 83-158, 1983-2 C.B. 159; LR 8141037.

§8.15.4. Depreciation and Depletion

For income tax purposes the value of a remainder interest in real property must take into account depreciation and depletion of the property. §170(f)(4). Under Reg. §1.170A-12(a)(1), depreciation is calculated on the straight-line method and depletion is determined by the cost recovery method. When a remainder consists of both depreciable and nondepreciable property, the depreciation or depletion is based only upon the fair market value of the depreciable or depletable interests. Thus, the fair market value of a residence must be allocated between the improvements, which are depreciable, and the land, which is not. The expected value of the property at the end of its life is also considered to be nondepreciable for this purpose. Reg. §1.170A-12(a)(2). The Regulations provide the formulas that are used to calculate the value of remainder interests following a single life, Reg. §1.170A-12(b), a term of years, Reg. §1.170A-12(c), and more than one life or a term of years concurrent with one or more lives, Reg. §1.170A-12(e). The method of valuation is illustrated by Example 8-14.

Example 8-14. *W*, a 60-year-old widow, gave the remainder interest in her residence to a public charity. At that time, the residence was worth $75,000, of which $25,000 was allocable to the land and $50,000 to the improvements. The improvements have a useful life of 45 years at the end of which they will be worth $5,000. For purposes of §170 the gift consists of $45,000 in depreciable property (the value of the house ($50,000) less the expected value of its improvements at the end of 45 years ($5,000)) and $30,000 in nondepreciable property (the value of the land ($25,000) plus the expected value of the improvements at the end of 45 years ($5,000)).

The value of the remainder interest in the nondepreciable property is discounted to present value by applying the appropriate factor to determine the value of a remainder interest following the life of a 60-year-old donor to the nondepreciable property.

The value of the remainder interest in the depreciable property is calculated in the same manner, but first the remainder factor must be reduced by a factor determined in the manner described in Reg. §1.170A-12(b)(2). The adjustment involves dividing (1) the difference between the R-factor for a donor aged 60 from column 2 of Table C of Reg. §1.170A-12 less the R-factor for the donor's terminal age (either 110 or the sum of the age of the life tenant and the estimated useful life of the depreciable property) by (2) the product of multiplying (a) the useful life of the property by (b) the D-factor for a donor aged 60 from column 3 of Table C. The R-factors for ages 60 and 105 are 718.0316 and .00543664 respectively and the D-factor is 261.1947.

$$\frac{718.0316 - .00543664}{45 \times 261.1947} = .06109$$

The value of the interest in the depreciable property is $8,730

($45,000 × (.25509 − .06109)). The total charitable deduction is $16,383 ($7,653 + $8,730).

§8.16. Undivided Portion of Donor's Entire Interest

An exception to the partial interest rule is also made for a gift of an undivided portion of the donor's entire interest in property. §§170(f)(3)(B)(ii), 2055(e)(2), 2522(c)(2). According to the IRS, a gift of an undivided interest made in trust does not fall within the exception although the statutes do not expressly impose that limitation. Reg. §§1.170A-7(b)(1), 20.2055-2(e)(2)(i), 25.2522(c)-3(c)(2)(i). The IRS position is illustrated by a ruling that denied an estate tax deduction where the decedent gave his residuary estate to a trust under which the income was payable in equal shares to his surviving spouse and a charity for the spouse's lifetime and, upon her death, the principal was distributable one-half to the charity and one-half to the decedent's heirs. Rev. Rul. 77-97, 1977-1 C.B. 285. The ruling noted that a deduction would have been allowed if the decedent had created two separate trusts: one for charitable purposes and one for private purposes. The IRS could just as easily have recognized that the charity's right to a specified share of the income and principal was a sufficiently distinct portion to justify treatment as a separate trust. *See* Reg. §20.2056(b)-5(c), which deals with the somewhat related problem of what constitutes a specific portion in the context of the marital deduction.

In order to qualify under this exception, the Regulations require that an undivided interest consist of a fraction or percentage of every substantial interest or right that the donor owns in the property, which must extend over the entire term of the donor's interest. Reg. §170A-7(b)(1)(i). Thus, when an individual has a remainder interest in a trust created by another person, a gift to charity of a fractional interest in the remainder would qualify as an undivided interest. Interestingly, the same Regulation treats a gift of the possession and control of property for a specified portion of each year as a gift of an undivided interest. Accordingly, a contribution of an undivided interest in an art collection to a museum is deductible when the collection remains in the donor's home if the museum has the right to possession and use during an appropriate portion of the year. *See* §8.10.1. *James L. Winokur,* 90 T.C. 733 (1988); LR 8333019.

Qualified Conservation Contribution. Charitable deductions are allowed for the value of certain partial interests in real property given to qualified charitable organizations. §§170(f)(3)(B)(iii) and (h), 2055(f), 2522(d). For income tax purposes, the contribution must be exclusively for conservation purposes as defined in §170(h)(4)(A), discussed below. §170(h)(1). But the 1986 Act relaxed the purpose requirement for estate and gift tax purposes. The rationale for the relaxation was stated in the Senate Finance Committee Report on the 1986 Act:

> The committee is concerned that applying the same conservation purpose standards for income, estate and gift tax deductions may cause undesirable results in some cases. If a conservation contribution is made and it later is established that the conservation purpose requirement for the contribution to be deductible is not satisfied, the donor loses his or her income tax deduction, and may also be subject to gift or estate tax. This is true notwithstanding the fact that a charitable organization owns the property interest and the donor may not have other property or funds with which to pay the gift or estate tax. S. Rep. No. 99-313, 99th Cong., 2d Sess. 284 (1986).

The amount of the gift of such an interest is equal to the amount by which it reduces the value of the property retained by the donor. *See* Rev. Rul. 76-376, 1976-2 C.B. 53; *Michael G. Hillborn,* 85 T.C. 677 (1985). It does not take into account any reduction in the value of the donor's contiguous property which results from the gift. *Leo A. Drey,* 535 F. Supp. 287 (E.D. Mo. 1982), *aff'd,* 705 F.2d 965 (8th Cir.), *cert. denied,* 464 U.S. 827 (1983). However, if the gift enhances the value of other property owned by the donor or related persons, the deduction is reduced by the increased value of the other property. Reg. §1.170A-14(h)(3)(i). Such a gift may generate a substantial income tax deduction and reduce the value of the donor's retained interests for real property tax purposes without interfering with the donor's use of the property. However, gifts for conservation purposes should be carefully planned in light of the provisions of §170(h). In addition, serious consideration should be given to the deleterious effect that perpetual restrictions could have on the property retained by the donor *and* on the broader community.

The partial interests for which a deduction may be claimed are defined in §170(h)(2) to include:

1. The entire interest of the donor other than his or her interest in subsurface oil, gas, or other minerals and the right of access to such minerals;
2. A remainder interest; and
3. A restriction (granted in perpetuity) on the use that may be made of the real property.

The last category covers easements and other interests in real property that have similar attributes under local law (*e.g.,* restrictive covenants).

In order to satisfy the requirements of §170(h), it is only necessary to meet one of four objectives listed under §170(h)(4)(A). They are limited to the following:

1. The preservation of land for outdoor recreation by the general public or for the education of the general public;
2. The protection of a relatively natural fish, wildlife, or plant habitat, or similar ecosystem;
3. The preservation of open space (including farmland and forest land) where the preservation is for the scenic enjoyment of the general public and will yield a significant public benefit or is pursuant to a clearly defined federal, state, or local government conservation policy and will yield a significant public benefit; and
4. The preservation of an historically important land area or a certified historic structure. *See also* Reg. §1.170A-14(d).

The qualified organizations to which contributions may be made are limited to governmental units and publicly supported charitable organizations. §170(h)(3), Reg. §1.170A-14(c).

§8.17. Donor's Entire Interest in Property

A deduction is allowed for a gift of the donor's entire interest in property, although it is only a partial interest. "Thus, if securities are given to *A* for life, with the remainder over to *B,* and *B* makes a charitable contribution of his remainder interest to an organization described in section 170(c), a deduction is allowed under section 170 for the present value of *B*'s remainder interest in the securities." Reg. §170A-7(a)(2)(i); Rev. Rul. 79-295, 1979-2 C.B. 349 (gift tax deduction allowable). But when a bequest of corporate stock is made to charity and the income during the period of administration of the estate is paid to a private donee, a split-interest gift is made and no deduction is allowable. Rev. Rul. 83-45, 1983-1 C.B. 7780. Similarly, a deduction is not allowed when the partial interest results from a division of the property that was made by the donor in order to avoid the restrictions imposed by §170(f)(3)(A). Rev. Rul. 79-295, 1979-2 C.B. 349. Thus, no deduction is allowed when the donor transfers a remainder interest in property to a private donee and immediately thereafter transfers the reserved life estate to a qualified charity. Id. A deduction is allowed, however, where the donor contributes all of the interests in a property to charities. Reg. §1.170A-7(a)(ii). For example, a deduction for the full value of the property is allowed where the donor gives an income interest in property to one charity and at the same time gives the remainder to another charity.

§8.18. Transfers Subject to a Condition or Power

A deduction is not allowed for a gift to a charity that may be defeated by the subsequent performance of some act or the happening of some event, unless the possibility of occurrence of the act or event is so remote as to be negligible. Reg. §§1.170A-1(e), 1.170A-7(a)(3). Thus, a deduction is allowable for a gift of land to a qualified charity for so long as it is used for park purposes only if the possibility that the land would be used for other purposes appears on the date of the gift to be so remote as to be negligible. Reg. §1.170A-1(e). However, because the test is essentially a factual one that may be questioned by the IRS, it is generally not desirable to give a defeasible fee interest to a charity. A gift of a defeasible fee is also undesirable because it may restrict the use of the property for generations, involve subsequent litigation, and require a substantial expenditure to trace the donor's successors. In this connection, see the discussion of *Brown v. Independent Baptist Church of Woburn,* 91 N.E.2d 922 (Mass. 1950) in W. Leach & J. Logan, Future Interests and Estate Planning 44 (1961).

A deduction is allowable for a contribution of land when mineral or timber rights are retained by the donor and exercise of the rights is unlikely or is subject to approval by the donee which is unlikely to be granted. Rev. Rul. 75-66, 1975-1 C.B. 85; Rev. Rul. 77-148, 1977-1 C.B. 63; *Nelda C. Stark,* 86 T.C. 243 (1986). But when the rights are exercisable solely by the donor, or when payments under an existing timber lease are retained by the donor, a deduction is not allowable. Rev. Rul. 76-331, 1976-2 C.B. 52. Also, no contribution deduction is allowable where voting shares are contributed if the donor retains the voting rights. Rev. Rul. 81-282, 1981-2 C.B. 78.

D. GIFTS IN TRUST

§8.19. General Limitations

For federal income, gift and estate tax purposes, charitable deductions are generally allowed for a post-1969 gift of a remainder interest in trust only if the trust is a charitable remainder annuity trust (CRAT), a charitable remainder unitrust (CRUT), or a pooled income fund. *See* §170(f)(2)(A). Note that the GSTT may apply to the noncharitable interests in any form of split interest trust. Of course, the GSTT is more likely to be a concern in the case of charitable lead trusts, which involve noncharitable remaindermen, than in the case of other types of split interest trusts.

Charitable remainder trusts and pooled income funds are discussed in §§8.20-8.30. Estate and gift tax charitable deductions are allowed for a gift of a current interest to a charitable organization only if the charitable interest is in the form of a guaranteed annuity or a unitrust interest. No income tax deduction is allowed to the donor for a gift of such an income interest unless the donor is treated as the owner of the trust under the grantor trust rules. *See* §170(f)(2)(B). Otherwise the transfer of property to a trust of which there is a charitable income beneficiary and private remaindermen does not qualify for any present charitable deduction. However, it is possible to structure the trust so that a transfer to it does not constitute a completed gift and that deductions will be available for income and gift tax purposes for the annual income distributions to charity. §8.33. Note that a transfer of a legal life estate to a spouse with remainder to a charity may qualify for the unlimited gift and estate tax marital deductions. §§2056(b)(7), 2523(f). On the death of the spouse the property is includible in his or her estate under §2044 and an offsetting charitable deduction is allowable under §2055. *See* §5.23.7.

The IRS has ruled that, where a possibility exists that federal estate or state death taxes may be paid out of the assets of a charitable remainder trust, no deduction is allowable. Rev. Rul. 82-128, 1982-2 C.B. 771. This ruling requires that trust instruments be drafted to preclude liability of the trust for death taxes in order to protect the charitable deduction. The ruling could be extended to apply to pooled income funds, charitable lead trusts, and charitable remainders in personal residences and farms. However, it may not apply to a charitable remainder trust where the only noncharitable beneficiary is the grantor's surviving spouse. §§2056(b)(8), 2523(g). Such a charitable remainder trust, if it is otherwise qualified, will be considered qualified for purposes of the marital deduction. Thus no federal estate or gift tax would be apportioned to the income interest in the trust. State taxes could still cause disqualification under the ruling.

A charitable remainder trust must function as such from the time of its creation. Reg. §1.664-1(a)(4). Under that Regulation, "the trust will be deemed to be created at the earliest time that neither the grantor nor any other person is treated as the owner of the entire trust under [§§671-678.]" In LR 9015049 the IRS held that if mortgaged property is transferred to a trust that will be responsible for making payments on the mortgage, the grantor will be treated as owner of the trust under §677. Applying the rule of Reg. §1.664-1(a)(4), the trust would not be a charitable remainder trust. Accordingly, no deduction would be allowed for the transfer to the trust. Also, the transfer of mortgaged property to a charitable remainder trust would be prohibited by the self-dealing rules unless the mortgage was placed on the property more than ten years prior to the transfer to the trust. §4941(d)(2)(A).

Software programs are available that calculate the value of the private and charitable interests in charitable remainder and charitable lead trusts. Extensive calculations can be made by using programs such as Planned Giving Manager, a relatively expensive program that is available from PG Calc, Inc., 129 Mount Auburn Street, Cambridge, Massachusetts. For those who do not have access to a suitable program, most values can be calculated by using the formulas and factors included in Actuarial Values, Alpha Volume, IRS Pub. No. 1457 and Actuarial Values, Beta Volume, IRS Pub. No. 1458.

§8.20. Charitable Remainder Trusts in General, §664(d)

A trust qualifies as a charitable remainder trust only if it satisfies the requirements of a charitable remainder annuity trust, §664(d)(1), or a charitable remainder unitrust, §664(d)(2). Those provisions are designed to assure that the charitable remaindermen will receive the full benefit of the remainder interest. The requirements, which are elaborated in the Regulations, severely restrict the nature and extent of the permissible noncharitable interests. Under prior law, the IRS disqualified trusts on picayune grounds. For example, it disallowed deductions for trusts that included "in terrorem" clauses (*i.e.,* one that would terminate the interest of any beneficiary who contested the validity of the will), LR 7942073, and ones that included a provision under which payments to an individual would terminate on remarriage, Rev. Rul. 76-291, 1976-2 C.B. 284. However, such provisions are allowable under §664(f), which was added by the 1984 Act and is effective for transfers after 1978. Under that provision the deductibility of the charitable interest in a trust is not jeopardized by the inclusion of a "qualified contingency." A qualified contingency is a provision under which the happening of a contingency would cause the noncharitable interest to expire no later than it would otherwise expire. §664(f)(3). The inclusion of a qualified contingency does not increase the amount of the charitable deduction — the valuation of the charitable contribution is made without regard to the qualified contingency. §664(f)(2).

§8.20.1. Double Deductions

A client who is charitably inclined may be influenced to make an inter vivos gift to a charitable remainder trust because it produces multiple charitable deductions — for income *and* gift and estate tax purposes. In contrast, a testamentary gift to a qualified charity supports only an estate tax charitable deduction. While the income tax deduction that is allowed for the value of the remainder interest may be relatively small, it is an important consideration for some taxpayers. An inter vivos gift may be more satisfying to the donor, who may receive some recognition for having made the gift. The gift may also stimulate gifts from others. In addition, as indicated in §8.20.2, a charitable remainder trust may appeal to some taxpayers because the trustee can sell appreciated assets and diversity investments without incurring any capital gains tax.

Note also that a testamentary gift to the surviving spouse may produce more tax benefits than a gift to charity. The marital deduction insulates the property given to a spouse from the estate tax. A gift to charity by the surviving spouse qualifies for both income and gift tax returns.

§8.20.2. Diversification of Investments

Charitable remainder trusts are exempt from the federal income tax, which allows them to sell appreciated property without incurring any tax liability. Accordingly, charitable remainder trusts are frequently used as an investment vehicle to increase the grantor's current cash flow: The taxpayer gets a current income tax deduction *and* the trustee sells appreciated assets and invests the proceeds in higher yielding forms of investment. Thus, a taxpayer who holds highly appreciated assets that generate a low rate of return may transfer them to a charitable remainder trust. Indeed, the tax-free status of charitable remainder trusts leads some taxpayers to transfer property to trusts that are designed to maximize the benefits to the taxpayer and minimize the benefits for charity. Under this approach the trustee, who might be the grantor, sells the appreciated assets and invests the entire proceeds in assets that provide the liquidity and security to support the required distributions to the grantor.

§8.20.3. Wealth Replacement Plans

A grantor may use part of the increased cash flow from a charitable remainder trust to "replace" the value of the principal that will pass to charity on the death of the grantor instead of being distributed to individual beneficiaries. The grantor may, for example, contribute part of the cash flow to an irrevocable trust to be invested in growth assets or used to make premium payments on life insurance on the grantor's life. Under a simple alternative the grantor makes annual gifts of a portion of his or her current income to his or her children. The children in turn use the funds to buy policies in insurance on the donor's life. In either case, the plan is designed to allow the insurance proceeds or other property to pass to the beneficiaries tax free (*i.e.,* the proceeds or other property is not included in the grantor's estate).

§8.20.4. Substitute for Tax-Exempt Retirement Plan

A charitable remainder trust can be used as a substitute for, or a supplement to, a retirement plan. In the simplest case a client transfers highly appreciated property to a charitable remainder trust, reserving substantial payments for life, or for the lives of the client and his or her spouse. Clements, Maximizing Capital Asset Returns Through Charitable Remainder Trusts, 3 J. Tax. Est. & Tr. 18 (1991). The plan may be economically attractive because of three factors: the gain on the trust's sale of the appreciated property is not taxed; the value of the charitable remainder will generate some income tax savings; and the donor's interest in the trust is not subject to the tax on excess distributions or accumulations. *See* §4980A; §12.26.3. Note, however, the excess of the charitable deduction for the contribution of the appreciated property over its basis is an item of tax preference.

Under another approach a client makes gifts to a charitable remainder unitrust over time, the income of which will accumulate free of tax. A unitrust is used because additional contributions cannot be made to a charitable remainder annuity trust. The unitrust would be an "income-only" unitrust (*i.e.,* one that provides for the annual distribution of the lesser of the actual income or a specified percentage of the value of the assets. Reg. §1.664-3(a)(1)(b)). If current income is less than the specified percentage, the trust would require the deficiency to be made up during periods when the current income exceeds the specified unitrust percentage. The growth in value of such a trust is sheltered from taxation until distributions are made to the grantor or other noncharitable beneficiary. Thus, a donor might contribute highly appreciated property to an income-only unitrust designed to have a relatively high payout where income was available for distribution. The transfer to the trust would support a small charitable deduction. After the property was transferred to the trustee, it would be sold and reinvested in assets that produce little if any income until after the donor retires and has a greater need for income. In the interim, the value of the trust assets would continue to increase, reflecting an investment strategy that was designed to defer the receipt of income and maximize growth. Greater income would be realized after the donor's retirement, as the trustee receives the delayed income on zero coupon bonds and other carefully selected investment. At that point, the trustee would change the investments of the trust in order to generate more current income to support current and make-up distributions to the grantor.

§8.20.5. Marital Deductions

The gift and estate tax marital deductions are generally available where the grantor's spouse is the only noncharitable beneficiary of a charitable remainder trust. §§2056(b)(8), 2523(g). The marital deduction is not available if the grantor's spouse is not a current beneficiary or is not a U.S. citizen. §2523(i). In either case the grantor can avoid the imposition of a gift tax by reserving the right by will to terminate the noncharitable interest of his or her spouse. *See* §8.21. If the trust is properly planned, an estate tax marital deduction will be available to the grantor's estate if he dies survived by his spouse and without having revoked her successive noncharitable interest. Of course, if the surviving spouse is not a U.S. citizen, the trust must meet the requirements of a qualified domestic trust under §2056A. *See* §5.25. The estate tax imposed by §2056A does not apply to distributions of income, such as distributions from an income-only unitrust.

§8.21. Charitable Remainder Annuity Trust (CRAT)

Charitable remainder trusts must make specified annual distributions to one or more beneficiaries, of whom at least one is a noncharity. However, the grantor may retain a power exercisable only by will to revoke or terminate the interest of any noncharitable beneficiary. The retention of such a power can be used to prevent the transfer of property to a CRAT from involving a gift to the holder of a successor noncharitable interest. Although a charity must have an irrevocable remainder interest in the trust, the grantor may reserve the right to change the charitable remainder beneficiary. The amount of the annual distributions is strictly limited by the Code and the Regulations. A CRAT must provide for an annual payout of a fixed sum that must be at least five percent of the initial net fair market value of the trust property. The amount may be expressed either as a specified dollar amount or as a percentage or fraction of the initial fair market value of the trust assets. In the latter case the trust must provide for appropriate adjustments to be made if the initial value of the trust is incorrectly determined. Reg. §1.664-2(a)(1)(iii). Because the amount of the payments is fixed at the outset, the payout may not vary from year to year and *no* additional property may be transferred to the trust.

In the case of a CRAT, the specified amount must be paid, not less often than annually, to one or more beneficiaries at least one of whom is not a charitable organization. Only an individual or a charitable organization may receive distributions for the life of an individual (*i.e.,* payments may not be made to noncharitable organizations). In any case the period of the payments cannot extend beyond either the life or lives of named individuals who are living at the time of creation of the trust or a term of years not to exceed 20 years. §664(d)(1)(A); Reg. §1.664-2(a)(5)(i). Specifically, the period for which the amount must be paid "begins with the first year of the charitable remainder trust and continues either for the life or lives of a named individual or individuals or for a term of years not to exceed 20 years." Reg. §1.664-2(a)(5). No amounts other than the required distribution may be paid to or for the use of any person other than the charitable remainderman. Thus, a trust may not allow invasions of principal to meet emergency needs of the individual beneficiaries. This limitation deters many prospective donors from establishing a CRAT.

Regulation §1.664-2(a)(5)(ii) indicates that the following are appropriate periods for payments to be made under a CRAT:

1. To *A* and *B* for their joint lives and then to the survivor for life;
2. To *A* for life or for a term of years not longer than 20 years, whichever is longer (or shorter);
3. To *A* for a term of years not longer than 20 years and then to *B* for life (provided *B* was living at the time the trust was created);
4. An amount to *A* for life and concurrently an amount to *B* for life (with amount distributable to each to terminate at death), provided that the amount paid to each is at least five percent of the initial fair market value of the property of the trust; or
5. An amount to *A* for life and concurrently an amount to *B* for life, and at the death of the first to die, the trust to distribute one-half of the then value of its assets to a charitable organization, if the total of the amounts given to *A* and *B* is not less than five percent of the initial fair market value of the property of the trust.

As noted later in this section, no charitable deduction is allowed if the distributions to the noncharitable beneficiary are so large that there is a greater than five percent probability that they will entirely exhaust the assets of the trust, leaving nothing for the charitable remainderman. *See* Rev. Rul. 77-374, 1977-2 C.B. 329.

Example 8-15. *D* transferred securities worth $200,000 to a trust from which *D* is entitled to an annual payment of $10,000 for life. The trust provides for the minimum 5% annual annuity payment required by §664(d)(1). The trust could have called for a larger annual payment, but not a smaller one.

The charitable interest in a CRAT is valued according to the actuarial tables printed in Actuarial Values, Alpha Volume, IRS Pub. No. 1457 (1989). Publication 1457 is available from the Superintendent of Documents at the address shown in §8.15.

§8.22. CHARITABLE REMAINDER UNITRUST (CRUT)

In general a charitable remainder unitrust (CRUT) must satisfy requirements similar to the ones that apply to a CRAT, except it must provide for a different type of payout. In particular, it must require a payout each year to the noncharitable beneficiaries of a fixed percentage of at least five percent of the annually determined net fair market value of its assets. Thus, the amount of the annual payment made from a unitrust will vary from year to year according to the value of the trust corpus. Unlike a CRAT, property may be added to a CRUT if the trust instrument contains provisions that require appropriate adjustments in the amount of the payout. *See* Reg. §1.664-3(b).

An exception made by §664(d)(3) recognizes a type of unitrust that provides for distributions based upon the net income of the trust. To qualify under this exception, the unitrust may be either: (1) an "income-only" unitrust, which provides for payment to the noncharitable beneficiary of only the net income of the trust in the years that it does not exceed a specified unitrust percentage of at least five percent, or, (2) an "income-with-make-up" unitrust, which provides for payment to the noncharitable beneficiary of only the income in years it does not exceed a specified percentage and such amount *plus* a make-up payment out of the net income for the current year above the unitrust percentage, to the extent that the payments for prior years were less than the specified unitrust amount for those years.

> **Example 8-16.** An income-with-make-up unitrust provided for distribution of the net income of the trust to the extent it did not exceed 5% of the value of the trust and so much of the net income for the current year in excess of 5% as may be required to make up for the deficiencies in distributions for prior years. The net income of the trust for the first year was $4,000 and the unitrust amount was $5,000. Accordingly, the trustee was required to distribute $4,000. The income of the trust for the second year was $6,000 and, the principal having the same value, the unitrust amount was $5,000. For the second year the trustee was required to distribute the full $6,000 in order to make up for the $1,000 deficiency in the first year.
>
> Setting the percentage at an amount below the anticipated income of the unitrust may result in greater overall distributions to the private beneficiaries. For example, assuming a 10% rate of return, the distributions from a 10% unitrust would remain the same. In contrast, because of the effect of compounding, distributions from an 8% unitrust would exceed the distributions from the 10% unitrust beginning in the 13th year. Over an extended period the total distributions from the 8% unitrust would be much

larger than distributions from the 10% unitrust. The differences would naturally be even greater in the case of unitrusts with even lower distribution rates. Note, too, that the charitable remainder will be worth more if the unitrust payment is lower than the annual rate of return.

An income-based unitrust may be appropriate where the current beneficiary will not need a stable flow of funds for support and the property contributed to the trust may generate little or no income in some years, particularly the early ones. It has been used by some planners, for example, in connection with gifts of appreciated real property that generate little, if any, current income. As indicated above, it may also be appropriate to delay distributions of income where the unitrust is part of the donor's retirement plan. The trustee could select growth-oriented investments during the donor's working years, and higher yielding investments after retirement. This would allow for larger make-up payments during the early retirement years.

Actuarial tables for valuing CRUTs are printed in Actuarial Values, Beta Volume, IRS Pub. No. 1458 (1989) at the address shown in §8.15. This volume may also be purchased from the Superintendent of Documents.

§8.23. Sample Declarations of Trust

The IRS has published sample declaration of trust forms for charitable remainder unitrusts and charitable remainder annuity trusts which meet the applicable requirements of federal law. Rev. Proc. 89-20, 1989-1 C.B. 841 (single life unitrust); Rev. Proc. 89-21, 1989-1 C.B. 842 (single life annuity trust). In 1990, sample forms were published based on two lives, Rev. Proc. 90-30, 1990-1 C.B. 534 (unitrust forms); Rev. Proc. 90-31, 1990-1 C.B. 539 (unitrust forms); Rev. Proc. 90-32, 1990-1 C.B. 546 (annuity trust forms). As noted below, the IRS has also published model forms of pooled income agreements. Rev. Proc. 88-53, 1988-2 C.B. 712. According to the Revenue Procedures the IRS will recognize a trust which "makes reference to this document and is substantially similar to the sample . . . provided the trust operates in a manner consistent with the trust instrument and provided it is a valid trust under applicable local law." A trust that omits any of the provisions or includes additional substantive provisions is not assured of qualification under the Revenue Procedures. Because of the complexity of the requirements and the potential that the IRS will take hypertechnical positions as it has in the past, charitable remainder trusts that deviate from the sample forms should be drafted very carefully — preferably with the participation of an expert.

The sample forms should not be taken as complete and sufficient in all respects. For example, the use of the specimen forms will involve a gift to the holder of a successive noncharitable interest. The completion of a gift can be avoided, however, by making the successive interest subject to termination by provision in the grantor's will.

Sample trust provisions were earlier published in Rev. Rul. 72-395, 1972-2 C.B. 340. However, the IRS interpretation of the requirements changed from time to time as indicated by a 1980 revenue ruling that made mandatory two of the previously optional provisions that appeared in Revenue Ruling 72-395. Rev. Rul. 80-123, 1980-1 C.B. 205.

In order to qualify for an estate tax charitable deduction, Revenue Ruling 80-123 requires a charitable remainder trust to provide that the obligation to pay the noncharitable beneficiary begins on the date of the decedent's death. Accordingly, there must be a make-up distribution to the beneficiary of an amount appropriate for the length of the period between the death of the trustor and the funding of the trust. Reg. §1.664-1(a)(5)(iv). Recognizing that the proper amount of the payments will not be finally established until a much later time in most cases, the governing instrument must also require corrective payments to be made by or to the trust in the case of an overpayment or underpayment to the beneficiary.

The requirements of Revenue Ruling 72-395 and Revenue Ruling 80-123 were further modified by Rev. Rul. 82-165, 1982-2 C.B. 117, and Rev. Rul. 88-81, 1988-1 C.B. 127. The latter ruling published new sample provisions dealing with the corrective payments that must be made in case of an incorrect valuation of an additional contribution made by will. Specifically, a corrective payment must be made by or to the trust within a reasonable time after the end of the year in which the trust is completely funded. Rather than specifying a particular rate of interest which must be paid, the sample forms in Revenue Ruling 88-81 refer to "the rate of interest that the federal income tax regulations under section 664 of the Internal Revenue Code prescribe for the trust for such computation for such period." The new corrective payment provision is not included in the model forms of charitable remainder trust referred to above, although it probably should be.

As Conrad Teitell has suggested, every charitable trust should include a provision authorizing the trustee to amend the trust for the purpose of complying with the relevant provisions of the Code and Regulations. Teitell, Philanthropy & Estate Planning Column, 128 Tr. & Est. 56 (1989). In particular, he recommends the use of the following type of form:

> The trustee shall have the power, acting alone to amend the trust for the sole purpose of complying with the requirements of the code [insert

section] and regulations [insert section] governing [insert type of split interest trust]. Id. at 57.

§8.24. Income Taxation of Charitable Remainder Trusts

The income taxation of charitable remainder trusts and their beneficiaries is governed by §664. To begin with, the trusts themselves are ordinarily exempt from taxation. §664(c). Amounts distributed to the beneficiaries are characterized as ordinary income to the extent of the trust's ordinary income for the current year plus any undistributed ordinary income for prior years. §664(b)(1). Next, the distributions are considered to be composed of capital gain to the extent the trust has capital gain for the year and undistributed gain for prior years. §664(b)(2). Finally, distributions are constituted of other income (*e.g.,* tax-exempt income) to the extent the trust has any for the current year and undistributed other income for prior years. §664(b)(3). Any remaining amount of a current distribution is considered to be composed of principal. §664(b)(4). Note that a trust with acquisition indebtedness, which may arise if mortgaged property is transferred to a charitable remainder trust, loses its tax exemption. §514(c)(2)(A).

Because charitable remainder trusts are generally exempt from the federal income tax, appreciated property that is transferred to a charitable remainder trust may be sold within two years of the transfer without generating any income tax liability. Section 644 taxes the sale of appreciated property that takes place within two years of transfer as if it had been sold by the grantor. Section 644 is a concern for charitable lead trusts, which are not exempt.

If there is depreciable property in the trust, depreciation deductions are allowed. The deductions are normally apportioned between the trustee and the beneficiaries on the basis of the trust income allocable to each. However, if the trust instrument provides otherwise, they may be allocated in another manner. LR 8610067; LR 8535048.

The transfer of property to a charitable remainder trust does not usually involve the realization of any gain or loss. Accordingly, a donor may increase the current yield generated by assets or achieve a degree of tax-free diversification by transferring appreciated assets to a charitable remainder trust that sells them and invests the proceeds in other assets.

Trust distributions to the noncharitable beneficiaries must be limited to the specified annuity or unitrust amounts. §§664(d)(1)(B), (2)(B). Thus, a trust will not qualify as a charitable remainder trust if it permits any other use or application of trust assets for the benefit of noncharities. The inability to distribute additional amounts in case of accident, illness, or other emergency is a major drawback that deters some individuals from establishing charitable remainder trusts.

Under Reg. §1.664-1(a)(3), a charitable remainder trust cannot "include a provision which restricts the trustee from investing the trust assets in a manner which would result in the annual realization of a reasonable amount of income or gain from the sale or disposition of trust assets." Accordingly, a trust generally should not direct the trustee to retain any particular asset or assets or impose any limits on the trustee's power to sell or dispose of trust assets.

Charitable remainder trusts may invest in tax-exempt securities, but pooled income funds may not. *See* §8.30. However, if there were an understanding or agreement that the trustee would sell the property transferred to a charitable remainder trust and invest in tax-exempt securities, the donor might be taxed on the gain. *See* Rev. Rul. 60-370, 1960-2 C.B. 203, dealing with the so-called Pomona College Plan.

§8.25 Valuing Charitable Remainders

For purposes of the income, gift, and estate tax charitable deductions, beginning May 1, 1989 the fair market value of a remainder interest in a CRAT following one life, two lives, or a term of years is determined under the unisex actuarial tables printed in Actuarial Values, Alpha Volume, IRS Pub. No. 1457. The valuation is based upon 120 percent of the Federal Midterm rate that was in effect during the month the gift was made or either of the preceding two months. *See* §7520. Between December 1, 1983 and May 1, 1989 the determinations were made according to the unisex 10 percent tables of Reg. §20.2031-7. Earlier transfers were valued according to gender-based actuarial tables based on a six percent return. Reg. §20.2031-10. These tables were held not unconstitutional. *Manufacturers Hanover Trust Co. v. United States,* 775 F.2d 459 (2d Cir. 1985).

Example 8-17. *D,* aged 50, contributed $200,000 in August 1990 to a CRAT which requires that an annual payment of $10,000 be made to *D.* (If the payments were made more frequently the payout rate would be adjusted by a factor from Table K of Alpha Volume.) Under §7520(a) *D* could choose to value the gift according to the interest rate for the month during which the gift was made or for either of the 2 preceding months. *D* chose to value the gift based upon an 11% rate which was in effect for June 1990. The factor for the value of an annuity for a person aged 50 is 8.0395 under Table S of the Alpha Volume. Thus, the charitable gift is $119,605 ($200,000 − ($10,000 × 8.0395)).

The value of the remainder interest in a CRUT after one life, two lives, or a term of years is calculated according to the actuarial tables printed in the Beta Volume, IRS Pub. No. 1458. The IRS will, upon request, furnish a factor for the value of remainder interests in a CRUT that cannot be calculated from the tables.

Example 8-18. On January 1 *D,* aged 60, transferred securities worth $500,000 to a charitable remainder unitrust. The trust called for the payment to *D* on December 31 of each year for *D*'s life of an amount equal to 5% of the fair market value of the trust as determined at the beginning of each tax year of the trust. The adjusted payout rate for the trust is determined by multiplying the 5% basic payout rate by the factor specified in Table F(5.0) of Beta Volume when the first valuation date precedes the first payout date by 12 months (.952381). In this case the adjusted payout rate is 4.7619%, the product of 5% × .9523811. The factor to be used to value the remainder for a trust having this adjusted payout rate is interpolated from the factors published in Table U(1) of Beta Volume for a donor aged 60.

Factor for donor aged 60, 4.6% payout	.43372
Factor for donor aged 60, 4.8% payout	.41992
Difference	.0138

$$\frac{4.7619 - 4.6\%}{4.6\% - 4.4\%} = \frac{X}{.0138}$$

$$X = .01117$$

Factor for donor aged 60, 4.6% payout	.43372
Less value of *X*	.01117
Interpolated factor	.42255
Present value of remainder in $500,000:	

$$\$500{,}000 \times .42255 = \$211{,}275$$

When the grantor of a charitable remainder annuity trust contributes the retained interest to a charitable beneficiary, the contribution qualifies for income and gift tax deductions. Rev. Rul. 86-60, 1986-1 C.B. 302.

No charitable deduction is allowed where the probability exceeds five percent that the noncharitable beneficiary of a CRAT will survive the exhaustion of a fund in which a charity has the remainder interest. Rev. Rul. 77-374, 1977-2 C.B. 329. The determination of whether the fund of an annuity trust will be exhausted prior to the life beneficiary's death is based upon the use of the appropriate actuarial tables. In Revenue Ruling 77-374, using the old gender-based tables and a six percent rate of return (applicable to decedents dying after November 30, 1983) the computations indicated that the annual payments of $40,000 per year for life from a fund of $400,000 to a 61-year-old female would completely exhaust the fund in less than 16 years was greater than 63 percent, therefore no charitable contribution was allowed. Applying an assumed ten percent rate of return would change this result since the fund would never be exhausted: the annual income and payout would be equal.

If, however, the annual payout were $48,000, using a ten percent rate, the fund would be exhausted in the nineteenth year. Under the current mortality table, 80CNSMT, Alpha Vol., Pub. No. 1457, Table 6-1, the probability that a 61-year-old would survive 19 years is 52 percent, the result of dividing the number of persons surviving to age 80 (43,180) by the number surviving to age 61 (82,581). Therefore, no deduction would be allowed since the probability of exhausting the fund is greater than five percent.

The Tax Court rejected the IRS's mechanical application of these tests in *Estate of George H. Moore,* 43 T.C.M. 1530 (1982). In it the Tax Court concluded that the chance the charitable remainder in two trusts would be exhausted was negligible where the probable return on assets was in excess of the assumed rate used in the Regulations, and using the rates in the Regulations, the chances of exhaustion were 7.63 percent and 7.09 percent, respectively.

§8.26. Private Foundation Rules

Charitable remainder trusts are "split-interest" trusts, the governing instruments of which must comply with the requirements of §508(e). §4947(a)(2). Accordingly, the instruments must prohibit the trustee from self-dealing, §4941(d), and making taxable expenditures, §4945(d). In addition, the instruments must ban any jeopardy investments, §4944, and excess business holdings, §4943, during any period that any annuity or unitrust amount is payable to a charity. *See* §§508(e), 4947(b)(3)(B); Reg. §53.4947-2(b)(1). Most states have adopted legislation under which charitable trusts are deemed to include the required provisions. However, it is prudent to include the prohibitions in the trust instruments themselves, if only to alert the trustees to their existence.

§8.27. Requests for Rulings

Having issued sample forms, the IRS has announced that it will not ordinarily issue rulings with respect to whether an inter vivos remainder trust for one or two measuring lives meets the requirements of §§664,

2055, or 2522. Sec. 4.01, Rev. Proc. 91-3, 1991-1 C.B. —. However, a planner should consider applying for a ruling if the provisions of a charitable remainder trust will be unusual or vary substantially from the standard forms. Requests should be prepared in accordance with the version of the procedural rules that are issued in the first Internal Revenue Bulletin each year. *E.g.,* Rev. Proc. 91-1, 1991-1 C.B. —. The rulings must include a completed checklist of the type published in Rev. Proc. 91-14, 1991-1 C.B. —. Requests may be hand delivered to Room 6561, 1111 Constitution Avenue, N.W., Washington, D.C. between 8:30A.M. and 4:00P.M. on working days or mailed to:

Internal Revenue Service
Associate Chief Counsel (Technical)
Attention CC:CORP:T
P.O. Box 7604
Ben Franklin Station
Washington, D.C. 20044

A request for a ruling must contain the data required by Revenue Procedure 91-1, including the checklist, Appendix A.

§8.28. Advantages of Charitable Remainder Trusts

A lifetime gift to a charitable remainder trust or pooled income fund is attractive mainly because it supports current income and gift tax charitable deductions though the charity will not have the beneficial use of the property until the expiration of the private interests. In the meantime the donor, or other noncharitable beneficiaries, may receive payments from the trust. As pointed out above, because charitable remainder trusts are not subject to taxation, §664(c), the trustee may sell the property that is transferred to it without incurring any income tax on the gain. Thus, the transfer of property to a trust may facilitate its sale and, in effect, the receipt of a higher net yield by the donor.

Example 8-19. *D,* age 55, is a successful executive with an adjusted gross income of $200,000. Some years ago, he invested $100,000 in a startup electronics company, and the stock which is now publicly traded is worth $480,000 although it pays no dividends. D expects to retire in 3 years, and would like to convert his investment to a more stable, income-producing asset (*e.g.,* U.S. Treasury bonds yielding 9%). *D* would also like to make a substantial contribution to the state university.

If *D* sells the electronics stock for $480,000, the capital gain will result in a tax of $106,400 (assuming the applicable tax rate is 28%), leaving $338,400 to invest. At 9% interest the fund will provide annual income to *D* of $30,456.

D may, instead, contribute the electronics stock to a CRAT and draw a 9% annuity ($43,200, which is an increase of $12,744 per year over the alternative above). In addition, D will be entitled to a charitable deduction, which would result in a significant income tax savings. The amount of the charitable deduction would be calculated according to the following formula, using the currently applicable life expectancy for a person aged 55: ($480,000 (the value of property transferred) − ($43,200 (the amount of the annuity) × the annuity factor from Table S of Alpha Volume).

The trustee may sell the electronics stock and reinvest the proceeds without subjecting the gain to taxation.

Additionally, a charitable remainder trust is useful when the donor wishes to provide support for another person who is in a lower income tax bracket. Because the income (annuity or unitrust payment) is taxable to the beneficiary and not the donor, the overall income tax burden may be reduced. In addition, the donor benefits from a current income tax deduction for the charitable contribution, subject to the applicable percentage limits of §170.

§8.29. Comparison of CRATs and CRUTs

CRATs and CRUTs are similiar in many respects; however, there are some important distinctions. Often a client's choice between them is based upon the client's judgment regarding the desirability of a trust that has a fixed payout or one that depends upon the annual value of the trust assets. The payout of a CRAT is stable — it neither increases if the value of the trust assets increases in an inflationary period nor decreases if the value of the assets falls during an economic downturn. A CRUT is generally considered to protect the beneficiary better against the ravages of inflation if the assets of the trust increase in value, which is not always the case.

The grantor may serve as trustee of a CRAT or CRUT provided that the trustee has no discretion regarding distributions to the noncharitable beneficiaries. However, the use of an independent trustee is almost always preferable. A CRAT or CRUT may give the grantor or another person the power to designate the charitable remaindermen or to substitute one qualified charitable organization for another. Rev. Rul. 76-8, 1976-1 C.B. 179 (power reserved by grantor); Rev. Rul. 76-7, 1976-1 C.B. 179 (power given income beneficiary).

The annual valuation of assets, which is required for a CRUT, may also be difficult and involve additional costs. However, the fact that a CRUT may provide for the subsequent addition of assets, but a CRAT cannot, is important to some clients. A CRAT may support a higher charitable deduction where the payout rate is less than the assumed rate of return. In such a case the excess of the assumed rate of return over the payout rate is attributed to the remainder that will pass to charity. However, in the case of a CRUT, the payout is assumed to increase each year by the specified percentage of the annual increase in principal (the excess of the assumed rate of return over the payout rate).

At various times in the past the valuation of the charitable remainder interests were based upon different assumed rates of return. Specifically, when the six percent gender-based mortality tables were replaced with ten percent unisex tables, effective December 1, 1983, the underlying earnings assumptions for a unitrust were not changed. Accordingly, between December 1, 1983 and May 1, 1989, when the new mortality tables became effective, the present worth of a unitrust remainder was less than an annuity trust remainder, all other factors being equal. For example, during that period if a donor aged 55 placed $100,000 in an annuity trust and drew an annuity of $8,000 for life, the annuity under Table A of Reg. §20.2031-7(f) was valued at $64,037. Thus, the remainder interest was valued at $35,963 ($100,000 − $64,037). In contrast, the charitable remainder of a $100,000 unitrust with an eight percent payout rate was valued at $25,899 as follows:

Adjusted payout rate: 8% × .90901 = 7.27208%
Interpolated factor for 7.27208%: .25899
Value of remainder: $100,000 × .25899 = $25,899

Also during that period, when a lead interest was given to charity (*see* §8.31), the difference in table values made a unitrust more attractive than an annuity trust.

§8.30. Pooled Income Fund, §642(c)(5)

Income, gift, and estate tax deductions are also available for the charitable remainder interest in property that is transferred to a pooled income fund, which is defined as a trust:

> (A) to which each donor transfers property, contributing an irrevocable remainder interest in such property to or for the use of [a public charity], and retaining an income interest for the life of one or more beneficiaries (living at the time of the transfer);
>
> (B) in which the property transferred by each donor is commingled with property transferred by other donors who have made or make similar transfers;

(C) which cannot have investments in securities which are exempt from the taxes imposed by this subtitle

(D) which include only amounts received from transfers that meet the requirements of this paragraph;

(E) which is maintained by the organization to which the remainder interest is contributed and of which no donor or beneficiary of an income interest is a trustee; and

(F) from which each beneficiary of an income interest receives income, for each year for which he is entitled to receive the income interest referred to in subparagraph (A), determined by the rate of return earned by the trust for such a year. §645(c)(5).

When property is transferred to a pooled income fund, participation units in the fund are allocated to the holder of the life interest. As in the case of a common trust fund, the number of units depends upon the value of the property transferred to the fund and the value of the fund's other assets. The Regulations contain detailed rules for the valuation of assets of the fund and allocation of units. *See* Reg. §§1.642(c)-5, 1.642(c)-6. The IRS has ruled that an exempt organization, as trustee, may commingle assets of pooled income funds with those of charitable remainder trusts. LR 8903019.

The IRS has published sample forms of pooled income fund trust and instruments of transfer. *See* Rev. Proc. 88-53, 1988-2 C.B. 712, discussed below. Earlier the IRS published sample provisions for inclusion in the governing instruments of pooled income funds. Rev. Rul. 82-38, 1982-1 C.B. 96, *as amplified by* Rev. Rul. 85-57, 1985-1 C.B. 182. Because of the complexity of the rules regarding pooled income funds, a donor should be hesitant to transfer property to a fund unless either (1) the pooled income fund and instruments of transfer are substantially in the form of the samples issued by the IRS, or (2) the charity has obtained a ruling from the IRS verifying that the fund meets the requirements of §642(c)(5).

A trust does not satisfy the requirements of §642(c)(5)(A) if the trustee is permitted to invest in depreciable property unless the governing instrument or the state law requires the trustee to establish a depreciation reserve with respect to depreciable property. Rev. Rul. 90-103, 1990-2 C.B. 159. Accordingly, a trust should either prohibit the trustee from holding depreciable property or require the trustee to establish a depreciation reserve. Revenue Ruling 90-103 amplifies Revenue Ruling 82-38 to approve the following sample provisions:

> If the trustee accepts or invests in depreciable or depletable property, it shall establish a depreciation or depletion reserve in accordance with Generally Accepted Accounting Principles (GAAP).
>
> The trustee shall not accept or invest in any depreciable or depletable assets.

The amount of the charitable deduction for property transferred to a pooled income fund depends upon the age of the income beneficiaries and the rate of return earned by the fund over the preceding three years. Under §642(c)(5) the life income interests are valued according to the highest rate of return earned by the fund in the preceding three years. Funds in existence before May 1, 1989 with less than three years of experience were deemed to have nine percent rate of return (six percent for transfers before December 1, 1983). Reg. §1.642(c)-(6)(b)(2). "[T]he first taxable year of a pooled income fund is the taxable year in which [it] first receives assets." Rev. Rul. 85-20, 1985-1 C.B. 183. Under Notice 89-60, 1989-1 C.B. 700,

> If a pooled income fund has been in existence less than three taxable years immediately preceding the taxable year in which the transfer or property to the fund is made, the highest yearly rate of return shall be deemed to be one percent less than the highest annual average of the monthly rates (prescribed by section 7520(a)(2) of the Code) for the 3 calendar years immediately preceding the year in which the fund is created (rounded to the nearest two-tenths of one percent). For funds created after April 30, 1989, and before January 1, 1990, the deemed rate of return is 9.4 percent.

Funds created in 1990 are deemed to have a 9.8 percent rate of return.

The donor may retain a testamentary power to revoke or terminate the income interest of any designated beneficiary other than the public charity. Reg. §1.642(c)-5(b)(2). However, the retention of such a power does not affect the valuation of the charitable remainder.

The present value of a remainder interest dependent upon the termination of one life or two lives is determined according to actuarial Table R(1) and R(2), respectively, of Alpha Volume, IRS Pub. No. 1457. When a life income interest terminates, the corresponding charitable remainder interest must be severed from the fund and paid over to or retained for the benefit of the designated public charity. Reg. §1.642(c)-5(b)(8).

No gain or loss is incurred by the donor when property is transferred to a qualified pooled income fund. However, gain may be recognized if the donor either receives any property from the fund in addition to the income interest or transfers encumbered property to the fund. Reg. §1.642(c)-5(a)(3). The fund and the beneficiaries are generally taxed according to the rules applicable to a noncharitable trust, except that the grantor trust rules do not apply. Reg. §1.642(c)-(5)(a)(2).

Overall, a pooled income fund offers an attractive way for a donor to make a charitable gift that would not justify the expense of establishing and operating a separate charitable remainder trust. The opportunity to achieve tax-free diversification of investments is an important advantage of a fund. However, unlike charitable remainder trusts, a fund cannot invest in tax exempt securities, §642(c)(5)(C), Reg. §1.642(c)-5(b)(4). Accordingly, none of the income received from a pooled fund is tax-exempt. Also, the statute bars a donor or beneficiary from serving as a trustee of the fund. §642(c)(5)(E). However, "[t]he fact that a donor of property to the fund, or a beneficiary of the fund is a trustee, officer, director or other officer of the public charity to or for the use of which the remainder interest is contributed ordinarily will not prevent the fund from meeting the requirements of section 642(c)(5) and this paragraph." Reg. §1.642(c)-5(b)(6).

A transfer to a pooled income fund could involve the GSTT if the donor's grandchildren or others in their generation are income beneficiaries of the fund.

In 1988 the IRS published sample forms of a pooled income fund trust and instruments of transfer. Rev. Proc. 88-53, 1988-2 C.B. 712. In Rev. Proc. 88-54, 1988-2 C.B. 715, the IRS announced that it would no longer issue rulings as to whether a pooled income fund qualified under §642(c)(5) or whether the contributions to the fund were deductible. However, in Revenue Procedure 88-53 the IRS announced that donors who transfer property to a pooled income fund that substantially complies with the model instruments are assured that the charitable remainder interests are deductible without obtaining a ruling. By issuing these procedures the IRS strongly encourages the use of the sample instruments.

§8.31. Gifts to Charitable Lead Trusts, §§170(f)(2)(B), 2055(e)(2)(B), 2522(c)(2)(B)

Charitable deductions are also allowed for a gift to charity of a current interest in a trust that is in the form of a guaranteed annuity or unitrust interest. *See* §8.32. A trust that provides for such current payments to charity is usually called a "charitable lead trust." A gift of a guaranteed annuity or unitrust interest is deductible for income tax purposes only if the income of the trust will be taxed to the donor under the grantor trust rules. §170(f)(2)(B). Thus, if the remainder interest is not retained by the grantor, but is vested in a noncharity, the gift of the income interest is nondeductible for income tax purposes. However, none of the income earned by the trust will be taxable to the donor. Instead, any accumulated income including capital gains is initially taxed to the trustee. The accumulations may later be taxed to the noncharitable remainderman, when distributed, under the "throwback" rules. §§666,667; *see* §10.4.10. The IRS has ruled that a charitable lead trust may provide that income in excess of the amount needed to make the required payments to charity may be accumulated for distribution to noncharities upon termination of the trust. Rev. Rul. 88-82, 1988-2 C.B.

336. No charitable deduction is available if the trust provides for current distribution of excess income to noncharitable beneficiaries.

Subject to the other limitations imposed by §170, including the 30 percent limit for gifts "for the use of" a qualified charity, Reg. §1.170A-8(a)(2), a donor is entitled to a present income tax deduction for the full value of a guaranteed annuity or unitrust interest given during the year to a qualified charity if the donor is treated as the owner of the trust for income tax purposes. A gift of a guaranteed annuity or unitrust amount also qualifies for a gift tax deduction, LR 8338108, and a bequest of an income interest similarly qualifies for an estate tax deduction.

A charitable lead trust may also be an attractive method for transferring appreciating property to private beneficiaries. The contribution to a trust can be structured to provide a charitable deduction for part or all of the assets contributed. The gift tax on the transfer to beneficiaries is based on the total asset value less the charitable contribution. Later, the appreciated remainder is distributed to designated beneficiaries free from the gift or estate tax.

A charitable lead trust may appeal to a client whose future income will be in lower tax brackets, since the gift accelerates the deduction for the future payments to the charity, while the income to fund those payments is taxed later when received. The rules prevent a donor from taking a large deduction at the outset and avoiding taxation on the trust income in later years by relinquishing the interests or controls that caused the donor to be treated as its owner under the grantor trust rules: If the donor ceases being treated as owner of the trust, he or she must recapture part of the deduction as current income. The amount recaptured is the excess of the deduction received for the gift, over the discounted value of the income that was taxed to the donor under the grantor trust rules. §170(f)(2)(B). The amount must be included in the donor's final income tax return if the donor ceases to be treated as owner of the trust by reason of death. Reg. §1.170A-6(c)(5), example 3.

A charitable lead trust is not tax-exempt. Accordingly, the trust instrument may direct that distributions to charity consist of ordinary income to the extent available, otherwise from capital gain (distributions of which would qualify for the §642(c) charitable deduction). *See* Rev. Rul. 83-75, 1983-1 C.B. 114; LR 8026032; LR 8030054.

If appreciated property is sold within two years after it is transferred to a charitable lead trust, the gain is taxed as if the grantor had made the sale. §644. Although the trust will pay the tax, it is imposed at the grantor's marginal rate.

The IRS has ruled that no charitable deduction is allowable with respect to a charitable lead trust that gives the trustee the power to commute and prepay the charitable beneficiary the value of the future annuity payments which it is entitled to receive. Rev. Rul. 88-27, 1988-

1 C.B. 331. The ruling reached that conclusion based on the provisions of Reg. §25.2522(c)-3(c)(2)(vi)(a), which define a "guaranteed annuity" as requiring the payment of a determinable amount for a specified term. The right of the trustee to commute and prepay the annuity deprives the charitable beneficiary of the right to receive payments of a fixed amount over a specified term. Accordingly, the trust failed to qualify for a charitable deduction.

Interestingly, a private letter ruling concluded that the termination of a charitable lead trust pursuant to a court decision which authorized commuting and prepaying the charitable beneficiary would not violate any of the private foundation rules. LR 8808031. The ruling did not consider whether or not the commutation and prepayment would jeopardize the charitable deductions that were allowed to the grantor 11 years before.

The rules regarding the determination of the GSTT inclusion ratio for charitable lead trusts was changed by the 1988 Act to prevent the ratio from being determined at the time the trust was created, which would have given the transferor the benefit of considerable leverage. *See* §2642(e). Specifically, for transfers taking place after October 13, 1987, the GSTT inclusion ratio of a charitable lead trust requires use of the "adjusted GSTT exemption" and the value of the property of the trust "immediately after the termination of the charitable lead annuity." Under §2642(e) the adjusted GSTT exemption (the amount of the $1 million GSTT exemption that was allocated to the trust adjusted by the interest rate that was applied to determine the amount of the charitable deduction purposes of §2055 (estate tax) or §2522 (gift tax)) is the numerator and the value of all of the property in the trust immediately after termination of the charitable lead annuity is the denominator.

§8.32. Guaranteed Annuity Interests and Unitrust Interests

Income, gift, and estate tax deductions are allowed for gifts of guaranteed annuity interests to charity. For this purpose a guaranteed annuity interest is an irrevocable right, pursuant to the trust, to receive an amount each year that is determinable on the date of the gift for a fixed term or for the life or lives of individuals who are living on the date of the gift. Reg. §1.170A-6(c)(2)(i)(A). An interest does not qualify unless it is a guaranteed annuity interest in all respects. Thus, the right to receive payments under an income-only unitrust (the lesser of a fixed amount or the actual income of the trust) does not qualify. Rev. Rul. 77-300, 1977-2 C.B. 352 (gift tax). Similarly, according to the Regulations, an interest does not qualify if a payment may be made from the trust for a private purpose prior to the expiration of the charitable annuity interest unless the payments must be made from assets that are devoted exclusively to private purposes. Reg. §20.2055-2(e)(2)(vi)(e), (vii)(e). However, the Tax Court held the Regulations invalid when a unitrust income interest is payable to charity following the death of one private beneficiary and prior to the distribution of the remainder interest on the death of the other private income beneficiaries. *Estate of Minnie L. Boeshore,* 78 T.C. 523 (1982), *acq.,* 1987-2 C.B. 1. Any income in excess of the annuity amount may also be payable to a charity, but it will not increase the amount of the allowable deduction for the year in which the income interest was gifted.

A charitable deduction is allowable for gift tax purposes when the charitable lead annuity trust accumulates any income that is not required to make annuity payments, and adds it to corpus. Rev. Rul. 88-82, 1988-2 C.B. 336. In Situation 2, Revenue Ruling 88-82 points out that if the excess income may be paid to a noncharitable beneficiary, the charitable interest is not a guaranteed annuity and no deduction is available. Finally, as noted in §8.31, the charitable beneficiary's right to receive annuity payments is not a guaranteed annuity if it can be commuted and prepaid.

A unitrust interest is an irrevocable right to receive payment each year of a fixed percentage of the net fair market value of the trust assets, determined annually. The value may be determined either on one date each year or by taking the average value on more than one date, provided that the same method is used each year. Reg. §1.170A-6(c)(2)(ii)(A). In general, the other rules applicable to a guaranteed annuity also apply to a unitrust interest.

> **Example 8-20.** *D* transferred $100,000 in trust to pay $5,000 a year for the first 5 years and $7,500 for the next 5 years to a qualified charity, *C.* At the end of the 10-year period the trust property will be distributed to *D*'s then living issue, per stirpes. The interest given to *C* is a guaranteed annuity, Reg. §1.170A-6(c)(2)(i)(B), but it is not deductible by *D* for income tax purposes unless *D* is treated as the owner of the trust under the grantor trust rules. Gift and estate tax deductions are available for the gift to *C* in any case. The interest would qualify as a unitrust interest if it were expressed as a fixed percentage (*e.g.,* 8%) of the fair market value of the trust assets determined on a specified date each year (*e.g.,* January 15). No annual exclusions are allowable with respect to the remainder interests in the trust.

§8.33. Gifts of Income Interests

An ordinary income interest in a trust does not qualify for the income, gift, or estate tax charitable deductions. However, the disallowance of the income tax deduction may be circumvented to some extent if the income is not taxed to the donor under the grantor trust rules.

> **Example 8-21.** *D* created a trust this year that provided for the net income to be paid to a qualified charity, *C,* for 10 years at the end of which the trust property will be distributed to *D'*s then living issue. The transfer to the trust does not qualify for an income tax deduction under §170. However, the income of the trust will not be taxed to *D* unless *D* is treated as the owner of the trust under the grantor trust rules. Importantly, the trust is entitled to a deduction for the amount distributed to charity each year. §642(c). Note that the transfer does not qualify for the gift tax charitable deduction because it is not in the form of a guaranteed annuity or fixed percentage of the fair market value of the property distributed annually. §2522(c)(2)(B). As explained below, the gift tax disadvantage would be eliminated if the gift of the income were incomplete when the trust was created. The gift would be incomplete if, for example, *D* retained the power each year to appoint the accumulated income to and among a class of charities. *See, e.g.,* LR 8338095.

A less satisfactory result follows where the donor is treated as the owner of the trust, as when the donor retains a reversionary interest in the corpus or income that exceeds five percent of the value of the corpus or income. §673(a). A donor who is required to report the income of the trust should be entitled to a deduction for the amount paid to charity, subject to the limits and other provisions of §170. However, the transfer to the trust would not qualify for the gift tax deduction.

The gift tax detriment of transferring property to a trust of which the income is payable to charity is avoided if the gift to the charity is not completed until the income is ready for distribution to the charity. *See, e.g.,* LR 8017058. For example, the gift is incomplete at the time of the initial transfer if the donor retains the right to designate the charity that will receive the net income earned by the trust during each year. *See* Rev. Rul. 77-275, 1977-2 C.B. 346. The grantor is not taxed on the income of a trust under the grantor trust rules merely because the grantor retains the power to allocate income or principal among charities. §674(b)(4); *see* §10.37.1. Importantly, the retention of such a power renders the gift incomplete until the power is exercised. Reg. §25.2511-2(c). When the donor designates the charity to receive the accumulated income, the gift is completed. The gift consists of the entire interest in the trust's accumulated income, which is not a split interest and for which an offsetting gift tax deduction is allowable under §2522(a). LR 8144051. Note that a gift tax deduction is not allowable where the donor designates the charity in advance of the receipt of the income. Rev. Rul. 77-275, *supra.* In such a case the designation gives the charity an income interest that does not qualify for the gift tax deduction. "No deduction is allowable under section 2522 of the Code with respect to such a completed gift due to [the donor's] retained right to reversion of the trust property upon termination and because the income right is not in the form prescribed by section 2522(c)(2)." §642(c)(1). The grantor of such a trust should instead retain the power to choose the charities to receive the net income for each year *after* the income is in hand. The payment to the charities is deductible under §642(c)(1) for income tax purposes even though it is paid after the close of the trust's taxable year. LR 8152078. Under that section, "[i]f a charitable contribution is paid after the close of [the] taxable year and on or before the last day of the year following the close of such taxable year, then the trustee or administrator may elect to treat such contribution as paid during such taxable year."

The slight differences between the charities described in §170(c) and those described in §§2055(a) and 2522(a) can also cause tax problems for the donor. For example, a gift tax deduction is not allowable where a trust permits the grantor, or another person, to designate the charitable recipient from among charitable organizations described in §170(c). In order to assure that a gift tax charitable deduction is also available, the selection must also be limited to charities that are described in §2522(a). The point is elaborated in LR 8017058 with respect to an irrevocable short-term trust. In most instances the authority to make distributions of trust property to undesignated charities should be limited to ones that meet the requirements of §§170(c), 2055(a), *and* 2522(a).

§8.34. Payments to Charity from a Trust upon Death of Grantor

For a variety of purposes it is important to distinguish between gifts made "in trust" and "not in trust." The distinction should be drawn in projecting the tax consequences that flow from the transfer of property to a trust from which payments will be made to charity following the grantor's death. The transfer of property to a revocable trust does not generally have any significant present income or gift tax consequences because of its revocable character. The grantor may safely provide for a distribution to be made to charity upon the grantor's death. By way of illustration, Rev. Rul. 75-414, 1975-2 C.B. 371, pointed out that a trust may be used as a conduit to make *outright* distributions of a specified percentage of the trust corpus to a charity upon the grantor's death. The Ruling allowed an estate tax deduction for a specified percentage of the trust property, augmented by a pour-over from the grantor's estate, which was payable to charity upon the grantor's death. A deduction was allowed because the gift constituted an outright transfer of an undivided interest in the trust property. An estate tax deduction is also allowable where a trust provides for payment of a specified sum to charity upon the grantor's death. In that case the gift would constitute the grantor's entire interest in that particular sum. Of course, a charitable deduction is allowable only to the extent that the property given to charity is included in the decedent's gross estates. §2055(d).

The transfer of property to an irrevocable trust that provides for a later distribution to charity may have very different consequences. For example, the transfer usually constitutes a completed gift for gift tax purposes. However, a charitable gift tax deduction is not allowed unless the charitable interest is in the form of a CRAT, a CRUT, or a guaranteed annuity or unitrust amount. Thus, some gift tax liability could be incurred at the time the charitable interest is created. The transfer to the trust also would not qualify for an income tax deduction unless it took one of those forms. Presumably the grantor's estate would be entitled to an estate tax charitable deduction for the value of the payment made from the trust at the time of the grantor's death. Recall that the marital deduction is available on an elective basis with respect to the full value of the property transferred to a trust in which the surviving spouse has a qualifying income interest for life. §§2056(b)(7), 2523(f). The value of such property is includible in the donee-spouse's estate under §2044. As noted above, if the remainder passes to charity upon the donee-spouse's death, the donee-spouse's estate will be entitled to an offsetting charitable deduction under §2055.

Alternatively, if the donor desires to make a substantial irrevocable transfer which will later be distributed to charity, it may be appropriate to create a private foundation to receive the contribution. This would facilitate income, gift, and estate tax deductions for the transfer without the use of a qualifying charitable remainder or lead trust. Private foundations are subject to the rules of §§4940-4948 as well as reporting requirements.

§8.35. Salvaging Charitable Deductions for Nonqualifying Interests

Gifts to charitable trusts sometimes fail to qualify for the intended income, gift, and estate tax deductions because of noncompliance with technical rules. There are, fortunately, two major methods by which the deductions may be salvaged. The first is the use of disclaimers to eliminate interests or powers that prevent a gift from qualifying.

> **Example 8-22.** *T* died leaving a will that gave her residuary estate to an individual, *X*, as trustee of a trust that was intended

> to qualify as a CRAT. However, the trust authorized *X* to distribute principal to or for the benefit of *T*'s husband, *H,* as required to maintain his standard of living. On the twentieth anniversary of *T*'s death the trust corpus is to be paid over to the C Church. The gift does not qualify for a charitable deduction under §2055 because of *X*'s power to distribute principal to or for the benefit of *H.* If *H* effectively disclaims the right to receive distributions of principal the value of C Church's remainder interest will be deductible.

The 1984 Act added provisions which establish the rules under which the reformation of charitable trusts, pooled income funds, and gifts of remainder interests in personal residences or farms will be recognized for purposes of the income, gift, and estate tax laws. Detailed rules regarding reformations are contained in §2055(e)(3), to which references are made in §§170(f)(5) and 2522(c)(4). The rules recognize the effect of "qualified reformation" of "reformable interests."

An overview of the provisions of §2055(e)(3) is provided by IRS News Release IR-84-101:

> In the case of a charitable interest created under a will executed or a trust created after December 31, 1978, the interest will generally qualify as a "reformable interest" only if all payment to noncharitable beneficiaries are expressed either in specified dollar amounts or in a fixed percentage of the fair market value of the property. If this requirement is not met, the interest may nevertheless qualify as a "reformable interest" if judicial proceedings are commenced on or before the later of (i) the 90th day after the last date for filing the estate tax return (including extensions); (ii) if no estate tax return is required to be filed, the 90th day after the last date for filing the first income tax return of the split-interest trust (including extensions); or (iii) on or before October 16, 1984.

In general a trust can be reformed if it would have qualified for the charitable deduction apart from the requirement that it be in the form of a CRAT, a CRUT, or a guaranteed annuity or unitrust interest (*i.e.,* under the pre-1969 rules). §2055(e)(3)(C)(i). In the case of post-1978 instruments, an interest is not reformable unless the noncharitable interests are specified in terms of a fixed percentage and a judicial reformation proceeding is initiated before the expiration of the estate tax limitations period. However, those requirements do not apply if the judicial proceedings are begun not later than the 90th day after the last date for filing the estate tax return (or, if no return is required, the 90th day after the last date for filing the income tax return for the first year of the trust). §2055(e)(3)(C)(iii).

In order to constitute a qualified reformation, it must be retroactive to the date of death (or creation of the trust). §2055(e)(3)(B)(iii). In addition, the reformation may not result in a change of more than five percent in the value of the reformable interest. §2055(e)(3)(B)(i). Also, the reformation cannot change the duration of the charitable and noncharitable interests — except for reducing the term of the noncharitable interest of more than 20 years to a term of 20 years. §2055(e)(3)(B).

E. SPECIAL TYPES OF TRANSFERS

§8.36. Bargain Sales to Charity, §1011(b)

A "bargain sale" (or part gift and part sale) occurs when property is sold to a charity for less than its fair market value. It may be an appropriate technique where a donor wants to recover part or all of his or her investment in an asset. For example, a client who does not want to make an outright gift of property to a charity may be willing to transfer it to the charity for an amount equal to its cost. The excess of the fair market value of the property over the consideration received by the donor (the "gift" portion) usually qualifies as a charitable contribution subject to the provisions of §170. *E.g.,* LR 8433061.

Under §1011(b), a portion of the seller's adjusted basis is disregarded for the purpose of determining gain on the sale:

> If a deduction is allowable under section 170 (relating to a charitable contribution) by reason of a sale, then the adjusted basis for determining the gain from such sale shall be that portion of the adjusted basis which bears the same ratio to the adjusted basis as the amount realized bears to the fair market value of the property. Id.

Thus, the following formula should be used to calculate the donor's adjusted basis under §1011(b):

$$\frac{\text{Amount realized}}{\text{Fair market value of property transferred}} \times \text{Adjusted basis} = \text{Adjusted basis to compute gain}$$

In the case of a bargain sale, the donor recognizes the same amount of gain as if he or she sold a separate portion of the property for its full value and made a gift of the remainder to the charity.

Where the elective reduction of §170(e)(1) is applied, and the reduction on the *whole* property sold exceeds the amount of gift, the regulations allow no §170 deduction, and allocate the whole of the basis to the portion of the property sold. Reg. §§1.170A-4(c)(2)(ii), 1.1011-

2(a)(1). The Tax Court held these Regulations invalid in *Estate of Bullard,* 87 T.C. 261 (1986) and instead allocated basis to the sale and gift portions of a bargain sale transaction on a pro rata basis under the general principles of §1011(b).

> **Example 8-23.** For more than a year, *D* has owned stock that cost $50,000 and has a fair market value of $150,000. *D* sold the stock to C Church for $60,000. The charitable contribution is $90,000, but since *D*'s contribution base is only $20,000 each year, *D* could only deduct $6,000 currently (30% × $20,000). Accordingly, *D* would probably not be able to make full use of the available deduction even with the benefit of the allowable five-year carryover. *D* might therefore elect to reduce the contribution by the capital gain element in accordance with §170(b)(1)(C)(iii) to take advantage of the 50% limitation and increase the annual deduction to $10,000. Under Reg. §1.1011-2(a)(1), the contribution is reduced by the capital gain portion as if the whole property had been sold to determine if there is an allowable deduction under §170:

Total contribution	$ 90,000
Capital gain portion	−100,000
Allowable deduction	0

> Reg. §1.170A-4(c)(2)(ii) therefore allocates all of the basis to the sale part of the property, and none to the gift part, thus eliminating the gift deduction:

Total sale	$ 60,000
Basis	− 50,000
Recognized gain on sale	$ 10,000
Gift	$ 90,000
Basis of gift	− 0
Capital gain element	$ 90,000
Gift reduced by capital gain element, to arrive at §170 deduction	0

> Under the Tax Court holding in *Estate of Bullard,* 87 T.C. 261 (1986), the basis would be ratably allocated between the gifted and sold portions of the property, resulting in a $40,000 capital gain ($60,000 − $20,000 basis) and a charitable contribution deduction of $90,000.

For purposes of §1011(b), if property is transferred subject to an indebtedness, the amount of the indebtedness is treated as an amount realized by the seller even though the transferee does not agree to assume or pay the indebtedness. Reg. §1.1011-2(a)(3). The principles of *Crane v. Commissioner,* 331 U.S. 1 (1947), apply to such a case, with the result that the donor may realize income as a consequence of making the gift. *Winston F. C. Guest,* 77 T.C. 9 (1981); *Ebben v. Commissioner,* 783 F.2d 906 (9th Cir. 1986). In *Ebben* the court stated, "we hold that every contribution of mortgaged property to a charity is a 'sale' and basis is computed under §1011(b)." 783 F.2d at 911. The income tax consequences of a bargain sale of encumbered property are also illustrated in Rev. Rul. 81-163, 1981-1 C.B. 433.

Under the pre-1970 law, if property were sold to a charity in a bargain sale, the proceeds were not taxable to the extent of the seller's entire adjusted basis in the property. In addition, the seller was entitled to a charitable deduction for the excess of the fair market value of the property over the sale price.

In the case of an outright transfer in connection with a bargain sale, the donor is entitled to a gift tax deduction in the amount of the gift portion. Similarly, the donor's estate is entitled to an estate tax charitable deduction if the property is included in the donor's gross estate. Where the donor makes a bargain sale of a partial interest in property, such as a remainder interest, a deduction is not allowed unless the interest falls within one of the exceptions to the split-interest rules. *See* §§8.14-8.18.

§8.37. Charitable Gift Annuities

Charitable deductions are also allowable when property is transferred to a charity in exchange for an annuity. The rate of the annuity is usually established in accordance with the recommendations of the Committee on Gift Annuities. Sample rates for single life annuities are:

Age	*Rate of Annual Income*	*Age*	*Rate of Annual Income*
50	6.5%	75	8.5%
55	6.7%	80	9.6%
60	7.0%	85	11.4%
65	7.3%	90 and over	14.0%
70	7.8%		

A donor who makes a transfer to a charity in exchange for an annuity is treated as having made a charitable gift of the amount by which the value of the transferred property exceeds the value of the annuity contract. For this purpose the annuity is valued according to the tables in Alpha Vol., IRS Pub. No. 1457. For transfers prior to May 1, 1989 the tables set forth in Reg. §§20.2031-7(f) and 25.2512-5(f) are used. *See* Rev. Rul. 84-162, 1984 C.B. 200.

Gift annuities that provide for current payments are generally of most interest to older clients. Some younger clients may be interested in deferred gift annuities — ones that provide for annuity payments to begin in the future. The donor of a deferred gift annuity is entitled to present federal income and gift tax deductions for the value of the interest given to charity (*i.e.,* the value of the property transferred less the present value of the annuity payments). The potential advantage of a deferred gift annuity is that, due to tax-free compounding during the deferral period, payments will be substantially larger when they begin than if payments had begun at the outset.

Example 8-24. *D,* 65 years old, transferred securities with a basis of $20,000 and a current value of $100,000 to a public charity, *C,* in exchange for its nonassignable promise to pay *D* $5,000 each year in monthly installments for life. Considering the appropriate interest rates for the current and immediate past 2 months, the donor chose to use an 11% rate for purposes of valuing the charitable interest. The value of the right to receive payments of $5,000 per year for the life of a 65-year-old is $35,131. That figure is determined by multiplying the amount of the annual payment ($5,000) by the factor for a 65-year-old from Table S of Alpha Vol. (6.6948) as increased by a factor from Table K of 1.0495 for monthly payments. *D* made a gift to *C* of the $64,869, the amount by which the value of the property transferred ($100,000) exceeded the value of the annuity ($35,131). *D* realized gain on the transfer, which is determined under the bargain sale rules and is usually reported over the life expectancy of the annuitant in the manner described below.

Example 8-25. A couple aged 50, *H* and *W,* transferred property worth $100,000 to a public charity in exchange for annuity payments to begin at at age 65. The payments would be $13,200 (13.2%). In addition, *H* and *W* would be entitled to an income tax deduction of $73,623. At a 31% rate the deduction would result in an income tax saving of $22,823. Of course, if appreciated property was transferred to the charity, the transaction will involve the realization of some gain.

The bargain sale rules apply to charitable gift annuity transactions that give rise to a charitable deduction under §170. Reg. §1.1011-2; LR 8117045. Accordingly, a donor will realize some gain when appreciated property is transferred to a charity in exchange for an annuity.

In this respect a gift annuity has less favorable income tax consequences than a gift to a charitable remainder trust or a pooled income fund. However, when the annuity contract is not assignable and the donor is one of the annuitants, the gain is not reported immediately. Instead, a portion of each payment is reported as gain over the period of the annuitant's life expectancy. Reg. §1.1011-2(a)(4). The portion treated as gain is determined by dividing the gain by the annuitant's life expectancy according to Table I or Table V of Reg. §1.72-9 depending on when the transfer to the charity took place. However, the gain is reported only from the portion of the annual payment that represents the return on the donor's investment in the contract as determined under §72. Otherwise, even if the annuitant lives longer than expected, none of the portion attributable to the annuitant's investment in the contract is taxed. The application of these rules is illustrated by Example 8-26, which is a slightly changed and updated version of Reg. §1.1011-2(c), example 8.

Example 8-26. A donor aged 65, *D,* transferred securities after May 1, 1986 which were worth $100,000 and had a basis of $20,000 to a public charity, *C,* in exchange for its nonassignable promise to pay *D* $5,000 per year in monthly installments for life. The present value of the annuity, calculated as described above is $35,131. Thus, *D* made a gift to *C* of $64,869. Under the bargain sale rules *D*'s adjusted basis in the securities was $7,026:

$$\frac{\$35{,}131}{\$100{,}000} \times \$20{,}000 = \$7{,}206$$

Accordingly, *D* realized a gain on the transfer of $28,105 ($35,131 − $7,026), which will be reported over the 20-year period the payments are expected to be made according to Table V of Reg. §1.72-9. *D* must report a gain of $1,405 each year out of the portion of the payment attributable to the investment in the contract. The portion of each payment that is attributable to *D*'s investment in the contract is determined by dividing the investment ($35,131) by the expected return on the contract ($100,000). The expected return is simply the amount of the annual payment ($5,000) multiplied by *D*'s life expectancy of 20 years determined under Table V of Reg. §1.72-9. *D*'s investment in the contract is $35,131, the present value of the annuity, or 35.1% of the expected return ($100,000). The annual payment of $5,000 is multiplied by the exclusion ratio (35.1%) to determine the amount that is excludible each year from *D*'s income ($1,755). However, the gain of $1,405 must be reported out of that portion of each payment until the full gain ($28,105) has been taxed. Thereafter, the full $1,755 is received tax free. The gain is the excess of *D*'s investment in the contract ($35,131) over the adjusted basis in the sale portion ($7,026). Each year *D* must report as ordinary income the amount ($3,245) by which the annuity payment ($5,000) exceeds the exclusion portion ($1,755).

A gift tax charitable deduction is allowable under §2522 for the excess of the value of the property transferred to the charity over the value of the annuity. Transfers made prior to May 1, 1989 were valued according to the former 10 percent unisex actuarial tables of Reg. §§20.2031-7 and 25-2512-5. Rev. Rul. 84-162, 1984-2 C.B. 200. The deduction is allowable although the gift does not take the form of a charitable remainder trust or pooled income fund because the donor did not retain an interest in the *same* property that was transferred to the charity. Rev. Rul. 80-281, 1980-2 C.B. 282. As is the case with other annuities, nothing is ordinarily includible in the donor-annuitant's gross estate at death. Some value would be included under §2039 if the annuity is payable to another person following the donor's death.

State Regulation. In many states charitable gift annuities are subject to insurance regulations. A few, such as Washington, exempt charities from regulation.

§8.38. Gift and Redemption of Appreciated Stock

An outright gift of closely-held stock to a charity, followed by a redemption of the stock, can be an effective way of making a charitable gift without reducing the shareholder's after-tax income. The redemption would prevent the shares from being transferred by the charity to outsiders. Also, a redemption may operate to increase the proportionate interests of the other shareholders without the imposition of a gift tax. In most cases, the valuation of the shares for income and gift tax purposes will require an appraisal by an expert. Of course, the amount paid in redemption of the shares is some evidence of their value. In order to avoid problems with the IRS or ethical problems, the amount claimed as a deduction should not exceed the amount for which the stock is redeemed.

The redemption of the shares is not taxed to the donor if the gift placed the shares beyond the donor's control and the donee was not obligated to surrender the shares for redemption, *Carrington v. Commissioner,* 476 F.2d 705 (5th Cir. 1973); *Palmer v. Commissioner,* 62 T.C. 684 (1974), *aff'd on another issue,* 523 F.2d 1308 (8th Cir. 1975); Rev. Rul. 78-197, 1978-1 C.B. 83. Such a redemption is not taxed even if the donor and donee discussed the redemption prior to the gift. The

IRS continues to stand by the principles of Revenue Ruling 78-197, under which a contribution of stock to charity with a subsequent redemption will not cause income from redemption to be attributed to the donor if the charity was not legally obligated to sell or redeem the shares. *E.g.*, LR 831014, LR 8639046. However, the Second Circuit in *Blake v. Commissioner,* 697 F.2d 473 (2d Cir. 1982), viewed Revenue Ruling 78-197 as reading too much into the *Carrington* and *Palmer* decisions. It held that a mere understanding that a redemption of shares would take place and that a subsequent purchase of another asset from the donor would follow was a "step transaction" requiring the donor to realize income on the redemption of shares. Further, when the redemption price is set well below fair market value, so that the effect of the charitable contribution and subsequent redemption is a shift of ownership and control between shareholders, the transaction is viewed by the IRS as a redemption of the donor's shares, and a gift of the proceeds. LR 8552009.

Example 8-27. *X* owns a majority interest in Zero, Inc., and *X*'s 2 children have minority interests. Zero, Inc. has excess cash, and *X* would like to make a charitable contribution of $100,000. Any dividends paid to *X* would be subject to an income tax rate of 31%. But, a $100,000 increase in dividends would be offset by the charitable contribution, allowing the dividend and contribution to take place without any tax to *X*. However, this would also require a dividend to other shareholders, the 2 children. *X* would prefer to increase the children's ownership, and avoid cash distributions to them. Therefore, *X* contributes stock worth $100,000 to the charity, and Zero, Inc. later redeems the stock. The gift has the effect of completing a $100,000 cash transfer to the charity but does not require payments to the other shareholders as a dividend payment would. The proportionate shareholdings of *X* and his children have been changed as well, since the number of shares owned by *X* has been reduced while the 2 children still own the same number of shares. There is an added bonus for *X* in that the charitable contribution deduction results in a tax savings of $31,000 (31% × $100,000).

This transaction could be compared to a salary increase, or a bonus to *X* of $100,000, which would be deductible to Zero, Inc. and would have the same tax result to *X* as a dividend, but would not require distributions to the other shareholders. There may be difficulty in justifying an additional $100,000 in compensation, however, and a challenge by the IRS could result in the additional compensation being classified as a dividend.

§8.39. Gift of Life Insurance

A person acquiring insurance on the life of another person is generally required to have an insurable interest in the life of the insured. *See* §6.2. In the case of close relatives, the requirement is fulfilled by love and affection; in the case of others, such as employers or creditors, it is fulfilled by the existence of a financial interest. In LR 9110016 the IRS concluded that under New York law a charity did not have an insurable interest in the life of a donor which might either allow the insurer to avoid payment of the policy proceeds or allow the insured's personal representative to recover the proceeds from the charity. Accordingly, the IRS ruled that no charitable income, gift, or estate tax deductions were available. Moreover, the insurance proceeds were includible in the estate of the insured under either §2035 or §2042(1). *See* Christensen, IRS Letter Ruling 9110016, Part of Controversy, Zeroes in on Policies Which Benefit Charities, 130 Tr. & Est. 73 (June 1991), which reports that "the Insurance Department of the State of New York has taken the position that the IRS has misconstrued New York Insurance Law Sec. 3205, which was the basis of the holding in Letter Ruling 9110016." The IRS revoked LR 9110011 following an amendment of the New York law. As noted in §6.2, the law of some states clearly allows the assignment of insurance that was originally issued to a person who had an insurable interest in the life of the insured to another person, such as a charity. 40 Pa. Stat. Ann. §512 (Purdon's 1971).

§8.40. Charitable Pledges

A charitable pledge generally does not involve a present transfer. Accordingly, it has no current income or gift tax consequences. However, deductions may be allowed when a pledge is fulfilled. For estate tax purposes a deduction is allowable under §2053(c) for an enforceable charitable pledge to the extent (1) the pledge was contracted bona fide for full consideration or (2) a deduction would have been allowed for the pledge under §2055 had it been a bequest. Reg. §20.2053-5. Clients who wish to make charitable contributions at death and qualify their estates for the benefits of §§303 and 6166 may benefit by making charitable pledges rather than bequests. A charitable pledge may be advantageous because qualification for the benefits of §§303 and 6166 depend upon the stock (or business interest) constituting more than 35 percent of the decedent's gross estate less deductions allowable under §§2053 and 2054. This point is elaborated at §11.17.

BIBLIOGRAPHY

Barwick & Watson, Retirement Planning: A New Wrinkle on Charitable Remainder Trusts, 5 Prob. & Prop. 31 (Mar.-Apr. 1991)

Knight & Knight, Obtaining Deductions for Contributions of Qualified Conservation Property, 4 J. Tax. Invest. 336 (1987)

Korman, Maximizing the Charitable Contribution Deduction: A Survey of Charitable Giving Techniques, N.Y.U., 43rd Inst. Fed. Tax., ch. 21 (1985)

McCue & Gary, Split-Interest Charitable Giving — Down but Not Out, U. Miami, 20th Inst. Est. Plan., ch. 8 (1986)

Moore, Estate Planning Under the Tax Reform Act of 1969: The Uses of Charity, 56 Va. L. Rev. 565 (1970)

Moore, Role of Charitable Dispositions in Estate Planning, U. Miami, 13th Inst. Est. Plan., ch. 6 (1979)

Muchin, Lubelchek & Grass, Charitable Lead Trusts Can Provide Substantial Estate Planning Benefits, 49 J. Tax. 2 (1978)

Note, It Pays to Give it Away — Sometimes: Inter Vivos Charitable Remainder Unitrusts in Estate Planning, 15 Pepp. L. Rev. 367 (1988)

Note, Taxation of Charitable Gift Annuities: Valuation and Policy Considerations, 67 Va. L. Rev. 1523 (1981)

Report of Committee on Tax Estate Planning — Pre-Death Planning Considerations for Charitable Contributions, 13 Real Prop., Prob. & Tr. J. 581 (1978)

Teitell, Charitable Gifts of Property — Tangible and Intangible, Real and Unreal, U. Miami, 20th Inst. Est. Plan., ch. 9 (1986)

Teitell, C., Charitable Lead Trusts (1991)

———, Deferred Giving (2 vols. 1991)

———, Outright Charitable Gifts (1991)

———, Planned Giving (1991)

Weithorn, Using the Charitable Remainder Trust as a Sophisticated Contribution Technique, N.Y.U., 43rd Inst. Fed. Tax., ch. 17 (1985)

CHAPTER 9

LIMITING ESTATE SIZE THROUGH INTRAFAMILY TRANSACTIONS

A. Introduction

§9.1. Overview
§9.2. Professional Responsibility

B. The Installment Sale

§9.3. General
§9.4. Gift Tax Consequences
§9.5. Estate Tax Consequences
§9.6. Income Tax Consequences
§9.6.1. Payments Received
§9.6.2. Alternative Minimum Tax (AMT)
§9.6.3. Inter Vivos Disposition of Obligation
§9.6.4. Disposition at Death
§9.6.5. Imputed Interest or Original Issue Discount
Table 9-1. Applicable Federal Rates
Table 9-2. Applicable Federal Rates for November, 1991
§9.6.6. Sale of Land to Family Member
§9.7. Resale by Related Person, §453(e)
§9.7.1. Related Person
§9.7.2. What Dispositions Constitute Resales?
§9.7.3. Involuntary Transfers
§9.7.4. Marketable Securities
§9.8. Self-Cancelling Installment Note (SCIN)
§9.8.1. Estate Tax
§9.8.2. Income Tax
§9.9. Installment Sales to Nonresident Aliens

C. The Private Annuity

§9.10. General
§9.10.1. Transfer to Trust in Exchange for Annuity

§9.10.2. Planning Considerations
§9.11. Nontax Considerations
§9.12. Income Tax Consequences of Transfer
§9.13. Income Taxation of Annuitant
§9.14. Income Taxation of Transferee
§9.14.1. Depreciation
§9.14.2. Gain or Loss
§9.15. Gift Tax Consequences
§9.16. Estate Tax Consequences

D. The Gift or Sale and Leaseback

§9.17. General
§9.18. Overall Consequences
§9.19. Income Tax Consequences of Transfer
§9.20. Income Tax Consequences of Rental Payments
§9.20.1. Economic Reality
§9.20.2. No Equity Interest
§9.20.3. Tax Court Requirements
§9.20.4. Suggested Approach
§9.20.5. Grantor Trust Rules
§9.21. Gift Tax Consequences
§9.22. Estate Tax Consequences
§9.22.1. Outright Gift and Leaseback
§9.22.2. Sale and Leaseback

E. The Widow's Election in Community Property and Common Law States

§9.23. Introduction
§9.24. Testamentary Elections
§9.25. Widow's Election Described
§9.26. Typical Widow's Election Plan
§9.27. Inter Vivos or Post-Mortem Election?
§9.28. "Voluntary" Widow's Election
§9.29. Nontax Consequences of a Forced Election
§9.30. Gift Tax Consequences
§9.30.1. Powers of Appointment
§9.30.2. Voluntary Election
§9.31. Income Tax Consequences
§9.31.1. The Trustee
§9.31.2. The Widow
§9.32. Income Tax Consequences of Trust Distributions
§9.33. Estate Tax: The Husband's Estate
§9.34. Estate Tax: The Widow's Estate
§9.35. GSTT

9. Limiting Estate Size Through Intrafamily Transactions

§9.36. Widow's Election Variations
§9.37. Widow's Election Insurance Trust
§9.38. State Tax Consequences
§9.39. Widow's Election Planning

F. Dividing Interests: Sale of Remainders, Joint Purchases, GRITs, and Qualified Personal Residence Trusts

§9.40. Introduction
§9.41. Sale of Remainder Interest
§9.41.1. Gift Tax Consequences
§9.41.2. Estate Tax Consequences
§9.41.3. Income Tax Consequences
§9.42. Joint Purchases
§9.42.1. Gift Tax Consequences
§9.42.2. Estate Tax Consequences
§9.42.3. Income Tax Consequences
§9.43. GRITs (Grantor Retained Interest Trusts)
§9.43.1. Gift Tax Consequences
§9.43.2. Qualified Interests
§9.43.3. Personal Residence Trusts
§9.43.4. Estate Tax Consequences
§9.43.5. Income Tax Consequences
§9.44. Conclusion

Bibliography

> First, inquiries into subjective intent, especially in intrafamily transfers, are particularly perilous. The present case illustrates that it is, practically speaking, impossible to determine after the death of the parties what they had in mind in creating trusts over 30 years earlier. Second, there is a high probability that such a trust arrangement was indeed created for tax-avoidance purposes. And, even if there was no estate-tax-avoidance motive, the settlor in a very real and objective sense did retain an economic interest while purporting to give away his property. Finally, it is unrealistic to assume that the settlors of the trusts, usually members of one family unit, will have created their trusts as a bargained-for exchange for the other trust. "Consideration," in the traditional legal sense, simply does not normally enter into such intrafamily transfers. *United States v. Estate of Grace,* 395 U.S. 316, 323-324 (1969).

A. INTRODUCTION

§9.1. Overview

This chapter covers several devices that are sometimes used as alternatives to gifts or more traditional estate planning techniques. Most are designed to limit or diminish the size of the estate of a senior family member. The devices are generically referred to as "estate freezes" although some may reduce rather than freeze the value of property. Outright gifts often produce the best overall tax results, particularly gifts within the allowable annual gift tax exclusions. They are followed closely by taxable gifts within the amount of the donor's unified credit and taxable gifts made more than three years prior to death.

Several of the devices reviewed in this chapter are, perhaps, most easily understood by analogizing them to commercial annuities: The client transfers property in exchange for an obligation that will expire on or before the client's date of death. If the transaction is properly planned no gift tax liability is incurred, none of the transferred property is includible in the client's estate, and the income tax costs are acceptable. The transfer involves shifting the risk of appreciation or loss to the "purchaser" in exchange for a fixed obligation — often one that expires on the transferor's death. Sales of remainders and joint purchases are simply variations on this theme. However, their use by related taxpayers has been made less attractive by the valuation rules of §2702, which may increase the gift tax cost, and the decision in *Gradow v. United States,* 11 Cl. Ct. 808 (1987), *aff'd,* 897 F.2d 516 (Fed. Cir. 1990), which may require the entire property to be included in the senior family member's estate less only the value of the consideration received, if any (*see* §9.34). Some techniques, including the installment sale and the family annuity, may result in significant tax savings if the transferred property appreciates substantially in value and it is not drawn back into the transferor's estate. Indeed, any transfer that removes an asset from the transferor's estate (*i.e.,* the transfer results in a "freeze") may result in a substantial tax saving if the asset greatly appreciates in value.

The installment sale is, perhaps, the best established and most widely used of the devices. However, changes in the income tax rules have limited its use. The private annuity has some advantages, but its tax and nontax disadvantages impair its attractiveness to clients. It is, however, free from some of the limitations that apply to installment sales, including the restrictions on resale by family members.

In recent years planners have given considerable attention to the so-called "joint purchase," which typically involves the purchase of an asset by a senior generation family member *and* a junior family member.

See §9.42. The senior member contributes an amount toward the purchase that equals the actuarially determined value of a life interest in the property and the junior member contributes the balance. The senior receives a life estate in the property and the junior receives a vested remainder. The arrangement may work very well if the interests are valued actuarially applying the tables issued under §7520. However, those tables do not apply if the purchasers of the term and remainder interests are members of the same family as defined in §2704(c)(2). If they are, the holder of the term interest is deemed to have purchased the entire property and transferred the remainder to the remainderman in exchange for the consideration contributed by the remainderman. That is, the life interest is treated as having no value whatsoever. In this connection note that nieces, nephews, cousins, aunts, and uncles are *not* considered to be members of the family. As indicated above, if the parties to a joint purchase are not family members and the transaction is properly structured, the acquisition of the property will not involve any gift and nothing will be includible in the estate of the purchaser of the life estate. In such a case the technique produces better tax results than an outright gift to the donee of an equivalent amount.

The grantor retained interest trust (GRIT) is a relative newcomer to the estate planning scene. It involves the transfer of property to a trust in which the transferor retains an interest for a term of years and the remainder is given to others. The special valuation rules of §2702 also apply to GRITs if the holder of the term interest and the remaindermen are members of the same family. If the parties are family members the general rule treats the term interest retained by the senior family member as having no value. However, the actuarially determined value of a retained term interest is recognized if it is in the form of a qualified interest. §2702(a)(2)(B). For this purpose, a qualified interest is the right to receive annually or more frequently either a fixed amount or an amount that is a fixed percentage of the value of the trust determined annually. §2702(b), §9.43.2. Under another important exception, the rules of §2702 do not apply to the transfer in trust "all of the property in which consists of a residence to be used as a personal residence by the persons holding the term interess." §2702(a)(3)(A)(ii), §9.43.3. If the grantor survives the term of the retained interest, none of the trust property is includible in his or her estate.

The gift (or sale) and leaseback and the widow's election each involve significant drawbacks. However, each is thoroughly explored because of its own significance and illustrative value. In some instances one or the other produces better overall tax results than an outright gift. *E.g., Hudspeth v. Commissioner,* 509 F.2d 1224 (9th Cir. 1975) (sale and leaseback of agricultural land recognized for tax purposes).

Each of the devices discussed in this chapter has attributes that make it more suitable for use in some cases than in others. Of the ones discussed here, the installment sale and the private annuity resemble each other the most. They are both frequently used to "cap" a client's estate by transferring appreciating property to a younger family member at little or no gift tax cost. If the transfer is properly planned and executed, the property is not includible in the transferor's estate. Joint purchases and GRITs are also intended to result in substantial gift and estate tax savings. However, the potential savings are reduced by §2702 unless the transferor and the donee of the remainder interest are not family members within the meaning of §2704(c)(2). The personal residence trust, §9.43.3, and some retained qualified interest trusts can produce attractive tax results. A gift (or sale) and leaseback may limit further growth in the donor-lessee's estate and produce limited income tax benefits. However, the advantage of shifting income from the donor-lessee to the donee-lessor is constrained by the compressed income tax rate structure. Also, income-shifting no longer takes place if the grantor or the grantor's spouse retains a reversionary interest in a trust worth more than five percent at the time of the transfer. *See* §673. *See also* §10.36.1. The widow's election is primarily a testamentary device, which distinguishes it from the others. While it is usually intended to produce gift and estate tax savings, it may generate some income tax savings.

§9.2. Professional Responsibility

A lawyer should be sensitive to the conflict-of-interest problems that are inherent in advising both parties to an intrafamily transfer for consideration. In some respects the conflicts are worse in a family setting, where one or both parties to a transaction may be less alert than in dealing with an unrelated party. In many instances it is appropriate for the same lawyer to represent multiple parties regarding estate planning matters, including parents and children. *See* DR 5-105; EC 5-14 through EC 5-18; MRPC 1.7 (conflict of interest) and MRPC 2.2 (lawyer as intermediary). However, in all such cases the lawyer should be sure the clients understand the consequences of the multiple representation and consent to the lawyer functioning in that capacity. In particular, they need to understand and agree that information regarding the common representation will be shared with all clients (*i.e.,* as between clients there will be no secrets regarding the subject of the common representation). The following passage from the Comment on MRPC 2.2 is relevant to the consideration of this issue:

> A lawyer acts as intermediary in seeking to establish or adjust a relationship between clients on an amicable and mutually advantageous basis; for example, in helping to organize a business in which two or

> more clients are entrepreneurs, working out the financial reorganization of an enterprise in which two or more clients have an interest, arranging a property distribution in settlement of an estate or mediating a dispute between clients. The lawyer seeks to resolve potentially conflicting interests by developing the parties' mutual interests. The alternative can be that each party may have to obtain separate representation, with the possibility in some situations of incurring additional cost, complication or even litigation. Given these and other relevant factors, all the clients may prefer that the lawyer act as intermediary.

The parties and the lawyer should appreciate the potential for conflict and disagreement — particularly if the transaction under consideration does not produce the anticipated benefits. For example, in a private annuity transaction the transferee may complain if the annuitant "lives too long" and the transferee winds up paying more for the property than if it had been purchased in an installment sale or by another method. On the other hand, the transferor may complain if the transferee is unable to make annuity payments and the transferor has no security interest in the property. Likewise, if the transferor dies "early," other members of the transferor's family may complain that the transferee did not pay enough for the property. At a minimum, the lawyer should point out the existence of the conflicts and the lawyer's inability to represent all parties with equal zeal. Everyone, including the lawyer, is better off if each party is represented by a separate competent lawyer.

B. THE INSTALLMENT SALE

> [T]he term "installment method" means a method under which the income recognized for any taxable year from a disposition is that proportion of the payments received in that year which the gross profit (realized or to be realized when payment is completed) bears to the total contract price. §453(c).

§9.3. General

The installment sale is a very useful device that allows owners of appreciated property to achieve a variety of planning goals. On the nontax side, an installment sale may help retain a unique asset within the family. The seller realizes some cash flow from the asset without subjecting the entire gain to taxation at the time of the sale. The responsibility for the property, and its future appreciation, are shifted to other (usually younger and more active) family members. The gain on an installment sale is deferred and taxed ratably as payments are received (or as the purchaser's notes are cancelled) unless the seller elects not to use the installment method of reporting. *See* §453(d); LR 8501014. An election may be made at any time up to the due date, including extensions, for filing the income tax return for the year of sale. A later election may be made with the permission of the IRS, which may be granted in case of a tax return preparer's unintended failure to make the election. Rev. Rul. 90-46, 1990-1 C.B. 107. In Revenue Ruling 90-46 the IRS indicated that it would not allow late elections which the taxpayer wished to make because of a change in the law or because of a change of mind.

Recognition of gain by the seller is accelerated in some cases where a related purchaser resells the property or an installment obligation is cancelled or otherwise terminated. §453(e). *See* §§9.6-9.8.

When property is sold for full and adequate consideration, only the value of the installment obligation is included in the seller's estate — any further appreciation in value of the property is excluded. Thus, an installment sale can effectively freeze the value of a portion of the seller's estate. Although the same goals may be achieved through use of a private annuity (*see* Part C, *infra*) the installment sale is superior in several respects. The most important differences between the two devices are:

1. The overall cost of the property and the duration of payments are known in the case of an installment sale, but not where the property is exchanged for a private annuity.
2. Without jeopardizing the income tax consequences the seller may retain a security interest in the property in the case of an installment sale. In contrast, the retention of a security interest will cause a private annuity to be taxed as a closed transaction (*i.e.,* all of the gain will be taxed at the time of sale).
3. Subject to the rule banning deductions for personal interest, §163(h), the purchaser may deduct interest payments made in connection with an installment sale, but no part of the payments made under a private annuity is deductible. Under §163(h) the interest deduction is allowed for interest on the purchase of a qualified residence, investment interest (to the extent of investment income), and for purchases allocable to a trade or business.

It is unclear whether or not the rules of §2702 apply to installment sales or private annuities. Arguably, they should not because the transferor has not retained an interest in the property transferred. If the rules do apply, perhaps the payments due the transferor will be treated as qualified interests. *See* §9.43.2.

The terms of §453 are broad enough to support taxing a private annuity transaction as an installment sale: "For purposes of this section — (1) In general. The term 'installment sale' means a disposition of property where at least 1 payment is to be received after the close of the taxable year in which the disposition occurs." §453(b). Also, the scope of the installment sales rules has been expanded to include sales where the sales price or the payment period is indefinite. *See* §453(j). However, private annuities may continue to be treated differently. The House Ways and Means Committee Report on the Installment Sales Revision Act of 1980 noted that private annuities were also used to make intrafamily sales of appreciated property. It continued to say that "[t]he bill does not deal directly with this type of arrangement." H.R. Rep. No. 1042, 96th Cong., 2d Sess., n.12 (1980). The possible extension of the installment sales rules to private annuities appears to have been left to the IRS. According to G.C.M. 39503, "In our view this [the above-quoted] language does not mean that private annuities are not installment sales; rather, it was meant to leave room for the Service to determine what constitutes an installment sale and what constitutes a private annuity. In other words, the Committee meant that the Act does not deal with private annuities as such, but does effectively deal with them to the extent that they are determined to be installment sales."

The tax consequences of an installment sale should also be compared with those of an inter vivos gift or a disposition at the owner's death. In general, better tax results flow from inter vivos gifts that qualify for the annual gift tax exclusion or are within the amount of the donor's unified credit. Of course, not all clients are able to make substantial inter vivos gifts that deprive them of the current use of the property and may require payment of state and federal gift taxes as well. The gift tax cost of transferring an asset is not necessarily reduced by making the gifts over a number of years. The interests retained by the donor may continue to increase in value until they are finally disposed of or the donor dies.

> **Example 9-1.** An unmarried taxpayer, *T,* owns property worth $100,000, which is appreciating at an annual rate of 10%. A gift of the entire interest to a single donee would result in a taxable gift of $90,000. Instead, *T* could transfer undivided 20% interests to the donee each year for 5 years. Assuming that no discount would be available for a gift of a fractional interest, the taxable gift in the first year would be $10,000 ($20,000 − $10,000). However, the 80% retained by *T* would be worth $88,000 at the end of the year (80% × $110,000). The next gift would have a value of $22,000 (20% × $110,000) and so on.

The installment sale allows the seller to transfer the property while retaining an interest and continuing to realize cash flow (interest and principal) from the property. But it does not precipitate a gift tax if the sale is for full value. Thus, a donor can freeze the value of the property by an installment sale, with later annual exclusion gifts which forgive part or all of the installment obligation.

Also, in the case of a gift, the donee usually takes only a carryover basis in the property. In contrast, a person who acquires property in an installment purchase has a basis equal to the purchase price, and a person who acquires property from a decedent will have a stepped-up basis determined under §1014. When the property is retained by the owner until death, the unrealized appreciation in its value will never be taxed for income tax purposes. In general, the gain on an installment sale *will* be taxed at some point. Gain will be taxed upon virtually any disposition of the obligation, whether or not any consideration is received by the seller. Thus, both the inter vivos cancellation of an installment obligation and the bequest of an obligation to the obligor are taxable dispositions. *See* §§453B(f) and 691(a)(5). *See also* §§9.6.3-9.6.4. The gain is also taxed if the obligation otherwise becomes unenforceable, as it might if the seller allows the statute of limitations to run with respect to its payment. In that case the seller would also have made a gift. *See* §9.4.

§9.4. Gift Tax Consequences

If property is transferred for less than adequate and full consideration, the amount by which the value of the property exceeds the value of the consideration is a gift, except when the transfer is made in the ordinary course of business. §2512(b); Reg. §25.2512-8. Accordingly, when the valuation of the property is subject to dispute, the sale price should be based upon a competent appraisal in order to reduce the risk that the transaction involves a gift. If an obligation with a fixed term carries a below-market rate of interest, it is worth less than its face value. Prior to the adoption of §483 the Tax Court held that for gift tax purposes an installment obligation with a fixed payment schedule is worth less than its face value if it carries a below-market rate of interest. *Gertrude H. Blackburn,* 20 T.C. 204 (1953) (gift tax case involving sale of real property to children for notes carrying 2¼ percent interest when market rate on similar notes was 4 percent). A demand note is probably worth its face amount regardless of the rate of interest it bears. Under §453(f)(4) a demand note is treated as a payment received in the year of sale, which would require the gain to be recognized at that time.

The effect of the "safe harbor" provisions of §483 was considered in *Ballard v. Commissioner,* 854 F.2d 185 (7th Cir. 1988), which held that the safe harbor rate of 6 percent applied for income *and* gift tax purposes. Accordingly, the court held that the installment obligation could not be discounted for gift tax purposes. Although §483 provides that it applies "for purposes of this title," the IRS and some courts agree that its safe harbor only applies for income tax purposes. *Lester H. Krabbenhoft,* 94 T.C. 887 (1990), *aff'd,* 939 F.2d 529 (8th Cir. 1991). Congress should resolve the conflict by making a clarifying amendment to §483.

A transfer nominally structured as a sale may be disregarded by the IRS and treated as a gift where it lacks substance. The IRS has frequently asserted that an intrafamily transfer of property in exchange for notes of the transferee is taxable as a gift where the transferor does not intend to enforce the notes. *E.g.,* Rev. Rul. 77-299, 1977-2 C.B. 343. *See* §7.24. It is questionable whether the gift tax outcome should turn upon a subjective matter such as the transferor's intent to forgive the notes in the future. The courts have generally disregarded the transferor's intent and characterized the transfer as a sale where valid, enforceable, interest-bearing notes are given in exchange for property. *See, e.g., Estate of J. W. Kelley,* 63 T.C. 321 (1974), *nonacq.,* 1977-2 C.B. 2; *Selsor R. Haygood,* 42 T.C. 936 (1964), *acq. in result,* 1965-1 C.B. 4, *acq. withdrawn and nonacq. substituted,* 1977-2 C.B. 2. The initial transfer of a remainder interest in unimproved, non-income-producing real property was held to be a gift where the transferor took back noninterest-bearing, unsecured demand notes that she subsequently forgave at the rate of $3,000 per year. *Minnie E. Deal,* 29 T.C. 730 (1958). Aside from the *Deal* case the IRS has generally been unsuccessful in the courts.

A gift also occurs if the transferor gratuitously transfers the obligation or cancels or forgives it. For this purpose allowing the statute of limitations to run is treated as a forgiveness. *Estate of Lang v. Commissioner,* 613 F.2d 770 (9th Cir. 1980). Of course, any such disposition of an installment obligation would also trigger recognition of gain by the transferor. *See* §9.6.3. Cancellation of accrued interest alone involves a gift of the interest. *Republic Petroleum Corp. v. United States,* 397 F. Supp. 900, 917 (E.D. La. 1975), *mod. on other issues,* 613 F.2d 518 (5th Cir. 1980).

§9.5. Estate Tax Consequences

If an installment sale is made for full and adequate consideration in money or money's worth, the property transferred is not includible in the transferor's estate. Instead, under §2033 the proceeds that were received are included in the transferor's estate (*i.e.,* the fair market value of the installment obligation). For estate tax purposes the value of the obligation may be discounted if it carries a below-market rate of interest. *Estate of G. R. Robinson,* 69 T.C. 222 (1977) ($1,120,000 unpaid balance of note for installment sale of stock carried 4 percent interest discounted by stipulation to yield 8½ percent, or $930,100); *see also* Reg. §20.2031-4.

Transferee's Estate. If the transferee's estate is liable for the indebtedness, the value of the property is includible in his or her estate, which is entitled to a deduction under §2053 for the amount of the obligation, including interest accrued to the date of death. Reg. §20.2053-7. However, where only a portion of the property is included in the transferee-decedent's estate, only a corresponding portion of the obligation is usually deductible. *Estate of Horace K. Fawcett,* 64 T.C. 889 (1975), *acq.,* 1978-2 C.B. 2. In most cases the full value of the property is includible in the transferee's gross estate and a deduction is allowable for the unpaid balance of the obligation.

If the transferee's estate is not liable for the indebtedness, only the value of the property less the amount of the indebtedness is includible in his or her estate. Reg. §20.2053-7. Thus, only the net value of the property is includible in the transferee's estate where the purchase was financed with a nonrecourse note.

> **Example 9-2.** *D* purchased Blackacre from *X* for $100,000, of which *D* paid $10,000 down and gave a note for $90,000. *D* and *D*'s estate were personally liable on the note. When *D* died, Blackacre was worth $150,000 and the note had been paid down to $40,000. Under Reg. §20.2053-7, the full value of Blackacre must be included in *D*'s estate, which is entitled to claim a deduction for $40,000. If *D*'s estate were not liable on the note, only the value of Blackacre net of the note would be reported on Schedule A of *D*'s estate tax return. The latter rule should be taken into account when arranging for the purchase of an asset with a situs in the United States by a nonresident alien. In the case of a nonrecourse loan only the net value of the property is includible in the nonresident alien's estate. Otherwise, the full value of the property is includible and only a portion of the indebtedness is allowable as a deduction. *See* §9.9.

§9.6. Income Tax Consequences

The tax deferral brought about by the income tax rules applicable to installment sales was significantly curtailed by the 1986 Act. For a discussion of the changes, *see* Roche, Installment Reporting After the Tax Reform Act of 1986, 66 J. Tax. 80 (1987). The most significant estate planning features of the installment sales rules are discussed below. Note that these restrictions do not apply to private annuities, which may make them more attractive to some clients. The income tax rules applicable to installment sales are intended to allow the gain on the sale of real property or a casual sale of personal property to be reported as payments are received. Gain on an installment sale is reported on the installment method unless the transferor makes a timely election not to use that method. §453(d). Further, an installment sale of depreciable real or personal property will result in recapture of depreciation in the year of sale, with other gain reported under the installment method. §453(i). A taxpayer might elect not to use the method where he or she has current losses that would offset the gain on the sale. The method does not affect the character of gain as capital gain or ordinary income. It also does not affect the way in which losses are reported — the installment method is totally inapplicable to losses.

In general, the installment method applies to any disposition of property where one or more payments will be received in future years. §453(b)(1). It is unavailable with respect to sales of stock or securities that are traded on an established securities market. §453(k)(2). Also, installment sales treatment does not apply to a sale of depreciable property between the taxpayer and a controlled (more than 50-percent-owned) entity, or two controlled entities. §453(g)(1); §1239(b). By reason of §1239 the gain recognized on a sale of depreciable property to a controlled corporation is ordinary income. Similarly, the gain on the sale of a noncapital asset to a controlled partnership is treated as ordinary income. §707(b)(2).

Under the installment method, the gain recognized for a tax year is "that proportion of the payments received in that year which the gross profit (realized or to be realized when payment is completed) bears to the total contract price." §453(c). Sometimes that proportion is called the gross profit ratio, which can also be expressed as a percentage. For purposes of the ratio, gross profit is calculated by reducing the gross selling price by the transferor's adjusted basis and the expenses of sale. For example, if property having a basis of $10,000 is sold for $50,000, the transferor's gross profit is $40,000. The total contract price is the amount the transferor will ultimately receive as a result of the sale, including cash, notes, and other property received, but not encumbrances on the property except to the extent they exceed the transferor's adjusted basis. Except where the property is sold subject to an encumbrance, the total contract price is essentially the sale price of the property. Temp. Reg. §15A.453-1(b)(2)(iii). The selling price does not include interest, whether stated or unstated or original issue discount. Temp. Reg. §15A.453-1(b)(2)(ii).

Example 9-3. *T* sold property to *X* that had a basis of $50,000, subject to a $20,000 mortgage. The purchase price was $100,000, of which $10,000 was paid in the year of sale and the balance of $70,000 was due in equal annual installments with a reasonable rate of interest over the following 7 years. *X* gave *T* a nonnegotiable promissory note for the balance. For purposes of the installment sale rules, *T*'s gross profit was $50,000 (the $100,000 selling price less *T*'s basis of $50,000). The total contract price is $80,000, which is the total amount *T* will receive disregarding the mortgage that is within the amount of *T*'s basis. Accordingly, 62.5% of each payment ($50,000 ÷ $80,000) must be recognized as gain. In addition, *T* must report the interest element of each payment. A purchaser such as *X* is ordinarily not entitled to deduct any portion of the payments made to the seller. Unless the property falls within one of the exceptions to §163(h) the interest payments by *X* will be personal interest expense which is nondeductible.

§9.6.1. Payments Received

In general, gain is recognized only as payments are received by the seller, or when the obligation is sold, exchanged, or otherwise disposed of by him or her. For the purposes of the installment sale rules, the word "payment" has a broad and somewhat undefined meaning. The planner must be alert to the circumstances under which the seller may be treated as having received payment without having actually received any cash or other property.

The receipt of an evidence of indebtedness of the purchaser is not ordinarily treated as payment. §453(f)(3). However, the receipt of an obligation that is payable on demand does constitute payment. §453(f)(4)(A). The receipt of a readily tradeable obligation issued by a corporation or government or political subdivision thereof is also treated as payment. §453(f)(4)(B). Assignment of the installment obligation as collateral security on a loan substantially equal to the amount of the installment obligation is also a disposition. Rev. Rul. 65-185, 1965-2 C.B. 153; *Bogatin v. United States,* 78-2 U.S.T.C. ¶9733 (W.D. Tenn. 1978); *but see* LR 8711002. The following paragraph reviews some other situations that have been found to involve the receipt of payment by the seller.

Security Interests and Escrow Accounts. The transferor's retention of a security interest in the property does not constitute a payment or otherwise jeopardize the application of the installment sale method. However, funds deposited in an escrow account for future distribution to the transferor are considered to be a payment unless there is a substantial restriction, other than the passage of time, upon the transferor's right to receive the sale proceeds. Rev. Rul. 73-451, 1973-2 C.B. 158. Thus, "the substitution of the escrow deposit for the deed of trust as collateral for the installment sale obligation represents payment of the remaining unpaid balance of the installment obligation." Rev. Rul. 77-294, 1977-2 C.B. 173, 174, *amplified by* Rev. Rul. 79-91, 1979-1 C.B. 179. In order to qualify as a substantial restriction upon the transferor's right to the proceeds, the provision "must serve a bona fide purpose of the purchaser, that is, a real and definite restriction placed on the seller or a specific economic benefit conferred on the purchaser." In *Rebecca J. Murray,* 28 B.T.A. 624 (1933), *acq.,* XII-2 C.B. 10 (1933), for example, receipt of the payments from the escrow account was contingent on the sellers refraining from entering a competing business for a period of five years." Rev. Rul. 79-91, 1979-1 C.B. 179.

Property Subject to Encumbrance. Where an existing mortgage is assumed by the purchaser, the mortgage is treated as a payment received only to the extent it exceeds the transferor's basis after adjustment for selling expenses. Reg. §15A.453-1(b)(3)(i). That treatment is consistent with the recognition of gain when the owner makes a gift of property that is subject to encumbrances in excess of its basis. *See* §7.13. Along the same line, the IRS earlier ruled that in the case of a casual sale of personal property, the buyer's assumption and payment of secured and general unsecured liabilities is not considered to be a payment received by the seller if the liabilities were incurred in the ordinary course of business and not to avoid the pre-1980 Act requirement that the initial payment not exceed 30 percent of the selling price. Rev. Rul. 73-555, 1973-2 C.B. 159.

§9.6.2. Alternative Minimum Tax (AMT)

Installment sales may create or increase the alternative minimum tax (AMT) liability in the year of sale. AMT liability may result because, under §56(a), the installment method does not apply to sales of certain property for purposes of computing alternative minimum taxable income. Under §56(a)(6), income from the sale of property described in §1221(1) is determined without regard to the installment method (§1221(1) refers to "stock in trade of the taxpayer or other property of a kind which would properly be included in the inventory of the taxpayer if on hand at the close of the taxable year, or property held by the taxpayer primarily for sale to customers in the ordinary course of his trade or business.") *See* §8.10.

§9.6.3. Inter Vivos Disposition of Obligation

Gain or loss is usually recognized whenever the seller sells, exchanges, or otherwise disposes of the installment obligation. §453B. However, transfers to spouses are excepted from this rule. §§453B(g), 1041. Also, the IRS concedes that the transfer of an obligation to the trustee of a trust is not a disposition if the income of the trust is taxable to the transferor under the grantor trust rules. Rev. Rul. 74-613, 1974-2 C.B. 153. Thus, there is not a §453B disposition where the grantor of the trust is considered the owner of the corpus under §677(a)(2) and therefore is taxable on the principal payments on the installment obligation, even if another taxpayer is the income beneficiary and is taxed on other income of the trust. LR 8450031. Accordingly, the installment sale rules should not deter the holder of an installment obligation from creating a revocable trust. *See* §10.32.3.

A change of underlying security, interest rate, and of the term of the note are not sufficient to be treated as a disposition. LR 8545010. Similarly, pledging installment receivables as security for a line of credit is not a disposition. LR 8711002.

For estate planning purposes perhaps the most important rule is one that treats the cancellation of an installment obligation as a taxable disposition. §453B(f). When a note is cancelled or otherwise becomes unenforceable, the seller is treated as having received the full face amount of the obligation where the obligor is a related person. §453B(f)(2). The term "related person" is discussed in the next section. §9.7.1. In effect, §453B(f) reverses *Miller v. Usry,* 160 F. Supp. 368 (W.D. La. 1958), which held that a father's forgiveness of his son's installment note did not constitute a disposition of the note for income tax purposes. Where the obligor is not a related party, gain or loss is limited to the difference between the seller's basis and the fair market value of the obligation. §453B(a), (f)(1).

> **Example 9-4.** *T* sold Blackacre, which had a basis of $10,000, to *X* for $100,000, represented by an interest-bearing note on which no principal payments were due until 5 years following the sale. *T* gave the note to *X* before any principal payments had been made. If *X* is a related party, *T* will recognize a gain of $90,000 in the year the note becomes unenforceable by reason of the gift. If *X* is not a related party, *T* will recognize gain in an amount equal to the excess of the fair market value of the note over his or her basis in it.

§9.6.4. Disposition at Death

In general, the rules regarding the inter vivos disposition of an installment obligation do not apply to the transmission of an installment obligation at death. §453B(c). Instead, the unreported gain attributable to an installment obligation is treated as an item of income in respect of a decedent. §691(a)(4). As such the gain component is barred by §1014(c) from acquiring a new basis by reason of the holder's death. For that reason the person who receives an installment obligation from a decedent is taxed on payments in the same manner the decedent would have been. §691(a)(1)(B). However, for income tax purposes, the seller's successor is allowed a deduction for the portion of the federal and state death taxes paid by the seller's estate with respect to the unreported gain. §691(c). Where an installment obligation is transferred by a trust to a remainderman by reason of the life tenant's death, the transfer is a disposition which triggers gain to the distributing trust. LR 8317050.

> **Example 9-5.** *T* bequeathed an installment note of an unrelated party to a child, *C.* The note had a value in *T*'s estate equal to its face amount, $20,000, of which $10,000 was attributable to the unreported long-term capital gain. *T*'s estate paid $4,000 in estate tax with respect to the unreported gain. If *C* receives payment of the entire amount due on the note in one year, $20,000, *C* must include the full $10,000 gain in gross income. However, *C* is entitled to a $4,000 deduction for the estate tax paid with respect to the gain. Thus, only $6,000 of the gain is ultimately subject to tax.

The rules cannot be avoided by bequeathing the obligation to the obligor or providing in the seller's will for cancellation of the obligation. Under the 1980 Act, any cancellation of the obligation or its transmission to the obligor triggers the recognition of gain "by the estate of the decedent (or, if held by a person other than the decedent before the death of the decedent, by such person)." §691(a)(5); LR 9108027 (testamentary forgiveness of balance of installment note causes recognition of income by decedent's estate). Although a self-cancelling installment note may work for estate tax purposes (*i.e.,* nothing is included in the seller's gross estate: *see* §9.8.1), the cancellation triggers recognition of the unrealized gain. Rev. Rul. 86-72, 1986-1 C.B. 253. *But see Banoff and Hartz,* Self-Cancelling Installment Notes: New IRS Rulings Expand Opportunities, 65 J. Tax. 146, 150, n.23, 151 (1986) which argues that the seller-decedent rather than the estate should recognize the remaining income. Where the decedent and the obligor are related parties, the obligation is treated as having a value that is not less than its face amount.

> **Example 9-6.** *T* sold capital gain property to a related party, *P,* in exchange for *P*'s note that was payable at the end of 10 years. *T* died prior to the payment of the note, which *T* bequeathed to *P.* Under §691(a) the bequest of the note to *P,* a related obligor, requires *T*'s estate to recognize all of the unreported gain on the sale. The same result would follow if the obligation were cancelled by *T*'s will. Of course, no gain would be recognized by *T*'s estate if the note were bequeathed to a person other than the obligor.

Because of this rule it is particularly important to plan carefully for the transmission of the installment obligation of family members. For example, the obligation might be bequeathed to the obligor's children or to a trust for their benefit instead of being left to the obligor. Even where the obligations will pass to the obligors, the tax cost can be reduced by cancelling or distributing them during a year in which the estate either has capital losses or other deductions to offset the gain or has little or no other income. The transfer of an installment obligation in satisfaction of a pecuniary marital deduction constitutes a disposition triggering gain. LR 9123036.

§9.6.5. Imputed Interest or Original Issue Discount

Intrafamily installment sale transactions must be planned in light of the imputed interest rules of §483 and the original issue discount (OID) rules of §§1272-1275. In general, these rules are designed to prevent the parties from converting the portion of deferred payments that would otherwise constitute interest into capital gain by increasing the purchase price and reducing or eliminating any provision for payment of interest. Thus, a seller cannot treat the full amount of deferred payments as the proceeds of sale and none of it as interest, and a seller usually cannot defer interest if the OID rules apply.

Section 1274 defines debt instruments to which the OID rules apply. These include, generally, debt instruments that are not publicly traded which are issued in exchange for property where there are payments due more than six months after the date of sale or exchange and there is unstated or deferred interest. Unstated interest occurs when the stated interest rate falls below the "test rate" (the "applicable federal rate" or AFR) at or about the time of the contract for sale.

Exempt Intrafamily Transactions. Fortunately the complex rules of §§1272-1275 do not apply to many common intrafamily transactions.

The following transfers are specifically exempted by §1274(c)(3) and are, therefore, subject to §483: (1) sales of farms for $1,000,000 or less by individuals, estates, testamentary trusts, and certain corporations and partnerships, (2) sales of a principal residence by an individual, (3) sales involving $250,000 or less in total payments (principal and interest), (4) sales of patents for a royalty, and (5) qualified sales of land to a family member as defined in §483(e).

Exception for Qualified Debt Instruments. Under §1274A the test and imputation rate to be applied to qualified debt instruments for purposes of §§483 and 1274 is the lesser of the AFR or nine percent compounded semiannually. A qualified debt instrument is one given in exchange for the sale of property other than new Section 38 property, the principal amount of which does not exceed $2.8 million. §1274A(b). For sales at prices in excess of $2.8 million and all sales of section 38 property the test rate is equal to the AFR. Table 9-1 shows the AFR for debt instruments of varying durations. §1274(d).

Section 483 only applies to payments that are due more than 6 months after a sale or exchange of property, one or more of which is due more than one year after the transaction. §483(c)(1)(A). Accordingly, no interest is imputed if all payments are due within one year of the sale. Reg. §1.483-1(b). The interest may be imputed on deferred payments when a sale results in a loss just as it would in the case of a sale at a gain.

Table 9-1
Applicable Federal Rates

Duration of Debt Obligation	*Applicable Federal Rate*
Not over 3 years	Short-term rate
Between 3 and 9 years	Mid-term rate
Over 9 years	Long-term rate

For both the imputed interest and OID rules, the AFR is used to test deferred payments made with respect to sales, exchanges, and contracts entered into after June 30, 1985. These rates are determined monthly under §1274(d) based on the market rates on U.S. obligations. Table 9-2 shows the semiannual compounded rates for November 1991. Rev. Rul. 91-57, 1991-44 I.R.B. 11.

The Proposed Regulations also include formulas that are used to determine whether the requisite test is satisfied. Prop. Reg. §1.483-2(b). Imputed interest is considered paid when payments are made on the contract for cash basis taxpayers, and accrues when payments are due for accrual basis taxpayers. LR 8545003.

Table 9-2
Applicable Federal Rates for November, 1991

Term	*Rate*
Short-term — up to 3 years	5.81%
Mid-term — more than 3 years, up to 9 years	7.09%
Long-term — over 9 years	7.69%

§9.6.6. Sale of Land to Family Member

Under a special provision, imputed interest on $500,000 of sale proceeds for sales or exchanges of land by an individual to a member of his or her family is limited to six percent compounded semiannually. §483(e). For this purpose the term "family" has the same meaning as it does in §267(c)(4) (*i.e.,* siblings, spouse, ancestors, and lineal descendants). However, the interest rate limit only applies to the extent the sales price for such sale (or sales) between the same individuals does not exceed $500,000 for the calendar year. The interest rate limit also does not apply if any party to the sale or exchange is a nonresident alien individual.

§9.7. Resale by Related Person, §453(e)

Prior to the enactment of the Installment Sales Revision Act of 1980 the installment sale was often used to transfer appreciated property to a family member or to the trustee of a trust established by the transferor, who would promptly sell the property for its full market value. In most cases, neither the original transferor nor the related buyer was required to recognize any gain at the time of the resale. *See, e.g., Rushing v. Commissioner,* 441 F.2d 593 (5th Cir. 1971); *William D. Pityo,* 70 T.C. 225 (1978). If the resale did not involve a payment to the original seller, the resale usually did not require him or her to recognize any gain. The related seller usually had no gain on the resale because his or her basis in the property was fixed by the installment sale. In effect, the installment sale technique allowed a family group to realize the gain without subjecting it to current taxation. Again, the restrictions imposed on installment sales do not apply to private annuities.

Changes made by the 1980 Act do not directly prohibit the use of the installment method of reporting gain on sales to related parties. Instead, §453(e) provides that the disposition of the property by a related purchaser triggers recognition of gain by the original transferor. In general, recognition is not triggered where the resale of property other than marketable securities occurs more than two years after the installment sale. (As noted below, after the 1986 Act marketable securities could not be sold on the installment method.) Where the resale rule applies, gain is recognized by the original transferor only to the extent the amount realized on the resale exceeds the total payments made on the original transaction. To that extent the gain flows through and is taxed to the original transferor as if the original transferor received the proceeds of the resale. If the original transferor is required to recognize gain because of a resale, any later payments received by him or her are not taxed until they equal the amount realized from the resale that triggered the acceleration of gain. §453(e)(5).

§9.7.1. Related Person

For purposes of §453, the term "related person" means one whose stock would be attributed to the original transferor under §318(a), excluding paragraph (4), or a person who bears a relationship described in §267(b) to the person disposing of the property. §453(f)(1). Accordingly, the term extends to spouses, brothers and sisters, ancestors and lineal descendants, as well as many trusts, partnerships, and corporations in which the transferor has a direct or indirect interest. For example, the trustee of a trust would be treated as a related party if any of the enumerated relatives of the original transferor is a beneficiary.

§9.7.2. What Dispositions Constitute Resales?

In general, the resale rule applies to voluntary dispositions made by the related party unless it is established to the satisfaction of the IRS that none of the dispositions had the avoidance of federal income tax as one of its principal purposes. §453(e)(7). Thus, the recognition of gain by the original transferor normally will be accelerated if the resale violates the basic rules. However, an exception insulates a corporation's sale of stock that it had purchased in an installment sale. §453(e)(6)(A). Also, a disposition following the death of the original transferor or the related party is not treated as a resale. §453(e)(6)(C). In this connection the Senate Report states that the death exception applies "after the death of either spouse when the spouses hold their interest in the installment obligation or the purchased property as community property or as equal undivided joint interests." S. Rep. No. 1000, 96th Cong., 2d Sess. 16 (1980).

Unfortunately, we have little guidance regarding the application of the nonavoidance exception to other voluntary transfers. According to the House Ways and Means Committee Report, the Regulations will provide definitive rules concerning its application. That Report indicates that most gifts and transfers to controlled corporations or partnerships will not constitute resales:

> In appropriate cases, it is anticipated that the regulations and rulings under the nontax avoidance exception will deal with certain tax-free transfers which normally would not be treated as a second disposition of the property, *e.g.*, charitable transfers, like-kind exchanges, gift transfers, and transfers to a controlled corporation or a partnership. H.R. Rep. No. 1042, 96th Cong., 2d Sess. 16 (1980).

However, a related party should be very cautious about making any gift of the property until the IRS position is established. A related party should also be slow to make an installment sale of the property, which the House Report indicates will be treated as a resale if it "would permit significant deferral of recognition of gain from the initial sale when proceeds from the resale are being collected sooner." Id. at 14.

> **Example 9-7.** *T* sold land with a basis of $20,000 and a fair market value of $100,000 to his son, *S,* in exchange for a $100,000 nonnegotiable promissory note that provided for 6% interest, compounded semiannually. Under the note no principal payments were due for 10 years. *S* sold the land for $100,000 cash immediately after he received it from *T.* Under the resale rule *T* must recognize the full $80,000 gain in the year in which *S,* a related party, sold it. *S* realized no gain on the sale because his cost basis in the land was $100,000. Any subsequent payments received by *T* are tax-free since all of the gain has been taxed to him already under the resale rule. If the second sale had occurred more than 2 years after the original transfer, *T* would not have been required to recognize any gain on the resale.

§9.7.3. Involuntary Transfers

Section 453(e)(6)(B) specifically exempts gain arising from an involuntary conversion if the original transfer occurred before the threat or imminence of the conversion. The House Report also indicates that other involuntary conversions will fall within the nonavoidance exception, including foreclosure by a creditor of the related party and bankruptcy of the related party. Id. at 14.

§9.7.4. Marketable Securities

For sales in tax years beginning after 1986, the installment method does not apply to sales of marketable securities. §453(k)(2). Under §453(f)(2), "the term 'marketable securities' means any security for which, as of the date of the disposition, there was a market on an established securities market or otherwise."

§9.8. Self-Cancelling Installment Note (SCIN)

It is possible that neither the value of the transferred property nor the value of the unpaid balance of the purchaser's obligation will be included in the seller's estate if the obligation terminates on the death of the seller. At least two cases have reached that result where the sale was bona fide and for full and adequate consideration and the provision for cancellation was bargained for by the parties. *Estate of John A. Moss,* 74 T.C. 1239 (1980), *acq.,* 1981-1 C.B. 2 (note given in connection with redemption of decedent's stock by corporation, the other stock in which was owned by unrelated employees of the corporation); *Ruby Louise Cain,* 37 T.C. 185 (1961) (note given in connection with redemption of decedent's stock by corporation, the other stock in which was owned by decedent's son and daughter-in-law). In order to be recognized as a SCIN it is important that the terms of the note reflect the fact that the self-cancelling feature was bargained for. In particular, the total purchase price should be higher than it otherwise would be.

General Counsel Memorandum 39503 states the following basic rules for determining whether a sale for deferred payments is an annuity or an installment sale:

> Where the conveyor of property receives a right to periodic payments for the remainder of his life, with no monetary limit . . . the payments represent an annuity and should be governed by section 72.
>
> When the terms of a property transaction are structured so that there is a stated maximum payout that will be achieved in a period less than the life expectancy of the transferor (as determined at the time of the transaction in accordance with Table I, Treas. Reg. §1.72-9), then the transaction will be characterized as an installment sale with a contingent sale price, and will be treated in accordance with the installment sale rules.

As a corollary of the second rule, when a sale under which a maximum sale price is to be paid over a period that extends beyond the seller's life expectancy, determined under the appropriate IRS table, the transaction will be characterized as an annuity. Thus, G.C.M. 39503 characterized the following transaction as an annuity: "*A* transfers property to *B* in return for *B*'s agreement to make annual payments of $10,000X to *A* until $100,000X is paid, or until *A*'s death, whichever occurs first. *A*'s actuarial life expectancy at the time of the agreement . . . is 9.1 years."

§9.8.1. Estate Tax

The use of SCINs received a boost in G.C.M. 39503, which states that SCINs and private annuities should be treated in the same way for federal estate tax purposes:

> We conclude that in the case of an installment sale, when a death-extinguishing provision is expressly included in the sales agreement and any attendant installment notes, the notes will not be included in the transferor's gross estate for Federal estate tax purposes.
>
> A private annuity also should not be included in the transferor's gross estate for Federal estate tax purposes. Thus, the estate tax consequences of a private annuity and an installment obligation with a death terminating provision are identical in our opinion.

If the transferor receives less than full and adequate consideration, there is some risk that the value of the property at the time of the transferor's death will be included in the transferor's estate under §§2035-2038. Because of the possibility that the consideration may not equal the value of the property, the transferor should not retain any interests or controls that could cause inclusion under those sections. Thus, an individual should not make sales to trusts over which he or she retains discretionary powers of distribution. However, in such a case the amount includible is limited to the excess of the value of the property on the appropriate estate tax valuation date over the consideration received by the transferor. §2043(a).

> **Example 9-8.** *T* sold Blackacre, which was worth $125,000, to a relative, *X,* for a total consideration of $125,000, of which $25,000 was paid at the time of transfer and $100,000 was represented by a note on which a reasonable rate of interest and $10,000 of principal was payable annually. *T* had a life expectancy of 30 years at the time of the sale. The note provided that if *T* died before it was fully paid, no further payments would be due. Under G.C.M. 39503 the note is a SCIN. Accordingly, if *T* dies before all payments are made on the note, under G.C.M. 39503 that note is not includible in *T*'s estate. However, for income tax purposes the cancellation of the note of a relative is treated as a

disposition of the note at its fair market value, which shall not be treated as less than its face amount.

§9.8.2. Income Tax

In some respects a SCIN resembles a private annuity. However, unlike an annuity, the termination of the obligation would probably cause the seller's estate or the seller-decedent to be taxed on the unreported portion of the gain. *See* §9.6.3. That position was taken in G.C.M. 39503: "Thus, the cancellation of the obligation would trigger recognition of gain under section 453B(f)." In connection with consideration of the *Moss* and *Cain* cases, note that the redemption of the stock might be treated as a distribution in the nature of a dividend unless it qualifies under one of the exceptions of §302(b). *See* §11.24.

§9.9. Installment Sales to Nonresident Aliens

For estate tax purposes the extent to which the installment indebtedness can be enforced against the transferee's estate is important, particularly in the case of nonresidents who are not citizens of the United States. If the loan is without recourse and can be collected only from the property and not from the debtor's estate as a whole, the estate may claim the full amount of the indebtedness as a deduction. *Estate of Harcourt Johnstone,* 19 T.C. 44 (1952), *acq.,* 1953-1 C.B. 3. Otherwise, the estate may deduct only that proportion of the indebtedness (and other §§2053 and 2054 items) "which the value of that part of the decedent's gross estate situated in the United States at the time of his death bears to the value of the decedent's entire gross estate wherever situated." Reg. §20.2106-2(a)(2).

C. THE PRIVATE ANNUITY

> A private annuity is generally an arrangement whereby an individual transfers property, usually real estate, to a transferee who promises to make periodic payments to the transferor for the remaining life of the transferor. A private annuity may also include a transaction whereby the transferee agrees to make periodic payments until a specific monetary amount is reached or until the transferor's death, whichever occurs first. Private annuity arrangements are often used for intra-family transfers whereby

> an older family member transfers appreciated property to a younger family member in order to gain tax advantages, *e.g.*, removal of the property from the transferor's gross estate. . . . Neither the statute nor the regulations prescribe any special or different rules where an annuitant uses property to purchase an annuity instead of using cash. G.C.M. 39503.

§9.10. General

As indicated in G.C.M. 39503, a private annuity is usually entered into between family members in order to achieve gift and estate tax savings. It may be used instead of the installment sale to lower the potential gift and estate tax costs of retaining a unique asset within the family. However, the tax and nontax risks of using a private annuity are formidable enough to deter most planners and clients.

In its simplest terms a private annuity involves the transfer of property from one person to another in return for a promise to pay the transferor a specified periodic sum for an agreed period. *Samuel v. Commissioner,* 306 F.2d 682 (1st Cir. 1962). Usually, appreciated property is transferred by an older to a younger family member. If the transaction is properly structured, the initial transfer does not give rise to any current income or gift tax liabilities and no part of the property is includible in the transferor's estate. Achieving a favorable gift tax result may hinge on whether or not the valuation rules of §2702 apply to private annuities and, if so, how the rules are applied. *See* §9.40. Unfortunately, the income tax rules applicable to such a transfer are also not entirely clear.

§9.10.1. Transfer to Trust in Exchange for Annuity

Where the transfer is made to the trustee of a trust created by the transferor, the transaction may be attacked by the IRS as a transfer with a retained income interest. A transfer in trust may be preferable to a transfer to an individual obligor, whose creditors may reach the property. If the transaction is treated as a retained interest trust, the income is taxable to the grantor under §677(a), *Weigl v. Commissioner,* 84 T.C. 1192 (1985); the transfer of the remainder in the trust is taxable as a gift, *Lazarus v. Commissioner,* 513 F.2d 824 (9th Cir. 1975); and the trust principal is includible in the grantor's estate, §2036(a). The degree of control the annuitant retains over the assets transferred was considered the most significant factor by the court in *Weigl,* while the use of the transferred property as the source of annuity payments was apparently considered the most significant factor in *Lazarus.* The Tax Court has rejected annuity treatment where the form of the transaction is disregarded by the annuitant to such an extent as to constitute a sham transaction. *Arthur W. Horstmier,* 46 T.C.M. 738 (1983). The Ninth Circuit Court of Appeals has overturned several decisions of the Tax Court that treated transactions with trusts as retained interest transfers rather than annuities.

Private annuity transactions have been upheld against IRS attack where the annuitant transferred appreciated stock to a foreign trust in exchange for an annuity of equal value. *Stern v. Commissioner,* 747 F.2d 555 (9th Cir. 1984); *Syufy v. United States,* 818 F.2d 1457 (9th Cir. 1987). Key factors in these decisions were: (1) the limited control exercised by the annuitant over the assets transferred to the trust; and (2) the fact that the trusts were not mere conduits for the income from the assets, but rather, assumed a risk that all of the assets would be consumed in paying the annuity. It is interesting to note that while control by the grantor over the trust was limited, there still was some evidence of control (*e.g.,* changing trustees, changing trust situs, selecting of new investment counselor, and loans to the grantors). In *Stern* the Ninth Circuit observed, in note 13, that, "[W]here there is no tie between the trust income and an annuity, the transaction should not be recharacterized as a transfer in trust unless the circumstances indicate that the taxpayers retain control or beneficial enjoyment of the trust assets."

The law now effectively precludes the use of foreign trusts, however. In particular, §1491 imposes an excise tax of 35 percent on transfers of appreciated assets to foreign entities. Also, foreign trusts with U.S. beneficiaries are treated as grantor trusts under §679.

§9.10.2. Planning Considerations

A private annuity is not subject to the limitations that apply to installment sales. Thus, the transferee (obligor) may promptly resell the property free of the resale rules that apply to installment sales. In addition, private annuities are not subject to the interest and OID rules. In structuring private annuities, favorable outcomes depend upon the proper valuation of the property transferred and of the annuity. Accordingly, property that does not have a ready market value should be valued by an expert. If an annuity is properly structured, the interest of the annuitant (valued according to the actuarial factors prescribed by the IRS) should have a value exactly equal to the transferred property. A private annuity transaction should not involve a gift element, particularly where a trust is the transferee-obligor. Where the property is transferred to a trust, the amount of the annuity should be fixed and not related to the income of the trust and the annuitant should not retain control over the trustee or of investments of the trust. *See,* Loftis, When Can a Trust Be Used to Fund a Private Annuity Without Creating a Retained Interest?, 14

Est. Plan. 218 (1987). The typical annuitant's interest, the right to receive specific amounts at least annually, should be a qualified interest for purposes of §2702.

A private annuity for a term of years may fit the circumstances of some clients better than an ordinary private annuity, installment sale, or SCIN. Hartz & Banoff, Planning Opportunities Available Using a Private Annuity for a Term of Years, 65 J. Tax. 302 (1986). For example, a private annuity for a term provides the annuitant with larger annual payments and limits the maximum number of payments the obligor is required to make.

A private annuity for a term of years calls for payments to be made to the annuitant for a period of years that exceeds the annuitant's normal life expectancy. Such an arrangement gives the transferee-obligor the assurance that the number of payments will not exceed the stated maximum. This type of annuity is almost indistinguishable from a SCIN, the main difference being a term in excess of the annuitant's life expectancy, while a SCIN has a term shorter than the transferor's life expectancy. *See* G.C.M. 39503. Some uncertainty exists regarding the proper life expectancy to use for this purpose: G.C.M. 39503 and Rev. Rul. 86-72, 1986-1 C.B. 253, refer to the tables under Reg. §1.72-9, while Rev. Rul. 86-32, 1986-1 C.B. 252, refers to U.S. Life Tables: 1969-1971. With the enactment of §7520 presumably the annuitant's life expectancy will be determined according to the Life Table for the Total Population, Table 1, U.S. Decennial Life Tables for 1979-81, referred to as Table 80CNSMT. That table is included in Actuarial Values, Alpha Vol., IRS Pub. No. 1457.

§9.11. NONTAX CONSIDERATIONS

As mentioned above, a private annuity may help preserve a farm, a business enterprise, or other unique asset within the family and free the transferor from the burdens and risks of management. A forced sale of the property to an outsider may be avoided if the family member-transferee can afford to make the necessary payments. However, the overall tax savings may be diminished if the transferee must sell the property in order to make payments or to meet other expenses.

The uncertain duration of the payments of an ordinary annuity may be a source of financial problems as well as family discord. When a parent and a child are parties to a private annuity, the arrangements may cause some resentment on the part of other children — particularly if the parent does not survive as long as expected according to the actuarial tables that were used to calculate the amount of the annuity payments. In that case the child-purchaser enjoys a windfall of sorts. On the other hand, the child-purchaser may become resentful if the annuitant "lives too long." These concerns may suggest the desirability of exploring the use of a private annuity for a fixed term of years.

Before entering into a private annuity, the parties should consider very carefully the financial, emotional, and domestic relations aspects of the transaction.

First, some risk is involved because of the requirement that the transferee's promise be unsecured in order to defer the taxation of the gain element. However, the risk caused by the unsecured nature of the obligation is reduced if a trust is the transferee-obligor. Second, the property may be entirely expended during the annuitant's lifetime and the transferee will be unable to make the required payments. The transferee might also be unable to make the required payments because of unrelated tort claims, business reverses, or other events. Third, continuation of the payments could be threatened if the transferee predeceases the annuitant. The obligation to continue the payments could deplete the transferee's estate, particularly if the annuitant lives longer than expected. However, these problems can be relieved to some degree by insuring the transferee's life. Fourth, the planned retention of the property within the family could be jeopardized by dissolution of the transferee's marriage. For example, a decree of dissolution may allocate the property between the transferee and the transferee's spouse. *See, e.g., Stanger v. Stanger,* 571 P.2d 1126 (Idaho 1977) (ranch received by husband in exchange for annuity is community property).

Substantial legal costs and other expenses may be incurred in connection with a private annuity. Because of the complex and evolving nature of the tax rules, it is almost always necessary for the planner to do some legal research. Additional time is also required to project the tax consequences and to prepare the necessary documents. The uncertainty of the tax rules and the overall complexity of the transaction may cause the fees to be significantly greater for a private annuity than for an inter vivos trust or an installment sale. As noted above, independent representation of the transferor and transferee is desirable because of the inherent conflict in their economic interests. It may also be desirable to obtain a professional appraisal of any property for which there is not a ready market.

§9.12. Income Tax Consequences of Transfer

No gain or loss arises at the time of the initial transaction (*i.e.,* when the property is transferred for an unsecured private annuity). According to the courts the transferee's obligation cannot be valued: "Where both the annuitant's life span and the obligor's ability to pay are uncertain no fair market value should be ascribed to the contract or obligation." *Commissioner v. Kann's Estate,* 174 F.2d 357, 359 (3d Cir. 1949).

Ordinarily gain or loss in a private annuity transaction is reported by the annuitant as annuity payments are received. *See* §9.13.

The same rules apply in the case of an annuity issued by a corporation that writes annuity contracts infrequently. *See 212 Corp.*, 70 T.C. 788, 799 (1978). In contrast, gain is recognized immediately by the transferor where appreciated property is transferred to a corporation, trust, or other organization that, from time to time, issues annuity contracts. Rev. Rul. 62-136, 1962-2 C.B. 12. In *Dix v. Commissioner,* 392 F.2d 313 (4th Cir. 1968), the court held that the ruling only applied to corporations that wrote enough annuity contracts to get a good spread of the actuarial risk.

In two cases a bare majority of the Tax Court held that the gain on a private annuity must be reported in the year of the transfer if the annuity is adequately secured. *212 Corp.*, 70 T.C. at 802-803; *Estate of Lloyd G. Bell,* 60 T.C. 469 (1973). According to those cases, where appreciated property is transferred for an annuity that has an actuarially determinable value in excess of the transferor's basis, "the exchange represents a 'closed transaction' and the resulting gain is taxable in the year of exchange." *212 Corp.*, 70 T.C. at 803. Presumably this approach would also apply where the transfer results in a loss. That is, where property with a fair market value below its adjusted basis is transferred in exchange for a secured annuity the loss would be deductible in the year of the exchange, subject to the other provisions of the Code, particularly §267. In the long run it seems likely that the Tax Court approach will be rejected in favor of one that allows the annuitant to report a pro rata part of each payment as gain. That approach was suggested by the dissenting judges in *Bell* and *212 Corp.*, who pointed out that the Regulations provide for proration where appreciated property is transferred to a charitable organization in exchange for an annuity. *See* §8.37. The mere fact that the annuity is secured should not cause such a radically different tax result.

Where the annuity is secured, it is unclear whether the transferor could invoke the revised installment sales rules to avoid reporting all of the gain in the year of transfer. As mentioned above, Congress apparently did not intend that private annuity transactions should be subject to the installment sales rules. *See* §9.3.

§9.13. Income Taxation of Annuitant

The tax treatment of annuity payments is simple enough where no gain results from the transfer of property in exchange for an annuity. That will occur, for example, when cash or property with a basis equal to its fair market value is transferred in exchange for an annuity. Since no gain results from the transfer, each annuity payment will consist of only two elements — a nontaxable recovery of capital, and a fully taxable annuity element. The amount allocated to each element depends upon the exclusion ratio, which is simply the investment in the contract divided by the expected return. In these "no gain" cases, the investment in the contract is the amount of cash or the value of the property transferred. The expected return is the amount of the annual payment multiplied by the life expectancy of the annuitant. Presumably the life expectancies provided in Table I or V of Reg. §1.72-9 are used for this purpose. *See* §8.37. In due course they should be revised on the basis of Table 80CNSMT. For annuities with starting dates after 1986, the total amount that may be excluded from gross income is limited to the investment in the contract. §72(b).

Example 9-9. *P,* 65 years old, transferred cash of $100,000 to child, *C,* in exchange for *C*'s unsecured promise to make a payment of $14,937.41 to *P* each year for life. The transaction was entered into in a month during which an 11% interest rate applied under §7520. Under Table S(11.0) the factor for valuing an annuity payable to a person aged 65 is 6.7764.

$$\$14,937.41 \times 6.7764 = \$100,000$$

Accordingly, the transfer does not involve any gift. For income tax purposes *P*'s investment in the contract is $100,000.

According to Table V, Reg. §1.72-9, *P*'s life expectancy is 20 years. Thus, the expected return is $298,748.20 ($14,937.41 × 20). The exclusion ratio applicable to each payment is 33.47% ($100,000 ÷ $298,748.20). *P* is entitled to exclude $4,999.99 (33.47% × $14,748.20) of each payment as a return of capital for up to 20 years. The other $9,937.42 is taxed as ordinary income, as is the full amount of all payments after 20 years. If *P* dies before all payments are made, a deduction will be allowed for any unrecovered exclusion on *P*'s final income tax return. *C* is not entitled to any deduction for the payments made to *P.*

The transaction described in Example 9-9 would involve a gift from *P* to *C* if the value of the property transferred exceeded the value of the annuity. In that case, *P* might incur some gift tax liability. *See* §9.15. Also, *C*'s basis in the gift portion of the property would be determined under §1015. *See also* Rev. Rul. 55-119, 1955-1 C.B. 352.

The proper income treatment of annuity payments is less clear where appreciated property is transferred to a noncharity in exchange for an unsecured annuity. In this case the annuitant is also entitled to exclude a portion of each payment based upon the exclusion ratio. However, the IRS has ruled that the investment in the contract is limited to the transferor's adjusted basis in the property transferred in exchange for the annuity and not its fair market value. Rev. Rul. 69-74, 1969-1 C.B. 43. It reasoned that "[s]ince the amount of the gain is not taxed in full at the time of the transaction, such amount does not represent a part of the 'premiums or other consideration' paid for the annuity contract." Id. According to the IRS, each payment is initially composed of three elements: a tax-free return of capital, a capital gain element, and a fully taxable ordinary income element. The tax-free element is determined by dividing the investment in the contract (the adjusted basis in the property transferred) by the expected return. The capital gain element is calculated by dividing the gain (the value of the annuity determined by applying the appropriate factor from Table S of IRS Pub. No. 1457 less the adjusted basis in the property) by the life expectancy of the annuitant according to Table V, Reg. §1.72-9. All of the gain is taxed if the annuitant survives as long as expected under the mortality table. According to Revenue Ruling 69-74, the capital gain element of any payments after expiration of life expectancy per the tables is taxed as ordinary income. Finally, the remainder of each payment is taxed as ordinary income (total payment − (return of capital + capital gain)). For annuities with starting dates after 1986, once the period of life expectancy originally projected has expired, all payments will be taxed as ordinary income as the full amount of invested capital and capital gain will have been recovered. §72(b).

Example 9-10. The facts are the same as those of Example 9-9, except that *P* transferred securities with a basis of $10,000 and a fair market value of $100,000 in exchange for the annuity payments of $14,937.41 each year. Under the approach taken in Revenue Ruling 69-74, the exclusion ratio would be 3.3473%, which would allow *P* to exclude $499.99 of each $14,937.41 annual payment as a return of capital. *P* would be required to report 30.1257% of each payment ($4,500.00) as capital gain until the full $90,000 gain is reported. The remainder of each annual payment ($9,937.40) is ordinary income. If *P* survives for 20 years the full amount of each subsequent payment would be taxable as ordinary income.

Revenue Ruling 69-74 conflicts with the 1939 Code rules as set forth in Rev. Rul. 239, 1953-2 C.B. 53. It also conflicts with the pre-1987 methods of taxing payments received under a gift annuity issued by a charitable organization. Reg. §1.1011-2(c), example 8. *See* §8.29 for a discussion of the gift annuity rules.

The exclusion ratio for charitable gift annuities is based on a "top down" approach. The fair market value of the property contributed, rather than its basis, is used to calculate the exclusion ratio, and the capital gain element is a portion of the exclusion. Reg. §1.1011-2(c), example 8. *See* §8.37.

Under Revenue Ruling 69-74, the exclusion ratio is computed according to the transferor's basis in the property, and the capital gain element is computed separately and in addition to the exclusion ratio. The significance of this difference is that under the pre-1987 provisions of §72(b) the exclusion ratio was nontaxable after the amount of the capital gain was recognized. Thus, an annuity resulting from a transfer to a charitable organization resulted in a larger total exclusion for transferors who survived beyond their normal life expectancy. Since the 1986 Act revised §72, the exclusion ratio applies only until the full amount of investment is recovered. This reconciles the differences between the above approaches to calculating the exclusion ratio. The change to §72 applies to annuities with starting dates after December 31, 1986.

A further difference between a charitable gift annuity and a private annuity results from the basis allocation rules of §1011(b). In a charitable gift annuity, the basis is allocated between the gift and the annuity elements. In other annuities, the basis is apparently allocated first to the annuity purchase, and then to the gift. This difference is demonstrated by Revenue Ruling 69-74 and Reg. §1.1011-2(c), example 8.

A transfer of appreciated property involves a gift from the transferor to the transferee-obligor where the value of the property transferred exceeds the value of the annuity. Unless such an exchange is an ordinary business transaction, Revenue Ruling 69-74 requires the excess to be disregarded in determining the income tax consequences to the transferor. The gift portion is significant when it comes to determining the transferee's basis for purposes of determining gain or loss or computing depreciation. *See* Rev. Rul. 55-119, 1955-1 C.B. 352. *See also* §9.14.

Finally, a private annuity could be used, in effect, to circumvent the resale rule of §453(e) that applies to installment sales. G.C.M. 39503. For example, if the family unit wishes to dispose of an asset, the gain on sale can still be recognized over a period of years if the asset is exchanged for an annuity and subsequently sold by the transferee. This could even be applied to marketable securities, which are not eligible for installment sale treatment. *See* §9.7.4.

§9.14. Income Taxation of Transferee

A transferee has not been allowed any income tax deduction for payments made to the annuitant even though the annuitant must report part of each payment as income. That rule prevailed prior to the amendment of §163(h), which prohibits deductions for personal interest. "Most courts hold that the entire amount of each annuity payment constitutes a payment of the purchase price of the assets received in exchange for the promise to pay the annuity. Thus the payments constitute capital expenditures, no part of which is excludible [deductible] as 'interest on indebtedness.' " *Dix v. Commissioner,* 392 F.2d 313, 318 (4th Cir. 1968). The denial of a deduction is consistent with the method for determining the transferee's basis in the assets, which takes into account the total amount of payments made by the transferee. *See, e.g., Perkins v. United States,* 701 F.2d 771 (9th Cir. 1983). Without a specific statutory basis for a deduction it is unlikely that a deduction for any part of the payments made by the transferee will be allowed. In contrast, in the case of an installment sale the actual or imputed interest paid by the purchaser is interest that is deductible to the extent it is not personal interest. *See* §163(h).

The general rules for calculating depreciation and gain or loss are set out in Rev. Rul. 55-119, 1955-1 C.B. 352, which was issued under the 1939 Code. Its rules applied to transactions arising under the 1954 Code. Rev. Rul. 72-81, 1972-1 C.B. 98. Presumably, they will also apply under the 1986 Code.

§9.14.1. Depreciation

The allowance for depreciation is initially based upon the value of the annuity contract determined under Table S of IRS Pub. No. 1457. Any annuity payments made in excess of that value are added to the basis of the property for the purpose of determining future depreciation. Once the annuitant dies, the depreciation allowance is fixed by the total amount of annuity payments made reduced by the amount of depreciation deductions previously allowed.

Example 9-11. *P,* a 70-year-old, transferred nondepreciable property worth $20,000 and depreciable real property worth $80,000 that had a useful life of 50 years and a salvage value of $10,000 to child, *C,* in exchange for *C*'s promise to pay *P* an annuity of $16,494.57 per year. The transfer was made during a period that an 11% interest rate was applicable. Using a factor from Table S, 6.0626, the value of the annuity is $100,000. *C* elects under §168(g)(7) to use the straight-line method for calculating depreciation. The prescribed useful life per §168(g)(2) is 40 years. *C* is entitled to claim a depreciation allowance of $1,750.00 per year, calculated as follows:

$$\frac{\frac{\$80{,}000}{\$100{,}000} \times \$100{,}000 - \$10{,}000}{40} = \$1{,}750.00$$

If *P* died after 5 years, the future depreciation allowance would be $1,456.52 per year, determined as follows:

$$\frac{\frac{\$80{,}000}{\$100{,}000} \times \$82{,}472.85 - (\$10{,}000 + \$8{,}750)}{35} = \$1{,}456.52$$

In the latter calculation the figure of $82,472.85 is the total amount of payments actually made to *P* and $8,750.00 is the total amount of depreciation deductions allowed for the period prior to *P*'s death.

§9.14.2. Gain or Loss

Where the property is disposed of by the obligor after the annuitant's death, for the purpose of determining gain or loss its basis is the total of the payments made under the contract, less the total amount of depreciation allowable to the transferor. Thus, in Example 9-11, if *C* sold the property for $100,000 one year after *P*'s death, the gain would be $27,733.67:

Sale price		$100,000.00
Less:		
Payments to *P*	$82,472.85	
Minus depreciation	−10,206.52	−72,266.33
Gain		$ 27,733.67

The computation of gain or loss is more complicated if the transferee disposes of the property prior to the annuitant's death. For the purpose of determining gain the transferee's basis is the total of payments made under the contract (reduced by the total amount of allowable depreciation) plus the value of future payments due under the contract. *See, e.g.,* LR 8102029. When it comes to calculating the amount of a loss, the basis is limited to the total amount of payments made to the time of sale reduced by the total amount of depreciation allowable. Additional gain or loss may be recognized by the transferee depending upon how many future payments are made by the time of the annuitant's death. For example, further gain is recognized if the annuitant dies before the transferee has made payments equal to the amount of the basis used for purposes of computing gain. In the case of a disposition that gives rise to a recognized loss, any subsequent payments made to the annuitant give rise to losses in the year or years made.

§9.15. Gift Tax Consequences

If the value of the property transferred exceeds the actuarially determined value of the annuity, the transfer involves a gift unless it is an ordinary business transaction. Rev. Rul. 69-74, 1969-1 C.B. 43; *LaFargue v. Commissioner,* 800 F.2d 936 (9th Cir. 1986). In the case of a transfer to an individual, any gift to the transferee should qualify for the annual exclusion. *See* §2503(b). On the other hand, the gift tax exclusion may not be available with respect to a transaction between an individual and a trustee. Of course, the transferor makes a gift to the annuitant when the annuity is payable to a person other than the transferor. Such a gift qualifies for the annual exclusion where the commencement of the annuity payments is not deferred. *See* Reg. §25.2503-3(b). The transaction will result in a gift by the transferee if the value of the annuity exceeds the value of the property transferred. Here again, the annual exclusion should be available if the annuity is payable currently.

Private annuity transactions are usually planned to avoid any gift element and to avoid inclusion in the transferor's estate. The rules of §2702 should not apply to private annuities entered into by members of the same family. However, if they do, perhaps the annual payments due under the annuity may be considered to be a qualified interest, the total value of which can be taken into account in determining the gift tax consequences of the transaction. The right to receive the annuity payment at least annually should constitute a qualified interest under §2702(b). In any case, the property to be transferred should be valued carefully. The amount of the annuity should be planned in light of the proper interest rate under §7520 (120 percent of the federal midterm rate for the month in which the transfer is made) and the appropriate factor from Table S. Before entering into a private annuity the parties should also consider the economic realities of the transaction, including the impact of income taxes on the transferor and transferee.

§9.16. Estate Tax Consequences

Significant estate tax problems are likely to arise in two situations: (1) where the value of the property transferred exceeds the value of the annuity and (2) where the annuity is payable to another person after the death of the transferor. As noted above, the transaction may be vulnerable when the annuity is issued by a trust, particularly when there is a tie-in between the amount of the trust income and the amount of annuity payments and the annuitants retain some control. Also, where the transferor retains use of the property for life through an implied agreement or understanding, the transferred property is includible in the gross estate under §2036. *Estate of Maria Bianchi,* 44 T.C.M. 422 (1982). In other situations the threat of inclusion in the transferor's estate is virtually eliminated because of the full adequacy of the consideration received in exchange for the property transferred (*i.e.,* the value of the annuity equals or exceeds the value of the property transferred). In this connection note that the valuation rules of §2702 only apply for gift tax purposes. If the value of the property transferred exceeds the value of the annuity, the amount includible in the transferor's estate is reduced by the value of the annuity at the time of transfer. §2043(a).

Where the annuity is payable to another person after the transferor's death, the amount includible in the transferor's estate is determined under §2039. The annuity is first valued under Table S. Next, the portion of the annuity value includible in the decedent's estate is determined by the proportion of the purchase price that he or she contributed. §2039(b). Thus, if the decedent had paid half of the cost of the annuity, only half of its value would be included in his or her gross estate. A marital deduction should be allowable where the successor annuitant is the decedent's surviving spouse who is a U.S. citizen. *See* §2056(b)(7)(C).

The property transferred to the obligor is includible in the obligor's estate. Of course, if the obligor predeceases the annuitant, the obligor's estate is entitled to a deduction for the actuarial value of the payments it is required to make to the annuitants. *Estate of Charles H. Hart,* 1 T.C. 989 (1943). However, where the annuitant dies prior to the time the obligor's estate tax return is filed, the deduction may be limited to the amount of the payments actually made. *Estate of Chesterton v. United States,* 551 F.2d 278 (Ct. Cl.), *cert. denied,* 434 U.S. 835 (1977).

D. THE GIFT OR SALE AND LEASEBACK

§9.17. General

The income tax changes made by the 1986 Act largely eliminated the attractiveness of a gift or sale and leaseback, which were previously very popular. Prior to the 1986 Act many high income individuals used the transfer and leaseback of business property to shift income to family members or trusts that would be subject to lower income tax rates. The tax advantages previously enjoyed by taxpayers who entered into such transactions are no longer available. First, the income tax advantage of shifting income to another family member is severely limited by the compressed income tax rate structure that was adopted in 1986. Second, the 1986 Act effectively destroyed the income tax advantage of creating a short-term irrevocable trust. Under §673 the grantor is treated as the owner of a trust if at the inception of the trust the reversionary interest of the grantor (or the grantor's spouse) has a value of five percent or more. The inability to retain a reversionary interest that will take effect after a relatively short period killed the interest of many taxpayers in the use of trusts — at least those who would be reluctant to give or sell the property to other family members or to trusts for the benefit of others. The attractiveness of the device was also limited by other changes, including the adoption of the Kiddie Tax. Prior to the 1986 Act the typical plan involved the transfer of property used in the transferor's business to the trustee of a short-term trust who leased the property back to the transferor. At the end of ten years (the minimum period required under the pre-1986 version of §673), the property would revert to the grantor. In the interim the grantor would deduct the lease payments made to the trustee, who would claim depreciation deductions on the income tax returns of the trust. With the change in §673 noted above, the income tax goals can be achieved only by making more permanent transfers. In earlier years the main problem with transfer-leasebacks, particularly in the case of short-term *Clifford* trusts, was the IRS challenge to the deductibility of rental payments by the transferor-lessee.

The chance that the IRS and the courts will allow the transferor's rental payments to be deducted is vastly greater where the lessee does not serve as trustee and does not retain any interest in the property. For example, in one case the IRS denied a deduction for rental payments made while the lessee held a reversionary interest in the property, but allowed a deduction for rental payments made after the lessee relinquished his reversionary interest. *C. James Mathews,* 61 T.C. 12, 15 (1973), *rev'd,* 520 F.2d 323 (5th Cir. 1975), *cert. denied,* 424 U.S. 967 (1976). In some instances the IRS had challenged the deduction although there was an independent trustee and the transferor did not retain a reversionary interest. *E.g., Skemp v. Commissioner,* 168 F.2d 598 (7th Cir. 1948).

Deductions were also challenged, but allowed, in one case where the transferees were minors and the transferor acted as their guardian. *Brooke v. United States,* 468 F.2d 1155 (9th Cir. 1972). The probability that deductions will not be allowed is also greater where the property is sold to a trust or another family member. Of course, the gift tax cost of an outright transfer and the economic effects of not retaining an interest in the property must also be considered.

Some circuits disallow rental deductions with respect to pre-March

2, 1986 transfers to short-term trusts, while five or more of the circuits and the Tax Court allow deductions when certain requirements are met. Kiley, The Evolving Gift-Leaseback Analysis in Light of *May* and *Rosenfeld,* 59 Notre Dame L. Rev. 921, 922 (1984). The IRS has also announced that it will not litigate three-party gift-leasebacks (*e.g.,* where property is gifted from one family member to another, and leased to a family-owned corporation). A.O.D. 1984-038.

An installment sale and leaseback is a variation on the theme that involves little or no gift tax cost. However, a sale and leaseback transaction is ordinarily more complicated than a gift and leaseback and could require the transferor to report a gain. The gain would be taxable as ordinary income to the extent it involved depreciation recapture under §§1245 and 1250. An installment sale and leaseback transaction may also involve annual forgiveness of the installment notes, as in *Hudspeth v. Commissioner,* 509 F.2d 1224 (9th Cir. 1975). In *Hudspeth* the parents avoided the 160-acre limit on the quantity of federally irrigated land that may be owned by one person (320 acres by a husband and wife) by making installment sales of the excess acreage to their children. The children in turn leased the purchased property to their parents. Installment payments were made by the children in part with rental payments from the parents and the balance with cash gifts from the parents. The Tax Court held that the original transfers to the children were not bona fide sales and, therefore, constituted gifts of the entire interest in the property. On appeal the Ninth Circuit reversed, holding that the transfers were sales and not gifts. "The parents were under no obligation to continue to make annual gifts to the children although they expected to do it. The children's obligation to make the annual payments continued regardless of whether the parents made these gifts." Id. at 1227.

On the negative side, an outright gift or sale of the property involves some of the same nontax risks as a private annuity. For example, the property is subject to disposition by the transferee and to the claims of the transferee's creditors. However, in the case of a sale the transferor could retain a security interest without significantly jeopardizing the outcome. The seller's interests might also be protected to some degree by the terms of the lease.

§9.18. Overall Consequences

Some current income tax savings may result from a gift and leaseback transaction if the transferee is subject to a lower income tax rate than the transferor. The Kiddie Tax eliminates the differential in some cases, but not where the rental income is received and retained by a trust for distribution to the transferor's minor children at a later time. Viewed most simply, the transaction will increase the income tax deductions available to the transferor by the excess of the annual rental cost over the otherwise allowable depreciation deduction. The taxes and interest paid by the transferor may also be deductible where he or she retains an interest in the property and is personally liable for them. *Walther v. Commissioner,* 316 F.2d 708 (7th Cir. 1963) (Indiana law; grantor is liable for and may deduct mortgage interest payments on property transferred to short-term trust).

The depreciation deduction for property held in trust is generally allocated between the beneficiaries and the trustee on the basis of the trust income allocable to each. §167(h). Where the income must be computed and distributed without regard to depreciation, the entire amount of the deduction is allowed to the beneficiary. In contrast, where local law or the instrument requires the establishment of a depreciation reserve, the deduction is allowed to the trustee and not to the beneficiary. Reg. §1.167(h)-1(b). The beneficiaries' cash flow position is enhanced if the deduction is available to them. A trust instrument should contain an appropriate provision dealing with this issue. The original Uniform Principal and Income Act, 7B U.L.A. 217 (1985), does not authorize a depreciation reserve. However, §13(a)(2) of the Revised Uniform Principal and Income Act, 7B U.L.A. 176 (1985), requires that a charge be made against income for depreciation where it is called for by generally accepted accounting principles.

In the case of a transfer in exchange for an annuity, or in a bargain sale for an annuity, the gift and estate tax consequences should be considered. In a bargain sale, gift tax may apply. If there is a reversionary interest, it is includible in the transferor's gross estate, and therefore, one cannot assume that an annuity transaction will reduce the size of the transferor's gross estate. *See* §9.22.

If the transaction takes the form of a sale, the savings are reduced to the extent the transferor must pay taxes on the gain. However, a sale does increase the basis against which the transferee may compute depreciation. A sale for the full market value of the property eliminates any taxable gift and prevents the property from being included in the transferor's gross estate if the rental is fair and the transaction is properly planned. *See* §9.22.2.

In evaluating the transaction, the lawyer and client must also consider the professional fees and other costs of carrying out the transaction. When those costs are aggregated with the offsetting tax considerations, the potential savings may be slight. The evaluation is incomplete unless the client also takes into account the nontax consequences of the transaction. For some, the loss of the ability to deal directly with the property is significant. Aggressive clients may savor the opportunity to duel with the IRS, while more cautious ones would prefer to avoid the anxiety of an audit and confrontation with the IRS.

§9.19. Income Tax Consequences of Transfer

A gift of business property to a trust or other beneficiary does not ordinarily require the transferor or the transferee to report any income. There are exceptions to the rule for special types of property. Thus, an early disposition of section 38 property requires investment credit recapture. *See* §47(a). In the case of a gift the transferor's basis in the property carries over to the transferee as provided in §§1015 and 1041 for purposes of depreciation and otherwise.

Where the transfer is made by sale, gain may be recognized by the transferor, which can be reported on the installment basis in appropriate cases. *See* Part B. Installment obligations arising in the sale-leaseback context are subject to more stringent interest rate rules under §1274. The minimum interest rate is 110 percent of the AFR (§1274(e)); the "lower discount rate" of 9 percent under §1274A(a) does not apply. *See* §9.6.5.

A sale at the market price of the property would avoid the imposition of any gift tax on the transaction and should avoid any threat of inclusion in the transferor's estate. However, a sale may involve depreciation recapture where §1245 (personal) property or §1250 (real) property is transferred. The rules of those sections apply to sale and leaseback transactions. Reg. §1.1245-1(a)(3).

> **Example 9-12.** Last year *T* sold equipment to an irrevocable trust for $8,000. *T* had paid $10,000 for the equipment and had taken depreciation deductions of $4,000 during the time *T* owned it. *T*'s gain on the sale was $2,000 — the difference between the $8,000 sale price and the $6,000 basis. The entire amount of the gain is ordinary income under §1245(a) and not gain realized from the sale of §1231 property. *See* Reg. §1.1245-1(b).

The gain would also be ordinary income where the sale is made between an individual and a controlled corporation. *See* §1239. Of course, under §267 losses on transfers to related taxpayers are not deductible.

§9.20. Income Tax Consequences of Rental Payments

If the transaction is properly structured the rental payments should be deductible. However, the IRS has taken a very narrow view of the circumstances in which rental payments are properly deductible in leaseback cases. Section 162(a)(3) allows a deduction as an ordinary and necessary business expense for

> (3) rentals or other payments required to be made as a condition to the continued use or possession, for purposes of the trade or business, of property to which the taxpayer has not taken or is not taking title or in which he has no equity.

Where there is a prearranged plan of transfer and leaseback, the IRS has argued that no deduction is allowable because the overall transaction lacks any valid business purpose. Thus, the rental payments made by the lessee are not ordinary and necessary expenses for which a deduction is allowable. Where the lessee retains a reversionary interest the IRS has sometimes also denied the deduction because the taxpayer had an equity interest in the property. *See* §162(a)(3).

Another view of the business purpose requirement has been taken by most courts:

> [W]e think that where, as here, a grantor gives business property to a valid irrevocable trust over which he retains no control and then leases it back, it is not necessary for us to inquire as to whether there was a business reason for making the gift. Admittedly there was none. Under such circumstances the test of business necessity should be made by viewing the situation as it exists after the gift is made. At that point, since Alden Oakes needed a building for practicing medicine, he agreed to rent the property from the trustee for a reasonable amount. Consequently, we believe there is a sound basis for holding that the rent paid by Oakes was, in terms of section 162, both "ordinary and necessary" and "required to be made as a condition to continued use . . . of property." *Alden B. Oakes,* 44 T.C. 524, 532 (1965).

The Tax Court and most appellate courts have rejected the IRS position, concluding instead that it is sufficient if the lease itself serves a valid business purpose. As the court observed in *Quinlivan v. Commissioner,* 599 F.2d 269, 273 (8th Cir.), *cert. denied,* 444 U.S. 996 (1979), "Congress had specified that the business purpose test is concerned with the 'continued use or possession' of the property. There is no justification for adding an inquiry into the origin of the lessor's title in applying this requirement." *See also Rosenfeld v. Commissioner,* 706 F.2d 1277 (2d Cir. 1983); *Brown v. Commissioner,* 180 F.2d 926 (3d Cir.), *cert. denied,* 340 U.S. 814 (1950); *Skemp v. Commissioner,* 168 F.2d 598 (7th Cir. 1948). On the other hand, the Fourth Circuit will not bifurcate the transfer and leaseback — it insists that the overall transaction have a valid business purpose. *Perry v. United States,* 520 F.2d 235 (4th Cir. 1975), *cert. denied,* 423 U.S. 1052 (1976).

§9.20.1. Economic Reality

The Fifth Circuit once championed the business purpose test. *Van Zandt v. Commissioner,* 341 F.2d 440 (5th Cir.), *cert. denied,* 382 U.S. 814 (1965). However, that court later stated that it was not enough to "conjure up some reason why a businessman would enter into this sort of arrangement." *Mathews v. Commissioner,* 520 F.2d 323, 325 (5th Cir. 1975), *cert. denied,* 424 U.S. 967 (1976). In *Mathews* the court focused on the substance of the overall transaction and held that no deduction is allowable unless it has some economic reality. Although "economic reality" is a term not infrequently used in appellate opinions, *e.g., May v. Commissioner,* 723 F.2d 1434 (9th Cir. 1984), its meaning is by no means clear. The *Mathews* opinion does state that economic reality is not present where there is a prearranged agreement to lease the property back to the transferor. According to the court, the prearrangement assures that the transferor will continue to have control over the property regardless of the independence of the trustee. The economic reality test could be very difficult to satisfy, particularly if the taxpayer must establish the absence of an express or implied prearrangement in the context of a family transaction. An analogous problem arises where a transferor continues to occupy a residence given to another family member. *See* §7.23.

§9.20.2. No Equity Interest

In order for rental payments to be deductible as rent, the statute requires that the taxpayer have no equity in the rental property. §162(a)(3). In several cases the IRS has argued that the statute bars a deduction where the lessee holds a reversionary interest in the property. The argument was rejected by most courts. However, it was accepted in two cases — *Chace v. United States,* 303 F. Supp. 513 (M.D. Fla. 1969), *aff'd per curiam,* 422 F.2d 292 (5th Cir. 1970), and *Hall v. United States,* 208 F. Supp. 584 (N.D.N.Y. 1962). The pertinent part of §162(a)(3) is ambiguous, but most courts agree that the requirement is intended to prevent taxpayers from converting a capital expenditure (purchase of asset) into a currently deductible expense (rent). For example, in *C. James Mathews,* 61 T.C. 12, 23 (1973), *rev'd on other grounds,* 520 F.2d 323 (5th Cir. 1975), *cert. denied,* 424 U.S. 967 (1976), the Tax Court said, "section 162(a)(3) should not be read to cause rental payments to become nondeductible merely by virtue of a lessee's property rights in an asset, which rights are not derived from the lessor or under the lease, and which will become possessory only after the lease expires." *See also Quinlivan v. United States,* 599 F.2d

269 (8th Cir.), *cert. denied,* 444 U.S. 996 (1979). This ban on deductions should not pose any problem for most gift and leaseback transactions.

§9.20.3. Tax Court Requirements

The Tax Court has established specific requirements that must be met in order to sustain the deductibility of rental payments in leaseback cases. *See Hobart A. Lerner, M.D., P.C.,* 71 T.C. 290 (1978); *C. James Mathews, supra,* 61 T.C. at 18-19; and *Richard R. Quinlivan,* 37 T.C.M. 346 (1978), *aff'd,* 599 F.2d 269 (8th Cir.), *cert. denied,* 444 U.S. 996 (1979). The requirements were also adopted by the Eighth Circuit in the appellate opinion in *Quinlivan,* 599 F.2d at 273, and by the Second Circuit in *Rosenfeld,* 706 F.2d at 1280:

1. The grantor must not retain "substantially the same control over the property that he had before" he made the gift;
2. The leaseback should normally be in writing and must require the payment of a reasonable rental;
3. The leaseback (as distinguished from the gift) must have a bona fide business purpose; and
4. The taxpayer must not possess a disqualifying equity interest in the property.

The first requirement implies the necessity of having an independent trustee, which has been stated explicitly in some cases. *E.g., Brooke v. United States,* 468 F.2d 1155 (9th Cir. 1972) (involving a guardianship and not a trust); *Alden B. Oakes,* 44 T.C. 524, 529 (1965). In *Lewis H. V. May,* 76 T.C. 7 (1981), *aff'd,* 723 F.2d 1434 (9th Cir. 1984), the Tax Court left open the question of whether there must be an independent trustee in all cases. Although some courts are willing to treat the lessee's lawyer or accountant as an independent party for this purpose, it is safer to use a corporate trustee.

§9.20.4. Suggested Approach

A leaseback from a family member or a trustee is subject to challenge by the IRS unless it is a three-party transaction covered by A.O.D. 1984-038. A deduction for rental payments will be upheld by most courts if the transaction has these characteristics:

1. The trustee is independent (preferably a corporate trustee);
2. The lease is written and enforceable under the local law;
3. The lease terms, including its duration and rental, are negotiated after the initial transfer;

4. The rental is reasonable — neither inadequate nor excessive;
5. The lease of the property serves a legitimate business purpose of the lessee; and
6. The lessor and lessee respect and enforce the terms of the lease.

The taxpayer's cause is helped immeasurably if there are valid nontax business purposes for the overall transaction. It is relatively simple to identify some plausible nontax motives where the initial transfer involves an outright gift or sale. For example, in *Brooke v. United States,* 468 F.2d 1155 (9th Cir. 1972), the nontax motives for a gift to minor children and leaseback from their guardian were found to be "abundant and grounded in economic reality." They included a desire to provide for the health and education of the minors, to avoid friction with medical partners, to withdraw assets from the threat of malpractice suits, and to diminish the ethical conflict arising from ownership of a medical practice and an adjoining pharmacy.

§9.20.5. Grantor Trust Rules

The benefit of the deduction is lost if the income of the trust is taxable to the transferor under §§671-677. For example, the income from transfers to a short-term trust is taxable to the transferor under §677(a) when an independent trustee has discretion to accumulate trust income for distribution to the transferor upon termination of the trust. *Duffy v. United States,* 487 F.2d 282 (6th Cir. 1973), *cert. denied,* 416 U.S. 938 (1974). The same applies to the income from any post March 1, 1986 transfers in trust where the reversionary interest exceeds five percent of the value of the transfer. §673(a). From the income tax point of view, treatment as a grantor trust should result in a wash — the grantor is allowed a deduction for the rent paid to the trust, but the income of the trust is taxed to the grantor under the grantor trust rules. Of course, such a taxpayer suffers some overall loss because of the costs incurred in creating the trust and the imposition of a gift tax on the transfer to the trust. The grantor trust rules are examined in detail in Part D of Chapter 10, §§10.30-10.41.

§9.21. Gift Tax Consequences

The initial transfer of property to a trust involves a gift to the extent the value of the transferred property exceeds the sum of the value of the interests retained by the transferor and the consideration received by the transferor. Ordinarily the transferor does not retain any interest in the trust. The trust is usually planned so that transfers to it will qualify for the maximum allowable number of gift tax annual exclusions. In this connection recall that where a trust is involved annual gift tax exclusions are available only if (1) the beneficiaries are entitled to current distributions of income, (2) the trust satisfies the requirements of §2503(c), or (3) the beneficiaries are given *Crummey* powers of withdrawal. *See* §§7.35-7.38. In appropriate cases the transfer could be structured to qualify for the marital or charitable gift and estate tax deductions. For example, the initial transfer might be made outright to a charity or to a charitable remainder trust or charitable lead trust. Great caution is required in planning a transfer to a charitable trust because of the complexity of the tax rules. *See* §§8.19-8.35.

The donee's interests are valued under the usual gift tax rules. Accordingly, term or other limited interests are valued by reference to the actuarial tables pursuant to §7520. However, when the rental is fixed at the time of the initial transfer, the value of the gift is "measured by the present worth of the right to receive the net rentals from the property during the term of the trust, provided the right to such rentals is under the terms of the transfer and applicable State law fixed or vested." Rev. Rul. 57-315, 1957-2 C.B. 624. The Ruling also points out that the gift of the rentals is complete at the time of transfer although the rentals are not deductible by the lessee for income tax purposes.

Where the gift is valued by reference to the actuarial tables, the transaction may result in either a partially nontaxable transfer or the imposition of an unnecessary gift tax (*i.e.,* where the rental payments are less than the actuarially determined value of the gift). The latter will occur if the reasonable rental payments under the lease are lower than the amount of income projected by applying the appropriate factor under §7520.

Example 9-13. At a time when an interest rate of 11% applied to the valuation of interests, *T* transferred a building worth $100,000 to the independent trustee of an irrevocable trust for a 10-year period. The income of the trust is distributable annually in equal shares to *T*'s 2 children. Applying the appropriate factor from Table B of IRS Pub. No. 1457, .647816, the term interest has a total value of $64,781.60 for gift tax purposes. To the extent the rental payments or other income of the trust exceed $11,000 (11% × $100,000) per year *T* will, in effect, make tax-free gifts to the children. On the other hand, if the income of the trust falls below $11,000 per year, for gift tax purposes *T* will have been treated as having made a gift that exceeded the value of the interest actually received by the children. However, note that excessive rental payments by *T* would probably involve further gifts to the beneficiaries of the trust.

In the past it was sometimes possible to make nontaxable gifts of term interests. Assets transferred to a trust often yielded much more than the six percent rate of return that was used for actuarial purposes prior to December 1, 1983. That is, prior to December 1, 1983, the value of a term interest in a trust was "understated" if the assets that are transferred to the trust or acquired by the trustee yielded more than six percent. Given the existing method of calculating the value of term interests and the grantor trust status of most short-term trusts, there is generally no tax advantage to creating short-term family trusts.

§9.22. Estate Tax Consequences

A gift to a trust may improve the donor's transfer tax position, at least if the trust will not be includible in his or her estate. On the other hand, no improvement is likely if the donor retains a reversionary interest in the property. In the latter case the gift tax applies to the actuarially determined value of the beneficial interests in the trust that were given to others. Moreover, if the grantor dies during the term of the trust the value of the grantor's reversionary interest is includible in his or her estate under §2033. The full value of the property may be included in the transferor's estate under §2036(a) if the lease was prearranged or the rental is not adequate. *See Estate of William du Pont, Jr.*, 63 T.C. 746 (1975) (inclusion where property transferred outright and leased back at inadequate rental); *Estate of Roy D. Barlow*, 55 T.C. 666 (1971), *acq.*, 1972-2 C.B. 1, 3 (no inclusion where property transferred outright more than three years prior to death and decedent paid fair rental under written leases). If the grantor survives termination of the trust, the trust property will be distributed to the grantor.

§9.22.1. Outright Gift and Leaseback

Where the transfer is made by outright gift all of the property may escape inclusion in the donor's estate if the donor leases the property back at a reasonable rental. The available annual gift tax exclusions and the unified credit may reduce or eliminate the out-of-pocket gift tax cost of transferring the property. If the gift and leaseback are beyond the reach of §2036, the property may be entirely excluded from the donor's gross estate. The gift and estate tax consequences of adopting this approach are illustrated by the following example, which should be compared with Example 9-13, *supra*.

Example 9-14. *O* transferred a new office building worth $200,000 to the independent trustee of an irrevocable trust of which *O*'s 4 children were the life income beneficiaries and their issue were the remaindermen. *O* did not retain any interest in the property and held no control over the trust. After the transfer *O* leased the building from the trustee on reasonable terms. At the time of the transfer to the trust *O* made gifts of the entire value of the property. Assuming that 4 $10,000 annual exclusions were available, the transfer resulted in taxable gifts of $160,000. If *O* had not previously made any taxable gifts, the gift tax on the transfer would be offset by *O*'s unified credit. Only the amount of the taxable gifts ($160,000) should be taken into account in later determining the tentative tax on *O*'s estate. However, the full value of the property is includible in *O*'s estate if *O* in effect retained the use of the property by paying an unreasonably low rental or if the transaction otherwise ran afoul of §§2036 to 2038. Note that the trust is subject to the GSTT. Accordingly, the grantor might choose to claim part or all of the $1 million exemption with respect to the transfer to the trust. §2631(a). Finally, note that the gift tax cost could be further reduced if *O*'s grandchildren were also given *Crummey* powers of withdrawal.

§9.22.2. Sale and Leaseback

If the initial transfer takes the form of a bona fide sale for the full value of the property, the property is not includible in the seller's estate. In this case the consideration received by the seller is includible in lieu of the property itself. The value of an installment note or other obligation received as consideration would depend upon a variety of factors, including the interest rate, security, and collectibility. *See* Reg. §20.2031-4. In this connection recall that more stringent interest rate rules apply to installment obligations in a sale-leaseback arrangement. *See* §9.19. If the sale price is inadequate the property may be included in the seller's estate under §§2035 to 2038. However, in such a case the estate would be entitled to an offset under §2043(a) for the consideration received.

E. THE WIDOW'S ELECTION IN COMMUNITY PROPERTY AND COMMON LAW STATES

§9.23. Introduction

Life or other limited interests in property are transferred for consideration in a wide variety of settings. Several of the most important litigated cases have involved the community property widow's election, which serves as the primary focus of this part. The tax consequences of the transfers are determined according to more or less universal rules that apply regardless of slight variations in the settings or relationships of the parties. For example, the purchaser of a life or other term interest in a trust acquired after July 27, 1989 is not entitled to amortize its cost for any period during which the remainder is held directly or indirectly by a related party. §167(e). Previously purchased life or other term interests may be amortized whether they were purchased from a decedent's estate in connection with a widow's election, *Estate of Christ v. Commissioner,* 480 F.2d 171 (9th Cir. 1973), or from the settlor of the trust, *Manufacturer's Hanover Trust Co. v. Commissioner,* 431 F.2d 664 (2d Cir. 1970). Also, the same estate tax rules apply whether the interest is acquired in the context of a will contest, *United States v. Righter,* 400 F.2d 344 (8th Cir. 1968), or a widow's election, *Estate of Vardell v. Commissioner,* 307 F.2d 688 (5th Cir. 1962). It is important to have a basic grasp of the tax rules and to be alert for circumstances in which they may apply — the rules can also be very helpful in planning other types of transactions. It is also important to be alert to the possible application of §2702 and of the GSTT.

The planning device under discussion was labelled the "widow's election" long ago. While it is equally applicable to spouses of either sex, the wife most often survives her husband. Consequently, this part generally refers to the first spouse to die as the "husband" and to the surviving spouse as the "widow." No suggestion of marital or sexual inequality is intended by this choice of language. The convention is adopted in the interest of brevity and consistency.

In community property states the term "widow's election" originally referred to the choice that a widow was forced to make when the deceased husband's will provided for the disposition of all of their community property. Such a will caused a problem because neither spouse has the right to dispose of the entire community interest. When confronted with this issue the courts could have limited the effect of the husband's will to his half of the community property. Instead they concluded that such a will required the widow to elect whether to (1) accept the provisions of the will and allow her share of the property to be disposed of in accordance with the decedent's will, or (2) give up her rights under the will and retain her share of the community property.

The widow's election was often used to establish a trust of all of the community property for the lifetime of the widow. Such a disposition was attractive because it resulted in the unified management of the community property, made the entire community property available for the support of the surviving spouse, and provided for the distribution of the property when she died. Typically the surviving spouse could not alter the disposition of the property upon her death.

§9.24. Testamentary Elections

A transfer for consideration may result from a testamentary election that is expressly or impliedly required by a decedent's will. For example, a testamentary gift may be conditioned upon the beneficiary transferring an asset he or she owns to another person. In other cases the necessity of making an election is implied rather than expressed directly in the will. Thus, *T* may make a gift to *X* and purport to give *Y* an item of property that is actually owned by *X*. In such a case *X* may elect either (1) to accept the gift from *T* and transfer the item of his or her property to *Y*, or (2) to reject the gift from *T* and not transfer any of his or her own property to *Y*. An election may also be required where the testator and the beneficiary of a testamentary gift are joint tenants in other property that the testator's will gives to a third party. *E.g., Estate of Waters,* 100 Cal. Rptr. 775, 778 (Cal. App. 1972).

> **Example 9-15.** *T* owned the entire interest in Blackacre, which *T*'s will devised to *X*. Although *T* and *X* owned Whiteacre as joint tenants with right of survivorship, *T*'s will purported to devise Whiteacre to *Y*. The devise of Blackacre to *X* may be construed by a court as being conditioned upon *X* transferring Whiteacre to *Y*.

§9.25. Widow's Election Described

The term "widow's election" has quite different meanings in common law and community property states. In common law property states, the term usually refers to the statutory right of a surviving spouse to elect to receive a specified share of the deceased spouse's estate (a so-called nonbarrable share) in lieu of taking under the decedent's will. *See, e.g.,* U.P.C. §2-201 (1990). The concept is an important one that may have significant tax consequences in some instances, such as cases involving the marital deduction.

In community property states the term usually refers to a plan under which the widow is given an interest in the deceased husband's share of the community property, conditioned upon her making a specified disposition of her share of the community property. The widow is forced to make an election because neither spouse can unilaterally dispose of more than one-half of the community property. *See* §3.28.2. As explained below, if the widow elects to take under the husband's will the tax cases generally treat her as having purchased the profferred interest in the husband's share of the community property by making the required transfer of her share of the community property.

The basic concept of the community property widow's election can be adapted for use in common law property states. For example, if each spouse owns a substantial amount of separate property, the husband's will can make a gift of an appropriate part of his property to a trust of which his wife is the life income beneficiary conditioned upon the transfer by her of a specified amount of her property to the trust, or to a similar, separate trust. Some commentators have suggested that a modified form of widow's election could be used where the wife does not have a substantial estate. They suggest that the husband's will could create a life estate-general power of appointment marital deduction trust and a residuary credit shelter trust. Then, the wife could be given the power to draw down the principal of the marital deduction trust and exchange part of it for a life income interest in the residuary trust. If she makes the exchange, presumably she would be treated as a purchaser of the income interest in the residuary trust. As such she might be entitled to the same tax benefits as the widow-beneficiary of a community property widow's election trust. However, the tax consequences of this approach are not established. In addition, the technique is subject to the same uncertainty as the community property widow's election regarding the application of §1001(e) to the sale by the residuary trust of a life interest to the widow. *See* §9.31.

The substantive law regarding the community property widow's election has evolved largely from cases that arose prior to the advent of significant income, gift, or estate taxes. *E.g., In re Estate of Smith,* 40 P. 1037 (Cal. 1895). The cases usually involved a husband's will that attempted to dispose of all of the community property, yet made some provision for his widow. Although a will is generally presumed to dispose of only the testator's property, where it was clear that he had attempted to dispose of all of the community property, the courts held that the widow was required to elect whether to accept the provisions of the will and allow her share of the community property to pass under the will or to reject the will and retain her share of the community property. *E.g., Herrick v. Miller,* 125 P. 974 (Wash. 1912). Litigation was frequently required in order to determine whether an election was required and whether the widow had made an election by accepting benefits under the will or by acquiescing in the distribution of some property in accordance with the terms of the will.

The uncertainties inherent in the original form of the widow's election device are generally avoided in modern wills, which usually require the election to be made in a particular way within a specified time following the testator's death. Modern wills also generally make a conditional gift to the widow of an interest in the trust funded with the husband's share of the property rather than attempting also to dispose directly of her interest in community property. However, some commentators still write of the election as if the husband were disposing directly of the entire interest in the community property.

§9.26. Typical Widow's Election Plan

Under a typical widow's election plan, the husband's will leaves his share of the community property to a trust, all of the income of which is distributable to his widow if she also transfers her share of the community property to the same trust, or to a separate trust that is subject to essentially the same terms. Their children are usually the remaindermen of the trust or trusts. The widow will receive no benefit from the trust of the husband's share of the community property unless she transfers her share to the trust. In any event the widow is usually entitled to receive specific bequests and a family allowance from the husband's estate.

The adoption of §2702 and the decision of the Court of Appeals in *Gradow v. United States,* 897 F.2d 516 (Fed. Cir. 1990), may cause future widow's election wills to be drawn differently, at least if the widow and the remaindermen are members of the same family. In particular, the entire value of the community property transferred by the surviving spouse should be exactly equal to the actuarially determined value of the life estate she receives in the trust established under her deceased husband's will. In such a case the transfer by the widow to the trust will not involve a gift to the remaindermen and none of the property she transferred to the trust will be included in her estate. This approach is dictated by §2702, which requires that the value of the widow's retained life interest in the property she transferred to the trust be disregarded entirely for gift tax purposes. Thus, a gift would result unless the life estate the widow received in the trust established by the husband was of equal value. Under *Gradow* the property transferred by the widow is includible in her estate unless the consideration she received (the life estate in the husband's share of the property) had a value at least equal to the full value of the property she transferred (not merely the value of the remainder interest in it). *See* §9.34.

The widow's election can be adapted for use in connection with an inter vivos trust or in connection with gifts to persons other than a spouse. *See, e.g., United States v. Righter,* 400 F.2d 344 (8th Cir. 1968) (estate tax approach of widow's election cases applied to trust created by decedent and others in settlement of will contest). However, this part generally focuses on testamentary widow's election plans involving married persons. The nontax considerations are discussed first, after which the tax consequences are developed in some detail. The tax concepts are discussed at some length because they may be applied in other contexts in community and common law states.

The husband and wife are each transferors for GSTT purposes, which requires some special planning. In particular, careful consideration should be given to the allocation of the GSTT exemption and the use of multiple trusts. There is a possibility that the widow's contributions to the trust may escape the GSTT. *See* §9.35.

§9.27. Inter Vivos or Post-Mortem Election?

The testator's spouse may agree during the testator's lifetime to accept the benefit of the plan and be bound by the terms of the will. *E.g., In Estate of Wyss,* 297 P. 100 (Cal. App. 1931); Rev. Rul. 69-346, 1969-1 C.B. 227. Use of a binding inter vivos election is generally unwise because it deprives the widow of the opportunity to evaluate the suitability of the plan after her husband's death. One of the attractive features of the traditional widow's election is the "second look" it gives the widow.

Where a plan involves an inter vivos election, the lawyer should seriously consider suggesting that each spouse be advised by independent counsel:

> There may be many cases where a single attorney is consulted and no question exists about the fairness or reasonableness of the agreement to both parties. The presence of advice from independent counsel is a desirable cautionary step, however, where there is a possibility that the fairness or reasonableness of the agreement will be subject to later attack. *Whitney v. Seattle-First National Bank,* 579 P.2d 937, 940 (Wash. 1978).

Ideally, the surviving spouse should also be advised by independent counsel where the election is made following the testator's death. In that way the scrivener of the will, who generally serves as counsel to the executor, will not be subject to a conflict of interest.

When the plan contemplates a post-mortem election, the husband's will should specify the period during which the widow may elect under the will. It is important that the widow be given ample time to consider the tax and nontax effects of an election before it must be made. For example, she might be permitted to elect at any time prior to final distribution of the testator's estate. The will should also specify whether the election may be made on the widow's behalf by her guardian (or her personal representative if she survives her husband, but dies before making an election). Even apart from such a provision, some states permit the widow's personal representative to make the election. *Estate of Murphy,* 544 P.2d 956 (Cal. 1976). In contrast, the U.P.C. does not permit an election to take a nonbarrable share to be made by the survivor's personal representative. U.P.C. §2-203 (1990).

§9.28. "Voluntary" Widow's Election

Some couples reject the use of a "forced" election of the type described above in favor of a noncoercive plan that permits the widow to add some or all of her property to the trust created under her husband's will. Under this plan the widow is not required to transfer any of her property to the trust in order to receive the income from her husband's share of the property. Instead, any property the widow transfers to the trust is typically held in a separate fund, which may be withdrawn by her at any time. Such a plan facilitates unified management of the community property, yet provides the surviving spouse with a high degree of flexibility. The husband's share of the community property is usually left to a trust that meets the requirements of a qualified terminable interest property trust under §2056(b)(7). Of course, the property of the trust is includible in the widow's estate under §2044 to the extent the husband's executor claims a marital deduction with respect to the trust. However, the plan does not produce any of the income or estate tax benefits that are typically sought through the use of the forced widow's election. In particular, the amount included in her estate will not be reduced by a consideration offset under §2043(a). *See* §9.30.2. Also, even apart from §167(e), the surviving spouse was not entitled to an amortization deduction.

§9.29. Nontax Consequences of a Forced Election

A widow's election plan may be attractive to some clients because of its nontax features. For example, the plan offers unified management of community assets, which is particularly helpful in the case of closely-held business interests. There may also be an advantage to having the entire community property managed by a trustee if the widow does not have any business experience or does not want to manage the property. The plan also assures that the community property, or at least the husband's share, will pass to the remaindermen named in his will. Furthermore, the property held in trust is not subject to an estate administration upon the widow's death. Of course, some of the advantages are available under the other plans, such as a voluntary widow's election.

A forced election plan is more complex than simple wills that transfer the community property to the surviving spouse or to a trust for her benefit. As a result it may be more difficult for clients to understand and more costly to implement. In addition, there is always a risk that some of the tax advantages sought by the parties will be challenged. Overall, the forced widow's election is not suitable for most clients. A widow's election plan should be used only if it is understood by the husband and wife and is completely acceptable to them. Otherwise, there is too great a risk that the widow will resent the plan and feel that she was not treated fairly by her husband or his planner. In short, the plan should be consensual and not imposed on a spouse who does not understand it or has some objection to it.

The nontax considerations are thoughtfully reviewed in a short article by Kahn & Gallo, The Widow's Election: A Return to Fundamentals, 24 Stan. L. Rev. 531 (1972). In general the authors favor a voluntary widow's election over a forced one.

§9.30. Gift Tax Consequences

For gift tax purposes in the typical widow's election, the widow is considered to have transferred a remainder interest in her share of the property in exchange for a life interest in the decedent's share. *Commissioner v. Siegel,* 250 F.2d 339 (9th Cir. 1957); *Zillah Mae Turman,* 35 T.C. 1123 (1961), *acq.,* 1964-2 C.B. 7. Under this approach the widow does not make a gift if the actuarially determined value of the life interest she receives is equal to or greater than the value of the remainder in the property she transfers. This approach will continue to apply to widow's election trusts that are not subject to the valuation rules of §2702, such as ones of which the remaindermen are not members of the widow's family. For purposes of §2704(c)(2) family members include lineal ascendants, lineal descendants, brothers and sisters, and their spouses. It does not include aunts, uncles, nephews, nieces, cousins and their spouses.

Example 9-16. *H*'s executor transferred his net share of the community property, worth $300,000, to a typical widow's election trust, the H trust. At a time when an 11% interest rate applied, the decedent's 75-year-old widow, *W,* elected to transfer her share of the community property, worth $375,000, to an identical trust, the W trust, in order to receive the income from both trusts for life. (*H*'s share is smaller because it was reduced by costs of administration, taxes, debts, and other expenses.) Upon *W*'s death the trust property is distributable by right of representation to the descendants of *W*'s brother *B.* At 11% interest the remainder transferred by *W* had a value of $154,493 ($375,000 × .41198). The life estate she received in the trust of *H*'s property had a value of $176,406 ($300,000 × .58802). Accordingly, *W*'s election did not involve a gift to the remaindermen of the trust. (Any gift of a remainder interest would be of a future interest that would not qualify for the annual gift tax exclusion.) Of course, if the remaindermen were family members within the meaning of §2704(c)(2), the life interest retained by *W* in her share of the community property would be valued at zero for gift tax purposes. *See* §2702. *See also* §9.43.

If the transfer made by a widow is subject to the valuation rules of §2702, the value of the widow's retained interest is disregarded unless it is a qualified interest (*i.e.,* an annuity or unitrust amount). Accordingly, in Example 9-16, if the remaindermen were family members (*e.g.,* lineal descendants of *H* or *W*), presumably the transfer by *W* would have resulted in a gift of $198,594, which is the amount by which the value of the property transferred by *W* ($375,000) exceeded the value of the life estate she received in the trust established under *H*'s will ($176,406).

§9.30.1. Powers of Appointment

An election to take under the husband's will does not result in a gift if the transfer is incomplete because the widow retained a power of appointment over the property she transferred to the trust. Reg. §25.2511-2(b). Thus, in LR 7746044 the IRS recognized that the widow's gift was not complete at the time of her election where she retained a special power of appointment over the property she transferred to the trust. However, the ruling concluded that under *Estate of Sanford v. Commissioner,* 308 U.S. 39 (1939), the gift became complete when she subsequently released the power of appointment. At that time she made a gift of the entire remainder value of the trust attributable to the property she transferred to the trust. The widow's gift in LR 7746044 was not reduced by the value of the life interest in her husband's share of the property which she had already received and was not affected by her release. The gift was larger because it took place later, which increased the value of the remainder interest, and because the widow received no consideration for the transfer. The analysis of LR 7746044 was followed by the Tax Court in *Myra B. Robinson,* 75 T.C. 346 (1980), *aff'd,* 675 F.2d 774 (5th Cir.), *cert. denied,* 459 U.S. 970 (1982).

The widow's retention of any power of appointment over the property she transfers threatens the treatment of the election as a transfer for value. As Professor Stanley Johanson has pointed out, where a power is retained the transaction more closely resembles a gratuitous transfer than a transfer for value. Johanson, Revocable Trusts, Widow's Election Wills, and Community Property: The Tax Problems, 47 Tex. L. Rev. 1247, 1309-1311 (1969). That is a serious problem because the principal tax advantages of the widow's election are lost if the transaction is not characterized as a transfer for value. In particular, the widow's estate will be unable to claim a consideration offset under §2043(a) for the value of the life estate she received. The Tax Court has held that the widow's estate is not entitled to a consideration offset where she held a general power of appointment over the property.

Estate of Bluma Steinman, 69 T.C. 804 (1978). Given the uncertainty regarding this issue, either the widow should not retain any power, or the power should be limited to a testamentary special power to appoint the corpus to and among their descendants or some other limited class.

§9.30.2. Voluntary Election

Where the election is a voluntary one, the widow receives no consideration in exchange for her transfer. Instead, she makes a gift of the full value of the remainder interest in her property. However, no completed gift occurs where she retains a general or special power of appointment over the property. Instead, the full value of the property is includible in the widow's estate and the amount of the taxable gift that she made at the time of the election is excluded in computing the estate tax on her estate. In effect, the widow can hold a general or special power of appointment without additional tax cost — the full value of the property is includible in her estate in any case. A power of appointment can add important flexibility to the estate plan. Of course, the widow's estate will not be entitled to a consideration offset under §2043(a).

§9.31. Income Tax Consequences

The holder of a life or other term interest acquired by gift, bequest, or inheritance cannot deduct any amount because of shrinkage in value of the interest due to the passage of time. §273. On the other hand, a life interest in a testamentary trust is treated as a capital asset for purposes of characterizing the gain realized on a sale or exchange of the interest. *McAllister v. Commissioner,* 157 F.2d 235 (2d Cir. 1946), *cert. denied,* 330 U.S. 826 (1947); Rev. Rul. 72-243, 1972-1 C.B. 233. Under §167(e) no depreciation or amortization deduction is allowable with respect to a term interest acquired after July 27, 1989 for any period during which the remainder is held by a related person as defined in §§267(b) and (e). For purposes of §267(b), family includes only "brothers and sisters (whether by the whole or half blood), spouse, ancestors, and lineal descendants." §267(c)(4). In the case of transfers prior to July 28, 1989, the purchaser of a life or other term interest is allowed to amortize its cost over its life, thereby reducing or eliminating the tax on income received from it. *Commissioner v. Fry,* 283 F.2d 369 (6th Cir. 1960), *aff'g,* 31 T.C. 522 (1958); *Bell v. Harrison,* 212 F.2d 253 (7th Cir. 1954); Rev. Rul. 62-132, 1962-2 C.B. 73. That rule would apply to later transfers if the remaindermen are not related within the meaning of §§267(b) and (e) (*e.g.,* in-laws, uncles, aunts, nieces, nephews, and cousins).

Prior to the 1969 Act, where a life estate or other term interest was sold, the seller's basis was determined by multiplying his or her entire basis by a factor to value the life estate. Rev. Rul. 72-243, 1972-1 C.B. 233. Under this rule the seller seldom realized any gain on the sale. Moreover, under the *McAllister* line of authority any gain would be capital gain and not ordinary income.

The 1969 Act added §1001(e), under which the seller's basis is disregarded to the extent it arises under §§1014, 1015, or 1041. As a result of this change, the full amount received by the seller of a term interest acquired by gift or bequest is gain where the sale takes place after October 9, 1969. The legislation only disadvantages the seller of a life or other term interest — it did not prevent the purchaser from amortizing the cost of the life interest.

> **Example 9-17.** *T*'s will left $100,000 in trust to pay the income to the beneficiary, *B*, for life. Upon *B*'s death the corpus is distributable to *X*. The income of the trust is taxable to *B*, who is barred by §273 from claiming any amortization deduction. *B*'s interest constitutes a capital asset for purposes of characterizing the gain realized on any sale or other disposition. If *B* sold his interest after October 9, 1969, *B*'s basis would be zero pursuant to §1001(e).

The legislative history of §1001(e) does not indicate whether or not Congress considered the possibility of applying the provision in the widow's election context. In the early 1970s it was rumored that the IRS would issue a ruling to the effect that §1001(e) would not apply to a widow's election unless a distribution from the estate was made in satisfaction of the widow's right to receive a specific dollar amount or a specific item of property. Committee Report, Estate Planning Through Family Bargaining, 8 Real Prop., Prob. & Tr. J. 223, 265 (1973). However, the ruling was never issued. The possibility that §1001(e) will apply to the widow's election deters some planners from recommending that a client use a forced widow's election plan. Neither the Code nor any identifiable considerations of tax policy prevent the application of §1001(e). Freeland, Lind & Stephens, What Are the Income Tax Effects of an Estate's Sale of a Life Interest?, 34 J. Tax. 376 (1971); Wilson, The Widow's Election Viewed in the Light of the 1976 Tax Reform Act and the 1975 California Probate Code Revision, 28 Hastings L.J. 1435, 1442 (1977).

§9.31.1. The Trustee

> In a situation involving a widow's election where the taxpayer exchanges the remainder interest in her community prop-

> erty for a life interest in her husband's community property, what actually occurs can be characterized as part gratuitous disposition-part sale or exchange. Where the wife received property worth more than the value of the property she transfers, the property received in excess should be viewed as a "bequest" from the husband which is not amortizable. But where the wife transfers property worth more than the value of that which she receives, she purchases property equivalent to the value of the "received" property and is deemed to have made a gift to the beneficiaries of the estate of [sic], and should pay a gift tax on, the excess. *Kuhn v. United States,* 392 F. Supp. 1229, 1239-1240 (S.D. Tex. 1975).

In the case of a forced widow's election trust the trust may realize a substantial gain if the plan is carried out and the widow transfers her share of the community property to the trust in exchange for a life interest in the decedent's share. The gain will occur if §1001(e) applies to the transaction and the trust's basis in the life interest transferred to the widow is disregarded to the extent it is determined under §1014. In most circumstances the full amount realized by the trust will constitute capital gain. The amount realized is equal to the actuarially determined value of the remainder interest the widow transferred to the trust. The rules of §2702, which only apply for gift tax purposes, will not affect the treatment of the transaction for income tax purposes. However, where the value of the remainder interest exceeds the actuarially determined value of the life interest transferred to the widow, the amount realized by the trust is probably limited to the value of the latter — the life interest. Lane, The Widow's Election as a Private Annuity: Boon or Bane for Estate Planners, 44 S. Cal. L. Rev. 74, 93 (1971). In determining the amount realized by the trust, this analysis properly ignores the gift element of the transaction. Such an approach is consistent with the cases that imposed a similar limit on the amount amortizable by the widow for income tax purposes in the case of transfers made prior to July 28, 1989. *Estate of Christ v. Commissioner,* 480 F.2d 171 (9th Cir. 1973).

Example 9-18. *H*'s executor transferred property worth $350,000 to a typical widow's election trust, the H trust, of which the children of *H* were the remaindermen. At the time the applicable interest rate was 11%. *H*'s 80-year-old widow, *W,* transferred property worth $400,000 to an identical trust, the W trust, as required by *H*'s will. Under §2702, if *W* retained only the right to receive the income from the *W* trust, the transfer involved a gift of $225,462 ($400,000 less $174,538, the value of the life estate she received in the H trust). However, for income tax purposes the amount realized by *H*'s trust is probably limited to $174,538, the value of the life estate *W* received in the exchange. In the case of a transfer prior to July 28, 1989, *W*'s amortization would probably be limited to the same amount. No amortization would be allowed for later transfers.

The gift by *W* would be smaller if the remaindermen were not members of *W*'s family or if §2702 otherwise did not apply in determining the gift tax consequences. Thus, if the remaindermen were *W*'s nephews, nieces, or cousins the gift would only be $25,990, which is the value of the remainder in the W trust, $200,528 ($400,000 × .50132), less the life estate she received in the H trust, $174,538 ($350,000 × .49868). The amount realized by the H trust and subject to amortization by *W* would probably be based on $174,538, the value of the amount she received in the exchange and not the full value of the remainder interest transferred by *W*. The excess constituted a gift from *W* to the remaindermen of the W trust.

If §1001(e) does not apply to a widow's election, the trust's basis will be determined under §1014. Accordingly, the trust will usually have little or no gain to report. Assuming that the amount realized by the trust is limited in the manner described above, the trust will seldom realize an amount greater than the trust's basis in the interest transferred. Under Reg. §1.1014-5 the trust's basis in the life interest transferred to the widow is determined by multiplying the adjusted basis of the decedent's share of the property by the factor for the widow's life estate. The widow's life interest will have an equivalent value if the assets held in the trust are valued for federal estate tax purposes on the date of the husband's death and the widow's election is effective on that date. Because of fluctuations in the value of the assets held by the trust, the life interest will have a different value if the valuation date and the date of the election are not the same.

Example 9-19. *H*'s executor transferred assets to a typical widow's election trust, the H trust, which had a total basis of $350,000 and a fair market value of $400,000 on the date they became subject to the trust. His 80-year-old widow, *W*, transferred property to an identical trust, the W trust, which had a fair market value of $450,000 on that date. For income tax purposes, based on an 11% interest rate, *W* would probably be treated as having transferred a remainder in the W trust that had a value of $225,594 ($450,000 × .50132) in exchange for a life estate in the H trust worth $199,472 ($400,000 × .49868). However, the trustee's basis in the life interest in the H trust is only $174,538 ($350,000 × .49868). Presumably the trustee realized a gain of $24,934 ($199,472 − $174,538).

The trust does not realize gain in the case of a voluntary widow's election because the widow's transfer of property to the trust is entirely gratuitous and does not involve any exchange or transfer for consideration.

The gain realized by the trust will probably be characterized as capital gain rather than ordinary income. Some commentators have suggested that the transaction might be treated as an assignment of income by the trust, in which case the gain would be ordinary income. *See* Freeland, Lind & Stephens, What Are the Income Tax Effects of an Estate's Sale of a Life Interest?, 34 J. Tax. 376 (1971); Lane, Widow's Election as a Private Annuity: Boon or Bane for Estate Planners, 44 S. Cal. L. Rev. 74, 93-95 (1971). However, the existing appellate court decisions support treating the gain as capital gain. They include a closely analogous case that involved the sale of a legal life estate that the seller carved out of a fee interest that he owned, *Estate of Johnson N. Camden,* 47 B.T.A. 926 (1942), *nonacq.,* 1943 C.B. 28, *aff'd per curiam,* 139 F.2d 697 (6th Cir. 1944), *nonacq.,* 1944 C.B. 34. Capital gain status was also recognized where the taxpayer sold a remainder interest in her ranch and retained a life estate. *Eileen M. Hunter,* 44 T.C. 109 (1965). Of course, if an amortization deduction is allowable to the widow under §167(e), any tax cost incurred as a result of the sale may be more than offset by the amortization deduction. *See* §9.32.

§9.31.2. The Widow

> [W]here the value of the rights surrendered [by the widow] exceeds the value of the rights received, only a portion of what is surrendered is allocated to the "purchase price" of the rights received and the rest is presumed to be a gift to the remaindermen. *Estate of Christ v. Commissioner,* 480 F.2d 171, 172 (9th Cir. 1973).

The widow may also realize a gain if she elects to transfer her share of the community property to the trust. In broad terms she is viewed as exchanging a remainder interest in her share of the community property for a life interest in her deceased husband's net share of the property. As a result of the exchange, she realizes an amount that cannot exceed the actuarially determined value of the life interest she receives. If the value of the life interest the widow receives exceeds the value of the remainder she transfers, the amount realized is probably limited to the value of the remainder. In such a case the amount by which the value of the life estate exceeds the value of the remainder is properly characterized as a bequest to the widow.

The amount of the widow's gain, if any, depends upon her basis in the property she transferred, which can only be determined after identifying the nature of the interest she transferred. Based upon the approach taken in the amortization cases (reflected in the quotation above), the widow will be treated as having transferred a remainder interest in her share of the community property, but only to the extent its value does not exceed the value of the life interest she received. Both of those values are determined by reference to the fair market value of the underlying assets and not their bases. She is considered to have made a gift to the remaindermen to the extent the remainder may have a greater value than the life interest.

Under §1014(b)(6) the widow is considered to have acquired her share of the community property from her deceased husband. Accordingly, the federal estate tax value of her husband's interest in the community property becomes the basis of her interest. When she transfers her share of the community property to the trust, the total basis should be allocated between her life estate and the remainder according to the respective actuarial factor for each. Such a method is applied to determine the bases of life estates and remainder interest in property acquired from a decedent. Reg. §1.1014-5. "Neither the Code nor the regulations prescribe a method for allocating a lump-sum basis when the owner of a fee simple interest conveys, inter vivos, a less-than-fee estate." *Eileen M. Hunter,* 44 T.C. 109, 115 (1965). Although *Hunter* involved a slightly different method of allocation, the Tax Court seemed to approve the approach taken in Reg. §1.1014-5, which had also been applied in an earlier case, *Estate of Johnson N. Camden,* 47 B.T.A. 926 (1942), *nonacq.,* 1943 C.B. 28, *aff'd per curiam,* 139 F.2d 697 (6th Cir. 1944), *nonacq.,* 1944 C.B. 34.

Example 9-20. *H*'s executor transferred property worth $650,000 to a typical widow's election trust, the H trust. His 65-year-old widow, *W,* transferred property with a basis and a value of $800,000 to an identical trust, the W trust, as required by *H*'s will. The interest rate used in valuing interests transferred was 11%. The factor for *W*'s life estate is .73643 and the factor for the remainder is .26357. Thus, the life estate in *H*'s share of the property was worth $478,680 ($650,000 × .73643) and the value (and basis of) the remainder in *W*'s trust is $210,856 ($800,000 × .26357). *W* should not recognize a gain on the transaction. Although the value of the life estate she received in the H trust exceeded the basis of the remainder in the property she transferred to the W trust, the excess constituted a bequest from *H* to *W. W* might have a gain, however, if *H*'s executor elected to use the alternate valuation date when the property had a lower value than on the date of distribution. Thus, *W* would have a gain in this example if her share of the community property had a value of

> $800,000 on the date it became subject to the trust and a basis of $700,000 (its value on the alternate valuation date). The value of the remainder transferred by *W,* which would limit the amount realized by her, would remain $210,856 but the basis allocable to the remainder would be reduced to $186,645. Presumably the $24,211 difference would constitute gain to *W.*

Any gain realized by the widow should be capital gain, just as it would be if realized by the trust. *See* §9.31.1.

§9.32. Income Tax Consequences of Trust Distributions

For income tax purposes the trust is recognized as a separate taxpaying entity. Under the basic income tax rules applicable to trusts, the income distributed to the beneficiaries is taxed to them and not to the trust, and the income retained by the trust is taxed to it. *See* §10.4. However, capital gains are taxed to the trust and not to the beneficiaries to the extent they are allocated to corpus and are not paid, credited, or required to be distributed during the taxable year. *See* §643(a)(3); Reg. §1.643(a)-3(a). Presumably distributions to the widow are taxed in accordance with those rules even though she is treated as a purchaser of the life interest in the decedent's share of the trust property.

An amortization deduction is barred by §167(e) unless either (1) the transfer was made prior to July 28, 1989 or (2) the remaindermen are not related to the widow — the holder of the term interest. If an amortization deduction is allowable, it is based on the cost of the life interest she purchased in her deceased husband's share of the trust. *Estate of Daisy F. Christ,* 54 T.C. 493 (1970), *aff'd,* 480 F.2d 171 (9th Cir. 1973); *Gist v. United States,* 296 F. Supp. 526 (S.D. Cal. 1968), *aff'd,* 423 F.2d 1118 (9th Cir. 1970); *Kuhn v. United States,* 392 F. Supp. 1229 (S.D. Tex. 1975). As yet no court has accepted the IRS's counterargument that the widow's life interest was acquired gratuitously and, hence, no deduction was allowable because of §273. "Interpreting §273 to prohibit amortization in a case such as this one could only occur by permitting form to conquer substance. The instant taxpayer does not receive income from the subject life estate as a result of a 'gift, bequest or inheritance.' She has acquired the life estate after exchanging valuable property, the right to which was undisputedly hers at the time of the exchange. She therefore will be permitted to amortize the cost basis of life estate payments received and reduce her taxable income by ratable annual deductions, pursuant to 26 U.S.C. §167(h)." *Kuhn,* 392 F. Supp. at 1240.

No amortization deduction is allowable to a widow who accepts the income interest in a trust established by her husband's will in lieu of a statutory share of his property. *Helvering v. Butterworth,* 290 U.S. 365 (1933). In that case the Court reasoned that by electing to accept the provisions of his will the widow waived her statutory rights instead of exchanging them for a life interest in the trust. The courts have thus far refused to follow the *Butterworth* approach in cases involving community property.

If an amortization deduction is allowable, it is determined by dividing the cost of the life interest the widow acquired by her life expectancy according to Table V, Reg. §1.72-9. *Gist v. United States, supra.* For this purpose the cost is the lesser of the actuarially determined values of (1) the remainder interest she transferred or (2) the life estate she received.

Example 9-21. *H*'s executor transferred property worth $200,000 to a typical widow's election trust established under *H*'s will, the H trust, the remaindermen of whom were not related to *W.* At a time when 11% interest rates applied *H*'s 70-year-old widow, *W,* transferred property worth $300,000 to an identical trust, the W trust, as required by *H*'s will. *W*'s life estate in the H trust is worth $133,378 and the remainder she transferred in the W trust is worth $99,933. Under Table V, Reg. §1.72-9, *W*'s life expectancy is 16 years. *W* may deduct $6,246 each year ($99,933 ÷ 16).

An amortization deduction not otherwise barred by §167(e) is allowable although the term interest that was purchased generates tax-exempt income. Section 265 denies deductions that are otherwise allowable under §212 for expenses of producing tax-exempt income. It does not affect amortization deductions, which are allowable under §167. *Manufacturer's Hanover Trust Co. v. Commissioner,* 431 F.2d 664 (2d Cir. 1970). Accordingly, a widow may be entitled to amortize the full cost of the life interest although it generates tax-exempt income.

No amortization deduction is allowable in the case of a voluntary election. The deduction is allowable only where the life interest was acquired for consideration.

The termination of a widow's election trust and distribution of all of its assets to the surviving spouse under a court order does not give rise to income to the surviving spouse where the trust instrument allowed the trustee to invade corpus for the surviving spouse's needs. LR 8335032.

§9.33. Estate Tax: The Husband's Estate

The use of a forced widow's election does not affect the amount of property included in the husband's gross estate on his death. Only his share of the community property is includible whether or not his widow elects to transfer her property in accordance with his plan. If the widow elects to accept an interest in the testamentary trust created by his will and to transfer her share of the community property to the trust, it does not augment his estate in any way. Instead, the widow's share passes directly from her to the trustee and does not become part of his estate. *Coffman-Dobson Bank & Trust Co.,* 20 B.T.A. 890 (1930), *acq.,* X-1 C.B. 13 (1931). The same rule applies where the transfer is made pursuant to an inter vivos election. *Pacific National Bank,* 40 B.T.A. 128 (1939), *acq.,* 1939-2 C.B. 28. If the widow elects to take under the husband's will, she receives a life income interest in the trust. The life interest in the husband's trust may constitute a qualifying income interest for life for which a marital deduction would be available under §2056(b)(7). Presumably, the amount of the deduction would be reduced by the value of the remainder interest that the surviving spouse was required to give up in her share of the property. *See* §2056(b)(4); *United States v. Stapf,* 375 U.S. 118 (1963). As indicated by Reg. §20.2056(b)-4(b), "if an obligation is imposed upon the surviving spouse by the decedent in connection with the passing of a property interest, the value of the property interest is to be reduced by the amount of the . . . obligation." Determining the amount allowable as a marital deduction in the husband's estate should not be affected by §2702.

§9.34. Estate Tax: The Widow's Estate

The widow should not hold any power over the property her husband transferred to the trust that might cause it to be included in her estate under §2041. Of course, any portion of the trust with respect to which a marital deduction was allowed to the husband's estate under §2056(b)(7) is includible in the widow's estate under §2044. Apart from those concerns, the main issue is the extent to which the property the widow transferred to the trust is includible in her estate under §2036(a)(1). Nothing is includible if the widow received full and adequate consideration in exchange for the property she transferred to the trust. According to the IRS and the decision in *Gradow v. United States,* 897 F.2d 516 (Fed. Cir. 1990), inclusion is required unless the consideration she received has a value at least equal to the full value of the property she transferred, not just a remainder in it. *See* §9.26. From the economic point of view the consideration should be sufficient if it equals the actuarially determined value of the remainder interest transferred by the widow.

> [F]or the purpose of evaluating whether [plaintiff's] election constituted full and adequate consideration within the meaning of §2036(a), the consideration flowing from Betty Gradow consists of the property which would otherwise have been included in her gross estate by virtue of her retention of a life estate — *i.e.,* her half of the community property. *Gradow,* 11 Cl. Ct. at 816, *quoted with approval in aff'g decision,* 897 F.2d 516, 518 (Fed. Cir. 1990).

Gradow is the first opinion in which a court has given extended consideration to identifying the property transferred by the widow for purposes of §2036(a). For purposes of determining the adequacy of the consideration received by the widow, the IRS has argued that the widow should be considered to have transferred the entire value of the property she transferred to the trust. Taxpayers have countered by arguing that the widow only transferred the remainder interest in her share of the property. *Gradow* is consistent with earlier decisions in which the courts seem to have concluded that the widow transferred the entire interest in her property in exchange for a life interest in the net amount of property her husband transferred to the trust. *United States v. Righter,* 400 F.2d 344 (8th Cir. 1968); *United States v. Past,* 347 F.2d 7 (9th Cir. 1965); *Estate of Lillian B. Gregory,* 39 T.C. 1012 (1963) (dicta).

The IRS approach totally ignores the value of the life estate the widow retained in her share of the property. It would be logical and consistent with the gift tax treatment to consider that the widow transferred only a remainder interest in her property in exchange for a life interest in the decedent's property, or that she transferred the entire interest in her property but is credited with receiving a life estate in all of the property transferred to the trust. The significance of the difference is illustrated in Example 9-22.

> **Example 9-22.** The community property estate of *H* and his wife, *W,* had a total value of $1,200,000 when *H* died. Under *H*'s will his net share of the property, $450,000, passed to the trustee of a widow's election trust, the H trust. All of the net income of the H trust was payable to *W* for life if she survived him and transferred her share of the community property to an identical trust, the W trust. Upon *W*'s death the remainder interests in both trusts were distributable to their children. If *W* did not transfer her share of the community property to the W trust, she would have received no benefit from the H trust. *W* was 77 when she elected to transfer her share of the community property, $550,000, to the W trust. At the time an 11.2% rate applied for purposes of valuing the interest. The factor for the life estate of a 77-year-old is .55830 and the factor for the remainder following her life is .44170. Thus, *W*'s life interest in *H*'s share of the property is worth $251,235

and the remainder is worth $198,765. *W*'s life interest in her share of the property is worth $307,065 and the remainder is worth $242,935.

Under the IRS approach, expressly approved in *Gradow, W* received only a life estate in H's property, worth $251,235, in exchange for the full value of her share of the property, $550,000. This approach ignores the value of the life interest *W* retained in her share of the property, which, at 11.2%, should yield her income with a present value of $307,065 over her lifetime. *W*'s estate must include the value of the W trust on the estate tax valuation date applicable to her estate less the consideration she received, valued in accordance with §2043(a) at the time of her election. This "frozen dollar" approach limits the consideration offset to $251,235 regardless of any increase in the size of the trust corpus. *See United States v. Past,* 347 F.2d 7 (9th Cir. 1965).

Under the alternative theory nothing is includible in *W*'s gross estate under §2036; *W* transferred an interest worth $242,935 for which she received an interest worth slightly more, $251,235.

The adequacy of the consideration received by the widow requires a comparison of the value of the interests she transferred with the value of the interests she received. If the widow did not receive full consideration, the portion of the trust attributable to her contributions to the trust is includible in her gross estate, valued on the date of her death, *less* the value of the interests she received in exchange. §2043(a).

The "frozen dollar" approach of §2043(a) is used to value the consideration received by the widow. This value is limited to its actuarial value on the date of her election. *United States v. Past,* 347 F.2d 7 (9th Cir. 1965). The consideration offset is not based on the actual amount of income she received (*i.e.,* the consideration offset is a fixed dollar amount and not a proportional part of the trust). Also, the value of the offset is determined by the actuarial tables in effect on the date of the election that were used to determine the gift tax consequences of the transfer, and not on subsequently adopted tables that assume a higher yield. *Estate of Elfrida G. Simmie,* 69 T.C. 890 (1978), *aff'd,* 632 F.2d 93 (9th Cir. 1980).

No offset is allowable in the case of a voluntary election because the widow does not receive any additional interests by reason of the election and transfer.

§9.35. GSTT

Given the arcane nature of the widow's election and its infrequent use, it is hardly surprising that the GSTT was adopted without any consideration of its potential application to widow's election trusts. Without any guidance other than the GSTT itself, the manner in which it will apply to widow's election trusts is far from clear. However, the probable results are suggested by matching the established estate and gift tax treatment of widow's election trusts with the provisions of the GSTT. The analysis should be equally applicable to transfers that do not involve community property.

First, in the case of a typical widow's election the husband will probably be treated as the transferor of the property that passes from his estate to the trust and the widow will be treated as the transferor of the property she transfers in trust. For GSTT purposes the husband is appropriately treated as the transferor of all of the property that passes from his estate to the widow's election trust although a life estate in it passes to the widow in exchange for the transfer of some of her property to a similar trust. Part or all of the husband's GSTT exemption could be allocated to his trust by making appropriate entries on Schedule R of his estate tax return. Reg. §5h.5(a)(3); Form 706 Instructions (rev. July 1990).

The widow is properly treated as the transferor of the portion of the trust attributable to her property if the transfer involves a taxable gift. That result flows from §2652(a) under which the donor is the transferor "in the case of any property subject to the tax imposed by chapter 12." The same result should follow even though the widow receives full consideration for her transfer, as a result of which the transfer of her property does not involve a taxable gift. Parenthetically, by reason of §2702 and the *Gradow* decision, widow's election trusts are likely to result in cash equivalency (*i.e.,* the widow will only be required to transfer property the total value of which is equal to the actuarially determined value of her life estate in the husband's trust). As indicated in the following examples the identity of the transferor may be different if a testamentary election involves outright transfers.

Example 9-23. *H* died leaving Blackacre, worth $1,000,000, to his widow, *W,* on condition that she transfer Whiteacre, worth $500,000, to their granddaughter, *D.* If *W* accepts the gift, *H* will be treated as having given $500,000 to *W* and $500,000 to *D. H*'s gift of $500,000 to *D* is a direct skip that is subject to the GSTT. *W* neither made a gift for gift tax purposes nor a transfer for GSTT purposes.

Example 9-24. *H* transferred Blackacre, worth $1,000,000, to a widow's election trust on condition that *W* transfer Whiteacre, worth $500,000, to a similar trust. Their granddaughter, *D,* is a contingent remainderman of the trust. For GSTT purposes if *W* accepts the condition *H* will probably be treated as the transferor of the $1,000,000 that passes to the trust. *W* will be treated as the transferor of $500,000.

Second, if each spouse transfers property to a separate trust, the separate existence of each trust will be recognized for GSTT purposes. Even if only one trust is created, the separate share rule of §2654(b) requires that the portion transferred by each spouse be treated as a separate trust. Under that subsection, "the portions of a trust attributable to transfers from different transferors shall be treated as separate trusts."

Third, under the GSTT apparently the amount of a generation-skipping transfer made by a widow's election trust will be determined without regard to any consideration given or received by the husband or the widow. Accordingly, the amount of a taxable distribution made from the wife's trust upon her death would be determined without regard to the value of the life estate she received in her husband's share of the property. Under the GSTT a consideration reduction is expressly allowed only for "the amount of any consideration provided by the transferee." §2624(d).

Example 9-25. Under a typical widow's election will *W* elected to accept a life estate worth $500,000 in a $1,000,000 trust established by her husband. Their grandchildren are the remaindermen of the trust. As required by the husband's will *W* transferred property worth $750,000 to a trust in which she retained a life estate worth $375,000. Presumably *H*'s executor could elect to claim a QTIP marital deduction for up to $625,000 — the $1,000,000 value of the property transferred to the trust less the $375,000 value of the remainder in *W*'s property that she was required to give up. For gift tax purposes §2702 requires that the value of *W*'s retained term interest be disregarded. Accordingly, *W* made a gift of $250,000 (the $750,000 value of the property she transferred, less the $500,000 value of the life estate she received). The transfer would not have involved a taxable gift if the value of the property she transferred had not exceeded the value of the life estate she received in her husband's trust. *W* could not allocate her GSTT exemption to the transfer because of the limitation of §2642(f). *See* §2.27.1. *W* died and was survived by her son, *S,* and *S*'s daughter, *D.* When *W* died the property of her trust, worth $1,000,000, passed outright to *D.* Under *Gradow* the value of the widow's trust is includible in her estate less the value of the consideration she received. If *H*'s executor elected to claim a QTIP marital deduction, a portion of *H*'s trust would also be includible in *W*'s estate under §2044. To that extent *W* would become the transferor of *H*'s trust for GSTT purposes. The distribution of its corpus to *D* would be subject to the GSTT. In addition, the distribution of the $1,000,000 corpus of *W*'s trust to *D* would be a taxable termination subject to the GSTT. *W*'s executor could allocate *W*'s GSTT exemption to the transfer. The distribution to *D* of the corpus of *H*'s trust is also a taxable termination subject to the GSTT.

As indicated in Example 9-25, §2624(f) prevents the widow from allocating her GSTT exemption to the transfer if the property transferred by her would be includible in her estate if she were to die immediately after the transfer. In such a case the allocation can only be made at the end of the estate tax inclusion period. *See* §2642(f) and §2.27.1. Under the *Gradow* approach (*see* §9.34), the property transferred by the widow would not be includible in her estate if the value of the life estate in the husband's trust was at least equal to the total value of the property she transferred. If the *Gradow* test is satisfied, presumably the widow could allocate her GSTT exemption in a gift tax return for the year in which the transfer was made. If so, the valuation of property for purposes of determining the inclusion ratio is its gift tax value. §2624(b)(1). The widow would argue that the value of the gift is its net value — determined after offsetting it by the value of the life estate received by the widow — zero. The value is the denominator of the applicable fraction. The amount of the GSTT exemption allocated to the transfer is the numerator. Thus, if she allocates $1 to the transfer the applicable fraction is 1. Accordingly, the inclusion ratio — one minus the applicable fraction — is zero. In response the IRS could be expected to argue that the value of the gift referred to in §2642(b)(1) is the value of the property transferred without regard to a consideration offset, even one that is allowed for gift tax purposes.

Example 9-26. The facts are the same as in Example 9-25, except *H*'s will only required *W* to transfer an amount of property equal in value to the actuarially determined value of her life estate in *H*'s trust. Electing to take under the will, *W* transferred property worth $500,000 to a trust in which her retained life estate was worth $250,000. *H*'s executor may claim a QTIP marital deduction of up to $750,000 ($1,000,000 less the $250,000 value of the remainder interest of *W* in the property that *W* was required to transfer to the trust). Under §2702 the value of *W*'s retained life interest is disregarded for gift tax purposes. Even so, *W* has made no gift because the value of the property she transferred, $500,000, does not exceed the value of the life estate she received. For GSTT purposes if *W* allocates $1 of her GSTT exemption to the transfer the inclusion ratio of the trust may be zero. As a protective matter she should file a gift tax return reporting the transfer to the trust, reflecting the offset for the consideration received, and electing to allocate $1 of her GSTT exemption to the trust. When *W* dies the *Gradow* approach will not require any of the property she transferred to be included in her estate. If *H*'s executor elected to claim a QTIP marital deduction with respect to *H*'s trust, a portion of it will be included in *W*'s estate under §2044. *W* would also be treated as the transferor of that portion of the trust. *W* could allocate a portion of her GSTT exemption to it. The distribution to *D* of the corpus of *W*'s trust is subject to the GSTT. However, *D* would argue that no GSTT is due because the trust has a zero inclusion ratio.

§9.36. Widow's Election Variations

Prior to the adoption of the unlimited marital deduction, planners showed considerable ingenuity in devising variations on the basic widow's election plan. Some plans, such as the voluntary measured election developed by Miller and Martin, are primarily concerned with reducing or eliminating the estate tax on the widow's share of the property. Voluntary Widow's Election: Nation-Wide Planning for the Million Dollar Estate, 1 Cal. W. L. Rev. 63 (1965). Under it the widow receives a life interest in the husband's net share of the property if she transfers property with an exactly equivalent value to their children or to a trust of which their children are the remaindermen. The object of the plan is to assure that the life interest the widow receives will constitute full and adequate consideration for the full value of the property she transfers. As a result, her transfer does not involve a gift and none of it will be included in her gross estate under §2036. *See* §9.34. However, the exchange will involve the same income tax consequences as the traditional election. Thus, the trustee may realize a substantial gain under §1001(e). The widow might also realize a small gain. Again, the widow would only be entitled to amortize the cost of the life interest if the remaindermen are not closely related to her.

Example 9-27. *H* left his residuary estate to the trustee of a testamentary trust who was authorized to sell a life interest in the trust to *W* in exchange for the transfer by *W* of property with a total value equal to the actuarial value of the life interest to the trustee of a separate trust for the benefit of their adult children. Under *H*'s will the life estate was required to be valued by multiplying the fair market value of the trust assets by the appropriate life interest factor based upon *W*'s age. For example, if *H* transferred property worth $500,000 to the trust, *W* was 65, and the interest rate used for valuation was 9.2%, *W*'s life estate in *H*'s trust would have a value of $344,950. Thus, *W* would be required to transfer property worth $344,950 to the trust in order to receive a life estate in *H*'s share of the property. The transfer by *W* would not involve a gift of any interest in the remainder. More important, for estate tax purposes *W* would have received full consideration in money or money's worth for the property she transferred to the trust.

Because of §1001(e) the trustee of *H*'s trust might realize a gain of the full amount, $344,950, as a result of the exchange. Section 167(e) would prevent *W* from claiming an amortization deduction. *W* might also realize a gain on the transaction, but it would probably be quite small because the basis in the property she transferred is adjusted to its estate tax value in *H*'s estate under §1014.

The adoption of the unlimited marital deduction largely eliminated the appeal of the "annuity" widow's election, described in detail in Professor Norman Lane's article, The Widow's Election as a Private Annuity: Boon or Bane for Estate Planners, 44 S. Cal. L. Rev. 74, 132-138 (1971). Under an annuity widow's election plan the husband leaves his share of the property to a discretionary trust in which the widow does not have any fixed rights. No marital deduction is allowable to the husband's estate, but no part of the trust will be includible in the widow's estate. The trustee of the trust is authorized to make distributions of principal and income to the widow after the separate trust funded with her share of the property is exhausted. The widow transfers her share of the community property to a trust of which she is the principal beneficiary. The "annuity" aspect is a feature of that trust: The widow retains a life income interest in the trust and the right to receive fixed annual payments of principal from it.

The overall objective of the annuity plan is to reduce or eliminate the amount of property that will be subject to inclusion in the widow's estate. That is accomplished by requiring her trust to be exhausted before she is entitled to any distribution from the husband's trust. The widow's transfer of property to her trust will involve some gift — which could be large if the remaindermen are family members and the value of the widow's retained life estate is disregarded under §2702 (*i.e.*, it is not a qualified interest). Of course, whatever remains of the trust at the time of the widow's death is includible in her estate. No consideration offset is available under §2043(a) because she did not receive any fixed consideration in exchange for the transfer of her property to the trust. Since the plan does not involve a sale or exchange, no gain or loss is realized on the transfer of the widow's property to the trust. Accordingly, wholly apart from §167(e) the widow would not be entitled to any amortization deduction.

The plan assumes that the widow will consume a substantial part of her share of the community property during her lifetime. The result is essentially the same as if she used her share of the community property to purchase an annuity. Indeed, such an approach has been suggested by other commentators. *See, e.g.,* Cohen, Recent Developments in the Taxation of Private Annuities, U.S.C., 16th Tax Inst. 491 (1964). Backup support for the widow is provided by a discretionary trust under the husband's will which, incidentally, would not qualify for a marital deduction under §2056(b)(7) in the husband's estate. The plan could generate some estate tax savings. However, the widow may feel insecure if future distributions to her depend upon an independent trustee's exercise of discretion.

§9.37. Widow's Election Insurance Trust

In the insurance trust approach, described in more detail at §6.22.4, the insured spouse transfers his community property interest in an insurance policy to an irrevocable insurance trust. The interest of the noninsured spouse is also transferred to the trust. However, her interest is revocable until she elects, following the death of the insured, either to withdraw her half of the insurance proceeds or to permit them to become a part of the irrevocable trust. In the latter case the surviving spouse will be entitled to receive the income from the entire trust.

The insured spouse may control the incidence of gift tax on the initial transfer by borrowing against the life insurance policies or by granting withdrawal powers to the beneficiaries. The uninsured spouse may make a gift to the remaindermen upon the death of the insured spouse, but her gift is reduced by the value of the life interest she receives in the insured's portion of the trust. A portion of the trust property may be included in her estate (the portion of the trust attributable to her transfers less the actuarial value of the life interest in the insured spouse's share of the trust). Note that the use of a measured election could eliminate the potential inclusion in the noninsured spouse's gross estate of any portion of the proceeds.

Section 1001(e) should not prove to be a problem to the trustee who sells an interest to the uninsured spouse, since the basis in the trust assets is not determined under §§1014, 1015, or 1041. For a further discussion of this type of trust, *see* Price, The Uses and Abuses of Irrevocable Life Insurance Trusts, U. Miami, 14th Est. Plan., ¶1111.3 (1980). *See also* §6.22.4.

§9.38. State Tax Consequences

The state income and transfer tax consequences of a widow's election should not be ignored at any stage. A widow's election plan may have an important impact on the state death tax when the husband dies. For example, the election may be taxed as if the deceased husband transferred his share of the community property to the remainderman of the widow's election trust. *In re Estate of Brubaker,* 98 Cal. Rptr. 762 (Cal. App. 1971) (former California inheritance tax law). The transfer may also result in a taxable gift from the widow to the remainderman. Finally, when the widow dies, some of the property she transferred to the trust will probably be subject to the death tax. Some states that impose inheritance taxes may not allow the widow's share of the property to be reduced by any consideration she received from her husband. *E.g., In re Estate of Patten,* 419 P.2d 157 (Wash. 1966) (former Washington inheritance tax law). Such states reason that a consideration analysis is inappropriate where the state tax is based upon the value of the property received by the transferee and not upon the value of the property to the decedent or to his or her estate.

§9.39. Widow's Election Planning

The forced widow's election is not suitable for most clients. Although the widow can be given the benefit of a second look at the plan after her husband's death, her options are very limited. In order for the election to qualify as a bargained-for exchange, the plan must be relatively inflexible and the widow must, in effect, be disinherited if she elects against the will. The overall tax consequences are moderately favorable, except for the possibility that §1001(e) will require the trust to realize a large gain if the widow elects to take under the will. That consideration alone is sufficient to deter many planners from recommending a forced widow's election plan. Some tax advantages remain, however, if the widow is only required to transfer an amount in trust equal to the actuarially determined value of the life estate she receives in the husband's trust. Such a transfer does not generate any gift or estate tax liability and may escape the GSTT as well. *See* §9.35.

A voluntary widow's election plan is consistent with the overall planning goals of many clients. The attractiveness of a voluntary plan is enhanced by the availability of the unlimited marital deduction for QTIP trusts. In particular, the estate tax on the deceased spouse's share of the community property may be deferred if the surviving spouse receives a qualifying income interest for life. §2056(b)(7). Unfortunately, however, such a trust cannot allow any distributions to be made to any other person during the widow's lifetime. Flexibility can be added to the plan if the husband transfers an amount equal to the amount sheltered by the unified credit to a discretionary trust from which distributions could be made to the widow and other family members. In addition, the widow could be given a special testamentary power to appoint the assets of one or both trusts. As noted above some commentators have encouraged the use of a voluntary widow's election instead of a forced one. *See, e.g.,* Kahn & Gallo, The Widow's Election: A Return to Fundamentals, 24 Stan. L. Rev. 531 (1972).

F. DIVIDING INTERESTS: SALES OF REMAINDERS, JOINT PURCHASES, GRITS, AND QUALIFIED PERSONAL RESIDENCE TRUSTS

§9.40. Introduction

Clients have attempted to transfer property at substantially reduced gift and estate tax cost through a variety of approaches that are based on the limited application of the estate tax to life interests in property and on the valuation of temporally divided interests in property according to assumed rates of return and mortality tables. Several key features of the law encouraged those approaches. First, upon the death of the owner of a life interest in property the value of the underlying property is ordinarily not includible in the decedent's estate. Second, with the exception of inter vivos transfers subject to §2702, annuities, life interests, term interests and remainders are all valued according to actuarial tables based upon 120 percent of the applicable federal rate. When current interest rates are high the actuarial tables place a correspondingly high value on life interests and term interests whether or not the income paid to the life or term tenant actually reaches the actuarially determined level. The more-or-less mechanical application of the valuation rules enhanced the appeal of some unusual estate planning techniques, particularly the sale of remainder interests, the joint purchase of property, and the transfer of property to trusts in which the grantor retained an interest for a term that was likely to end before his or her death. Each now looks less promising than before. The estate tax benefit of the sale of a remainder interest in property is threatened by the decision in *Gradow v. United States,* 897 F.2d 516 (Fed. Cir. 1990). *See* §9.34. The gift tax rules of §2702 severely restrict the ability to benefit from sales of remainders, joint purchases, and the use of most other devices that depend upon the retention of term interests. However, the creation of trusts in which the grantor retains a term interest in a personal residence is encouraged by an exception to the general rule. §2702(a)(3). *See* §9.43.3.

The general approach of §2702 is reflected in the following passages from Reg. §25.2702-1:

> (a) Scope of section 2702. Section 2702 provides special rules to determine the amount of a gift when an individual makes a transfer in trust to (or for the benefit of) a member of his or her family and the

individual or an applicable family member retains an interest in the trust. . . .

(b) Effect of section 2702. If section 2702 applies to a transfer, the value of any interest retained by the transferor or any applicable family member is determined under §25.2702-2(b). The amount of the gift, if any, is determined by subtracting the value of any interests retained by the transferor or any applicable family member from the value of the transferred property. If the retained interest is not a qualified interest . . . the retained interest is typically valued at zero, and the amount of the gift is the entire value of the property.

Note that §2702 only applies when the transferor *retains* an interest in the transferred property. This point is illustrated by Prop. Reg. §25.2702-2(d):

Example 3. D transfers property to an irrevocable trust under which the income is payable to *D*'s spouse for life. Upon the death of *D*'s spouse, the trust is to terminate and the trust corpus is to be paid to *D*'s child. *D* retains no interest in the trust. Although the spouse is an applicable family member of *D* under section 2702, the spouse has not retained an interest in the trust because the spouse did not hold the interest both before and after the transfer. Section 2702 does not apply because neither the transferor nor an applicable family member has retained an interest in the trust. The result is the same whether or not *D* elects to treat the transfer as a transfer of qualified terminable interest property under §2056(b)(7).

This interpretation of §2702 creates a loophole of sorts that is analogous to the spousal remainder trusts that were used to shift the income of a short-term trust until §672(e) was amended in 1986 to treat the grantor as holding any interest that was transferred to his or her spouse. While the transferor will be treated as having transferred the full value of the property in example 3 of Reg. §25.2702-2(d), the transferor and the donee may occupy the property for the donee's lifetime. Unless the transferor elects to claim the QTIP marital deduction with respect to the transfer, the property will not be included in the estate of the donor or the donee; unless a QTIP marital deduction is claimed, the property will not be included in the estate of the donee spouse, who received only a life interest in the property. Under this approach the use of the property may be retained for the donee's lifetime without taxing any appreciation in value that takes place over the donee spouse's lifetime.

§9.41. Sale of Remainder Interest

In the sale of a remainder interest, a senior family member who owns an asset sells a remainder interest in the property to a junior family member for its actuarially determined value. Such a sale made to a family member prior to October 8, 1990, the effective date of §2702, did not involve a gift. Of course, if the property had appreciated in value during the time it was owned by the senior family member some gain might result from the sale of the remainder interest. Some private letter rulings suggested that such a transfer of a remainder interest removed the asset from the owner's estate, which is a logical result. If the actuarial tables function properly the value of the consideration received in exchange for the remainder interest will grow to equal the value of the entire property at the expiration of the retained life estate. For example, LR 8145012 (TAM) concluded that,

> [O]n these facts we have determined that the sale of the remainder interest in the X Ranch, as described, would not result in the inclusion of any part of the value of the property in decedent's gross estate by reason of section 2036 of the Code. Of course, the proceeds of such a transfer, owned by the decedent at her date of death, would be includible in her estate under section 2033 of the Code.

Under the approach adopted in *Gradow v. United States,* 897 F.2d 516 (Fed. Cir. 1990) (*see* §9.34), the sale of a remainder interest in property does not remove the property from the owner's estate unless the owner receives consideration equal to the total value of the property. Accordingly, the sale of a remainder for its actuarially determined value would not remove the property from the seller's estate. Instead, the full value of the property would be included in the seller's estate under §2036(a) less the value of the consideration received in connection with the sale of the remainder, §2043(a). Unless there is a favorable outcome in other cases that raise the issue, the sale of a remainder interest holds little promise.

If a client decides to sell a remainder interest in property with the object of removing the asset from his or her estate, the planning requires a reliable determination of the fair market value of the property. In the case of publicly traded securities and some other properties, quotations are readily available. In other cases an expert appraisal should be obtained. The reason is simple: If the transferor receives less than the full fair market value of the property, the sale may involve a gift and the property may be included in the transferor's estate.

§9.41.1. Gift Tax Consequences

> *Sale of remainder interest and joint purchase of interests in property.* — Under the bill, the retention of a term interest (including a life estate) in property is treated like the retention of an

interest in trust. Moreover, a joint purchase of property is treated as an acquisition of the entire property by the holder of the term interest, followed by a transfer of the remainder interest. Thus, for purposes of determining the amount of the gift, the bill effectively treats the purchaser of a new life estate pursuant to a joint purchase as making a transfer of the entire property less the consideration paid by the remainderman. Senate Finance Committee Report, S. Rep. No. 3209, 101st Cong., 2d Sess., 136 Cong. Rec. §15629, 15629 (1990).

Under traditional analysis, the sale of a remainder interest involves a gift from the owner to the remainderman *only* if the remainderman pays too little for the remainder interest. Similarly, the transaction involves a gift from the remainderman to the seller if the remainderman pays too much for the remainder interest. Prior to October 9, 1990 the possibility of either party making a gift was avoided if the remainderman paid the actuarially proper amount for the remainder. Of course, if the seller were terminally ill at the time, the valuation of the remainder interest according to the actuarial tables would be inappropraite. *See Estate of James Stuart Pritchard,* 4 T.C. 204 (1944) (sale of insurance policy by terminally ill insured for cash surrender value was not made for full and adequate consideration). Reliance upon the actuarial tables in such a case might result in the seller making a gift the remainderman.

The valuation rules of §2702 apply to the sale of a remainder interest to a family member after October 8, 1990 (the effective date of §2702). The seller is treated as having transferred the entire property in exchange for the consideration paid by the remainderman. The resulting gift does not qualify for the annual gift tax exclusion. Note, however, that under §2702(c)(4) the fair market value of a retained term interest in nondepreciable tangible property is taken into account in determining the amount of the gift. Such an approach also applies to a joint purchase of such property by members of the same family. §2702(c)(2). *See* §9.42. Of course, the preexisting rules would continue to apply to the sale of remainder interests to persons who are not within the definition of family members in §2704(c)(2). Note also that the new rules do not apply to transfers of property that the transferor uses as a personal residence. *See* §9.43.3.

Example 9-28. Seller, *S,* sold a remainder interest in a commercial building to her cousin, *C,* for cash equal to its actuarially determined value. A cousin is not considered to be a family member for purposes of §2702. *See* §2704(c)(2). Accordingly, the valuation rules of §2702 do not apply to the sale. As the transfer was made for an amount equal to its actuarially determined value, the transfer did not involve a gift.

Section 2702 would have applied had the transfer been made

to a spouse, ancestor, lineal descendant, or brother or sister, or the spouse of any of them. If so, *S* would have been treated as having transferred the entire value of the property in exchange for only the value of the remainder interest. According to the Senate Committee Report the special rule of §2702(c)(4) does not apply to depletable or, presumably, depreciable, property. Finally, §2702 would not apply to the sale of a remainder interest in a personal residence used by the seller.

§9.41.2. Estate Tax Consequences

The most significant estate tax issue involved in the sale of a remainder interest is whether the decedent received full and adequate consideration in exchange for the transferred property. Under §2036(a) property transferred during lifetime in which the transferor retained a life interest is includible in the transferor's estate unless the transferor received "adequate and full consideration" in connection with the transfer. In the sale of a remainder, once the fair market value of the entire property is determined, the client must decide whether to adhere to the *Gradow* requirement that the transferor receive consideration equal to the full value of the property — not just the actuarially determined value of the remainder. *See* §9.34. Such a requirement does not appear to be required by the text of §2036(a). It requires the inclusion of "all property to the extent of any interest therein of which the decedent has at any time made a transfer (except in the case of a bona fide sale for an adequate and full consideration in money or money's worth)." Under the actuarial tables the transferor has received full consideration for a remainder interest if the transferor was paid an amount equal to the present value of the remainder interest (the right to the outright ownership of the property upon the transferor's death). A simple economic assumption underlies the valuation of life and term interests: The value of the right to receive property upon the death of a person of a certain age is the present value of that property, discounted by an appropriate interest rate. Stated in a different way: The present value of a remainder interest (*i.e.,* the right to receive the property at the end of a fixed period — the end of the life expectancy of the life tenant) is equal to the amount that, invested at the assumed rate, at the end of the fixed period would equal the present value of the property. The following example indicates the shortcomings of the *Gradow* approach.

Example 9-29. *T* owns Blackacre, which is worth $100,000. Based upon *T*'s age and the applicable interest rate, *T*'s life estate in Blackacre is worth $70,000 and the remainder is worth $30,000. The figures assume that if $30,000 were invested at the applicable interest rate for *T*'s lifetime, the fund would equal $100,000 at the time of *T*'s death. Under *Gradow* a sale of the remainder interest in Blackacre would not have been for adequate and full consideration unless *T* received an amount equal to its full fair market value, $100,000. If that were the appropriate approach, what must *T* receive in order to avoid the reach of §2036(a) if *T* later sells her retained life estate? Another $100,000, or, would $70,000 suffice?

Example 9-30. Father, *F*, owns Blackacre, a recreational residence, which has a basis of $50,000 and a fair market value of $150,000. Under the actuarial tables *F*'s life estate is worth $100,000 and the remainder following his life is worth $50,000. *F* proposes to sell Blackacre to his daughter, *D*, for $50,000, subject to a retained life estate in *F*. If the sale is made *F* would realize a gain on the sale. Presumably the transaction would not involve a gift under §2702 because of the exception for personal residences. *See* §2702(a)(3). *See also* §9.43.3. Most important, under *Gradow*, Blackacre would be includible in *F*'s estate under §2036(a) because the consideration received by *F* was not equal to the full value of Blackacre. However, the value of Blackacre includible in *F*'s estate would be reduced by $50,000 under §2043(a) — the value of the consideration received from *D*.

Under the economically sound approach, the seller of a remainder interest ordinarily receives adequate and full consideration if he or she receives an amount equal to the actuarially determined value of the remainder interest. As indicated above, that value is determined according to the transferor's age and the interest rate that applies to the valuation of term interests, life estates, remainders, and annuities for the month in which the transfer takes place.

§9.41.3. Income Tax Consequences

The sale of a remainder interest in appreciated property will result in a gain to the seller. The gain is determined according to the difference between the consideration received and the portion of the seller's basis attributable to the remainder interest. If the property is encumbered in an amount that exceeds that portion of the seller's basis, the seller will realize an additional amount of gain. Note that a loss in a sale to a related person would not be deductible by the seller. §267(a).

The seller, as life tenant, should be entitled to continue to claim depreciation with respect to the underlying property. Under the basic rule of §167(d) the life tenant is entitled to claim depreciation on the property. §167(d). The life tenant will not be able to amortize the remaining basis in the property as a cost of acquisition. §167(e).

The life tenant should be able to claim any losses that are generated by the property. Gain or loss on a sale of the underlying property is apportioned between them. Rev. Rul. 71-122, 1971-1 C.B. 224 (gain on condemnation of inherited life estate and remainders in real property taxed to life tenant and remaindermen). However, a life tenant with power of sale who is required to hold and reinvest the proceeds of sale for the ultimate benefit of the remaindermen may be treated as a trustee and required to file a Form 1041 with respect to the gain or loss. Rev. Rul. 61-102, 1961-1 C.B. 245.

§9.42. JOINT PURCHASES

The acquisition of divided interests in property not previously owned by the purchasers is involved in a joint purchase. In a joint purchase the senior family member contributes an amount toward the purchase price that is equal to the actuarially determined value of the life estate or other term interest that he or she will receive in the property. The junior family member contributes the balance of the purchase price. Presumably, nothing is includible in the senior's estate if the funds used by the junior to purchase the remainder did not originate with the senior. A joint purchase has a better chance than the sale of a remainder interest of preventing the property from being included in the senior purchaser's estate.

§9.42.1. Gift Tax Consequences

Prior to the adoption of §2702 a joint purchase by family members did not involve a gift if the interests were properly valued and each contributed an amount equal to the actuarially determined value of the interest acquired. This "old rule" will continue to apply with respect to joint purchases by persons who are not family members within the definition contained in §2704(c)(4). Effective after October 8, 1990, a joint purchase by family members (as defined in §2704(c)(2)) will almost certainly involve a gift from the senior to the junior. Under §2702(c)(2), if a joint purchase is made by family members, the holder of the term is treated as having acquired the entire interest in the property and having transferred the remainder in exchange for the consideration contributed by the remainderman. For purposes of §2702, the term "family member" does not include nieces, nephews, cousins, and more remotely related persons and their spouses.

Example 9-31. During a month when a 9.8% interest rate applied under §7520, Aunt, *A,* aged 71, and Nephew, *N,* purchased commercial real property for $200,000. *A* and *N* are not treated as family members under §2702(c)(4). Under Table S(9.8) *A*'s life estate had a value of .62000 and *N*'s remainder a value of .38000. Accordingly, *A* contributed $124,000 to the purchase price and *N* contributed $76,000. The joint purchase did not involve a gift by *A* or *N;* each contributed the required amount to the joint purchase.

Example 9-32. The facts are the same as in Example 9-31, except the parties are family members — Mother, *M,* aged 71, and Son, *S.* For gift tax purposes §2702(c)(2) requires that *M* be treated as having transferred the entire property, worth $200,000, in exchange for a consideration of $76,000. Thus, *M* is considered to have made a gift to *S* of $124,000. Query whether the gift would qualify for the annual exclusion. Presumably *M* would not be treated as having made a gift if the property acquired were a personal residence to be used by *M. See* §2702(a)(3). In the latter case *M* and *S* should enter into an ancillary agreement containing the provisions required for a qualified personal residence trust.

Section 2702(a)(3) might be construed broadly to bring the joint purchase of a personal residence by family members within the scope of the exception it creates. In order to satisfy the requirements of the Regulations, Reg. §25.2702-5, the parties should consider entering into a supplemental agreement containing the provisions required in the case of qualified personal residence trusts. In particular, the parties would have to enter into an agreement that included certain mandatory provisions. Thus, in Example 9-32 *M* and *S* might enter into an agreement ancillary to the purchase of the personal residence for *M* which contained the required terms. In order to reduce the risk that the residence would be included in *M*'s estate under §2036 she might purchase a term of years rather than a life interest in the property.

Term Interests in Tangible Property. Under §2702(c)(4) a special rule applies to the valuation of a term interest in tangible property, the use of which does not have a substantial effect upon the valuation of the underlying property. As explained in the following excerpt from the Senate Finance Committee Report, such a term interest is valued according to its market value.

A special rule applies to a term interest in tangible property where the non-exercise of the term-holder's rights does not substantially affect

> the value of the property passing to the remainderman. In that case, the value of the term interest is the amount for which the taxpayer establishes that the term interest could be sold to an unrelated third party. Such amount is not determined under the Treasury tables, but by reference to market norms, taking into account the illiquidity of such interests.
>
> For example, the rule could apply to the joint purchase of a painting or undeveloped real estate (the value of which primarily reflects future development potential). On the other hand, the rule would not apply to a joint purchase of depletable property. Treasury regulations would provide for the proper treatment of improvements or other changes in property governed by this special rule. S. Rep. No. 3209, 101st Cong., 2d Sess., 136 Cong. Rec. S15629, 15683-15684 (1991).

Presumably this section would apply to the transfer of a piece of jewelry or an art object that was transferred subject to the transferor's right to the exclusive use of the item for a fixed period. Of course, establishing the fair market value of the right to use a $2.5 million diamond necklace for ten years may be difficult. The application of this provision is illustrated by Reg. §25.2702-2(d), examples 8-10.

> **Example 9-33.** *A* and his child *B* purchased a painting for $1,000,000. *A* acquired a 10 year term interest and *B* the remainder. According to the actuarial valuation of their interests pursuant to §7520, *A* paid $400,000 of the purchase price and *B* paid the other $600,000. The painting is a type of property covered by §2702(c)(4). *A* established that an unrelated party would pay $100,000 for a 10 year term interest in the painting. *A* is treated as having made a gift of $300,000, the difference between his contribution to the purchase of the painting and the fair market value of the term interest.

§9.42.2. Estate Tax Consequences

The goal of excluding the property from the senior family member's estate may be achieved if (1) the property is acquired from a third party, (2) the property is properly valued, and (3) the senior and junior family members each contribute the actuarially appropriate amount toward the purchase price. If each party contributes the actuarially appropriate amount toward the purchase of the property from a third party, none of the underlying property should be included in the senior's estate. Note that inclusion should not be required under §2035(d)(2) if the purchase were made within three years preceding the life tenant's death. However, if the funds contributed by the remainderman are traceable to gifts received from the life tenant, the life tenant may be treated as having purchased the entire property and donated the remainder to the remainderman. If so, §2036(a) would require the entire property to be included in the senior's estate. The rules of §2702 regarding the treatment of joint purchases apply for gift tax purposes and *not* for estate tax purposes. In particular, §2702(a)(1) provides that, "Solely for the purpose of determining whether a transfer of an interest in trust (to or for the benefit of) a member of the transferor's family is a gift (and the value of such transfer), the value of any interest in such trust retained by the transferor or any applicable family member (as defined in section 2701(e)(2)) shall be determined as provided in paragraph (2)." In addition, the requirements of *Gradow* regarding the sufficiency of the consideration received by a transferor should not apply — in a joint purchase the senior family member has not transferred any interest.

§9.42.3. Income Tax Consequences

A joint purchase may involve significant income tax consequences that vary depending upon whether the joint purchase was made on or before July 27, 1989. To begin with, the initial purchase from a third party should not have any immediate income tax consequences. In addition, under the basic rules the senior family member is entitled to amortize the cost of acquiring the term interest. However, in the case of interests created after July 27, 1989, no amortization deduction is allowable "for any period during which the remainder interest is held (directly or indirectly) by a related person." §167(e)(1). Although no amortization deductions are allowed, the senior's basis is reduced and the remainderman's basis in the remainder is increased by the amount of the disallowed amortization deductions. §167(e)(3).

§9.43. GRITs (Grantor Retained Interest Trusts)

GRITs were used, beginning in the 1980s, to reduce the gift and estate tax costs of transferring property within the family. Under a typical plan a senior family member transferred securities or other valuable property to an irrevocable trust from which he or she was entitled to receive the income for a term of years with remainder to his or her children or other beneficiaries. At the end of the term the property would pass outright to the designated remaindermen. The gift of the remainder interest was a future interest that did not qualify for the annual gift tax exclusion. However, the gift tax cost of making the gift was reduced by the actuarially determined value of the term interest retained by the grantor. Of course, if the grantor died during the term of the trust it would be includible in the grantor's estate under §2036(a).

The enactment of §2702 seriously restricts the use of GRITs. Under it retained interests other than "qualified interests" are valued at zero in determining the gift tax consequences of transfers. For this purpose a qualified interest is (1) the right to receive a fixed annual payment (a grantor retained annuity trust, or GRAT); (2) the right to receive each year a fixed percentage of the value of the principal determined annually (a grantor retained unitrust, or GRUT); or (3) a noncontingent remainder interest following a GRAT or GRUT. Importantly, the rules of §2702 do not apply if (1) the remaindermen are not members of the grantor's family or (2) the only property transferred to the trust is a personal residence used by the grantor. As explained in §9.42.1, a special valuation rule applies to term interests in tangible property.

In order to allow the grantor some flexibility in meeting the tax problems that would arise if he or she died before the end of the term, grantors often retained a reversionary interest or a power of appointment in such a case. In particular, GRITs usually provided that if the grantor dies before the end of the term, the trust property would be distributed either (1) to the grantor's estate (*i.e.,* the grantor retained a reversionary interest) or (2) as the grantor appointed under a general power of appointment. In the case of a transfer creating a qualified interest the retention of a reversion or a general power of appointment apparently would not be assigned any value (*i.e.,* neither the reversion nor the power of appointment is not a qualified interest). Reg. §25.2702-3(e), example 1. Thus, the retention of such a power would not reduce the amount of the gift to the remaindermen. The retention of a reversion or general power of appointment may be desirable, although it has no value under §2702.

While the retained term interest in a traditional form of GRIT with a family member as remainderman will be valued at zero, it may be attractive to some clients who are interested in retaining some interest in the property while removing further appreciation in value from their estates. The arrangement, of course, will result in the inclusion of the property in the transferor's estate if the transferor dies during the term of the retained interest. Again, however, the risk of inclusion is eliminated if the term interest is transferred to the donor's spouse.

Example 9-34. Donor, *D,* owns all of the stock of D, Inc., which has a value of $5,000,000. *D* is unwilling to make an outright gift of a substantial portion of the stock, but is willing to transfer 20% of the stock to a trust in which *D* will hold an income interest for a 10-year term, at the end of which the trust will terminate and the property will be distributed to *D*'s children. Under §2702 *D*'s retained interest would be valued at zero for gift tax purposes. Recognizing discounts for lack of marketability and minority interest, the transferred stock would be valued at $600,000-700,000.

D's unified credit will offset most, if not all, of the gift tax on the transfer. If the value of D, Inc. were to grow at an annual rate of 7% compounded quarterly, the trust's porportionate interest would more than double in value in 10 years. The transfer may be particularly attractive if D, Inc. is likely to be acquired by another company or to go public and *D* is interested in an increased income stream. Of course, if *D* dies during the 10-year term the trust is all included in *D*'s estate.

§9.43.1. Gift Tax Consequences

The gift tax consequences of transferring property to a GRIT depend upon the time at which the GRIT was created, the relationship between the grantor and the remaindermen, and the type of property involved. The strict valuation rules of §2702 generally apply to transfers made after October 8, 1990 in which the grantor retains a term interest and the remainder is transferred to a member of the grantor's family. As indicated above, the term members of the family include the grantor's spouse, ancestors, lineal descendants, brothers and sisters, and the spouses of any of them. §2704(c)(2). In such cases the retained interest is generally treated as having a value of zero unless it is a qualified interest as defined in §2702(b).

For gift tax purposes if the rules of §2702 were applied without mitigation the same interest may be taxed more than once. For example, a retained term interest might be valued at zero under §2702 in connection with the transfer of a remainder interest in property, but be valued at fair market value when it is later transferred. In light of this possibility, the Regulations provide for a reduction in the total amount of an individual's taxable gifts if he or she transfers an interest that was previously valued under §2702, other than a qualified interest. Reg. §25.2702-6. The amount of the reduction is the lesser of (1) the increase in the individual's taxable gifts resulting from the interest being initially valued under §2702 and (2) the increase in the individual's taxable gifts (or taxable estate) resulting from the subsequent transfer of the interest. Reg. §25.2702-6(b)(1). In determining the increase in taxable gifts resulting from the subsequent transfer of the interest, the transferor's annual exclusion is considered to apply first to transfers other than the transfer of the interest previously valued under §2702. Id.

§9.43.2. Qualified Interests

The value of a qualified interest retained by the transferor is taken into account in determining gift tax consequences under §2702. For purposes of §2702 a qualified interest is an annuity interest, a unitrust interest, or a noncontingent remainder following an annuity or unitrust interest. In particular, under §2702(b) a qualified interest is:

1. Any interest which consists of the right to receive fixed amounts payable not less frequently than annually,
2. Any interest which consists of the right to receive amounts which are payable not less frequently than annually and are a fixed percentage of the fair market value of the property in the trust (determined annually),
3. Any noncontingent remainder interest if all of the other interests in the trust consist of interests described in paragraph (1) or (2).

The value of the grantor's retained annuity or unitrust interest is determined in accordance with §7520 (*i.e.,* according to the actuarial tables of IRS publications 1457 and 1458, based upon 120% of the applicable federal midterm rate for the month in which the transfer was made).

Example 9-35. Grantor, *G,* aged 50, transferred property worth $200,000 to a trust in which she retained the right to receive a payment of $20,000 each year for 15 years at the end of which the trust property would be distributed to her son, *S.* An assumed interest rate of 10.2% applied to the valuation of interests in the trust. According to Table B, the right to receive $1 each year for 15 years is worth 7.5200. Accordingly, *G*'s retained interest had a total value of $151,040. *G* made a gift of only $48,960. The transfer may be attractive to *G,* particularly if the property generates enough income to make the annual payments and be worth more than $200,000 at the end of the 15-year term.

Note that if *G* dies during the term the full value of the trust may not be includible in her estate. Instead, her estate would only include the value of property necessary to generate the annuity amount according to interest rate assumptions current at the time of her death. *See* §9.43.4. Thus, if *G* died during the term, at a time when the corpus had grown to $400,000 and a 12% rate applied, only $166,667 would be included in her gross estate.

The potential gift and estate tax savings are more dramatic if *G* transfers a much greater sum, say, $2,000,000. In that case *G*'s unified credit would be sufficient to cover the gift tax on the transfer if she had not made any prior taxable gifts.

Example 9-36. The facts are the same as in Example 9-35, except *G* retained a right to receive a payment each year equal to 10% of the value of the principal of the trust, determined annually. Under Table D of IRS Publication No. 1458, the remainder interest was worth .341007. Accordingly, *G*'s interest was worth the reciprocal or .658993 ($131,798.60). The gift in this case would be $68,201.40.

The amount distributable under a GRUT will vary from year to year according to the value of the principal of the trust. As the examples indicate, a GRUT will also produce a smaller remainder interest than a GRAT with a similar initial payout rate. Accordingly, the amount of the gift in a GRUT will be smaller. Distributions from a GRUT may keep up with inflation. However, that advantage is offset by the additional difficulty of having to value the trust property annually.

The Regulations define the criteria that must be met in order for a term interest to be treated as a qualified interest. Reg. §25.2702-3. Some of the requirements track those of charitable remainder trusts. The requirements include mandatory and optional provisions. Those applicable to qualified annuity interests are described in Reg. §25.2702-3(b); those applicable to qualified unitrust interests are described in Reg. §25.2702-3(c); and those applicable to both types of trusts are described in Reg. §25.2702-3(d). Among the requirements: an annuity trust must prohibit additions to the trust and all types of trusts must prohibit commutation of the interest of the transferor or applicable family member.

§9.43.3. Personal Residence Trusts

The valuation rules of §2702 do not apply if the only property transferred is a "residence to be used as a personal residence by persons holding term interests in such trust." §2702(a)(3). Under the Regulations the exception applies to a trust "the governing instrument of which prohibits the trust from holding for the original duration of the term interest, any asset other than one residence to be used or held for use as a personal residence by the term holder." Reg. §25.2702-2(b). A personal residence is defined as either the principal residence of the term holder as determined under §1034 or one other residence which would be treated as the term holder's dwelling under §280A(d)(1), without regard to §280A(d)(2), or an undivided fractional interest in either. Reg. §25.2702-5(b)(2). Under §280A(d)(1) a dwelling unit is treated as the taxpayer's residence if the taxpayer uses it more than the greater of 14 days or ten percent of the number of days it was rented during the taxable year. A residence may be rented for a portion of the year so long as the requirements of §280A are met. Reg. §25.2702-5(d), example 2. The personal residence may include appurtenant structures used by the term holder for residential purposes and adjacent land that is reasonably appropriate for residential purposes. Reg. §25.2702-5(b)(2)(ii). A personal residence may be subject to a mortgage, but may not include any personal property. Regulation §25.2702-5(b)(1) authorizes expenses, whether or not attributable to principal to be paid directly by the term holder. Spouses may transfer their interests in the residence to the same personal residence trust, provided that the governing instrument prohibits anyone other than a spouse from holding a term interest in the residence concurrently with the other spouse. Reg. §25.2702-5(b)(3). Thus, if one spouse dies the interest of the deceased spouse should not pass for the unexpired balance of his or her term interest to any person other than the surviving spouse. Beyond these requirements the Regulations give relatively little guidance regarding a personal residence trust. Importantly, the Regulations create a safe harbor for trusts that meet the requirements of a "qualified personal residence trust" and, therefore, are treated as personal residence trusts. Reg. §25.2702-5(a).

Two Personal Residence Limit. Under Reg. §25.2702-5(a) a trust of which the term holder is the grantor is not a personal residence trust (or a qualified personal residence trust) if, at the time of the transfer, the term holder of the trust already holds term interests in two trusts that are personal residence trusts (or qualified personal residence trusts) of which the term holder was the grantor. Accordingly, it appears that a husband and wife could participate in a maximum of three personal residence trusts: (1) one which is their principal residence (whether or not it is hers, his, or theirs); (2) one which is the wife's separate property; and, (3) one which is the husband's separate property.

Qualified Personal Residence Trust. A qualified personal residence trust must meet the requirements of Reg. §25.2702-5(c). In brief, the term personal residence is defined in the same way as above. Similarly, a qualified personal residence trust may include appurtenant structures, but no personal property such as furniture and furnishings. More important, the Regulations require the inclusion of certain terms and allow the inclusion of others. Most clients will probably prefer a trust that includes some of the optional terms — particularly ones that allow the proceeds of a sale, involuntary conversion, or destruction of a residence to be reinvested in a replacement residence or converted into a qualified annuity interest for the remainder of the term holder's interest.

In order to meet the requirements of a qualified personal residence trust, a trust *must*:

1. Require that any income of the trust be distributed to the term holder not less frequently than annually;
2. Prohibit the distribution of corpus to any beneficiary other than the grantor prior to the termination of the term interest;
3. Prohibit the trust from holding, for the entire term of the trust, any asset other than one residence. However, the trust may permit additions of cash to a separate account of the trust in amounts that do not exceed the costs of trust expenses for six months and improvements to be paid within six months. In addition, the trust may permit contributions to be made to finance the purchase of the initial residence within three months if the trustee has previously entered into a contract to purchase the residence. Similarly, additions may be made for the purchase of a residence to replace another residence within three months of the addition, provided that the trustee has already entered into a contract to purchase the residence.
4. Require, if the trust permits the addition of cash to the trust, the trustee to determine, not less often than quarterly, the amounts held by the trust for payment of expenses in excess of the amounts permitted. Any excess must be immediately distributed to the term holder.
5. Require, upon termination of the term holder's interest, the trustee to distribute outright to the term holder within 30 days of termination, any excess of additions to the trust not required to pay trust expenses due and payable on the date of termination.
6. Provide that the trust ceases to be a qualified personal residence trust if the residence ceases to be used or held for use as a personal residence by the term holder.
7. Provide that the trust ceases to be a qualified personal residence trust upon sale of the property if the trust does not permit the trust to hold the proceeds of sale in a separate account. A trust that allows the proceeds to be retained must provide that the trust ceases to be a personal residence trust with respect to the proceeds of sale (or the proceeds of involuntary conversion or insurance payments caused by damage or destruction of the residence) not later than the earlier of the date (a) two years after the sale; (b) the termination of the term holder's interest in the trust; and (c) the date on which a new residence is acquired by the trust.
8. Provide that no later than 30 days after the trust ceases to be a personal residence trust with respect to certain assets (*e.g.*, the proceeds of sale that are not used to purchase a replacement residence within two years), the assets must either be distributed outright to the term holder or be converted into a

> qualified annuity interest held in a separate share of the trust for the balance of the term holder's interest. Alternatively, the trustee may be given the sole discretion to make either such a distribution to the term holder or such a conversion to a qualified annuity interest.

Under the Regulations part or all of the proceeds of a sale, involuntary conversion or of the insurance proceeds resulting from damage or destruction of the residence may be used within two years of the sale, involuntary conversion, or damage or destruction of the residence, to acquire another residence for the term holder. Any excess cash must be distributed to the term holder or converted to a qualified annuity interest and held as a separate share of the trust. Reg. §25.2702-5(c)(8). The requirements for a qualified annuity interest are set out in Reg. §25.2702-5(c)(8)(ii).

If the grantor is treated as owner of the trust for income tax purposes, the trust should qualify for the benefits of §§121, 1033 and 1034 if the residence is sold or involuntarily converted. Under the approach taken by Rev. Rul. 85-13, 1985-1 C.B. 184, the trust might not realize any gain if the residence were sold to the grantor near the end of the term of the trust. *See* §10.32.8. The sale of a highly appreciated residence and the conversion of the proceeds into a qualified annuity interest might prevent the residence's appreciation in value from being included in the term holder's estate if he or she died during the balance of the term. *See* §9.43.4.

The Regulations do not prohibit the grantor from serving as trustee. Nonetheless, an independent trustee, who may be given broader discretion, is preferable. Put simply, if an independent party serves as trustee the trust is less likely to arouse suspicion by the IRS and more likely to accomplish its purposes unchallenged.

Following the death of the term holder a qualified personal residence trust might continue for the benefit of the remaindermen. Following the termination of the term holder's interest the trustee might lease the residence to him or her for fair market value. However, such a lease should not be prearranged or included as a part of the original trust, which might support an argument that the grantor-term holder had retained the use or occupancy of the residence for a period extending beyond his or her retained term interest. In most cases the owner of a residence should not enter into a qualified personal residence trust if it is critical that he or she have the use of the residence following the expiration of the term.

Retained Reversionary Interest. Several considerations may persuade a grantor to retain a partial or total reversionary interest in a personal residence trust, to take effect if he or she dies prior to the expiration of his or her term interest. First, the retention of such an interest will increase the value of the interests he or she retains in the trust and, correlatively, diminish the amount of the gift to the remaindermen. Second, it will also assure that the benefits of §§121, 1033 and 1034 will be available (*i.e.,* the grantor will be treated as owner of the trust income and principal under §§672-677). Third, the retention of a reversionary interest may enable the grantor better to address the estate tax problems that will arise if he or she dies during the term of the trust. In particular, if the grantor dies during the term without having retained a reversionary interest, the trust will be included in the grantor's estate, but he or she will have no power of disposition over the property. Thus, the trust might create a substantial estate tax liability without providing the grantor's estate with any resources with which to pay the tax. On the other hand, if the grantor retains a reversionary interest he or she would have the power to dispose of the property of the trust in a way that qualifies for the marital or charitable deduction. Alternatively, the grantor might choose to use the assets received as a result of the reversion to pay the expenses of his or her estate, including any estate tax liability that might arise on account of the personal residence trust.

§9.43.4. Estate Tax Consequences

If the grantor dies during the term of a trust in which the grantor has retained the income interest, the trust is fully includible in the grantor's estate under §2036(a). However, in the case of a GRAT the grantor's estate only includes so much of the trust property as is required to generate the specified annuity amount, using the appropriate assumed interest rate under §7520. *Marvin L. Pardee,* 49 T.C. 140 (1967), *acq.,* 1973-2 C.B. 3; Rev. Rul. 82-105, 1982-1 C.B.133 (charitable remainder annuity trust). This possibility suggests that a qualified personal residence trust should include an optioned provision that allows it to convert to a qualified annuity trust if the personal residence is sold during the term. Such a sale and conversion could be very advantageous if the grantor were likely to die before the end of the term and the residence had appreciated greatly in value. As indicated above, the gain on a sale may not be subject to the capital gains tax.

Under Revenue Ruling 82-105, in the case of a lifetime annuity the amount includible in the grantor's estate is determined according to the following formula:

$$\frac{\textit{Annuity Payable}}{\text{§7520 Interest Rate}} = \text{Amount Includible}$$

Revenue Ruling 76-273, 1976-2 C.B. 268, adopts a similar approach in the case of charitable remainder unitrusts, which should also apply to GRUTs. First, the equivalent income interest rate is calculated by dividing the unitrust adjusted payout rate by 1 minus that rate. If the equivalent income interest rate is equal to, or greater than, the adjusted payout rate, the full amount of the trust is includible in the grantor's estate. If the adjusted income interest rate is less than the adjusted payout rate, "then a correspondingly reduced proportion of the trust assets would be includible in the gross estate under §2036(a)(1)." The includible portion would be determined by dividing the equivalent income interest rate by the §7520 rate. Of course, if the grantor dies during the term of a GRIT, GRAT, or GRUT, any unified credit claimed by the grantor when the trust was established will be restored. In addition, the grantor will be allowed a credit for any gift tax paid with respect to the transfer of property to the trust. On the other hand, if the grantor survives the term of the retained interest, none of the property of the trust is includible in his or her estate.

As described in §9.43.3, the grantor may choose to retain a reversionary interest that will take effect if he or she dies during the term of the trust. By doing so, he or she may be able to ameliorate the tax effects of the trust being included in his or her estate.

§9.43.5. Income Tax Consequences

The transfer of property to a GRIT, GRAT, or GRUT does not have any immediate income tax consequences. For income tax purposes the grantor will be treated as the owner of the trust if the value of the grantor's reversionary interest exceeds five percent of the value of the trust property. Accordingly, the income and capital gains would be taxed to the grantor. In addition, the benefits of §§121, 1033, and 1034 will be available. Also, during the term of the grantor's interest the trust may hold the stock of an S corporation. §1361(c)(2)(A)(i).

§9.44. Conclusion

The adoption of §2702 and the decision in *Gradow, supra* §9.26, largely eliminate the potential tax benefits of the sales of remainder interests and joint purchases. Section 2702 also limits the tax benefits of some, but not all, GRITs. The previously enjoyed benefits of GRITs remain if either the holders of the term and remainder interests are not "family members" or the only property involved is a residence used by the holder of the term interest. Qualified personal residence trusts and residential GRITs involving nonfamily members offer attractive tax advantages. How long they will remain viable is another matter. As Professor Joseph Dodge has pointed out: "It is hard to see what nontax-avoidance purpose a GRIT would serve." Dodge, Rethinking Section 2036(c), 49 Tax Notes 199, 204 (1990).

BIBLIOGRAPHY

ALI-ABA, Study Materials, Estate Planning under Chapter 14 and the Proposed Regulations (1991)

Adams & Herpe, The 1990 Tax Act: Reading Between the Lines, 130 Tr. & Est. 20 (1991)

Committee on Tax and Estate Planning, Report: Predeath Estate Planning Through Family Bargaining, 8 Real Prop., Prob. & Tr. J. 223 (1973)

Emory & Hjorth, An Analysis of the Changes Made by the Installment Sales Revision Act of 1980, 54 J. Tax. 66, 130 (1981)

Fiore, Estate and Value Opportunity Shifting Through Installment Sales, Private Annuities and Interest Free Loans, U. Miami, 14th Inst. Est. Plan., ch. 7 (1980)

Freeland, Lind & Stephens, What Are the Income Tax Consequences of an Estate's Sale of a Life Interest? 34 J. Tax. 376 (1971)

Johanson, Revocable Trusts, Widow's Election Wills and Community Property: The Tax Problem, 47 Tex. L. Rev. 1247 (1969)

Lane, Widow's Election as a Private Annuity: Boon or Bane for Estate Planners, 44 S. Cal. L. Rev. 74 (1971)

Malloy & Bufkin, Critical Tax and Financial Factors that Must Be Considered When Planning a Private Annuity, 3 Est. Plan. 2 (1975)

McCaffrey, Asset Freezes — New Rules, U. Miami, 25th Inst. Est. Plan., ch. 8 (1991)

Moore, Grantor Retained Income Trusts — Fish or Fowl?, 130 Tr. & Est. 18 (1991)

Mulligan, New Tax Law Restricts GRITs and Related Planning Tools But Opportunities Remain, 18 Est. Plan. 66 (1991)

O'Sullivan, The Private Annuity: A New Look at an Old Estate Planning Tool, 17 Washburn L.J. 466 (1978)

CHAPTER 10

TRUSTS

A. Introduction

§10.1. Scope
§10.2. Encourage Flexibility
§10.3. Avoid Sham Trusts and Trusts with No Economic Substance
§10.4. Income Tax Summary
§10.4.1. Grantor Trust Rules, §§671-677
§10.4.2. Nongrantor Treated as Owner, §678
§10.4.3. Distributable Net Income, §643(a)
§10.4.4. Income Tax Consequences of Distributions, §§651, 652, 661, 662
§10.4.5. No Standard Deduction; Personal Exemptions
§10.4.6. Two Percent Floor on Miscellaneous Itemized Deductions, §67
§10.4.7. Passive Activity Losses (PALs)
§10.4.8. Rules Applicable to Simple Trusts, §§651, 652
§10.4.9. Rules Applicable to Complex Trusts, §§661, 662
§10.4.10. Throwback Rules, §§665-667
§10.4.11. Sale of Appreciated Property Within Two Years, §644
§10.4.12. Recognition of Loss, §267
§10.4.13. Section 1244 Stock
§10.4.14. S Corporation Stock
§10.4.15. Redemptions Under §303
§10.4.16. Taxable Year of the Trust
§10.4.17. Payment of Income Tax by Fiduciary
§10.4.18. Estimated Income Tax Payments
§10.5. Gift Tax Summary
§10.6. Estate Tax Summary
§10.6.1. Right to Vote Stock of Controlled Corporation, §2036(b)
§10.6.2. Benefits Under Qualified Plans, §2039

§10.6.3. General Power of Appointment, §2041
§10.6.4. Life Insurance Proceeds, §2042
§10.6.5. Alternate Valuation Date
§10.6.6. Deduction of Expenses Under §2053
§10.6.7. Deferral of Estate Tax
§10.6.8. Discharge of Executor and Other Fiduciaries from Personal Liability for Estate Tax
§10.6.9. Flower Bonds

B. The Revocable Trust

§10.7. Scope
§10.8. Reserving the Power to Revoke
Form 10-1. Reserved Power to Amend or Revoke
§10.9. Nontestamentary Nature of Revocable Trusts
§10.10. Validity of Pour-Over to Revocable Trust
Form 10-2. Residuary Clause for Pour-Over Will
§10.11. Claims of Creditors Against Grantor
§10.12. Principal Advantages of Revocable Trusts
§10.13. Principal Disadvantages of Revocable Trusts
§10.14. Summary of Tax Consequences
§10.15. Income Tax Considerations
§10.16. Gift Tax Considerations
§10.17. Estate Tax Considerations

C. Planning the Beneficiary's Interests in an Irrevocable Trust

§10.18. Scope
Table 10-1. Income Tax Rates Applicable to Trusts and Estates, 1991
Table 10-2. Income Tax Rates Applicable to Trusts and Estates, 1990
§10.19. Multiple Trusts
§10.20. Mandatory or Discretionary Distributions?
§10.20.1. Distribution or Accumulation of Income
§10.20.2. Sprinkling of Income
§10.20.3. Powers Held by Independent Trustee
§10.20.4. Powers Limited by an Ascertainable Standard, §674(d)
§10.20.5. Grantor as Trustee
§10.20.6. Beneficiary as Trustee
§10.20.7. "Absolute" or "Uncontrolled" Discretion
§10.20.8. Standards to Guide the Exercise of Discretion
§10.20.9. Transferability of the Beneficiary's Interest
§10.20.10. Discretionary Distribution Form
Form 10-3. Discretionary Distributions
§10.21. Spendthrift Clauses — Restricting the Transfer of a Beneficiary's Interests

§10.21.1. Form of Spendthrift Clause
Form 10-4. Spendthrift Clause
§10.21.2. Self-Settled Trusts
§10.22. General Powers of Appointment
§10.23. Special Powers of Appointment
Form 10-5. Special Testamentary Power of Appointment
§10.24. $5,000 or 5% Power of Withdrawal
Form 10-6. 5 or 5 Power of Withdrawal
§10.24.1. Income Tax
§10.24.2. "Hanging Power"
Form 10-7. Hanging Power of Withdrawal
§10.25. Power to Withdraw Trust Assets Limited by an Ascertainable Standard
Form 10-8. Power of Withdrawal Limited by an Ascertainable Standard
§10.26. Other Nongeneral Powers of Appointment
§10.27. Beneficiary as Trustee
§10.27.1. Income Tax
§10.27.2. Gift Tax
§10.27.3. Estate Tax
§10.28. Removal and Replacement of Trustee
§10.29. Planning Summary

D. Planning the Grantor's Interests in an Irrevocable Trust

§10.30. Scope
§10.31. Basic Income Tax Rules
§10.31.1. Adverse Party
§10.31.2. Jointly Exercisable Powers
§10.32. Grantor Treated as Owner of Trust Under Subchapter J
§10.32.1. Grantor Makes Free Gift of Income Tax on Trust
§10.32.2. Trust Holds S Corporation Stock
§10.32.3. Trust Holds Installment Obligations
§10.32.4. Grantor Trust Not Subject to Throwback Rules
§10.32.5. Capital Gains of Grantor Trust Offset by Grantor's Losses
§10.32.6. Exclusion of Gain on Sale of Grantor's Principal Residence
§10.32.7. Nonrecognition of Gain on Certain Dispositions
§10.32.8. No Gain on Sale of Trust Property to Grantor
§10.32.9. Grantor Trust May Sell Stock to ESOP
§10.33. Basic Gift Tax Rules
§10.33.1. Annual Exclusion
§10.33.2. Charitable Deduction
§10.34. Powers That Result in Transfers Being Incomplete
§10.34.1. Joint Power to Make Discretionary Distributions
§10.34.2. Joint Power to Terminate Trust

§10.34.3. Retained Testamentary Special Power to Appoint Remainder
§10.34.4. Retained Testamentary Power to Revoke Successive Private Interest
§10.35. Basic Estate Tax Rules
§10.35.1. §2036
§10.35.2. §2037
§10.35.3. §2038
§10.36. Retained Reversionary Interest
§10.36.1. Income Tax Consequences
§10.36.2. Gift Tax Consequences
§10.36.3. Estate Tax Consequences
§10.37. Retained Control of Beneficial Enjoyment
§10.37.1. Income Tax Consequences
§10.37.2. Gift Tax Consequences
§10.37.3. Estate Tax Consequences
§10.38. Administrative Powers
§10.38.1. Income Tax Consequences
§10.38.2. Gift Tax Consequences
§10.38.3. Estate Tax Consequences
§10.39. Power to Revest Title in Grantor
§10.39.1. Income Tax Consequences
§10.39.2. Gift Tax Consequences
§10.39.3. Estate Tax Consequences
§10.40. Retained Income Interests
§10.40.1. Income Tax Consequences
§10.40.2. Gift Tax Consequences
§10.40.3. Estate Tax Consequences
§10.41. Power to Appoint Successor Trustees
§10.41.1. Revenue Ruling 79-353
§10.41.2. Power to Remove Trustee and Appoint Self
§10.41.3. Factors in Planning Power to Appoint Successor Trustee
§10.41.4. Independent Trustee or Cotrustee
§10.41.5. Extent of Trustee's Discretionary Powers or Authority to Make Distributions That Satisfy Legal Obligations
§10.41.6. Prohibit Distributions That Satisfy Legal Obligations
§10.41.7. Income Tax Consequences of Distributions for Support
§10.41.8. Drafting Power of Grantor or Beneficiary to Remove and Replace Trustee with Tax-Sensitive Powers
§10.41.9. Prohibit Self-Appointment by Grantor or Beneficiary
§10.41.10. Disclaimers
§10.41.11. Releases
§10.41.12. Eliminating Powers by Court Order

E. Additional Issues

§10.42. Introduction
§10.43. Selection of Trustee
§10.43.1. Corporate Fiduciary
§10.43.2. Lawyer as Trustee
§10.43.3. Grantor as Trustee
§10.43.4. Beneficiary as Trustee
§10.43.5. Cotrustees
§10.43.6. Removal of Trustees
§10.44. Selection of Property to Transfer in Trust
§10.45. Provisions Regarding Trust Investments
§10.45.1. Investment Standard
§10.45.2. Trustees with Greater Skill
§10.45.3. Additional Directions Regarding Specific Assets
§10.45.4. Investment Advisor
§10.46. Exculpatory Clauses
§10.47. Power to Allocate Between Principal and Income
§10.47.1. Stock Splits and Stock Dividends
§10.47.2. Amortization of Bond Premium and Accumulation of Discount
§10.47.3. Depreciation
§10.47.4. Unproductive and Underproductive Property
§10.47.5. Annuity Trusts or Unitrusts
§10.48. Perpetuities Savings Clause
Form 10-9. Perpetuities Savings Clause

Bibliography

> The purposes for which trusts can be created are as unlimited as the imagination of lawyers. There are no technical rules restricting the creation of trusts. The trust can be and has been applied as a device for accomplishing many different purposes. One of the most important is and has always been the making of family settlements. Through the trust it is possible to separate the benefits of ownership from the burdens of ownership. The whole responsibility for the management of the property is thrown upon the trustee. It is possible to create successive interests which could not be effectively created by giving successive legal interests. It is possible to make the extent of the interests of the beneficiaries dependent upon the discretion of the trustee. It is possible, to a certain extent at least, to protect the beneficiaries in the enjoyment of their interests by making those interests inalienable and putting them beyond the reach of creditors. 1 A. Scott, Trusts §1 at 2 (4th ed. 1987).

A. INTRODUCTION

§10.1. Scope

This chapter surveys the most important and most common types of trusts, including the revocable trust, §§10.7-10.17; the beneficiary's interests in irrevocable trusts, §§10.18-10.29; and, the grantor's interests in irrevocable trusts, §§10.30-10.41. Some features of specialized types of trusts are reviewed in other chapters (*e.g.,* marital deduction trusts are discussed in Chapter 5, insurance trusts in Chapter 6, trusts for minors in Chapter 7, charitable remainder trusts in Chapter 8, and grantor retained interest trusts (GRITs), including qualified personal residence trusts and widow's election trusts, in Chapter 9).

The opening sections of this chapter summarize the basic income, gift, and estate tax consequences of establishing trusts. Some consideration is also given to GSTT planning, although it is considered primarily in Chapter 2, §§2.22-2.40, and in connection with other topics, such as *Crummey* powers, §7.37, and life insurance trusts, §6.23. This part also includes a review of the basic income tax rules applicable to trusts. Because the trust is widely used as a probate avoidance device, some comparisons are drawn between the tax treatment given trusts on the one hand and estates on the other. Some of the same tax points recur at later places in the chapter, particularly in the review of the grantor trust rules in §10.32.

The second part, Part B, takes a long look at the revocable trust, which is probably the most common form of trust. It includes a review of some of the substantive law regarding the use of the trust, proceeds to a discussion of the advantages and disadvantages of the trust, and concludes with a summary of the principal tax consequences of using that form of trust.

Planning the powers and interests of a beneficiary in an irrevocable trust is the subject of Part C, which extends from a consideration of the use of multiple trusts through the nature and transferability of the beneficiary's interest to the conferral of powers of appointment and the appointment of the beneficiary as fiduciary. Part D is a companion piece that is concerned with planning the grantor's interests in an irrevocable trust. Those parts also include a consideration of the grantor trust rules. Income tax rules were added in 1954 that define the circumstances under which the grantor would be treated as the owner of a trust, §§671-677. Until changes made by the 1986 Act the short-term irrevocable trust was a popular way to shift income from the grantor to others. It was attractive to many clients because it allowed the grantor to retain a reversionary interest in the property — so long as the reversion is not expected to take effect within ten years. Now, however, the grantor is treated as owner of any portion of a trust with respect to which the grantor has a reversionary interest the value of which exceeds five percent of the value of such portion. §673(a).

Part E, which concludes this chapter, briefly discusses the choice of trustee and the selection of property to transfer to the trustee. Although this book does not give detailed attention to trust administration (itself a substantial and complicated subject), Part E does discuss two matters about which additional directions should often be given: the investment of trust funds and the allocation of receipts and disbursements between income and principal. A planner must be concerned about a host of other matters regarding administration of the trust, of which these two serve as good illustrations. The part concludes with a discussion of the Rule Against Perpetuities and the use of perpetuities savings clauses.

§10.2. Encourage Flexibility

A carefully planned and drafted trust is a valuable estate planning tool. Particular care is required in the case of an irrevocable trust because the permanency of the arrangement may seriously limit its ability to meet the beneficiaries' long-term needs. In general, the planner is challenged to make the trust as flexible as possible without giving up any of the potential tax savings. The dual objectives of flexibility and tax savings can be attained if the client is willing to give discretionary powers over distributions to an independent trustee. Such discretionary powers are "tax sensitive" and cannot be safely retained by the grantor or given to a beneficiary. In general, only nondiscretionary powers can be retained by the grantor or held by a beneficiary. However, beneficiaries can generally be given special powers of appointment over the trust property without adverse tax effects. The ultimate balance between flexibility and tax savings should be struck by the client after receiving an adequate explanation from the planner. A client should not be permitted to create a trust unless he or she understands its terms and effect. Above all, a client must understand the extent to which the trust is revocable.

§10.3. Avoid Sham Trusts and Trusts with No Economic Substance

The planner and client should be wary of tax-saving trust plans that seem to lack economic reality or substance; the tax savings are often illusory. For example, no interest deduction is available to the grantor for interest paid to the trustee in a transaction involving a circular flow of funds that appears designed only to generate a tax deduction for the grantor. Rev. Rul. 86-106, 1986-2 C.B. 28 (when parent-grantor transferred $50,000 to trustee of trust for children with oral agreement that trustee would subsequently loan the same amount to grantor, no interest deduction allowed for annual payment of $7,500 to trust); *see also, Guaranty Trust Co. v. Commissioner,* 98 F.2d 62 (2d Cir. 1938); Rev. Rul. 87-69, 1987-2 C.B. 46 (gift to child, no trust involved); LR 8709001.

In the 1970s and 1980s many gullible taxpayers, often medical professionals and others with large personal service incomes, bought expensive trust packages that they hoped would insulate their income from taxation. Often those trust schemes did not work. Instead, the taxpayers were denied any deduction under §212 for the cost of the trust package, Rev. Rul. 79-324,1979-2 C.B. 119, taxed on the income of the trust, and held liable for a five percent penalty for "negligence or intentional disregard of rules and regulations." *E.g., Richard L. Wesenberg,* 69 T.C. 1005 (1978) (physician); *Louis Markosian,* 73 T.C. 1235 (1980) (dentist). In *Estate of Floyd G. Paxton,* 86 T.C. 785 (1986), the Tax Court recounted the income tax treatment of "so-called family trusts" in this estate tax case and held that the assets of such a trust were includible in the grantor's gross estate.

> In such cases, the trusts have been denied income tax effect on the grounds that the trusts were shams, *Holman v. United States,* 728 F.2d 462, 465 (10th Cir. 1984); *cf. Zmuda v. Commissioner,* 731 F.2d 1417, 1421 (9th Cir. 1984), *aff'g* 79 T.C. 714 (1982); were grantor trusts under secs. 671 to 677, *Vnuk v. Commissioner,* 621 F.2d 1318, 1321 (8th Cir. 1980), *aff'g* a Memorandum Opinion of this Court; or involved assignments of income, *Vnuk v. Commissioner,* 621 F.2d at 1320; *Hanson v. Commissioner,* 696 F.2d at 1234. In *United States v. Buttorff,* 761 F.2d 1056 (5th Cir. 1985), a promoter was enjoined from selling pure equity or family trust packages. The PFO trust involved in the instant case was held to be a grantor trust under secs. 676 and 677 in *Paxton v. Commissioner,* 520 F.2d 923 (9th Cir. 1975), *aff'g* 57 T.C. 627 (1972). *Paxton,* 86 T.C. at 801, n.7.

Trusts of the type involved in the *Wesenberg* and *Markosian* cases have been marketed under a variety of names. The arrangements typically call for the taxpayer to transfer all of his or her property and future services to a trust in which the taxpayer retains substantial interests and over which the taxpayer and other nonadverse parties hold significant controls. By some miraculous alchemy the income received by the trust is supposed to escape taxation. Quite to the contrary, because of the taxpayer's retained interests and controls, the income of the trust is taxed to the grantor under §§671-677. Rev. Rul. 75-257, 1975-2 C.B. 251. *See also, Paul G. Dubois,* 51 T.C.M. 895 (1986). For the same reason, the transfer of property to the trust is not a completed gift, Rev. Rul. 75-260, 1975-2 C.B. 376, and the property transferred to the trust is fully includible in the transferor's estate. *Estate of Floyd G. Paxton, supra;* Rev. Rul. 75-259, 1975-2 C.B. 361.

Another expensive but ineffective package involves the transfer of property to a "foreign tax haven double trust." Rev. Rul. 80-74, 1980-1 C.B. 137. The promoter of the "double trust" involved in Revenue Ruling 80-74 represented that the trust would radically reduce or eliminate the taxpayer's income tax liability, avoid probate, eliminate estate and gift tax liabilities, and avoid state and local taxes. The plan involves the creation of a trust in a foreign country by an agent of the promoter to which the taxpayer transfers income-producing property. The income of the trust is distributed to a second foreign trust that, in turn, makes distributions to the taxpayer and his family as directed by the taxpayer as trustee. Not surprisingly, Revenue Ruling 80-74 concluded that the creation of the trusts is a sham and will not be recognized for tax purposes. Instead, all of the income will be taxed to the grantor, who is not entitled to a deduction under §212 for the expenses incurred in connection with the establishment of the "double trust." *See, e.g., Zmuda v. Commissioner,* 79 T.C. 714 (1982), *aff'd,* 731 F.2d 1417 (9th Cir. 1984); *Professional Services v. Commissioner,* 79 T.C. 888 (1982).

§10.4. Income Tax Summary

For income tax purposes, a trust other than one that is treated as owned by its grantor is generally recognized as a separate taxable entity. Perhaps most important, a trust acts as a conduit with respect to amounts that are distributed to beneficiaries during the taxable year. In particular, a trust is allowed to deduct, and the beneficiaries are required to report, amounts that were properly distributed to beneficiaries. Otherwise, trusts are generally subject to the same basic tax rules that apply to individuals. Thus, a trust reports the same items of income and is usually entitled to the same types of deductions and credits as individuals. However, the two percent floor on the deductibility of miscellaneous itemized deductions does not apply to "the deductions for costs which are paid or incurred in connection with the administration of the estate or trust and which would not have been incurred if the property were not held in such trust or estate." §67(e)(1). A complex trust is also allowed a deduction for amounts of gross income paid to a charity. §642(c)(1). In addition, estates and trusts created prior to October 9, 1969 are allowed deductions for amounts permanently set aside for charitable purposes. §642(c)(2).

The optimum income tax results may be attained if a trustee is given discretion to sprinkle income among a class of beneficiaries or accumulate it for later distribution. *See* §10.20.2. Flexibility is increased if the trustee is also given authority to distribute trust principal to the beneficiaries. However, such powers should not be held by the grantor or a potential distributee because of the adverse income, gift, and estate tax consequences. An adroit sprinkling of income among beneficiaries may substantially reduce the overall income tax cost of trust distributions. The accumulation of income can result in some overall savings through deferral (*i.e.,* no interest is charged on the additional tax imposed on accumulation distributions). Of course, the throwback rules prevent a trust from permanently absorbing the entire tax liability on income that is accumulated after the beneficiary becomes 21 years old.

The current compressed income tax rate structure limits the tax savings that can be achieved by splitting income among multiple taxpayers. However, it is possible, and may be profitable, to split income between one or two discretionary trusts and a beneficiary under 21. In such a case the trustees can optimize the allocation of income among the taxpayers by accumulating or distributing the income of the trusts. Of course, the planner and the trustees must take into account the effect of the Kiddie Tax on distributions. Under it, unearned income in excess of $1,000 of a child under 14 is taxed at the marginal rate applicable to the child's parent. The trusts could, for example, authorize the trustees to make income distributions to a minor beneficiary or to a custodian for the minor under the Uniform Transfers to Minors Act or the Uniform Gifts to Minors Act. Such a distribution would enable an adult to retain control over the funds although they are treated as having been distributed to the minor. In any event the income accumulated during the beneficiary's minority will be taxed to the trust and will not be subject to the throwback rules when an accumulation distribution is made to the beneficiary.

§10.4.1. Grantor Trust Rules, §§671-677

The separate existence of a trust is largely disregarded to the extent the grantor or any other person is treated as owner of the trust under §§§671-678. The rules of those sections establish the exclusive means by which the income of a trust is includible in the income of a grantor or other person solely by reason of his or her dominion and control over the trust. Reg. §1.671-1(c). However, the rules do not govern the outcome of cases involving the assignment of income, whether or not the assignment is to a trust: "[F]or example, a person who assigns his right to future income under an employment contract may be taxed on that income even though the assignment is to a trust over which the assignor has retained none of the controls specified in sections 671 through 677." Id. Under §§671-677 the grantor is treated as the owner of a trust to the extent he or she retains any of the interests or controls proscribed by §§673-677 (*e.g.,* a reversionary interest in a portion of a trust that is worth more than five percent of that portion, §673; controls over the beneficial enjoyment of the trust, §674; extensive administrative controls, §675; or, a power to revoke the trust, §676). *See* §§10.30-10.41.

§10.4.2. Nongrantor Treated as Owner, §678

A person other than the grantor of a trust is treated as its owner to the extent he or she has the power, acting alone, to vest the corpus or income of the trust in himself or herself. §678(a). *See* §10.20.6. However, a person other than the grantor is not treated as the owner of any part of the trust of which the grantor is treated as the owner under §§671-677 (*i.e.,* these provisions prevail over those of §678). Where the grantor or another person is treated as the owner of the entire trust, a fiduciary income tax return (Form 1041) should not be filed for the trust. "Instead, all items of income, deductions, and credit from the trust should be reported on the individual's Form 1040 in accordance with its instructions." Reg. §1.671-4(b). In other cases, the income, deductions, and credits attributable to the part of a trust of which the grantor or another person is treated as the owner are not reported by the trust on its Form 1041, but should be shown on a separate statement attached to that form. Reg. §1.671-4(a).

§10.4.3. Distributable Net Income, §643(a)

The term "distributable net income" (DNI) is significant only in connection with the income taxation of estates and trusts and their beneficiaries. DNI is a concept that limits the deductions allowable to estates and trusts for amounts paid, credited, or required to be distributed to beneficiaries. It is also used to determine how much of an amount paid, credited, or required to be distributed to a beneficiary is includible in the beneficiary's gross income. Finally, it is also used to determine the character of distributions to the beneficiaries. DNI, for any taxable year, means "the taxable income (as defined in section 63) of the estate or trust, computed with the modifications set forth in Regs. §§1.643(a)-1 through 1.643(a)-7." Reg. §1.643(a)-0.

The taxable income of the trust is the starting point from which DNI is computed. No deductions are taken into account for the distributions to beneficiaries or for the personal exemption otherwise allowable under §642(b). §§643(a)(1), (2). Capital gains are excluded unless they are (1) allocated to income or (2) paid, credited, or required to be distributed to a beneficiary during the taxable year. However, capital gains are taken into account to the extent a charitable deduction under §642(c) was allowed with respect to the gains. §643(a)(3); Reg. §1.643(a)-3(a)(3). An exercise of discretion by a trustee, allocating capital gains to income and distributing them to the beneficiaries, will be recognized for income tax purposes. *See, e.g.,* LR 8728001. Losses from the sale or exchange of capital assets are excluded from DNI except to the extent they enter into the determination of any capital gains that are paid, credited, or required to be distributed to any beneficiary during the year. The treatment of capital gains and losses accords with normal trust accounting rules under which they do not enter into the computation of net income. Because of the compressed income tax rates the overall tax burden may be lessened if capital gains are distributed — at least in part. Capital gains are not subject to the throwback rules, which can be important when a trust and its distributees are subject to disparate tax rates. Gains and losses are taken into account in computing the DNI of a trust in some circumstances, such as the year in which the trust terminates or makes partial distributions. *See* Reg. §1.643(a)-3(d), examples 4, 5.

Under §643(a)(4), extraordinary dividends and taxable stock dividends received by a simple trust are excluded to the extent the trustee in good faith allocates them to corpus and does not pay or credit them to any beneficiary. Conversely, extraordinary dividends and stock dividends are included in computing DNI in the case of a complex trust or where the dividends are not allocated to corpus for trust accounting purposes. Here again the distinction parallels normal trust accounting rules.

The amount of tax-exempt interest received by the trust is included in computing DNI, reduced by the expenses attributable to it that are not deductible by reason of §265 (which bars the deduction of expenses under §212 to the extent they are incurred in connection with the production of tax-exempt income). §643(a)(5). The amount included in DNI is also reduced by a portion of the tax-exempt interest that is deductible under §642(c). The latter reduction is required because the full amount of the charitable deduction is allowed under §642(c). The computation of DNI under §643 is illustrated by the following example from Reg. §1.643(d)-2(a):

> *Example* (1). Under the terms of the trust instrument, the income of a trust is required to be currently distributed to *W* during her life. Capital gains are allocable to corpus and all expenses are charged against corpus. During the taxable year the trust has the following items of income and expenses:

Dividends from domestic corporations	$30,000
Extraordinary dividends allocated to corpus by the trustees in good faith	20,000
Taxable interest	10,000
Tax-exempt interest	10,000
Long-term capital gains	10,000

Trustee's commissions and
miscellaneous expenses allocable to corpus 5,000

(2) The "income" of the trust determined under §643(b) which is currently distributable to *W* is $50,000, consisting of dividends of $30,000, taxable interest of $10,000 and tax-exempt interest of $10,000. The trustee's commissions and miscellaneous expenses allocable to tax-exempt interest amount to $1,000 (10,000/50,000 × $5,000).

(3) The "distributable net income" determined under section 643(a) amounts to $45,000 computed as follows:

Dividends from domestic corporations		$30,000
Taxable interest		10,000
Nontaxable interest	$10,000	
Less: Expenses allocable thereto	1,000	9,000
Total		49,000
Less: Expenses ($5,000 less $1,000 allocable to tax-exempt interest)		4,000
Distributable net income		45,000

In determining the distributable net income of $45,000, the taxable income of the trust is computed with the following modifications: No deductions are allowed for distributions to *W* and for personal exemption of the trust (section 643(a)(1) and (2)); capital gains allocable to corpus are excluded . . . (section 643(a)(3)); the extraordinary dividends allocated to corpus by the trustee in good faith are excluded (section 643(a)(4)); and the tax-exempt interest (as adjusted for expenses) and the dividend exclusion . . . are included (section 643(a)(5) and (7)). . . .

§10.4.4. Income Tax Consequences of Distributions, §§651, 652, 661, 662

Trusts and estates are allowed deductions, not subject to the two percent floor, for amounts paid, credited, or required to be distributed to beneficiaries during the year. §§651(a), 661(a). in order to be "properly . . . credited" to a beneficiary for purposes of §661, the income must be allocated to the beneficiary beyond recall. *Commissioner v. Stearns,* 65 F.2d 371 (2d Cir.), *cert. denied,* 290 U.S. 670 (1933). A mere allocation to the beneficiary of the income on the books of the accountant or the fiduciary is not sufficient. *Estate of Keith W. Johnson,* 88 T.C. 225, *aff'd,* 838 F.2d 1202 (2d Cir. 1987). The deduction for distributions is limited, however, to the DNI of the trust. As explained above, DNI is the taxable income of the trust adjusted as provided in §643(a). The beneficiaries who receive distributions from a trust are required to report in their returns an amount equal to the total distribution deduction claimed by the trust. §§652(a), 662(a). However, tracking the provisions of §102, a trust is not allowed to deduct, and the beneficiaries are not required to report, a distribution made in satisfaction of a specific gift of money or other property that is payable all at once or in not more than three installments. §663(a). Not surprisingly, no distribution deduction is allowed to a noncharitable trust for the cost of providing care to specific animals. Rev. Rul. 76-486, 1976-2 C.B. 192. For purposes of the GSTT the interests of animals are also disregarded — a dog is not a person. LR 9036043.

Reflecting the conduit principle, a distribution has the same character in the hands of a beneficiary as it had in the hands of the trustee. §§652(b), 662(b). Specifically, a distribution is considered to consist of the same proportion of each class of items entering into the computation of the trust's DNI as the total of each class bears to the total DNI of the trust, unless the trust instrument or local law specifically allocates different classes of income to different beneficiaries. Trusts generally do not attempt to allocate specific classes of income to particular beneficiaries. However, some trusts do, particularly where there is a wide disparity in the income tax rates applicable to the beneficiaries or where there is a charitable beneficiary. Examples of provisions the IRS will recognize as specific allocations of income to different beneficiaries are set forth in Reg. §1.652(b)-2(b). The general allocation principles are described in Reg. §§1.652(b)-1, 1.662(b)-1, 1.662(b)-2.

§10.4.5. No Standard Deduction; Personal Exemptions

A trust is not entitled to a standard deduction and is not subject to the tax on self-employment income. §63(c). Limited personal exemptions are allowed to trusts: A trust that is required to distribute all of its income currently, has no charitable beneficiaries, and makes no distributions of principal during the year (a "simple" trust) is entitled to a $300 exemption; all other trusts ("complex" trusts) are entitled to $100 exemptions. Estates are generally subject to the rules applicable to complex trusts, but are entitled to a $600 personal exemption. §642(b).

§10.4.6. Two Percent Floor on Miscellaneous Itemized Deductions, §67

The nondeductibility of miscellaneous itemized deductions to the extent of two percent of adjusted gross income (AGI) adds a degree of complexity that is not likely to produce a commensurate amount of tax for the federal fisc. In brief, most trusts are unlikely to pay any tax because of §67. Most important, in computing AGI for trusts and estates deductions are fully allowable for distributions to beneficiaries under §§651 and 661, personal exemptions under §642(b), and administration expenses "which would not have been incurred if the property were not held in such trust or estate." §67(e). The floor will generally be of concern only to trusts (and beneficiaries of trusts) with large AGIs (*e.g.*, trusts with substantial capital gains).

First, almost all expenses of a trust may be deductible under §67(e) in computing AGI. The expenses of administration and related items are fully deductible because they would not have been incurred if the property were not held in trust. The fees of the trustee and the lawyer for the trustee fall into that category. So also do the fees of accountants required to prepare annual accountings and tax returns for the trust. Presumably, items such as safe deposit box fees and the costs of maintaining the residence of a trust beneficiary would not be deductible.

Second, the full allowability of the deduction for distributions to beneficiaries in computing AGI significantly diminishes the amount of the two percent floor.

Finally, the personal exemption ($300 for simple trusts, $100 for complex trusts, and $600 for estates) is available to absorb the two percent of miscellaneous itemized deductions that are not deductible in computing AGI. For example, in the case of a simple trust the $300 personal exemption offsets the disallowance of two percent of miscellaneous itemized deductions of $15,000. An estate's exemption of $600 offsets two percent of $30,000 and the $100 exemption of a complex trust absorbs two percent of $5,000.

§10.4.7. Passive Activity Losses (PALs)

> Simply stated, the interrelationship of the passive-activity loss limitation rules of Section 469 with Subchapter J, which establishes rules for taxation of fiduciaries and beneficiaries, is an unmitigated nightmare. Abbin, To Be [Active] or Not To Be [Passive]: That Is the Question Confronting Fiduciaries and Beneficiaries Trying to Apply the Passive Activity Loss (PAL) Rules, U. Miami, 23rd Inst. Est. Plan., ch. 3 (1989).

Changes made by the 1986 Act generally bar deductions for the net amount of passive losses incurred by individuals, trusts and estates, personal service corporations, and closely-held subchapter C corporations in connection with passive activities in any trade or business. §469(a). For purposes of applying §469 the income and losses from passive activities are netted for each year. More particularly, as defined in §469(d)(1) the term "passive activity loss" means the amount by which aggregate losses from all passive activities for the year exceed the aggregate income from passive activities for the year. Passive activities are ones that involve the conduct of a trade or business in which the taxpayer does not materially participate, §469(c)(1), including any rental activity, §469(c)(2), but not the ownership of oil and gas working interests, §469(c)(3). In order to constitute material participation the taxpayer must be involved in the operations of an activity on a basis which is "regular, continuous, and substantial." §469(h)(1). In the case of trusts and estates, presumably it is the fiduciary who must materially participate in the trade or business and not the beneficiaries. Except as otherwise provided by regulation, no limited partner is considered to have materially participated in the activities of a limited partnership. §469(h)(2).

Net losses are carried over from year to year and may be offset against the net income from passive activities in later years. §469(b). The disposition of a passive activity property is subject to special rules. First, a disposition by gift results in an increase in the basis of the property by the amount of the PALs allocable to it. However, the basis cannot exceed the fair market value of the property at the time of the gift. Second, under §469(g)(1) accumulated losses in a passive activity are fully deductible if the taxpayer's entire interest is disposed of in a fully taxable transaction to a person other than a related taxpayer described in §267(b) or §707(b)(1). Third, an installment sale of a passive activity allows a portion of the accumulated PALs allocable to the activity to be deducted. §469(g)(3). The deductible portion bears the same ratio to "all such losses as the gain recognized on such sale during such taxable year bears to the gross profit from such sale (realized or to be realized when payment is completed)." Id. Fourth, when a passive activity is transferred at death, the accumulated losses are deductible but only to the extent they exceed the amount of the increase of the basis in the property that took place upon the taxpayer's death. §469(g)(2). Fifth, it appears that distributions from trusts or estates do not carry out PALs to beneficiaries. Instead, under §469(j)(12) the basis of the property distributed is increased by the amount of PALs allocable to it. Such PALs are not allowable as a deduction for any taxable year.

Individual taxpayers are allowed to deduct up to $25,000 in PALs attributable to rental real estate activities in which they actively participated. However, the amount of this offset is reduced by 50 percent of the amount by which the taxpayer's adjusted gross income exceeds $100,000. §469(i). Also, under §469(i)(4) the estate of a taxpayer who was actively engaged in rental activities remains entitled to the $25,000 offset for two years following the taxpayer's death. The amount allowable to the estate is reduced to the extent the decedent's surviving spouse makes use of the offset.

§10.4.8. Rules Applicable to Simple Trusts, §§651, 652

A trust that requires the distribution of all of its income currently, does not provide for payment of any charitable gifts, and does not make any distribution other than of current income is a "simple" trust. §651; Reg. §1.651(a)-1. Income for this purpose has reference to its income as determined for trust accounting purposes. All other trusts are "complex" trusts. The classification, which affects the computation of DNI, the personal tax exemptions, *etc.,* is made each year. Accordingly, a trust that requries all income to be distributed currently and authorizes the trustee to make discretionary distributions of principal is a simple trust except for years during which it distributes principal. On the other hand, a trust that authorizes the trustee to accumulate income is necessarily a complex trust. Note that a trust is a complex trust in its final year and in the year in which it makes any partial distributions of corpus. Estates are subject to most of the rules applicable to complex trusts.

Under §651(a) a simple trust is entitled to deduct the amount it is required to distribute currently. However, the amount of the deduction cannot exceed the trust's DNI, reduced by the amount of items reflected in DNI, but not included in the trust's income (*e.g.,* life insurance excludable under §101(a) and municipal bond interest exempt under §103). §651(b). It is necessary to make the reduction so the trust will not benefit doubly from the items — once because they are excluded from income and again as the result of a distribution deduction. The application of the rule is illustrated in this example from Reg. §1.651(b)-1: "Assume that the distributable net income of a trust as computed under §643(a) amounts to $99,000 but includes nontaxable income of $9,000. Then distributable net income for the purpose of determining the deduction allowable under section 651 is $90,000 ($99,000 less $9,000 nontaxable income)."

The beneficiary of a simple trust includes in his or her income the amount of income required to be distributed currently for such year, whether or not actually distributed. §652(a); Reg. §652(a)-1. However, the amount includible in the beneficiary's income cannot exceed the trust's DNI for the year. When the amount required to be distributed exceeds DNI, each beneficiary includes in his or her income an amount equivalent to his or her proportionate share of DNI. Each item distributed to a beneficiary has the same character in his or her hands that it had in the hands of the trust. "For example, to the extent that the amounts specified in §1.652(a)-1 consist of income exempt from tax under section 103, such amounts are not included in the beneficiary's gross income." Reg. §1.652(b)-1. This exclusion is consistent with the disallowance of a distribution deduction for items excluded from the trust's income as noted above.

Amounts included in a beneficiary's gross income are treated as consisting of the same proportion of each class of items entering into DNI as the total of each class bears to DNI. A different result follows if the terms of the trust specifically allocate different classes of income to different beneficiaries. This point is illustrated by the following example from Reg. §1.652(b)-2(a):

> Assume that under the terms of the governing instrument beneficiary *A* is to receive currently one-half of the trust income and beneficiaries *B* and *C* are each to receive currently one-quarter, and the distributable net income of the trust (after allocation of expenses) consists of dividends of $10,000, taxable interest of $10,000, and tax-exempt interest of $4,000. *A* will be deemed to have received $5,000 of dividends, $5,000 of taxable interest, and $2,000 of tax-exempt interest; *B* and *C* will each be deemed to have received $2,500 of dividends, $2,500 of taxable interest, and $1,000 of tax-exempt interest. However, if the terms of the trust specifically allocate different classes of income to different beneficiaries, entirely or in part, or if local law requires such an allocation, each beneficiary will be deemed to have received those items of income specifically allocated to him.

Allocation of Deductions. In determining the nature of amounts distributed to the beneficiaries and included in their incomes, it is necessary to allocate the deductions of a trust that enter into the computation of DNI. The rules under which the allocations are made are described in Reg. §1.652(b)-3. First, all deductible items directly attributable to one class of income are allocated to it (with the exception of excludable dividends and interest). Examples include expenses incurred in carrying on a trade or business and expenses incurred in connection with the rental of property. Second, deductions not directly attributable to a specific class of income may be allocated to any class of income, including capital gains, that is taken into account in computing DNI. Examples of expenses that are not directly attributable to a specific class of income include trustee's commissions, safe deposit box rental, and state income and personal property taxes. Reg. §1.652(b)-3(c).

Example 10-1. The trust had income of $40,000, consisting of $10,000 of business income, $10,000 of rental income, $10,000 of taxable interest, and $10,000 of tax-exempt income. The trustee's commissions, not subject to the 2% floor, were $4,000. One-fourth of the commissions must be allocated to the nontaxable income. The trustee may allocate the balance of the deductions in his or her discretion among items included in DNI (*e.g.,* business income or rental income). The balance of $3,000 must be used to reduce the amount includible in the beneficiaries' income even though the governing instrument or local law treats a portion of the commissions as attributable to corpus because they relate to capital gains or other items not included in income for trust accounting purposes. Reg. §1.652(b)-3. In effect, charging a portion of the commissions to corpus increases the amount of income received tax free by the beneficiary. The increase, of course, comes at the expense of corpus, which bears the expense.

Third, if any deductions directly attributable to one class of income exceed that class of income, they may be allocated to another class of income. However, excess deductions attributable to nontaxable income may not be allocated to any other class of income. In general the same rules apply to complex trusts. Reg. §§1.662(b)-1, (b)-2. *See* §10.4.9.

§10.4.9. Rules Applicable to Complex Trusts, §§661, 662

In computing the taxable income of a complex trust, the trust is allowed a deduction under §661(a) of an amount equal to the sum of two classes (or *tiers*) of distributions. The first tier consists of the amount of income the trust is required to distribute currently, including the amount of an annuity or other item required to be paid currently out of income or corpus to the extent it is paid out of income for the current year. This amount corresponds to the deduction allowable to simple trusts. The second tier consists of any other amounts properly paid or credited or required to be distributed during the taxable year. It includes, for example, an annuity to the extent it is not payable out of current income, distributions of property in kind, and discretionary distributions of corpus. Of course, the distribution deduction cannot exceed the trust's DNI, reduced as in the case of a simple trust, by the amount of nontaxable items included in DNI (*e.g.,* life insurance proceeds excludable under §101(a), municipal bond interest that is tax-exempt under §103).

The character of the amounts deducted by the trust and includible in the beneficiaries' income is determined in essentially the same manner as in the case of a simple trust. Thus, the character of each distribution consists of a proportionate amount of each class of income. §§661(b), 662(b). However, adjustments may be required, depending upon the amount of the distributions, the tiers to which they belong, and the amount of the trust's DNI. In brief, first tier distributions are taken from DNI first in determining the consequences of the distributions. Thus, if the first tier distributions absorb the full amount of the trust's DNI, no income is carried out to the second tier beneficiaries. In such a case, each first tier beneficiary is taxed on a proportionate amount of the distribution.

Example 10-2. The trust provided for distribution of all current income in equal shares to *A, B,* and *C.* In addition, the trustee was authorized to make discretionary distributions of principal to the income beneficiaries, their spouses, or their children. Last year the trust income was $30,000 and its DNI was $27,000. The trustee distributed $10,000 to each of *A, B,* and *C.* He also made a discretionary distribution of $5,000 of principal to *B.* The trust has a distribution deduction of $27,000, (the amount of its DNI for the year), equal portions of which are reportable as income by *A, B,* and *C.* Under the tier system, *A, B,* and *C* each report $9,000 of income. The second tier distribution of $5,000 to *B* is neither deductible by the trust nor includible in *B*'s income.

When the distributions to the first tier beneficiaries are less than the trust's DNI, a proportionate amount of the excess is included in the income of the second tier beneficiaries. For example, had the DNI of the trust in Example 10-2 been $32,000, each first tier beneficiary would have included $10,000 in his or her income and the second tier beneficiary, *B,* would have included the remaining $2,000 in his income. As pointed out by Arthur Michaelson and Jonathan Blattmachr, "The rationale of the tier system is that first-tier distributions are more realistically distributions of income than are other distributions by the trust, and hence should be the first to be taxed as income and thus to absorb distributable net income." Income Taxation of Estates & Trusts 24-25 (13th ed. 1989).

Separate Share Rule, §663(c). The separate share rule of §663(c) applies to complex trusts that have more than one beneficiary with substantially separate and independent shares for the sole purpose of determining the amounts of DNI allocable to each beneficiary under §§661 and 662. The application of the rule is significant when income is accumulated for one beneficiary and a distribution is made to another beneficiary in excess of his or her proportionate share of income.

Example 10-3. A trust provided for the income to be divided into equal shares for the benefit of *A* and *B.* The trustee was authorized to distribute or accumulate each share and to make such distributions of principal as the trustee believed was in the best interests of the beneficiaries. Last year the trust income and its DNI was $20,000. The trustee accumulated *A*'s share of the income ($10,000) but distributed $10,000 to *B* along with principal of $5,000. Each share is treated as a separate trust. Thus, *B* received a distribution of only the DNI allocable to his share — he was not required to report any of the DNI allocable to the income accumulated in *A*'s share of the trust. However, the other $5,000 distribution to *B* might be a taxable accumulation distribution under the throwback rules. *See* §10.4.10.

The separate share rule does not permit the separate shares to be treated as separate trusts for any other purpose. Thus, it does not affect the filing of returns, the personal exemptions available, or the allocation of excess deductions on termination of the trust. The separate share treatment is mandatory, not elective. Reg. §1.663(c)-1(d). It is not applicable to estates. Reg. §1.663(c)-3(f).

§10.4.10. Throwback Rules, §§665-667

A complex trust initially bears the tax on any ordinary income it accumulates. As explained below, ordinary income that has already been taxed to the trust may be subject to an additional tax under the throwback rules of §§665-667 when it is distributed. The rules were adopted at a time when the income tax rates were much more progressive and considerable savings could be achieved if income could be permanently taxed to individuals or entities that were in lower tax brackets. In short, the throwback rules were designed to prevent trusts from being used to defeat the progressive character of the income tax by accumulating income for later tax-free distribution to higher bracket beneficiaries. The throwback rules do not apply to capital gains or to any distributions made by estates, which are less susceptible to tax avoidance through the accumulation of income. Income accumulated prior to the beneficiary's birth or his or her attainment of 21 years of age is also not subject to the throwback rules.

Accumulation distributions are taxed to the distributees under a special form of income averaging. The amount of an accumulation distribution includes any income tax paid by the trust with respect to the distribution (*i.e.,* the tax paid by the trust is "grossed up"). A distributee is allowed a credit for the taxes paid by the trust and treated as distributed to him or her. However, the credit can only be applied against the distributee's additional tax computed under the throwback rules — it cannot give rise to a refund or be used as a credit against the distributee's other tax liability. §666(e).

The throwback rules may impose an additional tax on an accumulation distribution by a trust that had undistributed net income for a preceding taxable year. The definitions of accumulation distribution and undistributed net income are critical to the application of the rules. Under §665(b) an accumulation distribution occurs where the amount of the second tier distributions (amounts properly paid, credited, or required to be distributed) exceeds the amount of DNI reduced by the amount of first tier distributions (amounts of income required to be distributed currently). A first tier distribution does not constitute an accumulation distribution although it exceeds the trust's DNI. Reg. §1.665(b)-1A(c)(3). For all practical purposes, income accumulated before the birth of the beneficiary or his or her attainment of 21 is not taken into account in applying the throwback rules. §665(b).

Undistributed Net Income. Undistributed net income is defined in §665(a) as the amount by which the trust's DNI for the year exceeds the sum of its first and second tier distributions and the amount of taxes borne by the trust on its DNI. For example, if a trust had DNI of $30,000 for the year, properly made distributions of $10,000 to beneficiaries, and paid a tax of $3,000 on its income, the trust would have an undistributed net income of $17,000 for the year ($30,000 − $10,000 + $3,000). Distributions made within the first 65 days following the end of a taxable year are taken into account to the extent provided in §663(b) in determining the undistributed net income and accumulation distributions of the trust. *See* Reg. §1.665(b)-1A(a).

When a beneficiary receives an accumulation distribution, the computation of the special tax requires several steps. First, the accumulation distribution is spread over the years the trust had undistributed net income, beginning with the earliest (but not prior to 1969) and moving forward. Second, the total amount of the accumulation distribution is divided by the number of years determined in step one over which the accumulation is considered to have taken place, excluding any year in which the undistributed net income was less than 25 percent of the average undistributed net income. §667(b)(3). Third, the average accumulation determined in step two is added to taxable income of the distributee for three of his or her five taxable years immediately preceding the year of the accumulation distribution (the years with the highest and the lowest taxable incomes are eliminated). §667(b)(1). Fourth, the distributee's tax for each of those three years is recalculated, with the inclusion of the average accumulation, and the additional amounts are added together and divided by three. Fifth, the average increase in tax is multiplied by the number of years used as the denominater in step two (the years during which the distribution was deemed to have been accumulated). The excess of that amount over the amount of taxes paid by the trust and deemed distributed to the distributee is the additional amount of tax imposed in connection with the accumulation distribution.

Example 10-4. This year *T* received an accumulation distribution of $24,000, representing undistributed net income of the trust for the preceding 7 years. The trust had paid $4,000 in income tax on the income represented by the accumulation distribution. The total accumulation distribution is $28,000, which is considered

> to have been accumulated at the rate of $4,000 for each of the preceding 7 years. The years of *T*'s highest and lowest taxable income during the 5 years immediately preceding the accumulation distribution are excluded and the average distribution of $4,000 is added to *T*'s taxable income for each of the remaining 3 years. The additional income tax attributable to the inclusion of the $4,000 is then calculated. The average increase in tax for the 3 years is determined by adding the amount of the additional income tax for each year and dividing by 3. *T*'s income tax liability is calculated by multiplying the resulting amount by 7, representing the years during which the income was accumulated. *T*'s tax liability is reduced by a credit for the $4,000 in tax previously paid by the trust. There is no throwback if the income had all been accumulated prior to *T*'s birth or his or her attainment of 21. There is also no throwback when the accumulated income of an estate is distributed. Of course, a distribution to an estate beneficiary may carry out the current DNI of the estate, which would be includible in the beneficiary's income.

The throwback rules discourage the creation of multiple accumulation trusts. First, in computing the special tax under §667(b)(1), the taxable income of a distributee includes the amount deemed distributed to him or her in prior years as a result of earlier accumulation distributions. §§667(b)(4). That is, the computation of the special tax takes prior accumulation distributions into account. Where accumulation distributions are made from more than one trust in the same taxable year the distributions are deemed to have been made consecutively in the order chosen by the distributee. §667(b)(5). Second, under §667(c) a special rule applies where a distributee receives accumulation distributions attributable to his or her same prior taxable year from more than two trusts. The accumulation distributions from the third and any additional trusts do not include any portion of the taxes paid by the trusts, nor is the distributee entitled to any credit for such taxes. An accumulation distribution is only taken into account for purposes of this rule where it, together with any other accumulation distributions deemed to have been made for the same year, amounts to $1,000 or more. §667(c)(2). Note that this de minimis rule may be satisfied by accumulation distributions made in more than one year. Similarly, the overall rule may come into play as a result of accumulation distributions made to the beneficiary in more than one of his or her taxable years. Note also that the special exclusion for income only accumulated prior to the distributee's birth or attainment of 21 does not apply to accumulation distributions received from more than two trusts with respect to the same prior taxable year of the distributee. §§665(b), 667.

Other Multiple Trust Rules. From time to time the IRS has sought, with little success, to consolidate multiple trusts for income tax purposes. In support of that effort, Reg. §1.641(a)-0(c) was adopted in 1972. That Regulation was struck down by the Tax Court in 1983, after which Congress came to the rescue by enacting §643(f). In *Edward L. Stephenson,* 81 T.C. 283 (1983), the Tax Court invalidated the Regulation on the ground that it exceeded the government's regulatory power. The invalidated Regulation provided as follows:

> (c) *Multiple trusts.* Multiple trusts that have —
> (1) No substantially independent purposes (such as independent dispositive purposes),
> (2) The same grantor and substantially the same beneficiary, and
> (3) The avoidance or mitigation of (a) the progressive rates of tax (including mitigation as a result of deferral of tax) or (b) the minimum tax for tax preferences imposed by section 56 as their principal purpose, shall be consolidated and treated as one trust for the purposes of subchapter J. Reg. §1.641(a)-0(c).

The courts have generally not supported efforts by the IRS to consolidate multiple trusts for tax purposes — at least not where the trustee has respected the separate character of the trusts by adminstering them separately and maintaining separate records. *See, e.g., Estelle Morris Trusts,* 51 T.C. 20 (1968), *aff'd per curiam,* 427 F.2d 1361 (9th Cir. 1970) (separate identity of ten trusts created for each of two minor beneficiaries upheld despite grantors' tax avoidance motivation). Multiple trusts have consolidated by the courts where they were not separately administered. *See Boyce v. United States,* 190 F. Supp. 950 (W.D. La.), *aff'd per curiam,* 296 F.2d 731 (5th Cir. 1961) (90 trusts with a total initial corpus of $17,400 were shams), and *Sence v. United States,* 394 F.2d 842 (Ct. Cl. 1968) (19 trusts).

Responding to *Stephenson,* in 1984 Congress accommodated the IRS by passing what is now §643(f):

> (f) *Treatment of Multiple Trusts.* — For purposes of this subchapter, under regulations prescribed by the Secretary, 2 or more trusts shall be treated as 1 if —
> (1) such trusts have substantially the same grantor or grantors and substantially the same primary beneficiary or beneficiaries, and
> (2) a principal purpose of such trusts is the avoidance of the tax imposed by this chapter.
> For purposes of the preceding sentence, a husband and wife shall be treated as 1 person.

§10.4.11. Sale of Appreciated Property Within Two Years, §644

When the capital gain throwback rule was abolished in 1976, §644 was adopted to deter the transfer of appreciated property in trust in order to shift the gain to the trust, where it would be subject to the trust's lower progressive tax rates. Section 644 applies (1) where property that has a fair market value in excess of its basis is transferred to a trust and (2) the property is sold at a gain by the trust within two years of its transfer to the trust. §644(a)(1). In such a case §644(a)(2) subjects the trust to a tax equal to the tax that would have been imposed had the grantor made the sale. The overall income tax result is essentially the same as if the grantor made the sale and transferred the net proceeds to the trust. Whether the gain is taxed as ordinary income or capital gain is also determined by reference to the character of the property in the hands of the grantor. §644(c). The rule does not apply to sales made following the grantor's death or sales made by a charitable remainder trust or pooled income fund. §644(e). Note, however, that §644 applies to sales by charitable lead trusts. The special rules of §§644(d) and (f) prevent circumvention of the tax through the making of short sales or installment sales.

§10.4.12. Recognition of Loss, §267

Section 267 bars a deduction for a loss arising from a sale to a related party. Insofar as trusts are involved, no deduction is allowed where property is sold by the fiduciary of a trust (1) to a beneficiary of the trust, §267(b)(6); (2) to the fiduciary of another trust created by the same grantor, §267(b)(5); or (3) to the beneficiary of another trust created by the same grantor, §267(b)(7). However, loss that is not allowable to the transferor under §267 may be utilized by the original purchaser for purposes of computing gain on a subsequent disposition of the property. §267(d). (Note that the benefit of this rule is only available to the *original* purchaser and not to his or her transferees. Reg. §1.267(d)-1(a)(3).)

Example 10-5. A trustee, *T,* sold stock with a basis of $1,500 to a beneficiary, *X,* of the trust for $1,000. *T* is not allowed to deduct the $500 "loss" on the sale to *X.* If *X* later sells the stock for $2,000, *X* realizes a gain of $1,000, but is required to recognize only $500, which is the excess of the realized gain ($1,000) over the loss ($500) not allowed to *T.* If *T* gave the stock to another person, the donee could not make use of the loss to offset any gain he or she realized on a subsequent sale or exchange.

In contrast, an estate is entitled to a deduction for the loss that is incurred when an estate sells property to a trust created by the decedent or to a party who was related to the decedent. Rev. Rul. 77-439, 1977 C.B. 85 (sale of property to executor, who is child of decedent); Rev. Rul. 56-222, 1956-1 C.B. 155 (sale of stock to a trust created by decedent). The same rule applies to losses incurred when an asset is distributed in satisfaction of a pecuniary legacy at a time when it is worth less than its adjusted basis. *Estate of Hanna v. Commissioner,* 320 F.2d 54 (6th Cir. 1963).

§10.4.13. Section 1244 Stock

A limited ordinary loss deduction is allowed under §1244 for loss on the sale or exchange of the stock in a qualifying small business corporation. However, the loss is only allowed to an individual or partner who held the stock continuously from the time of its original issue. In particular, "[a] corporation, trust, or estate is not entitled to ordinary loss treatment under section 1244 regardless of how the stock was acquired." Reg. §1.244(a)-1(b). Thus, the transfer of otherwise qualifying stock to a trust appears to cut off any possibility of obtaining an ordinary loss deduction under §1244. However, perhaps the deduction would be available if the grantor were treated as owner of the trust under the grantor trust rules. In other instances the grantor-owner has received the benefit of some tax rules. For example, the transfer of an installment obligation to a trust is not a disposition of the obligation where the grantor is treated as the owner of the trust. Rev. Rul. 74-613, 1974-2 C.B. 153.

§10.4.14. S Corporation Stock

Beginning in 1976 a series of amendments were made to the Code that permit certain trusts to be shareholders in S corporations. Under them certain types of trusts were allowed to be shareholders: (1) a trust of which the grantor is treated as the owner under §§671-677; (2) a voting trust; (3) a testamentary trust, but only for a 60-day period following the transfer of stock to it. §1361(c)(2).

Grantor Trusts. In 1978 the rules were liberalized to allow a grantor trust to be an eligible shareholder for 60 days following the death of the person who was treated as owner of the trust under §§671 to 677. §1361(c)(2)(A). Under §1361(c) the grantor is treated as the shareholder of the stock held in the trust, which may relieve the trustee of the necessity of filing a consent to the election not to be taxed as a corporation. If the entire corpus of the trust is includible in the grantor's gross estate, the trust is an eligible shareholder for a period of two years following the grantor's death. A grantor may deliberately make a trust "defective" in order to be treated as its owner, which will allow the trust to hold stock in an S corporation — and to be taxed on all of the income of the trust. *E.g.,* LR 9037011 (independent trustee held power in a nonfiduciary capacity to acquire property held by the trust by transferring property of equivalent value to the trust, §675(4)).

Nongrantor, §678, Trusts. Changes made by the 1981 Act allowed additional types of trusts to be shareholders. In particular, a trust, all of which is treated as owned by an individual other than the grantor under §678 is allowed to be a shareholder until 60 days following the individual's death. §1361(c)(2)(A). A trust of which a nongrantor was treated as the owner under §678 is a permitted shareholder for two years following the death of the nongrantor-owner if the entire corpus of the trust is includible in the grantor's gross estate. §1361(c)(2)(A).

Qualified Subchapter S Trust (QSST). Under the 1981 Act the individual beneficiary of a "qualified Subchapter S trust" (QSST) may elect to be a shareholder. Briefly, a QSST is one under which all of the income is payable currently to an individual who is a U.S. citizen or resident. In addition, the terms of the trust must provide that: (1) during the life of the current income beneficiary there shall only be one income beneficiary, (2) any corpus distributed during the lifetime of the current income beneficiary must be distributed to him or her, (3) the income interest of the income beneficiary shall terminate on the earlier of the death of the beneficiary or termination of the trust, and (4) upon termination during the life of the current income beneficiary, the trust shall distribute all of its assets to such beneficiary. A trust that will terminate and distribute its assets to persons other than the income beneficiary if the trust ceases to hold shares of an S corporation is not a QSST. Rev. Rul. 89-55, 1989-1 C.B. 168. Likewise, a trust is not a QSST if it provides that a portion of the corpus must be used to fund a separate trust for any grandchildren who are born after the creation of the trust. Rev. Rul. 89-45, 1989-1 C.B. 267.

Estates. The estate of a deceased shareholder is an eligible shareholder for so long as required to complete the administration of the estate. *See* §12.4. The IRS has recognized that an estate may remain an eligible shareholder during the period that payment of the estate tax is deferred under a prior version of §6166. Rev. Rul. 76-23, 1976-1 C.B. 264.

§10.4.15. Redemptions Under §303

Section 303 applies to distributions in redemption of stock included in a decedent's estate and held by any person at the time of redemption, including the trustee of a trust created by the decedent. Reg. §1.303-2(f). Where the value of the stock included in the decedent's estate constitutes more than 35 percent of the decedent's adjusted gross estate, a redemption distribution is treated as full payment in exchange for the redeemed stock. However, the amount that may be so treated is limited to the sum of the death taxes imposed on the decedent's estate and the amount of funeral and administration expenses that are deductible under §2053. §303(b)(2)(A). For this purpose the GSTT on a generation-skipping transfer that occurs at the time of the decedent's death is treated as a death tax. §303(d).

Note that §303 applies only to the extent that the interest of a redeeming shareholder is liable for payment of the taxes and administration expenses. §303(b)(3). Thus, stock that the parties might wish to redeem under §303 should not be transferred to a beneficiary or a trust that is not liable for payment of death taxes and expenses of administration. For a more complete discussion of redemptions under §303, *see* §§11.15-11.24.

§10.4.16. Taxable Year of the Trust

With the exception of tax-exempt trusts, changes made by the 1986 Act require trusts to report their income on the basis of a calendar year. §645. However, a trust that is treated as owned by the grantor for income tax purposes is not required to adopt a calendar year. Rev. Rul. 90-55, 1990-2 C.B. 161. The existence of such a trust is largely disregarded for income tax purposes. Under the prior law, testamentary trusts and revocable trusts that became irrevocable were allowed to select and use fiscal years, which allowed the income taxation of distributions to be deferred for a limited period. Now, fiscal years may only be used by tax-exempt trusts such as charitable remainder trusts. The designation of a fiscal year in a charitable remainder trust instrument (or its other selection) may still allow some deferral of taxation. Specifically, when a trust and its beneficiary have different taxable years, the amount the beneficiary is required to report as income in a particular year is based on the income and distributions made by the trust for the year (or years) that end within the beneficiary's taxable year. Reg. §1.664-1(d)(4)(i). The last cited Regulation provides, in part, that:

> If a recipient has a different taxable year (as defined in section 441 or 442) from the taxable year of the trust, the amount he is required to

include in gross income to the extent required by this paragraph shall be included in his taxable year in which or with which ends the taxable year of the trust in which such amount is required to be distributed. Reg. §1.664-1(d)(4)(i).

Under §664(b) distributions of charitable remainder trusts are deemed successively to have the following character: ordinary income, capital gains, other income, and corpus. Thus, the selection of the taxable year for a charitable remainder trust may result in some delay in the payment of income tax on distributions to the noncharitable beneficiaries.

Example 10-6. A charitable remainder trust was established on July 1, 1990 the first day of its taxable year. The noncharitable beneficiaries are cash basis taxpayers who file calender year returns. The amount of distributions reported by the beneficiaries in their returns for calendar 1991 are determined by the trust's return (Form 5227) for the year beginning on July 1, 1990, and ending on June 30, 1991. The same rule applies where the first year of the trust is a short one (*e.g.*, if the charitable trust were established on December 1, 1990).

The fiduciary of a trust may elect under §663(b) to treat any amount that is properly paid or credited to a beneficiary within the first 65 days following the close of the taxable year as an amount properly paid or distributed on the last day of such taxable year. This 65-day rule allows trustees to avoid the unintentional accumulation of income, which might otherwise be subject to the throwback rules of §§665-668. The election, of course, has an impact on the distribution deduction of the trust and the amounts reportable as income by the beneficiaries.

§10.4.17. Payment of Income Tax by Fiduciary

Trusts and estates are now subject to the same requirements when it comes to the time at which income tax liabilities must be paid. Specifically, the 1986 Act repealed §6152(a) under which estates were allowed to pay their income tax liabilities in four equal quarterly installments instead of a single payment.

§10.4.18. Estimated Income Tax Payments

Insofar as quarterly estimated tax payments are concerned, estates still enjoy an advantage. Under §6654(1) most trusts must make quarterly estimated payments of their income tax. In contrast, that requirement does not apply to estates with respect to any taxable year ending before the date two years after the date of the decedent's death. §6654(1)(2). (The same exemption applies to trusts of which the decedent was treated as the owner under the grantor trust rules and to which the residue of the decedent's estate will pass by will.) The estimated tax payments must be at least the lesser of 100 percent of the prior year's tax liability or 90 percent (increased from 80 percent in 1986) of the current taxable year liability. §6654(d)(1)(B). To the extent the estimated tax payments of the trust exceed its liability the trustee may allocate estimated tax payments to the beneficiaries. The allocation is made on the tax return for the trust. The tax credited to a beneficiary is considered to be a distribution and to have been paid as a part of the beneficiary's January 15 estimated tax payment.

§10.5. Gift Tax Summary

The transfer of property to a trust constitutes a gift *only* to the extent of the value of the interests that pass from the grantor's control. Reg. §25.2511-2(a), (b). Accordingly, the grantor's transfer of property to a revocable trust does not constitute a completed gift because the disposition of all interests in the property transferred to the trust remains subject to the grantor's control. The Regulations issued under the gift tax are helpful in determining what powers are sufficient to prevent a transfer from constituting a completed gift. Reg. §25.2511-2; *see also* §10.34.

Although there is no completed gift if the grantor retains a power of revocation, the Regulations require the grantor to file a gift tax return in such a case, specifying the reasons he or she believes the transfer is not taxable. Reg. §§25.2511-2(j), 25.6019-3(a). However, in practice gift tax returns are very seldom filed with respect to the transfer of property to a revocable trust. A gift is likewise incomplete if the grantor retains the power to change the beneficiaries. Reg. §25.2511-2(f).

Annual Gift Tax Exclusion. The annual gift tax exclusion has no significance with respect to transfers to revocable trusts, which do not involve a completed gift. An annual gift tax exclusion is available insofar as a trust beneficiary is entitled to the unrestricted right to "the immediate use, possession, or enjoyment of property or the income from property. . . ." Reg. §25.2503-3(b). *See* §2.5.2. In general, no exclusion is available with respect to the beneficiary's interests in a discretionary trust. However, transfers to a trust quality for the annual exclusion to the extent the beneficiary has a *Crummey* power that allows him or her to withdraw the transferred property for his or her own use.

For gift tax purposes the dispositions provided for in a revocable trust become complete if the power to affect the beneficial enjoyment of the property is released or otherwise terminates during the grantor's lifetime. *Estate of Sanford v. Commissioner,* 308 U.S. 39 (1939); Reg. §25.2511-2(f). However, the gifts probably do not become complete merely because the grantor becomes incompetent and may no longer exercise the retained power.

Example 10-7. *T* transfered Blackacre to *X* as trustee of an irrevocable trust. Under the terms of the trust the income of the trust is payable in the trustee's discretion to *T*'s siblings, *A, B,* and *C.* Upon the death of the survivor of *A, B,* and *C,* the trust assets are distributable to their then living issue. The transfer of Blackacre to the trust constituted a completed gift with respect to which no annual exclusions are available. The interests of *A, B,* and *C* in the income are not definite enough to support annual exclusions and the gift of the remainder is a future interest for which no annual gift tax exclusion is allowed. Annual exclusions would be available to the extent the beneficiaries were given *Crummey* powers of withdrawal. Note that the gifts would also be incomplete to the extent *T* retained a special power of appointment over the trust. *See* Reg. §25.2511-2(b).

§10.6. Estate Tax Summary

The value of assets held in a trust may be included in the grantor's estate under any of the provisions of §§2035 to 2038. In some cases a decedent's estate may be required to include part or all of a trust under §§2039, 2041, or 2042. Problems of inclusion most commonly arise under §§2036 or 2038 with respect to powers the grantor retained with respect to the disposition of trust property. Under §2036 and 2038, the trust is includible in the grantor's estate if a proscribed power is exercisable by the grantor alone *or* in conjunction with any other person. Note also that those sections make no exception for powers held by the decedent in a fiduciary capacity (*i.e.,* as trustee). A trust is, of course, includible in the grantor's estate under §2036(a)(1) to the extent he or she has directly or indirectly retained the use or benefit of the property.

§10.6.1. Right to Vote Stock of Controlled Corporation, §2036(b)

Shares of stock in a controlled corporation are includible in the grantor's estate if he or she retained the right to vote the shares. §2036(b). For this purpose a corporation is a controlled corporation if the decedent owned or had voting control of 20 percent or more of its stock within three years of decedent's death after giving effect to the attribution rules of §318. §2036(b)(2). Thus, stock in a controlled corporation that is transferred to a trust of which the transferor is the trustee and holds the power to vote the stock is includible in the transferor-trustee's gross estate.

§10.6.2. Benefits Under Qualified Plans, §2039

Interests in an employee benefit plan or an individual retirement arrangement are sometimes made payable to the trustee of an inter vivos or testamentary trust in order to consolidate the employee's assets in one trust for purposes of management and administration. Benefits are typically made payable to a bypass trust that will prevent the trust property from being included in the trust beneficiary's estate. The proceeds of insurance policies on the testator's life and the testator's residuary estate are also often made payable to the trustee of an inter vivos trust.

Under §205 of ERISA, as amended by the Retirement Equity Act of 1984, a surviving spouse is entitled to certain benefits under plans unless he or she has waived them in the required manner. In particular, if a covered employee dies prior to retirement his or her surviving spouse is entitled to an annuity equal to 50 percent of the value of the benefits accumulated by the decedent. However, this requirement does not apply to benefits provided by state plans.

In general, estate taxation of interests in plans is governed by §2039, of which only subsections (a) and (b) remain in force. In brief, §2039(a) requires the inclusion of the value of annuities or other payments receivable by any beneficiary by reason of having survived the decedent (other than insurance on the life of the decedent) if the annuity was payable to the decedent or if the decedent had the right to receive payments under it. However, the inclusion of qualified plan benefits in a deceased employee's estate may not be particularly hurtful. If the employee's surviving spouse is the only person entitled to receive annuity payments before the death of the surviving spouse, the marital deduction is available. *See* §2056(b)(7)(C). Of course, the marital deduction is not available to the extent it is subject to a legally binding obligation to pay estate expenses. *See* §2056(b)(4). Also, the marital deduction is not available with respect to plan benefits if the surviving spouse is not a U.S. citizen unless the benefits are settled in a manner that meets the requirements of qualified domestic trust under §2056A. If the decedent's spouse is not a citizen, the decedent's employer might cooperate by modifying the plan to meet those requirements or the surviving spouse might roll over the benefits into an IRA that does meet those requirements. Otherwise, withdrawing the funds and transferring them to a qualified domestic trust will subject them to income taxation, which generally should be avoided. The elections available with respect to the income and estate tax treatment of lump sum distributions are discussed at §§12.25.2-12.25.3.

§10.6.3. General Power of Appointment, §2041

Property transferred by another person to a trust that is revocable by the grantor is includible in the grantor's estate under §2041(a)(2) (with the exception of property subject to an unexercised power created before October 22, 1942). Of course, under §2041 the property of a trust is includible in the estate of a person other than the grantor who holds a power to withdraw the property. Similarly, the property is includible in the estate of a nongrantor who holds a power to appoint the property to himself, his creditors, his estate, or creditors of his estate.

§10.6.4. Life Insurance Proceeds, §2042

The proceeds of life insurance on the life of the grantor of a revocable trust are includible in the grantor's estate under §2042(2). Reg. §20.2042-1(c)(4). The proceeds of policies owned by other parties are also includible in the insured's estate to the extent they are "receivable by the executor" although the insured had no incidents of ownership in the insurance. §2042(1). *See* §6.26, *supra.* For that reason life insurance proceeds that are otherwise not includible in the insured's estate should not be made subject to a legally binding obligation to pay debts, taxes, and other expenses of the insured's estate. Where insurance proceeds are payable to a trust, the trustee might be given the discretionary power to use the proceeds to buy estate assets or make loans to the estate. Under the existing authorities, the trustee may also be given the discretionary power to use the proceeds to satisfy obligations of the estate. *See* §6.26.

§10.6.5. Alternate Valuation Date

Property held in a trust qualifies for alternate valuation just as do other assets that are included in the decedent's gross estate. *See* §12.19. However, property that is distributed, sold, exchanged, or otherwise disposed of within six months after the decedent's death is valued on the date of its distribution, sale, exchange, or other disposition. The provisions of a revocable trust regarding distributions should be drafted with an eye toward §2032 in order to preserve the full benefit of alternate valuation for the trust assets. *See* §12.19.

§10.6.6. Deduction of Expenses Under §2053

Section 2053(a) allows a deduction for administration expenses incurred with respect to property subject to an estate adminstration proceeding. Since 1954 a comparable deduction has been allowed by §2053(b) for expenses of administration incurred with respect to property includible in the decedent's gross estate (*e.g.,* property held in a revocable trust) but not subject to the claims of the decedent's creditors. The deduction is allowable to the extent that the costs are paid before expiration of the period of limitations for assessments under §6501 (*i.e.,* within three years following the date upon which the estate tax return is due). Deductions are limited to expenses "occasioned by the decedent's death and incurred in settling the decedent's interest in the property or vesting good title to the property in the beneficiaries. Expenses not coming within [this] description . . . but incurred on behalf of the transferees are not deductible." Reg. §20.2053-8(b).

§10.6.7. Deferral of Estate Tax

The estate tax attributable to a closely-held business interest that is includible in the decedent's estate may be deferred under §6166. *See* §§11.25-11.30 and 12.47. Deferral is available whether the business interest is held outright or in a trust. Where the business constitutes more than 35 percent of the decedent's adjusted gross estate, §6166 allows the tax to be paid in installments over a 10-year period, the first of which is due five years after the estate tax return is filed. Prior to 1982 the executor could elect to pay the estate tax on a closely-held business interest that constituted more than 35 percent of a decedent's gross estate or more than 50 percent of a decedent's taxable estate in ten annual installments under former §6166A.

§10.6.8. Discharge of Executor and Other Fiduciaries From Personal Liability for Estate Tax

Under §§3466-3467 of the Revised Statutes, 31 U.S.C. §3713 (1982), an executor or other fiduciary is personally liable for debts due the United States, including federal tax liabilities, to the extent the fiduciary disposes of the decedent's property without paying the debts due the

United States. *See* §12.49. An executor may apply for discharge from personal liability for the estate tax under §2204(a), in which case the government must notify the executor of the amount of the tax within nine months of the time the estate tax return must be filed. The executor is discharged from personal liability upon payment of the amount found to be due and upon furnishing bond for any amount the payment of which has been deferred under §§6161, 6163, or 6166. Section 2204 was amended in 1970 to extend essentially the same opportunity to fiduciaries other than executors. §2204(b). *See* Price, Recent Tax Legislation — The Excise, Estate and Gift Tax Adjustment Act of 1970, 47 Wash. L. Rev. 237, 273-279 (1972). Accordingly, since 1970 it has been possible for the trustee of a revocable trust to obtain a discharge from personal liability for the decedent's estate tax. The prior inability to obtain such a discharge was a matter of some concern to trustees. The change removed one of the obstacles to the use of a revocable trust as the principal dispositive instrument in an estate plan.

§10.6.9. Flower Bonds

Some United States Treasury bonds that are redeemable at par plus accrued interest in payment of the federal estate tax remain outstanding. *See* §12.43. Redeemable bonds were all issued prior to 1971. With the maturity date of the last outstanding issues approaching they sell at prices close to par despite their low interest rates. For federal estate tax purposes the bonds are valued at par plus accrued interest to the extent they are redeemable. Rev. Rul. 69-489, 1969-2 C.B. 172. However, not all bonds held in trust qualify for redemption. Under the applicable Treasury Regulations, 31 C.F.R. §306.28 (1990), bonds held in trust at the time of the decedent's death are redeemable only "(A) if the trust actually terminated in favor of the decedent's estate, or (B) if the trustee is required to pay the decedent's Federal estate tax under the terms of the trust instrument or otherwise, or (C) to the extent the debts of the decedent's estate, including costs of administration, State inheritance and Federal estate taxes, exceed the assets of his estate without regard to the trust estate." 31 C.F.R. §306.28(b)(1)(iii) (1973). Thus, some care must be taken in planning the terms of the grantor's will and trust where the trustee may acquire flower bonds for the purpose of redeeming them on the grantor's death. In particular, the will should not provide for payment of all death taxes from the residuary estate. In appropriate cases, the trust should provide that the trustee shall pay the federal estate tax liability of the decedent's estate. Alternatively, the trustee may be directed to pay so much of the tax as he or she may be asked by the decedent's executor to pay.

Special planning is also called for where the trust is funded with community property. Bonds that are held as community property are redeemable only to the extent of the decedent's one-half interest. This problem can be avoided by giving the trustee authority to partition some of the community property held in trust into equal units of separate property and to use a spouse's share of the property to purchase redeemable Treasury bonds for his or her separate account. Otherwise the trustee would be required to buy twice as many bonds as would be needed to satisfy the tax due on the death of the spouse.

B. THE REVOCABLE TRUST

§10.7. Scope

This part is concerned with the tax and nontax aspects of the revocable trust, which is one of the most important and flexible devices available to the estate planner. Altough a revocable trust has no current tax impact — it is "tax neutral" — its flexibility and substantial nontax advantages make it a favorite of many planners and their clients. The advantages of revocable trusts have been extolled for decades by leading academics and other proponents. *See, e.g.,* Casner, Estate Planning — Avoidance of Probate, 60 Colum. L. Rev. 108 (1960); H. Abts, The Living Trust (1989); N. Dacey, How to Avoid Probate (1965).

For income tax purposes, the grantor of a trust that is revocable by the grantor or a nonadverse party is treated as the owner of the trust. §676(a). The transfer of property to a trust that is revocable by the grantor alone or with the consent of a nonadverse party is not a completed gift. Reg. §25.2511-2(e); LR 8911028. Finally, the property of a trust that is revocable by the grantor alone or in conjunction with any other party is includible in the grantor's estate.

The opening sections of this part discuss some important matters of substantive law. They are followed by ones that review the basic advantages and disadvantages of revocable trusts. The concluding sections summarize the principal income, gift, and estate tax consequences of using a revocable trust in an estate plan.

A revocable trust may be funded or unfunded, but the funded variety receives most of the attention in this part. The revocable life insurance trust, discussed at §6.18.3, is one of the most common forms of the unfunded revocable trust.

Funded Revocable Trust. Perhaps most often a funded revocable trust is established to provide lifetime management of the grantor's property and to serve as a will substitute. The latter quality, which may enable the grantor's estate to "avoid probate," is a major selling point of revocable trusts — particularly in states which have statutory fee schedules for personal representatives and their counsel. When a revocable trust has a single grantor, it usually becomes completely irrevocable upon his or her death. The trust may include any of a wide variety of plans for the administration and distribution of the property following the grantor's death. A particular client's choice will depend upon the age, experience, and needs of his or her spouse and children. Thus, the assets of the trust may be distributed soon after the grantor's death or held in trust for a substantial period, such as the lifetime of one or more beneficiaries. A revocable trust that will continue following the grantor's death should be planned in view of the general considerations applicable to irrevocable trusts (*see* Parts C and D, *infra*).

Backup Will and Pour Over. A client may intend to transfer all of his or her property to the trust in order to avoid probate completely. Even in such a case the client should have a *backup will* to dispose of any property or claims that may not be included in the trust at the time of the client's death. A backup will usually provides for a gift of the grantor's residuary estate to the trustee of the revocable trust. The residuary estate is "poured over" to the trust and is not held in a separate trust under the will. The validity of the pour-over will is discussed at §10.10. Life insurance proceeds, employee benefits, and other property may also be made payable to the trustee. Such a program is attractive because it facilitates the unified management and administration of the grantor's property and the distribution of the property according to a single plan.

Pour Back or Reverse Pour Over. The grantor's assets are most frequently unified by a pour over of the type discussed above. However, in some cases the assets of a revocable trust are "poured back" and added to the probate estate for purposes of disposition. A pour back is less common because it reduces or eliminates some of the basic advantages of a revocable trust (*e.g.,* reducing probate costs, preserving secrecy). It also eliminates any uncertainty regarding the validity of the disposition, which might affect a pour over in some jurisdictions. The use of a pour back also allows the grantor to control the ultimate disposition of the property simply by changing the terms of his or her will, which is ambulatory and can be changed unilaterally. The trustee is not required to concur in such a change and need not know the terms of the grantor's will as it exists from time to time.

§10.8 Reserving the Power to Revoke

Under the law of most states a written trust is irrevocable unless the power to amend or revoke is expressly or impliedly reserved in the trust instrument. *Holmes v. Holmes,* 118 P. 733 (Wash. 1911); Restatement (Second) Trusts §330 (1959). However, the laws of California, Oklahoma, and Texas provide that a voluntary trust is revocable unless the instrument that creates the trust expressly provides that it is irrevocable. Cal. Prob. Code §15400 (West 1991 Supp.); Okla. Stat. Ann. tit. 60, §175.41 (West 1971); Tex. Prob. Code Ann. §112.051 (Vernon 1984).

Whatever the local law may be, a trust instrument should specify whether it is amendable or revocable or not. Otherwise there is some risk that the character of the trust might not be properly established or understood by the grantor. It is important to eliminate as many uncertainties as possible in order to avoid disputes with the client, the client's successors, and the tax authorities. For example, the failure of a Texas trust to provide that the trust was irrevocable caused the corpus of the trust to be included in the grantor's gross estate under §2038. *Estate of Alvin Hill,* 64 T.C. 867 (1975), *acq.,* 1976-2 C.B. 2, *aff'd by order,* 568 F.2d 1365 (5th Cir. 1978).

A reservation of the power to revoke the trust should include a suitable provision specifying the manner in which the power may be exercised and how the property will be disposed of upon revocation. The same paragraph often governs amendments of the trust. In Form 10-1, below, optional alternative sentences appear in brackets.

Form 10-1. Reserved Power to Amend or Revoke

The grantor reserves the power to amend or revoke this trust in whole or in part by an instrument in writing delivered to the trustee during the grantor's lifetime. However, without the trustee's consent an amendment may not substantially increase the duties or liabilities of the trustee or change the compensation of the trustee. If the trust is completely revoked, the trustee shall promptly deliver all of the trust fund to the grantor or as the grantor may designate. [This power is personal to the grantor and may not be exercised on the grantor's behalf by a guardian, custodian, or other representative.] [This power may be exercised by an attorney-in-fact for the grantor acting under a durable power of attorney or by a guardian of the grantor's estate.]

In order to be effective, an exercise of the power of revocation must comply with the terms of the trust. Under the provision in Form 10-1, for example, an oral revocation would be ineffective. A written revocation that is not delivered to the trustee during the grantor's lifetime, or otherwise does not comply with the terms of the trust, would also be ineffective. *See, e.g., In re Estate of Button,* 490 P.2d 731 (Wash. 1971); Restatement (Second) Trusts §330, comment j (1959).

The bracketed sentences are optional alternative provisions. One of them should be included regarding the exercise of the power by a representative of the grantor.

Community Property. Among the reasons for establishing a revocable trust, a husband and wife may wish to preserve the character of their respective interests in the property transferred to the trust. This reason is particularly important if they are moving to a state that has a different marital property regime. *See* §3.24. For example, a husband and wife who are moving from a community to a noncommunity property state may wish to transfer their community property to such a trust. The community property character of assets transfered to the trust is preserved if the trust satisfies the requirements of the local law. *See* §3.22; Rev. Rul. 66-283, 1966-2 C.B. 297 (decedent's estate includes only his one-half community property interest in the trust; step-up in basis under §1014(b)(6) also allowed for the survivor's interest in the trust). *See also Katz v. United States,* 382 F.2d 723 (9th Cir. 1967).

Revenue Ruling 66-283, *supra,* notes that "[u]nder California law, community property may also be held by a trustee without losing its character as such." The trust involved in that ruling provided (1) that the property transferred to the trust would retain its character as community property, (2) that the income would be paid to, or used for the benefit of, the grantors, and (3) that, during the lifetimes of *H* and *W,* the trust could be amended or revoked by the joint action of *H* and *W.* In addition, the trust specified that any property withdrawn from the trust will retain its community character. Following the death of one spouse the trust usually becomes irrevocable as to his one-half interest in the community property (and te entire interest in any separate property he or she contributed to the trust). The trust is usually structured so the surviving spouse will have a sufficient interest in the decedent's share to support a QTIP election. Following the death of the first spouse to die, the survivor usually has the power to amend or revoke the trust with respect to the portion of the trust attributable to the other one-half share of community property and any separate property that he or she contributed to the trust.

§10.9. Nontestamentary Nature of Revocable Trusts

Earlier in this century the validity of revocable trusts was sometimes challenged for failure to comply with the formal requirements of the Statute of Wills. Challengers argued that the grantor's retention of a life interest in the trust and an unrestricted power of revocation made the trust testamentary. To them, a revocable trust was comparable to a customary testamentary disposition that became operative only upon the death of the maker and did not affect the maker's title until that time. Most courts resolved the issue according to whether or not the establishment of the trust gave another person an interest in the property transferred to the trust. If an interest were created in another person, the trust was nontestamentary even though the grantor reserved a life interest and retained the power to revoke the trust. Restatement (Second) Trusts §57 (1959). The influential decision in *National Shawmut Bank v. Joy,* 53 N.E.2d 113 (Mass. 1944), put it this way: "The reservation by the settlor, in addition to an interest for life, of a power to revoke the trust, did not make incomplete or testamentary the gift over to the statutory next of kin." Id. at 124. More recent cases involving declarations of trust provided by mutual fund companies have generally reached the same result. *E.g., Farkas v. Williams,* 125 N.E.2d 600 (Ill. 1955). For the purpose of determining the validity of the trust, the interest of the beneficiary other than the grantor suffices if it is a contingent equitable remainder (*i.e.,* the beneficiary's interest is contingent upon surviving the grantor).

§10.10. Validity of Pour Over to Revocable Trust

Until the widespread adoption in the 1960s of the Uniform Testamentary Additions to Trust Act, 8A U.L.A. 599 (1983), the validity and effect of a testamentary addition to a revocable trust was uncertain. The Act, which validates pour overs to preexisting trusts, is included in the U.P.C. as §2-511. In one form or another the Act has been adopted by almost all states and the District of Columbia. 8A U.L.A. 204 (1989 Supp.). Because of local variations in the statute, the governing form should be examined carefully before drafting either a testamentary pour over or an amendment of a trust with respect to which a pour-over will has already been executed. Note that the Uniform Act authorizes a pour over to a trust created by the will of a person who predeceased the testator, but does not authorize a pour over to a trust provided for in the will of a living person. Also, remember that incorporation by reference or the doctrine of independent significance may be used in some cases to uphold a particular disposition. That is, the Uniform Act should not be considered the exclusive method by which the assets of a probate estate can be made subject to the terms of a previously written trust.

Under U.P.C. §2-511, property poured over to a preexisting trust will be administered in accordance with the provisions of the trust including any amendments made before or after the death of the testator. However, some states limit the pour over to the trust as it existed when the will was executed (*i.e.,* insofar as the pour over is concerned, no effect is given to subsequent amendments). Under the Uniform Act the testator's will may provide that the pour over shall also be subject to amendments to the trust made after the testator's death.

The Uniform Act provides that the pour over may be made to "a funded or unfunded life insurance trust, although the trustor has reserved any or all rights of ownership of the insurance contracts." On the other hand, it does not affect the validity of designating the trustee of a revocable trust as beneficiary of life insurance or pension benefits. Many states have statutes that validate such designations.

Form 10-2. Residuary Clause for Pour-Over Will

I give all of my property that is not effectively disposed of by the foregoing provisions of this will, excluding all property over which I hold a power of appointment (my "residuary estate"), to First Bank and its successors as trustee of the John Q. Client Revocable Trust dated June 11, 1988 as the terms of the trust exist at the time of my death, to be held and administered as a part of such trust. If for any reason the foregoing gift to First Bank and its successors is ineffective, I incorporate by reference the John Q. Client Revocable Trust, dated June 11, 1988, as the same shall on the date of this will and I give my residuary estate to First Bank as trustee to be held and administered as part of such incorporated trust.

§10.11. Claims of Creditors Against Grantor

The grantor's creditors can generally reach any beneficial interest the grantor retains in a trust. This rule applies although the trust includes a spendthrift clause that purports to restrict the voluntary or involuntary transfer of the grantor's interests. Restatement (Second) Trusts §156 (1959). As indicted below, courts in several states have allowed creditors to reach the assets of revocable self-settled trusts after the grantor's death.

Power of Revocation. In the absence of a statute, most courts have concluded that the grantor's creditors cannot reach the assets of a revocable trust that was established for others at a time when the grantor was solvent. *E.g., Guthrie v. Canty,* 53 N.E.2d 1009 (Mass. 1944); *Van Stewart v. Townsend,* 28 P.2d 999 (Wash. 1934). Of course, the creditors can reach the assets if the grantor revokes the trust and takes possession of them. Several important states have statutes that allow the grantor's creditors to reach the assets of a revocable trust. They include Florida, Indiana, Kansas, and Michigan. Fla. Stat. Ann. §726.105 (West 1988); Ind. Code Ann. §30-1-9-14 (Burns 1989); Kan.

Stat. Ann. §58-2414 (1983); Mich. Stat. Ann. §26.155(118) (Callaghan 1984).

Bankruptcy. Under §70(a)(3) of the former Bankruptcy Act, the trustee in bankruptcy could exercise any power that the bankrupt could have exercised for his own benefit. The language of the Revised Bankruptcy Act (the "Bankruptcy Code"), adopted in 1978 and codified in Title 11, U.S.C., is less explicit on the point, but presumably the rule continues to apply. This conclusion is supported by a negative implication drawn from §541(b) of the Bankruptcy Code: "Property of the [debtor's] estate does not include any power that the debtor may only exercise solely for the benefit of an entity other than the debtor." 11 U.S.C. §541(b) (Supp. 1982). Also, the leading treatise states that "[t]he same result would apply under the [Bankruptcy] Code." 4 Collier, Bankruptcy ¶541.21 at 541-101 (King ed. 1988).

General Power of Appointment. In some states creditors are allowed to reach property of a trust over which the grantor retained a general power of appointment. Others limit their reach to trusts in which the grantor also reserved a life interest. Where the grantor retained an inter vivos power that is exercisable in his or her own favor, the grantor's creditors should be able to reach the assets of the trust as the trustee in bankruptcy is permitted under the Bankruptcy Code.

Spouse's Elective Share. The extent to which the property of a revocable trust is subject to a surviving spouse's elective share varies according to the terms of the local law. Under U.P.C. §2-202(b)(2), property over which the decedent held a presently exercisable general power of revocation is included in the decedent's augmented estate. The New York law is to the same effect. N.Y. Est. Powers & Trusts Law §5-1.1(b)(1)(E) (West 1981). In the absence of statute, the outcome may turn on whether the court determines that a particular transfer in trust is "illusory" or a "fraud on the surviving spouse."

Other Creditors of a Deceased Grantor. The extent to which the grantor's creditors can reach the assets of a revocable trust following the grantor's death is uncertain in most jurisdictions. However, if the grantor retained a beneficial interest in the trust the creditors may be able to reach the assets.

> [W]here a person places property in trust and reserves the right to amend and revoke, or to direct disposition of principal and income, the settlor's creditors may, following the death of the settlor, reach in satisfaction of the settlor's debts to them, to the extent not satisfied by the settlor's estate, those assets owned by the trust over which the settlor had such

> control at the time of his death as would have enabled the settlor to use the trust assets for his own benefit. *State Street Bank & Trust Co. v. Reiser,* 389 N.E.2d 768,771 (Mass. App. 1979).

Under a common form of statute a self-settled trust is *void* as to existing and future creditors of the grantor. For example, in *Johnson v. Commercial Bank,* 588 P.2d 1096 (Or. 1978), the court held that such a statute allowed a creditor to reach the assets of a trust in which the grantor retained a life income interest and a power of revocation. The Oregon statute applied in the *Johnson* case provided that,

> All deeds of gift, all conveyances and all verbal or written transfers of goods, chattels or things in action made in trust for the person making the same, are void as against the creditors, existing or subsequent of such person. 588 P.2d at 1098.

Creditors of the deceased grantor are allowed to reach the assets of a revocable trust in some cases. *E.g., Ackers v. First National Bank of Topeka,* 387 P.2d 840 (Kan. 1963), *on reh'g,* 389 P.2d 1 (1964), and *In re Matter of Granwell,* 228 N.E.2d 779 (N.Y. 1967) (creditors of the deceased grantor allowed to reach the assets of the grantor's revocable trust). The latter decision was based on New York law, under which the grantor of a revocable trust is considered to have retained ownership of the trust assets until death insofar as creditors are concerned.

The possibility that the assets of a revocable trust cannot be reached by the grantor's creditors following the grantor's death is cited by some planners as an additional advantage of establishing a revocable trust. The interposition of a trust between creditors and the grantor's property no doubt makes it more difficult for the creditors. However, a revocable trust may not actually insulate the property from the claims of creditors. Instead, the "advantage" may prove to be more costly if the trustee is required to engage in litigation after the grantor's death.

§10.12. PRINCIPAL ADVANTAGES OF REVOCABLE TRUSTS

Revocable trusts offer a number of nontax advantages both during the grantor's lifetime and thereafter. The principal lifetime advantages arise from the trustee's management of, or availability to manage, the trust property. Although the grantor may start out as trustee, a successor trustee can assume the responsibility for managing the trust property if the grantor resigns or becomes unable or unwilling to act as trustee. The trust can also serve as an important probate avoidance device for assets located in the state of the grantor's domicile and in other states.

Inexperienced or Absent Grantor. A revocable trust may be suitable to provide for the management of property that belongs to a client who lacks investment experience or confidence. In such a case, the grantor's responsibility for investment of the trust fund can be increased as he or she gains experience. A revocable trust may be a suitable vehicle for the management of assets received by an individual when he or she reached the age for distribution of a custodianship or trust. The trustee's professional management of the trust property may also appeal to a client whose work, studies, or other activities will take him or her out of the country or otherwise make him or her unavailable for protracted periods.

Avoiding Guardianships. The establishment of a revocable trust is often especially attractive to older clients because the existence of the trust may obviate the necessity of having a guardian appointed if the grantor becomes incompetent or is otherwise unable or unwilling to manage property. By creating a trust the client can avoid the expense, complications, delays, and publicity of a guardianship proceeding. Also, the grantor is free to choose the trustee and successor trustees who will manage the property and make disbursements for his or her benefit in the event of disability or incompetency.

> The protective trust can be established with someone other than the donor [grantor] as the initial trustee, or can be created as a so-called convertible or standby trust in which the donor initially retains investment and management powers, with these powers passing to the other trustee or trustees at a later date under defined circumstances, as, for example, certification by a qualified physician that the donor is no longer capable. The mechanism should not be a court decree, which would usually subject the trust to then becoming a so-called court trust, defeating some of the purposes. In such a trust, the power of revocation should be reserved to the donor alone, as it would be disadvantageous, should the donor become incompetent, for a conservator or committee to revoke the trust and upset the donor's estate plan. Report, The Revocable Living Trust as an Estate Planning Tool, 7 Real Prop., Prob. & Tr. J. 223, 224 (1972).

The trust instrument should authorize the trustee to disburse funds to or for the benefit of the grantor at any time, including payment of the cost of providing for the grantor's care and support during any period he or she is disabled or incompetent. The trust may bar any amendment or revocation of the trust while the grantor is incompetent or may allow certain changes to be made by his or her attorney-in-fact under a durable power of attorney. For this purpose the trust should define what constitutes incompetency in a way that coordinates with the terms of any durable power of appointment executed by the grantor (*e.g.,* certification by two physicians, one of whom must be the grantor's attending physician, that he or she is unable to understand and manage financial affairs unassisted).

A durable power of attorney (*see* §4.35) may also obviate the necessity of a guardianship if the power is broad enough and a designated attorney-in-fact remains available to act for the principal. A trust offers more comprehensive protection and greater flexibility than a durable power of attorney. The devices can be coupled, however, to provide for the creation of a revocable trust if the principal becomes incompetent. Specifically, a durable power can authorize the attorney-in-fact to transfer the principal's property to the trustee of a revocable trust in the event of the principal's incapacity. Perhaps the surest method is to attach the form of the trust to be used to the durable power of attorney. *See* §4.35.

Maintaining Ownership Characteristics of Grantors' Property. As indicated above, a revocable trust may be used to preserve the character of the property owned by a husband and wife, which is particularly important if they are moving between states with different marital property regimes. For example, for residents moving to a community property state, it may be important to prevent the inadvertent commingling of assets and loss of their separate identity. It may also be important to maintain the separate character and identity of property where the husband or wife, or both, have children by prior marriages.

A "Trial Run." A revocable trust allows the grantor to observe the operation of the trust and the conduct of the trustee during the grantor's lifetime. The trust can be left in place if the grantor is satisfied. In many instances a revocable trust serves as the grantor's principal estate planning instrument. If it is, the grantor's insurance is made payable to the trustee, and the grantor's other assets can be poured over into the trust. If the grantor is not satisfied with the operation of the trust or the conduct of the trustee, the grantor can amend or revoke the trust or change the trustee.

Avoiding Delays; Providing Continuity. When the grantor dies, there is usually some unavoidable delay in the appointment of a personal representative and the management of the grantor's "owned" property. That property is subject to an estate administration proceeding, which in some states involves detailed court supervision, delays, and additional expenses. Property held in a revocable trust is not subject to administration. Accordingly, the assets of the trust may not be included in the base on which statutory fees are determined in the states whose laws provide for statutory fees for the grantor's personal representative or for the personal representative, or both.

The trustee may continue to invest and manage trust property without interruption following the death of the grantor. Thus, distributions of income and principal can continue to be made to the grantor's family. Subject to the liabilities of the trust for taxes, debts, expenses of administration, and the like, the trustee may also promptly distribute the assets of the trust. Of course, a trustee might be reluctant to make any large distributions soon after the grantor's death — the distribution of property would fix the alternate valuation date of any assets distributed and could subject the trustee to personal liability for the decedent's unpaid taxes. *See* §§12.15 and 12.49. The delays are minimized and the continuity is best if a person other than the grantor is serving as trustee at the time of the grantor's death.

In order to avoid unnecessary delays in filling the office of trustee, the trust should name at least one successor trustee. It is particularly important to do so where an individual is named as the initial trustee. Trusts frequently authorize the individual trustee or the adult beneficiaries of the trust to name a further successor trustee. Of course, if the trustee has discretion to make distributions, a beneficiary generally should not have the power to become successor trustee because of the potentially adverse income and estate tax consequences. *See* §10.20.6.

Secrecy. A revocable trust may also appeal to a person who does not want the disposition of his or her property to be a matter of public record. A relatively high degree of secrecy can be maintained with respect to the content of an inter vivos trust. However, in some jurisdictions the public has access to the state death tax file for an individual decedent, which may include a copy of any revocable trusts created by the decedent. Also, the trustee may be asked to provide a copy of the trust to a stockbroker or transfer agent in order to transfer securities held in the trust. However, such a request may be satisfied without providing a copy of the trust if the lawyer provides the stockbroker with a letter stating that the trust was validly created and is revocable by the grantor.

Wills and other documents involved in the administration of an estate are matters of public record. The wills of prominent individuals may be reported by the press or made the subject of subsequent books. Some publications routinely feature the "wills of the month."

Avoiding Ancillary Estate Administration Proceedings. In general, an estate administration proceeding must be conducted in each state in which a decedent owned real property. The necessity of conducting multiple proceedings can be avoided by transferring the properties to a revocable trust. Thus, a resident of California might transfer his or her condominium in Hawaii to a revocable trust. In order to facilitate disposition of the property the trustee should be given the power to sell or lease the property of the trust without court hearing or notice.

By using a trust, the grantor has some latitude in choosing the law that will apply to the construction and administration of the trust. The choice of law could have an important effect on the rights of creditors and the extent of a surviving spouse's right to claim an elective share of the grantor's property. *See* §9.25.

Avoiding Court Supervision. In some states testamentary trusts are subject to continuing court supervision, which may involve burdensome and expensive requirements to file annual reports and accounts with the court. A revocable trust is a noncourt trust that is generally not subject to those requirements either during or after the grantor's lifetime. In some circumstances it is beneficial for a trust to be treated as a "court trust" with prompt access to the court for instructions and settlement of disputes. However, the advantage of court trusts in this regard is slight. The court's jurisdiction over the parties concerned with a noncourt trust can usually be invoked by an action brought under the appropriate state's general declaratory judgments act, by another civil action, or by a judicial accounting proceeding.

Not all of the advantages apply in every case. Nonetheless, a revocable trust often provides a client with the most satisfactory way of organizing his or her property.

§10.13. Principal Disadvantages of Revocable Trusts

As a general rule the legal costs of preparing a revocable trust and a suitable pour-over will are higher than those for preparing a will that includes a comparable trust. The difference is traceable in part to the greater complexity of the revocable trust. However, it has been suggested that the difference is also due to the fact that "the charges of the profession for will drafting have notoriously lagged behind the actual cost and value of the service, in hopes of future benefit or otherwise." Report, The Revocable Living Trust as an Estate Planning Tool, 7 Real Prop., Prob. & Tr. J. 223, 227 (1972). The trustee's fees can also be a substantial additional cost, at least where there is a professional trustee. Subject to the two percent floor applicable to miscellaneous itemized deductions, the cost of establishing the trust is often deductible. More important, the costs of administering a trust that would not have been incurred if the property were not held in trust, are deductible in computing the adjusted gross income of the trust (*i.e.,* the two percent floor does not apply to them). On the other hand, the cost of preparing a will is a nondeductible personal expense. *See* §1.24.

Tax Returns and Recordkeeping. The trustee must obtain a taxpayer identification number for the trust. §6109; Rev. Rul. 63-178, 1963-2 C.B. 609. Also, the trustee will be required to prepare a statement of the income, deductions, and credits of the trust although the income is all taxable to the grantor. *See* §10.4.2.

The assets of the trust should be transferred into the name of the trustee of the particular trust (*i.e.,* "*X,* as trustee under trust agreement dated March 1, 1989"). In order to handle receipts and disbursements of the trust and to deal efficiently with the trust assets, it is generally necessary to open bank and brokerage accounts in the name of the trustee.

The trustee's fiduciary duties also require the assets of the trust to be segregated from other property and accounted for carefully. Accordingly, the trustee must keep accurate records of transactions affecting the trust. The overall accounting and bookkeeping requirements can be burdensome if performed by a family member as trustee and an unexpected cost if performed by someone hired by the family member. Again, however, the costs are generally deductible under §212. *See* §1.24.

Loss of Income Splitting. The opportunity to have post-mortem income taxed to the decedent's estate and not to the beneficiaries is generally lost to the extent that income-producing property is transferred by a revocable trust outside the decedent's estate. With proper planning, the income of an estate can often be permanently taxed to the estate and not to the beneficiaries. *See* §4.6. The throwback rules of §§665-667 deny such an opportunity in the case of trusts. Under them, virtually any subsequent distribution of property by the trust would be deemed to carry out accumulated income that would be taxed to the distributee as if it had been received by him or her in the year of its accumulation. *See* §10.4.10. However, so long as we have compressed income tax rates income splitting is less significant.

Miscellaneous. The transfer of property to a trust may also involve some other income tax disadvantages. The transfer of §1244 stock to a trust may prevent a subsequent loss in the stock from qualifying as an ordinary deduction. Also, §267 bars a deduction for a loss on a sale of trust property to a beneficiary. However, the transfer of property to a revocable trust will not trigger recapture of depreciation under §§1245 or 1250 or the recognition of gain on an installment sale under §453B.

§10.14. Summary of Tax Consequences

A revocable living trust is generally created for other than tax reasons. The creation of the trust has almost no immediate tax consequences, and is generally neutral as to taxes for the long run. The income is taxed to the grantor so long as the grantor holds the power to revoke. On the estate tax side, the transfer of assets to the trust does not remove them from the grantor's gross estate. The power to revoke and also the retained life estate require this result. Transfers to a revocable trust do not involve a taxable gift because of the grantor's retained power of revocation. On the grantor's death such a trust can split into marital deduction and family trusts in order to minimize overall estate tax costs. However, such a function could be accomplished as well by a testamentary trust. In short, revocable living trusts do not enjoy any particular tax advantage over other methods of disposition.

§10.15. INCOME TAX CONSIDERATIONS

In general, the creation of a revocable trust has no significant income tax consequences during the grantor's lifetime. Because the trust is revocable, its income is fully taxed to the grantor under the grantor trust rules regardless of whether it is distributed or accumulated. *See* §676. The transfer of property to a revocable trust generally does not constitute a taxable event or otherwise trigger the realization of gain. For example, the IRS has recognized that the transfer of an installment obligation to a revocable trust is not a "disposition" under §453B. Rev. Rul. 74-613, 1974-2 C.B. 153 (applying the pre-1980 rules of former §453(d)). In contrast, the transfer of an installment obligation to an irrevocable trust of which the grantor is not treated as the "owner" under §§671 to 677 is a disposition that triggers recognition of gain. Rev. Rul. 76-530, 1976-2 C.B. 132.

Subject to the two percent floor of §67, the legal and accounting costs of establishing a revocable trust are usually deductible by the grantor under §212(2). *See* §1.24. Of course, the cost of operating the trust is deductible by the trust without regard to the two percent floor. The costs are not deductible to the extent they are attributable to tax-exempt income. §265.

On the negative side, the grantor's estate is lost as a separate taxpayer to the extent income-producing property is transferred to the trust. *See* §4.6.

The transfer of stock to a revocable trust does not impair the ability to redeem the stock under §303. As noted above in §10.4.14, such a trust is an eligible stockholder of an S corporation during the grantor's lifetime. §1361(c)(2)(A)(i). It may also be an eligible shareholder following the grantor's death. *See* §1361(c).

The transfer of stock to a revocable trust may cause it to lose its character as section 1244 stock. Accordingly, any loss subsequently realized on the stock may not be deductible as an ordinary loss.

§10.16. Gift Tax Considerations

The transfer of property by the grantor to a revocable trust does not have any immediate gift tax consequences. Any gift provided for in the trust is incomplete at the time of transfer. Under Reg. §25.2511-2(c), "A gift is incomplete in every instance in which a donor reserves the power to revest the beneficial title to the property in himself." A gift is also incomplete if the power of revocation is exercisable in conjunction with a person whose interests are not adverse. Reg. §25.2511-2(e). As noted above, the Regulations require a gift tax return to be filed specifying the reasons the grantor of a trust believes the transfer is not taxable. Reg. §§25.2511-2(j), 25.6019-3(a).

The gifts provided for in a revocable trust become complete if the power to affect the beneficial enjoyment of the property is released or otherwise terminates during the grantor's lifetime. *Estate of Sanford v. Commissioner,* 308 U.S. 39 (1939); Reg. §25.2511-2(f). However, the gifts probably do not become complete merely because the grantor becomes incompetent and may no longer validly exercise the power. In analogous cases, the tax consequences of a power are generally determined without reference to the legal capacity of its holder. *See* §5.22.3. *See also,* Rev. Rul. 75-350, 1975-2 C.B. 366. A gift of course takes place when trust property is distributed to a person other than the grantor. As noted in §10.17, the IRS may contend that gifts made from a revocable trust within three years of death are includible in the grantor's estate under §2035(d)(2).

> **Example 10-8.** *T* transferred Blackacre to the trustee of a revocable trust. The income of the trust was payable to *T* for life and upon *T*'s death the corpus was distributable to *T*'s children, *A, B,* and *C.* The transfer of Blackacre to the trust did not constitute a complete gift. However, any distribution of property from the trust to *A, B,* or *C,* during *T*'s lifetime would constitute a gift. Also, the gift of the remainder interest to *A, B,* and *C* will become complete if *T* releases the power of revocation and does not retain any other power to affect the beneficial enjoyment of the trust.

§10.17. Estate Tax Considerations

The transfer of property to a revocable trust is largely unimportant insofar as the grantor's estate tax is concerned. The property of the trust is includible in the grantor's gross estate under §§2036(a)(2) and 2038(a)(1). Note that under both sections the property of the trust is includible in the grantor's estate if the power to revoke is exercisable by the grantor alone or in conjunction with any other person. The alternate valuation method is available with respect to property held in a revocable trust. *See* §2032. For alternate valuation purposes the division of the assets of a formerly revocable trust into separate trusts upon the death of the grantor constitutes a distribution. *See* Rev. Rul. 73-97, 1973-1 C.B. 404. *See also* §12.19.

A grantor who wishes to make a gift of property held in a revocable trust should withdraw the property first, then make a gift of it directly. Otherwise, if the grantor dies within three years of making the gift the IRS may argue that the property is includible in the grantor's gross estate under §2035(d)(2). The IRS ruled to that effect in a Technical Advice Memorandum in 1986, LR 8609005, and in a series of subsequent letter rulings and T.A.M.'s, *e.g.,* LR 9117003 (TAM), LR 9139002 (TAM). The IRS position is based upon a literal reading of §2035(d)(2) that requires the inclusion of property "which is included in the value of the gross estate under section 2036, 2037, 2038, or 2042 or would have been included under any of those sections if such interest had been retained by the decedent." Because of the retained power to revoke, the property of a revocable trust is includible in the grantor's gross estate under §§2036 or 2038. Thus, the argument runs, property transferred from a revocable trust within three years of the grantor's death "would have been included" in the grantor's gross estate. As a result, the IRS argues that the property transferred is includible in the grantor's gross estate. The result is a triumph of form over substance: It is preferable to recognize the substance of the transaction and reach the contrary conclusion. In substance the transfer of the property at the direction of the grantor is a withdrawal and gift by the grantor. In later rulings the IRS seems to distinguish between revocable trusts that permitted distributions to be made to persons other than the grantor and revocable trusts that did not permit distributions to others during the grantor's lifetime: Gifts made from the former within three years of the grantor's death are includible and gifts made from the latter within three years of the grantor's death are not includible in his or her estate. *E.g.,* LR 9010004; LR 9010005; LR 9016002.

A Technical Advice Memorandum did not require the inclusion of gifts made within three years of the grantor's death from a revocable trust that was includible in the grantor's estate under §2033. LR 8940003 (TAM). In that T.A.M. the grantor held all interests in the trust, the property of which was distributed to the grantor's estate when the grantor died. The gifts were not includible because §2038 was intended to apply to property that passed to others upon the grantor's death, "which would not otherwise be included in the decedent's gross estate under §2033."

Deductions are allowable for funeral expenses, debts, claims, and administration expenses actually paid from the property of the trust before the expiration of the period of limitation for assessment provided in §6501 (three years after the estate tax return is filed). §2053(b). Also, deductions are allowable for qualifying charitable transfers, §2055, and transfers to a surviving spouse, §2056.

C. PLANNING THE BENEFICIARY'S INTERESTS IN AN IRREVOCABLE TRUST

§10.18. SCOPE

This part is concerned with planning and drafting the powers and interests of a beneficiary of an irrevocable trust. The material is generally applicable to permanent irrevocable trusts, including testamentary trusts and trusts that begin life as revocable trusts. Issues regarding the grantor's powers and interests in irrevocable trusts are discussed in more detail in Part D. While some nontax considerations are mentioned, this part is primarily concerned with the federal tax consequences of giving the beneficiary certain important interests or powers. The coverage ranges from sections concerning multiple trusts and the mandatory or discretionary distribution of income to ones concerning the consequences of giving the beneficiary general or special powers of appointment and the appointment of the beneficiary as trustee.

In 1991, estates and trusts were subject to the income tax rates described in Table 10-1 (reflecting the adjustment for inflation). §1(e). The 1990 rates, also adjusted for inflation, are shown in Table 10-2.

The Conference Committee Report that accompanied the 1990 Act stated that the income tax rates applicable to trusts and estates were changed "in order not to increase the benefit of the lower brackets that might otherwise arise from the adoption of the 31-percent marginal tax rate bracket." The changes were "necessary to prevent additional

Table 10-1
Income Tax Rates Applicable to Trusts and Estates, 1991

Taxable Income					
From	*But Not More Than*	*Tax*	+	*Percentage on Excess*	*of the Amount Over*
$ 0	$ 3,450	$ 0		15%	$ 0
3,450	10,350	518		28%	3,450
10,350		2,450		31%	10,350

Table 10-2
Income Tax Rates Applicable to Trusts and Estates, 1990

Taxable Income					
From	*But Not More Than*	*Tax*	+	*Percentage on Excess*	*of the Amount Over*
$ 0	$ 5,450	$ 0		15%	$ 0
5,450	14,150	818		28%	5,450
14,150	28,320	3,254		33%	14,150
28,320		7,930		28%	28,320

undesirable incentives to create multiple trusts (*i.e.,* the benefit of the lower brackets to a trust will be a maximum of $726.00 per year compared with $708.50 under present law)."

§10.19. MULTIPLE TRUSTS

The enactment of the throwback rules in 1969 and the adoption of compressed income tax rates in 1986 eliminated much of the appeal of multiple trusts. In earlier days multiple accumulation trusts were frequently used to decrease a family's overall income tax liability by proliferating the number of separate taxpayers among whom income could be divided for tax purposes. Prior to 1969 the utility of accumulation trusts was based in large measure on rather broad exceptions to the throwback rules. For example, the rules did not apply to capital gains, to income accumulated more than five years prior to the current distribution, or where there had not been an addition to the trust for more than nine years. The advantage of using multiple trusts, of course, depended on recognition of the trusts as separate taxpayers. As noted above in §10.4, trusts that are administered separately have a good chance of being recognized by the courts as separate for income tax purposes.

The tax advantages of multiple trusts were diminished by the 1969 Act, which eliminated all of the former exceptions to the application of the throwback rules and subjected capital gains to the rules. Subsequently the rules were modified to eliminate their application to capital gains, §643(a)(3), and to income accumulated prior to the beneficiary's birth or attainment of 21 years of age, §665(b). Accordingly, the establishment of multiple trusts funded with appreciated capital assets or created for the benefit of minors can produce limited income tax benefits. It is important to note, however, that the gain on a sale of appreciated assets made within two years after the transfer of the assets to the trust is generally taxed under §644 as if the grantor had made the sale. *See* §10.4.11. While §644 does not apply to charitable remainder trusts, it does apply to charitable lead trusts.

§10.20. Mandatory or Discretionary Distributions?

The distributive provisions of each trust must be planned in light of the wishes of the grantor and the overall circumstances of the beneficiaries. One of the most important decisions to be made in planning a trust concerns the extent to which the trustee should be given discretionary authority to distribute income and principal. For example, a trust may prescribe a rigid scheme for the distribution of income or it may give the trustee discretion to accumulate income or to "sprinkle" income among several beneficiaries. A mandatory distribution trust may meet the needs of the income beneficiaries and remaindermen, but it is probably too inflexible to meet their long-range tax and nontax needs. In particular, the mandatory distribution of all of the income to one income beneficiary may subject the income to unnecessarily high income tax rates. The distributions also swell the beneficiary's estate, which may cause the imposition of an otherwise avoidable estate tax bite. The flexibility of the trust is enhanced and some income tax savings may be possible if the trustee is given discretion to distribute income among several beneficiaries and to accumulate undistributed income and add it to principal.

A discretionary trust may best provide for a beneficiary who is or may become the recipient of publicly provided care or benefits. Such a trust is intended to "supplement public welfare benefits without disqualifying the beneficiary and without subjecting the trust assets to reimbursing the public entity." Palmer, Estate Planning for Public Welfare Recipients, 2 Prob. & Prop. 43 (Mar./Apr. 1988).

Regardless of the provisions of the trust for the distribution of income, the capacity of the trust to meet the needs of the family over time is enhanced if the trustee is authorized to make discretionary distributions of principal to the beneficiaries (and, perhaps, to their issue). Of course, the terms of the trust and distributions must be planned in light of the generation-skipping tax. *See* §§2.22-2.40. Also, a trust will not qualify for the marital deduction under §2056(b)(7) if the trustee has discretion to distribute income to the surviving spouse or the trustee may distribute any income or principal to persons other than the decedent's surviving spouse during his or her lifetime. Note, however, that disclaimers may be used to eliminate interests that prevent a trust from qualifying for the marital deduction. §§12.32-12.35.

From the beneficiary's point of view a trust in which distributions depend upon the exercise of discretion by another person is less satisfactory than one that provides for mandatory distributions. However, the potential for conflict between the beneficiary and trustee is reduced if the trustee communicates frequently and effectively with the beneficiary regarding the needs of the beneficiary, the status of the trust, and the trustee's plans for making distributions. The security of the beneficiary is also enhanced if the beneficiary holds a limited power to withdraw trust assets, such as a "5 or 5" power of withdrawal (*i.e.,* the noncumulative power to withdraw each year the greater of $5,000 or five percent of the value of the trust property). *See* §10.24.

The indefiniteness of the beneficiary's interest in a discretionary trust generally prevents the beneficiary from transferring his or her interest. The indefiniteness of the interest also precludes the allowance of a previously taxed property credit to the beneficiary's estate for the estate tax paid in the grantor's estate. *See* §2013. As stated in Rev. Rul. 67-53, 1967-1 C.B. 265:

> Where a trustee possesses the power, in his or her absolute and uncontrolled discretion, to pay out net income to the income beneficiary of a trust or to accumulate such income, the beneficiary's interest cannot be valued according to recognized valuation principles as of the date of the transferor's death. Therefore, notwithstanding the fact that such income was actually paid to the decedent-transferee, the credit for tax on prior transfers under section 2013 of the Code is not allowable with respect to such an interest.

In contrast, a noncumulative power to withdraw the greater of $5,000 or five percent of the value of the trust property qualifies as property for purposes of the credit for tax on prior transfers to the extent of the value of the power on the date of the first decedent's death. Rev. Rul. 79-211, 1979-2 C.B. 319.

§10.20.1. Distribution or Accumulation of Income

A trust may simply authorize the trustee to pay the income to a named beneficiary or accumulate the income for later distribution. The potential for income splitting and some limited income tax saving is obvious where the beneficiary is under 21 and the accumulated income will not be subject to the throwback rules. *See* §665(b). Despite the compressed income tax rates, the accumulation of the income by the trust can result in some income tax deferral, depending upon the respective rates that apply to the trust and the beneficiary. More hopefully, the accumulated income will be subject to a lower rate of tax when it is distributed. That may occur if the distribution is made to the beneficiary from whom it was withheld after retirement or during a period of relatively lower income. A saving can also occur if the accumulated income is later distributed to other family members whose income is subject to lower rates. Such a distribution might be made, for example, following the death of the original beneficiary.

§10.20.2. Sprinkling of Income

More impressive income and estate tax savings are often possible where the trustee has discretion to "sprinkle" the income among a group of beneficiaries. In making distributions the trustee can take into account the needs of the beneficiaries and their respective income tax brackets. For example, an independent trustee of a family bypass trust can be given discretion to distribute income to and among a class of persons including the grantor's surviving spouse and children. In appropriate cases the class might also include the grantor's grandchildren, distributions to whom would implicate the GSTT. *See* §§2.22-2.40. In this connection note that distributions which are nontaxable gifts by reason of §2503(e) (direction tuition and medical expense payments) are not subject to the GSTT. §2642(c). Thus, a trustee could pay the tuition or medical care expenses of a grandchild of the grantor without incurring any GSTT liability. Of course, under §678 the income of a trust is taxed to a nongrantor to the extent he or she has the power, exercisable by himself or herself alone, to take the income or principal of the trust. This rule is avoided, however, if another person is required to consent to such distributions. Thus, the power to withdraw income or principal might require the concurrence of the power-holder's spouse. For estate tax purposes property that is subject to a power of withdrawal by a nongrantor is includible in the power-holder's estate unless the power is within one of the exceptions of §2041(b) (*i.e.,* limited by an ascertainable standard relating to the power-holder's health, education, support, or maintenance, or requires the consent of the creator or an adverse party).

Where the income exceeds the needs of the surviving spouse, or where he or she has no need for the income, the trustee holding such a power could distribute the trust income to children who are in lower tax brackets. Such distributions also avoid increasing the size of the surviving spouse's estate, which is an important consideration.

§10.20.3. Powers Held by Independent Trustees

The grantor is not treated as the owner of the trust for income tax purposes although the trustee or trustees may be given a free hand to distribute income or principal, or both, to the beneficiaries of the trust, provided that the grantor is not a trustee and no more than half of the trustees are "related or subordinate parties who are subservient to the wishes of the grantor." §674(c). The term "related or subordinate party" is defined in §672(c) as a nonadverse party who is

1. The grantor's spouse if living with the grantor;
2. Any one of the following: The grantor's father, mother, issue, brother, or sister; an employee of the grantor; a corporation or any employee of a corporation in which the stock holdings of the grantor and the trust are significant from the viewpoint of voting control; a subordinate employee of a corporation in which the grantor is an executive.

The definition of subordinate or related party is very helpful to grantors because of the limited class of persons who are included within it. In particular, a wide range of persons who are related to the grantor by affinity or consanguinity are not within its scope (*e.g.,* niece, nephew, cousin, son-in-law, mother-in-law, grandparent). Also, the term ordinarily does not include persons who perform professional services for the grantor, such as an accountant or lawyer. Given those definitions, a client can often find a suitable person to act as trustee who will not be classified as a related or subordinate party.

A related or subordinate party is deemed to be subservient to the grantor in the exercise of the powers held by him or her unless a preponderance of the evidence establishes that he or she is not subservient. §672(c).

The §674(c) exception permits an independent trustee to hold powers "(1) to distribute, apportion, or accumulate income to or for a beneficiary or beneficiaries or to, for, or within a class of beneficiaries; or (2) to pay out corpus to or for a beneficiary or beneficiaries or to or for a class of beneficiaries (whether or not income beneficiaries)." However, the exception does not apply if any person has a power to add beneficaries who are entitled to receive income or corpus, except to provide for after-born or after-adopted children. For this purpose the power of the beneficiary of a nonspendthrift trust to assign his or her interest is not consdered to be a power to add a beneficiary. Reg. §1.674(d)-2(b).

Example 10-9. *T* transferred property to a trust under which an independent trustee had the power to determine the amount of income to be distributed annually to each of the beneficiaries named in the trust. The grantor is not treated as owner of the trust by reason of the independent trustee's power to sprinkle income among the named beneficiaries. A contrary result would be reached if the grantor had the unrestricted power to remove the independent trustee and become trustee. *See* Reg. §1.674(d)-2.

§10.20.4. Powers Limited by an Ascertainable Standard, §674(d)

A trustee, other than the grantor or a spouse living with the grantor, can hold a power to "distribute, apportion, or accumulate income for a beneficiary or beneficiaries or to, for, or within a class of beneficiaries" if the power is limited by a reasonably definite external standard set forth in the trust instrument. §674(d). Under §674(d) a power is within the exception whether or not the conditions of §§674(b)(6) or (7) are satisfied. Thus, the power over income may be exercised by the trustee without regard to the age or competency of the beneficiaries or the ultimate disposition of the income or corpus. The powers permitted by this exception are very helpful where the requirements of §674(c) cannot be met (*e.g.,* the trustee is not independent), or the grantor does not wish to give the trustee broader discretion. The power is particularly appropriate where the trust will last beyond the minority of multiple beneficiaries, some of whom may need more income than others to provide for education, support, medical care, or emergency expenses. Reg. §1.674(b)-1(b)(5) describes powers that are limited by reasonably definite external standards in the following passage:

> It is not required that the standard consist of the needs and circumstances of the beneficiary. A clearly measurable standard under which the holder of a power is legally accountable is deemed a reasonably definite standard for this purpose. For instance, a power to distribute [income] for the education, support, maintenance, or health of the beneficiary; for his reasonable support and comfort; or to enable him to maintain his accustomed standard of living; or to meet an emergency, would be limited by an ascertainable standard. However, a power to distribute [income] for the pleasure, desire, or happiness of a beneficiary is not limited by a reasonably definite standard.

As in the case of §674(c), the exception does not apply if any person has a power to add beneficiaries, except where the power is limited to providing for after-born or after-adopted children.

§10.20.5. Grantor as Trustee

Because of the generally adverse income and estate tax consequences, great care must be exercised if the grantor will have any discretion to make distributions. To begin with, the possession of the power to make discretionary distributions of income or principal may cause the income to be taxed to the grantor under §674. *See* §10.37.1. As mentioned above, the grantor is taxable on the trust's income if a discretionary power of distribution is held by a nonadverse party other than an independent trustee within the exception of §674(c). Finally, where the grantor is trustee it is likely that any discretionary powers of distribution held by the trustee-grantor will cause the trust to be included in the grantor's estate under §§2036 and 2038. Thus, in *United States v. O'Malley,* 383 U.S. 627 (1966), the irrevocable trusts that the decedent established for his wife and daughters were included in his estate because of his power, as cotrustee, to pay out or accumulate the income of the trusts. Moreover, under §2038 the trust is includible in the grantor's estate where the grantor holds the power, as trustee, to accelerate the distribution of the trust property to the beneficiary. *Lober v. United States,* 346 U.S. 335 (1953).

§10.20.6. Beneficiary as Trustee

Unless the grantor is treated as the owner of the trust, a beneficiary-trustee is taxable on the income of the trust to the extent the beneficiary has the power, acting alone, to acquire the principal or income. See the discussion of §678 at §10.24.1. Thus, all of the income of a trust is taxed to a beneficiary-trustee who holds the power to distribute all of the income or principal to himself or herself. On the estate tax side, a trust over which a beneficiary-trustee holds a discretionary power to make distributions to himself or herself is to that extent includible in his or her estate under §2041. In contrast, a beneficiary can safely hold purely administrative powers. Reg. §20.2041-1(b).

§10.20.7. "Absolute" or "Uncontrolled" Discretion

The trust may provide that the trustee's discretion shall be "absolute," "unlimited," or "uncontrolled." Such a provision generally does not insulate the trustee's conduct from all court review, but it severely limits the court's supervisory role. According to the Restatement, in such a case the court will not consider whether the trustee acted beyond the bounds of reasonable judgment. Rather, the court will only consider whether the trustee acted in a state of mind contemplated by the trustor. Restatement (Second) Trusts §187, comment j (1959). Thus, a court's inquiry might be limited to determining whether the trustee acted arbitrarily or dishonestly. Because of the restricted review and reduced protection for the beneficiaries, it is generally undesirable to give the trustee such broad and unfettered discretion.

§10.20.8. Standards to Guide the Exercise of Discretion

It is helpful to the trustee and beneficiaries if the trust provides some guidance regarding the manner in which discretion should be exercised in making distributions. *See* Halbach, Problems of Discretion in Discretionary Trusts, 61 Colum. L. Rev. 1425 (1961). A trust might include, for example, a statement of the primary and secondary purposes of the trust. In addition, the trust should indicate whether priority should be given to one or another of the beneficiaries. For example, when it comes to making distributions of principal, the trustee is helped by an indication that the grantor was primarily (or secondarily) concerned with the needs of the current beneficiaries as opposed to the preservation of principal for the remaindermen.

The trust should also indicate the extent to which the resources or income of the beneficiaries should be taken into account in making a decision regarding distributions. The provisions may (1) require the trustee to consider the beneficiary's resources (or income), (2) authorize the trustee to consider them, or (3) direct the trustee to disregard them. In most instances it is appropriate to provide that the trustee should consider them to the extent known to him or her.

§10.20.9. Transferability of the Beneficiary's Interest

In the case of a discretionary trust other than a self-settled trust, a transferee or creditor of the beneficiary cannot force the trustee to make any payments of income or principal. Restatement (Second) Trusts §155(1) (1959). However, this rule only applies where the trustee has uncontrolled discretion to pay the income or principal of the trust to the beneficiary. Neither a transferee nor a creditor can require the discretion to be exercised in favor of making a payment. A transferee or creditor is generally entitled to the benefit of any payment the trustee decides to make unless the trust includes a valid restraint on alienation. Id. at §155(2). Thus, "if the trustee does pay over any part of the trust property to the beneficiary with knowledge that he has transferred his interest or after the trustee has been served with process in a proceeding by a creditor of the beneficiary to reach his interest, the trustee is personally liable to the transferee or creditor for the amount so paid, except so far as a valid provision for forfeiture for alienation or restraint on alienation has been imposed. . . ." Id. at §155, comment h.

The same general rule applies to the interest of a beneficiary in a trust that gives the trustee the discretion to make payments to a group of beneficiaries. Neither a beneficiary nor a transferee or creditor of a beneficiary can force the trustee to make any payment. However, the trustee may be liable if a payment is made to a beneficiary after the trustee receives notice that the interest of the beneficiary has been assigned.

Support Trust. The beneficiary's interest in a support trust is not transferable. "If by the terms of a trust it is provided that the trustee shall pay or apply only so much of the income and principal or either as is necessary for the education or support of the beneficiary, the beneficiary cannot transfer his interest and his creditors cannot reach it." Id. at §154. The rule requires that a distinction be drawn between a trust for support and a trust under which part or all of the income is payable to the beneficiary with a statement that the payments are to be used for education or support. Such a statement of purpose does not prevent the transfer of the beneficiary's interest.

§10.20.10. Discretionary Distribution Form

A provision authorizing discretionary distributions could be expressed in a variety of ways. The following represents one possible approach to the challenge of drafting the basic provision. The provision could be expanded to cover related matters, such as the extent to which unequal distributions of principal or income are to be taken into account upon a final distribution of the trust.

Form 10-3. Discretionary Distributions

Distributions. The trustee shall distribute so much of the income and principal of the trust to or for the benefit of my surviving spouse and issue as the trustee believes is desirable to provide for the comfortable support, maintenance, education, and general welfare of each of them. The trustee is authorized to make distributions to one or more of them in unequal amounts and to exclude one or more of the others of them from such distributions. In making decisions regarding distributions, I direct the trustee (1) to give primary consideration to the needs of my surviving spouse and secondary consideration to the needs of all others and (2) to give such consideration as the trustee deems appropriate to the resources and income of each beneficiary apart from the beneficiary's interest in this trust.

§10.21. Spendthrift Clauses — Restricting the Transfer of a Beneficiary's Interests

In the absence of a restriction imposed by the trust, the equitable interests of a beneficiary in the income and principal of an ordinary trust are freely alienable and may be reached by the beneficiary's creditors. As noted above, the beneficiary's interests in a support trust or a discretionary trust are not transferrable because of the limited nature of the beneficiary's interest. Restatement (Second) Trusts §§154, 155(1) (1959). Perhaps more importantly, most states recognize "spendthrift clauses" that restrict the right of a beneficiary to transfer an interest in the income or principal of a trust. Restatement (Second) Trusts §§152, 153 (1959). For example, Cal. Prob. Code §15300 (West 1991 Supp.) provides, with some exceptions, that "if the trust instrument provides that a beneficiary's interest in income is not subject to voluntary or involuntary transfer, the beneficiary's interest in income under the trust may not be transferred and is not subject to enforcement of a money judgment until paid to the beneficiary." Spendthrift clauses are not recognized in England and in three American states, New Hampshire, Ohio, and Rhode Island. G. Bogert, Trusts and Trustees §222 (2d ed. rev. 1979).

A spendthrift trust is one in which, either because of a direction of the settlor or because of statute, the beneficiary is unable to transfer his right to future payments of income or capital and his creditors are unable to subject the beneficiary's interest to the payment of their claims. Such a trust does not involve any restraint on alienability or creditor's rights with respect to property after it is received by the beneficiary from the trustee, but rather merely a restraint with regard to his rights to future payments under the trust. G. Bogert, *supra*.

The planner should advise a prospective grantor regarding the effect of including or excluding a spendthrift clause. The inclusion of a spendthrift clause is effective in most states to prevent the beneficiary from making any gift or sale of an interest in income or principal. For example, such a clause might prevent an immature beneficiary from transferring an interest to a religious cult, making an unwise sale of the interest, or otherwise dissipating the trust fund. A spendthrift clause is also usually effective to insulate the trust assets from the claims of most creditors. Many states allow the beneficiary's interests to be reached by certain preferred creditors including (1) a former spouse or dependents for support in accordance with a court order, (2) creditors who provide the beneficiary with the necessities of life, and (3) the United States or a state for taxes. *See* Restatement (Second) Trusts §157 (1959); G. Bogert, *supra,* at §224.

The inclusion of a spendthrift clause reduces the beneficiary's flexibility in dealing with trust interests. Thus, the clause prevents an income beneficiary from assigning his or her income interest to another person. Such a restriction could prevent the family from making a beneficial reallocation of the income within the family in order to reduce the overall income tax burden. However, a spendthrift clause generally does not prevent a beneficiary from disclaiming an interest in the trust. Many disclaimer statutes specifically provide that a beneficiary may disclaim an interest whether or not it is subject to a spendthrift provision or similar restriction. *E.g.,* U.P.C. §2-801(a); Cal. Prob. Code §15309 (West 1991 Supp.); Wash. Rev. Code §11.86.070 (1989).

§10.21.1. Form of Spendthrift Clause

A short form of spendthrift clause of the following type is adequate for most purposes:

Form 10-4. Spendthrift Clause

No interest of a beneficiary in the principal or income of this trust may be anticipated, assigned or encumbered, or subject to any creditor's claim or legal process prior to its actual distribution to the beneficiary.

A more detailed clause may require the trustee to pay the income or principal directly to or for the benefit of the beneficiary and not upon any written or oral direction or assignment by the beneficiary. Even if the trust prohibits the beneficiary from transferring the interest, the beneficiary may validly direct the trustee to distribute the interest in the trust to another person. In such a case the beneficiary's direction is recognized as a revocable authorization to pay. Restatement (Second) Trusts, §152, comment i (1959).

Planners should be aware of the extent to which the governing law exempts interests in trusts from the claims of creditors and the extent to which grantors can further restrict the voluntary or involuntary alienation of a beneficiary's interest. Many clients believe that a beneficiary's interest in a trust should be insulated from the beneficiary's own inexperience or imprudence. Their trusts should include provisions that prevent any voluntary or involuntary transfers of the beneficiary's interests in the trust.

§10.21.2. Self-Settled Trusts

The owner of property cannot insulate it from the reach of existing or subsequent creditors by transferring it to a trust of which the owner is a beneficiary. On the contrary, the beneficial interest of the owner in such a trust generally is transferrable and reachable by the owner's creditors. Restatement (Second) Trusts §156(1) (1959). Indeed, many states have statutes under which transfers in trust for the use of the transferor are void as to existing or future creditors. No gift occurs if the property of the trust can be reached by the grantor's creditors. *Commissioner v. Vander Weele,* 254 F.2d 895 (6th Cir. 1958).

The identity of the grantor and the extent of the grantor's interests are also important for federal gift and estate tax purposes. The reciprocal trust doctrine is sometimes applied to determine the true identity of the grantor of trusts established at the same time by related taxpayers for the benefit of each other. The doctrine is explained at §6.29. By applying the doctrine, the trusts are "uncrossed" with the result that the beneficiary of each trust is treated as its grantor. Accordingly, the trust assets may be fully includible in the beneficiary's estate under §§2036 or 2038.

The transfer of property to an irrevocable trust nominally for the benefit of others is an incomplete gift if the assets of the trust are subject to the claims of the grantor's creditors whenever the claims arise. *E.g.,* Rev. Rul. 76-103, 1976-1 C.B. 293. That ruling involved a trust that gave the trustee the absolute discretion to distribute income and principal to the grantor. Under the governing state law, the property of the trust was subject to the claims of the grantor's creditors. Accordingly, the transfer to the trust was incomplete for gift tax purposes and the trust property was includible in the grantor's estate because of the grantor's "retained power to, in effect, terminate the trust by relegating the grantor's creditors to the entire property of the trust." Id.

§10.22. General Powers of Appointment

"The term 'general power of appointment' means a power which is exercisable in favor of the decedent, his estate, his creditors, or the creditors of his estate. . . ." §2041(b) (1). A general power of appointment is the antithesis of a spendthrift restraint. Powers that might be characterized as general powers of appointment under §§2041 and 2514 should be seldom conferred except as required to qualify for a specific tax benefit such as the marital deduction under §2056(b)(5). The creation of general powers of appointment should be avoided because of the potentially adverse income, gift, and estate tax consequences for the holder: The income from property subject to a presently exercisable general power is taxable to the holder under §678 unless the grantor is treated as owner of the trust; the exercise or lapse of a general power is usually treated as a taxable gift, §2514; and property subject to a general power is includible in the power-holder's estate under §2041. Also, the grantor may not want to confer such a broad power of disposition on another person — a special power of appointment may provide sufficient flexibility.

The statutory definition of a general power of appointment is broad and encompasses "all powers which are in substance and effect powers of appointment regardless of the nomenclature used in creating the power and regardless of local property law connotations." Reg. §20.2041-1(b)(1). Importantly, the definition extends to powers held in a fiduciary capacity and to joint powers with the exception of joint powers held with either the creator of the power or a party with an interest that would be adversely affected by an exercise of the power, §§2041(b)(1)(C)(i), (ii). *See* §10.26. The trustee's power to distribute income among the members of a class that includes the trustee is a general power of appointment over the income. Also, the property of a trust is includible in the beneficiary's estate where the beneficiary and two other persons hold the power, as trustees, to terminate the trust and distribute the trust property to the beneficiary. *Maytag v. United States,* 493 F.2d 995 (10th Cir. 1974). Where the trustee has discretion to make distributions to the beneficiary, the beneficiary should not have the power to remove the trustee and become successor trustee, unless the beneficiary is barred from participating in the exercise of the discretionary powers. A person who has the power to become trustee is treated as having all of the powers of the trustee. Reg. §20.2041-1(b)(1). It is also risky if the beneficiary has the unlimited power to remove the trustee and appoint a successor trustee. *See* §10.41.

In some cases the conferral of a general power of appointment carries tax benefits that outweigh the disadvantages. Thus, the beneficiaries of a permanent irrevocable trust may be given *Crummey* withdrawal powers so the gift tax annual exclusion will be available with respect to property transferred to the trust. *See* §7.37. Giving a beneficiary a power that will require the trust to be included in his or her estate is sometimes done in order to support an increase in the basis of the assets of the trust under §1014. Thus, the power-holder and a nonadverse party might be given the power to terminate the trust and distribute the trust assets to the power-holder. It can also be used for GSTT purposes to change the transferor of the trust to the holder of the power. *See* §2.31.

§10.23. Special Powers of Appointment

Where it is consistent with the client's plan, a current beneficiary of the trust may be given a special power of appointment over the income or principal. The conferral of an appropriate special power substantially increases the flexibility of the trust at little or no additional gift or estate tax cost. For example, a surviving spouse may be given a testamentary special power to appoint the trust assets to and among the trustor's descendants rather than providing in the trust for a fixed method of distribution. In such a case the exercise of the power would not cause the trust to be included in the surviving spouse's estate. In order to avoid inclusion of the trust property in the beneficiary's estate, the power should expressly prohibit an appointment in favor of the beneficiary, "his estate, his creditors, or the creditors of his estate." §2041(b)(1).

A power is more flexible if it is exercisable during the beneficiary's lifetime. However, it is more common to create powers that are only exercisable upon the beneficiary's death (*i.e.,* a testamentary power). Such a limitation helps preserve the trust property during the beneficiary's lifetime and insulates the beneficiary from pressure by permissible appointees to exercise the power currently in their favor. Limiting the power to an exercise at death also eliminates the risk that the power might be characterized as a general power where it is exercisable in favor of persons for whom the power-holder has a lifetime legal obligation to support. *See* Reg. §20.2041-1(c). On the other hand, giving the beneficiary a currently exercisable power allows greater flexibility in meeting the economic and estate planning objectives of the family group. Thus, the holder may appoint trust property to family members in lieu of transferring "owned" property to the appointee. The appointment of trust corpus pursuant to a special power of appointment does not constitute a gift of the corpus. §2514(b), (c). However, where the power-holder is entitled to receive the income of the trust for life, an appointment of the corpus of the trust to another person constitutes a gift of a proportionate part of the holder's income interest. Reg. §25.2514-1(b)(2); Rev. Rul. 79-327, 1979-2 C.B. 342; *Estate of Ruth B. Regester,* 83 T.C. 1 (1984); *contra, Self v. United States,* 142 F. Supp. 939 (Ct. Cl. 1956).

From a future interest perspective, an income beneficiary's special power may be an invalid power appendant to the extent it applies to his or her right to the income from the trust. He or she holds that right apart from the purported power. Presumably no gift would occur in case of the exercise of a special power over the corpus if the power-holder were only entitled to receive distributions of income in the discretion of another person.

Under §678 the exercise of a power of appointment in favor of persons the power-holder is obligated to support is taxable to the power-holder only to the extent the distribution satisfies that obligation. On the other hand, that result is avoided if the trust requires the beneficiary to appoint an independent party to exercise such a power. Such an "add-a-trustee" approach was upheld in LR 9036048. Also, a beneficiary could safely be authorized to make distributions to his or her dependents for "super support" — items such as private lessons that the beneficiary is not obligated to provide to his or her dependents. LR 9030005.

The provision creating a power should indicate when and how the power is exercisable, whether the property may be appointed on a further trust, in whose favor it may be exercised, and whether the property may be appointed unequally or to the complete exclusion of some permissible appointees. In addition, the power should specify what will become of the trust property to the extent the power is not validly exercised. Form 10-5 is a sample of a testamentary special power of appointment.

Form 10-5. Special Testamentary Power of Appointment

Upon the death of the beneficiary, the trustee shall distribute the trust property, including the net income then in the hands of the trustee and all income then accrued but uncollected, to and among such of the beneficiary's spouse and issue as the beneficiary shall appoint by a will executed after the date this trust is created. An exercise of this power shall only be effective if it refers to the instrument by date and states expressly the beneficiary's intention to exercise the power. The beneficiary may appoint the trust property in such shares or interests and upon such terms and conditions as she/he chooses, either outright or upon a further trust. In exercising this power the beneficiary is authorized to appoint the trust property to or for the benefit of one or more of the possible appointees to the total exclusion of the other or others of them. However, in no event may this power be exercised in favor of the beneficiary, her/his creditors, her/his estate, or the creditors of her/his estate.

To the extent the beneficiary does not validly exercise this power, the trustee shall distribute the trust property to those of her/him issue who survive her/him, such issue to take by right of representation and not per capita. If none of the beneficiary's issue survive her/him, the trustee shall distribute the trust property to ______________________________.

In the case of an inter vivos power, the instrument should also specify how the power could be exercised inter vivos or upon the death of the holder of the power.

§10.24. $5,000 OR 5% POWER OF WITHDRAWAL

Under the basic estate and gift tax rule, the lapse of a post-1942 general power of appointment is treated as a transfer of the property subject to the power. §§2041(a)(2); 2514(b). However, a major exception to that rule allows a beneficiary to hold without substantial disadvantage a noncumulative, inter vivos power to withdraw a limited amount of property from the trust each year. The lapse of general powers of appointment during a calendar year is significant for gift tax purposes only to the extent that the total amount that could have been appointed exceeds the greater of $5,000 or five percent of the aggregate value of the assets out of which, or the proceeds of which, the exercise of the lapsed powers could have been satisfied. §2514(e). Under a parallel provision of the estate tax law, property with respect to which such a general power has lapsed is not includible in the power-holder's estate. §2041(b)(2). However, property subject to an unlapsed power of withdrawal at the time of the power-holder's death is includible in his or her estate although it is limited by the "5 or 5" standard. §2041(b)(2).

Powers of withdrawal, including *Crummey* powers, (*See* §7.37), are often tailored so the amount subject to withdrawal each year by a beneficiary does not exceed the 5 or 5 limit. According to the IRS the amount sheltered by this exception is limited to a total of $5,000 or five percent annually for all trusts. Rev. Rul. 85-88, 1985-2 C.B. 202. Thus, the planner must proceed with caution where the power-holder is, or may be, the beneficiary of more than one trust. However, the lapse of a power to withdraw an amount in excess of the 5 or 5 limit does not have any adverse gift tax consequences if the power-holder also has a general or special power of appointment over the remainder. In such a case Reg. §25.2511-2(b) indicates that the lapse would result in an incomplete gift: "[I]f a donor transfers property to another in trust to pay the income to the donor or accumulate it in the discretion of the trustee, and the donor retains a testamentary power to appoint the remainder among his descendants, no portion of the transfer is a completed gift." *See* LR 8229097; LR 8517052; LR 9030005.

Because of the favorable gift and estate tax treatment of 5 or 5 powers, it is common to give one to the surviving spouse or other life income beneficiary of an irrevocable trust. Giving the power obviously increases the flexibility of the trust and reduces the beneficiary's dependence on the trustee. It also increases the beneficiary's "comfort level," which can be important if the beneficiary and the trustee are to establish and maintain a good relationship. Some beneficiaries enjoy having the power to withdraw some amount each year as "mad money" to use as they wish.

If lapses of post-1942 general powers in any calendar year exceed the 5 or 5 limit, the excess is treated as a transfer by the power-holder, which may involve a taxable gift. Also, the excess is includible in the power-holder's estate if the lapse is "of such a nature that if it were a transfer of property owned by the decedent, such property would be includible in the decedent's gross estate under sections 2035 to 2038, inclusive." §2041(a)(2). Thus, the property in excess of the 5 or 5 limit over which a power had lapsed is includible in the power-holder's estate if he or she is entitled to receive the income from that property after the lapse.

Example 10-10. *B,* the life income beneficiary of a trust, had the power to withdraw $50,000 of principal in a specified calendar year. *B* did not exercise the power, as a result of which it lapsed. The principal of the trust was worth $800,000 at the end of that calendar year. *B* is treated as having transferred property worth $10,000 to the trust. That figure represents the excess of amount B could have withdrawn ($50,000) over the greater of $5,000 or 5% of the value of the property subject to the power (5% × $800,000 = $40,000). Accordingly, for estate tax purposes, *B* is treated as the grantor of 1/80 of the trust principal ($10,000/ $800,000). Thus, if the trust has a value of $1,200,000 at the time of his or her death $15,000 would be includible in *B*'s estate. Note also that the lapse of the power might involve a taxable gift to the remaindermen.

A 5 or 5 power is often given to a surviving spouse who is the beneficiary of a testamentary trust. It is appropriate to do so in the case of marital deduction trusts, including ones that meet the requirements of a QTIP trust under §2056(b)(7). As noted above, the power provides desirable flexibility to the trust and security to the surviving spouse.

Form 10-6. 5 or 5 Power of Withdrawal

Beneficiary shall have the power in each calendar year to withdraw from the principal of the trust, an amount not to exceed the greater of $5,000 or five percent of the value of the principal of the trust determined as of the end of the calendar year. This power may be exercised in whole or in part each year by a written notice delivered to Trustee. The power of withdrawal is noncumulative, so that the power of withdrawal with respect to a particular calendar year can only be exercised during the calendar year.

§10.24.1. Income Tax

Under §678(a)(1) the holder of a power of withdrawal exercisable by the power-holder alone is treated as owner of the portion of the trust subject to withdrawal. *See* §10.27.1. The rule only applies if the grantor is *not* treated as the owner of the trust under §§673-677. Also, the rule is of no concern if the power-holder is taxable on all of the income in any case.

The existence of such a power may cause the power-holder to be taxed on a portion of the income of a trust that is distributable to other beneficiaries. Rev. Rul. 67-241, 1967-2 C.B. 225 (surviving spouse with 5 or 5 power is taxable on proportionate part of income payable to decedent's two children). According to the IRS, "until the power is exercised, released or allowed to lapse, [the power-holder] will be treated as the owner for each year of that portion of [the trust] that is subject to the power of withdrawal." LR 9034004.

The power-holder may release a power of withdrawal which subjects the power-holder to taxation under §678(a). Of course, the release of such a power may have estate and gift tax consequences. Under §678(a)(2) a person who releases or otherwise modifies a power remains treated as owner of the trust if the power-holder retained "such control as would, within the principles of sections 671 to 677, inclusive, subject a grantor of a trust to treatment as the owner thereof." Thus, a beneficiary who had released an unlimited power of withdrawal would remain taxable on all of the income of the trust if, for example, a nonadverse trustee could make discretionary distributions of income to the beneficiary. A grantor to whom discretionary distributions could be made by a nonadverse party would be treated as owner of the trust under §677(a). On the other hand, a person who releases an unlimited power of withdrawal would not be treated as owner of the trust following release of the power if he or she retained no interest in the trust.

The question of whether or not the lapse of a power of withdrawal should be treated as a "release or modification" under §678(a)(2) has not been answered by the courts. Not surprisingly, the IRS equates the lapse of a power of withdrawal with a release. Accordingly, in a series of private letter rulings the IRS has ruled that a person who permits a noncumulative annual power of withdrawal to lapse is properly treated as the owner of a proportionate part of the trust under the principles of §§671 to 677. LR 9034004; LR 8545076; LR 8521060; LR 8517052; LR 8308033; LR 8142061. In effect the rulings treat the person whose power of withdrawal has lapsed as the grantor of that portion of the trust. Commentators have divided on the propriety of the IRS approach. Professor David Westfall supports the IRS "cumulativist" view. Westfall, Lapsed Powers of Withdrawal and the Income Tax, 39 Tax. L. Rev. 63 (1983). Others argue that the lapse of a power of withdrawal, such as a *Crummey* power, is not technically the equivalent of a release and that a beneficiary cannot properly be treated as having withdrawn and recontributed the portion of the principal that was subject to his power of withdrawal. *E.g.,* Early, Income Taxation of Lapsed Powers of Withdrawal: Analyzing Their Current Status, 62 J. Tax. 198 (1985); Lawrence, Structuring Irrevocable Trusts in Light of Tax Changes and Proposals, N.Y.U., 44th Inst. Fed. Tax., §55.03[1] [c] (1985).

The amount of the trust that will be considered as owned by a person whose power of withdrawal has lapsed in more than one year is determined in the manner indicated in LR 9034004:

> During each succeeding year in which *A* fails to exercise her power, *A* will be treated as the owner of an increasing portion of the corpus of

> *T* [the trust]. For purposes of determining the increase in her deemed ownership her current withdrawal power for any particular year will cause an increase in the amount of corpus which she is treated as owning equal to the product of the amount which she could withdraw multiplied by a fraction the numerator of which is the portion of trust corpus which she is not already treated as owning and the denominator of which is the total of trust corpus from which the withdrawal could be made. Discretionary distributions made by the trustee from corpus will be treated as coming from both the portion of corpus which the beneficiary is treated as owning and from the portion which she is not treated as owning in the same ratio as the fraction mentioned above.

Example 10-11. *X* is beneficiary of an inter vivos trust established 2 years ago by her uncle, *U.* Income of the trust is payable to *X* in the discretion of an independent trustee. Also, *X* has the annual noncumulative right to withdraw the greater of \$5,000 or 5% of the value of the trust property determined on the last business day of the year. In the first year *X*'s power to withdraw a maximum of \$10,000 lapsed. *X*'s power to withdraw \$10,000 in the second year also lapsed. At the end of the second year the trust had a total value of \$200,000. Under the IRS approach *X* is treated as owning a \$19,500/\$200,000 interest in the trust. The numerator of the fraction is the sum of the \$10,000 that could have been withdrawn by *X* in the first year and the portion (\$9,500) of the \$10,000 that could have been withdrawn in the second year from the part of the trust that she was not already treated as owning. The latter amount is determined as follows:

$$\$10{,}000 \times \frac{\$190{,}000}{\$200{,}000} = \$9{,}500$$

§10.24.2. "Hanging Power"

As indicated above, no adverse gift, estate or GSTT consequences result from the annual lapse of powers of withdrawal that do not, in the aggregate, exceed the 5 or 5 amount. *See* §7.37.4. A hanging power is designed to achieve two goals: (1) supporting the donor's qualification for a full \$10,000 annual gift tax exclusion by giving the beneficiary the power to withdraw the full \$10,000; and (2) preventing the beneficiary from experiencing any adverse gift or estate tax consequences by limiting the extent to which the power of withdrawal lapses each year to the sheltered 5 or 5 amount. Of course, the full amount of property subject to withdrawal at the time of the power-holder's death is subject to inclusion in the power-holder's gross estate. Thus, the use of a hanging power contemplates that the power-holder will live sufficiently long after the last gift to the trust to permit the power of withdrawal to lapse in full. A Technical Advice Memorandum, LR 8901004, held that the relatively simple form of hanging power there involved was an ineffective condition subsequent, which would be disregarded.

The use of a hanging power is particularly appropriate if the trust is likely to continue beyond the lifetime of the power-holder, as a result of which the portion of the trust attributable to lapses in excess of the 5 or 5 amounts would be includible in the power-holder's gross estate. Its use is less significant if the power-holder is most likely to survive termination of the trust and receive distribution of the trust property. In such a case, all of the trust property will be included in the power-holder's estate in any case.

A hanging power for a trust with a single beneficiary might be expressed as in Form 10-7.

Form 10-7. Hanging Power of Withdrawal

Grant of Withdrawal Right. The beneficiary shall have the right to withdraw so much of the property transferred to the trust by Grantor or any other person as Grantor or such other person shall designate at the time of the transfer. If no designation is made the beneficiary shall have the right to withdraw the full amount of the transferred property. [This will support the allowance of the annual gift tax exclusion up to $10,000 per donor for transfers to the trust, which is the principal objective of powers of withdrawal.]

Notice. The trustee shall promptly give written notice to beneficiary of the receipt by the trustee of any gratuitous transfer of property to the trust. If the beneficiary is a minor or otherwise lacks legal capacity, the notice shall also be given to the guardian of such beneficiary's estate if one has been appointed. [If the notice of a transfer is not given and the beneficiary does not learn of the transfer, the power of withdrawal may be disregarded by the IRS as illusory.]

Limitation. The beneficiary shall have the continuing cumulative right to withdraw property in accordance with paragraph 1, above. However, the power of withdrawal shall lapse on December 31 of each calendar year with respect to the greater of $5,000 or 5% of the total value of the trust property on the last day of the calendar year (or such greater amount as may be specified in IRC §2041(b)(2)). In no case shall the beneficiary's right to withdraw property transferred to the trust lapse until 30 days after notice to the beneficiary as provided in paragraph 2, above.

Exercise of Withdrawal Right. The beneficiary, or the beneficiary's guardian, may exercise the withdrawal right by delivering written notice to the trustee. Any property that is withdrawn by the beneficiary's guardian shall be held for the use and benefit of the beneficiary.

Example 10-12. *T* transferred $10,000 each year for 5 years to an irrevocable trust of which *T*'s adult child, *C,* was the beneficiary. *T* made no more transfers to the trust. Under the terms of the trust *C* had a hanging power of withdrawal in the form above. In the first year *C* had a power to withdraw $10,000, of which the power to withdraw $5,000 lapsed at the end of the year. The power to withdraw the other $5,000 carried over to the next year. In the second year *C* had the right to withdraw a total of $15,000, composed of the $5,000 carryover and the $10,000 transferred to the trust by *T.* If values remain constant and *C* makes no withdrawals, at the end of 5 years of $10,000 gifts to the trust the trust corpus will consist of $50,000, of which *C* has the power to withdraw $25,000. In subsequent years the power of withdrawal would lapse to the extent of $5,000 each year. If *C* died before the power of withdrawal lapsed entirely, the amount that remained subject to withdrawal at the time of her death would be included in her gross estate.

§10.25. Power to Withdraw Trust Assets Limited by an Ascertainable Standard

The flexibility of the trust can also be increased somewhat without significant adverse gift or estate tax consequences by giving the beneficiary a power to withdraw trust property, "which is limited by an ascertainable standard relating to the health, education, support, or maintenance" of the power-holder. §§2041(b)(1)(A), 2514(c)(1). Note that the standard must be ascertainable and must relate to the power-holder's health, education, support, or maintenance to qualify under this exception. Such a power is often most important because of the increased sense of security it gives to the power-holder. A beneficiary holding such a power may be treated as owner of the trust under §678.

A power only falls within the scope of this exception if it is subject to an ascertainable (*i.e.,* objective) standard and not an indefinite (*i.e.,* subjective) standard. State law determines the nature and extent of a right of withdrawal conferred by a trust. However, the Regulations contain helpful examples of provisions that are acceptable. They include powers that are exercisable "for the holder's 'support,' 'support in reasonable comfort,' 'maintenance in health and reasonable comfort,' 'support in his accustomed manner of living,' 'education, including college and professional education,' 'health,' and 'medical, dental, hospital and nursing expenses and expenses of invalidism.' " Reg. §20.2041-1(c)(2). The same Regulation points out that "[a] power to use property for the comfort, welfare, or happiness of the holder of the power is not limited by the requisite standard." Thus, in *Estate of John Russell Little,* 87 T.C. 599 (1986), the Tax Court held that a power to invade for purposes including "general happiness" was a general power of appointment.

A power that is intended to escape treatment as a general power because of this exception must be carefully drawn. The safest course is to couch the power in exactly the language of one of the examples set forth in the Regulation. Any deviation from the approved language creates a risk the IRS will treat the power as a general power of appointment. Thus, the IRS has argued that a power to invade corpus "in case of emergency or illness" was a general power. *Estate of Ida Maude Sowell,* 74 T.C. 1001, *rev'd,* 708 F.2d 1564 (10th Cir. 1980). On appeal, a sympathetic court rejected the IRS position. In another case, an uncontrolled right, power, and authority to use and devote such of the corpus of the trust from time to time as the beneficiary in her judgment believed necessary for her maintenance, comfort, and happiness was held to be limited by an ascertainable standard under Massachusetts law. *Estate of Brantingham v. United States,* 631 F.2d 542 (7th Cir. 1980). The IRS believes that the *Brantingham* case was incorrectly decided and has stated that it will not follow the holding. Rev. Rul. 82-63, 1982-1 C.B. 135.

Form 10-8. Power of Withdrawal Limited by an Ascertainable Standard

The beneficiary shall have the right, from time-to-time, to withdraw as much of the principal of the trust as may be required to provide for her/his health, education, and support in her/his accustomed manner of living.

§10.26. Other Nongeneral Powers of Appointment

The other two types of post-1942 powers of withdrawal that are not treated as general powers are of little use for planning purposes in typical circumstances. *See* §§2041(b)(1), 2514(c). The first exception is for a power only exercisable in conjunction with the creator of the power. §§2041(b)(1)(C)(i), 2514(c)(3)(A). Such a power is generally not used because the property subject to powers of distribution jointly exercisable by the grantor and another is includible in the creator's estate under §2038(a)(1). *Lober v. United States,* 346 U.S. 335 (1953); LR 9016079.

The exception is also unsuitable for planning purposes because it only applies during the lifetime of the creator of the power.

If it were possible for an independent party to be treated as the creator of a joint power for purposes of §2041(b), the first exception could allow additional flexibility to trusts. It is extremely doubtful that such a plan would work. For example, if *T* transferred his residuary estate in trust for the benefit of his daughter, *D,* an independent party, *I,* could be given the power to amend the trust to provide that *D* could, with the concurrence of *I,* withdraw an unlimited amount of the trust corpus. If *I* made such an amendment of the trust, a court is likely to conclude that *D*'s possession of the joint power would cause the full value of the trust to be included in *D*'s estate under §2041. It would reason that "creator" as used in §2041 means the grantor of the trust and that a post-transfer amendment of the trust would be treated under orthodox power of appointment analysis is relating back to the initial creation of the trust. Any other interpretation would expand the exception beyond the apparent intention of Congress.

The second exception is for a power that is only exercisable in conjunction with a person having a substantial interest in the property adverse to an exercise of the power by the beneficiary. §§2041(b)(1)(C)(ii), 2514(c)(3)(B). A leading commentator observed that "[t]his exception is of little or no use in estate planning because it is highly unlikely that the desired flexibility will be introduced into the estate plan where the decision as to whether a power will be exercised rests with one who will be adversely affected by the exercise." 3A A. J. Casner, Estate Planning 154-155 (5th ed. 1986). In LR 9030032 the surviving spouse and a child held a jointly-exercisable power to distribute corpus to the surviving spouse. The power was not limited by an ascertainable standard relating to the health, education, support and maintenance of the surviving spouse. However, because the child was entitled to an aliquot portion of the trust upon the death of the surviving spouse, the trust was not includible in the estate of the surviving spouse. The child, as remainderman, held an adverse interest in the trust.

§10.27. Beneficiary as Trustee

> [F]iduciary powers in the hands of the wrong persons may constitute dangerous powers for tax purposes either under the grantor rules of the income and estate tax laws or, in the case of a beneficiary serving as trustee, under various rules (especially those relating to general powers of appointment) of the estate, gift and income tax laws. Halbach, Discretionary Trusts and Income Tax Avoidance After the 1976 Tax Reform Act, U. Miami, 12th Inst. Est. Plan. ¶308 (1978).

The suitability of appointing a beneficiary as trustee or cotrustee depends primarily on family planning and tax considerations. Insofar as the trust law is concerned, the appointment of a beneficiary as trustee does not impair the validity of the trust so long as the trust has either another trustee or another beneficiary. Put somewhat differently: The sole beneficiary of a trust cannot be the sole trustee. As stated in Restatement (Second) Trusts §99 (1959),

> (1) One of several beneficiaries of a trust can be one of several trustees of the trust.
> (2) One of several beneficiaries of a trust can be the sole trustee of the trust.
> (3) The sole beneficiary of a trust can be one of several trustees of the trust.
> (4) If there are several beneficiaries of a trust, the beneficiaries may be the trustees.
> (5) The sole beneficiary of a trust cannot be the sole trustee of the plan.

The planner must recognize and attempt to deal with the potential conflict between the economic interests of the beneficiary and the duties of a beneficiary as trustee. One approach is to attempt to eliminate the sources of potential conflicts through the use of special trustees and the imposition of limits on the powers of the beneficiary-trustee. However, such an approach can cause the trust to be complicated and potentially confusing. (A special trustee is one who holds only limited powers over the trust — usually in order to insulate a beneficiary-trustee from adverse tax consequences that would result if they were held by the beneficiary-trustee.) Another, perhaps more common, approach is to refer to the existence of potential conflicts in the trust and to authorize the trustee to act with regard to those matters regardless of his or her personal interest.

The income, gift, and estate tax ramifications of appointing a beneficiary as trustee are considered in the following paragraphs. Giving the beneficiary power to remove the trustee and appoint a successor is reviewed in §10.27.3.

§10.27.1. Income Tax

The appointment of a beneficiary as trustee of an inter vivos trust can cause the income to be taxed to the grantor under the grantor trust rules unless the beneficiary-trustee is an adverse party as defined in §672 (*i.e.,* the holder of a substantial interest that would be adversely affected by the exercise or nonexercise of the power). The risk that the income will be taxed to the grantor arises primarily under §674, under which the grantor is generally treated as the owner of a trust to the extent the grantor or a nonadverse party has the power to control the beneficial enjoyment of the income or principal of the trust. However, as noted below, the exceptions of §674(b) permit the grantor or a nonadverse party to hold some limited, but important, powers regarding distributions. *See* §10.37.1.

If the grantor is not treated as owner of the trust, the appointment of a beneficiary as trustee may cause the income of the trust to be taxed to the beneficiary under §678. In general, §678(a) treats a person other than the grantor as owner of a trust if the person has a power, acting alone, to acquire the corpus or income. The rule does not apply to income that is taxable to the grantor under §§671 to 677. §678(b). Note that the risk of inclusion is elminated if a distribution to the beneficiary requires the consent of another person, who does not need to have an adverse interest.

> **Example 10-13.** *O* transferred property to a trust that is revocable by the joint action of *O* and *O*'s sister, *S.* The trustee of the trust is *O*'s brother, *B,* who has the power to distribute income each year to one or more members of a class that includes *B.* The power held by *B* is not within any of the exceptions created by §674(b). However, the income is not taxed to *O* under §674 because *B* is an adverse party as to the power over income. Instead, *O* is treated as the owner of the entire trust under §676 because of the power of revocation held jointly with *S,* a nonadverse party. Following the death of *O* the income of the trust will be taxed to *B* under §678.

Also, under §678(a) the income of the trust is taxable to a person who holds the power, acting alone, to use the income or corpus of the trust to satisfy his or her own legal obligations. Reg. §1.678(a)-1(b). However, a trustee is not taxed on the income of a trust merely because the trustee holds the power to apply the income to the support or maintenance of a person the trustee is legally obligated to support except to the extent the income is so used. §678(c). The latter rule is analogous to the one applicable to grantors under §677(b).

§10.27.2. Gift Tax

A taxable gift may occur if a beneficiary-trustee distributes any income or principal of the trust to another person. For example, a gift takes place if the beneficiary-trustee appoints income to which he or she is entitled to another person. Reg. §25.2514-3(e), example 1. In such a case, the beneficiary, in effect, exercises a general power of appointment in favor of the other person. The appointment of principal to others may also involve a taxable exercise of a general or special power of appointment under §2514. A gift would occur, for example, where the beneficiary-trustee distributes to others principal that he or she was free to distribute to himself or herself. The distribution of principal to others under a special power of appointment may involve a gift where the holder of the power is entitled to receive income distributions from the trust that will be diminished by the appointment. Reg. §25.2514-1(b)(2); Rev. Rul. 79-327, 1979-2 C.B. 342. *See* §10.23. A gift occurs when the holder of a general power of appointment over the corpus of one trust allows a recapitalization of the stock held by the trust, as a result of which a portion of the value of the stock is shifted to another trust with respect to which the power-holder does not have any power. Rev. Rul. 86-39, 1986-1 C.B. 301. If the power-holder is an income beneficiary of the second trust, the property transferred to the other trust is includible in the power-holder's estate under §2036 (transfer with retained life interest).

§10.27.3. Estate Tax

The property of the trust is includible in the estate of a beneficiary-trustee who holds a power, exercisable alone or in conjunction with others, to apply the principal of the trust for his or her own benefit. §2041(a)(2). However, as explained in §10.25, the rule does not apply to powers that are limited by certain ascertainable standards and to certain joint powers. Similarly, no inclusion is required if the beneficiary holds routine administrative powers. Reg. §20.2041-1(b)(1). Also, a surviving spouse may hold the power to veto the sale or disposition of the assets of the trust. LR 9042048.

In order to avoid a contest with the IRS, a person should not be authorized to use principal for the support of persons the power-holder is obligated to support (*e.g.,* minor or disabled children). The risk of confrontation arises because of Reg. §20.2041-1(c)(1), which provides, "A power of appointment exercisable for the purpose of discharging a legal obligation of the decedent or for his pecuniary benefit is considered a power of appointment exercisable in favor of the decedent or his creditors." In this connection note that the exception for powers limited by an ascertainable standard only applies to standards "relating to the health, education, support or maintenance of the *decedent.*" Reg. §20.2041-1(c)(2) (emphasis added). In particular, the exception does not apply to a power, limited by an ascertainable standard, to make distributions to the dependents of the power-holder. §2041(b)(1)(A). *See* §10.25.

§10.28. Removal and Replacement of Trustee

Giving a beneficiary the power to remove a trustee and replace the trustee with a person other than a beneficiary provides the beneficiary with valuable protection against an indolent or unresponsive trustee. However, the IRS has held that a beneficiary who holds such a power will be treated as having all of the powers of the trustee, although the beneficiary may not appoint himself or herself as trustee. LR 8916032. According to the IRS the trust is includible in the power-holder's estate under §2041 if the trustee had the power to make distributions that would satisfy a legal obligation of the beneficiary. The IRS position is based on an extension of Rev. Rul. 79-353, 1979-2 C.B. 366, which attributed to the grantor all of the powers that were held by an independent trustee who was subject to the grantor's power to remove and appoint another independent trustee in his place. The IRS position is not supported by the existing authorities and may not be sustained if it is challenged.

A beneficiary's power to remove and replace the trustee *will not* require the trust property to be included in the beneficiary's estate unless the powers held by the trustee would require inclusion in the beneficiary's estate under §2041 if they were held by the beneficiary. *See* LR 8922062. Accordingly, the IRS will argue that the assets of a trust are includible in the estate of a beneficiary who held an unrestricted power to remove and replace a trustee with discretion to make distributions to or for the benefit of the beneficiary or persons the beneficiary is obligated to support. *See* LR 8916032.

In some cases a client will wish to (1) authorize the trustee to make discretionary distributions to the beneficiaries and (2) authorize someone to remove and replace the trustee with an independent trustee. If so, the trust might be planned in a variety of ways. First, the power to remove and replace the trustee might be given to an independent party. Second, the power might be made exercisable only upon the presence of some external factor such as the trustee's failure to achieve a certain level of return on principal, the failure of the trustee to provide accurate and complete accountings on a timely basis, the commencement of litigation by a beneficiary against the trustee for a breach of trust, or a move by a beneficiary, or relocation by the trustee, that resulted in a beneficiary residing more than a specified distance from the trustee's principal place of business. Third, the discretionary powers of the trustee might be eliminated if the removal and replacement power were exercised.

The possibility of including a removal and replacement power should be thoroughly explored with the client, who may wish to give a removal and replacement power to an independent party or to make the exercise of the power conditional on the occurrence of particular events. Limitations should, of course, be imposed on the persons who could be appointed as successor trustees. It is often desirable to prohibit a beneficiary from becoming successor trustee because of the potentially adverse estate and income tax consequences.

A person who has the unlimited power to remove the trustee and appoint himself or herself as successor trustee is treated as holding all of the powers of the trustee. *See* Reg. §20.2041-1(b)(1). In the future the IRS might argue that a similar rule should apply under §678 for income tax purposes.

§10.29. Planning Summary

Adverse income and estate tax results are avoided if a nongrantor does not hold powers that are within the scope of §§678 or 2041. The reach of §678 is avoided if the beneficiary does not hold "a power exercisable solely by himself to vest the corpus or the income therefrom in himself." For example, a beneficiary who holds the power to distribute income to members of a class that includes the beneficiary would be taxed on the income of the trust. However, that result is avoided if the power is exercisable only with the consent of another person (including a spouse) who does not need to have an adverse interest. Because of the reach of §2041 a beneficiary should not hold a power to use or apply the income or corpus of the trust for his or her own benefit, except to the extent the power is protected by one of the exceptions: (1) a power limited by an ascertainable standard relating to the beneficiary's health, education, maintenance or support; (2) a noncumulative annual power limited to the greater of $5,000 or five percent of the trust; (3) a power exercisable only with the consent of its creator or an adverse party. In order to avoid a potential conflict with the IRS the beneficiary should not hold a power to remove and replace a trustee who holds any power that would require the trust to be included in the beneficiary's estate if it were held by the beneficiary. *See* LR 8916032. Finally, a beneficiary should not hold any power with respect to insurance on his or her life, including the power to remove and replace the trustee. *See* LR 8922003.

D. PLANNING THE GRANTOR'S INTERESTS IN AN IRREVOCABLE TRUST

Technical considerations, niceties of the law of trusts or conveyances, or the legal paraphernalia which inventive genius

> may construct as a refuge from surtaxes should not obscure the basic issue. That issue is whether the grantor after the trust has been established may still be treated as owner of the corpus. . . . And where the grantor is the trustee and the beneficiaries are members of his family group, special scrutiny of the arrangement is necessary lest what is in reality but one economic unit be multiplied into two or more by devices which, though valid under state law, are not conclusive so far as §22(a) [now §61(a)] is concerned. *Helvering v. Clifford,* 309 U.S. 331, 334-335 (1940).

§10.30. Scope

The income, gift, and estate tax consequences that flow from the grantor's retention of a power to revoke the trust are considered in Part B, §§10.15-10.17. The following sections examine the tax consequences that occur where the grantor retains other common interests or powers over the trust. Unfortunately, the criteria for determining the consequences of the retention of interests or powers are not the same for income, gift, and estate tax purposes. In fact, while the lack of coordination between the tax laws creates serious traps, they also create opportunities that taxpayers can sometimes exploit to their advantage.

§10.31. Basic Income Tax Rules

The grantor trust rules of §§671-677 are applied to determine whether or not the income of a trust is taxed to the grantor. Viewed differently, the rules specify the requirements that must be met in order to cause the income to be taxed to the trust or its beneficiaries and not to the grantor. Regulation §1.671-1(a) contains this concise statement of the circumstances under which the grantor will be treated as owner and taxed on the income:

> (1) If the grantor has retained a reversionary interest in the trust if, at the time of creation of the trust, the value of the reversionary interest exceeds 5%, §673;
>
> (2) If the grantor or a nonadverse party has certain powers over the beneficial interests under the trust, §674;
>
> (3) If certain administrative powers over the trust exist under which the grantor can or does benefit, §675;
>
> (4) If the grantor or a nonadverse party has a power to revoke the trust or return the corpus to the grantor, §676; or
>
> (5) If the grantor or a nonadverse party has the power to distribute income to or for the benefit of the grantor or the grantor's spouse, §677. Reg. §1.671-1(a).

The income of a trust is not taxed to the grantor to the extent it is taxable to the grantor's spouse under §71 (alimony and separate maintenance) or §682 (income of estate or trust payable to spouse in case of divorce or separate maintenance).

Under §678, if the grantor is not treated as the owner of the trust, the income is taxed to a nongrantor who has the sole power to vest corpus or income in himself or herself.

Prior to the 1986 Act the rules of §§671 to 677 usually involved irrevocable trusts in which the grantor's reversionary interest would take effect at the end of ten years or more. In the pre-1987 era short-term irrevocable "*Clifford*" or "ten-year" trusts were popular, principally because they could be used to shift income from grantors subject to high income tax rates to beneficiaries in substantially lower brackets. At that time, income-shifting was possible although the grantor retained a reversionary interest that would take effect at the end of a ten-year term. The compressed income tax rates established by the 1986 Act reduced the attractiveness of such trusts. More important, the 1986 Act amended §673 to require the grantor to be treated as owner of any portion of a trust in which he or she held a reversionary interest, if at the inception of the trust, the value of the reversionary interest exceeded five percent of the value of such portion. Accordingly, it is no longer possible to shift the income to the beneficiaries of ten-year trusts.

Another change made by the 1986 Act required the grantor to be treated as holding any interest or power held by his spouse, §672(e). That change eliminated the attractiveness of short-term irrevocable spousal remainder trusts which some individuals created in order to shift the income for periods of less than ten years. A spousal remainder trust usually gave the income to children for a short term, say two years, and the remainder to the grantor's spouse. The gift tax exposure was limited because of the short duration of the trust and the unlimited marital deduction, which sheltered the remainder from the gift tax.

Under the preexisting law the short-term irrevocable trust was a valuable estate planning tool because of its ability to shift income within the family without requiring the grantor to surrender all of his or her interests in the property. If the trust was properly prepared and administered, the income from the property was taxed to the beneficiary and not to the grantor. Also, the actual amount of the trust's income was not included in the grantor's estate. For example, a short-term trust could shift the income from a parent to a child who was in a lower tax bracket. The short-term trust lost some of its lustre because of the unification of the gift and estate tax laws that took place in 1976. However, it remained for the 1986 Act to eliminate its principal advantage — the grantor's retention of a reversionary interest that would become possessory in a relatively short time.

To the extent the grantor is treated as owner of the trust, he or she must report the items of income, deduction, and credit attributable to the trust. In such cases, the grantor's income is not limited to the distributable net income of the trust. Under Reg. §1.671-4 the trust does not report the income, deductions, and credits on its fiduciary income tax return (Form 1041): Instead they are shown on a separate statement attached to the trust's return. The trust must obtain a tax identification number although it is not required to file fiduciary income tax returns. *See* Reg. §1.671-4(b).

§10.31.1. Adverse Party

For purposes of §§671-677 (sometimes referred to as "Subchapter J"), the term "adverse party" is defined as "any person having a substantial beneficial interest in the trust which would be adversely affected by the exercise or nonexercise of the power which he possesses respecting the trust. A person having a general power of appointment over the trust property shall be deemed to have a beneficial interest in the trust." §672(a). A trustee is not an adverse party merely because of his or her interest as trustee. Reg. §1.672(a)-1(a). Powers over the trust are often sanitized for income tax purposes by making their exercise subject to the consent of an adverse party.

A beneficiary is ordinarily an adverse party. However, if the beneficiary only has the right to share in part of the income or corpus, the beneficiary may be an adverse party only as to that part. Reg. §1.672(a)-1(b). In addition, a person who is an adverse party with respect to the income interest in a trust, may or may not be adverse with respect to the exercise of a power over corpus. In determining whether or not a person is an adverse party, the critical question involves the effect of the exercise or nonexercise of the power on the power-holder's beneficial interests in the trust — not the effect on the grantor's interests. The last point is illustrated by Reg. §1.672(a)-1(d):

> [I]f the grantor creates a trust which provides for income to be distributed to *A* for 10 years and then for the corpus to go to *X* if he is then living, a power exercisable by *X* to revest the corpus in the grantor is a power exercisable by an adverse party; however, a power exercisable by *X* to distribute part or all of the ordinary income to the grantor may be a power exercisable by a nonadverse party (which would cause the ordinary income to be taxed to the grantor).

The proper identification of adverse parties is important because an adverse party is allowed to hold broad powers over a trust without causing the grantor to be treated as its owner. In particular, an adverse party may hold powers that (1) affect the beneficial enjoyment of the trust, §674; (2) cause a revocation of the trust and the return of the trust property to the grantor, §676; or (3) permit the income of the trust to be accumulated or distributed to or for the benefit of the grantor or the grantor's spouse, §677(a). The existence of such a power does not ordinarily cause any income, gift, or estate tax problems for the grantor. However, the mere existence of the power can have negative tax consequences for the power-holder. Specifically, if the grantor is not treated as owner of a trust, a person other than the grantor who holds the power "to vest the corpus or the income therefrom in himself" is treated as the owner of the trust under §678(a). In addition, the exercise or nonexercise of a power held by an adverse party may involve a gift to the other persons who are beneficially interested in the trust. *See* Reg. §25.2514-1(b)(2).

§10.31.2. Jointly Exercisable Powers

An adverse party who holds a power that is jointly exercisable with the grantor or another person generally escapes harsh income, gift, or estate tax treatment. *See* §§678(a), 2041(b)(1)(C), and 2514(c)(3). Specifically, the holder of a joint power is not treated as the owner of a trust under §678(a); that subsection only applies to powers that are exercisable solely by a person other than the grantor. For gift and estate tax purposes a joint power exercisable by the adverse party and the grantor is not a general power of appointment. *See* §§2041(b)(1)(C)(iv), 2514(c)(3)(A). Accordingly, the exercise or nonexercise of such a joint power should not ordinarily involve a gift of the entire interest by the adverse party. However, the grantor's retention of a joint power would cause the trust property to be included in the grantor's gross estate under §§2036 and 2038.

§10.32. Grantor Treated as Owner of Trust Under Subchapter J

The lack of coordination between the income and the gift and estate tax laws create opportunities as well as traps. A client usually wishes to avoid being treated as the owner of a trust under the grantor trust rules that would require the client to report the income, deductions, and credits attributable to the trust. However, in some circumstances a careful consideration of the client's objectives and the rules applicable to grantor trusts may suggest that the client should seek to be treated as owner of a trust. Thus, a nonresident alien who wishes to create a trust for the benefit of a U.S. citizen or resident might wish to be treated as owner of the trust. If so, the beneficiaries would not be taxed on distributions made from the trust. Rev. Rul. 69-70, 1969-1 C.B. 182. In this connection note that under the 1990 Act the beneficiary of a trust created by a foreign person is treated as grantor of the trust to the extent the beneficiary has transferred property directly or indirectly by gift to such foreign person. §672(f).

Of course, the "defect" in a defective trust must be carefully planned so that it will not require the trust to be included in the grantor's estate. Thus, the trust should not be revocable nor should the client have discretion to make distributions to the beneficiaries, which would cause inclusion under §§2036 and 2038. Ideally the trust should be planned so that the "defect" can be eliminated and the grantor status of the trust terminated without additional tax cost. For example, the holder of a power of administration that is exercisable in a nonfiduciary capacity without the approval or consent of any person in a fiduciary capacity should be authorized to release the power at any time. *See* §675(4)(C). Under that provision the grantor is treated as owner of a trust with respect to which a power "to reacquire the trust corpus by substituting other property of equivalent value" is exercisable by any person in a nonfiduciary capacity without the approval or consent of a person in a fiduciary capacity. The release of such a power should not have any adverse income, gift, estate or GST tax consequences for anyone.

Until recently irrevocable life insurance trusts were often deliberately made defective in order to allow the grantor to claim the interest deductions that arose because of borrowings made by the trust against the cash value insurance owned by the trust. The inability to deduct personal interest eliminated the attractiveness of that approach.

§10.32.1. Grantor Makes Free Gift of Income Tax on Trust

A grantor who is treated as owner of the trust under Subchapter J must pay the income tax on the income of the trust. As pointed out by Professor Halbach,

> [A] settlor sometimes wishes to be taxable on trust income that is nevertheless payable to an adult child whose tax bracket is comparable to that of the settlor. By paying the income tax that would otherwise be charged to the child, the settlor makes what amounts to an additional transfer to the child each year without having an additional taxable gift. Halbach, Tax-Sensitive Trusteeships, 63 Or. L. Rev. 381, 384 n.11 (1984).

Making such "free" gifts of the annual income tax imposed on the trust is clearly attractive to wealthy grantors who wish to make additional gifts without incurring any gift or GST tax.

Letter Ruling 9037011 illustrates a trust arrangement that causes the grantor to be treated as owner of the trust, but does not cause the trust to be included in the grantor's estate. The trust in LR 9037011 authorized the trustee in a "nonfiduciary capacity without approval or consent of any person acting in a fiduciary or nonfiduciary capacity, to acquire any property then held in Trust (or any succeeding trust) by substituting property of equivalent value." As indicated above, such a provision is a prohibited administrative power under §675(4). Accordingly, the grantor is taxable on the income. The grantor is also taxed on the income of the trust if the income may be accumulated for later distribution to the grantor's spouse, §677(a), or the property or the income or principal of the trust is borrowed by the grantor, §675(3).

§10.32.2. Trust Holds S Corporation Stock

A trust of which the grantor is treated as the owner is a permissible shareholder in an S corporation. §1361(c)(2)(A)(i). Letter Ruling 9037011 also recognized that because the grantor was treated as owner of the trust, the trust could hold S corporation stock. If the stock of an S corporation continued in trust after the death of the grantor-owner, the trust could be designed to continue to qualify as a qualified Subchapter S trust. *See* §1361(d).

§10.32.3. Trust Holds Installment Obligations

The transfer of an installment obligation to an irrevocable trust of which the grantor is *not* treated as the owner ordinarily triggers the recognition of gain by the grantor. Rev. Rul. 67-167, 1967-1 C.B. 107; Rev. Rul. 76-530, 1976-2 C.B. 132, both applying former §453(d). However, a transfer to a revocable trust, of which the grantor is treated as the owner, is not a disposition that triggers acceleration of the tax on an installment sale. Instead, the income remains taxable to the grantor.

§10.32.4. Grantor Trusts Not Subject to Throwback Rules

Income of a trust that is taxed to the grantor under the grantor trust rules is not subject to the other provisions of Subchapter J, including the throwback rules of §§665-668. *See* §671 and Reg. §1.671-2(b). The latter refers to the underlying principle that,

> Income of a trust over which the grantor or another person has retained substantial dominion or control should be taxed to the grantor or other

> person rather than to the trust which receives the income or to the beneficiary to whom the income may be distributed. Reg. §1.671-2(b).

The exclusivity of the grantor trust rules is also indicated by Rev. Rul. 69-70, 1969-1 C.B. 182, which held that the beneficiaries were not taxed on distributions made from a trust of which the foreign grantor was treated as the owner.

§10.32.5. Capital Gains of Grantor Trust Offset by Grantor's Losses

If the grantor is treated as the owner of a trust, the grantor's losses can be used to offset the gains of the trust. The gain on a sale of appreciated property by a grantor trust is taxed to the grantor. The grantor trust rules, in effect, carry out the policies of §644 that would otherwise apply to the sale of appreciated property by the trust within two years following its transfer to the trust. Depreciated property should not be transferred to a trust because the potential for a loss would be lost as a result of the transfer: Under §1015(a) the basis of property in the hands of the donee cannot exceed its fair market value at the time of the gift.

§10.32.6. Exclusion of Gain on Sale of Grantor's Principal Residence

The person who is treated as owner of a trust for income tax purposes is entitled to the benefit of the one-time exclusion of gain on the sale of a principal residence that is allowable under §121. Rev. Rul. 85-45, 1985-1 C.B. 183. Thus, the exclusion would be available with respect to a principal residence that is transferred to a personal residence trust, provided the requirements of §121 are met. *See* §9.43.3. Indeed, as noted in §10.32.8, if the residence is sold back to the grantor prior to the termination of the trust the gain on the sale may not be recognized. *See* §10.32.8.

§10.32.7. Nonrecognition of Gain on Certain Dispositions

If the grantor is treated as the owner of the trust, the nonrecognition provisions of §1033 (condemnation and replacement of property) and §1034 (sale of principal residence) also apply. Rev. Rul. 66-159, 1966-1 C.B. 162 (residential rollover); Rev. Rul. 70-376, 1970-2 C.B. 164.

Nonrecognition is permitted where property owned by the grantor was condemned and replacement property was acquired by a trust of which the grantor was treated as the owner. Rev. Rul. 88-103, 1988-2 C.B. 304. Revenue Ruling 88-103 treats the grantor as the taxpayer who acquired the property.

§10.32.8. No Gain on Sale of Trust Property to Grantor

According to the IRS the sale by a trust of property to a grantor who is treated as owner of the trust is not a sale that gives rise to gain or loss. Rev. Rul. 85-13, 1985-1 C.B. 184 (involving a grantor who had violated §675(3) by "borrowing" the corpus of the trust). In the view of the IRS, a grantor trust is not regarded as a taxpayer capable of engaging in a sales transaction with the grantor. Jonathan Blattmachr has suggested that the position of the IRS might be used to advantage in connection with a personal residence trust. Specifically, the trustee of a personal residence trust might sell the grantor's principal residence back to the grantor at its fair market value just before the termination of the grantor's reserved term. Under Revenue Ruling 85-13, the sale would not involve any gain. In that way the grantor could regain the residence in exchange for cash equal to its appreciated value. Note that the Second Circuit Court of Appeal rejected the IRS position in *Rothstein v. United States,* 735 F.2d 704 (2d Cir. 1984). The holding in *Rothstein* has been criticized by some commentators. Ascher, When to Ignore Grantor Trusts: The Precedents, a Proposal, and a Prediction, 41 Tax L. Rev. 253 (1986). This point is also discussed in §10.38.1.

§10.32.9. Grantor Trust May Sell Stock to ESOP

For purposes of §1042 a sale of qualified securities by a grantor trust to an employee stock ownership plan (ESOP) is treated as a sale by the grantor. LR 9041027. Accordingly, the grantor is the appropriate party to make the election not to recognize gain on the sale to the ESOP and the acquisition, by the trust, of qualified replacement securities.

§10.33. Basic Gift Tax Rules

The transfer of property to a trust constitutes a gift of the value of the property transferred, less the value of the donor's retained interest. Rev. Rul. 58-242, 1958-1 C.B. 251. In this connection note that a term interest retained by the grantor may be valued at zero. *See* §§9.40,

9.43. The actuarial tables prescribed by the IRS are used to value the income interests given to others under the trust unless their use would "violate reason and fact." Rev. Rul. 77-195, 1977-1 C.B. 295 (tables used to value income interest in stock the trustee was required to retain although it had historically yielded only a three percent return). However, the IRS has ruled that it is inappropriate to use the tables where the trustee has the power to retain common stock (or other property) that has historically produced little or no income. LR 8642028 (TAM). In LR 8801008 and LR 8806082 the grantors retained the power to replace unproductive assets of the trusts of which they were income beneficiaries for specified terms of years. The IRS ruled that the failure of the grantor of each trust to require the trustee to make the trust property productive resulted in a gift each year of the difference between the right to receive income of ten percent of the value of the trust corpus and the amount of income actually received from the trust. This approach, which has not been approved by any court, was adopted by the IRS to combat the attempt to use grantor retained interest trusts (GRITs) to take advantage of the actuarial tables to shift wealth to the remaindermen at little or no transfer tax cost. The valuation loophole that made GRITs attractive has largely been closed by §2702. §9.43.

The entire value of the transferred property may be treated as a gift where the trustee is empowered to distribute the trust principal as income, Rev. Rul. 76-275, 1976-2 C.B. 299, or when capital gains are allocable to income and capital losses to principal. Rev. Rul. 77-99, 1977-1 C.B. 295. The gift includes the amount of any appreciation in the property at the time of the transfer where the trustee may sell the property and distribute the gain to the income beneficiary. Accordingly, a trust ordinarily should not provide for distribution of capital gains to the beneficiary even though the grantor is taxed currently under §677(a)(1) on gains that are accumulated for later distribution to the grantor.

A gift also occurs if the period during which others are entitled to the income of the trust is extended by the grantor. Of course, the right to receive the income for an additional period is a future interest for which no annual exclusion is allowed. Rev. Rul. 76-179, 1976-1 C.B. 290.

As indicated above, the IRS has ruled that the grantor-income beneficiary's failure to exercise a power to compel the trustee to make the property of a trust productive results in an annual gift to the remaindermen of the trust. LR 8806082.

§10.33.1. Annual Exclusion

A transfer to a trust qualifies for the annual gift tax exclusion under §2503(b) to the extent the beneficiary's interest is a "present interest."

Rev. Rul. 58-242, 1958-1 C.B. 251. The beneficiary's income interest in a trust qualifies for the annual exclusion if income is distributable currently to the beneficiary, to a custodian for a minor beneficiary under the Uniform Transfers to Minors Act or the Uniform Gifts to Minors Act, or to a guardian for the minor beneficiary. *Jacob Konner, 35 T.C. 727 (1961), nonacq.,* 1963-2 C.B. 6, *withdrawn and acq. sub.,* 1968-2 C.B. 2 (§2503(c) trust); *see also Carl E. Weller,* 38 T.C. 790 (1962), *acq.,* 1963-1 C.B. 4, *withdrawn and nonacq. sub.,* 1963-2 C.B. 6, *withdrawn and acq. sub.,* 1968-2 C.B. 3.

When the income is currently distributable to a class of beneficiaries, such as the grantor's children, the gifts to the members of the class living at the time of the transfer are present interests. However, exclusions are allowable only to the extent the grantor can show that the present interests have present value. This burden is relieved a little by Rev. Rul. 55-678, 1955-2 C.B. 389, which states that "[i]n such cases it is not necessary that the exact value of the gift of the present interest in property be determinable on the basis of recognized actuarial principles." *See also* Rev. Rul. 55-679, 1955-2 C.B. 390. Nonetheless, in order to qualify for the annual exclusion, a trust with multiple beneficiaries should give each beneficiary a discrete interest in the income.

In any case, the value of the income interest in the trust should qualify for the annual exclusion if the beneficiary at the time the trust is created has the power to elect to receive the net income of the trust each year. *See* Price, Intrafamily Transfers: Blessed and More Blessed Ways to Give, U. Miami, 18th Inst. Est. Plan., ch. 6 (1984). Under a variation, the beneficiary might be given the noncumulative power to withdraw an amount each year equal to the trust's net income for the year. Both approaches are merely variations on the *Crummey* power to withdraw trust assets that is recognized as conferring a present interest on the beneficiary to the extent the power may be exercised currently. *Crummey v. Commissioner,* 397 F.2d 82 (9th Cir. 1968); Rev. Rul. 73-405, 1973-2 C.B. 321; *see also* §7.37.

Where nonincome-producing property is transferred to the trust, the IRS may contend that the income interest has no value. *See* Rev. Rul. 69-344, 1969-1 C.B. 225 (trustee authorized to invest in life insurance policies that are not considered to be income-producing property). The problem is most likely to arise if the trustee has no power to dispose of nonincome-producing assets and invest in income-producing property. *Berzon v. Commissioner,* 534 F.2d 528 (2d Cir. 1976). However, some courts have denied an annual exclusion for the beneficiary's income interest even though the trustee had the power to dispose of the property and invest the proceeds in income-producing property. *Fischer v. Commissioner,* 288 F.2d 574 (3d Cir. 1961); *Stark v. United States,* 477 F.2d 131 (8th Cir.), *cert. denied,* 414 U.S. 975 (1973); *Van*

Den Wymelenberg v. United States, 397 F.2d 443 (7th Cir.), *cert. denied,* 393 U.S. 953 (1968); *contra, Rosen v. Commissioner,* 397 F.2d 245 (4th Cir. 1968). The transfer of nonincome-producing property to a trust invites a challenge by the IRS — particularly if the trustee lacks the power to sell the property.

§10.33.2. Charitable Deduction

Caution must be exercised in making a charitable gift of an interest in a trust: Ordinarily a gift tax charitable deduction is not allowable where a simple income interest is given to charity. *See* §2522(c)(2). As explained in Chapter 8, the deduction is only available for a split interest given to charity when the interest is in the form of a "guaranteed annuity or . . . a fixed percentage distributed yearly of the fair market value of the property (to be distributed yearly)." §2522(c)(2)(B). However, this trap is avoided if the grantor retains the right to select the annual charitable recipient of the income until after it is received, which renders the initial gift incomplete. *See* §8.33 for a more complete description of the device. Of course, the grantor is only entitled to an income tax deduction for an "income" interest to the extent the grantor is treated as the owner of the trust under §671. §170(f)(2)(B). In essence, a present income tax deduction is available at the cost of being taxed on the future income of the trust.

§10.34. Powers That Result in Transfers Being Incomplete

In some circumstances a client may wish to transfer property to an irrevocable trust in a way that does not constitute a completed gift. For example, a client in declining health may wish to establish an irrevocable trust that places the property beyond his or her direct control, but does not require the payment of any gift tax that would deplete the amount available for his or her support. The client's retained interests would, of course, require the trust to be included in his or her estate. *See* §§2036 and 2038. The retention of powers that are exercisable jointly with another individual who does not have an adverse interest is often a satisfactory way to make the gift incomplete.

A client may wish to make a transfer to a trust incomplete for other reasons. For example, in connection with the establishment of a charitable remainder trust, the transferor may wish the transfer of a successive private interest in the trust to be incomplete.

§10.34.1. Joint Power to Make Discretionary Distributions

The grantor's retention of a joint power with a person or persons not having adverse interests to make discretionary distributions is treated in the same way as the grantor's retention of a sole power over distributions. Such a power causes the transfer of property to the trust to be incomplete for gift tax purposes. Rev. Rul. 75-260, 1975-2 C.B. 376; Reg. §25.2511-2(c). However, gifts become complete when property of the trust is distributed to others.

> A donor is considered as himself having a power if it is exercisable by him in conjunction with any person not having a substantial adverse interest in the disposition of the transferred property. . . . A trustee, as such, is not a person having an adverse interest in the disposition of the trust property or its income. Reg. §25.2511-2(e).

The retention of a *joint* power to make distributions may be adequate to insulate the property from improvident transfers by the grantor. It may also provide some protection against creditors. In contrast, the IRS contends that the transfer of property to an independent trustee who has complete discretionary power to make distributions to the grantor is a completed gift. Rev. Rul. 77-378, 1977-2 C.B. 347. Of course, the grantor would be treated as owner of the trust for income tax purposes and it would be included in his estate. Note also that gifts made from the trust within three years of the grantor's death pursuant to the joint action of the grantor and another party would almost certainly be includible in the grantor's estate under §2035(d)(2).

§10.34.2. Joint Power to Terminate Trust

The power exercisable jointly with a nonadverse party to terminate an otherwise irrevocable trust would also make the transfers to the trust incomplete. LR 8940008 (citing Reg. §25.2511-2(c), (e)). In LR 8940008, the grantor retained power to amend, modify, revoke, or terminate in whole or in part with approval of an independent trustee. The IRS appropriately concluded that the transfer was incomplete for gift tax purposes.

§10.34.3. Retained Testamentary Special Power to Appoint Remainder

The grantor's retention of a testamentary special power to appoint the remainder interest is sufficient to make the transfer of property to the trust incomplete for gift tax purposes. Reg. §25.2511-2(c), (e). In LR 9021017 the grantor retained the power to change the interests of the remainder beneficiaries. According to LR 9021017, "The retention of this power is sufficient, in and of itself, to render the transfer to the trust wholly incomplete for federal gift tax purposes." Thus, a retained power to appoint the remainder to and among lineal descendants or charitable organizations is sufficient to make a transfer incomplete.

§10.34.4. Retained Testamentary Power to Revoke Successive Private Interest

A client may wish to make a present transfer to a charitable remainder trust in which the client and the client's spouse or other relative is given a successive interest. In order to avoid the imposition of the gift tax or for a variety of nontax reasons the client may wish to make the successive interest terminable. If the donor retains the right by will to revoke the successive interest, the gift of the successive interest is incomplete, but the gift of the charitable remainder is complete. This device might also be of use where the donee of the successive interest is a noncitizen with respect to whom no gift tax marital deduction would be allowable. Indeed, it might be possible to structure the trust as an income-only unitrust, which could qualify on the client's death for the marital deduction under §§2056(b)(8) and 2056A if the client's spouse survives. *See* §5.24. Of course, distributions from a QDT, other than distributions of income or in cases of hardship, are subject to the §2056A tax. Presumably, the IRS would treat distributions made from an income-only unitrust as distributions of income.

§10.35. Basic Estate Tax Rules

If the grantor dies prior to termination of the trust, the value of any reversionary interest retained by the grantor is includible in the grantor's estate under §2033. Such a reversionary interest is valued in accordance with the valuation tables issued pursuant to §7520. The calculation is based in part on the interest rate, announced monthly in a revenue bulletin in the Internal Revenue Bulletin, based on 120 percent of the federal midterm rate, compounded annually (rounded to the nearest two-tenths of one percent). The actuarial tables appear in IRS Pub. No. 1457, Alpha Volume, (Remainder, Income and Annuity Factors for One Life, Two Lives and Term Interests; Interests Rates from 2.2 Percent to 26.0 Percent); and IRS Pub. No. 1458, Beta Volume (Unitrust Remainder Factors for One Life, Two Lives, and Terms Certain; Adjusted Payout Rates from 2.2 Percent to 26.0 Percent). If the tables are not available, the value of some interests can be calculated easily.

As pointed out in Internal Revenue Notice 89-24, 1989-1 C.B. 660, the applicable formula for calculating the value of a remainder interest following a term is:

$$\text{Remainder Factor} = \frac{1}{(1 + i)^t}$$

The income factor is simply 1.0 less the value of the remainder factor calculated according to the foregoing formula.

An unintended reversionary interest may arise under the Doctrine of Worthier Title where the grantor attempts to create a remainder in his or her own heirs. *See* §10.36.3. Fortunately, however, the Doctrine has been abolished in most states.

Of course, if the grantor survives termination of a trust, the property formerly held in the trust is includible in his or her estate. As explained below, inclusion may result under other sections, particularly §§2036 and 2038.

> **Example 10-14.** In 1985 *G* transferred property worth \$100,000 to a trust the income of which was payable to *G*'s sister, *S*, for 15 years, at the end of which the corpus would return to *G*. The transfer involved a gift to *S* of the actuarially determined value of the right to receive the income for 15 years. *G* died 7 years after the trust was established, at a time when the trust property had a value of \$150,000 and the applicable interest rate was 10.8%. The value of the right to receive \$150,000 at the end of 8 years, assuming an interest rate of 10.8% is \$66,035 (factor of .440232 × \$150,000). Accordingly, \$66,035 is includible in G's estate.

§10.35.1. §2036

Inclusion under §2036 could occur, for example, where the income of the trust is used to discharge the grantor's legal obligation to support a minor child or to make principal payments on a mortgage. Reg. §20.2036-1(b)(2); LR 9032002 (TAM) (dicta regarding inclusion because a trust discharged the grantor's support obligation). Of course, §2036(a)(2) mandates inclusion if the grantor retained the power to control beneficial enjoyment of the property (*e.g.,* to designate which of two beneficiaries will receive the income). Inclusion may also result if the decedent is identified as the grantor under the reciprocal trust doctrine and the grantor holds powers sufficient to cause inclusion under §§2036(a)(2) or 2038. *See Estate of Bruno Bischoff,* 69 T.C. 32 (1977). *See also* §6.29.

Example 10-15. *T* transferred securities worth $100,000 to a trust of which his sister, *S,* was the trustee and her 3 children were the beneficiaries. The trust instrument gave *S* as trustee discretion to sprinkle the income among the beneficiaries and to make distributions of principal to them for their comfort, welfare and happiness. *S* transferred $100,000 in securities to *T* as trustee of a similar trust for the benefit of his children. Under the reciprocal trust doctrine *T* will be treated as the grantor of the trust for the benefit of his children and *S* will be treated as the grantor of the trust for the benefit of her children. The principal of each "un-crossed" trust is includible in the gross estate of its grantor under §§2036 and 2038.

§10.35.2. §2037

Where the grantor retains a reversionary interest contingent on surviving the income beneficiary, the entire value of the property is includible in the grantor's estate under §2037 if the value of the reversionary interest immediately before the grantor's death exceeds five percent of the value of the property. *E.g.,* Rev. Rul. 76-178, 1976-1 C.B. 273 (real property transferred in trust to pay the income to the trust beneficiary for life, after which the property would be returned to the grantor if living, otherwise to the grantor's children). The threat of inclusion under §2037 can be avoided by drafting the trust to exclude the retention of any reversionary interest by the grantor.

§10.35.3. §2038

The trust corpus is includible in the grantor's estate under §2038(a) if the grantor at death holds a power to alter, amend, revoke, or terminate the trust, exercisable alone or in conjunction with any other person. Inclusion is also required where such a power is "relinquished during the 3-year period ending on the date of the decedent's death." §2038(a)(1).

Example 10-16. *T* transferred income-producing property worth $100,000 to an irrevocable trust. The trustee has discretion to distribute the income each year to and among *T*'s children, *A, B,* and *C.* The trust prohibits the trustee from making distributions to *A, B,* or *C* that would relieve *T* of any legal obligation. At the end of 10 years the trust property will be distributed to *T*'s brother, *X.* The transfer involves gifts to *A, B, C,* and *X,* none of whom qualifies for an annual gift tax exclusion. None of the trust property is includible in *T*'s gross estate. Note, however, that the full value of the trust property would be included in *T*'s gross estate if *T* retained the power to remove or discharge the trustee and appoint himself or herself as trustee. Reg. §20.2036-1(b)(2).

§10.36. Retained Reversionary Interest

The retention of a reversionary interest often has undesirable income and estate tax consequences. First, the grantor will be taxed on the income of the trust under §673, which requires the grantor to be treated as the owner of "any portion of a trust in which he has a reversionary interest in either the corpus or the income therefrom, if, as of the inception of that portion of the trust, the value of such interest exceeds 5 percent of the value of such portion." Second, the reversionary interest is includible in the grantor's estate under §2033. Of course, the value of the reversionary interest is includible under §2033 and may also cause inclusion under §§2037 or 2042.

§10.36.1. Income Tax Consequences

The utmost care must be exercised in planning the grantor's interest in any trust that is intended to shift the income liability to others. An exception to the general retained interest rule of §673 applies to a reversionary interest that might take effect upon the death of a beneficiary who is a lineal descendant of the grantor before such beneficiary attains age 21. §673(b).

The postponement of the date for reacquisition of the possession or enjoyment of the reversionary interest is treated as a new transfer commencing with the date on which the postponement is effective. §673(d). However, the grantor is not treated as the owner of the trust by reason of such a postponement where the grantor would not have been treated as owner apart from the postponement. §673(d).

§10.36.2. Gift Tax Consequences

The transfer of an income interest constitutes a gift to the extent of its actuarially determined value. The income interest qualifies for the annual gift tax exclusion if the income is payable currently to the income beneficiary or to a guardian or custodian for the beneficiary. Reg. §25.2503-3(b). A technique for maximizing the value of the beneficiary's income interest is illustrated by Example 7-16 at §7.38. No annual exclusion is available where the trustee may withhold payments of income from the beneficiary. Reg. §25.2503-3(c), example 1.

§10.36.3. Estate Tax Consequences

The actuarially determined value of a reversionary interest is includible in the grantor's estate under §2033. Inclusion is required whether the reversion was expressly retained or is deemed to have been retained under the Doctrine of Worthier Title. *See Beach v. Busey,* 156 F.2d 496 (6th Cir. 1946), *cert. denied,* 329 U.S. 802 (1947). Where the Doctrine has not been abolished judicially or legislatively, it exists as a rule of construction that prevents a transferor from creating a remainder in his or her own heirs. For a judicial repudiation of the Doctrine, *see Hatch v. Riggs National Bank,* 361 F.2d 559 (D.C. Cir. 1966). Under the Doctrine the grantor is considered to have retained a reversion where property is transferred in trust with a life estate in the grantor (or others) and a remainder to the heirs of the grantor. *See* Johanson, Reversions, Remainders and the Doctrine of Worthier Title, 45 Tex. L. Rev. 1 (1966).

As noted above, property in which the grantor retains a reversionary interest may be included in his or her estate under §2037. However, that section only applies where the possession or enjoyment of the property can, through the ownership of the transferred interest, be obtained only by surviving the grantor and the grantor retained a reversionary interest in the property that had a value immediately before the transferor's death in excess of five percent of the value of the property. It is unusual to create a trust that involves a reversionary interest that would subject it to §2037. Also, under §2042(2) a decedent is considered to have an incident of ownership in insurance with respect to which the decedent held a reversionary interest that had a value greater than five percent of the value of the policy immediately before the decedent's death. Because of this rule an insured person should not retain any interest in insurance policies that are owned by others. To be safe a policy rider should prevent the insured from acquiring any ownership interest in the policy.

§10.37. Retained Control of Beneficial Enjoyment

Adverse income and estate tax consequences may occur if the grantor retains control over the beneficial interests in a trust. First, under §674 the grantor may be treated as owner of the trust for income tax purposes. The retention of a power over the beneficial interests of a trust may prevent a transfer to the trust from being a completed gift. Reg.

§25.2511-2(c). Second, the trust may be included in the grantor's estate under §§2036 or 2038.

§10.37.1. Income Tax Consequences

Under §674(a) the grantor is treated as the owner of a trust if the beneficial enjoyment of the corpus or income is subject to the control of the grantor (or the grantor's spouse), a nonadverse party, or both, without the consent of an adverse party. Accordingly, the grantor is taxed on the income of a trust where the grantor or a nonadverse party holds the right to add or delete beneficiaries, to increase or decrease the shares of the beneficiaries in income or principal, or to determine when distributions will be made. However, the rigor of §674(a) is relaxed by important exceptions for (1) certain powers held by anyone including the grantor, §674(b), (2) powers held by an independent trustee, §674(c), and (3) powers held by a trustee or trustees, none of whom is the grantor or the grantor's spouse, that are limited by an ascertainable standard set forth in the trust instrument, §674(d). The exception for powers of distribution held by an independent trustee is discussed at §10.20.3. In general, the scope of each exception varies directly with the degree of the power-holder's independence (*i.e.,* the narrowest exception applies to the grantor or a nonadverse party and the broadest to a totally independent party). Some thoughtful commentators have proposed that the exceptions be narrowed, but their proposals have not been accepted. *See, e.g.,* Westfall, Trust Grantors and Section 674: Adventurers in Income Tax Avoidance, 60 Colum. L. Rev. 326 (1960). Others have suggested that income, gift, and estate tax consequences of grantor trusts should be more consistent.

The exceptions carved out by §674(b) allow the grantor or any other person to hold a variety of powers over income and corpus. Accordingly, the trust may permit some degree of flexibility over distributions. For example, the exceptions are broad enough to permit the grantor to act as trustee of a §2503(c) trust of which a dependent child is a beneficiary (the grantor would only be taxed on the income actually applied to discharge the grantor's obligation to support the child). Section 2503(c) trusts are discussed in more detail at §7.36.

The exceptions of §§674(b)(1) to (4) are of limited general significance in planning irrevocable trusts. Briefly, they permit the grantor or a nonadverse party to hold powers:

1. To apply income to the support of a dependent of the grantor to the extent the grantor would not be taxed under §677(b) (*i.e.,* the grantor is taxable only to the extent the income is

actually applied to satisfy his or her legally enforceable obligation to provide support);
2. To control the beneficial enjoyment of the trust only after the occurrence of an event such that the grantor would not be treated as the owner under §673 if the power were a reversionary interest, §674(b)(2);
3. To appoint the principal or income of the trust by will, other than income accumulated in the discretion of the grantor or a nonadverse party, or both, §674(b)(3); and
4. To allocate the principal or income among charitable beneficiaries. §674(b)(4).

The exception of §674(b)(1) does allow the grantor or a nonadverse party to hold the power to allocate income to the grantor's dependents without adverse income tax consequences except to the extent the power is actually exercised.

The exception of §674(b)(4) allows the creation of a specialized form of charitable income trust in which the grantor retains the power to designate each year the recipient of the income earned by the trust. *See* §8.33. In operation, the use of such a trust permits the grantor to make an unlimited charitable deduction: The grantor is not taxed on the income of the trust, which the trust is entitled to deduct in full for income tax purposes. Moreover, the creation of such a trust does not involve a completed gift because of the grantor's retained power to allocate the income among charitable organizations. Of course, the retention of such a power would require the trust property to be included in the grantor's gross estate under §2036(a).

The §674(b)(5) exception permits the grantor to hold the power to distribute corpus to or for any current income beneficiary if the distribution will be charged against the distributee's proportionate share of the trust fund as if the corpus constituted a separate trust. In addition, this subsection permits the grantor to distribute corpus to a beneficiary or a class of beneficiaries provided that the power is limited by a reasonably definite standard set forth in the trust instrument (*e.g.*, to defray costs of education or medical care).

Section 674(b)(6) allows the grantor to distribute or withhold income temporarily from a beneficiary if any accumulated income must be (1) ultimately paid to the beneficiary, to his or her estate, or to his or her appointees, or (2) distributed on termination of the trust to the current beneficiaries of the trust in shares irrevocably specified in the trust instrument. This exception provides a degree of flexibility that encourages creating trusts with separate shares.

Under §674(b)(7) the grantor may withhold income from a beneficiary during his or her incompetency or minority. To qualify under this exception it is not necessary that the accumulated income be payable to the beneficiary from whom it was withheld or to his or her estate or appointees. Reg. §1.674(b)-1(b)(7). Thus, income accumulated during the minority of a beneficiary may be added to corpus and ultimately distributed to others. Of course, provision for distribution to others could prevent the income interest from qualifying for the annual exclusion under §2503(c).

Finally, §674(b)(8) excepts a power to allocate receipts and disbursements between principal and income, even though expressed in broad language. This exception permits a desirable degree of flexibility regarding principal and income allocations.

§10.37.2. Gift Tax Consequences

The retention of powers that are within the exceptions of §674(b) may have adverse gift tax consequences for the grantor. For example, although the grantor retains the power to withhold income from the beneficiary, the gift will be complete for gift tax purposes. Reg. §25.2511-2(d). However, the income interest generally will not qualify for the annual gift tax exclusion unless the trust satisfies the requirements of a minor's trust under §2503(c). *See* §7.37.2. The retention of other powers could also prevent the trust from meeting the requirements of §2503(c). Under Reg. §25.2511-2(e), the donor is treated as holding a power if it is exercisable by the donor and a person not having a substantial adverse interest in the trust. For this purpose "a trustee, as such, is not a person having an adverse interest in the disposition of the trust property or its income." Id.

§10.37.3. Estate Tax Consequences

Perhaps more important, the retention of a power to distribute or withhold income or corpus would cause the trust to be included in the grantor's gross estate under §§2036 and 2038. *See Lober v. United States,* 346 U.S. 335 (1953). For this reason the grantor should not act as trustee of a §2503(c) trust. *See* §7.36.6. Also, recall that for estate tax purposes inclusion is required if a proscribed power is exercisable by the grantor alone or in conjunction with any other person. That is, there is no exception for powers that are jointly exercisable with a person who has an adverse interest in the trust. §§2036(a)(2), 2038(a)(1).

§10.38. Administrative Powers

The grantor's retention of routine powers of administration do not have adverse tax consequences, at least where they are exercisable in a fiduciary capacity. However, a grantor who retains unusually broad powers of administration may suffer adverse income and estate tax consequences. Indeed, under §675 adverse income tax consequences may result if certain administrative powers are exercisable by nonadverse parties or persons not acting in fiduciary capacities.

§10.38.1. Income Tax Consequences

The grantor is taxed on the income of a trust under §675 if certain powers of administration are held by the grantor or a nonadverse party. In general the powers are ones that indicate the trust may be operated substantially for the benefit of the grantor instead of the beneficiaries. A power may be present either because of the terms of the trust instrument or because of the manner in which the trust is operated. Reg. §1.675-1(a). The powers described in §675 are:

> (1) *Power to deal for less than adequate and full consideration.* A power exercisable by the grantor or a nonadverse party, or both, without the approval or consent of any adverse party [that] enables the grantor or any other person to purchase, exchange, or otherwise deal with or dispose of the corpus or the income therefrom for less than an adequate consideration in money or money's worth.
>
> (2) *Power to borrow without adequate interest or security.* A power exercisable by the grantor or a nonadverse party, or both, [that] enables the grantor to borrow the corpus or income, directly or indirectly, without adequate interest or without adequate security except where a trustee (other than the grantor) is authorized under a general lending power to make loans to any person without regard to interest or security.
>
> (3) *Borrowing of the trust funds.* The grantor has directly or indirectly borrowed the corpus or income and has not completely repaid the loan, including any interest, before the beginning of the tax year. The preceding sentence shall not apply to a loan that provides for adequate interest and security, if such loan is made by a trustee other than the grantor and other than a related or subordinate trustee subservient to the grantor.

In addition, under §675(4) the grantor is treated as the owner of any part of the trust in respect of which any person in a nonfiduciary capacity has, without the consent of any person in a fiduciary capacity:

> (A) a power to vote or direct the voting of stock or other securities of a corporation in which the holdings of the grantor are significant from the viewpoint of voting control;
>
> (B) a power to control the investment of the trust funds either by

directing investments or reinvestments, or by vetoing proposed investments or reinvestments, to the extent that the trust funds consist of stocks or securities in corporations in which the holdings of the grantor and the trust are significant from the viewpoint of voting control; or

(C) a power to reacquire the trust corpus by substituting other property of an equivalent value.

Note that the tests under §§675(1), (2) are whether "the grantor or a nonadverse party, or both" have certain powers over the trust property (or income). The grantor is treated as owner of any portion of the trust over which such a power exists. In contrast, §675(3) focuses on whether the grantor has borrowed the corpus or income of the trust. The grantor may be treated as owner of the *entire* trust if such a borrowing takes place. *See Larry W. Benson,* 76 T.C. 1040 (1981) (grantor borrowed entire income of trusts).

As noted in §10.32.8, in *Rothstein v. United States,* 735 F.2d 704 (2d Cir. 1984), a grantor was treated as owner of a trust from which he purchased stock in exchange for an unsecured promissory note that carried interest at five percent. The sale made by a subservient trustee on credit without adequate security was, in effect, a loan for purposes of §675(3). However, the trust was recognized as a separate taxpayer for purposes of determining the effect of the sale — the grantor obtaining a basis in the stock equal to the value of his note. In Rev. Rul. 85-13, 1985-1 C.B. 184, the IRS concluded that in such a case (where the grantor is treated as owner of the trust), the "sale" of the stock to the grantor should not be recognized because, for income tax purposes, the same person is the seller and the buyer. Revenue Ruling. 86-82, 1986-1 C.B. 253, held that under §675(3) the grantor-trustee is properly treated as the owner of a trust from which he borrowed the entire corpus at the market rate and with adequate security although the loan was repaid during the same year. The effect of borrowing only a portion of the corpus of the trust is not clear. Presumably the grantor-borrower would be treated as owner of only a proportionate part of the trust. *See O'Neil Bennett,* 79 T.C. 470 (1982) (borrowing of part of trust income by partnerships of which grantors were members was treated as indirect borrowing by grantors).

None of the powers proscribed by §675 are necessary for the legitimate administration of most trusts. In fact, the exercise of most of the powers described in §675 would constitute a breach of the trustee's fiduciary duties with respect to investments unless expressly authorized. Accordingly, §675 should cause no problems in the ordinary case. The simplest and most effective way to guard against an inadvertent violation of §675 is to provide expressly in the trust instrument that the trustee may not exercise any of the powers described in the section.

§10.38.2. Gift Tax Consequences

The retention of purely administrative powers does not render a gift incomplete although it necessarily has some impact on the beneficial enjoyment of interests in the trust. Thus, a gift is not incomplete merely because the grantor retains the power, exercisable in a fiduciary capacity, to control the investment of trust assets or to allocate receipts and disbursements between income and principal. A transfer is incomplete, however, if the grantor retains the power to change beneficial interests in the trust unless the power is a "fiduciary power limited by a fixed or ascertainable standard." Reg. §25.2511-2(c).

§10.38.3. Estate Tax Consequences

> We hold that no aggregation of purely administrative powers [retained by the grantor] can meet the government's amorphous test of "sufficient dominion and control" so as to be equated with ownership. *Old Colony Trust Co. v. United States,* 423 F.2d 601, 603 (1st Cir. 1970).

The rule set forth in the *Old Colony Trust Co.* case is consistent with the treatment of administrative powers in other contexts under the estate tax law. For example, administrative powers held in a fiduciary capacity do not constitute a general power of appointment for purposes of §2041. *See* Reg. §20.2041-1(b)(1).

The right to vote publicly traded stock transferred to a trust is usually an unobjectionable administrative power. However, the situation is different where the grantor retains the right to vote stock in a corporation in which the grantor and related persons own or have the right to vote 20 percent or more of the voting stock. In 1967 the IRS ruled that the retention of voting control of a corporation, combined with restrictions on the disposition of the transferred stock, was equivalent to retaining the right to control the enjoyment of the income of the trust. *See* Rev. Rul. 67-54, 1967-1 C.B. 269, *revoked,* Rev. Rul. 81-15, 1981-1 C.B. 457 (noting the control may have an effect on the value of the stock). However, when the issue was litigated, the Supreme Court rejected the IRS position. *United States v. Byrum,* 408 U.S. 125 (1972). In *Byrum* the Court held that the grantor's retained power "to affect, but not control" trust income was insufficient to cause the trust property to be included in his gross estate under §2036. In the Court's view the grantor's power to vote a majority of the stock was so constrained by the fiduciary duties applicable to majority shareholders and directors that it did not warrant inclusion of the stock in his estate.

Congress responded to the *Byrum* decision by enacting §2036(b) in 1976, which was modified in 1978. Under the so-called Anti-*Byrum* amendment, stock in a "controlled corporation" is included in the grantor's estate if the grantor retained the right to vote the stock. For this purpose, a "controlled corporation" is one in which the grantor owned or had the right to vote at least 20 percent of the voting stock at some time after the transfer of the stock and within three years of the grantor's death. The constructive ownership rules of §318 are applied in determining the ownership of stock in the corporation. §2036(b)(2). The new provisions are thoroughly reviewed in McCord, The 1978 Anti-*Byrum* Amendment: A Cruel Hoax, U. Miami, 14th Inst. Est. Plan., ch. 12 (1980).

Retention of the power to vote transferred stock may require the stock to be included in the transferor's estate under §2036(c). Thus, if a parent transfers common stock to a child, retaining the right to vote the stock, §2036(c) may require the stock to be included in the parent's gross estate. Presumably, that result would follow if a donor transferred stock of a controlled corporation to himself or herself as custodian for a minor donee.

§10.39. Power to Revest Title in Grantor

The grantor is treated as the owner of property held by a trust that can be revoked by the grantor. Thus, the income of a revocable trust is taxed to the grantor, transfers to the trust are not completed gifts, and the trust is includible in the grantor's estate. In order to remove any question regarding the revocability of a trust, the instrument itself should specify that the trust is irrevocable. This is particularly necessary if the trust might be subject to the laws of California, Oklahoma, or Texas, under which a trust is generally revocable unless otherwise specified in the trust instrument. *See* §10.8.

§10.39.1. Income Tax Consequences

Under §676(a) the grantor is treated as the owner of any portion of a trust "where at any time the power to revest in the grantor title to such portion is exercisable by the grantor or a nonadverse party or both." Thus, the grantor will be taxed on the income of the trust that is revocable by (1) the grantor, (2) a nonadverse party, or (3) the grantor and a nonadverse party. Apparently the grantor will not be treated as the owner of a trust where the power to revoke is held by an adverse party or may be exercised only with the consent of an adverse party. Thus, the existence of a power to revoke may be shielded by the involvement of an adverse party. However, a distribution to the grantor under such a power would probably involve a gift by the adverse party.

The general rule of §676(a) does not extend to powers that can only affect enjoyment of the income for a period commencing after the end of a period of sufficient duration that the grantor would not be treated as owner under §673 if the power were a reversionary interest. §676(b). However, because of the substantial change in §673 made by the 1986 Act this change is of little practical value. In contrast, under the prior provisions of §673, the grantor could retain a power to revoke the trust and recover title to the corpus provided that the power only becomes exercisable more than ten years after the property is transferred to the trust or after the death of the income beneficiary.

§10.39.2. Gift Tax Consequences

A gift is, of course, incomplete to the extent it is revocable by the grantor. For this purpose, a grantor is considered to have a power that is exercisable jointly with any person who does not have a substantial adverse interest in the property. Reg. §25.2511-2(e). The fact that a nonadverse party has the sole power to revest title in the grantor does not make the transfer incomplete.

§10.39.3. Estate Tax Consequences

Under §2038, property transferred to a trust is includible in the grantor's estate if the grantor retained the power, alone or in conjunction with any other person, to amend, revoke, or terminate the trust. The rule of §2038(a)(1) extends to powers held at death or relinquished within three years immediately preceding death. *See also* §2035(d)(2). The grantor's estate does not include the property of a trust merely because another person holds a power to amend, revoke, or terminate the trust. Understandably, where "the decedent had the unrestricted power to remove or discharge a trustee at any time and appoint himself trustee, the decedent is considered as having the powers of the trustee." Reg. §20.2038-(a)(3). Here again, some caution must be exercised in creating the power to remove and replace the trustee, even when the trustee must always be a corporation or trust company. The IRS has indicated that it will also treat the grantor as having the powers of the trustee where the trust appoints a corporate trustee and the grantor retains the power to remove the corporate trustee and appoint another corporate trustee. Rev. Rul. 79-353, 1979-2 C.B. 325. *See* §10.41.1. The position taken in the ruling remains of doubtful validity. However, to avoid a confrontation with the IRS, any such power should be drafted carefully. *See* §10.41.8.

§10.40. Retained Income Interest

A grantor may retain an income interest for valid nontax reasons — there are virtually no tax reasons for doing so. For example, a grantor may transfer property to such a trust in order to protect himself or herself against the unwise expenditure or waste of property. Of course, creditors can reach the interest of the grantor in a self-settled trust. *See* §§10.11, 10.21.2. For income and estate tax purposes such a transfer is largely ignored: The ordinary income of the trust is taxed to the grantor whether or not it is distributed; in addition, the entire value of the trust is includible in the grantor's estate under §2036(a).

§10.40.1. Income Tax Consequences

The basic income tax rule is a broad one: The grantor is treated as the owner of a trust if, without the consent of an adverse party, the income is or may be (1) distributed to the grantor or the grantor's spouse, (2) held or accumulated for later distribution to the grantor or the grantor's spouse, or (3) used to pay premiums on policies of insurance on the life of the grantor or of the grantor's spouse. §677(a). The latter rule is not avoided by including in the trust a term that prohibits use of trust income to pay premiums on policies insuring the life of the grantor. LR 8839008.

Under §677(a), the grantor is taxed on the ordinary income of the trust if the grantor or any nonadverse party, such as an independent trustee, has discretion to accumulate the income for later distribution to the grantor. *Duffy v. United States,* 487 F.2d 282 (6th Cir. 1973), *cert. denied,* 416 U.S. 938 (1974). Likewise, the grantor is taxed currently on capital gains that are allocable to corpus and will be distributed to the grantor or the grantor's spouse at the end of the trust term. Rev. Rul. 66-161, 1966-1 C.B. 164; Rev. Rul. 75-267, 1975-2 C.B. 254. However, capital gains are not taxed to the grantor where they are allocated to corpus and will *not* be distributed to the grantor or the grantor's spouse. Reg. §1.677(a)-1(g), example 1.

Section 677(a) also extends to the use of trust income to satisfy legal obligations of the grantor or of the grantor's spouse, such as contractual payments due from the grantor (*e.g.,* mortgage installments). Income that may be used to discharge the grantor's obligation to support a beneficiary other than the grantor's spouse is taxed to the grantor only to the extent it is actually used for that purpose. §§674(b)(1), 677(b). Income that is used to pay private school tuition of the grantor's minor child is taxed to the grantor if the grantor is expressly or impliedly obligated to make the payments. *Morrill v. United States,* 228 F. Supp. 734 (D. Me. 1964). However, in another case the Court of Claims held that where the local law did not require the grantor to send his children to a private day school, the income of the trust used to pay their tuition is not taxable to him. *Wyche v. United States,* 36 A.F.T.R.2d 75-5816 (Ct. Cl. Trial Judge's opinion, 1974) (South Carolina law). More recent cases from several states indicate that parents may be obligated to provide their children with private school educations and, hence, taxed on the income of trusts used to pay private school tuitions. *E.g., Frederick C. Braun, Jr. v. Commissioner,* 48 T.C.M. 210 (1984) (New Jersey law), and *Christopher Stone,* 54 T.C.M. 462 (1987) (California).

Income that might be used to pay premiums of policies insuring the life of the grantor or the life of the grantor's spouse is taxed to the grantor only if policies actually exist during the tax year, "upon which it would have been physically possible for the trustees to pay premiums." *Genevieve F. Moore,* 39 B.T.A. 808, 812-813 (1939), *acq.,* 1939-2 C.B. 25. *See* §6.39. "There were no existing policies upon which premiums might be paid, and no part of the income of the trust estate was used for that purpose. In this situation we have held that no part of the trust income is taxable to the grantor." *Corning v. Commissioner,* 104 F.2d 329, 333 (6th Cir. 1939). Where policies do exist, the reach of the statute is not defeated by a nominal requirement that income be distributed to an individual beneficiary or to another trust.

Example 10-17. *W* transferred income-producing property to Trust A, the income of which was payable in equal shares to her 3 children. At the same time she transferred policies of insurance on her life to Trust B, in which the children will each have a one-third interest. *W* will be taxed on the income of Trust A if it is paid to Trust B pursuant to the consent of the 3 children who are beneficiaries of Trust A. Rev. Rul. 66-313, 1966-2 C.B. 245. *See also L. B. Foster,* 8 T.C. 197 (1947), *acq.,* 1947-1 C.B. 2.

Under §677(b) the income of the trust that may "in the discretion of another person, the trustee, or the grantor acting as trustee or co-trustee" be applied "for the support or maintenance of a beneficiary (other than grantor's spouse) whom the grantor is legally obligated to support or maintain" is taxed to the grantor only "to the extent that such income is so applied or distributed." This provision prescribes the exclusive rule for the taxation of such support payments. Accordingly, the grantor is not treated as having a reversionary interest, within the meaning of §673, in a trust from which an independent trustee has discretion to make distributions for the support of his or her dependent children. Rev. Rul. 61-223, 1961-2 C.B. 125.

By reason of §§674(b)(1) and 677(b) the income of a trust such as a §2503(c) minor's trust is not taxed to the grantor merely because the income could be used to satisfy his or her legally enforceable obligation to support the beneficiary. Instead, the income is taxed to the grantor only to the extent it is actually used to discharge his or her support obligations. For this purpose, the extent of the grantor's obligation is measured by the applicable local law. *Brooke v. United States,* 468 F.2d 1155 (9th Cir. 1972); Rev. Rul. 56-484, 1956-2 C.B. 23. For example, the *Brooke* court did not require the parent-guardian to report the income that was used to pay for "private school tuition, musical instruments, music, swimming and public speaking lessons," the cost of an automobile for his oldest child, or the payment of travel expenses to New Mexico for an asthmatic child. The uncertain status of a parent's support obligation in most states and the consequent tax uncertainty would be relieved if a federal standard were adopted. *See* Nitzburg, The Obligation of Support: A Proposed Federal Standard, 23 Tax L. Rev. 93 (1967). As indicated by the cases discussed above, state law increasingly obligates parents to provide "extras" for their children, consistent with the family's standard of living.

In most states, trusts can still be used to provide the grantor's children with items of "super" support, such as private school tuition, music lessons, or the "luxuries" — which the grantor would otherwise pay out of his or her own after-tax dollars. However, the grantor will be taxable to the extent the trustee pays expenses that the grantor is obligated to pay. Thus, the grantor will be taxable to the extent the trustee pays for private school tuition that the grantor is contractually obligated to pay. As a protective measure trusts for the super support of children typically prohibit the trustee from using the funds to provide any item of support the local law required the grantor to furnish. Of course, it is generally preferable to give a trustee broad discretion to make distributions to beneficiaries.

§10.40.2. Gift Tax Consequences

For gift tax purposes, the transfer of property to a trust involves a gift of the actuarially determined value of any interest the grantor does not retain. In this connection recall the valuation rules of §2702. Of course, the gift of a remainder is incomplete and not presently taxable if the grantor retains the power to change the disposition of the remainder interest. *See* Reg. §25.2511-2(c). A gift of the remainder is a gift of a future interest that does not qualify for the annual gift tax exclusion. §2503(b).

There is some uncertainty regarding the gift tax consequences of the grantor's retention of the discretionary right to receive income. The Regulations suggest that the grantor has made a gift of the income interest. Reg. §25.2511-2(b). In Rev. Rul. 77-378, 1977-2 C.B. 347, the

IRS ruled that where the grantor's creditors could not reach any interest in the trust property, the grantor made a completed gift of the entire value of the property. However, where the income interest can be reached by the grantor's creditors, the transfer is not considered to involve a completed gift of the income interest. *Mary M. Outwin,* 76 T.C. 153 (1981); *Alice Spaulding Paolozzi,* 23 T.C. 182 (1954), *acq.,* 1962-2 C.B. 5; Rev. Rul. 76-103, 1976-1 C.B. 293.

§10.40.3. Estate Tax Consequences

A retained discretionary interest in income does not alone require the trust property to be included in the grantor's estate under §2036(a)(1). However, the property of such a trust is includible in the grantor's estate where the income is regularly distributed to the grantor, apparently by prearrangement. *Estate of Skinner v. United States,* 316 F.2d 517 (3d Cir. 1963). Property transferred outright more than three years prior to the transferor's death is likewise includible if the transferor continued to receive the income from the property by prearrangement. *Estate of McNichol v. Commissioner,* 265 F.2d 667 (3d Cir.), *cert. denied,* 361 U.S. 829 (1959). A prearrangement is not implied if the income is not regularly paid to the grantor. *Estate of Uhl v. Commissioner,* 241 F.2d 867 (7th Cir. 1957).

§10.41. Power to Appoint Successor Trustees

Trusts generally should provide a method for the selection of successor trustees. Indeed, in some instances it is desirable to provide a mechanism for the removal *and* replacement of trustees. However, provisions dealing with the removal and replacement of trustees should be drafted with care, particularly in light of Rev. Rul. 79-353, 1979-2 C.B. 325, and subsequent expansive letter rulings. If the trustee does not hold any tax-sensitive powers, the grantor or a beneficiary can hold an unrestricted power to remove and replace the trustee. Such an unrestricted power poses potential problems if the trustee holds any tax-sensitive powers, including the power to deal with policies of insurance on the life of the person holding such a power.

§10.41.1. Revenue Ruling 79-353

According to Revenue Ruling 79-353, the "reservation by the settlor of the power to remove the trustee at will and appoint another trustee is equivalent to reservation of the trustee's powers." The Ruling is unsupported by authority and is of questionable validity. Indeed, the extant authorities, including *United States v. Byrum,* 440 F.2d 949 (6th Cir. 1971), *aff'd,* 408 U.S. 125 (1972), suggest that the IRS position would not be upheld. *See also, Estate of Beckwith,* 55 T.C. 242 (1970), *acq.,* 1971-2 C.B. 1. In *Byrum* the court held that the trust was not includible in the grantor's estate although he held the power to remove and replace the trustee with a successor. While the income and estate taxes are not *in pari materia,* it is relevant to note that for purposes of Subchapter J the grantor is not considered to hold the powers of the trustee unless he or she has the power to appoint himself or herself as trustee. *See* Reg. §1.674(d)-2. Note that under Rev. Rul. 81-51, 1981-1 C.B. 458, the holding of Revenue Ruling 79-353 does not apply to irrevocable transfers made before the date of its publication, October 29, 1979. Subsequent letter rulings have indicated that the concepts of Revenue Ruling 79-353 were equally applicable to §§2041 and 2042. Letter Ruling 8916032, involving §2041, and Letter Ruling 8922003, involving §2042, are discussed below at §§10.41.4 and 10.41.5, respectively. In fairness the IRS should not attempt to apply the extension of Revenue Ruling 79-353 expressed in those letter rulings to irrevocable dispositions made prior to the issuance of explicit *published* rulings. Letter rulings are hardly the way to communicate new interpretations of the tax laws.

Although Revenue Ruling 79-353 may ultimately be invalidated, clients must be informed of the risks inherent in employing approaches that contravene the terms of Revenue Ruling 79-353. In the ordinary case, the grantor should not retain the power to remove and replace a trustee or cotrustee without cause — the risks are simply too great. However, in the case of a trust that is to be included in a client's will, the client may wish to give a beneficiary the power to remove and replace an independent trustee who holds discretionary powers. The client may reason that either the courts will not extend the application of Revenue Ruling 79-353 to powers of removal and replacement held by a beneficiary or the beneficiary could eliminate the risk of inclusion by disclaiming the power under §2518. A beneficiary's disclaimer of a power to remove and replace a trustee should be effective.

§10.41.2. Power to Remove Trustee and Appoint Self

A grantor or other person who holds the power to remove the trustee and appoint *himself or herself* as successor trustee is appropriately treated as holding the powers of the trustee. Reg. §20.2036-1(b)(3) (grantor); Reg. §20.2038-1(a)(3) (grantor); Reg. §20.2041-1(b)(1) (nongrantor). Indeed, the grantor may be treated as holding the powers of the trustee if the grantor has the *contingent* power to appoint himself as trustee if the original trustee resigns, is removed, or becomes unable to act. For example, in Rev. Rul. 73-21, 1973-1 C.B. 405, inclusion was required under §2036 where grantor held contingent power to appoint a successor trustee, including himself, and the trustee had power to vary distributions. In this connection it is interesting to note that G.C.M. 34730 indicated that the IRS was not confident that Revenue Ruling 73-21 would be upheld by the courts:

> Although we agree that the proposed revenue ruling [73-21] currently reflects the law, we believe that the position taken in the revenue ruling will be a hazardous one to defend in litigation.

§10.41.3. Factors in Planning Power to Appoint Successor Trustee

Drafting a power to appoint successor trustees must be done in light of the other provisions of the trust. The extent to which a power of removal and replacement may be held by the grantor or a beneficiary depends largely upon the extent to which the trustee has discretion to make distributions to or for the benefit of the grantor or the beneficiaries. If the trustee has only nondiscretionary power to make distributions, the grantor or a beneficiary can safely serve as trustee — or hold the power to remove and replace the trustee with anyone. Rev. Rul. 73-143, 1973-1 C.B. 407.

Overall, the following tax-related factors should be considered: (1) the choice of trustee (tax-sensitive powers can more safely be given to an independent trustee or cotrustee); (2) the extent to which the trustee is authorized to make discretionary distributions or distributions that satisfy the legal obligation of the grantor or a beneficiary; (3) the circumstances under which the grantor or beneficiary has the power to remove and replace a trustee; (4) the limits, if any, on the appointment of the grantor or beneficiary as trustee; and (5) the extent to which the grantor or beneficiary is prohibited from taking any action affecting any life insurance on his life that may be held in the trust, including the appointment of a trustee of the trust.

§10.41.4. Independent Trustee or Cotrustee

An independent trustee or cotrustee can be given discretion to make distributions without causing the property to be included in the estate of the grantor or a beneficiary. Although an independent trustee may not be needed at the outset, the trust may provide that one should be added in order to avoid an otherwise adverse tax result. Thus, at some point — say, the birth of children — an independent trustee might be added to the trust to make decisions regarding discretionary distributions. Under a variation of this approach a beneficiary-trustee might be given the power to appoint a special trustee to exercise the power to make distributions to persons the beneficiary is legally obligated to support. LR 9036048 (trust not included in the beneficiary's estate under §2041 where she was authorized to appoint, but not to remove, a special trustee who would have authority to make distributions to the beneficiary's minor children). In short, an independent trustee with tax-sensitive powers should not be subject to unrestricted removal and replacement by the grantor or a beneficiary.

Tax-sensitive powers should be exercisable *only* by an independent trustee — *not* by such a trustee *and* the grantor or beneficiary. A grantor who holds discretionary powers to make distributions would be treated as the owner of the trust for income tax purposes unless the powers were within the exceptions of §674(b). Note in this connection that for estate tax purposes the grantor cannot safely hold a *joint* power to make discretionary distributions. In LR 8916032 the IRS stated, "For purposes of sections 2036 and 2038, it is immaterial whether a power is exercisable by the decedent alone or in conjunction with persons having an adverse interest."

Similarly, a beneficiary's joint power to distribute to himself causes inclusion under §2041 unless the coholder of the power is the creator of the power or an adverse party. §2041(b)(1)(C)(ii). In practical terms the exception for such powers is of limited utility, as explained in §10.41.9.

§10.41.5. Extent of Trustee's Discretionary Powers or Authority to Make Distributions That Satisfy Legal Obligations

The grantor or a beneficiary can safely serve as trustee if the trustee has no discretion to make distributions or exercise other tax-sensitive powers. However, in order to increase the flexibility of trusts it is often desirable to allow the trustee some discretion in making distributions. As suggested above, tax-sensitive powers should generally be entrusted only to an independent trustee or third party who is not subject to removal and replacement by the grantor or a beneficiary. Otherwise, the IRS is likely to contend that the grantor should be treated as holding all of the powers of a trustee who can be removed and replaced by the grantor without cause even though the grantor cannot appoint himself trustee. Thus, if an independent trustee who held discretionary powers to distribute income or principal was subject to removal and replacement by another independent trustee chosen by the grantor, the theory of Revenue Ruling 79-353 would require the trust to be included in the grantor's estate under §§2036 and 2038. The IRS also contends that life insurance held by the trust is includible in the grantor's estate under §2042 if the grantor held the unrestricted power to remove and replace the trustee. LR 8922003.

Because of the threat of inclusion under §2041 indicated in LR 8916032 a trust beneficiary should not be given the unlimited power to remove and replace a trustee who holds discretionary powers. In contrast, Reg. §20.2041-1(b)(1) indicates that §2041 only deals with instances in which a donee may have power to remove or discharge the trustee and appoint *himself or herself* as successor trustee:

> A power in a donee to remove or discharge a trustee and appoint himself may be a power of appointment. For example, if under the terms of a trust instrument, the trustee or his successor has the power to appoint the principal of the trust for the benefit of individuals including himself, and the decedent has the unrestricted power to remove or discharge the trustee at any time and appoint any other person including himself, the decedent is considered as having a power of appointment.

On the other hand, a trust is not includible in the grantor's estate merely because the grantor holds nondiscretionary powers to vary distributions to persons whom the grantor is not obligated to support. Rev. Rul. 73-143, 1973-1 C.B. 407. The IRS has ruled that a trust is not includible under §2041 in the estate of a beneficiary who holds a joint power to remove and replace the trustee where the trustee's power to make distributions to the beneficiary is limited by an ascertainable standard relating to maintenance, education, support or health. LR 9043052. According to the IRS, part of a trust would be included in the estate of a beneficiary who held the power to remove and replace an independent trustee who was authorized to make distributions to persons the beneficiary was obligated to support. LR 8916032. *See also,* Rev. Rul. 79-154, 1979-1 C.B. 301 (life insurance fund subject to withdrawal by surviving spouse to support adult children was not includible in her estate, but would have been includible if it could have been used to discharge surviving spouse's legal obligation to support dependent children).

§10.41.6. Prohibit Distributions That Satisfy Legal Obligations

Another important safeguard is to prohibit the trustee from making any distribution that satisfies a legal obligation of the trustee or anyone holding the power to remove and replace the trustee. Such a provision may avert an inclusion that would otherwise be required by §§2036 or 2041. Without such a limitation, inclusion might be required under §2036 if the grantor held such a power or the right to appoint those who do. Reg. §20.2036-1(b)(2). As indicated in §10.41.5, there is a risk of inclusion under §2041 in the estate of a nongrantor who holds, individually or as guardian of minors, the majority power to remove and replace a trustee who has discretion to make distributions that might satisfy beneficiary's obligation to support minors. LR 8916032. In this connection consider the text of Reg. §20.2041-1(c)(1):

> A power of appointment exercisable for the purpose of discharging a legal obligation of the decedent or for his pecuniary benefit is considered a power of appointment exercisable in favor of the decedent or his creditors.

In Rev. Rul. 79-154, 1979-1 C.B. 301, the IRS stated by way of dicta that a decedent who held the power to make appointments from an insurance fund that would meet her obligation to support her minor children would be treated as holding a general power of appointment over the fund. In such a case the threat of inclusion arises because the power is limited by a standard relating not to the power-holder herself, but to a person the power-holder is legally obligated to support. Inclusion in the power-holder's estate would not have been required under §2041 if the power had been limited by an ascertainable standard relating to *her* own maintenance, education, support, or health. Inclusion under this theory can be blocked by including in the trust a provision that prohibits the trustee from making distributions that would satisfy any legal obligation of the trustee (or of any person who holds the power to appoint a successor trustee), including the duty to support a distributee. Of course, the local law may preclude a fiduciary from expending funds to meet his obligation to support a beneficiary if the fiduciary has the means to satisfy the obligation himself or herself.

§10.41.7. Income Tax Consequences of Distributions for Support

The power of the trustee to make distributions that satisfy the grantor's obligation to support a dependent is not generally taken into account for income tax purposes. Thus, under §677(b) only the amount actually distributed by a trustee in ways that satisfy the grantor's legal obligation of support is taxable to the grantor under §677(b). Similarly, under §678(c) the power of a nongrantor to make distributions of income that satisfy the power-holder's obligations of support and maintenance require him or her to be treated as owner of the trust only to the extent the income is so applied. Here again, allowing the power-holder to make distributions to his or her dependents subject to an ascertainable standard probably would not prevent inclusion in the power-holder's income to the extent the distributions satisfy his or her obligation of support.

§10.41.8. Drafting Power of Grantor or Beneficiary to Remove and Replace Trustee with Tax-Sensitive Powers

If a grantor wishes to create a discretionary trust *and* retain the power to remove and replace the trustee, the grantor should consider taking steps that may blunt the reach of Revenue Ruling 79-353 and related private letter rulings. In any case the grantor or beneficiary should be prohibited from appointing himself. Several drafting strategies are discussed in the following paragraphs.

First, the trust might limit the circumstances under which a grantor or beneficiary could remove and replace the trustee. This approach has some promise, as Revenue Ruling 79-353 is premised upon the existence of an unrestricted power to remove and replace the trustee. By way of illustration, the grantor or beneficiary might be empowered to remove an independent trustee and appoint a successor independent trustee if certain objective criteria were satisfied. Thus, such a power might be exercisable if the income generated by the trust fell below a certain level, if there were litigation between a beneficiary and the trustee involving the administration of the trust, or if the principal residence of one or more beneficiaries was more than a specified distance from the principal place of business of the independent trustee. The last condition might be satisfied if either the beneficiary or the trustee relocated.

Second, if the grantor or beneficiary exercised a power of removal the powers of the successor trustee might be limited. For example, the successor trustee might be limited to making nondiscretionary distributions. In effect, the removal and replacement of the trustee would cause the trust to shift from a discretionary one to a nondiscretionary one.

Third, the powers of removal and replacement might be given to different beneficiaries. Thus, the trust might authorize one beneficiary to remove the trustee and another beneficiary to appoint an independent successor. Presumably such a division of authority would be recognized.

Fourth, the power of removal and replacement might be exercisable by the grantor or a beneficiary only in a fiduciary capacity. Although subsequently limited by Congress, *United States v. Byrum,* 408 U.S. 125 (1972), indicates that the courts are, to some extent, sensitive to the capacity in which powers are held. On the other hand, it is clear that the grantor's retention of some powers is fatal although the powers are held in a fiduciary capacity. *See* LR 9131006 (TAM). For example, a retained power to vote the stock of a controlled corporation in a fiduciary or nonfiduciary capacity requires inclusion under §2036(b). Similarly, the retained power to exercise incidents of ownership in life insurance in a fiduciary or nonfiduciary capacity will require inclusion under §2042.

Fifth, the power to remove and replace the trustee of a discretionary trust might spring into existence only if Revenue Ruling 79-353 is withdrawn or invalidated. In effect, the power would be a conditional one.

Overall, it is safest to authorize an independent party to remove and replace the trustee. Presumably the grantor's accountant or lawyer could hold such a power without creating a substantial risk that the trust would be included in the grantor's estate. If the named accountant or lawyer were no longer available, presumably the power to designate a successor could be given to the managing partner of the accounting or law firm or its successor. However, as a practical matter a client might well be chary of binding the trust to the firm in such a fashion. Unfortunately, the continued availability of trustworthy and reliable independent parties to exercise such a power is rare.

§10.41.9. Prohibit Self-Appointment by Grantor or Beneficiary

> [T]he course that best combines flexibility with simplicity and safety is to exclude the settlor from the role of trustee. Halbach, Tax-Sensitive Trusteeships, 63 Or. L. Rev. 381, 397 (1984).

Tax problems are most likely to arise if the grantor serves as trustee or retains the power to appoint himself or herself as successor trustee. The regulations treat the grantor as holding the powers of the trustee if the grantor has the power to remove the trustee and appoint himself. In addition, the IRS has treated a grantor as holding the powers of the trustee where the grantor held the *contingent* power to appoint himself successor trustee upon the death, resignation or removal of the original trustee. Rev. Rul. 73-21, 1973-1 C.B. 405. Accordingly, if the trustee holds any discretionary powers of distribution, the trust generally should not permit the grantor to appoint himself as successor under any circumstances. As suggested above, if a trustee holds any discretionary powers as a general rule the beneficiaries should also be prohibited from serving as trustee.

At least one court has applied the theory of Revenue Ruling 73-21 where the grantor had a contingent power to appoint himself as successor trustee. In *First National Bank of South Carolina v. United States,* 81-2 U.S.T.C. ¶13,422 (D. S.C. 1981), the grantor held the power to appoint himself as successor trustee upon the resignation of the corporate trustee. A comparable problem arises under §2041 if a beneficiary has the power to remove the trustee and to appoint himself as successor trustee and the trustee has power to make discretionary distributions to the beneficiary or to make distributions that satisfy the legal obligations of the beneficiary. Note that Reg. §20.2041-1(b)(1) limits inclusion to cases in which the power existed at the time of the decedent's death:

> [I]f under the terms of a trust instrument, the trustee or his successor has the power to appoint the principal of the trust for the benefit of individuals including himself, and the decedent has the unrestricted power to remove or discharge the trustee at any time and appoint any other person including himself, the decedent is considered as having a power of appointment. However, the decedent is not considered to have a power of appointment if he only had the power to appoint a successor, including himself, under limited conditions which did not exist at the time of his death, without an accompanying unrestricted power of removal.

This language should be contrasted with the text of LR 8916032, in which §2041 is applied to a beneficiary who is a member of a committee that was empowered to remove and replace a trustee who could make distributions that would satisfy the beneficiary's obligation to support her minor children. According to LR 8916032, inclusion would be required if the beneficiary acting individually and as the guardian of her minor children held a majority of the votes on the committee. It thus disregards the fact that as guardian the beneficiary would be acting in a fiduciary capacity. This seems incorrect under the rationale of *United States v. Byrum,* 408 U.S. 125 (1972).

A grantor is also treated as holding the powers of a trustee who may be jointly removed by the grantor and another party and replaced by a successor chosen by them, including the grantor. LR 8606002. For purposes of §§2036 and 2038, a joint power is fatal regardless of the adversity of the interests of the decedent and the joint power-holder. As pointed out above, both of those sections require inclusion if the transferor may exercise a prohibited power or control in conjunction with *any* other person. In LR 8606002 (TAM) the trust was included in the grantor's estate under §§2036 and 2038 because of a retained joint power to require the trustee to make distributions to the primary beneficiary that were not subject to an ascertainable standard.

In *First National Bank of Denver v. United States,* 648 F.2d 1286 (10th Cir. 1981), the court refused to include the trust under §2041 in the estate of a beneficiary who had the power to remove the trustee and appoint a successor other than himself. However, despite the text of Reg. §20.2041-1 and the outcome in *First National Bank of Denver,* the IRS seems intent to apply the theory of Revenue Ruling 79-353 in other cases as indicated by LR 8916032.

§10.41.10. Disclaimers

Adverse tax results of holding a power to remove and replace a trustee may be avoided if the holder disclaims the power. LR 8122075. However, in order for the disclaimer to be a qualified disclaimer, the disclaimant must give up all discretionary powers to control the disposition of any property affected by the power. Specifically,

> [A] disclaimer of a power of appointment with respect to property is a qualified disclaimer only if any right to direct the beneficial enjoyment of the property which is retained by the disclaimant is limited by an ascertainable standard. Reg. §25.2518-3(a)(1)(iii).

See also, Reg. §25.2518-3(d), example 9. Finally, note that the IRS will not recognize an attempted disclaimer by a fiduciary of a power to invade corpus for a specific beneficiary if the disclaimer is not effective for state law purposes. Rev. Rul. 90-110, 1990-52 I.R.B. 18.

§10.41.11. Releases

The threat of inclusion in the grantor's estate may be reduced if the offending power is released. Of course, inclusion would be required if the grantor dies within three years after releasing a tax-sensitive power. §§2035(d)(2), 2038(a)(1). It is more difficult for a beneficiary to eliminate the threat of inclusion by releasing a power. Under §2041(a)(2), the property is includible if the

> [D]ecedent has at any time exercised or released such a power of appointment by a disposition which is of such nature that if it were a transfer of property owned by the decedent, such property would be includible in the decedent's gross estate under sections 2035 to 2038, inclusive.

Thus, a beneficiary's release of a power of appointment would not insulate the property from inclusion in his or her estate if he or she retained an income interest in the trust. Inclusion would be required because the retention by a transferor of an income interest in a trust would require the trust to be included in his or her estate under §2036.

§10.41.12. Eliminating Powers by Court Order

A favorable outcome may also result if the power of the grantor or beneficiary is terminated by a court decree during his lifetime. The IRS recognized the effectiveness of a court order terminating the grantor's power to appoint himself as trustee although the decree was inconsistent with existing state law:

> A lower state court construed the trust instrument to mean that the decedent had reserved the right to remove and appoint a trustee only once, that this power did not include the right to appoint himself; and that once having exercised that power, decedent would have exhausted his reserved powers. Rev. Rul. 73-142, 1973-1 C.B. 405.

Subsequent to the decree the decedent removed the trustee and appointed a successor other than himself. As a result, according to the court decree, which was binding on the decedent, the decedent no longer held the power to remove and replace the trustee. After the decree became final the decedent's power was, according to Revenue Ruling 73-142, "effectively extinguished."

E. ADDITIONAL ISSUES

§10.42. Introduction

This part is concerned with several additional matters that the planner and the client should consider in planning trusts. They include: the selection of trustees, §10.43; the selection of property to transfer to the trust, §10.44; provisions regarding investment of trust funds, §10.45; directions regarding the allocation of receipts and disbursements between principal and income, §10.47; and the use of a perpetuities savings clause, §10.48. The topics discussed do not exhaust the matters that should receive the serious attention of the planner and client. They are, however, fairly illustrative of the breadth of concerns that must be considered from the tax and the nontax points of view.

§10.43. Selection of Trustee

Except as limited by law, any individual, association, partnership, or corporation that has the capacity to take and hold property may act as a trustee. Restatement (Second) Trusts §§89, 96-98 (1959). Practically speaking, the choice is generally between an individual, such as the grantor or a beneficiary, and a corporate trustee. The choice may be dictated, however, by economic or family circumstances: In the case of a small trust, the appointment of a corporate trustee may be uneconomical. On the other hand, there may be no suitable family member or other individual available to serve as trustee. Some jurisdictions, including provinces of Canada, provide a public trustee who may be appointed in such cases. However, the concept has not caught on in the United States. The needs of some clients are best met by using multiple trustees (*e.g.*, an individual and a corporate trustee or two or more individual trustees). The practice of appointing co-fiduciaries may be too expensive — at least in jurisdictions such as New York, that allow a full statutory fee to each fiduciary.

A lawyer and a client who intends to create a trust should discuss the role of the trustee in some detail before the client chooses a trustee. The client's choice should be made in light of all relevant factors including the purposes of the trust, the extent of the duties imposed on the trustee, the complexity and probable duration of the trust, and the reliability and experience of the beneficiaries and other family members. The lawyer can usually help the client make an appropriate choice by pointing out the advantages and disadvantages of the alternatives. The availability of a convenient local office of a corporate trustee is important to some clients.

§10.43.1. Corporate Fiduciary

A corporate fiduciary may be chosen as trustee or cotrustee because of its financial responsibility, its continuity of life, and its overall administrative capabilities. Those considerations are particularly important in the case of large trusts, which usually require more attention to administrative details, investment decisions, and accounting matters. However, an individual trustee may be authorized to retain accountants, investment advisors, attorneys, and others who may provide the trust with essentially the same services that are available from a corporate fiduciary. Indeed, some corporate fiduciaries will provide some administrative support services to individual trustees on a contract basis. In choosing a corporate fiduciary, the client should review the investment performance and investment philosophy of the ones under consideration. Corporate fiduciaries will typically wish to have authority to invest the assets of all but the largest trusts in common trust funds, of which they may offer a variety designed to serve varying investment objectives. Thus, a corporate fiduciary may offer common trust funds that are designed to maximize income, to generate a balance of income and growth, or to produce maximum growth.

A trust that is likely to endure for a long period usually requires either the appointment of a corporate trustee or the establishment of a suitable mechanism for the selection of successor individual trustees. Where a corporate trustee is appointed trustee of a long-term trust it is often desirable to provide some mechanism for the removal and replacement of the trustee. Because of the generally disadvantageous tax consequences a beneficiary generally should not be empowered to remove the trustee and appoint himself or herself as successor trustee. *See* §10.28. In the case of individual trustees, the trust might name several successor individual trustees or cotrustees and authorize the survivor of them (or other responsible persons) to appoint further successors.

The quality of services provided by a corporate fiduciary varies according to the ability and interest of the personnel assigned to the trust. Special provisions can be used if a client wants a particular trust officer to work on the account. For example, a trust may express the grantor's wish that the designated trust officer work on, or supervise, the account and provide that the trust should follow the trust officer if he or she later moves to a different corporate trustee. Of course, such a provision introduces a degree of instability and could result in the imposition of additional trustees' fees if the designated trust officer changes employment.

§10.43.2. Lawyer as Trustee

The appointment of the scrivener as fiduciary is discussed in some detail in §1.18. Although a lawyer may serve as trustee, it is unwise unless he or she has the necessary expertise and is willing to take the time to apply it for the benefit of the trust. In general a lawyer should not serve as trustee unless there is no qualified corporate or individual trustee available. The lawyer should be aware of the ethical issues involved in accepting an appointment as fiduciary, the most serious of which are conflicts of interest and the appearance of impropriety. Concerns that accepting such an appointment involves offensive solicitation of business have largely abated.

Ethical Consideration 5-6 is concerned with appointment of the draftsman as fiduciary:

> A lawyer should not consciously influence a client to name him as executor, trustee, or lawyer in an instrument. In those cases where a client wishes to name his lawyer as such, care should be taken by the lawyer to avoid even the appearance of impropriety.

Rule 1.8 of the MRPC does not expressly prohibit such an appointment. However, the appointment would be subject to the general conflict of interest provision in MRPC 1.7 and the specific requirements of MRPC 1.8. *See* Wash. Ethics O. 86-1, Wash. State Bar Assn., Resources 96 (April 1988).

In order to eliminate most questions regarding the efficacy of the appointment, a client who wishes to appoint his or her lawyer as fiduciary should obtain legal advice from an independent lawyer. The independent lawyer should draw the trust instrument, or at least the part designating the trustees. Some states bar lawyers from drafting instruments in which they are appointed as fiduciaries (a practice frequently condemned by courts in other states). *E.g., Estate of Shaughnessy,* 702 P.2d 132 (Wash. 1985).

If a client is considering the appointment of his or her lawyer as fiduciary, the lawyer should discuss the relevant factors with the client. Specifically, the lawyer should point out that the trustee will usually require legal representation, which is not included in the fee for the trustee's services. In short, the appointment of the lawyer as trustee may not save any fees.

§10.43.3. Grantor as Trustee

It is common for the grantor to serve as trustee or cotrustee of a revocable trust, which generally does not involve any tax disadvantages. *See* §§10.15-10.17. In such a case the trust should designate a successor to serve following the grantor's death or disability. For example, another person might be named to serve as cotrustee with the grantor and as sole trustee following the grantor's death or disability. Under another approach the surviving trustee is given the power to appoint a person to fill the vacancy and serve as cotrustee. A corporate fiduciary may be reluctant to serve following an individual trustee unless its potential liability for acts of its predecessor is eliminated by the terms of the trust, an accounting, or agreement of the beneficiaries.

In the case of an irrevocable trust, the grantor can serve as trustee without tax disadvantage if the grantor's powers are appropriately circumscribed. *See* §§10.31-10.35. Serious tax disadvantages may arise, however, if the grantor retains the power, alone or in conjunction with any other person, to make discretionary distributions. *See* §§2036(a)(2), 2038(a)(1). The grantor may be willing to take that risk where the trust is relatively small and will probably terminate during the grantor's lifetime. For example, a grantor might decide to serve as trustee of a §2503(c) trust although doing so would cause the trust to be included in the grantor's estate he or she were to die prior to distribution of the trust. A similar issue exists with respect to a discretionary trust that will terminate when the beneficiary attains a relatively young age. Along the same lines, the grantor may choose to serve as custodian of a gift under the Uniform Transfers to Minors Act or the Uniform Gifts to Minors Act.

§10.43.4. Beneficiary as Trustee

An individual beneficiary, such as the primary income beneficiary, can serve as trustee. The appointment of a beneficiary is logical because of the beneficiary's obvious interest, but it is generally unwise unless the beneficiary is reliable, has reasonably good judgment, and has a modicum of financial or business experience. The planner should be alert to the possibility that the appointment of one beneficiary as trustee may cause concern on the part of other beneficiaries. On the tax side, care must be exercised not to give the beneficiary any powers that would cause unwanted income, gift, or estate tax consequences. *See* §§10.27-10.27.3. The planner should be particularly careful not to give the beneficiary-trustee a power that might be construed as a general power of appointment under §2041, such as an unlimited power to invade trust principal for the beneficiary's own benefit. A beneficiary-trustee could, however, be given powers to invade the trust principal that are (a) "limited by an ascertainable standard relating to [his or her] health, education, support or maintenance," §2041(b)(1)(A), or (b) limited to a noncumulative power to withdraw the greater of $5,000 or five percent of the value of the trust corpus, §2041(b)(2). *See* §§10.24-10.25.

§10.43.5. Cotrustees

If the grantor or a beneficiary is a trustee, the appointment of a cotrustee may be of some tax benefit. For example, the appointment of a trustee with an adverse interest may prevent the grantor from being treated as the owner of a trust for income tax purposes. Similarly, the appointment of a cotrustee may prevent a nongrantor from being treated as owner of the trust under §678.

The appointment of a cotrustee is often most important for a variety of nontax reasons. For example, a corporate fiduciary might be appointed as a cotrustee because of its superior administrative capacity and immortality. On the other hand, an individual might be appointed because of his or her familiarity with the beneficiaries. In order to reduce the risk of conflict and avoid the threat of a deadlock, each cotrustee can be given exclusive authority over specific activities of the trust. For example, one of the cotrustees might be given exclusive power to make certain decisions (*e.g.,* discretion to make distributions) or to act with respect to certain property. Doing so may avoid the adverse tax consequences that would follow if the power were shared with the other trustee. *See* §6.27.11. Before appointing cotrustees, some thought should also be given to the rate and manner of their compensation. Depending on the circumstances, each trustee may receive a full fee, a single fee may be divided between them, or the individual trustee may forego receiving any compensation. However, it is generally unwise to set forth a rigid compensation schedule in the trust instrument because of the difficulty in anticipating the services that may be required of the trustee and the difficulty of obtaining approval of any change in such a schedule.

§10.43.6. Removal of Trustees

In most states it is difficult if not impossible to obtain the judicial removal of a trustee unless the trustee has engaged in an egregious breach of trust. Accordingly, the grantor may wish to give a responsible person the power to remove and replace a trustee. The power is particularly valuable in the case of a corporate trustee, which otherwise might serve indefinitely. Again, a beneficiary ordinarily should not have the power to appoint himself or herself, unless the beneficiary could have acted from the outset without adverse tax consequences. Because of Rev. Rul. 79-353, 1979-2 C.B. 325, and later letter rulings, care must be exercised in planning and drafting a power to remove and replace a trustee. *See* §§10.41.3, 10.41.8.

§10.44. Selection of Property to Transfer in Trust

The choice of property to transfer to the trustee is very important, especially in the case of an irrevocable inter vivos trust. In general the same factors that must be considered in selecting property to transfer by way of inter vivos gift, §§7.12-7.17, must be taken into account when it comes to selecting property to transfer in trust. In brief, the grantor should avoid transferring property that will cause the recognition of income (*e.g.,* an installment obligation) or will have other adverse income tax consequences. A grantor who creates an irrevocable trust for the benefit of others might fund it with appreciated stock rather than municipal bonds that produce tax-exempt income. The trustee must exercise care in selling property transferred to the trust. Where appreciated property is sold by the trust within two years following its addition to the trust, the gain is taxed as if the sale had been made by the grantor. §644. The grantor should also avoid giving away any business interests that might prevent the grantor's estate from qualifying for the benefits of §§303, 2032A, and 6166. *See* §7.10. The grantor should also be aware that the potential availability of some income tax advantages may be lost if stock in a small business corporation is transferred to a trust. In particular, the ordinary loss deduction that is allowed under

§1244 for a loss suffered on small business stock is allowed only to the original shareholder — not to a trust or other successor shareholder. *See* Reg. §1.1244(a)-1(b). Also, a trust generally cannot be a shareholder in a Subchapter S corporation unless the grantor is treated as its owner under §§671-677 or the trust is a Qualified Subchapter S trust. §1361(c)(2), (d).

The selection of property to transfer to a revocable trust is usually much less significant because the grantor will be treated as the owner of the property for tax purposes. For example, the transfer of an installment obligation to such a trust is not treated as a disposition that triggers recognition of gain. *See* §9.6.3. Similarly, property held in the trust is included in the grantor's gross estate. Hence it may be used to fund a marital gift, and is counted for purposes of meeting the percentage requirement of §§303, 2032A, and 6166.

§10.45. Provisions Regarding Trust Investments

"The little match girl realized too late what her mistake had been. She had failed to diversify."

A trust generally should not restrict the *types* of property in which the trustee may invest. Indeed, many lawyers prefer to list in the trust instrument the types of property in which the trustee is authorized to invest, although the same types of property may be authorized in a local statute. The lawyer may believe that including the list will cause the trustee to keep them in mind. In addition, either the list may change in the future or the trust may be moved to another jurisdiction. Overall, imposing a limit on permissible investments can unduly restrict the trustee's ability to respond to changing economic circumstances and can impair the value of the trust. Of course, a court may authorize the trustee to deviate from an investment restriction where there has been an unanticipated change in circumstances and adherence to the restriction would result in substantial losses to the trust and frustrate accomplishment of trust purposes. *See, e.g., In re Trusteeship Under Agreement with Mayo,* 105 N.W.2d 900 (Minn. 1960); Restatement (Second) Trusts §167 (1959).

Where the trust is intended to qualify for the marital deduction the trustee should not be prevented, directly or indirectly, from investing in income-producing property. In fact, because of the requirements of §§2056(b)(5), (b)(7), and 2523(f), the decedent's (or donor's) spouse should be given the power to compel the trustee to invest in income-producing property. Along the same lines, a charitable remainder trust should not restrict the trustee from making investments that would produce a reasonable amount of income or gain. *See* Reg. §1.664-1(a)(3). *See also* §8.24.

§10.45.1. Investment Standard

A trustee is required to make the trust property productive within a reasonable time. Restatement (Second) Trusts §181 (1959). Under Cal. Prob. Code §16007 (West 1991 Supp.), "The trustee has a duty to make the trust property productive under the circumstances and in furtherance of the purposes of the trust." In making investments, however, the trustee must not prefer the interests of one beneficiary over another (*i.e.,* the trustee must be impartial). Cal. Prob. Code §16003 (West 1991 Supp.). Here it is worth noting that the interests of the current and future beneficiaries are less likely to conflict if the trustee has discretion to distribute income *or* principal to the current beneficiaries. Of course, the same is true if the current beneficiary is entitled to receive a fixed amount each year (an annuity) or a fixed percentage of the current value of the trust property (a unitrust amount). In the case of the discretionary trust, an annuity trust, or a unitrust, the trustee need not be particularly concerned with the extent to which the investments produce current income. Instead, the trustee can concentrate on the overall increase in the value of the trust. In contrast, if the current beneficiaries are only entitled to receive the current income of the trust, the trustee must invest with a view toward the production of income. Of course, in any case the investments must be consistent with the terms and purposes of the trust. As indicated above, the types of permissible investments may be defined in the trust.

In most states the appropriateness of an investment is measured by the *prudent person rule.* That is, the trustee is permitted to make any investment that a prudent person "would make of his own property having in view the preservation of the estate and the amount and regularity of the income to be derived." Restatement (Second) Trusts §227(a) (1959). From its origins in *Harvard College v. Amory,* 26 Mass. (9 Pick.) 446 (1830), the prudent person rule has evolved in a way that focuses on the propriety — principally the safety — of each investment. It has emphasized the necessity of avoiding the risk of loss as to each investment rather than considering its place in the trust's portfolio and its role in fulfilling the overall investment strategy of the trust. Thus, a trustee who makes an investment that itself does not meet the prudent person standard could be surcharged for any loss that resulted.

In contrast, the Restatement and the law of some states now consider the appropriateness of an investment in light of the purposes of the trust and its overall portfolio.

California Probate Code §16040 (West 1991 Supp.) illustrates the new trend:

> (a) The trustee shall administer the trust with the care, skill, prudence, and diligence under the circumstances then prevailing that a prudent person acting in a like capacity and familiar with such matters would use in the conduct of an enterprise of like character and with like aims to accomplish the purposes of the trust as determined from the trust instrument.
>
> (b) When investing, reinvesting, purchasing, acquiring, selling, and managing trust property, the trustee shall act with the care, skill, prudence, and diligence under the circumstances then prevailing, including but not limited to the general economic conditions and the anticipated needs of the trust and its beneficiaries, that a prudent person acting in a like capacity and familiar with such matters would use in the conduct of an enterprise of like character and with like aims to accomplish the purposes of the trust as determined from the trust instrument. In the course of administering the trust pursuant to this standard, individual investments shall be considered as part of an overall investment strategy.
>
> (c) The settlor may expand or restrict the standards provided in subdivisions (a) and (b) by express provisions in the trust instrument. A

trustee is not liable to a beneficiary for the trustee's good faith reliance on these express provisions.

A similar approach is reflected in Wash. Rev. Code §11.100.020(1) (1989), which provides that "a fiduciary, in determining the prudence of a particular investment, shall give due consideration to the role that the proposed investment or investment course of action plays within the overall portfolio of assets."

The prudent person rule was generally recognized as requiring a trustee to diversify the investments of a trust. Restatement (Second) Trusts §228 (1959). Diversification is also an essential ingredient of the overall portfolio approach reflected in Cal. Prob. Code §16040. Indeed, modern portfolio theory emphasizes the need to diversify in order to minimize the risk of loss due to unforeseen events. In either case, a trustee should not concentrate trust investments in the stock of a single company or industry. Among other things a trustee might invest as broadly as possible, which would avoid risks associated with most eventualities — oil shortages, recessions, labor problems, tax changes, inflation, and so forth. Overall a trust might best be protected by investing in a broad range of assets, including ones that when viewed in isolation might be too risky (speculative), but actually add to portfolio stability. Some have suggested that the best refuge is in stock index funds — against which the performance of a trustee might be measured.

§10.45.2. Trustees with Greater Skill

The prudent person standard represents a minimum standard that may be increased if the trustee has greater skill than a person of ordinary prudence or where the trustee holds himself or herself out to possess such skill. Cal. Prob. Code §16014(b) (West 1991 Supp.); Wash. Rev. Code §11.100.020 (1989) ("if the fiduciary has special skills or is named trustee on the basis of representations of special skills or expertise, the fiduciary is under a duty to use those skills"); U.P.C. §7-302, 8 U.L.A.§7-302 (1983); Restatement (Second) Trusts §176, comment a (1959). *See also, Estate of Beach,* 542 P.2d 994 (Cal. 1975), *cert. denied,* 434 U.S. 1046 (1978); *In re Estate of Killey,* 326 A.2d 372 (Pa. 1974). Of course, the terms of the trust can vary the obligations of the trustee, including duties regarding the investment of trust property. Of course, the trust may authorize (or direct) the trustee to retain specific assets and attempt to relieve the trustee from any liability that would otherwise attach for failure to dispose of the assets. Regardless of the terms of such a provision, the trustee cannot be completely relieved of all responsibility for trust investments. Despite a direction to retain particular assets, at some point it may be necessary for the trustee to take steps to dispose of them or face the possibility of a surcharge.

The grantor may authorize or direct the trustee to make otherwise improper investments or may prohibit the trustee from making otherwise lawful investments. Thus, a grantor who does not want a corporate trustee to invest in a common trust fund may prohibit it from doing so. Along the same lines, a grantor may prohibit an individual trustee from investing in mutual funds (which, naturally, pay a management fee to their investment advisor). Most grantors recognize that it makes little sense to prevent a trustee from making investments that are broadly diversified — and best protect the trust against loss. In addition, from a practical point of view, restrictive or unusual investment directions may discourage a trustee from accepting a trusteeship or may result in the imposition of higher annual fees than normal. If an individual is appointed as trustee, it may be desirable to authorize him or her to obtain investment advice at the expense of the trust, and to rely upon the advice without any duty to inquire regarding the reliability of the advice provided by the investment advisor.

§10.45.3. Additional Directions Regarding Specific Assets

The nature of the trust property, the relationship of the parties, or other factors sometimes make it desirable to give the trustee more specific directions or authorization. It is particularly appropriate to do so if the trust will hold the stock of a closely-held family business. The trustee needs and deserves some specific direction regarding the retention of the stock and the operation of the business and, perhaps, exoneration from liability for retention of the stock. In such a case the planner should also attempt to deal with the conflicts of interest that might arise between the trustee, the beneficiaries, nonbeneficiary shareholders, and other persons who are interested in the business. It may also be necessary to give the trustee some specific directions regarding the allocation of receipts and disbursements between income and principal. *See* §10.47.

Conflicts regarding investments can arise where the trust and the trustee are both interested in the same business or other property. Likewise, the interests of a trustee-beneficiary may conflict with the interests of other beneficiaries, including remaindermen. The planner must be alert to potential conflicts and should discuss any that can be identified with the grantor and, when possible, with the intended trustee. An instrument can identify a particular conflict and authorize the trustee to act with respect to the matter without liability. The problem might arise, for example, where the real property transferred to the trust is leased to the intended trustee or a business in which he or she is interested. In such a case the trust might specifically authorize the trustee to lease the property from the trust upon the same terms and conditions (or upon such other terms and conditions as the trustee deems appropriate). In the case of a corporate trustee, the trust may authorize it to retain and vote any of its own stock that is originally transferred to the trust. It is generally undesirable to authorize a corporate trustee to acquire more of its shares for the account of the trust.

§10.45.4. Investment Advisor

Where the grantor has particular confidence in the skill of a particular investment advisor, the trustee may be directed to accept the investment directions given by the advisor. In such a case the trustee may be required to follow the instructions of the advisor. *See* Restatement (Second) Trusts §185 (1959). Presumably a trustee subject to such directions is substantially relieved of investment responsibilities *and* liabilities. A person who has authority to direct or control the investments of the trust may be treated as a fiduciary. Under a fairly common approach, such a person is "deemed to be a fiduciary and shall be liable to the beneficiaries of said trust and to the designated trustee to the same extent as if he were a designated trustee in relation to the exercise or nonexercise of such a power or authority." Wash. Rev. Code §11.100.130 (1989). Some investment advisors are, understandably, unwilling to act in such a capacity and assume the responsibilities of a trustee.

§10.46. Exculpatory Clauses

The grantor may wish to exonerate an individual trustee from liability for loss to the trust except for intentional misconduct or gross negligence, particularly if the trustee is a family member serving without compensation. *See* §4.26.6 (exculpatory clause for executors). In this connection, note that the trustee is likely to be held to the same standard of performance whether or not the trustee is compensated. *See* Cal. Prob. Code §16041 (West 1991 Supp.). With regard to exculpation, the Restatement (Second) Trusts explains, "[I]f by the terms of the trust it is provided that the trustee shall not be liable 'except for his wilful default or gross negligence,' although he is not liable for mere negligence, he is liable if he intentionally does or omits to do an act which he knows to be a breach of trust or if he acts or omits to act with reckless indifference as to the interests of the beneficiary." Restatement (Second) Trusts, §222, comment a. Exculpatory clauses should be used sparingly and only in exceptional circumstances in the case of professional fiduciaries, of whom a higher standard of performance is reasonably required. It is also generally inappropriate for an exculpatory clause to be included in an instrument that appoints the scrivener as fiduciary.

§10.47. Power to Allocate Between Principal and Income

The trustee generally should be given discretion to allocate receipts and disbursements between principal and income. An allocation is necessary because of the bifurcated nature of the beneficial interests in a typical trust — the income and principal beneficiaries generally are not the same. The income of the trust is usually payable to one beneficiary (or group of beneficiaries) upon whose death the principal is distributable to another beneficiary (or group of beneficiaries). Two-thirds of the states have responded to the allocation problem by adopting either the Uniform Principal and Income (1931) Act, 7B U.L.A. 187 (1985) (the "Original" Act), or the Revised (1962) Uniform Principal and Income Act, 7B U.L.A. 145 (1985) (the "Revised" Act). The rules prescribed by the Uniform Acts are generally fair and workable. However, as explained below, they do not satisfactorily resolve all allocation problems.

> [T]he subject is highly technical in nature and . . . the trustees should have broad discretion for their own protection and for the maximum efficiency of the program. The grant of this discretion is valid, although there may be certain limits on its exercise. J. Farr &. J. Wright, An Estate Planner's Handbook, §35 at 219 (4th ed. 1979).

Planners often meet the allocation problem by giving the trustee discretion to allocate receipts and disbursements between income and principal as the trustee believes is reasonable and equitable under the circumstances. Such a power gives the trustee more flexibility in dealing with the complex problems of principal and income allocations while carrying out the terms of the trust and meeting the needs of the beneficiaries.

Section 2 of the Original and Revised Acts recognizes that the trustee may be given discretion to make allocations of principal and income. When the trustee is given such discretion, "no inference of imprudence or partiality arises from the fact that the trustee has made an allocation contrary to a provision of this Act." §2(b), 7B U.L.A. 151 (1985). Importantly, such a discretionary power exercisable in a fiduciary capacity is not treated as a general power of appointment for federal estate tax purposes: "The mere power of management, investment, custody of assets, or the power to allocate receipts and disbursements as between income and principal, exercisable in a fiduciary capacity, whereby the holder has no power to enlarge or shift any of the beneficial interests therein except as an incidental consequence of the discharge of such fiduciary duties is not a power of appointment." Reg. §20.2041-1(b)(1). Similarly, the existence of such a power does not jeopardize the allowance of the marital deduction for an otherwise qualifying interest in a trust. Reg. §20.2056(b)-5(f)(3), (4); Prop. Reg. §20.2056(b)-7(c).

It is often desirable to give the trustee some specific directions (or additional authorization) regarding certain allocation matters. The directions in a particular case may run counter to the basic provisions of the Uniform Acts. The following paragraphs discuss some of the matters about which trusts commonly provide additional guidance. They include the treatment of stock splits and stock dividends, the amortization of bond premium, and the accumulation of discount, unproductive or underproductive property, and the handling of depreciation.

§10.47.1. Stock Splits and Stock Dividends

The lawyer may find it necessary or desirable to specify a rule regarding allocation of stock splits and stock dividends contrary to the basic rule of the Uniform Acts. Under §5 of the Original Act and §6 of the Revised Act, all stock splits and stock dividends of the issuing corporation are entirely allocated to principal. That rule prejudices current income beneficiaries where the trust includes stock in corporations that regularly issue small stock dividends in lieu of cash dividends or in addition to small cash dividends. This problem can be met by providing that the trustee may allocate stock dividends to income in accordance with a formula such as the New York statutory formula. Under N.Y. Est. Powers & Trusts Law §11-2.1(e)(3) (McKinney 1967), stock distributions of six percent or less are allocated to income whether the distribution is called a stock split or a stock dividend. Such a rule fairly meets the needs of the beneficiaries and those of the trustee.

§10.47.2. Amortization of Bond Premium and Accumulation of Discount

Corporate and municipal bonds usually carry a fixed rate of interest that is payable semiannually until redemption at face value upon maturity. Because the market rate of interest fluctuates, the current market price of a bond typically depends on two factors: (1) the length of time until the maturity of the bond and (2) the difference between the current market rate of interest and the rate specified in the bond. Thus, a bond that carries a rate of interest above the going rate will sell at a price in excess of its redemption value (*i.e.*, it will sell at a premium). If a bond is purchased at a premium and held until maturity, the principal account will be depleted unless an amount equal to the premium is recovered from income. The problem can be met by allocating a portion of each income payment to principal (*i.e.*, the premium is amortized over the life of the bond). However, the Revised Act prohibits amortization unless the instrument provides otherwise or the trustee is empowered to make discretionary allocations between principal and income. The Original Act also does not provide for amortization or accumulation of discount.

> **Example 10-18.** At a time when the going rate of interest was 8%, Trustee paid $5,500 for a $5,000 bond that carried a 12% rate. Under §7(a) of the Revised Act, the full amount of each semiannual interest payment would be allocated to income. 7B U.L.A. 165 (1985). If the bond were held until maturity the proceeds of $5,000 would be allocated to principal, resulting in a "loss" of $500.

Section 7(a) of the Revised Act also prevents accumulation of discount when a bond is purchased for less than its redemption value. 7B U.L.A. 165 (1985). That is, when the trustee purchases a bond for less than its redemption value and holds it until maturity, none of the appreciation received is allocable to income. In this case the income account is disadvantaged by the purchase of a bond that carried an interest rate below the market rate at the time of purchase.

The rules of the Original and Revised Acts are unduly restrictive. They may discourage the trustee from making otherwise attractive investments or result in unfairness to one class of beneficiaries. However, because interest rates and bond prices fluctuate over time, it may be equally undesirable to require the amortization of premium or the accumulation of discount. Instead, the trust may be drafted to give the trustee discretion to deal with the bonds as required to avoid unfairness to the income beneficiaries or the remaindermen according to overall circumstances.

§10.47.3. Depreciation

Under §13(a)(2) of the Revised Act, the trustee is required to make a reasonable charge against income for depreciation where it is appropriate to do so under generally accepted accounting principles. However, no charge for depreciation is required for the "portion of real property used by a beneficiary as a residence or for . . . any property held by the trustee on the effective date of this Act for which the trustee is not then making an allowance for depreciation." 7B U.L.A. 175 (1985). Of course, if depreciation is charged, a smaller amount of income will be available for distribution to the income beneficiaries.

For income tax purposes, the depreciation deduction is allocated between the trustee and the beneficiaries on the basis of the income allocable to each. §167(h); Reg. §1.167(h)-1(b). However, the depreciation deduction is first allocated to the trustee to the extent the income is set aside for a depreciation reserve. Reg. §1.167(h)-1(b). Overall, it is preferable to give the trustee discretion regarding the establishment of a depreciation reserve.

§10.47.4. Unproductive and Underproductive Property

> Unless it is otherwise provided by the terms of the trust, if property held in trust to pay the income to a beneficiary for a designated period and thereafter to pay the principal to another beneficiary produces no income or an income substantially less than the current rate of return on trust investments, and is likely to continue unproductive or underproductive, the trustee is under a duty to the beneficiary entitled to the income to sell such property within a reasonable time. Restatement (Second) Trusts, §240 (1959).

> (1) Unless it is otherwise provided by the terms of the trust, if property held in trust to pay the income to a beneficiary for a designated period and thereafter to pay the principal to another beneficiary is property which the trustee is under a duty to sell, and which produces no income or an income substantially less than the current rate of return on trust investments, or which is wasting property or produces an income substantially more than the current rate of return on trust investments, and the trustee does not immediately sell the property, the trustee should make an apportionment of the proceeds of the sale when made, as stated in Subsection (2).
>
> (2) The net proceeds received from the sale of the property are apportioned by ascertaining the sum which with simple interest thereon at the current rate of return on trust investments from the day when the duty to sell arose to the day of the sale would equal the net proceeds; and the sum so ascertained is to be treated as principal, and the residue of the net proceeds as income. Restatement (Second) Trusts §241 (1959).

Where the interests in a trust are divided between beneficiaries entitled to the current income and others entitled to receive the principal at some time in the future, the trustee is ordinarily obligated to make the trust property productive within a reasonable time following the creation of the trust. However, in some instances the retention of property that produces little or no income is authorized, directed, or is otherwise proper. In such a case the economic interests of the income beneficiaries are disadvantaged.

The Restatement addresses the problem by allocating a portion of the net proceeds received upon the sale of the property to the income beneficiaries. Section 11 of the Original Act and §12 of the Revised Act provide a similar remedy as to trust property that has not produced an average net income of at least one percent per year. Under the Original Act upon sale of the property the amount allocated to principal is equal to the amount which, "had it been placed at simple interest at the rate of five per centum per annum for the period during which the change was delayed, would have produced the net proceeds at the time of change." The Revised Act provides for the allocation to principal to be based upon a four percent rate. The California version of the underproductive property section does not apply to "securities listed on a national securities exchange or traded over the counter if the securities are held in a broadly diversified portfolio designed to produce a reasonable rate of return appropriate to the purposes of the trust." Cal. Prob. Code §16311(d) (West 1991 Supp.).

Example 10-19. An unproductive parcel of real property was acquired by the trust on January 1, 1988. The property was sold for $130,000 on January 1, 1993. Expenses and taxes of $10,000 were paid during the time the property was owned by the trust. Under the Revised Act $100,000 of the net proceeds will be allocated to principal and the balance ($20,000) to income. The amounts are determined according to the following formula:

$$\text{Principal} = \frac{\$130{,}000 - \$10{,}000}{1 + (5)(4\%)}$$

§10.47.5. Annuity Trusts or Unitrusts

Under a unitrust instrument, all income as received would be combined with principal in a single fund and there would be no distinction between income and principal. All items received, whether they be dividends, rents or splits, would be termed "receipts" and all items paid out would be termed "payouts." The payout would be direction in fractions or in specific dollar amounts — for example, five percent of the market value of the total fund as of the first day of the fiscal year, but no more (or less) than a specific dollar amount — and no one interested in the trust would have merely an interest in income or principal.

> The unitrust thus removes any conflict of interest between the parties beneficially interested in the trust. Many advantages result. There is no longer any need to allocate receipts and expenditures between principal and income since these separate funds are irrelevant to any purpose or need of the trust or its beneficiaries. Accounting requirements are simplified and time and money saved. More important, any requirement that the trustee must invest for yield is eliminated: the trustee is no longer required to produce a reasonable income. DelCotto & Joyce, Taxation of a Unitrust, 23 Tax L. Rev. 229, 260 (1968).

The necessity of differentiating between income and principal is largely eliminated if the interests of the current trust beneficiaries are discretionary or are defined as a specified amount payable annually (an annuity) or as a percentage of the value of the trust determined annually. In the future, private annuity trusts or unitrusts may be created more frequently by reason of the valuation rules of §2702, which take into account the value of a retained interest in the form of a qualified annuity trust or a qualified unitrust. *See* §9.43.2. In the past some commentators have suggested that a private unitrust could be used to avoid problems of allocating between principal and income. *E.g.,* Lovell, The Unitrust: A New Concept to Meet an Old Problem, 105 Tr. & Est. 215 (1966). The tax consequences of the proposal were explored in a three-part article, DelCotto & Joyce, Taxation of the Trust Annuity, 23 Tax L. Rev. 231 (1968). A unitrust also substantially eliminates the clash of interests between current beneficiaries and remaindermen regarding investments: Their interests are not affected by the characterization of a receipt or disbursement as income or principal. Instead, the total annual amount of distributions to the current beneficiaries of a unitrust would be based on a specified percentage of the annually determined value of the trust assets. Thus, the unitrust would not require any allocation between income and principal and the interests of both the current and ultimate beneficiaries would be served by a growth-oriented investment policy. By way of illustration, a unitrust might provide for the payment to the current beneficiary of an amount each year equal to eight percent of the total value of the trust assets on the last business day of the preceding calendar year.

A trust that incorporates the unitrust concept should include some specific directions regarding investments. In particular, the trust might expressly authorize the trustee to make investments without regard to the amount of income they generate (the "probable income" to be derived from an asset is one element of the generally applicable prudent person investment standard). Put positively, the trustee might be authorized to invest for the overall return produced by the trust without regard to the income produced by the assets.

§10.48. Perpetuities Savings Clause

The lawyer should also be alert to the problems that might arise under the applicable form of the Rule Against Perpetuities. The Rule varies somewhat from state to state in terms of both its basic provisions and the availability of remedial devices. For example, the common law rule tests the validity of interests at the time of creation while the Uniform Statutory Rule Against Perpetuities, 8A U.L.A. 159 (1990 Supp.), waits for *90* years. The Uniform Act has been adopted in several jurisdictions, including Connecticut, Florida, Michigan, Minnesota, Montana, Nebraska, Nevada, Oregon and South Carolina. Indeed, the Uniform Rule combines a 90-year wait-and-see period with a judicial reformation of interests that are determined to be invalid under the common law rule as applied at the end of the 90-year period. Because of the uncertainty regarding the rule that might apply, modern trusts typically include a perpetuities savings clause appropriate to the jurisdiction. It is desirable to include a savings clause in most trusts although the rigors of the Rule have been relaxed significantly in a number of states by judicial decisions and statutory modifications of the common law Rule.

A common savings clause simply provides for the vesting of any interest in the trust that has not vested within the period allowable under the local law (most often 21 years after the death of the survivor of a reasonable number of designated individuals who are alive when the period of the rule begins to run). This approach vests any interests that are not vested according to the terms of the trust at the end of the common law period. Accordingly, at the time the trust is created it can be said with certainty that all unvested interests will fail or vest within the period of the Rule. Of course, the savings clause should provide expressly for the disposition of the interests involved to the extent they do not vest within the allowable period. The alternative dispositive plan must describe interests that vest at the end of 21 years after the death of the named individuals referred to in the savings clause. For example, a leading commentator has suggested that a will include a clause along the lines of Form 10-9. A. J. Casner, 3 Estate Planning 245-246 (5th ed. 1986).

Form 10-9. Perpetuities Savings Clause

If this trust has not terminated within 21 years after the death of the survivor of my issue living on my death, it shall terminate at the end of such 21-year period, and the trust property shall be distributed outright to my issue then living, such issue to take per stripes.

The persons who are designated to take the property on termination of the trust could be a different class or could be designated differently (*e.g.,* "in equal shares to the persons then entitled to receive distributions of income from the trust"). Another approach, suggested by Professors Leach and Logan, involves giving a corporate fiduciary authority to reform an interest that offends the Rule in a manner that carries out the grantor's intent. *See* Leach & Logan, Perpetuities: A Standard Saving Clause to Avoid Violations of the Rule, 74 Harv. L. Rev. 1141 (1961). The approach taken by Leach and Logan gives a corporate trustee a cy pres power similar to ones that have been given to the courts by some statutes in recent years and ones that have been exercised by some courts on their own. *E.g., In re Estate of Chun Quan Yee Hop,* 469 P.2d 183 (Hawaii 1970) (reducing a 30-year contingency to 21 years).

In drafting a savings clause of the first type described above, the planner must recognize the difference in the effective dates of a will and an irrevocable trust. A will is effective and the period of the Rule begins to run only upon the testator's death, but an irrevocable trust is effective and the period of the Rule begins to run from the date the trust is created. Because a revocable trust is subject to change or revocation until the time of the grantor's death, it is treated in the same way as a will. Thus, a savings clause that provides for termination of a trust 21 years after the death of the survivor of a class of persons living at the time of the grantor's death is suitable for inclusion in a will, but is not suitable in the case of an irrevocable inter vivos trust. Instead, the clause used in an irrevocable trust should provide for termination of the trust 21 years after the death of the last survivor of designated persons or a class of persons living at the time the trust was created or who are designated by name. It is easy to overlook the difference in the effective dates and to include an improper clause in an irrevocable trust.

It is best, of course, to understand the local Rule and to draft with a view toward its provisions. Such preventive drafting is desirable although a savings clause, statute, or judicial doctrine might "save" an offending interest. Overall, preventive drafting is clearly the best approach. In particular, a planner should view with suspicion any gift that is contingent upon the attainment of an age greater than 21 and avoid making gifts when an event in the administration of an estate or trust takes place (*e.g.,* when all debts are paid or the estate is distributed). Note in this connection that gifts subject to an administrative contingency may fail to qualify for the marital deduction.

BIBLIOGRAPHY

I. Books and Treatises

Bogert, G., Trusts and Trustees (2d ed. rev. 1979)

Calif. CEB, Drafting California Irrevocable Living Trusts (2d ed. 1987)

Calif. CEB, Drafting California Revocable Living Trusts (2d ed. 1987)

Casner, A. J., Estate Planning (5th ed. 1986)

Gallo, Drafting and Exercising Powers of Appointment, 120 Tr. & Est. 41 (1981)

Michaelson, A. & Blattmachr, J., Income Taxation of Trusts (13th ed. 1989)

Peschel, J. & Spurgeon, E., Federal Taxation of Trusts, Grantors and Beneficiaries (2d ed. 1990)

Restatement (Second) Trusts (1959)

Scott, A., Trusts (4th ed., Fratcher ed. 1987)

II. Articles

II.

Brachtl, Problems of Fiduciaries as Powerholders, U. Miami, 17th Inst. Est. Plan., ch. 17 (1983)

Barr, Berall & Ross, Drafting Trustee-Removal Power to Avoid the Adverse Consequences of Rev. Rul. 79-353, 10 Est. Plan. 30 (1983)

Friedman, Right to Remove Trustee and Other Problem Powers of Grantors, Beneficiaries and Trustees, U. So. Cal., 33rd Tax Inst., ch. 16 (1981)

Halbach, Problems of Discretion in Discretionary Trusts, 61 Colum. L. Rev. 1425 (1961)

Halbach, Powers of Distribution, Invasion and Appointment, U. So. Cal., 32nd Tax Inst., ch. 14 (1980)

Halbach, Tax-Sensitive Trusteeships, 63 Or. L. Rev. 381 (1984)

Hayes, Protecting the Fiduciary by Drafting in Anticipation of Administration, U. Miami, 24th Inst. Est. Plan., ch. 15 (1990)

Horn, Whom do You Trust: Planning, Drafting and Administering Self and Beneficiary-Trusteed Trusts, U. Miami, 20th Inst. Est. Plan., ch. 5 (1986)

Keydel, Trustee Selection, Succession, and Removal: Ways to Blend Expertise With Family Control, U. Miami, 23rd Inst. Est. Plan., ch. 4 (1989)

Moore, New Horizons in the Grant and Exercise of Discretionary Powers, U. Miami, 15th Inst. Est. Plan., ch. 6 (1981)

Nagel, Income and Estate Tax Consequences of Removal and Replacement of Corporate Fiduciaries, N.Y.U., 39th Inst. Fed. Tax., ch. 52 (1981)

Pennell, Estate Planning: Drafting and Tax Considerations in Employing Individual Trustees, 60 N.C. L. Rev. 799 (1982)

Price, Powers to the Right People: Flexibility Without Taxability, U. Miami, 25th Inst. Est. Plan., ch. 7 (1991)

Report, Rights of Creditors to Reach Assets of a Revocable Trust After the Death of the Grantor — The Missouri Approach, 20 Real Prop., Prob & Tr. J. 1189 (1985)

Strauss, Drafting Trustee Substitution Clauses to Avoid the Adverse Impact of Rev. Rul. 79-353, 53 J. Tax. 66 (1980)

Strauss & Thornburgh, IRS Rationale on Trustee Substitution May Spread to Powers of Appointment, 55 J. Tax. 224 (1981)

Wade, The New California Prudent Investor Rule: A Statutory Interpretive Analysis, 20 Real Prop., Prob. & Tr. J. 1 (1985)

Waggoner, The Uniform Statutory Rule Against Perpetuities, 21 Real Prop., Prob. & Tr. J. 569 (1986)

Weinstock, Nontaxable Grantor and Beneficiary Powers, N.Y.U., 43rd Inst. Fed. Tax., ch. 51 (1985)

CHAPTER 11

Closely-Held Business Interests

A. Introduction

§11.1. Overview
§11.2. Nontax Features of Corporations
§11.3. Income Taxation of Subchapter C Corporations
§11.4. Subchapter S Corporations
§11.4.1. One Class of Stock
§11.4.2. Election to Be S Corporation
§11.4.3. Termination of S Corporation Status
§11.4.4. Income, Distributions, and Basis
§11.4.5. Pre-1987 S Corporation Strategy
§11.5. Partnerships

B. Buy-Sell Agreements

§11.6. Overview
§11.7. Nontax Considerations
§11.8. Entity Purchase or Cross-Purchase?
§11.9. Redemptions by C Corporations
§11.10. Redemptions by S Corporations
§11.11. Valuation
§11.12. Funding the Purchase
§11.12.1. Installment Payments
§11.12.2. Medium of Payment
§11.12.3. Accumulated Earnings Tax
§11.13. Ethical Considerations
§11.14. Community Property Aspects

C. Redemptions Under §303

§11.15. Overview
§11.16. Introduction to §303

§11.17. Thirty-five Percent Requirement, §303(b)(2)(A)
§11.18. Stock in Two or More Corporations, §303(b)(2)(B)
§11.19. Maximum Amount Redeemable, §303(a)
§11.20. Time Limit on Redemptions, §303(b)(1), (4)
§11.21. What May Be Distributed
§11.22. Inter Vivos Planning for Redemptions Under §303
§11.23. Worksheet for §303
§11.24. Redemptions That Do Not Qualify Under §303
§11.24.1. Redemption Not Essentially Equivalent to a Dividend, §302(b)(1)
§11.24.2. Substantially Disproportionate Redemption, §302(b)(2)
§11.24.3. Complete Termination of Interest, §302(b)(3)
§11.24.4. No Waiver of Entity Attribution

D. Deferral of Estate Tax Under §6166

§11.25. Overview
§11.26. Closely-Held Business
§11.26.1. Who Is Counted as a Partner or Shareholder
§11.26.2. Trade or Business
§11.26.3. Passive Assets, §6166(b)(9); Farmhouses, §6166(b)(3)
§11.26.4. Partnerships and Stock That Is Not Readily Tradeable, §6166(b)(7)
§11.26.5. Holding Companies, §6166(b)(8)
§11.27. Qualification Under §6166
§11.27.1. Protective Election
§11.27.2. Acceptance or Rejection of Election
§11.27.3. Overpayments
§11.27.4. Deficiencies
§11.28. Installment Payments Under §6166
§11.29. Acceleration Under §6166(g)
§11.29.1. Distribution Under Will, §6166(g)(1)(D)
§11.29.2. Withdrawals of Money or Other Property, §6166(g)(1)
§11.29.3. Estate Has Undistributed Income, §6166(g)(2)
§11.29.4. Failure to Pay Income and Principal on Time, §6166(g)(3)
§11.30. Worksheet for Making §6166 Calculations

E. Recapitalizations

§11.31. Overview
§11.32. Application and Effect of §2701
§11.33. Scope and Effect of §2704
§11.34. Income Tax Treatment of Recapitalizations
§11.34.1. Business Purpose of Recapitalization

§11.34.2. Boot
§11.34.3. Section 306 Stock
§11.34.4. Section 305 Problems
§11.34.5. Redemption Premium, §305(c)
§11.35. Recapitalization Tax Freezes Not Subject to §2701
§11.35.1. Valuation Problems
§11.35.2. Gift or Additional Compensation?
§11.36. Other Tax Considerations
§11.37. Recapitalization Strategies

F. Family Partnerships and Partnership Freezes

§11.38. Overview
§11.38.1. Suitable Assets
§11.38.2. Income Tax Advantages
§11.38.3. Tax Uncertainties
§11.38.4. Valuation Problems and Costs
§11.38.5. Scrutiny by IRS
§11.38.6. Ethical Considerations
§11.39. Creation of Partnership Is Not a Taxable Event
§11.40. Family Partnership Rules
§11.40.1. Capital as a Material Income-Producing Factor
§11.40.2. Trustees and Minors as Partners
§11.40.3. Allocation of Income
§11.40.4. Retained Control by Donor
§11.41. Planning a Frozen Partnership Interest
§11.41.1. Liquidation Preference
§11.41.2. Income Interest
§11.41.3. Management and Control
§11.42. Conclusion

Bibliography

A. INTRODUCTION

§11.1. Overview

Planning for the management and disposition of a client's interests in a family business is a vital element in the formulation of the client's estate plan. The business may be a sole proprietorship, a partnership or a closely-held corporation. Changes made by the 1986 Act have led family business enterprises increasingly to take the form of Subchapter S corporations, one of the main subjects of this chapter. Along the way the chapter also considers planning for traditional Subchapter C business corporations ("C corporations") and partnerships. Regardless of the legal form of a family business, the planner is confronted with many of the same tax and nontax problems. Nontax factors regarding the personal liability of the owners are among the most important. Of course the client's dispositive plans and the circumstances of the client's family are crucial in planning for the continuation and disposition of a business. In particular, the age, health, interests, experience, and capacities of children may dictate whether it is feasible for the business to be continued within the family after the client's death. The planner must also recognize and deal with the valuation and liquidity problems that may arise on the death of the owner of a substantial interest in a business.

Tax and nontax considerations generally support the preparation and execution of a buy-sell agreement covering the stock or partnership interests in the business. *See* §§11.6-11.14. On the tax side, an agreement may serve to establish the value of the decedent's interest in the business. Without such an agreement, the valuation of the interest may be the subject of intense controversy with the IRS. The difficulty of valuing small business interests under the "willing buyer-willing seller" test is legendary. The frustrations of attempting such a valuation are suggested by an English jurist's plaint:

> The result is that I must enter into a dim world peopled by the indeterminate spirits of fictitious or unborn sales. It is necessary to assume the prophetic vision of a prospective purchaser at the moment of the death of the deceased, and firmly to reject the wisdom which might be provided by the knowledge of subsequent events. *Holt v. Inland Revenue Commissioners,* [1953] All E.R. 1499, 1501.

A plan may also call for a client to dispose of some or all of the client's business interests by way of inter vivos gifts to family members or to charities. Outright gifts remain perhaps the simplest and most effective lifetime estate planning technique. Gifts of minority interests usually qualify for substantial valuation discounts that reduce the tax cost of making the gifts. The following example illustrates the transfer tax savings that may result from lifetime gifts of stock.

Example 11-1. *W*, who has not previously made any taxable gifts, owned 100% of the common stock of *W,* Inc., which was worth a total of $4,000,000. In 1991 *W* transferred 10% of the stock to each of her 2 children, *D* and *S*. Discounting the gifts for lack of marketability and their minority nature, the stock given to each child had a value of $310,000. *W*'s annual gift tax exclusions reduced the gifts to $300,000 each. The gift tax imposed on the gifts was completely offset by *W*'s unified credit. The gifts effectively removed one-fourth of the value of *W,* Inc. from *W's* estate ($800,000) at no out-of-pocket tax cost. Of course, any increase in the value of the transferred stock will also be excluded from *W's* estate. Note, too, that the gifts also removed from her estate any income that the gifted stock might generate in the future. On the negative side, *W's* basis in the stock carries over to *D* and *S* — it will not be stepped up when *W* dies.

The planning for a client's interest in a closely-held corporation is also often concerned with the post-mortem redemption of stock under §303 and the deferral of estate taxes under §6166. *See* §§11.15-11.30.

Finally, a recapitalization of the corporation or partnership may be desirable in order to facilitate divided ownership and the transfer of interests by the owner in ways that meet the differing needs and interests of family members. For example, common stock might be distributed to family members who are active in the business and preferred stock to those who are inactive. The use of recapitalizations is restricted. S corporations can only have one class of stock and C corporations suffer income tax disadvantages that deter their use. Under Prop. Reg. §1.1361-1(l), (m), a corporation is treated as having only one class of stock if "all outstanding shares of stock of the Corporation confer identical rights to distribution and liquidation proceeds." Differences in voting rights are disregarded. With the enactment of Chapter 14, §§2701-2704, the gift and estate tax advantages of using a recapitalization to "freeze" the value of a senior family member's interest were severely restricted. However, various changes in the form of the business may remain attractive to some clients. As explained below, the adoption of §2701 also limits the freeze potential of family partnerships.

§11.2. Nontax Features of Corporations

Several important nontax features of the corporate form make it attractive in many planning contexts. The limited liability of the shareholders of a corporation is foremost, particularly when contrasted with the unlimited liability of a general partner or sole proprietor. Of course, limited partners also generally enjoy limited liability. Unlimited liability extends to S corporations although they are treated as conduits for federal income tax purposes. Corporate shares are almost always nonassessable, which means that the shareholder is liable only for the initial cost of shares purchased from the corporation. The free transferability of interests in a corporation is another important feature of corporations that is often a critical element of an estate plan. Of course, the transfer of shares in a closely-held corporation is commonly restricted by the terms of its articles, bylaws, or a buy-sell agreement or other arrangement. Note, however, that the theoretical free transferability of shares may be of very little value in the case of a minority shareholder. From a practical point of view unless the minority shareholder and his or her successors are protected by the terms of a buy-sell agreement they are largely at the mercy of the majority.

As indicated by Example 11-1, *supra,* gifts of stock can be used to spread the income and the future growth in value of the stock among members of the owner's family and trusts. However, note that the transfer of shares may have some negative tax consequences, such as the loss of qualification of the stock under §1244. Under that section only the *original* owner is entitled an ordinary loss deduction for a loss incurred with respect to stock in a small business — successive owners are not. In contrast, if a loss is characterized as a capital loss, it can only be used to offset capital gains or be deducted to the extent of $3,000. §1211. Finally, the corporation has a potentially indefinite existence, unrelated to the life of any shareholder. Thus, a corporation can continue to function without interruption following the death of a shareholder.

§11.3. Income Taxation of Subchapter C Corporations

The maximum income tax rate generally applicable to individuals (31 percent) is now lower than the maximum income tax rate applicable to corporations (34 percent). (As noted below, a marginal rate of 39 percent applies to corporate income at one level.) From the income tax point of view it is no longer attractive to incorporate for the purpose of accumulating income within the corporation in order to shelter the income from higher individual income tax rates. For federal income tax purposes corporations other than S corporations are taxed as separate entities at rates which increase from 15 percent on the first $25,000 to 34 percent on taxable income over $75,000. An additional tax of five percent is imposed on taxable income from $100,000-$335,000, a maximum of $11,750. A C corporation is not allowed a deduction for dividends distributed to shareholders. Thus, the income of profitable C corporations may be subject to a form of double taxation: The income of a C corporation that is distributed to shareholders is subject to income taxation at both the corporation *and* the individual levels.

Example 11-2. The income of *X* Corp. last year was subject to an effective federal income tax rate of 34%. Thus, *X* Corp. paid $34 on every $100 of taxable income. Later *X* Corp. paid a cash dividend to its shareholders. A dividend of $66 was to be paid to an individual shareholder, *A,* whose income was subject to a marginal income tax rate of 31%. Accordingly *A* paid a tax of $20.46 with respect to the dividend. Thus, a total tax of almost 55% was paid on the corporation's $100 of taxable income.

A form of double taxation may result if *X* Corp. retains its earnings because the increase in value will result in a capital gain when *A* sells the shares of *X* Corp. Of course, if *A* holds the shares until death, the basis in the shares will be stepped up to their federal estate tax value without the imposition of any income or gains tax.

In contrast to the nondeductibility of dividend distributions, a corporation is entitled to a deduction for interest paid on indebtedness. Not surprisingly the IRS and taxpayers frequently clash over whether a particular arrangement is debt or a species of stock.

The amount taxed to a family C corporation is reduced to the extent salaries are paid to employee-shareholders. The income tax liability of a profitable corporation is also reduced by the wide range of fringe benefits that are deductible by the corporation, but are not currently taxable to the employees. They range from contributions to qualified retirement plans (which is generally the most important benefit) to payment of the cost of health and group life insurance coverage to the extent of $50,000 and club dues and membership fees. In contrast, fringe benefits for shareholders of S corporations are generally not deductible by the corporation. §1372. When all is said and done, the present income tax law discourages the use of ordinary business corporations.

Clients must also recognize that earnings of a C corporation may be impossible to withdraw for the benefit of the shareholders without attracting income tax liabilities (*i.e.,* virtually any distribution is taxable as a dividend if the corporation has any accumulated earnings and profits). This is not a problem for newly formed S corporations, which will have no accumulated income. While most assets can be transferred to a corporation tax-free under §351, distributions from a C corporation to the shareholders are usually treated as dividends, subject to taxation as ordinary income. Under the *General Utilities* doctrine, which was repealed by the 1986 Act, a corporation generally did not recognize gain or loss when appreciated property was distributed to shareholders in a partial or total liquidation. *See General Utilities & Operating Co. v. Helvering,* 296 U.S. 200 (1935). Now, under §311(b), a corporation recognizes gain when appreciated property is distributed to a shareholder. Paraphrasing a popular epigram: Incorporate in haste; repent at leisure.

§11.4. Subchapter S Corporations

Most new family corporations elect to be taxed under Subchapter S, §§1361-1379, under which a domestic corporation with only one class of stock and 35 or fewer shareholders is not taxed as a corporation. In effect an S corporation is treated as a conduit, much like a partnership, through which the income and losses flow to the shareholders on a current basis. Under §1366(b) the character of income, loss, deduction, or credit is passed through to the shareholder. More complicated rules apply to corporations that shift from the status of a regular corporation to S corporation status, including ones that did so during the transition period following the 1986 Act.

For purposes of determining the number of shareholders, a "husband and wife (and their estates) shall be treated as 1 shareholder." §1361(c)(1). This rule is similar to the ones applicable for purposes of determining qualification under §§303 and 6166. In general, §1361(b) bars an S corporation from having any foreign or institutional shareholders. However, an estate may be a shareholder during the period required for administration of the estate, §1361(b)(1)(b), including the period the estate tax is deferred under §6166. Rev. Rul. 76-23, 1976-1 C.B. 264 (involving the predecessor of §6166).

Voting trusts, grantor trusts, and qualified Subchapter S trusts (QSSTs) may also be shareholders. §1361(c), (d). *See* §10.4.14. As explained in §10.32-10.32.2, a trust may purposefully be made "defective" under the grantor trust rules for the purpose of causing the grantor to be treated as the owner and taxed on all of the income of the trust. Such a grantor trust may be a shareholder in an S corporation although the trust does not meet the requirements of a QSST. For example, so long as the trust is treated as a grantor trust it may have multiple shareholders. Of course, if the trust ceases to be a grantor trust the S election will terminate after a period of time, §1361(c)(2)(A)(ii), (iii), unless the trust becomes a QSST. Under §1361(d) a QSST is a trust which requires that (1) the income beneficiary be the only beneficiary for his or her lifetime, (2) any principal that is distributed during the lifetime of the income beneficiary may only be distributed to him or her, (3) the income interest terminates when the income beneficiary dies or the trust earlier terminates, and (4) if the trust terminates during the lifetime of the income beneficiary, all of the trust assets must be distributed to the beneficiary. Note that the requirements of a QTIP and a QSST are consistent. That is, a QTIP can be drafted to meet the requirements of a QSST. Thus, an inactive spouse may leave stock in an S corporation to a QTIP trust for the benefit of the surviving spouse who is active in the business.

At base, an S corporation combines the attributes of a partnership with the limited liability and greater legal certainty of the corporate legal form. Under §1372 an S corporation is treated like a partnership for purposes of the income tax treatment of employee fringe benefits. Thus, an owner of two percent or more of the stock of an S corporation cannot exclude from income the corporation's payment of life, accident, and health insurance and employer-provided meals and lodging. There are, however, important differences between S corporations and partnerships. Among them are the limited character and number of shareholders an S corporation may have and the requirement that it have only one class of stock. In contrast, a partnership can have an unlimited number of members of varying types (*e.g.,* estates, trusts, and other corporations). In addition, partners can have differing interests in income and capital.

§11.4.1. One Class of Stock

Although an S corporation can have only one class of stock, it is not "treated as having more than 1 class of stock solely because there are differences in voting rights among the shares of common stock." §1361(c)(4); Prop. Reg. §1.1361-1(*l*)1. This rule allows an S corporation to be structured in a way that allows a parent to retain voting control while giving a majority of the common stock to family members or charities. The retention of voting stock does not subject the transferred nonvoting stock to inclusion under §2036(b). Likewise, bona fide stock purchase or redemption agreements are generally disregarded. Prop. Reg. §1.1361-1(*l*)(2)(iii). Also, note that the valuation rules of §2701 do not apply if the retained and the transferred interests are of the same class of equity. §2701(a)(2)(B).

Straight Debt. Shareholders or others may make loans to an S corporation without the indebtedness being treated as a second class of stock if the debt qualifies as "straight debt" under §1361(c)(5). Straight debt is defined as an unconditional written promise to pay a fixed amount on demand or on a specified date which is not convertible into stock, the interest rate is not contingent on profits, the borrower's discretion, or similar factors and the creditor is "an individual (other than a nonresident alien), an estate, or a trust" which is a permissible S corporation shareholder.

§11.4.2. Election to Be S Corporation

All of a corporation's shareholders must consent to make a Subchapter S election. §1362(a). An election is effective for the following taxable year except an election made in the first two and a half months of a taxable year is effective on the first day of the taxable year. §1362(b). Once an election is effective the income, losses, deductions, and credits of the corporation flow through to the shareholders automatically. §1366(b). The beneficiary of a QSST must consent to an election within two and a half months, §1361(d).

§11.4.3. Termination of S Corporation Status

A Subchapter S election may be terminated in three ways. First, a majority of the taxpayers may elect to revoke the status. §1362(d)(1). Second, S corporation status terminates automatically if the corporation ceases to qualify (*e.g.*, it issues a second class of stock or has more than 35 shareholders or an alien, estate, nonqualified trust, or corporation becomes a shareholder). §1362(d)(2). In addition termination will result if an S corporation with earnings and profits accumulated during the time it was a C corporation has excess passive income. §1362(d)(3). By definition a newly-formed S corporation is not subject to termination under this provision. A buy-sell agreement can be drafted to prevent termination of the election through the issuance of a second class of stock or the addition of too many shareholders to an S corporation or the addition of nonqualifying shareholders (*e.g.*, a trust that is not eligible to be a shareholder).

§11.4.4. Income, Distributions, and Basis

A shareholder of an S corporation is treated as having received a proportionate share of an S corporation's income for the taxable year whether or not actually distributed. Accordingly, a shareholder may be taxed on income he or she did not actually receive. To the extent the current income is not distributed to a shareholder, the matter is adjusted by increasing the shareholder's basis in the S corporation stock. In particular, under §1367(a)(1) a shareholder's basis in the stock of an S corporation is increased by the amount of income that is taxed to the shareholder under §1366. Consistently, a shareholder's basis is reduced, but not below zero, by the amount of distributions. §1367(a)(2)(A). However, under §1368(b)(2) a distribution in excess of basis is treated "as gain from the sale or exchange of property."

Example 11-3. *Y* contributed $10,000 to *Y* Corp., in exchange for which *Y* received all of its stock. *Y* Corp. made a timely election to be treated as an *S* corporation, to which *Y* consented as required by §1362(a). In its first year of operation *Y* Corp. had earnings of $1,000 which were not distributed to *Y*. *Y* was required to report the earnings of *Y* Corp. as income. However, as the earnings were not distributed *Y*'s basis was increased by an equal amount, to $11,000.

As indicated above, losses and deductions also pass through to shareholders on a current basis. The amount of losses and deductions which flow through to a shareholder reduce the basis in the S corporation stock. However, a shareholder's basis cannot be reduced below zero. §1366(d).

> **Example 11-4.** The facts are the same as in Example 11-3, *supra.* In its second year of operation *Y* Corp. had deductions of $2,000, but no earnings and made no distributions to *Y*. The deductions were passed through and reported by *Y*. The deductions reduce *Y*'s basis by $2,000 to $9,000.

Except as otherwise provided, the rules of Subchapter C apply to S corporations and their shareholders. §1371(a). Applying the rules of Subchapter C, distributions of appreciated property generate gain to the S corporation as sales or exchanges which is taxed to the shareholders. §311(b). The gain flows through to the shareholder, who must report it as income. The distribution has no effect on the basis of the shareholder — while the shareholder's basis is increased in the amount of the gain, it is reduced an equivalent amount on account of the distribution. §1367(a).

> **Example 11-5.** The facts are the same as in Example 11-3, *supra.* In its third year of operation *Y* Corp. distributed property to *Y* which had a basis of $2,000 and a fair market value of $3,000. *Y* Corp. has a gain of $1,000 as a result of the distribution, which is passed along to *Y*. Accordingly, *Y* is taxed on the $1,000 gain. *Y*'s basis is reduced by a net of $2,000 on account of the distribution. (While *Y*'s basis is increased by $1,000 on account as a result of *Y* being taxed on the gain, *Y*'s basis is reduced by $3,000 because of the distribution.)

§11.4.5. Pre-1987 S Corporation Strategy

Prior to 1987, when the regular corporate income tax rates were lower than individual income tax rates, taxpayers often elected to claim S corporation status in the early years of a corporation's existence in order to give the shareholders the current income tax benefit of its losses. If the corporation became profitable the shareholders typically shifted status from an S corporation to a C corporation in order to shelter the income in the corporation. With the inversion of the income tax rates this type of shift is no longer being made.

§11.5. Partnerships

A general or limited partnership is frequently used to operate closely-held businesses. As indicated above, beginning in 1986 the inversion of the personal and corporate tax rates made the use of partnerships or S corporations more attractive. In gross terms a limited partnership can emulate the income tax consequences of an S corporation. However, in some respects the partnership form is preferred. In particular, a partnership can have more than 35 partners, the capital interests of the partners and their rights to receive income can vary (*i.e.,* there can be more than one type of partnership equity interest), and a partnership may include nonresident aliens and other persons who may not be shareholders in S corporations. Partnerships are also not subject to the special taxes on personal holding company income, §§541-547, the tax on unreasonable accumulation of earnings, §§531-537, and the taint that attaches to some corporate stock by reason of §§305 and 306.

The general income tax treatment of a partnership as a conduit means that the partners and not the entity bear the tax consequences. Within this context it is important to bear in mind the flexibility of partnerships in providing for management and, within the limits of §704, in allocating items of income, loss, credit, and deduction. Thus, a partnership may consist of two classes of interests: a preferred ("senior") interest and an ordinary ("junior") interest. The senior interest is typically entitled to a specified annual payment, the right to participate in income above a certain annual level, and a fixed preference upon liquidation. The junior interest is usually entitled to a participation in income after the senior preference is satisfied and to the remainder of the assets upon liquidation. Management responsibilities may be assigned to the holders of the senior interests, which they would be required to exercise in a fiduciary capacity. Under *United States v. Byrum,* 408 U.S. 125 (1972), there is little risk that any junior interests that had been transferred by the managing partners would be included in the managing partners' estates under §2036(a). Regulations issued under §704 do impose some restrictions on allocations, particularly in the case of family partnerships. *See* Reg. §1.704-1(e).

Although the valuation rules of §2701 may increase the gift tax cost, in some circumstances the partnership form remains an attractive vehicle for achieving a tax freeze. For example, a multiclass partnership, with future appreciation allocated to the holders of the junior partnership interests, might be used in connection with the initial formation of a partnership that had a potential for considerable appreciation in value. Likewise, an existing partnership that generated substantial earnings might be recapitalized with the senior family members receiving interests that carried fixed rights to periodic payments that met the requirements of qualified payments under §2701(c)(3).

B. BUY-SELL AGREEMENTS

§11.6. Overview

This part reviews the basic tax and nontax considerations involved in drafting buy-sell agreements that either obligate the corporation to purchase a deceased or retiring owner's stock or partnership interest (an "entity-purchase" agreement) or obligate the other owners to purchase his or her interest (a "cross-purchase" agreement). The pros and cons of the two types of agreements are reviewed in §11.8. Either form of agreement can serve important nontax needs of shareholders in closely-held businesses. In addition, a properly drafted agreement can establish the value of a deceased decedent's stock or partnership interest, which may limit the liability for the payment of state and federal death taxes. The worst case occurs if an agreement fixes a relatively low value on a decedent's interest for purposes of the agreement and a much higher value is placed on the interest for federal estate tax purposes.

Pre-§2703 Rules. Prior to the October 9, 1990 effective date of §2703, the extent to which a buy-sell agreement would fix the value of an interest in a closely-held business for estate tax purposes was determined under §20.2031-2(h).

> Another person may hold an option or a contract to purchase securities owned by a decedent at the time of his death. The effect, if any, that is given to the option or contract price in determining the value of the securities for estate tax purposes depends upon the circumstances of the particular case. Little weight will be accorded a price contained in an option or contract under which the decedent is free to dispose of the underlying securities at any price he chooses during his lifetime. Such is the effect, for example, of an agreement on the part of a shareholder to purchase whatever shares of stock the decedent may own at the time of his death. Even if the decedent is not free to dispose of the underlying securities at other than the option or contract price, such price will be disregarded in determining the value of the securities unless it is determined under the circumstances of the particular case that the agreement represents a bona fide business arrangement and not a device to pass the decedent's shares to the natural objects of his bounty for less than an adequate and full consideration in money or money's worth. Reg. §20.2031-2(h).

Broken down into its constituent elements, the Regulation provides the value of a decedent's interest established by an option or agreement will be recognized if the option or agreement:

1. Fixed the price of the shares directly or by way of a formula;
2. Restricted the decedent's power to dispose of the interest during his or her lifetime;
3. Obligated the decedent's successors to sell the shares for that price following his or her death;
4. Was a bona fide business arrangement; and,
5. Was not merely a device for passing the interest to the natural objects of the decedent's bounty for less than an adequate and full consideration.

Whether or not the first three requirements are satisfied can be determined from the face of an option or agreement. In contrast, the latter two elements require the consideration of other factors.

Regulation §20.2031-2(h) builds on a prior published ruling that held that an agreement was effective to fix the value of the shares if (1) it was a bona fide business arrangement and (2) either required the corporation or the other shareholders to purchase the decedent's shares *or* gave the corporation or the other shareholders the option to purchase the shares. Rev. Rul. 157, 1953-2 C.B. 255.

No doubt Reg. §20.2031-2(h) will continue to apply to agreements entered into *prior* to October 9, 1990 *and* to agreements that are not subject to §2703. Presumably it will also apply to restrictions subject to §2703 except to the extent it was affected by §2703. Thus, the Regulation and related authorities provide valuable guidance regarding the effect that will be given to future agreements. The legislative history indicates that the new provisions were otherwise not intended to change the requirements for giving recognition to a buy-sell agreement. *See* S. Rep. No. 3209, 101st Cong., 2d Sess. (1990), *reprinted in* 136 Cong. Rec. S15629, S15683 (1990). For example, it leaves intact present rules requiring that an agreement have lifetime restrictions in order to be binding on death. *E.g.,* LR 8634004 (agreement which did not specify price at which decedent would be allowed to sell stock to new employees is not binding for federal estate tax purposes). On the positive side, the IRS and courts should continue to recognize that various purposes, including continued family control of a corporation, are bona fide business purposes for having a buy-sell agreement.

The IRS will not recognize a price fixed by an agreement that does not have a bona fide business purpose. LR 8710004 (TAM) (redemption agreements between uncle and two nephews to whom he had given shares of stock in two corporations were not devices for transferring interests in the corporations to his nephews for less than adequate and full consideration and were not bona fide business arrangements). *See also St. Louis County Bank v. United States,* 674 F.2d 1207 (8th Cir.) (agreement must be bona fide business arrangement *than* not a device for transferring value to family members for less than full consideration).

Section 2703. Options, agreements, and other restrictions affecting the valuation or disposition of property that are entered into or substantially modified *after* October 8, 1990 are subject to the provisions of §2703. Act §11602(e)(1)(A)(ii). Under §2703 options, agreements to acquire property or ones restricting the right to sell or use property (the "provision") will be recognized for estate, gift, and generation-skipping transfer tax purposes only if they satisfy the tripartite test of §2703(b):

1. It is a bona fide business arrangement;
2. It is not a device to transfer property to members of the decedent's family for less than full and adequate consideration; and
3. Its terms are comparable to similar arrangements entered into by persons in an arms' length transaction.

The first two requirements are essentially restatements of the substantive requirements of Reg. §20.2031-2(h). They should be construed and applied in light of the Regulation and related authorities. They adopt the reasoning of *St. Louis County Bank,* which requires that an agreement be a bona fide business arrangement *and* not be a device to transfer wealth.

The third requirement of §2703 is a new one. The rigor of the requirement is relaxed to some extent by the report of the Conference Committee on the 1990 Act, which states that,

> The conferees do not intend the provision governing buy-sell agreements to disregard such an agreement merely because its terms differ from those used by another similarly situated company. The conferees recognize that general business practice may recognize more than one valuation methodology, even within the same industry. In such situations, one of several generally accepted methodologies may satisfy the standard contained in the conference agreement. H. Conf. Rep. No. 101-964, 101 Cong. 2d Sess. 1137 (1990).

Reflecting that intention the Proposed Regulations provide that "A right or restriction is comparable to similar arrangements entered into by persons in an arms' length transaction if the right or restriction is one that *could have been obtained in a fair bargain among unrelated parties in the same business dealing with each other at arm's length.*" Prop. Reg. §25.2703-1(b)(4)(i) (emphasis added). In making the latter determination, consideration will be given to factors including "the expected term of the agreement, the current fair market value of the property, anticipated changes in value during the term of the arrangement, and the adequacy of any consideration given in exchange for the rights granted." Id.

According to the Senate Committee Report, "the bill does not otherwise alter the requirements for giving weight to a buy-sell agreement. For example, it leaves intact present law rules requiring that an agreement have lifetime restrictions in order to be binding on death." S. Rep. No. 3209, *supra,* at S15683.

Safe Harbor for Agreements Among Unrelated Parties. The Regulations create a safe harbor for agreements among parties, if a majority of the interests are held by unrelated parties. In particular, under Reg. §25.2703-1(b)(3), a right or restriction is considered to meet all three requirements if "more than 50 percent by value of the property subject to the right or restriction is owned directly or indirectly . . . by individuals who are not members of the transferor's family."

Substantial Modification. Changes in the terms of rights or restrictions established under options, articles, buy-sell agreements, and other arrangements entered into prior to October 9, 1990, should be made in light of the provisions of §2703. A substantial modification of a preexisting right or restriction will subject it to the terms of §2703. Under the Regulations a right or restriction is substantially modified if there is a discretionary modification of the right or restriction other than a de minimis one. A mandatory change in value is not treated as a subsequent modification. Importantly, "the addition of any family member as a party to a right or restriction is considered a substantial modification" unless the addition is mandatory or the added family member is assigned to a generation no lower than the lowest generation of the persons who are already parties to the right or restriction. Reg. §25.2703-1(c). A gift of an interest to a child (a discretionary transfer) as a result of which the child must become a party to a buy-sell agreement may be a substantial modification — at least to the extent of the interests affected by the child's joinder. Id. In contrast, the gift of an interest to the donor's spouse — a person in the same generational level — is not "a substantial modification of the right or restriction." Reg. §25.2703(d), example 2.

§11.7. Nontax Considerations

The interests of all owners are protected by an agreement that provides a fair method of valuing the stock of a deceased, disabled, or terminated party. Without such an agreement a disabled or terminated owner or the family of a deceased minority owner may lack the bargaining power necessary to negotiate a satisfactory agreement with the business or the remaining owners for the disposition of the decedent's interest. Of course, an agreement also provides important protection for the remaining owners. Thus, an agreement can prevent the transfer of interests to unwanted or hostile outsiders. Restrictions on transfers are important in the case of an S corporation in order to prevent the corporation from exceeding the permissible number of shareholders (35) and from adding ineligible shareholders such as corporations, nonresident aliens, or unqualified trusts. In addition, an agreement might also be used to obligate the shareholders to continue the S election. The IRS long ago recognized that entry into a restrictive agreement does not constitute a second class of stock that would terminate an S election. Rev. Rul. 73-611, 1973-2 C.B. 312. Finally, under Prop. Reg. §1.1361-1(*l*)(2)(iii) a bona fide buy-sell agreement is generally disregarded in determining whether there is more than one class of stock.

The preparation of an agreement is also beneficial in that it requires the parties to consider the long-term plans for the business and the need to generate funds with which to purchase the interest of a deceased shareholder. As indicated below, funds are typically provided either by insurance on the lives of owners or by earnings of the business that are accumulated in another form. In any case, the liquidity crunch is eased somewhat if the agreement permits an installment purchase of a deceased owner's interest.

§11.8. Entity Purchase or Cross-Purchase?

The type of agreement to be used in any given case depends upon the preference of the parties and a number of tax and nontax factors. Particular care must be exercised in choosing the type of agreement where the ownership of stock and control of the corporation is balanced between two or more groups. In such a case a redemption of a decedent's shares might disrupt the balance more than the pro rata purchase of the decedent's shares by the remaining stockholders. Of course, a preexisting balance might also be upset if the surviving shareholders purchase pro rata interests in the decedent's shares. Note that the IRS would probably not accept a valuation made under an agreement that provided for the sale of shares only to a decedent's nuclear family to the exclusion of other shareholders. Such an agreement would be vulnerable to attack as an effort to shift the stock to the natural objects of the decedent's bounty at a bargain price. From the tax viewpoint, perhaps the greatest flexibility is provided if the corporation and the other shareholders successively have the right to purchase the shares of a deceased shareholder.

A buy-sell agreement is also useful to close a partnership's tax year. In the absence of an agreement the tax year does not terminate on the death of a partner. §706(c)(1). Closing the tax year at the time of a partner's death, which ends the decedent's final income tax year, can be helpful for income tax purposes. The tax year terminates as to a deceased partner "when such partner's interest (held by his estate or other successor) is liquidated or sold or exchanged. . . ." Reg. §1.706-1(c)(2).

Entity Purchase. Some planners prefer an entity-purchase agreement because a purchase by the business (redemption of the stock or liquidation of a partner's interest) is simpler and more easily accomplished than the purchase of the decedent's interest by a number of other owners under a cross-purchase agreement. Also, purchase of insurance or other provision for funding by an entity (the business) may be surer and more easily arranged and maintained than purchases by several owners. However, for C corporations life insurance has significant alternative minimum tax (AMT) implications. The AMT does not apply to S corporations. First, the annual internal build-up in value of life insurance is taken into account in determining adjusted current earnings. §56(g)(4)(B)(ii). Second, the excess of death benefits over the basis in the policy is also included in adjusted current earnings. Reg. §1.56(g)-1(c)(5)(v). From the shareholder's basis perspective, a redemption of the stock of a deceased shareholder may be less attractive. A redemption does not increase the bases of the interests of the surviving owners. However, basis is increased by the payment of premiums and on the receipt of proceeds — but both increases should not be allowed. The increase in basis resulting from a cross purchase can be an important factor if the surviving owners intend to sell their interests. In addition, insurance proceeds paid to a business may be depleted by claims of creditors and other obligations. On the other hand, it may be more economical for a business to purchase a single policy of insurance on the life of each owner than it would be for each owner to purchase a pro rata amount of insurance on the life of each other owner. Recall in this connection that neither the corporation nor the shareholders is able to deduct the premiums on the insurance for income tax purposes. *See* §6.56.

Insurance proceeds received by the business are not generally includible in the estate of the insured shareholder or partner. However, the proceeds may be includible in unusual circumstances. For example, LR 8943082 held that insurance proceeds in excess of the amount required to purchase the decedent's stock were includible because they were payable to a beneficiary designated by the insured, to his spouse, or to his estate. In LR 8943082 the IRS reasoned that the "excess" proceeds were includible under §2038 because the decedent, by executing the buy-sell agreement, had made a transfer of an interest in the insurance but retained the right to control the disposition of the "excess" proceeds. For income tax purposes LR 8943082 held that the excess proceeds were taxable as an employee benefit under §101(b) except to the extent of $5,000.

Unless life insurance is used as a funding mechanism there is perhaps a greater risk that when an owner dies the corporation will lack sufficient surplus or other funds that the local corporate law allows to be used to redeem stock. However, if financing is required, it may be less expensive for a business to obtain the financing necessary to purchase a decedent's interest.

Payments in liquidation of a retiring or deceased partner's interest are treated as distributions that are categorized for income tax purposes according to §736. As explained in McKee, Nelson & Whitmire, Federal Taxation of Partnerships and Partners §22.01[4][b] (2d ed. 1990), "All payments that are not §736(b) payments are §736(a) payments." Under §736(b) distributions made in exchange for the retired or deceased partner's interest in partnership property, other than unrealized receivables and goodwill, result in capital gain or loss. *See* Reg. §1.736-1(b). A reasonable payment made with respect to a partner's share of goodwill is within the scope of §736(b) to the extent provided in an agreement. Reg. §1.736-1(b)(3). In contrast, distributions of partnership income or guaranteed payments are ordinary income as provided in §736(a). *See* Reg. §1.736-1(a)(4). The latter types of payments either reduce the taxable income attributable to the remaining partners or are deductible by the partnership under §162(a). Id. The remaining partners generally benefit to the extent distributions are subject to §736(a).

Cross-Purchase. If a decedent's interest in a corporation or partnership is sold to the remaining owners, the transaction is treated as a sale or exchange. A sale may result in gain or loss to the estate based upon the difference between the selling price and the estate's basis in the stock or partnership interest. However, little, if any, gain or loss usually results from such a sale because the price fixed in the buy-sell agreement will usually determine the basis of the interest in the decedent's estate and the sale. The gain, if any, on the sale of a decedent's interest is ordinarily capital gain. However, in the case of a partnership, any gain attributable to unrealized receivables and substantially appreciated inventory of a partnership is not classified as capital gain. §§741, 751(a). The remaining partners usually benefit if a substantial portion of the sale price is allocated to unrealized receivables and substantially appreciated inventory, which reduces their future ordinary income.

The basis of the purchasers of a decedent's interest is determined by reference to the sale price. Under §742 the cost of a purchased interest in a partnership is its basis. Reg. §1.742-1. The cross-purchase of a decedent's interest in a corporation or partnership is generally attractive because it increases the overall bases of the purchasers. In the case of an S corporation the increased bases will shelter more distributions from taxation under §1368 and decrease the amount of gain that would be realized on a sale of the stock. In contrast, an entity purchase (redemption) does not increase the bases of the surviving shareholders.

In the case of a C corporation the cost of cross-owned insurance is lower if the funds necessary to support the agreement are made available to the shareholders as salaries, which are deductible by the corporation. Salaries, which are only subject to taxation at the shareholder level, are preferable to dividends, which are diluted by income taxes at the corporate *and* shareholder levels. In some cases split-dollar insurance that is provided to shareholder-employees as additional compensation produces the same overall result as a salary increase. *See* §6.71 for a discussion of split-dollar insurance.

Shifting from an Entity- to a Cross-Purchase Agreement. Changes in the tax rules, including the inclusion of insurance proceeds in the adjusted current earnings of a C corporation for AMT purposes, has led some corporations to shift from an entity to a cross-purchase form of agreement. The potential application of the transfer for value rule, which would cause the insurance proceeds to be included in the income of the recipient(s), §101(a)(2), is a serious concern if the corporation assigns existing policies to the shareholders. *Monroe v. Patterson,* 197 F. Supp. 146 (N.D. Ala. 1961). The transfer for value rule is discussed in detail at §6.53. It is important to note that the transfer for value rule does not apply to transfers that are made to the insured, to a partner of the insured, to a partnership in which the insured is a partner, or to a corporation in which the insured is a shareholder or officer. §101(a)(2)(B). Thus, the transfer for value rule does not apply to policies that were distributed by a corporation to its shareholders who were partners in a bona fide partnership. LR 9045004; LR 9012063. The distribution of an existing policy to the insured shareholder is exempt from the transfer for value rule. While LR 8906034 held that the transfer for value rule would not apply if the policy were subsequently transferred by gift to another shareholder, §101(a)(2)(A), it noted that the outcome depended upon a determination that the insured's subsequent transfer of the policy was a gift, which was a question of fact on which the ruling expressed no opinion. Letter Ruling 8906034 offers little comfort because the outcome hinges on a factual determination which the IRS would probably contest. Under the approach taken in *Monroe v. Patterson,* a court might conclude that the subsequent transfer was a transfer for value and not a gift which involved a carryover of the donor's basis.

§11.9. Redemptions by C Corporations

A redemption by a C corporation is taxed as a dividend to the distributee except to the extent the redemption is treated as a sale or exchange under §303 or one of the exceptions of §302(b). *See* §§11.15-11.24. If the redemption is treated as a sale or exchange, the distributee usually recognizes little gain, if any, because the decedent's death caused the basis of the shares to be adjusted under §1014 (*i.e.,* the basis of the shares is changed to their federal estate tax value in the decedent's estate). Of course, a distribution is not a dividend if the corporation has no earnings and profits. §316(a). However, if appreciated property is distributed, the corporation will recognize gain under §311(b), which will increase its earnings and profits. A distribution treated as a dividend reduces the corporation's earnings and profits. §312(a). On the other hand, a redemption treated as an exchange reduces earnings and profits only to the extent of a ratable share of the corporation's earnings and profits. §312(n)(7).

> **Example 11-6.** When *X* died in 1992 she owned 1,000 shares of *X* Corp. common stock that were worth $1,000,000 for federal estate tax purposes. *X* Corp. is a C corporation with substantial accumulated earnings and profits. Her shares of *X* Corp. qualified for redemption under §303 to the extent of $500,000 (the sum of death taxes imposed by reason of her death and funeral and administration expenses for which deductions were allowable under §2053). *X* Corp. redeemed 500 shares of *X* Corp. stock from *X*'s estate in exchange for a payment of $500,000. Under §303 the payment by *X* Corp. is treated as a distribution in exchange for the stock and not as a dividend. Accordingly, *X*'s estate received no income and realized no capital gain as a result of the redemption. A redemption of the remainder of *X*'s shares would be treated as a distribution in the nature of a dividend unless it qualified for one of the exceptions of §302. As explained in §11.24.3, the distribution might qualify under §302(b)(3) as a complete termination of the shareholder's interest in *X* Corp.

§11.10. Redemptions by S Corporations

In determining the income tax consequences that result from redeeming a deceased shareholder's stock in an S corporation, the redemption is first classified under the C corporation rules as either a sale or exchange under §§302 or 303 or a distribution in the nature of a dividend. If the redemption is treated as a sale or exchange, the gain or loss of the redeeming shareholder is determined in the same way as in the case of a redemption by a C corporation: The gain or loss is determined according to the difference between the amount of the redemption proceeds and the redeeming shareholder's basis in the redeemed stock. Although such a redemption does not require the distributee to report any dividend income, it results in a proportionate reduction in the S corporation's accumulated adjustment account, §1368(e)(1)(B), and earnings and profits, if any, §1371(c)(2). If the corporation has earnings and profits, such a redemption benefits the remaining shareholders by reducing the corporation's earnings and profits, which will reduce the amount ultimately taxable to them.

The tax consequences of a redemption by an S corporation that does not qualify as a sale or exchange are determined under §1368. Under §1368(b), if the corporation has no earnings and profits the distribution is not included in the distributee's gross income to the extent of the distributee's adjusted basis in the stock (*i.e.,* basis is recovered first, tax-free). In this connection bear in mind that the basis in the stock will have been stepped up (or down) to its federal estate tax value by reason of the decedent's death. Any excess is treated as gain from the sale or exchange of property. If the corporation has accumulated earnings and profits, the redemption distribution is treated as a tax-free return of basis to the extent of the corporation's accumulated adjustments account, then as a dividend to the extent of the accumulated earnings and profits of the corporation, and finally, as a sale or exchange as to the remainder. §1368(c).

A redemption distribution made by an S corporation does not give rise to any gain unless appreciated property is distributed. The distribution of appreciated property causes the corporation to realize gain under §311(b). Under the conduit rules applicable to S corporations, the gain flows through to *all* shareholders, including the redeeming shareholder. However, the flow through of the gain is of limited significance to the redeeming shareholder, whose basis was stepped up by (1) the federal estate tax value in the decedent's estate *and* (2) the portion of the gain that flowed through as a result of the distribution of appreciated property. In effect, the gain that flows through to the redeeming shareholder is offset by the loss which results from the receipt of a redemption distribution worth less than the redeeming shareholder's basis.

Example 11-7. *T* owned half of the shares of *S* Corp. They had an estate tax value of $500,000. In redemption of *T*'s stock *S* Corp. distributed an asset which had a basis of $100,000 and a fair market value of $500,000. The distribution resulted in a gain of $400,000 to *S* Corp. Half of that gain ($200,000) flowed through to each of the shareholders. The unredeemed shareholder has a gain of $200,000. The flow through of the gain increased the basis of *T*'s estate in the stock to $700,000. The distribution of property worth $500,000 to *T*'s estate in redemption of the stock resulted in a loss of $200,000 ($700,000 − $500,000). The loss offset the gain of an equal amount that flowed through to the estate as a result of the distribution.

Under §1377(a)(2), if the interest of a shareholder is terminated during the taxable year, the remaining shareholders may elect to end the taxable year of the terminating shareholder on the date of the termination of his interest.

§11.11. VALUATION

> Certainly, an owner wants to avoid a situation where, upon his death, his successors are contractually bound to sell the business interest at the Agreement's price, while the tax authorities successfully ignore that price and use a higher value for tax purposes. Gorman, The Buy-Sell Agreement as a Dispositionary Device: Tax and Valuation Problems in Transferring Corporate, Partnership and Real Estate Interests at Death, N.Y.U., 34th Inst. Fed. Tax., 1591, 1594 (1976).

For tax and nontax reasons careful consideration must be given to the selection of a method for fixing the value of the shares that are subject to the agreement. Of course, under §2703 the agreement cannot be a device for transferring the property to the natural objects of a stockholder's bounty (*i.e.,* the shareholder's intestate successors under the local law) for less than full and adequate consideration. Fixing the purchase price at the current value of the shares without provision for future adjustment is usually inappropriate because changes in value will inevitably take place before a sale occurs. When the need to purchase the shares arises, the price set forth in the agreement may be either too high or too low. Thus, an agreement that establishes a current price should provide for periodic adjustments of the price and include a backup method of valuation should the parties fail to agree upon an adjustment in the future.

An agreement may provide for the value of the shares to be fixed by reference to a single factor, such as their book value or the capitalized earnings of the corporation. However, the use of a single factor is also inappropriate because it can distort the value of the shares. For example, in *St. Louis County Bank v. United States,* 674 F.2d 1207 (8th Cir. 1982), a formula based solely on a multiple of net earnings was fair at the time the agreement was entered into. However, the moving and transfer business was sold and the proceeds invested in rental real estate. Application of the formula to the new business produced a value of $0 for the decedent's interest, although it had a $200,000 book value. Some parties are content to leave the valuation to one or more appraisers named in the agreement or later to be designated by the parties. In any case, the agreement can provide for arbitration if a dispute arises. Often the best choice is to provide for valuation of the shares under a multifactor formula that takes into account factors such as the corporation's book value, its average earnings for the most recent three- to five-year period, and the price-earnings ratio of publicly traded corporations in the same line of business.

A requirement that the corporation or other shareholders purchase all of the shares of a deceased shareholder should be used with caution. Such a provision is particularly dangerous because the sale or other disposition of all of a decedent's shares will prevent the decedent's estate from deferring the time for payment of any portion of the estate tax under §6166. It will also accelerate the time for payment of any estate tax that had been deferred under §6166. *See* Part D, *infra.* Because of that problem, it may be desirable to limit the number of shares that must be sold at the outset. The limit might be based upon the maximum number of shares that could be disposed of without triggering an acceleration under §6166 or exceeding the amount redeemable under §303. Where appropriate, the corporation or the other shareholders could be given an option to purchase the remainder of the shares. A contract for the sale of the shares might be drawn in a way that attempts to fix the price of the shares to be sold without having the contract treated as a disposition of the shares for purposes of §6166. Such a contract should provide for transfer of the stock certificates at the specified future times, prior to which the seller would be entitled to vote the stock, receive the dividends, and so forth. Alternatively, the number of shares to be redeemed by a corporation with earnings or profits might be limited in order to avoid the risk that the redemption of all of a decedent's stock would cause part of the distribution to be taxed as a dividend. Thus, the agreement might limit the mandatory purchase to a number of shares that have a value equal to the maximum amount redeemable under §303 (*i.e.,* equal to the sum of the state and federal death taxes, and the funeral and administration expenses that are deductible under §2053). *See* §11.16. As explained below, the redemption of some shares is treated as a sale or exchange where the stock comprises more than 35 percent of the excess of the value of the decedent's gross estate over the amounts allowable as deductions under §§2053 and 2054. *See* §§11.17-11.18. Any excess distribution made in redemption of the stock will be taxed as a dividend under §301 unless it qualifies under one or more of the three exceptions created by §302(b). *See* §11.24. It may be difficult to fit within one of the exceptions where a family corporation is involved because of the application of the stock attribution rules of §318. The exceptions are discussed further in §11.24.1.

Buy-sell agreements that were applicable only upon the death or retirement of a party have generally not been effective to fix the value of the shares for gift tax purposes. Although the price fixed in an agreement may establish the price for the shares for nontax purposes, it will not be binding for gift tax purposes unless it gives the other parties the right to purchase the gifted shares. *See Commissioner v. McCann,* 146 F.2d 385 (2d Cir. 1944) (restrictive provision in by-laws); *Krauss v. United States,* 140 F.2d 510 (5th Cir. 1944) (restrictive provision in charter).

§11.12. FUNDING THE PURCHASE

Insurance on the lives of shareholders is often used to fund a buy-sell agreement because of its positive characteristics: liquidity, reliability, and general availability. Unfortunately, however, the exact amount required to fund a purchase may not be known until a shareholder dies and it becomes possible to value his or her shares under the agreement. The problem is more difficult if one or more of the shareholders is, or becomes, uninsurable. In some cases the corporation may establish a reserve for the purpose of funding the agreement, which could be invested in liquid assets other than cash value insurance. Of course, the alternative minimum tax problem described in §11.8 discourages the use of insurance owned by the corporation. Earnings accumulated in the year of a shareholder's death or thereafter are exempt from the accumulated earnings tax to the extent needed to redeem the decedent's stock, but not in excess of the maximum amount redeemable under §303. §537. Note that §537 does not insulate earnings retained in prior years from the reach of the accumulated earnings tax.

Maintaining the necessary number of insurance policies is usually simple enough when an entity purchase agreement is involved and the policies are owned by the corporation or partnership. In such a case, the business ordinarily acquires and owns one policy on the life of each shareholder. Under §264(a) the business is not allowed a deduction for premiums paid on such policies. The insurance proceeds received by the business are not subject to the income tax. §101(a).

The value of the insurance on a shareholder's life that is payable to the corporation is not directly includible in his or her gross estate. Under Reg. §20.2042-1(c)(6), if the proceeds are paid to the corporation, the corporation's incidents of ownership are not attributed to the sole or controlling shareholder. *See* Rev. Rul. 82-85, 1982-1 C.B. 137. *See also* §6.28. Instead, the proceeds received by the corporation may be reflected in the value of the decedent's interest in the corporation. However, the value of the decedent's interest should be controlled by the agreement, which is not necessarily related to the amount of the insurance proceeds. If the insurance is taken into account in valuing the stock in the corporation, the decedent's shares may be worth more, thereby increasing the amount to be received by the decedent's successors. Also, the value of the decedent's shares, including a proportionate share of the insurance proceeds, may be discounted because of a lack of marketability.

The proceeds of insurance owned by and payable to a partnership should not be directly or indirectly included in the estate of a deceased insured partner. In order to achieve this result the individual partners should not hold any incidents of ownership over the policies which might require inclusion under §2042. The receipt of the proceeds will not affect the valuation of the decedent's interest in the partnership if its value is effectively fixed in a binding buy-sell agreement. Again, the proceeds should not be included in the income of the partnership. §101(a).

Where a cross-purchase agreement is involved, each owner must own a policy on the life of each other owner. An almost unmanageable number of policies is required if there are more than three or four owners. For example, 30 policies of insurance are required if there are six owners (each owner must own policies on the lives of the other five). The problem is exacerbated if the owners own unequal interests in the business, which requires them to own policies of varying amounts. Complications may also arise in disposing of policies held by a deceased owner on the lives of the survivors. A sale of policies to the surviving partners would fall within an exception to the transfer for value rule. §101(a)(2)(B). However, a sale of policies the decedent owned on the surviving shareholders is not excepted from the transfer for value rule only for transfers to the persons insured. Accordingly, the proceeds of the policies may be subject to taxation under §101(a)(2). *See* §6.53. In general, an owner should avoid purchasing a policy on his or her own life, which would subject the entire proceeds to the estate tax. The payment of premiums on individually-owned policies on the lives of other owners is not deductible for income tax purposes. If a corporation pays the premiums on policies owned by the shareholders, they will be considered to have received a constructive dividend unless they are employees and the premium payments are treated as additional compensation.

§11.12.1. Installment Payments

A deceased shareholder's stock may be redeemed on the installment basis. *See, e.g.,* LR 8043030. The immediate cash requirements of a redemption are reduced if the agreement provides for payment of the purchase price in installments or if a deceased shareholder's successors are willing to sell the decedent's stock on that basis. *See* LR 7941037. The installment payment of the purchase price could also reduce the tax cost to the redeeming shareholder, which could be very important if the redemption does not qualify as a sale or exchange of the stock (*i.e.,* if the proceeds were taxed as dividends). The circumstances in which an installment sale is feasible depend upon the financial stability of the company and the shareholders, the relationships between the shareholders, and the needs of the decedent's successors. In some cases the sellers may feel it is necessary to obtain some further assurance that payments will be made when due, such as a guarantee by individual shareholders or others. An installment sale must also be planned carefully in light of the tax circumstances of the decedent's estate. Consideration must be given to the fact that an installment sale would ordinarily involve a disposition of the decedent's stock that could accelerate the time for payment of any estate tax deferred under §6166. *See* §11.29. Finally, interest will be imputed on the unpaid balance unless the purchaser pays at least the rate required by §483 or the original issue discount rules of §§1271-1275. *See* §9.6.5.

§11.12.2. Medium of Payment

In some cases the parties do not take any steps to provide that the required funds will be available upon the death of a shareholder. Instead, they are content to rely upon the availability of borrowed funds or the distribution of appreciated assets in exchange for the shares. However, neither of those methods is sufficiently reliable in most cases. It may be impossible or very expensive to borrow the necessary funds under the circumstances that exist at the time of a shareholder's death. The distribution of appreciated property in redemption of a decedent's stock is generally not attractive because it requires the corporation to recognize gain. §311(b).

§11.12.3. Accumulated Earnings Tax

The retention of earnings by a C corporation for the purpose of funding an entity purchase agreement may be subject to the tax on unreasonable accumulated earnings. *See* §§531-537. The risk exists whether or not the earnings are invested in insurance on the lives of the shareholders. *See* Rudolph, Stock Redemptions and the Accumulated Earnings Tax — An Update, 4 J. Corp. Tax. 101 (1977). The tax is imposed at a flat rate of 28 percent of accumulated taxable income. §531. However, an operating company may accumulate $250,000 ($150,000 in the case of professional service corporations) without being subject to the tax. §535(c)(2). Importantly, the tax only applies if the accumulation was made to avoid the income tax with respect to the shareholders. §532(a). An S corporation (the income of which flows through to its shareholders) is normally not concerned with the accumulated earnings tax. However, the tax might come into play if a C corporation with unreasonable accumulated earnings elected to be treated as an S corporation.

A corporation may accumulate earnings for the purpose of redeeming a decedent's shares under §303, provided the accumulations take place in the year of the shareholder's death or later. §537(b)(1). Accumulations made prior to the shareholder's death may be subject to the tax. In most cases the tax should not apply, however, because an accumulation of earnings for the purpose of funding a buy-sell agreement is within the reasonable needs of the corporation. Also, such accumulations are not generally made in order to permit the shareholders to avoid income taxation.

§11.13. Ethical Considerations

A lawyer who advises the owners of a business regarding the preparation of a buy-sell agreement must recognize the potential for conflicts of interest between them. Accordingly, the lawyer should explain to them at the outset the desirability of having independent counsel and the difficulty of representing any of them adequately to the extent their interests conflict. *See* §1.14. Independent counsel should also be recommended in connection with a corporate recapitalization or the formation or restructuring of a partnership. *See* Part E, *infra.* The lawyer can represent more than one party if they all consent to the multiple representation and it is clear that the lawyer can represent them without adversely affecting their interests. *See* MRPCs 1.7(b) and 2.2.

§11.14. Community Property Aspects

Additional factors must be taken into account where the shares are community property, including the events which will trigger a sale or redemption. For example, the parties may wish to provide for the sale of all of the stock belonging to a husband and wife upon the death of the spouse who is active in the business. A sale or redemption of the stock will serve the tax and nontax interests of the other shareholders and of the surviving spouse. The other shareholders generally prefer to eliminate the surviving spouse as a shareholder, who most often prefers to be cashed out rather than "locked in." A properly drawn agreement will fix the estate tax value of the stock, which may be important. Of course, the immediate estate tax concerns are ameliorated if the decedent's interest in the stock passes in a way that qualifies for the marital deduction.

A husband and wife and the other shareholders might not want to require the sale of the stock upon the death of a spouse who is not active in the business. Such a sale could deprive the surviving active spouse of important control and equity interests in the business.

The estate tax valuation of the stock is not fixed by a buy-sell agreement unless the stock is subject to a binding obligation to sell. As noted above, a husband and wife will usually want to make the marital deduction available upon the death of either in order to defer the payment of estate tax until the death of the surviving spouse. For example, they may wish to provide for a QTIP trust, which allows the executor to elect the extent to which the marital deduction will be claimed. *See* §5.23. In any case they will want to preserve the value of a deceased spouse's unified credit. Accordingly, if it is consistent with the couple's overall plans, the will of the inactive spouse should dispose of his or her interest in the stock in a way that will not inadvertently subject it to estate taxation again upon the death of the active spouse. Such a disposition is most important where their stock taken together represents control of the corporation. For example, the interest of an inactive spouse in the stock may be left to a bypass trust of which the active spouse is the beneficiary and over which the active spouse has some degree of control. They should also take into account the benefits available under §§303 and 6166 if a deceased spouse's estate pays some tax. In particular, the redemption of stock within the limits of §303 is treated as a sale or exchange and not as a dividend. §§11.15-11.24. In addition, payment of the estate tax attributable to interests in a small trade or business may be deferred under §6166. §§11.25-11.30.

C. REDEMPTIONS UNDER §303

> The key to successful estate planning in general and to successful planning for redemptions in particular is anticipation. From the moment it becomes apparent that an individual owns a substantial block of corporate stock, the practitioner should determine whether a redemption of the shares will be a likely feature in the administration of the individual's estate. A redemption which qualifies for capital gain treatment is almost always desirable for an estate since it offers the decedent's heirs an opportunity to withdraw large amounts of cash from a corporation without dividend treatment. As long as estates receive a basis in stock equal to estate tax value . . . redemptions which avoid dividend treatment provide an unparalleled opportunity for tax-free distribution of corporate cash. Fox, Options Available to a Corporation Acquiring Its Own Stock from Estate of Deceased Shareholder, 7 Est. Plan. 206, 210-211 (1980).

§11.15. Overview

Congress has been sensitive to the problems of generating funds to pay estate settlement costs where an interest in a closely-held trade or business is a major asset of an estate. The present relief provisions are embodied in §§303 and 6166. Under §303, the redemption of stock included in a decedent's estate is treated as a sale or exchange if the stock was worth more than 35 percent of the decendent's gross estate less allowable deductions under §§2053 and 2054. The estate tax attributable to a closely-held business interest may be deferred and paid in installments over 15 years under §6166 if the value of the business interest exceeds 35 percent of the value of the decedent's adjusted gross estate. For this purpose, a closely-held business includes a proprietorship and certain partnership and corporate interests.

The 1981 Act liberalized and coordinated the provisions of §§303 and 6166. Most significant, the 1981 Act reduced the percentage tests of §§303 and 6166 to the same amount, 35 percent of the decedent's gross estate less deductions allowable under §§2053 and 2054. §6166(a). In addition, both §§303 and 6166 were amended to allow the decedent's stock in two or more corporations to be aggregated for the purpose of satisfying the percentage test if the decedent's estate includes 20 percent or more of the value of each corporation. *See* §11.18. Finally, the 1981 Act liberalized several of the acceleration provisions of §6166(g). Most important was the increase from one-third to one-half in the amount of stock that could be disposed of, or the amount that could be withdrawn from the business, without accelerating the time for payment of the tax. *See* §11.29.

In planning a redemption program the parties must consider at least two important nontax questions. First, will the redemption result in an undesirable shift of corporate control? Second, will the distribution of funds in redemption of the stock unduly hamper corporate operations or growth? If the answer to either question is "yes," the parties should consider redeeming fewer shares or adopting an alternative plan for raising funds.

§11.16. Introduction to §303

Section 303 largely eliminates the income tax cost of withdrawing enough funds from a closely-held business to pay the death taxes and administration expenses incurred by a deceased shareholder's estate. If the stock exceeds 35 percent of the decedent's gross estate less deductions allowable under §§2053 and 2054, the redemption of a limited amount of stock is treated as a sale or exchange the proceeds of which qualify for capital gains treatment. Little, if any, gain is usually realized upon a redemption because the stock will have acquired a basis equal to its estate tax value in the decedent's estate. §1014(a). Treatment as a sale or exchange extends to all qualifying redemptions — it does not depend upon need. Thus, a redemption may be made with respect to qualifying stock although the decedent's estate is awash with cash and does not need the proceeds of redemptions to pay the taxes and expenses. Without the benefit of §303 the redemption of a decedent's stock would be treated as a dividend unless it fell within one of the exceptions of §302(b). *See* §11.24.

The provisions of §303 extend to the redemption of "new" stock, the basis of which is determined by reference to the "old" stock that was included in the decedent's estate. §303(c); Reg. §1.303-2(d). Thus, nonvoting common stock or preferred stock received in connection with a reorganization under §368, a tax-free exchange under §1036 or a distribution under §305(a), can be redeemed under §303. The opportunity to redeem "new" stock can be of particular value where the shareholders wish to maintain the pre-mortem balance of voting stock among the families of shareholders. *E.g.,* Rev. Rul. 87-132, 1987-2 C.B. 82 (distribution of nonvoting common to decedent's estate and surviving shareholder was nontaxable under §305(a), the carryover of basis provisions of §307(a) apply to the distribution, and the distributed stock is redeemable by the estate under §303).

Amount Redeemable. The amount redeemable under §303 is limited to the sum of the state and federal death taxes, including penalties and interest and the funeral and administration expenses that are deductible under §2053. §303(a). However, the 1976 Act added a provision under which a redemption *only* qualifies to the extent "the interest of the shareholder is reduced directly (or through a binding obligation to contribute) by any payment" of death taxes and funeral and administration expenses. §303(b)(3). Accordingly, shares specifically bequeathed to one party may not be redeemed under §303 where the obligation to pay death taxes and funeral and administration expenses is imposed on another party. Because of the marital deduction, shares that pass to a surviving spouse are not normally subject to a charge for a portion of the death taxes and expense. If the shares passing to a surviving spouse were subject to an agreement to contribute, the marital deduction would be reduced by a similar amount. *See* §2056(b)(4).

Transfers Within Three Years of Death, §2035(d)(3). For purposes of determining whether the 35 percent requirement is satisfied, a decedent's estate is treated as including property transferred within three years of death. §2035(d)(3). Note that all property transferred within three years of death is included for this purpose. Thus, the inclusion of property transferred within three years of death may qualify or disqualify an estate for the benefit of §303. In particular, stock transferred within three years of death is taken into account for purposes of the percentage requirement of §303(b), although it is not included in the decedent's estate. However, stock not actually included in the decedent's gross estate cannot be redeemed under §303. Rev. Rul. 84-76, 1984-1 C.B. 91. In order to be redeemed under §303 the stock *must* be included in the decedent's estate. §303(a). In short, the ability of an estate to meet the percentage requirement of §303 cannot be enhanced by deathbed transfers.

Example 11-8. In 1992 *T* transferred stock in ABC, Inc. worth $1,000,000 to a child, *C*. *T* died in 1993 leaving an estate of $4,000,000 of which $1,000,000 was stock in ABC, Inc. Deductions allowable under §§2053 and 2054 amounted to $500,000. For purposes of the percentage requirement of §303(b) *T*'s estate is treated as also including the stock transferred to *C* in 1992. Thus, *T*'s estate is treated as having an overall value of $5,000,000, including ABC, Inc. stock worth $2,000,000. The value of the stock ($2,000,000) is greater than 35% of the value of *T*'s gross estate ($5,000,000) less allowable deductions ($500,000). The ABC, Inc. stock actually included in *T*'s estate may be redeemed under §303 up to an amount equal to the total of all death taxes and allowable funeral and administration expenses. *See* Rev. Rul. 84-76, 1984-1 C.B. 91.

Example 11-9. In 1992 *T* transferred Blackacre, worth $600,000, to his children. *T* died in 1993 leaving an estate of $2,000,000, of which $800,000 was stock in XYZ, Inc. Deductions allowable under §§2053 and 2054 amounted to $200,000. *T*'s estate would meet the 35% requirement of §303(b) if the gift of Blackacre were not considered:

$$\frac{\$800{,}000}{(\$2{,}000{,}000 - \$200{,}000)} = 44.44\%$$

However, including Blackacre as required by §2035(d)(3), the XYZ, Inc. stock does not constitute a large enough percentage of *T*'s estate:

$$\frac{\$800{,}000}{(\$2{,}600{,}000 - \$200{,}000)} = 33.33\%$$

Transfers made within three years of death are also included for purposes of §2032A, §2035(d)(3); §6166, §2035(d)(4); and the lien provisions of subchapter C of Chapter 64; §2035(d)(3).

Redemptions More Than Four Years After Death. The use of the proceeds of a redemption made within four year of the decedent's death is not restricted. §303(b)(1). Most later redemptions qualify under §303 only where the payment of the estate tax has been deferred under §6166 (or former §6166A) and the amount distributed is applied within one year toward payment of the death taxes and funeral and administration expenses. §303(b)(4). Redemptions made more than four years after the decedent's death must be carefully coordinated with payment of the estate tax installments under §6166 (or former §6166A).

Redemptions of Stock Subject to GSTT. Stock subject to the generation-skipping transfer tax (GSTT) by reason of a generation-skipping transfer occurring at or after the death of an individual may also be redeemed under §303. §303(d). For purposes of applying §303 the stock is considered to be included in the gross estate of the individual; the relationship of the stock to the decedent's estate is measured by reference to the amount of the generation-skipping transfer; the GSTT and similar taxes are treated as an estate tax imposed by reason of the individual's death; and the period within which distribution may be made in redemption of the stock is measured from the date of the generation-skipping transfer. The application of §303 to generation-skipping transfers should be clarified after regulations are issued as contemplated by §303(d).

§11.17. Thirty-Five Percent Requirement, §303(b)(2)(A)

Stock included in a decedent's gross estate qualifies for redemption under §303 *only* if its federal estate tax value exceeds 35 percent of the decedent's gross estate less the amount of deductions allowable under §§2053 and 2054. §303(b)(2)(A). For purposes of this computation the amounts deducted under §§2053 and 2054 (*i.e.,* debts, funeral and administration expenses, and casualty losses) are taken into account whether or not they are claimed as deductions for federal estate tax purposes. §303(b)(2)(a)(ii). *See* Rev. Rul. 56-449, 1956-2 C.B. 180 (declared obsolete by Rev. Rul. 80-367, 1980-2 C.B. 386). Note that the amount of the charitable and marital deductions do not figure into the computation.

Example 11-10. *T*'s gross estate was $1,000,000 including stock in *X* Corp. that had an estate tax value of $475,000. The deductions allowable to *T*'s estate under §§2053 and 2054 amounted to $80,000. The 35% requirement is met in this case because the value of the stock included in *T*'s gross estate ($475,000) comprised more of *T*'s estate than required by §303(b)(2)(A):

$$\frac{\$475{,}000}{\$1{,}000{,}000 - \$80{,}000} = 51.63\%$$

Special planning may be called for if a client wishes to make a gift to charity at death and qualify under §303 (or §6166). A charitable bequest *does not* reduce the amount of the gross estate for purposes of determining whether the 35 percent requirement is met. However, a deduction is allowable under §2053 for an enforceable charitable pledge to the extent it was contracted bona fide and would have been deductible if it had been a bequest. Reg. §20.2053-5. The allowability of the deduction under §2053 reduces the amount of the 35 percent threshold.

Example 11-11. *X* died leaving a gross estate of $5,000,000, which included stock in *X* Corp. worth $1,400,000. *X*'s will left $1,000,000 to a tax-exempt charity. Deductions allowable under §§2053 and 2054 amounted to $100,000. *X*'s estate could not redeem any stock under §303 because the value of *X*'s stock in *X* Corp. ($1,400,000) is only 28.57% of *X*'s gross estate less deductions allowable under §§2053 and 2054 ($5,000,000 − $100,000). Note that *X*'s stock in *X* Corp. would have exceeded the 35% threshold had *X* made an enforceable pledge of $1,000,000 to the charity instead of making a bequest.

In planning the administration of the estate the personal representative must recognize that the valuation of the stock and other assets may determine whether or not the 35 percent test is satisfied.

§11.18. Stock in Two or More Corporations, §303(b)(2)(B)

Stock of two or more corporations may be combined for purposes of satisfying the 35 percent requirement if at least 20 percent in value of the outstanding stock of each corporation is included in the decedent's gross estate. §303(b)(2)(B). In order to qualify for aggregation, the decedent's estate must include at least 20 percent of the total value of all issues of each corporation's stock. That is, the test does not require that the decedent's estate include 20 percent of each issue of stock. Thus, the stock in corporations *A* and *B* is considered to be the stock of a single corporation for purposes of the 35 percent requirement if the decedent's estate includes common or preferred stock of each corporation that has a value of more than 20 percent of all of its stock. In this connection remember that the value of a minority block of closely-held stock is usually subject to valuation discounts.

Example 11-12. *T*'s gross estate had a federal estate tax value of $900,000, including 30% of the outstanding stock of *A* Corp. and 25% of the outstanding stock of *B* Corp. A total of $100,000 was allowable to *T*'s estate as deductions under §§2053 and 2054. *T*'s stock in *A* Corp. was worth $200,000 of its total value of $950,000, and *T*'s stock in *B* Corp. was worth $100,000 of its total value of $450,000. Thus, more than 20% in value of the stock of both corporations was included in *T*'s gross estate. The total value of the stock in the two corporations included in *T*'s estate ($300,000) exceeds 35% of the value of *T*'s gross estate reduced by deductions allowable under §§2053 and 2054 ($900,000 − $100,000). Accordingly, the 35% requirement of §303(b)(2) is satisfied.

For purposes of the 20 percent test, the surviving spouse's interest in stock held by the decedent and the surviving spouse as community property, joint tenants, tenants by the entirety, or as tenants in common is considered to be included in the decedent's gross estate. §303(b)(2)(B); *cf.*, Rev. Rul. 61-91, 1961-1 C.B. 714 (comparable issue under former §6166A). However, the surviving spouse's interest in such stock is not included in the decedent's estate. In particular, the value of the surviving spouse's stock cannot be counted for purposes of satisfying the basic 35 percent test.

§11.19. Maximum Amount Redeemable, §303(a)

Under §303(a) the maximum amount that can be received in redemption of qualifying stock is the sum of the death taxes imposed by reason of the decedent's death and the amount of funeral and administration expenses deductible under §2053. As indicated above, the funeral and administration expenses are included in the computation whether they are taken as estate tax or as income tax deductions. Note, however, that the amount of debts and casualty losses is not included in determining the ceiling.

Care must be exercised in planning the sequence of distributions in redemption of a decedent's stock. Where more than one distribution takes place, the distributions are applied against the total amount that is redeemable under §303 in the order in which the distributions are made. Reg. §1.303-2(g)(1). Redemption distributions in excess of the amount redeemable under §303 are taxable as dividends unless they fall within one of the exceptions to §302. *See* §11.24. Rev. Rul. 71-261, 1971-1 C.B. 108.

Example 11-13. A maximum of $500,000 of stock was redeemable under §303 from *T*'s estate by *X* Corp. On January 15 of this year *X* Corp. distributed $400,000 to *T*'s son, *S*, in redemption of shares *T* had transferred to a trust and that were included in *T*'s estate under §2036. In February *X* Corp. redeemed

$200,000 shares held by the executor of *T*'s will. Under the local estate tax apportionment law all of the shares of *X* Corp. were required to contribute proportionately to payments of estate tax. The first $500,000 received in redemption of the estate's shares qualifies under §303. Half of the distribution received by *T*'s executor ($100,000) does not qualify under §303.

§11.20. Time Limit on Redemptions, §303(b)(1), (4)

Under the basic limitation of §303(b)(1) a redemption must take place within three years and 90 days after the date the federal estate tax return is filed. §303(b)(1)(A). The proceeds of a redemption made within that period may be used for any purpose. If a petition for redetermination of estate tax by the Tax Court is timely filed, a redemption may be made at any time within 60 days after the Tax Court decision becomes final. §303(b)(1)(B). Also, where the payment of the estate tax is deferred under §6166, a redemption may be made within the time determined under that section for payment of the estate tax in installments. §303(b)(1)(C).

A redemption made more than four years after the decedent's death qualifies only to the extent it does not exceed the lesser of (1) the amount of death taxes and funeral and administration expenses that remained unpaid immediately before the distribution and (2) the amount paid toward those expenses within one year following the date of the distribution. §303(b)(4). Of necessity the latter amount is always the lesser. In planning a redemption program the parties should consider the restrictions imposed on the use of the proceeds of redemptions made more than four years after the decedent's death. It is particularly important to do so where payment of the estate tax has been deferred under §6166 because of the acceleration provision of that section. *See* §11.29.

§11.21. What May Be Distributed

Cash is ordinarily distributed in a redemption under §303. Until amended in 1986 the provisions of §311 allowed appreciated property to be distributed by a corporation in redemption of stock without recognition of gain. In addition, the taxpayer did not recognize any gain on the distribution. Effective January 1, 1987 a corporation recognizes gain if appreciated property is distributed in a stock redemption. In addition, the property that is distributed must be selected carefully to avoid distributions that have other adverse tax consequences. For example, the distribution of §§1245 or 1250 property triggers depreciation recapture by corporations other than S corporations.

§11.22. Inter Vivos Planning for Redemptions Under §303

The shareholder and the corporation should ordinarily both do some careful advance planning where a shareholder's stock holdings may meet the requirements of §303. To begin with, the shareholder should avoid making any inter vivos gifts or other dispositions of the stock that might reduce the value of his or her holdings below the required 35 percent. (Of course, reducing a shareholder's stock holdings to a minority block that qualify for a minority discount might be best in overall tax terms.) If the stock might be below the 35 percent threshold, steps might be taken to increase the value of the stock relative to the value of the shareholder's other assets. For example, assets that the shareholder owns outright might be transferred to the corporation, tax free, in exchange for additional shares of stock. Such a transfer does double duty by reducing the value of assets outside the business and increasing the amount of stock the shareholder holds.

A change in the beneficiary designation of corporate-owned life insurance may also boost the value of the shareholder's stock. Where the shareholder has control of a majority of the corporation's stock, its incidents of ownership are attributed to the shareholder and the proceeds are includible in the shareholder's estate under §2042 if the proceeds are payable to a beneficiary other than the corporation. *See* Reg. §20.2042-1(c)(6). In contrast, the proceeds are taken into account in valuing the shareholder's stock where the proceeds are payable to the corporation. Rev. Rul. 82-85, 1982-1 C.B. 137.

Special care must be exercised when the shareholder owns stock in several corporations, the holdings in none of which is by itself sufficient to satisfy the 35 percent test. Of course, the stock of two or more corporations can be aggregated for this purpose where more than 20 percent in value of each corporation is included in the shareholder's estate. §303(b)(2)(B). *See* §11.18. More sophisticated planning may be called for where the client's stock holdings in any one corporation are not large enough to satisfy the 35 percent requirement and aggregation is prevented because the shareholder owns less than 20 percent of the stock of each corporation. The effect of aggregation could be approximated, however, if the corporations in which the shareholder-owned stock are merged or consolidated prior to the shareholder's death. As a result, the value of the stock in the surviving corporation might be more than adequate to satisfy the 35 percent test. Stock in two or more corporations could, of course, be transferred to a holding company in exchange for some of its stock. Such a step might also allow the estate to defer payment of the estate tax under §6166(b)(8), which is slightly less advantageous than deferral under the basic provisions of §6166. *See* §11.26.5.

The planner should also consider whether it is necessary or desirable to obtain a commitment from the corporation to redeem the stock through an entity purchase agreement or similar arrangement. *See* §§11.6-11.14. The potential for future problems may be reduced if all shareholders are informed of the plans and approve of them. Some consideration must also be given to the availability of liquid assets to the corporation for the purpose of financing the redemption. A redemption may be adequately financed if, for example, retained earnings are used to purchase insurance on the shareholder's life or to invest in some other relatively liquid form. In any case, the corporation should avoid the imposition of the accumulated earnings tax under §§531 to 537. As noted above, §537 permits a corporation to accumulate funds in the year of a shareholder's death or later, for the purpose of funding a redemption under §303. For purposes of §537 the accumulation of earnings in years prior to the stockholder's death for the purpose of funding a redemption may not be considered a reasonable business need.

The planner should also inquire into any restrictions that may be imposed on redemptions by the local law or by the corporation's financing arrangements. Some states restrict redemptions to the amount of the corporation's earned surplus. However, a redemption may be made under §6.40 of the Model Business Corporation Act so long as the corporation is not insolvent, and the net assets of the corporation are not reduced below the amount payable to the shareholders who would have prior or equal rights to the assets of the corporation if it were liquidated.

As mentioned in §11.16, the stock to be redeemed should only be given to a person whose interest in the stock will be chargeable for death taxes and funeral and administration expenses allowable under §2053. The stock qualifies under §303 only if the interest of the shareholder is reduced by payment of the death taxes and other expenses. §303(b)(3).

§11.23. Worksheet for §303

In the planning process it is important to determine whether a particular shareholder's stock meets the requirements of §303 and, if so, how much might be redeemed. It is safer and more efficient if the planner uses computer software or a worksheet of the following type to make the necessary calculations:

Section 303 Worksheet
(For decedents dying after December 31, 1981)

Part I. Qualifications

1. Adjusted Gross Estate

   Gross estate (estimate or enter from Form 706, page 1, line 1; include property transferred within 3 years of death per §2035(d)(3)) $

   Less: Deductions allowable under §§2053 and 2054 – ________

   Adjusted Gross Estate (item 1) ________

2. Value of stock in corporation, including stock transferred within 3 years of death (the value of 2 or more businesses may be aggregated under §303(b)(2)) (item 2) ________

3. Divide item 2 by item 1. (If the closely held business, item 2, has a value of more than 35% of the adjusted gross estate, item 1, the requirements of §303 are met.) ________

Part II. Amount Redeemable

4. Death taxes, including interest and penalties, paid by reason of decedent's death, §303(a)(1): ________

   a. Federal estate tax (estimate or enter from Form 706, page 1, line 10)

   b. State death tax + ________

   Total (item 4) ________

5. Funeral and administrative expenses allowable as deductions under §2053, whether or not claimed on Form 706 (§303(a)(2)) (item 5) + ________

6. Total amount redeemable (item 4 plus item 5) ________

Caveat. See §303(b)(1) regarding the time within which the redemptions must be accomplished.

§11.24. Redemptions That Do Not Qualify Under §303

> The congressional purpose underlying §302 is to allow exchange treatment for those redemptions that resemble a sale to an outsider. Redemptions that do not significantly change the shareholder's interest in the corporation are more akin to dividend distributions and generally do not qualify for exchange treatment. E. Hood, S. Kurtz, & J. Shors, Closely Held Corporations in Business and Estate Planning §7.7.2 (1982)

A redemption that does not qualify under §303 will be treated as a distribution in the nature of a dividend unless it qualifies under one of the three exceptions of §302(b). The exceptions apply to redemptions that are (1) not essentially equivalent to a dividend, §302(b)(1); (2) substantially disproportionate, §302(b)(2); or (3) result in a complete termination of the shareholder's interest, §302(b)(3).

§11.24.1. Redemption Not Essentially Equivalent to a Dividend, §302(b)(1)

The first exception establishes a subjective test under which a redemption is treated as a sale or exchange if it is "not essentially equivalent to a dividend" in light of all of the facts and circumstances. §302(b)(1). Unfortunately, the scope of the exception is unclear, which makes it of little use in planning. Court decisions, the Regulations, revenue rulings, and private letter rulings provide some guidance, albeit somewhat contradictory.

In the leading case, *United States v. Davis,* 397 U.S. 301 (1970), the Supreme Court held that the exception does not apply unless the redemption results in a *meaningful reduction* in the shareholder's proportionate interest in the corporation. In *Davis* the corporation needed to increase its capital by $25,000 in order to qualify for a loan from the Reconstruction Finance Corporation. The taxpayer transferred $25,000 to the corporation in exchange for 1,000 shares of $25 par preferred stock with the understanding that the preferred stock would be redeemed after the loan was repaid. Later, when the preferred stock was redeemed the taxpayer and members of his family owned all of the corporation's stock. Under the family attribution rules of §318(a)(1) the taxpayer was considered to own all of the corporation's common stock before and after the redemption of the preferred stock. The redemption was treated as a dividend although there had been a valid business purpose for the original issuance of the preferred stock.

What constitutes a meaningful reduction in the shareholder's proportionate interest in the corporation is not clear. In Rev. Rul. 75-502, 1975-2 C.B. 111, the IRS listed three interests of a shareholder that are relevant for purposes of the meaningful reduction test: "(1) the right to vote and thereby exercise control; (2) the right to participate in current earnings and accumulated surplus; and (3) the right to share in net assets on liquidation." Nonetheless, the authorities are difficult to reconcile. For example, Rev. Rul. 78-401, 1978-2 C.B. 127, holds that a reduction from 90 percent to 60 percent was not meaningful because no action was contemplated which required a two-thirds affirmative vote. On the other hand, in *Henry T. Patterson Trust v. United States,* 729 F.2d 1089 (6th Cir. 1984), the court held that a reduction from 80 percent to 60 percent was meaningful. Indeed, under the unique facts of the case the court stated that a decrease in stock ownership from 97 percent to 93 percent was a "meaningful reduction."

Not surprisingly, the Regulations are consistent with the meaningful reduction test articulated in *Davis.* In particular, Reg. §1.302-2(b) indicates that a pro rata redemption does not qualify where only one class of stock is outstanding. ("All distributions in pro rata redemptions of a part of the stock of a corporation will be treated as distributions under section 301 if the corporation has only one class of stock outstanding.") However, a pro rata redemption might qualify as a partial liquidation under §302(b)(4). The Regulations also provide that a redemption of all of one class of the stock of a corporation is not within the exception of §302(b)(1). Reg. §1.302-2(b). As illustrated by *Davis* the family attribution rules make it difficult for a family-owned corporation to meet the requirements of §302(b)(1).

Example 11-14. When Magma, Inc. was incorporated, its 15,000 shares of common stock were issued equally to *H* (7,500) and *W* (7,500). Subsequently *H* and *W* each sold 2,500 shares to a key employee, *C,* who was unrelated to them. When *H* died, Magma redeemed *H*'s remaining 5,000 shares from his estate in accordance with the terms of a buy-sell agreement that bound all of the shareholders regarding the disposition of their shares. The redemption reduced the estate's actual ownership of Magma stock from one-third to zero and its constructive ownership of stock from two-thirds to one-half. The IRS has ruled that such a redemption is not essentially equivalent to a dividend. LR 8044034. The redemption would not fall within the terms of this exception if *C* were a beneficiary of *H*'s estate because the estate would be treated as the constructive owner of *C*'s shares as well. *See* §318(a)(3); Reg. §1.318-3(a).

Attribution Rules. Whether or not a redemption qualifies under the exceptions of §302(b) often depends upon an application of the attribution rules. Without thoroughly exploring the complexity and subtlety of the rules, some features should be noted. First, family attribution under §318(a)(1) is limited to spouses, children, grandchildren, and parents. Thus, there is no attribution between siblings. Also, while there is attribution from grandchild to grandparent, there is no attribution from grandparent to grandchild. Importantly, the operating rules of §318(a)(5)(B) bar double attribution under the family attribution rules. For example, stock owned by a parent cannot be attributed to a child and then attributed from the child to the child's spouse.

> **Example 11-15.** All of the stock of *X* Corp. is owned by *X* (50%) and *X*'s children, *D* (25%) and *E* (25%). If *X* Corp. redeems all of *X*'s stock the family attribution rules will prevent the redemption from reducing *X*'s interest in *X* Corp. Specifically, *X* will be treated as owning the stock of both of his children. Accordingly, the redemption would not result in a meaningful reduction in *X*'s interest. However, the redemption would qualify as a complete termination of *X*'s interest under §302(b)(3) if the family attribution rules can be waived under §302(c)(2).

Second, under the entity attribution rules the stock owned by an estate, trust, partnership or corporation may be attributed pro rata to its beneficiaries, partners or shareholders. Third, stock owned by a beneficiary, partner, or shareholder may be attributed to the entity. Again, the operating rules of §318(a)(5)(C) prevent the double attribution of stock through an entity. That is, stock attributed to an entity may not be reattributed to its beneficiaries, partners or shareholders. Fourth, a person who holds an option to acquire stock is treated as owning the stock. §318(a)(4). In this connection note that stock which may be considered as owned by an individual under the family attribution rules of §318(a)(1) or the option rule of §318(a)(4) will be considered as owning the stock under the option rule. §318(a)(5)(D).

Hostility between family members does not prevent application of the attribution rules. *David Metzger Trust v. Commissioner,* 76 T.C. 41 (1981), *aff'd,* 693 F.2d 459 (5th Cir.), *cert. denied,* 463 U.S. 1207 (1982); *Michael N. Cerone,* 87 T.C. 1 (1986) ("Family hostility does not prevent application of the attribution rules.")

§11.24.2. Substantially Disproportionate Redemptions, §302(b)(2)

The second exception applies if the redemption is "substantially disproportionate with respect to the shareholder." §302(b)(2). In order to qualify under this exception the redemption must satisfy three mathematical tests. Again, satisfying the tests is made difficult by the application of the stock attribution rules. §§302(c)(1), 318. In brief, the tests require that immediately after the redemption the shareholder must own *less* than:

1. 50 percent of the combined voting power of all classes of stock,
2. 80 percent of the voting stock that the shareholder owned immediately before the redemption, and
3. 80 percent of the common stock (whether voting or nonvoting) that the shareholder owned immediately before the redemption.

Because of the second of the tests, "Section 302(b)(2) only applies to a redemption of voting stock or to a redemption of both voting stock and other stock. Section 302(b)(2) does not apply to the redemption solely of nonvoting stock (common or preferred)." Reg. §1.302-3(a). Where a redemption is one of a series, the applicability of this exception is determined by the aggregate effect of the redemptions and not the effect of the one redemption alone. A redemption is not disproportionate if all of the stock of one class is redeemed or if the same percentage of each shareholder's stock is redeemed. It is also significant that §302(b)(2) does not impose any percentage test with respect to nonvoting preferred stock.

Example 11-16. *W, X, Y,* and *Z* each owned 100 shares of the 400 outstanding shares of the common stock of Comet Corp. In addition, *X* and *Y* each owned 100 shares of the outstanding 200 shares of Comet's nonvoting preferred stock. The shareholders were not related parties within the meaning of the attribution rules of §318(a). Comet Corp. redeemed 60 shares of common stock from *W,* 25 shares from *X,* and 15 shares from *Y.* In order to qualify under §302(b)(2), after the redemption a shareholder must own less than 20% (80% times 25%) of the 300 shares of common stock that remain outstanding. No test is imposed with respect to the nonvoting preferred stock, none of which was redeemed. After the redemption *W* owned 40 shares (13.33%); *X* owned 75 shares (25%); and *Y* owned 85 shares (28.33%). Accordingly, the redemption is disproportionate only with respect to *W.* See the example in Reg. §1.302-3(b).

§11.24.3. Complete Termination of Interest, §302(b)(3)

Finally, §302(b)(3) treats a redemption of the entire interest of a shareholder as an exchange. This exception is superficially easy to satisfy, but it is complicated by the application of the attribution rules. However, the family attribution rules of §318(a)(1) can be waived for purposes of §302(b)(3) if the requirements of §302(c)(2) are met. Waiver is allowed under §302(c)(2) if the following requirements are satisfied: (1) after the redemption the former shareholder has no interest in the corporation (including an interest as officer, director, or employee) other than as a creditor; (2) the former shareholder acquires no interest in the corporation for a period of ten years other than by bequest or inheritance; and (3) the former shareholder agrees to inform the Treasury of the acquisition of any interest in the corporation within that period. §302(c)(2)(A). In addition, attribution may not be waived if, within the preceding ten years, the former shareholder either acquired any of the redeemed stock from a person whose stock would be attributed to the former shareholder under §318(a) or transferred any stock in the corporation to a person whose stock is attributable to the former shareholder under §318(a). However, the forgoing additional rules do not apply if the avoidance of the federal income tax was not one of the principal purposes of the acquisition or transfer of the shares.

Under a change made by the 1982 Act, the family attribution rules of §318(a)(1) may be waived by an entity such as a trust or estate if some additional requirements are met. §302(c)(2)(C). In particular, all of the persons through whom stock might be attributed to the entity must meet the requirements of §302(c)(2)(A)(i), (ii) and (iii) and agree to be jointly and severally liable for any deficiency that may result from the acquisition of an interest within ten years (other than by bequest or inheritance). The IRS had previously taken the view that where shares were redeemed from a trust or estate (or other entity), the family attribution rules could not be waived by the entity. Under the IRS approach it was much more difficult to qualify under this exception where closely-held stock was to be redeemed from a trust or estate.

In effect the 1982 Act codified the Tax Court holding in *Lillian M. Crawford,* 59 T.C. 830 (1973), *nonacq.,* 1974-2 C.B. 5, *app. dismissed* (9th Cir. 1973), *acq.,* 1984-2 C.B. 1 (*nonacq. withdrawn*). In *Crawford* the Tax Court held that the redemption of all of the shares owned by the deceased shareholder's estate and by his widow, who was its sole beneficiary, constituted a complete termination although his children continued to own the remainder of the shares. Specifically, the court found that the waiver agreement filed by the decedent's estate was effective to bar the attribution of the children's stock to the widow and, through her, to the estate. It was concerned that the IRS position "merely put a premium on tax planning and set a trap for the unwary." Id. at 837. *See also Rodgers P. Johnson Trust,* 71 T.C. 941 (1979), *acq.,* 1984-2 C.B. 1, which permitted a trust to waive the family attribution rules. The IRS position was clearly wrong as a matter of policy and of law. The qualification of a redemption under §302(b)(3) should not have depended upon whether the decedent's shares were redeemed from the estate or from its sole shareholder.

Example 11-17. *H* and his daughter, *D,* were the only shareholders in Alpha Corp. *H* died survived by *W,* his widow and the sole beneficiary under his will. *H*'s interest in Alpha Corp. did not constitute a sufficient portion of his estate to qualify for the redemption under §303. A redemption of the shares formerly owned by *H* will qualify as an exchange only if the redemption of the estate's stock will qualify under one of the exceptions to the basic rule of §302. A complete termination of the estate's interest, §302(b)(3), is possible if *D*'s shares are not attributed to *W* and from *W* to *H*'s estate. Section 302(c)(2)(C) would allow *H*'s estate to waive family attribution of *D*'s shares to *W* under §318(a)(1) so that there would be no shares to attribute from *W* to the estate.

Under another approach, *H*'s shares of Alpha Corp. might be distributed by his estate to *W.* A redemption of all of the shares owned by *W* would qualify as a complete termination under §302(b)(3) if the family attribution from *D* to *W* could be waived under §302(c)(2). Even prior to the 1982 Act the IRS treated such a redemption as a complete termination of *W*'s interest. Rev. Rul. 79-67, 1979-1 C.B. 128.

§11.24.4. No Waiver of Entity Attribution

Attribution to or from an entity under §318(a)(2) and (3) cannot be waived. Thus, a trust, estate, partnership, or corporation will be treated as owning all of the stock held by its beneficiaries, partners or stockholders. §318(a)(3). Conversely, beneficiaries, partners, or stockholders will be considered to own a pro rata interest in the trust, estate, partnership, or corporation. Under the operating rules of §318(a)(5) stock that is attributed to an entity is not considered as owned by it for purposes of attributing ownership to a beneficiary, partner or shareholder. Thus, an interest of a beneficiary that is attributed to a trust cannot be reattributed to another beneficiary. Of course, the stock owned by one beneficiary may be attributed to another beneficiary under the family attribution rules of §318(a)(1).

Example 11-18. A brother and sister, *X* and *Y,* each own 20% of the stock of ABC, Inc. The other 60% is owned by the XYZ Partnership in which *X, Y,* and *Z* are equal partners. Under the family attribution rules stock owned by one sibling is not attributed to another. While the stock owned by one sibling may be attributed to a parent under the family attribution rules, the operating rules of §318(a)(5)(B) prevent the stock from being reattributed to the other sibling (or any other family member). Stock owned by *X* and *Y* is attributed to the XYZ Partnership under the attribution-to-entity rule of §318(a)(3). Again, the operating rules of §318(a)(5)(C) prevent the stock attributed to the Partnership from being reattributed to individual partners. However, the stock actually owned by the XYZ Partnership is attributed equally to *X*, *Y*, and *Z*. Thus, *X* and *Y* are each considered to own 40% of the stock of ABC, Inc.

Prior to the 1982 Act the IRS and the Tax Court had concluded that entity attribution could not be waived. *David Metzger Trust,* 76 T.C. 42 (1981), *aff'd,* 693 F.2d 459 (5th Cir. 1982), *cert. denied,* 463 U.S. 1207 (1983). However, the Fifth Circuit allowed entity waiver in an earlier poorly reasoned and much maligned opinion, *Rickey v. United States,* 592 F.2d 1251 (5th Cir. 1979). While *Rickey* created some uncertainty regarding this issue, the Conference Report that accompanied the 1982 Act made it clear that entity attribution could not be waived.

D. DEFERRAL OF ESTATE TAX UNDER §6166

§11.25. Overview

Payment of the portion of the estate tax attributable to a closely-held business interest may be deferred under §6166 if the value of the closely-held interest exceeds 35 percent of the decedent's adjusted gross estate. For this purpose the term "adjusted gross estate" means the gross estate reduced by the deductions allowable under §§2053 and 2054 (funeral and administration expenses, debts, and losses). §6166(b)(6). The amount of those items is taken into account whether or not they are claimed as deductions on the federal estate tax return. The percentage test is, of course, the same as is imposed under §303. As noted above in connection with §303, a legally enforceable charitable pledge is deductible under §2053, which reduces the size of the decedent's gross estate and the amount of the 35 percent threshold. *See* §11.17.

The estate's ability to meet the 35 percent requirement is affected by the inclusion of assets in the estate and the estate tax valuation of assets. §6166(b)(4). Accordingly, the executor must carefully consider decisions that affect the valuation of assets, including the use of the alternate valuation and special use valuation methods. The latter method allows the value of "qualified real property" to be reduced by as much as $750,000. *See* §12.19. In general an election may be made to value qualified real property under §2032A where the real and personal property used in the business constitute 50 percent or more of the adjusted value of the gross estate and the qualified real property constitutes 25 percent or more of the adjusted value of the gross estate. Because of the requirements of §6166, an executor should not make an election under §2032A without first determining whether it will prevent the estate from satisfying the 35 percent test.

Interests held by the decedent in two or more businesses may be aggregated if 20 percent or more in value of each is included in his or her gross estate. §6166(c). Presumably the decedent's interests in a partnership and a corporation could be combined under this rule. *See* LR 9015009 (decedent's interests in partnership and corporation could not be combined where partnership was not engaged in an active trade or business). Also, for purposes of §6166(c), the surviving spouse's interest in property held by a husband and wife as community property, joint tenants, tenants by the entirety, or as tenants in common is treated as included in the decedent's gross estate.

> **Example 11-19.** *H*'s gross estate had a value of $2,000,000, including his interest in the stock of Corporations One and Two. The funeral and administration expenses, debts, and other deductions allowable under §§2053 and 2054 amounted to $100,000. *H* and *W* held stock in Corporation One as joint tenants, which represented 20% ($800,000) of its voting stock. *H* and *W* also owned 30% in value ($700,000) of the voting stock of Corporation Two as tenants in common. *H*'s estate includes only 10% in value of the stock of Corporation One. (The stock constitutes a qualified joint interest under §2040(b), as a result of which only one-half is includible in *H*'s gross estate.) *H*'s estate also includes only half of the stock owned by *H* and *W*, 15% in value, of the stock of Corporation Two. The entire percentage interests of *H* and *W* in the stock of both corporations is considered to be owned by *H* for purposes of satisfying the 20% threshold necessary to allow them to be considered as one corporation. As a result, the value of *H*'s one-half interests in Corporation One ($400,000) and Corporation Two ($350,000) may be aggregated for purposes of the 35% test. Because their total value ($750,000) exceeds 35% of *H*'s adjusted gross estate ($1,900,000), the tax attributable to *H*'s interest in the two corporations may be deferred under §6166.

Note that the value of the stock owned by *H* and *W* cannot be combined in order to satisfy the 35% requirement.

§11.26. Closely-Held Business

Various ownership interests in a trade or business qualify for the benefits of §6166 including the interest of a sole proprietor. §6166(b)(1)(A). As noted in §11.26.2, a decedent's interest in a trust that is engaged in a trade or business may qualify for deferral under §6166. An interest in a partnership also qualifies if 20 percent or more of the capital interest in the partnership is included in the decedent's gross estate *or* the partnership had 15 or fewer partners. §6166(b)(1)(B). Similarly, stock in a corporation engaged in a trade or business qualifies if 20 percent or more of the voting interest in the corporation is included in the decedent's gross estate or there are 15 or fewer shareholders. §6166(b)(1)(C). A determination of whether an estate satisfies the requirements of the section is determined as of the time immediately before the decedent's death. The limits should be borne in mind in planning the capital structure of a new enterprise or making changes in existing ones (*e.g.,* mergers, recapitalizations, and the restructuring of partnerships).

§11.26.1. Who Is Counted as a Partner or Shareholder

Importantly, for purposes of determining whether the decedent's interest qualified as a closely-held business, the stock or partnership interests held by a husband and wife as community property or as cotenants (joint tenants, tenants in common, or tenants by the entirety) is considered to be owned by only one person. §6166(b)(2)(B). As noted above, the same rule applies in determining whether interests in two or more closely-held businesses can be treated as one under §6166(c). Thus, the community property or joint tenancy interests of a decedent and his or her spouse in two or more active businesses could be combined and treated as owned entirely by the decedent. However, while the community property and cotenancy interests of both spouses are taken into account for purposes of §6166(b), only the value of the interests actually included in the decedent's estate is considered for purposes of the 35 percent requirement of §6166(a).

Example 11-20. *W* died owning 25% in value of the voting stock of ABC, Inc. In addition, *W* and her spouse, *H,* owned 30% in value of the voting stock of XYZ, Inc. as joint tenants.

Neither *W*'s 25% interest in ABC, Inc. nor her 15% interest in XYZ, Inc. has a value in excess of 35% of her adjusted gross estate. However, the combined value of her interests in the two corporations exceeds the 35% requirement. Under §6166(c) *W* is treated as owning 20% or more of the value of both corporations which are treated as "an interest in a single closely-held business." Accordingly, her interests in them, 25% and 15% respectively, can be combined for purposes of the 35% requirement of §6166(a).

Family Attribution. A broader attribution rule provides that, "All stock and all partnership interests held by the decedent or by any member of his family (within the meaning of section 267 (c)(4)) shall be treated as owned by the decedent." §6166(b)(2)(D). For purposes of determining the number of partners or shareholders, a decedent is treated as owning all of the partnership interests or stock held by the decedent's spouse, siblings, ancestors, or descendants. Id. (The decedent is not treated as holding the interests of family members for purposes of the percentage ownership tests of §§6166(b)(2)(B) and (C). *See* §11.26.4.)

Indirect Ownership. Under §6166(b)(2)(C) each person who holds an interest in a corporation, partnership, trust, or estate is considered to own a proportionate interest in the property it owns. Thus, the number of partners or shareholders is not reduced by transferring interests to a trust or other entity. According to the staff report, this provision was included to prevent avoidance of the shareholder and partner limits by the use of partnerships, trusts, and tiers of corporations. General Explanation of the 1976 Act 548.

Example 11-21. *W* and her husband, *H,* hold stock in XYZ, Inc. as joint tenants. There are 13 other unrelated individual shareholders. In addition, shares of XYZ, Inc. are owned by a trust of which there are 5 current income beneficiaries. For purposes of §6166, *H* and *W* are considered to be one shareholder. Accordingly, other than the trust there are 14 shareholders. However, under the indirect ownership rule of §6166(b)(2)(C) each of the beneficiaries of the trust is considered to be a shareholder. Thus, XYZ, Inc. has 19 shareholders.

§11.26.2. Trade or Business

Section 6166 of the Code was not intended to protect the continued management of income producing property or to

> permit the deferral of tax merely because the payment of tax may make the sale of income producing assets necessary. Only in cases where these types of assets form an active enterprise producing business income, rather than income solely from property ownership, can an estate elect to pay its tax in installments under section 6166 of the Code. Because Partnership only collects rent on the property, it is merely managing income producing property. Thus, Partnership is not carrying on a trade or business within the meaning of section 6166(b)(1) of the Code. LR 9015009.

Deferral is available only for interests of a proprietor, partner, or stockholder in a "trade or business." §6166(b)(1). The term is not defined in the Code. However, several revenue rulings that were issued regarding former §6166A during the time it was designated as §6166 indicate that the trade or business must be an active one in order to qualify for deferral. Additional guidance is provided by some recent letter rulings.

Under the published rulings a farming, manufacturing, or service enterprise is a trade or business, but a collection of investment assets (as in a holding company) is not. "[S]ection 6166 was intended to apply only with regard to a business such as a manufacturing, mercantile, or service enterprise, as distinguished from management of investment assets." Rev. Rul. 75-365, 1975-2 C.B. 471. However, farm real estate constitutes a trade or business where it is operated by tenant farmers under rental agreements whereby the decedent receives a portion of the rental and bears a portion of the expenses and participates in management decisions. Rev. Rul. 75-366, 1975-2 C.B. 472. Real estate development and sales also qualify as a trade or business. Rev. Rul. 75-367, 1975-2 C.B. 472. *See also* Rev. Rul. 61-55, 1961-1 C.B. 713 (ownership, exploration, development, and operation of oil and gas properties was a trade or business, but mere ownership of royalty interests was not). However, the rental of real estate to children in exchange for their agreement to pay taxes and other expenses of the property does not qualify as a trade or business. LR 8020101.

In some cases a decedent's interest in a trade or business that is held in a trust will qualify as an active trade or business. For example, in LR 9015003, deferral was allowed with respect to a grantor's one-third interest in timber property that was held in trust. The trustee who directly managed the timber property was considered to be an agent for the three grantors, all of whom participated "in the decision process in running the timber business."

§11.26.3. Passive Assets, §6166(b)(9); Farmhouses, §6166(b)(3)

The value of passive assets owned by a business is not taken into account in determining whether the 35 percent requirement of §6166(a)(1) has been satisfied. §6166(b)(9). For this purpose a passive asset is any asset other than one used in the trade or business. §6166(b)(9)(B)(i). By way of example, the IRS has treated the proceeds of a policy that insured the life of a sole proprietor and that was used from time to time as security for business loans as a passive asset. LR 8848002 (TAM). On the other hand, the proceeds received by a real estate corporation in eminent domain were not passive assets if reinvested within three years. LR 8829013. If the eminent domain proceeds were not reinvested, they would be treated as a disposition as of the first day of the replacement period.

Stock in any other corporation is generally treated as a passive asset. §6166(b)(9)(B)(ii). However, stock in another corporation does not constitute a passive asset in two cases. The first applies where a §6166(b)(8) holding company election is involved; the other where the other corporation is closely held and 80 percent or more of the value of both corporations is involved in an active trade or business.

Stock is not considered a passive asset if the stock is treated as held by the decedent as a result of an election under §6166(b)(8) and the stock constitutes 35 percent or more of the value of the decedent's adjusted gross estate. §6166(b)(9)(B)(ii).

The second exception applies if a corporation owns 20 percent or more of the value of the voting stock of another corporation *or* the other corporation has 15 or fewer shareholders *and* 80 percent or more of the value of the assets of each corporation is attributable to assets used in a trade or business. In such a case the corporations are treated as one for purposes of §6166(b)(9)(B)(ii). Accordingly, there is no "stock in another corporation" for purposes of applying the passive asset rule.

For purposes of the 35 percent requirement of §6166(a) a closely-held business which is engaged in farming "includes an interest in residential buildings and related improvements on the farm which are occupied on a regular basis by the owner or lessee of the farm or by persons employed by such owner or lessee for purposes of operating or maintaining the farm." §6166(b)(3).

§11.26.4. Partnerships and Stock That Is Not Readily Tradeable, §6166(b)(7)

Deferral on less favorable terms may be available for the estates of decedents which include interests in partnerships or stock that are not readily tradeable but do not qualify for deferral under the basic provisions of §6166. In particular, a form of deferral may be available although a decedent's interest does not qualify as a closely-held business under §6166(b)(2)(B) or (C). Deferral is available under §6166(b)(7) if the decedent is treated as having owned 20 percent or more of the value of the partnership or corporation *after* the application of the entity ownership and family attribution rules of §6166(b)(2). If an executor elects to claim the benefits of §6166(b)(7), he or she is treated as having elected to make the first payment on the date the federal estate tax return is due. That is, the executor may not elect to defer making the first installment payment, which otherwise could be deferred for five years. In addition, the special four percent rate of interest, that otherwise applies to the first $153,000 in tax attributable to the closely-held business does not apply.

Under §6166(b)(7)(B) stock qualifies as not readily tradeable if there was no market for the stock on an exchange or in an over-the-counter market at the time of the decedent's death.

> **Example 11-22.** When *T* died she owned 10% in value of the voting stock of TNT, Inc., which had 50 shareholders. Thus *T*'s estate did not satisfy the alternate requirements of §6166(b)(1)(C). *T*'s sister *S* owned an additional 10% in value of the voting stock of TNT, Inc. There was no market for stock in TNT, Inc. on any exchange or on the over-the-counter market. *T*'s gross estate had a total value of $4,200,000, of which the stock in TNT, Inc. comprised $2,000,000. Items allowable as deductions under §§2053 and 2054 amounted to $200,000. *T*'s interest in TNT, Inc. does not meet the requirements of §6166(b)(1)(C). However, *T* is treated as owning the 10% of the stock held by her sister *S*. If *T*'s executor elects to take advantage of §6166(b)(7) *T* will be treated as owning 20% in value of the stock of TNT, Inc., which satisfies the requirement of §6166(b)(2)(C). In addition, the TNT, Inc. stock owned by *T* and included in her estate more than satisfies the percentage requirement of §6166(a)(2) — the value of her stock represents 50% of her adjusted gross estate ($2,000,000 ÷ ($4,200,000 − $200,000)). Thus, half of the estate tax due from *T*'s estate (50% × $1,648,000) may be paid in installments. §6166(a)(2). The first installment is due on the date provided for payment of the federal estate tax and the special 4% rate of interest does not apply to any portion of the deferred tax.

§11.26.5. Holding Companies, §6166(b)(8)

The 1984 Act added §6166(b)(8) which clarified the extent to which deferral is allowable under §6166 with respect to a decedent's interest in a holding company. Previously it was unclear whether or not the ownership of shares in a holding company could constitute the conduct of an active trade or business required by §6166. For purposes of §6166(b)(8) "the term 'holding company' means any corporation owning stock in another corporation," and "the term 'business company' means any corporation carrying on a trade or business." §6166(b)(8)(D). Note, however, that no stock is taken into account if there is a market for it on a stock exchange or in an over-the-counter market. §6166(b)(8)(B).

Under §6166(b)(8) a decedent's executor may elect to treat "the portion of the stock of any holding company which represents direct ownership (or indirect ownership through 1 or more other holding companies) by such company in a business company" as stock in such business company. In effect, if an election is made under §6166(b)(8), a decedent who owned shares in a holding company is treated as owning a proportional interest in each business in which the holding company held an interest.

Deferral under the special provisions of §6166(b)(8) is only available if the stock which the decedent is deemed to have owned in the business company meets the percentage requirements of §6166(b)(1)(C). For this purpose §6166(b)(8)(C) provides that the stock the decedent is deemed to have owned is "treated as voting stock to the extent that . . . the holding company owns directly (or through the stock of 1 or more other holding companies) voting stock in the business company." As indicated in the Temporary Regulations, if an election is made under §6166(b)(8), "then the special 4-percent interest rate of section 6601(j) and the 5-year deferral of principal payments of section 6166(a)(3) are not available." Temp. Reg. §5h.4(k)(1).

Deferral under §6166(b)(8) is only available with respect to the estates of decedents dying after July 18, 1984. Under §1021(d)(2) of the 1984 Act, a special, more limited rule applies to holding company stock owned by decedents who died prior to July 19, 1984.

Pre-1984 Act Rule. Under the pre-1984 law one could have argued that a decedent who owned stock in a holding company should have been treated as owning a proportionate interest in the operating companies in which the holding company owned stock. In brief, an executor could have argued that the decedent's interest in the holding company should qualify as a trade or business under §6166 if the companies in which the holding company owned interests were themselves operating companies. That is, the rule of §6166(b)(2)(C), which treats the property of a corporation as being owned proportionately by its shareholders, should be applied to such a case. Thus, if a decedent owned 50 percent of the stock of a holding company, the decedent should have been treated as owning half of its assets, including stock it owned in active businesses.

§11.27. Qualification Under §6166

The election must be made no later than the time the estate tax return is required to be filed, taking into account any extensions of time that are granted for filing the return. §6166(d).

> If it is made at the time the estate tax return is filed, the election is applicable both to the tax originally determined to be due and to certain deficiencies. If no election is made when the estate tax return is filed, up to the full amount of certain later deficiencies (but not any tax originally determined to be due) may be paid in installments. Reg. §20.6166-1(a).

An election must contain the following:

1. the decedent's name and taxpayer identification number;
2. the amount of tax to be paid in installments;
3. the date for payment of the first installment;
4. the number of installments in which the tax is to be paid;
5. the properties shown on the estate tax return that constitute the closely-held business; and
6. the facts that form the basis of the executor's conclusion that the estate qualifies for payment of the tax in installments. Reg. §20.6166-1(b).

§11.27.1. Protective Election

Although an estate does not appear to satisfy the requirements of §6166 when the return is filed, the executor may make a protective election to defer payment of any portion of the tax remaining unpaid at the time values are finally determined and any deficiencies that are attributable to the closely-held business. "A protective election is made by filing a notice of election with a timely filed estate tax return stating that the election is being made." Reg. §20.6166-1(d).

§11.27.2. Acceptance or Rejection of Election

The District Director is responsible for determining whether an election meets the requirements of §6166. Rev. Proc. 79-55, 1979-2 C.B. 539. Under Revenue Procedure 79-55, if the District Director determines that an election satisfies the requirements of §6166 no notice will be given to the executor. If the District Director determines that an election is not proper, the executor will be notified. Upon request the determination can be reviewed at an appellate conference. The IRS will communicate the decision on appeal to the executor. Also under Revenue Procedure

79-55, "An executor, etc., may request that the issue of whether the election under section 6166 . . . is proper be referred to the National Office for technical advice on the grounds that a lack of uniformity exists as to the disposition of the issue, or that the issue is so unusual or complex as to warrant consideration by the National Office."

The Tax Court does not have jurisdiction over a §6166 determination made by the IRS. *Estate of Floyd Sherrod,* 82 T.C. 523 (1984), *rev'd on other grounds,* 774 F.2d 1057 (11th Cir.), *cert. denied,* 479 U.S. 814 (1986). However, the Tax Court does have jurisdiction to determine the deductibility of interest payments as expenses of administration, which may have an effect on the qualification of the estate for deferral under §6166. *Estate of Dorothy H. Meyer,* 84 T.C. 560 (1985).

§11.27.3. Overpayments

The overpayment of an installment will be applied against future installments. An estate may not obtain a refund of an excess payment and enjoy the privilege of deferred payment of the balance of the estate tax. *Estate of Laura V. Bell,* 92 T.C. 714, *aff'd,* 928 F.2d 901 (9th Cir. 1991).

§11.27.4. Deficiencies

If an estate tax deficiency is asserted, the estate qualifies for deferral, and the executor has made no prior election, the executor may elect to defer under §6166(a). §6166(h)(1). However, deferral is not available with respect to deficiencies due to negligence, intentional disregard of rules, or fraud with intent to evade taxes. The election must be made not later than 60 days after the IRS issues a notice of deficiency. §6166(h)(2).

If an election is made to defer payment of a deficiency, the deficiency is prorated to the installments which would have been due had the election been timely made when the estate tax return was filed. §6166(h)(3). The portion of the deficiency prorated to installments which would already have been due must be paid at the time the election is made. Id.

§11.28. Installment Payments Under §6166

Under §6166(a)(2), the maximum amount of the estate tax (reduced by credits against the tax) that can be paid in installments is determined by the ratio of the value of the closely-held business to the adjusted gross estate. Thus, the formula is:

$$\frac{\text{Value of Closely-Held Business}}{\text{Adjusted Gross Estate}} \times \text{Net Estate Tax} = \text{Amount Subject to Deferral}$$

Again, for purposes of §6166 the term "adjusted gross estate" means the gross estate reduced by the amount of deductions allowable under §§2053 and 2054, whether or not actually claimed as deductions. §6166(b)(6). The tax may be paid in two to ten equal annual installments, the first of which is due not more than five years after the date on which the federal estate tax was due to be paid. §6166(a)(3). Each succeeding installment is due on or before a date one year after the due date for the preceding payment.

If the executor elects to take advantage of the maximum deferral, only interest is paid for a maximum of four years following the date on which the estate tax was due to be paid. §6166(f)(1). Interest and principal payments are due in each of the following years until all of the installment payments have been made. A preferential four percent interest rate applies to the greater of (1) $345,800 less the amount of the unified credit applicable to the decedent's estate (a maximum of $153,000 in 1987 and later years) and (2) the amount of the estate tax that was deferred under §6166. §6601(j). Thus, the four percent rate applies to a maximum of $153,000, which is equal to the estate tax on the first $1 million of the closely-held business included in the decedent's estate less the amount of the unified credit. The balance is subject to a rate equal to the short-term federal rate plus three percent. §6621(a)(2).

Each principal payment of tax reduces proportionally the amounts that are subject to the two interest rates. Specifically, each principal payment reduces the portion of the tax that is subject to the four percent rate by an amount that bears the same ratio to the amount of the principal payment as the original amount of the four percent portion bears to the total amount of tax deferred under §6166. A formula puts it more concisely:

$$\text{Amount of installment payment of tax} \times \frac{\text{Amount subject to 4\% rate}}{\text{Total amount of tax deferred}} = \text{Annual Reduction in 4\% portion}$$

Deduction for Interest Payments. Annual payments of interest on the deferred tax are deductible as administration expenses under

§2053(a)(2). Rev. Rul. 78-125, 1978-1 C.B. 292. However, the deduction is only allowed for interest actually paid — not for estimated future payments. *Estate of Pierre L. Bailly,* 81 T.C. 246 (1983), *on reconsideration,* 81 T.C. 949 (1983). The allowance of additional deductions for interest payments of course reduces the amount of estate tax, including the amount of future installments. As each interest payment is made the estate should file a supplemental Form 706, captioned "Supplemental Information." Rev. Proc. 81-27, 1981-2 C.B. 548. According to the IRS the supplemental 706 can be filed with the annual installment payment or later.

§11.29. ACCELERATION UNDER §6166(g)

The deferral election is terminated and the date for payment of the tax is accelerated under a variety of circumstances enumerated in §6166(g). Acceleration occurs if one-half or more in value of the decedent's interest in the business is redeemed, sold, exchanged, or otherwise disposed of. Thus, the sale of a decedent's interest in a closely-held business pursuant to a buy-sell agreement would accelerate the time for payment of the tax. However, acceleration does not occur as a result of certain dispositions. Corporate reorganizations and tax-free exchanges are exempted by §6166(g)(1)(C). A liquidation under §331 after which the same business is continued by a partnership in which the estate and other parties will have the same proportionate interest as before does not constitute a disposition or withdrawal of assets. LR 8103066. Similarly, a liquidation under §331 and distribution of the corporation's assets to a family trust was not treated as a disposition or withdrawal of assets for purposes of §6166(g). LR 8829013.

The sale of a portion of the assets of a business, such as a farm, in order to pay mortgages on the property is treated as a transaction in the ordinary course of business that does not constitute a disposition that would trigger acceleration. LR 8441029. In contrast, the sale by one beneficiary to another of real property used in the farming business is a disposition. LR 8730006.

§11.29.1. Distribution Under Will, §6166(g)(1)(D)

Acceleration is not triggered by a distribution of an interest in a decedent's business to a person entitled to receive it by reason of the decedent's will, the law of intestate succession, or a trust created by the decedent. §6166(g)(1)(D). *See, e.g.,* LR 8339023 (division of farm into 2 parcels by decedent's heirs does not trigger acceleration, but discontinuance of use of property as a farm would accelerate). Likewise, a transfer by reason of the subsequent death of a person who received the property from the decedent (or a transferee of such person) is also exempt, provided that each transferee is a family member (within the meaning of §267(c)(4)) of the transferor. Id.

The transfer by a distributee of an interest in the decedent's business to a grantor trust is not a disposition that will trigger acceleration. LR 8326023. The result reached in LR 8326023 is consistent with that reached in other contexts. For example, the transfer of an installment obligation to a grantor trust is not treated as a disposition under §453B. *See* §9.6.3.

§11.29.2. Withdrawals of Money or Other Property, §6166(g)(1)

The time for payment of the tax is accelerated if withdrawals of money and other property from the business equal or exceed half of its value. §6166(g)(1)(A). However, a redemption that qualifies under §303 is not counted for purposes of the one-half withdrawal rule if an amount equal to the redemption distribution is paid on the remaining balance of the estate tax within one year of the distribution. §6166(g)(1)(B). Instead, under this exception the amount of the redemption reduces the base against which the one-half is calculated. Id.

Example 11-23. *D*'s adjusted gross estate had a value of $3,100,000 upon which a net estate tax of $1,000,000 was due after giving effect to all allowable credits. *D*'s interest in a closely-held corporation was worth $2,100,000 or about 67.75% of *D*'s adjusted gross estate. Pursuant to an election made by *D*'s executor, the time for payment of $677,500 of the tax was deferred under §6166. Under §6166(g) time for payment of the tax would be accelerated if one-half or more in value of the stock were redeemed, sold, exchanged, or otherwise disposed of. Thus, the estate could not redeem or dispose of $1,050,000 of *D*'s stock unless some payments were made on the estate tax liability. However, amounts received in a distribution that met the requirements of §303 are not counted if they are applied in payment of the tax. Thus, if $300,000 of *D*'s stock were redeemed under §303 and the proceeds were applied in payment of the tax, the amount of the redemption would not be counted toward the one-half limit. Instead, the base for computing the one-half limit would be reduced from $2,100,000 to $1,800,000. In effect the withdrawal and application of funds in payment of the principal amount of the tax only causes a one-half reduction in the amount that can be withdrawn without restriction as to its use.

Until 1986 it was unclear whether the exception of §6166(g)(1)(B) would be applied on a "redemption-by-redemption" basis, a "cumulative" basis, or both. The redemption-by-redemption approach requires the estate to pay the amount or a §303 redemption toward the estate tax and interest within one year following the receipt of the redemption distribution. An estate might experience difficulty in satisfying this test — funds received in a §303 redemption could be required for other purposes, such as the payment of debts or expenses of administration. Under the cumulative approach the total of all §303 redemptions may not exceed the total of all estate tax and interest payments made within one year following the redemption distribution. The application of the funds received in a particular redemption is disregarded. Happily, in Rev. Rul. 86-54, 1986 C.B. 356, the IRS ruled that it will "permit the cumulative approach and the redemption-by-redemption approach to be used interchangeably. Estates, therefore, may qualify for the exclusion under section 6166(g)(1)(B) if a section 303 redemption (or each of a series of redemptions) qualifies under either approach."

§11.29.3. Estate Has Undistributed Income, §6166(g)(2)

If the estate has undistributed net income for a taxable year ending on or after the date for payment of the first installment, the estate must pay an amount equal to the undistributed income toward the tax on or before the date the income tax return must be filed for the year. §6166(g)(2).

§11.29.4. Failure to Pay Income and Principal on Time, §6166(g)(3)

If any payment of principal or interest is not made on time, the unpaid portion of the tax must be paid upon notice and demand from the Secretary. §6166(g)(3). However, if the delinquent amount is paid within six months of the time it was due, acceleration does not occur. Instead, the preferential four percent rate does not apply to the payment and a penalty is imposed of five percent of the amount of the payment for each month the payment was late. §6166(g)(3)(B).

§11.30. WORKSHEET FOR MAKING §6166 CALCULATIONS

Software programs such as the BNA Estate Tax Spreadsheet allow projections and calculations involving §6166 to be made. A program should make the interrelated computations that are required in order to take into account the deductibility of the interest paid by the estate on the amount of the tax deferral. If a program is not readily available the following form can be used to make an estimate.

Section 6166 Worksheet (Fifteen-year deferral)

Part I. Qualifications

1. Gross estate (estimate or enter from Form 706, page 1, line 1, including the value of property transferred within 3 years of death per §2035(d)(3)) (item 1) __________
2. *Less:* Deductions allowable under §§2053 and 2054, whether or not claimed on Form 706:
   a. Debts, funeral, and administrative expenses (allowable under §2053) __________
   b. Casualty losses (allowable under §2054) +__________
   Total (item 2) −__________
3. Adjusted gross estate (item 1 less item 2) (item 3) __________
4. Value of closely-held business (a proprietorship, partnership, or corporation carrying on a trade or business in which decedent was one of 15 or fewer owners or in which decedent owned 20% or more of the capital interest. §6166(b). Two or more businesses may be aggregated if at least 20% of the total value of each business is included in the shareholder's estate. §6166(c)). (item 4) __________
5. Divide item 4 by item 3. (If the closely-held business repre-

sents more than 35% of the adjusted gross estate, item 3, the requirements of §6166 are met.) (item 5) __________

Part II. Amount to be deferred

6. Net federal estate tax (estimate or enter from Form 706, line 21) (item 6) __________
7. Enter percentage from item 5 above (item 7) __________
8. Maximum deferrable amount (item 6 × item 7) (item 8) __________
9. Years over which payments to be made (2–10) (item 9) __________

(The executor may elect to pay part or all of the amount of tax shown at item 9 in 2–10 equal installments, the first of which is due no more than 5 years after the date prescribed for payment of the tax (9 months after death). Each succeeding installment is due one year after the preceding installment. §6166(a)(3).)

10. Amount of annual principal installments (divide item 8 by item 9) (item 10) __________

Part III. Interest rates

11. Amount of tax deferred (item 8 above) (item 11) __________
12. Amount subject to special 4% interest rate (not to exceed the larger of the amount of tax deferred under §6166, or $345,800 reduced by the amount of the unified credit). §6601(j)(2). (item 12) __________
13. Initial amount subject to variable rate (item 13) __________

Part IV. Amount of payments years 1-4 (Estimated)

14. Estimated annual interest payments years 1-4:
    Item 12 × 4% ________
    Item 13 × estimated variable rate +________ __________
15. Estimated total payments years 1-4 (item 14 × 4) __________

Part V. Payments in years 5-14 (Estimated)
Unless payments are accelerated voluntarily or involuntarily, the amount of each successive annual payment of principal will be slightly less. The reduction will result when the basis estate tax liability of the estate is recalculated. A recalculation will be made because the payment of interest on the outstanding balance of tax due is a deductible expense of administration under §2053. Because the IRS will not allow the deduction until the interest has actually been paid, the amount of the federal estate tax must be recalculated after each payment. *See* §12.13. Each principal payment reduces the amount subject to each interest rate by a proportionate amount. *See* §6601(j)(3).

E. RECAPITALIZATIONS

> In a typical recapitalization the parents, who have a substantial interest in the family business, retain preferred stock, and perhaps some common stock, transferring the bulk of the common stock, or all of that stock, to their children. As a result, the value of their interest in the corporation will stay static, since preferred stock is much like a mortgage in terms of economics if not in terms of legal theory. The common stock will carry the growth of the business to the children. The transfer of the common stock can either be done by gift or by sale. To the extent the company grows in value faster than the amount of the dividends paid on the preferred, wealth inures to the children or to trusts that have been established for their benefit. Panel Discussion (and Outlines), The Estate Freezing Rage: A Practical Look at Planning Opportunitites and Potential Problems, 15 Real Prop. Prob. & Tr. J. 19, 34 (1980) (statement of John Cohan).

§11.31. OVERVIEW

Recapitalizations of the type described above were intended to shift all of the future growth in value of the business to the donees at little or no gift tax cost. The success of the arrangement depended upon substantially all of the value of the corporation being absorbed by the preferred stock which was retained by the donor-parents. In order to create preferred stock of sufficiently high value the preferred stock had to carry high dividend rates. Taxpayers often tried to squeak by with noncumulative preferred, but the cumulative feature was typically required in order to support a sufficiently high valuation of the preferred stock. As a practical matter, preferred stock recapitalizations were out of reach for most closely-held corporations simply because they could not afford to pay high annual dividends on preferred stock. The payment of preferred stock dividends was costly because the payments were not deductible by the corporation for income tax purposes but they were includible in the recipients' income. The concern of the IRS that the retained preferred stock be properly valued led to the publication of Rev. Rul. 83-119 1983-2 C.B. 57, and Rev. Rul. 83-120, 1983-2 C.B. 170. In particular, Revenue Ruling 83-120 emphasized that the valuation of preferred stock was primarily dependent upon its dividend rate and preference; the capacity of the corporation to pay the dividends and the extent of the liquidation protection and preference. It also pointed out the extent to which the preferred stock had voting rights might increase its value. Finally, Revenue Ruling 83-120 noted that the common stock would have a substantial value if all future appreciation in value was allocated to the common stock.

Continuing concerns about abusive valuations used in recapitalizations and similar wealth-shifting techniques led to the enactment of former §2036(c) in 1987. Section 2036(c) was an extraordinarily complex attempt to control the use of estate freezes through the estate tax. In simplest terms, §2036(c) required the inclusion in a decendent's estate of interests in an enterprise that were transferred during lifetime if (1) they were entitled to a disproportionate share in the appreciation of the enterprise, and (2) the transferor retained an interest in the income or rights in the enterprise. The uncertainty generated by the statute led to the eventual publication of an explanatory notice (Notice 89-99, 1989-2 C.B. 422) of unusual complexity and difficulty. In 1990 Congress responded to the outcry over §2036(c) by repealing it retrospectively and substituting an approach based on the gift tax that requires objectively supportable valuation of retained interests for valuation purposes. The provisions of particular relevance to the valuation of interests arising in a recapitalization of a corporation or partnership are found in §§2701 and 2704, which are designed to eliminate the potential for abusive valuations. Section 2702, which is concerned with the valuation of retained interests in trusts, is examined in Chapter 9; §2703, which is concerned with the effect of options, buy-sell agreements, and other rights to acquire property at less than its fair market value, is reviewed in Part B of this chapter.

A corporation that is recapitalized will have two or more classes of stock. Accordingly, it would no longer qualify as an S corporation. The loss of S corporation status is one of the factors that a client must consider in deciding whether or not to recapitalize. Because of the tax advantages of S corporations and the advent of the new valuation rules of §2701, the use of recapitalizations will probably continue to decline.

§11.32. Application and Effect of §2701

> Generally, section 2701 applies when an interest in a corporation or partnership is transferred to a member of the transferor's family and the transferor or an applicable family member retains a certain type of interest senior to the transferred interest (an "applicable retained interest"). Notice of Proposed Rulemaking, 56 Fed. Reg. 46,244, 46,246 (Sept. 11, 1991).

Section 2701 requires that the value of a transferred interest be determined according to the subtraction method (*i.e.,* by subtracting the value of the retained interest from the value of the entire entity). *See* Notice of Proposed Rulemaking, 56 Fed. Reg. 46244, 46246 (Sept. 11, 1991). The rules of §2701 are also designed to require retained interests to be valued according to certain fixed criteria if the donor gives interests of a different class to family members. The goal is to prevent the inflated valuation of retained interests that do not have fixed cumulative rights to distributions (*i.e.,* noncumulative preferred stock). Such distribution rights are valued at zero under §2701(a)(3)(A). On the other hand, the value of cumulative preferred stock and other interests that carry the right to receive fixed annual cumulative payments ("qualified payments") is taken into account. §2701(c)(3).

Section 2701 does not apply to retained interests (1) for which market quotations are readily available on an established securities market, §2701(a)(2)(A); (2) that are of the same class as the transferred interest, §2701(a)(2)(B); or (3) that are proportionately the same as the transferred interest without regard to nonlapsing differences in voting power (or nonlapsing differences with respect to the management of a partnership), §2701(a)(2)(C). Also, note that §2701 does not apply to gifts made (1) prior to October 9, 1990 or (2) to donees who are not family members. For this purpose the term "family member" only includes "the transferor's spouse, a lineal descendant of the transferor or the transferor's spouse, and the spouse of any such descendant." §2701(e)(1). Thus, transfers to siblings and their descendants and uncles and aunts and their descendants are subject to the "old" rules and not §2701.

Section 2701(e)(6) requires the Secretary to issue regulations that provide for an appropriate adjustment where there is a subsequent transfer of an applicable retained interest that was valued under the special valuation rules of §2701. Proposed Regulation §25.2701-5 does so by allowing the transferor's estate a nonrefundable credit against the estate tax. The amount of the credit is the amount of the gift tax payable on the property valued under §2701 multiplied by a fraction, the numerator of which is the amount by which taxable gifts were increased pursuant to §2701 and the denominator of which is the amount of the transfer determined under §2701.

The adjustment provided for in Prop. Reg. §25.2701-5 is flawed in two respects. First, the availability of the credit is postponed until the death of the transferor. It should be available if the retained interest is transferred inter vivos. Second, under the credit approach the transferor's estate may be subject to marginal tax rates that are higher than they should be. That occurs because when the transferor dies the value of the initial transfer determined under §2701 remains a part of his or her tax base together with the estate tax value of the retained interest. The allowance of a credit equal to a portion of the gift tax paid on the initial transfer is insufficient. Instead, the amount by which taxable gifts were increased as a result of the application of §2701 should be deleted from the transferor's tax base. Alternatively, the credit could be based upon the amount of estate tax imposed on an amount by which taxable gifts were increased pursuant to §2701. The Regulations under §2702 provide for an adjustment based upon a reduction in the aggregate amount of taxable gifts. Reg. §25.2702-6.

Under §11602(e)(1) of the 1990 Act, the provisions of §§2701 and 2702 apply to transfers made after October 8, 1990. However, in the case of property transferred prior to October 9, 1990, the failure to exercise a right of conversion, a failure to pay dividends, or a failure to exercise other rights specified in the Regulations is not to be treated as a subsequent transfer. Act §11602(e)(1)(B).

§11.33. Scope and Effect of §2704

> The conference agreement provides that the lapse of a voting or liquidation right in a family-controlled corporation or partnership results in a transfer by gift or an inclusion in the gross estate. The amount of the transfer is the value of all interests in the entity held by the transferor immediately before the lapse (assuming the right was nonlapsing) over the value of the interests immediately after the lapse. The conference agreement grants the Secretary of the Treasury regulatory authority to apply these rules to rights similar to voting and liquidation rights. H.R. Conf. Rep. 101-964, 101st Cong., 2d Sess. 1137 (1990).

Section 2704 prescribes two independent rules. First, under §2704(a) the lapse of voting or liquidation rights in a family-controlled corporation or partnership is treated as a transfer of value for gift and estate tax purposes. See Reg. §25.2704-1. Thus, any reduction in value that results from the lapse of voting or liquidation rights in a family-controlled business will be subject to the gift or estate tax. The use of voting or liquidation rights that lapse upon the death of the owner of an interest in a partnership or corporation is sometimes appropriate for nontax reasons. Section 2704 is designed to prevent such a lapse from depressing the value of the owner's interest for gift or estate tax purposes. *See* Reg. §25.2701-1(d).

A voting right of a liquidation right may be conferred by or lapse by reason of state law, a corporate charter or bylaws, an agreement, or any other means. Reg. §25.2704-1(a)(4). In general, "a transfer of an interest that results in the lapse of a liquidation right is not subject to this section if the rights with respect to the transferred interest are not restricted or eliminated." Reg. §25.2704-1(c).

Second, under §2704(b) the value of an interest in a family-controlled corporation or partnership that is transferred to a member of the transferor's family is determined without regard to certain restrictions on liquidation ("applicable restrictions"). The rule of §2704(b) applies to restrictions that prevent the transferee from liquidating the corporation or partnership. §2704(b)(2). In effect, the transferred interest is to be valued as if the corporation or partnership did not impose any restrictions on the transferee's right to liquidate. Both the statute and the Regulations indicate that the rules do not apply to a commercially reasonable restriction on liquidation imposed by an unrelated person providing financing to the entity for trade or business operations. §2704(b)(3); Reg. §25.2704-2(b). They also do not apply to any restriction imposed by state or federal law. Id. Also, note that according to the Conference Committee Report, "These rules do not affect minority discounts or other discounts available under present law." H.R. Conf. Rep. 91-964, 101st Cong., 2d Sess. 1137 (1990). Thus, unmarketability and minority discounts will continue to be available in valuing interests in closely-held businesses.

According to the Conference Committee Report, §2704 was adopted in order to overturn *Estate of Daniel J. Harrison,* 52 T.C.M. 1306 (1987), which permitted the lapse of a liquidation right at the death of the decedent to diminish substantially the value of the interest included in the decedent's estate. Id. The lapse of the decedent's liquidation right reduced the value of his interest from almost $60 million to $33 million — costing the federal fisc about $16 million.

The operation of §2704 is illustrated by Example 11-24, Example 11-25, and Example 11-26, which were adapted from the Conference Committee Report.

Example 11-24. *X* and her child, *C,* control a corporation. The voting rights associated with *X*'s stock will terminate on her death. Under §2704(a) the federal estate tax value of *X*'s stock is determined without regard to the lapse of her voting right. *See* Reg. §25.2704-1(a).

Example 11-25. *X* owns a general interest in a partnership and her daughter, *D,* owns a limited interest. Under the terms of the partnership agreement the general partner has the right to liquidate the partnership, which expires after 10 years. When the liquidation right of the general partnership interest lapses, *X* is treated as having made a gift to *D.* The gift is equal to the excess of (1) the value of the general partnership interest before the lapse over (2) the value of the general partnership interest after the lapse.

Example 11-26. *X* and her daughter, *D,* are the only partners of a general partnership. The partnership agreement provides that the partnership cannot be terminated by one partner alone. *X* left her partnership interest to her son, *S. D* and *S* acting together could remove the restriction on termination of the partnership. The federal estate tax value of *X*'s partnership interest is determined without regard to the restriction on termination. However, the interest might qualify for a fragmentation discount.

§11.34. Income Tax Treatment of Recapitalizations

Since 1921, recapitalizations have been recognized as a permissible form of tax-free corporate reorganization. §368(a)(1)(E) (an E-type reorganization). Neither the Code nor the Regulations define the term "recapitalization"; however, the Regulations do provide some terse examples. For the estate planner, the most important example is this one: "A corporation issues preferred stock, previously authorized but unissued, for outstanding common stock." Reg. §1.368-2(e)(3). The Supreme Court has described a recapitalization as a "reshuffling of a capital structure within the framework of an existing corporation." *Helvering v. Southwest Consolidated Corp.,* 315 U.S. 194, 202 (1942).

Simply put, a recapitalization involves an exchange of stock or securities of a corporation for other stock or securities of the same corporation. Thus, the controlling shareholder in a closely-held corporation is permitted to exchange some or all of his or her common stock for preferred stock without incurring any current tax liability. Such an exchange gives a shareholder greater flexibility in transferring his or her interests inter vivos or at death. For example, it may be desirable to transfer common stock to relatives who are active in a family business and preferred stock to those who are not.

§11.34.1. Business Purpose of Recapitalization

In order to qualify as a tax-free recapitalization, the change in the corporation's capital structure must serve a valid business purpose. This requirement is met if, for example, the recapitalization either shifts control to the persons active in the management of the corporation, LR 8033025, or encourages the shareholders to remain active in the conduct of the company's business. Some courts have found that it is sufficient if the recapitalization serves the business needs of the shareholders as opposed to the needs of the corporation. See *Estate of Parshelsky v. Commissioner,* 303 F.2d 14 (2d Cir. 1962). However, the IRS and most courts require the recapitalization to serve the business needs of the corporation. See *Rafferty v. Commissioner,* 452 F.2d 767 (1st Cir. 1971), *cert. denied,* 408 U.S. 922 (1972); Rev. Rul. 77-321, 1977-2 C.B. 98. The distinction between corporate and personal purposes is highly artificial where closely-held businesses are concerned. As the court noted in *Parshelsky,* "It is not only difficult but often purely formalistic to distinguish between corporate and personal benefit." 303 F.2d at 19. In most cases it is simple enough to identify a corporate business purpose that is served by a proposed recapitalization. The IRS will not issue rulings regarding whether or not a transaction involving a closely-held corporation constitutes a corporate recapitalization within the meaning of §368(a)(1)(E). Rev. Proc. 91-3, 1991-1 C.B. 364.

§11.34.2. Boot

Gain may be recognized in connection with a recapitalization if "boot" is received as a result of the exchange. For example, gain is recognized where securities (*i.e.,* bonds) are issued to a shareholder who surrendered no securities. §356(a)(1). The gain in such a case is ordinary income if the distribution of the securities had the effect of a dividend. §356(a)(2). A similar result occurs if the principal amount of the securities received exceeds the principal amount of the securities surrendered. §354(a).

§11.34.3. Section 306 Stock

The rough equivalence of the tax rates applicable to capital gains and to ordinary income diminishes the significance of stock being classified as section 306 stock. Some important differences remain, which will increase if the differential in the tax rates applicable to ordinary income and capital gains increases significantly.

Preferred stock issued in connection with a recapitalization is sometimes classified as section 306 stock, which may cause adverse income tax consequences for the distributees. The receipt of section 306 stock does not itself have any immediate adverse income tax consequences. Instead, the characterization of the stock carries forward and may cause the shareholder to realize some ordinary income when the stock is sold or exchanged. For example, a sale of part of a shareholder's section 306 stock would give rise to ordinary income to the extent the amount received would have been treated as a dividend had the corporation distributed cash instead of the preferred stock. The ordinary income element is limited to the amount by which the earnings and profits of the corporation at the time of distribution exceeded the shareholder's allocated basis in the shares that were transferred. Any additional amount the shareholder receives is capital gain. The classification of the proceeds as ordinary income in such a case would also limit the amount allowable as a charitable deduction if the stock were contributed to charity. *See* §170(e)(1)(A); Reg. §1.170A-4(b)(1). *See also* §8.9.

By way of background, §306 was added to the Code in 1954 to block the use of the preferred stock bailout as a device for withdrawing funds from the corporation in the form of capital gains rather than ordinary income. Congressional action was hastened when the bailout won judicial approval in *Chamberlin v. Commissioner,* 207 F.2d 462 (6th Cir. 1953), *cert. denied,* 347 U.S. 918 (1954). A bailout, such as the one involved in *Chamberlin,* typically involved the following steps:

1. The corporation issued redeemable preferred stock as a stock dividend on the outstanding common stock. The receipt of the stock dividend was not taxable by reason of the predecessor of §305.
2. The common shareholders sold the preferred stock for an amount close to its redemption value to third-party investors, who expected the corporation to redeem the stock promptly. Prior to the adoption of §306 the gain on the sale was characterized as capital gain, which would almost always be long-term capital gain because the holding period of the common stock also applied to the preferred stock.
3. The corporation redeemed the preferred stock from the third parties, who usually recognized a small gain on the transaction.

What Is Section 306 Stock? Stock distributed as a tax-free stock dividend is classified as section 306 stock except for common stock that is received as a distribution on common stock. §306(c)(1)(A). More important for present purposes, stock distributed in connection with a recapitalization is classified as section 306 stock if the effect of the transaction is substantially the same as a stock dividend or is received in exchange for section 306 stock. §306(c)(1)(B). In this connection,

Reg. §1.306-3(d) provides, "Ordinarily, section 306 stock includes stock which is not common stock received in pursuance of a plan of reorganization (within the meaning of section 368(a)) . . . if cash received in lieu of such stock would have been treated as a dividend. . . ." Accordingly, the classification of the preferred stock received in a recapitalization in part turns upon the application of the rules of §302. *See* §11.15. Applying the rules of §302, preferred stock received by a shareholder in exchange for *all* of the shareholder's common stock would not be classified as section 306 stock if the distribution of cash in case of such a complete termination would not be treated as a dividend. *See* §302(b)(3); Rev. Rul. 59-84, 1959-1 C.B. 71. However, for purposes of determining whether or not the shareholder surrendered all of his or her stock, the 1982 Act amended §306(c)(4) to require that the attribution rules of §318 be applied. Accordingly, a stockholder exchanging common stock for preferred stock will be considered to own the common stock held by his or her spouse, children, grandchildren and grandparents. As a result, in a family recapitalization the stock received by the senior family member will often be classified as section 306 stock. Prior to the 1982 Act, the IRS would not apply the attribution rules of §318 where a shareholder surrendered all of his or her common stock in exchange for the preferred. Accordingly, preferred stock issued to a shareholder in exchange for all of his or her common stock was not classified as section 306 stock, although other family members continue to own common stock in the same corporation. *See, e.g.,* LR 7730008; LR 8018068; LR 8020124.

Dispositions Not Reached by §306. The §306 taint is less significant if the shareholder plans to retain the stock until the time of his or her death, after which the stock will no longer be classified as section 306 stock. Regulation §1.306-3(e) recognizes that "[s]ection 306 stock ceases to be so classified if the basis of such stock is determined by reference to its fair market value on the date of the decedent-shareholder's death or the optional valuation date under section 1014." Also, the proceeds of the sale of the shareholder's entire interest to an unrelated party are not taxed as ordinary income. §306(b)(1)(A); Rev. Rul. 77-455, 1977-2 C.B. 93. Liquidations and certain other dispositions are also excepted by section 306(b) from treatment as ordinary income. Despite the exceptions, if ordinary income tax rates are high the holder of section 306 stock may feel substantially "locked in" by the tax rules applicable to the stock.

§11.34.4. Section 305 Problems

Section 305 governs the income tax treatment of distributions made by a corporation of its own stock, or rights to acquire its stock. Under the general rule of §305(a), a pro rata stock dividend paid to common shareholders is not includible in their gross income. However, a wide range of actual or constructive distributions are taxable as dividends under §§305(b) and (c). For example, a distribution of stock is taxable under §305(b)(1) if it is payable at the election of any shareholder in money or property instead of stock. Also, a distribution is taxable if it has the result of the receipt of cash or other property by some shareholders and an increase in the proportionate interests of other shareholders in the assets or the earnings and profits of the corporation. §305(b)(2). However, §305 does not extend to nonvoting preferred stock that was issued to the decedent's estate and the surviving shareholder in connection with a post-mortem recapitalization and was subsequently redeemed by the corporation under §303. Rev. Rul. 87-132, 1987-2 C.B. 82. Importantly, virtually any distribution of stock with respect to preferred stock is treated as a dividend. §305(b)(4).

Most reorganizations of closely-held family corporations will not involve a distribution that will be treated as a dividend under §305. However, a problem may be encountered under §305(b)(4) if the preferred stock is redeemable at a premium after a specified period.

§11.34.5. Redemption Premium, §305(c)

Most commonly the preferred stock issued in connection with the recapitalization of a closely-held corporation is not callable by the corporation. Because of the rules of §305(c), special care must be exercised when the preferred stock is redeemable at a premium after a specified period of time. Under Reg. §1.305-5(b) the preferred stock may carry a reasaonable redemption premium without giving rise to a distribution in the nature of a dividend. In particular, the Regulations provide that "a redemption premium not in excess of ten percent of the issue price on stock which is not redeemable for 5 years from the date of issue shall be considered reasonable." Reg. §1.305-5(b)(2). If a redemption premium is excessive, the preferred shareholders will be considered under §305(c) to have received a distribution of additional stock on the preferred stock over the period of time during which the preferred stock could not be called for redemption. Reg. §1.305-5(b)(1). In Rev. Rul. 83-119, 1983-2 C.B. 57, the IRS ruled on a recapitalization in which the corporation issued preferred stock that was redeemable on the holder's death at a price in excess of 110 percent of the issue price. It held that the excess was a distribution subject to §305(b)(4). Accordingly, the excess was considered to be constructively received ratably over the shareholder's life expectancy.

Example 11-27. Zero Corp. issued preferred stock worth $100 per share in exchange for common stock in a recapitalization.

> The preferred stock did not provide for the payment of dividends and is redeemable at the end of 5 years for $185 per share, with yearly increases thereafter of $15 per year. Under the circumstances a call premium in excess of $10 cannot be justified. The $75 excess of the call premium ($85) over the amount of a reasonable premium ($10) is considered to have been received on each share of preferred stock in equal portions over the 5-year call period. Each subsequent increase of $15 per year is considered to be an additional distribution on the preferred stock. *See* Reg. §1.305-5(d), example 5.

The 1990 Act amended §305(c) to require the IRS to issue regulations treating redemption premiums in excess of certain guidelines as taxable to the owner of the preferred stock on an economic accrual basis. If the issuer is required to redeem the stock at a specified time or if the holder has the option to require the issuer to redeem the stock, a redemption premium resulting from such requirement or option is treated as reasonable only if the premium does not exceed an amount determined under the principles of §1273(a)(3) (the original issue discount rules, or "OID rules"). According to the House Committee Report, under the OID rules an amount is reasonable if it does not exceed the product of "(1) one-quarter of one percent of the redemption price and (2) the number of complete years to maturity)." H.R. Rep. No. 101-881, 101st Cong., 2d Sess. 347 (1990). If stock is callable by the issuer, the OID rules do not apply. Instead, "if such premium is considered to be unreasonable under regulations in effect without regard to this provision . . . the entire call premium will be accrued over the period of time during which the preferred stock cannot be called for redemption." Id. at 348.

Prior to the 1990 Act the redemption premium problem could be avoided by the parties in a variety of ways. Some of the same opportunities may remain. For example, the redemption premium could be eliminated entirely or the stock could be made immediately redeemable or never redeemable. *See, e.g.,* LR 8020124. Under the preexisting regulations, where the preferred stock is redeemable at a premium after a fixed period of time, the premium is commonly limited to the amount permitted under the Regulations (*i.e.,* ten percent on stock that is not redeemable for five years). The amount of a redemption premium will, of course, affect the value of the stock gift and estate tax value of the preferred stock.

§11.35. Recapitalization Tax Freezes Not Subject to §2701

The use of a recapitalization to shift future appreciation in the value of a corporation to younger generation family members at a reduced gift tax cost was relatively routine prior to the 1987 Act. Preferred stock freezes were possible because the preferred stock would not increase in value although the corporation prospered in the future. Instead, all of the future growth was reflected in the value of the common stock.

The opportunity to engage in a traditional preferred stock freeze remains with respect to transfers that are not subject to §2701 (*i.e.,* recapitalizations in which the transferees are *not* members of the transferor's family as defined by §2701(e)(1)). Members of the family include the transferor's spouse; lineal descendants of the transferor and the transferor's spouse; and the spouses of such descendants. Thus, the term does not include siblings, nieces and nephews, cousins, and ascendant relatives.

> **Example 11-28.** Cosmos, Inc. had 1,000 shares of voting common stock outstanding all of which were owned by *X*. *X* wished to turn over more management responsibilities to his nieces, who were employed by Cosmos. In order to encourage their continued participation in the business of Cosmos, the capital structure was reorganized so his nieces would be the primary beneficiaries of any future growth. Specifically, *X* exchanged his 1,000 shares of common stock for 10,000 shares of voting $100 par value 10% cumulative preferred stock and 5,000 shares of common stock. *X* gave the common stock to his nieces. In similar cases the IRS has ruled that the exchange of the preferred stock for common stock was a tax-free recapitalization under §368(a)(1)(E). *See, e.g.,* LR 8044021.
>
> The gifts of common stock are not subject to §2701 because the transferees are not members of *X*'s family. Accordingly, the common stock gifted by *X* is valued according to its fair market value. The value was traditionally fixed at the amount by which the value of the preferred stock received by *X*, determined according to its fair market value, was less than the value of the common stock that *X* exchanged for it.
>
> If the gifts had been made to children or other family members, the amount of *X*'s gifts would be determined under §2701 according to a similar subtraction method. That is, the gift would be equal to the total value of Cosmos reduced by the value of the "distribution rights" retained by *X*. *See* Reg. §25.2701-1(a)(2). However, the value of any distribution right in a controlled corporation is zero unless it is a qualified payment right. Under

§2701(c)(3), a fixed cumulative dividend is a qualified payment right. Accordingly, the value of the preferred stock retained by *X* would be taken into account in determining the amount of *X*'s gift. In any case, however, the common stock would have a value equal to 10% of the total value of all equity interests in Cosmos. §2701(a)(4)(A).

§11.35.1. Valuation Problems

> Fundamentally, I look at a standard preferred stock as though it were a Christmas tree. The tree is simple. It has straight lines. And it is easy to understand. But then we start to put ornaments on this Christmas tree, all kinds of ornaments. We give it a low dividend rate, or a high dividend rate, or a high call price, or we make it noncumulative, and so on. As a matter of fact, we have so many ornaments that we can't see the tree. . . . But, I warn you, someone has to value the preferred stock. If you insist on putting so many ornaments on this tree that it is not possible to value it, you are exposing your client to a significant risk.
>
> This brings me the principal point I want to make on preferred stock valuations. No matter how you dress up the preferred stock with ornaments, you just can't get virtually one hundred percent of the value of the company into the preferred stock. I know you would like to do that. And I know your clients would like to do that; believe me, I sympathize with the problem. But there is just no way that a valuation expert can substantiate a conclusion that the value of the preferred stock is equal to 100 percent of the value of the company. Panel Discussion (and Outlines), The Estate Freezing Rage: A Practical Look at the Planning Opportunities and Potential Problems, 15 Real Prop., Prob. & Tr. J. 19, 54 (1980) (statement of Robert Meyers).

A recapitalization that is not subject to §2701 confronts the planner with serious problems regarding the valuation of the corporation and of the preferred stock issued in connection with the transaction. The valuation of the stock of a closely-held corporation is controversial enough without adding the difficulty of placing a value on preferred stock issued in a recapitalization of the corporation. Of course, the valuation of the stock is a factual matter upon which the IRS will not issue an advance ruling. As indicated above, rulings are not generally issued concerning the recapitalization of closely-held corporations. In general, recapitalizations should be planned with the advice of a valuation expert, who will be available to testify if the taxpayer's valuations are challenged.

§11.35.2. Gift or Additional Compensation?

Although a recapitalization qualifies under §368(a)(1)(E), the exchange of stock may have gift, income, or estate tax consequences under other sections of the Code. For example, where the value of the preferred stock received by a shareholder is less than the value of the common stock surrendered by the shareholder, the recapitalization will involve a gift to the other shareholders or the payment of additional compensation to them. Where the other shareholders are unrelated, the transaction may be treated as a bona fide business transaction that does not give rise to any gift tax liability. *See* Reg. §25.2512-8. If the exchanging shareholder is related to the other shareholders, the IRS will almost certainly charge that the recapitalization involved a gift to the others. The opposite result occurs where the value of the preferred stock received by a shareholder exceeds the value of the common stock he or she surrendered: Either the other shareholders made a gift to the exchanging shareholder or additional compensation was paid to him or her. The IRS has stated that it would apply that analysis to recapitalizations:

> However, if *A* receives shares of preferred stock having a fair market value in excess of the fair market value of the common stock surrendered, or surrenders shares of common stock having a fair market value in excess of the fair market value of the preferred stock received, the amount representing such excess will be treated as having been used to make gifts, pay compensation, satisfy obligations of any kind, or for whatever purpose the facts indicate. Rev. Rul. 74-269, 1974-1 C.B. 87.

If a post-1981 exchange involves an outright gift, presumably none of the value of the common stock is includible in the exchanging shareholder's estate although he or she dies within three years of the exchange. Of course, any common stock included in the shareholder's estate under §§2035(d)(2), 2036(b), or other provision of the Code will be valued on the estate tax valuation date applicable to the shareholder's estate. However, the shareholder's estate should be entitled to an offset under §2043 for the value of the stock that the decedent received in exchange. *See* Ehrlich, Corporate Recapitalization as an Estate Planning Business Retention Tool, N.Y.U., 34th Inst. Fed. Tax., 1661, 1669-1971 (1976).

> **Example 11-29.** *X,* the controlling shareholder of Titan, Inc., exchanged 1,000 of the outstanding 1,500 shares of Titan common stock for 10,000 shares of 8% noncumulative voting preferred stock that had a par value of $100. The recapitalization assumed

that *X*'s common stock and the preferred stock he received were each worth $1,000,000, which was roughly two-thirds of the total value of Titan ($1,500,000). The exchange qualified as a tax-free recapitalization under §368(a)(1)(E). The other common shareholders in Titan at the time of the exchange were related to *X* but were not members of his family within the meaning of §2701(e)(1). The exchange would involve a gift by *X* to the extent the value of the common stock that he surrendered exceeded the value of the preferred stock he received. In such a case, presumably only the value of the preferred stock would be included in *X*'s estate.

§11.36. Other Tax Considerations

A recapitalization will deprive the parties of two tax advantages otherwise available to small business corporations. Their significance will depend in part on the profitability of the corporation under consideration. First, a corporation is not eligible for Subchapter S treatment if it has more than one class of stock. §1371(a)(4). Thus, a recapitalization will prevent the corporation from electing Subchapter S treatment and will terminate an existing election. When income tax rates are lower for individuals than for corporations, S corporations are more attractive than C corporations. Second, an ordinary loss deduction is available under §1244 only with respect to common stock. §1244(c)(1). Accordingly, a loss suffered on the sale or exchange of preferred stock cannot be claimed as an ordinary loss under §1244 even though the common stock originally qualified under that section. Of course, the disqualification is of limited significance for profitable corporations.

The preferred stock issued in connection with a recapitalization typically carries the right to a large cumulative dividend. It may be impractical or undesirable for a corporation to undertake such a substantial cash drain. Before proceeding with a recapitalization the parties should also understand that the preferred stock dividends are ordinary income to the recipient but are not deductible by the corporation. This consideration often deters clients from adopting recapitalization plans.

§11.37. Recapitalization Strategies

A carefully planned recapitalization remains a valuable estate planning tool — particularly for nontax purposes. For example, recapitalization can be used in order to allocate a fixed interest (preferred stock) to family members who are not active in the business, and equity interests (common stock) to the family members who play an active part in the business. In the latter case, often only the common stock would carry the right to vote. In any case, the terms of a recapitalization should be based upon valuations made by a qualified expert. In some cases the income tax advantages will make it desirable to use an S corporation. Although an S corporation may only have one class of stock, it may be divided into voting and nonvoting shares.

In some circumstances a recapitalization may have an attractive estate freezing potential, particularly if §2701 does not apply. For exmaple, transfers made to donees who are not family members are not subject to the cumbersome and disadvantageous rules of §2701. In addition, a preferred stock recapitalization may result in significant overall tax savings where the corporation has a cash flow sufficient to support substantial preferred stock dividends and it is likely to grow in value. Planners should not ignore the simple expedient of making gifts of interests in a corporation or partnership without undergoing a recapitalization. The gift approach typically qualifies for valuation discounts (*e.g.,* lack of marketability and minority interest), is simpler, involves fewer costs, and is the easier to understand. A client's particular circumstances may indicate that a more exotic approach, such a "reverse freeze," should be considered. In a reverse freeze, a preferred interest is transferred to a younger generation family member while the donor retains a junior equity interest. A reverse freeze could have beneficial estate tax results if the business grows slowly or declines in value.

F. FAMILY PARTNERSHIPS AND PARTNERSHIP FREEZES

> A partnership capital freeze, simply stated, is nothing more than the creation of a new partnership, or a restructuring of an existing partnership, that results in at least two classes of partnership interest. A "regular partnership interest" is similar to that well understood by those dealing with a normal type of partnership in its typical structure, *i.e.,* a pro rata sharing of income (including loss and capital) or any other allowable allocation and derivation thereof. A "frozen partnership interest," on the other hand, is substantially different in that it will have a fixed liquidation value and will carry a preferred income distribution position. In many respects the "frozen partnership interest" is comparable to the senior position of preferred stock in corporate equity ownership. Abbin, The Partnership Capital Freeze — An Alternative to Corporate Recapitalization, U. Miami, 13th Inst. Est. Plan., ¶1801.1 (1979).

§11.38. Overview

Family partnerships with more than one type of capital interest (multiclass partnerships), such as limited partnerships, have been used for a wide variety of tax and nontax purposes. When individual income tax rates were steeply progressive family partnerships were used as income-shifting devices. However, the compaction of income tax rates and the adoption of the Kiddie Tax reduce the incentive to shift income within the family. The inversion of corporate and individual income tax rates and the repeal of the *General Utilities* doctrine (*see* §11.3) generated greater interest in the use of partnerships in lieu of C corporations. In addition, through the 1980s multiclass partnerships were sometimes used instead of multiclass corporations to achieve an estate freeze. Partnership freezes and multiclass corporations were usually intended to cap the value of the senior family member's estate, to assure him or her of a steady flow of income, and to shift some of the income from the business to other family members. The senior family member may be entitled to a fixed basic payment and a participation in additional profits, which provides some protection against inflation.

A partnership freeze, like a preferred stock recapitalization, may involve a substantial gift to donees who receive the junior equity interests. The enactment of Chapter 14 virtually assures that a family partnership freeze will involve a substantial gift. *See* §11.32. In particular, under §2701 retained interests may be valued at zero for gift tax purposes and under §2704 lapsing voting or liquidation rights may be disregarded. Recall, however, that §2701 does not apply to gifts of interests that are of the same class as the transferred interest. §2701(a)(2). The senior family member whose partnership interest is frozen can retain effective control of the business, but the estate tax risk of doing so is probably greater in the case of a partnership than of a corporation. Overall, partnerships are often considered to be more attractive because of their greater flexibility and freedom from some of the income tax complications that plague corporations. Also, corporations may be subject to franchise and other taxes that do not apply to partnerships. Although the gift and estate tax dynamics have changed, family partnerships have an income tax advantage over C corporations and the nontax advantage of incredible flexibility.

§11.38.1. Suitable Assets

A multiclass partnership is a particularly attractive vehicle for the management and disposition of interests in assets that are likely to appreciate substantially in value (*e.g.,* improved real property or a family farm). Of course, as a general rule the assets must be capable of generating sufficient income to support the fixed payout on the frozen interest. A partnership is less suitable for some other types of assets. For example, the overall limited liability of the corporate form may be critically important where the business involves risks that deplete family assets (*e.g.*, building construction) or that could exceed insurance limits (*e.g.*, manufacture, transportation, or disposal of toxic substances).

§11.38.2. Income Tax Advantages

Some planners and clients are attracted to the partnership form because of its perceived income tax advantages over corporations. The advantages are largely traceable to the fact that a partnership, unlike a corporation, is not a taxpaying entity. Instead, a partnership is a conduit through which the income flows to the partners currently. §701. Accordingly, there is no risk of the double taxation of income that may occur in the case of a corporation unless a Subchapter S election is in effect. Recall in this connection that a Subchapter S election cannot be made with respect to a corporation with more than one class of stock. On the other hand, as a result of the flow-through characteristic of a partnership, the taxpayers have less control relative to a C corporation over the time the partnership's income is taxed to them. Also, a partnership is not subject to the special taxes on personal holding company income, §§541 to 547, and on the unreasonable accumulation of earnings, §§531 to 537. Finally, partnership interests are not subject to the taint that attaches to some corporate stock by reason of §§305 and 306. Of course, the Kiddie Tax applies to the unearned income of children under 14, including income generated by a partnership.

§11.38.3. Tax Uncertainties

On the negative side, the use of a family partnership involves some tax risks because of the lack of certainty regarding the application of some income, gift, and estate tax rules. While the risk is relatively slight, a multiclass partnership might be treated as an assocation taxable as a corporation under Reg. §301.7701-2. The risk can be virtually eliminated by carefully drafting the partnership agreement. *See Phillip G. Larson,* 66 T.C. 159 (1976), *acq.,* 1979-1 C.B. 1; *Zuckman v. United States,* 524 F.2d 729 (Ct. Cl. 1975). Under the cited Regulation a business is treated as an association taxable as a corporation if it possesses a majority of these four characteristics: (1) continuity of life, (2) centralization of management, (3) limited liability, and (4) free transferability of interest. There is also some uncertainty regarding the application of the family partnership rules of §704(e) to a multiclass partnership.

The uncertainty regarding the application of §§2036 and 2038 to the senior family member's estate is particularly troubling. For example, are there circumstances in which the income rights of the frozen interest may be treated as a retained income interest in the contributed property under §2036(a)(1)? It is also unclear the extent to which controls held by the senior family member over the affairs of the partnership might subject the transferred property to inclusion in his or her estate under §§2036(a)(2) or 2038. However, the estate tax risks are reduced if the interests are properly valued at the time the partnership is formed (or restructured), the partnership agreement is carefully planned and drafted, and the terms of the agreement are followed by the parties. Also, under state law the controls held by the senior family members are generally exercisable in a fiduciary capacity. Under the rationale of *United States v. Byrum,* 408 U.S. 125 (1972), the senior family member's retention and exercise, in a fiduciary capacity, of ordinary business controls should not require inclusion of the interests held by junior family members. *See* LR 9131006 (TAM).

§11.38.4. Valuation Problems and Costs

Wholly apart from Chapter 14, the proper valuation of the assets contributed to a partnership and of the frozen interest is essential. For estate tax purposes the risks of encountering problems under §§2035 to 2038 are diminished if no gifts are involved in a transfer of partnership interests. Note that since §2701 only applies for gift tax purposes, its valuation rules should not be applied in determining whether the transfer involved a transfer for inadequate consideration. As in the case of a recapitalization, the services of an expert appraiser in fixing values are indispensable. However, the cost of an expert in addition to the lawyer's fees and other expenses of a partnership freeze may be too much for the client. Scheifly, Partnership Recapitalization: Achieving a Capital Freeze, U. So. Cal., 32nd Tax. Inst., §511.8 (1980).

§11.38.5. Scrutiny by the IRS

Family partnerships are subject to close scrutiny by the IRS for income and transfer tax purposes because of their potential for abuse. The concern of the IRS is reflected in the following passage from the income tax regulations dealing with the reality of a family member's partnership interest:

> A donee or purchaser of a capital interest in a partnership is not recognized as a partner under the principles of section 704(e)(1) unless

such interest is acquired in a bona fide transaction, not a mere sham for tax avoidance or evasion purposes, and the donee or purchaser is the real owner of such interest. To be recognized, a transfer must vest dominion and control of the partnership interest in the transferee. The existence of such dominion and control in the donee is to be determined from all the facts and circumstances. A transfer is not recognized if the transferor retains such incidents of ownership that the transferee has not acquired full and complete ownership of the partnership interest. *Transactions between members of a family will be closely scrutinized, and the circumstances, not only at the time of the purported transfer but also during the periods preceding and following it, will be taken into consideration in determining the bona fides or lack of bona fides of the purported gift or sale.* Reg. §1.704-1(e)(1)(iii) (emphasis added).

§11.38.6. Ethical Considerations

The interests of the parties to a partnership freeze are sufficiently divergent that a single lawyer should be cautious about representing those with conflicting interests. The lawyer who represents the party who initiates the plan, usually the senior family member, should recommend that the other parties retain independent counsel. The use of independent counsel relieves the conflict-of-interest problem and the potential for future disputes and litigation. While additional counsel may increase the initial cost, they provide valuable protection and may also make valuable contributions to the development of plans for the partnership. As noted in §1.14, a lawyer cannot represent parties with conflicting interests unless the lawyer can adequately represent the interests of each and each consents to the representation after full disclosure. *See* MRPC 1.7.

§11.39. Creation of Partnership Is Not a Taxable Event

A multiclass partnership can usually be formed or an existing partnership restructured without the imposition of any income tax liability. The contribution of property to a partnership in exchange for a partnership interest is not a taxable event. §721. Instead, the partner has a basis in the partnership interest equal to the amount of money and the basis of other property that he or she contributed to the partnership. §722. Consistently, the partnership takes a carryover basis in the contributed property. §723. The distinction between a partner's basis in his or her partnership interest (the outside basis) and the partnership's basis in the property it owns (the inside basis) is particularly important in postmortem planning. Upon the death of a partner the value of his or her partnership interest is adjusted under §1014, but the basis of the partnership property is unaffected unless a timely election is made under §754. *See* §12.5.

Converting Partnership Interests. An existing partnership may be restructured to create preferred and regular capital interests without the imposition of any tax. Thus, in Rev. Rul. 84-52, 1984-1 C.B. 157, the IRS recognized that a general partnership interest could be converted into a limited partnership interest, or a limited into a general interest, without the imposition of any tax. Earlier, the IRS held that such a conversion did not involve a sale or exchange:

> The conversion of the general partnership into a limited partnership will not constitute a sale or exchange of a partnership interest by any of the partners. No gain or loss will be recognized in connection with the conversion except to the extent that any decrease in a partner's share of the liabilities of the partnership, or any decrease in a partner's individual liabilities by reason of assumption by the partnership of such liabilities, exceed the adjusted basis of the partner's interest in the partnership. LR 7948063.

Thus, some partners may convert general interests into limited interests, while other partners retain their general interests. The risk of challenge by the IRS is decreased if the restructuring has a recognized business purpose, such as encouraging continued participation of younger generation partners.

Exchanges of Partnership Interests. The exchange of an interest in one partnership for an interest in another partnership made after March 31, 1984 is not a tax-free exchange under §1031(a). However, the committee reports that accompanied the 1984 Act indicated that an exchange of interests in the same partnership was within §1031(a). In LR 8912023, the IRS cited the congressional reports, stating that "Congress intended, therefore, to deny like-kind treatment to the exchange of interests in *different* partnerships, and not to deny like-kind treatment to the exchange of interests in the same partnership. H.R. Rep. No. 98-432, 98th Cong., 2d Sess., Pt. 2 (1984), pp. 1231-1234." Curiously, LR 8912023, which approved the tax-free exchange of interests in the same partnership was later revoked without explanation by LR 8944043.

On April 25, 1991 the IRS issued Reg. §1.1031-1(a)(1) which specifies that §1031(a) does not apply "to any exchange of interests in a partnership regardless of whether the interests exchanged are general or limited partnership interests or are interests in the same partnership or in different partnerships." Under Reg. §1.1031-1(e), the portion of the Regulation dealing with the exchange of partnership interests applies to transfers made on or after April 25, 1991.

Congress amended §1031(a) effective with respect to transfers made after July 18, 1984 to bar the tax-free exchange of interests in partnerships that had been permitted by the courts. For example, the Tax Court had held that §1031(a) applied to the exchange of a general interest in one partnership for a general interest in another partnership where the underlying assets of the partnerships were of like kind. *Arthur E. Long,* 77 T.C. 1045 (1981); *contra,* Rev. Rul. 78-135, 1978-1 C.B. 256. However, the Tax Court had held that a general interest in one partnership could not be exchanged tax-free for a limited partnership interest in another partnership (*i.e.,* the two interests were not of like kind as required by §1031). *Estate of Rollin E. Meyer, Sr.,* 58 T.C. 311 (1972), *nonacq.,* 1975-1 C.B. 3, *aff'd per curiam,* 503 F.2d 556 (9th Cir. 1974).

§11.40. Family Partnership Rules

The family partnership rules of §704(e) must be borne in mind in structuring a family partnership freeze. The basic rules are relatively simple, but some uncertainties remain regarding their application.

Since 1951 the income tax law has provided for the recognition of family partnerships in which capital is a material income-producing factor. §704(e)(1). Prior to that time the law was quite confused and family partnerships were often disregarded as mere assignments of income. If capital is not a material income-producing factor, the partnership may be disregarded and the income "taxed to the person who earns it through his own labor and skill and the utilization of his own capital." Reg. §1.704-1(e)(1)(i).

Example 11-29. *X,* who receives substantial fees for lecturing on inner peace and self-fulfillment, formed a partnership with his 2 minor children, *A* and *B*. *X* contributed a nominal amount of capital to the partnership on behalf of *A* and *B*. In exchange *A, B,* and *X* each received an equal one-third interest in the partnership. The interests of *A* and *B* are held by an independent guardian. The partnership assumed the responsibility of booking *X*'s lectures, received the lecture fees, paid *X* a fixed amount (usually one-half of the total fee), and divided the balance of the income equally between *A, B,* and *X*. Under the circumstances capital is not a material income-producing factor for the partnership. Accordingly, the partnership would be disregarded under §704(e)(1) and all of the income would be taxed to *X,* whose personal services generated all of the income.

§11.40.1. Capital as a Material Income-Producing Factor

Under the current Regulations capital constitutes a material income-producing factor if,

> [A] substantial portion of the gross income of the business is attributable to the employment of capital in the business conducted by the partnership. In general, capital is not a material income-producing factor where the income of the business consists principally of fees, commissions, or other compensation for personal services performed by members or employees of the partnership. Reg. §1.704-1(e)(1)(iv).

Of course, even where capital is a material income-producing factor, a family member is not recognized as a partner "unless such interest is acquired in a bona fide transaction, not a mere sham for tax avoidance or evasion purposes, and the donee or purchaser is the real owner of such interest." Reg. §1.704-1(e)(1)(iii). The reality of a donee's ownership is determined from all of the circumstances, beginning with the execution of legally sufficient deeds or other instruments of gift. However, the actual conduct of the parties is an important factor. Some of the other most important factors are considered in the following subsections. *See also* Reg. §1.704-1(e)(2).

§11.40.2. Trustees and Minors as Partners

A trustee who is unrelated to and independent of the grantor is usually recognized as legal owner of the partnership interests that are held in trust. Reg. §1.704-1(e)(2)(vii). Presumably the IRS or a court would look to the grantor trust rules of §672 for the purpose of determining who is unrelated and independent. Where the grantor is trustee or the trustee is amenable to the will of the grantor, all of the circumstances will be taken into account in determining whether or not to recognize the trustee as legal owner of the interest. In such a case the trustee will be recognized as a partner only if the trustee actively represents the interests of the beneficiaries in accordance with the obligations of a fiduciary and does not subordinate their interests to those of the grantor. Overall, it is most desirable to have an independent trustee, such as a bank or trust company.

A minor child who is competent to manage his or her own property will be recognized as a partner. Under the Regulations a minor is competent if he or she has "sufficient maturity and experience to be treated by disinterested persons as competent to enter business dealings and otherwise to conduct his [or her] affairs on a basis of equality with adult persons, notwithstanding legal disabilitites of the minor under State law." Reg. §1.704-1(e)(2)(viii). If the minor does not satisfy that test, he or she generally will not be recognized as a partner unless the partnership interest is controlled by another person as fiduciary for the sole benefit of the minor, subject to judicial supervision. An independent guardian would suffice for this purpose. Presumably a custodian under the Uniform Gifts to Minors Act or the Uniform Transfers to Minors Act would also suffice. *Joseph A. Garcia,* 48 T.C.M. 425 (1984). All things considered, a trust is preferable to a guardianship or custodianship.

§11.40.3. Allocation of Income

The allocation of income made in the partnership agreement generally controls for income tax purposes. However, where a partnership interest is acquired by gift, the allocation is respected only when (1) the donor partner is allocated reasonable compensation for services he or she renders to the partnership and (2) the share of the income allocated to the donated capital of the donee is not proportionately greater than the share of the income allocated to the donor's capital. §704(e)(2). For purposes of this rule, an interest purchased from a family member is treated as having been acquired by gift. §704(e)(3). An individual's family includes "his spouse, ancestors, and lineal descendants, and any trusts for the primary benefit of such persons." Id. Thus, the income allocation cannot initially be structured in a way that unduly favors a partner who is a family member. However, the Regulations permit the allocation to take into account the fact that "a general partner, unlike a limited partner risks his credit in the partnership business." Reg. §1.704-1(e)(3)(ii)(C). In light of the recognition of the differences in their interests, presumably the income share of the donee general partners can be allowed to grow if the partnership prospers without any increase in the share of the senior limited partner. Note also that the income tax rules of §704(e) do not bar the allocation of future appreciation in value of the partnership property to a donee partner. Such an allocation is, of course, the raison d'etre of the partnership freeze.

§11.40.4. Retained Control by Donor

The family partnership rules allow the donor to retain controls over the business that are "common in ordinary business relationships" provided the donee "is free to liquidate his interest at his discretion without financial detriment." Reg. §1.704-1(e)(2)(ii)(d). Accordingly, the terms of a buy-sell agreement must avoid terms that would diminish the economic value of a donee's interest. A right of first refusal should not be objectionable. In any case, however, the donee should not be obligated to transfer his or her interest to another party at less than its fair market value. Although a donor is permitted to retain ordinary controls, the donor may not retain undue control over the distribution of income. In addition, the donor may not retain control over assets that are essential to the business. Thus, the donor may not retain assets that are required for the conduct of the business and lease them to the partnership. The Regulations also point out that consideration will be given to the existence of controls that may be exercised indirectly through a separate business organization, estate, trust, individual, or other partnership. Reg. §1.704-1(e)(2)(iii). The estate tax problems generated under §§2036(a)(2) and 2038 by the retention of control over the partnership must also be considered.

§11.41. Planning a Frozen Partnership Interest

The creation of a multiclass family partnership requires decisions regarding the structuring of capital interests, rights to income, and management of the partnership. The allocation of capital in large measure determines the extent to which the creation of the partnership involves gifts to the junior members. For example, a gift obviously occurs if the senior family member contributes $500,000 to a multiclass partnership, of which $300,000 is allocated to his or her capital account and $100,000 is allocated to the capital account of the donees. Of course, if §2701 applies, the donor may have made $500,000 in gifts because the interest he or she retained is valued at zero. A gift of partnership interests should qualify for the annual exclusion if the donees are currently able to use and enjoy them — even though they are subject to some restrictions on transfer. *See* LR 9131006 (TAM). If the interests are not transferable and do not have any right to receive current distributions of income, perhaps no annual exclusion would be allowed. *See Berzon v. Commissioner,* 534 F.2d 528 (2d Cir. 1976) (annual exclusion not allowed for gift of stock in trust where the trustee could not freely dispose of the stock and it had paid no dividends for 5 years). *See also* §2.5.6.

The creation of the partnership would be "cleaner," and the gift tax consequences more certain, if the donor made gifts of cash or property to the donees *before* the partnership was formed. Under such an approach the annual exclusion is unquestionably available with respect to the initial gifts.

§11.41.1. Liquidation Preference

The value of the senior's interest and the presence of absence of a gift are also affected by the extent of his or her right to a liquidation preference upon withdrawal from, or termination of, the partnership. Again, in the case of interests transferred to a member of the donor's family a liquidation preference is disregarded in valuing the transfer if it may be removed by the donor or members of the donor's family. For purposes of §2704, "family" means: the donor's spouse; lineal ascendants and descendants of the donor and the donor's spouse; siblings of the donor; any spouse of a sibling or of lineal ascendants and descendants of the donor and the donor's spouse. §2704(c)(2). If §2704 does not apply the amount of the liquidation preference and, hence, its "frozen" value, is usually equal to or less than the amount of the capital allocated to the senior. The value of the frozen interest is also affected by the extent to which it is protected by the net worth of the partnership assets in excess of the amount of the preference. In order to function properly the interest should be frozen regardless of the gains or losses of the business. As one commentator pointed out, "If the segregated interest bears its share of losses and depreciation, but is restricted from sharing in gain and appreciation, there has likely been no 'freeze,' but merely an assignment of income (not losses) as such income is realized." Scheifly, Partnership Recapitalization: Achieving a Capital Freeze, U. So. Cal., 32nd Tax. Inst., ¶503.3 (1980).

§11.41.2. Income Interest

The provisions of the agreement regarding the payment of income also affect the valuation of the frozen interest. A frozen interest is usually entitled either to a fixed annual payment regardless of the income of the partnership (a guaranteed payment) or to a fixed annual payment out of the profits of the partnership. Under §707(c) a guaranteed payment is ordinary income to the payee and is deductible by the other partners. A payment to be made only out of the profits of the partnership may be cumulative or noncumulative, which will also have an impact on the valuation of the frozen interest. In deciding between the two approaches the parties must consider the sufficiency of the income and other resources of the partnership to support the payments and expenses of operating the partnership.

Apart from §2701 the creation of the multiclass partnership may involve a gift if the frozen interest is not entitled to a sufficient portion of the partnership's income. A gift may occur, for example, where the income currently generated by the property contributed to the partnership by the senior family member exceeds the income allocable to his or her frozen interest. In such a case the value of the frozen interest may not be established by its liquidation preference alone. On the other hand, a serious retained income problem may arise under §2036(a)(1) if the frozen interest is entitled to all or substantially all of the income from the contributed property. For example, where the decedent was entitled to substantially all of the income from the farm under an agreement with the limited partners, who received their interests from the decedent by gift, the IRS ruled that the entire value of the farm was includible in the decedent's estate under §2036. LR 7824005.

A frozen interest often carries the right to participate in some partnership income in addition to the fixed amount. This approach is suggested because one of the indicia of a partnership is the sharing of profits. There is some risk that a person who is only entitled to a fixed amount each year regardless of the amount of the partnership's profits or losses (*i.e.,* there is no sharing of profits) would not be recognized as a partner. W. McKee, W. Nelson & R. Whitmire, Federal Taxation of Partnerships and Partners §3.02[5][a] (2d ed. 1990). The transfer of property to the partnership by such person in exchange for interests in the partnership's income and capital might constitute a taxable event. Nelson, The Partnership Capital Freeze: A Précis, 15 Real Prop., Prob. & Tr. J. 99, 104 (1980).

§11.41.3. Management and Control

The retention of control by the senior family member must be carefully considered in light of tax and nontax considerations. The senior typically wishes to participate in the business as a limited partner in order to enjoy limited liability. However, under §7 of the Uniform Limited Partnership Act, the limited liability is lost by a partner who participates in control of the business. 6 U.L.A. 582 (1969). Section 303 of the Revised Limited Partnership Act is to the same effect, but enumerates some specific actions that a limited partner can take without losing that status. 6 U.L.A. 325-326 (1991 Supp.). Because of the unlimited liability of a general partner the senior may not wish to hold a regular interest, however slight.

In order to avoid adverse income tax consequences the donor's retained controls should be drafted in light of the family partnership rules. *See* §11.40.

Where the formation of the partnership involves a gift according to estate tax principles (*i.e.,* apart from §2701), consideration must also be given to the potential inclusion of the gifted interests under §§2036(a)(2) and 2038. However, as indicated above, under *United States v. Byrum,* 408 U.S. 125 (1972), the retention of controls consistent with ordinary business practices should not require inclusion of the partnership interests held by others. *See also* LR 9131006 (TAM). On the other hand, inclusion may result if the donor may exercise control in a nonfiduciary capacity or retains controls over the donee's use and enjoyment of the interest.

§11.42. Conclusion

Partnerships offer some important tax and nontax advantages for ownership and management of family businesses. Relative to other entities partnerships continue to offer limited income tax advantages and flexibility regarding allocations. On the gift and estate tax side §§2701, 2703 and 2704 complicate matters, but opportunities still exist for estate freezes — particularly where substantial valuation discounts appear to be available, there is significant current cash flow, and a potential for substantial future appreciation in value. Of course, planning is simpler and opportunities may be greater if §§2701 and 2704 are not applicable because either only one class of capital interest is involved or the transferees are not family members. On the nontax side partnerships allow differing interests to be created and transferred and permit a simple centralized management structure.

BIBLIOGRAPHY

I. General Discussions of Planning for Closely-Held Businesses

ALI-ABA, Study Outline, Estate Planning Under New Chapter 14 and the Proposed Regulations (1991)

Bittker, B. & Eustice, J., Federal Income Taxation of Corporations and Shareholders (5th ed. 1987)

Freeman, D., Estate Tax Freeze (1988)

Grant, I. & Christian, W., Subchapter S Taxation (1990)

Hood, E., Kurtz, S., & Shors, J., Closely Held Corporations in Business and Estate Planning (1982)

Kelley, Formation and Maintenance of Business Organizations — After TRA 1986, N.Y.U., 47th Inst. Fed. Tax., ch. 22 (1989)

Lay, Estate Planning for the S Corporation Shareholder, N.Y.U., 48th Inst. Fed. Tax., ch. 10 (1990)

Russo, Hodges, Ellis, Edwards & Coghill, Estate Planning and Closely Held Stock Transactions and S Corporations, 242-3rd Tax Mgmt. Port. (1986)

II. Buy-Sell Agreements

Bonn, Buy-Sell Agreements, N.Y.U., 48th Inst. Fed. Tax., ch. 24 (1990)

Gamble, Buy-Sell Agreements, Transfer Restrictions and Section 2703: Have Buy-Sells Gone Bye-Bye?, N.Y.U., 50th Inst. Fed. Tax., ch. 19 (1992)

Gamble, How Do We Handle Buy-Sell Agreements Under Chapter 14?, 130 Tr. & Est. 38 (1991)

Gorman, The Buy-Sell Agreement as a Dispositionary Device: Tax and Valuation Problems in Transferring Corporate, Partnership and Real Estate Interests at Death, N.Y.U., 34th Inst. Fed. Tax. 1591 (1976)

Jacobowitz, Structuring and Funding a Buy-Sell Agreement for the Closely Held Corporation, N.Y.U., 49th Inst. Fed. Tax., ch. 3 (1991)

III. Redemptions Under §303 and Estate Tax Deferral Under §6166

Blum, Estate Tax Payment and Liabilities, BNA 219-3rd Tax Mgmt. Port. (1986)

Blum & Trier, Planning for Maximum Benefits of 303 Redemptions with Estate Tax Deferral, 53 J. Tax. 236 (1980)

Knickerbocker, Corporate Stock Redemption — Section 303, BNA 91-5th Tax Mgmt. Port. (1986)

IV. Planning with Partnerships and S and C Corporations

Abbin, The Partnership Capital Freeze — An Alternative to Corporate Recapitalization, U. Miami, 13th Inst. Est. Plan., ch. 18 (1979)

Blatt, The Effect of Sec. 2701 on Preferred Interest Freezes, 130 Tr. & Est. 8 (1991)

Dees, The Slaying of Frankenstein's Monster: The Repeal and Replacement of Section 2036(c), 64 Taxes 151 (1991)

Donald, Corporate Buy-Out Agreements, 106-5th Tax Mgmt. Port. (1990)

Eastland & Christian, Proposed Valuation Regulations Provide Harsh Results Under Adjustment and Lapse Rules, 75 J. Tax. 364 (1991)

Fiore, Dual Capital Partnerships as an Estate Planning Device, N.Y.U., 39th Inst. Fed. Tax., ch. 54 (1981)

Gardner, Estate Freezes in 1990 and Beyond: The Story of the Repeal of Section 2036(c) and the Valuation Rules That Took Its Place, 64 Taxes 3 (1991)

Harris, Family Tax Planning Using Partnerships, N.Y.U., 49th Inst. Fed. Tax., ch. 14 (1991)

Bibliography

Klein & Gardner, Sales and Liquidations of S Corporations, N.Y.U., 47th Inst. Fed. Tax., ch. 9 (1989)

Kuntz, S Corporation Operating Problems, N.Y.U., 47th Inst. Fed. Tax., ch. 10 (1989)

Massey & O'Connell, Keeping It All in the Family: Use of Family Partnerships and Section 704(b)(2) Special Allocations to Control Estate Tax Evaluation, 33 U. Fla. L. Rev. 1 (1980)

Nash, Family Partnerships: A Viable Planning Alternative, U. Miami, 13th Inst. Est. Plan., ch. 10 (1979)

Schrieber, I. & Traum, S., The S Corporation: Planning and Operation (1983, 1991)

CHAPTER 12

Post-Mortem Planning

A. Introduction

§12.1. Scope
§12.2. Initial Steps
§12.2.1. Memorandum for the Personal Representative
§12.2.2. Cash Needs
§12.2.3. Federal Tax Notices

B. Income Tax

§12.3. The Decedent's Final Income Tax Return: General
§12.3.1. Election to File a Joint Return
§12.3.2. Advantages of Filing a Joint Return
§12.3.3. Disadvantages of Filing a Joint Return
§12.3.4. Deduction of Medical Expenses, §213
§12.3.5. Passive Activity Losses, §469
§12.3.6. Miscellaneous Itemized Deductions, §67
§12.3.7. Election to Report Accrued Interest as Income, §454
§12.4. Subchapter S Election, §1362
§12.5. Partnership Elections, §§754, 732(d)(4)
§12.5.1. Extensions to Make Election, Reg. §1.9100
§12.5.2. Section 732 Election
§12.5.3. Partnership Agreements
§12.6. Declaration and Payment of Estimated Tax
§12.7. Selection of a Taxable Year for an Estate or Trust, §441
§12.8. Waiver of Fees

C. Estate Tax and Income Tax Deductions

§12.9. General
§12.10. Deductions in Respect of a Decedent
§12.11. Deductions Allowed Only for Estate Tax Purposes
§12.12. Deductions Allowed Only for Income Tax Purposes

§12.13. Deductions Allowable Either for Income or Estate Tax Purposes
- §12.13.1. Miscellaneous Itemized Deductions, §67
- §12.13.2. Expenses of Sale: Capital Gain Offset or Estate Tax Deduction, §642(g)
- §12.13.3. Planning Considerations
- §12.13.4. IRS Access to Attorney's Time Records
- §12.13.5. Comparative Tax Benefits of Deductions
- §12.13.6. Community Property Administration Expenses

§12.14. Equitable Adjustments

D. Elections Affecting Estate and GST Taxes

§12.15. Alternate Valuation Method, §2032
- §12.15.1. Limits on Use of Alternate Method
- §12.15.2. Income Tax Impact of Using Alternate Method
- §12.15.3. Property Affected by Alternate Method
- §12.15.4. Effect on Special Use Valuation
- §12.15.5. Alternate Valuation Election
- §12.15.6. Distributed, Sold, Exchanged, or Otherwise Disposed of
- §12.15.7. Alternate Method and GSTT

§12.16. Penalties for Incorrect Valuation of Assets on Returns Due Prior to January 1, 1990
- *Table 12-1. Penalties for Underpayment of Estate or Gift Tax, Pre-1990*
- *Table 12-2. Penalties for Underpayment of Income Tax, Pre-1990*

§12.17. Incorrect Valuation of Assets on Estate or Gift Tax Returns Due After 1989, §6662

§12.18. Avoid Incurring Valuation Penalties

§12.19. Special Use Valuation, §2032A
- §12.19.1. Election
- §12.19.2. Protective Election
- §12.19.3. Maximum Reduction in Value of Property
- §12.19.4. Basic Requirements
- §12.19.5. De Minimis Interests Passing to Nonqualified Heirs
- §12.19.6. Ownership, Use, and Material Participation
- §12.19.7. Cropshare Leases
- §12.19.8. Special Use Valuation Methods
- §12.19.9. Recapture
- §12.19.10. Additional Tax
- §12.19.11. Involuntary Conversion and Like Kind Exchanges
- §12.19.12. Personal Liability
- §12.19.13. Special Lien
- §12.19.14. Practical Concerns
- §12.19.15. Planning for Special Use Valuation and Marital Deduction

§12.19.16. Impact of Special Use Valuation on Other Provisions
§12.20. Marital Deduction QTIP Election, §2056(b)(7)
§12.20.1. Partial Election
§12.20.2. Formula Elections
Form 12-1. Formula QTIP Election
§12.20.3. Making the QTIP Election
§12.20.4. Protective Election
§12.20.5. Professional Responsibility
§12.21. Marital Deduction QDT Election, §2056A
§12.22. Reverse QTIP Election for GSTT Purposes, §2652(a)(3)
§12.23. Allocation of GSTT Exemption, §2631(a)
§12.24. Consent to Split Gifts, §2513
§12.24.1. Time of Consent
§12.24.2. Revocation of Consent
§12.24.3. Deceased Spouse Was Donor
§12.24.4. Gifts Not Included in Decedent's Gross Estate
§12.24.5. Surviving Spouse Was the Donor
§12.25. Qualified Plan Benefits
§12.25.1. Special Exceptions
§12.25.2. Lump Sum Distribution to Surviving Spouse
§12.25.3. Income Taxation of Lump Sum Distribution
§12.25.4. Five-Year Forward Averaging
§12.26. Tax on Excess Distributions and Excess Accumulations of Qualified Plans, §4980A
§12.26.1. Grandfather Election
§12.26.2. Lump Sum Distributions
§12.26.3. Excess Accumulations
§12.26.4. No Deductions or Credits Allowable
§12.26.5. Computation of Tax on Excess Accumulations
§12.27. Life Insurance Proceeds

E. Reordering the Distribution of Property

§12.28. General
§12.29. Family Awards and Allowances
§12.29.1. Estate Tax
§12.29.2. Income Tax
§12.30. Widow's Election
§12.31. Disclaimers: General
§12.32. Qualified Disclaimers, §2518
§12.32.1. Powers
§12.32.2. Disclaimer of Benefit of Tax Clause
§12.32.3. Pre-1977 Transfers
§12.32.4. Statutory Requirements for Qualified Disclaimers
Form 12-2. Acknowledgment for Receipt of Disclaimer
§12.32.5. Disclaimers Not Recognized by Local Law
§12.33. Disclaimer of Joint Tenancy Interests

§12.33.1. Revocable Transfers
§12.33.2. Property Subject to Partition
§12.34. Disclaimer of Partial Interests
§12.35. Disclaimer Planning

F. Planning Estate Distributions

§12.36. General
§12.36.1. Basic Rule
§12.36.2. Distributable Net Income (DNI)
§12.36.3. Tier System
§12.36.4. Specific Gifts
§12.36.5. Timing of Distributions
§12.36.6. Distributions to Trusts
§12.36.7. In Kind Distributions
§12.37. Distributions That Do Not Carry Out DNI, §663(a)(1)
§12.37.1. Annuities and Similar Payments from Income
§12.37.2. Specifically Devised Real Property
§12.38. Distribution in Kind
§12.39. Non-Pro Rata Distributions
§12.39.1. Fiduciary Duty of Impartiality
§12.39.2. Community Property
§12.40. Trapping Distributions

G. Payment of Estate and GST Taxes

§12.41. Introduction
§12.42. Source of Payment of Estate Tax
§12.42.1. Recovery of Estate Tax from Estate and Beneficiaries, §2205
§12.42.2. Recovery of Estate Tax from Insurance Beneficiaries, §2206
§12.42.3. Recovery of Estate Tax from Property Subject to General Power, §2207
§12.42.4. Recovery of Estate Tax on QTIP, §2207A
§12.42.5. Recovery of Estate Tax on §2036 Property, §2207B
§12.42.6. Transferee Liability
§12.43. Extension of Time to File Estate Tax or GSTT Return, §6081
§12.44. Extension of Time to Pay Estate Tax, §6161
§12.45. Deferral of Estate Tax on Reversions and Remainders, §6163
§12.46. Estate Tax Deferred Under Former §6166A
§12.47. Deferral of Estate and GST Taxes Under §6166
§12.48. Payment of Estate Tax with "Flower Bonds"
§12.48.1. Bonds Purchased by an Agent for an Incompetent Principal

§12.48.2. Income Tax Consequences and Community Property Issues
§12.48.3. Community Property Planning
§12.48.4. List of Redeemable Bonds
§12.48.5. Procedure for Redemption
§12.49. Release from Liability for Taxes
§12.49.1. Request for Prompt Determination of Estate Tax, §2204
§12.49.2. Request for Discharge from Personal Liability for Income and Gift Taxes, §6905
§12.49.3. Request for Prompt Assessment of Income and Gift Taxes, §6501(d)
§12.50. Checklist of Post-Mortem Matters

Bibliography

A. INTRODUCTION

§12.1. SCOPE

Post-mortem estate planning offers the lawyer challenging opportunities to minimize the overall tax costs incurred by reason of the decedent's death and to preserve the maximum amount of property for his or her intended beneficiaries. The plan adopted during a client's lifetime fixes the basic pattern for the disposition of his or her property at death. However, the tax consequences of carrying out the plan can vary substantially depending upon the post-mortem elections made (and other actions taken) by the executor (which includes for the purposes of this chapter the decedent's personal representative or trustee). The executor may make elections regarding matters that range from the treatment of medical expense deductions on the decedent's final income tax return to the payment or deferral of the federal estate tax. Importantly, the distribution of property may be rearranged to a certain degree through the use of disclaimers and applications for family awards and allowances. A comprehensive checklist of post-mortem matters is included at the end of this chapter in §12.50.

This chapter first reviews the opportunities that arise by reason of the executor's obligation to file a final income tax return for the decedent, §§12.3-12.8. Where the decedent leaves a surviving spouse, one of the most important matters to consider is whether the decedent's final income tax return should be a joint one filed with the surviving spouse. Other income tax elections concern the use of medical expense deductions and the accrual of interest income. The decisions made regarding the decedent's final income tax return also have an impact on the income tax planning for his or her estate. That planning includes decisions that are very important to the estate and the beneficiaries, especially the choice of the estate's taxable year and the elections regarding expenses that may be claimed as deductions on the estate's income tax return, the estate tax return, or on both, §§12.9-12.14.

Decisions that directly affect the value of property includible in the estate are discussed in Part D, including the use of the alternate valuation method, §12.15, and the special use valuation of real property used in a farm or closely-held business, §12.19. That part also covers a number of other elections, including ones that are available with respect to the treatment of qualified plan benefits, §12.25, and the effect of life insurance settlement options, §12.27.

Part E deals with devices by which the distribution of property may be reordered and reviews the use of family awards and allowances and the so-called widow's election, §§12.28-12.30. It concludes with a discussion of the law regarding disclaimers, including a section on planning for the use of disclaimers, §§12.31-12.35. The importance of disclaimers has grown substantially since the federal estate and gift tax treatment of disclaimers was clarified by the enactment of §2518 as a part of the 1976 Act.

The planning and income tax consequences of estate distributions are reviewed in Part F, §§12.36-12.40. Estates are generally subject to the same income tax rules that apply to complex trusts. *See* §§10.4, 10.4.3-10.4.18. As noted below, distributions by an estate have important tax consequences. If the distributions from an estate are carefully planned they may minimize the overall income tax burdens of the estate and the beneficiaries. Part F includes a discussion of the consequences of making distributions, which can be used to spread the estate's income among several taxpayers. Under the basic rule applicable to distributions, the distributable net income of the estate is carried out to the extent of the lesser of the basis of the property or its fair market value at the time of distribution. Applying it, the basis of the estate in the distributed property carries over to the distributee. However, under §643(e) the executor may elect to treat an in kind distribution as a taxable event resulting in recognition of gain or loss as if the property had been sold to the distributee. If the election is made, the basis of the distributee is increased to the fair market value of the property. The consequences of non-pro rata distributions of community property are also discussed in this part.

The final part is concerned with the payment of the federal estate and GST taxes, including the general rules regarding the allocation of the obligation to pay the tax. The various opportunities for deferring the tax are reviewed in §§12.45-12.47. The chapter concludes with sections that deal with the payment of the estate tax with "flower bonds," §12.48, the release of personal representatives from liability for federal taxes, §12.49, and the checklist of post-mortem matters, §12.50.

§12.2. Initial Steps

It is very important for the lawyer who represents the executor to establish a good rapport with the personal representative and persons who are beneficially interested in the estate. The lawyer's relationship with them is likely to be better if the lawyer provides them with an adequate explanation of the steps that will be involved in settling the estate and communicates with them regularly throughout the administration of the estate.

§12.2.1. Memorandum for the Personal Representative

At the outset the lawyer should give the personal representative a memorandum that outlines his or her duties, reviews the important steps in the estate proceeding, and estimates the state and federal death taxes that will be due. In appropriate cases the memorandum should mention the possible use of disclaimers by the beneficiaries of the estate. The memorandum or a contemporaneous letter should outline the legal services that will be performed and repeat the terms of their agreement regarding the amount and payment of the lawyer's compensation. (Under MRPC Rule 1.5 the lawyer should provide the client with a written explanation of the basis upon which the lawyer's fee will be determined.) It may also be useful and appropriate for the lawyer to communicate directly with the beneficiaries. However, the lawyer should make it clear to the beneficiaries that he or she does not represent them directly.

§12.2.2. Cash Needs

At an early stage the lawyer should prepare and provide the personal representative with a projection of the estate's cash needs and the time at which funds will be required for payment of taxes, administration expenses, legacies, and other purposes. The amount of some items such as cash legacies will be known, but others, such as the amount of taxes, can only be estimated. If the decedent had an accountant or other financial advisor, the information and the help he or she can provide should not be overlooked. In many cases it is helpful if the personal representative retains the same person to keep the books for the estate and to prepare or assist in preparing the estate's fiduciary income tax returns and the estate tax return. His or her help is useful even when the lawyer's office will keep the books and use its computer to produce the necessary cash projections and accountings.

Once the cash projection is prepared, the personal representative, the accountant, and the lawyer must consider the steps that should be taken to raise the necessary funds. In that connection they must take into account the tax and nontax impact that each step will have on the estate and the beneficiaries. For example, the respective income tax brackets of the estate and the beneficiaries should be taken into account in planning the tax year the estate will use, how long the estate will remain open, and the policies that should be adopted regarding sales and distributions. The projection provides the factual base upon which many decisions are made. Accordingly, it should be prepared with care and updated as circumstances require. The parties should all recognize that it is only a projection, which is only as reliable as the assumptions upon which it is based (*e.g.,* estimates of the amount of taxes, value of assets).

§12.2.3. Federal Tax Notices

The lawyer should also counsel the personal representative regarding the filing of Form 56, Notice Concerning Fiduciary Relationship (rev. Feb. 1989), which also serves as notice of qualification of executor. *See* §§6036 and 6903. Also, under the regulations the notice required by §6036 is satisfied by filing the estate tax return as required by §6018. Reg. §20.6036-2. If a notice is filed under §6903, the IRS must communicate directly with the fiduciary regarding the tax liabilities of the decedent. In contrast, if the notice is not filed, the fiduciary may not receive direct notice of a deficiency assessed against the decedent and mailed by the IRS to his or her last known address. Some lawyers advise against filing the notice because it may trigger an audit of the decedent's income and gift tax returns and no penalty is imposed if the notice is not filed. Nevertheless, it is generally advisable to file the notice if the personal representative and the lawyer are not too familiar with the decedent's business affairs.

§12.2.4. Extensions of Time

Under Temp. Reg. §301.9100-1T(a), the Commissioner may for good cause shown grant extensions of time within which to make an election in respect of any tax under all subtitles of the Code except E, G, H and I. An extension may be granted if the time for making the election is not specified in a statute, the request is filed with the Commissioner within a reasonable time, and granting the extension will not jeopardize the interests of the government. Thus, an extension may be granted in order to make a partnership election under §754, §12.5.1, or to perfect a QTIP election under §2056(b)(7). LR 9151002 (TAM).

B. INCOME TAX

§12.3. The Decedent's Final Income Tax Return: General

A final personal income tax return must be filed for the period beginning with the first day of the decedent's taxable year and ending on the day of his or her death. §443(a)(2). The same rates and personal exemption apply although the final year is a short one (*i.e.,* less than 12 full months). The return for the final year must be made by the decedent's "executor, administrator, or other person charged with the property of such decedent." §6012(b)(1). The due date for the final return is the same as if the decedent had lived through the entire taxable year. §6072(a); Reg. §1.6072-1(b). Thus, the final return for a calendar year decedent is April 15 of the year following death. In the unlikely event of a decedent who filed on the basis of a fiscal year, the decedent's final return is due on the fifteenth day of the fourth month following the close of the decedent's regular taxable year. The final return of a resident decedent is filed with the district director, or the service center, for the district in which the personal representative resides or has his or her principal place of business. §6091(b)(1)(A); Reg. §1.6091-2(a)(1).

Note that if a decedent dies early in the year, it may be necessary for the personal representative to file an income tax return for the preceding calendar year.

> **Example 12-1.** *X* died on February 20, prior to filing an income tax return for the preceding calendar year. The return for that year must be filed by *X*'s personal representative on or before April 15. The return for *X*'s final, short taxable year (January 1-February 20) must be filed on or before April 15 of the following year.

The tax due with respect to a decedent's return must be paid when the return is due. However, the time for payment of the tax may be extended for up to six months where payment would result in "undue hardship." §6161(a)(1); Reg. §1.6161-1(b). For taxable years beginning before January 1, 1987, former §6152(b)(1) allowed a personal representative to elect to pay the income tax due with respect to an estate's return in four equal quarterly installments instead of a single payment without the imposition of any penalty or interest. Now an estate is required to file a declaration and make estimated tax payments with respect to any tax year ending two years or more after the decedent's death. §6654(*l*). *See* §12.6.

§12.3.1. Election to File a Joint Return

Under §6013(a)(2) a joint return may be filed for the decedent and his or her surviving spouse if the surviving spouse does not remarry before the end of the year and the length of the tax year of either has not been shortened by reason of a change of accounting period under §443(a)(1). A joint return for a decedent and his or her surviving spouse includes the income of the decedent through the date of death and the income of the surviving spouse for the entire taxable year. Reg. §1.6013-1(d)(1). Where a personal representative is appointed prior to the last day for filing the return, the joint return must be made by both the surviving spouse and the personal representative. §6013(a)(3). If no return has been filed for the decedent and no personal representative has been appointed, the surviving spouse may file a joint return. However, if the surviving spouse files such a joint return, a later-appointed personal representative for the decedent may disaffirm it within one year of the last day for filing the surviving spouse's return. Id.

§12.3.2. Advantages of Filing a Joint Return

The principal tax advantage of filing a joint return is traceable to the somewhat more favorable "split" rates that apply to joint returns. Of course, a surviving spouse who files a separate return may take advantage of the same rates for two years following the decedent's death if the surviving spouse is supporting a dependent child or stepchild. §§1(a), 2(a).

Filing a joint income tax return will produce a lower overall income tax liability than if separate returns were filed in several circumstances. That result will follow where, for example, an individual received a large amount of income in his or her final taxable year and the surviving spouse will have little or no income for the taxable year. A similar tax saving is available in the converse case (*i.e.,* where the decedent had little or no income but the survivor will receive a large amount of income during the year).

A joint return often allows the parties to make better use of the income tax deductions attributable to a decedent's final taxable year.

In some cases the deductions, which cannot be carried over to the decedent's estate, would be wasted if a joint return were not filed. For example, an individual may have made charitable contributions prior to death which exceed the amount that is deductible when measured by the decedent's contribution base alone. If a joint return were filed, a larger charitable deduction would be allowable because the percentage limitations would be applied to a contribution base that includes the combined income of the decedent and the surviving spouse. If a joint return were not filed, the portion of the charitable contribution in excess of the amount allowable as a deduction on the decedent's final return would be wasted: in such a case the excess cannot be carried over and used by the deceased donor's estate. *See* Reg. §1.170A-10(d)(4)(iii). A like advantage of filing a joint return exists where the decedent realized a net capital loss in his or her final taxable year and the surviving spouse had a net capital gain during the year. A net capital loss is deductible only to the extent of $3,000 ($1,500 in the case of married taxpayers filing separately). §1211(b)(1). More importantly, a decedent's excess capital loss cannot be carried over and claimed on the returns filed by the decedent's personal representatives. However, if a joint return were filed, the decedent's net loss could offset any capital gains realized by the surviving spouse during the taxable year, before or after the decedent's death. *Cf.* Rev. Rul. 74-175, 1974-1 C.B. 52 (capital and net operating losses sustained by a decedent during the decedent's final taxable year are deductible only on the decedent's final return). If the surviving spouse's income would not otherwise be sufficient to absorb the full amount of the deductions, the surviving spouse's income might be increased by making distributions to the surviving spouse from the decedent's estate. Such distributions would carry out some of the estate's distributable net income to the surviving spouse. Of course, the distributions would be of assistance in this regard only if the estate's taxable year ended within the taxable year of the surviving spouse for which the joint return is being filed.

Example 12-2. *H* died on January 31 of this year survived by his wife, *W*. Earlier in January *H* suffered a long-term capital loss of $50,000. Apart from the capital loss deduction, *H*'s adjusted gross income for his short final tax year would be $10,000. *W* expects to have an income of about $50,000 this year aside from any income she may receive from *H*'s estate. *W* has owned some publicly traded securities for more than a year that have a current value of $40,000 over their bases. *H*'s personal representative and *W* should consider filing a joint income tax return for the year. If they do, *H*'s capital loss could be used to offset the full $40,000 of capital gain that *W* would realize if she sold the publicly traded securities that she owns. Otherwise, the tax benefit of *H*'s capital loss would be wasted except for the $3,000 deduction that could be claimed on his final return.

§12.3.3. Disadvantages of Filing a Joint Return

The principal disadvantage of filing a joint return is the joint and several liability that attaches to the estate and the surviving spouse for the amount of taxes, interest, and penalties. §6013(d)(3). Thus, if a joint return is filed, the assets of the estate may be liable for deficiencies and penalties attributable to the survivor's negligence or misconduct. This disadvantage is, of course, not present where the surviving spouse is the personal representative and the principal beneficiary of the decedent's estate.

Under the "innocent spouse" provisions of §6013(e), an estate may not be liable where the personal representative did not know and had no reason to know that the joint return substantially understated the income of the surviving spouse attributable to grossly erroneous treatment of items of income, deductions, credits, or bases.

§12.3.4. Deduction of Medical Expenses, §213

Under §213(a) individuals are allowed a deduction for income tax purposes of uncompensated medical expenses paid during the taxable year to the extent that the expenses exceed 7.5 percent of the taxpayer's adjusted gross income. A remedial provision added in 1958 permits medical expenses that are paid within one year following the decedent's death to be treated as if they had been paid when they were incurred. §213(c)(1). As a result, expenses paid within that period may be deducted on the decedent's income tax return for the appropriate taxable year or years. So long as there is no duplication of the deductions claimed, a portion of the medical expenses may be claimed for estate tax purposes and the remainder for income tax purposes. In order to be entitled to claim the expenses as income tax deductions, the estate must file both a statement that the "amount paid" has not been allowed as a deduction for estate tax purposes under §2053 and a waiver of any right to claim it as a deduction under §2053. §213(c)(2). In any case, no refund or credit will be allowed for any taxable year for which the statutory period for filing a claim has expired. Reg. §1.213-1(d)(1). A decedent's estate realizes income in respect of a decedent to the extent it is reimbused by insurance for amounts deducted on the decedent's final return. Rev. Rul. 78-292, 1978-2 C.B. 233.

According to the IRS, where the expenses are claimed as deductions for income tax purposes, the amount within the nondeductible threshold (*i.e.,* 7.5 percent of the decedent's adjusted gross income) is not deductible for income or estate tax purposes. Specifically, in 1977 the IRS ruled that the statement and waiver must recite that the "amount paid" has not been nor will it be at any time allowed as a deduction under §2053. Rev. Rul. 77-357, 1977-2 C.B. 328. This contrasts with the treatment of some other types of expenses for which no income tax deduction is allowed, but which are deductible for estate tax purposes. For example, in Rev. Rul. 59-32, 1959-1 C.B. 245, the IRS ruled that the portion of expenses attributable to tax-exempt income, which is not deductible for income tax purposes, may be deducted on the estate tax return.

> **Example 12-3.** *T* died last December, after a 3-month illness during which medical expenses of $20,000 were incurred. The expenses were paid by *T*'s executor in January of this year. In order to reduce the potential estate tax liability of *T*'s estate to zero, *T*'s executor claimed an estate tax deduction for $5,000 of the expenses under §2053. The necessary statement and waiver were filed with regard to the other $15,000 of expenses that were claimed on the decedent's final income tax return, which showed an adjusted gross income of $100,000. Under these circumstances, an estate tax deduction of $5,000 is allowable together with an income tax deduction of $7,500. The latter amount represents the excess of the expenses claimed for income tax purposes ($15,000) over 7.5% of the decedent's adjusted gross income for the period ($7,500). According to the IRS, no income or estate tax deduction is allowable for the other $7,500, which is within the 7.5% floor.

§12.3.5. Passive Activity Losses, §469

When passive activity property is transferred at death, the accumulated passive activity loss allocable to the property is deductible on a decedent's final income tax return as a loss not from a passive activity. The deduction is limited to the amount by which the total loss exceeds the excess of the basis of the property in the hands of the transferee (its stepped-up basis) over the adjusted basis of the property in the hands of the decedent immediately prior to death. §469(g)(2). As noted in §10.4.7, other dispositions are subject to different rules. For example, if passive activity property is disposed of in a fully taxable transaction, the accumulated passive losses are deductible in full. §469(g)(1).

§12.3.6. Miscellaneous Itemized Deductions, §67

The 1986 Act amended §67(a) to provide that miscellaneous itemized deductions are allowable to individual taxpayers only to the extent that they exceed two percent of the taxpayer's adjusted gross income. Section 67(b) defines "miscellaneous itemized deductions" negatively by enumerating thirteen deductions that are not "miscellaneous." Among the nonmiscellaneous deductions are ones for interest, taxes, charitable gifts, and medical expenses. Estates and trusts are subject to the same rules except that they are allowed deductions under §§642(c), 651, and 661 and "for costs which are paid or incurred in connection with the administration of the estate or trust and would not have been incurred if the property were not held in such trust or estate shall be treated as allowable in arriving at adjusted gross income." §67(e).

The joint return strategy with respect to miscellaneous deductions is the same as with medical deductions: A joint return is appropriate where the decedent's deductions will exceed his or her income and the deductions can be used to shelter from taxation some of the income of the surviving spouse.

§12.3.7. Election to Report Accrued Interest as Income, §454

The periodic increase in value of a Series EE United States Savings Bond, or similar obligation, does not constitute income to a cash basis taxpayer. However, a cash basis taxpayer may elect to report the increase in redemption value as income for the period in which it accrues. §454(a). If the election is made, the taxpayer must report all of the accrued increase in value of all such bonds (Series EE, H and HH United States Bonds) in the electing taxpayer's income tax return for the year in which the election is made. Thereafter an electing taxpayer must report the amount that accrues each year as income, unless the Secretary permits the taxpayer, under whatever conditions the Secretary deems necessary, to change the method of reporting such items. Id.

In the case of obligations owned by a decedent, the accrued interest may be reported on (1) the decedent's final return, (2) a return filed for the estate, or (3) on a return filed by the distributee of the bonds. The IRS recognizes that the person who is obligated to file the decedent's final income tax return may elect to report all of the accrued increase in value as income on that return. Rev. Rul. 68-145, 1968-1 C.B. 203. If such an election is made with respect to the decedent's final return, it does not bind any other taxpayer (*e.g.,* the decedent's estate or the ultimate recipient of the bonds). If the election is made, it may increase the income tax due on the decedent's final return, which is deductible for estate tax purposes. *See* Reg. §20.2053-6(f). In such a case there will be no income in respect of a decedent attributable to the accrued interest and no deduction will be allowable under §691(c).

The IRS has allowed a decedent's executor to make an election under §454(a) although the decedent had transferred the bonds to a revocable trust. Rev. Rul. 79-409, 1979-2 C.B. 208. The IRS reasoned that because the grantor could have made the election regarding bonds in the trust (the interest on which was taxable to him under §676), the fiduciary required to file the deceased grantor's final income tax return "assumed the powers and duties of [the decedent] for this purpose, including the right to make an election under section 454(a) of the Code." Id.

If the election is not made, the unreported increment in value reflected in the redemption value of Series E bonds as of the date of the decedent's death constitutes income in respect of a decedent. Rev. Rul. 64-104, 1964-1 C.B. 223. As such, the taxpayer who must ultimately include the income in his or her income is entitled to a deduction under §691(c) for the state and federal death taxes that are attributable to it. In this connection note that the §691(c) deduction is not a miscellaneous itemized deduction that is subject to the two percent floor discussed above. §67(b)(8).

The decedent's personal representative, or the distributee of the bonds, may elect under §454(a) to report as income the amount that accrued during the decedent's lifetime. If the election is made, the taxpayer must report as current income the increment in value that accrues in each subsequent year. If no election is made the entire amount of accrued interest is reported in the year in which the bonds are disposed of, redeemed, or reach final maturity. Rev. Rul. 64-104, 1964-1 C.B. 223.

The election is typically made when it will cause the accrued interest to be reported on a return that has relatively little or no income. Depending upon the circumstances, that return might be the decedent's final return, the estate's first or last return, a return for a testamentary trust, or a return for an individual distributee. The key is to be aware of the options and to make the necessary decisions in a timely fashion.

The full value of bonds, including accrued interest, is includible in the decedent's gross estate whether or not an election is made under §454.

§12.4. Subchapter S Election, §1362

At an early point the lawyer should determine whether or not an election has been made under §1362 with respect to estate's stock in small business (Subchapter S) corporations. Under §§1361-1368, certain domestic small business corporations are permitted to elect that their income should be taxed directly to their shareholders rather than to themselves. In general, an electing corporation may not have more than one class of stock, §1361(b)(1)(D), or more than 35 shareholders, §1361(b)(1)(A), all of whom must be individuals, estates, or trusts described in §1361(c)(2).

An estate may be a shareholder of an electing corporation whether the election is made before or after the decedent's death. Where the election is made after the decedent's death, the estate and all other shareholders must give their consent. §1362(a)(2); Temp. Reg. §18.1362-2(b).

The death of a shareholder does not affect an election that was previously made. In contrast, under prior law the decedent's personal representative was allowed to terminate an election by "affirmatively refusing to consent" to the election. Former §1372(e)(1)(A). A personal representative no longer has such a power: Now an election may be terminated by the action of "more than one-half of the shares." §1362(d)(1).

An estate may continue as a shareholder of a Subchapter S corporation for the entire period the estate is under administration. The IRS has recognized, for example, that an estate may remain a shareholder during the period that payment of the estate tax is deferred under the predecessor of §6166. Rev. Rul. 76-23, 1976-1 C.B. 264. Certain trusts may also be shareholders during and following the grantor's death. *See* §10.4.14.

§12.5. Partnership Elections, §§754, 732(d)(4)

A deceased partner's interest in a partnership is includible in his or her gross estate. The basis of the partnership interest in the hands of the decedent's estate or successors is equal to its federal estate tax value under §1014, increased by the successors' share of partnership liabilities and decreased to the extent that the value of the interest is attributable to items of income in respect of a decedent. §742; Reg. §1.742-1. The basis in the decedent's partnership interest (the so-called outside basis) is used to determine the income tax consequences of transactions involving the decedent's partnership interest (*e.g.*, sales or liquidations).

A partnership may elect under §754 that the basis of partnership property will be adjusted upon the transfer of an interest in the partnership by sale or exchange, upon the death of a partner, or upon the distribution of partnership property. Under Reg. §1.754-1(b) the election must be made in a written statement filed with the partnership return for the taxable year in which the partnership interest is transferred (*i.e.*, the year of the partner's death). If such an election is in effect, on the death of a partner the interest of the partner's estate or successors in each item of partnership property is increased or decreased in order to reflect the federal estate tax value of the deceased partner's interest in the partnership. Importantly, the adjustment also extends to a surviving spouse's interest in a community property partnership interest. Rev. Rul. 79-124, 1979-1 C.B. 225. The Regulations make it clear that the adjustment is only made with respect to the interests of the estate or successors of a deceased partner: "The amount of the increase or decrease constitutes an adjustment affecting the basis of partnership property with respect to the transferee [or deceased] partner only. Thus, for purposes of depreciation, depletion, gain or loss, and distributions, the transferee partner will have a special basis for those partnership properties which are adjusted under section 743(b). . . ." Reg. §1.743-1(b).

As noted above, in the absence of an election under §754, the death of a partner does not affect the basis of the assets held by the partnership (the so-called inside basis). In such cases, a deceased partner's estate or successors will have a stepped-up basis in the decedent's partnership interest, but the bases of the partnership assets will be unchanged. Thus, the sale of an appreciated partnership asset may require the partnership and, derivatively, the surviving partners and the deceased partner's estate or successors, to recognize gain on the sale. Unless an effective election is made under §754, the outside basis is generally disregarded in determining the income tax consequences of transactions involving partnership assets. On the other hand, if an election under §754 is in effect, the inside basis is adjusted up or down with respect to the interest of the decedent partner's estate or his successors. Accordingly, if the partnership property has appreciated in value, such an election and adjustment may increase the depreciation deduction or reduce the gain allocated to the estate or the successors.

The inside-outside basis distinction is, in effect, extinguished if a decedent's partnership interest is completely liquidated. In the case of such a liquidation, the decedent's estate or successors take a basis in the distributed assets equal to their basis in the partnership, reduced by the amount of any cash received. §732(b).

The estate or the successors of a deceased partner are most likely to benefit from a §754 election where the partnership interest will not be liquidated and the fair market value of the partnership assets exceed their bases. Unless an election is made under §754, the income tax rules do not provide any current tax advantages where a deceased partner's estate or successors remain in the partnership. In particular, their bases in the partnership assets are not adjusted for purposes of computing gain or loss, depreciation or depletion, and so forth. §743(a).

Example 12-4. *X*'s one-third interest in the XYZ partnership was valued at $100,000 in *X*'s estate. The partnership owned 3 parcels of real property, each of which had a basis of $10,000 and a fair market value of $100,000. If no election is made under §754, the sale of Parcel One for $100,000 would result in a gain of $30,000 to each partner. On the other hand, if the partnership makes a timely election under §754, the basis of *X*'s estate or successors in Parcel One would be increased to $33,333. Accordingly, the estate (or successors) would realize no gain as a result of its sale.

§12.5.1. Extension to Make Election, Reg. §1.9100

If a taxpayer establishes good cause for failure to make an income tax election within the period of time required by a Regulation, the Commissioner may grant an extension under Reg. §1.9100-1. Reg. §1.754-1(b). The election must relate to the income, gift, estate, or generation-skipping transfer (GST) tax, the time for making the original election must be specified in the Regulations, the request must be filed within a reasonable time, and the Commissioner must be satisfied that granting the extension will not prejudice the government's interests. Originally, extensions were limited to income tax elections. However, Temp. Reg. §301.9100-1T, adopted April 5, 1991, extended the relief to gift, estate, and GST taxes. §12.2.4. Extensions to make a §754 election are granted under Reg. §1.9100-1. *See, e.g.,* LR 8912011; LR 8910038; LR 8910039. Of course, in some instances, the application for such an extension is denied. *E.g.,* LR 8331012; LR 8337024. In passing on a request for an extension under Reg. §1.9100-1, the IRS will take into account all relevant factors, including the following as given by Rev. Proc. 79-63, 1979-2 C.B. 578:

1. Due diligence of the taxpayer;
2. Prompt action by the taxpayer;
3. Intent of the taxpayer;
4. Prejudice to the interests of the government; and
5. Statutory and regulatory objectives.

The IRS will, for example, consider a request for an extension of time to make an election under §754 where the failure to do so was not discovered until after the partnership terminated. Rev. Rul. 86-139, 1986-2 C.B. 95.

§12.5.2. Section 732 Election

If a partnership does not make an election under §754, some relief may be provided by §732(d) to the extent property other than cash is distributed to the estate or to other successors within two years of the deceased partner's death. The estate or other successor must make an election under §732 for the year of the distribution if the distribution includes any property subject to depreciation, depletion, or amortization. Otherwise, the election must be made for the first taxable year of the transferee partner in which the basis of any distributed property is pertinent in determining his or her income tax. An election under §732 should be considered if an election under §754 would have been valuable but was not made by the partnership. Also, if the sale of an appreciated partnership asset occurs within two years of the deceased partner's death and no section 754 election is in effect, the successors of the deceased partner are allowed to elect to have their share in the sale proceeds given the basis it would have taken had a section 754 election by the partnership been in effect. §732(d); Reg. §1.732-1(d).

§12.5.3. Partnership Agreements

A properly drawn partnership agreement should specify whether or not the partnership is obligated to make a section 754 election if a partnership interest is sold or exchanged or a partner dies. Some partnership agreements require the partnership to make the election at the request of the personal representative of a deceased partner. The failure to make a section 754 election can subject the estate of a deceased partner to the imposition of substantial income tax liabilities that might otherwise be deferred or avoided. *See Estate of Ernest D. Skaggs,* 75 T.C. 191 (1980), *aff'd per curiam,* 672 F.2d 756 (9th Cir.), *cert. denied,* 459 U.S. 1037 (1982). (Large income tax deficiencies upheld against widow and deceased husband's estate on income from farming partnership. No section 754 election was made; widow and estate improperly assigned stepped-up basis to crops sold and depreciable assets of partnership.)

A partnership may be reluctant to make a section 754 election because of the permanency of the election, which at some future time might prove to be disadvantageous. (An election may only be revoked with the approval of the IRS.) An election might, for example, require a downward adjustment in the value of partnership property that had declined in value. An election also imposes additional administrative burdens on the partnership, which must keep separate records with respect to the interests of each affected partner — transferees and future admittees.

§12.6. Declaration and Payment of Estimated Tax

For taxable years beginning prior to 1987 neither an estate nor a trust was required to file a declaration of estimated tax. Former §6015(h) (repealed 1986). Changes made by the 1986 Act require estates to make estimated tax payments with respect to any taxable year beginning after December 31, 1986 and ending two years or more after the date of the decedent's death. §6654(*l*). The same subsection requires all trusts to make estimated tax payments with respect to taxable years beginning after 1986. Note that the 1986 Act also repealed §6152, which permitted estates to pay the income tax in four equal installments beginning with the due date of the estate's fiduciary income tax return.

The application of §6654 to an estate is illustrated by Example 12-5.

> **Example 12-5.** *D* died on January 31, 1992. The personal representative of *D*'s estate elected to report the estate's income on the basis of a fiscal year ending June 30. No estimated tax payment is due with respect to the estate's initial short taxable year (February 1, 1992 - June 30, 1992) or its second full taxable year (July 1, 1992 - June 30, 1993). Estimated tax payments would be due, however, with respect to the estate's third taxable year, beginning July 1, 1993, unless the estate is closed and its final taxable year ends prior to January 31, 1994.

An addition to tax is imposed in the case of the underpayment of an installment of estimated tax. The addition to tax is calculated by multiplying the amount of the underpayment by the underpayment rate established by §6621(a)(2) for the period of the underpayment. No addition to tax is imposed where (1) the tax liability, less the credit allowable under §531, was less than $500 for the current year or (2) the taxpayer had no tax liability for the preceding taxable year of 12 months. §6654(e)(1), (2).

No payment of estimated tax need be made on account of a decedent following the date of the decedent's death. However, a surviving spouse remains liable for the payments shown on a joint declaration of estimated tax unless he or she files an amended declaration. Where payments of estimated tax were made on a joint declaration, the surviving spouse and the decedent's personal representative are free to allocate the payments between the surviving spouse and the decedent. If they cannot agree on an allocation, the surviving spouse is allocated an amount that bears the same relation to the total payments as the amount of income tax that would be due on the surviving spouse's separate income tax return bears to the total amount of income tax due on the surviving spouse's separate return and the final return of the decedent. Reg. §1.6015(b)-1(c)(2). If a sufficient amount of the payments are allocated to the surviving spouse and the surviving spouse files an amended declaration, it may be unnecessary for the surviving spouse to make any further payments of estimated tax for the year.

A trust making estimated tax payments may elect on a return filed within 65 days of the close of its taxable year to assign any amount of its quarterly payments to one or more of the beneficiaries of the trust. §643(g). The amount subject to the election is treated as a distribution that carries out distributable net income to the beneficiaries on the last day of the taxable year of the trust. Accordingly, the trust is eligible for a §661 deduction if it makes a valid election under §643(g).

§12.7. Selection of a Taxable Year for an Estate or Trust, §441

The estate of a decedent is treated as a separate taxpayer for federal income tax purposes. An income tax return must be filed for each taxable year in which the estate has gross income of $600 or more. §6012(a)(3).

As a new taxpayer, the personal representative may choose a taxable year for the estate. The estate's income may be reported on a calendar year basis or on the basis of a fiscal year ending on the last day of any month within 12 months of the decedent's death. §441(b).

An estate's fiduciary income tax return (Form 1041) must be filed on or before the fifteenth day of the fourth month following the close of the taxable year. §6072(a). The election of a taxable year is made by timely filing a return for the taxable year on the basis of which the return was prepared. For example, if the decedent died on May 15, the personal representative could elect to report the estate's income on the basis of a calendar year or on the basis of a fiscal year ending on the last day of any month from May through April. The personal representative could elect to use the calendar year by filing a return on or before the following April 15, reporting the income of the estate for the period from April 15 through December 31. The first taxable year of the estate will ordinarily be a short one. *See* §443(a)(2). However, succeeding taxable years must consist of 12 months, except for the last taxable year of the estate, which ends on the day the administration of the estate is completed. Reg. §1.441-1T(b)(1)(i)(B); §443(a)(2). The selection of a taxable year for the estate should be based upon the overall circumstances of the estate and its beneficiaries. In particular, the personal representative should project the receipt of income by the estate, the length of time the estate will remain open, the amount of deductions that may be claimed for income tax purposes, and the time at which distributions will be made. The planning should also take into account the circumstances and tax brackets of the beneficiaries, which will affect policy decisions that are made regarding such things as distributions and deduction of expenses.

In selecting a taxable year for the estate the overall objective of minimizing the tax costs to the estate and its beneficiaries often calls for the adoption of a taxable year that will result in the division of the estate's income into as many taxable years as possible. Such an approach provides the estate with the maximum number of $600 exemptions, one of which is allowed for each taxable year the estate is in existence. §642(b). It may also help prevent bunching of too much income in the estate's initial taxable year and equalize the amount of income that is taxable to the estate in each taxable year.

> **Example 12-6.** *T* died in February 20 and the executor received a large payment on March 15 that constituted income in respect of a decedent. The estate is expected to remain open for 18 months. If no distributions of income-producing property are made, the gross income of *T*'s estate is expected to remain relatively constant over the period the estate is open. The executor should adopt a tax year that ends soon after receiving the March 15 payment in order to minimize the other income that the estate will report for the period. Thus, the executor might adopt a fiscal year ending on March 31. Such an election would spread the estate's income over 3 taxable years instead of 2, such as would occur if the executor adopted a calendar year. Based upon a fiscal year ending March 31, the 3 taxable years would be:
>
> Year One: Date of death through March 31.
> Year Two: April 1 through March 31.
> Year Three: April 1 through August 20.

In selecting the taxable year and planning distributions, the personal representative may also seek to defer the income taxation of income that is carried out to the beneficiaries as a result of making distributions to them. The opportunity to defer exists if the selection of a taxable year and distributions are carefully planned. The governing rule requires a beneficiary to report income that is carried out by an estate distribution in the year that includes the end of the estate's taxable year during which the distribution was made, §662(c). The rule sounds complicated, but it is really rather simple, as indicated by the following example:

> **Example 12-7.** *T* died on January 10, 1992. *T*'s personal representative elected to file income tax returns for the estate on

> the basis of a fiscal year ending on February 28. Any income that was carried out by distributions made to a beneficiary during the estate's first taxable year (January 10 - February 28, 1992) would be included in the income of the beneficiary for that year. Income carried out by distributions made during the remainder of that calendar year (March 1 - December 31, 1992) would not be included in the beneficiary's 1992 return. Instead, those distributions would be reflected on the estate's return for the period March 1, 1992 - February 28, 1993 and reported in the beneficiary's 1993 return. Thus, a calendar year beneficiary who received a distribution on March 15, 1992 would report income arising from the distribution in the beneficiary's return for 1993 unless the estate terminated prior to January 1, 1993. If the estate did not terminate during 1992, its taxable year for the period during which the distribution was made would end on February 28, 1993. In that case the tax on the distribution would not have to be paid until April 15, 1994, more than 2 years after the distribution was made.

The rules described in this paragraph applied to trusts for taxable years that began prior to January 1, 1987. Under the current rules, all trusts except those described in §675(h) (trusts exempt from tax or charitable trusts) must be calendar year taxpayers. §645(a). This provision essentially eliminates the possibility of enabling the beneficiaries to defer the payment of the income tax attributable to distributions from trusts.

Short Final Tax Year. The personal representative may plan for a short final taxable year for the estate in which a large portion of the estate administration expenses will be paid in order to maximize the amount of the estate's nonbusiness deductions that can be carried out to the beneficiaries under §642(h). *See* §12.13.5. The excess deductions are carried out to the "beneficiaries succeeding to the property of the estate or trust," §642(h), who are usually the residuary beneficiaries. Reg. §1.642(h)-3(c), (d). Distributions of the estate may be planned, together with the selection of a tax year and payment of estate expenses, in a way which maximizes the tax benefit of the excess deductions.

The deductions carried out to a beneficiary will largely be miscellaneous itemized deductions for purposes of §67. They, together with other miscellaneous itemized deductions, will be deductible by the beneficiary only to the extent they exceed two percent of the individual beneficiary's adjusted gross income. The overall tax burden may be lower if a deduction for these items is claimed on the federal estate tax return where they are not subject to any floor.

Estates and trusts are generally taxed as individuals. However, as noted in §12.6, estates are not required to make estimated tax payments with respect to taxable years that end within two years after the date of the decedent's death. The income taxation of trusts is summarized at §10.4.

§12.8. Waiver of Fees

At an early stage of the proceedings the lawyer should discuss with the personal representative the question of whether he or she will accept or waive the right to receive fees for serving as personal representative. A family member who serves as personal representative often waives the right to receive a fee either to avoid conflict with other beneficiaries or to optimize the tax results. A personal representative who is receiving social security payments may choose to waive part or all of the fee in order not to exceed the amount of earned income that may be received without reducing the amount of social security payments. On the other hand, a personal representative with a modest income might choose to accept payment of a fee each year that would support an equivalent deductible annual contribution to an IRA. The right to receive compensation may be waived without risk of adverse gift or income tax consequences provided the waiver is made at a sufficiently early stage.

Amounts paid to a personal representative for serving as personal representative are earned income and are generally deductible by the estate for either income or estate tax purposes. *See* §12.13. The tax impact of accepting compensation for serving as personal representative can be ameliorated if the fee is paid in installments over two or more tax years. Of course, if no fees are paid, the personal representative is usually not required to report any amount as compensation and the estate is not entitled to any deduction. Under Rev. Rul. 56-472, 1956-2 C.B. 21, a fiduciary may waive all or a portion of the fees he or she is entitled to receive. A waiver should be executed promptly if the personal representative decides to forego receiving his or her fee. Otherwise the personal representative could face a costly tax conflict with the IRS.

> The crucial test of whether the executor of an estate or any other fiduciary in a similar situation may waive his right to receive statutory commissions without thereby incurring any income or gift tax liability is whether the waiver involved will at least primarily constitute evidence of an intent to render a gratuitous service. If the timing, purpose, and effect of the waiver make it serve any other important objective, it may then be proper to conclude that the fiduciary has thereby enjoyed a realization of income by means of controlling the disposition thereof, and at the same time, has also effected a taxable gift by means of any resulting transfer to a third party of his contingent beneficial interest in a part of the assets under his fiduciary control. Rev. Rul. 66-167, 1966-1 C.B. 20.

The ruling concludes that the requisite intent to serve gratuitously will be deemed to have been established if the fiduciary, within six months of his or her initial appointment, delivers a formal waiver of the right to any compensation to one or more of the estate's primary beneficiaries. The ruling also indicates that an intent to serve gratuitously may be implied where the fiduciary fails to claim fees or commissions at the time of filing the tax returns and accounts and if all of the other facts and circumstances evidence a fixed and continuing intent to serve gratuitously. For this purpose the claiming of fees as a deduction on one or more of the estate's tax returns is considered to be inconsistent with a fixed and definite intent to serve without compensation.

In *George M. Breidert,* 50 T.C. 844 (1968), *acq.,* 1969-2 C.B. xxiv, the Tax Court refused to follow the test set out in Revenue Ruling 66-167 and held that the taxpayer had not realized any income despite an ineffective waiver of executor's fees and despite an actual award of fees by the probate court. The taxpayer did not, in fact, receive the fees and the court found sufficient intent to waive the fees so as to avoid subjecting them to tax.

Example 12-8. *D* died last year, leaving all of his property in equal shares to his unmarried nephew, *N,* and his cousin, *C. N* is the executor of *D*'s will for which he is entitled to receive a fee this year of $10,000. *D*'s taxable estate, apart from any executor's fee paid to *N,* will be $750,000. *N* expects to have a taxable income of $60,000 this year including any fee he receives from *D*'s estate. If *N* does not waive the right to receive the fee, he will have $10,000 more of income, subject to the federal income tax at a 31 percent rate. On the other hand, *D*'s taxable estate will be reduced by $10,000, which would otherwise be subject to tax at a 37 percent rate. Thus, the total amount of federal taxes paid by *D* and *N* will be $500 less if the fee is paid. However, if the fee received by *N* were subject to other taxes such as a state income tax or the self-employment tax, the overall taxes might be higher than if no fee were paid. As indicated above, a timely waiver of the fee would not involve any gift from *N* to the other beneficiary.

C. ESTATE TAX AND INCOME TAX DEDUCTIONS

§12.9. General

This part is concerned with the deductibility of various costs, expenses, and losses for estate tax and income tax purposes. One class of deductions, called "deductions in respect of a decedent," can be claimed for both estate and income tax purposes. §12.10. From the planning perspective, perhaps the most important items are those that may be deducted on either return but not both. Such alternatively deductible items give the planner an opportunity to affect the amount of the marital and charitable deductions, to defer the payment of some taxes, and to achieve overall tax savings by carefully allocating the deductions among the estate's tax returns. The planner should recognize that the elections open to the personal representative sometimes involve serious conflicts of interest — ones that may invite court intervention and litigation. It is necessary to make an equitable adjustment of accounts between beneficiaries when the deductions are claimed for income tax purposes and, perhaps, in other cases. *See* §12.14. An equitable adjustment of the classic type relieves the residuary beneficiaries of the burden of the increase in the federal estate tax that results from claiming the alternatively deductible expenses that are paid from the residue as income tax rather than estate tax deductions. Of course, such elective use of the deductions will be relatively rare when the income tax rate applicable to an estate is below the lowest marginal estate tax rate.

Planning for the decedent's final return also involves consideration of the income tax consequences for the decedent's estate and its beneficiaries. The income tax rules applicable to complex trusts reviewed in §10.4 generally apply to estates. As in the case of trusts, the concept of distributable net income (DNI) limits the tax consequences of distributions by an estate to its beneficiaries. *See* §§10.4.3, 12.36.2. A complex trust or an estate is entitled to deduct the amounts paid, credited, or required to be distributed to beneficiaries during the year. §§10.4.4, 12.36.1. The distribution deduction is limited, however, to the amount of the estate's DNI. For their part, the beneficiaries who receive distributions must report an amount equal to the distribution deduction allowed to the trust. The allocation among beneficiaries is refined by the application of the tier system under which distributions carrying out DNI are first allocated to beneficiaries who are entitled to receive the income required to be distributed currently. *See* §§10.4.9, 12.36.3. If any DNI remains, it is allocated to the other beneficiaries (the second tier). Distributions to beneficiaries have the same character in the hands of the beneficiaries as they did in the hands of the estate. Planning for distributions is reviewed in §§12.36-12.40. An estate is entitled to an exemption of $600. *See* §10.4.5. Providentially, the throwback rules do not apply to estates — once income is taxed to an estate it will not be taken into account in determining the income tax consequences of making distributions to beneficiaries.

§12.10. DEDUCTIONS IN RESPECT OF A DECEDENT

Both income and estate tax deductions are allowed for taxes, interest, business expenses, and some other items for which the decedent was liable, but which were not properly allowable as deductions on the decedent's final income tax return. The dual deductibility of deductions in respect of a decedent is recognized in Reg. §1.642(g)-2, which provides that deductions accrued at the date of the decedent's death "are allowable as a deduction under section 2053(a)(3) for estate tax purposes as claims against the estate, and are also allowable under section 691(b) as deductions in respect of a decedent for income tax purposes. However, section 642(g) [denial of double deductions] is applicable to deductions for interest, business expenses, and other items accruing after the date of the decedent's death so that they are allowable as deductions for estate tax purposes only as administration expenses under section 2053(a)(2)." Of course, the deductions for interest and taxes are allowable only to the extent the respective requirements of §§163 and 164 are satisfied.

Beginning in 1987 an income tax deduction has been allowed for miscellaneous itemized deductions only to the extent they exceed two percent of the taxpayer's adjusted gross income. §67. For purposes of §67, miscellaneous itemized deductions includes all itemized deductions other than ones allowed under 13 Code sections enumerated in §67(b) including §163 (interest), §164 (taxes), §165(a) (losses), §170 (charitable contributions), and §642(c) (amounts paid or permanently set aside for a charitable purpose). The overall tax burden may be lessened by claiming any administration expenses that might be subject to the two percent floor as deductions on the federal estate tax return. That approach makes full use of the deductions and may simultaneously reduce the amount of the marital deduction that must be claimed on the decedent's return in order to eliminate the necessity of paying any estate tax. Of course, a reduction in the amount of the marital deduction also reduces the amount that may be includible in the surviving spouse's estate.

The estate is usually the taxpayer entitled to claim deductions in respect of a decedent. §691(b)(1)(A). However, if the estate is not liable to discharge an obligation, the deduction is allowed to the person who succeeds to the decedent's property subject to the obligation. §691(b)(1)(B).

The IRS has allowed a decedent's estate both income and estate tax deductions for periodic payments made by the estate to the decedent's exspouse under a divorce decree. The estate tax deduction for the commuted value of the payments was allowable under §2053(a)(3) as a claim against the estate. Payments to the former spouse were deductible under §661 as distributions for income tax purposes. *See* Rev. Rul. 67-304, 1967-2 C.B. 224.

§12.11. Deductions Allowed Only for Estate Tax Purposes

Some expenses are deductible under §2053 for estate tax purposes but not for income tax purposes. This category includes: funeral expenses; gift taxes; property taxes that accrued before the decedent's death and were an enforceable obligation of the decedent; federal income taxes due in connection with the decedent's final return or any prior return; the debts and obligations of the decedent. Also, because of the limitation imposed by §265, administration expenses attributable to tax-exempt income are not deductible for income tax purposes. Rev. Rul. 59-32, 1959-1 C.B. 245. However, such expenses are deductible for estate tax purposes.

An item is deductible on the estate tax return only to the extent the requirements of §2053 are satisfied. In general, an expense must be: (1) actually paid, (2) reasonable in amount, and (3) properly allowable under the local law. The last requirement is one that frequently causes a deduction to be denied. For example, no deduction is allowable for funeral expenses imposed on and paid by the surviving spouse in accordance with local law. Rev. Rul. 76-369, 1976-2 C.B. 281. Similarly, only half of the amount of the funeral expenses is deductible in community property states that impose the liability for payment of the expenses upon the entire community. *Estate of Lang v. Commissioner,* 97 F.2d 867 (9th Cir. 1938) (Washington law); Rev. Rul. 70-156, 1970-1 C.B. 190 (pre-June 17, 1970 California law). Because of that rule Texas, California, and New Mexico amended their laws to relieve the surviving spouse from any obligation to pay the funeral expenses of a deceased spouse, making an estate tax deduction allowable for the full amount. Rev. Rul. 71-168, 1971-1 C.B. 271 (California); Rev. Rul. 69-193, 1969-1 C.B. 222 (Texas); N.M. Stat. Ann. §45-2-804. Under Idaho law the decedent's funeral expenses are also fully deductible. *Estate of W. S. Lee,* 11 T.C. 141 (1948), *acq.,* 1948-2 C.B. 3. Because of the availability of the unlimited marital deduction since 1981, the issue has decreased in importance.

Note that an enforceable charitable pledge may be deductible under §2053(c), which may be of more advantage to the estate than a charitable deduction under §2055. Reg. §20.2053-5. In particular, such a deduction may assist the estate in qualifying for the benefits of §§303 and 6166. *See* Parts C and D of Chapter 11.

§12.12. DEDUCTIONS ALLOWED ONLY FOR INCOME TAX PURPOSES

Some expenses incurred after death are deductible for income tax purposes, but not for estate tax purposes. They include state income taxes on the estate's post-mortem income, real estate taxes that accrue after death, and interest that accrues after death to the extent it is not allowable as an expense of administration under local law. Note, however, that interest accrued after death may be deductible as an expense of administration under §2053(a)(2). *See* §12.13.

The IRS has generally resisted allowing a deduction for post-mortem interest on loans outstanding at the time of the decedent's death. *See* Rev. Rul. 77-461, 1977-2 C.B. 324. However, the Tax Court has allowed a deduction in such instances where the interest was paid to extend debts incurred by the decedent. *Estate of William M. Wheless,* 72 T.C. 470 (1979), *nonacq.,* 1982-1 C.B. 1; *Estate of Jane deP. Webster,* 65 T.C. 968 (1976), *acq. and nonacq.,* 1977-2 C.B. 2. According to the Tax Court in the *Wheless* case, "the expenses sought to be deducted as administration expenses must be actually and necessarily incurred in the administration of the estate and they must be allowable administration expenses under local law." 72 T.C. at 479. Similarly, an interest deduction is allowable for interest actually paid with respect to the amount of estate tax that is deferred under §6166 or that was deferred under former §6166A. Rev. Rul. 78-125, 1978-1 C.B. 292; Rev. Rul. 80-250, 1980-2 C.B. 278 (deduction under §2053(a)(2) disallowed for estimated future tax expense under §6166A); Rev. Proc. 81-27, 1981-2 C.B. 548. Post-mortem interest on income tax deficiencies accrued while contesting decedent's income tax liabilities is also deductible. Rev. Rul. 69-402, 1969-2 C.B. 176.

Estates are generally bound by the same rules on business and capital losses as individuals. These areas were changed substantially by the 1986 Act. Capital gains and losses retain their distinct character, separate from ordinary income. Also, as before, capital losses are first netted against capital gains. The rules now require that a capital asset be held for 12 months or more for gain or loss on sale or exchange to be characterized as long-term.

The 1986 Act also introduced a new category of loss: the passive activity loss. §469. *See* §12.3.5. An activity is characterized as passive where the taxpayer is involved in a trade or business in which the taxpayer does not materially participate, including any rental activity whether or not the taxpayer materially participates. An activity is characterized as passive whether it is conducted by an individual, estate, trust, pass-through entity, or closely-held Subchapter C corporation. Passive activity losses are generally only allowable against passive activity income. However, losses from real estate rental activity are allowed to offset up to $25,000 of ordinary income for any "natural person." §469(i). The offset available to natural persons is phased out for those with adjusted gross incomes exceeding $100,000. Importantly, this offset is not allowed to estates or trusts.

§12.13. Deductions Allowable Either for Income or Estate Tax Purposes

Administration expenses and casualty losses are deductible either for income tax or estate tax purposes, but not both. Administration expenses include the fees of the personal representative and of the attorney, which together often account for the bulk of an estate's deductions. For that reason, the executor's election regarding the use of the deductions is very important. As noted below, where all of the community property is subject to administration upon the death of a spouse, only a portion of the expenses of administration are deductible. Under §642(g) an income tax deduction is allowable only if a statement is filed in duplicate to the effect that the items have not been allowed as deductions from the gross estate of the decedent under §§2053 or 2054 and that all rights to claim the items as deductions under those sections are waived. Reg. §1.642(g)-1. That Regulation permits the statement to be filed at any time before the expiration of the limitations period for the taxable year for which the deduction is sought. However, an income tax deduction is not allowable if an estate tax deduction has been finally allowed. Id. Filing the statement prevents the executor from changing the plan and claiming the items instead as estate tax deductions. Accordingly, some commentators suggest that the statement and waiver should not be filed because it limits the executor's future flexibility. They reason that the executor can file the statement at any time until the expiration of the limitations period, after which the IRS could not disallow the deductions in any case.

The Regulations permit alternatively deductible items to be claimed wholly on either return or partly on one return and partly on the other. "One deduction or portion of a deduction may be allowed for income tax purposes if the appropriate statement is filed, while another deduction or portion is allowed for estate tax purposes." Reg. §1.642(g)-2. Of course, a cash basis taxpayer may only deduct the expenses for income tax purposes on the return for the year in which they were paid.

An estate tax deduction is allowed for the accrued interest on the unpaid federal estate tax when an estate has elected to make deferred payment of the federal estate tax. Rev. Rul. 84-75, 1984-1 C.B. 193. *See* §12.47. The interest incurred on the unpaid portion of the estate tax is deductible as an expense of administration under §2053(a)(2). However, the deduction is only allowed if it is actually and necessarily incurred and is allowable under local law. LR 9046002 (TAM) (involving taxes deferred under §6166 and taxes not deferred under §6166). In this connection note that post-mortem interest on delinquent estate and inheritance taxes is deductible when attributable to late filing of the returns. Rev. Rul. 81-154, 1981-1 C.B. 170 (four months late); LR 9051002 (TAM) (five years late). Penalties are not deductible.

§12.13.1. Miscellaneous Itemized Deductions, §67

The two percent floor for miscellaneous itemized deductions, §67, does not apply to administration expenses of trusts and estates that would not otherwise have been incurred. *See* §10.4.6. In particular, §67(e) provides that for purposes of computing the adjusted gross income of an estate or trust, deductions are allowable "for costs which are paid or incurred in connection with the administration of the estate or trust and which would not have been incurred if the property were not held in such trust or estate." In addition, in computing adjusted gross income, §67(e) allows the deductions described in §642(b) (personal exemption) and §§651 and 661 (distribution deductions). As indicated above, the overall tax burdens may be lightened if miscellaneous itemized deductions that would be within the two percent floor are claimed on the estate tax return.

§12.13.2. Expenses of Sale: Capital Gain Offset or Estate Tax Deduction, §642(g)

Under the pre-1977 law, the expenses of selling property of an estate were allowable both as an offset against the selling price for the purpose of determining gain or loss and as a deductible expense of administration for estate tax purposes. Rev. Rul. 71-173, 1971-1 C.B. 204 (declared obsolete by Rev. Rul. 89-75, 1989-1 C.B. 320, as to tax years ending after October 4, 1976), *following Estate of Viola E. Bray,* 46 T.C. 577 (1966), *acq.,* 1971-2 C.B. 2, *aff'd,* 396 F.2d 452 (6th Cir. 1968). The 1976 Act amended §642(g) to provide that for tax years ending after October 4, 1976, an item may not be used to offset the sales price for income tax purposes if it is deducted for estate tax purposes. Accordingly, an executor must choose whether to claim the item as an offset to the capital gain or as an estate tax deduction. Where the estate will pay any estate tax it is generally preferable to claim it as an estate tax deduction.

§12.13.3. Planning Considerations

The planner should make a decision regarding the return on which the administration expenses and casualty losses will be taken as deductions only after considering carefully the impact on the estate and the beneficiaries. In particular, the planner should note that casualty losses claimed on the estate's income tax return are subject to §67 (the two percent floor for miscellaneous itemized deductions). As noted above, §67(e) exempts costs incurred for estate administration which would not otherwise have been incurred. Thus, the estate should be allowed fully to deduct executor's and attorney's fees. However, the IRS handbook for estate tax audits suggests at §(15)42 that accounting fees are to be disallowed as deductions if the services rendered are part of an executor's normal duties, and suggests at §52 that the agent obtain an affidavit stating what legal services were performed, how long the services took, and who did the work.

§12.13.4. IRS Access to Attorney's Time Records

An evolving body of case law indicates that the IRS may subpoena an attorney's time records and other documents that justify the attorney's fees for which an estate tax deduction is claimed, *United States v. White,* 853 F.2d 107 (2d Cir. 1988), *cert. dismissed as improvidently granted,* 493 U.S. 5 (1989). According to *White* the subpoena must be issued if the IRS meets the requirements of *United States v. Powell,* 379 U.S. 48 (1964). They are: "(1) the investigation will be conducted pursuant to a legitimate purpose; (2) the inquiry may be relevant to the purpose; (3) the information sought is not already within the Commissioner's possession; and (4) the administrative steps required by the Code have been followed."

§12.13.5. Comparative Tax Benefits of Deductions

In order to determine the return upon which deductions will be claimed, the planner should compare the marginal estate tax and income tax rates that will apply. Of course, under the existing rate structure the marginal federal estate tax rate is almost invariably higher than the marginal income tax rate. Accordingly, alternatively deductible items are most often claimed as deductions on the estate tax return. Where the overall tax costs are essentially the same the benefit of the deductions may be maximized by splitting them between the two returns. In other cases, it may be beneficial to claim the deductions all on one return or the other. Consideration must also be given to other impacts of claiming the deductions on one return or the other. They include the applicability of state income taxes, the effect on the marital deduction and other gifts, and the effect on the beneficiaries of the estate.

The planning should also take into account the possibility of carrying out to the estate's beneficiaries the estate's excess income tax deductions in its final taxable year. *See* §642(h). *See also* §12.7 (selection of tax year); §12.36.5 (distributions). The benefit of the carryover of the deductions is usually maximized if the estate's final taxable year is a short one, during which it has little income. As noted above, expenses are deductible by the estate for income tax purposes only in the year they are paid. Here again the planner should be alert to the possible impact of §67: It seems to apply the two percent floor to deductions carried out by §643(h) even where it would not apply to the same deduction were it claimed by the estate.

In light of this problem, the planner should consider that in some cases the combined income tax liability of the estate and the beneficiaries will be reduced if excess deductions arise in the estate's final taxable year and are carried out to the estate's beneficiaries. §642(h). Excess deductions may arise where, for example, substantially all of the lawyer's and executor's fees are paid in the estate's final, short taxable year. In order to plan most effectively for the payment of the fees and closure of the estate the lawyer must be aware of the income tax position of the beneficiaries. Where it will assist the beneficiaries, the lawyer may agree to defer payment of his or her fee until the estate's final taxable year. The deferral, of course, conflicts with the lawyer's interest in being paid currently. A lawyer may be willing to defer payment of a fee where it produces a significant tax saving. However, the possibility that payment of the fee might be deferred should be discussed with the executor at the outset along with other matters relating to the lawyer's compensation. They might agree, for example, that interest should be paid by the estate on any portion of the fee that is unpaid for more than a specified period after it is earned and billed. However, it may be inappropriate to do so, particularly where the local law prescribes a statutory fee which is customarily not paid until termination of the estate. Charging interest might be questionable unless the lawyer charges interest on the unpaid balance of fees owed by other clients. In any case, the lawyer should be cautious in dealing with the matter because of conflict-of-interest problems. Whether or not there is a technical conflict of interest, the beneficiaries are interested parties whose interests and concerns should be taken into account. Overall, however, it seems doubtful that a lawyer would be required to forego payment of the fee for a protracted period in order to confer a tax advantage on the beneficiaries of an estate.

§12.13.6. Community Property Administration Expenses

Where only the decedent's interest in the community property is subject to administration, the full amount of expenses of administration are deductible under §2053. *Estate of William G. Helis,* 26 T.C. 143 (1956), *acq.,* 1956-2 C.B. 6. In contrast, where all of the community property is subject to administration upon the death of a spouse, only the expenses of administration attributable to the deceased spouse's share of the community property are deductible. The IRS has recognized that, "expenses which can be specifically allocated to the decedent's share of the community property, such as attorney's fees incurred in the determination or litigation of estate and inheritance taxes in connection with his share of the property, are fully deductible." The leading case on the subject allowed the estate to deduct half of the ordinary expenses of administration and the full amount of attorney's fees and expenses incurred in connection with the settlement and adjustment of death taxes. *Estate of Lang v. Commissioner,* 97 F.2d 867 (9th Cir. 1938) (Washington law). In *Ray v. United States,* 385 F. Supp. 372 (S.D. Tex. 1974), *aff'd on other issues,* 538 F.2d 1228 (5th Cir. 1976), the court allowed the estate to deduct (1) attorney's fees incurred in connection with determining state and federal death taxes and income taxes and those incurred in performing ordinary probate services for the decedent's estate, which together amounted to 95 percent of the attorney's fees, and (2) administration expenses that would not otherwise have been incurred, including appraisal fees and costs of selling the decedent's interest in property.

§12.14. Equitable Adjustments

> An equitable adjustment is a reallocation of assets from the account of one beneficiary, or from some other person beneficially interested in a trust or estate, to the account of another to compensate for disproportionate sharing of a tax burden. Generally, reallocations are made when tax elections by trustees, executors, administrators, and other fiduciaries otherwise would have disparate impacts on beneficiaries. Since the enactment of the Internal Revenue Code of 1954, there has been increasing discussion and debate concerning this concept. Carrico & Bondurant, Equitable Adjustments: A Survey and Analysis of Precedents and Practice, Tax L. Rev. 545 (1983).
>
> Equitable adjustment is a form of equitable apportionment, a doctrine that requires fiduciaries, in order to deal with beneficiaries fairly, to reallocate or reapportion benefits or burdens re-

ceived in an initially unfair form under standard accounting rules. Dobris, Equitable Adjustments in Post-mortem Income Tax Planning: An Unremitting Diet of *Warms,* 65 Iowa L. Rev. 103, 148 (1979).

In some cases an election made by an executor gives some beneficiaries an economic benefit while it causes others to suffer an economic loss. Where the election involves claiming administration expenses as an income tax deduction, some states require an equitable adjustment to be made in the absence of contrary direction in the will. As pointed out in the comprehensive and very helpful article by Carrico and Bondurant, *supra,* there is no uniformity among the states regarding equitable adjustments: Several states require certain adjustments and others restrict the availability of some adjustments.

Thus far courts have been reluctant to recognize claims for adjustment based on losses allegedly suffered as a result of the executor's election regarding the use of the alternative valuation date or the distribution of property in kind in satisfaction of bequests. For example, income beneficiaries may benefit from an executor's election to use the valuation date that produces the higher valuation and higher bases for estate assets, although the election results in a higher estate tax payment borne by others.

In making tax elections the fiduciary is often subject to conflicting duties. Primary among them are the duties to be impartial as among beneficiaries and to minimize taxes. A will or trust should give the fiduciary some guidance in making the elections. Instead, many wills and trusts attempt to relieve the executor from the necessity of making any adjustments by waiving the necessity of making any adjustments, by waiving any obligation that the executor do so, or by giving the executor discretion to make an appropriate adjustment. However, it may be unwise to give the executor discretion in the matter where it would subject him or her to a serious conflict of interest (*e.g.,* when the executor is also a beneficiary). Where an election may result in a disparate impact on beneficiaries the executor should consider presenting the matter to the court for guidance. Obtaining directions from the court is especially appropriate where the executor is in a conflict-of-interest position.

Most of the reported cases have involved an executor's election to claim administration expenses as a deduction on the estate's income tax return instead of on the estate tax return. Such a use of the deductions is proper where it will result in an overall tax saving (*i.e.,* where the income tax liability will be reduced by a larger amount than the resulting increase in the estate tax liability). The claim for an adjustment arises where the beneficiaries whose share of the estate bears the cost of the administration expenses *and* the additional estate tax that results from claiming the expenses on the income tax return do not benefit from the income tax saving. Essentially the same problem is presented where an estate distribution carries out distributable net income of the estate, but is characterized as principal for trust accounting purposes. An adjustment is appropriate in the case of such a "trapping distribution" because the income tax on the distribution is borne by principal, but benefits the income beneficiaries of the estate. *See* §12.40.

> **Example 12-9.** *X* died leaving a will that gave income-producing securities to his widow, *W,* and gave the residue of his estate to his child, *C.* Under the local law *W* was entitled to the income from the securities, reduced only by the income taxes and other expenses directly attributable to them. The local law also required the administration expenses and the estate tax to be paid out of the residuary estate. *C* will have a claim for an equitable adjustment to the extent the estate tax is increased by deducting the administration expenses on the estate's income tax return in a way that only benefits *W.*

In cases similar to the foregoing example, the courts have typically required that the residuary beneficiaries be reimbursed from estate income in an amount equal to the increase in the estate tax that resulted from claiming the expenses as income tax deductions. The leading cases are *Estate of Bixby,* 295 P.2d 68 (Cal. App. 1956), and *Estate of Warms,* 140 N.Y.S.2d 169 (Surr. Ct. 1955). Statutes in some states require a similar adjustment. *See* Md. Est. & Trusts Code Ann. §11-106(a) (1974); N.Y. Est. Powers & Trusts Law §11-1.2(A) (McKinney 1991 Supp.). Under such an approach the income beneficiaries do enjoy the *net* saving in taxes.

It is not necessary to make any adjustment where the administration expenses are claimed as a deduction on the estate tax return. In that case the deduction benefits the beneficiaries whose share of the estate bore the expenses that generated the deduction. Of course, the executor may be subject to criticism if a greater overall tax saving would result if the expenses had been claimed as a deduction on the estate's income tax return.

D. ELECTIONS AFFECTING ESTATE AND GST TAXES

§12.15. ALTERNATE VALUATION METHOD, §2032

Until 1935 the gross estate was valued on the date of death and the federal estate tax was due one year later. As a result of the steep decline in property values that took place during the Great Depression of the 1930s the tax often claimed a disproportionately large portion of the estate on the payment date. The alternate valuation method was added to the Code in 1935 in order to prevent the virtual confiscation of estates when there was a sudden decline in market values. Revenue Act of 1935, §202, 49 Stat. 1022. Under it the assets of the estate could be valued on the date of death or as of a date one year after death. In order to permit an estate to take full advantage of the alternate valuation date, the date for payment of the tax was extended from one year after death to 15 months after death. S. Rep. No. 1240, 74th Cong., 1st Sess. (1935), *reprinted at* 1939-1 C.B. 651. Effective January 1, 1971, the alternate valuation date and the date for payment of the tax were both advanced by six months as a part of a plan to accelerate tax collections. *See* Price, Recent Tax Legislation — The Excise, Estate and Gift Tax Adjustment Act of 1970, 47 Wash. L. Rev. 237 (1972).

Under §2032, property included in the gross estate is valued as of the time of the decedent's death unless the executor makes a timely election on the estate tax return to value the gross estate according to the alternate valuation method. An election is not effective, however, unless the decedent's gross estate is sufficiently large to require a federal estate tax return to be filed. Reg. §20.2032-1(b)(1).

If the alternate valuation method is elected, all items are valued as follows:

1. Property distributed, sold, exchanged, or otherwise disposed of within six months of the decedent's death is valued as of the date of distribution, sale, exchange, or other disposition.
2. Property not distributed, sold, exchanged, or otherwise disposed of within six months after the decedent's death is valued as of the date six months after the decedent's death.
3. Items that are affected by the mere lapse of time are included at their values as of the date of death (instead of the later date), adjusted for any differences in value that are not due to the mere lapse of time. *See* §2032(a).

The choice of valuation date affects the valuation of assets for estate tax purposes, which directly affects the size of the gross estate.

Derivatively, the election affects the amount of the credit for state death taxes and the amount of the federal estate tax itself. It may also determine whether the estate meets the percentage requirement of §303 (*see* §§11.15-11.24), §2032A (*see* §12.19), or §6166 (*see* §11.25-§11.30).

The estate tax valuation of assets also establishes their bases for income tax purposes. §1014(a). Thus, the use of the alternate valuation date will have an impact on the income tax liability of estates and distributees. The gain or loss realized on the sale of property acquired from the decedent is long-term by reason of §1223(11). Under that provision a person to whom property passed from a decedent within the meaning of §1014 is considered to have held the property for more than one year.

§12.15.1. Limits on Use of Alternate Method

Effective with respect to decedents dying after July 18, 1984, the alternate valuation date may be elected only if the election will decrease both the value of the gross estate and the sum of the estate tax and the GSTT. §2032(c). Thus, the executor may not elect to use the alternate method if it will cause an overall increase in the value of the decedent's gross estate. *E.g.,* LR 9001001 (TAM). This limitation is consistent with the original purpose of the alternate valuation date — to offer estates some protection against precipitous declines in value. It was adopted largely to prevent use of the alternate valuation date to increase the income tax basis of assets in estates that would pay no estate tax because of the unlimited marital deduction.

§12.15.2. Income Tax Impact of Using Alternate Method

If the alternate valuation method is used, all assets that are sold, exchanged, distributed, or otherwise disposed of within six months immediately following the decedent's death are valued at their respective values on the date or dates of their disposition. Thus, where the alternate valuation method is elected, the estate will not recognize any gain or loss on sales or exchanges that are made within six months following death. Where the election is made, all assets that are not sold or otherwise disposed of during the six months immediately following death are valued according to their respective fair market values at the end of that period.

Example 12-10. *T* died last year leaving a gross estate that consisted of the following items, each of which is followed by its date of death and alternate date values:

Asset	*Date of Death Value*	*Alternate Date Value*
Cash	$ 50,000	$ 50,000
Life insurance	300,000	300,000
Residence	125,000	150,000
Blackacre	100,000	75,000
ABC Co. stock	250,000	175,000
XYZ, Inc. stock	150,000	100,000
Municipal bonds	50,000	40,000
Total	$1,025,000	$890,000

Within 6 months of *T*'s death the ABC stock was sold for $175,000 and the residence was distributed at a time when it was worth $150,000. If the date of death values are used in valuing the estate, the estate will realize a loss of $75,000 on the sale of the stock. No gain or loss would be realized on the distribution of the residence unless it was distributed in satisfaction of a pecuniary bequest. Instead, the estate tax valuation would generally carry over and become the basis of the devisee in the residence. (However, distribution of the residence might carry out some or all of the estate's distributable net income to the distributee.)

If the alternate valuation date is elected, the gross estate will be $890,000. In such a case, the estate will realize neither any loss on the sale of stock nor any gain on the distribution of the residence. In addition, the devisee would take a $150,000 basis in the residence.

§12.15.3. Property Affected by Alternate Method

Property that forms a part of the decedent's gross estate at the time of death is "included property," which is subject to alternate valuation under §2032. Such property remains included even though it may change form during the alternate valuation period. On the other hand, property earned or accrued after the date of death is generally "excluded property," which is not taken into account for purposes of §2032. Thus, interest or rent accrued *prior* to death is *included* property, but interest or rent accrued *after* death is *excluded* property. Likewise, dividends declared and payable to stockholders of record prior to the decedent's death are included property, but dividends declared to shareholders of record after the decedent's death are excluded property. In either case the item would constitute income to the recipient. However, an included item might constitute income in respect of a decedent for which the recipient would be entitled to a deduction under §691(c) for the estate tax attributable to it.

The statute and the regulations provide some guidance for the alternate valuation of items whose value changes merely due to the lapse of time. An item, such as a patent, life estate, remainder or term of years, is included in the decedent's gross estate at its value on his or her date of death, adjusted as required for any difference in value not due to the mere lapse of time. §2032(a)(3). The nature of the adjustment is illustrated by Example 12-11, which is based on Reg. §20.2032-1(f)(1).

> **Example 12-11.** *D* owned a life estate and *S* a vested remainder in Blackacre. *S* died survived by *D,* who was then 40 years old. When *S* died Blackacre was worth $100,000. On the alternate valuation date applicable to his estate Blackacre was worth $50,000. The vested remainder is includible in *S's* gross estate under §2033. Its date of death value is determined by multiplying the date of death value of Blackacre ($100,000) by the factor for valuation of a remainder interest following the life interest of a person aged 40. The value of the vested remainder on the alternate valuation date is determined by multiplying the value of Blackacre on the alternate valuation date ($50,000) by the same factor. The approach takes into account the change in value of the underlying asset, but no change is made in the factor for the life estate, remainder, or other limited interest.

If the executor elects to use the alternate valuation method a mortgage or similar obligation included in the decedent's estate is returned at its value on the alternate valuation date. However, in such a case the estate must also include any principal payments received between the date of death and the alternate valuation date. Rev. Rul. 58-576, 1958-2 C.B. 625. Special rules applied in the case of other assets. Rev. Rul. 58-436, 1958-2 C.B. 366, *modified,* Rev. Rul. 64-289, 1964-2 C.B. 173 (livestock and crops); Rev. Rul. 71-317, 1971-2 C.B. 328 (mineral interests).

§12.15.4. Effect on Special Use Valuation

An estate may elect to use both the alternate valuation method and special use valuation, discussed at §12.19. Rev. Rul. 88-89, 1988-2 C.B. 333. If an estate makes both elections, the special use calculations must be based on values on the alternate valuation date. Id.

§12.15.5. Alternate Valuation Election

Under §2032(d) and Temp. Reg. §5h.4, an election to use the alternate valuation date must be made on the estate tax return. An election is allowed only if it is made on a return filed within one year of the date it is due, including extensions. An election once made is irrevocable. However, if a "return that fails to make the election is filed, this election may not be made on a subsequent return unless the subsequent return is filed by the due date (including extensions) of the original return." Temp. Reg. §5h.4(b)(1).

§12.15.6. Distributed, Sold, Exchanged, or Otherwise Disposed of

In general, the phrase "distributed, sold, exchanged, or otherwise disposed of" describes all possible ways by which property ceases to form a part of the gross estate. Reg. §20.2032-1(c). However, the term does not extend to transactions that are mere changes in form. Thus, it does not apply to a tax-free exchange of stock in a corporation for stock in the same corporation or in another corporation such as in a merger, reorganization, or other transaction described in §§355 or 368(a), with respect to which no gain or loss is recognized for income tax purposes under §§354 or 355. Id. The existing authorities have evolved a test that turns on whether the assets have been placed beyond the dominion and control of the fiduciary or surviving cotenant, or have been the subject of a decree that shifts the economic benefit of the property to a successor. *See Hertsche v. United States,* 244 F. Supp. 347 (D. Or. 1965), *aff'd per curiam,* 366 F.2d 93 (9th Cir. 1966).

The economic benefit analysis of *Hertsche* was followed in Rev. Rul. 78-378, 1978-2 C.B. 229, which was concerned with whether the passage of property by operation of law to a decedent's devisee constituted a distribution of the property where it remained subject to claims against the estate until a final court order. Under the ruling,

> The delivery of property to the distributee that is subject to a subsequent court decree is not a delivery within the meaning of section 20.2032-1(c)(2)(iii) of the regulations. Under these circumstances, there is not a shifting of economic benefits until the court decree.

For purposes of §2032 property may be sold, exchanged, or otherwise disposed of by the executor, a trustee, or other donee to whom the decedent transferred the property inter vivos; an heir or devisee to whom the property passes directly under local law; a surviving joint tenant; or any other person. Reg. §20.2032-1(c)(3). Entering into a binding contract for the sale, exchange, or other disposition of property constitutes a sale, exchange, or other disposition of the property on the effective date of the contract where the contract is subsequently carried out substantially in accordance with its terms. For example, property that is sold by a trustee or surviving joint tenant within six months of the decedent's death will be valued on the date of sale if the executor elects to use the alternate valuation date. On the other hand, the transfer of property by a surviving joint tenant to a revocable trust is not considered to be a sale, exchange, or other disposition because for tax purposes the surviving joint tenant is not considered to have relinquished any authority or power of ownership over the property. Rev. Rul. 59-213, 1959-1 C.B. 244.

The IRS has ruled that the division of the corpus of a revocable trust into two equal parts upon the grantor's death in order to facilitate the payment of income to two income beneficiaries did not constitute a distribution. Rev. Rul. 57-495, 1957-2 C.B. 616. A contrary result was reached in Rev. Rul. 73-97, 1973-1 C.B. 404, where the corpus of the original trust was divided into two separate trusts upon the grantor's death. Under the latter ruling, "when the trustee divided the corpus of the original trust into separate trusts, he effectuated a 'distribution' within the meaning of section 2032 of the Code." Revenue Ruling 73-97 indicates that the difference in the outcome of the two rulings resulted because the original trust involved in Revenue Ruling 57-495 continued after the division of the corpus into shares whereas the trust involved in Revenue Ruling 73-97 ceased to exist when its corpus was divided and transferred to the trustee of the successor trusts. The distinction is consistent with an earlier ruling that held that the bookkeeping division of estate assets into three separate accounts, which corresponded to three separate trusts created by the decedent's will, did not constitute a distribution within the meaning of §2032 where the executor retained control over the property held in the accounts. Rev. Rul. 71-396, 1971-2 C.B. 328. Under Rev. Rul. 78-431, 1978-2 C.B. 230, a division of community property into two shares, followed by the transfer of the surviving spouse's share into a separate trust, does not constitute a distribution for purposes of §2032. That result is reached because the share of the community property that was included in the decedent's estate remained in the original trust, subject to the control of the original trustee.

§12.15.7. Alternate Method and GSTT

For GSTT purposes, the value of property that is included in the transferor's gross estate and passes as a direct skip is the same as its value for purposes of the estate tax. §2624(b). If one or more taxable terminations occur at the same time as, and as a result of the death of an individual, an election may be made to value all property included in such termination in accordance with §2032. §2624(c). Where two or more members of the same generation have present interests in the same trust, a taxable termination does not occur until the last of the interests terminates. §2612(a)(1). In that case the alternate valuation date may be used to value all of the trust assets when the final interest terminates.

Example 12-12. *T*'s will transferred property to a trust that provided for the income to be distributed among *T*'s children *A*, *B*, and *C*. Upon the death of the last survivor of *A*, *B*, and *C*, the trust property is to be distributed to *T*'s then living grandchildren. Under §2612(a)(1) a taxable termination will take place upon the death of the survivor of *A*, *B*, and *C*. At that time the trustee may elect to value all of the trust property according to the alternate valuation method.

§12.16. Penalties for Incorrect Valuation of Assets on Returns Due Prior to January 1, 1990

Former §6660 imposed an addition to tax where an estate or gift tax was underpaid by $1,000 or more because of an undervaluation of property. For this purpose, there was a valuation understatement if the value of any property reported on the return was 66⅔ percent or less of its correct value. The addition to tax was an applicable percentage of the underpayment, determined according to Table 12-1.

Table 12-1
Penalties for Underpayment of Estate or Gift Tax, Pre-1990

If the Valuation Claimed was the Following Percent of the Correct Valuation —	*The Applicable Percentage was:*
50% or more but not more than 66⅔%	10%
40% or more but less than 50%	20%
Less than 40%	30%

The addition to tax could be waived by the IRS if the taxpayer showed that there was a reasonable basis for the valuation claimed on the return and that the claim was made in good faith. Former §6660(e). Basing the claim upon a valuation by a qualified expert probably constitutes a reasonable basis for a valuation by the executor.

Section 6659 imposed a penalty in the form of an addition to tax where the overvaluation of property by an individual, a closely-held corporation, or a personal service corporation results in the underpayment of income tax by $1,000 or more in any taxable year. No penalty applied, however, unless the valuation was 150 percent or more of its correct valuation. In general, §6659(e) permits all or any part of the penalty to be waived if the taxpayer established that there was a reasonable basis for the valuation or adjusted basis claimed on the return and that the claim was made in good faith. However, the authority to waive any portion of the penalty is limited where the underpayment was the result of an overvaluation of property contributed to charity.

Under §6659(b) the addition to tax was an increasing percentage of the underpayment caused by an overvaluation, based upon the following table:

Table 12-2
Penalty for Underpayment of Income Tax, Pre-1990

If the Valuation Claimed is the Following Percent of the Correct Valuation —	*The Applicable Percentage is:*
150% or more, but not more than 200%	10%
More than 200%, but not more than 250%	20%
More than 250%	30%

The addition to tax was a flat 30 percent where property contributed to charity was overvalued. The IRS could waive the underpayment penalty for overvaluation of property contributed to charity only if (1) the claimed value of the property was based on a qualified appraisal made by a qualified appraiser, and (2) the taxpayer made a good faith investigation of the value of the property. §6659(f)(2).

Revenue Ruling 85-75, 1985-1 C.B. 376 holds that the addition to tax applies where an individual adopts as his adjusted basis an overvaluation of property shown on a federal estate tax return. It involved a building which had a fair market value of 2,000*x* dollars, but was valued at 3,500*x* dollars in the estate tax return of the taxpayer's (*H*'s) deceased wife (*W*). Because the entire estate qualified for the marital deduction under §2056, no estate tax was due from *W*'s estate. *H* claimed accelerated depreciation for the building on his individual income tax return based on its federal estate tax value. As a result, *H* underpaid his income tax by $1,000. As stated in the ruling, the overvaluation penalty will apply unless waived by the IRS because the $1,000 underpayment of *H*'s income tax was due to a valuation of the property of 150 percent of its correct value. The penalty may be waived. However, "The fact that the adjusted basis of the building on *H*'s income tax return is the same as the value on *W*'s estate tax return does not of itself show that *H* had a reasonable basis to claim the valuation." Id.

§12.17. Incorrect Valuation of Assets on Estate or Gift Tax Returns Due After 1989, §6662

The 1989 Act consolidated the penalties for underpayments of tax due to inaccurate valuations in §6662. In case of an underpayment of tax described in §6662, an amount equal to 20 percent of the underpayment is imposed as an addition to tax. §6662(a). In the case of gross valuation misstatements the addition to tax is 40 percent. §6662(h). Underpayments subject to §6662 include ones due to negligent disregard of rules or regulations, substantial understatements of income tax, and any substantial estate or gift tax understatement. §6662(b)(1), (2), (5).

No addition to tax is made if the underpayment of estate or gift tax due to a substantial valuation understatement is $5,000 or less. §6662(g)(2). For this purpose there is a substantial valuation understatement if the property is valued at 50 percent or less of its correct value. §6662(g)(1). However, a gross valuation misstatement is made if the property is valued at 25 percent or less of its correct value. §6662(h)(2)(C).

An addition to tax for underpayment of income tax may be imposed if the amount of the understatement exceeds the greater of ten percent of the tax or $5,000. §6662(d). The amount of an understatement is reduced by the portion attributable to a position for which there is substantial authority or with respect to which the facts were adequately disclosed. §6662(d)(2)(B).

An addition to tax may be made under §6662(e) if the income tax is underpaid by more than $5,000 due to an overstatement of the value of property. For this purpose there is an overstatement if the property is valued at 200 percent or more of its correct value. There is a gross valuation misstatement, subject to a 40 percent addition to tax, if the property was valued at 400 percent or more of its correct value. §6662(h).

§12.18. Avoid Incurring Valuation Penalties

Where the valuation of a substantial estate asset is uncertain, the executor should obtain a written appraisal by a qualified expert. A good faith valuation made in accordance with an appraisal by an expert may avoid the imposition of an addition to tax under §6662 if the property is incorrectly valued. *See* Prop. Reg. §1.6664-4(b).

§12.19. Special Use Valuation, §2032A

> The Act provides that, if certain conditions are met, the executor may elect to value real property included in the decedent's estate which is devoted to farming or closely held business use on the basis of that property's value as a farm or in the closely held business, rather than its fair market value determined on the basis of its highest and best use. General Explanation of the 1976 Act, 537.

In 1976 Congress enacted a complex provision, §2032A, which permits the executor to elect to value real property that was used as a farm or in connection with a closely-held business ("qualified real property") according to its actual use rather than its highest and best use. The maximum allowable reduction under §2032A is $750,000. Ordinarily the value of property included in the gross estate is based upon its fair market value, which takes into account the highest and best use to which the property can be put. Congress was concerned that valuation of real property used for farming or other closely-held business purposes at its fair market value could result in unreasonably high estate taxes and make "continuation of farming, or the closely held business activities, not feasible because the income potential from these activities is insufficient to service extended tax payments or loans obtained to pay the taxes. Thus, the heirs may be forced to sell the land for development purposes." General Explanation of the 1976 Act, at 537.

A special use election may be made only if the decedent was a U.S. citizen or resident at the time of his or her death. §2032A(a)(1)(A). In addition, the election is available only with respect to qualified real property, which means "real property located in the United States which was acquired from or passed from the decedent to a qualified heir of the decedent and which, on the date of the decedent's death was being used for a qualified use by the decedent or a member of the decedent's family." §2032A(b)(1). The election is also conditioned on satisfying two percentage tests. First, the adjusted value of real or personal property used for qualified purposes on the date of the decedent's death must constitute 50 percent or more of the adjusted value of the gross estate (the gross estate less the amount of unpaid mortgages or indebtedness in respect of property). §2032A(b)(1)(A). Second, 25 percent or more of the adjusted value of the gross estate must consist of the adjusted value of real property that for a period of at least five of the eight years immediately preceding the decedent's death was owned and used by the decedent or a family member who materially participated in the operation of the farm or other trade or business. For purposes of the percentage tests, apparently the entire value of qualified real property that is held as community property is taken into account. *See*

§2032A(e)(10). If so, it would only be logical to include the full value of all community property to determine if the tests were satisfied.

§12.19.1. Election

An election to value qualified real property under the special use method must be made on the decedent's estate tax return. §2032A(d). In addition, the executor must file an agreement to the election signed by all parties having an interest in the property that is binding under the local law. Originally the election could only be made on a timely filed estate tax return. However, an amendment made by the 1981 Act allows the election to be made on a late return, if it is the first estate tax return filed by the executor. Once made, an election is irrevocable.

Under §2032A(d)(3) the IRS is required to establish procedures that allow an executor a reasonable period of time (not exceeding 90 days) to perfect an election that was timely filed and substantially complied with the Regulations. This opportunity exists where (1) the notice of election does not contain all required information or (2) the agreement consenting to application of the recapture tax is missing some signatures or the agreement does not contain some required information such as social security numbers and addresses of the qualified heirs and copies of written appraisals of the property.

§12.19.2. Protective Election

An executor may make a protective election by following the instructions for completion of Form 706. Under the October, 1991 version the executor is instructed to check the "Yes" block on line 2 of Part 3 of Form 706 and to complete Schedule A-1. In case of a protective election the executor must complete the Form 706 by valuing all property at its fair market value. If it is later determined that the estate qualified for special use valuation, the executor must file an amended Form 706 within 60 days of that determination.

§12.19.3. Maximum Reduction in Value of Property

The maximum reduction in the value of qualified real property allowable as a result of the special use valuation method is $750,000. In the case of community property, the limit applies to the decedent's share of the property regardless of the ownership interest of the surviving spouse. Rev. Rul. 83-96, 1983-2 C.B. 156; §2032A(e)(10). *See also* LR 8301008; LR 8229009. The special use value establishes the basis of the qualified real property for income tax purposes. However, if a recapture tax is imposed because of disposition of the qualified real property or cessation of the qualified use, the basis of the qualified real property may be increased to its fair market value on the estate tax valuation date applicable to the decedent's estate. §1016(c). If the qualified heir elects this basis adjustment, interest must be paid at the floating rate of §6621 on the amount of the recapture tax from a date nine months after the decedent's death until the due date of the recapture tax. §1016(c)(5)(B).

§12.19.4. Basic Requirements

The valuation requirements of §2032A are relatively simple. Real property used in a farm or other business qualifies for special use valuation if the adjusted value of the real *or* personal property used in connection with the farm or business accounts for at least 50 percent of the value of the adjusted value of the gross estate. In addition, the adjusted value of the real property must amount to at least 25 percent of the value of the adjusted gross estate. §2032A(b)(1)(B). (The election to value property under the special use method may be made with respect to a portion of the decedent's real property "but sufficient property to satisfy the [25 percent] threshold requirements of section 2032A(b)(1)(B) must be specially valued under the election." Reg. §20.2032A-8(a)(2).) The IRS takes the position that §2035(d)(3)(B) allows the decedent's estate to use property transferred within three years of death to meet the 50 percent requirement of §2031(b)(1) if it remained qualified property until the time of death, as long as other property in the estate meets that section's 25 percent requirement. Rev. Rul. 87-122, 1987-2 C.B. 221.

Some other relatively simple requirements are also imposed by §2032A. As indicated above, the decedent must have been a citizen or resident of the United States, §2032A(a)(1)(A), and the real property must be located in the United States, §2032A(b)(1). The real property must also pass to a member of the decedent's family, including the decedent's ancestors (*e.g.,* parents and grandparents) or spouse; lineal descendants of the decedent or of the decedent's spouse or parents (*e.g.,* nieces or nephews); or the spouse of any lineal descendant (a "qualified heir"). §2032A(e)(1), (2).

§12.19.5. De Minimis Interests Passing to Nonqualified Heirs

Under the Regulations, all interests must pass to qualified heirs. Reg. §20.2032A-8(a)(2). However, the courts have rejected the IRS position that the passage of a remote de minimis interest to a nonqualified heir disqualifies the property from §2032A valuation. For example, in *Estate of Davis,* 86 T.C. 1156 (1986), the Tax Court held that the gift over of the real property to charities (*i.e.,* entities that were not qualified heirs) if the decedent's children were to die not leaving descendants was so remote as not to preclude an election under §2032A. A Federal District Court reached a similar result regarding a de minimis remote interest that passed to persons who were not qualified heirs. *Smoot v. Commissioner,* 1988-1 U.S.T.C. ¶13,748 (D.C. Ill. 1988). In *Smoot* the court also held that the special use election could be made although the decedent's surviving spouse held a special testamentary power of appointment that could be exercised in favor of persons who were not qualified heirs.

§12.19.6. Ownership, Use, and Material Participation

More complex requirements relate to the ownership, use, and material participation in the management of the property. Unfortunately the liberalizing amendments made by the 1981 Act added to the already staggering complexity of §2032A. The complexity has not been relieved by subsequent acts. On the date of the decedent's death the real property must have been in use by the decedent or a family member as a farm or for other business purposes. In addition, for at least five of the last eight years preceding the decedent's death, the decedent or family member must have (1) owned the real property and (2) used the real property for farming or other business purposes. §2032A(b)(1)(C). The decedent or a family member must also have materially participated in the operation of the farm or other business for at least five of the last eight years preceding the decedent's date of death, disability, or commencement of social security retirement benefits. §2032A(b)(1)(C), (4). Importantly, real property owned indirectly through the ownership of an interest in a partnership, corporation, or trust qualifies for special use valuation to the extent the requirements of the Regulations are satisfied. §2032A(g); Reg. §20.2032A-3(f).

§12.19.7. Cropshare Leases

Both the decedent's and the qualified heirs' use and material participation in the management of farm property may be satisfied although the property is subject to a cropshare lease, which may relieve the owner of much of the labor required to conduct farming operations on the property. Under the Regulations, "physical work and participation in management decisions are the principal factors to be considered in determining whether material participation is present." Reg. §20.2032A-3(e)(2). The Regulation continues, pointing out that, "[a]s a minimum, the decedent and/or a family member must regularly advise or consult with the other managing party on the operation of the business." For a case involving a crop lease with respect to which the lessor's conservator was sufficiently involved in the farming operation to constitute material participation, *see Mangles v. United States,* 828 F.2d 1324 (8th Cir. 1987). For a helpful discussion of cropshare leases, *see* Dennis-Strathmeyer, The IRC §2032A Cropshare Lease, 2 Prob. and Prop. 36 (May-June 1988). *See also* §12.19.9.

§12.19.8. Special Use Valuation Methods

Section 2032A provides three methods for valuing farm property for farming purposes. Where comparable land is located in the same locality, from which the average gross cash rental can be calculated, the executor may value the real property by dividing (1) the excess of the average annual gross cash rental for comparable land over the average annual state and local taxes by (2) the average annual effective interest rate for all new Federal Land Bank loans. §2032A(e)(7)(A). Under a provision added by the 1981 Act, if there is no comparable land from which the average cash rentals may be calculated, the value may be based on the average net share rentals received by the lessors of comparable land in the same locality. §2032A(e)(7)(B). Finally, if there is no comparable land in the same locality from which the average cash or net share rentals can be calculated, the real property will be valued according to a multifactor formula. §2032A(e)(8). It is based upon the following factors:

1. Capitalization of income;
2. Capitalization of fair rental value for special use purposes;
3. Assessed land values in states that provide a differential or use value assessment law;
4. Comparable sales of other farm or closely-held business property in the same area; and
5. Any other factor that fairly values the farm or closely-held business use of the property.

§12.19.9. Recapture

The tax benefit of the special use valuation is recaptured if the qualified heir disposes of the real property or ceases to use it for the qualified use within ten years following the decedent's death and before the death of the qualified heir. §2032A(c)(1). The recapture period was originally fifteen years, with a declining percentage subject to recapture in the final five years. No disqualification results if the qualified heir commences to use the qualified real property within two years following the decedent's death. §2032A(c)(7)(A).

Cessation of the qualified use may occur if the qualified heir and members of his or her family fail to participate materially in the management of the real property for an aggregate of more than three years of any eight-year period ending after the date of the decedent's death. §2032A(c)(6). The qualified heirs' one-year cash lease of qualified farm property to a nonrelative constituted a cessation of the qualified use that triggered recapture of the tax. *Martin v. Commissioner,* 783 F.2d 81 (7th Cir. 1986). In such a case the heirs become passive investors for the duration of the lease, without any stake in the productivity of the farm or in the prices for which its produce were sold. However, the *Martin* court noted that the government had conceded that "if the lease had been on a sharecropping basis so that part of the risk of the farming remained on the heirs rather than being totally shifted to the lessee, the case would be different." As explained above, if a qualified heir leases farm property to others under a cropshare lease, the heir's participation may still suffice to avoid the recapture penalty. The 1988 Act added a sentence to §2032A(b)(5) that provides that the decedent's "surviving spouse shall not be treated as failing to use such property in a qualified use solely because such spouse rents such property to a member of such spouse's family on a net cash basis."

§12.19.10. Additional Tax

The amount subject to recapture is the lesser of (a) the excess of the amount realized upon disposition of the interest (or, in the absence of a bona fide sale or exchange, the fair market value of the interest) over the special use value of the interest, or (b) the excess of the estate tax liability that would have been incurred had the special use valuation method not been used over the estate tax liability based upon special use valuation. This amount is called the "additional tax." §2032A(c)(2).

§12.19.11. Involuntary Conversions and Like Kind Exchanges

An involuntary conversion of the qualified real property during the recapture period does not trigger recapture of the tax where the proceeds are completely reinvested in qualified replacement property. §2032A(h). In general, the replacement property must meet the requirements of

§1033(a) (*i.e.,* qualify for special use valuation). §2032A(h)(3)(B). The recapture period is extended by any period beyond the two-year period referred to in §1033(a)(2)(B)(1) during which the qualified heir was permitted to replace the converted property. §2032A(h)(2)(A).

Like kind exchanges of qualified real property also do not trigger the recapture tax except to the extent that property is received in the exchange other than real property that is used for the same qualified use as the original property. §2032A(i).

§12.19.12. Personal Liability

A qualified heir is personally liable for the amount of the tax that is subject to recapture with respect to his or her interest in the property. §2032A(c)(5). The personal liability terminates (1) when the qualified heir dies, (2) when the recapture period passes, or (3) if he or she provides a bond in an amount equal to the maximum amount attributable to his or her interest that might be recaptured. *See* §2032A(e)(11). A qualified heir may request that the IRS advise him or her of the maximum amount of additional tax attributable to his or her interest. The IRS must notify the heir of that amount within one year of the request. In determining the maximum amount the IRS may not consider any interest on the amount for which the heir might be personally liable.

§12.19.13. Special Lien

If special use valuation is employed, §6324B imposes a lien on the special use property in the amount of the maximum additional tax.

§12.19.14. Practical Concerns

The special use valuation provides some estate tax relief for estates that include sufficient amounts of qualified real property. However, many planners are reluctant to advise a client to elect to use the method because of its complexity, the potential for recapture, the personal liability of the qualified heir, and the special lien. Where there are multiple qualified heirs there is also the risk that they may disagree regarding the use or disposition of the property.

§12.19.15. Planning for Special Use Valuation and Marital Deduction

Careful consideration must be given to the interrelationship between special use valuation and the unlimited marital deduction. The planner must bear in mind that the surviving spouse will be treated as the transferor of property for which the marital deduction was claimed in the estate of the deceased spouse. Accordingly, special use valuation will not be available if the property passes on the death of the surviving spouse to beneficiaries who are not members of the surviving spouse's family (*e.g.*, where the surviving spouse is the beneficiaries' step parent).

In some instances the interested parties will not elect to make use of special use valuation (with the consequent limitation on basis) where the real property passes to a surviving spouse in a way that qualifies for the unlimited marital deduction. On the negative side, however, if the estate does not use special use valuation, a much larger marital deduction must be claimed in order to eliminate the estate tax liability of the estate. That amount is subject to inclusion in the estate of the surviving spouse. Thus, not taking advantage of special use valuation may unnecessarily increase the amount of property subject to inclusion in the gross estate of the surviving spouse.

> **Example 12-13.** *H* died survived by his wife, *W*. *H*'s will leaves an estate which has a value of $2,000,000, of which $1,000,000 consists of real property that could be valued at $500,000 under §2032A. *H*'s will makes a formula gift to a trust for *W* of an amount sufficient to reduce to zero the estate tax liability of his estate. If special use valuation is elected, *H*'s gross estate will have a value of $1,500,000 of which $900,000 must be transferred to the marital deduction trust. The other $600,000 is sheltered by *H*'s unified credit. On the other hand, if special use valuation is not used, $1,400,000 must be transferred to the trust in order to avoid payment of any estate tax by *H*'s estate.

Transferring appreciated qualified real property in satisfaction of a pecuniary marital deduction gift may result in the realization of gain by the estate. However, under §1040(a) the amount is limited to the excess of the fair market value of the property on the date of distribution over the federal estate tax value of the property, not taking into account its special use valuation.

§12.19.16. Impact of Special Use Valuation on Other Provisions

Note that an election to use the special use valuation method may affect the ability of the estate to qualify for benefits available under other provisions of the Code. For example, special use valuation may disable the estate from meeting the requirements for stock redemptions under §303, or the 15-year deferral of estate taxes under §6166. *See* §12.47.

§12.20. Marital Deduction QTIP Election, §2056(b)(7)

The 1981 Act added §2056(b)(7), which makes the marital deduction available on an elective basis for the value of property in which a surviving spouse is given a "qualifying income interest for life." *See* §5.23. A qualifying income interest for life is defined as one in which (1) the surviving spouse is entitled to all of the income for life, payable at least annually, and (2) no person has a power to appoint any of the property to a person other than the surviving spouse so long as he or she lives. §2056(b)(7)(B)(ii). The House Report notes that "income interests granted for a term of years or life estates subject to termination upon remarriage or the occurrence of a specified event will not qualify under the committee bill. The bill does not limit qualifying income interests to those placed in trust. However, a qualifying life income interest in any other property must provide the spouse with rights to income that are sufficient to satisfy the rules applicable to marital deduction trusts under present law. (Treas. Reg. §20.2056(b)-(f))." H.R. 4242, 97th Cong., 1st Sess. 161 (1981). The Regulations recognize that a legal life estate constitutes a qualified life income interest if the surviving spouse is entitled to the exclusive and unrestricted use of the property. Prop. Reg. §20.2056(b)-7(e), example 1. The IRS has ruled that installment distributions from an IRA to a QTIP trust may qualify for the marital deduction. LR 8728001.

§12.20.1. Partial Election

A QTIP election can be made with respect to all or part of any separate property (including a trust) in which the surviving spouse has a qualifying income interest for life. An election cannot be made if the existence of the spouse's qualifying income interest depends upon the election. LR 8611006.

The allowance of a partial election with respect to separate property is recognized by §2056(b)(7)(B)(iv), which provides that "[a] specific portion of property shall be treated as separate property." Proposed Regulation §20.2056(b)-7(b) recognizes that an election may relate to any part of property that passes from the decedent in which the surviving spouse has a qualifying income interest for life. However, "any partial election shall relate to a fractional or percentile share of the property so that the elective part will reflect its proportionate share of the increment or decline in the whole of the property for purposes of applying sections 2044 or 2519." Id.; Temp. Reg. §22.2056-1(b)(2). Thus, an election could relate to a percentage or fraction of the entire trust (*e.g.,* one-half or 50 percent). With respect to partial elections the Regulations provide that "the trust may be divided into separate trusts to reflect a partial election that had been made or is to be made." Prop. Reg. §20.2056(b)-7(b).

§12.20.2. Formula QTIP Elections

The fraction or percentage may be defined by a formula, which is a useful approach because it can automatically adjust for changes in the value of assets or the allowance of deductions for federal estate tax purposes. As indicated by the Proposed Regulations, an election may be made with respect to a pecuniary amount of a trust, provided that the trust is later divided into separate shares based upon the election and the current fair market value of the assets of the trust. This presumption is based upon Prop. Reg. §20.2056(b)-(7)(e), example 11, which allowed the marital deduction where "*D*'s will directs the executor to elect qualified terminal interest treatment for the minimum amount of property necessary to reduce estate taxes on *D*'s estate to zero, directs the executor to divide the residuary estate into two separate trusts to reflect the election and directs that any payments of principal to [the decedent's surviving spouse] shall be charged first to the marital deduction trust." The latter point is an important feature to remember in drafting QTIP trusts — invasions of principal should diminish the amount of the marital deduction share that is potentially includible in the gross estate of the surviving spouse. *See* §5.23.4. Note also that LR 8602005 suggests that the election may be made with respect to specified assets held in the trust.

> **Example 12-14.** *W* died survived by her husband, *H. W* left the residue of her estate to a trust, all of the income of which was payable quarterly or more frequently to *H.* None of the trust property could be distributed to anyone other than *H* during his lifetime. *W*'s executor may elect to claim a marital deduction with respect to a fractional share of the residuary estate by using language along the following lines: "The executor provides that the numerator of the fraction is the amount of deduction necessary to reduce the Federal estate taxes to zero (taking into account any specific bequests or liabilities of the estate paid out of the residuary estate) and the denominator of the fraction is the final estate tax value of the residuary trust (after taking into account any specific bequests or liabilities of the estate paid out of the residuary estate)." Prop. Reg. §20.2056(b)-7(e), example 8. *See also* Prop. Reg. §20.2056(b)-7(e), example 9.

In this connection it is important to note that the opportunity to disclaim property exists in addition to the election allowed by §2056(b)(7).

In case of a partial election with respect to a trust, the trust may be divided into separate shares to which assets are allocated in accordance with the election. As noted above, the regulations generally require a partial election to be made with respect to a fraction or percentage of the whole trust. However, once the election is made, it should be possible to allocate entire assets to each of the separate shares in accordance with their respective fair market values at the time. *See* Reg. §20.2056(b)-(7)(e), example 11.

If a formula election is made, the estate tax return need not indicate the assets or portions of assets that will be allocated to the marital deduction share. LR 9116003 (TAM).

The text of the formula QTIP election in Form 12-1 is based on the model form of pecuniary marital deduction gift discussed at §5.35. It is consistent with the example in the Proposed Regulations discussed above.

Form 12-1. Formula QTIP Election

Executor elects the QTIP marital deduction with respect to the smallest amount of the trust, which if allowable as a marital deduction for Federal Estate Tax purposes, will result in no Federal Estate Tax being due from decedent's estate taking into account all other deductions allowed decedent's estate for Federal Estate Tax purposes and the amount of the unified credit and other credits allowable to decedent's estate, and the amount of gift tax payable with respect to decedent's post-1976 taxable gifts, and the state death tax credit. However, the state death tax credit shall be taken into account only to the extent that it does not increase the amount of tax due to any state from decedent's estate.

A QTIP formula election can be expressed in the form of a percentage or a fraction of the trust. Proposed Regulation §20.2056(b)-7(e), example 8, upholds a fractional election:

> *D*'s executor elects to deduction under section 2056(b)(7) a fractional share of the residuary estate. The executor provides that the numerator of the fraction is the amount of deduction necessary to reduce the Federal estate tax to zero (taking into account final estate tax values) and the denominator of the fraction is the final estate tax value of the residuary trust (after taking into account any specific bequests or liabilities of the estate paid out of the residuary estate). The formula election is of a fraction share. The value of such share qualifies for the marital deduction even though the executor's determinations to claim administration expenses as estate or income tax deductions and the final estate tax value will affect the amount of the fractional share.

A fractional formula may be expressed in other ways. Thus, the following language from Prop. Reg. §20.2056(b)-7(e), example 9, is treated as a valid formula fractional election: "I elect that portion of the residuary trust, up to 100 percent, necessary to reduce the Federal estate taxes to zero, after taking into account the available unified credit, final estate tax values and any liabilities paid out of and specific bequests funded out of the residuary estate."

§12.20.3. Making the QTIP Election

Under §2056(b)(7)(B)(v), a QTIP election is made by the executor on Schedule M of the federal estate tax return. According to the October 1991 Form 706 the election is made by listing the QTIP on Schedule M and deducting its value. In previous forms the executor was required to check a box on line 2 of Schedule M and list the QTIP in part 2 of the schedule. Here, note that the election is made by the decedent's executor, not the decedent's surviving spouse. The election must be made on "the last estate tax return filed by such executor on or before the due date of the return, or if a timely return is not filed by such executor, the first estate tax return filed by the executor after the due date." Prop. Reg. §20.2056(b)-7(b). An election, once made, is irrevocable. §2056(b)(7)(B)(v). The decedent may authorize or direct the executor to exercise the election in a particular way. *See* Reg. §20.2056(b)-7(e), example 11.

As a general rule, an executor should plan the election in a manner that preserves the full benefit of the decedent's unified credit. An "over election" will cause an unnecessarily large portion of the property to be included in the surviving spouse's estate. Thus, where the decedent's surviving spouse receives a qualifying income interest for life in the decedent's entire estate, the executor should not elect to claim a deduction with respect to all of the property. Instead, the executor's decision should preserve the benefit of the decedent's unified credit. The executor should, of course, take into account all relevant considerations including the size of the surviving spouse's estate, the age and health of the surviving spouse, and the advantages of equalizing the sizes of the spouses' taxable estates.

Example 12-15. *H* died recently leaving his entire $1,000,000 estate to a trust that satisfies the requirements of §2056(b)(7). *W, H*'s widow, is in good health, and has an estate of similar size. *H*'s executor should not treat more than $400,000 as QTIP. In that way the portion of the trust that is sheltered by *H*'s unified credit ($600,000/$1,000,000) will not be included in *W*'s estate under §2044. *W* would, of course, be treated as the transferor of the remainder of the trust. On a related point, keep in mind that *H*'s executor may elect under §2652(a)(3) to have *H* treated as the transferor of the trust for GSTT purposes and to allocate *H*'s $1,000,000 GSTT exemption to the trust. *See* §§12.22-12.23.

§12.20.4. Protective Election

The executor may choose to make a protective QTIP election in order to protect against the imposition of an estate tax if the size of the gross estate increases substantially or if the amount of allowable deductions decreases substantially. Because of inherent uncertainties the protective election should be in the form of a formula. A protective formula QTIP election may be expressed in the language of Form 12-1, *supra,* which is consistent with the examples in the Regulations. *See* Example 12-14, *supra;* Reg. §2056(b)-7(e), examples 8-9.

§12.20.5. Professional Responsibility

An executor is subject to a general duty to preserve estate assets and to minimize taxes. *See, e.g., Estate of Bixby,* 295 P.2d 68 (Cal. App. 1956) (alternative deduction of administration expenses, application of equitable adjustment); Ascher, The Fiduciary Duty to Minimize Taxes, 20 Real Prop., Prob. & Tr. J. 663 (1985). The election to claim a marital deduction with respect to a QTIP may reduce overall current tax liabilities. However, a greater estate tax may be due later — which may be payable out of the interests of beneficiaries who did not benefit from the deferral of the tax. Put bluntly, an election may have an adverse effect on the interests of some beneficiaries. In such a case the executor is in a difficult position — the executor's duty to minimize taxes conflicts with the duty of impartiality among beneficiaries. *See* Ascher, The Quandary of Executors Who Are Asked to Plan the Estates of the Dead: The Qualified Terminable Interest Property Election, 63 N.C. L. Rev. 1 (1984). This dilemma is relieved to some extent if the decedent authorized or directed the executor to make a QTIP election. *See* §5.23.

§12.21. Marital Deduction QDT Election, §2056A

The 1988 Act amended §2056 to provide that no marital deduction is allowable if the surviving spouse of the decedent is not a U.S. citizen. §2056(d). However, the bar does not extend to "property passing to the surviving spouse in a qualified domestic trust." §2056(d)(2). Note that under the terms of §2056(d) the effect of the exception is simply to remove the disqualification imposed by the general rule of §2056(d). That is, in order to qualify for the marital deduction for a transfer to a QDT the trust must meet other requirements of §2056. Accordingly, in order to sustain the allowance of the marital deduction, a transfer to a QDT must satisfy one of the exceptions to the terminable interest rule (*e.g.,* it may be a QTIP trust or a life income-general power of appointment trust). As described below the marital deduction is allowable with respect to a QDT only if the executor so elects on a decedent's estate tax return.

Under §2056A a QDT must meet the following requirements:

1. The trust instrument requires that at least one trustee be an individual citizen of the United States or a domestic corporation and provide that no distribution other than income may be made from the trust unless such trustee has the right to withhold from such distribution the tax imposed by §2056A on such distribution.
2. The trust must meet the requirements prescribed by the Secretary in order to ensure payment of the estate tax imposed upon the trust. According to the Conference Committee Report, "it is expected that the Treasury regulations will require that sufficient trust assets be subject to U.S. jurisdiction so as to ensure collection of estate tax with respect to the trust. The regulations might, for example, require that a portion of trust property to be [*sic*] situated in the United States or that the trustee be an institution with substantial U.S. assets."
3. The executor must make an irrevocable election with respect to the trust on the estate tax return.

The election in effect defers payment of the tax on the QDT until (1) the property is distributed to the surviving spouse or (2) the death of the surviving spouse. In contrast to other types of marital deduction transfers, the tax on the property of a QDT is imposed at the marginal rate applicable to the estate of the deceased spouse. Such a method of determining the tax may be advantageous in some circumstances.

Example 12-16. At the time of *H*'s death he was married to *W,* who was not a U.S. citizen. Each of them owned property worth $1,000,000. *H*'s will established a credit shelter trust of $600,000 and a QDT trust of $400,000. No estate tax was payable by *H*'s estate. When *W* dies the property of the QDT will be taxed at the marginal rate applicable to *H*'s estate. Her gross estate will not be increased by the property of the QDT as it would if a QTIP trust were involved. Accordingly, in this instance *H*'s executor would elect to treat the trust for *W* as a QDT.

Section 2056A(b) imposes an estate tax on (1) any distribution from a QDT before the death of the surviving spouse and (2) the value of the property remaining in the trust on the date of the death of the surviving spouse. The tax does not apply to a distribution of income to the surviving spouse or a distribution made to the surviving spouse on account of hardship. §2056A(b)(3). Each trustee is personally liable for payment of the tax. §2056A(b)(6). The tax is due on the 15th day of the fourth month following the end of the calendar year in which the taxable event occurs (*i.e.,* April 15). The benefits of §§303, 2032, 2032A, 2055, 2056, 6161(a)(2) and 6166 are available for purposes of the tax imposed by §2056A. In addition, any tax that is imposed under §2056A on a distribution is treated as a gift tax that may result in an adjustment to basis under §1015. §2056A(b)(13).

§12.22. Reverse QTIP Election for GSTT Purposes, §2652(a)(3)

As explained in §2.26, if a reverse QTIP election is made, the decedent who created the QTIP trust continues to be treated as transferor of the trust for GSTT purposes although the trust is included in the estate of the surviving spouse under §2044. LR 9002014. Unfortunately, §2652(a)(3) does not permit a partial reverse election to be made — the election must relate to the entire trust with respect to which it is made.

Under the GSTT rules the transferor of property is the person who was the donor of the property for gift tax purposes or in whose estate the property was included for estate tax purposes. §2652(a)(3). In the case of QTIP the deceased spouse is treated as the transferor until the property is treated as having been transferred by the surviving spouse for gift or estate tax purposes. Upon the death of the surviving spouse the QTIP is includible in his or her estate under §2044. Accordingly, in the ordinary case the surviving spouse becomes the transferor of the property for GSTT purposes. Such a shift in the identity of the transferor may result in a waste of the GSTT exemption of the spouse first-to-die. That result can be avoided by making an election under §2652(a)(3) to treat the property as if the QTIP election had not been made for GSTT purposes. Temporary Regulation §5h.5(a)(3) provides that the election, which is irrevocable, is made by attaching a statement to the appropriate tax return (*i.e.,* the gift tax return of the donor spouse or the estate tax return of the spouse first-to-die). The statement must identify the taxpayer, the election, the Code section under which the election is being made, and the property to which the election relates.

Example 12-17. *T* died recently leaving an estate of $2,000,000. *T*'s will left $600,000 to a family trust for the benefit of his wife, *W,* and their children, $400,000 to a QTIP, and the residue ($1,000,000) to a separate QTIP trust. *T*'s executor elected to claim the marital deduction with respect to both QTIP trusts. In order to maximize the value of *T*'s GSTT exemption, *T*'s executor allocated it to the family trust ($600,000) and the smaller QTIP trust ($400,000). *T*'s executor preserved the value of the GSTT exemption allocated to the latter trust by making a reverse QTIP election with respect to it. Thus, *T* continues to be treated as the transferor of that trust for GSTT purposes. Of course, the reverse QTIP election does not affect the estate tax treatment of the smaller QTIP trust — it is includible in *W*'s gross estate under §2044.

The same result could be reached if *T* had only created 2 trusts — a $600,000 family trust and a $1,400,000 QTIP trust. If authorized to do so by *T*'s will, *T*'s executor could divide the QTIP trust into 2 trusts — one consisting of $400,000 and the other of $1,000,000. *T*'s executor could then apply *T*'s GSTT exemption to the family trust and the smaller QTIP trust. *See* LR 9050022; LR 9101013. *See also* §2.26.

In the unusual circumstances presented in LR 8837031, the IRS treated an estate as if a reverse QTIP election had been made. The ruling concerned an estate that, under the transition rules, was not subject to the new GSTT (decedent died before January 1, 1987 leaving a will executed prior to October 22, 1986). Decedent's estate elected to claim a QTIP marital deduction with respect to a trust, the principal of which would ultimately be distributed to his grandchildren. Under the GSTT rules the surviving spouse would be treated as the transferor of the QTIP trust for GSTT purposes unless a reverse QTIP election had been made. In this instance there was no procedure for making such an election at the time decedent's federal estate tax return was due. Because of the unusual circumstances the IRS appropriately agreed to treat the trust as if a valid reverse QTIP election had been made.

§12.23. Allocation of GSTT Exemption, §2631(a)

The executor may allocate any unused portion of a decedent-transferor's $1 million GSTT exemption. §2631(a). The allocation must be made within the time allowed to file the federal estate tax return, including extensions, regardless of whether such a return is required to be filed. §2632(a). The allocation is made on Schedule R of the federal estate tax return. An allocation, once made, is irrevocable. §2631(b). However, an election that the deemed allocation rules of §2632(b) *not* apply to lifetime transfers may be revoked. Thus, the executor might choose to allocate a portion of the decedent's exemption to a lifetime transfer. In the absence of a direction from the transferor regarding allocation of the exemption the executor may have to balance conflicting duties to treat beneficiaries impartially and to minimize overall tax burdens.

Example 12-18. *T* died and is survived by her daughter, *D,* who is 30 and in good health, and her son, *S,* who is 40, unemployed, and an alcoholic. *D* and *S* each have 2 children. *T* had not used any part of her $1,000,000 exemption during her lifetime. *T*'s will left $1,000,000 to a trust to pay the income to *D* until she becomes 35 when the trust will terminate and the trust property will be distributed to her. If *D* dies before becoming 35 the trust will continue for the benefit of her issue. *T* also left $1,000,000 to a trust to pay the income to *S* for life. When *S* dies the property of the trust is distributable by right of representation to those of his issue who survive him. *D* will probably survive to age 35 when the property of her trust will be distributed to her. A distribution to *D* would not be a generation-skipping transfer as she is not a skip person. On the other hand, if *D* did not survive termination of the trust, a generation-skipping transfer is likely to take place on her death. (A generation-skipping transfer would not take place on her death if she was not survived by issue and the property of her trust was added to the trust for *S.*) When *S* dies, a generation-skipping transfer of his trust is likely to take place.

Pursuing strict impartiality *T*'s executor might allocate *T*'s $1,000,000 exemption one-half to the trust for *D* and one-half to the trust for *S.* However, it is likely that any of the exemption that is allocated to the trust for *D* will be wasted (*i.e., D* will survive to age 35 and receive distribution of the trust property). More taxes are likely to be saved if *T*'s exemption is allocated entirely to the trust for *S,* as a result of which it would have an inclusion ratio of zero. The termination of the trust for *S* will almost certainly involve a generation-skipping transfer.

The parties might reach an agreement that maximizes the value of *T*'s exemption and protects the interests of *D.* For example, they might agree that (1) *T*'s entire exemption be allocated to the trust for *S* and (2) the trustee of the trust for *S* would reimburse *D*'s trust for one-half of the amount of any GSTT that is imposed on it if *D* dies prior to termination of the trust. (The trustee might acquire term insurance on *D*'s life to insure against any loss.)

Deemed Allocations Under §2632(c). Any portion of a decedent-transferor's GSTT exemption that is not allocated within the time allowed is deemed allocated in accordance with the provisions of §2632(c). Under them the exemption is deemed allocated first proportionally among direct skips occurring at the decedent's death and second proportionally among trusts of which the decedent is the transferor and from which a taxable distribution or a taxable termination might occur after the decedent's death. Deemed allocations may not make the most effective use of the exemption. Accordingly, the executor must give careful consideration to the preparation of Schedule R.

> **Example 12-19.** Under the facts of Example 12-18, *supra,* if *T*'s executor does not allocate *T*'s exemption, it will be allocated proportionately to the 2 trusts under the rules of §2632(c). Thus, *T*'s exemption would be equally divided between the 2 trusts, giving each an inclusion ratio of 50%. As *D* is in good health and will most likely survive another 5 years, the portion of *T*'s exemption allocated to *D*'s trust will probably be wasted. As suggested in Example 12-18, the parties might agree to an allocation that maximizes the benefit provided by the exemption, yet protects *D*'s trust against loss by reason of *T*'s exemption being entirely allocated to the trust for *S.*

§12.24. Consent to Split Gifts, §2513

Under §6019 the donor's executor is responsible for reporting taxable gifts for which no return has been filed. If both spouses give their written consent, under §2513 all gifts made by them to others during the calendar year are considered to be made one-half by each of them, provided both are U.S. citizens or residents at the time of the gifts. Note in this connection that the effect of splitting gifts is recognized for purposes of the GSTT. §2652(a)(2). ("If, under section 2513, one-half of a gift is treated as made by an individual and one-half of such gift is treated as made by the spouse of such individual, such gift shall be so treated for purposes of this chapter.") Following the death of a spouse, the surviving spouse and the decedent's personal representative may elect under §2513 to split gifts made during the decedent's lifetime. Reg. §25.2513-2(c). The election can only apply to gifts that were completed prior to the decedent's death. Rev. Rul. 55-506, 1955-2 C.B. 609 (1939 Code). The surviving spouse may execute the consent on behalf of the decedent when the decedent did not leave an estate subject to administration and no personal representative was appointed. When the gifts are split the surviving spouse and the decedent's estate are jointly liable for the tax. §2513(d).

§12.24.1. Time of Consent

A consent to split gifts may be signified at any time following the close of the year in which the gift was made. However, a consent may not be given after either spouse has filed a gift tax return for the same year. Consent may be given after April 15 if neither spouse has filed a gift tax return for the year. Consent may not be given after either spouse has received a notice of deficiency with respect to the gift tax for the year. A Technical Advice Memorandum, LR 8843005, held that gifts could not be split where the initial returns filed on behalf of the husband and wife did not report a large gift that resulted from a noninterest-bearing loan to their son. It distinguished *Alex Frieder,* 28 T.C. 1256 (1957), *acq.,* 1958-2 C.B. 5, which concerned gifts made by the wife prior to marriage and by the husband after marriage. Briefly, the Tax Court held that a gift tax return reporting only the wife's gift, which was filed by an agent on her behalf, did not bar the husband and wife from filing subsequent "spouse" returns that split the gifts. The Tax Court also pointed out that the wife ratified the return filed by her son as agent *after* the gift tax returns were filed by her and her husband that split the gifts.

§12.24.2. Revocation of Consent

A consent may be revoked by filing duplicate signed statements of revocation before April 15th of the year following the year in which the gift was made. §2513(c); Reg. §25.2513-3(a). There is no right to revoke a consent that is filed after April 15 of the year following the year in which the gift was made. §2513(c)(2).

§12.24.3. Deceased Spouse Was Donor

Subject to the rules described above, the surviving spouse may consent to split gifts made by the decedent prior to his or her death. The question of whether or not consent should be given requires consideration of a number of factors, such as (1) the includibility of the gift(s) in the decedent's estate, (2) the relative sizes of the spouses' estates, and (3) the availability of annual gift tax exclusions and unified credits.

§12.24.4. Gifts Not Included in Decedent's Gross Estate

A lifetime gift may not be includible in the donor's gross estate. If the amount of the gift exceeds the allowable annual exclusion the executor is required to file a gift tax return reporting the gift. If a return is required, the executor and the surviving spouse must consider whether or not gifts made by the decedent and the surviving spouse should be split.

In this connection note that under §2035(c) the decedent's gross estate is increased by the amount of any gift tax paid by the decedent or the decedent's estate on any post-1976 gift made by the decedent or the decedent's spouse during the three-year period ending on the date of the decedent's death. However, an offsetting deduction is available under §2053 for the amount of gift tax payable by the decedent's estate. If a gift is not included in the decedent's gross estate, splitting the gift may reduce the estate tax payable by the decedent's estate and increase the amount of property available for distribution to the beneficiaries of the decedent's estate. In effect, part of the tax burden is shifted to the surviving spouse. If the surviving spouse does consent to be treated as donor of half of the decedent's gifts, the surviving spouse may assume the responsibility for payment of the transfer tax attributable to one-half the amount of the decedent's gifts. That result follows because a splitting of the gifts would reduce the amount of the decedent's adjusted taxable gifts otherwise includible in the decedent's tax base under §2001(b) in computing the estate tax on the decedent's estate. Of course, the tax attributable to such a gift is not shifted to the surviving spouse if the gift is entirely drawn back into the decedent's estate under §2035. However, outright gifts of property other than life insurance made within three years of the donor's death are ordinarily not includible in the donor's estate.

When the surviving spouse is treated as the donor of half of the decedent's gifts, the decedent's estate is given the benefit of any gift tax the surviving spouse paid with respect to gifts that are included in the decedent's estate. *See* §2001(b)(2). Under the statute, the total amount of the gift taxes paid by both spouses with respect to such gifts is deducted from the tentative tax in determining the amount of estate tax on the donor's estate.

Example 12-20. *T* made outright gifts of $210,000 to each of his 3 children shortly before his death (a total of $630,000). Previously neither *T* nor his wife, *W,* had made any taxable gifts. Apart from the gifts, *T*'s taxable estate is $1,400,000. If the gifts are not split with *W,* the tentative tax on *T*'s estate would be based on the total amount of adjusted taxable gifts ($600,000) plus the amount of any gift tax paid by *T* with respect to the gifts ($0) and the amount of *T*'s taxable estate ($1,400,000). The gross tax on *T*'s estate would be $780,800, which would be reduced by the unified credit and the appropriate state death tax credit. On the other hand, if *W* consented to split the gifts, she would be treated as having made gifts of $285,000 in the year of his death (($630,000 ÷ 2) − $30,000). In such a case, for purposes of determining the unified tax applicable to *T*'s estate, *T*'s tax base would be reduced by the amount of one-half of the gifts ($315,000) to $1,685,000. The gross tax would be $639,050. Thus, the election could reduce the estate tax currently payable by *T*'s estate by about $140,000. Of course, by making the election *W* would be treated as having made taxable gifts of $285,000. However, assuming that *W* had not already used her unified credit, a taxable gift of that size would not require the payment of any gift tax.

Upon the death of the consenting spouse an adjustment is made where the entire amount of a split gift is included in the donor's estate by reason of §2035. In particular, under §2001(e) the amount of such a gift is not included as an adjusted taxable gift in computing the tentative tax on the consenting spouse's estate. Unfortunately, none of the unified credit used by the surviving spouse is restored to him or her in such a case. Also, the amount of gift tax treated as payable by the consenting spouse is not allowed under §2001(b)(2) as an offset in calculating the estate tax on his or her estate. The amount of gift tax paid by the consenting spouse is includible in the gross estate of a consenting spouse who dies within three years of the date of the gifts. §2035(c).

By splitting gifts a surviving spouse may increase the amount of property that passes to the beneficiaries of the deceased donor's estate where the splitting requires the surviving spouse to pay some gift tax. This occurs because the tax paid by the survivor in effect reduces the amount of estate tax payable by the donor's estate. As a result, the amount that passes to the donor's beneficiaries is increased. Here, again, the survivor's payment of the tax on the split gift does not appear to constitute a gift. *See* Reg. §25.2511-1(d).

§12.24.5. Surviving Spouse Was the Donor

The deceased spouse's executor may consent to split gifts that were made by the surviving spouse prior to the decedent's death. Reg. §25.2513-2(c). However, the estate of a deceased spouse may not consent to split gifts after a gift tax return was filed by the donor spouse for the year in which the gifts were made. That rule applies although the return filed by the donor spouse did not report the gift at issue. LR 8843005. In some cases, an overall tax saving will result if a decedent's executor consents to split the gifts. Such a consent makes the decedent's annual gift tax exclusions and unified credit available with respect to the gifts. On the other hand, the decedent's share of any taxable gifts will increase the tax base on which the tentative tax payable by his or her estate is computed. If the consent results in the imposition of a gift tax liability on the decedent's estate, an offsetting deduction may not be allowed under §2053.

Example 12-21. *T* made a gift of $100,000 to his daughter, *D*. Shortly thereafter *T*'s wife, *W*, died. *W*, who had not made any taxable gifts during her lifetime, left her entire gross estate of $300,000 to *D. W*'s personal representative may consent to split the gift made by *T.* If the consent is given, *W* will be treated as the donor of half of the gift ($50,000), but the estate tax applicable to her estate will be within the amount of her unified credit. Most important, the personal representative's consent to split the gift would preserve some of *T*'s unified credit, which could be used later.

A tax saving may also result where the consent would increase the estate tax payable by the decedent's estate by a smaller amount than the corresponding decrease in the gift tax payable by the donor. However, the personal representative should be reluctant to subject the decedent's estate to a greater transfer tax liability unless the donor is also the person who bears the burden of the increase in the estate tax. Needless to say, a serious conflict of interest arises where the donor spouse serves as the deceased spouse's personal representative and the estate tax burden is borne by others.

§12.25. Qualified Plan Benefits

The 1982 Act limited (to a maximum of $100,000) the previously unlimited exclusion of the value of benefits payable to survivors under qualified plans that was formerly available under §2039(c). The 1984 Act eliminated the exclusion entirely with respect to persons dying after 1984.

The 1984 amendment greatly simplified §2039 by repealing all but subsections (a) and (b). Under the basic rules of §2039, an annuity or other payment under a qualified plan is included in the decedent's estate to the extent it is receivable by any beneficiary by reason of surviving the decedent and if the decedent had a right to payment under the annuity contract or agreement. §2039(a). Any part of the annuity attributable to either the employee's or the employer's contributions is deemed to be contributed by the employee and taxed under this section. §2039(b).

The community property interest of a deceased nonemployee spouse in a qualified plan is includible in the decedent's estate under §2033 if the nonemployee spouse dies first. The Department of Labor has ruled that the plan administrator is not required to follow a probate court order directing the disposition of the nonemployee spouse's community property interest in the plan. *See* Dept. of Labor AO 90-46A (1990); Dept. of Labor AO 90-47A (1990). *See also* §4.20.6. The marital deduction is available if the decedent's interest passes to the employee spouse. If, despite AOs 46A and 47A, the decedent's interest passes to others, the marital deduction is not available.

§12.25.1. Special Exceptions

Under the 1984 Act the unlimited exclusion is available with respect to a person dying after 1982 who had irrevocably elected the form of benefit payable under the plan (including survivor's benefits) before 1983 and whose plan was in pay status on December 31, 1982. Similarly, the unlimited exclusion remains available to a decedent dying after 1984 to the extent that the decedent participant had irrevocably elected the form of benefits payable under the plan (including survivor's benefits) before July 18, 1984 and the decedent's interest was in pay status on December 31, 1984. See Temp. Reg. §20.2039-1T. Under the 1986 Act the unlimited exclusion was restored for the qualified plan benefits of decedents who separated from service before 1982 and do not change the form of benefits prior to death. In addition, the limited $100,000 exclusion is available with respect to decedents who separated from service before 1985 and do not change the form of benefits prior to death.

In LR 8728001 the IRS ruled that the marital deduction may be available with respect to installment distributions from an IRA to a QTIP trust.

§12.25.2. Lump Sum Distribution to Surviving Spouse

A surviving spouse who receives a lump sum distribution may elect to defer income taxation of the distribution by rolling it over to an IRA under §402(a)(7). Otherwise the distribution is subject to taxation presently, subject to five-year forward averaging. A spousal rollover is allowed for a partial distribution from a qualified plan, provided the distribution is equal to 50 percent or more of the balance to the participant's credit and is not one of a series of periodic payments. §402(a)(5)(D). Note also that §408(d)(3) permits surviving spouse to rollover a distribution received from a deceased spouse's IRA. Letter Ruling 8911006 permitted such a rollover where the IRA was payable to the estate of the decedent husband and his widow was the sole beneficiary under his will.

In order to defer the income taxation of the distribution, the rollover to an IRA must be made within 60 days following receipt of the distribution. In making the decision the surviving spouse should take into account the fact that the income of an IRA accumulates free of income tax until it is distributed. It is also significant that a contributor may retain investment direction over property held in an IRA. Note that after 1981 an individually directed account cannot invest in "collectibles such as works of art, rugs, antiques, metals, gems, stamps, coins, and alcoholic beverages." §408(m). However, the 1986 Act created an exception to the rule against collectibles, allowing investment in gold or silver coins minted under Title 31. §5112.

§12.25.3. Income Taxation of Lump Sum Distributions

A lump sum distribution from a qualified plan will consist of one or more of the following three parts: (1) a part attributable to the employee's previously taxed contributions, which is not taxable, (2) a part attributable to the employer's pre-1974 contributions, which is taxed as ordinary income unless the distributee elects to treat it as capital gain, and (3) a part attributable to the employer's post-1973 contributions, which is taxed as ordinary income.

The 1986 Act repealed §402(a)(2) for distributions after 1986; thereafter, unless the taxpayer qualifies to elect such treatment, lump sum distributions may not be treated as capital gain. However, the transition rules of Pub. L. No. 99-514, §1122(h)(3)-(6), 100 Stat. 2470-2472, allow the taxpayer to elect capital gains treatment for distributions made after 1986. The first provides that where distribution takes place after December 31, 1986 and before January 1, 1992, any distributee may elect to have a percentage of the pre-1974 portion of the distribution characterized as long-term capital gain. The percentage in 1989 was 75 percent, which declined annually in 25 percent increments until it reaches zero in 1992. Under this election, the capital gain portion of the distribution was includible in gross income but may be offset by the distributee's capital losses. If this treatment of the distribution was elected, the distribution was not eligible for five-year forward averaging.

The other election allowed under the 1986 Act is available only to taxpayers who attained the age of 50 before January 1, 1986. For such taxpayers, the requirement of §402(e)(4) that they be 59½ years old before receiving distributions does not apply. Qualifying taxpayers may elect to have the pre-1974 portion of the distribution taxed at a 20 percent rate instead of at the income tax rate. They may further elect to have the post-1974 portion of the distribution taxed under the either the old ten-year or the current five-year forward averaging method. Such taxpayers may also choose to forgo capital gains treatment altogether and elect to use the ten-year forward averaging method for the entire distribution.

§12.25.4. Five-Year Forward Averaging

Under §402(e)(4) the distributee may elect that the ordinary income component be taxed under a special five-year averaging method. A distribution would be taxed in the following way assuming that an election is made to use five-year averaging:

1. The amount of the distribution that is taxable is calculated.
2. A minimum distribution allowance is deducted from the taxable portion of the payment. The allowance is the lesser of $10,000 or one-half of the distribution, less 20 percent of the amount by which the taxable distribution exceeds $20,000. Thus, there is no allowance where the taxable distribution is $70,000 or more.
3. The portion of the estate tax attributable to the remaining value is deducted at this point. *See* §691(c).
4. The balance is subject to a specially computed tax. The tax is equal to five times the tax that would be imposed on one-fifth of the balance had it been received by a single taxpayer who had no other income except an amount equal to the zero bracket amount. In essence the tax is imposed at the lowest rates applicable to an individual taxpayer if the distribution were received in five equal annual installments. §402(e)(1)(B). (If five-year averaging is not available the balance is taxed as ordinary income in the year of the distribution.)

§12.26. Tax on Excess Distributions and Accumulations of Qualified Plans, §4980A

In the 1986 Act, Congress added §4980A (originally designated as §4981A), which imposes a 15 percent tax on excess distributions from and, at death, the excess accumulations of, qualified retirement plans. The tax on excess distributions is imposed in addition to the income tax that otherwise applies. Note, however, that in order to avoid the imposition of both the excess accumulation tax and excess distribution tax from applying to the same fund, §4980A(c)(2)(A) exempts from the tax on excess distributions any distribution with respect to an individual made after that individual's death. Thus, the tax on distributions may have no impact on post-mortem tax planning. However, a surviving spouse who receives all of a deceased spouse's interests in an excess retirement accumulation may elect that the excess accumulations tax not apply and that the surviving spouse instead be treated as owning such interests. §4980A(e)(5). Thus, subsequent distributions would be subject to the excise tax on excess distributions as if the surviving spouse had been the plan participant.

§12.26.1. Grandfather Election

A taxpayer for whom qualified plan benefits (including IRAs) of more than $562,500 had accrued on August 1, 1986 was allowed to elect to grandfather the value of benefits accrued as of August 1, 1986. §4980A(f). The grandfathered amount is exempt from the tax on the excess distributions tax; at death, it is exempt from the tax on excess accumulations to the extent the exempt amount was not treated as distributed during the participant's lifetime. The grandfather election was made by filing Form 5329 with the taxpayer's income tax return (Form 1040) for the year 1987 or 1988.

A taxpayer who made the grandfather election gave up the right to use the fixed $150,000 amount that would otherwise be exempt from the tax on distributions and as the basis for determining the amount subject to the tax on excess accumulations. Instead, in determining the amount subject to the tax on excess distributions, the taxpayer is limited to the alternate amount ($112,500 indexed for inflation) less the portion attributable to the grandfathered amount under the method of calculation chosen by the taxpayer. §4980A(f)(2)(A). In effect, the taxpayer is given the advantage of the larger of (1) the portion of the grandfathered amount that is considered distributed to the taxpayer during the year under the method of calculation elected by the taxpayer, or (2) $112,500, indexed for inflation. Similarly, for purposes of the tax on excess accumulations, the amount exempt from tax is determined by calculating the value of a hypothetical annuity based upon an annual payment in the alternate amount ($112,500 indexed for inflation) reduced by the present value of the grandfathered amount that had not been treated as distributed. For purposes of the tax on excess accumulations, the exempt amount is the greater of the portion of the grandfathered amount that remained undistributed at the time of the taxpayer's death, §4980A(f)(1), or the value of an annuity of $112,500, indexed for inflation, that is payable for the period of the decedent's actuarially determined life expectancy on the date of his or her death.

§12.26.2. Lump Sum Distributions

If the recipient of a lump sum distribution as defined in §402(e)(4)(A) elects income averaging with respect to the distribution, the tax on excess distributions applies to the amount by which the distribution exceeds five times the applicable annual exemption (*i.e.*, the greater of $150,000 or $112,500 indexed for inflation). §4980A(c)(4). The distribution within a single taxable year of the participant's entire interest in a qualified plan is a lump sum distribution if it is payable (1) after the participant attains age 59½, (2) on account of the participant's separation from service, (3) on account of the participant's disability, or (4) by reason of the participant's death. Again, the amount recoverable with respect to a taxpayer who elected grandfathering is the greater of the unused grandfathered amount or the value of a distribution of five times $112,500 indexed for inflation.

§12.26.3. Excess Accumulations

The 15 percent estate tax of §4980A(d) applies to excess accumulations where the decedent died after December 31, 1986. Under the tax, which is levied independently of the estate tax, the estate or the beneficiary must pay a 15 percent tax on the decedent's excess retirement accumulation. §4981A(d)(1). As indicated above, a surviving spouse who is the sole beneficiary of the decedent's excess accumulated retirement benefits may elect that the decedent's interests not be subject to the tax. If the election is made the surviving spouse will be treated as the plan participant for purposes of the tax on excess distributions. §4980A(d)(5).

The amount subject to the tax on excess accumulations is the amount by which the value of the decedent's qualified retirement benefits exceeds the present value determined under the new actuarial tables of a single life annuity for a person of the decedent's age at the time of death of an amount equal to the maximum annual distribution that could be made under §4980A(c) without the imposition of the excise tax on excess distributions (*i.e.,* the greater of $150,000 or $112,500 indexed for inflation). As indicated above, if the decedent had made a valid grandfather election, the exempt amount is the greater of (1) the amount of the grandfathered amount that had not been distributed and (2) a life annuity in the amount of $112,500, indexed for inflation, for a person with the decedent's actuarially determined life expectancy on the date of his or her death.

§12.26.4. No Deductions or Credits Allowable

The tax may not be offset by any estate tax credits or deductions. Most important, no marital deduction is allowable in determining the new tax.

§12.26.5. Computation of Tax on Excess Accumulations

The tax is calculated as follows:

1. Add the aggregate value of the decedent's interests in all qualified employer and individual retirement plans as of the date of death (or alternate valuation date, if elected by the estate under §2032). Do this without regard to the community property law. From this figure, subtract amounts listed in Temp. Reg. §54.4981A-1T(d), Q&A d-6, such as the decedent's unrecovered investment in any plan or the excess amount payable (because of the decedent's death) under a life insurance contract over the contract's cash surrender value before death.
2. Calculate the present value of a hypothetical single life annuity for a person of the decedent's age at the time of death of an amount equal to the maximum annual payment, using the new actuarial tables. The annual payment is the amount determined under §4981A(c) for the year of death, which is the greater of $150,000 or $112,500 indexed for inflation. If the decedent had made a valid grandfather election, the exempt amount is the larger of (1) the portion of the grandfathered amount that remained undistributed at the time of the taxpayer's death or (2) an annuity for a person of the decedent's age at the time of death of $112,500 indexed for inflation.
3. Subtract the amount derived in Step 2 from the amount determined in Step 1.
4. The tax is 15 percent of the amount determined in Step 3.

If the retirement plan benefits go to the decedent's spouse, the spouse can elect to roll the benefits into an IRA. If the IRA was created by the rollover and no other assets are in the IRA, any distributions from that account will not be subject to the excess distribution tax. This treatment is also allowed the spouse if the spouse elects to treat an inherited IRA as the spouse's own and makes no further contributions to that account. These rules apply to other beneficiaries if they meet certain requirements. Temp. Reg. §54.4981A.1T(d), Q&A d-10.

§12.27. Life Insurance Proceeds

A beneficiary of a life insurance policy may accept the benefits under the policy or disclaim the right to receive them. Also, a beneficiary is usually free to receive the proceeds outright or to leave them with the insurer under a settlement option. A beneficiary who elects a settlement option is treated as having received the proceeds outright and having transferred them back to the insurer in exchange for its commitment to make payments under the option. The estate and income tax consequences of electing an optional settlement mode are described at §§6.39 and 6.52.

> **Example 12-22.** *H*'s life was insured under a policy that designated his wife, *W,* as the beneficiary. Following *H*'s death *W* elected to receive the policy proceeds in monthly installment payments over a 20-year period. If *W* died prior to the end of the 20-year period, the commuted value of any remaining payments would be made to her surviving children. *W*'s election was not a disclaimer. Instead, *W* will be treated as if she had received the proceeds outright and transferred them to the insurer in exchange for its commitment to make payments to her for a 20-year period. The interest element of each payment will be taxed to *W.* The exclusion of up to $1,000 each year from the spouse's income under §101(d) has been repealed where the insurance proceeds are payable with respect to deaths occurring after the date of enactment of the 1986 Act. If *W* dies prior to the end of the 20-year period, the amount that will be paid to her children is includible in her gross estate under §2036. *See* §6.39.

The settlement options are usually based upon a low guaranteed rate of interest. Some options do provide for the interest payments to be augmented at the election of the insurer. A beneficiary may receive a higher net return by taking the proceeds outright and investing them in secure, higher yielding, relatively liquid investments (*e.g.,* certificates of deposit, corporate or municipal bonds). The election to leave the funds with the insurer may be attractive to a beneficiary, assuming the insurer is financially sound, because it will not require any further supervision or any payment of fees or commissions.

E. REORDERING THE DISTRIBUTION OF PROPERTY

§12.28. General

This part deals with several important devices by which the distribution of property can be reordered after a decedent's death. The family awards and allowances available to a surviving spouse or to minor children are discussed first. The awards and allowances are usually quite limited in amount but can provide important economic protection for the survivors. Next, the focus shifts to the option that most states give a surviving spouse to receive a statutory share of the decedent's property in lieu of the provisions made for him or her in the decedent's will. The concluding sections review the law regarding disclaimers and the circumstances in which they may be used to advantage.

§12.29. Family Awards and Allowances

The share of a decedent's estate that passes to the decedent's surviving spouse or minor children may be increased if they take advantage of the family awards and allowances that are allowed by local law. The family awards generally include a limited probate homestead allowance and a limited allocation of exempt property. *See* U.P.C. §§2-402, 2-403. They usually prevail over any contrary testamentary disposition made by the decedent. However, a surviving spouse may be barred from claiming the awards if the right to them was waived in connection with a property settlement agreement. The awards are often of special value because they are usually exempt from creditors' claims against the decedent *and* the surviving spouse or dependent children.

Most states permit a surviving spouse or minor or dependent children to claim a homestead or award in lieu of homestead and an allocation of exempt property. However, the awards are usually limited to pitiful amounts. By way of illustration, the U.P.C. suggests a homestead award of $15,000, §2-402, and an exempt property allocation of $10,000, §2-403. In addition, the spouse and children are usually entitled to claim a reasonable allowance in money out of the estate for their support during the period of administration. *E.g.,* U.P.C. §2-404. However, some states limit the duration or amount, or both the duration and amount, of family allowance payments. A family allowance is typically payable to the surviving spouse for his or her support and the support of the minor or dependent children. If the decedent did not leave a surviving spouse, it is payable to the children or to the persons who have the care and custody of them. The family allowance is also generally exempt from all claims of the decedent's creditors. If a decedent leaves a small estate the protection from creditors can be very important to the family.

The awards and allowances are generally allowable in addition to any property the survivors are entitled to receive by will, intestate succession, or otherwise. However, a testamentary gift to a survivor may be conditioned upon the survivor not claiming a family award or allowance. If so, the beneficiary may not be entitled to receive the gift if he or she makes such a claim. Also, a surviving spouse might be barred from claiming an award or allowance by reason of the provisions of a prenuptial or post-nuptial agreement with the decedent.

§12.29.1. Estate Tax

Homestead and exempt property awards of the type provided for in the U.P.C. vest in the survivors upon the decedent's death and qualify as deductible interests for purposes of the estate tax marital deduction. *See* §5.16. Accordingly, use of the awards could play a role in deferring some of the taxes that would otherwise be payable by reason of the decedent's death. In contrast, the family support allowances are usually terminable interests that do not qualify for the marital deduction.

§12.29.2. Income Tax

A homestead or exempt property award should be treated as an inheritance that is not subject to taxation by reason of §102(a) and that does not constitute a distribution for purposes of §§661 and 662. By reason of the latter feature, such an award does not entitle the estate to a deduction or require the recipient to report any income. A different rule applies in the case of family support allowances. Under Reg. §1.661(a)-2(e), the estate is entitled to a deduction for family allowance payments made from income or principal. A recipient is, of course, required to report family allowance payments as income to the extent of the recipient's share of the estate's distributable net income. Reg. §1.662(a)-2(c). The income tax consequences of family allowance payments must be taken into account in, for example, selecting the estate's tax year or making distributions. The lawyer should explain the income tax impact of the payments to the surviving spouse in order to facilitate planning for any income tax liability that may result from them.

§12.30. Widow's Election

Under the law of most noncommunity property states a surviving spouse may elect to receive a specified share of the decedent's property outright in lieu of the property he or she is entitled to receive under the decedent's will. Zaritsky, Attack of the Surviving Spouse: The Evolving Problems of the Elective Share, U. Miami, 23rd Inst. Est. Plan., ch. 4 (1989). *See also* §9.25. Neither Georgia nor South Carolina provides for an elective share, although dower is allowed to a widow. Am. C. Tr. & Est. Couns., Study #10 (1985). The size of the elective share, the property from which it is payable, and the election procedure vary from state to state. Perhaps the most extensive protection is provided the surviving spouse by the U.P.C., which greatly expands the property base that is used for computing the elective share. Under U.P.C. §2-202, the surviving spouse is entitled to claim a portion of the "augmented estate," which includes the surviving spouse's net estate *and* the decedent's probate estate and reclaimable estate. The elective share of the surviving spouse increases with the length of the marriage to a maximum of 50 percent after 15 years. U.P.C. §2-201. However, the share the survivor is entitled to receive is reduced by the value of property received from the decedent during lifetime or at death. The augmented estate concept serves both to prevent a person from transferring property to others in a way that would defeat a spouse's right to a share in the property and to prevent a surviving spouse from claiming a share in the probate estate where he or she had already received a substantial amount of property from the decedent.

The interests in a decedent's property that a surviving spouse receives pursuant to an election against the decedent's will are considered to pass to the surviving spouse from the decedent for marital deduction purposes. Reg. §20.2056(e)-2(c). When the surviving spouse receives outright interests in property as a result of the election, the interests normally qualify for the marital deduction. According to the Regulations, if the surviving spouse does not elect against the will, "then the dower or other property interest relinquished by her is not considered as having passed from the decedent to his surviving spouse." Reg. §20.2056(e)-2(c). Prior to 1982 an uncommuted common law dower interest in property was treated as a nondeductible terminable interest. In the case of decedents dying after 1982, the surviving spouse might have a qualifying income interest for life in the property subject to his or her dower interest. If so, the value of the property would be deductible under §2056(b)(7) at the executor's election. *See* §§5.23, 12.20. The commuted value of a survivor's dower interest, if requested and paid in accordance with state law, is a deductible nonterminable interest. Rev. Rul. 72-7, 1972-1 C.B. 308. Thus, a marital deduction is allowable for a dower interest that is an absolute interest that vests at death under state law. Rev. Rul. 72-8, 1972-1 C.B. 309 (Florida law). Also, the commuted value of the survivor's dower interest that is paid under a negotiated, bona fide settlement of the interest is also deductible under §2056 if the amount is no more than would have been received in a court proceeding; a court decree is not needed. Rev. Rul. 83-107, 1983-2 C.B. 159. From the estate planning perspective, a decision regarding the exercise of the spouse's election should only be made after projecting the overall tax and nontax consequences. In some cases the election may help salvage the estate from the ravages of an unwise or ineffective estate plan.

§12.31. Disclaimers: General

A disclaimer (or "renunciation," as it is sometimes called) is an unequivocal refusal to accept an interest in, or a power over, property to which one is otherwise entitled by lifetime or deathtime transfer or operation of law. Disclaimers were part of the common law of many states. However, an increasing number of states have recently adopted more or less comprehensive statutes on the subject. A disclaimed interest in property generally passes as if the disclaimant had predeceased the attempt to transfer the property to him or her. Because a disclaimed interest usually passes along to another person, a disclaimer can be used to decrease the amount of property passing to a named beneficiary and to increase the amount passing to others (*e.g.,* the disclaimant's children, the decedent's surviving spouse, a charity). The opportunity to reorder the distribution of property free of tax is one of the most important tools available to the estate planner.

A small number of states have adopted the comprehensive Uniform Disclaimer of Property Interests Act (1978), 8A U.L.A. 86 (1983), or its more limited companions, the Uniform Disclaimer of Transfers by Will, Intestacy or Appointment Act (1978), 8A U.L.A. 96 (1983), and the Uniform Disclaimer of Transfers Under Nontestamentary Instruments Act (1978), 8A U.L.A. 111 (1983). Other forms of disclaimer statutes have been enacted by a number of other states.

State laws generally require a disclaimer to be made without consideration and within a reasonable time of the original transfer. The acceptance of any benefit from a transfer generally precludes a valid disclaimer. The underlying theory is that an individual should be relatively free to accept or reject an interest that others attempt to transfer to him or her. However, in order to protect creditors, some states prohibit insolvent persons from disclaiming interests in property.

The federal gift and estate tax consequences of a disclaimer are determined by federal law. It was clarified considerably by the adoption of §2518 in 1976, which introduced the concept of a qualified disclaimer (*i.e.,* one that satisfies federal requirements for a disclaimer). The 1981 Act went further and, in effect, established a national standard for disclaimers that was largely independent of state law. *See* §2518(c)(3). Prior to 1977 the tax consequences of disclaimers were determined according to a scattered and uncoordinated group of statutes and regulations, augmented by a few judicial decisions. In general, a disclaimer was considered to be effective if it was valid under the governing state law and was made within a reasonable time after the disclaimant learned of the attempted transfer to him or her. Because of the wide differences in state law, identical refusals to accept property made in different states sometimes had different federal gift and estate tax consequences.

A disclaimer must be distinguished from a release, which involves the relinquishment of a power or interest that had been accepted. The difference in concept is recognized by Reg. §20.2041-3(d)(6)(i):

> A disclaimer or renunciation of a general power of appointment created after December 31, 1976, in the person disclaiming is not considered a release of the power if the disclaimer or renunciation is a qualified disclaimer as described in section 2518 and the corresponding regulations. If the disclaimer or renunciation is not a qualified disclaimer, it is considered a release of the power by the disclaimant.

Although a disclaimed power ordinarily does not pass to another person, powers can be validly disclaimed under §2518.

Before recommending that a client execute a disclaimer the lawyer must learn of the client's family circumstances and be aware of the impact of all of the relevant state laws. For example, in *Webb v. Webb,* 301 S.E.2d 570 (W. Va. 1983), a son's disclaimer of an intestate interest did not cause the disclaimed property to pass to his mother as intended. Instead, the property passed to the disclaimant's infant daughter, of whose existence he neglected to inform his counsel. Under the intestate succession law of West Virginia the disclaimed intestate share passed to the infant daughter, who lived with the son's former wife. The court refused to set aside the disclaimer, which was executed because of the negligence of the son and his counsel: "We are of the opinion that counsel's mistake, like that of the appellant, arises from a lack of diligence. We believe that, in the circumstances presented, counsel had a duty to inquire of the appellant whether he had any children before advising him to execute the disclaimer." 301 S.E.2d at 576. As indicated in Example 12-23, *infra,* a state's anti-lapse statute may similarly cause a disclaimed bequest to pass to the issue of the disclaimant. Finally, "a disclaimer that is wholly void or that is voided by the disclaimant's creditors cannot be a qualified disclaimer." Reg. §25.2518-1(c)(2). However, the mere fact that a disclaimer is *voidable* by the disclaimant's creditors has no effect on the determination of whether or not it is a qualified disclaimer. Also, where the transferor did not direct the disposition of the property in the event of disclaimer, the consequences of a disclaimer may be affected by the local anti-lapse statute.

> **Example 12-23.** *T* died leaving a will which bequeathed the residue of his estate to his 2 daughters. The daughters felt obligated to make the funds available to their mother, *T*'s widow, for her support. The daughters disclaimed their right to receive the residue with the intent that it pass to their mother under the local intestate succession law. Instead, the residuary estate passed to the daughter's minor children by reason of the local anti-lapse statute. Under the local law, in the absence of contrary direction

by the decedent, a bequest to a beneficiary who was related to the testator passes to the beneficiary's descendants by right of representation if the beneficiary predeceases the testator. LR 7833008. *See also* LR 8926001 (TAM).

§12.32. Qualified Disclaimers, §2518

> [T]he disclaimer of all or an undivided portion of any separate interest in property may be a qualified disclaimer even if the disclaimant has another interest in the same property. In general, each interest in property that is separately created by the transferor is treated as a separate interest. For example, if an income interest in securities is bequeathed to *A* for life, then to *B* for life, with the remainder interest in such securities bequeathed to *A*'s estate . . . *A* could make a qualified disclaimer of either the income interest or the remainder, or an undivided portion of either. *A* could not, however, make a qualified disclaimer of the income interest for a certain number of years. Reg. §25.2518-3(a)(1).

Section 2518 added the term "qualified disclaimer" to the estate planner's vocabulary. In brief, a disclaimer that meets the requirements of §2518(b) is a "qualified disclaimer" that will be recognized as effective for gift and estate tax purposes. Under §2518(a), if a person makes a qualified disclaimer with respect to an interest in property, the gift and estate tax laws apply as if the interest had never been transferred to the disclaimant. The provisions of §2518 apply to taxable transfers made after December 31, 1976 that create an interest in the party attempting to disclaim the interest. Reg. §25.2518-1(a). Interests created by pre-1977 transfers are subject to the prior law.

§12.32.1. Powers

A power with respect to property is generally treated as an interest in that property, and may therefore be disclaimed. §2518(c)(2). A power, such as a general power of appointment, that is disclaimed normally terminates. However, as in the case of other interests, a power may be partially disclaimed. *See* Reg. §25.2518-3(d), example 21 (qualified disclaimer of testamentary power to appoint one-half of the trust corpus). As noted in the Regulations, "a disclaimer of a power of appointment with respect to property is a qualified disclaimer *only* if the right to direct the beneficial enjoyment of the property which is retained by the disclaimant is limited by an ascertainable standard" (emphasis added). In contrast, a disclaimer is ineffective if the disclaimant retains a discretionary power to allocate the property among the beneficiaries. *See* Reg. §25.2518-2(d)(2); Reg. §25.2518-3(a)(1)(iii). Example 7 of Reg.

§25.2518-2(e)(5) suggests that an otherwise valid disclaimer is not disqualified by reason of the disclaimant's retention of a 5 or 5 power of withdrawal (*i.e.,* the power to withdraw the greater of $5,000 or five percent of the value of the trust). In some cases a disclaimed power may pass to another party — which is acceptable so long as the disclaimant cannot direct the transfer of the power. Reg. §25.2518-2(e). However, a trustee may not unilaterally make a qualified disclaimer of a power to invade trust corpus for the benefit of a specified beneficiary unless authorized to do so by the trust or state law. Rev. Rul. 90-110, 1990-2 C.B. — .In order to save the marital deduction a surviving spouse may disclaim the lifetime power to appoint the principal of a trust to and among her children. LR 8935024.

§12.32.2. Disclaimer of Benefit of Tax Clause

The right to have estate taxes on property passing outside of the probate estate paid out of the residuary estate in accordance with the provisions of the tax clause of a will may be disclaimed. *Estate of Boyd,* 819 F.2d 170 (7th Cir. 1987). That outcome is consistent with the general rule that treats "each interest with respect to property that is separately created by the transferor" as a separate interest subject to disclaimer. Reg. §25.2518-3(a)(1)(i).

§12.32.3. Pre-1977 Transfers

The disclaimer of an interest created under a pre-1977 transfer will be recognized for gift and estate tax purposes if (1) it is unequivocal and effective under state law and (2) it is made within a reasonable time after knowledge of the transfer. Reg. §25.2511-1(c)(2). The "transfer" referred to in the Regulations occurs when the interest is created and not later when it vests or becomes possessory. *Jewett v. Commissioner,* 455 U.S. 305 (1982).

§12.32.4. Statutory Requirements for Qualified Disclaimers

In order to constitute a qualified disclaimer under §2518, Reg. §25.2518-2(a) requires that:

> (1) The disclaimer must be irrevocable and unqualified;
> (2) The disclaimer must be in writing;
> (3) The writing must be received by [the transferor or his legal representative] not later than the date that is 9 months after the later of —
> (i) The date on which the transfer creating the interest in the disclaimant is made, or

(ii) The day on which the disclaimant attains age 21;

(4) The disclaimant must not have accepted the interest disclaimed or any of its benefits; and

(5) The interest disclaimed must pass either to the spouse of the decedent or to a person other than the disclaimant without any direction on the part of the person making the disclaimer.

Each of the requirements is considered briefly in the following paragraphs.

Irrevocable and Unqualified. The requirement that the disclaimer be irrevocable and unqualified will ordinarily not create any problem for the planner. In order to avoid any question on this point, a disclaimer should state that it is irrevocable and is not subject to any qualifications or conditions.

In Writing. The requirement that the disclaimer be in writing is unlikely to cause any serious problems. However, the planner should be sure that the disclaimer also satisfies the local law regarding formalities of execution. For example, some state laws require that disclaimers be acknowledged, witnessed, or recorded.

Received Within Nine Months. Under §2518(b)(2) the disclaimer must be received by the transferor within nine months after the date on which the original transfer was made. Under the Regulations, a timely mailing will be treated as a timely delivery if the mailing requirements of Reg. §301.7502-1(c)(1), (c)(2), and (d) are met. Reg. §25.2518-2(c)(2). A disclaimer can be drafted to provide evidence of the date on which it was received by the transferor. For example, the disclaimer could include a form of receipt to be signed by the transferor such as that found in Form 12-2.

Form 12-2. Acknowledgment for Receipt of Disclaimer

Receipt of this disclaimer on ____________________199____, is acknowledged.

____

[*Transferor*]

Under the Regulations the time limit is generally computed separately with respect to each taxable transfer. Reg. §25.2518-2(c)(3). In general, a taxable transfer occurs when there is a completed transfer for federal gift or estate tax purposes. However, a disclaimer that is executed within nine months of a taxable transfer will not be effective if the disclaimant previously accepted an interest in the property.

In most situations the time period within which disclaimer must occur starts at the time of the original taxable transfer. For example, if the remaindermen of a QTIP trust wish to disclaim, they must do so within nine months of the creation of the trust, not nine months after the corpus of the trust is subject to taxation under §2044 or §2519. *See* Reg. §25.2518-2(c)(3). Similarly, a "person who receives an interest in property as the result of a qualified disclaimer of the interest must disclaim the previously disclaimed interest no later than nine months after the date of the taxable transfer creating the interest in the preceding disclaimant." Id. In contrast, those who take through the exercise or lapse of a general power of appointment may disclaim within nine months of its exercise or lapse. Of course, the holder of that power must disclaim within nine months of the creation of the power. Id.

No Acceptance of Benefits. A qualified disclaimer cannot be made if the disclaimant accepted the interest or any of its benefits, expressly or impliedly, prior to making the disclaimer. As the Regulations state, "Acts indicative of acceptance include using the property or the interest in the property; accepting dividends, interest or rents from the property; and directing others to act with respect to the property or interest in the property. However, merely taking delivery of an instrument of title, without more, does not constitute acceptance." Reg. §25.2518-2(d)(1). For purposes of this rule, a disclaimant is treated as having accepted a benefit from the property if the disclaimant receives any consideration in exchange for the disclaimer, including the agreement of another party to dispose of the property in a way specified by the disclaimant. *See* Reg. §25.2518-2(d)(1). However, actions taken by the disclaimant in a fiduciary capacity to preserve or protect the property do not constitute an acceptance of benefits. For example, an executor may direct the harvesting of a crop or the general maintenance of a building. Reg. §25.2518-2(d)(2). A disclaimant is not treated as having accepted property merely because the title to the property vests in the disclaimant under the local law immediately upon the owner's death. The exercise to any extent of a power of appointment by the donee of the power is an acceptance of its benefits. Id.

The acceptance of a distribution from a gift or bequest is treated as an acceptance of a proportionate part of the income earned by the bequest or gift. Accordingly, the acceptance of partial distribution may not bar a subsequent disclaimer of a pecuniary amount of the gift or bequest. The principle is illustrated by Reg. §25.2518-3(c) and Reg. §25.2518-3(d), example 17. Thus, the receipt of a distribution of a portion of a brokerage account only bars the recipient from disclaiming that proportion of the account. Id.

Pass to Surviving Spouse or Others Without Direction. The requirement that the property pass to the decedent's surviving spouse or to a person other than the disclaimant without any direction on the disclaimant's part can be troublesome, particularly where trusts are involved. A disclaimant may have to disclaim the right to receive a particular interest by more than one method in order to satisfy this requirement. For example, the disclaimer by a residuary beneficiary (other than a surviving spouse) of the right to receive a decedent's estate would not be a qualified disclaimer if the disclaimant were entitled to receive the residuary estate under the intestate succession law. Reg. §25.2518-2(e)(5), example 3.

A disclaimer by a surviving spouse is not a qualified one if he or she retains the right to direct the future beneficial enjoyment of the property in a transfer that will not be subject to the federal gift or estate tax. A surviving spouse can validly disclaim an outright bequest if the property will pass to a trust over which the spouse holds no power of appointment. However, such a disclaimer would not be a qualified one if the spouse were to retain a special power of appointment over the trust. Reg. §25.2518-2(e)(5), example 5. In such a case, the surviving spouse must also disclaim the power.

§12.32.5. Disclaimers Not Recognized by Local Law

Changes made by the 1981 Act effective with respect to interests created after 1981 provide that a written transfer which does not qualify as a disclaimer under local law will be recognized as a qualified disclaimer if it meets the requirements of §§2518(b)(2) and (3) and the transferred property passes to the persons who would have received the property had the transferor made a qualified disclaimer. Under §§2518(b)(2) and (3), the attempted disclaimer must be timely (*i.e.,* made within nine months after the transfer to the present transferor), §2518(b)(2), and that the present transferor must not have accepted the interest or any of its benefits, §2518(b)(3).

Finally, partial disclaimers are allowed under the federal law but the interests that may be partially disclaimed are limited. *See* §12.34.

§12.33. Disclaimer of Joint Tenancy Interests

The tax position of the survivors is often improved if a joint tenancy interest is validly disclaimed. Unfortunately, the state laws are often unclear regarding the ability of a surviving joint tenant to disclaim an interest in the joint tenancy property. The common law generally did not permit joint tenancy interests to be disclaimed because the survivor's title was acquired by operation of law and not by transfer from the decedent at his death. However, the Uniform Disclaimer of Property Interests Act (1978), 8A U.L.A. 86 (1983), and some state disclaimer statutes expressly allow survivorship interest to be disclaimed. Even where a joint tenancy interest cannot be disclaimed under local law, a surviving joint tenant may be able to execute a qualified disclaimer if the requirements of §2518(c)(3) are met.

The Regulations say little regarding the disclaimer of interests in joint tenancies. The general rule of Reg. §25.2518-2(c)(4) simply provides that "a qualified disclaimer under section 2518(a) or an interest or any portion of an interest in a joint tenancy or a tenancy by the entirety must be made no later than 9 months after the transfer creating the tenancy." The same Regulation properly notes that a joint tenant cannot disclaim any portion of a joint interest that is attributable to consideration provided by him or her. The Regulations helpfully recognize that, "[i]n the case of residential property, held in joint tenancy by some or all of the residents, a joint tenant will not be considered to have accepted the joint interest merely because the tenant resided on the property prior to disclaiming his interest in the property." Reg. §25.2518-2(d)(1). In the case of a "revocable" joint tenancy the nine-month period during which a disclaimer must be made runs from the time of death of one of the tenants. *Dancy v. Commissioner,* 872 F.2d 84 (4th Cir. 1989).

§12.33.1. Revocable Transfers

A disclaimer need not be made within nine months of the original transfer of property into a joint tenancy that is revocable by the transferor. Typical forms of revocable joint tenancies include joint bank accounts and joint brokerage accounts. A joint bank account is revocable if the governing law allows a party who transfers funds into a joint bank account to withdraw his or her contributions without a duty to account to the other tenant(s). *See* Reg. §25.2518-2(c)(5), example 9. This outcome is consistent with the recognition that the creation of a joint tenancy bank account does not constitute a taxable transfer for gift tax purposes. *See* §3.14.1. Note that a joint brokerage account opened by the transferor and to which he made all of the contributions is also treated as revocable. LR 8824033.

Example 12-24. *H* and *W* both signed a joint and survivor signature card in connection with the establishment of a savings account in a financial institution. *H* deposited $10,000 in the account. Six months prior to *H*'s death he received a distribution of $10,000 from the estate of his father, *F,* which he also deposited in the account. *W* could make a qualified disclaimer of part or all of the interests in the account within 9 months following *H*'s death.

Under the circumstances of Example 12-24, the survivor has the right to disclaim the entire $20,000 unless she had accepted some benefit from the account. The disclaimer of the original amount in the account or of an undivided portion or a pecuniary amount out of the account should be possible if the requirements of Reg. §25.2518-3 are met.

§12.33.2. Property Subject to Partition

Several courts have held that the transfer of property to a joint tenancy that is subject to partition by the tenants should be treated the same way as revocable transfers are. In such instances a surviving joint tenant could disclaim his or her survivorship interest at any time within nine months following the death of the first tenant to die.

> The regulations do not discuss the effects of a power to partition. Yet the prospect of partition means that only the one-half undivided interest has been transferred irrevocably; the survivorship interest may be withdrawn at will, just as funds in a joint account may be. *Kennedy v. Commissioner,* 804 F.2d 1332, 1335 (7th Cir. 1986).
>
> There is no principled distinction between a joint tenancy with right of survivorship that is subject to partition by either cotenant and a joint bank account with right of survivorship that can be depleted through withdrawals by either cotenant. In both instances it is impossible to ascertain whether a cotenant has any right of survivorship until the other cotenant dies. *Dancy v. Commissioner,* 872 F.2d 84, 88 (4th Cir. 1989).

The Eighth Circuit reached a similar result in *McDonald v. Commissioner,* 853 F.2d 1494 (8th Cir. 1988), *cert. denied,* 490 U.S. 1005 (1989), as did the Fourth Circuit in *Dancy v. Commissioner, supra.*

§12.34. Disclaimer of Partial Interests

Special care must also be exercised in disclaiming partial interests in property, particularly where a trust is involved. On the federal side, §2518(c)(1) permits the disclaimer of an "undivided portion" of an interest. *See* Reg. §25.2518-3(a) and (b). The position taken by the IRS on this issue has important implications for marital planning, including the use of the election under §2056(b)(7) to claim a deduction with respect to part of the property in which the surviving spouse has the requisite life interest. *See* §5.23.

Separate Interests. The Regulations recognize that a separate interest in property can be validly disclaimed even though the disclaimant has another interest in the same property. For example, where an income interest in property is bequeathed to *A* for life, then to *B* for life, remainder to *A*'s estate, *A* may disclaim either the income interest, or the remainder interest, or an undivided portion of either. Reg. §25.2518-3(a)(1)(i). However, a disclaimer cannot be used to create separate interests in property. Thus, if property is bequeathed to *A* outright, *A* cannot disclaim it yet reserve a life interest or a remainder. Reg. §25.2518-3(b). The Regulations also permit the disclaimer of severable property, such as the disclaimer of some of the shares of stock bequeathed to the disclaimant. Reg. §25.2518-3(a)(1)(ii). For this purpose severable property is defined as that "which can be divided into separate parts each of which, after severance, maintains a complete and independent existence." Id. *Boyd v. Commissioner,* 819 F.2d 170 (7th Cir. 1987) (*see* §12.32.2) recognized the effectiveness of a disclaimer of the benefits of a tax apportionment clause made by the sole beneficiary under the decedent's will. The court analogized the benefits of such a tax clause as equivalent to a direct pecuniary bequest of an equivalent amount.

Pecuniary Amount. A specific pecuniary amount can be disclaimed out of a pecuniary or nonpecuniary bequest or gift, provided that the disclaimant receives no income or other benefit from the disclaimed amount before or after the disclaimer. Reg. §25.2518-3(c). The final form of the disclaimer regulations allow the disclaimer of a pecuniary amount of a residuary gift. Reg. §25.2518-3(d), examples 18 and 19. As indicated below, a pecuniary amount determined by a formula can be disclaimed.

Interests in Trusts. More complex rules apply where a trust is involved. A beneficiary may disclaim his or her entire interest in a trust, whether that interest is in the income, corpus, or both. Alternatively, a beneficiary may disclaim an undivided portion of his or her interest. Reg. §25.2518-3(a)(2). For example, an income beneficiary of a trust who also holds a general testamentary power of appointment over the corpus of the trust may disclaim the power to appoint one-half of the trust corpus. Reg. §25.2518-3(d), example 21. In general, the beneficiary of a trust cannot disclaim the income interest or the income and remainder interests in a particular trust asset *and* retain the right to receive income from the trust unless the disclaimer results in the removal of the asset from the trust. Reg. §25.2518-3(a)(2). According to the cited Regulation, a disclaimer of interests in specific trust assets is only effective if "as a result of such disclaimer, such assets are removed from the trust and pass, without any direction on the part of the disclaimant, to persons other than the disclaimant or to the spouse of the decedent." Where property is transferred to the trust at different times, a qualified disclaimer can be made with respect to each transfer.

Undivided Interests. The Regulations also permit the disclaimer of undivided portions of the disclaimant's separate interests in property (including powers). However, in such a case the disclaimer must extend to a fraction or percentage of *all* interests the disclaimant holds in the property. Reg. §25.2518-3(b). In addition, the disclaimer must cover the entire term of the disclaimant's interest in the property. Id. Thus, the beneficiary of a life income interest could not validly disclaim the right to receive the income for a period of years. Reg. §25.2518-3(a).

> **Example 12-25.** *T* devised Whiteacre and Blackacre in trust, to pay the income to *X* for life, remainder to *Y*. *X* may disclaim all or a fractional or percentage portion of the income interest in the trust. *X* may also disclaim the right to receive the income from Whiteacre (or Blackacre), provided that Whiteacre is removed from the trust and distributed without any direction by *X*. *Y* could disclaim all or part of the interests in the remainder of the trust.

Disclaimer by Formula. The Regulations and several letter rulings recognize the validity of disclaimers of fractional shares or pecuniary amounts determined by formula. For example, Reg. §25.2518-3(d), example 20, recognizes the effectiveness of a disclaimer of a fractional share of a decedent's residuary estate. *See also* LR 8514095 (disclaimer by decedent's child of portion of fractional share of her intestate interest in the decedent's estate). Disclaimers of pecuniary amounts determined by formula are also effective, as indicated by LR 8502084 (disclaimer by surviving spouse of an amount equal to the credit equivalent).

§12.35. Disclaimer Planning

A disclaimer can be used effectively in a wide variety of circumstances. Some common opportunities that involve federal tax benefits include:

1. *Skipping a Generation.* A financially secure child may disclaim the right to receive an outright bequest, as a result of which the property will pass to the disclaimant's children outright or to a trust for their benefit. Of course, such a disclaimer would subject the bequest to the GSTT (*i.e.,* the transfer to the disclaimant's child would be a direct skip).
2. *Decreasing (or Increasing) Gifts to a Surviving Spouse.* A

surviving spouse may disclaim the right to receive property that would be sheltered from federal taxation by the decedent's unified credit. A disclaimer in such a case will help control (*i.e.,* limit) the size of the surviving spouse's gross estate. Reg. §20.2056(d)-1(a). *See* LR 8429085 and LR 8443005 (which involve disclaimers by children in order to qualify trusts for the marital deduction). A disclaimer by the guardian of minor grandchildren was recognized in LR 8701001 where it would support a larger marital deduction.

3. *Perfecting or Increasing Charitable Gifts.* A wealthy beneficiary may disclaim a life interest in a trust, as a result of which the property will pass outright to the designated charitable remainderman in a way that will qualify for the charitable deduction under §2055. Of course, outright gifts may also be disclaimed in favor of charitable alternate takers.
4. *Eliminating a Generation-Skipping Transfer.* A grandchild or more remote descendant may disclaim a bequest in a way that will prevent a generation-skipping transfer from taking place. Moreover, the GSTT does not apply to direct skips made under wills executed prior to the effective date of the GSTT if the testator was incompetent on that date and did not regain competency prior to death. Thus, the GSTT does not extend to bequests under such a will that pass outright to grandnephews and grandnieces (*i.e.,* direct skips) as a result of qualified disclaimers by the testator's nephews. LR 9111011.
5. *Eliminating Nonqualified Heirs.* Where an estate qualifies for special use valuation under §2032A but for the interests passing to nonqualified heirs, the nonqualified heirs may disclaim their interests.
6. *Avoiding Multiple Administrations and Unnecessary Taxation.* If a beneficiary dies within nine months of the decedent, the beneficiary's personal representative may disclaim the right to receive property from the decedent's estate in order to avoid multiple administrations and multiple taxation of the same property (the previously taxed property credit may be inadequate protection against multiple taxation).
7. *Terminating a Trust.* A disclaimer by the life income beneficiary may cause the remainder to accelerate, resulting in distribution of the trust corpus and termination of the trust. In some cases a disclaimer by the remainderman may result in termination of the trust. Termination would also usually result if all beneficiaries disclaim their interests.

A planner can provide valuable help to clients by alerting them to the possibilities offered by disclaimers. Indeed, the failure to advise beneficiaries of the availability and consequences of a disclaimer by the surviving spouse may constitute actionable professional malpractice under the local law. *Linck v. Barokas & Martin,* 667 P.2d 171 (Alaska 1983). Advice to clients should, of course, include appropriate caveats regarding the uncertainties and limitations regarding the use of disclaimers. Finally, the planner should also be sensitive to the conflicts of interest that may arise in advising parties regarding disclaimers. For example, a lawyer should exercise great care in undertaking to advise grandchildren regarding the use of disclaimers if the lawyer represents their parents, who will receive any property the grandchildren disclaim.

The planner should also watch for situations in which it may be advantageous to use a disclaimer even though it will not produce any federal tax benefits. For example, differences between the state and federal transfer tax laws may cause a disclaimer to result in a state tax saving although no federal tax is saved. Finally, it may be desirable to use a disclaimer to help rearrange property ownership even where it will not save any taxes. For example, a disclaimer could be made by a guardian ad litem to deflect property from a beneficiary to a trust for the disclaimant's benefit where an outright transfer would subject the property to an expensive and cumbersome guardianship. Of course, such a disclaimer can be made only where authorized by local law and often only with court approval.

F. PLANNING ESTATE DISTRIBUTIONS

> The 1954 Code policy adverted to can be both a serious trap for the unwary and an important post-mortem tax planning tool in the hands of the sophisticated fiduciary; a tax trap in that the unwary estate practitioner familiar only with fiduciary accounting principles may suddenly find that the distribution of a family automobile results in income to the recipient. On the other hand, the sophisticated use of distributions in creating multiple entities such as testamentary trusts, has significant tax saving possibilities. . . . *Estate of Holloway,* 327 N.Y.S.2d 865, 866 (Surr. Ct. 1972).

§12.36. GENERAL

Estate distributions have important estate and income tax consequences. For estate tax purposes distributions have a particularly important impact on the alternative valuation of assets. *See* §12.15. The income tax consequences of distributions remain significant despite the compressed rate structure adopted in the 1986 Act. Overall, the proper planning of estate distributions is at the very heart of post-mortem income tax planning. Distribution planning must be considered in connection with the selection of the estate's tax year (*see* §12.7) and the payment of estate expenses (*see* §12.13).

The proper treatment of some payments by an estate or trust is not always clear. For example, the payment of the costs of maintenance of a personal residence used by a beneficiary may be treated as an expense of the estate incurred in order to maintain a capital asset rather than a distribution. *See Henry Bradley Plant,* 30 B.T.A. 133 (1934), *acq.,* 1976-1 C.B. 1, *aff'd,* 76 F.2d 8 (2d Cir. 1935); LR 8341005.

The opportunities for creative post-mortem income tax planning arise in large part because the estate is recognized as a separate taxpaying entity. Insofar as current income is concerned, an estate generally acts as a conduit for estate income. In brief, an estate is taxed on any income that is neither currently distributed nor required to be distributed to its beneficiaries. As a result, all of the income received by an estate during a taxable year net of deductions is taxed to the estate to the extent it does not make any nonspecific distributions during the year. Because the so-called throwback rules of §§665-667 do not apply to estates, the executor has considerable flexibility in "splitting" the estate's income between the estate and its distributees (*e.g.,* trusts and beneficiaries). Generally speaking, once an item of income is taxed to an estate its origin as an item of income has no significance in determining the income tax consequences of future distributions to the beneficiaries.

Example 12-26. The estate of *T* had a taxable income of $25,000 in its second taxable year, during which it made no distributions. The estate closed early in the following year during which it distributed all of its assets before it received any income. The distribution of the estate's assets, including the $25,000 of accumulated income, is not taxed to the distributees. Under §642(h), the estate's beneficiaries are entitled to the benefit of the estate's deductions for its final taxable year in excess of its gross income and the estate's net operating loss and capital loss carryovers. However, under §67 miscellaneous itemized deductions are generally subject to the 2% floor in the hands of the beneficiaries.

§12.36.1. Basic Rule

An estate is allowed deductions for income required to be distributed currently and "other amounts" properly paid, credited, or required to be distributed during the taxable year. §661(a). Rounding out the picture, the amounts that are deductible by the estate must be reported as income by the beneficiaries. §662(a). Each item distributed retains its particular character in the hands of the beneficiaries (*e.g.,* dividends and tax-exempt interest). In general, each distribution is considered to consist of a proportionate part of each item. §662(b); Reg. §1.662(b)-1.

§12.36.2. Distributable Net Income (DNI)

The amount deductible by the estate and reportable by the beneficiaries is limited to the distributable net income of the estate, a concept that is significant mainly for that purpose. DNI is basically the taxable income of the estate, computed without regard to the distribution deduction and adjusted for capital gains that are added to principal and for certain other items. *See* §643. *See also* §10.4.3.

§12.36.3. Tier System

Under the so-called tier system, DNI is allocated first to beneficiaries who are entitled as a matter of right to receive distributions of income. §662(a)(1). It is allocated to the first tier beneficiaries in the same proportion that the income required to be distributed currently to each bears to the total amount required to be distributed currently to all beneficiaries. *See* Reg. §1.662(a)-2(b). Where DNI exceeds the amount distributable currently to first tier beneficiaries the excess is allocated to the second tier beneficiaries in proportion to the distribution each of them receives. *See* §10.4.9. Under this method of allocation, a distribution of principal may require the distributee to report a portion of the estate's income, depending upon whether DNI is completely absorbed by first tier distributions.

Example 12-27. *X* and *Y* are each entitled to receive $10,000 of current income from the estate each year. *X* and another beneficiary, *Z,* are entitled to receive equal shares of the corpus of the estate. During a year in which estate's DNI was $20,000, the executor distributed $20,000 to *X,* $10,000 to *Y,* and $10,000 to *Z. X* and *Y* are each taxable on $10,000. Apart from the statute the income might be taxed in proportion to the value of each distribution (*i.e.,* 50% to *X,* 25% to *Y,* and 25% to *Z*). As it is, the $10,000 of the amount distributed to *X* and the $10,000 distributed to *Z* are not taken into account because the estate's DNI was exhausted by the distributions of income that were required to be made to the first tier beneficiaries, *X* and *Y.* Had the estate's DNI been $30,000, then *X* would be taxed on a total of $15,000, *Y* on $10,000, and *Z* on $5,000. In that event, the additional $10,000 of DNI would be taxed to the second tier beneficiaries, *X* and *Z*, in proportion to the amount of corpus distributed to each of them.

§12.36.4. Specific Gifts

Distributions in satisfaction of gifts of specific sums of money or of specific items of property that are paid all at once or in three or fewer installments are neither deductible by the estate nor includible in the distributee's income. *See* §663(a). *See also* §12.37. In order to qualify under this provision, the amount of money or the identity of specific property must be ascertainable under the terms of the will on the date of the testator's death. Reg. §1.663(a)-1(b).

Example 12-28. *T*'s will left $10,000 to *X*, 1,000 shares of ABC stock to *Y*, and the residue of his estate to *Z*. The estate had income of $25,000 during the year, which was accumulated and added to corpus for estate accounting purposes. During the year the executor distributed $10,000 to *X*, 1,000 shares of ABC stock to *Y*, and nothing to *Z*. The distributions to *X* and *Y* are neither deductible by the estate nor includible in the income of *X* or *Y*. However, any distribution of residue made to *Z* during the year would have carried out the estate's DNI to him or her to the extent of the distribution.

Distributions in satisfaction of a formula pecuniary gift carry out DNI unless the amount of the gift was specifically ascertainable on the date of death. Reg. §1.663(a)-1(b). Because of uncertainties about the amounts that will be claimed for various deductions the amount that will be distributable to a credit shelter trust or under a pecuniary marital deduction formula clause is not ascertainable at the time of the decedent's death.

§12.36.5. Timing of Distributions

Combined with the opportunity to select a fiscal year for the estate and the election regarding the use of the alternate valuation date, carefully planned distributions can help to minimize the overall income tax burden of the estate and the beneficiaries. The timing of distributions has an important impact on the taxation of the estate and the beneficiaries. For example, nonspecific distributions can often be accelerated or deferred to generate the most desirable tax results for the estate and the beneficiaries (*e.g.*, distributions that will carry out DNI might be made during a year in which the estate will have little or no income to carry out to the distributees). Of course, in some circumstances it is desirable to make distributions that carry out income (*e.g.*, when the beneficiaries have excess deductions available to offset the income carried out to them by reason of the distributions). A determination of whether or not an amount is properly paid or credited for purposes of §§661 and 662 depends upon the terms of the governing instrument and the state law. *See Bohan v. United States,* 456 F.2d 851 (8th Cir. 1972), which the IRS has announced it will not follow, Rev. Rul. 72-396, 1972-2 C.B. 312.

Distributions can be planned and made in ways that maximize the benefit of deductions for estate administration expenses and other items. Careful planning can, for example, allow excess deductions to be carried out to the distributee who will benefit the most from them. A distribution should be adequately documented (with a court order, if required by state law). *See, e.g., Bohan, supra.* In particular a distribution supported only by informal workpapers prepared in the ordinary course of business is insufficient to evidence "a commitment to set aside funds beyond the recall of petitioner, its creditors, and its other beneficiaries," which is the relevant test. *Estate of Keith W. Johnson,* 88 T.C. 225, 236, *aff'd,* 838 F.2d 1202 (2d Cir. 1987).

Example 12-29. *T*'s will left his residuary estate in equal shares to 4 charities and an individual, *X.* No estate tax is due from *T*'s estate, which has relatively little income, but will pay substantial expenses of administration. The expenses of administration could be paid in its final, short tax year, when most of them could be carried out to the residuary distributees. The amount of the expenses carried out to *X* will be maximized if the distributions in satisfaction of the charitable bequests are made in the estate's last full tax year. By doing so, *X* will be the only residuary beneficiary to whom distributions are made, and to whom excess deductions are carried out, in the estate's final tax year. Making the distributions to the charities earlier than the distribution to *X* may be a superficial violation of the executor's duty of impartiality. However, by so arranging the distributions the executor has also preferred *X.* If asked, *X* would no doubt consent to the plan.

§12.36.6. Distributions to Trusts

The composition and timing of distributions to trusts are also important, particularly when a distribution can be used to carry out DNI to a trust, where it will be "trapped" and not taxed to the trust beneficiaries. (The use of trapping distributions is discussed in §12.40.)

§12.36.7. In Kind Distributions

In some cases it is helpful to the beneficiaries to make in kind distributions. However, consideration must be given to the tax consequences. The planner should recall that by reason of changes made in 1984, in kind distributions can no longer be used to effect a tax-free increase in the basis of the property. §643(e). However, §643(e) allows an executor to elect to recognize gain or loss on the distribution as if the property distributed had been sold to the distributee at its fair market value. In such a case, the distributee takes a basis equal to the fair market value of the property. The election should be made with respect to the distribution of appreciated property if the estate has losses on other sales which would offset any gain resulting from the distribution. In addition, the distributee would receive an increased basis in the property.

In planning distributions it is important to bear in mind that non-pro rata in kind distributions to residuary beneficiaries can involve a taxable exchange between the distributees. *See* §12.39. However, they may involve a tax-free exchange of property under §1031. *See* LR 8404099. In kind distributions require the estate to recognize gain where appreciated property is distributed in satisfaction of a pecuniary gift. §12.38. An estate, but not a trust, may deduct a loss that is incurred as a result of satisfying a pecuniary bequest with property that has a fair market value lower than its basis.

§12.37. Distributions That Do Not Carry Out DNI, §663(a)(1)

Distributions can be made in satisfaction of most specific gifts without affecting the income taxation of the estate or of the distributees. Specifically, under §663(a)(1) a distribution in satisfaction of a gift of a specific sum of money or of specific property does not carry out the estate's DNI if it is paid or credited all at once or in not more than three installments. This exclusion is traceable to the basic rule of §102 that gross income does not include gifts, bequests, and inheritances. In order to come within the ambit of this rule, the specific sum of money or the specific property must be ascertainable under the terms of the decedent's will at the date of death. Reg. §1.663(a)-1(b)(1). Thus, gifts of $10,000 or of 100 shares of XYZ, Inc. stock both qualify as specific gifts, but a gift of one-half of the residue of the estate does not. A bequest of assets in cash or in kind equal to a specific dollar amount is a bequest of a sum of money for purposes of §663. Rev. Rul. 86-105, 1986-2 C.B. 83.

As pointed out above, pecuniary formula marital deduction gifts are not treated as specific bequests for purposes of §663 because the amount of the gifts depends upon the exercise of the executor's discretion regarding a number of matters including the valuation of estate assets and the return upon which administration expenses would be claimed. *See* Reg. §1.663(a)-1(b)(1). Any distribution made in satisfaction of such a pecuniary gift is subject to the ordinary distribution rules of §§661 and 662 (*i.e.*, it would carry out the estate's DNI to the distributee).

§12.37.1. Annuities and Similar Payments from Income

The Regulations also provide that the specific gift rule does not apply to annuities or other amounts that are payable only from the income of an estate. Reg. §1.663(a)-1(b)(2). The Regulations illustrate the application of this rule to a trust by the following example:

> *Example (3)*. Under the terms of a trust instrument, income is to be accumulated during the minority of *A*. Upon *A*'s reaching the age of 21, $10,000 is to be distributed to *B* out of income or corpus. Also, at that time, $10,000 is to be distributed to *C* out of the accumulated income and the remainder of the accumulations are to be paid to *A*. *A* is then to receive all the income until he is 25, when the trust is to terminate. Only the distribution to *B* would qualify for the exclusion under section 663(a)(1). Reg. §1.663(a)-1(b)(2), example 3.

In this example the distribution to *B* qualifies for the exclusion because it could be satisfied out of income or principal. In contrast, no exclusion is available for the distribution to *C*, which was payable solely out of accumulated income. However, if the distributions in the example were from an estate rather than a trust, no tax would be levied on the distributions of accumulated income to *A* and *C* by reason of the throwback rules of §§665 to 667, which do not apply to estates.

§12.37.2. Specifically Devised Real Property

Specifically devised real property that passes directly to the devisee under local law is not taken into account for purposes of applying the rules of §§661 and 662. Regs. §§1.661(a)-2(e), 1.663(a)-1(c)(1)(ii). In such a case the real property does not form a part of the Subchapter J estate and is not paid, credited, or required to be distributed by the estate. Accordingly, the devisee and not the estate is required to report the income, deductions, and credits attributable to the real property from the time of the decedent's death. Presumably the same rule applies to any property that passes directly from the decedent to another person under local law. *See* Rev. Rul. 68-49, 1968-1 C.B. 304.

The rules of §663(a)(1) should be borne carefully in mind at all stages. Proper drafting can give the estate plan valuable additional flexibility. Also, the income tax consequences of various types of distributions must be taken into account in the post-mortem phase when it comes to planning and making distributions from the estate.

§12.38. Distributions in Kind

The income tax consequences of in kind distributions changed significantly in 1984 with the adoption of §643(e). Formerly the distributee who received property in kind in satisfaction of a nonpecuniary bequest took a basis in the property equal to its fair market value. Such a distribution and free step-up in basis could be achieved without incurring any income tax liability. That opportunity was eliminated by §643(e). Under it, the distributee takes a basis equal to the property's adjusted basis in the estate prior to distribution, adjusted for any gain or loss recognized by the estate on the distribution. Where a distribution in kind is made, the amount of the distribution, for purposes of §§661 and 662, is generally deemed to be the lesser of the basis in the hands of the distributee or the fair market value of the property. However, §643(e) allows the estate to elect to recognize gain or loss upon such distributions "in the same manner as if such property had been sold to the distributee at its fair market value." If the election is made, the fair market value of the property is taken into account for purposes of §§661 and 662. Under §643(e)(3)(B) the election, which is made on the income tax return of the trust or estate, applies to all distributions made during the year. Finally, §643(e) does not apply to any distribution described in §663(a) (gifts or bequests of specific property or specific amounts of money). §643(e)(4).

An estate which had incurred losses for the year might distribute appreciated property in order to benefit from making an election under §643(e). In such a case the losses could be used to offset the gains that the estate would recognize as a result of the distributions. In addition, the basis of the distributee would be increased as a result of the election. Note that §267 may bar a trust from recognizing losses arising from distributions. Also, recall that under §663(a) a distribution in kind made in satisfaction of a right to receive the specific property distributed does not carry out DNI to the distributee.

Example 12-30. This year *T*'s estate has DNI of $20,000. *T*'s executor plans to distribute property worth $10,000 to a residuary beneficiary, *B*. The distribution will give *B* some needed cash and will carry out half of the estate's income to *B*. Such a distribution would effectively split the estate's income between the estate and *B*. The executor might distribute cash of $10,000 or 1,000 shares of XYZ, Inc., which have an estate tax value of $5,000 and a present value of $10,000. In the latter case the executor must decide whether to make an election under §643(e). If the election is not made, *B* will take the estate's basis in the XYZ, Inc. stock ($5,000), which is the amount that will be taken into account for purposes of §§661 and 662. On the other hand, if an election is made, the estate will realize a gain of $5,000 on the distribution; *B* will have a basis of $10,000 in the shares; and $10,000 is the amount taken into account for purposes of §§661 and 662.

As indicated in Example 12-30, the basis of the distributee is affected by whether or not the estate makes an election under §643(e). In this connection note that the distributee's basis is determined without regard to the estate's DNI. While the extent of the estate's DNI determines the amount of the estate's distribution deduction under §661 and the amount taken into the beneficiary's income under §662, it does not affect the beneficiary's basis in the property. In brief, the estate's DNI is irrelevant to the calculation of the distributee's basis under §643(e).

Example 12-31. *T*'s will made a bequest of $10,000 to a friend, *F*. *T*'s will authorized his executor to satisfy cash gifts by making distributions in kind, with distributions valued at their fair market value at the time of the distributions. The executor plans to satisfy the gift to *F* by distributing property that has an estate tax value of $5,000 and a current fair market value of $10,000. Presumably such a distribution is not subject to §643(e) by reason of the exception described in §643(e)(4). The prior rules probably continue to apply — the estate will recognize a gain of $5,000 if the appreciated property is distributed to *F* in satisfaction of the gift. Of course, under §1223(11) the gain on the sale would be long term. *F* would have a basis of $10,000 in the property.

The cancellation of an installment obligation upon the death of the payee accelerates the recognition of gain by the payee's estate. Rev. Rul. 86-72, 1986-1 C.B. 253. Similarly, the transfer of an installment obligation to the obligor is treated as a transfer that triggers the recognition of gain. §691(a).

§12.39. NON-PRO RATA DISTRIBUTIONS

A personal representative should be cautious about making non-pro rata distributions to the residuary beneficiaries unless such distributions are authorized either by the decedent's will or by the governing state law. In the absence of such authorization a non-pro rata distribution may involve a taxable exchange between the residuary beneficiaries and possibly a violation of the personal representative's fiduciary duty of impartiality. In a letter ruling the IRS has held that an equal but non-pro rata distribution to three estate beneficiaries did not result in any gain where the decedent's will authorized such a distribution. LR 8119040.

A non-pro rata distribution may be treated as a taxable exchange when it is made pursuant to an agreement among the residuary beneficiaries and not by reason of the executor's authority. The problem arises because each residuary beneficiary is generally entitled to a proportionate interest in each asset of the residuary estate. The nature of the problem is illustrated in Example 12-32.

> **Example 12-32.** *T*'s will gave his residuary estate "in equal shares to those of my children who survive me." *T* was survived by 2 children, *D* and *S*. *T*'s residuary estate consists of $10,000 and 100 shares of XYZ, Inc. stock, which was worth $5,000 on the estate tax valuation date and $10,000 on the date of distribution. Under the local law *D* and *S* are each entitled to receive $5,000 and 50 shares of XYZ, Inc. stock. If the executor distributes $10,000 to *S* and 100 shares of stock to *D* pursuant to their agreement, the distribution may be taxed as if *S* sold "his" 50 shares of stock to *D* for "her" $5,000. If so, *S* would be required to report a gain of $2,500 on the transaction ($5,000 sale proceeds, less $2,500 basis under §1014). The gain would be long-term under §1223(11). As purchaser, *D* would have a basis of $5,000 in the 50 shares she purchased from *S* and a basis of $2,500 in the other 50 shares. No loss could result from such an exchange between related taxpayers because of the provisions of §267.

In Rev. Rul. 69-486, 1969-2 C.B. 159, the IRS held that a non-pro rata in kind distribution to the two beneficiaries of a trust involved a taxable exchange between the beneficiaries where the distribution was made pursuant to their agreement and was not authorized by the trust.

> Since the trustee was not authorized to make a non-pro rata distribution of property in kind but did so as a result of the mutual agreement between *C* and *X*, the non-pro rata distribution by the trustee to *C* and *X* is equivalent to a distribution to *C* and *X* of the notes and common stock pro rata by the trustee, followed by an exchange between *C* and *X* of *C*'s pro rata share of common stock for *X*'s pro rata shares of notes. Id.

Presumably no taxable exchange would have been involved if the trust or the local law had authorized the trustee to make a non-pro rata in kind distribution.

§12.39.1. Fiduciary Duty of Impartiality

An unauthorized non-pro rata distribution may violate the fiduciary's duty of impartiality toward the beneficiaries. Without the consent of the beneficiaries, or authorization in the instrument or by the governing law, the in kind non-pro rata distribution of assets to the two beneficiaries of an estate is a questionable practice even though the assets received by each are of equal value on the date of distribution. Distributing all of asset *A* to one beneficiary and all of asset *B* to another beneficiary without their consent invites criticism by one or both beneficiaries because of inherent differences in the properties. A violation would certainly occur if the persons who were entitled to an equal share of the bequest did not receive assets of equal value on the date of distribution. The extent to which a fiduciary may be required to take the income tax bases of the assets into account in making a distribution is not settled in most states. In some the courts have refused to take the income tax bases of assets into account in the context of a marital dissolution. A careful fiduciary should take the bases of assets into account in planning sales and distributions.

§12.39.2. Community Property

Following the death of a spouse, the surviving spouse generally continues to own a one-half interest in the assets previously owned by them as community property. In general, a husband or wife may only dispose by will of his or her interest in the community property. An attempt to dispose of a greater interest in the property may involve the rules applicable to widow's election arrangements. *See* §§9.23-9.39.

Under the item theory of community property, each spouse owns and is entitled to dispose by will of an equal interest in each community property asset. *See Estate of Patton,* 494 P.2d 238 (Wash. App. 1972). Where the item theory applies, the surviving spouse and other persons who are beneficiaries under the will of the deceased spouse will hold the former community property as tenants in common. A non-pro rata distribution of the former community property to the surviving spouse and the beneficiaries under the will of the deceased spouse might be treated as a taxable exchange under Revenue Ruling 69-486, *supra.* Recognition of a loss arising from such a distribution-exchange is barred by §267. It is doubtful that such a non-pro rata division would be treated as a nonrecognition transfer "from an individual to (or in trust for the benefit of) — (1) a spouse. . . ." §1041(a). Section 1041 was adopted in order to make the tax laws less intrusive with respect to transfers between spouses or former spouses. There is no indication that it was intended to apply after the death of one or both of the spouses.

Example 12-33. *H* and *W* owned Blackacre and Whiteacre as their community property. When *H* died, he devised his one-half interest in Blackacre and Whiteacre to their daughter, *D,* and left the residue of his estate to *W. W,* of course, would continue to own a one-half interest in each parcel. After the death of *H,* Blackacre and Whiteacre would be owned by *D* and *W* as tenants in common. A taxable exchange might take place if, pursuant to an agreement between *D* and *W,* a fee interest in Blackacre were distributed to *D* and the fee interest in Whiteacre were distributed to *W* (or vice versa).

In several Private Letter Rulings the IRS has indicated that a taxable exchange does not occur if the surviving spouse and the successors of the deceased spouse receive non-pro rata distributions of assets equal in value. LR 8037124; LR 8016050. If the Letter Rulings are followed, no gain would result from the distribution described in the foregoing example. The Rulings are based largely upon Rev. Rul. 76-83, 1976-1 C.B. 213, which held that an equal division of the fair market value of community property between spouses made in the context of a separation or divorce was not a taxable event. *See also, Jean G. Carrieres,* 64 T.C. 959 (1975), *aff'd per curiam,* 552 F.2d 1350 (9th Cir. 1977), *acq. in result only,* 1976-2 C.B. 1. The extension of the holding of Revenue Ruling 76-83 to dispositions at death is desirable because of the flexibility it gives the parties, its fairness, and its simplicity of administration. The case for not taxing such a distribution is strengthened if the executor of a deceased spouse has the power to administer all of the community property and is given authority to make non-pro rata distributions of community property assets. Perhaps the best protection is provided if the spouses enter into an inter vivos agreement under which the executor of the spouse first to die has the power to make non-pro rata distributions of the entire interest in community property in satisfaction of residuary bequests. However, such an agreement might cause the estate of a deceased spouse to lose its claim to a discount in the value of the decedent's one-half community property share in closely-held stock if the agreement required the decedent's interest to be valued at one-half of the entire community property interest. That is, the agreement might overcome the favorable holdings of *Estate of Bright,* 658 F.2d 999 (5th Cir. 1981), and *Estate of Elizabeth Lee,* 69 T.C. 860 (1978), *nonacq.,* 1980-1 C.B. 2.

A non-pro rata distribution in which the surviving spouse and the successors of the deceased spouse each receive assets of equal value would not involve a taxable exchange if the aggregate theory of community property is followed. Under it, the spouses do not each have a fixed and equal interest in each community property asset. Instead, each of them is merely entitled to receive assets that have a value equal to one-half of the total value of all of the community property. For an application of this theory in the gift tax context, *see Kaufman v. United States,* 462 F.2d 439 (5th Cir. 1972), discussed at §6.47.

§12.40. Trapping Distributions

A *trapping distribution* is a distribution from an estate to a trust that carries out DNI to the trust, where the income is "trapped" and taxed to the trust. Cornfeld, Trapping Distributions, U. Miami, 14th Inst. Est. Plan., ch. 14 (1980); Income Tax Opportunities and Pitfalls in Estate Distributions, 13 Real Prop., Prob. & Tr. J. 835, 868-871 (1978). The typical case involves a distribution of property that is characterized as principal under the local law. As principal the property is not distributable by the trustee to the income beneficiaries of the trust. The income carried out in a trapping distribution is taxed to the trust permanently or temporarily depending on the provisions of the trust regarding distributions. Carefully planned trapping distributions permit an estate's income to be split among the maximum number of taxpayers: the estate, individual distributees of the estate, the trust, and the beneficiaries of the trust. The compressed income tax rates adopted in 1986 severely restrict the utility of trapping distributions. Because the rates applicable to trusts and estates escalate rapidly, there is little opportunity to trap income at a favorable rate in an estate or trust.

The ultimate tax consequences of a trapping distribution depend to a large extent on whether the distributee trust is a simple trust or a complex trust. The difference arises because the throwback rules do not apply to simple trusts (*i.e.,* ones required to distribute all of their income currently and to make no distribution of principal during the year). *See* Cohan & Frimmer, Trapping Distributions — The Trap That Pays, 112 Tr. & Est. 766 (1973). A trapping distribution is generally effective to trap the distributed income permanently in a simple trust. The distribution of the principal of a simple trust upon termination will not involve a throwback of the trapped income except to the extent it consists of income in respect of a decedent (IRD) or unrealized accounts receivable. *See* Reg. §1.665(e)-1A(b), example 1. Consequently, the executor should avoid distributing IRD to a trust where the intent is to achieve a permanent trap. In the case of a complex trust, the trapped income will be taxed to the beneficiaries when the trust makes an accumulation distribution to them. Of course, the throwback rules do not apply to income accumulated prior to the beneficiary's birth or prior to his or her becoming 21. *See* §10.4.10. Those exceptions permit the trapped income to escape taxation under the throwback rules where the trapping distribution by the estate was made prior to the beneficiary's birth or during the beneficiary's minority. Trapped income is subject to taxation under the throwback rules where an accumulation distribution is made to beneficiaries other than charities.

The technique of making trapping distributions is of some limited value in minimizing the impact of income taxes. Where it is desirable to do so, some estate income can be deflected to the trust, or trusts, each year by making appropriate distributions that would be characterized as principal under local law. Of course, income-splitting can be extended to the trust's beneficiaries where the distribution it receives from the estate includes items that are properly characterized as income of the trust that can be distributed to the beneficiaries of the trust.

When a trapping distribution is made the income tax liability imposed on the trust should be charged to the trust account to which the distribution is allocated under the local law. Thus, the income tax is appropriately paid from the principal account where the trapping distribution is characterized as principal. Conversely, it is chargeable to income where the distribution is characterized as income. In the latter case, it may be necessary to make an equitable adjustment to the principal and income accounts where the tax liability is initially paid from principal. *Estate of Holloway,* 327 N.Y.S.2d 865 (Surr. Ct. 1972), *mod'g,* 323 N.Y.S.2d 534 (Surr. Ct. 1971).

G. PAYMENT OF ESTATE AND GST TAXES

§12.41. Introduction

The next section reviews the rules that govern the allocation of the estate tax burden. Succeeding sections examine the options that are available to the executor in making payment of the federal estate tax, most of which involve deferral of payment of the estate tax. Payment of the tax or a deficiency in the estate tax may be deferred under §6161 for reasonable cause. In addition, portions of the tax may be deferred under §6163 (remainder and reversionary interests) and §6166 (closely-held business interests). Finally certain issues of United States Treasury bonds ("flower bonds") may be redeemed at par in payment of the estate tax imposed by reason of the owner's death. The last section

(§12.50) is a checklist of post-mortem matters. The rules governing the payment of the GSTT are discussed in §§2.22-2.40.

§12.42. Source of Payment of Estate Tax

The federal estate tax must be paid by a decedent's executor. §2002. Presumably the executor is also liable for payment of the additional 15 percent estate tax imposed by §4980A(d) on the amount of excess retirement accumulations. The term "executor" is defined in §2203 as the decedent's executor or administrator or, if none, any person in actual or constructive possession of the decedent's property. The executor in turn must be sure that the proper parties bear the burden of the tax. A person is generally free to designate in his or her will or trust the source of funds that should be used to pay the tax. When no source is designated, the state law determines how the tax should be paid. Many states have a form of apportionment law that allocates the burden among the beneficiaries according to the value of the property each of them receives from the decedent. *See* U.P.C. §3-916. *See also* §4.25. The common law of other states generally requires the tax to be paid from the residuary estate in the absence of contrary direction by the decedent. However, courts in a few states have required equitable apportionment of the federal estate tax.

Five Code sections deal with the question of where the federal estate tax burden will fall in the absence of contrary direction by the decedent. Those sections and the apportionment acts adopted by many states both recognize that directions by the decedent prevail over their provisions. In some instances the provisions of the federal and local law conflict; the federal law would prevail. In this connection, see the discussion in *McAleer v. Jernigan,* 804 F.2d 1231 (11th Cir. 1986). *McAleer* allowed the decedent's personal representative acting under §2206 to recover a portion of the federal estate tax from the recipient of proceeds of life insurance that were includible in the decedent's gross estate. The personal representative's right to do so prevailed over a state statute that directed all estate taxes to be paid from the residuary estate and relieved the personal representative from recovering any portion of the tax from the recipients of any other property including life insurance.

§12.42.1. Recovery of Estate Tax from Estate or Beneficiaries, §2205

Under the first section, §2205, if a person other than the executor pays any portion of the tax, that person may be entitled to reimbursement from the estate or contribution from the other beneficiaries of the estate. The provision is intended primarily to assure the tax is paid from the appropriate source, whether payment occurs prior or subsequent to distribution of the estate. The section recognizes rights to reimbursement, but it does not attempt to establish a particular rule of contribution by the beneficiaries.

§12.42.2. Recovery of Estate Tax from Insurance Beneficiaries, §2206

In the absence of a contrary direction in the decedent's will, the second section, §2206, allows the executor to collect a proportionate part of the estate tax from the beneficiary of life insurance proceeds that were included in the gross estate. If there is more than one beneficiary, the amount recoverable from each is calculated according to the following formula:

$$\frac{\text{Proceeds of Policy}}{\text{Taxable Estate}} \times \text{Total Tax} = \text{Amount Recoverable}$$

However, the section does not allow a recovery from a surviving spouse to the extent that a marital deduction is claimed and allowed with respect to the property. As indicated in *McAleer, supra,* the right to recover a portion of the tax from the payee of a life insurance policy on the decedent's life may prevail despite a contrary state statute.

§12.42.3. Recovery of Estate Tax from Property Subject to General Power, §2207

The third section, §2207, similarly allows an executor to recover a proportionate part of the estate tax from persons who receive property that was included in the decedent's estate under §2041 by reason of the exercise, nonexercise, or release of a power of appointment. Under it the executor has the right to recover from the recipients "unless the decedent directs otherwise in his will." As in the case of §2206, however, it is inapplicable to the extent the property qualifies for the marital deduction.

§12.42.4. Recovery of Tax on QTIP, §2207A

Under the fourth section, §2207A, the executor has the right to recover from the recipients of qualified terminable interest property any additional estate tax imposed because the property was included in the decedent's estate under §2044. The provision also extends to penalties and interest attributable to the additional estate tax incurred by reason of the inclusion of the property. §2207A(d). Subsection 2207A(a)(2) provides that the executor's right of recovery "shall not apply if the decedent otherwise directs by will." Thus, the surviving spouse (the "decedent" under §2207A) can assume the responsibility for payment of any additional tax. For that reason care must be exercised regarding the type of tax clause included in the surviving spouse's will. A boilerplate tax clause directing the payment of "all death taxes from the residue of my estate" may be sufficient to overcome the executor's right of recovery under §2207A.

The executor's failure to exercise the right of recovery available under §2207A constitutes a constructive addition to the trust for GSTT purposes. Temp. Reg. §26.2601-1(b)(1)(v)(C). Query whether an express direction by the surviving spouse to pay the tax imposed by §2044 would similarly result in a constructive addition to the trust for purposes of the GSTT. If so, presumably the surviving spouse would be treated as the transferor of the addition.

§12.42.5. Recovery of Tax on §2036 Property, §2207B

Finally, under §2207B if property is included in the decedent's gross estate under §2036, the decedent's estate is entitled to recover a proportionate amount of the tax from the person receiving the property. A contrary direction in the decedent's will (or revocable trust) prevails over the general rule only if it specifically refers to §2207B. §2207B(a)(2). The decedent's estate has no right of recovery against a charitable remainder trust. §2207B(e).

By relieving the charitable remainder of any obligation to contribute to payment of the estate tax, §2207B(e) avoids the problem of determining which interest should be charged with the estate tax attributable to the nondeductible current interest. A problem arises because of the conflict between two general rules. Under the first, where income and remainder interests are involved, the estate tax is entirely chargeable to the remainder interest. *See, e.g., Estate of Williamson,* 229 P.2d 312 (Wash. 1951). State apportionment acts typically exempt temporary interests from being charged with any part of the estate tax. Of course, payment of the tax from principal operates to reduce the amount of the income that is distributable.

The second general rule exempts charitable interests from any obligation to contribute to payment of the estate tax in the absence of contrary direction by the decedent. In *Estate of Anne B. Leach,* 82 T.C.

952 (1984), *aff'd per curiam,* 782 F.2d 179 (11th Cir. 1986), the Tax Court held that the estate tax on a charitable remainder annuity trust was entirely recoverable from the charitable remainder. *Leach* involved the Florida Apportionment Act, which does not specify how the tax is to be charged when an annuity interest is involved. In contrast, the New York apportionment law does not exempt a common law annuity interest from contributing toward payment of the estate tax. N.Y. Est. Powers & Trusts Law §2-1.8(b) (McKinney 1981 Supp.).

§12.42.6. Transferee Liability

Note that the foregoing sections do not restrict the *government's* right to collect the tax from any person who received property from the decedent. For example, in *Horne v. United States,* 519 F.2d 51 (5th Cir. 1975), the government recovered a portion of the unpaid estate tax by levying upon all of the insurance proceeds paid to the decedent's minor daughter although his will directed that the tax be paid from his probate estate. The court pointed out that the daughter's right to contribution from other recipients of the decedent's property was fundamentally a question of state law.

§12.43. Extension of Time to File Estate Tax or GSTT Return, §6081

Under §6081 an executor may apply for an extension of time to file an estate tax or GSTT return by filing Form 4768 (Application for Extension of Time to File U.S. Estate Tax Return and/or Pay Estate Tax). That form may also be used to request an extension of time within which to pay the estate tax or GSTT. Both requests may be made on a single form. An extension under §6081 is limited to six months unless the executor is out of the country. The Regulations provide that the application for extension "should be made before the expiration of time within which the return otherwise must be filed and failure to do so may indicate negligence and constitute sufficient cause for denial." Reg. §20.6081-1(b). Form 4768 should be filed with the internal revenue officer with whom the federal estate tax return is required to be filed. Id.

An extension of time within which to file an estate tax or GSTT return does not extend the time for payment of the tax. Accordingly, unless the executor also requests an extension of time within which to pay the tax, Form 4768 should be accompanied by payment of the estimated amount of tax due.

§12.44. Extension of Time to Pay Estate Tax, §6161

The 1976 Act substituted a "reasonable cause" standard for the "undue hardship" standard that previously applied for purposes of the discretionary ten-year extension of time to pay the estate tax. §6161(a)(2). Under that provision an extension may also be granted with respect to the payment of any installment of tax deferred under §6166. The explanation prepared by the staff of the Joint Committee of Taxation states that "for this purpose, the term 'reasonable cause' is to have the same meaning as the term is used for granting discretionary extensions of up to twelve months (regs. §20.6161-1(a))." General Explanation of the Tax Reform Act of 1976, 546 (1976). The Regulation referred to in the quotation provides that an extension may be granted if an examination of all the facts and circumstances shows that there is reasonable cause. Reg. §20.6161-1(a). The Regulation also presents several helpful examples of situations that are recognized as constituting reasonable cause for this purpose.

An extension may be applied for by submitting a request that must include a statement of the period of the extension requested and a declaration that it is made under penalties of perjury. The request should be made on Form 4768 and filed with the Internal Revenue officer with whom the estate tax return must be filed. Reg. §20.6161-1(b).

If an extension is granted the district director may require the executor to furnish bond for payment of the deferred amount of the tax. Reg. §20.6165-1(a). However, the bond may not exceed double the amount of the deferred tax. Interest is charged at the annually adjusted rate under §6621 on the amount of the unpaid tax.

§12.45. Deferral of Estate Tax on Reversions and Remainders, §6163

Where a reversionary or remainder interest in property ("the future interest") is included in the decedent's gross estate, the executor may elect to defer payment of the estate tax attributable to the future interest until six months after all of the precedent interests terminate. §6163(a). Under the Regulations the election is made by filing a notice with the district director before the date prescribed for payment of the tax. Reg. §20.6163-1(b). The notice may be in the form of a letter to the district director accompanied by a certified copy of the will or other instrument under which the future interest was created. Where the duration of the precedent interest is dependent upon the life of any person, the notice must also show the date of birth of that person. Again, interest is charged at the annually adjusted rate on the amount of tax that is deferred.

Regulations issued under §6165 require payment of the tax and accrued interest to be secured by a bond equal to double the amount of the tax and accrued interest for the estimated duration of the precedent interest. Reg. §20.6165-1(b). If the duration of the precedent interest is indefinite, the bond must be conditioned upon the principal or surety promptly notifying the district director when the precedent interest terminates and upon his or her notifying the district director in September of each year as to the continuance of the precedent interest.

When the decedent's estate includes both a future interest and other property, the amount of tax that can be deferred is determined by the following formula, described in Reg. §20.6163-1(c):

$$\frac{\text{Adjusted value of future interest}}{\text{Adjusted value of gross estate}} \times \text{Estate tax} = \begin{array}{c}\text{Tax that}\\\text{may be}\\\text{deferred}\end{array}$$

For purposes of the calculation the value of the future interest is reduced by (1) the amount of outstanding liens on the interest, (2) losses deductible under §2054 with respect to the interest, (3) amounts deductible in respect of the interest as charitable transfers under §2055, and (4) amounts deductible in respect of the interest as a marital deduction under §2056. Similar reductions are made in the value of the gross estate.

§12.46. Estate Tax Deferred Under Former §6166A

In the case of decedents dying prior to 1982, an executor could elect to pay the estate tax attributable to the decedent's interest in a closely-held business in equal annual installments over a period not to exceed ten years. Under this provision the first payment had to be made when the estate tax was regularly due (*i.e.,* nine months after death). Interest is payable each year on the unpaid balance of the tax at the quarterly adjusted rate determined under §6621 — the Federal short-term rate determined as provided in §6621(b) plus three percentage points. §6621(a)(2). (In the period between 1978 and 1990 the rate ranged between 7 and 20 percent.) Deferral was available under §6166A only where the value of the business interest included in the decedent's estate exceeded 35 percent of the decedent's gross estate or 50 percent of the decedent's taxable estate. §6166A(a).

The time for payment of the deferred portion of the estate tax is accelerated in certain instances described in §6166A(h). In particular, acceleration occurs if 50 percent or more in value of the business interest is (1) withdrawn from the business or (2) sold, exchanged, or distributed. Transactions affecting the business should of course be carefully planned in order to avoid an inadvertent acceleration.

§12.47. Deferral of Estate and GST Tax Under §6166

In the case of decedents dying after December 31, 1981, §6166 allows the estate tax attributable to a closely-held business interest to be paid in ten installments, the first of which is due five years after the federal estate tax return is due. Deferral under §6166 is allowed if the value of the closely-held business interest exceeds 35 percent of the decedent's gross estate less the amount of deductions allowable under §§2053 and 2054. (The percentage requirement was 65 percent for decedents who died between 1976 and 1982.) Again, recall that a deduction is allowable under §2053 and not §2055 for enforceable charitable pledges. *See* §11.17. For purposes of §6166, the decedent's interests in two or more businesses may be aggregated if 20 percent or more of the value of each of them is included in the decedent's estate. In essence, the 1981 Act made the more impressive benefits of §6166 available to estates that met the less onerous percentage requirement of the former §6166A. For a more detailed discussion of §6166, *see* §§11.25-11.30. Under §6166(i) the GSTT on direct skips of closely-held businesses is treated as an additional estate tax imposed under §2001.

Interest is paid each year on the unpaid amount of the tax. However, the tax on the first $1 million in value of the business interest is subject to interest at only four percent. §6601(j). The amount subject to this special rate is the lesser of (1) $153,000 ($345,800, the amount of the estate tax on $1 million, minus $192,800, the amount of the unified credit allowable under §2010(a)) or (2) the amount of the tax extended under §6166. The remainder of the tax is subject to the quarterly adjusted rate. Deferral of more than the four percent amount may not be particularly attractive when the floating rate is high.

The interest incurred on the unpaid portion of the estate tax is deductible as an expense of administration under §2053(a)(2). *See* §12.13. However, the deduction is only allowed as the interest is paid — an anticipatory deduction is not allowed. Accordingly, as additional interest is paid a Form 706 with the supplemental information should be filed as provided in Rev. Proc. 81-27, 1981-1 C.B. 548. *See* §11.28. A similar procedure should be followed in order to claim a credit under §2011 for deferred payment of state death taxes. Also, note that the entire amount of interest might be deductible if the executor borrowed the funds with which to pay the tax and the interest were paid in advance (*i.e.*, if the interest were deducted from the loan at the outset).

The 1981 Act also made the more lenient acceleration provisions of former §6166A applicable to tax that is deferred under §6166 by estates of decedents dying after December 31, 1981. *See* §6166(g). Tax deferred by the estates of persons dying prior to 1982 is subject to acceleration if one-third or more in value of the business interest is (1) withdrawn from the business or (2) sold, exchanged, or distributed.

§12.48. Payment of Estate Tax with "Flower Bonds"

A few United States Treasury bonds issued prior to March 31, 1971, are redeemable at par, plus accrued interest, in payment of the federal estate tax on their owner's death. Reg. §20.6151-1(c). The bonds all carry low interest rates as a result of which bonds formerly often sold at substantial discounts. Redeemable bonds are called "flower bonds" because they "blossom" into full value upon the owner's death. However, the bonds are redeemable only to the extent they are included in the decedent's gross estate. Also, the bonds may be redeemed at par only to the extent of the net amount of the federal estate tax after taking all allowable credits into account. Rev. Rul. 76-367, 1976-2 C.B. 259.

The redemption of bonds held in trust or in joint ownership at the time of the decedent's death is restricted by Treasury Circular No. 300, 31 C.F.R. 306.28 (1990) ("Circular 300"). Under it, bonds held in joint ownership are redeemable only to the extent that (1) the bonds became property of the decedent's estate or (2) the surviving joint owner was required to contribute toward payment of the federal estate tax on account of the bonds and other jointly owned property. Bonds held in trust are redeemable under Circular 300 "(a) if the trust actually terminated in favor of the decedent's estate, or (b) if the trustee is required to pay the decedent's Federal estate tax under the terms of the trust instrument or otherwise, or (c) to the extent the debts of the decedent's estate, including costs of administration, State inheritance and Federal estate taxes, exceed the assets of his estate without regard to the trust estate." Because of these limitations it is particularly important to exercise care in drafting trusts and in purchasing flower bonds.

§12.48.1. Bonds Purchased by an Agent for an Incompetent Principal

The government has vigorously resisted redemption of bonds purchased for an incompetent individual by another person acting under an ordinary (*i.e.*, nondurable) power of attorney. It has argued that the bonds purchased under such a power of attorney were not part of the principal's estate because the agent's authority terminated when the principal became incompetent. The validity of the actions taken by the agent is, of course, a question of state law. *Campbell v. United States,* 657 F.2d 1174 (Ct. Cl. 1981). *Campbell* and most other cases have found that actions taken by an agent for a comatose principal are voidable and not void. Hence, they have allowed redemption of the bonds. *See United States v. Manny,* 645 F.2d 163 (2d Cir. 1981). The most famous case upheld the estate's claim for damages as a result of the government's refusal to redeem $4.7 million in bonds tendered by the estate of Arthur Watson, the late chairman of IBM's board. *Estate of Watson v. United States,* 81-2 U.S.T.C. ¶13,421 (Ct. Cl. 1981). Bonds purchased by an agent acting within the scope of a durable power of attorney for a comatose principal would not be vulnerable to the government's argument. *See* §4.35.4.

Cavanagh v. United States, 87-2 U.S.T.C. ¶13,727 (Cl. Ct. 1987), likewise concluded that the failure to redeem the bonds of a comatose principal was a breach of contract. The decision adopts the theory that the government breached its contract at the time the bonds were rejected. According to the court, at the time that the bonds were tendered they were constructively redeemed at par value. When the estate later paid the amount of the estate tax in cash there was an overpayment of estate tax, after which the estate was entitled to statutory interest. In addition, the estate was entitled to recover the amount of penalties and interest imposed by the IRS for the period between the date the bonds were first tendered and the date the estate tax was paid.

A bond that is redeemable at par in payment of the estate tax is includible in the decedent's gross estate at its redemption value plus accrued interest whether or not it is submitted for redemption. *Bankers Trust Co. v. United States,* 284 F.2d 537 (2d. Cir. 1960), *cert. denied,* 366 U.S. 903 (1961); Rev. Rul. 69-489, 1969-2 C.B. 172. However, flower bonds in excess of the amount redeemable in payment of the estate tax are valued at their fair market values, not their par values. Id. Bonds are also valued at par that could have been redeemed in payment of an estate tax deficiency that was determined after the estate disposed of the bonds it held in excess of the amount of the tax as shown on the estate tax return. *Estate of Fried v. Commissioner,* 54 T.C. 805 (1970), *aff'd,* 445 F.2d 979 (2d Cir. 1971), *cert. denied,* 404 U.S. 1016 (1972); *Estate of Elfrida G. Simmie,* 69 T.C. 890 (1978), *aff'd,* 632 F.2d 93 (9th Cir. 1980). However, an unreported district court decision held that the disposal of the "excess" bonds prior to issuance of a deficiency made them unavailable for use in payment of the deficiency and, therefore, it was proper to include them in the gross estate at their market value instead of at their redemption value. *Colorado National Bank of Denver v. United States,* 71-1 U.S.T.C. ¶12,781, 27 A.F.T.R.2d 71-1827 (D. Colo. 1971).

§12.48.2. Income Tax Consequences and Community Property Issues

Under §1014, the estate's basis in a flower bond is increased to its estate tax value. Accordingly, the estate does not recognize any gain when the bond is redeemed at its par value. Only the deceased spouse's interest in a community property flower bond is redeemable. The surviving spouse's one-half interest in a community property bond is not stepped-up under §1014(b)(6) to the estate tax value of the decedent's one-half interest. Instead, the survivor's basis in a community property flower bond is the fair market value of the surviving spouse's interest in the bond on the federal estate tax valuation date. *Ann F. Neuhoff,* 75 T.C. 36 (1980); Rev. Rul. 76-68, 1976-1 C.B. 216.

§12.48.3. Community Property Planning

In order to make available to the estate of one spouse an amount of redeemable community property bonds of an appropriate amount, a husband and wife might purchase double the amount of bonds that might be redeemed on the death of one spouse (*i.e.,* double the amount of the estimated estate tax to be due). Such a double purchase may be avoided, however, if the bonds are purchased with the separate property of the spouse whose estate is expected to make use of the bonds. Separate property can be created by partitioning some community property into two equal units of separate property. (Of course, in such a case there is no step-up in the value of the surviving spouse's separate property just as the survivor's one-half interest in community property bonds would not be increased to their par value). Under another approach one spouse can give to the other spouse his or her community property interest in the bonds or in funds to be used to purchase the bonds.

Flower bonds or other property purchased on the separate credit of one spouse alone are the separate property of that spouse. For an illustration of how the credit extended by a cooperative bank can cause the bonds that were purchased for a decedent to be characterized as separate, see *Ray v. United States,* 385 F. Supp. 372 (S.D. Tex. 1974), *aff'd per curiam,* 538 F.2d 1228 (5th Cir. 1976).

§12.48.4. List of Redeemable Bonds

The following is a list of the issues of bonds that remain outstanding and are redeemable in payment of estate taxes:

Series		*Issue Date*	*Due*
4¼'s	1987-92	Aug. 15, 1962	Aug. 15, 1992
4's	1988-93	Jan. 17, 1963	Feb. 15, 1993
4⅛'s	1989-94	Apr. 18, 1963	May 15, 1994
3's	1995	Feb. 15, 1955	Feb. 15, 1995
3½'s	1998	Oct. 3, 1960	Nov. 15, 1998

§12.48.5. Procedure for Redemption

Bonds should be submitted for redemption with Form PD 1782, Application for Redemption of Treasury Bonds for Federal Estate Tax Credit, to a Federal Reserve Bank, the Office of the Treasurer, or to the Bureau of the Public Debt. *See* Rev. Proc. 69-18, 1969-2 C.B. 300. The executor may request redemption as of the date the federal estate tax is due or as of a date prior or subsequent to that date. The bonds and Form PD 1782 should be submitted a month prior to the date requested for redemption. Bonds received after the redemption date requested on Form PD 1782 will be redeemed as of the date of receipt. Inquiries regarding redemption of bonds should be addressed to:

Bureau of the Public Debt
Division of Loans and Currency
Treasury Department
Washington, D.C. 20226

§12.49. Release from Liability for Taxes

A representative of a person or estate is liable for the payment of claims of the government (including taxes). The liability is based upon 31 U.S.C. §3713, which codified the provisions of §§3466 and 3467 of the Revised Statutes. Subsection 3713(a) provides that "claim of the United States Government shall be paid first when — . . . (B) the estate of a deceased debtor, in the custody of the executor or administrator, is not enough to pay all debts of the debtor." Under subsection 3713(b) "A representative of a person or estate . . . paying any part of a debt of the person or estate before paying a claim of the Government is liable to the extent of the payment for unpaid claims of the Government."

Potential liability under §3713 is of concern to fiduciaries because federal tax liabilities are considered to be debts due the United States and the Regulations treat the distribution of property to a beneficiary as the payment of a debt. Reg. §20.2002-1. Funeral expenses, costs of administration, a family allowance, and a limited number of other items are not considered to be debts. *See, e.g., United States v. Weisburn,* 48 F. Supp. 393 (E.D. Pa. 1943), and *Malcolm D. Champlin,* 6 T.C. 280 (1946) (estate administration expenses). Accordingly, they may be paid without risk. On the other hand, expenses of the decedent's last illness are considered to be debts. The risk of personal liability naturally discourages fiduciaries from distributing estate property before the tax liabilities are settled.

The problem of the fiduciary's potential liability is relieved somewhat by §2204, which permits the executor or other fiduciary to apply for prompt determination of the estate tax liability. Also, §6905 establishes a procedure under which the executor can obtain a discharge from personal liability for the decedent's income and gift taxes.

§12.49.1. Request for Prompt Determination of Estate Tax, §2204

Section 2204 allows an executor or other fiduciary to apply for prompt determination of estate tax liability and discharge from personal liability for the tax. In the case of an executor, the IRS is generally required to notify the executor of the amount of the tax within nine months of the time the estate tax return must be filed. The executor is discharged from personal liability upon payment of the amount of which he or she is notified (other than any amount the time for payment of which is extended under §§6161, 6163 or 6166) and upon furnishing any bond that may be required for any amount, the payment of which has been extended. If not timely notified, the executor is discharged from personal liability for any deficiency thereafter found as to the executor's personal assets. Reg. §20.2204-1(a). A fiduciary other than an executor can obtain a release from personal liability for estate tax on essentially the same terms. §2204(b). An agreement that meets the requirements of §6324A (relating to the special lien for estate tax deferred under §6166) is treated as the furnishing of a bond for purposes of §2204.

By filing an application for prompt determination of estate tax, the estate tax liability of the estate must be fixed within 18 months following a decedent's death. Many executors and other fiduciaries file requests under §2204 in order to facilitate the early distribution of assets from estates and trusts. However, some planners are reluctant to file a request under §2204 because they believe that filing such a request increases the probability the decedent's estate tax return will be audited.

§12.49.2. Request for Discharge from Personal Liability for Income and Gift Taxes, §6905

An executor can also apply under §6905 for discharge from personal liability for the decedent's income and gift tax liabilities. Such a request is filed with the same office as the decedent's federal estate tax return if one was filed — otherwise where the decedent's final income tax return was required to be filed. Reg. §301.6905-1(a). If such a request is filed, the executor is released from personal liability if he or she is not notified of the amount due within nine months of the receipt of the executor's request. Otherwise, the executor is released upon payment of the amount of which he or she is notified.

§12.49.3. Request for Prompt Assessment of Income and Gift Taxes, §6501(d)

An executor may limit the assessment of any deficiency for income or gift taxes by filing a request for prompt assessment under §6501(d). The possibility of filing a request with respect to the GSTT is not clear. The text of §6501(d) appears to permit such a request to be made. Its language is inclusive enough to include the GSTT: "any tax (other than the tax imposed by chapter 11 of subtitle B relating to estate taxes) for which return is required in the case of a decedent, or by his estate during the period of administration. . . ."

The provisions of §6501(d) require that income or gift tax liabilities of a decedent must be assessed within 18 months after receipt of a request for prompt assessment. In the ordinary case, if the 18 months pass without an assessment being made, the executor cannot be held personally liable for the taxes unless he or she had personal knowledge of the liability, or had such knowledge as would put a reasonably prudent person on inquiry. Again, the filing of such a request may trigger an audit of the decedent's income or gift tax returns.

§12.50. CHECKLIST OF POST-MORTEM MATTERS

I. Income Tax
   A. Decedent's final income tax return
      1. Joint return with surviving spouse, §6013(a)(2), (3), §12.3.1
      2. Medical expenses paid within 1 year of death, §213(d)(1), §2053, §12.3.4
      3. Miscellaneous itemized deductions, §67, §12.3.6

4. Accrued interest on Series EE bonds and similar obligations, §454, §12.3.7

B. Estate's income tax return

5. Election of tax year, §441(b), §12.7
6. Estate administration expenses, §642(g) §12.13
7. Estate selling expenses, §642(g), §12.13.2
8. Distributions of estate assets and excess deductions in final year, §642(h), §§12.36-12.40
9. Distribution of installment obligation to obligor, §691(a)(5), §9.6
10. Redemption of stock under §303, §§11.15-11.24

C. Other income tax elections

11. Subchapter S status, §1362(d)(1), §12.4
12. Partnership election to increase basis in assets in which decedent had proportionate interest, §754, (if election not made in time, apply for extension under Reg. §1.9100-1), §12.5
13. Waiver of the personal representative's fees, Rev. Rul. 66-167, 1966-1 C.B. 20; §12.8
14. Rollover of lump sum payments to surviving spouse, §402(a)(7), §12.25.2

II. Estate Tax

15. Alternate valuation, §2032, §12.15
16. Special use valuation, §2032A, §12.19
17. Marital deduction, qualified terminable interest property §2056(b)(7), §12.20
18. Marital deduction, qualified domestic trust election, §2056A, §12.21
19. Estate administration expenses and expenses of selling estate assets, §642(g), items 6 and 7 above
20. Payment of tax with flower bonds (Form PD 1782), §12.48
21. Application for extension of time to file Estate Tax Return (Form 4768), §12.43
22. Application for extension of time to pay estate tax (Form 4768), §12.44
23. Deferral of estate tax on reversions and remainders, §6163, §12.45
24. Reformation of charitable interests, to qualify for deductions, §2055(e)(3), §8.25
25. Election for deferred payment of tax, §6166, §12.47
26. Election of surviving spouse that additional estate tax on excess retirement accumulations not apply, §4980A(d)(5), §12.26.3

III. Generation-Skipping Transfer Tax
27. Alternate valuation on taxable termination at death, §2624(c), §12.15.7
28. Application for extension of time to file GSTT return, §6081, §12.43
29. Application for extension of time to pay GSTT, §6081, §12.43
30. Allocation of GSTT exemption, §2631(a), §12.23
31. Reverse QTIP election, §2652(a)(3), §12.22
32. Election to defer payment of GSTT on direct skips of closely-held business, §6166(i), §12.47

IV. Other Tax Notices and Elections
33. Application for employer identification number (Form SS-4), §6109
34. Notice concerning fiduciary relationship (Form 56) also serves as notice of qualification of executor under §6036. Ann. 86-78; §12.2.3
35. Request for prompt assessment of gift, income, and GST taxes, §6501(d), §12.49.3
36. Application for discharge for personal liability of estate tax, §2204, §12.49
37. Consent to split gifts of decedent or surviving spouse, §2513, §12.24
38. Notice of termination of fiduciary relationship (Form 56 may be used for this purpose), §6903, Ann. 86-78, §12.2.3

V. Reordering Distribution of Property
39. Disclaimers, §2518, §§12.31-12.35
40. Surviving spouse's election against will, §12.30
41. Family awards and allowances, §12.29
42. Optional settlement of life insurance proceeds, §101(d), §§6.35, 12.27

VI. Extension of Time for Most Tax Elections
43. Application for extension of time. Temp. Reg. §301-9100-1T. §12.2.4

BIBLIOGRAPHY

I. General

Brackney, Post-Mortem Tax Planning for Estates, 15 Wake Forest L. Rev. 581 (1979)

Cornfeld, Fiduciary Elections, U. Miami, 18th Inst. Est. Plan., ch. 10 (1984)

Ferguson, C., Freeland, J. & Stephens, R., Federal Income Taxation of Estate and Beneficiaries (1970)

J. Kasner, Post Mortem Tax Planning (1988)

Mariani, Executors' Elections, vol. 12, No. 2 ALI-ABA Course Materials J. 59 (1987)

Moore, Post-Mortem Planning and Administration for Unlimited Marital Deduction Estates, U. Miami, 20th Inst. Est. Plan., ch. 12 (1986)

II. Disclaimers

Frimmer, A Decade Later: Final Disclaimer Regulations Issued Under Section 2518, U. Miami, 21st Inst. Est. Plan., ch. 6 (1987)

Moore, The Ever-Expanding Use of Disclaimers in Estate Planning: An Update, U. Miami, 24th Inst. Est. Plan., ch. 17 (1989)

Ramlow, Qualified Disclaimers: Planning Considerations Under the Final Regulations, 24 Idaho L. Rev. 413 (1987-88)

III. Estate Distributions

Barnett, The Taxation of Distributions in Kind — What Hath the President and Congress Designed? U. Miami, 20th Inst. Est. Plan., ch. 15 (1986)

Freeland, Maxfield & Sawyer, Estate and Trust Distribution of Property in Kind After the Tax Reform Act of 1984, 38 Tax L. Rev. 449 (1985)

IV. Estate Tax Payment

Hirschson & Bochner, §6166 and All That, U. Miami, 25th Inst. Est. Plan., ch. 16 (1991)

V. Miscellaneous

Belcher, The Closely Held Business in Estate Administration: A Lesson in Defensive Driving for the Fiduciary, U. Miami, 22nd Inst. Est. Plan., ch. 13 (1988)

Blattmachr, The Tax Effects of Equitable Adjustments: An Internal Revenue Code Odyssey, U. Miami, 18th Inst. Est. Plan., ch. 14 (1984)

Carrico & Bondurant, Equitable Adjustments: A Survey and Analysis of Precedents and Practice, 63 Tax L. 545 (1983)

Dobris, Limits on the Doctrine of Equitable Adjustment in Sophisticated Postmortem Tax Planning, 66 Iowa L. Rev. 273 (1981)

Kasner, The "Optimum" Marital Deduction — Pay Now or Pay Later?, N.Y.U., 43rd Inst. Fed. Tax., ch. 54 (1985)

Moore, Recognition and Uses of Federal Estate Tax Credits in Estate Planning and Administration, U. Miami, 21st Inst. Est. Plan., ch. 8 (1987)

Report, Current Problems in Administration and Distribution of Tangible, Collectible Property in the Estate of a Decedent, 16 Real Prop., Prob. & Tr. J. 320 (1981)

GLOSSARY

Abatement. The appropriation of assets disposed of by will to satisfy the testator's debts. In the absence of testamentary direction the usual order of abatement is: (1) intestate property, (2) residuary estate, (3) general bequests, and (4) specific bequests. *See* U.P.C. §3-902.

Active management. For special use valuation purposes under §2032A, active management means the making of management decisions of a business other than daily operating decisions. §2032A(e)(12).

Ademption. A common law doctrine under which a specific gift fails if the specifically bequeathed property is not owned by the testator at the time of his or her death. *See* U.P.C. §2-606; §4.15.1.

Advancement. An inter vivos gift made to an heir apparent as an advance on the amount the donee may be entitled to receive as an intestate share of the donor's estate. *See* U.P.C. §2-109.

Alternate valuation date. A date, six months after death, on which decedent's executor can elect to value the assets of the decedent's estate. If the election is made, assets sold or otherwise disposed of within six months of death are made on the date or dates of distribution. Under §2032(c) the election can only be made if it will result in a reduction of the value of the gross estate and the sum of the estate and GST taxes applicable to assets included in the decedent's gross estate. *See* §2032; §§2.13, 12.15.

Alternative minimum tax (AMT). A tax that is tentatively calculated at a rate of 24 percent on the amount of a taxpayer's alternative minimum taxable income (AMTI) in excess of the applicable exemption. The AMT for a taxpayer is the tentative tax less the amount of regular income tax paid for the year. §8.10.

Alternatively deductible expenses. Expenses paid by a decedent's estate that are deductible either for income or estate tax purposes. §12.13.

Anatomical gifts. Gifts of a decedent's body or body parts for transplantation or medical research. Usually made pursuant to the Uniform Anatomical Gifts Act. *See* §4.38.

Ancillary administration. The administration of a decedent's estate carried out in a jurisdiction other than the one in which the decedent was domiciled at the time of his or her death.

Annual gift tax exclusion. Under §2503(b) an annual gift tax exclusion of $10,000 is allowed with respect to transfers of present interests to each donee. *See* §2.5.

Annuity. A fixed amount payable to the annuitant for life or for a fixed period. A private annuity, defined below, is an example. *See* §9.10.

Ante-nuptial agreement. An agreement entered into between a man and a woman in contemplation of marriage. Such an agreement usually attempts to fix the character of the property acquired by them or either of them during marriage and the rights each of them will have in such property. §1.14.2.

Anti-*Byrum* rule. Congress enacted §2036(b) to overturn *Byrum v. United States,* 408 U.S. 125 (1972). Under §2036(b) a deceased transferor's estate includes stock in a controlled corporation over which the decedent retained the right to vote in any capacity. §2.17.1.

Anti-lapse statutes. Statutes under which the interest of a beneficiary who predeceases the testator is distributed to the beneficiary's lineal descendants unless otherwise directed in the will. Anti-lapse statutes typically apply only to testamentary gifts made to relatives of the testator other than the testator's spouse. *See* U.P.C. §2-603; §4.15.

Applicable family member. Defined in §2701(e)(2) as the transferor's spouse, an ancestor of the transferor or the transferor's spouse, or the spouse of any such ancestor. *See* Family members.

Applicable federal rate. Under §1274(d) the applicable federal rate for debt instruments of various terms is fixed by the average market yield for marketable obligations with various terms of the United States. Annuities, term interests, remainders, and reversions are valued by applying a rate equal to 120 percent of the federal mid-term rate (*i.e.,* for U.S. obligations with terms of between three and nine years). §7520(a).

Applicable fraction. For GSTT purposes, a fraction used in determining the inclusion ratio. The numerator of the fraction is the amount of the transferor's GSTT exemption allocated to the trust or other disposition; the denominator is the value of the property transferred less the death taxes recovered from such property and any charitable deduction allowed with respect to it. §2642(a); §2.24.

Applicable rate. For GSTT purposes, the product of multiplying the maximum federal estate tax rate by the inclusion ratio. §2641(a).

Applicable restriction. A restriction, described in §2704(b)(2), on the right of a partnership or corporation to liquidate that either lapses after a transfer or may be removed by the transferor and members of his or her family. Applicable restrictions are disregarded under certain circumstances in determining the value of a transferred interest in a corporation or partnership controlled by the transferor and members of his or her family.

Applicable retained interest. Either (1) an interest in a partnership or corporation with respect to which there is a liquidation, put, call, or conversion right or (2) an interest with respect to which there is a distribution right in a corporation or partnership controlled by the transferor and applicable family members. §2701(b).

Ascertainable standard. A limitation applicable to the exercise of a power to invade, consume, or use property or the income from property. For purposes of §2041 "a power is limited by such a standard if the extent of the holder's duty to exercise and not to exercise the power is reasonably measurable. . . ." Reg. §20.2041-1(c)(2). Property subject to a power to consume that is limited by an ascertainable standard relating to the decedent's health, education, support, or maintenance is not includible in his or her estate under §2041.

Attorney-in-fact. A person designated in a power of attorney to act as agent for the principal. *See* §4.35.

Attribution rules. Rules under §318 and similar provisions by which the ownership of stock is attributed from one person or entity to another person or entity. Attribution is required to determine, *inter alia,* whether a decedent had control of a corporation for purposes of §2036(b).

Bargain sale. The sale of property for less than its fair market value. In the case of a bargain sale to charity, for purposes of determining gain the adjusted basis of the property is reduced as provided in §1011(b). §8.36.

Basis. For income tax purposes the basis of property is generally its cost. §1012. The donor's basis in property generally carries over the donee under §1015. The basis of property acquired from a decedent is fixed by its federal estate tax value in the decedent's estate. §1014. As provided in §1016, the basis of property is adjusted for post-acquisition expenditures, receipts, depreciation, losses, and other items.

Below-market loan. A loan made at a below-market interest rate on which interest may be imputed, resulting in income and gift tax liability under §7872. *See* §7.18.

Buy-sell agreement. An agreement under which interests in a partnership or corporation will be purchased by the other owners or by the entity when an owner dies or another triggering event occurs. The agreement may be a cross-purchase agreement (*i.e.*, one that calls for the other owners to purchase the interest of a deceased party) or an entity-purchase agreement (*i.e.*, one that calls for the corporation or partnership to purchase the decedent's interest). §§11.6-11.14.

Bypass trust. A trust that will not be includible in the estate of the decedent's surviving spouse (or of the other initial beneficiary). The amount placed in the trust is often fixed by formula at the amount of the decedent's credit equivalent. *See* also Credit shelter trust and Unified credit.

Byrum v. United States. *See* Anti-*Byrum* rule.

C Corporation. A C corporation is a corporation that, for federal income tax purposes, is not an S corporation. §1361(a)(2); §11.3.

Capital gains (losses). The difference between the amount realized upon the sale or exchange of an asset and its adjusted basis. Gains and losses are short term if the asset was held for less than one year prior to sale and long term if it was held for one year or more. §1222.

Carryover basis. For purposes of determining gain or loss, the donor's basis in property generally carries over to the donee, adjusted as provided in §1015.

Charitable contribution carryover. Charitable contributions that exceed the maximum amount deductible in the current tax year may generally be carried over for the next five years. §8.5.

Charitable lead trust. A split-interest trust in which a charity holds the right to receive current distributions of a guaranteed annuity or unitrust amount.

A guaranteed annuity is a determinable amount, payable at least annually for a fixed term or for the life or lives of designated persons who are living at the time of the transfer. Reg. §1.170A-6(c)(2)(i)(A). A unitrust is a fixed percentage of the fair market value of the property determined annually. §8.31.

Charitable remainder annuity trust (CRAT). A split-interest trust that provides for the annual distribution to a noncharitable beneficiary or beneficiaries of a fixed amount, not less than five percent of the initial value of the trust property. The remainder must be held by a qualified charity. §664. *See* §8.21.

Charitable remainder trust. A split-interest trust in which a current interest meeting the requirements of §664 is held by a noncharity and the remainder is held by a charity. Income, gift, and estate tax deductions are allowed for interests in charitable remainder trusts that are either a charitable remainder annuity trust or a charitable remainder unitrust as defined in §664. §8.20.

Charitable remainder unitrust (CRUT). A split-interest trust that must provide for the payout each year to a noncharitable beneficiary of a fixed percentage (at least five percent) of the annually determined net fair market value of its assets. The remainder must pass to a qualified charity. §664; §8.22.

***Clifford* trust.** A short-term irrevocable trust of which the grantor was treated as owner under *Helvering v. Clifford,* 309 U.S. 331 (1940). Sections 671-677, adopted in 1954, now govern the income tax treatment of grantor trusts. §10.4.1. *See* Short-term trust.

Closely-held corporation. A corporation, the stock of which is held by a small number of shareholders — often members of a single family. The shares of a closely-held corporation are not publicly traded, as a result of which they may be valued by applying a discount for lack of marketability.

Code. The Internal Revenue Code of 1986.

Common trust fund. A trust fund maintained by a financial institution exclusively for the collective investment of funds held by it in a fiduciary capacity (*i.e.*, as personal representative, trustee, custodian under Uniform Gift (Transfer) to Minors Act). An institution typically maintains several funds, each with a different investment objective. §584.

Community property. A marital property regime followed by eight western and southwestern states and Wisconsin under which a husband and wife own equal interests in property onerously acquired during marriage. §3.23.

Community property agreement. An agreement between husband and wife regarding the disposition of community property upon the death of either or both of them. Such agreements are recognized as valid in some community property states. §3.30.

Community property joint tenancy. In several community property states the property held in a joint tenancy by a husband and wife is presumed to be their community property. §§3.12.5, 3.20.6.

Complex trust. For income tax purposes, a trust that either is not required to distribute all of its income currently, provides for the payment of charitable gifts or distributes amounts other than income. *See* §661 and §10.4.5.

Controlled corporation. A corporation in which an individual or entity is treated as having control over the requisite interest in the stock after applying one or another form of the attribution rules. §318. For purposes of §2036(b) a corporation is controlled if the decedent had the right to vote 20 percent or more of its stock while §2703 defines control as 50 percent or more.

Credit equivalent. The taxable amount ($600,000) that can be transferred by a donor or decedent without the payment of any federal gift or estate tax by reason of the unified credit. §2010; §2.3.

Credit shelter trust. A trust funded with a portion of the decedent's estate equal to the credit equivalent. The trust is usually drafted to avoid any portion being included in the estate of the decedent's surviving spouse. §2.45.

Cross-owned life insurance. A husband and wife may each own policies of insurance on the life of the other. Such cross-ownership of life insurance can result in substantial estate tax savings if the husband and wife die simultaneously. §6.21.1.

Cross-purchase agreement. A buy-sell agreement which obligates the other shareholders or partners to buy the interest of a deceased or withdrawing owner. The agreement may fix the value of the interest of the deceased or withdrawing owner. §2703; §11.8.

***Crummey* power (*Crummey* trust).** A beneficiary's noncumulative power to withdraw property transferred to a discretionary trust that enables the donor to claim the annual gift tax exclusion with respect to the transfer. Such a power is named after *Crummey v. Commissioner,* 397 F.2d 82 (9th Cir. 1972), which allowed an annual gift tax exclusion for assets transferred to a discretionary trust for a minor. §7.37.

***Cruzan* case.** *Cruzan v. Director, Missouri Department of Health,* 110 S. Ct. 2841 (1990). The decision that recognizes the constitutionally protected liberty interest of an individual to refuse medical treatment, presumably including artificial nutrition and hydration. However, the decision upheld a state law requirement that a patient's desire to refuse treatment be established by clear and convincing evidence. §4.35.3.

Custodian. Under the Uniform Gift (Transfer) to Minors Act, the custodian is the person in whose name property may be registered in order to make an irrevocable gift to a minor. The custodian is a fiduciary having broad powers to manage and distribute the property for the benefit of the minor. §7.34.

Date of distribution value. Assets that are distributed in kind in satisfaction of a pecuniary gift are ordinarily valued on the date or dates they are distributed. This method of valuation, also called "true worth," may be used in satisfying a pecuniary marital deduction gift. §5.37.2.

Death benefit only (DBO) plan. An arrangement under which an employer makes a payment upon the death of an employee to designated members of the employee's family. Benefits paid under a DBO plan are generally not includible in the employee's gross estate. §6.78.

Decedent's final return. A decedent's income tax return for the income tax year in which he or she died. The return may be filed jointly with the decedent's surviving spouse. §12.3.

Defective trust. A trust that is deliberately drafted in a way that causes the grantor to be treated as owner of the trust for income tax purposes but without causing the property to be included in his or her estate. §10.32.

Direct skip. For GSTT purposes a direct skip is a transfer to a skip person (including a trust all of the interests of which are held by skip persons). §§2612(c), 2613(a).

Directive to physicians. *See* Living will.

Disclaimer (or renunciation). *See* Qualified disclaimer. A refusal by a donee to accept a gift, bequest, or other attempted transfer. Disclaimers must be contrasted with assignments and releases, which are premised on acceptance by the donee: Once accepted, the property received may be assigned or a power released. §12.31.

Discretionary trust. A trust which gives the trustee discretion to make distributions of income (or principal) to one or more beneficiaries. The annual gift tax exclusion is not allowed for transfers to such a trust unless the beneficiary holds a *Crummey* power of withdrawal. *See* §7.37.

Distributable net income (DNI). For income tax purposes DNI limits the amount deductible by estates and trusts for amounts paid, credited, or distributed to beneficiaries. §643(a). It also fixes the character of the distributions to the beneficiaries and limits the amount reportable by the beneficiaries as income. *See* §643(a); §10.4.3.

Distribution deduction. The amount, limited to the distributable net income of a trust or estate, that it is allowed to deduct with respect to amounts required to be distributed currently to beneficiaries and other amounts properly paid, credited, or required to be distributed to beneficiaries. The beneficiaries are required to include the same amount in their income. §§651, 652, 661, 662.

Diversification. A principle, often considered to be a part of the prudent person rule, that investments of a trust should be diversified. *See* §10.45.1.

Durable power of attorney. A power of attorney that remains effective although the principal becomes incompetent. *See* §4.35.

Durable power of attorney for health care (DPAHC). A durable power of attorney that authorizes the agent to make health care decisions for the principal if he or she is incompetent. §4.35.

Equalization clause. A marital deduction formula clause under which the surviving spouse is given a portion of the decedent's estate sufficient to equalize the sizes of their estates for federal estate tax purposes. Such a clause normally directs that the surviving spouse be presumed to have died immediately after the decedent and that the estate of the surviving spouse be valued as of the same date and in the same manner as the decedent's estate. §5.7.1.

Equitable adjustment. An adjustment between the principal and income accounts of an estate or trust that is equitably required by reason of an election made by a fiduciary. The adjustment originated in order to compensate the principal account for the loss suffered when administration expenses paid by principal were claimed as income tax deductions rather than estate tax deductions. §12.14.

Estate freeze techniques. Devices, such as installment sales, by which assets which might increase in value are converted into ones with fixed values. §2.44.

Estate tax value. The value of an asset for estate tax purposes. The fair market value of an asset on the date of its owner's death or on the alternate valuation date if it is elected by the owner's executor.

Estate trust. A type of marital deduction trust under which all of the income and principal will pass to the estate of the surviving spouse upon her death. §2056(b)(1); §5.21.

Excess accumulation tax. An additional estate tax is imposed at a 15 percent rate on the amount by which the value of the decedent's interest in qualified retirement plans exceeds the present value of a single life annuity with annual payments equal to the greater of $150,000 or $112,500 adjusted as provided in §4980A(c). §12.26.

Excess distribution tax. An additional tax of 15 percent is imposed on the amount of retirement distributions during any year that exceed the greater of $150,000 or $112,500 adjusted as provided in §4980A(c). §12.26.

Exculpatory clause. A provision, often narrowly construed by the courts, that exonerates a fiduciary from liability. §§4.26.6, 10.46.

Exemption equivalent. *See* Credit equivalent.

Exoneration. The right of the devisee of real property to have an encumbrance discharged by the estate. §4.20.1.

Family members. For gift and estate tax purposes family members are persons who are related in certain ways by blood or marriage to a donor or decedent. *E.g.*, §§2032(e)(2), 2704(c)(2).

Five or five power. A power to withdraw the greater of $5,000 or five percent of the total value of property subject to withdrawal. The lapse or release of such a power is not a gift and does not require inclusion in the powerholder's estate of the property with respect to which the power has lapsed. Giving a trust beneficiary such a power increases the flexibility of the trust. §§2041(b)(2), 2514(e); §10.24.

Flower bonds. Certain issues of U.S. Treasury bonds issued before 1971 that are redeemable at par in payment of the federal estate tax. §§10.6.9, 12.48.

Formula clauses. Clauses of a will or trust that express the extent of a beneficiary's interest by reference to a formula. The interest passing to a surviving spouse or to a marital deduction trust for the benefit of a surviving spouse is commonly determined by reference to a pecuniary formula clause or a fractional share formula clause. §§5.32-5.40. Elections, such as a QTIP election, may also be made by reference to a formula. §12.20.2.

Fractional interest discount. A discount in the valuation of real property for federal transfer tax purposes that is allowed because two or more persons hold interests in the same asset. §2.43.1.

Fractional share formula. A fractional share formula clause is used in marital deduction planning to fix the percentage in a pool of assets, typically the testator's residuary estate, that must pass to the surviving spouse in order to reduce to zero the amount of federal estate tax payable by the decedent's estate. §§5.32-5.40.

Free step-up (or down) in basis. *See* Stepped-up basis.

GST. A generation-skipping transfer, such as an outright gift or bequest to a grandchild or other skip person or a taxable distribution or taxable termination.

GSTT. The generation-skipping transfer tax, which is imposed by Chapter 13, §§2601-2663. §§2.22-2.35.

GSTT exemption. For purposes of determining the inclusion ratio, each transferor is allowed an exemption of $1 million that may be allocated to any property with respect to which the individual is the transferor. §2631; §2.25.

General power of appointment. A power that may be exercised in favor of the "decedent, his estate, his creditors, or the creditors of his estate." §§2041(b)(1), 2514(c).

***General Utilities* doctrine.** A doctrine traceable to *General Utilities & Operating Co. v. Helvering,* 296 U.S. 200 (1935), under which a corporation did not recognize gain or loss on a distribution of assets to shareholders in partial or total liquidation. The 1986 Act repealed the doctrine, as a result of which gain or loss is generally recognized by a corporation when it makes a liquidating distribution or sale of assets. *See* §311(b).

Generation assignment. For GSTT purposes, the generational assignment of a person is determined by his or her relationship to the transferor or by his or her age relative to the age of the transferor. §2651.

Gift splitting. Under §2513 a husband and wife who are both U.S. citizens may elect to report gifts made by them during the calendar year as made one-half by each. §2.7.

Grantor retained annuity trust (GRAT). A trust in which the grantor retains the right to receive a fixed amount payable not less frequently than annually. §2702(b)(1); §9.43.2. The value of the grantor's retained interest in GRAT is taken into account for gift tax purposes.

Grantor retained income trust (GRIT). A trust in which the grantor retains an income interest for life or for a term of years. For gift tax purposes the value of the grantor's retained interest is determined according to §2702 if the remaindermen are members of the grantor's family. §2702; §9.43.2.

Grantor retained interest trust (GRIT). A generic term for trusts in which the grantor has retained an interest. §9.43.2.

Grantor retained unitrust (GRUT). A trust in which the grantor retains the right to receive amounts that are payable not less frequently than annually and are a fixed percentage of the fair market value of the property in the trust (determined annually). §2702(b) (2); §9.43.3. The value of grantor's retained interest in a GRUT is taken into account for gift tax purposes.

Grantor trust. A grantor trust is one of which the grantor is treated as owner for income tax purposes. §§671-677; §10.4.1. *See* Short-term trust.

Group life insurance. Life insurance that is made available to members of a particular group, such as the members of a particular voluntary association.

Group-term life insurance. Group-term life insurance that is made available to employees by their employer under a non-discriminatory plan that meets the requirements of §79. Employers are not taxed on the first $50,000 of group-term life insurance. §6.72.

Hanging power. A cumulative power of withdrawal that lapses each year at the maximum rate allowed without potentially adverse gift and estate tax consequences to the power-holder (*i.e.*, the power lapses with respect to the greater of $5,000 or five percent of the value of the property subject to withdrawal). §7.37.4.

Heirs. The persons who are the intestate successors of a decedent. §4.14.

Imputed interest. Interest that is imputed to the seller in an installment sale if the installment obligation does not carry the interest rate required by §§483 or 1274. §9.6.5.

Incidents of ownership. Interests in, or controls over, the economic benefits of life insurance that will cause it to be included in the insured's gross estate. §2042(2); §§6.27-6.28.

Inclusion ratio. For GSTT purposes, the excess of 1 over the applicable fraction. §2642(a); §2.24.

Income in respect of a decedent (IRD). Income a decedent was entitled to receive at the time of his or her death. IRD is taxed to the decedent's estate or to the other persons receiving payment; they are entitled to deduct the portion of the federal and state death taxes paid by the decedent's estate with respect to the IRD. §691.

Individual Retirement Account (IRA). A tax-exempt trust created in the United States exclusively for an individual or his or her beneficiaries. §408.

Installment gift. The sale of property followed by the staged forgiveness of the purchaser's obligation. The amount forgiven each year is often equal to the amount of the annual gift tax exclusion. §7.24.

Installment sale method. The gain on a sale of property in which the purchase price is received in more than one taxable year of the seller is reported ratably as payments are received. A seller may elect to report all of the gain in the year of sale. The installment sale is a classic form of estate freeze (*i.e.*, the seller's estate will include only the proceeds of the sale — not any further appreciation in value of the property). §453; §§9.3-9.9.

Inter vivos trust. *See* Irrevocable trust. A trust created during the grantor's lifetime; frequently a revocable inter vivos trust used as a will substitute. An irrevocable trust is largely neutral for income, gift, estate, and GST tax purposes. §§10.7-10.17.

Insurable interest. An insurance contract is valid only if the owner has an economic interest in the life of the insured. Close family members are presumed to have the requisite interest. §6.2.

Irrevocable trust. A type of inter vivos trust that cannot be revoked or terminated by the grantor. Irrevocable trusts are frequently created for the benefit of persons other than the grantor in order to remove the property from the grantor's gross estate. §§10.18-10.29. Insurance on the grantor's life is often transferred to, or acquired by an irrevocable trust. §6.23.

Joint account. A multiparty account in a financial institution that may be with or without right of survivorship. *See* U.P.C. §6-201; §3.12.1.

Joint or survivorship life. A policy of insurance insuring the life of the later to die of two persons, usually a husband and wife. Joint life policies can have favorable premiums. They are often acquired by irrevocable life insurance trusts. §6.75.

Joint purchase. A technique by which a senior family member and a junior family member join in the purchase of an asset. The senior receives a life estate for which he or she pays the portion of the purchase price equal to the actuarially determined value of the life estate. The younger family member contributes the balance of the cost. Joint purchases are subject to the valuation rules of §2702. §9.42.

Joint return. An income tax return filed by a husband and wife on which all of their income is reported. A joint return may be filed by the surviving spouse and the personal representative of a deceased spouse. §12.3.1.

Joint tenancy with right of survivorship. A form of coownership under which two or more individuals own undivided interests in real or personal property. Upon the death of a tenant the surviving tenant or tenants become the exclusive owners of the property. §§3.11-3.12.

Junior equity interest. Under §2701(a)(4)(B) a junior equity interest is an interest in a corporation or partnership whose rights to income and capital are junior to all other classes of equity.

Kiddie tax. A provision added by the 1986 Act under which unearned income in excess of $1,000 of a child under 14 years of age is taxed at the highest marginal rate applicable to his or her parent. §2.42.

Lapse. The termination of a power of withdrawal such as a *Crummey* power for failure to exercise the power within the time allowed. Also, the failure of a testamentary gift due to the death of the beneficiary before the death of the testator. §4.15. The lapse of a voting or liquidation right held by an individual in a corporation or partnership controlled by the transferor and members of his family is treated as a transfer of an amount equal to the difference in value of the transferor's interest before and after the lapse. §2704(a).

Life income-general power of appointment trust. A type of marital deduction trust that meets the requirements of §2056(b)(5). §5.22.

Living will. A document in which an individual expresses his or her wishes regarding the use or nonuse of medical treatments that prolongs vital bodily functions if he or she is terminally ill and incompetent. Living wills are statutorily authorized in some states; in some legislation they are called "directives to physicians." §4.36. *See* Durable power of attorney for health care.

Lock-in effect. The impetus to retain appreciated property that is created by the combined effect of the capital gains tax and the free step-up in basis that occurs at death.

Lump sum distribution. A distribution of a participant's interest in a qualified plan in a single payment. Lump sum distributions qualify for some special income tax benefits, including a tax-free rollover by a surviving spouse into an IRA under §402(a)(7). §§12.25.2-12.25.3.

Marital deduction. A gift tax deduction is allowed for outright transfers and interests in certain types of trusts given to a spouse who is a U.S. citizen. *See* §2523 and §5.11. A similar deduction is allowed for estate tax purposes. §2056; §5.10. The estate tax marital deduction is allowable for transfers to a surviving spouse who is not U.S. citizen if the transfers are made to a QDT. §2056A; §5.25.

Marital property. The Wisconsin equivalent of community property. §3.23. *See* Community property.

Marketable retained interest. A right with respect to an applicable retained interest for which market quotations are available on an established exchange. §2701(a)(2).

Minority discount. A discount typically allowed in the valuation of minority interests in closely-held corporations. §2.13.

Miscellaneous itemized deductions. Under §67 an individual may only deduct miscellaneous itemized deductions to the extent they exceed two percent of his or her adjusted gross income. §10.4.6.

National service life insurance (NSLI). *See* Veteran's life insurance.

Net gift. A gift with respect to which the donee assumes the obligation of paying the portion of the donor's gift tax attributable to the gift. The amount of the gift is reduced to the extent of that obligation. The obligation is also considered to be an amount realized by the donor for capital gains purposes. §7.25.

No-interest loan. *See* below-market loan.

Nonpublic charities. Charitable organizations other than public charities, contributions to which qualify for smaller maximum income tax deductions. §8.4.

Nonskip person. A person who is not a skip person. *See* Skip person. §2613(b); §2.23.1.

Nontaxable gifts. For GSTT purposes, a transfer that is not treated as a taxable gift by reason of the annual gift tax exclusion or the exclusion for qualified transfers under §2503(e). §2642(c)(3).

Nontestamentary transfers. Transfers effective at death that are not required to comply with the requirements of the Statute of Wills. See U.P.C. §6-101.

One-lung trust. A single trust in which there are separate shares, one of which is usually intended to qualify for the marital deduction.

Option. A right to acquire specified property upon terms fixed in the option. Under §2703 an option or similar right to acquire property for less than its fair market value may be disregarded.

Orphan grandchild exclusion. In determining whether a transfer is a direct skip for GSTT purposes, a grandchild of the transferor (or of the transferor's spouse) is treated as a child of the transferor if the grandchild's parent who is a child of the transferor (or of the transferor's spouse) is deceased at the time of the transfer. §2612(c); §2.40.7.

Part gift-part sale. *See* Bargain sale. A transfer of property in exchange for less than full consideration. §7.27.

Partnership election. An election by a partnership that the basis of partnership property will be adjusted upon the transfer of an interest in the partnership by sale or exchange, upon the death of a partner, or upon the distribution of the partnership property. §754; §12.5.

Partnership freeze. A type of estate freeze involving the creation of a partnership, equity interests in which are typically transferred to younger generation members of the donor's family. The valuation rules of §2701 severely restrict the opportunities to utilize partnership freezes. §11.38.42.

Passive activity losses (PAL). The amount by which the aggregate passive activity losses for the year exceed the aggregate income from passive activities. As defined in §469(b), a passive activity is any activity involving the conduct of a trade or business in which the taxpayer does not materially participate. No deductions are allowed for PALs incurred by individuals, trusts and estates, personal service corporations, and closely-held C corporations. §469; §10.4.7.

Personal interest. Interest for which no deduction is allowed to taxpayers other than corporations by reason of §163(h); specifically, interest other than investment interest, interest with respect to a trade or business, interest taken into account for purposes of §469, and qualified personal residence interest.

Personal residence trust. Under §2702(a)(3), for gift tax purposes a trust "all of the property of which consists of a residence to be used as a personal residence by persons holding term interests in such trust." §9.41.3. *See* Qualified personal residence trust.

Pick-up tax. A state death tax imposed in an amount equal to the state death tax credit allowable under §2011. §2.15.

Pooled income fund. A type of split-interest trust maintained by a charity, in which property contributed by individual donors is commingled. Donors are entitled to retain a proportionate part of the income for the life of one or more beneficiaries and the remainder is held by the charity. A pooled income fund is similar to a common trust fund in which the property transferred by donors is commingled. §642(c)(5); §8.30.

Power of appointment. A power that allows the power-holder to designate, in the manner and within the limits prescribed, who is to receive the property subject to the power. *See* General power of appointment and Special power of appointment.

Preferred stock recapitalization (freeze). A type of estate tax freeze involving the recapitalization of a closely-held corporation which results in the corporation having both common and preferred stock. Under the plan a senior generation family member exchanges his or her common stock for preferred stock of roughly equivalent value and new common stock having presumably little, if any, value. The common stock, which represents the entire equity interest in the company, is given to younger generation family members. The valuation rules of §2701 severely restrict the use of this type of estate freeze. §11.31.

Pretermitted child. A child who is not mentioned or provided for in the will of a parent. Such a child may be entitled to receive an intestate share of the deceased parent's estate. In some states the right is limited to children born after the execution of the parent's will. §4.14.

Private annuity. A transaction, usually between family members, in which property is transferred from one person to another in exchange for the other's promise to pay a fixed amount each year for a term of years or for the life of the annuitant. The tax and nontax consequences of private annuities are complex and not entirely favorable. §§9.10-9.16.

Private letter ruling (PLR). A ruling is a written statement issued by the IRS at the request of a taxpayer that interprets and applies the tax laws to a specific set of facts. Reg. §301.6110-2(d). A PLR is not authority and may not be cited. §6110(j)(3). The first Revenue Procedure issued by the IRS each year relates to the issuance of rulings and defines the areas in which rulings will and will not be issued.

Protective elections. Tax elections that are contingent upon one or more factors, such as the size of a decedent's estate. For example, an executor may make a contingent election to defer the payment of a portion of the estate tax under §6166 if the estate meets the necessary requirements.

Prudent person rule. The standard by which the investments of trustees have traditionally been measured. Under it, each investment made by a trustee must satisfy the standard or the trustee may be liable for any loss incurred by the trust. §10.45.

Public charities. Charitable organizations described in §170(b)(a)(A). Contributions to them qualify for the maximum allowable income tax deductions. §8.3.

Qualified disclaimer. A disclaimer that meets the requirements of §2518. The person making a qualified disclaimer is not treated as having transferred the property with respect to which it was made. §2518; §12.32.

Qualified domestic trust (QDT or QDOT). Property transferred to a QDT for the benefit of a surviving spouse who is not a U.S. citizen qualifies for the marital deduction. §2056A; §5.25.

Qualified heir. For purposes of special use valuation under §2032A, a qualified heir is a member of the decedent's family who acquired the property from the decedent. §2032A(e)(a); §12.19.

Qualified interest. Under §2702(b), for gift tax purposes, a qualified interest is a right to receive a fixed amount payable annually (a qualified annuity interest) or the right to receive a fixed percentage of the fair market value of the property determined annually (a qualified unitrust interest), or a noncontingent remainder. §9.43.2.

Qualified joint interest. A tenancy by the entirety or a joint tenancy with right of survivorship in which a husband and wife are the only joint tenants. §2040(b); §3.16.

Qualified payments. Amounts payable on a periodic basis at a fixed rate, such as ones payable with respect to cumulative preferred stock or an equivalent interest in a partnership. §2701(a)(2).

Qualified personal residence trust. A trust of a personal residence that meets the requirements of Prop. Reg. §25.2702-5(e). The actuarially determined value of a retained interest in a qualified personal residence trust is taken into account for gift tax purposes. §§2702(a)(3); §9.43.3.

Qualified plan. Employer-created trust formed as a part of a stock bonus, pension, or profitsharing plan for the exclusive benefit of employees that meets the minimum participation, nondiscrimination, and other requirements. §§401-409. Excess accumulations or distributions from qualified plans are subject to a special additional tax under §4980A. §12.26.

Qualified real property. For purposes of special use valuation under §2032A qualified real property is real property located in the United States that passed from the decedent to a qualified heir and was being used for a qualified use. In addition, the percentage requirements of §2032(b)(1) must be satisfied. §12.19.

Qualified Subchapter S Trust (QSST). A type of trust, defined in §1361(d), that may be a shareholder in an S Corporation. §11.4.

Qualified terminable interest property (QTIP). Property in which the surviving spouse has a qualifying income interest for life (*i.e.*, he or she is entitled to all of the income for life, payable annually or more frequently and with respect to which no person has a power to appoint any part of the property to any other person during the surviving spouse's lifetime). The marital deduction is allowed with respect to QTIP to the extent the decedent's executor elects to claim the marital deduction. §2056(b)(7); §5.23.

Qualified transfer. For gift tax purposes amounts paid directly as tuition to an educational institution or directly to any person providing medical care to the donee. §2503(e); §2.6.

Qualified use. For special use valuation under §2032A, qualified use is the use of property as a farm or for farming purposes or use in a trade or business other than farming. §2032A(b)(2), §12.19.

Qualifying income interest for life. See qualified terminable interest property.

Quasi-community property. Property acquired during the marriage of a husband and wife while domiciled in another state that would have been community property had they been domiciled in California, Idaho, or Washington. §3.38.

Reciprocal trust doctrine. Where two or more trusts are created by related parties and the nominal grantor of one trust is the beneficiary of another, for federal transfer tax purposes the trusts are "uncrossed." As a result, each person is treated as grantor of the trust of which he or she is the beneficiary. §6.29.

Renunciation. *See* Disclaimer.

Retained interests. *See* Applicable retained interests. Interests retained by a transferor. Under §2702, for gift tax purposes, term interests retained by the grantor of a trust are valued at zero unless they are qualified interests.

Revenue Procedure 64-19. An important pronouncement of the IRS with regard to the circumstances under which the marital deduction is allowable with respect to formulas that provide for property distributed in kind to be valued at its federal estate tax value. *See* §5.37.3.

Revenue Ruling. A statement published by the IRS with respect to the treatment that will be given to a particular transaction for federal tax purposes. Rulings are published weekly in the Internal Revenue Bulletin and semiannually in collected form in the Cumulative Bulletin.

Reverse QTIP election. For GSTT purposes an election that the deceased spouse be treated as the transferor of a QTIP trust. §2652(a)(3); §2.26. If such an election is not made, the surviving spouse will be treated as the transferor of the QTIP.

Reverse split-dollar insurance plan. A split-dollar insurance plan in which the employee is the financing party and the employer controls the disposition of the risk portion of the insurance. §6.71.1.

S Corporation. A small business corporation of 35 or fewer shareholders with a single class of stock that elects not to be subject to the income tax. The income of an S corporation flows through and is taxed to its shareholders whether or not distributed. §§1361-1379; §11.4.

Sale of remainder. The sale, by the owner of property, of a remainder interest in the property for its actuarially determined value for the purpose of excluding the property from his or her estate at death. The sale of a remainder interest to a family member is subject to §2702. §9.41.

Savings clause. A direction in a will or trust that it be construed in accordance with the maker's intention that it meet the requirements of a specified provision of the tax laws. For example, it is common for such a provision to be included with regard to a marital deduction trust. §5.27.

Self-proving affidavit (or will). An affidavit, or declaration under penalty of perjury, of the witnesses to a will, establishing its due execution. Many states authorize its use in lieu of personal appearance of the witnesses. §4.31.

Separate property. In community property states the property owned by a husband or wife that is not community property (*e.g.,* propterty owned prior to marriage or acquired thereafter by gift or inheritance). §3.23.

Separate trusts. For GSTT purposes the portions of a trust attributable to different transferors and the portions of a trust that are held for a beneficiary or beneficiaries substantially separate and distinct from other portions of the trust are treated as separate trusts. §2654(b). For purposes of determining distributable net income, substantially separate and distinct shares held for different beneficiaries are treated as separate trusts. §663(c).

Short-term trust. An irrevocable trust in which the grantor retains a reversionary interest that becomes possessory at the end of ten years or more. As a result of a 1986 amendment of §673, for income tax purposes the grantor is treated as the owner of such a trust. Prior to the amendment short-term trusts were widely used to shift income from the grantor to the beneficiaries of the trust.

Simple trust. A trust that is required to distribute all of its income currently, has no charitable beneficiaries, and makes no principal distributions during the year. Reg. §1.651(a)-1; §10.4.5.

Skip person. For GSTT purposes a skip person is (1) a person assigned to a generation that is two or more below the transferor's generation, (2) a trust in which all interests are held by skip persons, or (3) a trust if there are no persons holding an interest in it or at no time may a distribution be made from the trust to a nonskip person. §2613(a). All other persons are nonskip persons. For example, a transferor's grandchild is a skip person if his or her parent is a child of the transferor and is living at the time of the transfer. §2.23.1.

Special power of appointment. A power of appointment other than a general power of appointment. Property that is subject to a nongeneral power of appointment is not includible in the power-holder's estate under §2041. See General power of appointment and Ascertainable standard.

Special trustee. A trustee who holds a specific power or powers that for tax purposes cannot be safely held by a beneficiary-trustee. For example, a special trustee may be designated to deal with policies of insurance on the life of the trustee. §6.27.11.

Special use valuation. A valuation method by which the executor can elect to value real property used as a farm or in connection with a closely-held business for estate tax purposes according to its actual use rather than its highest and best use. §2032A; §12.19.

Spendthrift clause. A provision that prevents a beneficiary from transferring his or her interests in a trust and prevents the beneficiary's creditors from reaching them. §10.21.

Split-dollar insurance plan. A plan under which the interests in a cash value insurance policy are divided between a financing party (usually the insured's employer) and the insured (usually the employee). The insured pays a portion of the premium attributable to the cost of the insurance proceeds controlled by him or her.

Status agreement. An agreement between a husband and wife regarding the separate or community property status of the property owned by them or either of them. §3.29.

Stepped-up (or down) basis. In general, property acquired from a decedent takes a basis equal to its value on the date of the decedent's death or on the alternate valuation date applicable to the decedent's estate. §1014. The tax-free increase in basis at death should be contrasted with the carryover of basis that applies to gifts.

Straight debt. Nonconvertible debt held by an individual (other than a nonresident alien), an estate, or certain trusts, that has a fixed maturity date, a fixed interest rate, and fixed payment dates. Straight debt does not constitute a second class of stock for S corporation purposes. §1361(c)(5).

Substituted judgment doctrine. A doctrine under which a guardian or conservator is permitted to make gifts of the property of a ward.

Survivorship community property. A husband and wife may create survivorship community property in Nevada and survivorship marital property in Wisconsin. Upon the death of either spouse property so held belongs entirely to the surviving spouse. §3.31.

303 Redemption. If the stock included in a decedent's estate was worth more than 35 percent of the decedent's gross estate less deductions under §§2053 and 2054, the redemption of an amount not to exceed the sum of the state and federal death taxes and funeral and administrative expenses, is treated as a sale or exchange of the stock and not a dividend. §11.16.

2503(c) trust. A trust for the benefit of a donee who is under 21, that meets the requirements of §2503(c), transfers to which will not be treated as future interests for purposes of the annual gift tax exclusion. §7.36.

2% Floor. Under §67, miscellaneous itemized deductions are not allowable to the extent of two percent of the taxpayer's adjusted gross income. §10.4.6.

Taxable distribution. For GSTT purposes, any distribution from a trust to a skip person, other than a taxable termination or direct skip. §2612(b).

Taxable termination. The termination by death, lapse, time, or otherwise of an interest in property held in a trust unless either (1) immediately after the termination, a nonskip person has an interest in such property or (2) at no time after the termination may any distribution to a skip person be made. §2612(a)(1).

Technical Advice Memorandum (TAM). A TAM is a written statement issued by the National Office to a district director with respect to the examination of a taxpayer's return or a consideration of a taxpayer's claim for refund or credit. Reg. §301.6110-2(f).

Tenancy by the entirety. Form of joint ownership with right of survivorship by husband and wife in noncommunity property states. §3.13.

Tenancy in common. A form of coownership without right of survivorship in which each tenant owns an undivided interest in the subject property. §3.2.

Term interest. For gift tax purposes a term interest is defined in §2702(c)(3) as a life interest in property or an interest in property for a term of years. For purposes of determining gain or loss on the disposition of a term interest, an income interest in a trust is also included. §1001(e).

Testamentary power of appointment. A power of appointment that is exercisable only by the will of the power-holder.

Tier system. For income tax purposes amounts distributed are divided into classes (or "tiers") of distributions. The first consists of amounts of income the trust is required to distribute currently. The second consists of all other amounts properly paid, credited, or required to be distributed. Distributions to first tier beneficiaries are deducted from DNI. If distributions to first tier beneficiaries exhaust the DNI of the trust, no income is carried out to second tier beneficiaries. Otherwise, distributions to second tier beneficiaries will carry out the balance of the DNI. §10.4.9.

Transferor. For GSTT purposes the transferor is the decedent in the case of a transfer subject to the estate tax and the donor in the case of a transfer subject to the gift tax. §2652(a)(1).

Trapping distribution. A distribution from an estate or trust to a trust that carried out DNI, where the income is "trapped" and taxed to the trust. §12.40.

Underproductive or unproductive property. For principal and income purposes, property that has not yielded the required average rate of return during the time it was held in trust. *See* §10.47.4. A trust that is required to retain such property may not qualify for the marital deduction. §§5.22-5.23.

Unified credit. Each citizen or resident is allowed a credit of $192,800 against the gift tax imposed on lifetime transfers, §2505, or against the estate tax imposed on his or her estate, §2010. §2.3.

Uniform Gifts to Minors Act (U.G.M.A.). Provisions under which irrevocable gifts to minors can be made by transferring property into the name of a custodian for the minor. *See* Uniform Transfer to Minors Act.

Uniform Probate Code (U.P.C.). A comprehensive code governing wills, trusts, intestate succession, and related subjects.

Uniform Simultaneous Death Act. An act containing rules that apply where the title to property or its disposition depends upon the priority of death and there is no sufficient evidence that the persons have died otherwise than simultaneously. §6.80.

Uniform Transfer on Death (TOD) Security Registration Act. Act permitting transfer on death registration of securities. §3.12.2.

Uniform Transfer to Minors Act (U.T.M.A.). An act, similar to the U.G.M.A., under which a broader range of property may be transferred to a custodian for a minor.

Unrelated business taxable income (UBTI). UBTI is the gross income of an exempt organization derived from any trade or business the conduct of which is not substantially related to the organization's conduct of its exempt function. §512-513.

Veteran's life insurance. Life insurance made available in limited amounts upon very favorable terms to persons who have served in the U.S. armed forces. §6.77.

Widow's election. In noncommunity property states the right of a surviving spouse to elect to receive a statutory share of a deceased spouse's estate in lieu of the benefits provided by the decedent's will. In community property states the right of a surviving spouse to retain his or her share of the community property rather than disposing of it in accordance with the will of his or her deceased spouse. *See* §§9.23-9.39.

Table of Cases

(references are to sections)

Ablamis v. Roper, 937 F.2d 1450 (9th Cir. 1991), 3.32, 4.20.6
Ackers v. First Natl. Bank of Topeka, 387 P.2d 840 (Kan. 1963), *on reh'g* 389 P.2d 1 (1964), 10.11
Addison v. Addison, 399 P.2d 897 (Cal. 1965), 3.38
Aetna Life Ins. Co. v. Wadsworth, 689 P.2d 46 (Wash. 1984), 6.15.2, 6.15.3
Alexander, C. S., Estate of, 82 T.C. 34 (1984), *aff'd in unpubl. op.* (4th Cir. 1985), 5.22.1
Allard v. French, 754 S.W.2d 111 (1988), *cert. denied,* 109 S. Ct. 788 (1989), 3.32
Aloy v. Mash, 696 P.2d 656 (Cal. 1985), 1.30.5
Alperstein, Estate of, v. Commissioner, 613 F.2d 1213 (2d Cir. 1979), *cert. denied sub nom.,* Greenberg v. Commissioner, 446 U.S. 918 (1980), 5.22.3
American Natl. Bank & Trust Co. v. United States, 832 F.2d 1032 (7th Cir. 1987), 6.32.5
Anderson, Estate of, v. Smith, 316 N.E.2d 592 (Ind. App. 1974), 1.7
Armstrong's Estate, In re, 366 P.2d 490 (Cal. 1961), 4.27.1
Arnold v. Carmichael, 524 So. 2d 464 (Fla. App. 1988), 1.2
Arnold v. United States, 180 F. Supp. 746 (N.D. Texas 1959), 6.64
Auric v. Continental Casualty Co., 331 N.W.2d 325 (Wis. 1983), 1.2
Avery v. Commissioner, 111 F.2d 19 (9th Cir. 1940), 6.64

Bagley, Estate of, v. United States, 443 F.2d 1266 (5th Cir. 1971), 5.22.3
Bagley, Nancy R., 8 T.C. 130 (1947), *acq.,* 1947-1 C.B. 1, 1.24
Bailly, Pierce L., Estate of, 81 T.C. 246 (1983), 11.28
Ballard v. Commissioner, 854 F.2d 185 (7th Cir. 1988), 9.4
Bankers Trust Co. v. United States, 284 F.2d 537 (2d Cir. 1960), *cert. denied,* 366 U.S. 903 (1961), 12.48.1
Baratta-Lorton, Mary, Estate of, 49

T.C.M. 770 (1985), *aff'd without opinion* (9th Cir. 1986), 6.33
Barlow, Roy D., Estate of, 55 T.C. 666 (1971), *acq.,* 1972-2 C.B. 1, 9.22
Barrett, W. Stanley, 42 T.C. 993 (1964), *aff'd,* 348 F.2d 916 (1st Cir. 1965), 6.68
Beach v. Busey, 156 F.2d 496 (6th Cir. 1946), *cert. denied,* 329 U.S. 802 (1947), 10.36.3
Beach, Estate of, 542 P.2d 994 (Cal. 1975), *cert. denied,* 434 U.S. 1046, 10.45.2
Bean, Bourne, 14 T.C.M. 786 (1955), 6.53.3
Beauregard, Theodore E., Jr., Estate of, 74 T.C. 603 (1980), 6.27.10
Beckwith, Estate of, 55 T.C. 242 (1970), *acq.*, 1971-2 C.B. 1, 10.41.1
Bel v. United States, 452 F.2d 683 (5th Cir. 1971), *cert. denied,* 406 U.S. 919 (1972), 6.32.3
Belcher, Estate of, 83 T.C. 227 (1984), 8.6
Bell, Laura V., Estate of, 92 T.C. 714, *aff'd,* 928 F.2d 901 (9th Cir. 1991), 11.27.3
Bell, Lloyd G., Estate of, 60 T.C. 469 (1973), 9.12
Bell v. Harrison, 212 F.2d 253 (7th Cir. 1954), 9.31
Benson, John T., 37 T.C.M. 989 (1978), 7.25.1
Benson, Larry W., 76 T.C. 1040 (1981), 10.38.1
Berzon v. Commissioner, 534 F.2d 528 (2d Cir. 1976), 2.5.2, 10.33.1, 11.41
Biakanja v. Irving, 320 P.2d 16 (Cal. 1958), 1.2
Bianchi, Maria, Estate of, 44 T.C.M. 422 (1982), 9.16
Bill v. Payne, 25 A. 354 (Conn. 1892), 4.15.2
Biltoft v. Wootten, 157 Cal. Rptr. 581 (Cal. App. 1979), 6.15.2
Bintliff v. United States, 462 F.2d 403 (5th Cir. 1972), 6.26
Bischoff, Bruno, Estate of, 69 T.C. 32 (1977), 6.29, 10.30.5
Bixby, Estate of, 295 P.2d 68 (Cal. App. 1956), 12.14, 12.20.6
Blackburn, Gertrude H., 20 T.C. 204 (1953), 9.4, 7.24
Blackford, Eliza W., Estate of, 77 T.C. 1246 (1981), *acq. in result,* 1983-2 C.B. 1, 8.15.3
Blair v. Commissioner, 300 U.S. 5 (1937), 2.42.2
Blais v. Colebrook Guar. Sav. Bank, 220 A.2d 763 (N.H. 1966), 7.31
Blake v. Commissioner, 697 F.2d 473 (2d Cir. 1982), 8.38
Bloch, Harry, Jr., Estate of, 78 T.C. 850 (1982), 6.27.11
Boatmen's Natl. Bank v. United States, 705 F. Supp. 1407 (W.D. Mo. 1988), 2.10.3
Bodine v. Commissioner, 103 F.2d 982 (3rd Cir.), *cert. denied,* 308 U.S. 576 (1939), 6.64
Boeshore, Minnie L., Estate of, 78 T.C. 523 (1982), *acq.,* 1987-2 C.B. 1, 8.32
Bogatin v. United States, 78-2 U.S.T.C. ¶9,733 (W.D. Tenn. 1978), 9.6.1
Bogert, Estate of, 531 P.2d 1167 (Idaho 1975), 3.12.5
Bohan v. United States, 456 F.2d 851 (8th Cir. 1972), *nonacq.,* 72-396, 1972-2 C.B. 312, 12.36.5
Bonness, Estate of, In re, 535 P.2d 823 (Wash. App.), *rev. denied,* 85 Wash. 2d 1015 (1975), 3.12.1
Bordenave v. United States, 150 F. Supp. 820 (N.D. Cal. 1957), 3.20.7, 3.35.4
Bowling, Roger, Estate of, 93 T.C. 286 (1989), 5.23.8
Boyce v. United States, 190 F. Supp. 950 (W.D. La.), *aff'd per curiam,* 296 F.2d 731 (5th Cir. 1961), 10.4.10
Boyd v. Commissioner, 819 F.2d 170 (7th Cir. 1987), 12.32.2, 12.34
Brantingham, Estate of, v. United States, 631 F.2d 542 (7th Cir. 1980), 10.25
Braun, Frederick C., 48 T.C.M 210 (1984), 7.34.3, 10.40.1
Bray, Viola E., Estate of, 46 T.C. 577 (1966), *aff'd,* 396 F.2d 452 (6th Cir. 1968), *acq.,* 1971-2 C.B. 2, 12.13.2

Breidert, George M., 50 T.C. 844 (1968), *acq.,* 1969-2 C.B. xxiv, 12.8
Brenner, Estate of, 547 P.2d 938 (Colo. App. 1976), 4.27.4
Bright, Estate of, v. Commissioner, 619 F.2d 407 (5th Cir. 1980), *rev'd in part en banc,* 658 F.2d 999 (5th Cir. 1981), 6.28.1, 12.39.2
Brinley v. Commissioner, 782 F.2d 1326 (5th Cir. 1986), 8.4.2
Brooke v. United States, 468 F.2d 1155 (9th Cir. 1972), 9.17, 9.20.3, 9.20.4, 10.40.1
Brown v. Commissioner, 180 F.2d 926 (3d Cir.), *cert. denied,* 340 U.S. 814 (1950), 9.20
Brown v. Independent Baptist Church of Woburn, 91 N.E.2d 922 (Mass. 1950), 8.18
Brubaker, In re Estate of, 98 Cal. Rptr. 762 (Cal. App. 1971), 9.38
Bucquet v. Livingston, 129 Cal. Rptr. 514 (Cal. App. 1976), 1.31.3
Bullard, Estate of, 87 T.C. 261 (1986), 8.36
Burkett v. Mott, 733 P.2d 673 (Ariz. App. 1986), 4.18.5
Button, In re Estate of, 490 P.2d 731 (Wash. 1971), 10.8

Cain, Ruby Louise, 37 T.C. 185 (1961), 9.8
Camden, Johnson N., Estate of, 47 B.T.A. 926 (1942), *nonacq.,* 1943 C.B. 28, *aff'd per curiam,* 139 F.2d 697 (6th Cir. 1944), *nonacq.,* 1944 C.B. 34, 9.31.1, 9.31.2
Cameron v. Montgomery, 225 N.W.2d 154 (Iowa 1975), 1.39
Campbell v. United States, 657 F.2d 1174 (Ct. Cl. 1981), 12.48.1
Carlton, Estate of, v. Commissioner, 298 F.2d 415 (2d Cir. 1962), 6.27.8
Carpenter v. Commissioner, 322 F.2d 733 (3d Cir. 1963), *cert. denied,* 375 U.S. 992 (1964), 6.60
Carpenter v. United States, 338 F.2d 366 (Ct. Cl. 1964), 1.24
Carrieres, Jean C., 64 T.C. 959 (1975), *aff'd per curiam,* 552 F.2d 1350 (9th Cir. 1977), *acq. in result only,* 1976-2 C.B. 1, 3.35.3, 12.39.2
Carrington v. Commissioner, 476 F.2d 704 (5th Cir. 1973), 8.38
Cassidy, Sara C., Estate of, 49 T.C.M. 580 (1985), 8.15
Castleberry, Winston, Estate of, 68 T.C. 682 (1977), *rev'd,* 610 F.2d 1282 (5th Cir. 1980), 6.39
Cavanagh v. United States, 87-2 U.S.T.C. ¶13,727 (Cl. Ct. 1987), 12.48.1
Century Wood Preserving Co. v. Commissioner, 69 F.2d 967 (3d Cir. 1934), 6.63.2
Cerone, Michael N., 87 T.C. 1 (1986), 11.24.1
Chace v. United States, 303 F. Supp. 513 (M.D. Fla. 1969), *aff'd per curiam,* 422 F.2d 292 (5th Cir. 1970), 9.20.2
Chamberlin v. Commissioner, 207 F.2d 462 (6th Cir. 1953), *cert. denied,* 347 U.S. 918 (1954), 11.34.3
Champlin, Malcolm D., 6 T.C. 280 (1946), 12.49
Chenoweth, Dean E., Estate of, 88 T.C. 1577 (1987), 2.13, 5.5.2
Chesterton, Estate of, v. United States, 551 F.2d 278 (Ct. Cl.), *cert. denied,* 434 U.S. 835 (1977), 9.16
Chiu, Robert C., 84 T.C. 722 (1985), 8.7
Chown, Estate of, v. Commissioner, 428 F.2d 1395 (9th Cir. 1970), 6.80
Christ, Estate of, v. Commissioner, 480 F.2d 171 (9th Cir. 1973), 6.22.4, 9.23, 9.31.1, 9.31.2, 9.32
Chrysler, Jack F., Estate of, 44 T.C. 55 (1965), *acq.,* 1970-2 C.B. xix, *rev'd on other issues,* 361 F.2d 508 (2d Cir. 1966), 7.36.5
Citizens' Natl. Bank of Waco v. United States, 417 F.2d 675 (5th Cir. 1969), 7.25.1
City Bank of Cleveland v. United States, 371 F.2d 13 (6th Cir. 1966), 6.39
Clay, Lee J., Estate of, 86 T.C. 1266 (1986), 6.33

Coe, In re, 731 P.2d 1028 (Or. 1987), 1.18
Coffin, Estate of, 499 P.2d 223 (Wash. App.), 4.21.1
Coffman-Dobson Bank & Trust Co., 20 B.T.A. 890 (1930), *acq.,* X-1 C.B. 13 (1931), 9.33
Coleman, Inez G., Estate of, 52 T.C. 921 (1969), *acq.,* 1978-1 C.B. 1, 6.32.3
Collier v. Collier, 242 P.2d 537 (Ariz. 1952), 3.12.5
Colorado v. James, 502 P.2d 1105 (Colo. 1972), 1.6
Colorado Natl. Bank of Denver v. United States, 71-1 U.S.T.C. ¶12,781, 27 A.F.T.R.2d 71-1827 (D. Colo. 1971), 12.48.1
Commissioner v. Beck's Estate, 129 F.2d 243 (2d Cir. 1942), 7.1
Commissioner v. Duberstein, 363 U.S. 278 (1960), 3.35.2, 6.78.9
Commissioner v. Fry, 283 F.2d 869 (6th Cir. 1960), 9.31
Commissioner v. Hogle, 165 F.2d 352 (10th Cir. 1947), 7.22
Commissioner v. Kann's Estate, 174 F.2d 357 (3d Cir. 1949), 9.12
Commissioner v. McCann, 146 F.2d 385 (2d Cir. 1944), 11.11
Commissioner v. Mills, 183 F.2d (9th Cir. 1950), 3.7.2, 3.35.3
Commissioner v. Estate of Noel, 380 U.S. 678 (1965), 6.27, 6.27.1
Commissioner v. Stearns, 65 F.2d 371 (2d Cir.), *cert. denied,* 290 U.S. 670 (1933), 10.4.4
Committee on Professional Ethics v. Randall, 285 N.W.2d 161 (Iowa 1979), *cert. denied,* 446 U.S. 946 (1980), 1.16
Commonwealth v. Terjen, 90 S.E.2d 801 (Va. 1956), 3.36
Connecticut Gen. Life Ins. Co. v. Peterson, 442 F. Supp. 533 (W.D. Mo. 1978), 6.1
Connelly, Estate of, v. Commissioner, 551 F.2d 545 (3d Cir. 1977), 6.27.2
Cooke, Estate of, 524 P.2d 176 (Idaho 1974), 3.12.5
Corning v. Commissioner, 104 F.2d 329 (6th Cir. 1939), 6.58, 10.40.1
Cox v. United States, 286 F. Supp. 761 (W.D. La. 1968), 6.47.1
Crane v. Commissioner, 331 U.S. 1 (1947), 6.53.1, 7.26, 8.36
Crawford, Estate of, 730 P.2d 675 (Wash. 1986), 1.14.2
Crawford, Lillian M., 59 T.C. 830 (1973), *nonacq.,* 74-2 C.B. 5, *app. dismissed* (9th Cir. 1973), *acq.,* 1984-2 C.B. 1 (*nonacq. withdrawn*), 11.24.3
Cristofani, Estate of Maria, 97 T.C. — (1991), 7.37.5, 7.37.8
Crocker, Gertrude H., Estate of, 37 T.C. 605 (1962), 6.63
Crummey v. Commissioner, 397 F.2d 82 (9th Cir. 1968), 7.35, 10.33.1
Cruzan v. Director, Missouri Dept. of Health, 110 S. Ct. 2841 (1990), 4.35.3, 4.35.8, 4.36

Dancy v. Commissioner, 872 F.2d 84 (4th Cir. 1989), 12.33, 12.33.2
Danforth, N. Loring, 18 B.T.A. 1221 (1930), 6.56
Davis, David, Estate of, 86 T.C. 1156 (1986), 12.19.5
Davis, Kenneth W., Estate of, 30 T.C.M. 1363 (1971), *aff'd per curiam,* 469 F.2d 694 (5th Cir. 1972), 7.25.1
Davis, Platt W., Estate of, 79 T.C. 503 (1982), 1.24
Davis v. United States, 110 S. Ct. 2014 (1990), 8.4.2
Deal, Minnie E., 29 T.C. 730 (1958), 7.24, 9.4
Dean, J. Simpson, 35 T.C. 1083 (1961), *nonacq.,* 1973-2 C.B. 4, 6.59, 6.60.1
DeMarco, Paul J., Estate of, N.Y.L.J. at 15 (Mar. 1, 1988), 1.18
Depas v. Mayo, 49 Am. Dec. 88 (Mo. 1848), 3.36
Dependahl v. Falstaff Brewing Corp., 491 F. Supp. 1188 (E.D. Mo. 1980), *aff'd on this issue,* 653 F.2d 1208, *cert. denied,* 454 U.S. 968 (1981), 6.78.12
D'Ercole v. D'Ercole, 407 F. Supp. 1377 (D. Mass. 1976), 3.13

Detroit Bank & Trust Co. v. United States, 467 F.2d 964 (6th Cir. 1972), *cert. denied,* 410 U.S. 929 (1973), 6.32.3
Dickman v. Commissioner, 465 U.S. 330 (1984), 2.42.1
Diedrich, Victor P., 39 T.C.M. 433 (1979), *rev'd,* 643 F.2d 499 (8th Cir. 1981), *aff'd,* 457 U.S. 191 (1982), 7.25.1
Diedrich v. Commissioner, 643 F.2d 499 (8th Cir. 1981), *aff'd,* 457 U.S. 191 (1982), 7.25.1
Dillingham, Elizabeth C., Estate of, 88 T.C. 1569 (1987), *aff'd,* 903 F.2d 760 (10th Cir. 1990), 8.6
DiMarco, Anthony F., Estate of, 87 T.C. 653 (1986), 6.78.8
Dimen, Alfred, Estate of, 72 T.C. 198 (1979), *aff'd mem. (unpubl. op.),* 633 F.2d 203 (2d Cir. 1980), 6.71.4
Dix v. Commissioner, 392 F.2d 313 (4th Cir. 1968), 9.12, 9.14
Doss v. Kalas, 383 P.2d 169 (Ariz. 1963), 4.20.4
Draper v. Commissioner, 536 F.2d 944 (1st Cir. 1976), 6.26
Drey, Leo A., 535 F. Supp. 287 (E.D. Mo. 1982), *aff'd,* 705 F.2d 965 (8th Cir.), *cert. denied,* 464 U.S. 827 (1983), 8.16.1
Driver v. United States, 38 A.F.T.R.2d 6315 (W.D. Wisc. 1976), 7.16
Duarte, Henry D., 44 T.C. 193 (1965), 7.29.3
du Pont, In re, 194 A.2d 309 (Del. Ch. 1963), 7.5
du Pont, William, Estate of, 63 T.C. 746 (1975), 9.22
Dubois, Paul G., 51 T.C.M. 895 (1986), 10.3
Duffy v. United States, 487 F.2d 282 (6th Cir. 1973), *cert. denied,* 416 U.S. 938 (1974), 9.20.5, 10.40.1
Dunham v. Dunham, 528 A.2d 1123 (Conn. 1987), 1.16

Ebben v. Commissioner, 783 F.2d 906 (9th Cir. 1986), 8.36
Edwards v. Edwards, 233 P. 477 (Okla. 1924), 3.36
Edwards v. Greenwald, 217 F.2d 632 (5th Cir. 1954), 7.26
Effron, Estate of, 173 Cal. Rptr. 93 (4th Dist. 1981), 1.22
Ekins, Estate of, v. Commissioner, 797 F.2d 481 (7th Cir. 1986), 6.31
Elam v. Hyatt Legal Services, 541 N.E.2d 616 (Ohio 1989), 1.36, 4.26.1
Ellis First Natl. Bank of Bradenton v. United States, 550 F.2d 9 (Ct. Cl. 1977), 8.15
English v. United States, 284 F. Supp. 256 (N.D. Fla. 1968), 2.7
Enright, M. A., 56 T.C. 1261 (1971), 6.72.8
Estate of __________. *See* name of party.
Evangelista v. Commissioner, 629 F.2d 1218 (7th Cir. 1980), 7.25.1
Exchange Bank & Trust Co. v. United States, 694 F.2d 1261 (Fed. Cir. 1982), 7.34.2

Farkas v. Williams, 125 N.E.2d 600 (Ill. 1955), 10.9
Farver v. Department of Retirement Systems, 644 P.2d 1149 (Wash. 1982), 3.32, 4.20.6
Fawcett, Horace K., Estate of, 64 T.C. 889 (1975), *acq.*, 1978-2 C.B. 2, 9.5
Fein, Estate of, v. United States, 730 F.2d 1211 (8th Cir.), *cert. denied,* 469 U.S. 858 (1984), 6.31
First Natl. Bank of Denver v. United States, 648 F.2d 1286 (10th Cir. 1981), 10.41.9
First Natl. Bank of Kansas City v. Commissioner, 309 F.2d 587 (8th Cir. 1962), 6.63
First Natl. Bank of Oregon v. United States, 488 F.2d 575 (9th Cir. 1973), 6.32.3
First Natl. Bank of South Carolina v. United States, 81-2 U.S.T.C. ¶13,442 (D. S.C. 1981), 10.41.9
Fischer v. Commissioner, 288 F.2d 574 (3d Cir. 1961), 10.33.1
Fittro v. Lincoln Natl. Life Ins. Co.,

757 P.2d 1374 (Wash. 1988), 6.72.11
Flaherty v. Weinberg, 492 A.2d 618 (Md. 1985), 1.2
Fletcher, Estate of, v. Jackson, 613 P.2d 714 (N. M. Ct. App. 1980), 1.28
Fox, Agnes I., 43 B.T.A. 895 (1941), 6.60.1
Fox v. Smith, 531 S.W.2d 654 (Tex. Civ. App. 1975), 3.4
Foster, L. B., 8 T.C. 197 (1947), *acq.*, 1947-1 C.B. 2, 10.40.1
Fried, Estate of, v. Commissioner, 54 T.C. 805 (1970), *aff'd,* 445 F.2d 979 (2d Cir. 1971), *cert. denied,* 404 U.S. 1016 (1972), 12.48.1
Frieder, Alex, 28 T. C. 1256 (1957), *acq.*, 1958-2 C.B. 5, 12.24.1
Frost v. Frost, 88 N.E. 446 (Mass. 1909), 6.18.4
Fruehauf, Estate of, v. Commissioner, 427 F.2d 80 (6th Cir. 1970), 6.27.11
Fusz, Firmin D., Estate of, 46 T.C. 214 (1966), *acq.,* 1967-2 C.B. 2, 6.78.1

Gall v. United States, 521 F.2d 878 (5th Cir. 1975), *cert. denied,* 425 U.S. 972 (1976), 7.36.4
Gallun v. Commissioner, 327 F.2d 809 (7th Cir. 1964), 6.63
Gamble, George E. P., Estate of, 69 T.C. 942 (1978), *acq.*, 1981-2 C.B. 1, 7.11
Garcia, Joseph A., 48 T.C.M. 425 (1984), 11.40.2
Germundson, In re, 724 P.2d 793 (Or. 1986), 1.18
Gesner v. United States, 600 F.2d 1349 (Ct. Cl. 1979), 6.27.11
Gilchrist, Estate of, v. Commissioner, 630 F.2d 340 (5th Cir. 1980), 5.22.3
Giovanazzi v. State Bar of California, 619 P.2d 1005 (Cal. 1980), 1.17.1
Gist v. United States, 296 F. Supp. 526 (S.D. Cal. 1968), *aff'd,* 423 F.2d 1118 (9th Cir. 1970), 9.32
Glaser v. United States, 306 F.2d 57 (7th Cir. 1962), 3.8, 3.18
Goldberg v. Frye, 217 Cal. App. 3d 1258 (4th Dist. 1990), 1.36
Goldfarb v. Virginia State Bar, 421 U.S. 773 (1975), 1.22
Goldsborough, Marcia P., Estate of, 70 T.C. 1077 (1978), 3.15.2
Goldwater, Estate of, v. Commissioner, 539 F.2d 878 (2d Cir.), *cert. denied,* 429 U.S. 1023 (1976), 5.14
Goodman v. Commissioner, 156 F.2d 218 (2d Cir. 1946), 6.46
Goodnow v. United States, 302 F.2d 516 (Ct. Cl. 1962), 6.39
Gorby, Max, Estate of, 53 T. C. 80 (1969), *acq.,* 1970-1 C.B. xvi, 6.72.11
Gradow v. United States, 1987-1 U.S.T.C. ¶13,711, 11 Ct. Cl. 808 (1987), *aff'd,* 897 F.2d 516 (Fed. Cir. 1990), 6.24.1, 6.34, 9.1, 9.26, 9.34, 9.40, 9.41, 9.41.2, 9.44
Grant, Frances D., 39 T.C.M. 1088 (1980), *rev'd sub. nom.,* Diedrich v. Commissioner, 643 F.2d 499 (8th Cir. 1981), 7.25.1
Grant, W. W., 84 T.C. 809 (1985), *aff'd,* 800 F.2d 260 (4th Cir. 1986), 8.4.2
Granwell, In re Matter of, 228 N.E.2d 779 (N.Y. 1967), 10.11
Gray v. United States, 541 F.2d 228 (9th Cir. 1976), 6.27.10
Gregory, Lillian B., Estate of, 39 T.C. 1012 (1963), 9.34
Grimes v. Commissioner, 851 F.2d 1005 (7th Cir. 1988), 4.7.1, 5.17.6
Grynberg, Jack J., v. Commissioner, 83 T.C. 255 (1984), 8.11
Guaranty Trust Co. v. Commissioner, 98 F.2d 62 (2d Cir. 1938), 10.3
Gudelj v. Gudelj, 259 P.2d 656 (Cal. 1953), 3.28.5
Guest, Winston F. C., 77 T.C. 9 (1981), *acq.,* 1982-2 C.B. 1, 8.7, 8.36
Guggenheim v. Rasquin, 312 U.S. 254 (1941), 6.43
Gutchess, Allen D., Estate of, 46 T.C. 554 (1966), *acq.,* 1967-2 C.B. 1, 7.23
Guthrie v. Canty, 53 N.E.2d 1009 (Mass. 1944), 10.11

Guynn v. United States, 437 F.2d 1148 (4th Cir. 1971), 7.23
Gwinn, D. Byrd, Estate of, 25 T.C. 31 (1955), *acq.*, 1956-2 C.B. 4, 7.26

Hacker, Alcy S., 36 B.T.A. 659 (1937), 6.53.3
Hale v. Croce, 744 P.2d 1289 (Or. 1987), 1.2
Hale v. Hale, 539 A.2d 247 (Md. App.), *cert. denied,* 542 A.2d 857 (1988), 1.14.2
Hall v. United States, 208 F. Supp. 584 (N.D.N.Y. 1962), 9.20.2
Hall v. United States, 78-1 U.S.T.C. ¶9126, 41 A.F.T.R.2d 78-367 (Ct. Cl. Tr. Div.), *aff'd,* 78-1 U.S.T.C. ¶9420 (Ct. Cl. 1977), 1.24
Halsted, Harbeck, 28 T.C. 1069 (1957), *acq.,* 1958-2 C.B. 5, 6.44.2
Hanna, Estate of, v. Commissioner, 320 F.2d 54 (6th Cir. 1963), 5.37.2, 10.4.12
Harrison, Daniel J., Estate of, 52 T.C.M. 1306 (1987), 11.33
Harrison v. Schaffner, 312 U.S. 579 (1941), 2.42.2
Hart, Charles H., Estate of, 1 T.C. 989 (1943), 9.16
Harvard College v. Amory, 9 Pick. (26 Mass.) 446 (1830), 4.24.5, 10.45.1
Harwood Investment Co., 82 T.C. 239 (1984), *aff'd without opinion,* 786 F.2d 1174 (9th Cir.), *cert. denied,* 479 U.S. 1007, (1986), 2.13
Hass, Robert W., Estate of, 51 T.C.M. 453 (1986), 6.33
Hatch v. Riggs Natl. Bank, 361 F.2d 559 (D.C. Cir. 1966), 10.36.3
Hawaiian Trust Co. v. Kanne, 172 F.2d 74 (9th Cir. 1949), 2.42.2
Haygood, Selsor R., 42 T.C. 936 (1964), *acq. in result,* 1965-1 C.B. 4, *acq. withdrawn and nonacq. substituted,* 1977-2 C.B. 2, 7.24, 9.4
Haynes v. First Natl. Bank, 87 N.J. 163, 432 A.2d 890 (1981), 1.8, 1.14.1
Headrick, Eddie L., Estate of, 93 T.C. 171 (1989), *aff'd,* 918 F.2d 1263 (6th Cir. 1990), 6.23.1, 6.31.4, 6.32.4
Helis, William G., Estate of, 26 T.C. 143 (1956), *acq.,* 1956-2 C.B. 6, 12.13.6
Helvering v. Butterworth, 290 U.S. 365 (1933), 9.32
Helvering v. Clifford, 309 U.S. 331 (1940), 10.30
Helvering v. Gregory, 69 F.2d 809 (2d Cir. 1934), *aff'd,* 293 U.S. 465 (1935), 1.31
Helvering v. Horst, 311 U.S. 112 (1940), 2.42.2
Helvering v. Hutchings, 313 U.S. 393 (1941), 2.5.2, 6.44.2
Helvering v. Southwest Consol. Corp., 315 U.S. 194 (1942), 11.34
Hendricks, In re, 580 P.2d 188 (Or. 1978), 1.17.1
Henry, Douglas, Estate of, 69 T.C. 665 (1978), 7.25.1
Heringer v. Commissioner, 235 F.2d 149 (9th Cir.), *cert. denied,* 352 U.S. 927 (1956), 2.5.5
Herr, Arlean I., 35 T.C. 732 (1961), *nonacq.,* 1962-2 C.B. 6, *withdrawn and acq. substituted,* 1968-2 C.B. 2, *aff'd,* 303 F.2d 780 (3d Cir. 1962), 7.36.1
Herrick v. Miller, 125 P. 974 (Wash. 1912), 9.25
Hertsche v. United States, 244 F. Supp. 347 (D. Or. 1965), *aff'd per curiam,* 366 F.2d 93 (9th Cir. 1966), 12.15.6
Higgins, John T., Estate of, 91 T.C. 61 (1988), *aff'd on other grounds,* 897 F.2d 856 (6th Cir. 1990), 5.23.7
Hill, Alvin, Estate of, 64 T.C. 867 (1975), *acq.,* 1976-2 C.B. 2, *aff'd by order,* 568 F.2d 1365 (5th Cir. 1978), 10.8
Hill v. Nevada Natl. Bank, 545 P.2d 293 (Nev. 1976), 4.27.4
Hillborn, Michael G., 85 T.C. 677 (1985), 8.16.1
Hirst, Edna Bennett, 63 T.C. 307, *aff'd,* 572 F.2d 427 (4th Cir. 1978), 7.25.1

Holbrook v. Holbrook, 403 P.2d 12 (Or. 1965), 3.2
Hollingsworth, CTUW Georgia Ketteman, 86 T.C. 91 (1986), 2.5.5
Holloway, Estate of, 327 N.Y.S.2d 865 (Surr. Ct. Nassau Cty. 1972), 12.36, 12.40
Holmes v. Holmes, 118 P. 733 (Wash. 1911), 10.8
Holt v. Inland Revenue Commissioners, 2 All E.R. 1499 (1953), 2.43.1, 11.1
Hooper, Mathilde B., 41 B.T.A. 114 (1940), *acq. in valuation issue,* 1940-1 C.B. 3, 7.16
Hop, Chin Quan Yee, Estate of, 469 P.2d 183 (Hawaii 1970), 10.48
Hope v. United States, 691 F.2d 786 (5th Cir. 1982), 6.23.1, 6.23.3
Horlock v. Horlock, 533 S.W.2d 52 (Tex. Civ. App. 1975), 7.6
Horne v. Peckham, 158 Cal. Rptr. 714 (1979), 1.7, 1.30.7
Horne v. United States, 519 F.2d 51 (5th Cir. 1975), 12.42.6
Horstmier, 46 T.C.M. 738 (1983), 9.10.1
Howard, Lindsay C., 23 T.C. 962 (1955), *acq.,* 1955-2 C.B. 6, 4.16.3
Howard v. Commissioner, 910 F.2d 633 (9th Cir. 1990), 5.22.2
Hudspeth v. Commissioner, 509 F.2d 1224 (9th Cir. 1975), 9.1, 9.17
Hunt v. United States, 59-2 U.S.T.C. ¶11,891, 4 A.F.T.R.2d ¶6051, (E.D. Texas 1959), 6.77
Hunter, Eileen M., 44 T.C. 109 (1965), 9.31.1, 9.31.2
Hunter v. United States, 624 F.2d 833 (8th Cir. 1980), 6.27.11
Huntsman, John L., Estate of, 66 T.C. 861 (1976), *acq.,* 1977-1 C.B. 1, 6.28, 6.28.1, 6.71.4
Hutson, Hugh C., Estate of, 49 T.C. 495 (1968), 6.77

Illinois Natl. Bank of Springfield v. United States, 91-1 U.S.T.C. ¶60,063 (C.D. Ill. 1991), 7.36.2
In re ____________. *See* name of subject.

Industrial Trust Co. v. Broderick, 94 F.2d 927 (1st Cir.), *cert. denied,* 304 U.S. 572 (1938), 6.64

Jackman, D. S., 44 B.T.A. 704 (1941), *acq.,* 1942-1 C.B. 9, 7.26
Jackson v. Seder, 467 So. 2d 422 (Fla. App.), *rev. denied,* 479 So. 2d 118 (Fla. 1985), 1.14.2
Jensen v. Jensen, 665 S.W.2d 107 (Tex. 1984), 3.28.5
Jewitt v. Commissioner, 455 U.S. 305 (1982), 12.32.3
John F. Kennedy Memorial Hosp. v. Bludworth, 452 So. 2d 921 (Fla. 1984), 4.36
Johnson v. Commercial Bank, 588 P.2d 1096 (Or. 1978), 10.11
Johnson v. Commissioner, 495 F.2d 1079 (6th Cir.), *cert. denied,* 419 U.S. 1040 (1974), 6.23.6, 7.13, 7.25.1, 7.26
Johnson, Keith W., Estate of, 88 T.C. 225, *aff'd,* 838 F.2d 1202 (2d Cir. 1987), 10.4.4, 12.36.5
Johnson, Rodgers P., Trust, 71 T.C. 941 (1979), *acq.,* 1984-2 C.B. xx, 11.24.3
Johnstone, Harcourt, Estate of, 19 T.C. 44 (1952), *acq.* 1953-1 C.B. 3, 9.9
Jones v. Commissioner, 231 F.2d 655 (3d Cir. 1956), 6.55

Karagheusian, Estate of, v. Commissioner, 233 F.2d 197 (2d Cir. 1956), 6.27.6
Katz v. United States, 382 F.2d 723 (9th Cir. 1967), 3.25, 10.8
Kaufman, In re Estate of, 155 P.2d 831 (Cal. 1945), 4.10
Kaufman v. United States, 462 F.2d 439 (5th Cir. 1972), 6.47, 12.39.2
Kay, Murray, 44 T.C. 660 (1965), 6.76
Kelley, J. W., Estate of, 63 T.C. 321 (1974), *nonacq.,* 1977-2 C.B. 2, 7.24, 9.4
Kelsey, Henry B., 27 T.C.M. 337 (1968), *aff'd mem.,* 1969-2 U.S.T.C. ¶9619, 23 A.F.T.R.2d 69-1481 (2d Cir. 1969), 6.55.1

Kennedy v. Commissioner, 804 F.2d 1332 (7th Cir. 1986), 12.33.2
Kern v. United States, 491 F.2d 436 (9th Cir. 1974), 3.33, 6.21.3
Keystone Consol. Publishing Co., 26 B.T.A. 1210 (1932), 6.63.2
Killey, In re Estate of, 32 A.2d 372 (Pa. 1974), 10.45.2
King v. King, 236 P.2d 912 (Cal. 1951), 3.12.5
Klaskin v. Klepack, 534 N.E.2d 971 (Ill. 1989), 1.16
Klein v. Mayo, 367 F. Supp. 583 (D. Mass. 1973), *aff'd mem.,* 416 U.S. 953 (1974), 3.13
Knetsch v. United States, 364 U.S. 361 (1960), 6.60
Knipp, Frank H., Estate of, 25 T.C. 153 (1955), *aff'd,* 244 F.2d 436 (4th Cir.), *cert. denied,* 355 U.S. 827 (1957), *nonacq. on insurance issue,* 1956-2 C.B. 10, *withdrawn and acq. in result substituted,* 1959-1 C.B. 4, 6.28.2
Koenig v. Bishop, 409 P.2d 102 (Idaho 1965), 3.28.2
Konner, Jacob, 35 T.C. 727 (1961), *nonacq.,* 1963-2 C.B. 6, *withdrawn and acq. sub.,* 1968-2 C.B. 2, 10.33.1
Koussevitsky, Nathalie, Estate of, 5 T.C. 650 (1945), *acq.,* 1945 C.B. 4, 3.17
Krabbenhoft, Lester H., 94 T.C. 887 (1990), *aff'd,* 939 F.2d 529 (8th Cir. 1991), 9.4
Kramer v. United States, 406 F.2d 1363 (Ct. Cl. 1969), 6.78.2, 6.78.7
Krause, Victor W., 56 T.C. 1242 (1971), 7.25.1
Krauss v. United States, 140 F.2d 510 (5th Cir. 1944), 11.11
Krawczyk v. Stingle, 543 A.2d 733 (Conn. 1988), 21.6
Kroloff v. United States, 487 F.2d 334 (9th Cir. 1973), 6.21.3
Kuhn v. United States, 392 F. Supp. 1229 (S.D. Tex. 1975), 9.31.1, 9.32
Kurihara, Tetsuo, Estate of, 82 T.C. 51 (1984), 6.23.1, 6.30, 6.32.3, 6.33
Kyle, Henry H., Estate of, 94 T.C. 829 (1990), 5.16.1
LaFargue v. Commissioner, 800 F.2d 936 (9th Cir. 1986), 9.15
Lambert v. Peoples Natl. Bank, 574 P.2d 738 (Wash. 1978), 1.28
Landorf v. United States, 408 F.2d 461 (Ct. Cl. 1969), 6.27.4
Lang, Estate of, v. Commissioner, 613 F.2d 770 (9th Cir. 1980), *acq.,* 1981-2 C.B. 2, 7.11, 9.4, 12.11, 12.13.6
Lang's Estate v. Commisioner, 97 F.2d 867 (9th Cir. 1938), 3.33.1
Larson, Estate of, 694 P.2d 1051 (Wash. 1985), 1.22, 1.36, 4.26.1
Larson, Phillip G., 66 T.C. 159 (1976), *acq.,* 1979-1 C.B. 1, 11.38.3
Laurin, Estate of, v. Commissioner, 645 F.2d 8 (6th Cir. 1981), 5.7.1
Layton v. State Bar, 789 P.2d 1026 (Cal. 1990), 1.18
Lazarus v. Commissioner, 513 F.2d 824 (9th Cir. 1975), 9.10.1
Leach, Anne B., Estate of, 82 T.C. 952 (1984), *aff'd per curiam,* 782 F.2d 179 (11th Cir. 1986), 12.42.5
Leder, Joseph, Estate of, 89 T.C. 235 (1987), *aff'd,* 893 F.2d 237 (10th Cir. 1989), 6.23.1, 6.30, 6.32.2, 6.32.4
Lee, Elizabeth, Estate of, 69 T.C. 860 (1978), *nonacq.,* 1980-1 C.B. 2, 6.28.1
Lee, W. S., Estate of, 11 T.C. 141 (1948), *acq.,* 1948-2 C.B. 3, 12.11
Lehner v. Estate of Lehner, 547 P.2d 365 (Kan. 1976), 4.21.2
Lerner, Hobart A., M.D., P.C., 71 T.C. 290 (1978), 9.20.3
Levin, Stanton A., Estate of, 90 T.C. 723 (1988), *aff'd without opinion,* 891 F.2d 281 (3d Cir. 1989), 6.78, 6.78.3, 6.78.5, 6.78.7
Levine v. Commissioner, 526 F.2d 717 (2d Cir. 1975), 7.36.2
Levine, Estate of, v. Commissioner, 72 T.C. 780 (1979), *aff'd,* 634 F.2d 12 (2d Cir. 1980), 7.25.1, 7.26
Levine, Estate of, v. United States, 10 Cl. Ct. 135 (1986), 6.32.2
Levy, Milton L., Estate of, 70 T.C. 873 (1978), 6.28

Liberty Natl. Life Ins. Co. v. First Natl. Bank, 151 So. 2d 225 (Ala. 1963), 7.34
Lidbury, Estate of, v. Commissioner, 800 F.2d 649 (1986), 4.7.1
Linck v. Barokas & Martin, 667 P.2d 171 (Alaska 1983), 1.36, 12.35
Linderme, Emil Sr., Estate of, 52 T.C. 305 (1969), 7.23
Lio, Peter J., 85 T.C. 56 (1985), *aff'd sub nom.,* Orth v. Commissioner, 813 F.2d 837 (7th Cir. 1987), 8.7
Lion, Estate of, v. Commissioner, 438 F.2d 56 (4th Cir.), *cert. denied,* 404 U.S. 870 (1971), 5.20
Lipsitz v. Commissioner, 220 F.2d 871 (4th Cir.), *cert. denied,* 350 U.S. 845 (1955), 3.20.1
Little, John Russell, Estate of, 87 T.C. 599 (1986), 10.25
Little v. United States, 191 F. Supp. 12 (E.D. Tex. 1960), 7.29.3
Lober v. United States, 346 U.S. 335 (1953), 7.36.5, 10.20.5, 10.26, 10.37.3
Logan v. Barge, 568 S.W.2d 863 (Tex. Civ. App. 1978), 7.6
Lohm, Estate of, In re, 269 A.2d 451 (Pa. 1970), 1.39
London Shoe Co. v. Commissioner, 80 F.2d 230 (2d Cir. 1935), *cert. denied,* 298 U.S. 663 (1936), 6.64
Long, Arthur E., 77 T.C. 1045 (1981), 11.39
Lucas v. Earl, 281 U.S. 111 (1930), 2.42.2
Lucas v. Hamm, 364 P.2d 685 (Cal. 1961), *cert. denied,* 368 U.S. 987 (1962), 1.2
Lumpkin, Estate of, v. Commissioner, 474 F.2d 1092 (5th Cir. 1973), 6.27.2

Madden, Richard V., 52 T.C. 845 (1969), *aff'd per curiam,* 440 F.2d 784 (7th Cir. 1971), 3.20.3
Magee v. State Bar of California, 374 P.2d 807 (Cal. 1962), 1.16
Malone v. United States, 326 F. Supp. 106 (N.D. Miss. 1971), *aff'd per curiam,* 455 F.2d 502 (5th Cir. 1972), 7.26
Mangles v. United States, 828 F.2d 1324 (8th Cir. 1987), 12.19.7
Maniscalco v. Commissioner, 632 F.2d 6 (6th Cir. 1980), 8.9
Mann v. Bradley, 535 P.2d 213 (Colo. 1975), 3.3
Mann v. Commissioner, 35 F.2d 873 (D.C. Cir. 1929), 8.6
Manufacturer's Hanover Trust Co. v. Commissioner, 431 F.2d 664 (9th Cir. 1970), 6.24.1, 9.23, 9.32
Manufacturer's Hanover Trust Co. v. United States, 775 F.2d 459 (2d Cir. 1985), 8.25
Mapes, In re Estate of, 738 S.W.2d 853 (Mo. 1987), 1.16
Margrave v. Commissioner, 618 F.2d 34 (8th Cir. 1980), 6.26
Markosian, Louis, 73 T.C. 1235 (1980), 10.3
Marriage of Hadley, 565 P.2d 790 (Wash. 1977), 5.28
Marriage of Smith, 705 P.2d 197 (Or. 1985), 3.3
Martin v. Commissioner, 783 F.2d 81 (7th Cir. 1986), 12.19.9
Mathews, C. James, 61 T.C. 12 (1973), *rev'd,* 520 F.2d 323 (5th Cir. 1975), *cert. denied,* 424 U.S. 967 (1976), 9.17
Matter of Peeples, 374 S.E.2d 674 (S.C. 1988), 1.16
Matter of Rentiers, 374 S.E.2d 672 (S.C. 1988), 1.16
Matter of Totten, 71 N.E. 748 (1904), 7.32
Matthews v. Commissioner, 520 F.2d 323 (5th Cir. 1975), *cert. denied,* 424 U.S. 967 (1976), 9.20.1
May v. Commissioner, 723 F.2d 1434 (9th Cir. 1984), 9.20.1
May, Lewis H. V., 76 T.C. 7 (1981), *aff'd,* 723 F.2d 1434 (9th Cir. 1984), 9.20.3
Mayo, In re Trusteeship Under Agreement with, 105 N.W.2d 900 (Minn. 1960), 10.45
Maytag v. United States, 493 F.2d 995 (10th Cir. 1974), 10.22
McAleer v. Jernigan, 804 F.2d 1231 (11th Cir. 1986), 12.42
McAllister v. Commissioner, 157 F.2d 235 (2d Cir. 1946), *cert. denied,* 330 U.S. 826 (1947), 9.31

McCarty v. McCarty, 453 U.S. 210 (1981), 1.30.5
McCurdy v. McCurdy, 372 S.W.2d 381 (Tex. Civ. App. 1963), *writ refused,* 3.28.5, 6.15.1
McDonald v. Commissioner, 853 F.2d 1494 (8th Cir. 1988), *cert. denied,* 490 U.S. 1005 (1989), 12.33.2
McDonald v. Morely, 101 P.2d 690 (Cal. 1940), 3.3
McKee, Ray, Estate of, 37 T.C.M. 486 (1978), 6.39
McNichol, Estate of, v. Commissioner, 265 F.2d 667 (3d Cir.), *cert. denied,* 361 U.S. 829 (1959), 10.40.3
Meeske, Fritz L., Estate of, 72 T.C. 73 (1979), *aff'd sub. nom.,* Estate of Laurin v. Commissioner, 645 F.2d 8 (6th Cir. 1981), 5.7.1
Mellon Bank v. United States, 762 F.2d 283 (3d Cir. 1985), *cert. denied,* 475 U.S. 1032 (1986), 8.2
Meltzer, Estate of, v. Commissioner, 439 F.2d 798 (4th Cir. 1971), 6.80
Merians, Sidney, 60 T.C. 187 (1973), 1.24
Metzer, David, Trust, 76 T.C. 42 (1981), *aff'd,* 693 F.2d 459 (5th Cir.), *cert. denied,* 463 U.S. 1207 (1983), 11.24.1, 11.24.4
Meyer, Dorothy H., Estate of, 84 T.C. 560 (1985), 11.27.2
Meyer, Rollin E., Sr., Estate of, 58 T.C. 311 (1972), *nonacq.,* 1975-1 C.B. 3, *aff'd per curiam,* 503 F.2d 556 (9th Cir. 1974), 11.39
Miller v. Usry, 160 F. Supp. 368 (W.D. La. 1958), 9.6.3
Minahan, Victor I., 88 T.C. 492 (1987), 7.16
Minnis, Robert W., 71 T.C. 1049 (1979), *nonacq.,* 1979-2 C.B. 2, 6.59.1
Minotto, Idamay Swift, Estate of, 9 T.C.M. 556 (1950), 6.39
Mittleman v. Commissioner, 522 F.2d 132 (D.C. Cir. 1975), 1.31.3
Modern Woodmen of America v. Gray, 299 P. 754 (Cal. App. 1931), 6.15.2
Monroe v. Patterson, 197 F. Supp. 146 (N.D. Ala. 1961), 6.5.3, 11.9
Mooneyham, Nancy M., 60 T.C.M. — (1991), 7.16
Moore, Genevieve F., 39 B.T.A. 88 (1939), *acq.,* 1939-2 C.B. 25, 10.40.1
Moore, George H., Estate of, 43 T.C.M. 1530 (1982), 8.25
Morales v. Field, 160 Cal. Rptr. 239 (1st Dist. 1979), 1.36
Morgan, Annette S., Estate of, 37 T.C. 981 (1962), *aff'd,* 316 F.2d 238 (6th Cir.), *cert. denied,* 375 U.S. 825 (1963), 7.25.1, 7.26
Morgan v. Roller, 794 P.2d 1313 (Wash. App. 1990), 1.8.1
Morrill v. United States, 228 F. Supp. 734 (D. Me. 1964), 7.34.3, 10.40.1
Morris, Estelle, Trusts, 51 T.C. 20 (1968), *aff'd per curiam,* 427 F.2d 1361 (9th Cir. 1970), 10.4.10
Morris, In re, 281 A.2d 156 (N.H. 1971), 7.5
Morton v. United States, 457 F.2d 750 (4th Cir. 1972), 6.45.1
Moseley, Ned W., 72 T.C. 183 (1979), *acq.,* 6.61
Moser v. Moser, 572 P.2d 446 (Ariz. 1977), 5.28
Moss, John A., Estate of, 74 T.C. 1239 (1980), *acq.,* 1981-1 C.B. 2, 9.7.4
M.S.D., Inc. v. United States, 39 A.F.T.R.2d 77-1393 (N.D. Ohio 1977), *aff'd without opinion,* 611 F.2d 373 (6th Cir. 1979), 6.78.11
Murphy, Estate of, 544 P.2d 956 (Cal. 1976), 9.27
Murphy, Elizabeth, Estate of, 60 T.C.M. 645 (1990), 7.16
Murphy v. Commissioner, 342 F.2d 356 (9th Cir. 1965), 3.20.7, 3.35.4

National Shawmut Bank v. Joy, 53 N.E.2d 113 (Mass. 1944), 10.9
Neugass, Estate of, v. Commissioner, 555 F.2d 322 (2d Cir. 1977), 5.17.2
Neuhoff, Ann F., 75 T.C. 36 (1980), *aff'd,* 69 F.2d 291 (5th Cir. 1982), 12.48.2
Nilssen, Estate of, v. United States,

322 F. Supp. 260 (D. Minn. 1971), 6.78.9
Northeastern Pa. Natl. Bank & Trust Co. v. United States, 387 U.S. 213 (1967), 5.22.1

Oakes, Alden B., 44 T.C. 524 (1965), 9.20.3
Old Colony Trust Co., 39 B.T.A. 871 (1939), 6.26
Old Colony Trust Co. v. United States, 423 F.2d 601 (1st Cir. 1970), 10.38.3
Old Kent Bank & Trust Co. v. United States, 430 F.2d 392 (6th Cir. 1970), 6.80
Opal, Estate of, v. Commissioner, 450 F.2d 1085 (2d Cir. 1971), 4.7.1, 5.17.6
Oursler v. Armstrong, 179 N.E.2d 489 (N.Y. 1961), 1.4
Outwin, Mary M., 76 T.C. 153 (1981), 10.40.2

Pacific Natl. Bank, 40 B.T.A. 128 (1939), *acq.,* 1939-2 C.B. 28, 9.33
Paley v. Bank of America, 324 P.2d 35 (Cal. App. 1958), 3.38
Palmer v. Commissioner, 627 T.C. 684 (1974), *aff'd on another ground,* 523 F.2d 1308 (8th Cir. 1975), *acq.,* 1978-2 C.B. 2, *nonacq.,* 1978-2 C.B. 4, 8.38
Palmer, Estate of, v. Commissioner, 839 F.2d 420 (8th Cir. 1988), 8.7
Paolozzi, Alice Spaulding, 23 T.C. 182 (1954), *acq.,* 1955-2 C.B. 5, *acq. withdrawn, nonacq.,* 1957-2 C.B. 8, *acq. reinstated,* 1962-1 C.B. 2, 10.40.2
Parshelsky, Estate of, v. Commissioner, 303 F.2d 14 (2d Cir. 1962), 11.34.1
Parsons, Charles Cutler, 16 T.C. 256 (1951), 6.68
Patten, In re Estate of, 419 P.2d 157 (Wash. 1966), 9.38
Patterson, Henry T., Trust v. United States, 729 F.2d 1089 (6th Cir. 1984), 11.24.1
Patton, Estate of, 494 P.2d 238 (Wash. App.), *rev. denied,* 80 Wash. 2d 1009 (1972), 4.13, 12.39.2
Paxton, Floyd G., Estate of, 86 T.C. 785 (1986), 10.3
Pennell, Helen S., Estate of, 4 B.T.A. 1039 (1926), 1.24
People v. Bejarano, 358 P.2d 866 (Colo. 1961), 3.36
Perkins v. United States, 701 F.2d 771 (9th Cir. 1983), 9.14
Perry, Frank M., Estate of, 59 T.C.M. 65 (1990), *aff'd,* 927 F.2d 209 (5th Cir. 1991), 6.23.1, 6.23.4
Perry, Estate of, v. United States, 931 F.2d — (5th Cir. 1991), 6.32.4
Perry v. United States, 520 F.2d 235 (4th Cir. 1975), *cert. denied,* 423 U.S. 1052 (1976), 3.10, 9.20
Phillips, Jesse S., 12 T.C. 216 (1949), 6.44.2
Phillips v. Wellborn, 552 P.2d 471 (N.M. 1976), 6.15.3
Pityo, William D., 70 T.C. 225 (1978), 9.7
Plant, Henry Bradley, 30 B.T.A. 133 (1934), *acq.,* 1976-1 C.B. 1, *aff'd,* 76 F.2d 8 (2d Cir. 1935), 12.36
Poling v. North America Life & Casualty Co., 593 P.2d 568 (Wyo. 1979), 6.72.11
Porter, Bernard L., Estate of, 54 T.C. 1066 (1970), *aff'd,* 442 F.2d 915 (1st Cir. 1971), 6.78.4
Pritchard, James Stuart, Estate of, 4 T.C. 204 (1944), 6.34, 6.43.5, 9.41.1
Pritchard v. Estate of Tuttle, 534 S.W.2d 946 (Tex. Civ. App. 1976), 3.4
Proctor, Commissioner v., 142 F.2d 824 (4th Cir.), *cert. denied,* 323 U.S. 756 (1944), 7.37.4
Professional Services v. Commissioner, 79 T.C. 888 (1982), 10.3
Propstra v. United States, 680 F.2d 1248 (9th Cir. 1982), 2.43.1, 6.28.1, 7.16
Puget Sound Natl. Bank v. Burt, 786 P.2d 300 (Wash. App. 1990), 4.35
Pyle, Estate of, v. Commissioner, 313 F.2d 328 (3d Cir. 1963), 6.39
Pyle v. United States, 766 F.2d 1141

(7th Cir. 1985), *cert. denied,* 475 U.S. 1015 (1986), 4.7.1

Quinlivan v. Commissioner, 37 T.C.M. 346 (1978), *aff'd,* 599 F.2d 269, (8th Cir.), *cert. denied,* 444 U.S. 996 (1979), 9.20, 9.20.2, 9.20.3

Rafferty v. Commissioner, 452 F.2d 767 (1st Cir. 1971), *cert. denied,* 408 U.S. 922 (1972), 11.34.1
Ramp v. St. Paul Fire & Marine Ins. Co., 269 So. 2d 239 (La. 1972), 1.39
Rapelje, Adrian K., Estate of, 73 T.C. 82 (1979), 7.23
Rath, Estate of, v. United States, 608 F.2d 254 (6th Cir. 1979), 6.53.3, 6.71.2
Ray v. United States, 385 F. Supp. 372 (S.D. Tex. 1974), *aff'd per curiam on other issues,* 538 F.2d 1228 (5th Cir. 1976), 3.33.1, 12.13.6, 12.48.3
Reed, Estate of, 672 P.2d 829 (Wyo. 1983), 1.8.1
Regester, Ruth B., Estate of, 83 T.C. 1 (1984), 10.23
Reilly v. Sageser, 467 P.2d 358 (Wash. App. 1970), 3.3
Republic Petroleum Corp. v. United States, 397 F. Supp. 900, (E.D. La. 1975), *modified on other issues,* 613 F.2d 518 (5th Cir. 1980), 9.4
Reynolds, Pearl G., Estate of, 55 T.C. 172 (1970), *acq.,* 1971-2 C.B. 2, 7.18, 7.24
Rickey v. United States, 592 F.2d 1251 (5th Cir. 1979), 11.24.4
Robinson, G. R., Estate of, 69 T.C. 222 (1977), 5.37.1, 9.5
Robinson, Myra B., 75 T.C. 346 (1980), *aff'd,* 675 F.2d 774 (5th Cir.), *cert. denied,* 459 U.S. 970 (1982), 9.30.1
Rockefeller v. Commissioner, 676 F.2d 35 (2d Cir. 1982), 8.4.2
Rockwell, Estate of, v. Commissioner, 779 F.2d 931 (3d Cir. 1985), 6.27.8
Rose v. United States, 511 F.2d 259 (5th Cir. 1975), 6.27, 6.27.11
Rosen v. Commissioner, 397 F.2d 245 (4th Cir. 1968), 10.33.1
Rosenblatt, Estate of, v. Commissioner, 633 F.2d 176 (10th Cir. 1980), 5.22.3
Rosenfeld v. Commissioner, 706 F.2d 1277 (2d Cir. 1983), 9.20, 9.20.3
Ross v. Caunters, [1979] 3 All E.R. 580, 1.2
Ross, Cornelius A., 71 T.C. 897 (1979), *aff'd,* 652 F.2d 1365 (9th Cir. 1981), 7.36.4
Rothstein v. United States, 735 F.2d 704 (2d Cir. 1984), 10.32.8, 10.38.1
Rupp v. Kahn, 55 Cal. Rptr. 108 (Cal. App. 1966), 3.12.4
Rushing v. Commissioner, 441 F.2d 593 (5th Cir. 1971), 9.7
Rushton v. Commissioner, 498 F.2d 88 (5th Cir. 1974), 7.16

Salsbury, Joseph E., Estate of, 34 T.C.M. 1441 (1975), 6.26
Salvatore v. Commissioner, 434 F.2d 600 (2d Cir. 1970), 7.9.2
Salvini, Estate of, 397 P.2d 811 (Wash. 1964), 3.4
Samuel v. Commissioner, 306 F.2d 682 (1st Cir. 1962), 9.10
Sandifur v. United States, 64-2 U.S.T.C. ¶9,817, 14 A.F.T.R.2d 5882 (E.D. Wash. 1964), 7.29.3
Sanford, Estate of, v. Commissioner, 308 U.S. 39 (1939), 2.4.3, 9.30.1, 10.5, 10.16
Saunders, Estate of, 317 P.2d 528 (Wash. 1957), 6.80.1
Sbicca, Frank, Estate of, 35 T.C. 96 (1960), 3.38
Schelberg, Estate of, v. Commissioner, 612 F.2d 25 (2d Cir. 1979), 6.78.1
Schnack v. Commissioner, 848 F.2d 933 (9th Cir. 1988), 6.32.3, 6.33
Schwager, Eleanor M., 64 T.C. 781 (1975), 6.27.8
Scott v. Commissioner, 374 F.2d 154 (9th Cir. 1967), 6.15, 6.22.3
Sears v. Austin, 292 F.2d 690 (9th

Cir.), *cert. denied,* 368 U.S. 929 (1961), 4.20.4
Seattle First Natl. Bank v. Whitney, 560 P.2d 360 (Wash. App. 1977), *aff'd,* 579 P.2d 937 (Wash. 1978), 1.14.2
Self v. United States, 142 F. Supp. 939 (Ct. Cl. 1956), 10.23
Seligmann, Grace R., 9 T.C. 191 (1947), *acq.,* 1947-2 C.B. 4, 6.46
Sence v. United States, 394 F.2d 842 (Ct. Cl. 1968), 10.4.10
Shaughnessy, Estate of, 702 P.2d 132 (Wash. 1985), 10.43.2
Shaw, Estate of, 572 P.2d 229 (Okla. 1977), 4.32
Sheaffer, Craig R., Estate of, 37 T.C. 99 (1961), *aff'd,* 313 F.2d 738 (8th Cir.), *cert. denied,* 375 U.S. 818 (1963), 7.25.1
Sherrod, Floyd, Estate of, 82 T.C. 523 (1984), *rev'd,* 774 F.2d 1057 (11th Cir. 1985), *cert. denied,* 479 U.S. 814 (1986), 11.27.2
Siegel, Commissioner v., 250 F.2d 339 (9th Cir. 1957), 6.24.1, 9.30
Siegel, Murray J., Estate of, 74 T.C. 613 (1980), 6.78.1, 6.78.7
Silverman, Morris, Estate of, 61 T.C. 338 (1973), *acq.,* 1978-1 C.B. 2, *other issues aff'd,* 521 F.2d 574 (2d Cir. 1975), 6.35
Simmie, Elfrida G., Estate of, 69 T.C. 890 (1978), *aff'd,* 632 F.2d 93 (9th Cir. 1980), 9.34, 12.48.1
Simon v. Zipperstein, 512 N.E.2d 636 (Ohio 1987), 1.2
Skaggs, Ernest D., Estate of, 75 T.C. 191 (1980), *aff'd per curiam,* 672 F.2d 756 (9th Cir.), *cert. denied,* 459 U.S. 1037 (1982), 12.5.3
Skemp v. Commissioner, 168 F.2d 598 (7th Cir. 1948), 9.17, 9.20
Skifter, Estate of, v. Commissioner, 468 F.2d 699 (2d Cir. 1972), 6.27.11
Skinner, Estate of, v. United States, 316 F.2d 517 (3d Cir. 1963), 10.40.3
Skouras v. Commissioner, 188 F.2d 831 (2d Cir. 1951), 6.44.1
Smead, James, Estate of, 78 T.C. 43 (1982), 6.27.5
Smith, In re Estate of, 40 P. 1037 (Cal. 1895), 9.25
Smith v. Lewis, 530 P.2d 589 (Cal. 1975), 1.30.5
Smith v. St. Paul Fire & Marine Ins. Co., 366 F. Supp. 1283 (M.D. La. 1973), *aff'd per curiam,* 500 F.2d 1131 (5th Cir. 1974), 1.39
Smith, Charles C., Estate of, 23 T.C. 367 (1954), 6.46
Smith, Frederick R., Estate of, 94 T.C. 872 (1990), 2.10.3
Smith, John, 73 T.C. 307 (1979), 6.27.6
Smoot v. Commissioner, 1988-1 U.S.T.C. ¶13,748 (D.C. Ill. 1988), *aff'd,* 892 F.2d 597 (7th Cir. 1989), 12.19.5
Sowell, Ida Maude, Estate of, 74 T.C. 1001 (1980), *rev'd,* 708 F.2d 1564 (10th Cir. 1983), 10.25
Spalding, Estate of, v. Commissioner, 537 F.2d 666 (2d Cir. 1976), 5.14
Staley, A. E., Sr., Estate of, 47 B.T.A. 260 (1942), *aff'd,* 136 F.2d 368 (5th Cir.), *cert. denied,* 320 U.S. 786 (1943), 7.25.1
Standard Brewing Co., 6 B.T.A. 980 (1927), 6.64
Stanger v. Stanger, 571 P.2d 1126 (Idaho 1977), 5.28, 9.11
Stark, Nelda C., 86 T.C. 243 (1986), 8.18
Stark v. United States, 477 F.2d 131 (8th Cir.), *cert. denied,* 414 U.S. 975 (1973), 10.33.1
State v. Gulbankian, 196 N.W.2d 733 (1972), 1.34.1, 4.32
State Street Bank & Trust Co. v. Reiser, 389 N.E.2d 768 (Mass. App. 1979), 10.11
Steffke, Estate of, v. Commissioner, 538 F.2d 730 (7th Cir.), *cert. denied,* 429 U.S. 1022 (1976), 5.14
Steinman, Bluma, Estate of, 69 T.C. 804 (1978), 9.30.1
Steinway v. Bolden, 460 N.W.2d 306 (Mich. App. 1990), 1.36
Stephenson Trust, Edward L., 81 T.C. 283 (1983), 10.4.10
Stern v. Commissioner, 747 F.2d 555 (9th Cir. 1984), 9.10.1

Stewart v. United States, 512 F.2d 269 (5th Cir. 1975), 4.21.1
St. Louis County Bank v. United States, 674 F.2d 1207 (8th Cir. 1982), 11.6, 11.11
St. Mary's Church of Schuyler v. Tomek, 325 N.W.2d 164 (Neb. 1982), 1.2
Stockman, Arthur, 3 T.C. 664 (1944), 6.58
Stone, Christopher, 54 T.C.M. 462 (1987), 7.34.3, 10.40.1
Story, Nelson III, 38 T.C. 936 (1962), 7.24
Stuit v. Commissioner, 452 F.2d 190 (7th Cir. 1971), 7.34.2
Sullivan, Estate of, v. Commissioner, 175 F.2d 657 (9th Cir. 1949), 3.18
Sulovich, Estate of, v. Commissioner, 587 F.2d 845 (6th Cir. 1978), 7.32
Sumpter, Estate of, 419 N.W.2d 765 (Mich. App. 1988), 1.14.2
Swan v. Walden, 103 P. 931 (Cal. 1909), 3.13
Sweeney, Margaret L., 54 T.C.M. 1003 (1987), 6.78.9
Syufy v. United States, 818 F.2d 1457 (9th Cir. 1987), 9.10.1

Tarien v. Katz, 15 P.2d 493 (Cal. 1932), 3.4
Terriberry v. United States, 517 F.2d 286 (1975), *cert. denied,* 424 U.S. 977 (1976), 6.27.11
Thornton, Estate of, 33 P.2d 1 (Cal. 1934), 3.38
Tingley, Frank E., Estate of, 22 T.C. 402 (1954), *aff'd sub. nom.,* Starrett v. Commissioner, 223 F.2d 163 (1st Cir. 1955), 5.22.2
Tomerlin, James O., Estate of, 51 T.C.M. 831 (1986), 6.27.9
Tonsic, Estate of, 235 N.E.2d 239 (Ohio App. 1968), 7.31
Towne, William S., 78 T.C. 791 (1982), 6.72.6
Truax v. Southwestern College, Oklahoma City, Oklahoma, 522 P.2d 412 (Kan. 1974), 7.31
Tully, Estate of, v. United States, 528 F.2d 1401 (Ct. Cl. 1976), 6.78.2, 6.78.3, 6.78.5, 6.78.8
Tulsa Professional Collection Services, Inc. v. Pope, 485 U.S. 478 (1988), 4.5
Turman, Zillah Mae, 35 T.C. 1123 (1961), *acq.,* 1964-2 C.B. 7, 9.30
Turner, Richard H., 49 T.C. 356 (1968), *aff'd per curiam,* 410 F.2d 752 (6th Cir. 1969), *nonacq.,* 1971-2 C.B. 3, 7.25.1
212 Corp., 70 T.C. 788 (1978), 9.12

Uhl, Estate of, v. Commissioner, 241 F.2d 867 (7th Cir. 1957), 10.40.3
United States v. Allen, 293 F.2d 916 (10th Cir.), *cert. denied,* 368 U.S. 944 (1961), 6.34
United States v. Byrum, 408 U.S. 125 (1972), 2.5.7, 2.17.1, 6.28, 6.78.5, 10.38.3, 10.41.1, 10.41.8, 11.5, 11.38.2, 11.41.3
United States v. Chandler, 410 U.S. 257 (1973), 7.5, 7.30.2
United States v. Davis, 397 U.S. 301 (1970), 11.24.1
United States v. Denison, 318 F.2d 819 (5th Cir. 1963), 2.15
United States v. Goodson, 253 F.2d 900 (8th Cir. 1958), 4.27.5
United States v. Gordon, 406 F.2d 332 (5th Cir. 1969), 6.39
United States v. Grace, Estate of, 395 U.S. 316 (1969), 9.1
United States v. Heasty, 370 F.2d 525 (10th Cir. 1966), 3.18
United States v. Manny, 645 F.2d 163 (2d Cir. 1981), 12.48.1
United States v. O'Malley, 383 U.S. 627 (1966), 10.20.5
United States v. Past, 347 F.2d 7 (9th Cir. 1965), 6.33, 9.34
United States v. Powell, 379 U.S. 48 (1964), 12.13.4
United States v. Rhode Island Hosp. Trust Co., 355 F.2d 7 (1st Cir. 1966), 6.27, 6.27.1
United States v. Righter, 400 F.2d 344 (8th Cir. 1968), 9.23, 9.26, 9.34
United States v. Ryerson, 312 U.S. 260 (1941), 6.43.5, 6.44.1
United States v. Stapf, 375 U.S. 118 (1963), 9.33
United States v. Weisburn, 48 F.

Supp. 393 (E.D. Pa. 1943), 12.49
United States v. White, 853 F.2d 107 (2d Cir. 1988), *cert. denied,* 493 U.S. 5 (1989), 12.13.4

Van Den Wymelenberg v. United States, 397 F.2d 443 (7th Cir.), *cert. denied,* 393 U.S. 953 (1968), 10.33.1
Van Stewart v. Townsend, 28 P.2d 999 (Wash. 1934), 10.11
Van Zandt v. Commissioner, 341 F.2d 440 (5th Cir.), *cert. denied,* 382 U.S. 814 (1965), 9.20.1
Vander Weele, Commissioner v., 254 F.2d 895 (6th Cir. 1958), 10.21.2
Vardell, Estate of, v. Commissioner, 307 F.2d 688 (5th Cir. 1962), 9.23
Victor v. Goldman, 344 N.Y.S.2d 672 (Sup. Ct. Rockland Cty., 1973), *aff'd mem.,* 351 N.Y.S.2d 956 (App. Div. 2d Dept., 1974), 1.6

Wade, Estate of Charles Howard, 47 B.T.A. 21 (1942), 6.26
Wadewitz, Edward H., Estate of, 39 T.C. 925 (1963), *aff'd on other grounds,* 339 F.2d 980 (7th Cir. 1964), 6.78.2
Walther v. Commissioner, 316 F.2d 708 (7th Cir. 1963), 9.18
Ward v. Arnold, 328 P.2d 164 (Wash. 1958), 1.34
Warms, Estate of, 140 N.Y.S.2d 169 (Surr. Ct. 1955), 12.14
Warner, Commissioner v., 127 F.2d 913 (9th Cir. 1942), 6.72.12
Waters, Estate of, 100 Cal. Rptr. 775 (Cal. App. 1972), 9.24
Watson, Estate of, v. United States, 81-2 U.S.T.C. ¶13,421 (Ct. Cl. 1981), 12.48.1
Webb v. Webb, 301 S.E.2d 570 (W. Va. 1983), 12.31
Webster v. Commissioner, 120 F.2d 514 (5th Cir. 1941), 6.26
Webster, Jane DeP., Estate of, 65 T.C. 968 (1976), *acq. and non-acq.,* 1977-2 C.B. 2, 12.12
Wedemeyer, Estate of, 240 P.2d 8 (Cal. App. 1952), 6.80.1
Weeden, Norman D., Estate of, 39 T.C.M. 699 (1979), *rev'd,* 685 F.2d 1160 (9th Cir. 1982), 7.25.1
Weigl v. Commissioner, 84 T.C. 1192 (1985), 9.10.1
Weinstock, Estate of, 386 N.Y.S.2d 1 (1976), 1.18
Wesenberg, Richard L., 69 T.C. 1005 (1978), *nonacq.,* 1978-2 C.B. 4, 10.3
Weller, Carl E., 38 T.C. 790 (1962), *acq.,* 1963-1 C.B. 4, *withdrawn and nonacq. sub.,* 1963-2 C.B. 6, *withdrawn and acq. sub.,* 1968-2 C.B. 3, 10.33.1
Wheless, William M., Estate of, 72 T.C. 470 (1979), *nonacq.,* 1982-1 C.B. 1, 12.12
White v. United States, 725 F.2d 1269 (10th Cir. 1984), 8.4.2
Whitney v. Seattle First Natl. Bank, 579 P.2d 937 (Wash. 1978), 9.27
Wien, Estate of, v. Commissioner, 441 F.2d 32 (5th Cir. 1971), 6.80
Williamson, Estate of, 229 P.2d 312 (Wash. 1951), 12.42.5
Wilmot, Dorothy C., Estate of, 29 T.C.M. 1055 (1970), 6.29
Winokur, James L., 90 T.C. 733 (1988), *acq.,* 1989-2 C.B. —, 8.10.1, 8.16
Wissner v. Wissner, 338 U.S. 655 (1950), 6.77
Withers, Lavar, 69 T.C. 900 (1978), 8.8
Wolder v. Commissioner, 493 F.2d 608 (2d Cir. 1974), *cert. denied,* 419 U.S. 828 (1974), 1.23
Wong, Arthur K., 58 T.C.M. 1073 (1989), 1.24
Wooley v. United States, 1990-1 U.S.T.C. ¶60,013 (S.D. Ind. 1990), 2.5.7.
Worrell, Re, 8 D.L.R. 3d 36 (Ontario Surr. Ct. 1969), 1.8
Wyche v. United States, 36 A.F.T.R.2d 75-5816 (Ct. Cl. 1971), 10.40.1
Wycoff, Estate of, v. Commissioner, 506 F.2d 1144 (10th Cir. 1974), *cert. denied,* 421 U.S. 1000 (1975), 5.22.1

Wyly, Charles J., Estate of, 69 T.C. 227 (1977), *rev'd,* 610 F.2d 1282 (5th Cir. 1980), 6.39
Wyss, In re Estate of, 297 P. 100 (Cal. App. 1931), 9.27

Yee Hop, Chon Quan, In re Estate of, 469 P.2d 183 (Hawaii, 1970), 10.48
Youle, George W., Estate of, 56 T.C.M. 1594 (1989), 8.15.2

Zander v. Holly, 84 N.W.2d 87 (1957), 3.2
Zmuda v. Commissioner, 79 T.C. 714 (1982), *aff'd,* 731 F.2d 1417 (9th Cir. 1984), 10.3
Zuckman v. United States, 524 F.2d 729 (Ct. Cl. 1975), 11.38.3

Table of Internal Revenue Code Sections

(references are to sections)

1(a) 12.3.2
1(e) 10.18
1(g) 7.91
1(g)(3)(c) 7.9.2
1(g)(7) 7.9.1
1(i) 2.42
2(a) 12.3.2
47(a) (former) 3.20, 7.17, 9.19
47(b) (former) 7.17
47(e) 3.20
55(b)(1) 8.10.1
55(d)(1)(A) 8.10.1
56 8.10.1
56(a) 9.6.2
56(a)(6) 9.6.2
56(g)(4)(B)(ii) 11.9
57 8.10.1
57(a) 8.10.1
57(a)(6) 8.10.1
58 8.10.1
63 10.4.3
63(b) 8.1
63(c) 10.4.5
63(c)(5) 7.9.1
67 1.20, 1.24, 10.4.6, 10.15, 12.3.6, 12.7.1, 12.10, 12.13.1, 12.13.3, 12.13.5, 12.36, 12.50
67(a) 12.3.6
67(b) 12.3.6, 12.10
67(b)(8) 12.3.7
67(e) 10.4.6, 12.3.6, 12.13.1, 12.13.3
67(e)(1) 10.4
71 6.55.1, 10.31
72 6.49, 6.50, 6.54, 6.59.1, 6.61, 6.66, 6.78.10, 8.37, 9.13
72(b) 6.64, 6.78.10, 9.13
72(b)(2) 9.13
72(d) 6.78.10

72(e) 6.74
72(e)(1) 6.61
72(e)(1)(B) 6.59.1
72(e)(2)(B) 6.49, 6.50, 6.59.2, 6.75
72(e)(3)(A) 6.74
72(e)(4)(A) 6.50, 6.59.2, 6.74
72(e)(4)(B) 6.50, 6.61
72(e)(5) 6.49, 6.66
72(e)(5)(E) 6.64
72(e)(6) 6.59.2
72(e)(10)(A) 6.74
72(h) 6.64
72(m)(3) 6.54, 6.57
72(m)(3)(B) 6.54
72(m)(3)(C) 6.51, 6.54
72(v) 6.50
79 6.28, 6.28.2, 6.56, 6.72, 6.72.1, 6.72.2, 6.72.6, 6.72.13
79(a)(1) 6.72, 6.72.3
79(b)(1) 6.72
79(b)(2) 6.72
79(c) 6.72.9
79(c) (former) 6.72.9
79(d)(1) 6.72.3
79(d)(2) 6.72.3
79(d)(3)(B) 6.72.4
83 6.72.13
83(e)(5) 6.72.13
89 6.72.5
91(c) 12.15.3
101(a) 10.4.8, 10.4.9, 11.12
101(a)(2) 6.2, 11.12, 11.9
101(a)(2)(A) 11.9
101(a)(2)(B) 11.2
101(d) 12.27, 12.50
102 3.20.9, 3.35.2, 3.35.3, 6.78.9, 10.4.4, 12.37
102(a) 12.29.2
102(c) 6.78.9
103 10.4.8, 10.4.9
121 7.23, 9.43.3
151 7.9.1
162 1.24, 6.56, 6.72
162(a) 6.56, 11.8
162(a)(3) 9.20, 9.20.2
163 6.55.3, 6.60, 12.10
163(h) 6.59.1, 6.59.3, 6.73, 9.3, 9.6, 9.14
163(h)(5) 6.60
164 2.30.2, 12.10
164(a) 2.23.3
164(b)(4) 2.23.3, 2.30.2
165 8.8
165(a) 12.10
165(c)(1) 8.8
165(c)(2) 6.64, 8.8
167 9.32
167(d) 9.41.3
167(e) 9.23, 9.31, 9.32, 9.36, 9.41.3
167(e)(1) 9.42.3
167(e)(3) 9.42.3
167(h) 9.18, 10.47.3
167(h)(5) 6.60.1
167(r) 6.24.1
167(r)(3) 9.42.3
168(g)(2) 9.14.1
168(g)(7) 9.14.1
170 5.24, 6.55.2, 6.72, 8.1, 8.4.1, 8.13, 8.15.4, 8.28, 8.31, 8.33, 8.36, 8.37, 12.10
170(a) 8.1
170(a)(3) 8.13
170(b)(1) 8.5
170(b)(1)(A) 8.2.1, 8.3, 8.4, 8.4.1
170(b)(1)(A)(ii) 2.6
170(b)(1)(B) 8.4, 8.5
170(b)(1)(C) 8.10
170(b)(1)(C)(i) 8.10
170(b)(1)(C)(iii) 8.10.1, 8.11, 8.36
170(b)(1)(C)(iv) 8.10
170(b)(1)(D) 8.10
170(b)(1)(D)(ii) 8.5
170(b)(1)(E) 8.3
170(b)(1)(F) 8.2.1
170(c) 8.2, 8.2.2, 8.33
170(c)(2) 8.1, 8.3
170(c)(2)(A) 8.1
170(d) 8.4
170(d)(1) 8.5, 8.10
170(d)(1)(D)(i) 8.10

170(e)	8.9, 8.10, 8.11	267	2.4, 3.35.2, 5.37.2, 7.14, 9.12, 10.4.12, 10.13, 12.38, 12.39, 12.39.2
170(e)(1)	8.10, 8.11, 8.36	267(a)	9.41.3
170(e)(1)(A)	8.9, 11.34.3	267(b)	8.13, 9.7.1, 9.31, 10.4.7
170(e)(1)(B)	8.13	267(b)(5)	10.4.12
170(e)(1)(B)(i)	8.12	267(b)(6)	10.4.12
170(e)(1)(B)(ii)	8.12	267(b)(7)	10.4.12
170(e)(5)	8.10	267(c)(4)	9.6.6, 9.31, 11.26.1, 11.29.1
170(f)(2)(A)	8.19	267(d)	10.4.12
170(f)(2)(B)	8.19, 8.31, 10.33.2	267(e)	9.31
170(f)(3)(A)	8.17	273	9.31, 9.32
170(f)(3)(B)(i)	8.15	280A(d)(1)	9.43.3
170(f)(3)(B)(ii)	8.16	301	11.11, 11.24.1
170(f)(3)(B)(iii)	8.16.1	302(b)	9.8.2, 11.9, 11.16, 11.24
170(f)(4)	8.15.4	302(b)(1)	11.24, 11.24.1
170(f)(5)	8.35	302(b)(2)	11.24, 11.24.1, 11.24.2
170(g)	8.4.2	302(b)(3)	11.9, 11.24, 11.24.1, 11.24.3, 11.34.3
170(h)	8.16.1	302(b)(4)	11.24.1
170(h)(1)	8.16.1	302(c)(1)	11.24.1
170(h)(2)	8.16.1	302(c)(2)	11.24.1, 11.24.3
170(h)(4)(A)	8.16.1	302(c)(2)(A)	11.24.3
170(i)	8.1	302(c)(2)(A)(i)	11.24.3
170(j)	8.4.2	302(c)(2)(A)(ii)	11.24.3
170(k)	8.4.2	302(c)(2)(A)(iii)	11.24.3
172	8.2.1	302(c)(2)(C)	11.24.3
212	1.24, 9.32, 10.3, 10.4.3, 10.13	303	2.16, 2.36.4, 4.27.4, 6.4, 6.20, 6.24.3, 7.7, 7.10, 7.16, 10.4.15, 10.15, 10.44, 11.1, 11.9, 11.10, 11.11, 11.12, 11.12.3, 11.14, 11.15, 11.16, 11.19, 11.21, 11.23, 11.24, 11.24.3, 11.25, 11.29.2,
212(1)	1.24		
212(2)	1.24, 10.15		
212(3)	1.24		
213	2.6, 12.3.4		
213(a)	12.3.4		
213(c)(1)	12.3.4		
213(c)(2)	12.3.4		
213(d)(1)	12.50		
215	6.55.1		
262	1.24		
263	1.24		
264	6.60, 6.60.2		
264(a)	6.71.2, 6.72, 6.73, 11.12		
264(a)(1)	6.56, 6.71.1		
264(a)(2)	6.60.2		
264(a)(3)	6.60.2, 6.60.3		
264(a)(4)	6.60, 6.71		
264(c)	6.60.3		
264(c)(1)	6.60.3, 6.73		
264(c)(2)	6.60.3		
264(c)(3)	6.60.3		
264(c)(4)	6.60.3		
265	9.32, 10.4.3, 10.15, 12.11		
265(1)	6.55		

	11.34.4, 12.15, 12.19.16, 12.21, 12.50
303(a)	7.10, 11.16, 11.19
303(a)(1)	11.23
303(a)(2)	11.23
303(b)	11.16
303(b)(1)	11.16, 11.20, 11.23
303(b)(1)(A)	11.20
303(b)(1)(B)	11.20
303(b)(1)(C)	11.20
303(b)(2)	11.23
303(b)(2)(A)	7.10, 10.4.15, 11.17
303(b)(2)(A)(ii)	11.17
303(b)(2)(B)	7.10, 11.18, 11.22
303(b)(3)	10.4.15, 11.16, 11.22
303(b)(4)	11.16, 11.20
303(c)	11.16
303(d)	11.16
305	11.34.3, 11.34.4
305(a)	11.16, 11.34.4
305(b)	11.34.4, 11.35.2
305(b)(1)	11.34.4
305(b)(2)	11.34.4
305(b)(4)	11.34.4, 11.34.5
305(c)	11.34.4, 11.34.5, 11.35.2
306	8.9, 11.34.3
306(b)	11.34.3
306(b)(1)(A)	11.34.3
306(c)(1)(A)	11.34.3
306(c)(1)(B)	11.34.3
303(c)(4)	11.34.3
307(a)	11.16
311	11.21
311(b)	11.3, 11.4.4, 11.10, 11.12.2, 11.9
312(a)	11.9
312(n)(7)	11.9
316(a)	11.9
318	2.17.1, 6.72.3, 10.6.1, 10.38.3, 11.11, 11.24.2, 11.34.3
318(a)	9.7.1, 11.24.2, 11.24.3
318(a)(1)	11.24.1, 11.24.3, 11.24.4
318(a)(2)	11.24.4
318(a)(3)	11.24.1, 11.24.4
318(a)(4)	11.24.1
318(a)(5)	11.24.4
318(a)(5)(B)	11.24.1, 11.24.4
318(a)(5)(C)	11.24.1, 11.24.4
318(a)(5)(D)	11.24.1
331	11.29
341	8.9
351	11.3
354	12.15.6
354(a)	11.34.2
355	12.15.6
356(a)(1)	11.34.2
356(a)(2)	11.34.2
368	11.16
368(a)	11.34.3, 12.15.6
368(a)(1)(E)	11.34, 11.34.1, 11.35, 11.35.2
401	5.37.3
401(g)	6.65.3
401(k)	5.25.2
402(a)(2)	12.25.3
402(a)(5)(D)	12.25.2
402(a)(7)	12.25.2, 12.50
402(e)(1)(B)	12.25.4
402(e)(4)	12.25.3, 12.25.4
402(e)(4)(A)	12.26.2
403(b)	6.65.3
408(d)(3)	12.25.2
408(m)	12.25.2
419	6.72.13
419A(c)	6.72.13
419A(e)	6.72.13
419A(e)(1)	6.72.13
441	12.7
441(b)	12.7, 12.50
441(c)(1)	7.37.2
443(a)(1)	12.3.1
443(a)(2)	12.3, 12.7
453	9.3, 9.7.1
453(b)	9.3
453(b)(1)	9.3
453(b)(1)	9.6
453(c)	9.6
453(e)	9.3, 9.7, 9.13
453(e)(5)	9.7
453(e)(6)(A)	9.7.2

453(e)(6)(B) 9.7.3
453(e)(6)(C) 9.7.2
453(e)(7) 9.7.2
453(f)(1) 9.7.1
453(f)(2) 9.7.4
453(f)(3) 9.6.1
453(f)(4) 9.4
453(f)(4)(A) 9.6.1
453(f)(4)(B) 9.6.1
453(g)(1) 9.6
453(i) 9.6
453(j) 9.3
453(k)(2) 9.6, 9.7.4
453B 3.20, 3.35.3, 7.17, 9.6.3, 10.13, 10.15, 11.29.1
453B(a) 9.6.3
453B(c) 9.6.4
453B(f) 9.3, 9.6.3
453B(f)(1) 9.6.3
453B(f)(2) 9.6.3
453B(g) 3.20, 9.6.3
454 7.30, 12.3.7, 12.50
454(a) 7.30.1, 12.3.7
469 10.4.7, 12.3.5, 12.12
469(a) 10.4.7
469(b) 10.4.7
469(c)(1) 10.4.7
469(c)(2) 10.4.7
469(c)(3) 10.4.7
469(d)(1) 10.4.7
469(g)(1) 10.4.7, 12.3.5
469(g)(2) 10.4.7, 12.3.5
469(g)(3) 10.4.7
469(h)(1) 10.4.7
469(h)(2) 10.4.7
469(i) 10.4.7, 12.12
469(i)(4) 10.4.7
469(j)(12) 10.4.7
483 9.4, 9.6.5, 11.12.1
483(c)(1)(A) 9.6.5
483(e) 9.6.5, 9.6.6
501(c) 8.12, 8.13
501(c)(3) 6.59.1
505(b) 6.72.13
508(e) 8.26
509(a)(1) 8.2.1, 8.3
509(a)(2) 8.2.1, 8.3
509(a)(3) 8.2.1, 8.3
514(c)(2)(A) 8.24
531-537 11.38.2
531 11.12.3, 12.6
532(a) 11.12.3
535(c)(2) 11.12.3
537 11.12, 11.22
537(b)(1) 11.12.3
541-547 11.38.2
642(b) 4.6, 10.4.3, 10.4.5, 10.4.6, 12.7, 12.13.1
642(c) 8.31, 8.33, 10.4.3, 12.3.6, 12.10
642(c)(1) 8.33, 10.4
642(c)(2) 10.4
642(c)(5) 8.30
642(c)(5)(C) 8.30
642(c)(5)(E) 8.30
642(e)(3) 4.17.3
642(g) 5.33, 12.13, 12.13.2, 12.50
642(h) 12.7.1, 12.13.5, 12.36, 12.50
643 10.4.3, 12.36.2
643(a) 10.4.3, 10.4.4
643(a)(1) 10.4.3
643(a)(2) 10.4.3
643(a)(3) 9.32, 10.4.3, 10.19
643(a)(4) 10.4.3
643(a)(5) 10.4.3
643(e) 5.21, 12.1, 12.36.7, 12.38
643(e)(3)(B) 12.38
643(e)(4) 12.38
643(f) 10.4.10
643(g) 12.6
644 7.9.2, 7.25.1, 7.28, 7.34.3, 7.36.6, 7.37.10, 8.24, 8.31, 10.4.11, 10.19, 10.32.5, 10.44
644(a)(1) 10.4.11
644(a)(2) 10.4.11
644(c) 7.25.1, 10.4.11
644(d) 10.4.11
644(e) 10.4.11
644(f) 10.4.11

645	10.4.6
645(a)	12.7
651	10.4.4, 10.4.6, 10.4.8, 12.3.6, 12.13.1
651(a)	10.4.4, 10.4.8
652	10.4.4, 10.4.8
652(a)	10.4.4, 10.4.8
652(b)	10.4.4
661	10.4.4, 10.4.6, 10.4.9, 12.3.6, 12.6, 12.10, 12.13.1, 12.29.2, 12.36.5, 12.37, 12.37.2, 12.38
661(a)	10.4.4, 10.4.9, 12.36.1
661(b)	10.4.9
662	10.4.4, 10.4.9, 12.29.2, 12.36.5, 12.37, 12.37.2, 12.38
662(a)	10.4.4, 12.36.3
662(a)(1)	12.36.3
662(b)	10.4.4, 10.4.9, 12.36.1
662(c)	12.7
663	4.20, 12.37
663(a)	10.4.4, 12.36.4, 12.38
663(a)(1)	4.17.2, 12.37, 12.37.2
663(b)	10.4.10, 10.4.16
663(c)	10.4.9
664	4.16.1, 5.18, 8.24, 8.27
664(b)	10.4.16
664(b)(1)	8.24
664(b)(2)	8.24
664(b)(3)	8.24
664(b)(4)	8.24
664(c)	8.24, 8.28
664(d)	8.20
664(d)(1)	8.4.1, 8.20, 8.21
664(d)(1)(A)	8.21
664(d)(1)(B)	8.24
664(d)(2)	8.20
664(d)(2)(B)	8.24
664(d)(3)	8.22
664(f)	8.20
664(f)(2)	8.20
664(f)(3)	8.20
665	2.42, 5.21, 10.4.10, 10.4.16, 10.13, 10.32.4, 12.36, 12.37.1
665(a)	10.4.10
665(b)	10.4.10, 10.19, 10.20.1
665(b)	4.21.5, 7.28, 7.36.6
666	2.30.2, 2.42, 5.21, 8.31, 10.4.10, 10.4.16, 10.13, 10.32.4, 12.36, 12.37.1
666(e)	10.4.10
667	2.42, 5.21, 8.31, 10.4.10, 10.4.16, 10.13, 10.32.4, 12.36, 12.37.1
667(b)(1)	10.4.10
667(b)(3)	10.4.10
667(b)(4)	10.4.10
667(b)(5)	10.4.10
667(c)	10.4.10
667(c)(2)	10.4.10
668	2.42, 10.4.16, 10.32.4
671	6.28, 6.60.1, 7.17, 7.36.3, 7.37.10, 7.38.2, 9.20.5, 10.1, 10.3, 10.4.1, 10.4.2, 10.4.14, 10.15, 10.24.1, 10.27.1, 10.31, 10.32.4,

	10.33.2, 10.44
672	6.28, 6.60.1, 7.17, 7.36.6, 7.37.10, 7.38.2, 9.20.5, 10.1, 10.3, 10.4.1, 10.4.2, 10.4.14, 10.15, 10.24.1, 10.27.1, 10.31, 10.44, 11.40.2
672(a)	10.31.1
672(c)	10.20.3
672(e)	9.40, 10.31
672(f)	10.32
673	2.42.2, 6.28, 6.60.1, 7.17, 7.36.6, 7.37.10, 7.38.2, 7.39, 9.1, 9.17, 9.20.5, 10.1, 10.3, 10.4.1, 10.4.2, 10.4.14, 10.15, 10.24.1, 10.27.1, 10.31, 10.36, 10.36.1, 10.37.1, 10.39.1, 10.40.1, 10.44
673(a)	2.42.1, 8.33, 9.20.5, 10.1
673(b)	10.36.1
673(d)	10.36.1
674	6.28, 6.60.1, 7.17, 7.32, 7.36.6, 7.37.10, 7.38.2, 9.20.5, 10.1, 10.3, 10.4.1, 10.4.2, 10.4.14, 10.15, 10.20.5, 10.24.1, 10.27.1, 10.31, 10.31.1, 10.37, 10.44
674(a)	10.37.1
674(b)	10.27, 10.37.1, 10.37.2, 10.41.4
674(b)(1)	10.37, 10.41.4
674(b)(2)	10.37.1
674(b)(3)	10.37.1
674(b)(4)	8.33, 10.37.1
674(b)(5)	6.27.3, 7.36.6, 10.37.1
674(b)(6)	7.36.6, 10.20.4, 10.37.1
674(b)(7)	7.36.6, 10.20.4, 10.37.1
674(b)(8)	10.37.1
674(c)	10.20.3-10.20.5, 10.37.1
674(d)	10.20.4, 10.37.1
675	6.28, 6.60.1, 7.17, 7.36.6, 7.37.10, 7.38.2, 9.20.5, 10.1, 10.3, 10.4.1, 10.4.2, 10.4.14, 10.15, 10.24.1, 10.27.1, 10.31, 10.38.1, 10.44
675(1)	10.38.1
675(2)	10.38.1
675(3)	10.32.1, 10.32.8, 10.38.1
675(4)	10.4.14, 10.38.1
675(4)(c)	7.21, 10.32, 10.32.1
676	6.18.3, 6.28, 6.60.1, 7.4, 7.17, 7.36.6, 7.37,10, 7.38.2, 9.20.5, 10.1, 10.3, 10.4.1, 10.4.2, 10.4.14, 10.15, 10.24.1,

	10.27.1, 10.31, 10.31.1, 10.44, 12.3.7
676(a)	10.7, 10.39.1
676(b)	10.39.1
677	6.18.3, 6.28, 6.60.1, 7.17, 7.25.1, 7.26, 7.34.3, 7.36.6, 7.37.10, 7.38.2, 9.20.5, 10.1, 10.3, 10.4.1, 10.4.2, 10.4.14, 10.15, 10.24.1, 10.27.1, 10.31, 10.44
677(a)	6.23.5, 6.60.1, 9.10.1, 9.20.5, 10.31.1, 10.32.1, 10.33, 10.40.1
677(a)(2)	9.6.3
677(a)(3)	6.58, 6.79
677(b)	7.38.2, 10.27.1, 10.37.1, 10.40.1, 10.41.7
678	5.22.3, 6.28, 7.37.4, 7.37.8, 7.37.10, 10.4.2, 10.4.14, 10.20.2, 10.20.6, 10.22, 10.23, 10.25, 10.27.1, 10.28, 10.31, 10.43.5
678(a)	10.4.2, 10.24.1, 10.27.1, 10.31.1, 10.31.2
678(a)(1)	6.22.3, 7.37.10, 10.24.1
678(a)(2)	10.24.1
678(b)	7.37.10, 10.27.1
678(c)	10.27.1, 10.41.7
679	9.10.1
682	10.31
691	6.78.9, 7.30
691(a)	6.78, 9.6.4, 12.38
691(a)(1)(B)	9.6.4
691(a)(2)	5.37.6
691(a)(4)	9.6.4
691(a)(5)	4.16.4, 9.3, 9.6.4, 12.50
691(b)	8.11
691(b)(1)(A)	12.10
691(b)(1)(B)	12.10
691(c)	5.37.6, 6.78, 6.78.10, 9.6.4, 12.3.7, 12.25.4
701	11.38.2
704	11.5
704(e)	11.38.2, 11.40, 11.40.3
704(e)(1)	11.38.5, 11.40
704(e)(2)	11.40.3
704(e)(3)	11.40.3
706(c)(1)	11.8
707(c)	11.41.2
707(b)	8.13
707(b)(1)	10.4.7
707(b)(2)	9.6
721	11.39
722	11.39
723	11.39
732	12.5.2
732(b)	12.5
732(d)	12.5.2
732(d)(4)	12.5
736	11.8
736(a)	11.8
736(b)	11.8
741	11.8
742	11.8, 12.5
743(a)	12.5
751(a)	11.8
754	11.39, 12.5, 12.5.1-12.5.3, 12.50
873(b)(2)	8.1
1001(a)	8.8
1001(c)	8.8
1001(e)	6.24.1, 9.25, 9.31, 9.31.1, 9.36, 9.37, 9.39
1011(b)	7.27, 8.36, 9.13

1012	3.20.3, 7.27
1014	5.9, 5.23, 5.31, 5.37.3, 7.8.2, 7.12, 7.14, 7.23, 9.3, 9.31, 9.31.1, 9.36, 9.37, 11.9, 11.34.3, 11.39
1014(a)	2.35, 11.16
1014(b)(6)	9.31.2
1014(b)(10)	5.23
1014(c)	9.6.4
1014(e)	5.9, 5.31
1015	2.4, 2.35, 3.20.3, 6.22.5, 7.8.2, 7.23, 7.25.1, 7.27, 9.13, 9.19, 9.31, 9.37, 12.21
1015(a)	3.35.4, 7.9.2, 7.14, 10.32.5
1015(d)	7.12
1015(d)(6)	2.35, 3.20.3, 7.8.2, 7.12, 7.14, 7.25.1
1016	1.31.1
1016(c)	12.19.3
1016(c)(5)(B)	12.19.3
1031	11.39, 12.36.7
1031(b)	6.66
1031(c)	6.66
1031(d)	6.66
1033	9.43.3, 10.32.7
1033(a)(2)(B)(1)	12.19.11
1034	9.43.3, 10.32.7
1035	6.59.1, 6.62, 6.65, 6.65.2, 6.65.3, 6.65, 6.66, 6.68
1035(d)	6.65
1036	3.20
1040	5.37.2
1040(a)	5.37.2, 12.19.5
1040(c)	5.37.2
1041	3.20, 3.35.1, 3.35.2, 3.35.3, 6.53.2, 9.6.3, 9.19, 9.31, 9.37, 12.39.2
1041(a)	3.34.3, 3.35.1, 12.39.2
1041(b)	3.35.1
1041(d)	3.35.1
1042	10.32.9
1122(b)(3)	12.25.3
1211	11.2
1211(b)(1)	12.3.2
1221	9.6.2
1222	6.64
1223	7.9.2, 7.25.1, 7.27, 12.15, 12.38, 12.39
1231(b)	8.10
1239	9.6, 9.19
1239(b)	9.6
1244	10.4.13, 10.13, 10.15, 10.44, 11.2, 11.36
1244(c)(1)	11.36
1245	3.20, 7.17, 9.17, 9.19, 10.13, 11.21
1245(a)	9.19
1245(b)(1)	7.17
1250	3.20, 7.17, 9.17, 9.19, 10.13, 11.21
1251(d)(1)	7.17
1271	11.12.1
1272	9.6.5, 11.12.1
1273	9.6.5, 11.12.1
1273(a)(3)	11.34.5
1274	9.6.5, 9.19, 11.12.1
1274(c)(3)	9.6.5
1274(d)	9.6.5
1274(e)	9.19
1274A	9.6.5
1274A(a)	9.19
1274A(b)	9.6.5
1275	9.6.5, 11.12.1
1361	12.4
1361(b)(1)	7.17
1361(b)(1)(A)	12.4
1361(b)(1)(B)	11.4
1361(b)(1)(D)	12.4
1361(c)	10.4.14, 10.15
1361(c)(1)	11.4
1361(c)(2)	10.4.14, 10.44, 12.4
1361(c)(2)(A)	10.4.14
1361(c)(2)(A)(i)	9.43.3, 10.15, 10.32.2
1361(c)(2)(A)(ii)	11.4
1361(c)(2)(A)(iii)	11.4

1361(c)(4) 11.4.1
1361(c)(5) 11.4.1
1361(d) 10.32.2, 10.44, 11.4, 11.4.2
1362 12.4
1362(a) 11.4.2, 11.4.4
1362(a)(2) 12.4
1362(b) 11.4.2
1362(d)(1) 11.4.3, 12.4, 12.50
1362(d)(2) 11.4.3
1362(d)(3) 11.4.3
1363 12.4
1364 12.4
1365 12.4
1366 11.4.4, 12.4
1366(b) 11.4, 11.4.2
1366(d) 11.4.4
1367 12.4
1367(a) 11.4.4
1367(a)(1) 11.4.4
1367(a)(2)(A) 11.4.4
1368 11.8, 11.10, 12.4
1368(b) 11.10
1368(b)(2) 11.4.4
1368(c) 11.10
1368(e)(1)(B) 11.10
1371(a) 11.4.4
1371(a)(4) 11.36
1371(c)(2) 11.10
1372 11.3
1372(e)(1)(A) (former) 12.4
1377(a)(2) 11.10
1433(b)(3) 2.39
1491 9.10.1
2001 5.7
2001(a) 2.11
2001(b) 2.11, 2.15, 2.19.1, 3.18, 3.21, 8.13, 12.24.4
2001(b)(2) 2.3, 12.24.4
2001(b)(2)(D) 2.24
2001(c) 2.2, 2.3, 2.11, 5.3
2001(c)(3) 2.3, 5.5, 5.7, 5.8
2001(e) 12.24.4
2002 4.27.1, 12.42
2010 2.15
2010(a) 2.3
2011 2.3, 2.11, 2.15, 5.25.2, 5.34.1, 7.11
2012 2.11, 2.15
2013 2.3, 2.11, 2.15, 3.17, 4.15.4, 5.5, 5.7, 5.19, 5.20, 5.22.3, 5.25.2, 10.20
2013(d)(3) 2.15
2014 2.3, 2.11, 2.15, 5.25.2
2015 2.15
2016 2.15
2031 2.12, 2.13, 6.28.1
2031(a) 2.13
2031(b)(1) 12.19.4
2032 2.12, 2.13, 2.29, 3.35.4, 5.25.2, 5.33, 10.6.5, 10.17, 10.44, 12.15, 12.15.3, 12.15.6, 12.15.7, 12.21, 12.26.5, 12.50
2032(a) 12.15
2032(a)(3) 12.15.3
2032(c) 2.13, 12.15.1
2032(d) 12.15.5
2032A 2.12, 2.13, 2.16, 2.29, 5.25.2, 5.29, 5.33, 5.37.2, 6.4, 6.20, 6.24.2, 7.7, 7.10, 7.16, 11.16, 11.25, 12.15, 12.19, 12.19.4, 12.19.5, 12.19.6, 12.19.8, 12.19.15, 12.35, 12.50
2032A(a)(1)(a) 12.19, 12.19.4
2032A(a)(2) 7.10
2032A(b)(1) 7.10, 12.19, 12.19.4
2032A(b)(1)(A) 12.19
2032A(b)(1)(B) 12.19.4
2032A(b)(1)(C) 12.19.6

2032A(b)(5) 12.19.9
2032A(c)(1) 12.19.9
2032A(c)(5) 12.19.12
2032A(c)(6) 12.19.9
2032A(c)(7)(A) 12.19.9
2032A(d) 12.19.1
2032A(d)(3) 12.19.1
2032A(e)(1) 12.19.4
2032A(e)(2) 12.19.4
2032A(e)(7)(A) 12.19.8
2032A(e)(7)(B) 12.19.8
2032A(e)(8) 12.19.8
2032A(e)(10) 12.19, 12.19.3
2032A(e)(11) 12.19.12
2032A(g) 12.19.6
2032A(h) 12.19.11
2032A(h)(2)(A) 12.19.11
2032A(h)(3)(B) 12.19.11
2032A(i) 12.19.11
2033 2.11, 2.12, 3.8, 3.17, 3.33, 5.16, 6.15.1, 6.78.2, 6.80, 7.11, 7.29.2, 7.30.1, 7.32, 9.5, 9.22, 10.17, 10.35, 10.36, 10.36.3, 12.15.3, 12.25
2034 2.11, 2.12
2035 2.7, 2.11, 2.12, 2.16, 2.17.1, 2.20.2, 2.43, 3.17, 6.23.1, 6.23.6, 6.25, 6.30, 6.31, 6.32, 6.34, 6.36, 6.37, 6.37.1, 6.38, 6.72.11, 6.78.3, 6.78.4, 7.8, 7.16, 7.29.2, 8.39, 9.8.1, 9.22.2, 10.6, 12.24.4
2035(b) 7.8
2035(c) 2.16, 7.8, 7.8.1, 7.11, 12.24.4
2035(d)(1) 7.25.3
2035(d)(2) 2.16, 6.23.1, 6.72.11, 7.8, 7.25.3, 7.37, 9.42.2, 10.16, 10.17, 10.34.1, 10.34.3, 10.41.11, 11.35.2
2035(d)(3) 2.16, 5.29, 11.16, 11.23
2035(d)(3)(B) 12.19.4
2035(d)(4) 11.16
2035(d)(5) 11.30
2035 (former) 6.31.2, 6.36
2036 2.11, 2.12, 2.17, 2.20, 2.20.2, 2.20.3, 2.44, 3.18, 3.28.3, 4.27.3, 5.29, 6.22.4, 6.23.1, 6.23.5, 6.23.6, 6.24.1, 6.26.7, 6.37, 6.39, 6.78.3, 6.78.5, 7.23, 7.25.3, 7.29.2, 7.32, 7.34.2, 7.36.5, 7.37, 8.13, 9.1, 9.8.1, 9.16, 9.22.1, 9.22.2, 9.34, 9.35, 10.6, 10.17, 10.20.5, 10.21.2, 10.27.2, 10.31.2, 10.34, 10.35, 10.35.1, 10.37.3, 10.38.3, 10.41.2, 10.41.6, 10.41.9, 10.41.11, 11.38.3, 11.38.4, 11.41.2, 12.27, 12.42.5
2036(a) 2.17, 2.27.1,

	5.23.6, 6.28, 7.36.5, 9.10.1, 9.22, 9.34, 9.41, 9.41.2, 9.42.2, 9.43, 9.43.2, 10.37, 10.40, 11.5
2036(a)(1)	6.23.5, 6.26, 6.29, 6.39, 6.78.5, 9.34, 10.6, 10.40.3, 11.38.3, 11.41.2
2036(a)(2)	2.17, 6.27.3, 6.78.5, 7.36.5, 10.17, 10.35.1, 10.37.3, 10.43.3, 10.43.6, 11.38.3, 11.40.4, 11.41.3
2036(b)	2.17.1, 6.28, 10.6.1, 10.38.3, 10.41.8, 11.4.1, 11.35.2
2036(b)(2)	2.17.1, 10.6.1, 10.38.3
2036(b)(3)	2.17.1
2036(c)	2.12, 2.13, 2.17.2, 2.44, 10.38.3
2037	2.11, 2.12, 2.20.2, 2.20.3, 6.23.1, 6.37.1, 6.78.3, 6.78.6, 9.8.1, 9.22.2, 10.6, 10.35.2, 10.36, 10.36.3, 11.38.4
2037(a)	6.78.6
2037(b)(1)	6.78.6
2038	2.7, 2.11, 2.12, 2.17, 2.20, 2.20.2, 2.20.3, 2.38, 4.24.1, 6.23.1, 6.23.5, 6.24.3, 6.27.2, 6.28.1, 6.37.1, 6.78.3-6.78.5, 6.78.7, 6.79, 7.4, 7.25.3, 7.32, 7.34.2, 7.37, 9.8.1, 9.22.1, 9.22.2, 10.6, 10.8, 10.17, 10.20.5, 10.21.2, 10.31.2, 10.34, 10.35, 10.35.1, 10.35.2, 10.37, 10.37.3, 10.39.3, 10.41.5, 10.41.9, 11.38.3, 11.38.4, 11.40.4, 11.41.3
2038(a)	10.35.2
2038(a)(1)	2.17, 6.27.3, 6.37, 6.78.7, 7.36.5, 10.17, 10.26, 10.35.3, 10.37.3, 10.39.3, 10.41.11, 10.43.3, 10.43.6
2039	2.11, 2.12, 2.18, 5.23.5, 5.23.7, 6.78.1, 8.37, 9.16, 10.6, 10.6.2, 12.25
2039(a)	6.78.1, 9.16, 10.6.2, 12.25
2039(b)	10.6.2, 12.25
2039(c) (former)	6.26, 12.25
2040	2.11, 2.12, 2.19, 3.16, 3.17, 3.18, 3.20.3,

	3.20.7, 6.28, 7.30.2, 7.33.1
2040(a)	2.19.1, 3.8, 3.14.2, 3.15, 3.15.1, 3.18, 3.20.3
2040(b)	2.19.2, 3.8, 3.15.1, 3.15.2, 3.16, 3.17, 3.18, 7.30.3, 7.33.1, 11.25
2040(c)	2.19.2
2040(d)	2.19.2
2040(e)	2.19.2
2040(b) (former)	3.14.2
2040(c) (former)	2.19.2, 3.16
2040(d) (former)	2.19.2, 3.16
2041	2.2, 2.11, 2.12, 2.20, 2.20.1, 2.40.5, 4.24.1, 4.35.4, 5.16, 5.22, 5.22.3, 5.23.3, 6.23.4, 6.23.5, 6.24.1, 6.26, 7.32, 7.34.2, 7.36.3-7.36.5, 7.37.4, 7.37.8, 7.38.2, 9.34, 10.6, 10.6.3, 10.20.6, 10.22, 10.26, 10.28, 10.38.3, 10.41.1, 10.41.4-10.41.6, 10.41.9, 10.43.4, 12.42
2041(a)	4.21.1
2041(a)(1)	2.20.1
2041(a)(2)	2.20.2, 7.36.5, 10.6.3, 10.24, 10.27.3, 10.41.11
2041(a)(3)	2.31, 2.40.8
2041(b)	10.20.2, 10.26
2041(b)(1)	2.20, 2.31, 5.7.2, 10.22, 10.23, 10.26
2041(b)(1)(A)	2.20.1, 5.7.2, 10.25, 10.27.3, 10.43.4
2041(b)(1)(B)	5.23.3
2041(b)(1)(C)	2.20.1, 10.31.2
2041(b)(1)(C)(i)	10.26
2041(b)(1)(C)(ii)	10.26, 10.41.4
2041(b)(1)(C)(iv)	10.31.2
2041(b)(2)	2.20.3, 5.7.2, 5.22.3, 5.23.3, 7.37.2, 7.37.4, 7.37.6, 7.37.11, 10.24, 10.24.2, 10.43.4
2042	2.2, 2.11, 2.12, 2.16, 2.38, 10.6, 10.6.4, 10.36, 10.41.1, 10.41.5, 10.41.8, 11.22
2042(1)	2.21, 8.39, 10.6.4
2042(2)	2.21, 5.13, 6.39, 10.6.4, 10.36.3
2043	2.11, 2.12, 11.35.2
2043(a)	6.24.1, 6.39.1, 9.8.1, 9.16, 9.22.2, 9.28, 9.30.1, 9.30.2, 9.34, 9.36, 9.41, 9.41.2
2043(b)	6.27.10
2044	1.32, 2.9.2, 2.11, 2.12, 2.26, 2.27.3, 2.36.1, 2.40.1, 3.27, 4.16.1, 4.21.2, 4.27, 4.27.2, 5.3.2, 5.7.2, 5.23.3,

Section	Paragraph
	5.23.4, 5.23.7, 5.23.8, 5.23.11, 6.23.5, 8.13, 8.19, 8.34, 9.28, 9.34, 9.35, 12.20.4, 12.22, 12.32.4, 12.42.4
2044(a)	4.16.1
2044(b)	4.16.1
2044(c)	5.23.7
2045	7.34.2
2046	2.12, 3.19, 5.16.2
2053	1.25, 2.11, 2.14, 3.33.1, 3.33.2, 5.2.2, 5.13, 5.34.2, 6.27.10, 10.4.15, 10.6.6, 11.9, 11.11, 11.15-11.19, 11.23, 11.25, 11.26.4, 11.28, 11.30, 12.3.4, 12.11, 12.13, 12.13.6, 12.24.4, 12.24.5, 12.30, 12.47, 12.50
2053(a)	10.6.6
2053(a)(2)	11.28, 12.12, 12.13
2053(a)(3)	6.27.10, 12.10
2053(a)(4)	6.27.10
2053(b)	10.6.6, 10.17
2053(c)(1)	6.27.10
2053(e)	6.27.10
2054	2.11, 2.14, 3.33.1, 3.33.2, 5.2.2, 7.10, 9.9, 11.15-11.18, 11.25, 11.26.4, 11.28, 11.30, 12.13, 12.45, 12.47
2055	2.11, 2.14, 3.33.1, 4.15.4, 5.2.2, 5.23.7, 5.24, 5.25.2, 8.1, 8.13, 8.19, 8.27, 8.31, 8.34, 8.35, 10.17, 12.35, 12.45
2055(a)	2.14, 8.2, 8.13, 8.33
2055(a)(2)	8.1
2055(c)	4.27.7
2055(d)	8.2, 8.34
2055(e)(2)	2.14, 4.16.1, 5.3.2, 8.15, 8.16
2055(e)(2)(B)	8.31
2055(e)(3)	8.35, 12.50
2055(e)(4)	8.12
2055(e)(3)(B)	8.35
2055(e)(3)(B)(i)	8.35
2055(e)(3)(B)(ii)	8.35
2055(e)(3)(C)(i)	8.35
2055(e)(3)(C)(ii)	8.35
2056	2.2, 2.11, 2.12, 2.14, 2.19.2, 7.33.1, 10.17, 12.16.1, 12.21, 12.30.1, 12.45
2056(a)	8.19
2056(b)(3)	4.15.4
2056(b)(4)	9.33, 10.6.2, 11.16
2056(b)(5)	7.36.4, 10.22, 10.45
2056(b)(6)	5.22
2056(b)(7)	1.32, 2.12, 2.14, 2.26, 3.27, 4.7.1, 4.16.1, 4.21.2, 4.27.5, 4.27.10, 6.22, 6.22.1, 6.23.5, 6.78.7, 8.13, 8.19, 8.34, 9.28, 9.33, 9.36, 9.39, 10.20, 10.24, 10.45, 12.2.4, 12.20, 12.20.2, 12.20.4,

	12.30.1, 12.34, 12.50
2056(b)(7)(B)(ii)	12.20
2056(b)(7)(B)(iv)	12.20.1
2056(b)(7)(B)(v)	12.20.4
2056(b)(7)(C)	2.18, 9.16, 9.34, 10.6.2
2056(b)(8)	2.14, 8.19, 8.20.5, 10.34.4
2056(c)	5.2.3, 5.3.1, 5.15, 5.32
2056(c)(1)(A)	3.33.2
2056(c)(1)(C)	3.33.2
2056(d)	2.14, 5.10, 5.25, 12.21
2056(d)(1)(B)	2.19.2, 3.15.1, 3.16
2056(d)(2)	12.21
2056(d)(3)	5.25.2
2056(d)(4)	5.15, 5.25
2056A	2.14, 3.15.1, 5.15, 5.25, 5.25.1, 5.25.2, 5.25.3, 8.20.5, 10.34.4, 12.21, 12.50
2056A(a)	5.25.1
2056A(b)	5.25.1, 5.25.2, 12.21
2056A(b)(3)	5.25.2, 12.21
2056A(b)(5)(A)	5.25.2
2056A(b)(5)(B)	5.25.2
2056A(b)(6)	5.25.2, 12.21
2056A(b)(8)	5.25.2
2056A(b)(12)	5.25, 5.25.3
2056A(b)(13)	12.21
2056A(d)	5.25.1
2056A(d)(2)(A)	5.25
2056A(d)(2)(B)	5.25
2056A(d)(5)(A)	5.25
2057	2.14
2101	2.15
2102	2.15
2106(a)(2)	8.1
2203	5.23.1, 12.42
2204	12.49, 12.49.1, 12.50
2204(a)	10.6.7
2204(b)	10.6.7, 12.49.1
2205	4.27.9, 12.41.1
2206	4.27.9, 12.42, 12.42.2, 12.42.3
2207	4.21.1, 4.27.9, 6.23.4, 12.42.3
2207(c)	5.23.11
2207A	2.38, 4.27, 4.27.2, 4.27.9, 12.42.4
2207A(a)	5.23.11
2207A(a)(1)	5.23.11
2207A(a)(2)	12.42.4
2207A(b)	5.23.10, 5.23.11
2207A(d)	5.23.11, 12.42.4
2207B	4.27.3, 4.27.9, 12.42.5
2207B(a)(2)	4.27.3, 12.42.5
2207B(e)	12.42.5
2501(a)(1)	2.4
2501(a)(2)	2.4.1
2502(d)	2.4, 7.25.1
2503	2.5.1, 2.28, 6.44.2
2503(b)	2.5, 2.5.8, 2.10, 2.28, 6.44.3, 6.78.8, 7.23, 7.30.1, 7.36.7, 7.38, 9.15, 10.33.1, 10.40.2
2503(c)	2.5.4, 6.44.2, 7.36.5, 7.2.3, 7.35, 7.36, 7.36.1, 7.36.2, 7.36.3, 7.36.4, 7.36.5, 7.36.6, 7.36.7, 7.36.8, 7.37.10, 7.37.11, 9.21, 10.33.1, 10.37.1-10.37.3, 10.40.1, 10.43.3
2503(e)	2.6, 2.10, 2.28, 2.40.3, 4.35.4, 6.44.3, 7.2.1,

	7.36.7, 10.2.2
2504(c)	2.10.3
2511(a)	2.4, 2.4.1
2512	2.43.1
2512(b)	7.24, 9.4
2513	2.5, 2.7, 2.10, 2.25, 2.28, 2.40.3, 7.20, 7.34.1, 7.34.2, 7.36.7, 12.24, 12.50
2513(a)(1)	2.7
2513(c)	12.24.2
2513(c)(2)	12.24.2
2513(d)	12.24
2514	4.35.4, 7.36.3, 7.37.4, 7.37.8, 10.22, 10.27.2
2514(b)	2.20.2, 10.23, 10.24
2514(c)	10.23, 10.26
2514(c)(1)	5.23.2, 10.25
2514(c)(3)	10.31.2
2514(c)(3)(A)	10.26, 10.31.2
2514(c)(3)(B)	10.26
2514(e)	5.22.3, 5.23.3, 6.44.2, 7.36.5, 7.37.2, 10.24
2515	2.19.2, 2.24, 2.30.1, 3.14.2
2515(a)	3.14.2
2515(c)	3.14.2
2515A	2.19.2
2516	6.27.10
2516(1)	6.27.10
2518	2.12, 3.19, 3.30, 5.16.2, 5.21, 10.41.1, 12.1, 12.31, 12.32, 12.32.4, 12.50
2518(a)	12.32
2518(b)	5.16.2, 12.32
2518(b)(2)	12.32.4, 12.32.5
2518(b)(3)	12.32.5
2518(c)(1)	12.34
2518(c)(2)	12.32.1
2518(c)(3)	12.31, 12.33
2519	5.23.10, 12.32.4
2519(a)	5.23.10
2521	2.10.3
2522	2.8, 5.24, 6.42, 8.1, 8.27, 8.31, 8.37
2522(a)	2.8, 8.2, 8.33
2522(a)(2)	8.1
2522(a)(3)	8.2
2522(b)	8.1
2522(c)(2)	5.3.2, 6.45.2, 8.13, 8.15, 8.16, 10.33.2
2522(c)(2)(B)	8.31, 8.33, 10.33.2
2522(c)(3)	8.12
2522(c)(4)	2.8, 8.35
2522(d)	8.16.1
2523	2.9, 2.9.1, 2.10, 3.7, 3.34, 5.2.3, 5.11, 5.24, 6.42, 6.46
2523(a)(2)	5.3.1
2523(a)(2)(A)	2.9
2523(a)(2)(B)	2.9
2523(b)	2.9, 3.14, 5.17
2523(d)	3.14
2523(e)	5.22.3, 6.45.2
2523(f)	2.9, 2.9.2, 2.12, 5.3.1, 5.3.2, 6.45.2, 8.15.1, 8.19, 8.34, 10.45
2523(f)(2)	5.3.2
2523(g)	5.3.2, 5.24, 8.19, 8.20.5
2523(i)	2.5.8, 2.9, 3.7, 8.20.5
2523(i)(1)	5.11
2523(i)(2)	2.9, 5.11
2523(i)(3)	2.19.2
2603(a)	2.36
2603(a)(1)	2.30.2
2611(b)	2.28, 2.40.6
2611(b)(1)	2.6
2612	6.40
2612(a)	2.23.2
2612(a)(1)	12.15.7
2612(b)	2.23.3
2612(c)	2.23.1, 2.40.7
2612(c)(2)	2.23.1, 2.40.6, 2.40.7
2613	2.23.1, 6.41
2613(a)	2.23.1, 2.32
2613(b)	2.23.1

2621 2.30, 2.30.2
2622 2.30, 2.30.3
2622(b) 2.30.3
2623 2.24, 2.30
2624 2.29
2624(b) 2.29, 12.15.7
2624(c) 2.29, 12.15.7, 12.50
2624(d) 2.29, 9.35
2631(a) 2.23, 2.25, 9.22.1, 12.23, 12.50
2631(b) 2.25, 12.23
2632(a) 12.23
2632(b) 2.2.7, 2.27.3, 12.23
2632(b)(3) 2.27
2632(c) 2.27.3, 12.23.1
2632(c)(2)(A) 2.27.3
2641(a) 2.24
2642 2.24, 2.38
2642(a)(2)(A) 2.24
2642(a)(2)(B) 2.24
2642(b)(1) 2.24, 6.23.4, 9.35
2642(b)(2) 2.26, 2.27.3
2642(b)(3) 2.24
2642(c) 2.28, 2.40.3, 6.23.4, 6.41, 6.75, 7.36.7, 7.37, 7.37.9, 10.20.2, 6.41.1
2642(c)(1) 2.28, 7.36.7
2642(c)(2) 2.5.3, 2.28, 2.40.3, 6.22.4, 6.41, 6.44.1, 6.44.3, 7.37.2
2642(c)(3) 2.6, 4.35.4, 7.2.1, 7.63
2642(d) 2.34
2642(e) 2.27.2, 8.31
2642(f) 2.27.1, 9.35
2642(f)(3) 2.27, 9.35
2651 2.32
2651(b)(1) 2.32
2651(b)(2) 2.32
2651(c)(1) 2.32
2651(c)(2) 2.32
2651(d)(1) 2.32
2651(d)(2) 2.32
2652 2.25
2652(a) 9.35, 12.20.3
2652(a)(1)(A) 2.31
2652(a)(1)(B) 2.31
2652(a)(2) 2.7, 12.24
2652(a)(3) 2.26, 5.26, 12.22, 12.50
2652(b) 2.38
2652(b)(1) 2.36.2, 6.23.4
2652(b)(3) 6.23.4, 6.41
2652(c) 2.23.2
2653 7.37.2
2653(b) 2.31
2654(a) 2.35
2654(a)(1) 2.35
2654(a)(2) 2.30.3, 2.35
2654(b) 2.26, 6.41, 6.41.1, 9.35
2654(b)(1) 2.33
2654(b)(2) 2.33
2662 2.36
2662(a)(1) 2.36
2662(a)(2)(A) 2.36.4
2701 2.13, 2.17.2, 2.44, 11.1, 11.31, 11.32, 11.35, 11.37, 11.38, 11.38.4, 11.41, 11.41.2, 11.41.3, 11.42
2701(a)(2) 11.38
2701(a)(2)(A) 11.32
2701(a)(2)(B) 11.4.1, 11.31, 11.32
2701(a)(2)(C) 11.32
2701(a)(3)(A) 11.32
2701(a)(4)(A) 11.35
2701(c)(3) 11.5, 11.32, 11.35
2701(e)(1) 11.32, 11.35, 11.35.2
2701(e)(2) 9.42.2
2702 2.5.2, 2.13, 2.17.2, 2.44, 4.7.1, 6.24.1, 6.42, 7.24, 9.1, 9.3, 9.10, 9.10.2, 9.15, 9.23, 9.26, 9.30, 9.31.1, 9.33, 9.35, 9.36, 9.40, 9.41, 9.41.1, 9.41.2,

9.42.1, 9.43, 9.43.1, 9.44, 10.32.8, 10.33, 10.40.2, 11.1, 11.4.1, 11.31, 11.32, 11.38, 11.38.4, 11.42
2702(a)(1) 9.42.2
2702(a)(2)(B) 9.1
2702(a)(3) 9.41.2, 9.42.1, 9.42.2, 9.43.3
2702(b) 9.1, 9.3, 9.15, 9.43.1, 9.43.2
2702(c)(2) 9.41.1, 9.42.1, 9.43.1
2702(c)(4) 9.41.1, 9.42.1
2703 2.13, 2.17.2, 2.44, 11.1, 11.6, 11.11, 11.31, 11.32, 11.38, 11.38.4, 11.42
2704 2.13, 2.17.2, 2.44, 11.1, 11.31, 11.38, 11.38.4, 11.41.1, 11.42
2704(a) 11.33
2704(b) 11.33
2704(c)(2) 9.1, 9.30, 9.41.1, 9.42.1, 9.43.1, 11.41.1
3466 10.6.8
3467 10.6.8
4940 8.3, 8.34
4941 8.3, 8.34
4941(d) 8.26
4941(d)(1)(A) 6.55.2
4941(d)(2)(A) 8.19
4942 8.3, 8.34
4942(j)(3) 8.3
4943 8.3, 8.26, 8.34
4944 8.3, 8.26, 8.34
4945 8.3, 8.34
4945(d) 8.26
4946 8.3, 8.34
4947 8.3, 8.34
4947(a)(2) 8.26
4947(b) 6.55.2
4947(b)(3)(B) 8.26
4948 8.3, 8.34
4980A 8.20.4, 12.26
4980A(c) 12.26.5
4980A(c)(4) 12.26.2
4980A(d) 12.26.3, 12.42
4980A(d)(5) 12.26.3, 12.50
4980A(e)(5) 12.26
4980A(f) 12.26.1
4980A(f)(1) 12.26.1
4980A(f)(2)(A) 12.26.1
5112 12.25.2
6019 2.10, 3.34, 12.24
6019(a) 2.5, 2.10
6012(a)(3) 12.7
6012(b)(1) 12.3
6013(a)(2) 12.3.1, 12.50
6013(a)(3) 12.3.1, 12.50
6013(d)(3) 12.3.3
6013(e) 12.3.3
6015 (former) 12.6
6018 12.2.3
6036 12.2.3, 12.50
6050L 8.7.3
6072(a) 12.3, 12.7
6075(b)(3) 2.10
6081 12.43, 12.50
6091(b)(1)(A) 12.3
6091(b)(4) 2.10.2
6109 10.13, 12.50
6151(a) 2.10.3
6152 (former) 12.6
6152(a) (former) 10.4.17
6152(b)(1) (former) 12.3
6161 2.10.4, 5.25.2, 10.6.8, 12.41, 12.44, 12.49.1
6161(a) 2.10.3
6161(a)(1) 12.3
6161(a)(2) 12.21, 12.44
6163 2.15, 10.6.8, 12.41, 2.45, 12.49.1, 12.50
6163(a) 12.45
6165 12.45
6166 2.15, 2.16, 2.46, 5.25.2, 5.29, 6.4, 6.20, 6.24.3, 7.7,

	7.10, 7.16, 10.6.7, 10.6.8, 10.44, 11.1, 11.4, 11.11, 11.12.1, 11.15-11.17, 11.20, 11.22, 11.25, 11.26.4, 11.26.5, 11.27, 11.27.2, 11.28, 11.30, 12.4, 12.12, 12.13, 12.15, 12.19.16, 12.21, 12.41, 12.44, 12.49.1, 12.50
6166(a)	11.15, 11.26.1, 11.26.3, 11.27.4
6166(a)(1)	7.10, 11.2.3
6166(a)(2)	11.26.4, 11.27.4, 11.28
6166(a)(3)	11.28, 11.30
6166(b)	11.26.1, 11.30
6166(b)(1)	11.26.2
6166(b)(1)(A)	11.26
6166(b)(1)(B)	11.26, 11.26.4
6166(b)(1)(C)	11.26, 11.26.4, 11.26.5
6166(b)(2)	11.26.4
6166(b)(2)(B)	11.26, 11.26.4
6166(b)(2)(C)	11.26.1, 11.26.4, 11.26.5
6166(b)(2)(D)	11.26.1
6166(b)(3)	11.26.3
6166(b)(4)	11.25
6166(b)(6)	11.25, 11.28
6166(b)(7)	11.26.4
6166(b)(7)(B)	11.26.4
6166(b)(8)	11.22, 11.26.3, 11.26.5
6166(b)(8)(B)	11.26.5
6166(b)(8)(C)	11.26.5
6166(b)(8)(D)	11.26.5
6166(b)(9)	11.26.3
6166(b)(9)(B)(i)	11.26.3
6166(b)(9)(B)(ii)	11.26.3
6166(c)	7.10, 11.25, 11.26.1, 11.30
6166(d)	11.27
6166(f)(1)	11.28
6166(g)	11.15, 11.29, 11.29.2, 12.47
6166(g)(1)(A)	11.29.2
6166(g)(1)(B)	11.29.2
6166(g)(1)(C)	11.29
6166(g)(1)(D)	11.29.1
6166(g)(2)	11.29.3
6166(g)(3)	11.29.4
6166(g)(3)(B)	11.29.4
6166(h)	2.36.3, 2.46
6166(h)(1)	11.27.4
6166(h)(2)	11.27.4
6166(h)(3)	11.27.4
6166(i)	12.47, 12.50
6166(j)	7.10
6166A (former)	10.6.7, 11.1, 11.18, 11.26.2, 12.12, 12.46, 12.47
6166A(c) (former)	12.46
6166A(h) (former)	12.46
6324	5.25.3
6324A	12.49.1
6324B	12.19.13
6501	10.6.6, 10.17
6501(d)	12.49.3, 12.50
6601(a)	2.10.4
6601(j)	2.46, 11.26.5, 11.28, 12.47
6601(j)(2)	11.30
6601(j)(3)	11.30
6621	2.10.4, 12.19.3, 12.44
6621(a)(1)	2.10.4
6621(a)(2)	2.10.4, 2.46, 11.28, 12.6, 12.46
6621(b)	12.46
6651	2.10.4
6651(a)(1)	2.10.2
6651(a)(2)	2.10.4
6652(a)(1)	2.10.4
6652(b)	2.10.4
6652(d)	2.10.4
6654	12.6

6654(d)(1)(B) 10.4.18
6654(e)(1) 12.6
6654(e)(2) 12.6
6654(*l*) 12.3, 12.6, 10.4.18
6654(*l*)(2) 10.4.18
6659 12.16
6660 (former) 12.16
6660(e) (former) 12.16
6661 1.13
6661(b)(2)(B) 1.13
6662 2.10.3, 8.7, 8.7.2, 12.17, 12.18
6662(a) 12.17
6662(d) 12.17
6662(d)(2)(B) 12.17
6662(e) 12.17
6662(e)(1) 8.7.2
6662(g) 2.10.4
6662(g)(1) 12.17
6662(g)(2) 12.17
6662(h) 12.17
6662(h)(2)(C) 12.17
6664(c) 2.10.4
6903 12.23, 12.50
6905 12.49, 12.49.2
7503 2.10.2
7520 1.31.1, 5.19, 5.23.5, 6.24.1, 7.38, 9.1, 9.10.2, 8.25, 9.13, 9.15, 9.21, 9.42.1, 9.43.1, 9.43.3, 9.43.4, 10.35
7520(a) 8.25
7702 6.9.3, 6.49, 6.51
7702(b)(1) 6.49
7702(b)(2)(A) 6.49
7702(b)(2)(B) 6.49
7702(b)(2)(C) 6.49
7702(c)(1) 6.49
7702(c)(4) 6.49
7702(d)(2) 6.49
7702(f)(7) 6.49, 6.66
7702(g) 6.69
7702(g)(1)(A) 6.49
7702(g)(2) 6.49
7702A 6.9.3, 6.50, 6.59.1, 6.74
7702A(c)(3) 6.50
7702A(d) 6.50
7815(d)(16) 3.15.1
7871(a) 8.2
7872 2.42.1, 7.19
7872(a) 7.19
7872(b)(1) 7.19
7872(c)(2) 7.19
7872(d) 7.19
7872(d)(1)(A) 7.19
7872(d)(1)(B) 7.19
7872(f)(3) 7.19

Table of Treasury Regulations

(references are to sections)

1.47-2(a)(1)	7.17
1.56(g)-1(c)(5)(v)	11.9
1.61-2(d)(2)(ii)(a)	6.56
1.61-2(d)(2)(ii)(b)	6.72.2
1.61-7(d)	6.61
1.72-9	6.78.10, 8.37, 9.10.2, 9.13, 9.32
1.72-11(b)(1)	6.61
1.79-0	6.72.7, 6.72.8
1.79-2(c)(3)	6.72
1.79-3(d)(2)	6.43.1, 6.72.2, 6.72.9
1.79-3(f)(2)	6.72.2
1.79-3T	6.72.9
1.79-4T	6.72.5
1.101-1(a)	6.51
1.101-1(b)(4)	6.53
1.101-1(b)(5)	6.53.2
1.101-3(a)	6.53
1.101-4(b)(3)	6.52
1.167(h)-1(b)	9.18
1.170A-1(b)	8.6
1.170A-1(c)	8.7, 8.8
1.170A-1(c)(2)	8.7
1.170A-1(e)	8.18
1.170A-4(b)(1)	8.9
1.170A-4(b)(3)	8.12
1.170A-4(c)(2)(ii)	8.36
1.170A-5	8.13
1.170A-6(c)(2)(i)(A)	8.31
1.170A-6(c)(2)(i)(B)	8.32
1.170A-6(c)(2)(ii)(A)	8.32
1.170A-6(c)(5), Example (3)	8.31
1.170A-7(a)(2)(i)	8.17
1.170A-7(a)(2)(ii)	8.17
1.170A-7(a)(3)	8.18
1.170A-7(b)	8.15
1.170A-7(b)(1)	8.16
1.170A-7(b)(1)(i)	8.12, 8.16
1.170A-7(b)(3)	8.15
1.170A-7(b)(4)	8.15
1.170A-8(a)(2)	8.4.1, 8.31
1.170A-9(g)	8.3
1.170A-9(h)	8.3
1.170A-10(c)(1)(ii)	8.10
1.170A-10(d)(4)(iii)	8.11, 12.3.2
1.170A-12, Table C	8.15.4
1.170A-12(a)(1)	8.15.4
1.170A-12(a)(2)	8.15.4
1.170A-12(b)	8.15.4
1.170A-12(b)(2)	8.15.4
1.170A-12(c)	8.15.4
1.170A-12(e)	8.15.4
1.170A-13(b)(1)	8.7.1

1.170A-13(b)(2)	8.7
1.170A-13(b)(3)	8.7, 8.7.1
1.170A-13(b)(4)	8.7
1.170A-13(c)(2)(B)	8.7.1
1.170A-14(h)(3)(i)	8.16.1
1.212-1(k)	1.24
1.213-1(d)(1)	12.3.4
1.262-1(b)(1)	6.55
1.264-2	6.60.2
1.264-4(d)(3)	6.60.3
1.264-4(d)(4)	6.60.3
1.267(d)-1(a)(3)	10.4.12
1.302-2(b)	11.24.1
1.302-3(a)	11.24.2
1.302-3(b)	11.24.2
1.303-2(d)	11.16
1.303-2(f)	10.4.15
1.303-2(g)(1)	11.19
1.305-5(b)(2)	11.34.5
1.305-5(d), Example (5)	11.34.5
1.306-3(d)	11.34.3
1.306-3(e)	11.34.3
1.318-3(a)	11.24.1
1.368-2(e)(3)	11.34
1.441-1T(b)(1)(i)(B)	12.7
1.453-4(c)	9.6.1
1.453-9	7.17
1.509(a)-3	8.3
1.509(a)-4	8.3
1.641(a)-0(c)	10.4.10
1.642(c)-5	8.30
1.642(c)-5(a)(2)	8.30
1.642(c)-5(a)(3)	8.30
1.642(c)-5(b)(2)	8.30
1.642(c)-5(b)(4)	8.30
1.642(c)-5(b)(6)	8.30
1.642(c)-5(b)(8)	8.30
1.642(c)-6	8.30
1.642(c)-6(b)(2)	8.30
1.642(g)-1	12.13
1.642(g)-2	1.25, 12.10, 12.13
1.642(h)-3(c)	12.7.1
1.642(h)-3(d)	12.7.1
1.643(a)-0	10.4.3
1.643(a)-1	10.4.3
1.643(a)-3(a)	9.32
1.643(a)-3(a)(3)	10.4.3
1.643(a)-3(d)	10.4.3
1.643(a)-7	10.4.3
1.643(d)-2(a)	10.4.3
1.651(a)-1	10.4.8
1.651(b)-1	10.4.8
1.652(a)-1	10.4.8
1.652(b)-1	10.4.4, 10.4.8
1.652(b)-2(a)	10.4.8
1.652(b)-2(b)	10.4.4
1.652(b)-3	10.4.8
1.652(b)-3(c)	10.4.8
1.661(a)-2(c)	12.29.2
1.661(a)-2(e)	12.29.2, 12.37.2
1.661(a)-2(f)(1)	4.16.3, 5.39
1.661(a)-2(f)(3)	5.21, 5.39
1.662(a)-2(b)	12.36.3
1.662(b)-1	10.4.4, 10.4.8, 12.36.1
1.662(b)-2	10.4.4, 10.4.8
1.663(a)-1(b)	12.36.4
1.663(a)-1(b)(1)	12.37
1.663(a)-1(b)(2)	12.37.1
1.663(a)-1(c)(1)(ii)	12.37.2
1.663(c)-1(d)	10.4.9
1.663(c)-3(f)	10.4.9
1.664-1(a)(3)	8.24, 10.45
1.664-1(a)(4)	8.19
1.664-1(a)(5)(iv)	8.23
1.664-1(d)(4)(i)	10.4.16
1.664-2(a)(1)(iii)	8.21
1.664-2(a)(5)	8.21
1.664-2(a)(5)(i)	8.21
1.664-2(a)(5)(ii)	8.21
1.664-3(a)(1)(B)	8.20.4
1.664-3(b)	8.22
1.665(b)-1A(a)	10.4.10
1.665(b)-1A(c)(3)	10.4.10
1.665(e)-1A(b)	12.40
1.671-1(a)	10.31
1.671-1(c)	10.4.1
1.671-2(b)	10.32.4
1.671-4	10.31
1.671-4(a)	10.4.2
1.671-4(b)	10.4.2, 10.31
1.672(a)-1(a)	10.31.1
1.672(a)-1(b)	10.31.1
1.672(a)-1(d)	10.31.1
1.674(b)-1	10.37.1
1.674(b)-1(b)(5)	10.20.4
1.674(b)-1(b)(7)	10.37.1
1.674(d)-2	10.20.3, 10.41.1
1.674(d)-2(b)	10.20.3
1.675-1(a)	10.38.1
1.677(a)-1	10.40.1
1.678(a)-1(b)	10.27.1
1.704-1(e)	11.5
1.704-1(e)(1)(i)	11.40

1.704-1(e)(1)(iii)	11.38.5	20.2031-4	9.5, 9.22.2
1.704-1(e)(1)(iv)	11.40.1	20.2031-7	1.31.1, 8.25, 8.37
1.704-1(e)(2)	11.40.1		
1.704-1(e)(2)(ii)(d)	11.40.4	20.2031-7(f)	8.29, 8.37
1.704-1(e)(2)(iii)	11.40.4	20.2031-8	1.31.1, 6.22.3
1.704-1(e)(2)(vii)	11.40.2	20.2031-8(a)(2)	6.34
1.704-1(e)(2)(viii)	11.40.2	20.2031-10	1.31.1, 2.13
1.704-1(e)(3)(ii)(c)	11.40.3	20.2032-1(b)	3.20.3
1.706-1(c)(2)	11.8	20.2032-1(b)(1)	12.15
1.732-1(d)	12.5.2	20.2032-1(c)	12.15.6
1.736-1(a)(4)	11.8	20.2032-1(c)(3)	12.15.6
1.736-1(b)	11.8	20.2032-1(f)(1)	12.15.3
1.736-1(b)(3)	11.8	20.2032A-3(e)(2)	12.19.7
1.742-1	11.8, 12.5	20.2032A-3(f)	12.19.6
1.743-1(b)	12.5	20.2032A-8(a)(2)	12.19.4, 12.19.5
1.754-1(b)	12.5, 12.5.1		
1.1001-1(a)	8.8	20.2035-1(b)	2.17
1.1001-1(e)(1)	7.27	20.2036-1(b)(2)	10.35.1, 10.35.3, 10.41.6
1.1001-2(a)(4)(i)	6.63.1		
1.1011-2	8.37		
1.1011-2(a)(1)	8.36	20.2036-1(b)(3)	6.78.5, 10.41.2
1.1011-2(a)(3)	7.26, 8.36		
1.1011-2(a)(4)	8.37	20.2038-1(a)(3)	10.39.3, 10.41.2
1.1011-2(c)	9.13		
1.1011-2(c), Example (8)	8.37	20.2039-1(b)(ii)	6.78.1
		20.2040-1(a)	3.15, 3.18
1.1014-4(a)(3)	5.39	20.2040-1(a)(2)	3.15
1.1014-5	9.31.1, 9.31.2	20.2040-1(c)(4)	3.15.2
1.1015-4(a)	7.27	20.2040-1(c)(5)	3.15.2
1.1015-4(a)(1)	7.25.1	20.2040-1(c), Example (7)	3.15.3
1.1015-5(b)(2)	7.12		
1.1031(d)-1(b)	6.66.1	20.2040-1(c), Example (8)	3.15.3
1.1034-1(c)(3)	9.43.3		
1.1035-1(c)	6.68	20.2041-1	10.41.9
1.1041-1T(d)	3.35.1	20.2041-1(b)	10.20.6
1.1223-1(b)	7.9.2	20.2041-1(b)(1)	10.22, 10.27.3, 10.28, 10.38.3, 10.41.5, 10.41.9, 10.47
1.1244(a)-1(b)	10.4.13, 10.44		
1.1245-1(a)(3)	9.19		
1.1245-1(b)	9.19		
1.6013-1(d)(1)	12.3.1		
1.6015(b)-1(c)(2)	12.6		
1.6072-1(b)	12.3		
1.6091-2(a)(1)	12.3	20.2041-1(b)(1)(C)(i)	10.22
1.6161-1(b)	12.3	20.2041-1(b)(1)(C)(ii)	10.22
1.9100	12.5.1	20.2041-1(b)(2)	2.20
1.9100-1	12.5.1, 12.50	20.2041-1(c)	10.23
20.0-2(a)	2.11	20.2041-1(c)(1)	10.27.3, 10.41.6
20.2002-1	12.49		
20.2016-2(a)(2)	9.9	20.2041-1(c)(2)	4.21.2, 10.25, 10.27.3
20.2031-1(a)	2.12		
20.2031-1(b)	1.31.1, 2.13	20.2041-3(d)(3)	7.36.5
20.2031-2	1.31.1	20.2041-3(d)(4)	7.36.5
20.2031-2(f)	6.71.4	20.2041-3(d)(6)(i)	12.31
20.2031-2(h)	11.6	20.2042-1(b)	2.21, 6.26

20.2042-1(c)(2)	2.21
20.2042-1(c)(4)	10.6.4
20.2042-1(c)(6)	11.12, 11.22
20.2053-3(b)(2)	4.26.8
20.2053-3(c)	1.25
20.2053-5	11.17
20.2053-6(f)	12.3.7
20.2053-7	9.5
20.2053-8	1.25
20.2053-8(b)	10.6.6
20.2055-2(e)(1)(ii)	8.12
20.2055-2(e)(2)	8.15
20.2055-2(e)(2)(i)	8.16
20.2055-2(e)(2)(ii)	8.15
20.2055-2(e)(2)(iii)	8.15
20.2055-2(e)(2)(vi)(e)	8.32
20.2055-2(e)(2)(vii)(e)	8.32
20.2055-3(a)	4.27.7
20.2056(a)-2(b)(2)	5.13
20.2056(b)-1(b)	5.17.1
20.2056(b)-1(e)(1)	5.17.2
20.2056(b)-1(g)	5.17.4
20.2056(b)-1(g)(8)	5.16
20.2056(b)-2	5.17.5
20.2056(b)-3	5.22.3
20.2056(b)-3(a)	4.15.4, 5.19
20.2056(b)-3(d)	5.20
20.2056(b)-4(a)	4.27.7, 5.22.2
20.2056(b)-4(b)	9.33
20.2056(b)-4(c)(1)	4.27.7
20.2056(b)-5(a)	5.22
20.2056(b)-5(c)	8.16
20.2056(b)-5(c)(1)	5.22.1
20.2056(b)-5(c)(3)	5.22.1
20.2056(b)-5(e)	5.22.2
20.2056(b)-5(f)	5.22.2, 5.23.2
20.2056(b)-5(f)(3)	5.22.2, 10.47
20.2056(b)-5(f)(4)	5.21, 5.22.2, 10.47
20.2056(b)-5(f)(5)	5.21, 5.22.2, 5.23.2
20.2056(b)-5(f)(7)	5.22.2, 5.23.10
20.2056(b)-5(f)(8)	5.22.2
20.2056(b)-5(f)(9)	5.22.2
20.2056(b)-5(g)(1)(iii)	5.22.2
20.2056(b)-7(b)	12.20.4
20.2056(b)-7(e), Example (8)	12.20.2
20.2056(b)-7(e), Example (9)	12.20.3
20.2056(b)-7(e), Example (11)	12.20.2, 12.20.4
20.2056(d)-1(a)	12.35
20.2056(d)-1(b)	5.16.2
20.2056(e)-2	4.15.3
20.2056(e)-2(a)	5.16
20.2056(e)-2(b)	5.18
20.2056(e)-2(b)(1)	5.2.1
20.2056(e)-2(c)	5.16, 12.30.1
20.2056(e)-2(d)	5.16
20.2056(e)-2(e)	5.20
20.2056(e)-3	5.21
20.2204-1(a)	12.49.1
20.6036-2	12.2.3
20.6081-1(b)	12.43
20.6151-1(c)	12.48
20.6161-1(a)	12.44
20.6161-1(b)	12.44
20.6163-1(b)	12.45
20.6163-1(c)	12.45
20.6165-1(a)	12.44
20.6165-1(b)	12.45
20.6166-1(a)	11.27
20.6166-1(b)	11.27
20.6166-1(d)	11.27.1
25.2503-3(a)	2.5.1, 6.44
25.2503-3(b)	2.5.2, 6.44.2, 9.15, 10.5, 10.36.2
25.2503-3(c)	10.36.2
25.2503-3(c), Example (2)	6.42, 6.44.2, 6.72.12
25-2503-3(c), Example (6)	6.21.4, 6.42, 6.44, 6.46
25-2503-4(b)	7.36.4
25.2503-4(b)(1)	7.36.2
25.2503-4(c)	7.38
25.2511-1(a)	2.4
25.2511-1(c)	2.4
25.2511-1(c)(2)	12.32.3
25.2511-1(d)	7.20, 12.24.4
25.2511-1(e)	7.24
25.2511-1(g)(1)	7.8
25.2511-1(h)(1)	2.5.5
25.2511-1(h)(4)	7.30.2, 7.33.1
25.2511-2	2.4.3, 4.7.1, 5.25, 10.5
25.2511-2(a)	10.5
25.2511-2(b)	7.37.2, 9.30.1, 10.5, 10.24, 10.40.2
25.2511-2(c)	7.4, 7.32, 8.33, 10.16, 10.34.2, 10.34.3, 10.37,

	10.38.2, 10.40.2
25.2511-2(d)	10.37.2
25.2511-2(e)	6.78.8, 10.7, 10.16, 10.34.1, 10.34.2, 10.34.3, 10.37.2, 10.39.2
25.2511-2(f)	6.78.8, 10.5, 10.16
25.2511-2(h)	7.5.1
25.2511-2(j)	10.5, 10.16
25.2512-1	2.13
25.2512-2	1.31.1, 2.4.3
25.2512-5	1.31.1, 8.32, 8.37
25.2512-5(f)	8.37
25.2512-8	3.7.1, 9.4, 11.35.2
25.2512-9	1.31.1
25.2513-1(c)	2.7
25.2513-2(a)(1)(i)	2.7
25.2513-2(c)	12.24
25.2513-3(a)	12.24.2
25.2514-1(b)(2)	10.23, 10.27.2, 10.31.1
25.2514-3(c)	7.36.5
25.2514-3(e), Example (1)	10.27.2
25.2518-1(a)	12.32
25.2518-1(c)(2)	12.31
25.2518-2(a)	12.32.4
25.2518-2(c)(2)	12.32.4
25.2518-2(c)(3)	12.32.4
25.2518-2(c)(4)	12.33
25.2518-2(c)(5), Example (9)	12.33.1
25.2518-2(d), Example (21)	12.32.1
25.2518-2(d)(1)	12.32.4, 12.33
25.2518-2(d)(2)	12.32.1, 12.32.4
25.2518-2(e)	12.32.1
25.2518-2(e)(5), Example (3)	12.32.4
25.2518-2(e)(5), Example (5)	12.32.4
25.2518-2(e)(5), Example (7)	12.32.1
25.2518-3	12.33.1
25.2518-3(a)	12.34
25.2518-3(a)(1)	12.32
25.2518-3(a)(1)(i)	12.32.2, 12.34
25.2518-3(a)(1)(ii)	12.34
25.2518-3(a)(1)(iii)	10.41.10, 12.32.1
25.2518-3(a)(2)	12.34
25.2518-3(b)	12.34
25.2518-3(c)	12.32.4, 12.34
25.2518-3(d), Example (9)	10.41.10
25.2518-3(d), Example (17)	12.32.4
25.2518-3(d), Example (18)	12.34
25.2518-3(d), Example (19)	12.34
25.2518-3(d), Example (20)	12.34
25.2518-3(d), Example (21)	12.34
25.2522(b)-1	2.8
25.2522(c)-3(c)(1)(ii)	8.12
25.2522(c)-3(c)(2)	8.15
25.2522(c)-3(c)(2)(i)	8.16
25.2522(c)-3(c)(2)(ii)	8.15
25.2522(c)-3(c)(2)(iii)	8.15
25.2522(c)-3(c)(2)(vi)(2)	8.31
25.2523(e)-1(f)(4)	6.45.2, 6.46
25.2701-1(a)(2)	11.35
25.2702-1	9.40
25.2702.2(b)	9.43.3
25.2702-2(d)	9.42.1
25.2702-3(c)	9.43.2
25.2702-3(d)	9.43.2
25.2702-3(e), Example (1)	9.43
25.2702-5	9.42.1
25.2702-5(a)	9.43.3
25.2702-5(b)(1)	9.43.3
25.2702-5(b)(2)	9.43.3
25.2702-5(b)(2)(ii)	9.43.3
25.2702-5(b)(3)	9.43.3
25.2702-5(c)	9.43.3
25.2702-5(c)(8)	9.43.3
25.2702-5(c)(8)(ii)	9.43.3
25.2702-5(d), Example (2)	9.43.3
25.2702-6	9.43.1, 11.32
25.2702-6(b)(1)	9.43.1
25.2704-1	11.33
25.2704-1(a)	11.33
25.2704-1(a)(4)	11.33

25.2704-1(c)	11.33
25.6019-3(a)	10.5, 10.16
25.6161-1(b)	2.10.4
26.2601-1(b)(1)(ii)(B)	2.38
26.2601-1(b)(1)(iv)	2.38
26.2601-1(b)(1)(v)	4.27.2
26.2601-1(b)(1)(v)(A)	2.38, 7.37.2
26.2662-1(c)	2.36, 2.36.2
26.2662-1(c)(1)	2.36.1
26.2662-1(c)(2)	2.36.2
31.3401(c)-1	6.72.8
31.3401(f)	6.72.8
53.4942(b)-1	8.3
53.4942(b)-2	8.3
53.4947-2(b)(1)	8.26
301.6905-1(a)	12.49.2
301.7502-1(a)	2.10.2
301.7502-1(c)(1)	12.32.4
301.7502-1(c)(2)	12.32.4
301.7502-1(d)	12.32.4
301.7701-2	11.38.3

Proposed Regulations

1.483-2(b)	9.6.5
1.1361-1(l)(1)	11.1, 11.4.1
1.1361-1(l)(2)(ii)	11.7
1.6664-4	2.10.4
1.6664-4(a)	8.7.2
1.6664-4(b)	8.7.2, 12.18
20.2056(b)-7(b)	12.20.1, 12.20.3
20.2056(b)-7(c)	10.47
20.2056(b)-7(e), Example (1)	12.20
20.2056(b)-7(e), Example (8)	12.20.2, 12.20.5
20.2056(b)-7(e), Example (9)	12.20.2, 12.20.5
20.2056(b)-7(e), Example (11)	12.20.2, 12.20.4
25.2701-1(b)(3)	11.6
25.2701-1(b)(4)(i)	11.6
25.2701-1(c)	11.6
26.2601-1(b)(1)(v)(A)	2.40.5

Temporary Regulations

1.1041-T(d), Q10	3.35.1
1.1041-T(d), Q11	3.35.1
5h.4	12.15.5
5h.4(k)(1)	11.26.5
5h.5(a)(3)	9.35, 12.22
15A.453-1(b)(2)	9.6
15A.453-1(b)(3)(i)	9.6.1
18.1362-2(b)	12.4
20.2039-1T	12.25.1
22.2056-1(b)(2)	12.20.1
26.2601-1(b)(1)(v)(C)	12.42.4
26.2601-1(b)(3)	2.40.5
54.4981A-1T(d), Q&A d-6	12.26.5
54.4981A-1T(d), Q&A d-10	12.26.5
301.9100-1T	5.10, 12.5.1
301.9100-1T(a)	12.2.4

C.F.R. (Non-Treasury Regs.)
31 C.F.R.

10	1.13
10.22	1.13
10.51(a)	1.13
10.51(b)	1.13
10.51(d)	1.13
10.51(j)	1.13
306.28	10.6.9, 12.48
315.5	7.30
315.6(c)	7.30.2
315.7(b)	7.30
315.37	7.30.2
315.51	7.30.2
315.62	7.30.1
315.63	7.30.1
315.70	7.30.2

Table of Internal Revenue Rulings

(references are to sections)

157, 1953-2 C.B. 255 11.6
239, 1953-2 C.B. 53 9.13
54-264, 1954-2 C.B. 57 6.68
54-327, 1954-2 C.B. 50 7.30
55-38, 1955-1 C.B. 389 2.42.2
55-119, 1055-1 C.B. 352 9.13, 9.14
55-278, 1955-1 C.B. 471 7.30.2
55-506, 1955-2 C.B. 609 12.24
55-518, 1955-2 C.B. 384 5.22.3
55-605, 1955-2 C.B. 82 3.33
55-622, 1955-2 C.B. 622 6.77
55-678, 1955-2 C.B. 389 10.33.1
55-679, 1955-2 C.B. 390 10.33.1
55-709, 1955-2 C.B. 609 3.7.2
55-747, 1955-2 C.B. 228 6.57, 6.71.2
56-60, 1956-1 C.B. 443 3.20.3
56-215, 1956-1 C.B. 324 3.20.3
56-222, 1956-1 C.B. 155 10.4.12
56-397, 1956-2 C.B. 599 6.28.2, 6.29
56-400, 1956-2 C.B. 116 6.56
56-408, 1956-2 C.B. 600 2.7
56-437, 1956-2 C.B. 507 3.20.9, 3.35.3
56-449, 1956-2 C.B. 180 11.17
56-472, 1956-2 C.B. 21 12.8
56-484, 1056-2 C.B. 23 7.34.3, 10.40.1
57-315, 1957-2 C.B. 624 7.3, 9.21
57-441, 1957-2 C.B. 45 6.61
57-495, 1957-2 C.B. 616 12.15.6
58-65, 1958-1 C.B. 13 7.29.3
58-153, 1958-1 C.B. 43 6.78.10
58-242, 1958-1 C.B. 251 10.33, 10.33.1
58-436, 1958-2 C.B. 366 12.15.3
58-576, 1958-2 C.B. 625 12.15.3
59-9, 1959-1 C.B. 232 2.15
59-32, 1959-1 C.B. 245 12.3.4, 12.11
59-84, 1959-1 C.B. 71 11.34.3
59-213, 1959-1 C.B. 244 12.15.6
59-357, 1959-2 C.B. 212 7.34.1, 7.34.2, 7.34.3
60-87, 1960-1 C.B. 286 5.40
60-370, 1960-2 C.B. 203 8.24
61-55, 1961-1 C.B. 713 11.26.3
61-91, 1961-1 C.B. 714 11.18
61-102, 1961-1 C.B. 245 9.41.3
61-134, 1961-2 C.B. 250 6.51.2
61-223, 1961-1 C.B. 125 10.40.1
62-132, 1962-2 C.B. 73 9.31

62-136, 1962-2 C.B. 12 9.12
63-178, 1963-2 C.B. 609 10.13
64-104, 1964-1 C.B. 223 7.30, 12.3.7
64-289, 1964-2 C.B. 173 12.15.3
64-328, 1964-2 C.B. 11 6.71, 6.71.2
65-144, 1965-1 C.B. 442 5.27
65-185, 1965-2 C.B. 153 9.6.1
66-60, 1966-1 C.B. 221 3.17
66-79, 1966-1 C.B. 48 8.2
66-110, 1966-1 C.B. 12 6.71.1, 6.71.2
66-116, 1966-1 C.B. 198 7.34.3
66-120, 1966-1 C.B. 14 6.55.3
66-159, 1966-1 C.B. 162 10.32.7
66-161, 1966-1 C.B. 164 10.40.1
66-167, 1966-1 C.B. 20 4.26, 7.22, 12.8, 12.50
66-203, 1966-2 C.B. 104 6.56, 6.71.2
66-248, 1966-2 C.B. 303 3.20
66-283, 1966-2 C.B. 297 3.25, 10.8
66-298, 1966-2 C.B. 48 6.76
66-313, 1966-2 C.B. 245 10.40.1
67-53, 1967-1 C.B. 265 10.20
67-54, 1967-1 C.B. 269 10.38.3
67-167, 1967-1 C.B. 107 10.32.3
67-228, 1967-2 C.B. 331 6.29
67-241, 1967-2 C.B. 225 7.37.10, 10.24.1
67-270, 1967-2 C.B. 1 7.36.2
67-304, 1967-2 C.B. 224 12.11
67-396, 1967-2 C.B. 351 2.4.3
67-463, 1967-2 C.B. 327 6.35
68-49, 1968-1 C.B. 304 12.37.2
68-80, 1968-1 C.B. 348 3.34.2, 3.35.4, 3.36, 3.39
68-145, 1968-1 C.B. 203 12.3.7
68-174, 1968-1 C.B. 81 8.6
68-227, 1968-1 C.B. 381 7.34.3
68-235, 1968-1 C.B. 360 6.66
68-269, 1968-1 C.B. 399 7.30.1, 7.30.2
68-334, 1968-1 C.B. 403 6.72.11
68-554, 1968-2 C.B. 412 5.21
68-648, 1968-2 C.B. 49 6.59.1
68-670, 1968-2 C.B. 413 7.36.1
69-54, 1969-1 C.B. 221 6.27.4, 6.72.11
69-70, 1969-1 C.B. 182 10.32, 10.32.4
69-74, 1969-1 C.B. 43 9.13, 9.15
69-80, 1969-1 C.B. 65 8.2
69-148, 1969-1 C.B. 226 3.14.1
69-187, 1969-1 C.B. 45 6.53.1
69-193, 1969-1 C.B. 222 3.33.1, 12.11
69-344, 1969-1 C.B. 225 6.44.2, 10.33.1
69-345, 1969-1 C.B. 226 7.36.2
69-346, 1969-1 C.B. 227 3.34.3, 4.7.1, 9.27
69-402, 1969-2 C.B. 176 12.12
69-486, 1969-2 C.B. 159 4.27.6, 5.38.5, 12.39
69-489, 1969-2 C.B. 172 10.6.9, 12.48.1
69-577, 1969-2 C.B. 173 3.8, 3.18
69-657, 1969-2 C.B. 189 6.72.8
70-155, 1970-1 C.B. 189 7.23
70-156, 1970-1 C.B. 190 3.33.1, 12.11
70-237, 1970-1 C.B. 13 4.26
70-348, 1970-2 C.B. 193 7.34.2
70-376, 1970-2 C.B. 164 10.32.7
70-400, 1970-2 C.B. 196 5.19, 5.20
70-428, 1970-2 C.B. 5 7.30
71-122, 1971-1 C.B. 224 9.41.3
71-168, 1971-1 C.B. 271 3.33.1, 12.11
71-173, 1971-1 C.B. 204 12.13.2
71-261, 1971-1 C.B. 108 11.19
71-268, 1971-1 C.B. 58 3.20.2
71-317, 1971-2 C.B. 328 12.15.3
71-355, 1971-2 C.B. 334 7.11
71-396, 1971-2 C.B. 328 12.15.6
71-433, 1971-2 C.B. 337 2.5.5
71-497, 1971-2 C.B. 329 6.35, 6.37
72-7, 1972-1 C.B. 308 5.17.2, 12.30.1
72-8, 1972-1 C.B. 309 5.17.2, 12.30.1
72-81, 1972-1 C.B. 98 9.14
72-153, 1972-1 C.B. 309 5.16.1
72-193, 1972-1 C.B. 58 6.64
72-243, 1972-1 C.B. 233 9.31
72-307, 1972-1 C.B. 307 6.27.4, 6.27.5, 6.72.11
72-333, 1972-2 C.B. 530 5.21
72-358, 1972-2 C.B. 473 6.65.2, 6.66
72-395, 1972-2 C.B. 340 8.23
72-545, 1972-2 C.B. 179 1.24
72-609, 1972-3 C.B. 199 6.60.3

73-21, 1973-1 C.B. 405 10.41.2, 10.41.9
73-97, 1973-1 C.B. 404 10.17, 12.15.6
73-124, 1973-1 C.B. 200 6.65.3
73-142, 1973-1 C.B. 405 10.41.12
73-143, 1973-1 C.B. 407 10.41.3, 10.41.5
73-174, 1973-1 C.B. 43 6.72
73-287, 1973-2 C.B. 321 7.36.3
73-327, 1973-2 C.B. 214 6.78.9
73-404, 1973-2 C.B. 319 6.26
73-405, 1973-2 C.B. 321 7.37.1, 10.33.1
73-451, 1973-2 C.B. 158 9.6.1
73-482, 1973-2 C.B. 44 6.60.1
73-555, 1973-2 C.B. 159 9.6.1
73-611, 1973-2 C.B. 312 11.7
74-43, 1974-1 C.B. 285 7.36.3
74-175, 1974-1 C.B. 52 12.3.2
74-269, 1974-1 C.B. 87 11.35.2
74-492, 1974-2 C.B. 298 5.16
74-556, 1974-2 C.B. 300 2.7, 7.34.2
74-613, 1974-2 C.B. 153 7.17, 9.6.3, 10.4.13, 10.15
75-8, 1975-1 C.B. 309 3.13
75-63, 1975-1 C.B. 294 7.11
75-66, 1975-1 C.B. 85 8.18
75-70, 1975-1 C.B. 301 6.27.8
75-72, 1975-1 C.B. 310 7.25.2
75-128, 1975-1 C.B. 308 5.21
75-142, 1975-1 C.B. 256 3.20.5
75-257, 1975-2 C.B. 251 10.3
75-260, 1975-2 C.B. 376 10.3, 10.34.1
75-267, 1975-2 C.B. 254 10.40.1
75-350, 1975-2 C.B. 366 5.22.3, 7.36.4, 10.16
75-351, 1975-2 C.B. 365 5.22.3, 7.36.4
75-365, 1975-2 C.B. 471 11.26.2
75-366, 1975-2 C.B. 472 11.26.2
75-367, 1975-2 C.B. 472 11.26.2
75-414, 1975-2 C.B. 371 8.34
75-440, 1975-2 C.B. 372 5.27
75-502, 1975-2 C.B. 111 11.24.1
76-7, 1976-1 C.B. 179 8.29
76-8, 1976-1 C.B. 179 8.29
76-23, 1976-1 C.B. 264 11.4, 12.4
76-49, 1976-1 C.B. 294 7.25.2
76-83, 1976-1 C.B. 213 3.35.3, 12.39.2
76-103, 1976-1 C.B. 293 10.21.2, 10.40.2
76-113, 1976-1 C.B. 276 6.27.10
76-143, 1976-1 C.B. 63 6.71.3
76-166, 1976-1 C.B. 287 5.16.1, 5.20
76-178, 1976-1 C.B. 273 10.35.2
76-179, 1976-1 C.B. 290 10.33
76-200, 1976-1 C.B. 308 6.45.2, 6.71.3
76-261, 1976-2 C.B. 276 6.27.11
76-274, 1976-2 C.B. 278 6.28, 6.71.4
76-275, 1976-2 C.B. 299 10.33
76-291, 1976-2 C.B. 284 8.20
76-303, 1976-2 C.B. 266 3.17
76-331, 1976-2 C.B. 52 8.18
76-357, 1976-2 C.B. 285 8.15
76-367, 1976-2 C.B. 259 12.48
76-369, 1976-2 C.B. 281 12.11
76-376, 1976-2 C.B. 53 8.16.1
76-380, 1976-2 C.B. 270 6.78.1
76-486, 1976-2 C.B. 192 10.4.4
76-490, 1976-2 C.B. 300 6.21.4, 6.23.5, 6.43.1, 6.71.3, 6.72, 6.72.12, 6.72.13
76-530, 1976-2 C.B. 132 10.15, 10.32.3
77-97, 1977-1 C.B. 285 8.16
77-99, 1977-1 C.B. 295 10.33
77-148, 1977-1 C.B. 63 8.18
77-169, 1977-1 C.B. 286 8.15.3
77-195, 1977-1 C.B. 295 10.33
77-275, 1977-2 C.B. 346 8.33
77-294, 1977-2 C.B. 173 9.6.1
77-299, 1977-2 C.B. 343 7.24, 9.4
77-321, 1977-2 C.B. 98 11.34.1
77-346, 1977-2 C.B. 340 5.22.2
77-357, 1977-2 C.B. 328 12.3.4
77-359, 1977-2 C.B. 24 3.7.3, 3.34.1
77-374, 1977-2 C.B. 329 8.21, 8.25
77-378, 1977-2 C.B. 347 10.34.1, 10.40.2
77-439, 1977-2 C.B. 85 5.37.2, 10.4.12
77-455, 1977-2 C.B. 93 11.34.3
77-461, 1977-2 C.B. 324 12.12
78-38, 1978-1 C.B. 67 8.6
78-125, 1978-1 C.B. 292 11.28, 12.12
78-129, 1978-1 C.B. 67 8.6
78-135, 1978-1 C.B. 256 11.39

78-197, 1978-1 C.B. 83 8.38
78-292, 1978-2 C.B. 233 12.3.4
78-303, 1978-2 C.B. 122 8.15.2
78-378, 1978-2 C.B. 229 12.15.6
78-379, 1978-2 C.B. 238 6.27.10
78-401, 1978-2 C.B. 127 11.24.1
78-409, 1978-2 C.B. 234 7.23
78-420, 1978-2 C.B. 67 6.71.2, 6.71.3
78-431, 1978-2 C.B. 230 12.15.6
79-7, 1979-1 C.B. 294 7.16
79-14, 1979-1 C.B. 309 5.22.1
79-41, 1979-1 C.B. 124 6.60.2
79-46, 1979-1 C.B. 303 6.27.6
79-47, 1979-1 C.B. 312 6.71.3, 6.72.12
79-50, 1979-1 C.B. 138 6.71.2
79-86, 1979-1 C.B. 311 5.22.2
79-87, 1979-1 C.B. 73 6.9.5, 6.51
79-91, 1979-1 C.B. 179 9.6.1
79-124, 1979-1 C.B. 225 12.5
79-129, 1979-1 C.B. 306 6.71.4
79-154, 1979-1 C.B. 301 10.41.5, 10.41.6
79-187, 1979-1 C.B. 95 6.55.3
79-202, 1979-2 C.B. 31 6.57
79-211, 1979-2 C.B. 319 10.20
79-231, 1979-2 C.B. 23 6.72.1
79-295, 1979-2 C.B. 349 8.17
79-303, 1979-2 C.B. 332 6.80.1
79-324, 1979-2 C.B. 119 10.3
79-327, 1979-2 C.B. 342 10.23, 10.27.2
79-353, 1979-2 C.B. 325 4.24.1, 6.27.7, 10.28, 10.39.3, 10.41, 10.41.1, 10.41.5, 10.41.8, 10.41.9, 10.43.6
79-372, 1979-2 C.B. 330 3.15.2
79-398, 1979-2 C.B. 338 2.4.2, 7.25.2
79-409, 1979-2 C.B. 208 12.3.7
80-33, 1980-1 C.B. 69 8.9
80-74, 1980-1 C.B. 137 10.3
80-80, 1980-1 C.B. 194 2.5.2
80-123, 1980-1 C.B. 205 8.23
80-132, 1980-1 C.B. 255 6.55.2
80-242, 1980-2 C.B. 276 6.15.1
80-250, 1980-2 C.B. 278 12.12
80-255, 1980-2 C.B. 272 6.27.3
80-261, 1980-2 C.B. 279 7.37.9
80-281, 1980-2 C.B. 282 8.37
80-289, 1980-2 C.B. 270 6.32.5, 6.72.11
80-36, 1980-2 C.B. 386 11.17
81-6, 1981-1 C.B. 385 7.37.10
81-7, 1981-1 C.B. 474 7.37.6
81-14, 1981-1 C.B. 456 6.36
81-15, 1981-1 C.B. 457 10.38.3
81-31, 1981-1 C.B. 475 6.78.8
81-51, 1981-1 C.B. 458 6.27.7, 10.41.1, 10.43.6
81-126, 1981-1 C.B. 206 6.59.1
81-128, 1981-1 C.B. 469 6.27.2
81-154, 1981-1 C.B. 170 12.13
81-163, 1981-1 C.B. 433 8.36
81-164, 1981-1 C.B. 458 6.71.4
81-166, 1981-1 C.B. 477 6.26, 6.42, 6.47
81-198, 1981-2 C.B. 188 6.71.3
81-221, 1981-2 C.B. 178 6.39
81-223, 1981-2 C.B. 189 7.25.2
81-253, 1981-2 C.B. 187 7.16
81-282, 1981-2 C.B. 78 8.18
81-302, 1981-2 C.B. 170 7.11
82-13, 1982-1 C.B. 132 6.72.11
82-23, 1982-1 C.B. 139 5.7.1
82-38, 1982-1 C.B. 96 8.30
82-63, 1982-1 C.B. 135 10.25
82-98, 1982-1 C.B. 141 2.6
82-85, 1982-1 C.B. 137 6.71.4, 11.12, 11.22
82-128, 1982-2 C.B. 771 8.19
82-141, 1982-2 C.B. 209 6.32.2
82-145, 1982-2 C.B. 213 6.71.4
82-165, 1982-2 C.B. 117 8.23
83-45, 1983-1 C.B. 233 8.17
83-75, 1983-1 C.B. 114 8.31
83-96, 1983-2 C.B. 156 12.19.3
83-107, 1983-2 C.B. 159 12.30.1
83-119, 1983-2 C.B. 57 11.31, 11.34.5
83-120, 1983-2 C.B. 170 11.31
83-147, 1983-2 C.B. 158 6.28.2
83-148, 1983-2 C.B. 157 6.28.2
83-158, 1983-2 C.B. 159 8.15.3
84-9, 1984-2 C.B. 196 8.15.2
84-61, 1984-1 C.B. 40 8.4.2
84-75, 1984-1 C.B. 193 12.12, 12.13
84-76, 1984-1 C.B. 91 11.16
84-130, 1984-2 C.B. 194 6.27.5
84-147, 1984-2 C.B. 201 6.43.1
84-162, 1984-2 C.B. 200 8.37
84-179, 1984-2 C.B. 195 6.27.11
85-13, 1985-1 C.B. 184 9.43.3, 10.32.8, 10.38.1
85-20, 1985-1 C.B. 183 8.30
85-24, 1985-1 C.B. 329 7.37.5

Table of Internal Revenue Rulings

85-45, 1985-1 C.B. 183	10.32.6
85-57, 1985-1 C.B. 182	8.30
85-75, 1985-1 C.B. 376	12.16
85-88, 1985-2 C.B. 202	10.24
85-184, 1985-2 C.B. 85	8.2
86-32, 1986-1 C.B. 252	9.10.2
86-39, 1986-1 C.B. 301	10.27.2
86-54, 1986-1 C.B. 356	11.29.2
86-60, 1986-1 C.B. 302	8.25
86-72, 1986-1 C.B. 253	9.6.4, 9.10.2, 12.38
86-82, 1986-1 C.B. 253	10.38.1
86-105, 1986-2 C.B. 83	12.37
86-106, 1986-2 C.B. 28	10.3
86-139, 1986-2 C.B. 95	12.5.1
87-37, 1987-1 C.B. 295	8.15.2
87-69, 1987-2 C.B. 46	10.3
87-98, 1987-2 C.B. 206	3.12.5, 3.20.6, 3.35.4
87-122, 1987-2 C.B. 221	12.19.4
87-132, 1987-2 C.B. 82	11.16, 11.34.4
88-27, 1988-1 C.B. 331	8.31
88-31, 1988-1 C.B. 302	12.15.4
88-81, 1988-1 C.B. 127	8.23
88-82, 1988-2 C.B. 336	8.31, 8.32
88-89, 1988-2 C.B. 333	12.15.4
88-103, 1988-2 C.B. 304	10.32.7
89-45, 1989-1 C.B. 267	10.4.14
89-51, 1989-1 C.B. 89	8.4.2
89-55, 1989-1 C.B. 268	10.4.14
89-75, 1989-1 C.B. 319	12.13.2
89-77, 1989-1 C.B. 266	9.6.5
90-3, 1990-1 C.B. 175	5.34
90-21, 1990-1 C.B. 172	6.28, 6.32.2
90-46, 1990-1 C.B. 107	9.3
90-55, 1990-2 C.B. 161	10.4.16
90-103, 1990-2 C.B. 159	8.30
90-109, 1990-2 C.B. —	6.65
90-110, 1990-2 C.B. 209	5.23.8, 10.41.10, 12.32.1

Revenue Procedures

59-31, 1959-2 C.B. 949	8.2.1
69-18, 1969-2 C.B. 300	12.48.5
79-55, 1979-2 C.B. 539	11.27.2
79-63, 1979-2 C.B. 578	12.5.1
81-27, 1981-2 C.B. 548	11.28, 12.12
82-39, 1982-1 C.B. 759	8.2.2
88-53, 1988-2 C.B. 712	8.23, 8.30
88-54, 1988-2 C.B. 715	8.30
89-20, 1989-1 C.B. 841	8.23
89-21, 1989-1 C.B. 842	8.23
90-30, 1990-1 C.B. 534	8.23
90-32, 1990-1 C.B. 539	8.23
90-32, 1990 C.B. 546	8.23
90-64, 1990-2 C.B.	7.9.1
91-1, 1991-1 C.B.	8.27
91-3, 1991-1 C.B.	11.34.1
91-14, 1991-1 C.B.	8.2.2, 8.27

IRS Notices

89-24, 1989-1 C.B. 660	6.20, 10.35
89-60, 1989-1 C.B. 700	8.30
89-99, 1989-2 C.B. 422	11.31

Private Letter Rulings and Technical Advice Memoranda

7730008	11.34.3
7734048	12.6
7752001	7.25.1, 7.27
7802002	6.78.6
7810001	4.7.1
7821150	3.35.2
7824005	11.41.2
7826050	7.37.7
7827008	5.37.1
7833008	12.31
7842068	7.25.2
7906051	6.54
7909031	6.60.1
7935006	7.37.8
7935091	6.44.2, 7.37.7
7935115	2.5.5
7941037	11.12.1
7946007	7.37.6
7946080	3.14
7947066	7.37.8
7948063	11.39
8003033	7.37.3
8003152	7.37.2, 7.37.3
8004172	7.37.8
8006048	7.37.6, 7.37.7, 7.37.8
8006109	6.72.12, 7.37.7
8009027	8.12
8016050	3.35.3, 5.38.5, 12.39.2
8017058	8.33

8018068	11.34.3	8440037	5.27
8020124	11.34.3, 11.34.5	8441029	11.29
8021058	6.44.2, 6.72.12	8443005	5.23.8, 12.35
8022048	7.37.2	8445004	2.5.7, 7.37.7
8026032	8.31	8450031	9.6.3
8030054	8.31	8501012	6.65, 6.66
8034017	6.72.11	8501014	9.3
8037124	5.33.5, 12.39.2	8509005	6.32.2
8043030	11.12.1	8514095	12.34
8044021	11.35	8515063	6.65.2
8044034	11.24.1	8517052	7.37.2, 10.24, 10.24.1
8102029	9.14		
8103066	11.29	8521060	10.24.1
8103130	7.24	8521155	5.23.10
8117045	8.37	8526038	6.65.3
8119040	4.27.6, 12.39	8532006	5.23.10
8122075	10.41.10	8535048	8.24
8128005	6.27.10	8545003	9.6.5
8141037	8.15.3	8545010	9.6.3
8142061	10.24.1	8545076	10.24.1
8143029	8.12	8552009	8.38
8144001	6.51.2	8602005	12.20.5
8144051	8.33	8604033	6.59.1, 6.65, 6.65.2, 6.66
8145012	9.41		
8152078	8.33	8606002	10.41.9
8202023	5.22.3	8609005	10.17
8229009	12.19.3	8610067	8.24
8229097	7.37.2, 10.24	8610068	6.27.1
8229107	6.65.2	8611004	2.5.7
8301008	12.19.3	8611006	12.20.1
8308033	10.24.1	8634004	11.6
8310033	6.65.3	8639046	8.38
8317050	9.6.4	8642028	10.33
8320007 (TAM)	2.5.2, 2.5.4	8701001	12.35
8326023	11.29.1	8701003	6.78.5, 6.78.7
8331012	12.5.1	8709001	10.3
8333019	8.10.1, 8.16	8710004	6.71.4, 11.6
8335032	9.32	8711002	9.6.3
8335033	5.23.1	8723007	2.5.5
8337024	12.5.1	8724014	6.35
8338095	8.33	8727003	7.37.5
8338108	8.31	8728001	10.4.3, 12.20, 12.25.1
8339023	11.29.1		
8341005	12.36	8730006	11.29
8343010	6.65.3	8801008	10.33
8349034	6.9.5	8806004	6.34, 6.38
8403010	2.5.5	8806082	10.33
8404099	12.36.7	8808031	8.31
8424010	6.65.3	8816015	6.65, 6.66
8427085	6.9.5	8819001	6.27.3, 6.32.5
8429085	12.35	8824033	12.33.1
8433024	7.37.8	8829013	11.26.3, 11.29
8433035	6.65.2	8834005	5.16
8433061	8.36	8837031	12.22

Table of Internal Revenue Rulings

8839008	10.40.1
8843005	12.24, 12.24.5
8848002 (TAM)	11.26.3
8901004	7.37.4, 10.24.2
8903019	8.30
8905004	6.68
8906002	6.28, 6.32.2
8906034	11.9
8910038	12.5.1
8910039	12.5.1
8911006	12.25.2
8911028	10.7
8912011	12.5.1
8916032	10.28, 10.29, 10.41.1, 10.41.4-10.41.6, 10.41.9, 10.43.6
8922003	6.27.7, 10.29, 10.41.1, 10.41.5
8922062	7.37.5, 7.37.6, 7.37.12, 10.28
8926001	12.31
8935024	5.23.8, 12.32.1
8940003	10.17
8940008	10.34.2
8943005	5.23.3, 5.29
8943082	6.28.1, 11.9
8944005	2.15
8944009	2.9.2, 5.23.6
8949009	5.9
8952005	5.25
9001001	12.15.1
9002014	2.26, 2.40.2, 12.22
9005001	8.2.3
9008017	5.23.7
9010004	10.17
9010005	10.17
9012063	6.53.3, 11.9
9015003	11.26.2
9015009	11.25, 11.26.2
9015049	8.19
9016002	10.17
9016079	10.26
9021017	10.34.3
9021037	5.25
9030005	7.34.3, 7.37.2, 7.37.6, 10.23, 10.24
9030032	10.26
9032002	10.35.1
9034004	7.37.10, 10.24.1
9046043	10.4.4
9036048	10.23, 10.41.4
9037011	10.4.14, 10.32.1, 10.32.2
9038015	5.23.5
9040003	8.2
9041027	10.32.9
9042048	10.27.3
9043016	4.16.1
9043045	5.38.5
9043052	10.41.5
9043054	5.23.5
9043070	5.25
9044072	5.25
9045002	7.37.5
9045004	11.9, 12.6
9046002	12.13
9048001	5.3.3
9050004	5.5.2
9051002	12.13
9104024	2.5.5, 2.5.7
9105006	2.30.1
9108027	9.6.4
9109003	5.21
9110016	6.2, 8.39
9111011	2.40.5, 12.35
9111028	6.27.11
9113009	7.18
9114023	2.5.5
9114024	2.23.1
9116003	12.20.2
9117003 (TAM)	10.17
9123036	9.6.4
9128008	6.27.9
9131006 (TAM)	2.5.7, 10.41.8, 11.38.3, 11.41, 11.41.3
9139001 (TAM)	5.17
9139002 (TAM)	10.17
9141008	7.37.5
9147065 (TAM)	5.17
9147040	6.2
9151002 (TAM)	12.2.4

Table of Miscellaneous Federal Citations

(references are to sections)

ADVISORY OPINIONS (*A.O.*) (DEPARTMENT OF LABOR)

AO 90-46A	3.32, 4.20.6, 12.25
AO 90-47A	3.32, 4.20.6, 12.25

ACTIONS ON DECISION (*A.O.D.*) IRS

1984-038	9.17, 9.20.4
1990-14	5.3.3
1990-026	6.78.8
1991-012	6.31, 6.32. 6.32.5

GENERAL COUNSEL'S MEMORANDA (*G.C.M.*) IRS

34730	10.41.2
39503	9.3, 9.8, 9.8.1, 9.8.2, 9.10, 9.10.2, 9.13

INTERNAL REVENUE SERVICE PUBLICATIONS

Cumulative List of Organizations Described in I.R.C. §170(c)

78	8.2.3

Actuarial Values, Alpha Volume (1989)

1457	6.10, 7.38, 8.19, 8.21, 8.25, 8.37, 9.13, 9.21, 9.43.1, 10.35

Actuarial Values, Beta Volume (1989)

1458	8.19, 8.22, 8.25, 9.43.1, 10.35

Actuarial Values, Gamma Volume (1989)

1459	8.15

General Explanation of the 1976 Act

537	12.19
546	12.44
548	11.26.1

IRS Handbook for Estate Tax Audits

15(42)	12.13.3
15(52)	12.13.3

IRS News Releases

IR-84-101	8.35

IRS Forms

56	12.2.3, 12.50
706	5.3.3,11.23,11.30,11.28, 12.19.2, 12.20.4
709	2.10
1041	10.4.2, 10.31, 12.7
4768	12.43, 12.44, 12.50
5227	10.4.16
5329	12.26.1
8282	8.7.3
8283	8.7, 8.7.1
PD 1782	12.48, 12.50
SS-4	12.50

TABLE OF STATUTES

(references are to sections)

FEDERAL STATUTES

11 U.S.C. (Bankruptcy Code)

541(b) 10.11
70(a)(3) (former) 10.11

31 U.S.C.

3713 10.6.8, 12.49
3713(a) 12.49
3713(b) 12.49

38 U.S.C.

765 6.77
777 6.77
777(b) 6.77

PUBLIC LAWS

P.L. 93-289, 88 Stat. 168, 5(a)(5) 6.77
P.L. 99-514, 100 Stat. 2470-72 12.25.3

ACTS OF CONGRESS

Employee Retirement Income Security Act of 1974 (ERISA)

Generally 3.32, 4.20.6
205 10.6.2

Retirement Equity Act of 1984

Generally 10.6.2

Revenue Act of 1932

202 12.15

Tax Reform Act of 1976 (1976 Act)

Generally 2.2, 2.3, 5.2.3

Economic Recovery Tax Act of 1981 (1981 Act)

Generally 2.3, 2.9.2

Tax Reform Act of 1982 (1984 Act)

Generally 12.25, 12.25.1

Tax Reform Act of 1986 (1986 Act)

Generally 12.25, 12.27

Revenue Act of 1987 (1987 Act)

Generally 2.17.2

Technical Corrections and Miscellaneous Revenue Act of 1988 (1988 Act)

Generally 2.17.2

Revenue Reconciliation Act of 1989 (1989 Act)

Generally 6.22.4

Revenue Reconciliation Act of 1990 (1990 Act)

11602(e)(1) 11.32
11602(e)(1)(B) 11.32
11602(e)(1)(A)(ii) 11.6

STATE STATUTES

Alaska

Statutes Annotated

13.11.277 5.3.3

Arizona

Revised Statutes

25-318 3.38

Arkansas

Code Annotated

9-11-402 1.14.2

California

Business and Professions Code

6148 1.19

Civil Code

683 3.3, 3.12
683.2 3.3
1386.2 4.21.1
4800.1 3.4, 3.7.2, 3.12.5, 3.26
4800.8 3.32
4803 3.38
5103 3.29
5110.150 3.25
5110.730 3.29
5125 3.28.2
5125(b) 7.9

Probate Code

101 3.38
700 4.5
901 1.22
3905 4.17.1
6142 4.21.1
6220-6247 4.3
6320-6330 6.18.2
6324 4.21.4, 6.18.2
6401 4.4.2
8480 4.26.7
9050 4.5
9100 4.5
10500 4.26.9
15300 10.21
13500 et seq. 4.21.2
15400 10.8
15408 4.24.6
15411-154 4.24.7
16003 10.45.1
16007 10.45.1
16014(b) 10.45.2
16040 4.24.5, 10.45.1, 10.46

16311(d)	10.47.4
20100 et seq.	4.27.1
21523	5.3.3

Delaware

Code Annotated

Tit. 12, 3302(a)	4.24.5
Tit. 25, 501	2.31

Florida

Statutes Annotated

689.15	3.3
710.102	4.17.1
726.105	10.11
732.102	4.4.1
732.102(1)	4.4.1
732.513	4.21.4
732.517	4.29
732.607	4.21.1
732.701	4.7
733.808	4.21.4

Idaho

Code

15-2-201(a)	3.38
15-2-201(b)	3.38
15-6-201	3.30
32-906	3.28.3
32-906A	3.25

Illinois

Annotated Statutes

Ch.110-½, 4-5	4.21.4, 6.18, 6.19

Indiana

Annotated Code

27-1-12-16	6.18.2, 6.19
29-1-5-3(c)	4.32
30-1-9-14	10.11

Iowa

Code Annotated

633.211-.212	4.4.1

Kansas

Statutes Annotated

58-2414	10.11

Louisiana

Civil Code Annotated

Art. 2336	3.34.2
Art. 2339	3.25, 3.28.3
Art. 2341	3.34.2
Art. 2343	3.34.1

Maine

Revised Statutes Annotated

18-A, 2-514	4.3

Maryland

Estate & Trusts Code Ann.

11-106(a)	12.14

Michigan

Statutes Annotated

25.131	4.20.4
25.132	3.3
26.155(118)	10.11

Montana

Revised Code

72-2-202(1)	4.4.1

Nevada

Revised Statutes

111.060	3.3, 3.12
111.064	3.12.5, 3.30
123.070	3.29
163.280	4.24.3

New Mexico

Statutes Annotated

40-3-8	3.4, 3.12.5
45-2-804	12.11

New York

Estates, Powers and Trusts Law

2-1.8	4.27.1
2-1.8(b)	12.42.5
2-1.8(d)	4.27.4
3-3.3	4.15
3-4.5	4.15.1, 4.20.2
4-1.1	4.4.1
5.1.1(b)(1)(E)	10.11
7-4.9	4.17.1
6-2.2(a)	3.3, 3.12
6-2.2(b)	3.3
6-2.2(c)	3.3, 3.13
10-6.1(a)(4)	4.21.1
11-1.2(A)	12.14
11-2.1(e)(3)	10.47.1
13-3.3	6.19
13-3.3(a)(1)	6.18.2
13-3.3(a)(2)	6.18.2

Surrogate's Court Procedure Act

710	4.26.7
2111	4.26.1
2307	4.26.4
2309	4.26.4

North Carolina

General Statutes

39-13.3	3.13
41-2	3.12

Ohio

Revised Code

1339.63	4.20.4
5402.20(c)(5)	3.3

Oklahoma

Statutes Annotated

Tit. 15, 178	4.26.4, 6.1
Tit. 60, 175.41	10.8
Tit. 84, 186	5.3.3

Oregon

Revised Statutes

93.180	3.2, 3.12

Pennsylvania

Statutes Annotated

Tit. 40, 512	6.2, 8.39

South Carolina

Code

62-5-501(c)	4.35.1

Texas

Constitution

art. xvi, 15	3.28.3, 3.29, 3.30, 6.39

Family Code

3.63	3.38
3.632	4.20.4

Insurance Code

3.49-3	4.21.4

Probate Code

89	4.21.2
117	4.25
145	4.26.9
155	4.21.2
193	4.25
194	4.26.7
195	4.26.7
450	3.30
451 et seq.	3.12.5, 3.30
452	3.12.5
456(a)	3.30
458	3.30

Property Code

112.051	10.8

Utah

Code Annotated

75-2-613	5.3.3
75-7-501	5.3.3

Virginia

Code Annotated

64-1-62.1	5.3.3

Washington

Revised Code

11.04.015(1)(a)	4.4.2
11.04.071	3.13
11.12.110	4.15
11.86.070	10.21
11.88.080	4.25
11.94.010	4.35.2
11.100.020	4.24.5, 10.45.2
11.100.020(1)	10.45.1
11.100.130	10.45.4
11.100.23	4.24.5
11.108.040	5.3.3
26.16.030(2)	7.9, 3.28.2
26.16.120	3.29, 3.30
26.16.220-.250	3.38
26.16.230	3.38
48.18.030	6.2
48.18.375	6.72.11
48.18.450	6.18.2
48.18.452	4.21.4, 6.18.2
64.28.020	3.13
64.28.040	3.12.5, 3.26
64.28.087	3.12

Wisconsin

Statutes Annotated

766.01	3.23
766.001(2)	3.23
766.17	3.29
766.31(3)	3.28.2, 3.32
766.31(4)	3.28.3
766.31(5)	3.25
766.31(6)	3.28
766.53	3.28.2
766.58	1.14.2, 3.29, 3.30
766.59	3.25
766.60(4)(a)	3.7.2
766.60(5)	3.12.5, 3.30
766.60(5)(a)	3.30
766.61	3.28.5
766.61(b)(3)	3.28.5
766.61(c)	3.28.5
766.61(d)	3.28.5
766.75	3.3
851.055	3.38
852.01	4.4.2
853.50-853.62	4.3
861.01(2)	3.4
861.02	3.38

UNIFORM ACTS

Anatomical Gift Act
8A U.L.A. 15 (1983)

Generally	4.11, 4.34, 4.38
3	4.38.2
4(a)	4.38.3
4(b)	4.38.3
4(c)	4.38.2
4(d)	4.38.3
4(e)	4.38.3
6(a)	4.38.4
6(b)	4.38.4
6(c)	4.38.4

7(a)	4.38.5
7(b)	4.38.5
7(c)	4.38.5
7(d)	4.38.5
11(c)	4.38

Disclaimer of Property Interests Act
8A U.L.A. 86 (1983)

Generally	12.31, 12.33

Disclaimer of Transfers by Will, Intestacy or Appointment Act (1978)
8A U.L.A. 96 (1983)

Generally	12.31

Disclaimer of Transfers Under Nontestamentary Instruments Act (1978)
8A U.L.A. 111 (1983)

Generally	12.31

Disposition of Community Property Rights at Death Act
8A U.L.A. 121 (1983)

Generally	3.36, 4.4.1

Durable Power of Attorney Act
8A U.L.A. 77 (1991 Supp.)

Generally	4.34, 4.35

Gifts to Minors Act
8A U.L.A. 317 (1983)

Generally	4.17.1, 6.29, 6.44.2, 7.2.2, 7.2.3, 7.28, 10.4, 10.33.1, 10.43.3, 11.40.2
2(a)(2)	7.34
2(a)(4)	6.79
3(b)	7.34
4(b)	7.34
4(d)	7.34
4(e)	7.34

Limited Partnership Act
U.L.A. 582 (1969)

7	11.41.3

Limited Partnership Act (Revised)
6 U.L.A. 325-26 (1991 Supp.)

303	11.41.3

Marital Property Act
9A U.L.A. 97 (1987)

Generally	3.23
4(c)	4.4.2

Parentage Act
9A U.L.A. 287 (1987)

2	4.14

Premarital Agreement Act
9B U.L.A. 369 (1987)

Generally	1.14.2

Principal and Income Act
7B U.L.A. (1985)

Generally	9.18, 10.47, 10.47.1, 10.47.2, 10.47.4
3(c)(1)	4.24.3
6(a)	4.24.3

Principal and Income Act (Revised) (1962)
7B U.L.A. 145 (1985)

Generally	10.47, 10.47.1-10.47.4

Probate Code

Generally	4.35.7, 7.31, 7.32, 7.33.1
Art. VI, Part 2	3.12.1
2-102	4.4.1
2-102A	4.4.2
2-104	4.15.4, 5.20
2-201	9.25
2-202(b)(2)	3.11
2-202(1)(ii)	10.11
2-203	9.27
2-401	5.16.1, 12.29
2-402	5.16.1, 12.29
2.403	5.16.1, 12.29
2-501	1.8.1, 4.35.7
2-502	4.32
2-504	4.31
2.505(b)	4.30
2-506	4.30
2.508	4.20.5
2.510	4.18.1
2.511	4.21.4, 10.10
2-512	4.18.2
2-513	4.17.3, 4.18.4
2-514	4.7
2-603	4.15
2-603(b)(3)	4.15
2-604(a)	4.15
2-605	4.19
2.606	4.15.1
2-606(a)(3)	4.20.2
2-607	4.12, 4.20.1
2-608	4.21.1
2-609	4.16.2
2-702	4.15.4, 5.20
2-703	4.21.7
2-804	4.20.4, 6.1
3-603	4.26.7
3-715	4.26.9
3-803	4.5
3-902	4.12
3-905	4.29
3-916	4.27.1, 12.42
3-916(e)(2)	4.27.7
5-202	4.25
5-209(c)(2)	4.25
5-501 et seq.	4.35
5-501	4.35, 4.35.1
5-503(a)	4.35.1
5-503(b)	4.35.1, 4.35.2
5-504(a)	4.35
5-504(b)	4.35
6-101	3.1, 3.21, 3.30, 4.16.4, 4.21.4
6-205	7.33.1
6-211(b)	7.33.1
6-212(a)	7.33.1
6-211	3.12.1
6-212(a)	3.12.1
6-215	3.11.1
6-301(1)	3.12.2
6-302	3.12.2
6-310	3.12.2
7-302	10.45.2

Rights of the Terminally Ill Act
9B U.L.A. 609 (1987)

Generally	4.34, 4.36.3
2(c)	4.36.3

Simultaneous Death Act
8A U.L.A. 575 (1983)

Generally	3.12.3

Statutory Rule Against Perpetuities Act
8A U.L.A. 159 (1990 Supp.)

Generally	10.48

Statutory Wills Act
8A U.L.A. 196 (1990 Supp.)

Generally	4.3

Testamentary Additions to Trust Act
8A U.L.A. 599 (1983)

Generally	10.10

Transfer on Death Security Registration Act
8 U.L.A. (1990 Supp.)

6-301	3.12.2
6-305	7.33.2

Transfer to Minors Act 8A U.L.A. 207 (1989 Supp.)

Generally 4.2, 4.17.1, 4.24, 4.24.6, 6.44.2, 7.2.8, 11.40.2
5 4.21.6
6 4.17.1
9 6.79, 7.34
11(c) 7.34
12(b) 7.34
14(a) 7.34
14(c) 7.34
20 4.21.6, 7.34

Trustees' Powers Act

Generally 4.24.3

FOREIGN STATUTES

United Kingdom

U.K. Finance Act 1975

20.2 2.43.1

Finance Act of 1976

115-117 7.22

MODEL RULES OF PROFESSIONAL CONDUCT

1.1 1.7
1.2 1.5, 1.31
1.2(d) 1.13
1.3 1.6
1.4 1.5, 1.8.3
1.4(b) 1.31
1.5 12.2.1
1.5(a) 1.20
1.5(b) 1.19
1.6 1.7, 4.26
1.6(a) 1.14.1
1.7 1.14, 1.14.3, 1.36, 9.2
1.8 1.17, 10.43.2
1.8(a) 1.15
1.8(c) 1.16, 1.18
1.8(f) 1.21
1.10(a) 1.14.4, 1.16
1.14(a) 1.8.1
2.1 1.9
2.2 1.14, 1.14.3, 9.2
3.1-3.9 1.13
3.3 4.26.1
4.1 1.13
5.1 1.11
5.3 1.11
5.5 1.12

CODE OF PROFESSIONAL RESPONSIBILITY

Canons

9 1.14

Disciplinary Rules

1-102(A)(4) 1.13
2-106(B) 1.22
3-101(A) 1.34
3-101(B) 1.12
4-101 1.7, 1.14.1
4-101(D) 1.11
5-104(A) 1.15, 1.17
5-105 1.14, 9.2
5-107(A) 1.7.3
5-107(B) 1.21
6-101 1.7
7-102(A)(1) 1.13
7-102(A)(5) 1.13

Ethical Considerations

2-18 1.20
2-19 1.19
4-2 1.7
4-4 1.14.1
5-3 1.17
5-5 1.16
5-6 1.18, 4.26.1, 10.43.2
5-14-5-18 9.2, 11.38.6
5-15 1.14
5-16 1.14
5-17 1.14
7-8 1.9, 1.31

RESTATEMENTS

Conflict of Laws (Second) (1971)

259	3.36

Property (1940)

312(2)	4.21.7
325	5.21

Trusts (Second) (1959)

57	10.9
89	10.43
96	10.43
97	10.43
98	10.43
99	10.27
152	10.21
152 (comment i)	10.21.1
153	10.21
154	10.20.9, 10.21
155 (comment h)	10.20.9
155(1)	10.20.9, 10.21
155(2)	10.20.9
156	10.11
156(1)	10.20.2
157	10.21
167	10.45
176 (comment a)	10.45.2
181	10.45.1
185	10.45.4
187 (comment j)	10.8, 10.20.7
222 (comment a)	10.46
227(a)	10.45.1
228	10.45.1
240	10.47.4
241	10.47.4
303	10.8

INDEX

(references are to sections)

Ademption, 4.15.1
Alternate valuation date. *See* Estate tax
Anatomical gifts, 4.11, 4.38
  action by others, 4.38.5
  disposition of remains, 4.11
  donees, 4.38.2
  donor card, 4.38.7
  planning, 4.38.6
  revocation and amendment, 4.38.4
  ways of making gifts, 4.38.3
Annual exclusion. *See* Gift tax
Ante-nuptial agreement, 1.14.2
Anti-lapse statutes, 4.15
Appreciated property acquired from a decedent, 3.35.5
Attorneys. *See also* Clients, Conflicts of interest, Malpractice and Professional responsibility
  advice to, record of, 1.10, 1.31.3
   letter, 1.3, 1.32
  assisting client's decision, counselling, 1.9, 1.31
  associating others, 1.1, 1.5
  beneficiary, lawyer as, 1.16
  business arrangements with client, 1.17
  client relations, 1.4
  competence, 1.5
  confidentiality, duty of, 1.7, 1.30.6
  conflicts. *See* Conflicts of interest
  continuing supervision or services, 1.34.1
  counselling client, 1.9, 1.31
  diligence, 1.6
  efficiency, 1.6
  engagement letter, 1.10
  fees
   bequest, payment by, 1.23
   fee schedules, 1.22
   for estate administration services, 1.22, 1.25
   for lifetime estate planning services, 1.20, 1.24
   guidelines, 1.22
   hourly rates, 1.20
   income tax deductibility, 1.24
   informing client, 1.19
   payment by nonclient, 1.21
   referral fees, kickbacks, 1.7.3
   satisfying the fee, 1.23
  fiduciary, lawyer as, 1.18, 4.26.1

Attorneys (*continued*)
gifts to, 1.16
imputed disqualification, 1.14.4
incompetent client, protection of, 1.8.1
intermediary, acting as, (MRPC 2.2), 1.14.3
procrastination by, 1.6
relationship to beneficiaries, 1.36
Automation in estate planning
document production, 1.33

Bargain sales
charity, to, 8.36
Below-market loans, 7.18
Bequests and devises. *See also* Marital deduction, Wills
condition of survivorship for a specified period, 4.15.2
exoneration, 4.12, 4.20.1
pecuniary, 4.16
residuary, 4.20
specific property, 4.15
tangible personal property, 4.17
corporate securities, 4.19
disposition by later list, 4.18.4
Buy-sell agreements, 11.6
accumulated earnings tax, 11.12.3
C corporation, 11.9
community property, 11.14
cross purchase, 11.8
entity purchase, 11.8
ethical considerations, 11.13
funding, 11.8, 11.12
accumulated earnings tax, 11.12.3
cross-purchase agreement, 11.12
installment payment, 11.12.1
life insurance, 11.8, 11.12
modification, 11.6
nontax considerations, 11.7
S corporation, by, 11.10
section 2703, 11.6
shifting from entity purchase to cross purchase, 11.8
valuation, 11.11
Bypass trust
reducing the size of the estate, 2.45

Charitable deduction
estate tax, 2.15
bargain sale, 8.36
cash bequests, 4.6.1
charitable pledges, 8.4
conditional transfer, 8.18
future interests in tangible personal property, 8.13. *See also* Charitable trusts
lead trusts. *See* Charitable trusts
partial interests, 8.14
donor's entire interest, 8.17
remainder in personal residence or farm, 8.15
qualified conservation contribution, 8.16
undivided portion of interest, 8.16
pooled income fund. *See* Charitable trusts
qualified charities, 8.2
tangible personal property, 8.12
trusts. *See* Charitable trusts
gift tax, 2.8
bargain sale, 8.36
charitable gift annuities, 8.37
conditional transfer, 8.18
future interests in tangible personal property, 8.13. *See also* Charitable trusts
income interest, 8.33
lead trusts. *See* Charitable trusts
life insurance, 8.39
partial interests, 8.14
donor's entire interest, 8.17
remainder in personal residence or farm, 8.15
undivided portion of interest, 8.16
pooled income fund. *See* Charitable trusts
qualified charities, 8.2
tangible personal property, 8.12
trusts. *See* Charitable trusts
income tax, 8.1
bargain sale, 8.36
capital gain property, 8.10
election to reduce gift amount, 8.11
carryover deduction, 8.5
charitable gift annuities, 8.37
conditional transfer, 8.18
depreciated property, 8.8
future interests in tangible personal property, 8.13
income interest, 8.33

lead trusts. *See* Charitable trusts
life insurance, 8.39
limit, 8.2, 8.3
nonpublic charities, 8.4
ordinary income property, 8.9
partial interests, 8.14
donor's entire interest, 8.17
remainder in personal residence or farm, 8.15
undivided portion of interest, 8.16
pooled income fund, 8.30. *See* Charitable trusts
public charities, 8.3
qualified charities, 8.2
remainder interest, 8.4, 8.15
time of gift, 8.6
trusts. *See* Charitable trusts
valuation, 8.7
Charitable gifts, 8.1
annuities, 8.37
federal tax consequences. *See* Charitable deduction
gift and redemption of appreciated stock, 8.38
not in trust, 8.14, 8.15
part sale, part gift, 8.36
qualified conservation contribution, 8.16
remainder interest in farm or residence, 8.15
trusts. *See* Charitable trusts
Charitable trusts, 8.2
lead trusts, 8.31
remainder trusts, 8.20, 8.21
advantages of, 8.28
annuity trust, 8.21
addition prohibited, 8.21
minimum annual payout, 8.21
minimum remainder value required, 8.21
required distribution, 8.21
valuation, 8.21
disqualification, risk of, 8.20
diversify investment, used to, 8.20.2
double deductions, 8.20.1
income-only unitrust, 8.22
income taxation, 8.24
lead trust, 8.31
tax consequences, 8.32
marital deduction, 5.25, 8.20.5
mortgaged property, 8.19
pooled income fund, 8.30
requirements, 8.30
valuation, 8.30
private foundation rules, 8.26
requests for rulings, 8.27
requirements, 8.20
restrictions on distributions, 8.20
restrictions on investments, 8.19
retirement plan, substitute for, 8.20.4
sample forms, 8.23
unitrust, 8.22
income-only, 8.22
income with makeup, 8.22
minimum annual payout, 8.22
required distributions, 8.22
valuation, 8.25
wealth replacement plans, 8.20.3
Checklists. *See* Worksheets, forms, and checklists
Clients. *See also* Attorneys
attorneys continuing supervision or services to, 1.34.1, 1.34.2
beneficiaries as, 1.36
competence of, 1.8
counseling, 1.9, 1.31
data summary, 1.10.1
document summary, 1.10.2
engagement letter, 1.10.1, 1.30.6
estate or trust as, 1.36
fiduciary as, 1.36
independent representation, 1.14
initial conference with, 1.29, 1.30
facilitating communication with, 1.5, 1.30-1.30.4
multiple, 1.14
recommending fiduciaries, 1.5
recording advice to, 1.10, 1.31.3
subsequent communication with, 1.34.1, 1.34.2
testamentary capacity, 1.8
transactions with, 1.37
transference by, 1.30
Closely-held businesses. *See also* Gifts, Partnerships, Recapitalizations
deferring payment of estate tax, 2.46
gifts of interests, 7.7-7.11
Community property
agreements governing disposition at death, 3.30

Community property (*continued*)
agreements regarding character of property, 3.29
buy-sell agreements, 11.14
character and ownership of property, 3.25, 3.28
confirming character of testator's property, 4.13
conflict of laws, 3.36
conversion
community property into tenancy in common, 3.7.2
tenancy in common into community property, 3.7.3
elections, 4.13
employee benefits, 3.32
ERISA, 3.32
terminable interest rule, 3.32
estate planning with, 3.24, 3.27
preserve character of, 3.25
preserve availability of stepped-up basis, 3.26
estate tax, 3.33
credits, 3.33.3
deductions, 3.33.1
life insurance, 3.33
marital deductions, 3.33.2
"flower bonds," 4.35.4
gifts of, 2.10.1, 3.28.2
gift tax, 3.34
conversion of future income into separate, 3.34.3
partition of community into separate, 3.34.2
transfer of separate into community, 3.34.1
history, 2.3, 3.23
income from, character of, 3.25
income tax, 3.35
appreciated property acquired from a decedent, 3.35.5
basis following death of a spouse, 3.12.5, 3.26, 3.35.4
conversion of community into separate, 3.35.3
conversion of separate into community, 3.35.2
transfers between spouses, no gain or loss on, 3.35.1
intestacy, 4.4
joint tenancy, 3.12.5, 3.20.6
life insurance, 6.15, 6.80
apportionment rule, 6.15.2
characterization, 6.15
inception-of-title rule, 6.15.1
irrevocable trusts, 6.23.6
receivable by the estate, 6.26
risk payment doctrine, 6.15.3
simultaneous death, 6.80
veteran's life insurance, 6.77
widow's election insurance trust, 6.24.1
marital deduction, 5.7.2
post-mortem income, 4.6
presumption in favor of, 3.28.4
protecting migratory spouses, 3.39
retirement plans, 4.20.6
revocable trusts of, 3.25, 3.39
separate and community distinguished, 3.28
basic presumption, 3.28.4
special characterization problems, 3.28.5
survivorship agreements, 3.30
tenancy in common, 3.4
survivorship form, 3.12.5, 3.31
tracing, 3.28.3
transfers between spouses, 3.35.1
widow's election, 3.27. *See* Widow's election
Complex trust
defined, 10.4.9
income tax exemption, 10.4.9
Conditional wills, 4.7.3
Confidentiality. *See also* Professional responsibility
ethical considerations, 1.7, 1.14
Conflict of laws
basic rules, 3.36, 4.4.1
quasi-community property, 3.38
trust administration, 10.10
Conflicts of interests, 1.14. *See also* Professional responsibility
buy-sell agreements, 11.13
corporate fiduciary, 1.15
gifts to lawyer, 1.16
husband and wife, 1.14.2
intergenerational planning, 1.14.1
partnerships, 11.38.6
representation of multiple parties, 1.14
transfers for consideration, 9.2
Contractual wills, 4.7
Corporations, 11.2-11.4
buy-sell agreements. *See* Buy-sell agreements
C corporations, 11.2-11.3

double taxation, 11.2
gifts to, 2.5.5
S corporations, 10.4.14, 11.4
trapped assets, 11.3
Credits. *See also* Unified credit
foreign death tax, 2.15
previously taxed property, 2.15
state death tax, 2.15
unified, 2.2, 2.15
Crummey power
annual exclusion, 2.5.3, 7.37
discretionary trust with, 7.37
form of, 7.37.12
lapse of power of withdrawal, 7.37, 7.37.10-7.37.11
power of appointment, 7.37
Cruzan case, 4.35.3
health care powers of attorney, 4.35.3

Defective trusts, 10.32
Directive to physicians, 4.36. *See* Living will
Disclaimers, 12.28
acknowledgment form, 12.32.4
GSTT, 12.35
joint tenancy, gift tax, 12.33
marital deduction, increasing or decreasing, 5.16.2
partial interests, 12.34
planning, 12.35
powers, 12.32.1
pre-1977 transfers, 12.32.3
qualified, 12.32
requirements of qualified disclaimer, 12.34.4
requirements when not authorized by local law, 12.34.5
Distributable net income (DNI), 10.4.3, 12.36
basic rule, 10.2, 12.36.1
community property, 12.39.2
distributions
in kind, 12.36.7
non-pro rata, 12.39
not effecting, 12.37
timing, 12.36.5
sale or exchange, 12.38
specific gifts, 12.36.4, 12.37
tier system, 10.4.9, 12.36.3
trapping distributions, 12.40
Domicile, 4.9
Durable power of attorney
creation, 4.35.1
effective date, 4.35.7
"flower bonds" purchased under, 4.35.4, 12.48.1
health care decisions, 4.35.3
limitations, 4.35.6
power to make gifts, 4.35.4
recordation, 4.35.1
revocable trusts, power to transfer property to, 4.35.5
revocation, 4.35.1
scope and use, 4.35.2
springing power, 4.35.7
tax matters, 4.35.2

Elections
alternate valuation, 2.13, 10.6.5, 12.15
community property, 4.13
defer payment of estate tax, 11.27
QDT, 5.25
QTIP, 5.23.9
special use valuation, 12.19
taxes, power to make, 4.27.10
widow's election. *See* Widow's election
Engagement letter, 1.10, 1.30.6
Equalization clause, 5.7.1. *See* Marital deduction
Equitable adjustments, 12.14
ERISA, 4.20.6, 6.78.12
Estate administration
income splitting between estate and survivors, 4.6
protects against creditors, 4.5
unsupervised, 4.21.2
Estate freezes, 2.44
grantor retained interest trusts, 9.43
gifts, 7.7-7.11, 11.2
installment sale, 9.3-9.9
partnership freeze. *See* Partnership freeze
qualified interests, 9.43.2
qualified personal residence trust, 9.43.3
recapitalization. *See* Recapitalization
Estate planning
inter vivos planning, 1.1, 1.4

Estate planning (*continued*)
  assisting client's decisions, 1.9, 1.31
  basic lifetime strategies, 2.41-2.46
  charitable gifts. *See* Charitable gifts
  charts, 1.33.3
  client objectives, 1.30.4
  communications with client, 1.5
  community property, 3.24
  conference, initial, 1.29, 1.39
  confidential data form, 1.28
  documents to review, 1.30.5, 1.33.3
  drafts, 1.33.3
  durable powers of attorney. *See* Durable powers of attorney
  engagement letter, 1.10, 1.30.6
  executive estate planning, 1.20
  follow-up, 1.34.1
  forms, 1.33-1.33.3
  gifts, use of, 7.7-7.11. *See* Gifts
  health care. *See* Durable powers of attorney, *Cruzan* case, Living will
  implementing the plan, 1.34
  informed consent, 1.5
  installment sales, 9.3-9.9
  international, 1.14.1
  joint tenancy, 3.21
  lawyer's duty to collect data, 1.28
  legal assistance, use of in, 1.28
  life insurance. *See* Life insurance
  marital deduction, use of, 5.5-5.9
  partnership freeze, 11.38
  private annuities, 9.10-9.16
  producing the documents, 1.33, 1.33.4
  recording advice to clients, 1.10, 1.31.3
  redemptions under §303, 11.15
  scope, 1.2
  self-cancelling installment notes, 9.8
  stages involved, 1.27
  subsequent communications with client, 1.34.1
  tax estimates, 1.31.2, 1.32
    estimate form, 1.32
    letter regarding, 1.32
    tax estimate worksheet and forms, 1.21, 1.22
    timetable, 1.33.2
    trusts, 10.1
    valuation of property, 1.31.1
  post-mortem planning, 1.35
    alternate valuation, 12.15
    cash projection, 1.38
    checklist, 12.50
    closing the estate, 1.40
    deductions, income and estate tax, 12.9-12.14
    disclaimers. *See* Disclaimers
    deferred payment of estate tax, 11.25
    estate distributions, 12.36-12.40
    estimated income tax, 12.6
    family awards and allowances, 12.29
    qualified plan benefits, 12.25
    reordering property distributions, 12.28.-12.35
    self-dealing, 1.16
    special use valuation, 12.19
    split gifts, consent to, 12.20
    stages involved, 1.26
    strategies, 2.41
      bypass estates of survivors, 2.45
      defer payment of taxes, 2.46
      freeze values, 2.44
      reduce size of estates, 2.43
      shift income, 2.42
    tax planning, 1.31-1.32
    tax returns, 1.39
    tax year, 12.7
    tenancy in common, 3.10
    valuation. *See* Valuation
    who attorney represents, 1.16
Estate tax, 2.11
  administration expense deduction, 2.14, 12.13
  alternate valuation, 2.13, 10.6.5, 12.15
  annuities and other death benefits, 2.18
  beneficiary as trustee, 10.20.6
  casualty loss deduction, 12.13
  charitable deduction. *See* Charitable deduction
  community property, 3.33
  computation of, 2.2
  contractual wills, 4.7
  credits, 2.15
  Crummey trust, 7.37

deductions, 2.14, 12.9-12.14. *See also* Marital deduction, Charitable deduction
  equitable adjustments, 12.14
  in respect of a decedent, 12.10
deferral of, 2.46, 10.6.7, 11.25-11.30
  acceleration, 11.29
  closely-held business, 11.25-11.30
  election, 11.27
  installment payments, 11.30
  protective election, 11.27.1
  qualification under §6166, 11.28
  reversions and remainders, 12.45
  section 6166, 11.27, 12.47
  section 6166A (former), 12.46
  trade or business, 11.26.3
  worksheet, 11.30
disclaimers. *See* Disclaimers
distributions in kind, 4.16.3, 4.17.3
family allowances, 5.16.1, 12.29
"flower bonds," 10.6.9, 12.48
freezes, 2.44. *See* Gifts, Partnerships, Recapitalizations
  legislation, anti-freeze, 2.17.2
funeral expense deduction, 12.11
gift and income tax deduction, 12.13
gifts to minors, 7.28-7.39
  Crummey trust, 7.37
  outright gifts, 7.29
  section 2503(c) trust, 7.36
  Uniform Gifts (Transfers) to Minors Act, 7.34
gross estate, 2.12
  items included in gross estate, 2.12
  valuation, 2.13, 12.15-12.19
GSTT. *See* Generation-skipping transfer tax
historical note, 2.2
installment sales, 9.5
joint tenancy, 2.19. *See* Joint ownership
  husband and wife, 2.19.2
life insurance, 6.25-6.39
  death benefit only (DBO) plans, 6.78
  group-term assignment, 6.72
  history, 6.25
  incidents of ownership, 6.27-6.28
    attribution, 6.28
    beneficiary, power to change, 6.27.3
    cancellation, power to prevent, 6.27.6
    contract, powers under, 6.27.9
    convert, power to, 6.27.5
    held as fiduciary, 6.27.11
    reciprocal trust doctrine, 6.28, 7.34.2
    remove and replace trustee, power to, 6.27.2
    reversionary interests, 6.27.10
    terminate, power to, 6.27.4
    veto, power to, 6.27.8
    transfer within three years of death, 6.38
  irrevocable trusts, 6.23-6.24
  receivable by estate — community property, 6.26
  receivable by, or for benefit of, the estate, 6.26
  retained life interest, 6.39
  split-dollar life insurance, 6.71
  state death taxes, 6.40
  transfer within three years of death, 6.30
    of incidents of ownership, 6.38
    premiums paid within three years of death, 6.37
marital deduction. *See* Marital deduction
nature and computation of tax, 2.11
payment of, 12.41-12.48
  deferral
    on reversions and remainders, 12.45
    under former §6166A, 12.46
    under §6166, 11.25-11.30, 12.47
  extension of time limit, 12.44
  "flower bonds," 4.35.4, 10.6.9, 12.48
  life insurance proceeds, 12.42.2
  powers of appointment, 12.42.3
  qualified terminable interest property, 4.27.2, 12.42.4
  release from liability, 12.49
  source of, 12.42
power of appointment, 2.20. *See* Power of appointment
private annuity, 9.16

Estate tax (*continued*)
qualified plan benefits, 12.25
quasi-community property, 3.38
retained interests and powers, 2.17
retained voting rights, 2.47.1
sale and leaseback, 9.22
selling expenses, 12.13.2
source of funds, 4.27.1
special use valuation, 2.13, 12.19
tenancy in common, 3.8
transfers within three years of death, 2.16, 6.30, 6.38
trusts, summary, 10.6-10.6.9
alternate valuation date, 10.6.5
deferral of estate tax, 10.6.7
expenses, deductibility, 10.6.6
fiduciary, discharge of liability, 10.6.8
life insurance proceeds, 10.6.8
qualified plans, interests in, 10.6.2
stock in a controlled corporation, 10.6.1
unification of transfer tax system, 2.3, 2.15
unified credit, 2.3
valuation, 2.13
changes in, 2.10.3
widow's election, 9.23-9.29, 12.30
worksheet, 1.40
Estimates, tax, 1.31, 1.31.2
worksheet, 1.40
Ethics
appointment as fiduciary, 1.18, 4.26.1
attorney's fees, 1.19-1.25
basic elements, 1.3.2
buy-sell agreements, 11.13
competence, 1.7
confidentiality, 1.7, 1.14
conflicts of interests, 1.14-1.18, 9.2, 11.13
discussing fees with clients, 1.19
experts, use of, 1.7
gifts to attorney, 1.16
intrafamily transfers for consideration, 9.2
loans to attorney, 1.17
partnership freeze, 11.38.6
retention of wills, 4.32
supervise subordinates, 1.11
tax return preparation, 1.13
widow's election, 9.27
Excess accumulations tax, 12.26
Excess distributions tax, 12.26
Exculpatory clauses, 4.26.6
Executors
alternate, 4.26.5
appointment, 4.26
authority to settle estate, 4.26.9
bond, 4.26.7
coexecutors, 4.26.4
compensation, 4.26.8
corporate fiduciary, 4.26.2
estate tax, release from liability, 12.49
exculpatory clauses, 4.26.6
family-member fiduciary, 4.26.3
fees, 12.8
fiduciary duties, 12.14, 12.20.5, 12.23, 12.24.5, 12.36.5, 12.39, 12.39.1
lawyer fiduciary, 4.26.1
successor, 4.26.5
waiver of fees, 12.8
Exoneration, 4.20.1
Experts, 1.7
fees, 1.7.1

Fees
attorney's, 1.19-1.25
executor's, 12.8
trustee's, 1.7.1
5 or 5 powers, 10.24
estate tax treatment, 2.20.3, 10.24
gift tax treatment, 10.24
hanging power, 7.37.4 , 10.24.2
income tax, 10.24.1
lapse of, 2.20.3, 7.37.4, 7.37.10-7.37.11
marital deduction, use with, 5.22.3
QTIP, use with, 5.22.3
"Flower bonds," 10.6.9, 12.48
community property, 10.6.9, 12.48.2
durable power of attorney, 4.35.4
held under trust, 10.6.9
income tax consequences, 12.48
list of, 12.48.4
payment of estate tax, 12.48
purchased by agent, 4.35.4, 12.48.1
redemption, procedure, 12.48.5
Forms. *See* Worksheets, forms and checklists

Funeral arrangements, 4.11
Future interests. *See* Gift tax

Generation-Skipping Transfer Tax (GSTT) of 1986
  alternate valuation, 2.29, 12.15
  applicable fraction, 2.24
  applicable rate, 2.24
  background and scope, 2.22
  deferral on closely-held business, 2.26.3
  direct skips, 2.23.1
  exclusions, 2.28
  exemption, $1 million, 2.25
    allocation, 2.27
    allocation, deemed, 2.27, 2.27.3
    charitable lead trusts, 2.27.2
    inter vivos allocation, 2.27.2
  Gallo amendment, $2 million exemption, 2.39
  effective date, 2.38
  generation assignments, 2.32
  historical note, 2.2
  inclusion ratio, 2.24
  layered trusts, 2.27.3, 2.40.6
  liability for tax, 2.30
  life insurance. *See* Life insurance
  marital deduction, coordination with, 2.40.2
  multiple transfers, 2.34
  nonskip persons, 2.23.1
  nontaxable gifts, 2.28, 2.40.3
  orphan grandchild exclusion, 2.23.1, 2.40.7
  planning and drafting techniques, 2.25, 2.40
    coordination, 2.40.2
    exemption, $1 million, use of, 2.40.1
    inter vivos direct skips, 2.40.4
    nontaxable gifts, 2.40.3
    nontaxable gift, §2503(c) trust, 7.37.4
    orphan grandchild exclusion, use of, 2.40.7
    preserve tax-exempt status of preexisting trusts, 2.40.5
    trustee, amendments by, 2.40.8
  redemption of stock to pay, 2.36.4
  reverse QTIP election, 2.26, 12.22
  separate trusts, 2.33
  skip persons, 2.23.1
  special use value, 2.29
  taxable amount, 2.30
    direct skip, 2.30.1
    taxable distribution, 2.30.2
    taxable termination, 2.30.3
  taxable distribution, 2.23.3
  taxable termination, 2.23.2
  tax returns, 2.36
  valuation, 2.29
Gifts
  charitable. *See* Charitable gifts
  closely-held stock, 7.10, 11.3, 11.31
  community property, 7.6
  lifetime
    causa mortis, 7.4
    elements, 7.5
      acceptance, 7.5.2
      delivery, 7.5.1
    inter vivos, 7.4
    local property law, significance, 7.3
    nontax considerations, 7.2
    tax objectives, 7.7-7.11
      annual exclusion gifts, 7.8.1
      carryover of donor's basis, 7.8.2
      freeze estate value of assets, 7.8
      minimize state transfer tax costs, 7.11
      reduce nonbusiness assets, 7.10
      shift income from donor to donee, 7.9
        kiddie tax, 7.9.1
        shifting capital gains, 7.9.2
  marital deduction, 2.9. *See* Marital deduction
  minors, to, 7.28-7.39
    importance of, 7.28
    in trust, 7.34-7.39
      Crummey trust, 7.36
      estate tax, 7.37.11
      gift tax, 7.37.1
      hanging power, 7.37.4
      income tax, 7.37.10
      mandatory distribution of income trust, §2503(b), 7.38
      section 2503(c) trusts, 7.36
        estate tax, 7.36.6
        GSTT, 7.36.8
        gift tax, 7.36
        income tax, 7.36.7

Gifts (*continued*)
joint accounts, 7.33
bank accounts, 7.33.1
securities accounts, 7.33.2
outright gifts, 7.29
payable on death (POD) bank accounts, 7.30
series EE bonds, 7.30
minor as beneficiary, 7.30.3
minor as coowner, 7.30.2
minor as sole owner, 7.30.1
tentative (Totten) trust, 7.32
Uniform Gifts (Transfers) to Minors Act, 7.34. *See* Uniform Gifts to Minors Act
specialized techniques, 7.18-7.27
below-market loans, 7.19
encumbered property, gifts of, 7.26
free services and use of property, nongifts, 7.22
gift of residence with continued occupancy by donor, 7.32
grantor pays income tax of trust, 7.21
guaranty of note, 7.18
installment gifts, 7.24
net gifts, 7.25
part gift and part sale, 7.27
payment by one spouse of entire income or gift tax liability, nongifts, 7.20
split gifts, consent to, 2.7, 12.24
tax factors in selecting property to give, 7.12-7.17
adverse income tax consequences to donor, 7.17
appreciated property, 7.12
property subject to an encumbrance in excess of its basis, 7.13
property that reduces value of assets retained by the donor, 7.16
property with a basis exceeding current fair market value, 7.14
property with positive tax characteristics, 7.15
to attorney, ethical considerations, 1.16
use in estate planning, 2.4, 7.7-7.11

Gift tax, 2.4-2.10
annual exclusion, 2.5
gifts in trust, 2.5.2, 11.5
Crummey powers, 2.5.3
discretionary trusts, 2.5.2
gifts to corporations, 2.5.5
indirect gifts by shareholder-donor, 2.5.6
gifts to noncitizen spouse, 2.5.8
gifts to partnership, 2.5.7
appreciated property, basis, 7.12
beneficiary as trustee, 10.20.6
charitable deduction. *See* Charitable deduction
community property gifts, 2.10.1, 3.28.2
contractual wills, 4.7
Crummey trusts, 7.37
definition of "gift," 2.4
disclaimers. *See* Disclaimers
exclusion, medical care expenses, 2.6
exclusion, tuition, 2.6
exemption, replaced by credit, 2.4.2
gift splitting, 2.7, 12.24
gifts, completed, 2.4.3
gifts by nonresidents, 2.4.1
gifts to minors, 7.28-7.39
joint accounts, 7.33
outright gifts, 7.29
section #2503(c) trusts, 7.36
Uniform Gifts (Transfers) to Minors Act, 7.34.1
historical note, 2.2
indirect, 2.5.6
installment gifts, 7.24
installment sales, 9.4
joint tenancy, 3.14
lapse, power of withdrawal, 7.37.2
life insurance, 6.42-6.47
annual exclusion, 6.44
charitable deductions, 6.45.2
cross-owned, 6.21.1
death benefit only (DBO) plans, 6.78.8
group-term assignments, 6.72.10
group-term, valuation, 6.43.1
irrevocable beneficiary designation, 6.45.1
marital deductions, 6.45.2
premiums, payment of, 6.46
proceeds, payment of, 6.47.8

split-dollar life insurance, 6.71.3
term, valuation, 6.43.1
transfer of policy, 6.45
trusts, 6.18.2
irrevocable, 6.23
revocable, 6.18.3
testamentary, 6.13.4
widow's election, 6.24.1
valuation of policies, 6.43
local law, significance of, 7.3
marital deduction. *See* Marital deduction (gift tax)
net gifts, 7.25.2
part gift and part sale, 7.27
payment and penalties, 2.10.4
private annuity, 9.15
property with a basis exceeding its current fair market value, 7.14
qualified terminal interest property (QTIP), 5.23
recapitalization, 11.35.2
returns, 2.10
community property gifts, 2.10.1
manner and time of filing, 2.10.2
sale and leaseback, 9.21
tenancy in common, 3.7
conversion from community property into, 3.7.2
conversion into community property from, 3.7.3
termination of, 3.7.1
trusts, summary, 10.5
unification of transfer tax system, 2.3
unified credit, 2.2, 2.15
valuation, 1.31.1
changes in, 2.10.3
widow's election, 9.30
Grantor trust
beneficiary as trustee, 10.27
income tax, 10.27.1
"defective" trusts, 10.32
income tax summary, 10.4.1, 10.31
S corporations and, 10.32.2
tax consequences, 10.32
Grantor retained annuity trust (GRAT), 9.43.2
Grantor retained income trust (GRIT), 9.43.2
Grantor retained interest trust (GRIT), 9.43.2
Grantor retained unitrust (GRUT), 9.43.3
Gross estate. *See* Estate tax
Group-term life insurance. *See* Life insurance

Hanging power, 7.37.4
Heirs, 4.14
Homestead, 5.16.1, 12.29

Incidents of ownership. *See* Life insurance
Income shifting, 2.42
between estate and survivors, 4.6
Income tax
accrued interest deduction, 12.10
administration expense deduction, 12.13
beneficiary as trustee, 10.20.6
below-market loan, general, 7.19
below-market loan, small, 7.19
casualty loss deduction, 12.13
charitable deduction. *See* Charitable deduction
community property, 3.35
Crummey trust, 7.37.10
decedents final income tax return, 12.3-12.8
accrued interest as income, election, 12.7
estimated tax, declaration and payment, 12.6
extensions to make elections, 12.5.1
joint return, 12.3
advantages, 12.3.2
disadvantages, 12.3.3
medical expense deduction, 12.3.4
miscellaneous itemized deductions, 12.3.6
partnership election, 12.5
passive activity losses, 12.3.5
subchapter S election, 12.4
taxable year, selection of, 12.7
deductions
estate planning fees, 1.24-1.25
equitable adjustments, 12.14
for expenses occurring after death, 12.13
in respect of a decedent, 12.10
encumbered property, gift of, 7.26

Income tax (*continued*)
family allowances, 12.29
"flower bonds," 12.48
gift of a residence, 7.23
gifts to minors, 7.27-7.39
Crummey trust, 7.37.10
outright gifts, 7.29.3
section #2503(c) trust, 7.36.7
Uniform Gifts (Transfers) to Minors Act, 7.34.1
gift of a residence, 7.23
grantor as trustee, 10.20.5
installment sales, 9.6
alternative minimum tax, 9.6.2
disposition at death, 9.6.4
disposition inter vivos, 9.6.3
imputed interest, 9.6.5
nonresident alien, 9.9
resales by related parties, 9.7
joint tenancy, 3.20
life insurance, 6.48-6.69
death benefit only (DBO) plans, 6.78.9
dividends, 6.61
grantor trusts, 6.59
interest on, deductibility of, 6.60
limitations, 6.60.2
modified endowment contract, 6.50
policy loans, 6.59
policy purchases by a qualified plan, 6.54
premiums, payment of, 6.55
proceeds, payment of, 6.51
deferred payment, 6.51.1
paid to shareholder-beneficiary, 6.51.2
settlement options, 6.52
split-dollar life insurance, 6.71.2
transfer for value, 6.53
transfer of policies, 6.62-6.68
exchange of policies, 6.65-6.68
sale, 6.62
surrender of policies, 6.64
lump sum distributions, qualified plans, 12.25.2, 12.25.3
marital deduction, formula gifts, 5.33-5.38
net gifts, 7.25.1
part gift and part sale, 7.27
power of withdrawal, 10.4.2, 10.24.1
post-mortem income, 4.6, 12.6
private annuity, 9.11-9.14
qualified plan lump sum distributions, 12.25.2, 12.25.3
real estate tax deduction, 12.11
recapitalization, 11.31
income tax problems
boot, 11.34.2
business purposes, 11.34.1
redemption premium, 11.34.5
section 305, 11.34.4
section 306 stock, 11.34.5
strategies, 11.37
subchapter S ineligibility, 11.31
redemption of stock under §303. *See* Redemption under §303
S corporations, 10.4.14, 11.4
election, 11.4.2
income distributions and basis, 44.4.4
termination, 11.4.3
sale and leaseback, 9.19-9.20
selling expenses, 12.13.2
tenancy in common, 3.9
trusts. *See* Income tax (trusts)
widow's election, 9.23-9.39
Income tax (estates), 12.36
basic rule, 12.36.1
community property, 12.39.2
deductions, 12.9-12.14
deductions in respect of a decedent, 12.10
distributions in kind, 12.36.7
distributable net income (DNI), 10.4.3, 12.36.2
distributions, non-pro rata, 12.39
distributions not effecting, 12.37
estimated tax, declaration and payment, 12.6
planning, 12.36
sale or exchange, 12.38
specific gifts, 12.37
tier system, 10.4.9, 12.36.3
trapping distributions, 12.40
Income tax (trusts), 10.4-10.4.18
appreciated property, sale within two years, 10.4.1
Crummey trust, 7.37.10
distributable net income (DNI), 10.4.3
distributions, 10.4.4
estimated tax payments, 10.4.18

grantor trust, 9.20.5, 10.4.1. *See also* Grantor trust
loss recognition, 10.4.12
multiple trusts, 10.4.10
payment by fiduciary, 10.4.17
qualified subchapter S Trust (QSST), 10.4.14
redemptions under §303, 10.4.15
section 1244 stock, 10.4.13
taxable year, 10.4.16
throwback rules, 10.4.10
accumulation distributions, 10.4.10
application, 10.4.10
calculation of partial tax, 10.4.10
multiple trusts, 10.4.10
Installment gifts, 7.24
Installment sales, 9.3-9.9
estate tax consequences, 9.5
gift tax consequences, 9.4
income tax consequences, 9.6
AMT, 9.6.2
disposition at death, 9.6.4
disposition inter vivos, 9.6.3
imputed interest, 9.6.5
resale by related party, 9.6.5
sale to family member, 9.6.6
self-cancelling installment note, 9.8
Insurable interest, 6.2
Intestacy
common law states, 4.4.1
community property states, 4.4.2
Intrafamily transfers for consideration, 9.1
installment sale, 9.3-9.7
estate tax consequences, 9.5
gift tax consequences, 9.4
income tax consequences, 9.6
resale by related persons, 9.7
joint purchase
estate tax, 9.42.2
gift tax, 9.42.1
income tax, 9.42.3
private annuity, 9.10-9.16
estate tax consequences, 9.16
gift tax consequences, 9.15
income tax consequences, 9.12-9.14
annuitant, 9.13
nontax considerations, 9.11
transfer, 9.12
transferee, 9.14
professional responsibility, 9.2
sale and leaseback, 9.17-9.22
estate tax consequences, 9.22
gift tax consequences, 9.21
income tax consequences, 9.19-9.20.5
rental payments, 9.20
transfer, 9.19
widow's election, 9.23-9.39
described, 9.25
election, 9.29
forced, 9.29
inter vivos, 9.27
post-mortem, 9.27
voluntary, 9.28
estate tax consequences, 9.33-9.34
husband's estate, 9.33
widow's estate, 9.34
GSTT, 9.35
gift tax consequences, 9.24
income tax consequences, 9.31-9.32
background, 9.31
trustee, 9.31.1
trust distributions, 9.32
widow, 9.31.2
life insurance trust plan, 9.35
nontax consequences, 9.29
state tax consequences, 9.38
testamentary elections, 9.24
typical plan, 9.26
variations, 9.36
voluntary, 9.28

Joint (or Survivorship) life insurance, 6.75
Joint ownership
community property. *See* Community property
estate taxes, 2.19
joint tenancy (and tenancy by the entirety), 3.10-3.11, 3.21
advantages, 3.11.1
disadvantages, 3.11.2
community property, 3.20.6-3.20.7
states, 3.12.5, 3.20.8
confirmation in will, 4.13
conversion into tenancy in common, 3.3, 3.8, 3.20.9
creditor's rights, 3.11
estate tax, 2.19, 3.15

Joint ownership (*continued*)
contributions by surviving tenant, 3.15.1
disclaimers, 3.19. *See* Disclaimers
general rule, 3.15
joint tenancies between husband and wife, 3.16
marital deduction, 3.16
qualified joint interests, 3.16
simultaneous death, 3.17
termination of joint tenancy, 3.18
features, 3.12
gift tax, 3.14
disclaimers, 3.19. *See* Disclaimers
revocable transfers, 3.14.1
severance, 3.14
income tax, 3.20
basis, 3.20.3
depreciation adjustment, 3.20.5
planning with, 3.20.8
deductions, 3.20.2
income from joint tenancy property, 3.20.1
termination, 3.20.9
multiparty accounts in financial institutions, 3.12.1
planning with, 3.21
severance creates tenancy in common, 3.3, 3.14
simultaneous death, 3.12.3
state death taxation, 3.20
tenancy by the entirety, 3.13
tenancy in common, 3.2
community property states, 3.4
conversion of joint tenancy into, 3.3, 3.8, 3.20.9
creation, 3.3
creditor's claims, 3.6
estate planning use, 3.10
estate tax, 3.8
gift tax, 3.7
conversion of community property into, 3.7.2
conversion of tenancy in common into community property, 3.7.3
termination, 3.7.1
income tax, 3.8
partition, 3.5
substantive law summary, 3.2
Joint purchase, 9.42
Joint tenancy. *See* Joint ownership

Kiddie tax, 2.42, 7.9.1

Lapse
anti-lapse statutes, 4.15
bequest of specific property, 4.15
Legal assistants, 1.28
ethical considerations, 1.28
Life insurance, 6.1
accidental death, 6.11.1
agents, 6.13
beneficiary change by will, 4.18.4, 4.20.4
buy-sell agreements, funding
cross purchase, 11.8
entity purchase, 11.8
cash value (whole life), 6.8, 6.9
common policy riders, 6.11
community property
characterization, 6.15, 6.33
apportionment rule, 6.15.2
inception-of-title rule, 6.15.1
risk payment doctrine, 6.15.3
gift tax — payment of proceeds, 6.47
irrevocable life insurance trusts, 6.23
receivable by the estate, 6.26
retained life interests, 6.39
simultaneous death, 6.80
veterans' life insurance, 6.77
data collection form, 6.3
death benefit only (DBO) plans, 6.78
ERISA, 6.78.12
estate tax consequences, 6.78.1-6.78.7
gift tax consequences, 6.78.8
income tax consequences, 6.78.9
defined, 6.49
definitions, 6.2
divorce, effect of, 4.20.4, 4.18.4
endowment insurance, 6.9.3
estate planning, 6.16-6.24
cross-owned policies, 6.21.1, 11.8
for wealthier clients, 6.20-6.24
irrevocable life insurance trusts, 6.23-6.24

marital deduction gifts, 6.22
ownership by person other than the insured, 6.21
trusts, use of, 6.18, 6.23-6.24
estate tax, 6.25-6.39
history, 6.25
incidents of ownership, 6.27-6.28
attribution, 6.28
beneficiary, power to change, 6.27.3
cancel, power to, 6.27.6
contract powers under, 6.27.9
convert, power to, 6.27.5
powers held as fiduciary, 6.27.11
remove and replace trustee, power to, 6.27.7
reversionary interests, 6.27.10
terminate, power to, 6.27.4
transfer within three years of death, 6.38
veto power, 6.27.8
obligation to pay, 6.26
receivable by, or for benefit of, the estate, 6.26
reciprocal trust doctrine, 6.29, 7.34.2
retained life interest, 6.27.10
split-dollar life insurance, 6.71
state death taxes, 6.40
transfer within three years of death, 6.30
exchange of policies, 6.33
insurance on life of a person other than the decedent, 6.36
insured transfers funds used to pay premiums, 6.32.3
of incidents of ownership, 6.38
owner transfers policy, 6.32.1
post-1981 law, 6.32
pre-1982 law, 6.32.3
premiums paid within three years of death, 6.22
functions, 6.4
generation-skipping transfer tax, 6.41
annual exclusion gifts, 6.44.3
irrevocable life insurance trusts, 6.23.4
nontaxable gifts, 6.44.3
gift tax, 6.42-6.47
annual exclusion, 6.44
charitable deductions, 6.45.2
form 712, 6.43.6
group-term assignments, 6.72.10
group-term valuation, 6.43.1
irrevocable beneficiary designation, 6.45.1
marital deductions, 6.45.2
premium payments, 6.46
proceeds payment, 6.47
split-dollar life insurance, 6.71
term insurance, valuation, 6.43.1
transfer of policy, 6.45
valuation of policies, 6.43
group-term, 6.72
amount includible in income, 6.72.9
assignment, 6.72.10
basic requirements, 6.72.6
employees defined, 6.72.8
estate tax, 6.72.11
gift tax, 6.72.12
nondiscrimination rules, 6.72.3, 6.72.5
retired lives reserve (RLR), 6.72.13
planning with, 6.72.1
spouses and children, 6.72.2
valuation, 6.43.1
how much to buy, 6.5
income tax, 6.48-6.69
alternative minimum tax, 6.69
death benefit only (DBO) plans, 6.78.9
dividends, 6.61
grantor trusts, 6.58
policy loans, 6.59
deductibility generally, 6.60
deductibility limitations, 6.60.2
interest on, 6.60
policy purchased by a qualified plan, 6.54
premium payment, 6.55
alimony, as, 6.55.1
charitable deduction, 6.55.2
discount, 6.55.3
employer, by, 6.56
proceeds payment, 6.51
deferred payment, 6.51.1
paid to shareholder-beneficiary, 6.51.2

Life insurance (*continued*)
settlement options, 6.52
split-dollar life insurance, 6.71.1
transfer for value, 6.53
transfer for value, exceptions, 6.53.1
transfer of policies, 6.62-6.68
exchange of policies, 6.65-6.68
sale, 6.63
surrender of policies, 6.64
insurable interest, 6.2
insurer's financial condition, 6.14
irrevocable life insurance trusts, 6.23, 6.24
beneficiary designations, 6.22.1
community property, 6.23.4
community property widow's election trust, 6.24.1
drafting considerations, 6.23.5
estate tax, 6.23.1
GSTT, 6.23.4
gift tax, 6.23.2
premium payments, 6.22.2
successive ownership, 6.22.3
survivorship policies, 6.23.3
leased life insurance, 6.76
limited pay life, 6.92
minimum deposit, 6.73
modified endowment contract, 6.50
ordinary life, 6.9.1
participating and nonparticipating, 6.12
planning techniques, 6.7, 6.16
combined estates less than $600,000, 6.17
combined estates less than $1.2 million, 6.18
protect minors, 6.18.1
revocable trusts, 6.18.3, 6.19
testamentary trusts, 6.18.4, 6.19
use trusts, 6.18.2
combined estates more than $1.2 million
applications and assignments, 6.21.2
beneficiary designations, 6.21.5
community property, 6.21.3
cross-owned, 6.21.1
marital deduction, 6.22
ownership by others, 6.21
premium payments, 6.21.4
successor ownership, 6.21.6
reverse split-dollar, 6.71.1
settlement options, 6.52
single premium, 6.74
split-dollar, 6.71-6.71.4
estate tax, 6.71.4
gift tax consequences, 6.71.3
income tax consequences, 6.71.2
spouse insurance, 6.6
survivorship (joint lives) insurance, 6.75
term insurance, 6.8, 6.10, 6.43.1
decreasing term, 6.10.1
group-term, 6.10.2, 6.72
trusts, other, 6.24
business uses, 6.24.2
charitable, 6.24.3
community property widow's election, 6.24.1
types of, 6.8
Uniform Gifts (Transfers) to Minors Act, 6.79
Uniform Simultaneous Death Act, 6.80
universal life insurance, 6.9.4
variable life insurance, 6.9.5
veteran's life insurance, 6.77
community property, 6.77.1
waiver of premiums, 6.11.2
will, provisions affecting, 4.18.4, 4.20.4
whole life, 6.9.1
Living will, 4.36. *See also Cruzan* case, Durable powers of attorney
family member, 4.36.4
immunity, civil and criminal, 4.36.2
nutrition and hydration, 4.36.4
physicians, discussions with, 4.36.4
sources of information, 4.37
who may make, 4.36.1
Loans
below-market, 6.19
lawyer, by client to, 1.17
tax consequences, 7.19

Malpractice, 1.3, 1.39
Marital deduction (estate tax)
allocating assets to marital deduction gift, 5.37.6

closely-held stock, 5.37.6
income in respect of a decedent (IRD), 5.37.6
charitable remainder trust, use with, 5.24, 5.32
choosing trust form, 5.26
community property, 3.33.2
contractual wills, 4.7
credit, previously taxed property, 5.5
disclaimers, 5.16.2, 12.28
disclaimer-QTIP approach, 4.21.2, 5.23.8, 5.32
division of trusts, 2.26, 4.24.7
equalization clause, 5.7.1
ERTA (1981) changes, 5.3
estate trust, 5.21
family awards and allowances, 5.16.1
form of trust to use, 5.56
formula gifts, 5.32-5.40
assessment of, 5.33
transitional rule (pre-1982 formulas), 5.3.3
fractional share formulas
allocating income and capital gains and losses, 5.38.3
expressing the fraction, 5.38.1
income tax aspects, 5.39
model fractional share gift, 5.38.2
planning of, 5.38
true residue provision, 5.38.4
fractional share formula clause and pecuniary formula compared, 5.40
history, 5.2
life insurance proceeds, 5.22
life interest-power of appointment trust, 5.22
5 or 5 power, 5.22.3
income interest, 5.22.2
investment criteria, 4.24.5
power of appointment, 5.22.3
specific portion, 5.22.1
stub income, 5.22.2
unproductive assets, 5.22.2
pecuniary formula, 5.34
credits, 5.34.1
funding of, 5.37
model formula pecuniary marital deduction gift, 5.35
model formula pecuniary nonmarital deduction gift, 5.36
nondeductible principal charges, 5.34.2
planning of, 5.37
pecuniary formula clause and fractional share formula compared, 5.48
planning for use of, 5.5
basic approach, 5.5
community property, 5.7.2
disclaimers, 5.16.2
equalizing estate, 5.7
equalization clauses, 5.7.1
equalization gifts, 5.23.6
general objectives, 5.6
minimize tax — defer payments, 5.8
tax estimates, 5.5.1
unified credit, take advantage of, 5.9
valuation of assets, 5.5.2
power of appointment, 5.22.3
qualified domestic trust (QDT), 5.25
distributions, tax on, 5.25
requirements, 5.25
qualified terminable interest property (QTIP), 5.3.1, 5.23, 5.23.1, 5.32
annuity interests, 5.23.6
charitable remainder trust, in, 5.23.2
disclaimers, use with, 5.23.8
election, 5.23.9, 12.20, 12.50
gift tax consequences, 5.23.10
qualifying income interest for life, 5.23.2
tax on surviving spouse's death, 5.23.11
trust, form of, 4.22
requirements. *See also* Terminable interests, this heading.
citizen, surviving spouse a, 5.10, 5.11, 5.15, 5.25
deductible interest, 5.33-5.38
gross estate, included in, 5.13
pass to surviving spouse, 5.16
surviving spouse, 5.14
savings clauses, 5.27
simultaneous deaths, 5.20
specific portion, 5.22.1
surtax on large estates, 5.5

Marital deduction (estate tax) (*continued*)
surviving spouse becomes a citizen, 5.25.3
tax payable by QTIP distributees, 5.23.11
terminable interests, 5.17
basic rule, 5.17
exceptions to disqualification, 5.18
charitable remainder trust, 5.24
estate trust, 5.21
life income-general power of appointment trust, 5.22
limited survivorship, 5.19
qualified terminal interest property, 5.23, 12.20
executor purchase rule, 5.17.4
requirements, 5.17
passes to another person, 5.17.2
subsequent enjoyment, 5.17.3
terminable interest, 5.17.1
unidentified or "tainted" asset rule, 5.17.5
unlimited amount, 5.2.3, 5.31
valuation of assets, 5.5.2
valuation of assets distributed in kind, 5.37.1
date of distribution value ("true worth"), 5.37.2
estate tax value (Rev. Proc. 64-19), 5.37.3
fairly representative, 5.37.5
minimum value, 5.37.4
widow's election, 12.30
Marital deduction (gift tax)
community property, 5.7.2
generally, 2.9, 5.11, 5.28
post-1981, 2.9.2
pre-1981, 2.9.1
history, 5.2
lifetime QTIP planning, 5.23.6
objectives of inter vivos gifts, 5.6, 5.29
equalizing estates, 5.7, 5.23.6, 5.30
unified credit, use of, 5.23.6, 5.31
minority discount. *See* Valuation
planning, 2.9.3
requirements, 5.11
citizen, donee spouse a, 5.11, 5.12
Minors. *See also* Uniform Gifts to Minors Act
distribution of bequest to, 4.17, 4.17.1
gifts in trust, 7.35-7.39
Crummey trust, 7.37
mandatory distribution of income trust, §2503(b), 7.38
section 2503(c) trusts, 7.36
lifetime gifts to, 7.27-7.39
importance of, 7.28
joint accounts, 7.33
outright gifts, 7.29
payable on death bank accounts, 7.30
series EE bonds, 7.29
tentative (Totten) trust, 7.32
Uniform Gifts (Transfers) to Minors Act, 7.34. *See also* Uniform Gifts to Minors Act
minors' trust, 4.21.6, 4.23
testamentary gifts to custodians for, 4.17.1
Minors' trust, 4.21.6

Net gifts, 7.25
estate tax, 7.25.3
gift tax, 7.25.2
income tax, 7.25.1
Nonresident aliens
gifts by, 2.4.1
gifts to, 2.5.8
marital deduction, 5.11, 5.25

Part gift-part sale, 7.27
Partnership, gifts to, 2.5.7
Partnership freeze, 11.38
advantages, 11.38.2
converting interests, 11.39
creation not taxable, 11.39
ethical considerations, 11.38.6
family partnership rules, 11.40
allocation of income, 11.40.3
capital as material income-producing factor, 11.40.1

retained control by donor, 11.40.4
trustees and minors as partners, 11.40.2
gifts of, 11.38, 11.41
multiclass partnerships, 11.38
one class of equity, 11.4, 11.42
personal holding company rules inapplicable, 11.38.2
planning aspects, 11.41
income interest, 11.42.2
liquidation preference, 11.41.1
management and control, 11.41.3
section 2701, 11.5, 11.42
suitable assets, 11.38.1
summary, 11.42
tax uncertainties, 11.38.3
valuation, 11.5, 11.38.2
Passive activity losses, 10.4.7
Personal residence trust, 9.41.3
Pooled income fund, 8.30
Power of appointment, 2.20. *See also Crummey* power
ascertainable standard, limited by, 10.25
competency to exercise, 5.22.3
estate taxes, 2.20
payment of, 12.42.3
exercise in residuary bequest, 4.21.1
5 or 5 power, 5.22.3, 10.21
general, 10.22
lapse, 2.20.3, 7.37.10-7.37.11
marital deduction, 5.22.3
release, 2.20.2
special, 10.23
Power of attorney. *See* Durable power of attorney
durable, 4.35
Present interest exclusion, 2.5. *See* Gift tax
gifts to noncitizen spouse, 2.5.8
joint tenancy, 3.14
transfers in trust, 2.5.2
transfers to a corporation, 2.5.5
transfers to a partnership, 2.5.7
Private annuity, 9.10
estate tax, 9.16
gift tax, 9.15
income tax
annuitant, 9.13
transfer, 9.12
transferee, 9.14
nontax considerations, 9.11
Probate estate. *See* Estate administration
Professional responsibility. *See also* Attorneys, Conflicts of interest, Ethics, Fees
basic elements, 1.2.2
buy-sell agreement, 11.13
Code of professional responsibility (CPR), 1.2.1
competence of lawyer, 1.7
conflicts of interest. *See* Conflicts of interest
corporate fiduciaries, 1.15
disbarment, 1.6
fees, 1.19-1.25
gifts to lawyer, 1.16
intrafamily sales, 9.2
Model Rules of Professional Conduct (MRPC), 1.2.1
multiple clients, 1.14
multijurisdictional problems, 1.12
partnerships, 11.38.6
subordinates, duty to supervise, 1.11
tax practice and, 1.13
unauthorized practice, 1.12

Qualified domestic trust (QDT), 5.25. *See also* Marital deduction
Qualified interest, 9.43.2
Qualified joint interest, 3.16
Qualified personal residence trust, 9.41.3
Qualified retirement plans
estate tax, 12.25
excess accumulations, tax on, 12.26
excess distributions, tax on, 12.26
income tax, 12.25.3
lump sum distributions, 12.25.3
lump sum distributions, rollover by spouse, 12.25.2
premium payments, income tax effects, 6.57
purchase of life insurance, income tax effects, 6.54
Qualified subchapter S trust (QSST), 10.4.14

Qualified terminable interest property (QTIP), 5.23. *See also* Marital deduction
Qualified use, 12.19
Qualifying income interest, 5.23
Quasi-community property
  conflict of laws, 3.36, 3.38
  defined, 3.38
  estate tax, 3.38
  protecting migratory spouses, 3.39

Recapitalization, 11.31. *See* Buy-sell agreements, Estate freezes, Partnership freezes
  economic considerations, 11.31
  income tax, 11.34
    boot, 11.34.2
    business purpose, 11.34.1
    redemption premium, 11.34.5
    section 305, 11.34.4
    section 306, 11.34.3
  loss deduction, preferred stock, 11.12
  section 1244 inapplicable, 11.36
  section 2701, 11.5, 11.35
  section 2704, 11.5
  subchapter S ineligibility, 11.36
  valuation, 11.31, 11.35.1
    gift or additional compensation, 11.35.2
Reciprocal trust doctrine, 7.34.2
  life insurance, 6.29
Redemption under §303, 11.15
  disqualified redemptions, 11.24
  distributable property, 11.21
  entity attribution, no waiver, 11.24.4
  exceptions of §302(b)
    complete termination of interest, 11.24.3
    not equivalent to a dividend, 11.24.1
    substantially disproportionate, 11.24.2
  inter vivos planning for, 11.22
  maximum amount, 11.19
  thirty-five percent requirement, 11.18
    stock in two or more corporations, 11.18
  worksheet, 11.23
Remainder, sale of, 9.41
Renunciation. *See* Disclaimer
Reverse QTIP election, 2.26, 12.22
Reverse split-dollar insurance, 6.71.1
Rule against perpetuities
  savings clause, 10.48

S corporation, 10.4.14, 11.4
Sale and leaseback, 9.17-9.18
  estate tax, 9.22
  gift and leaseback, 9.22.1
  gift tax, 9.21
  income tax, 9.19
    rental payments, 9.20
      economic reality, 9.20.1
      grantor trust rules, 9.20.5
      no equity interest, 9.20.2
      suggested approach, 9.20.4
      Tax Court rules, 9.20.3
    transfer, 9.19
  sale and leaseback, 9.22.2
Savings clause, 5.27
Section 303 redemption. *See* Redemption under §303
Simple trust
  defined, 10.4.5
  income tax exemption, 10.4.5
Simultaneous death
  bequest of specific property, 4.15.3
  joint tenancy, 3.12.3
    estate tax, 3.15
  marital deduction, 5.20
  Uniform Probate Code, 5.20
Skip person, 2.23.1
Spendthrift clause, 10.21
Split-dollar insurance, 6.71

Tenancy by the entirety. *See* Joint ownership
Tenancy in common. *See* Joint ownership
Tier system, 10.4.9, 12.36.3
Transfers within three years of death. *See* Estate tax, Life insurance
Trapping distributions, 12.40
Trusts
  absolute discretion, 10.20.7
  allocation between income and principal, 10.47

alternate valuation date, 10.6.5
annual gift tax exclusion, 10.5
appreciated property, sale of, 10.4.11
ascertainable standard, powers limited by, 10.20.4
beneficiary as trustee, 10.20.6, 10.43.4
beneficiary's interest, transferability, 10.21
bypass, 2.45
charitable. *See* Charitable trusts
complex. *See* Complex trust
controlled corporation, stock of, 10.6.1
cotrustees, 10.43.5
creation in residuary bequest in a will, 4.21
Crummey trusts, 7.37
deductions, estate tax, 10.6.6
deferral, estate tax, 10.6.7
discretion to make distributions, standards, 10.20.8
discretion to make distributions, form, 10.28.10
distribution or accumulation of income, 10.20.1
divide, power to, 4.24.7
estate tax summary, 10.6
exculpatory clause, 10.46
5 or 5 power of withdrawal, 10.24
  hanging power, 10.24.2
  income tax, 10.24.1
flower bonds, 10.6.9
GSTT. *See* Generation-skipping transfer tax
general power of appointment, 10.6.3, 10.22
gift tax summary, 10.5
gifts to minors. *See* Gifts, minors
grantor as trustee, 10.20.5
grantor trust. *See* Grantor trust
income tax summary, 10.4. *See also* Income tax (trusts)
investment advisor, 10.45.4
investments, provisions regarding, 10.45
irrevocable trust, grantor's interest in, 10.30-10.41
  administrative powers, 10.38
  beneficial enjoyment, retained control, 10.37
  defective trust, 10.32
  estate tax, 10.35
  gift tax, 10.33, 10.34
  grantor treated as owner, 10.32
  incomplete gifts, 10.34
  jointly held powers, 10.31.2, 10.34
  power to revest title in grantor, 10.39
  retained income interest, 10.40
  retained reversionary interest, 10.36
  support obligation, 10.41.6
lawyer as trustee, 10.43.2
legal obligations, distributions that satisfy, 10.41.6
liability for taxes, discharge from, 10.6.8
life insurance, 6.18, 6.19, 6.23, 10.6.4
marital deduction. *See* Marital deduction
merger of similar trusts, 4.24.7
minor's trust, 4.21.6, 4.23
multiple accumulation trusts, 10.4.10
  recognition of separate status, 10.4.10
  throwback rules, 10.4.10
nongrantor treated as owner of trust, 10.4.2
perpetuities savings clause, 10.48
planning, 10.1
powers held by independent trustees, 10.20.3, 10.37
preference over contractual wills, 4.7.2
property, selection of, 10.44
QDT. *See* Marital deduction
QTIP. *See* Marital deduction
revocable trust, 10.7-10.17
  advantages, nontax, 10.12
  community property, 10.8
  creditors' claims against grantor, 10.11
  disadvantages, nontax, 10.13
  estate tax considerations, 10.17
  funded, 10.7
  gift tax considerations, 10.16
  income tax, 10.15
  nontestamentary nature, 10.9
  pour-over wills, 10.10
  power to revoke, 10.7
  property, selection of, 10.44

Trusts (*continued*)
reasons for, 10.7
reverse pour-over, 10.7
residuary trust, 4.21.2, 4.21.3
Rev. Rul. 79-353, 10.41.1
selection of trustees, 10.43
shams, 10.3
simple. *See* Simple trust
special power of appointment, 10.23
spendthrift clause, 4.24.8, 10.21
sprinkling of income, 10.20.2
stock splits and dividends, 10.47.1
successor trustee, 4.24.1
support trusts, 10.20.9
section 2503(c) trusts, 7.36
tentative (Totten), 7.32
termination of small trusts, 4.24.6
throwback rules, 10.4.10, 10.32.4
trustee
removal and replacement, 10.41
selection, 1.18, 4.26.1, 10.43
trustees' bond, 4.24.2
trustees' powers, 4.22.3
trustees' discretion to distribute income and principal, 10.20
uncontrolled discretion, 10.20.7
unified management of trust assets, 4.24.4

Unified transfer tax system, 2.2
Unified credit, 2.2-2.3, 2.15
marital deduction planning, 5.9
Uniform Anatomical Gift Act, 4.38
Uniform Disposition of Community Property at Death Act, 3.37
Uniform Gifts to Minors Act and Uniform Transfers to Minors Act, 7.34
gifts of life insurance, 6.79
gifts of Series EE Bonds, 7.30
gifts to custodian, 4.17.1
Uniform Marital Property Act, 4.4.2
Uniform Probate Code
bequests of corporate securities, 4.19
condition of survivorship, 4.15
durable power of attorney, 4.35
exercise of powers of appointment in residuary bequest, 4.21.1
exoneration, 4.12, 4.20.1
facts or acts of independent significance, 4.18.2
family awards, 5.16.1, 12.29
informal lists, 4.18.4
intestacy provisions, 4.4.1, 4.4.2
joint accounts, 7.33.1
marital deduction, limited survivorship, 5.19
payable on death (POD) bank accounts, 7.31
pour-over wills, 10.10
revocation by change of circumstances, 4.20.5
satisfaction, 4.16.2
simultaneous death, 5.20
support allowance, 12.29
tentative (Totten) trust, 7.32
testamentary appointment of guardian, 4.25
widow's election, 9.25, 12.30
will contracts, 4.7
Uniform Rights of Terminally Ill Act, 4.36.3
Uniform Simultaneous Death Act
life insurance, 6.80
marital deduction, 5.20
Uniform Testamentary Additions to Trusts Act, 10.10
Uniform Transfer on Death (TOD) Security Registration Act, 3.12.2
Uniform Transfers to Minors Act. *See* Uniform Gifts to Minors Act
Unproductive or underproductive property, 5.22-5.23, 10.47.4

Valuation of property, 1.31.1, 2.13
alternate valuation, 2.13, 12.15
distributed, sold or disposed of, 12.15.6
election, 12.15.5
GSTT, 12.15.7
income tax impact, 12.15.2
limits, 12.15.1
assets distributed in kind, marital deduction, 5.37
buy-sell agreements, 11.11
changes in, 2.10.3

discounts, 2.13
fractional interests, 2.43.1
lack of marketability, 2.13
minority business interest, 2.13
estate tax, 12.15-12.19
gross estate, 2.12
partnership freeze, 11.38.2
recapitalization, 11.31, 11.35.1
special use, 2.13, 12.19
basic requirements, 12.19.4
election, 12.19
maximum reduction in value, 12.19.3
personal liability, 12.19.12
practical concerns, 12.19.14
protective election, 12.19.2
recapture, 12.19.9

Widow's election, 9.23-9.39, 12.30
estate tax, 9.33-9.34
husband's estate, 9.33
widow's estate, 9.34
gift tax, 9.30
GSTT, 9.35
income tax, 9.31-9.32
trust distributions, 9.32
trustee, 9.31.1
widow, 9.31.2
inter vivos or post-mortem election, 9.27
marital deduction, 9.33
measured elections, 9.36
nontax consequences, 9.29
planning, 9.39
power of appointment, 9.30.1
state tax consequences, 9.38
testamentary elections, 9.24
voluntary election, 9.30.2, 9.39
Wills, 4.1
ademption of specific gifts, 4.15.1
adoption, effect of, 4.14
attestation clause, 4.30.1
bequests and devises
condition of survivorship for a specified period, 4.15.2
corporate securities, 4.19
exoneration, 4.20.1
insurance policies, 4.20, 4.20.2, 4.20.3
pecuniary, 4.16
distribution in kind, 4.16.3, 4.17.3
satisfaction, 4.16.2
residence, 4.20
retirement plan, interests in, 4.20.6
specific property, 4.13, 4.15
tangible personal property, 4.17
specific gifts and cash legacies, 4.17.2
testator's subsequent directions, 4.18
bequest with request, 4.18.3
facts or acts of independent significance, 4.18.2
incorporation by reference, 4.18.1
informal lists, 4.18.4
bond, waiver, 4.24.2
capacity to make, 1.8
character of property, 4.13
charitable gifts, 4.16.1
citizenship, 4.9
clause stating no will contract, 4.28
community property, 4.13
conditional wills, 4.7.3
consolidate property in one trust, 4.21.4
contractual wills, 4.7
debts, directions regarding, 4.12, 4.27
definitions included, 4.14
descendants v. issue, 4.14
heirs, use of term, 4.14
devises. *See* Bequests and devises, this heading
disclaimer-QTIP plan, 4.21.2
elections, power to make, 4.27.10. *See also* Elections
execution, 4.30-4.32
executors, appointment, 4.26. *See also* Executors
exoneration, 4.12, 4.20.1
expenses of administration, directions regarding, 4.27
family status, 4.14
funeral arrangements, 4.11
guardian of minor children, 4.25
indebtedness, forgiveness of, 4.16.4
intestacy, avoiding, 4.4
introduction, 4.9
joint tenancy confirmation, 4.13
joint wills, 4.7
letter to client regarding, 4.33

Wills (*continued*)
life insurance, beneficiary designation change by, 4.18.4, 4.20.4
living will, 4.36
marital deduction, 4.21.1, 4.22, 4.27.7. *See also* Marital deduction
minors, gifts to, 4.17
minors trust, 4.23
mutual wills, 4.7
no contest clause, 4.29
non-pro rata distributions, 4.27.6
organization and content, 4.8
pour-over, 4.21.4
pretermitted child, 4.14
QTIP trust, 4.21.2
QTIP trust, form of, 4.22
reciprocal wills, 4.7
residuary bequest, 4.21
exercise of powers of appointment, 4.21.1
minors' trust, 4.21.6, 4.23
trust, 4.21. *See also* Trusts
trusts for children, 4.21.3
trust provisions, 4.22
ultimate disposition of residue, 4.21.7
revocation, prior wills and codicils, 4.10
revocation by change in circumstances, 4.20.5
satisfaction, 4.26.2
self-proving affidavit, 4.29
simultaneous deaths, 4.15.3
spendthrift clause, 4.24.8
spouse, all to, 4.21.2
state inheritance tax, payment, 4.27.8
statutory wills, 4.3
super will, 4.1
table of contents, 4.8
taxes
directions regarding, 4.27.1, 4.27.7
elections, power to make, 4.27.10
trust administrative provisions, 4.24
trustees
divide or merge trust, power to, 4.24.7
powers, 4.24.3, 4.24.5
successors, 4.24.1
terminate trust, power to, 4.24.6
uses, 4.1
widow's election, 4.13, 9.23-39, 12.30
Worksheets, forms, and checklists
5 or 5 Power of Appointment (Form 10-6), 10.24
Acknowledgment for Receipt of Disclaimer (Form 12-2), 12.32.4
Annual Lapse of Hanging Power (Form 7-3), 7.37.4
Annual Premium, Five-Year Renewable $250,000 Term Policy (Graph 6-1), 6.10
Appointment of Executors (Form 4-20), 4.26
Appointment of Guardian (Form 4-19), 4.25
Attestation Clause (Form 4-26), 4.30
Cash Corridor Test of §7702(d)(2) (Table 6-1), 6.49
Cash Gift to Charity (Form 4-7), 4.16
Checklist of Post-Mortem Matters, 12.50
Confidential Estate Planning Data Form (Form 1-5), 1.40
Crummey Power for Trust with One Beneficiary (Form 7-4), 7.37.12
Date of Distribution (True Worth) Funding Clause (Form 5-8), 5.37.2
Date Power Becomes Effective (Form 4-31), 4.35.8
Declarations Under the Uniform Rights of the Terminally Ill Act (1989) (Form 4-32), 4.36.3
Discretionary Distributions (Form 10-3), 10.20.10
Disposition of Assets Under Will (Chart 4-1), 4.8
Disposition of Estate Under Will (Chart 1-1), 1.33.3
Disposition of Property upon Death of Married Insured (Moderate Size Estates) (Chart 6-1), 6.17
Distributive Provisions of §2503(c) Trust (Form 7-1), 7.36.5

Estate Tax Deferral Worksheet, 11.30
Estate Tax Value, Fairly Representative (Form 5-10), 5.37.5
Exculpatory Clause (Form 4-22), 4.26.6
Execution Clause (Form 4-25), 4.30
Executor Authorized to Make Partial or Total QTIP Election (Form 5-3), 5.23.9
Family Status and Definitions (Form 4-4), 4.14
Federal Estate and Gift Tax Rates Prior to 1993 (excluding surtax) (Figure 2-1), 2.3
Federal Estate Tax Worksheet (Form 1-6), 1.40
Formula Fractional Share Marital Deduction Gift (Form 5-11), 5.38.2
Formula Pecuniary Marital Deduction Gift (Form 5-6), 5.35
Formula Pecuniary Nonmarital Deduction Gift (Form 5-7), 5.36
Formula QTIP Election, (Form 12-1), 12.20.2
Gift of Corporate Securities (Form 4-11), 4.19
Gift of Residence, Life Insurance, and Employee Benefits (Form 4-12), 4.20
Gift of Specific Item of Personalty (Form 4-5), 4.15
Gift of Tangible Personal Property (Form 4-8), 4.17
Gift of Tangible Personal Property by List (Form 4-9), 4.18
Hanging Power of Withdrawal, (Form 10-7), 10.24.2
Income Tax Rates Applicable to Trusts and Estates, 1990 (Table 10-2), 10.18
Income Tax Rates Applicable to Trusts and Estates, 1991 (Table 10-1), 10.18
Increases in Unified Credit and Credit Equivalent (Table 2-1), 2.3
Introduction to Will (Form 4-2), 4.9
Letter of Transmittal (Form 4-27), 4.33
Letter to Client After Initial Conference (Form 1-2), 1.30.6
Letter to Client Describing Recommended Plan (Form 1-3), 1.32
Letter to Client Regarding Initial Conference (Form 1-1), 1.29
Life Insurance Data Collection Form, 6.3
Limitation of Power of Withdrawal (Form 7-2), 7.37.3
List of Gifts of Tangible Personal Property (Form 4-10), 4.18.4
Marital Deduction Savings Clause (Form 5-4), 5.27
Minimum Worth Funding Clause (Form 5-9), 5.37.4
Nonformula Pecuniary Nonmarital Deduction Gift (Form 5-5), 5.32
Payment of Debts, Taxes, and Expenses (Form 4-23), 4.27
Payment of Income to Surviving Spouse (§2056(b)(5) Trust) (Form 5-1), 5.22.2
Penalties for Underpayment of Estate or Gift Tax, Pre-1990, (Table 12-1), 12.16
Perpetuities Savings Clause (Form 10.9), 10.48
Post-Mortem Problem Checklist, 12.50
Pour-Over to Inter Vivos Trust (Form 4-14), 4.21.4
Power of Withdrawal Limited by an Ascertainable Standard (Form 10-8), 10.25
Power to Make Gifts to Family Members (Form 4-30), 4.35.4
Power to Make Heath Care Decision (Form 4-29), 4.35.3
Power to Represent Principal with Respect to Federal Tax Matters (Form 4-28), 4.35.2
QTIP Trust (Form 4-16), 4.22
Reserved Power to Amend or Revoke (Form 10-1), 10.8
Residuary Clause for Pour-Over Will (Form 10-2), 10.10
Residuary Gift (Form 4-13), 4.21

Worksheets, Forms, and Checklists (*continued*)
- Revocation of Prior Wills (Form 4-3), 4.10
- Section 303 Worksheet (for decedents dying after December 31, 1981), 11.23
- Section 6166 Worksheet (15-year deferral), 11.30
- Special Testamentary Power of Appointment (Form 10-5), 10.22
- Spendthrift Clause (Form 10-4), 10.21.1
- Statutory Benefits Under §§303, 2032A, and 6166 (Table 7-1), 7.10
- Surviving Spouse's General Testamentary Powers of Appointment (§2056(b)(5) Trust) (Form 5-2), 5.22.3
- Table of Contents, John Q. Public Will (Form 4-1), 4.8
- Tax Estimates (Form 1-4), 1.32
- Trust Administrative Provisions (Form 4-18), 4.24
- Trust for Descendants (Form 4-15), 4.22
- Trust for Minor Distributees (Form 4-17), 4.23
- Uniform Donor Card (Anatomical Gifts) (Form 4-33), 4.38.7
- Uniform One-Year Term Premiums for $1,000 Life Insurance Protection (Table 6-2), 6.71.2
- Uniform Premiums for $1,000 of Group-Term Life Insurance Protection (Table 6-3), 6.72.9
- Waiver of Confidentiality by Executor (Form 4-21), 4.26
- Wills Not Contractual (Form 4-24), 4.28